THEOLOGICAL INDEX.

REFERENCES

TO THE

PRINCIPAL WORKS

IN EVERY DEPARTMENT OF

RELIGIOUS LITERATURE.

EMBRACING NEARLY

SEVENTY THOUSAND CITATIONS,
ALPHABETICALLY ARRANGED UNDER TWO THOUSAND HEADS.

BY

HOWARD MALCOM, D.D., LL.D.

"*Scire ubi aliquid possis invenire, magna pars eruditionis est.*"

BOSTON:
GOULD AND LINCOLN,
59 WASHINGTON STREET.
LONDON: TRÜBNER & CO.
60 PATERNOSTER ROW.
1868.

ROCKWELL & ROLLINS, STEREOTYPERS AND PRINTERS,
122 Washington Street, Boston.

PREFACE.

NOTHING was further from my mind, in commencing this body of references, than the idea of making it available to others as well as myself. On assuming the pastorship of a church in 1820, I purchased, under the guidance of my honored instructors in theology, Drs. Staughton, Alexander, and Miller, about two thousand volumes. But to many of them I was a stranger, and often found that I had help at hand when it was too late for my purpose. For my own convenience, I arranged the entire contents of my library in the manner here exhibited. For aid in future investigations, references were added, as important books came under my notice—in Reviews, or elsewhere. Lying constantly on my desk for over forty years, and receiving almost daily additions, the book grew, without any sensible deduction of time from my proper pursuits; and since my retirement from professional life, I have found pleasant occupation in endeavoring to give it completeness.

So far as I know, the work is unique, so that whatever may be its deficiences, it will be useful as far as it goes. There are bibliothecas, each of which was received favorably by the learned, but all so different in design from this, that it will lose none of its value when placed by their side. Few of them can now be had, and nearly all of them were published more than a century ago, when there were few valuable theological books in the English language. Such as desire to consult them, are referred to the head "Bibliography."

Theology has become the most voluminous of all the sciences. A minister now can read through very few of the teeming productions of the press, while there are many he must consult. In the English language alone, there are, I suppose, a quarter of a million of religious books. To become familiar with these, to say nothing of an equal number in Latin, German, and French, would require a thousand lives. Hence the absolute need of an aid like this, to enable the student to consult just those books, or parts of books, which will furnish him the required assistance.

Persons who have given special attention to some one topic, will probably be acquainted with authors on that point which are not here adduced. But such will not forget that other parts of the book, and perhaps that very part, will render them good service.

The omission which they discover may have been through my ignorance or oversight, but in thousands of cases, such omission is the result of self-imposed restraint. The book may be out of print, or very rare, or superseded by a better, or of small value compared with those which are mentioned. My aim is not to preserve the whole sum of theological literature from that oblivion which much of it merits, but to furnish ready reference to what is still both valuable and accessible. Nor am I willing to hide meritorious authors in a crowd; nor to waste a student's time in searching for books which he cannot find; nor by amassing references, useless or merely curious, to give my book a scholarly and complete appearance, and destroy its utility. Zealous bibliographers enumerate every title they can find, though the book may be nowhere in existence, and love to append to their notice, "rare;" "very rare;" "only fifty copies printed;" "unnoticed hitherto," etc. But I desire neither the credit of authorship, nor the gratification of the learned, and have no other ambition than to help the industrious. No small labor, therefore, has been spent in making careful omissions, and many more would have been made, were it not that a book may be of signal use, though not the best on the subject; and may be within reach, when a better one is not. On a few subjects, such as "English Bible," and "New Version," all the writers which have come to my knowledge are named.

"The Fathers" are constantly referred to, though the subjects may have been much better handled by others. This respect seems due to antiquity. In all cases, their testimony as to facts is important. It is desirable also to keep open the original sources of controversial theology, and to trace the succession of sacred literature. That so many of the references are to old books, will be no objection to scholars. On some of the subjects, nearly all the literature is old; and the aggregate of the good theology of all past ages, is vastly greater than the amount produced in our single age. The zeal of publishers keeps new books before the public, and the student is much less likely to be ignorant of these than of those of older date.

Lists of editions of the Hebrew and Greek scriptures, and of the Septuagint, Vulgate, and other versions, are omitted, because not only are the "Biblia" named separately in booksellers' catalogues, but there are numerous compilations of this sort, which leave nothing to be done in that department. I have mentioned the best of these under "Bibliography," and "Printed editions."

Bodies of Divinity, Bible Dictionaries, Church Histories, and Commentators, are named in their proper places; but as they are themselves works of general reference, they are not referred to under the several topics they embrace, except they discuss some one particularly and largely. The inquirer will, of course, consult such of them as are within his reach.

The abridgement of titles is the result of much reflection, and has cost much labor. To have given them in full would have trebled the cost of the book, without increasing its value. Enough of each title is given to preclude embarrassment or uncertainty.

To assort books accurately is impossible, for some may properly be placed under divers heads; but all inconvenience on this score is obviated by the references to kindred heads.

References are not made to volumes and pages, because the diversity of editions would make them not only useless but perplexing. When a work is divided into parts and chapters, the number is given. Single sermons and pamphlets are omitted, because generally ephemeral, and always difficult to find.

The date of the first publication of a book is given,* where it seemed desirable, as under Commentators, Common Prayer, Concordances, English Bible, Geography, Histories, Missions, Palestine, Theology, etc. The date given in catalogues is only that of the edition there mentioned, and in some of the best, dates are not given at all. Let the owner of this book undertake to put the date of the first editions to the works named under any single head, and he will be convinced of the folly of attempting it for all. To do it as far as I have, has been very troublesome, and in many cases it required an examination of the biography of the author. In Law, Medicine, or Science, the date of a publication may be useful; but theology has a positive basis in Revelation, and he who in any age writes well on sacred subjects, writes for all ages. If the student finds the aid he requires, it is enough. Besides, there are few important books which have not been reprinted, perhaps more than once; and some of the oldest are still being reproduced, often with valuable editorial improvements. Whenever a book relates to "the present time," or the state of a country at a certain period, the date is given, if possible; † and when some particular edition is greatly preferable, it is designated.

Observations on the comparative value of books are sparingly introduced, preferring to omit works of small merit, if there are good ones on that topic, not too rare, except when it seemed well to put the reader on his guard. The little reliance which can be placed on such notices is illustrated by the specimens below, selected because they are the utterances of well-known men in regard to well-known books.

Wake's New Version of the Psalms. "Well drawn up." "Notes judicious."—British Critic. "No value."—Orme.

McKnight on the Epistles. "Luminous and valuable."—Parkhurst. "Not often paralleled."—British Critic. "Translation rash, uncouth, and

---

* Some of these dates are disputed by scholars. I have intended to give those most usually assigned.

† Guild, in his useful *"Librarian's Manual,"* discriminates between intellectual and natural bibliography. The former term he applies to the consideration of the contents of books; the latter, to notices of the number of volumes, date, size, price, and rarity of editions or of particular copies. My tastes do not lead me to the latter class of inquiries, and if they did, I should not mingle both in one book.

often ungrammatical. The notes tend more to perplex than enlighten."—Loundes. "With two exceptions, scarcely any doctrine is rightly stated." —Orme.

Draper's Lectures on the Liturgy. "Perspicuous, sensible, and evangelical."—Eclectic Review. "No small portion is jargon."—Critical Review.

Burnet's History of the Reformation was honored, as no other book ever was, by a vote of thanks in the British Parliament. "Impartial, liberal, laborious."—Prof. Smyth. "Burnet is, without doubt, the English Eusebius."—Apthorpe. "One of the most thoroughly digested works of the century."—Prof. Spalding. "The style is mere chit-chat. I do not believe that Burnet intentionally lied, but he was so much prejudiced, that he took no pains to find out the truth."—Dr. Johnson, *in Boswell's Life.*

Dr. Samuel Clarke's Essays. "The most serious treatises Dr. C. ever wrote." "Very useful in all families."—Whiston. "Destitute of originality and acuteness; nor is there any thing in the style to compensate for the mediocrity of thought."—Cunningham.

Quaresmii Elucidatio terrae sanctae. "Not much esteemed."—Walch. "The most valuable work on biblical geography ever printed."—Orme.

Gifford's Translation of Juvenal. "The best version ever made of a classical author."—Sir Walter Scott. "The baldest, and in many parts the most offensive of all the translations of Juvenal."—Hazlitt.

Aikins' General Biography. "Evinces sound judgment, manly freedom, and correct taste."—Roscoe. "A worthless compilation."—Gifford.

Echard's General Eccles. History, to A. D. 313. "The best of its kind." —Prideaux. "Of little value."—Lowndes.

Jortin's Remarks on Eccles. History. "Pithy, learned, candid, and acute." —Dibdin. "Full of manly sense, ingenious strictures, and profound erudition."—Vicess. Knox. "A vulgar caricature, distinguished not more for heartlessness and the absence of every noble feeling, than for the author's shameful ignorance of the subject."—Dowling. "There are few authors to whom I am so much indebted."—Dr. Parr.

Fuller's Church History of Britain. "Even the most serious and authentic parts are so interlaced with pun and quibble, that it looks as if he had designed to ridicule our Church."—Bishop Nicholson. "Simply a caricature of history, and a systematic violation of all its proprieties. Never was there such a medley."—Henry Rogers. "There are only two writers of the genuine history of our Church who deserve the name of historians—Collier and Fuller."—Bishop Warburton. "One of the most remarkable books in the language; the varied powers of learning, sagacity, pathos, wit, humor, and imagination, all animating the pages of a Church history."—Henry Reed. "Sensible, pious, candid."—Bickersteth.

Prettyman's Elements of Theology. "Well arranged, the reasoning clear and solid, well adapted for students in theology, and may be read with advantage by the most experienced divine."—Bishop Marsh. "Merely shows how a creed may be made to signify any thing or nothing."—Williams.

Milner's Church History. "Eminently pious; an estimable treatise in the very spirit of the sacred writers."—Bickersteth. "Milner was destitute of the information necessary to an ecclesiastical historian."—Dowling. "The book has no intrinsic value, and will sink into total and merited neglect."—Dr. Hugh J. Ross.

Dunlop's History of Fiction. "He has executed a defective plan in rather a superficial manner."—LOND. QUART. REVIEW. "An agreeable miscellany, which discovers uncommon information and learning."—EDINB. REVIEW.

Beattie's Essay on Truth. "Beattie's Essay is, I believe, every day more liked; at least, I like it more, as I look upon it more."—DR. JOHNSON, *in Boswell's Life.* "Beattie's book is even more remarkable for being abusive and acrimonious, than for its defects in argument and originality."—EDINBURG REVIEW.

Hallam's Constitutional Hist. of England. "Acrimonious, arrogant, unjust, ill-tempered." "The production of a decided partisan."—SOUTHEY, *in Lond. Quart. Review.* 37 : 194. "Eminently judicial." "Its whole spirit is that of the bench, not of the bar." "Calm, steady, acute, profound. The most impartial book we ever read."—T. B. MACAULEY, *Edinb. Rev.* 48 : 96.

The following are the prominent features which distinguish this undertaking from any other of its kind.

1. The alphabetical arrangement of topics, with writers annexed, instead of the usual alphabetical arrangement of authors, with their writings annexed.

2. The multiplication of heads, so as to comprehend not only principal subjects, but the widest range of theological literature. The number of heads, not counting those which merely refer to others, is over two thousand.

3. The magnitude of the work, comprising, as it does, about seventy thousand citations.* This number is perhaps nearly doubled by the extensive lists of books, which are adduced under particular heads. See the table of such heads at the end of the book.

4. The including of the great Reviews, secular and religious. Unlike pamphlets and single sermons, these are bound, and accessible. A large amount of the best theological literature is thus made available.

5. The analytical arrangement of the best English sermons. These contain a great treasure of both doctrinal and practical theology, and the number of my references to them is proportionably large, some articles consisting mainly of such, though only bound volumes are noticed.

6. The introduction of a wide range of authors not theological Nearly every head contains such references, and some are made up of them almost entirely.†

7. The insertion of the names of prominent characters, scriptural and ecclesiastical, with their biographies, works, and the critics

---

* Lowndes' Bibliographer's Manual, though embracing *all* departments of knowledge, contains but about fifty thousand authors. Allibone's Dictionary of Authors, designed to name *every* writer in the English language, even of an ephemeral pamphlet, embraces but thirty thousand authors.

† See Budhism, Capital punishment, Eleusinian mysteries, Ethnology, Geology, Hinduism, Mesmerism, Phrenology, Palestine, etc. etc.

upon them. Great assistance is thus furnished for investigating the history of sects and doctrines.

8. The separation of writers on controverted subjects into three divisions, viz.: for, against, and historical. Every order, sect, and school, ancient or modern, is fairly presented, as far as is in my power. Leading men, of existing sects, have been written to for lists of their best writers, and the result, though sometimes helpful, has shown how much even they needed such a book of reference.

9. The numerous references to books which do not, by their titles, indicate their subject; thus furnishing aid which no ordinary catalogues could supply.

10. The work is brought down to recent publications

To three classes of persons I hope good service is here rendered.

1. To *authors*, in furnishing them both assistance and restraint. To write well, a man must know to what extent and in what manner his subject has been treated by others. He may be wise, but writers, of whom he is ignorant, may have been more so. He may think he will enlighten the world, when his theme has been already better handled. It is not uncommon for an author to say in his preface that had he known the existence of a certain book, he would have made his own better, or not written at all. Active minds often adopt views unlike those of their cotemporaries, and perhaps lead off a party, not aware that similar notions have been published, refuted, and forgotten. Want of extensive reading is the root of many heresies and superstitions.

2. To *students*, in showing them where they may find desired knowledge. Without such aid, they may stand in a large library, or even in their own, with all needed assistance at hand, and yet be helpless. Next to knowing a thing, is to know where to obtain the information; and as no one can know much, the latter attainment, if extensive, is, on the whole, the better. The student is here introduced to the great minds of the past and the present, and taught who of them and what portions of their works will answer his inquiries or resolve his doubts.

3. *Purchasers of books* for public or private theological libraries, or the theological department of general libraries, will here be shown how to make the collection symmetrical (a quality which few libraries possess), as well as comprehensive and complete.

I am quite conscious of having made a very imperfect book. One life is not long enough, nor one man's knowledge of books extensive enough, to make such a work complete. But as the owner becomes familiar with this volume, he will find the undesirable omissions both fewer and less important than he suspected; for books which might have been named under several heads, are given but under one, and the apparent omission is supplied elsewhere. I present the result of my labors for just what it is—an arranged catalogue of many thousand books, in a single department of literature. These are books which theologians will never discard, so that what I have done is done forever. Future publications will be added by future editors, but they will add, from past publications, few of those which I have omitted.

I do not presume that my book will incur no censures but such as it deserves. Some will think many of the references should have been omitted, and some, that many more should have been added. Some will find fault for the sake of seeming to know more than the author, and some for the love of fault-finding. Some out of ignorance, or lack of reflection, will condemn real excellencies; and some will judge me by a standard which cannot be reached. I have pursued my work in full view of such considerations, content to provide for future theologians a labor-saving apparatus.

> "Si quid novisti rectius istis,
> Candidus imperti: si non, his utere mecum."
> HORACE. EP. VI.

PHILADELPHIA, 1868.

NOTICE.—The Latin titles occurring among English writers, are not there by mistake. It was once customary to give such titles to books in our own language.

When a writer's name is in brackets, it indicates that the book was published anonymously.

Some Reviews have several times commenced a "New Series," and some have been reprinted with altered paging. This has made some unavoidable confusion as to such references; but the only alternative was to insert them with this disadvantage, or omit them altogether.

"A Bibliotheca, or account of books in English, continued to the present day, is a desideratum."—*Bickersteth.*

"A book which treats only of other books, is the touchstone of a genuine lover of literature. He will handle it with gentle reverence, and keep it at his right hand for frequent consultation; while mere readers would throw the book aside as a dull and worthless catalogue."—*London Quarterly Review.*

"Book Catalogues are to men of letters what the compass and lighthouse are to the mariner, the digested index to the lawyer, the dispensatory to the physician, the sign-post to the traveller: in short, they are the concordances of literature."—*Western Memorabilia.*

"Books can give new views of life, and teach us how to live. They soothe the grieved, the stubborn they chastise. Fools they admonish, and the wise confirm."—*Crabbe.*

"A library is not like a dead city of stones, yearly crumbling, and needing repair: but like a spiritual tree. There it stands and yields its precious fruit, from year to year, and from age to age:—thaumaturgic, for it can persuade men."—*Carlyle.*

"Theology is by far the most voluminous of all the sciences. There is none that comes nearly up to it, in the amount, or what may be termed the dimensions of its authorship. It is a colossus of most precious and solid material, brought together by the multiplied efforts of a most prodigious industry, and elaborated into form by the skill of many thousand intellects; some of which equal, both in power and achievement, the most gigantic of those spirits that ever signalized themselves in any of the walks of philosophic investigation."—*Chalmers.*

"Hi sunt magistri qui nos instruunt sine virgis et ferula, sine pane et pecunia. Si accedis, non dormiunt; si inquiris, non se abscondunt; non remurmurant si oberres; cachinnos nesciunt si ignores."—*Richard de Bury.*

THEOLOGICAL REFERENCES.

Aaron. See BIOGRAPHY.
Taylor's (Dr. T.) Types of the Old Test.

Abelard.
Abelardi Opera (Various editions).
Ouvrages inedits d'A. Ed. Cousin. 1836.
Bohringer, die Kirche Christi.
Gervaise, Vie de Abeillard.
Frerich de A. doctrina et morali.
Goldhorn de Summis principiis theol. A.
Schlosser's Leben e. schwärmers u. e. philos.
Berington's Hist. of Abelard and Eloisa.

Ability. See MORAL ABILITY.

Abraham. See BIOGRAPHY, FAITH OF THE PATRIARCHS, OFFERING OF ISAAC, PATRIARCHS.
Benson's (C.) Lectures. Lect. 14, 15.
Beza's Tragedy of Abraham.
Blunt's Lectures on the hist. of Abraham.
Bowdler's (Tho.) Sermons.
Buddicom's Friendship with God. (40 sermons on the life of Abraham.)
Calvin's Sermons.
Conybeare's (Bp.) Sermons.
Cooper's (E.) Sermons.
Gilbank's Scripture hist. of Abraham.
Gilfillan's Alpha and Omega. Chap. 8.
Jebb's (Bp.) Sermons.
Macduff's Sunsets on the Hebrew mountains.
Milner's (Joseph) Sermons.
Secker's (Abp.) Sermons.
Short's (William) Sermons.
Stebbing's Hist. of A. and its meaning.
Thompson's (F. E.) Lent lectures.
Warburton's Divine legation of Moses.
Wilson's (Tho.) Sermons.

Abipones. See MISSIONS.
Dobrizhofferi Historia de Abiponibus. (Highly praised by SOUTHEY.)
Peramas de Vita sex sacerdotum Paraguay.
Dobrizhoffer's Account of the Abipones: tr. by Mrs. S. H. Coleridge.
The same: tr. by Dr. Southey, 1822.

Abrahamic Covenant. See INFANT BAPTISM.
Limborchii Theologia.
Witsii Economia Fœderis.

Abrahamic Covenant—*continued.*
Barrington's (J. S.) Theological works.
Bowden's Covenant right of infants.
Buddicom's Friendship with God.
Gregg on Infant church-membership.
Janeway on the Abr. covenant.
Kelly's (John) Congregational lectures.
Maye's Technobaptist.
MacKnight on the Abrahamic covenant.
Presbyterian Review. 3: 529.
Taylor on the Covenant of grace.
Watt's Harm. of the Div. dispensations.
Worcester on the Abr. covenant.

Abrahamists. See PAULICIANS.

Abrogation of the Ceremonial Law. See CEREMONIAL LAW.
Bialloblotsky de Legibus Mosaicæ.
Limborchii Collatio cum Tryphone.
Benson's (Dr. Geo.) Critical dissertations.
Berriman's Boyle lectures. 1831.
Hooker's Ecclesiastical polity.
Jeacock's Vindic. of the Apostle Paul.
Jennings' Jewish Antiquities.
Leland's Answer to Morgan.
Priestley's Letters to the Jews.
Sykes on Christianity.
Warburton's Julian.
Witsius on the Covenants.

Absolution. See AURICULAR CONFESSION, POPERY.
Cladenius de Natura absolutionis.
Hannekenii Dissertationes.
Krackewitzii Absolutio ministeriali.
Luther (M.) von dem Schlüssen.
Pfaffii Dissertationes.
Quistorpii Dissertationes.
Schubert's Erlautertes nein auf die frage.
Wernsdorfii Dissertationes.
Allen's (Will.) Defence of the power of the priesthood to forgive sins.
Andrews' (Lancelot) Sermons.
Burton's Bampton lectures. 1829.
Church Review. 2: 573.
Luther (M.) on the Use of the Keys.
Maskell's Doctrine of Church of England.
Salter's Hall Sermons. Ser. by Burroughs.

Abstinence. See FASTING, MODERATION.

Abstinence from Blood. See PROHIBITION.

Acacians. See EUTYCHIANS.

Acephali. See MONOPHYSITES.

Acquaintance with God.

Atterbury's (Bp.) Sermons.
Beveridge's (Bp.) Sermons.
Blunt's (Henry) Sermons.
Dalgleish's (Wm.) Sermons.
D'Oyly's (George) Sermons.
Girdlestone's (Chas.) Sermons.
Hampden's (R. D.) Sermons.
Hinton's (J. H.) Sermons.
Sanderson's (Bp.) Sermons.
Sherman's Guide to Acquaintance with God.
Van Mildert's (Bp.) Sermons.

Adamites.

Augustinus de Hæresiis.
Epiphanius de Hæresiis.
Baronii Annales ecclesiastici.
Evagrii Historia ecclesiastici. L. 1, c. 21.

Adessenarians. See CONSUBSTANTIATION.

Adiaphorists. See GOOD WORKS, INTERIM.

Aepini Epistola a. Joach. Westphalo.
Andreæ Forum Adiaphorum.
Bachmeisteri Acta Philipica.
Amsdorf's Kunstliche, spætische, &c., oration.
Flacius Leipsiger interim, mit scholien.
——— Scripta duorum doctorum.
——— Omnia Latina scripta contra A.
Galli (N.) Disputationes.
——— Erklarung d. religious treite, &c.
Melanothonis (P.) Doctrina de pœnitentia.
Pfeffingerus de Traditionibus et ceremoniis.
Schmid (C. F.) Observ. ad naturam peccati.
Schmid's (K. E. C.) Untersuch. philos. theol.
Westphali (Joach.) Opera.
Plank's History of Protestant theology.
Ranke's History of the Reformation.
Wirth's System of speculative ethics.

See list of writers in FLACIUS, above cited.

Admonition. See REPROOF.

Blair's (James) Sermons.
Edward's (Bp.) Works.
Hamilton on Zeal.
Hammond on Friendly Correction.
Hopkins' (Ezek.) Miscellaneous Sermons.

Adoptians. See HERESY.

Alexandri (Natalis) Dissertationes.
Bassnage (Benj.) Observationes.
Dorner's Entwicklunggeschichte der person Christi.
Mabillonii Observationes.
Trellendus de Felicis et Elipandi errore.
Voightii Bibliotheca.
Walchii (C. G. F.) Historia Adoptiniarum.

For a full literary history of the controversy, see WALCH, as above.

Adoption.

Brackenbury's (Edward) Discourses.
Charnock's Works.
Cotton's (Rich. L.) Sermons.
Dwight's Discourses. Disc. 82.
Flavel's Works.
Kattern's (Dan.) Sermons.
Kollock's (Shepard K.) Sermons.
Oram's (Will.) Discourses.
Stewart's (James H.) Sermons.
Witsius on the Covenants.
Walton (Dan.) on the Witness of the Spirit.

Adultery. See COMMANDMENTS, CONCUPISCENCE, UNCLEANNESS.

Augustin de adulterinis conjugiis.
Brackenbury's (Edward) Sermons.
Burnaby's (And.) Sermons and charges.
Burnet (Bp.) Sermons.
[Comber's] Inquiry into the cause of the prevalence of adultery at the present time, (1810. Written under the name of Philaretes.)
Dwight's (Timothy) Discourses. (Powerful.)
Evans' (Dr. John) Sermons.
Foster's (Dr. James) Sermons.
Hall's (Bp.) Practical works.
Hopkins' (Bp.) Sermons.
McLean's Apostolical commission.
Morgan (H. D.) on Adultery and Divorce.
Paley's Moral Philosophy.
Parsons on the Catechism.
Reynolds' God's revenge against adultery.
Secker (Abp.) on the Catechism.
Smith's (Sydney) Sermons.
Tebbs' Scr. doct. of adultery and divorce.
Whitaker's (Edw. W.) Sermons.
Wollaston's Religion of nature. Sect. 6.

Advancement of Society. See HUMAN PROGRESS.

Advent of Christ. See INCARNATION, JESUS CHRIST, BIRTH OF, NATIVITY.

Adversity. See AFFLICTION.

Advocacy of the Spirit. See HOLY SPIRIT, OPERATIONS.

Arnold de Sp. S. in oratione fidelium efficaci.
Guntherus de Clamore Sp. S. in cordibus.
Hoepfner de Advocatione Spiritus Sancti.
Jockius de Spiritu precum.
Ketner de Advocatione majestica et gemitu ineffabili Spiritus Sancti.
Velthemius de Gemitu Spiritus Sancti.
Wendlerus de Sp. S. pro sanctis intercessione.

Æons. See BASILIDIANS, GNOSTICS.

Aëtians. See EUNOMIANS.

Affection. See BROTHERLY LOVE, FRIENDSHIP

Affections. See PASSIONS.

Amer. Bib. Repos. 3d series. 2 : 445.
Blackwood's Magazine. 33 : 124, 391.
Buckminster's (Joseph S.) Sermons.
Edwards on the Religious affections.

Maclauren's Essays.
Pike and Hayward's cases of conscience.
Sharp's (Abp.) Sermons.
Tottie's Sympathizing Affections.

Affiliation of Languages. See ORIGIN OF LANGUAGES, PHILOLOGY.

Adelungii Mithridates. ("One of the most learned and valuable works of the age.") BALBI. 1806–1817.
Balbi, Atlas ethnographique du globe.
Bopp's Vergleichende grammatik. (Traces the European languages to the Sanscrit.)
Chamberlainii's Oratio Dominica. (A survey of very many languages, with valuable dissertations.)
Cluverii Germania antiqua.
Crucigori Harmonia linguarum.
Denina, la Clef des lang. (European only.)
Eichoff, Parallèle des lang. de l'Europe et de l'Inde. (Very learned.)
Engelmann's Bibliothek der neuerin sprachen. (Finnish, Icelandic, Albanian, Hungarian, &c.)
Gebelin, Histoire de la parole.
Hennequin, sur l'analogie des langues.
Henselii Philologia universa.
Hornemanni Observ. de harmonia linguarum Orientalium, Ebraicæ, Syriacæ, Chaldaicæ, et Arabicæ.
Hottingeri Etymologicum Orientale.
Humbolt's Kawi-sprache auf d. Java.
Klaprothii Asia polyglotta.
——— Apperçu de origine des diverses ecritures de l'ancien monde. (Two noble works.)
Kuhn und Schleicher's Vergleichden sprachforschung auf dem Gebeite der Arischen, Celtischen, und Slawischen sprachen.
Pileur, Tableaux synoptiques.
Krusenstern's Worter-sammlungen. (Asia and America.)
Leibnitz, de Variis linguis.
Maupertius Réflexions philosophique.
Memoires de la Société Ethnologique.
Meriam, Principes de l'etude comparatif des langage.
Morini (S.) Exercitationes.
Nicholson de Universis orbis linguis.
Pallas, Ling. totius orbis vocabularia.
Potts' Etymologische forschuchungen, &c.
Relandi Ægyptiaca.
Stephan, Conformitè du langue Françoais avec le Grec.
Surenhusii Dissertationes.

Adelung's general survey of languages.
American Institute of Instruction Period. Boston. (Many good articles.)
Bibliotheca Marsdeniana. (A catalogue of books and manuscripts, with vocabularies; collected for the purpose of comparing languages.)
Bibliotheca Sacra. 14 : 753. 15 : 543.
Bunsen's (Chev.) Philos. of history, as applied to languages.

Affiliation of Languages—*continued.*

Craik's Characteristics of the leading lang. of Asia and Europe.
Cramp's Philosophy of language.
Edinburg Review. 51 : 529.
Fearn's Analysis of language.
Foreign Quart. Rev. 1 : 377, 2 : 475.
Forster's One primæval lang. traced through ancient inscriptions. Plates.
——— Sinai photographed. (Appendix.)
Fry's Pantographia. (Copies all the known alphabets.)
Gyll (G. W. J.) on Language.
Higgins on Nations, languages, &c.
Jamieson's Hermes Scythicus. (Origin and affinities of the languages of Asia and Europe. Plates.)
Jones' (Rowland) Origin of languages, hieroglyphically, etymologically, and topographically defined.
Kennedy's Origin and affinities of the principal languages. (Many plates of alphabets and fac-similes.)
Llewellyn's Remarks on the English lang.
McPherson's Philological system.
——— Japhetic languages.
Malcom's Antiquities of Britain and Ireland. (Traces an affinity between the languages of the ancient Britons, and that of the Americans at the isthmus of Darien.)
Monthly Review. 117 : 143.
Minsher's Guide into tongues.
Müller's (Max) Science of language.
Murray's (A.) Affinities of the Teutonic, Greek, Celtic, Sclavonic, and Indian languages.
New York Review. 1 : 109.
Nolan's Harmonial Grammar.
Parsons' (J.) Remains of Japhet. Plates. (European languages.)
Piries' Dissertation on Hebrew roots.
Proceedings of the Lond. Philosoph. Soc.
Quarterly Review. 10 : 250. 14 : 128.
Sharp's (Gregory) Origin, division, and relation of languages.
Southern Lit. Messenger. 14 : 521.
Trench (R. C.) on the Study of words.
Weston's (S.) Conformity of European languages, especially the English, with the Oriental.
Winning's Comparative philology. (Comprises all Indo-European languages, according to Bopp and Pott.)

Affliction. See BEREAVEMENT, COMFORT, CONTENTMENT, MOURNERS, PATIENCE, RESIGNATION, SICKNESS, TROUBLE.

Drelincourt, les Visites charitables.

Allestree's (Rich.) Sermons.
Alexander's (J. W.) Discourses.
Addington on Affliction.
Ambrose's Looking to Jesus.
Anderson's (James) Light in Darkness.
Arnold's (Tho.) Sermons.
Atterbury's (Francis) Sermons.

Affliction—*continued.*

Ball's Power of godliness.
Baxter's Directions for spiritual comfort.
Beddome's (Benj.) Village Sermons.
Berens' (Edw.) Sermons for the sick.
Berriman's (Wm.) Sermons.
Bethune's Word to the afflicted.
Black's (David) Sermons.
Blair's (James) Sermons.
Blundell's (Tho.) Sermons.
Bolton's Instructions for right comforting.
Boston's Crook in the lot. (Excellent.)
Bradley's (Cha.) Sermons.
Brady's (N.) Sermons.
Brookes' Mute Christian.
Brown's (J.) Heart's ease in trouble.
Buchanan's (J.) Comfort in affliction.
———— Improvement of affliction.
Buddicom's Practical Sermons.
Bull's (Bp.) Sermons.
Bundy's (R.) Sermons. (Instructive.)
Burder's (Henry F.) Sermons.
Butcher's (Edm.) Sermons.
Butler's (Alban) Sermons.
Capp's Devotional discourses.
Carrington's Temporal afflictions advantageous.
Carr's (George) Sermons.
Case's (Tho.) Correction instruction.
Charnock's Works.
Clarke's (Dr. Sam.) Sermons.
Christian Observer. 11:203.
Close's (F.) Sermons.
Cooper's (E.) Sermons.
Cunningham's (J. W.) Sermons.
Dealtry's (Will.) Sermons.
Delme's Christian under affliction.
Donne's (J.) Sermons.
Dodd's Comfort to the afflicted.
Drysdale's (Dr. John) Sermons.
Dykes' Two treatises on Philemon.
Fisk's (Geo.) Sermons.
Farrington's Sermons.
Fell's (Hunter F.) Sermons.
Fiddes' (Rich.) Sermons.
Franklin's (T.) Sermons. (Excellent.)
Froude's (Rich. H.) Sermons.
Fuller's Tract for the afflicted.
Gahan's (Will.) Sermons.
Gardner's Memoirs of tried Christians.
Gilpin's (Rich'd) Sermons.
Girdlestone's (Cha.) Sermons.
Grotius' Mourner comforted.
Greenham's Comfort and cure of the afflicted.
Hacket's (Bp.) Christian consolations.
Hale's (Sir M.) Contemplations.
Hall's (Bp.) Practical works.
Hickman's (Bp.) Sermons.
Hale's (James) Sermons.
Hill's (John) "Is it well?"
Holdsworth's (R.) Sermons.
Hooker's Four treatises.
Hopkins' (Bp.) Works.
Horne's (T. H.) Manual for the afflicted.
Howard's (Leonard) Sermons.
Hunter's Sermons.

Affliction—*continued.*

Howe's (John) Sermons.
Hutchinson's (Roger) Works.
Hurd's (Bp.) Sermons.
Jay's (Wm.) Sermons.
Johnson's (John) Sermons.
Joles' Word to afflicted consciences.
Jones' (Will., of Nayland) Sermons.
Jortin's (Dr. John) Sermons.
Kemp's (Henry W.) Sermons.
Kennaway's Sermons.
Kennedy's Comfort to the afflicted.
Kirwan's (W. B.) Sermons.
Knowles' (Jas.) Sermons for families.
Lavington (John) on the 77th Psalm.
Major's Honey on the rod. (Small, but sweet.)
Mannering's Christian consolation.
Manning's (H. E.) Thoughts for mourners.
Mant's (Bp.) Sermons.
Masillon's Sermons.
Mede's (Bp.) Sermons.
Morehead's (R.) Discourses. Dis. 19 and 20.
Murray's (L.) Power of religion.
Newman's (J. H.) Sermons.
Pearce's (Bp.) Sermons.
Penn's (Will.) No cross, no crown.
Pierson's Expos. of Psalms 27, 84, 85, and 87.
Quarle's Judgment and mercy.
Richardson on Religious conversation.
Russel's Letters, practical and consolatory.
Rutherford's Letters. (A treasure.)
Sanderson's (Bp.) Sermons.
Scattergood's (Sam.) Sermons.
Seed's (Jer.) Sermons.
Sheddan's Blessings in disguise.
Shuttleworth's (P. N.) Sermons.
Sibb's Bruised reed.
——— Soul's comfort.
Smallbridge's (Bp.) Sermons.
Smith's (D.) Chamber of affliction.
Smith's (Henry) Sermons.
Smith's (Theyre) Sermons.
Stennet's (Sam.) Sermons.
Sumner's (Bp.) Sermons.
Tappan's Sermons.
Taylor's (Jer.) Sermons.
Thelwell's Thoughts in affliction.
Thornton's (J.) Christian consolation.
Townsend's (Geo.) Sermons.
Vidal's (Bp.) Sermons.
Vincent on Affliction.
Walker's (T. H.) Companion for the afflicted.
Waples' Sermons.
Warren's (Sam.) Sermons.
Watson's Divine cordial.
Willison's Afflicted man's companion.
Yonge's (James) Sermons. Second series.
Young's (R.) Counter poysen; or soverain antidote against all griefe.

Agapæ. See LOVE FEASTS.

Aged. See OLD AGE.

Age of the World. See COSMOLOGY, CREATION, GEOLOGY, HARMONY OF SCIENCE AND RELIGION.

Agonistici. See DONATISTS.

Agur's Prayer. See POVERTY, RICHES.

Agar's (Wm.) Sermons.
Brady's (Nich.) Sermons.
Brown's (Will. Laurence) Sermons.
Brownrig's (Bp.) Sermons.
Burnet's (Gilbert) Sermons.
Carr's (Geo.) Sermons.
Carter's (Benj.) Sermons.
Cosins' (Dr. John) Sermons.
Fidde's (Rich.) Sermons.
Foster's (James) Sermons.
Hart's (Abp.) Sermons.
Harvest's (Geo.) Sermons.
Heylin's (John) Sermons. (2 on this subject.)
Hoadley's (Bp.) Sermons.
Horts' (Josiah) Sermons.
Jortin's (John) Sermons.
Kidder's (Bp.) Sermons.
Laurie's (Dr. Tho.) Sermons.
Mede's Works.
Morning Exercises at Cripplegate. Vol. 3. (Sermon by John Oakes.)
Newton's (Bp.) Dissertations.
Roger's (John) Sermons.
Smith's (James) Sermons.
Stebbings' (H.) Sermons.
Zollikoffer's Sermons on prevalent errors.

Albanenses. See MANICHEES.

Albigenses. See WALDENSES.

Barrau et Daragon, Hist. des croisades contre les Albigeois.
Benoit, Histoire des Albigeois. To 1690.
Chassanion, Histoire des Albigeois.
Chatel, Histoire de Languedoc.
Fauriel, Hist. de la croisade contre les heretiques Albigeois.
Gay, Hist. des schismes et hérésies.
Langlois, Hist. des croisades contre les A.
Limborchii Codex Inquisitione Tolosanæ.
Lucas, de Altera vita.
Parctelaine, Hist. de la guerre contre les A.
Perrin, Hist. des Vaudois et Albigeois.
Petri, Hist. A. et belli in eos, A. D. 1209. (Bitter.)
Sernay, Histoire des Albigeois.
Tillet, Hist. de la guerre contre les A.

Allix's History of Piedmont.
Baird's (Robt.) Hist. of the Albigenses.
Blackwood's Magazine. 52:534.
Jones' Church History.
Maitland's Hist. of the ancient Albigenses.
Maturin's History of the Albigenses.
Morland's Evang. Churches of Piedmont. 1658.
Monthly Review. 106:170.
Sismondi's Crusades against the Albigenses in the 13th century.

Aleim. See ELOHIM.

Alexandrian Version. See SEPTUAGINT.

Allegory. See FIGURATIVE LANGUAGE.

Almost Christian. See DECISION, INDECISION.

Almsgiving. See PAUPERISM.

Ambrose, Lectiones variæ.
Chrysostom, Homiliæ.
Cyprian, Opera. (De opere.)

Baumgarten's Versuch über die apostelg.
Hiffling's Lehre die altest.

Barrow's (Dr. Isaac) Sermons.
Bennet on Christian charity.
Beveridge's (Bp.) Sermons.
Blackall's (Offspring) Sermons.
Bosanquet's Rights of the poor
Butler's (Alban) Sermons.
Chalmer's Sufficiency of the parochial system.
Christian Observer. 13:695.
Fowle's (J. W.) Sermons.
Frier's Advocate of the poor.
Fuller's (And.) Miscellaneous works.
Girdlestone's (Cha.) Parochial sermons.
Gouge's Surest and safest way of thriving.
Hicks' (Dr. Geo.) Sermons.
Hertzog's Real encyclopedia. (Able article.)
Horseley's (Bp.) Sermons.
Johnson's (Dr. Sam.) Sermons.
Kidder's (Bp.) Charity directed.
Massilons' Sermons.
Munkhouse's (R.) Occasional discourses.
Nicholson's (Will.) Sermons.
Paley's Moral philosophy.
Pascall's Provincial letters.
Saurin's Sermons.
Stebbing's Sermons. Ser. on 1 John 3:17.
Taylor's (John) Sermons.
Tennison's Discretion in giving alms.

Altars.

Heylin's Antidotum Lincolniense.
Mede's (Jos.) Discourses.
Owen's (Jas.) History of the consecration of altars, temples, and churches.
Pecklington's Dead vicar's plea.
Thorndike's Treatises relating to the Ch.
Williams' (Bp.) Holy table.

Ambition. See LOVE OF PRAISE.

Bourdaloue, Sermons. (Dimanches.)
Abercrombie's Philosophy of the moral feelings. Part 1, Sec. 1.
Chalmer's (Thomas) Sermons.
Christian Observer. 17:517.
Dwight's Sermons. Sermon 132.
Enfield's (Will.) Sermons.
Munkhouse's (Rich.) Practical sermons.
Smith on the Love of praise.
Webb's (F.) Sermons.

Ambrose.

Ambrosii Opera, ab Codices Vaticanos, &c. Studio Benedictini.
Baronii (C.) Vita Ambrosii.
Bartholomæ Milleloquium.
Bohringer, Kirchengesch in biographien.

Costerii Vita Ambrosii.
Erasmi Prefatio ad Ambrosii opera.
Heinze's Beschr. d bücher A. de officiis.
Hermance, Vie de Saint Ambrose.
Marcelli Oratio de Ambrosio.
Michelseni de A. fidei adv. Arianos vindice.
Paulini Vita Sanctæ Ambrosii. (This life is prefixed to the famous Benedictin Edition of the works of Saint Ambrose.)

Ammonians. See NEOPLATONISM.

Amos. See BIOGRAPHY.

Michaelis Dissertationes.

Amusements. See DANCING, PLEASURE, RECREATION, SOBRIETY, STAGE PLAYS.

Barbeyrac, Questions de droit morale.
Thiers (J. B.), Divertissements qui peuvent etre permis.
Witting, Ueber das Kartenspiel.

Anderson's (Geo.) Use and abuse of diversions. 1733.
Bedell's (Greg. T.) Renunciation of worldly amusements.
Bourdaloue, Sermons. (3 on this subject.)
Burton's Anatomy of melancholy. Part 3.
Burder's (George) Sermons.
Christian Examiner. 8 : 201. 45 : 157.
Combe on Health.
Declaration of King James, concerning lawful sports on Sunday. (Recommends dancing, vaulting, &c. &c.)
[Gilpin] on the Amusements of clergymen.
Grove's (Henry) Sermons and tracts.
Henry (Tho. C.) on the Consistency of popular amusements with a profession of Christianity.
Hill's (R.) Warning to professors.
Jebbs' (Bp.) Works.
More (Hannah) on Education.
Northbroke on Dicing, dancing, plays, &c. (An interesting work, giving a large insight into the manners of his age. 1579.)
Paley's (William) Sermons.
Porteus' (Bp.) Sermons.
Seed's (Jeremiah) Sermons.
Smith's (Sam. Stanhope) Sermons.
Stillingfleet's (Edward) Sermons.
Strutt's Sports of England, from the earliest times to the present, 1810. 40 plates.
Thompson on Fashionable amusements.
Wesley's (John) Sermons.
Woodward on Preaching against amusements.
Zollikoffer's (George J.) Sermons.

Anabaptists. See BAPTISTS, MENNONITES, MUNZER, SECTS.

Pro.

Menno Simonis Opera theologica.
Munzer's Ordnung des deutschen amts zu alsted.
——— Testificatio.
——— Deutsche evangelische messe.

Anabaptists—*continued.*

Kiffin's Reasons of the Anabaptists for their separation.
——— Right to church communion.
Stennet's Answer to Russen's Anabaptists.

Con.

Botsaccus' Wiederlefung der wiedertäufferischen lehre.
Bullinger, adv. omnia Catabaptistarum.
——— Widertäufferen; ursprung, furgang, Secten, wasen, artickel, &c. 1561.
Cloppenburgii Gangrena theologiæ.
Calvin, Instruction contre les Anabapt.
Gebser de Primordiis studior. Anab. Sæc. 16.
Hoornbeckii Summa controversiarum.
Hortensius (L.) de Anabaptistis.
John a Lasco, Defensio, &c. (Reply to Menno.)
Klupfelii Institutiones theologicæ. Par. 2.
Melancthonis Corpus doctrinæ theol.
Menius' vom Geist der Wiedertäuffer.
Müller's Wiedertäuffer irthum.
Pantheon, Anabaptisticum et enthusiasticum. (Includes Venner, Peters, Cromwell, Hobbes, Fludd, Naylor, &c.)
Spanheimii (Fred.) Disputationes.
Ulrich's Christlichen ermahnung aus Gottes wort.
Vandervelde, les Anabaptistes—les Hussites.
Vossenhol's Gesprache mit d. Wiederdöperen.
Wigandi Refutatio dogm. Anabaptistarum.
Wills' Geschichte de Deutchland.
Zuingle de Officio concionandi.
——— Elenchus in Catabapt. strophas.

Asheton's Conference with an Anabaptist.
Bullinger's Counter-poyson.
——— Dialogue between an Anabaptist and a Christian.
Calvin's Miscellaneous works.
Russel's Fundamentals without a foundation.
Whitgift's (Abp.) Works.

Beside the books written professedly against the Anabaptists, their tenets are unfavcrably discussed in the works of Luther, Calvin, Melancthon, Œcopampadius, Guy de Bres, Hunnius, Osiander, &c.

Anabaptists, History of.

Bullinger's Wiedertäuffern. ursprung, &c.
Bussiere, Histoire de Luthéranisme.
Catrou, Hist. des A. et leur opinions.
Fuszlin's Kirch d. Schweizerlands.
Gobil's Geschichte der Wiedertäufer.
Harenburgii Historia Anabaptistica.
Hast's Geschichte der Wiedertäuffer.
Heresbachii Historia Anabaptistica.
Kessenbroick's Gesch. d. Wied. zur Munster.
Krohn's Gesch. der fanat. Wiedertäufer.
Meshow, Histoire des Anabaptistes.
Modæus de Initiis sectæ Anabaptistarum.
Nibsert's Urkunden zur gesch. der Wiedert.
Ottii Hist. universalis de Anabaptist.
Schyn, Historia Christianorum.

Anabaptists, History of—*continued.*

Spanheim, de Origine, progressu, &c.
Starcke's Taufe und Taufgesinnten.
Wills' Gesch. des Anabapt. Deutschland.
Winter's Gesch. der Wiedert. in 16 Jahr.

Baum's Life of Beza.
Benedict's History of the Baptists.
Henry's Life of John Calvin.
Herzog's Life of Œcolampadius.
Motley's Dutch Republic. (Fair and candid.)
Robinson's (Robt.) Eccles. researches.

These are all, with a few exceptions, opponents of the Anabaptists. Many more have written their history in a spirit equally bitter.

Analogy of Faith.

Buchanan's Analogy as a guide to truth.
Govet's Gospel analogies.
Horne's Introduction to the S. Script.

Analogy of Religion to Nature.
See CHRISTIANITY ADAPTED TO MAN, PHILOSOPHY OF RELIGION, NATURAL RELIGION, LAW OF NATURE.

Schmitz's Religion u. die naturforschung.

Adam's (A.) Arrangement of passages, &c.
Barton's Anal. of Div. wisdom to the natural, moral, and spiritual worlds.
Baseley's Glory of the heavens.
Brown (Bp. Peter) on Things divine.
Budinger's (M.) Way of faith.
Burnet's (C. M.) Power and goodness of God.
Butler's Analogy of religion and nature. (Edited, with notes, conspectus, and index, by Howard Malcom.)
Christian Examiner. 61 : 321.
Gabel's Accordance of religion with nature.
Graves' (Dr. Richard) Sermons.
Grinfield's Connection of nat. and rev. relig.
Hampden's Philos. evidence of Christianity.
Mill's Bampton lectures.
Morehead's (Robert) Dialogues.
Owen's (Henry) Sermons.
Parkinson's Hulsean lecture. 1837.
Powell (Baden) Connection of natural and divine truth.
Ragg's Creation's testimony to its God.
Reid's (Tho.) Works. Essay 1. Chap. 1.
Shuttleworth's Consist. of rev. with reason.
Valpy on the Course of nature.
Wood's Bampton lectures. 1838.

Analyses of the Bible.
See INTRODUCTIONS.

Cornis Pomphearium. (A digest of the whole Bible under alphabetical heads.)
Griesbachii Synopsis evangeliorum.
Heideggeri Enchiridion biblicum. (A minute analysis of each book.)
Kahl's Biblisch real concordanz.
Marlorati Thesaurus.
Musculi Loci communes. ("Opus divinum." —ADAM.)

Analyses of the Bible—*continued.*

Perkinsii Specimen digesta.
Van Till, Opus analyticum.

Adam's (A.) Passages under distinct heads.
Bird's Texts, arranged according to their tenor.
Bogart's Threats and punishments of Scrip.
Budinger's (M.) Way of faith.
Burnet's Analysis of the New Testament.
Butcher's (E.) Holy Scriptures methodized.
Clarke's (Sam.) Christian's inheritance. (Commonly called "Clarke on the promises." A favorite little manual of devotion.)
Craddock's Hist. of the O. Test. methodized.
Cruden's Compend of the Bible. (A conspectus of each chapter.)
Dale's Analysis of all the epistles.
Dodd's (W.) Commonplace book.
Eadie's Analytical concordance.
Farrand's Christian system.
Gaston's Collection of texts. (Needed by every minister.)
Gastrel's Christian institutes.
Inglis' (James) Bible cyclopædia.
Jones' (Jos.) Analytical view of the Bible.
Knight's (W.) Axiomatical concordance.
Latham's (H.) Harmonia Paulina. (A system of Divinity in the language of Paul.)
Locke's (John) Commonplace book.
Lloyd's (Bp.) Index to the Bible.
Longhurst's Companion to the New Test.
Martin's (R. M.) Social duty of man.
Maurice's Unity of the New Testament.
Musculus' Commonplaces.
Neligan's (James) Bible in miniature.
Pilkington's Rational concordance.
Pinnock's Analysis of Scripture history.
Priestley's (Jos.) Index to the Bible.
Roes' Analytical arrang. of the Scriptures.
Sarcerus' Commonplaces tr. by R. Taverner.
Shaw's Heads of relig. in the words of S. S.
Stroud's (Wm.) Analytical index to the Gospels and Acts.
Strutt's Commonplace book. (Recent editions are much improved, and are truly valuable.)
Talbot's Analysis. (Scarce, and well deserves to be re-printed.)
Townsend's Chronological arrangement.
Warden's Digest of the system of religion in the express words of S. Sc. ("Executed with singular ability."—HORNE.)
West's Complete anal. (Many editions.)
Wheeler's Analysis and summary. (With notes; Historical, Geographical, an. Antiquarian.)
Whewell's Analogy of the O. and N. Test.
Wilson's (H. B.) Index to the Bible.
Wirgman's Divarication of the N. Test into doctrine and history.

Anarchy. See CIVIL GOVERNMENT.

Mudges' (Zech.) Sermons.

Ancient Armor. See ARMOR, ARCHÆOLOGY, BIBLICAL HISTORY.

Ancient History. See ARCHÆOLOGY, BABYLON, CHRISTIAN ANTIQUITIES, EGYPT, JEWISH ANTIQUITIES, ORIGIN OF NATIONS, &C.

Andrew, Life of.

Hammerschmidii Cruciger apostolicus.
Hanckii Dissertationes.
Lemmii Memoria.
Saussay de Gloria sancti Andreæ apostoli.
Woogius de Martyris S. Andreæ.

Angel of the Covenant. See LOGOS, JESUS.

Markii Dissertationes Sacræ.
Witsii Economia Fœderis.

Barrington on the Divine dispensations.
Clarke on the Trinity.
Fleming's Christology.
Lowman's Civil govern. of the Hebrews.
Tennison on Idolatry.
Tompkins' Sober appeal.

Angels. See APPARITIONS, CHERUB, MINISTERING SPIRITS, GUARDIAN.

Augustini Opera.
Blasche's Kritik. d. modernen geisterglaub.
Brochmandi (C. E.), Dissertationes. (Good and bad angels, their fall, &c.)
Carpzovii varia Historia angelorum, ex Epiphania et aliorum.
Casmani (Otto) Angelographia. ("Curious.")
Clotzii (Stephan.) Angelographia.
Cotta (Jo. Frider.) Disputationes. Disp. 2.
Dionysius (Areop.) de Celesti hierarchia.
Dorchii Singularium angelic. septenarius.
Eisemenger's Entdecktes Judenthum.
Eusebii Preparatio evangelica.
Fabricii Dissertationes sacræ.
Gfrorer's Jahrenhundert des heils.
Hackspanii Disput. theol. et philologicæ.
Heideggeri (Joan. Henric.) Disputationes.
Horst (G. K.) Theurgie.
Huetius in Origianis.
Keil, Opuscula academica.
Krug (W. T.) über die geisterwelt.
Limborchii Theologia Christiana.
Loersii (J. Ch.) Dissertationes.
Marckii Diss. ad selectos textos Vet. Test.
Maimonides de fundamen. legis. Cap. xi.
Ode, Commentarius de angelis. (A scholarly work, in which, whatever is said on the subject, in the Scriptures, classics, rabbins, and modern authors, is collected.)
Petavius de Angelis, bonis et malis.
Platinæ Prelectiones theologicæ.
Remigii Demonolatria.
Schmidii (Sebastian.) in Senario angelico.
Schulthess' Engelwelt, engelgesetz, &c.
Spanheimii Disputationes theologicarum.
Suiceri Thesaurus.
Stilling's (Jung) Theorie der Geisterkunde.
Stuckii (T. G.) Meditationes.

Angels—*continued.*

Vitus de Corporibus angelorum.
Voetii Disputationes theologicæ.

Arnold's (Thomas) Sermons.
Barrow's (Isaac) Works.
Baxter's (Richard) Works.
Biblical Repository. Vol. 12.
Bibliotheca Sacra. 1:88. 2:108.
Blundel's (Thomas) Sermons.
Bull's (Bp.) Sermons.
Calmet's Preface to Gospel of Luke.
Camfield's (Benj.) Discourses.
Charnock's Works.
Conybeare's (John) Discourses.
Clayton's (Geo.) Angelology. (Agency, rank, titles, characteristics, residence, employment, &c.)
Doddridge's Lectures. Lect. 210 to 214.
Dwight's Discourses. Disc. 18 and 19.
Edward's (Bp.) Works.
Farmer's Dissertation on miracles.
Franklin's (Tho.) Sermons.
Gale's Court of the Gentiles.
Gill's Body of Divinity.
Gilpin on Temptation.
Hall's (Robt.) Notes of sermons.
Hammond's (Henry) Works.
Heber's (Bp.) Sermons.
Horne's (Bp.) Sermons.
Horts' (Josiah) Sermons.
Killen's our Companions in glory.
Lawrence on our Communion and war with angels.
Mason's (Wm.) on Paul's use of the word angel.
Mede's Works. (Apostacy of latter times.)
Newton's (Bp.) Dissertations.
Reynolds' Economy of the angelic worlds.
Ridgeley's Body of Divinity.
Robinson's Scripture characters.
Salkeld's Treatise on angels.
Sanderson on the Nature, office, &c.
Saunder's Pneumatologia.
Scattergood's (Sam.) Sermons.
Shepard's (T.) Sermons. (Several on this subject.)
Simpson (T.) on the Nature of angels.
Steir's Words of the angels.
Stuart's (M.) Sketches. (Bibl. Sacra, No. 1.)
Timson's Angels of God, their nature, &c.
Wesley's (John) Sermons.
Whateley's Scriptural review concerning a future state.
——— on Good and evil angels.
Wheeler's (Prof. B.) Theological lectures.
Wilkin's World in the moon.

Angelolatria. See WORSHIP OF ANGELS.

Anger. See FORGIVENESS, HATRED, PASSIONS.

Basilii Homiliæ.

Abernethy's (Bp.) Sermons.
Berens' (Edward) Village sermons.
Blair's (Jas.) Sermons.

Anger—*continued.*

Boston's (Tho.) Sermons.
Burgess' (Dan.) Hastiness to anger disgraced.
Christian Observer. 18:145.
Davies' (Thomas) Sermons.
Fawcett's (Dr. John) Essay on anger.
Felton's (Henry) Sermons.
Foster's (Dr. James) Sermons.
Franklin's (Thomas) Sermons.
Gale's (Dr. John) Sermons. 3 on this subj.
Gilpin's (William) Sermons.
Hale's (Sir M.) Contemplations.
Jortin's (John) Sermons.
Jowett's (Jos.) Fifty-two short sermons.
Mant's (Bp.) Sermons.
Newton's (Bp.) Dissertations.
Paley's Moral philosophy.
Scott's (Thomas) Sermons.
Seed's (Jer.) Sermons.
Secker's (Abp.) Sermons.
Seneca's Morals.
Whitaker's (Edward W.) Sermons.
Wynyard's (J. M.) Sermons on Chris. duties.
Zollikoffer on Festivals and fasts. Vol. 2.

Animal Food, Lawfulness of.

Pro.

Clarke's Origin of evil.
Doddridge's Lectures. Part 3. Prop. 52.
Edinburg Review. 2 : 128.
Fitzosborn's Letters. Letter 8.
Magee on Atonement.
Puffendorf's Law of nations.
Reynold's Letter to a Deist.
Thompson's Seasons. Lines 336 to 378, and 1089 to 1124.

Con.

Cheyne's Philosophical conjectures.
Holwell on the Use of animal food.
Oswald on Animal food.
Ritson's Essays on the use of animal food.

Animal Magnetism. See MESMERISM.

Annihilation of the Wicked. See DESTRUCTIONISTS, IMMORTALITY OF THE SOUL.

Anointing the Sick. See EXTREME UNCTION.

Launoius de Sacramentis. (Gives the statements of many early writers, as to this custom as it existed in the first ages of the church.)

Answers to Prayer. See PRAYER.

Buchanan's Modern atheism. Chap. 5.
Fincher's Achievements of prayer. (Instances answers of prayer from the Bible.)
Goodwin's (Tho.) The return of prayers. (How to discern answers to prayer.)
Harding's (J.) Sermons. (Unanswered prayer.)
King's Origin of evil.
Leechman on Prayer.
Ogden's (S.) Sermons.
Stevenson on Prayer.

Antediluvians. See BIBLICAL HISTORY.

Bebelii Ecclesia, vera et falsa.
Clarkson's (Thomas) Researches.
Hall's (Robert) Notes of sermons.
Winning's Essays on the antediluvian age.

Anthropomorphists. See EXISTENCE OF GOD.

Cyril (Alex.) Κατα ανθρωπομορφιτων.
Schroederi Dissertationes historicæ.
Vogtii Observationes de Audianismo ante Audiam.
Kitto's Journal. 1 : 9.

Antiburghers. See ASSOCIATE CHURCH, CHURCH OF SCOTLAND, SECESSION CHURCH.

Antichrist. See COMMENTATORS ON THE APOCALYPSE, POPERY, PROPHECY, NUMBER 666.

Augustini Opera.
Abboti Demonstratio. (Against Bellarmin.)
Asili Tyrannis Antichristi.
Balduini Diatribe Theologica.
Batti (Bartholom.) Disputationes.
Bocharti Opera. (Dissert. xxviii.)
Cocceji Repetitio locorum V. et N. T. (Great.)
Danæus de Antichristo.
Danhaveri Antichristosophia.
Dorschæi (Jo. Georg.) Dissertationes.
Downami Diatribe de Antichristo.
Du Moulin, Œuvres.
Gerlachii Disput. theologicæ. Dis. xxv.
Gomari (Francisc.) Disputationes.
Grotii Com. ad loca quædam N. Test. quæ de Antichristi agere pertantur.
Gualtheri Homiliæ quinque. (Powerful.)
Heerbrandi (Jacob) Disputationes.
Hippolyti Demonstratio de Antichristo.
Hunnii (Ægid.) Dissertationes.
Huss (Joh.) de Anatomia Antichristi.
Karlii (Bern.) Dissertationes.
Koenigii Antichristus revelatus.
Laurentius, in Hugo Grotio papizante.
Lesii (Leonard.) Opuscula varia.
Luther's (M.) Sammtliche Scriften.
Lyserus (Guil.) de Antichristo.
Maresii Dissertationes. (Against Grotius.)
Nicolai de Mahumate et Pontifice.
——— L'Antiochrist rencontre.
Osiandri Enchiridion controvers. relig.
Rabani Mauri Opera. (His opinion is adopted by Mede, Sir I. Newton, and others.)
Schlichtingii Commentatio in 2 Thess. ii.
Sohnii (Georg.) Opera.
Spanheimii Dissertationes. Par. I.
Thomson (G.), Chasse de la Bete Romaine. (A very ancient and curious work, by a Scotchman.)

Antichrist—*continued.*

Thummii (Theodor.) Opera.
Tilenus de Papa Romana.
Venemæ Prelectio. de methodo prophetica.
Whitakeri (Guil.) Opera.
Wigandi Synopsis Antichristi Romani.
Abbot's Antichrist demonstrated.
Apthorp's Warburton lectures. 1786.
Bagot's Sermons at Lincoln's inn chapel.
Bales' (John) Pageant of Popes.
Barlow's (Bp.) Genuine remains.
Beard's Pope of Rome the true Antichrist.
Blondell's Sibyline oracles.
Bonar's Development of Antichrist.
Brightman on the Apocalypse.
Brown's (J. H.) Character of Antichrist.
Calmet's Dissertations.
Cassel's Christ and Antichrist.
Cunninghame's Apostacy of the ch. of Rome.
Danæus on Antichrist.
Davies' (J.) Two Antichrists. (Infidelity and Romanism.)
Downame (Bp.) on Antichrist.
Elliott's Warburton lectures. 1856.
Faber's (G. S.) Dissertations.
Fleming on the fall of Antichrist.
Frith's (John) Revelation of Antichrist.
Glas' (John) Notes on Scripture texts. (Time of his reign.)
Greenfield's (Edmund) Works.
Gregory's (W.) Trial of Antichrist.
Gault's (R.) Man of sin. Prize essay. 1852.
Gavazzi's Lectures in New York. 1853.
Grotius on Antichrist.
Gualther's Homilies.
Halifax's (Bp.) Sermons.
Hammond's Commentary on Revelations.
Hardy (Sam.) on Prophecy.
Hoffman (Chr.) de Religione Christiana. (Condemned to be burnt.)
Holland on the Revelation of John.
Hurd's (Bp.) Sermons.
Hutchinson's Religion of Satan.
Jewell's Rise and fall of Antichrist.
Jones' (Will.) Church history.
Juriu's Accomplishment of Sc. prophecy.
Keach's (Benj.) Antichrist stormed.
Keith on the Signs of the times.
Knight's Lectures on certain prophecies.
Legget's (Rich.) Evangelical providences.
Limborch's Theology.
——— Reply to Grotius.
Malvenda on Antichrist.
Manton's 18 Sermons on 2 Thess. ii.
Marcus' Reply to Grotius.
Mede on the Apocalypse.
More's Mystery of iniquity.
Morning Exercises at Cripplegate. Vol. 6.
Moseley on the Fall of Babylon.
Nelson's Perfect description of Antichrist. (Makes him to be Oliver Cromwell.)
Ness' Person and period of Antichrist.
Newton (Bp.) on the Prophecies.
Newton (Sir I.) on the Prophecies.
Pike's (J.) Antichrist unmasked.

Antichrist—*continued.*

Quarterly Review. 70:197.
Rabet on the Name and number of the Beast.
Ramsay's (W.) The Lord of Rome the Antichrist, proved from the writings of Solomon and Isaiah.
Richard's (Dr. Wm.) Corruptions of Christianity.
Riland's (John) Antichrist: Papal, Protestant, and Infidel.
Robinson's Premonitions of the doom of Papacy.
Rutherford's Spiritual Antichrist: Opening the Secrets of Familism, Antinomianism, &c. (Describes curious events in New England.)
Sharp's Looking glass for the Pope.
Simpson's Key to the prophecies.
Smith (Ethan) on the Prophecies.
Sohn's True description of Antichrist.
Squire's Exposition of 2 Thess. ii. 2.
[Symson's] Growth of the Roman Antichr.
Taylor (Henry) on the Grand apostacy.
Tazewell on Antichrist. (Maintains him to be the Quakers.)
Todd's (J. H.) Donnellan lectures. 1838.
Tuckney's Prelections.
Warburton's (Bp.) Sermons.
Ward's Three sermons on prophecy.
Whitley's Scheme of prophecy. (Makes Mahomet Antichrist.)
Williams' (Bp.) Antichrist revealed. (Maintains him to be the Presbyterians.)
Winthrop (J.) on Antichrist.

The writers on this subject are a great multitude; the valuable thoughts selected from them all might be contained in half a dozen volumes.

Antimasonry. See FREEMASONRY.

Antinomianism. See GOOD WORKS, IMPUTATION, MORAL ABILITY, PAUL AND JAMES.

*Pro.**

Allen's (John) Spiritual exposition of the Bible.
Agricola (John) on Luke and the 19th Ps.
Archer's (Henry) Works. (Publicly burnt, by order of the Westminster Assembly.)
Brine's Tracts.
Crisp's (Tobias) Sermons. (Great and devout.)
Crisp's (S.) Christ made sin.
Eaton's Honeycomb of free justification. (One of the first, if not the first writer on this side. 1642.)
——— Discovery of a dead faith.
Edwards' (Tho.) Gospel truth.
——— Baxterianism barefaced.

* Those here set down as Antinomians, are so considered by theological writers generally; but no body of Christians accepts this designation.

Antinomianism—*continued.*

Edwards' (Tho.) Review of Crispianism unmasked.
Goodwin's (John) Imputatio fidei.
Hussey's Glory of Christ unveiled. (An able and candid book, strong against Socinians.)
Richardson's Justification by Christ alone.
——— Answer to Holmes.
——— Divine consolations.
Saltmarsh's Free grace.
——— Shadows flying away. (Reply to Gataker.)
——— Smoke in the Temple.
——— Sparkles of glory.
Smith's (Zephaniah) Sermons.
——— Doom of heretics.
Spiritual Magazine. 2:271.
Toplady's Scheme of Christian necessity.
Town's Assertion of grace.
——— Re-assertion of grace.
——— Monomachia.
Twisse's Animadversions on J. Armenius.
——— Vindicat. of grace and providence.
——— Riches of God's love.
——— Treatise on reprobation.
——— on the Scientia Media.
Wilk's Fearless def. of leading doctrines.

Con.

Bullii Defensio fidei Nicænæ.
Hoornbeckii Summa controversia.
Petavii Dogmata.
Witsii Animadversiones Irenicas.
——— de Foedere.

Allen (Thos.) on the Two covenants.
Bates' Observations on important points.
Baxter on Justification and the covenant.
——— on Catholic theology.
Bellamy's Works. (Dialogues, Essays.)
Bull on the Nicene creed.
——— Harmonia apostolica.
Burder's (Sam.) Moral law a rule of life.
Burton's Law and gospel reconciled.
Chase's A. unmasked. (Fine preface by Robert Hall.
Chauncey's Neononianism unmasked.
——— Antidote to Neonomian bane.
Christian Observer. 16:413. 18:531.
Cottle's Strictures on Antinomianism.
Edwards' (Jno.) Crispianism unmasked.
——— (Various other treatises.)
Faber on the Prophecies.
Flavels' Rise and growth of A. errors.
Fletcher's Four checks. (Often reprinted.)
Fuller's (And.) Dialogues. Dial. 7.
——— A. contrasted with the rel. of Scrip.
——— Perpetuity of the moral law.
——— Rule and conduct of believers.
Gataker's A. discovered and confuted.
——— Antidote to error.
——— Shadow without substance.
Geree's Antinomians confuted.
Giles' Antinomian reclaimed.

Antinomianism—*continued.*

Hall's Help to Zion's travellers. (An excellent work for all unlearned Christians.)
Hall's (Robt.) Works.
Hallifax on the Prophecies.
Hampson's Blow at the root of pretended Calvinism.
Hankinson's (Tho. E.) Sermons.
Hardy on the Prophecies.
Hawker's (R.) Portrait of Antinomianism.
Huntingdon's (W.) Lamentations of Satan.
Hutchinson (Mrs.) on Antinomians.
Knollys' (Hanserd) Flaming fire in Zion.
Moore's Mystery of godliness.
Neale's History of the Puritans. Vol. 7.
Ridgeley's Body of Divinity.
Rutherford's Spiritual Antichrist.
Sedgwick's Antinomianism anatomized.
Sharp's (Granville) Mystic Babylon.
Sherlock's Knowledge of Jesus Christ.
Simon's (Jno.) Letter on certain errors.
Stephen's Doctrinal A. refuted.
Stillingfleet on the Satisfaction of Christ.
Taylor (Henry) on the Grand apostacy.
Thomas' (John) Sermons.
Tillotson's (Abp.) Sermons.
Weld's Rise and ruin of the A. and Familists.
White's (Hugh) Profession and practice.
Williams' (Dan.) Gospel truth vindicated.
Witsius' Conciliatory animadversions on the controversies in Great Britain. 1700.

Antiquity of Man. See NATURAL HISTORY OF MAN.

Antislavery. See SLAVERY.

Anxiety. See PEACE OF MIND, TROUBLE, TRUST.

Atterbury's (Francis) Sermons.
Baxter's (Arthur G.) Sermons.
Beachcroft's (Robt. P.) Sermons.
Beveridge's (Bp.) Sermons.
Blackall's (Dr. O.) Sermons.
Blair's (James) Sermons.
Bloomfield's (George B.) Sermons.
Buddicom's (Robert P.) Sermons.
Butcher's (William) Sermons.
Cappe's (Newcombe) Devotional discourses.
Carmichael's (Frederick) Sermons.
Clarke's (Dr. Sam.) Sermons.
Farringdon's (Anthony) Sermons.
Franklin's (Thomas) Sermons.
Gataker's (Thomas) Sermons.
Gisbourne's (Thomas) Sermons.
Girdlestone's (Charles) Sermons.
Horne's (Bp.) Discourses.
Hough's (Dr. John) Sermons and charges.
Howe (J.) on Thankfulness for to-morrow.
Lowth's (Bp.) Sermons.
Morrison's (Dr. Robt.) Sermons.
Secker's (Abp.) Sermons.
Sharp's (Abp.) Sermons.
Smith's (Sydney) Sermons.
Spincke's (N.) on Casting our care on God.
Stanhope's (George) Sermons.

Summerfield's (John) Sermons.
Verchoyle's (H.) Sermons.
Zollikoffer on the Festivals and fasts.

Aphthardocetæ. See MONOPHYSITES.

Apocalypse. See COMMENTATORS.

Apocrites. See MANICHEANS.

Apocrypha. See CANON, ENOCH, JASHER.

Apelii (H. E.) Libri vet. test. Apocryphi.
Arens de Evangeliorum apocr. in canonicis, usu, historico, critico, exegetico.
Augusti Libri Apocryphi.
Beausobre, Hist. critique des dogmes.
Bernard, Republique des lettres.
Beckhaus' Bemerkungen über d. Gebrauch der Apokryphen.
Bibliandri Protevangelion.
Bretschneider's Dogmatik der Apocryphen.
Chrytæi Interpretatio librorum Apoc.
Codex Apocryphus Nov. Test. (Collected and edited by Dr. Giles.)
Dallæus de Pseudepigraphis apostolicis.
Dupin, Prolegomena sur la Bible.
Eichorn's Einleitung in die Apok. des A. T.
Fabricii Codex pseudepigraphis Vet. Test.
——— Codex pseudepigraphis Nov. Test. (This collection contains every fragment of such productions; with important remarks on their character, evidence, &c.; from which Lardner, Jones, and others, have drawn largely.)
Fritzsche und Grimm's Kurzgefasstes exegetisches Handbuch.
Frankelii Hagiographa posteriora.
Gaab's Philologischen Verstehen.
Gerardi Loci theologici.
Gutmann's Apocryphen d. Alt. Testament.
Grotii Interpretatio librorum Apoc.
Henckii Dissertationes. (One of these is on the use of the O. T. apocryphal writings in our New Testament.)
——— Introd. ad libros apoc. vet. test.
Henock's Vollständiger übersetzung.
Hauff's Griechisch profanscriben.
Henzel's Erklarend. anmerk. anhang, &c.
Himmelii Librorum Apoc. analysis.
Hottingeri Censura libror. Apoc. V. Test.
Ittigius de Pseudepig. Christi, V. Mariæ, &c.
Janii libri Apocryphi Vet. Testament.
Kluge's Stellung u. bedentung der Apoc.
Kuinoel, Observ. ad N. T. ex libris apoc.
Kunzgefasstes Exigetisches handbuch.
Keerl's Apocryphenfrage m. berücksicht. der darauf bezugl. schriften Stier's und Hengstenberg's, &c.
Le Clerc (or Clerici), Dissertationes.
Lemmischii Interpretatio libror. Apoc.
Leusdeni Libri V. T. Apocryphi omnes.
Millii Prolegomena ad Nov. Testamentum.
Morus de Canone Scripturæ.
Mosheim, adversus Tolandum.
Mouline, sur les livres Apoc. Ancien Test.
Neander (M.), Apocrypha.
Pellicani Interpretatio libror. Apoc.

Apocrypha—*continued.*

Rainoldi Censura libror. Apoc. V. Test.
Reus' Diss. de libris V. T. apocryphis.
Schmidii Corpus Vet. Apocryphorum.
——— Corpus Nov. Apocryphorum.
Spanheimii Interpretatio libror. Apoc.
Stier, über die Apokryphen.
Thilonis Codex Apocryph. (Exact text.)
Turretini Theologia elenctica.
Vatabulus, Interpretatio libr. Apocryph.
Volkmar's Handbuch d. einleitung in die A.
Wahl, Clavis librorum Vet. Test. Apoc.
Waltheri Officina Biblica.
Wolfii (Chris.) Bibliotheca. Par. II.

Arnold's Crit. Com. with dissertations.
Bunsen's History of the Apocrypha.
Burnet's (Benj.) Discourses against Popery.
Burnet (Gilbert) on the 39 articles.
Christian Examiner. 14:1.
Christian Observer. 22:1. 65:129.
Dick (John) on Inspiration.
Diodati's Comment. on the Scriptures.
Eusebius' Ecclesiastical History.
Goodwin's Translation of the Apocrypha.
Gill's Dissertation on the Apocrypha.
Gorham's Impropriety of circulating the A. (Gives valuable historical facts.)
Gray & Percy's Key to the O. Test. Apocry.
Hone's Apocryphal New Test. (*All* extant pieces, translated into English.)
Jones' (Jer.) Full method of settling the canon, &c. (Describes the Apoc. books of the New Testament.)
Lardner's Credibility of the gospel.
Lewis' Antiquities. Bk. 8. Ch. 46.
Prideaux's Connection of the O. and N. T.
Princeton Review. 17:268.
Quarterly Review. 25:346. 30:472.
Wake's Preliminary discourses to the canonical epistles of the Apostolic Fathers.
Whiston's Genuine collect. of the A. books.
Wilson's (C.) Crit. and histor. observations. (Introductory discourses to each book.)
Wordsworth's Hulsean lectures. 1847.

Esdras.

Laurence, Versio Æthiopica in medium prolata et Latine angliceque reddita.
Lee's Dissertation on Esdras.
Laurence's Trans. with critical disquisitions.

Tobit.

Bedæ Explicationes allegorica.
Drusii (Joan.) Opera.
Fagii Tobias Hebraicæ.
Munsteri (Sebast.) Codex Judæorum.
Reusch's Ueberset. und erklärung.
Sengelman's Buch T. erklärung.

Judith.

Montfaucon, la Verité de l'hist. de Judith.
Rabanus Maurus, Opera.

Wisdom of Solomon.

Bauermeister, Commentarius.

Apocrypha—*continued.*

Bibliandri Annot. in libro Sapientiæ.
Bretschneideri Versio emend. et comment.
Dieterici (Conrad.) Annotationes.
Faber (J. M.) Dissertationes ix. in sap. Sal.
Gilse de lib. S. argumento, doctr. foute, &c.
Grim de libri sapientiæ Alexandrina indole.
Schmidii (Sebast.) Annotationes.
Strigelii (Victor) Commentaria.
Thilom's Exercitationes crit. in sap. S.

Arnold's (Rich.) Critical commentary.

Ecclesiasticus.

Bretchneideri Liber de Jesu Siracidæ. 1806. (Great.)
Camerarii Annotationes in libro Eccles.
Drusii (Joan.) Annotationes in libro Eccles.
Fagii (Paul.) Annotationes in libro Eccles.
Sarceri (Erasm.) Annotationes in libro E.
Strigelii (Victor.) Annotationes in libro E.

Arnold's (Rich.) Critical commentary.
Howard's Trans. from the Vulgate. With notes.

Baruch.

Grunebergii (Jo. Petr.) Exercitationes.
Ursinus de libri Baruchi.

Song of the Children.

Polycarp Interp. Cantici trium puerorum.

Lyseri Cant. triumph. trium puerorum.
Sike, Evangelium Infantae.

Howard's Translation and notes.

Susanna.

Chrysostom, Gregory Naz.

Bernhard Interpretatio hist. Susannæ.
Witstein (J. J.) Dissert. philol. theologica.

Howard's Translation and notes.

Maccabees.

Bertheau, Dissertations.
Gentilis (Scipio) Disputationes.
Sanctii Comment. in librorum Maccab.
Strigelii (Victor.) Dissertationes.
Thomæ (Aq.) in libros. M. explicatio.
Verhorstii Commentaria.
Wernsdorf, de Fide historica librorum M.

Cotton's (H.) Five books of Maccab. (New trans. and notes.)

Twelve Patriarchs.

Nitzschii Comm. critica.

Grosthead's (Bp.) Test. of the twelve Patriarchs. "Englished by A. G" [olding]. (18 queer wood cuts.)

Enoch.

Dillman's Buch Henock, übersets. u. erklart.
Hoffmann's Enleit. überset. und com.

Bruce's Travels in Abyssinia. Vol. 2.
Biblical Repertory. Jan. 1840.
Dutt on the Genuineness of the book of E.
Foreign Quarterly Review. 24:251.
Lawrence's Trans. with preliminary diss.

Apocrypha—*continued.*

Murray's Attempt to separate from the books of Enoch the book quoted by Jude.
Overton's Inquiry into the truth and use of the book of Enoch.

New Testament.

Codex Apoc. Nov. Testam. J. C. Thilo.
Codex Apoc. Nov. Testam. J. A. Fabricio.
Lörsbach's Beitrage d. Apoc. d. N. T.
Sike, Evangelium infantiæ.
Tischendorfii Evangelia Apocrypha.

Hone's Apocryphal N. T. With notes.
Quarterly Review. 25:348. 30:472.
Warrin's Trans. of Nicodemus, his gospel.
Wright's Contributions to the Apocryphal literature of the N. Test. Collected from Syriac MSS.

The various editions of the Apocrypha, collective and separate, are described in MASCH, *Biblioth. Sac.*, and HORNE, *Introduction.*

Apollinarians. See HERESIES, JESUS CHRIST, INCARNATION.

Athanasius de Incarnatione Christi.
Chrysostomi Epist. ad Cæsarium.
Gregorii (Naz.) Orationes.
Gregorii (Nys.) Epistolæ.
Theodoreti Dialogi.

Bassnage Historia hæresis Apollinaris.
Damasii Epistolæ contra sectatores.
Dorner's Lehre von der person Christi.
Schrœderi (J. J.) Dissertationes.
Wernsdorfii (Gottl.) Dissertationes.

Bayle's Crit. and historical dictionary.

Apollonius Tyanæus. See FALSE MIRACLES.

Beroaldi Vita Apollonii.
Eunapius, in Vitis Sophistarum. Procem.
Eusebius adversus Hieroclem. Cap. IV.
[Dupin,] Hist. d'Apollone de Tyane. (Pub. under the name of De Claireval.)
Müller (E.) Apoll. von Tyana, ein weiser.
Philaleutheri [Zimmerman] de Miraculis.
Philostratus de Vita Apollonii.
Philostrate, Vita A. traduit par Vigenere.
Tillemont, Vie de Apollone.

Berwick's Life of A. from Philostratus.
Blount's Translation of Philostratus.
Bradley's Truth of Christianity.
Cudworth's Intellect. system. Ch. 4, Sec. 15.
Doddridge's Course of lectures. Part 6.
Douglass' Criterion of miracles.
Fleetwood on Miracles.
Jackson (John) on Credulity.
Jenkins' Confutation of pretences against natural religion.
Lardner's Testimonies.
Quarterly Review. 3:417.
Tillemont's Life of A.: Tr. by Robt. Jenkins.

See a great list of such authors, few of

which are now extant, in HOUTEVILLE'S *Critical and historical discourse on the principal writers for and against Christianity.* 1690.

Apologetics. See AUTHENTICITY OF SCRIPTURE, DEISM, INSPIRATION.

Ambrose, de Fide resurrectionis.
Arnobius, Adversus Gentes.
Athenagoras, Apologia pro. Christianis.
Augustin, de Doctrina Christiana.
——— de Civitate dei.
——— contra Academicos.
Clemens, (Alexandrinus) stromata.
Cyprian, de Idolorum vanitate.
Justin M., Dialogus cum Triphone Judæo.
——— Apologiæ pro Christianis.
Lactantius, Institutionum divinarum.
Origen, contra Celsum.
Theodoret, de Curandis Græcor. affectibus.
Theophylus, Libri tres ad Autolycum.
Tertullian, Apologeticus adversus gentes.
——— Liber ad Scapulam.

Apollinaris ad Marcum Antoninum.
Arnobius, adversus Gentes.
Clausen, Apol. eccl. christianæ ante Theodosiani.
Eusebii Preparatio et Demonstratio.
Gourcy, Suite des anciens apologistes.
Havercampi Tertulliani apologia perpetuo commentaria.
Melito, Apologia pro Christianis.
Minutii Felicis Opera.
Mosheim de Vera ætate apologetici.
Orosius, adversus Paganos.
Senden's Geschichte der Apologetik.
Tzschirner's Geschichte der Apologetik.
Woodman's Tertulliani liber apologeticus. (With English preface and notes.)

Betty's Translation of parts of Tertullian and Theophilus.
Bolton's Evidences of Christianity, as exhibited in the writings of the Apologists.
Chevalier's Tr. of Justin M. and Tertullian.
Cunningham, on Origen cont. Celsus.
Dalrymple's Translation of the Octavius.
Dodson's Apologetics of Tertullian.
Frank's (G. S.) New system of apologetics.
Glass' Trans. of Origen contra Celsus.
Haverkamp's Comm. of the A. of Tertullian.
Humphrey's Apologetics of Athanagoras.
Lorrain's Translation of the Octavius.
North British Review. 15:172.
Reeve's Translation of the apologies of Justin, Tertullian, and Minutius. With notes.
Sack's Christian apologetics.

Apostacy. See BACKSLIDING, PERSEVERANCE.

Abernethy's (Bp.) Sermons.
Brameld's (G. W.) Sermons.
Bridges' (Will.) Sermons.
Charnock's (Stephen) Works.
Cochrane's (James) Sermons.
Cruso's (Timothy) Sermons.

Apostacy—*continued.*

Fisk's (George) Sermons.
Hall's (Bp.) Polemic works.
Hall (Robert) on Apostacy.
Haynes' Illustrations of faith and practice.
Kidd's Danger of apostacy from Christ.
Owen's (John) Nature and causes of A.
Pike (G.) on Apostacy.
Trapp's (Joseph) Sermons.
Wallis' (Benj.) Sermons.

Apostles.

Buddæi Ecclesia Apostolica.
Burmanni Disputationes decem.
Bucher's Leben Jesu, und der apostels.
Capelli (Lud.) Hist. apostolica illustrata.
Erasmi Peregrinationes apostolorum.
Fabricii Hist. J. Christi et Apostolorum.
Hypolitus de Duodecem Apostolis.
Lampe (J.) de Eruditione Apostolorum.
Lechler das Apostolische und das nachapostolische, &c. (The "Baptist Theological Association of Haarlem, offered a prize for an essay to meet the destructive doctrines of Tübingen. This was the successful one.)
Mayer's Geschichte und schriften der Apos.
Mesner's Lehr der Apostels.
Nicetas, Orationes.
Perionius de Rebus gestis, vitisque, &c.
Sagittarii Introductio ad Hist. eccles.
Sandani Historia Apostolica.
Spanheimii (Fred.) Dissertationes.
Wilhelmi Christi. apos. u. erste bekenner.

Ashwell's (Dr. Geo.) Faith of the Apostles.
Bacon's (D. F.) Lives of the Apostles.
Barrington's Miscellanea sacra.
Benson's (C.) Lectures.
Baumgarten's Apos. history: tr. by Morris.
Bradford's History of the Apostles.
Cave's Antiquitates apostolicæ.
Craddock's Apostolical history. (Gives the time and occasion of each epistle.)
Crosthwaite's (J. C.) Sermons.
Dealtry's (Will.) Sermons.
Frank's (James C.) Hulsean lectures. 1823.
Grave's (R.) Character of the Apostles.
Kitto's Bible illustrations.
Lardner's Lives of the Apostles.
Mant's Biographical notices.
Marshall's (N.) Sermons.
Merivale's (L. A.) Christian records
Milman's Bampton lectures. 1827.
Nares' Veracity of the Evangelists.
Rhees' (Abraham) Sermons.
Shepherd's (John) Horæ Apostolicæ. (A digested narrative of the acts and writings of the Apostles.)
Sumner's (Bp.) Apos. preaching considered.

Apostles' Creed. See CREEDS.

Apostolians. See MENNONITES.

Apostolical Constitutions.

Barratieri Opera.

Apostolical Constitutions—*Cont.*

Brun's Canones Apost. (Pref. by Neander.)
Buddæi Isagoge in Theologiam.
Beveridgii Synodicon.
Capelli Epitome Apost. Constitutionum.
Cellier, Hist. generale, des auteurs sacrés.
Conradi (C.) Kritik der christlichen Dogmen.
Dallæus de Const. apostolic, apocryphis.
Drey's Untersüchungen über d. Kanones.
Fabricii Bibliotheca Græca.
Janus de Antiq. canon. Apost. in qua J. Dallæi et G. Beverigii sententia inter se comparantur.
Ittigius de Pseudepigraphis Apostolicis.
King (P.) Hist. symboli Apostolicorum.
Krabbe's Uber d. Ursprung u. d. Inhalt, &c.
Oleviani Expositio symbolorum apostol.
Richardson Prelectiones ecclesiasticæ.
Ultzen, Textum Græcum, et annotationes.

Bibliotheca Sacra, 5 : 296.
Bunsen's Hypolitus and his age.
Christian Examiner, 44 : 223.
Christian Review, 1 : 536. 13 : 201. 15 : 505.
Chace's (Ira) Tr. of the Apostolical Const.
Doddridge's Lectures. Lect. 119.
Grabbe's Historical and Critical Essay on the Apostol. Const. (Answer to Whiston.)
Jones (William) on the Canon.
Lardner's Works. Part 2.
Platt's (J. P.) Ethiopic Didascalia. (A tran. of the Ethiopic version.)
Princeton Review. 21 : 42.
Saurin's (James) Sermons.
Smallbrook's Pretended authority of the Apostolical Constitutions confuted.
Theological and literary Journal. 1 : 174.
Turner on the pretended Apostol. Const.
Whiston's Primitive Christianity.
——— Demonst. that the Apostol. Constitutions were written in the 1st century.

Apostolical Fathers. See BARNABAS, CLEMENS ROM., HERMAS, IGNATIUS, POLYCARP, JUSTIN MARTYR.

Ittigii Patres Apost.	cum annotat,		1700.
Clerici	do.	do.	1700.
Russel,	do.	do.	1746.
Horneman,	do.	do.	1816.
Jacobson,	do.	do.	1840.
Hefele,	do.	do.	1851.

There are many other editions; but any of the above are sufficient.

Ceillier, Histoire generale des autres sacres.
Gerhardi Patrologia.
Maréchal, Concordance des SS. PP.
Olearii Abacus patrologicus.
Sandius de Vet. scriptoribus ecclesiast.
Tentzelii (Guil. Ernesti) Exercitationes.
Varenius de Scriptoribus eccl. sec. primi.

Cave's Fathers of the first 3 centuries.

Apostolical Succession. See EPISCOPACY, ORDINATION.

Pro.

Benzelii Dissertationes academicæ.

Apostolical Succession—*Continued.*

Fennell, Memoires sur la validité des ordinations des Anglois. (Argues that the clergy of the English church are mere laymen.)
Masoni Vindiciæ Ecclesiæ Anglicana.
Brett's Divine right of Episcopacy.
Chapin's Order of the Primitive church.
Cook's History of the Apost. succession.
Courayer's Validity of English Ordination.
Dublin Review, 5 : 285. 7 : 139. (To show that the English church has no claim to Apostolical succession.)
Faber on the Apostolical succession.
Fry (H. P.) on the Apos. succ. (As able as anything on this side of the question, from the Tractarian school.)
Houghton's (Wm.) Theology of the Anglican reformers.
Harrington (E. C.) on Apostol. succession.
Irons (W. J.) on the Apostol. succession.
Lawrence (R.) Lay Baptism invalid.
Palmer's (Wm.) Episcopacy in the British Churches.
Percival (A. P.) on Apostolical succession.
Sinclair (John) on the Episcopal succession.
Stopford's Weapons of Schism.
Tracts for the Times. Nos. 4, 15, 18, 74.

Con. See CONGREGATIONALISM, NAG'S-HEAD PRESBYTERIANISM.

Boardman's Doct. of Apostol. succession.
Brown's (D. J.) Claims of the Puseyites.
Campbell's (John) Puseyism and Popery.
Carey on the Doct. of the Apostol. Succ.
Cater's Great Fiction of the Times.
Davison's Protestant Minister's mission.
Goode's Divine rule of faith and practice.
Powell on Apostolical succession. (Replies to Percival.)
Princeton Review. 14 : 129. 19 : 539. 28 : 1.
Prynne on Independency.
Snodgrass on Apostolical succession.
Smyth's (Tho.) Doct. of Apost. succession.
——— Presbytery not Prelacy.
Stratton on the Apostolical succession.
Whiston's Proof. that all persons solemnly, though irregularly, set apart, are real clergymen; or else there are none such in the world.
Wisner's Lectures on prelacy and parity.

Apostolicals. See WALDENSES.

Apotactites. See ENCRATITES.

Apothegms of Scripture.

Delvii Adagia sacra, V. et N. Testament.
Drusii Classes duæ in quibus explicantur, etc.
Schottii Adagia sacra N. Testament.

Apparent Contradictions. See CHRONOLOGY, DIFFICULTIES, QUOTATIONS.

Althameri, Conciliationes locorum S. S. qui inter se pugnare videntur. (Excellent.)
Beconi, Opera.

Apparent Contradictions—*continued.*

Broughton, Concensus sacræ scripturæ.
Macri, sive Magrii, Antilogiæ.
Mayeri, Manuale biblicum.
Manassah ben Israel, de conventia locorum S. S. quæ inter se pugnare videntur.
Matthæi Antilogia biblica.
Mettingeri Harmonia in utroque Test.
Thaddei Scrip. sacra a se non diversa.
Turrettini Theologia Elenctica.
Waltheri Harmonia biblica.

Boyer's Critical conjectures, &c.
Burnett's Four discourses.
Calamy's (Edward) Sermons.
Cooper's Four hundred texts explained.
Cox's (J. H.) Harm. of Scrip. vindicated.
Doddridge's Lectures. Part 6.
Falconer's Bampton lectures. 1810. (Dissonance of the Four Evangelists.)
Fuller's (And.) Works. (A judicious and learned discussion.)
Hallet's (Joseph) Notes on texts.
Jenkins' Reasonableness of Christianity.
Kennicott's State of the printed text.
——— Remarks on select passages.
Lindo's (E. H.) The Conciliator.
Man's 3000 Seeming contrad. reconciled.
Manassah ben Israel, The Conciliator.
Paley's Evidences. Part 3.
Ridgeley's Body of divinity.
Sykes' Trnth of the Christian religion.
[Thaddeus' (Jno.)] Reconciler of the Bible. (Notices 2000 seeming contradictions.)
Whately's (Rich.) Essays. Essay 7.
Wood's (Prof.) Works.

Most works of this class find apparent contradictions in a multitude of passages where there are none.

Apparitions. See MAGIC, SUPERSTITION.

Bekker, le Monde enchante.
Brierre, Hist. raisonnee des Apparations.
Boisardus de Spiritum apparitionibus.
Cahagnet Arcanes de la vie future.
Calmet, sur les angels, demons, &c.
Grasse's Wissenschaftlich Geordnete, &c.
Kerner's Seherin von prevorst.
Jung Stilling's Theorie der Geisterkunde.
Lavater de Spectris.
Lenglet Dufresnoy, sur les Revelations particuliéres.
Loyer (P.), des Spectres.
Melancthoni Epistolæ ad Hubert.
Meisneri Dissertationes.
Salverte des Sciences occultes.
Stelling (W.), Geheimnissvolle Jenseits.
Thyræi (Pet.) Opera.
Wierus de Angelis et Demonibus.
Zanchii (Hieron.) Dissertationes.

Alderson & Hibbert on Apparitions.
Abercrombie on the Intellectual powers.
Analytic Magazine. 2 : 338.
Aubrey's (John) Miscellanies.
Baxter's Histor. treatise on apparitions.
Berington's (Simon) Dissertations.

Apparitions—*continued.*

Berthogg on the Nature of spirits.
Bigland's Essays. Essay 7.
Boismont (B.) on Hallucinations.
Brewster on Natural magic.
Burrowes' (E. J.) Hours of devotion.
Calmet's Dissertations.
——— Phantom world. Tr. by Christmas.
Casaubon on Witches and apparitions.
Christian Examiner. 12 : 106.
Crowe's Night side of nature.
De Foe's Secrets of the invisible world.
Drelincourt on Death. (Preface.)
Eclectic Magazine. 3 : 71.
Edwards' (Bp.) Theologia reformata.
Ferrier's Theory of apparitions.
Frazier's Magazine. 2 : 33. 34 : 231.
Glanvill's Sadduceismus triumphatus.
——— Demon of Tedworth.
——— Essays in philos. and religion.
Hammond's (Henry) Discourses.
Hibbert's Philosophy of apparitions.
Jackson (Tho.) on the Apostles' creed.
Jung Stilling's Theory of pneumatology. Tr. by Jackson. (Gives many remarkable accounts, including one related by John Wesley.)
Lawton's (Edward) Lectures.
Littell's Living Age. 13 : 529.
London Retrospective Review. 11 : 66.
Mather's (Cotton) Magnalia.
Mather's (Increase) Remarkable providences. (Furnishes an instructive picture of the state of society among the early settlers of America.)
Moore's (Henry) Divine dialogues.
Morton's Secrets of the invisible world.
Museum of Foreign literature. 7 : 157.
New England Magazine. 2 : 8.
North British Review. 9 : 393.
Quarterly Review. 9 : 304. 48 : 287.
Radcliffe s Origin and nature of the belief in the supernatural.
Saunders on Angels and an angelic life.
Sinclair's Invisible world discovered. (Curious narratives, given as authentic.)
Telfair's Actings of a spirit which infested the house of A. Mackie. 1695.
Toplady's Sermons.
Taylor's (Joseph) Mystery of ghosts.

Appearance of Evil. See DEPORTMENT.

Fawcett's (James) Sermons.
Rogers' (John) Sermons.
Secker's (Abp.) Sermons.
Smallridge's (Bp.) Sermons.

Appetites. See MORAL SCIENCE.

Baxter's Practical works.
Hutchinson on the Nature of virtue.
——— on the Passions.

Ararat. See ARK, GEOGRAPHY.

Amer. Biblical Repository. 7 : 390.
Blackwood's Magazine. 28 : 24. 65 : 577.
Foreign Quarterly Review. 15 : 288.

Southern Literary Messenger. 10:131.
Westminster Review. 51:199.

Archangel. See PHILOLOGY.

Stengelii Hist. archangelorum. Plates.
Witsii Miscellanea sacra. Tom. 2. Exer. 4.

Clayton's (Bp.) Miscellaneous works.
Rudd's Is Michael our Saviour?
Simpson on the Language of scripture.

Archæology. See CHRISTIAN ANTIQUITIES, JEWISH ANTIQUITIES, COINS, EGYPT, HIEROGLYPHICS, VESTMENTS.

Ackermanni Archæologia biblica. (Chiefly from Jahn.)
Alliolis' Biblischen Alterthumskunde.
Augusti's Denkwürdigkeiten aus der christlichen Archäologie.
Baumgarten-Crusius' Dogmengeschichte.
Bauer's Hebräische Mythologie.
——— Beschreibung die Gottesdienstlichen Verfassung der alten Hebräer.
Bibliothèque archæologique. (Periodical.)
Bohlen das alte Indien und Egypt.
Bruningii Compar. antiq. Græcæ. ("Executed with great learning and judgment." —HARWOOD.)
Cremeri Antiquitates Sacræ.
Donati Roma: vetus et recens. (1725.)
Grævii Thesaurus antiq. Romanorum.
——— Idem. Italiæ, Siciliæ, Sardiniæ. (Two very valuable works, in 60 volumes.)
Gronovii Thesaurus antiq. Græcorum.
Hattemer's Denkmahl des mittel alters.
Keil's Handbuch der biblischen Archæologie.
Kinkel's Alte christliche Kunst.
Kleem's Cultur Geschichte.
Jablonski, Opuscula varia.
Jahn, Archæologia Biblica.
Lamy, Apparatus biblicus.
Millii Dissertationes.
Montfaucon, l'Antiquité expliquée.
Muller de Vitiis archæologiæ biblicæ.
Nouvelle Encyclopédie theologique.
Revue Archéologique. (Periodical.)
Rosenmuller's Biblisch Alterthumskunde.
Schilteri Thesaurus antiq. Teutonicarum. (A vast collection of curious matter.)
Suiceri Thesaurus ecclesiasticus.
Waltoni Biblia Polyglot. (Prolegomena.)

Archæologia of Lond. Antiq. Society. 1770 to 1820. (Many hundred engravings. The contributors were among the first scholars in England.)
Archæological Journal. (Begun 1844.)
Bruce's State of society in the age of Homer.
Bryant's Observations and enquiries.
Burton's Phraseology, manners, history, &c., of Eastern nations; as illustrating the sacred Scriptures.
Cory's Fragments of ancient Phœnician, Chaldæan, Egyptian, Carthagenian, Indian, Persian, and other writers.
Cumberland's Sanchoniatho's Phœnician History, translated.
——— Origin of the most ancient nations.

Archæology—*continued.*

Fosbrook's Elements of Archæology. (An excellent book for general reference.)
Gale's Court of the Gentiles. (Origin of literature and philosophy, the ancient Jewish Scriptures, &c.)
Godwin's Moses and Aaron. (Elucidates many passages of Scripture by Jewish rites.)
Gray's (Robt.) Con. between the sacred writings and the literature of the Jewish and Heathen authors. ("Profound and elegant."—ORME.)
Guerickè's Christian antiquities.
Hager on the Newly discovered Babylonian inscriptions. 1801. (Plates.)
Halliwell's Journal of antiq. science.
Heeren's Politics, intercourse, &c., of the principal nations of antiquity. ("As learned as a professed commentary, and as entertaining as a book of travels."—EDINB. REVIEW.)
Jackson's Antiq. of the most anc. nations.
Jahn's Biblical Archæology. Tr. by Upham.
Jones' Asiatic researches.
Kennet's Roman antiquities.
Landseer's Sabæan researches. (Lectures on the engraved hieroglyphics of Chaldea.)
Layard's Ruins of Nineveh and Babylon.
Maurice's Indian antiquities. (Hindus, Persians, &c.)
——— Ruins of Babylon. As in 1815.
Montfaucon's Antiquity explained. (Trans. by Humphreys. A library in itself; and wholly reliable.)
Nuttal's Archæological Dictionary.
Osborn's Monumental hist. of Egypt.
Prideaux's Connection of the O. and N. Test.
Potter's Greek antiquities.
Proceedings of the Archæological Society of Great Britain and Ireland.
Shaw's (H.) Alphabets, numerals, and devices of the middle ages.
Smith's (Geo.) Gentile nations.
Wait's (D. G.) Jewish, Oriental, and Classical antiquities. (Able illustrations of Scrip.)
Walsch's (Jno.) Heb. and Egyp. antiquities.
Whately on Difficult passages of the N. T.

See many other citations in FABRICII *Bibliographia Antiquaria.*

Architecture. See CHURCH ARCHITECTURE.

Areopagus.

Cicero ad Atticum. Lib. 1. Epist. 14.
Witsii Meletemata.

Roscoe's Boyle lectures.

Arianism. See COUNCIL OF NICE.

Pro.

Arii Epistola ad Eusebium Nicomed.
——— θαλεια.
Febingeri Demonstrationes Christianæ.
——— die Lehre von Gott und Christ.
Sandii Confessio fidei.
——— Nucleus hist. ecclesiasticæ.
Voetii Apologia equitis Poloni.

Arianism—*continued.*

Pro.

Belsham's (Tho.) Review of Wilberforce.
Bruce's (Will.) Sermons.
Carpenter on the Doctrines of revelation.
——— on the Works of creation.
Chandler's (Dr. Sam.) Sermons and commentaries.
Chubbs' Supremacy of God the Father.
Clarke's (Dr. S.) Scrip. doct. of the Trinity. (Takes up every text in the New Test. in which the subject is mentioned.)
[Clayton (Bp.)] on the Spirit. (This book drew out more than thirty replies, mostly pamphlets.)
Cornish on the Pre-existence of Christ.
Drummond's (Geo. H.) Theological works.
Emlyn's Scripture account of Jesus Christ.
——— Vindic. of the worship of Christ.
——— Remarks on Mr. Boyse.
——— Supreme deity of the Father.
——— Three tracts in reply to Leslie.
——— (Many other treatises.)
Harwood's (Edward) Five dissertations.
[Hopkins' (Will.)] Appeal to common sense.
Price's (Richard) Sermons.
Sykes on the Epistle to the Hebrews.
Taylor's Apology of Ben Mordecai.
Theological Repository. 4:153.
Tompkins' Mediator.
Whiston's Primitive Christianity.
——— Sermons and essays.

Con.

Ambrose, de Fide; ad Gratianum.
Athanasii Disputationes et Orationes.
Augustine, contra Sermonem Arianorum.
Basil, Rationes syllogisticæ.
Chrysostom, de Natura Dei.
Cyrill (Alex.), de Sancta Trinitate.
Epiphanius, Epistolæ.
Gregory (Naz.), Oratio adv. Arianos.
Jerome, Epistolæ.

Bezæ Tractationes theologicæ.
——— Orthodoxæ fidei explicatio.
Bulli Defensio fidei Nicenæ.
Cocceji Examen apol. equitis Poloni.
Fulgentius contra Arianos.
Grotius de Satisfactione Christi.
Hilarius de Trinitate.
Hoornbeckii Apparatus ad controversiam.
Langii (S.) Hæresis Arii.
Meisneri (Jo.) Disputationes.
Petavii Dogmatica Theologia.
Porti Orthodoxæ fidei defensio.
Smiglecii Nova monstra.
Ursini Tractationes theologicæ. (Powerful.)
Virgilii Altercatio: sive dialogi, &c.
Wuchereri (Jo. F.) Prolusiones.

Abbadie's Antidote against socin. poison.
Allix's (Peter) Remarks on Mr. Whiston's books.
Athanasius' Four disputations: trans. by S. Parker.
Bennet's Reply to Clarke's Scrip. doctrine.
Biley (Edw.) on the 12th ch. of Revelations.

Arianism—*continued.*

Con.

Bishop's Moyer lectures. 1724, 1725.
Blackmore on the Arian hypothesis.
Bogue & Bennet's Hist. of Dissenters.
Boyse's (Joseph) Sermons.
Bull's Defence of the Nicene creed.
Burrell's Mystery of God.
Carson's (Alex.) Works.
Clagget's (John) Arianism anatomized.
Edwards' (John) Reply to S. Clarke.
Eusebius' Life of Constantius.
Felton's Moyer lectures. 1728. (Powerful.)
Gastrell's Reply to Dr. S. Clarke.
Gataker's (Thomas) Sermons.
Hancock's Ante-Nicene Fathers.
Hawker's (Robt.) Sermons.
Hey's (John) Lectures in Divinity.
Jones' (Will.) Answer to Clayton.
Kirby (John) on the Trinity. (Reply to Clayton.)
Knight's Reply to Clarke's Scrip. doctrine.
Knowles' (Thomas) Reply to Clayton.
Leslie's Short method.
Lowth's Excerpts from eccles. history.
McDonald's Answer to Hopkins' appeal.
May's Reply to Dr. Samuel Clarke.
Miller (Dr. G.) on the Doctrines of Christ'y.
Moyer lectures. (Many excellent treatises.)
Paul's (Dr. John) Refutation of Arianism.
Pike's Reply to Dr. Samuel Clarke.
Pearson (Bp.) on the Creed.
Scott's (John) Doct. of the Trinity.
Skelton's Dialogue of the gods. (Ironical.)
Smallbrook's Idolatry of Arianism.
——— Pretended authority of the Clementine constitutions.
Taylor's (Abraham) Doct. of the Trinity.
Thyrwitt's Commentaries and essays.
Tillotson on the Incarnation.
Trapp's (Jos.) Summary view of the controv.
Warren's Antidote to Arianism.
Waterland's Answer to Dr. S. Clarke.
Well's Answer to Dr. Samuel Clarke.
Whitaker's Origin of Atheism.
Wynperse's Divinity of Christ. (A masterly little manual.)

See "An account of all the considerable books and pamphlets written on either side of the controversy from 1712 to 1719." Pub. at London, 1720; and Wilson's History of Dissenting Churches.

Arians, Hist. of. See HIST. OF DOCTRINES.

Bebelii (Balthas.) Dissertationes.
Fabricii Lux salutaris evangelii.
Hanneckii Historia Arianismi.
Koenigii Historia Arianismi.
Langii Hæresis Arii.
Lupus, Vie, mors, erreurs, &c.
——— sur les Semi-ariens.
Maimbourg, Histoire de l'Arianisme, avec l'origine des Sociniens.
Meisneri (Joann.) Disputationes.
Osiandri Arianismi antiq. et novi.

Arians—*continued.*

Sandii Nucleus hist. ecclesiasticæ. (Collects from reliable sources all that is important on this subject.)
Wetzeri Restitutio veræ chronol. rerum ex controver. Arianis; ab. A. D. 315 ad 350.
Wietrowski (Soc. Jesu) Hist. de Ariana.
Zeltneri Crypto-socinismus Altorfinæ.

Berriman's Hist. of the Trinitarian controv.
Cave's Lives of the Fathers.
Christian Examiner. 12:298.
Christian Monthly Spectator. 4:192.
Hey's (Dr. John) Lectures. Bk. 4.
Jortin's (John) Works.
Lardner's Credibility of the gospel history.
Life of St. Athanasius.
Lowth's Excerpta. (Extends from the Council of Nice to that of Armenium.)
Maimbourg's History of A. Tr. by Webster.
Newman's (J. H.) Arians of the 4th century.
Spirit of the Pilgrims. 4:420.
Tillemont's Hist. of the A. Tr. by Deacon.
Webster's (W.) Hist. of A. From 306 to 1666.
Whiston's Arian heresy in England.

Ark of Noah. See ARARAT, DELUGE.

Buteorus de Arca. (In Crit. Sacra.)
Hosti (Matth.) Dissertationes.
Kircheri (Athanas.) Dissertationes.
Pelletierii (Laurent.) Dissertationes.
Relandi (Adrian) Dissertationes.

Bedford's Chronology. (Appendix.)
Calmet's Dictionary.
Montanu's Jewish antiquities.
Saurius' Dissertations.
Stillingfleet's Origines Sacræ.
Wells' Geography of the Old Test.
Wilkins (Bp.) Real character, &c.

Ark of the Covenant. See CHERUBIM, ILLUSTRATIONS, JEWISH ANTIQUITIES.

Buxtorfii Exercitationes.
Sennerti (Andr.) Dissertationes.
Thaleman de Nube super arca.
Ugolini Thesaurus antiquit. sacrorum.
Van Till, (Salom.) Dissertationes.

Deyling's Sacred observations.
Hamm's Philological dissertations.

Armenian Church.

Assemanni Bibliotheca Orientalis.
Aywasowski, Catéchisme Armenien.
Bembi Ritus Armeniorum.
Bonucci Vita Gregorii Archiepiscopi.
Bredenbachius de Armeniorum.
Celsii (O.) Dissertationes.
Cianciani Hist. Armeniorum. (To 1784.)
De la Croix, Etat des nations Grecque. 1686.
Fridonis Statu ecclesiæ Armeniæ.
Galani Conciliatio eccles. A. cum Romana.
——— Historia Armena.
Gerhardi (Joann.) Dissertationes.
Gravinus de Chris. religione in Armenia.
Kemp, de Statu Arm. eccles. et polit. 1665.
La Croze, Hist. du Christianisme.

Armenian Church—*continued.*

Paulini India Orientalis.
Ricaut, Hist. de l'etat present, &c. 1679.
Stierner de hodierno Statu eccles. A. 1726.

Buchanan's Researches in Asia. 1811.
Dwight's (H. G. O.) Christianity in the East. 1850.
Etheridge's Syrian Churches. (History, liturgies, literature, &c.)
Ricaut's State of the A. Church. 1679.
Simons' Religion of Eastern nations.
Smith & Dwight's Missionary researches.
Stanley's Hist. of the Eastern Church.
Yeates' Indian Church history.

Arminianism. See FIVE POINTS, PELAGIANISM, REMONSTRANTS, SYNOD OF DORT, &C.

Pro.

Arminii Disputationes.
——— Declaratio sententiæ.
——— Analysis Rom. ix.
——— do. do. vii.
——— Collatio cum Junio.
——— (Many other works. He would, by some modern writers, be charged with Calvinism.)
Batelerii Examen disputationis Voetii.
Clerici (Joann.) Commentationes.
——— Delineatio Christ. religionis.
Confessio Sententiæ pastorum qui in fœderato Belgio, "Remonstratensis" vocantur. (This is the Arm. confession of faith, drawn up by Episcopius. 1622.)
Corvini Defensio sententiæ J. Arminii.
Curcellii Institutio rel. christianæ.
Episcopii Opera theologica.
Herbert, Instructiones ex sacra scriptura.
Le Clerc, Bibliotheque.
——— Entretiens sur matieres de theol.
Limborch, Theologiæ christianæ.
Molinæi (Jo.) Armamentarium spirituale.
Nicole, Prejugez legitimès.
Poelenburgii Fred. Spanheimii Disputatio.
Tileni (Dan.) Canones Synodi Dordracænæ.
Vorstius de Natura et attributis Dei.
——— (Opera varia.)
Wetstein, Prolegomena.

Arminius' Works. Trans. by J. Nichols. (Excellent prolegomena and notes.)
Baillie's Offspring of Scotch Calvinism.
Copplestone on the Doctrine of Necessity.
Edwards (Tho.) on Irresistible grace.
Fellows' Christian philosophy.
——— Religion without cant.
Fletcher's (John W.) Works. (Very pious.)
Gleig's (Bp.) Sermons.
Goodwin (John) on Justification.
——— Expos. of Romans, 9th ch.
——— Redemption redeemed. (Very able.)
Heylin's Judgment of the Western churches.
——— Removal of the stumbling block.
Hoard's Doct. of eternal decrees.
Moorhouse's Arminianism and Calvinism compared.

Arminianism—*continued.*

Pro.

Nichols' Calv. and Armin. compared.
Playfere's Appello evangelium. (Very moderate.)
Sancroft's (Abp.) Predestinated Thief.
Taylor's Key to the Epistles.
——— Doct. of original sin.
Tomline's (Bp.) Calvinism refuted.
Watson (Rich.) on Redemption.
Wesley's (John) Works.
Wesley's (Cha.) Works.
Wheedon (D. D.) on the Freedom of the will.

Con.

Acta Synodi Dordrecti.
Amesii Antisynodalia.
——— Opera varia.
Amyraldi Declaratio fidei.
Bradwardine de causa Dei.
Capelli Theses theologicæ.
Du Moulin, Anatomie Arminianisme.
Eckardi Fasciculus controv. theol. (Exhibits the opinions of Zuingle, Calvin, Beza, Zanchius, and many others, under the different points of the controversy.)
Fraxani Specimen notarum in loca, &c.
Gomari (Francisc.) Opera.
Luberti Com. ad 99 errores C. Vorstii.
Maresii (Samuel.) Dissertationes.
Molinæii (Pet.) Anatomie Arminianisme.
Musæi Disputationes.
Peltii Harmonia Remonstrantium et Socinianorum.
Spanheimii Disputationes.
Twisse, Vindiciæ graciæ Divinæ.
——— Animadversiones ad Armin.
——— de Scientia media.
Vedelii (Nic.) Arcana Arminianismi.
Zanchius de Religione christiana.

Baillie's Antidote of Arminianism.
Bates on Important points in divinity.
Beausobre's Defence of the Reformed doct.
Beza on Predestination.
Biblical Repository. Apr. 1831.
Bledsoe's Theodicy. (Able.)
Brown's (H.) Arminian inconsistencies.
Booth's Reign of grace.
Brine's (John) Works.
Burgess on the Moral law.
Claude's Defence of the Reformation.
Coles on Divine sovereignty. (Excellent.)
Du Moulin's Anatomy of Arminianism.
Edwards' (Pres.) Works.
Edwards' (Dr. John) Answer to Dr. Whitby.
Gill's Cause of God and truth. (Reply to Whitby.)
——— on the Five points.
Hill's (Sir Rich.) Review of Wesley's doctrine. (Replies to Fletcher.)
Hussey's Glory of Christ. (Reply to Hoard.)
Kendall's Theocratia. (Reply to Goodwin.)
Lamb's Freedom from sin by Christ. (Reply to Goodwin.)

Arminianism—*continued.*

Con.

Owen's (John) Display of Arm. (Reply to Goodwin.)
——— (Other works on the subject.)
Princeton Review. 28:38.
Prynne's (W.) Anti-arminianism.
——— God no impostor.
Resberry's Stop to the gangrene.
——— Lightless star. (Reply to Goodwin.)
Rutherford's Apology for Divine grace.
Scott's (Tho.) Reply to Tomline.
Smith's (John) Letters to his brother.
Toplady's Historical proof.
——— Church of England vindicated.
Twisse on the Grace and power of God.
Webster's (C.) Arminianism.

Arminians, Hist. of. See ARMINIUS.

Cattenburgii Bibliotheca scrip. Remonstran.
De Vry, Hist. of te Kort und wærachtig verhael van de oorspronck.
Epistolæ ecclesiasticæ. (These letters of Arminius, Vorstius, Episcopius, Grotius, &c., furnish a very good history of the period immediately after the synod of Dort.)
Limborch de Origine et progressu, &c.
Salomo Theodoctus [Ægidius] de Secti Belgii.
Sandii Bibliotheca.
Staudlin Ges. der theol. Wissenschaften.
Theodoti (sive Afhacker) Ευωτικον.
Triglandii Antapologia.

Amer. Biblical Repository. 1:226.
Eclectic Review. New Series. 9:532.
Lord's Literary and Theol. Review. 6:337.
Methodist Quart. Review. 4:425, 556.

See an account of Foreign Arminian writers, in CATTENBURG, *Biblioth. scriptorum Remonstrantium,* and KOECKER, *Biblioth.* theol. symbolicæ. SALOMONIS THEODOCTUS [his real name is Ægidius], in his Secti Belgii, professes to give a complete list of the writers on both sides.

Arminius.

Arminii Opera.
Brantii Vita Jacobi Arminii.
Armenius' Works, with Memoir. Trans. by Nichols and Bagnal.
——— Trans. by J. Guthrie.
Bangs' Life of Arminius.
Brandt's Life of Arminius.
Jones' Christian biography.

Armor, Ancient.

Edinburg Review. 39:346.
Grose's Military antiquities. 150 plates.
Quarterly Review. 30:335.
Meyrick's Crit. enquiry into ancient armor. (Three folios, with many fine plates.)

Armor of God. See FIGHT OF FAITH.

Bennett's (Will.) Miscellaneous sermons.
Brackenbury's (Edward) 53 Discourses.
Butts' (Thomas) Sermons.

Armor of God—*continued.*

Dale's (Thomas) Sermons.
Girdlestone's (Charles) Sermons.
Glassebrook's (James) Sermons.
Gurnall's Christian in complete armor.
Gleig's (George) Sermons.
Hastings' (J.) Sermons at the University of Cambridge.
Horne's (Bp.) Discourses.
Latimer (Bp.) Sermons.
Scott's (John) Sermons.
Smith's (Sydney) Sermons.
Sullivan's (W. H.) Parish sermons.
Trench's (Richard C.) Sermons.
Vaughn's (Henry) Sermons.
Venner's (Richard) Panoplia.
Wilson's (Bp.) Sermons.

Arnoldists. See WALDENSES.

Bernhardi Epistolæ.
Boulay, Histoire academ. Parisiensis.
Chaupefied, Dictionnaire historique.
Murator, Droits de l'Empire.

Jones' Church history.

Arrangement of Scripture. See ANALYSES.

Artificial Memory. See MNEMONICS.

Ascension of Christ. See JESUS CHRIST.

Affelmani Disputationes.
Flaccii Explicationes.
Henrici Aphorismi triumphales.
Hoornbeckii Theologia practica. lib. v.
Koeppenii (Joann. Ulric.) Dissertationes.
Loescheri (Caspar) Dissertationes.
Mayeri (Joan. Frid.) Dissertationes.

Allison's (Archibald) Sermons.
Amory's (Thomas) Sermons.
Bibliotheca Sacra. 1:152.
Blair's (Hugh) Sermons.
Bloomfield's (G. B.) Sermons.
Blundell's (T.) Sermons.
Chandler's (Samuel) Sermons.
Cooper's (William) Sermons.
Dehon's (Bp. T.) Sermons.
Hall's (Bp.) Contemplations.
Hurrion on the Knowledge of Christ.
Noel's (Gerard T.) Sermons.
Riddle's (J. E.) Sermons.
Townsend's (George) Sermons.

Asceticism. See ESSENES, MORTIFICATION, MONASTICISM, THERAPEUTÆ.

Ashamed of Christ.

Arnold's (Thomas) Sermons.
Milner's (Isaac) Sermons.
Stillingfleet's (Bp.) Sermons.
Van Mildert's (Bp.) Sermons.
Whichcot (Benjamin) Sermons.

Ash Wednesday. See FASTS.

Andrews' (Bp.) Sermons.
Calamy's (Benjamin) Sermons.
Dehon's (Bp.) Sermons.

Gordon's (Adam) Sermons.
Higgins' (Francis) Sermons.
Lowth's (Bp.) Sermons.
Marshal's (N.) Sermons.
Secker's (Abp.) Sermons.

Associate Church. See SECEDERS.*

Pro.

Acts of the Assoc. Presb. Church, on renewing the Covenant, &c. 1766.
Anderson (John) on Saving faith.
Anderson's (Abraham) Theology.
Associate Presbytery, Acts of. 1766.
Associate Presbytery, Brief account of. 1796.
Constitution and Standards of the A. Ch.
Erskine's (Ralph) Works.
Erskine's (Ebenezer) Works.
Fisher's (James) Catechism.
Gib's Display of the Secession testimony.
Hall (A.) on the Burgess Oath.
McKerrow's Hist. of the Secession Church.
Miller's Sketches of the A. Church in Amer.
Proceedings of the A. Synod.

Associate Reformed Church.

Pro.

Assoc. Ref. Church Const. and Standards.
——— Synodical Reports.
Blakie's Philos. of sectarianism.
Carothers, Life of. By A. Ritchie.
Claybaugh's Christian profession.
Constitution and standards of the A. R. Church in North America. 1799.
Dales' (J. B.) Christian instructor.
Harper's (R. D.) Memorial church.
Lawson's (Geo.) Works.
McDill's Exposition of the Conf. of faith.
Pressly's (John T.) Letters on Psalmody.
Proudfit, Life of. By J. Forsyth.

Assurance. See FAITH.

Barclay's Assurance vindicated.
Baxter's (Richard) Sermons.
Bellamy's Letters and dialogues.
Biddulph's Lectures on the 51st Psalm.
Brackenbury's (Edward) Discourses.
Bowers' (Dean) Sermons.
Brine's (John) Sermons. (All excellent.)
Brooks' Heaven upon earth.
Burgess' (Anthony) 141 Sermons on grace.
Charnock's (Stephen) Works.
Coles' (Nath.) Godly man's assurance.
East (T.) on the Forgiveness of sin.
Edwards' (Prest.) Works.
Erskine's (Ebenezer) Sermons.
Erskine's (Thomas) Essay on faith.
Fawcett's (John) Sermons. (3 on this subj.)
Fuller's Gospel its own witness.
Hall's (Bp.) Sermons.
Henry's (Philip) Sermons.
Horæ Solitariæ.

* The Associate and Associate Reformed Churches in the United States became united in 1859, under the name of United Presbyterian Church.

Assurance—*continued.*

Hervey's Theoron and Aspasio.
Jones' (Tho.) The true Christian.
Jay's (Will.) Sermons.
Keckerman on Heavenly knowledge.
McLean's Apostolical commission.
Marshall on Sanctification.
Mason's (Jno. M.) Sermons.
Maunder on Full assurance.
Mills' (Tho.) Light of life.
Owen on the Spirit.
Polhill's Mystical union between Christ and believers.
Roberts' (Arthur) Sermons.
Rogers' Righteous man's evid. for heaven.
Saurin's (James) Sermons.
Stewart's (J. H.) Sermons.
Thorn on the Assurance of faith.
Toplady on the Assurance of faith.
Vaughn's (Henry) Sermons.
Wardlaw's (Ralph) Sermons.
——— Essays. Ess. 1.
Watts' (Isaac) Sermons.
Wilks' (Sam. C.) Christian Essays.
Zanchius on How one may know he is a child of God.

Astrology. See DIVINATION.

Pro.

Alchabitii Scientia judic. astronom.
Bartolomæi Coclitis Bononiensis.
Belin, Figures astrales.
Cardini Metopocopia.
Eschiudii Astrologia judicialis.
Grunpeckii Speculum visionis.
Hagecii Astrol. opuscula antiqua.
Wendelini Contemplationum physicarum.
Nostradami Centuriæ.

Barret's Celestial Intelligencer.
Bishop's Manual of Astrology.
Boyse's Pantheon. (Appendix.)
Case's Angelical Guide.
Coley's Key to Astrology.
Dariot's Briefe and most easie jntrod. to yᵉ iudgement of yᵉ stars.
Heydon's (Chris.) on Judicial astronomy.
Heydon's (John) Holy guide.
Holwell's (John) Discourses.
Kirby's Marrow of astrology.
Lillie's Guide to Astrologers.
Middleton's Practical astrology.
Penseyre's Guide to Astrology.
Raphael's Oracle of the future.
Ramsay on Judicial Astrology.
Sibley's (Eben.) Trans. of Placidus.
——— Key to physic.
Wharton's (Geo.) Works. (Very curious.)
Wing's Astronomy and Nature.
Worsdale's Celestial Philosophy.
Zadkiel's Horoscope.

Con.

Limborchii Theologia. Lib. v. cap. 25.
Luther (Martin) de Astrologia.
Turrettini Institutiones. Loc. v. quest. 7.

Astrology—*continued.*

Calvin (J.) on Judicial astrol. Tr. by Gilby.
Chambers on Astrology. (Reply to Heydon.)
Carleton's Exam. of Heydon's defence.
Edwards' (Dr. John) Cometomantia.
Howe's (John) Works.
Jennings' Jewish Antiquities.
Melton's (John) Astrologaster.
Moody's Complete refutation of A.
Prideaux's Connection of the O. and N. Test.
Quarterly Review. 26:180.
Rowland on Judicial Astrology.

Astronomy. See COSMOLOGY.

Athanasian Creed. See CREEDS.

Athanasius. See FATHERS.

Athanasii Opera omnia. Ed. Benedictini.
Athanasii Vita ex Photio.
——— Vita ex Aretini.
——— Vita ex Benedictinorum.
——— Vita ex Bernardi de Montfaucon.
——— Vita ex Papebrocii.
——— Vita ex Simeonis.
Boeringer Kirchengeschichte in biographien.
Goetze de Dubiis Athanasii scriptis.
Hermance. Vie de St. Athanase. (Includes a history of Arianism.)
Kalleri Dissertationes.
Mansius de Epochis conciliorum Sardic et Sirmiens.
Möhler's A. und die kirche sein Zeit.
Renaudot, Hist. de patriarc. Alexandriæ. (Collects all the accounts of Athanasius by Oriental writers.)
Valesii Observationes Ecclesiasticæ.

Athanasius' Festal epistles. Tr. from the Syriac, with notes and indexes. Oxford, 1854.)
Christian Monthly Spectator. 4:244.
Kaye's Account of the Council of Nice.
Lardner's Credibility of the Gospels. Part 2.
Parker's Trans. of the orations of A.
Thirlby's Answer to Mr. Whiston.
Whiston's Athanasius convicted of forgery.

Atheism. See EXISTENCE OF GOD.

Pro.

Baur's (F. C.) Ges. des Christenthums.
——— Kritische untersuchungen.
——— (Other works.)
Beregardi Circulus Pisanus.
Brunus de Immenso et innumerabilibus.
Cæsalpini Questionum peripateticarum.
D'Holbach, le Christianisme devoilé.
——— Lois du monde.
——— La contagion sacrée.
Hekel's Encyklopädie.
Mettrie, L'homme machine.
——— Reflexions philosophique.
——— Nouvelle liberté de penser.
——— Hist. naturelle de l'ame.
——— (Other works.)
Mocenici Contemplationes.

Atheism—*continued.*

Pro.

Spinoza, Tractatus theologico-politicus.
——— Opera posthuma.
Vanini Amphitheatrum æternum.
Wolfii (Jo. Chris.) Opera.
Atkinson's Letters on the laws of man.
Blount's Oracles of reason.
Collins on Free-thinking.
D'Holbach's Christianity exposed.
Investigator. Periodical. Lond. 1855, et seq.
Holyoake (Geo. J.) on the Atonement.
——— Types of religion.
——— Discussion with Rev. B. Grant. 1853.
——— (Other treatises.)
Laws' (Tho. L.) Philosophical meditations.
Leroux (J. J.), Opera.
Mandeville's Free thoughts.
Martineau's (Harriet) Letters.
Mettrie's Natural hist. of the soul.
——— Liberty of thinking.
Mirabeau's System of nature.
Reasoner, The. Edited by Holyoake.
Spinoza, Tractatus theologico-politicus.
Toland's Nazarenus.
——— Infinite and eternal universe.
——— Amyntor.
——— Christianity not mysterious.
——— Pantheisticon.
——— Tetradymus.
——— (Other works.)

Several of these writers are by some ranked as Deists.

Con.

Abbadie, de la Religion chretienne.
Abichtius de damno Atheismi in republica.
Assonlevilla, Atheomastix.
Barchovichii Dissertatio de Deo.
Baumeisteri Exercitationes. (An philosophus possit esse Atheus?)
Bellarmin de adscensione mentis in Deum per scalas creaturum.
Benoist, Melange de remarques crit.
Buddei Thesis theologicæ.
——— de orig. gentis Ebrææ. (Ag. Toland.)
Carpzovii Programma. (Against Toland.)
Cuperi Arcana Atheismi revelata.
Cudworth, Systema intellectuale hujus Universi. (This trans., by Mosheim, is more valuable than the English original, on account of the numerous learned notes.)
Deylingii Observationes. (Against Toland.)
Donatus, num Deum esse, per se, notum?
Elsneri Dissertationes. (Against Toland.)
Fabricii Apologet. pro genere humana.
——— Delectus Argumentorum, &c. (A comprehensive review of writers against Atheists, Deists, Jews, &c.)
Fenelon, Demonstra. de l'existence de Dieu.
Frankii Atheus convictus.
Gisbert Coquei Hobbianismi anatomea.
Grappius, an Atheismus necessario ducat ad corruptionum morum?
Kortholtus de Atheismo.

Atheism—*continued.*

Con.

La Croze, Diss. sur les Athées modernes.
Langii Causa Dei et religionis.
Lassenii Arcana politico-atheistica.
Mangii Animadversiones.
Maret's (H. L. C.) Pantheismus in d. modernen gesellschaften. 1842.
Martinii Dissertationes.
Menkenii Diss. de Hobbesii Epicureismo.
Mosheimii Vindicatio antiquæ christianorum disciplinæ.
Mulleri Atheismus devictus.
Niemanni Atheismus refutatus.
Nieuentyt, het rect Gebruyk der Wereltbeschouwingen.
Noesselt's Vertheidigung d. christl. Relig.
Phillips, de Atheismo.
Raphsoni Demonstratio de Deo.
Rechenbergii Fundamenta veræ religionis.
Reiserus de Orig., progressu, &c., Atheismi.
Riemani Hist. Atheismi et Atheorum.
Seligmanni (G. F.) Exercitationes academ.
Spanheimii Opera.
Staalkopfius de Atheismi habitu ad vitam civilem.
Thomasii Historia atheismi.
Tiezmanni (Henric.) Disputationes.
Varenii Remedio therapeutico atheologiæ.
Voetii (Gisbert.) Disputationes.
Volder, Disputationes philosophicæ.
Vossius de theologia gentili, et physiologia christiana.
Wagneri Examen atheismi speculativi.
Wittichii Adnotationes. (Agt. Des Cartes.)
Adams on the Existence of God.
Alexander's (J.) Observations. (Ag. Hobbes.)
Allen's Oracles of reason.
Allen's (Thomas) Modern Atheism.
Balguy's Sermons and Tracts.
Batchellor's (Henry) Logic of Atheism.
Baxter's (Andrew) Works.
Bayle's Dictionary. (Under Diagorus, Theodorus, Vaninus.)
Beecher's (Lyman) Atheism considered theologically and politically.
Bentley's (Richard) Sermons.
Berkeley's (Bp.) Works.
Boyle Lectures. (From 1692 to the present.)
——— Inquiry into received notions.
——— Essay on final causes.
Buchanan's Modern Atheism: as exhibited under the forms of Pantheism, Materialisms, Secularism, and Development. 1855.
Carleton's Darkness of Atheism.
Charnock's Works.
Cheyne's Philosophical Principles.
Christian Examiner. 50:309. 78:
Clarendon's Reply to Hobbes.
Clarke on the Being and Attributes of God.
Cudworth's Intellectual System.
——— ——— ——— Abridged by Dr. Wise.
Cumberland's Law of nature.
Delaney's Revelation examined with candor.
Doddridge's Lectures. Part II.

Atheism—*continued.*

Con.

Dix's (Morgan) Lectures on Pantheism.
Durham's Demonstration.
Dwight's Discourses. Disc. 1, 2, and 3.
Eclectic Review. New series. 7:329.
Edwards on the Visible struct. of the world.
Elliot's Folly of Atheism.
Estlin's Nature and causes of Atheism.
Foster (James) on Natural Religion.
Fotherby's Atheomastix.
Gardner's Doom's-day book.
Grant's (Brewin) Public discussion with G. J. Holyoake, in 1854.
Godwin's Lectures on the A. controversy.
Gregory's Modern Atheism.
Grew's Cosmologia Sacra.
Hale's (Sir Matthew) Origin of man.
Hall's (Robt.) Modern Infidelity.
Harris on Atheistical objections.
Hattecliffe's God or nothing.
Hill's Lectures and Reflections.
Howel's Spirit of prophecy. (Agt. Hobbes.)
Howe's (John) Works.
Hunt's Essay on Pantheism.
Jenyn's (Soame) Disquisitions.
Lectures on Secularism, by Gregory, Condor, Savage, and Mellor.
Lesser's Insecto-theology.
Lewis' (Tayler) Plato against the Atheists.
Locke's Works.
McAll's Logic of Atheism.
McLaurin's Essays.
McCullock's (John) Sermons.
Mills on the Attempted application of Pantheistic principles to the historic criticism of the Gospel.
Monthly Review. 54:163.
More's (Henry) Philosophical works. Part 1.
Nelson's Cause and cure of infidelity.
Nieuentyt's Religious philosopher.
Nichols' Conference with a Theist.
Parker on God and Providence.
Pattison's Anti-Nazarenus.
Pilling on the Existence of God.
Pironett's Disquisitions. (Against Hobbes.)
Phillips' Diss. Historico-philosophica.
Ray's Physico-theology. (Great, and most useful.)
Saisset's Modern Pantheism. 1863.
Seed's (Jeremiah) Sermons.
Sparks' Antidote of Atheism.
Talmot's (Bp.) Sermons.
Temple's Doctrine of Leviathan.
Tennison's (Abp.) Sermons. (Agt. Hobbes.)
Thompson's (R. A.) Christian Theism.
Tower's Atheismus vapulans.
Tullock's Theism. Burnett prize essay. 1854.
Vaughn's (J.) Lectures. Lect 4.
Vince's Laws and constitutions of the heavenly bodies. (Uses profound astronomical knowledge, in the simplest language.)
Ward's (Bp.) Essay toward an eviction, &c.
Whish on the First Cause.
Wise's (Tho.) Reason and Philosophy of A.
Wisheart's (William) Sermons.
Wharton (Francis) on Theism.
Woolsey's Unreasonableness of Atheism.

The above are a very small specimen of the numerous writers on this subject.

Atheism, History of.

Brucker de Stratonis Atheismo.
Buddeus de A. et superstitione. Cap. 1.
Burgman, de Stoa.
Fabricii Delectus argumentorum.
Foppii Atheis philosophorum gentilium celebriorum.
Gregoire, Hist. des sectes religieuses.
Jenkin (Tho.), Historia Atheismi.
Parker, Disputationes de Deo. Disp. I.
Phillips, Historia Atheismi.
Riemanni Hist. Universalis Atheorum.
Rieserus de Origine, progressu, &c.
Treverus de Theologia Luciana.
Triller, in Hippocrate.
Upmark, Atheomastix.
Wagner, Examinatio, A. Speculatio. Cap. 4, 5.
Zimmermanni Dissertationes.

Amer. Biblical Repository. 2d series. 2:320.
Christian Examiner. 40:108.
Eclectic Review. 4th series. 9:85.
New England Magazine. 7:500.

Athenagoras.

Athenagoræ Opera, cum notis, &c. Rechenbergio.
La Crose de Fabula erotica.
Leyserus de Athanag. Athen. philosopho.
Mosheim, de Vera ætate libelli ab Athan. conscripti.
Tentzelii Exercitationes.
Veyssierii Epistola ad Wolfium, de fabula erotica quæ sub Athenag. nomine prodiit.
Athenagoras' Apologetics. Translated by D. Humphreys.
Conybeare's Bampton lectures. 1839.
Humphrey's Trans. of the Apologetics.

Atonement. See DEFINITE ATONEMENT, IMPUTATION, POLEMIC THEOLOGY, REDEMPTION, SUFFERINGS OF CHRIST, UNITARIANISM, &C.

Callixtus de Sacrificio Christi.
Grotius de Satisfactione Christi.
Jaegerus de Christo sponsore.
Mayerus de Officio Christi sacerdoti.
Outram de Sacrificiis.
Stapferi Institutiones Theologicæ.
Turretini Disputatio de Satisfactione.

Adams' Letter to Gannet.
Amer. Bibl. Repository. 2d series. 10:110. 12:177. 3d series. 4:86.
Appleton's Works. Lect. 33 to 35.
Balguy (Thomas) on Atonement.
Bampton Lectures.
Barrow on the Creed.
——— Sermons on Redemption.
Bates' (William) Works.
Bradford's Boyle Lectures. 1699.
Bibliotheca Sacra. 13:130. 15:132. 18:284.

Atonement—*continued.*

Beveridge's Thesaurus theologicus.
Blundell's Sermons.
Brown's (E. H.) Sermons.
Burton's (Hezekiah) Sermons.
Burton's (Edward) Sermons.
Calamy's (Benjamin) Sermons.
Candlish's (R.) Cross of Christ.
——— on the Atonement.
Carson (A.) on the Atonement.
Chalmers' Discourses.
Charnock's Works.
Christian Monthly Spectator. 2:21, 82, 139. 6:475, 659.
Christian Review. 1:215.
Christian Observer, 1861, p. 160.
Close's (Fr.) Sermons.
Coles on Divine Sovereignty.
Daubeney's (Charles) Discourses.
Dewar's Nature, reality, efficacy, &c.
Dwight's Discourses. Disc. 55–57.
Eclectic Review. 4th series. 18:249.
Edwards' (Prest.) Works.
Evans' (Dr. Caleb) Christ crucified.
——— 4 Discourses on the Atonement.
Fuller's Gospel its own witness.
Gibert's Basis, nature, bearings, &c.
Haldane's (J. A.) Nature, &c., of the A.
Hampton on the Atonement.
Hare's (A. W.) Sermons.
Hoadley's (Bp.) Sermons.
Hervey's Theoron and Aspasius.
Hopkins' (Bp.) Works.
Hurd's (Bp.) Sermons.
Jamieson's Sacred History.
Jerram's Letters on the Atonement.
Jenkin on the Atonement. (Infirm.)
Jones on the Mediation of Christ. (A beautiful epitome of the gospel.)
Juke's (H.) The Law of the Offerings.
Kirk's (Edw. N.) Sermons.
Kitto's Journal of Sacred Literature. 3:74.
Lumley's Letters.
Magee on A. and sacrifice. ("One of the profoundest writers of the age."—Bp. Jebb.)
Mann's (Bp.) Essay on the Atonement.
Marshall's Divine purpose of the A.
Mant's (Bp.) Lectures.
Methodist Quarterly Review. 6:392. 7:379.
Newton's (B. Will.) The Perfect Sacrifice.
Outram on Sacrifices. (No work is so satisfactory on the typical relations of Jewish sacrifices.)
Owen on the Satisfaction of Christ.
Paley's (William) Sermons.
Parks on the A. (A collection of tracts.)
Pearson on the Creed.
Penrose's Moral principle of the A.
Princeton Review. 8:201.
Quaif's Necess. and efficacy of the A.
Reynolds on Reconciliation.
Scattergood's (Samuel) Sermons.
Seabury's (Bp.) Sermons.
Seed's (Jer.) Sermons.
Shedd's (W. G. T.) Discourses and Essays.

Atonement—*continued.*

Sherlock's (Bp.) Sermons.
Short's (T. V.) Sermons.
Shuttleworth's (P. N.) Sermons.
Simpson's Plain Thoughts.
Skelton's (P.) Sermons.
Spirit of the Pilgrims. 2:25.
South's (Robt.) Sermons.
Stanhope's Boyle Lectures. 1702.
Stevenson's (Geo.) Essay on the A.
Stillingfleet's (Bp.) Works.
Symington on the A. and Intercession.
Taylor's Apology of Ben Mordecai.
Taylor's (John) Scripture doctrine of the A.
Thompson's Bampton Lectures. 1853.
Tillotson's (Abp.) Sermons.
Townsend's (George) Sermons.
Treffry's Letters. (Highly esteemed, especially by Methodists.)
Trench's (R. C.) Sermons.
Turner's Boyle Lectures. 1708.
Turrettin on the A. Tr. by J. R. Wilson.
Urwick's Person and A. of Christ.
Venn's (Henry) Sermons.
Veysie's Bampton Lectures. 1795.
Walker's (Geo.) Letters.
Wardlaw's (R.) Nature of the Atonement.
Watt's (Isaac) Sermons.
West's (Steph.) Scripture doct of the A.
Willson's History of opinions on the A.
Winslow's (Octav.) View of the Atonement.
Wintles' Bampton Lectures. 1794.
Witsius on the Covenants.

Attributes of God. See under THE SEVERAL ATTRIBUTES.

Doederlini Theologia.
Gerhardi Loci theologici.
Lessii Opuscula varia.
Parkeri (Sam.) Disputationes.
Turrettini Instit. Theologiæ elencticæ.
Vorstius de Deo.
Zanchius de natura Dei.

Abernethy's (John) Sermons.
Balguy's Moral and theological tracts.
Bibliotheca Sacra. 7:686.
Barrows' (Isaac) Sermons.
Bates' Harmony of the Divine attributes.
Boyle Lectures. (Several.)
Brown on the Being and attributes of God.
Bryant's Truth of the Christian religion.
Burder (Geo.) on the Divine perfections.
Burder's (H.) Scripture character of God.
Charnock's Discourses. ("One of the most inestimable productions that ever did honor to the sanctified judgment and genius of a human being."—Toplady.)
Christian Family Library. Vol. 15. (Comprising selections from Charnock, Wisheart, Bates, and Goodwin.)
Clarke's (Sam.) Demonstration of the exist. of God.
——— Sermons. (Grand.)
Clark's (Adam) Discourses.
Dick's (T.) Philosophy of religion. Chap. 1.

Attributes of God—*continued.*

Drew (Sam.) on the Being and attrib. of God.
Duncan on the Attributes of God.
Dwight's (Timothy) Discourses.
Erskine's (Ralph) Sermons. (Excellent.)
Gastrell's Christian Institutes.
Graves' (Dr. Richard) Sermons.
Grinfield on the Attributes of God.
Harris' (John) Refutation of objections agt. the being and attributes of God.
Harris' (Robert) Sermons.
Haynes' Attributes and worship of God.
Hickman's (Bp.) Sermons.
Hunt's (Jeremiah) Sermons.
Jackson's Divine essence and attributes.
Jamieson's Sacred history.
Knight's Being and attrib. of God demonstr.
Knowles' (Thos.) Discourses.
Law's Limit of human enquiry.
Leigh's (Sir E.) Discourses.
Limborch's Christian theology.
London Eclec. Review. 4th series. 3 : 37.
McCulloch (John) on the Attrib. (Physical argument.)
Moore's Divine Dialogues.
Morton (Bp.) on the Nature of God.
Phillip (R.) on the Attributes of God.
Preston on the Divine essence.
Saurin's (James) Sermons.
Skelton's (P.) Deism revealed.
——— Sermons.
Sumner on the Moral attributes of God.
Tillotson's (Abp.) Sermons.
Toplady's Preliminary discourse.
Tucker's Light of nature pursued.
Veysie's Bampton Lectures. 1795.
Vizard's Principles of Religion and Philos.
Watts' Glory of Christ as God. (Often reprinted.)
Whitby's 33 Sermons.
Wilson on the Attributes of God.
Wisheart's (George) Sermons. (Precious.)

Audæans. See ANTHROPOMORPHISTS.

Augustine, de Hæresibus.
Epiphanius, adversus lxxx. hæreses.
Theodoret, de Fabula hæreticorum.
Schrœder, de Hæresi Audianorum.
Voght, de Audianismo ante Audium.

Audianists. See AUDÆANS.

Augsburg Confession. See CREEDS, LUTHERANISM.

Altingii Exegesis August. confessionis.
Auzeigung und Bekentniss des glaubens und Lehre, so die adpellierenden stende Key. First German edition. 1530.
Batti Disputationes Theologicæ.
Baumgarten (M.), Disputationes.
Calovii Criticus Sacer.
Carpzovii Isagoge in libros ecclesias.
Chytræi Hist. Augustanæ confessionis.
Cyprian (E. S.), Hist. der Augsb. Confes.
Deylingius de Auctoritate Aug. Confes.
Feverlini de Libris hypognosticon.

Augsburg Confession—*continued.*

Feverlini Observationes in Aug. Confession.
Finck, de omnibus artic. Aug. Confessionis.
Gerhardi Confessio Catholica.
Graveri Prelectiones in August. Conf.
Hanneckenii Declarationes theologicæ.
Hasei Libri symbolici ecclesiæ evang.
Heilbrunner's Augspurgischen Conf.
Hoeneg, Apologia pro beato Luthero.
Hoffman, com. in August. Conf.
Hutteri Analysis artic. conf. August.
Kœcher de Veritate ac præstantia religionis evangelico Lutheranæ.
Kromayeri Comm. didactico-elenchticus.
Kuzmany's Praktische Theol. d. evangelisch. Kirche.
Lobeschii Disputationes Theologicæ.
Martini Collegio in August. Confessionem.
Mentzeri Exegesis Augustanæ Confessionis.
Meyer (L.), les Principes fondamentaux de l'eglise.
Moltheri Disputationes XXII.
Muller der Augspurgischen Confession.
Mylii Explicatio Aug. Confessionis.
Osiandri Coll. theologic. in Aug. Confes.
Pappii Commentar. in confes. fidei.
Reinbeck's Betrachtungen über die A. C.
Ritteri Disputationes XXII.
Rohr's Glaubenssätze der evang. Kirche.
Rotermund Geschichte des Reichstages.
Rudelbach Historisch-kritische einleitung.
Ruzicka's Gesch. Augsburg. Confession.
Salig's Historie der A. Confession.
Schleiermacker's Predigten auf die feier der Uebergabe, &c.
Semleri Apparatus in lib. symbol. Lutheranæ.
Shelvig's Erklærung der Aug. Confession.
Siegwartii Disputationes.
Titius Vindicatio A. Confessionis.
Vittman's Augsburgische Confession.
Verpootennii Positiones Theologicæ.
Villers' (C.) Précis historique sur la presentation de la Conf. d'Augsbourg a l'Empereur Charles V.
Weber's Geschichte der Augs. Confession.
Winer's Darstellung.
Wirtembergensium Theologorum Scripta. (These were J. Andreas, E. Bidembachius, J. Magirus, L. Osiander, J. Brent, Martin Crusius, &c.)

Burrow's Translation of the Augsb. Conf.
Okeley's 21 Dissert. upon the Aug. Conf.
Salig's Hist. of the Augsburg Confession.
Zinzendorf's Discourses on the A. Conf.

Augustan Confession. See AUGSBURG.

Augustine.

Augustini Opera.
Bindeman's Leben des A. seit seiner Täufe.
Boehringer, der Kirche Christi, und ihre Zeugen.
Busch, Epistolæ et sermones A.
Carpzovii Disputationes.
Clausenii A. scripturæ sac. interpres.
Gastii (Jacob.) Commentaria.

Augustine—*continued.*
Godeau, Vie de St. Augustine.
Jordani Vita Augustini.
Lancilotti Vita St. Augustini.
Laval, Instructions tirées de St. August.
Maieri Augustini Vita.
Orse, Vie de St. Augustine.
Posidii Vita et indiculus scriptorum A.
Riseri Augustinus; contra Bellarmin. ("Luculentum et egregium."—BUDDÆUS.)
Rivii Vita A. ex operibus concinnatæ.
Surii Vitæ sanctorum.

Augustine's Confessions. Tr. by W. Watts.
——— ——— Tr. by E. B. Pusey.
——— ——— Tr. by Shedd.
——— ——— Tr. by Bickersteth.
Augustine's Meditations. Tr. by G. Stanhope.
Augustine's City of God. Tr. by Vives.
Amer. Bibl. Repository. 2d series. 7:375.
Baillie's Memoir of Augustine.
British Quart. Review. 6:213.
Christian Review. 5:64.
Princeton Review. 8:567. 26:437.
Schaff's (Philip) Life and labors of A.
Trench's A. as an interpreter of Scripture.

PANZER enumerates over 200 editions of Augustine's works, in whole or in part, previous to A. D. 1500, many of them with notes.

Augustinism. See CALVINISM.

Auricular Confession. See POPERY.

Pro.

Antonini Summa Confessionem.
Boileau, Hist. confes. auric. ex antiquis scripturæ, patrum, pontificum, et conciliorum monumentis.
Bohn, Animadversiones ad hist. conf. auric.
Hullinghofii Antiq. confessionis privatæ.
Latonus de Confessione secreta.
Maillard, La Confession generale.
Mangin, la Science des Confesseurs.
Nider, Manuale confessorum.
Tammarthan Traité de la confession.
Theramo, Consolatio peccatorum.
Thyræi Disputationes theologicæ.
Valentine de Rebus controversis.

Brownson's Quart. Review. 3:327.
Fourth Council of Lateran.

Con.

Abechtii (Joann. Georg.) Dissertationes.
Daillæi (Joann.) Disputationes.
Kamperi Hist. Indulgentiarum.
Lasteyrie, Hist. de la conf. sous ses rapports religieux, moraux, et politique.
Schmidt, Lettres sur la conf. auriculaire.
Titus de Confessione privata.

Ace (Dan.) on the Tenet of A. confession.
Beard (J. R.) on the Confessional.
Beamish on Auricular confession.
Eclectic Magazine. 5:413.
Eclectic Review. 4th series. 7:668. 19:72. 23:690.
Evans' (B.) Modern Popery. 1855.

Auricular Confession—*continued.*

Con.

Foreign Quarterly Review. 35:188.
Goodman on Auric. conf., as prescribed by the Council of Trent.
Hopkins' History of the Confessional.
Kitto's Journal. New series. Vol. 3.
Lasteyrie's History of Auricular confession. Tr. by C. Cocks. (A tremendous blow.)
Mendham on Indulgences and pardons.
Peace (W.) on Auric. conf. and absolution.
Poole's Dialogues bet. two Protestants.
Reading on the Principal controversies.
Salter's Hall sermons. Ser. by J. Burroughs.
Taylor's (Jer.) Polemic Discourses.
Todd on Confession and absolution.
Young's (John) Lectures.

Authenticity of the Scriptures. See CANON, DEISM, INSPIRATION, INTERNAL EVIDENCE, PROPHECY AS A PROOF OF REVELATION, REVELATION.

Athenagoræ Legatio pro Christianis.
Augustine, de civitate Dei.
Clemens (Alex.) Cohortatio ad Græcos.
Justin Martyr, Apologia.
——— Cohortatio ad Græcos.
Theophilus ad Autolycum.

Arnobius, adversus Gentes.
Bocharti Epistola ad Tapinum.
Bullingerus de S. S. auctoritate, &c.
Callixtus de Auctorit. majestasque S. S.
Cellerier, de Origine, &c., de S. S.
Coccejus de Potentia Scrip. sacræ.
Curcellii Opera.
De la Mothe, de l'Inspiration, &c.
Duvoisin, Demonstration évangélique.
Edvardus de auctor, stilo, et perfect. S. S.
Gausenius de Verbo Dei.
Hollman dem Ueberzengenden Vörtrag von Gott, &c.
Hornii Tractatus theologica de S. S.
Hauteville, la Relig. chrêtien prouvée.
Huetii Demonstratio evangelica.
Hunnius de Majestate, auctoritate, &c.
Hutteri (Leonard.) Disputationes.
Jaquelot, la Verité des livres du N. Test.
Kœppen, die Bibel. (Edited by Schreibel, in 1837.)
Kromayer de Auctoritate Sac. Scripturæ.
Limborch, collatio cum credito Judæo.
Maii (Jo. Henric.) Dissertationes quatuor.
Meisneri (Balthas.) Disputationes.
Monot, Erreurs de Voltaire.
Musæi Introductio in Theologiam.
——— Questiones theo. de syncretismo.
Paræus de Sc. præstantia, auctoritate, &c.
Quenstedii Exercitationes Theologici.
Saubertii Disputationes.
Sohnius de verbo Dei.
Spanheim de Div. Scrip. origine et auctor.
Thumii (Theodor.) Disquisitiones.
Whitakeri (Guil.) Disputationes.
Zelleri Historia Scripturæ sacræ.
Addison on the Evidences, &c.
Amer. Biblical Repository. 11:265.

Authenticity of Scriptures—*cont'd.*

Amer. Monthly Review. 2:466.
Bampton Lectures. (Annual since 1780. Most of them by the ablest Divines.)
Bannerman's Divine authority of S. S.
Bates' (William) Works.
Bayley's Antiquity, evidence, &c.
Blackwood's Magazine. 18:160.
Blunt's Veracity of the Gospels. (Argued from the undesigned coincidences.)
Bogue's Div. authority, &c. ("One of the best books on the subject."—ORME.)
Bolton's Evidences as exhibited in the apologists, down to Augustine.
Bonnett's Philosoph. and crit. enquiries.
Boyle Lectures. (Annual since 1692.)
British Quart. Review. 7:431.
Burnett's (Tho.) Demonstr. of the true rel.
Cellerier's Auth. of the O. T. Tr. by Wreford.
Christian Examiner. 14:181. 17:155. 20:307. 22:321. 36:145, 359. 41:216. 43:148.
Christian Review. 3:53. 11:229.
Christian Spectator. 5:126.
Clark's Div. authority of S. Scripture.
Constable's Miscellany. Vol. 26.
Davidson on Prophecy.
Debate between R. D. Owen and Alexander Campbell.
Delany's Revelation examined.
Dodd's (William) Evidences, &c.
Doddridge's (Philip) Discourses.
Dublin University Magazine. 6:231.
Edinburg Review. 86:210.
Faber's Horæ Mosaicæ.
Finlay's Vindication. (Agt. Voltaire.)
Fotherby's Atheomastix.
Frèsinous' Def. of Christ'y. Tr. by Jones.
Giles' Christian Records.
Graves on the Pentateuch.
Gregory's (Olynthus) Letters to a friend.
Gurney's (Joseph) Essays.
Haldane's (Robt.) Authority of Scripture.
Hampden's Philos. evidence. (A worthy companion to Butler's Analogy.)
Hengstenberg's Egypt and the Pentateuch.
Hedge's (John) Sermons on the evidences.
Hulsean Lectures. (Annual since 1819. See especially those of Benson, 1820, Franks, 1821, Benson, 1826, Blunt, 1831, Parkinson, 1837, Smith, 1840.
Jesse (Will.) on the Holy Scriptures.
Keith's Evidence from prophecy.
Knox's Evid. of the Christian religion.
Lawrie's Evidence from prophecy.
Leland's Authority of the O. and N. Test.
Levi's (David) Letters to Thomas Paine.
Lilienthall's Divine rev. vindicated.
Literary and Theolog. Review. 2:436.
Lowth on the Divine authority, &c.
McKnight's Truth of the gospel history.
Mial's Bases of belief.
Michaelis' Introduction to the N. T.
Miller's (John) Authority of Scripture.

Authenticity of Scriptures—*cont'd.*

Monthly Lectures on the evidences. (By Orme, Collier, Burder, Stratton, Reed, J. Pye Smith, Fletcher, &c.)
Murray's Rev. demonstrated. (By monuments, sculptures, gems, coins, &c.)
Nares' Veracity of the Evangelists.
New Englander. 4:401.
New York Review. 4:428.
Noesselt's Divinity of the Christian religion.
North American Review. 36:345. 42:206. 58:39.
Norton's (A.) Genunineness of the Gospels.
Olshausen's Genuineness, &c. Tr. by Fosdick.
Osborn's Ancient Egypt. (Proofs from inscriptions, pictures, &c.)
Pascal's (Blaise) Thoughts.
Princeton Review. 16:359.
Rawlinson's Historical Evidences, &c. (Has particular reference to modern discoveries at Nineveh, Babylon, &c.)
Redford's Scrip. verified by science, history, and human consciousness.
Ross (Earl of), Truth of Revelation.
Sack's Christian Apologetics.
Simpson's (David) Sacred Literature.
——— Plea for religion. (Ag. Tom Paine.)
Steele's (Jas.) Philosophy of the evidences.
Stillingfleet's Origines Sacræ.
Taylor's (Isaac) Historical proofs.
Thompson (Edw.) on the Prophecies, types, miracles, &c.
Tredgel's Historic evid. of the authorship.
Wellwood's Authority of the N. Test.
Wilson's (Dan.) Lectures on the evidences. (A good family book.)
Woolsey on Scripture belief.

Avarice. See COVETOUSNESS.

Avignon. See POPES OF AVIGNON.

Baal.

Oort's Worship of Baalim in Israel.

Baalzebub. See SATAN.

Babel. See TOWER.

Babylon. See APOCALYPSE, POPERY, PROPHECY.

Caulfield's Fall of Babylon.
Cunningham's Apostacy of the Ch. of Rome.
Ettrick's Second Exodus.
Fulke's (W.) Proof that Babylon is Rome.
Hardy on the Principal prophecies.
Keith's (Alex.) Signs of the times. 1823.
Lee (Prof.) on the Interpret. of prophecy.
Sergrove's Lectures on Popery.
Tower's Illustrations of prophecy.
Weaver's Fulfilment of Scripture.

Babylonish Captivity.

Abrami Pharo Veterum Testamentum.
Calmeti Dissertationes.
Cellarii Dissertationes.
Crenii Fasciculus ad historiam sacram.
Behmii de Termino a quo, et ad quem.
Vorstii Exercitationes Academicæ.

Backbiting. See SLANDER.

Backsliding. See APOSTACY.

Baker's (John) Sermons.
Brine's (John) Works.
Buddicom's (Robert) Sermons.
Cecil's (Richard) Sermons.
Cooper's (Edward) Sermons.
Cunningham's (J. W.) Sermons.
Erskine's (Ebenezer) Sermons.
Fenner's (W.) Sermons.
Ford's Laodicea.
Fuller's (Andrew) Backslider.
Gahan's (William) Sermons.
Godwin's Child of light walking in darkness.
Heurtley's (Charles) Parochial Sermons.
Hogg on Declension in religion.
Jay's (William) Sermons.
Leifchild's (John) Discourses.
Sibbs' (Rich.) Sermons. (Tender and pointed.)
Udal's Sermons. (Fall of Peter.)
Wesley's (John) Sermons.
Winslow on Personal declensions and revivals in religion.
Woods' Religious declension: its nature, causes, effects, and means of recovery.
Woodhouse's Careless Christian.

Bad Company. See EVIL COMPANY.

Balaam. See BIOGRAPHY.

Bartolocci Bibliotheca Rabbinica.
Deylingii Observationes Sacræ.
Hengstenberg's Geschichte Bileams, und seine Weissagungen Erlantert.
Mœbii Historia Balaam.
Selden de Diis Syris.
Velleri Annot. in hist. Balaam.
Wellemeri Dissertationes Theologicæ.

Anderson's Life and character of Moses.
Arnold's (of Rugby) Sermons.
Attersoll's Hist. of Balaak and Balaam.
Bibliotheca Sacra. 3:347, 699.
Blencoe's (Edward) Sermons.
Bryant's Observ. on passages of Scripture.
Butler's (Bp.) Sermons.
Carter's (N.) Sermons.
Collyer's (W. B.) Lectures on Scripture facts.
Dehon's (Bp.) Sermons.
Gilpin's (William) Sermons.
Girdlestone's (Charles) Sermons.
Hall's (Bp.) Contemplations.
Hill's (Bryan) Sermons.
Jortin's (Dr. J.) Sermons.
——— Dissertations. Diss. 5.
McKnight on the Epistles. (2 Peter ii. 15.)
Newman's (J. H.) Sermons.
Owen on the Spirit.
Percival's (A. P.) Sermons.
Richardson's (William) Sermons.
Riddle's (J. E.) Sermons.
Shuckford's Connection of Sac. and profane history.
Spencer's (Bp.) Sermons.
Theed's (Richard) Sermons.
Wilberforce's (Bp.) Sermons.
Williams' (Alfred) Sermons.
Wrangham on Passages of Scrip. (Abridged from Bryant.)

Bangorean Controversy.

Pro.

Dalrymple's Letters to Dr. Sherlock.
Hoadly's Measure of submission.
——— Origin of civil government.
——— Common rights of subjects.
Balguy's Tracts, moral and theological.
——— Sermons and charges.
Lowman's Remarks on Sherlock's "Answer."
——— Defence of Dissenters.
Pyle's Vind. of the Bp. of Bangor.
Sykes' (A. A.) Letters to Bp. Sherlock.
Whitby's Defence of the Bp. of Bangor.

Con.

Earbury's Rev. of the Bp. of B.'s answer, &c.
Hare's (Bp.) Scripture vindicated.
Law's Letters to the Bp. of Bangor.
Nicholson's (Wm.) Collection of papers.
Potter's (Abp.) Theological works.
Sherlock's Answer to the Bp. of Bangor.
——— Considerations.
——— (Various other tracts.)
Snape's Letter to the Bp. of Bangor.
Smith's Review of Hoadly's ans. to Snape.
Stebbings (Bp.) on Religious Sincerity.
——— Defence of Religious Sincerity.
Trapp's (Joseph) Sermons.

See HEARNES' *Account of all the considerable pamphlets published on either side*, to 1718, and NICHOL'S *Collection of tracts*, on the Bangorean controversy.

Baptism, History of.

Büshing de Procrastinatione baptismi apud veteres, ejusque causis.
Du Viel, Acta Apostolorum.
Faes de Cereis baptismalibus.
Gutbieri Dissertationes Historicæ de controversia circa rebaptizationem.
Hildebrandi Rituale baptism. veteris.
Jundt de Susceptorum baptismalium origine.
Köhler von den Christl. Taufzeugen.
Leschnertus de Baptismate vicario.
Polchow (C. P.) Dissertationes.
Pontanus de Ritu Mersionis.
Reische de Baptismatis origine.
Schmid (J. A.) de B. per arenam.
Schwazii (Ch. G.) Dissertationes.
Van Mastricht, de Susceptoribus infantium, eorum origine, usu, et abusu.
Vicecomes de Antiquis B. ritibus.
Walchii (J. G.) Ritus B. seculi 2.
Wegner (G.), Disputationes Historicæ, de alba veste baptizatorum.
Wodderkamp, de Baptisteriis veterum.
Zeibich de Ritu baptiza. in mortem Christi.
Zeltner de Mersione in baptismo apostolica.
Hinton's History of Baptism.
Jones' (Wm.) Church History.
Kingsford's Centenary traces of B.
Robinson's (Robt.) History of Baptism.

Baptism for the Dead.

Bocharti Dissertationes.
Du Viel, Acta Apostolorum. (Spanheim's learned Dissertation is often affixed to this Commentary.)
Deylingii Observationes Sacræ.
Harduini Questio triplex de baptismo.
Markii Scripta in Selecta Scripturæ.
Mulleri Dissertationes.
Otto's (C. W.) Decalogische Untersüchungen. (Anhang.)
Spanheimii Dissertationes.
Zeibach de Ritu Baptizandi.

Calmet's Dissertations.
Christian Review. 17:296.
Cochrane's Discourses on difficult texts.
Du Viel on the Acts of the Apostles.
Ellis' Fortuita Sacra.
Kitto's Journal of Sacred Literature. 5:396.

Baptism of the Holy Ghost.

Christian Repository. 1:45.
Kitto's Jour. of Sac. Literat. 3:162. 4:135.
Wade (J.) on the Baptism of the Spirit.

Baptismal Regeneration.

Pro.

Conrius de Statu paruvlorum, sine baptismo decedentium.
Reische, de Baptismi origine.

Aitkin's Teaching of the Types.
Barters' (W. B.) Defence of the Church.
Benson's (C.) Discourses on Baptism.
Bethel's (Bp.) Apology for the ministers of the Church of England.
——— View of the doctrine of regeneration.
Blackburn's Doct. of baptismal regeneration.
Bradford (Bp.) on Regeneration.
Bramhall's (Abp.) Works. (Discourse on persons dying without baptism.)
Budd's (Henry) Infant Baptism the means of national reformation.
Bugg (Geo.) on Spiritual Regeneration.
Burgess' The Regeneration of elect infants, as professed by the Church of England.
Christian Observer. 2:276, 403. 19:656.
Comber's (Thomas) Works.
Cooper's Letters to a clergyman.
——— Vindication of "Letters," &c.
Croly's (Geo.) Theory of Baptism. (As able as any on this side.)
Dakeyne on Baptismal regeneration.
Davison's (John) Remarks on bapt. regen.
Donne's (J.) Four sermons preached at a christening.
French's (R. C.) Sermons.
Gardent's History and benefits of baptism.
Gibson's Testimony of sacred Scripture and the early Church.
Goode's Doct. of the Church of England.
Hare's Mission of the Comforter.
Hickes' (George) Case of infant baptism.
Hull (W.) on Baptismal regeneration.

Baptismal Regeneration—*continued.*

Pro.

Irons' (W. J.) Theological Treatises. (Gives the judgment of 1. The Court of arches. 2. The Privy council. 3. The English bishops. 4. The Scotch bishops.)
Jerram's Conversations on infant baptism.
Joly's Friendly address on baptism.
Jones' (of Nayland) Works.
Lawrence's (Rich.) Doct. of the Ch. of Eng.
Mant's (Bp.) Sermons.
——— Sense of the Church of England.
Marsh's Letters to Rev. C. Simeon.
Mercersburg Review. (Various articles.)
Millenial Harbinger. Periodical. Bethany, Virginia.
Morgan's Regeneration distinct from renovation.
Mosley's Primitive doct. of regeneration.
Napper's Doctrines of the Ch. of England.
Newman's (J. Henry) Sermons.
Patrick's (Bp.) Aqua genitalis.
Pusey's Scripture views of baptism.
Ridley's Lady Moyer's Lectures. 1742.
Tracts for the Times. Nos. 67, 68, 69, 82.
Vaux's Bampton Lectures. 1826.
Walford's Holiness of a Christian Child.
Wellford on the Baptismal service of the Church of England.
Wickham's Synopsis of the doct. of baptism.
Wilberforce's (R. J.) Doct. of holy baptism.
——— 24 Sermons on the new birth.

Con.

Armitage (J.) on Baptism.
Barker's Regeneration and its counterfeits.
Beamish's Truth spoken in love.
Bennet (John) on Baptismal regeneration.
Biddulph on Bapt. regen. (Reply to Mant.)
Brookes (Tho.) on Baptismal regeneration.
Burder's (George) Village Sermons.
Butts on the Doctrines of the Chur. of Engl.
Christian Observer. 1:767. 16:709.
Eclectic Review. 4th Series. 26:478.
Faber (George S.) on Regeneration.
Gresley's Real danger of the Ch. of E. 1856.
Hobden (Samuel) on Regeneration.
Holloway on Baptismal regeneration.
Hughes on Baptismal regeneration.
Jukes' Way which some call heresy.
Life of John Foster. Pp. 107–117.
Molyneaux on Baptismal regeneration.
New Englander. 2:397. 9:76.
Nicholson's Letters on Regeneration.
Parker's Bible, Church of England, and reason, on Regeneration.
Scott (John) on the Effects of baptism.
Spurgeon's (Cha. H.) Sermons. 8th Series.
Stovell (C.) on Baptismal regeneration.

See MOZLEY'S *Review of the baptismal controversy.* 1862.

Baptists. See ANABAPTISTS, CLOSE COMMUNION, INFANT BAPTISM, PROSELYTE BAPTISM.

Pro.

Abrahami Apologia pro Protestantibus.

Baptists—*continued.*

Pro.

Abrahami Introd. in scientiam christiani.
——— Smegna Hollandicum contra maculas quas P. Bontemps adspersit Mennonitis.
Arnoldi Epist. ad Fred. Spanheimium.
——— Elenchus Controversiarum.
Dooregeest's Unterricht in der christlichen Lehre.
Du Viel, Opera. 1680.
Eeghemii Theologia Christiana.
Frederici Catechesis. 1698.
Frankii Epistolæ.
Kat's Kurtzer Begrief von der Lehre der Wahrheit nach den sinn der taufgesinten christen.
Knuyt, Brevis confessio fidei. 1623.
Lechler's Apostolische u. d. nachapostolische Zeitalter.
Menno Simon, Opera Theologica. 1540.
Munzeri Opera.
Nicolai Præcipuorum dogmatum conf. 1624.
Petri Dissertationes Moralium.
Phillipi Enchiridion christianæ doct. 1578.
Riessius de Recto usu linguæ.
Schyn's Erster Anfang des christlichen Gottesdiensts.
Togeri Christianæ Theologiæ systema.
Toombs' Refutatio positionis. H. Savage.
Twisckius de Religionis Libertate. 1609.
Ubon's Bekentniss.
Vangent's Anfang und Fortgang de Uneinigkeiten.
Van Huyzen, Catechesis. 1705.
Verduin's Unterweisung im glauben.
Wybrantius in Symbolum Apostol. 1640.
Zeltner de Mersione in baptismo apostolica.

Anderson's (G. W.) Plea for principles.
Andrews' Vindication of the Baptists.
Ashdowne's Design of the New Covenant.
Backus' Letter to Rev. Benjamin Lord.
Bailey's Believer's baptism from heaven.
Baldwin (Thomas) on Baptism.
Barker's Duty and benefits of baptism.
Birt's Vindication of the Baptists.
Blackwall's Sea of Absurdity.
Blackwood's Storming of Antichrist.
Booth's Pedobaptism examined.
——— Defence of "Pedobaptism examined."
——— Apology for the Baptists.
Braidwood's Letters on the grace of God.
Brantley on the Covenant of circumcision.
Brine's (John) Works.
Brown's (J. Newton) Baptismal balance.
Bull's (S.) Baptisms of Scripture.
Burroughs (J.) on Positive Institutions.
Byron's Doctrine of Baptism.
Campbell's (Alex.) Baptism, with its antecedents and consequents.
Carson's Mode and subjects of baptism. (Reply to Ewing.)
Chapman (Edwin) on the Subjects and mode of baptism.
Chase (Ira) on the Design of baptism.

Baptists—*continued.*

Pro.

Christian Review. 1:430, 514. 3:84, 196, 333. 6:302. 11:1, 186, 278. 12:529, 605. 13:609. 14:1, 217. 15:1. 16:506. 17:48, 296.
Chrystal's Hist. of the modes of baptism.
Collins on Believer's baptism.
——— Sandy foundation shaken.
Conant's (T. J.) Meaning of *baptizein.*
Confessions of Faith. Published at various times. Of which, see those of John de Reis and Lubert Gerard, 1580; of the elders and brethren, London, 1643 and 1688; of the Philadelphia Baptist Association, in 1742; and the New Hampshire Baptist Convention, in 1833. All these agree with the Savoy and Westminter Confessions, as to points of doctrine.
Cox (F. A.) on Baptism. (Reply to Ewing, Dwight, and Wardlaw.)
Cox's (Neh.) Discourses on the Covenants.
Coxhead (B.) on Baptism. (Ans. to Thorn.)
Craps' Concise view of Christian baptism.
Crawley on Baptism. (Reply to W. Elder.)
Curtis' Progress of Baptist principles.
Cutting's Historical Vindications.
D'Anvers on Baptism. (One of the oldest and ablest works of the kind. 1673.)
Davyes' (Thomas) on Baptism.
Dell's (Wm.) Doctrine of baptisms reduced from its ancient and modern corruptions.)
Dore's Antipedobaptism and female communion consistent. (Reply to passages in P. Edwards.)
Duke on the Christian Covenant.
Dyke's The Baptist's answer to Mr. Willis.
Eaton's (D.) Scripture the only relig. guide.
——— Practical uses of Christian baptism.
Edwards' (Morgan) Anti-pedorantism.
——— Antiped. defended. (Reply to Prest. Finley.)
Ellison on Baptism as instituted of God.
Evans' (C.) Address to serious professors.
Evans' (John) History of baptism.
Ewar's (Sam.) Answer to David Hitchin.
Fisher's Baby Baptism meer babism. Fol. 1563.
——— Christendom unchristened. (Reply to Baxter, Featley, Holmes, Marshall, Blake, Cook, &c.)
Foote's (Wm.) Plain account of the ord. of B.
——— Primitive baptism defended.
Foster's (Benj.) Divine rite of immersion.
Francis' Salopian Zealot.
Frey's Essays on Christian baptism.
Fuller's (Andrew) Works.
Gale's Reflections on Wall's hist. of inf. bap.
——— Sermons. (7 on this subject.)
Gamble's (John) Familiar letters on baptism.
General Bap. Magazine. Periodical. London.
Gibb's (Geo. A.) Defence of the Baptists.
Gilchrist (James) on Baptism.
Gill's Testimony of ancient writers.
——— Infant baptism a pillar of Popery

Baptists—*continued.*

Pro.

Gill's Essay on Scripture baptism.
——— Reply to Towgood. (Tradition.)
——— (Other treatises.)
Gotche's Critical exam. of βαπτιζω, in ancient and modern versions.
Grant (Peter) on Baptism.
Grantham's Loyal Baptist.
——— Assemblies of baptized believers the true Church of Christ.
Graves' (J. R.) Tri-lemma.
Haggar's (H.) Foundation of the font.
Hague's Baptismal question.
Haldane (James) on Baptism.
Haldane (Alex.) on Baptism.
Hinton's (J. T.) History of baptism.
Hiscox's Baptist Church Directory.
Hurthouse's Remarks on Penisten Booth's "Friendly advice."
Ingham's Handbook on Christian baptism.
Innis' (Wm.) The Reign of heaven.
——— Conversations on baptism.
Jacobs' Babel of Pædobaptists.
Jenkins' Def. of the B. (Reply to P. Edwards.)
——— Beauty of believer's baptism.
——— Calm reply to De Courcy.
Jewitt on the Mode and subjects of baptism.
Jones' (Wm.) History of the Church.
——— Facts opposed to fiction.
Jones' (David) Candid reasons examined. (Reply to P. Edwards.)
Judson's Sermon at Lall-bazar Chapel.
Keach's (Benj.) Baptism in its purity.
——— Antidote to a late counterfeit. 1694. (Answer to Shute.)
——— Axe laid to the root. (Answer to Flavel, Rothwell, and Exel.)
Kiffin's Reasons for separation.
Killingsworth's Answer to Bulkeley's plea.
——— Supplement to Salter's Hall's serm.
Kinghorn on Baptism. (Rep. to P. Edwards.)
Kingsford's Vindication of the Baptists.
——— Three letters to John Wesley.
——— Centenary traces of the Baptists.
Knott's Dialogues on Baptism. (Reply to Shrubsole.)
——— Letters on B. (Reply to P. Edwards.)
Leach's Strictures on J. W. Wood.
McGregor on Baptism. (Reply to Addington.)
——— Believer's baptism.
——— Nature and import of baptism.
McLean's Apostolical Commission.
Martin's Nine letters to John Horsey.
Maye's Tecknobaptist. (Keen and scholarly.)
Merrill's Sermons on baptism.
Morell's New dissert. on an old controversy.
New Baptist Mag. London. 1825 to 1832.
New Baptist Miscel. Lond. 1827 to present.
Newman's Immersion defended.
Noel's (B.) Essay on Christian baptism.
Norcott's Baptism plainly discovered.
Norton's Dispassionate thoughts.
Palmer's Serious address to Christians.
Pearce (Samuel) on Baptism.

Baptists—*continued.*

Pro.

Pendleton's Reasons why I am a Baptist.
Pengilly's Scripture guide to baptism.
Remington's (S.) Reasons for being a Bapt.
Richards' History of Antichrist.
Richardson's Reply to Featley.
Ripley's (H. J.) Reply to Prof. Stuart.
Rush (Judge) on Christian baptism.
Russel's Vindic. of baptized churches.
——— Epistle on baptism.
——— Vindic. of Christ and the Apostles.
Ryland's Candid statement of reasons, &c.
Scott (John) on the Effects of baptism.
Shilgberie's God's ordinance the saint's privilege.
Smith's (J. Torrey) Reply to Abs. Peters on B.
Southern Baptist Review. Since 1855.
Stennett's (Joseph) Answer to Russen.
Stennett's (Sam.) Defence of the Baptists.
——— Reply to Addington.
Stovell (Cha.) on Christian discipleship. (Reply to Holley.)
——— The Baptismal reconciliation. (2d reply to Holley.)
Taylor (Jer.) Baptists justified; with notes, by Anderson.
Taylor's (Dan.) Humble essay on baptism.
Thomas' (D. E.) The Action and subjects of Baptism.
Toombs' Felo de se. (Reply to Baxter.)
Toulmin (Dr. Joshua) on Baptism.
Towgood's (M.) Dissertations.
Turney's Scriptural law of baptism.
Wallin (Benj.) on Baptism.
Wayland's Princip. and practices of the B.
Westlake on the Mode and subjects, &c.
——— Extracts from various authors.
Wiberg's Baptism in the words of the Bible.
Wilson's (Sam.) Scripture Manual.
——— Plain representation of baptism.
Woolsey's Doctrine of baptism.

Con.

Borkensii Auctoritate patrum collectæ.
Bugenhagius contra Anabaptistas.
Cloppenburgii Gangrena Theologiæ.
Hoffman's (W.) Taufe und Wiedertaufe.
Hottingeri Bibliotheca.
Hoornbeckii Summa Controversiarum.
Martensen's Baptistische frage. (1860.)
Matthies (C. S.), Baptismatis Expositio.
Melancthonis Refutatio erroris Serveti.
Meyerus (J. A.) de Baptismo.
Morling (S.) de Baptismo per immersionem.
Spanheimii Disputationes.
Sylvii Corpus controversiarum.
Vossius de Baptismo.
Zuinglius contra Catabaptistos.
Addington's Christian minister's plea.
Allen's Serious and friendly address.
Allestree's (Richard) Sermons.
American Biblical Repository. 2d Series. 3:288. 11:222.
Armstrong's (G.) Doct. of baptisms.

Baptists—*continued.*

Con.

Austin's Reply to Merrill on baptism.
Baillie's Anabaptism the true fountain of independency, &c.
Baker's (Dan.) Scriptural view of baptism.
Barnes' Baptist Exclusivism.
Barrow (Isaac) on the Sacraments.
Barry's Falseness of Anabaptism.
Beckwith's (J. H.) Immersion not baptism.
Beecher (Edw.) on the Meaning of βαπτιζω.
Berriman's (Will.) Sermons.
Beveridge's (Bp.) Sermons.
Bibliotheca Sacra. 1:703. 15:29.
Biden's (J.) Truths maintained.
Bickersteth on Baptism.
Blake's (T.) Covenant of God with mankind.
Bostwick (D.) on Baptism.
Bradbury's Duty and doct. of baptism.
Buckminster's (Joseph S.) Discourses.
Calvin's Instruct. for arming the faithful.
Carpenter's (Rich.) Anabaptist washed, and shrunk in the washing.
Cave's Primitive Christianity.
Christian Monthly Spectator. 10:340, 590.
Clinton on Baptism.
Colling's Message from the Lord.
Cotton (John) on Baptism.
Couch's (John) Ans. to a Kentish Anabapt.
Cragge's Arraignment of Anabaptism.
Crofton (Z.) on Baptism.
Cummings' (D. J.) Baptismal Font.
D'Assigny's Pernicious errors of the dipping sect.
De Courcey on Baptism.
——— Rejoinder to Jenkins.
Drierburg on Baptism.
Edwards' (Peter) Candid reasons, &c.
Elliot's Dipping not baptizing.
Eltringham's Baptist against Baptist.
——— Remarks on the B. vindication.
Ewing's (Greville) Essay on baptism.
Fairchild (A. G.) on Mode and subjects of B.
Featley's Dipper dipt, or Baptists ducked over head and ears. (Queer plates.)
Fleming's (Caleb) Mode and subjects of bap.
Fowle's (J. H.) Baptism examined.
Gamble's (H.) Scripture baptism.
Greenfield's (Edmund) Works.
Hall's (Edwin) Law of baptism.
Halley's (R.) Nature of Christian baptism.
Hemmenway (Moses) on Baptism.
Henry (Matthew) on Baptism.
Hibbard's (F. G.) Mode, obligation, &c.
Houghton's Antidote agt. Haggar on bapt.
Hunt's (T. P.) Bible Baptist.
Hurd's (Bp.) Sermons.
Irving's (Edw.) Homilies on baptism.
Johnson's Three treatises agt. Anabaptists.
Kennaway's Manual of baptism.
Kerr (Jas.) on Baptism. (The mode only.)
Kingdon's (T. H.) Baptism considered.
Knox's (John) Answer to the blasphemous cavillations of an Anabaptist.
Lathrop's (Dr. J.) Church of God defended.

Baptists—*continued.*

Con.

Lawrence's (Rich.) Doct. of the Ch. of Eng.
Levington's Scripture baptism defended.
Llewellyn on Baptism.
Lothrop's Four sermons on baptism.
Maskell (W.) on Baptism.
Mason's Boasting Baptist dismounted.
Mather (Increase) on Baptism.
——— First principles of New England.
Maurice's Plunging into water no scripture baptism.
Mayo's True scripture doctrine.
Mede's (Bp.) Sermons.
Methodist Quar. Review. 4:325. 10:554.
Middleton's Vind. of the ordinance of bapt.
Miller (Samuel) on Baptism.
Munro's Mod. immersion opposed to baptism.
——— Enquiry into the principal questions between Baptists and Pædobaptists.
Newman's (J. H.) Sermons.
Osgood's (Dr. D.) Discourses on baptism.
Parsons on Baptism.
Patrick's (Bp.) Sermons.
Peters' (Absalom) Sprinkling the only mode of baptism.
Pirie (Alex.) on Baptism.
Pond (Enoch) on Christian baptism.
Porter's (David) Essay on baptism.
Powers on Household baptism.
Pressley's (John T.) Lectures on baptism.
Priestley's Letters to an Antipædobaptist.
Princeton Review. 19:34. 30:347. 33:215, 446, 680.
Potts' (Archdeac.) Observations on the cont.
Pusey's (E. B.) Scriptural views of baptism.
Rice's (N. L.) Design, mode, subjects, &c.
Ricraft's Looking-glass for Separatists.
Russen's Fundamentals without foundation.
——— Picture of the Anabaptists.
Schomberg's Doctrine of baptism.
Scott (Thomas) on Baptism.
Sheppard's New England's lamentation.
Shrubsole's Minister's defence of his flock.
Shute's Antidote.
Smith's Reasons agt. baptizing elder people.
Smith's B. sophistry discovered. (Quaker.)
Somes' (R.) Godly treatise ag. the execrable fancies of Henry Barrow, John Greenwood, and others of the Anabaptistical order. 1589. (These two men were martyred at Tyburn, April 6, 1593.)
Spirit of the Pilgrims. 1:295. 5:539.
Stephens' (John) Baptism accomplished.
Steward's (Geo.) Baptism explained.
Stock's (John) Essay on baptism.
Stuart's (Moses) Is the mode of baptism prescribed in the New Testament?
Taylor's (C.) Facts and evidences on bapt.
Thorn's (Wm.) Immersion not Scripture B.
Toulmin (Joshua) on Baptism.
Tower's Sacrament of baptism.
Turner's Preservative against the poison of Pelagius.
Tyerman's (Dan.) Essay on baptism.

Baptists—*continued.*

Con.

Walker's (W.) Doctrine of baptism.
Whiston's (W.) Address to the Baptists.
Whitehead's Dipper plunged, &c.
Wickham's (J. A.) Synopsis on baptism.
Williams' Nature, design, mode, &c.
Wills' Appeal to the B. (Against Danvers.)
Wood's (Dr. J.) Familiar treatise on baptism. (Plates.)

Mr. SAM. AGNEW, of Philadelphia, has made a list of the titles of works on baptism, which now amounts to nearly four thousand! Of these, he has about twenty-seven hundred in his possession.

Baptists, History of. See ANABAPTISTS, MENNONITES, WALDENSES.

Bracht [or Van Bracht] Theatrum Martyrum. 1660.
Corvinus de Miserabili monasteriensium Anabaptistarum obsidione.
Dale [seu Van Dale], Historia Baptismorum.
Loescheri Com. de Munzeri doct. et fatis.
Marc (L.), le Baptême dans l'eglise réf. comparé avec le bapt. dans l'eglise apost.
Memoirs de Trevoux.
Ottii Annales Anabaptistica.
Polchow (C. P.) Dissertationes.
Pontanus de Ritu mersionis in baptismate.
Racine, Source et fondement des Anab.
Rose, Disquisitio Historica.
Schmid (J. A.) de Baptismo per arenam.
Schyn, Historia Christianorum.
Spanheim de Origine, progressu, &c.
Theobald's Bericht was jammer die Wiedert.
Van Bracht's Bloodigh toonel der Doopsgesinde. 1660. (Many editions.)
——— Theatrum Martyrum.
Vanhuysen's Hist. Erzehlung von dem Ursprung und Fortgang, &c.
——— de Ortu et progres. Catabaptistarum.
Walchii Specimen historiæ Anabapt.
——— Ritus baptismales seculi II.
Wedderkamp de Baptisteriis veterum.

Adams' (John Q.) Baptists thorough reformers.
Amer. Quarterly Register. 11:44. 13:182. 14:42, 370.
Anderson (Mrs. M. F.), Baptists in Sweden.
Ashmead's (Joseph) Progress of religious sentiment. 1852.
Backus' History of New England Baptists.
Benedict's Hist. of Baptists in America.
——— Fifty years among the Bapt. 1864.
Bogue & Bennet's History of Dissenters.
Burrows' Am. Bapt. Reg. (Statistics of 1852.)
Christian Examiner. 10:20.
Christian Review. 10:384. 11:1. 14:517, 556. 17:481.
Cox's (F. A.) Baptists in America.
Crosby's History of English Baptists.
Cutting's (S. S.) Historical vindications.
Davis' (J.) History of Welch Baptists. (From A. D. 63 to 1770.)

Baptists, History of—*continued.*

Duncan's (W. C.) Hist. of the early Baptists.
Eclectic Review. 4th Series. 12:637.
Eddy's Roger Williams and the Baptists. (Traces them from the time of Christ.)
Edward's Baptists of New Jersey. 1792.
——— Baptists of Pennsylvania.
——— Materials toward a history of American Baptists.
Haynes' The Baptist denomination.
Hinton's (Isaac T.) History of baptism.
Ivemy's Hist. of English Baptists. To 1800.
Jones' (Wm.) Church History.
Lewis' Rise and progress of Anab. in Engl.
Mann's Lectures on Non-conformity.
Millet's Hist. of the B. in Maine, U. S.
Murch's History of Baptists in England.
Orchard's Hist. of foreign Baptists; from the New Testament, Fathers, and writers of all ages.
Peck & Lawton's Origin and progress of the Baptists in Central and Western New York. (To 1837.)
Peck (J. M.), Life of: by R. Babcock. 1860.
Phillippo's Past and pres. of Jamaica. 1840.
Quarterly Review. 1:109.
Rippon's Baptist Annual Register. London.
Robinson's (of Camb.) History of Baptism.
Semple's History of the Virginia Baptists.
Sleidan's Hist. of the German Anabaptists.
Spanheim's Origin and prog. of Anabaptists.
——— England's warning by Germany's woe.
Stoupas' Religion of the Hollanders.
Taylor's (A.) History of English Baptists.
Thomas' History of the Welch Baptists. (1650 to 1790.)
Underhill's Martyrology of the Churches of Christ, commonly called Baptist, during the Reformation.
Westminster Review. 39:407.
Worcester's (N.) Progress of the Baptists.

The above list comprises both friends and foes—mostly foes. Other old writers on Baptism and the Baptists, are mentioned in MOSHEIM, *Sec.* 3, *Part* 2, *Ch.* 3.

Barbets. See WALDENSES.

Bardesanes. See HERESIES.

Beausobre, Hist. du Manichæisme. Lib. 4. Ch. 9.
Origen, Dialogus contra Marcionitas.
Strunzii Historia Bardesanistarum.

Barnabas. See LIVES OF THE FATHERS.

Barnabæ Epistolæ. (Many editions.)
Heffele's Sendschreiben des Apost. B.
Henke de Epist. quæ Barnabæ tribuiter.
Le Moyne, Exercitatiuncula.
Menardus de St. B. et ejus epistolæ.
Papebrochii Acta et passio Barnabæ. (Acta sanctorum.)
Puccinell, Vita de St. B. Milano.
Roidan, de Authentia epistolæ B.
Saxe, de Adventu Mediolanum B. apost.

Ulman's Studien und Kritiken.
Burton's (Edward) Lectures.
Davidson's Sacred Hermeneutics.
Lardner's Works.
Wake's Genuine epistles of the Fathers.

See a list of all the editions in CEILLIER, *Hist. generale des auteurs sacrés.*

Bartholomew. See MASSACRE.

Basil. See FATHERS.

Assemanni Bibliotheca Orientalis.
Baertii Vità S. Basilii.
Basilii Opera.
Bohringer's die Kirche christi.
Ducæi Basilii opera, cum notis.
Erasmi Epistolæ. Epis. 7.
Feisseri Diss. hist. theolog. de vita B.
Georgii Vita et doctrina Basiliæ.
Gregory (Nyssen) Orationes. Orat. 20.
Hermance, Vie de St. Basile le grand.
Werenberg, Diss. de prudentia B. in refutandis hæreticis.

Barksdale's Basil on Solitude.
Berker's Exhortations of St. Basil.
Oudin's Life and writings of Basil.

Basilidians.

Beausobre, Hist. du Manicheism. Lib. 4, c. 1.
Chifletii Abraxas proteus.
Grabbii (Joan. Ernest) Dissertationes.
Macarii Abraxas.
Massnetii Dissertatio in Ireneum.
Mosheim, de Rebus chris. ante Constantin.
Passeri Dissertatio de gemmis.
Uhlhorn's Basilidianische System.

Baxterians. See CALVINISM.

This name was given to writers who relaxed the Calvinist system; but no body of Christians is so called.

Beatitudes. See SERMON ON THE MOUNT; and also the various GRACES.

Gregory (Nys.) Orationes.

Anderson's (James S. M.) Discourses.
Anderson's (Robt.) Discourses. 8 on this sub.
Blackall's (Bp.) Discourses.
Blair's (James) Sermons.
Brewster's Lectures on the Beatitudes.
Buck (Jas.) on the Beatitudes.
Butcher's (William) Sermons.
Butt's (Thomas) Sermons.
Caunter's Sermons on the Beatitudes.
Cennick's (John) Discourses.
Clow's (J.) Sermons.
Cobden's (Edward) Sermons.
Cook's (John) Sermons.
Crum's (Geo.) Mount of blessing.
Cunningham's Morning Thoughts.
Edward's (Dr. John) Theologia Reformata.
Farrar's Bampton Lectures. 1803.
Garbett's (Jas.) Lectures in Lent.
Gardner's Exposition of the Beatitudes.
George's Blessing of Chris. philosophy.

Beatitudes—*continued.*

Good's (E.) Lectures on the Beatitudes.
Graves' (Rich.) Sermons. (4 on this subj.)
Grove's (Henry) Sermons.
Hambleton's (John) Sermons.
Harris' (Robert) Twenty-four sermons.
Horneck's (Anthony) Sermons.
James' Index of passages from the Fathers upon every verse of Matt. v.
Johnson's (Samuel) Sermons.
Jortin's (John) Sermons.
Latimer's (Bp.) Sermons.
Liefchild's Lectures on Christian temper.
Mackay's (M.) Expos. of Matt. v. 1–10.
Mather's (Increase) Sermons.
Moberly's (Geo.) Sermons.
Monsel (J. S. B.) on the Beatitudes.
Norris (John) Sermons.
Naylor's (Tho.) 8 Sermons on the B. 1828.
Orr's (John) Discourses.
Piggot's (Hugh) The blessed life.
Prince's (Thomas) Ten Lectures in Lent.
Smith's (Dean) Sermons.
Watson's (T.) Sermons on the Beatitudes.
Wintle's Christian Ethics.

Beghards, or Beguins. See FRATRICELLI.

Hemmerlini Tractatus contra Validos.
Mosheim, de Beghardis et Beguinibus.

Behemoth. See NATURAL HISTORY.

Baieri (Joann. Guil.) Dissertationes.
Bochartii Hierozoicon.
Kirchmayeri (Joann. Chris.) Dissertationes.
Mulleri Theologica Biblicæ.

Behmen. See BŒHMEN.

Belgic Confession.

Benthem's Hollandischen Kirchen.
De Bress, Confessio Belgicæ.
Maresii Fœderatum Belgium orthodoxum.

Beelzebub. See SATAN.

Benedictines. [Black Friars.]

Acta Sanctorum ordinis Benedicti, in sæculorum classes distributa. 10 folios.
Armelii Bibliotheca.
Bucelini Annales Benedictini.
Bulteau, Abregé de l'hist. de l'ordre St. B.
Dacherii Acta Sancti Benedicti.
Francois, Biblioth. generale des ecrivans de l'ordre de St. Benoit.
Gregoris (Magni) Benedicti Vita.
Jepes, Hist. general de l'ordre, &c.
Le Cerf, Bibliothéque historique et critique.
Mabilloni, Annales ordinis St. B. 9 v. fol.
Pezii Bibliotheca B. (Lives and writings.)
Reyneri Apostolatus Bened. in Anglia.
Richardson (J.), Prælectiones Ecclesiasticæ.
Schamel's Hist. d. alt. Benedictinerklos.
Sczygielski, Aquila Polono Benedictino.
Spittler's Geschichte des Benedictiner.
Weissii Lyceum Benedictinum.

Edinburg Review. 89:1.
Eclectic Magazine (same article). 16:433.
Littell's Living Age (same article.) 20:433.
Stephens' (Sir James) Eccles. Biography.

ZEIGELBAUER, *Hist. rei literariæ ord. St. B.* In 4 vols., fol. Gives not only the entire history of the order, but the lives of its principal members, and a classified list of books written by them, with a critical notice of each.

Beneficence. See BENEVOLENCE.

Allen on Christian Beneficence.
Christian Review. 16:200, 254.
Clarke's Faithful Steward. (Prize essay.)
Dick on Christian Beneficence.
Fawcett's (James) Sermons.
Gold and the Gospel. (Ulster prize essay.)
Gouge's Riches increased by giving.
Johnson's (Dr. Sam.) Sermons.
Mason on the Human virtues.
Simpson's Essay on Beneficence.
Tennison's Sermons. (B. to posterity.)
Wayland's (Francis) Occasional discourses.
Zollikoffer's Sermons on education.

Benevolence.

Amer. Biblical Repository. 2d Series. 9:1.
Amer. Quarterly Register. 8:241.
Balguy's (Dr. Tho.) Discourses.
Barnes' (Albert) Practical Sermons.
Besley's Doctrinal Discourses.
Black's (David) Sermons.
Brown's Essay on Shaftesbury's characterist.
Christian Examiner. 2:241. 13:137.
Christian Monthly Spectator. 1:569. 4:113, 522, 617. 7:367.
Christian Review. 2:85. 9:583.
Dick's Philosophy of Religion.
Doddridge's Lectures. Lec. 65.
Dyer's (Geo.) Theory and practice of benev.
Eden's Harmony of Benevolence.
Fellow's Picture of Chris. philosophy.
Ferguson's Sermons.
Foster's (Dr. James) Sermons.
Franklin's (Thomas) Sermons.
Fuller's (And.) Socinian and Calvinistic Systems. Letter 8.
Guardian, The. No. 61.
Greathead on the Regard we owe to each other.
Hale's Contemplations.
Hall's (Robt.) Sermons.
Housman's Principles and extent of benev.
Hutchinson on the Passions.
Jebb's (John) Excellency of Benevolence.
Johnson's (Samuel) Sermons.
Literary and Theolog. Review. 4:373.
McCalla's Sermons.
New Englander. 9:14.
Pamphleteer. 13:391. 14:65.
Puffendorf's Law of Nature. Lib. 4, c. 3.
Stanford's (John) Sermons.
Tucker's Light of nature pursued. Ch. 34.
Tutty's Duty of universal benevolence.
Wayland's Elements of moral science. Bk. 2.

Benevolence of God. See ATTRIBUTES.

Allestree's (Richard) Sermons.
Amory's (Thomas) Sermons.
Appleton's (Nathaniel) Works. Lect. 6 and 7.
Balguy's Divine benevolence asserted.
Baye on Divine benevolence.
Bonnet's Contemplations of nature.
Bradford's (The Martyr) Works.
Carr's (George) Sermons.
Carter's (Nicholas) Sermons.
Cooper's (Edward) Sermons.
Davies' (Prest.) Sermons.
Doddridge's Lectures. Part 3.
Dwight's (Tim.) Discourses. Disc. 8, 9.
Emmons' (Will.) Sermons.
Foster's (Dr. James) Sermons.
Gales' (John) Sermons.
Hallett (Joseph) on Scripture.
Grove on the Wisdom of God. (Refers Divine benevolence entirely to wisdom.)
Harris' (Robert) Sermons.
Hopkins' System of Divinity.
Johnson's (Dr. Sam.) Sermons.
Jortin's (John) Sermons.
Langhorn's Sermons.
Leland's (Tho.) Sermons.
Pettitpierre's Thoughts on Divine goodness.
Robinson's Christian System.
Saurin's (James) Sermons.
Scott's (John) Sermons.
Scott's (Will.) Sermons.
South's (Robert) Sermons.
Strong on the Benevolence of God.
Taylor's (John) Sermons.
Venn's (John) Sermons.
Wilder's (John) Sermons.
Wood's (Prof.) Sermons.
Wollaston's Religion of Nature.

Benevolent Institutions. See EDUCATION SOCIETIES, ENDOWMENTS, VOLUNTARY ASSOCIATIONS.

Butler's (Bp.) Sermons.
Christian Examiner. 2:241. 7:307.
Chris. Quart. Spect. 9:255. (On agents.)
Edinburg Review. 1:578. 33:109.
Gifford's Public charities of Eng. and Wales.
Hazlitt on the Principles of charitable institutions.
New Englander. 5:28.
Pamphleteer. 13:1.
Quarterly Review. 53:249.
Westminster Review. 2:97.
Woodrow's Rise and progress of London religious societies.

Bereavement. See MOURNERS.

Allet's Christian's Support.
Baker's (Arthur) Sermons.
Beren's (E.) Sermons. (Death of children.)
Brown's Comfortable Words.
Coverdale's Book of Death.
Dehon's (Bp.) Sermons. (Death of children.)
East's Memoir of Miss Humphrey.
Edwards' (Prest.) Sermons.
Erskine's (Ebenezer) Discourses.

Bereavement—*continued.*

Gataker's (Tho.) Sermons. (Death of children.)
Hall's (Bp.) Practical works.
Harris' (Robt.) Sermons. (Death of children.)
Logan's Comfort for bereaved parents.
Lucas' (Rich.) Sermons. (Death of children.)
Macfarlane's Why weepest thou?
Orton's (Job) Discourses to the aged.
Patrick's (Bp.) Discourses.
Russell's Letters, practical and consolatory.
Shaebotham's Lamentat. in Rama hushed.
Smyth's Bereaved parents consoled.
Thompson's consolation for mourners.

Berengarians. See WALDENSES.

Alexandri (Hieron.) Dissertationes.
Dassovii (Theodor.) Dissertationes.
Haberkornii (Pet.) Dissertationes.
Lupi (Christian.) Dissertationes.
Mabilloni Prefatio ad Acta Benedicti.
Mulleri Hist. Berengarianismi. vet. et novi.
Oudinus de Scriptoribus Ecclesiasticis.
Roy, de Vita, hæres., et penitent., Bereng.
Vernous, contre le père Sirmond.
Voigtii (Gottfr.) Bibliotheca.

See an account of various treatises on the controversy between Beringer and the Papists, touching the Lord's Supper, in LUPUS, and OUDIN.

Berkeley's Theory. See IDEAS.

Pro.

Berkeley's Principles of human knowledge.

Con.

Baxter (Andrew) on the Soul.
Beattie's Immutability of Truth.
Doddridge's Lectures. Part 2. (Appendix.)
Hamilton's Lectures on Metaphysics.
Kaimes on the Principles of virtue.
McIntosh's Hist. of ethical philosophy.
Reid on the Intellectual Powers.

Besetting Sins. See TEMPTATION.

Collison's (M. A.) Sermons.
Cunningham's (J. W.) Sermons.
Mason on Self-knowledge. Ch. 7.
Newton's (Bp.) Dissertations.
North American Review. 4:187.
Pamphleteer. 6:269.
Quarterly Review. 4:68. 36:1.
Smith's (Dr. H.) Sermons.

Beza.

Bezæ Opera.
Baum's Th. Beza nach Handscriftlichen quellen Dargestellt.
Bolseci Historia de vita, doctrina, &c.
Bibliotheca Sacra. 7:501.

Bible. See ENGLISH BIBLE, REVISION, TRANSLATIONS.

Bible Dictionaries. See DICTIONARIES.

Bible in Common Schools. See USE, &C.

Bible Societies.

Amer. Quarterly Register. 2:29.
Blackwood's Magazine. 18:161.
Brown's History of the British and Foreign Bible Society. 1859.
Christian Disciple. 5:146.
Christian Monthly Spectator. 2:429, 483. 6:36, 62, 142.
Christian Review. 1:299. 2:585.
Dudley's Analysis of the system of the Brit. and For. Bib. Soc. 1822. (Gives forms of constitutions, blanks, by-laws, &c., for every sort of auxiliary.)
Haldane's Review of the conduct of the Brit. and Foreign Bible Society.
——— Second Review of the same.
Hall's (Robert) Works.
Monthly Review. 103:499. 124:1.
Owen's Hist. of the Brit. and For. Bib. Soc.
Pamphleteer. 1:47, 81, 151. 6:269.
Phelan's The Bible, not the Bible Society.
Quarterly Review. 1:354.
Strickland's Hist. of the Am. Bib. Soc. 1849.
Timson's Bible triumphs. (A valuable hist. of the British and Foreign Bible Society.)
Warner's Hist. of the Br. and For. Bib. Soc.
Wyckoff's Origin, history, &c., of the Amer. and Foreign Bible Society.

Biblical Antiquities. See ARCHÆOLOGY, BIBLICAL HISTORY, ILLUSTRATIONS OF SCRIPTURE, JEWISH ANTIQUITIES.

Biblical Criticism. See DIFFICULTIES, FIGURATIVE LANGUAGE, HEBREW LANGUAGE, HERMENEUTICS, IDIOMS, PHILOLOGY, POETRY, PRINTED EDITIONS, QUOTATIONS, STYLE, SYNONYMS, VARIOUS READINGS, VOWEL POINTS.

Abichtii Ars distincte interpretandi.
Baumgarten-Crusius, Exegetische Schriften zum Neue Testament.
Bengelii Apparatus Criticus ad N. T.
——— Gnomon Novum Testamentum.
Berger's Unterricht von der Deutch. Bibeln.
Bloomfield, Recensio Synoptica.
Bootii Animadversiones Sacræ.
Boston, Tractatus Stigmologicus.
Cameroni Myrothecium Evangelicum.
Capelli (L.) Observationes in Nov. Test.
——— Commentaria crit. in V. T.
Carpzovii Critica Sacra in V. et N. Test. (Not only profound and satisfactory himself, but gives references to the best writers on particular points.)
Clerici Ars Critica.
——— de Optimo genere interp. S. S.
Cocceii Opera Exigetica.
Crellii Opera Exegetica.
Critica Sacra. (An invaluable collection, in nine thick folios, of the writings of the best biblical critics previous to 1700.)
Crowæi Elenchus Scriptorum, &c.
Dathii Opuscula.
De Dieu, Animadversiones in Nov. Test.

Biblical Criticism—*continued.*

Deylingii Observationes Sacræ. (Quotes all the principal critics up to 1748; sustaining or refuting their opinions.)
Eichhorn's Allgemeine Bibliothek.
——— Kritische Schriften, &c.
Elsneri Observationes Sacræ.
Ewald's Gesch. der altesten Auslegung und Spracherklarung des Alt. Test.
Fabricii Bibliotheca Græca.
Greisbachii Prolegomena.
——— Com. criticus in Textum N. T.
——— Symbolæ Criticæ.
Grawitz, These critique sur la lang. de Matthieu. (Asserts the Hebrew original.)
Hageman Nachricht von der vörnehmsten Uebersetzungen.
Hegelmair Chaldaismi biblici fundamenta.
Heideggeri Dissertationes Selectæ.
——— Labores Exegeticæ.
——— Enchiridion Biblicum.
Hezel's Gesch. der bibl. Kritik des alten T.
Hitzig's Kurtzgefastes exegetisches.
Hodius de Bibl. textibus originalibus.
Houbiganti Prolegomena in S. Script.
Hulsius de Heb. textu. (Against Vossius.)
Hyperius de Sac. Script. lectione.
Ikenii Dissertationes. ("Egregiæ." WALCH.)
Jerhovii Conjectanea in titulos psalmos.
Kluit, Vindiciæ articuli ὁ, ἡ, τό, in N. T.
Knappii Scripta var. exegetica.
Kortholti Tractationes theologico-philol.
Krebsii Observationes in N. Testamentum.
Kuinoel, Commentationes Theologicæ.
Kype, Observ. in N. T. ("Nothing superior, or, indeed, equal."—MICHAELIS.)
Le Clerc, Bibliotheq. ancienne et moderne.
Le Long, Bibliotheca Sacra.
Leigh, Critica Sacra.
——— Supplementa.
Lightfoot, Opera.
Limborch, de Scriptura Sacra.
Lindanus de Optimo genere interpret.
Markii Exercitationes textualis.
Millii Dissertationes.
Montani (Arias) Prolegomena.
Montfaucon, Hexaplorum Originis, &c.
Muntingii Expositio critica V. T. (A compend of the most valuable critics.)
Noesselti Opuscula.
——— Exercitationes.
Norberg (M.), Opuscula Academica.
Polli Synopsis Criticorum. (This work, in 5 folios, is an abridgement and improvement of the Critica Sacra.)
Reuschii Syrus interpres cum fonte N. Test. Græco collatus.
Rosenmulleri Scholia in V. Test. (25 vols.).
——— Scholia in N. Test. (8 vols.)
Schnurrer, Dissertationes. (On the age of manuscripts, and on various difficult texts.)
Scholz, Curæ Criticæ.
Schulten's Animadv. philolog. et crit.
——— de Utilitate dialector. orient. ad tuendam integritatem codicis, &c.

Biblical Criticism—*continued.*

Sciopius de Ars Critica.
Simonis Historia critica.
Spitzneri Inst. ad analyticam textus.
Storr, Dissertationes.
——— Opuscula Academica.
Tischendorf, Novum Testamentum cum apparatu et prolegomenis.
Venemæ Dissertationes Sacræ.
Wokenius de Elipsibus e textu Hebraice.
Wolfburgii Observationes in N. T. (A valuable supplement to Leigh's Critica Sacra.)
Wölfii Bibliotheca Hebræa.
——— Cura philolog. et crit. in N. T.
Alexander's (F.) Ecclesiastical Hist. (Interspersed with numerous learned and important dissertations.)
Alford's Greek Testament. (A revised text, digest of various readings, prolegomena, and critical commentary.)
American Biblical Repository. 3d Series. 2:124. 3:95, 323.
Bates on the Integrity of the Heb. text.
Bengel's Gnomon. Trans. by Fausset.
Benson on the Unity of sense.
Bentley's Proposals for printing a new edition of the Greek Testament. 1721.
Berriman's Moyer Lectures. 1741. (Critical dissertations on 1 Tim. iii. 16. Defends the received reading, and gives an acc. of 100 Greek manuscripts not before collated.)
Biblical Cabinet. 1832, and since. An Edinburgh periodical, embracing the works of Ernest, Planch, Tholuck, Tittman, Pareau, Storr, and others.
Blackwell's Sacred Classics defended.
Bloomfield's Digest of annot. on the N. T.
Bowyer's Critical conjectures. (A collection of valuable observations.)
Burton's Greek Test. with English notes.
Butler's Horæ Biblicæ. (A series of notes on the Heb. and Greek texts, versions, and printed editions.)
Calmet's Dissertations on the Sac. Scrip.
Campbell's Four gospels, with Preliminary dissertations.
Carson (Alex.) on Biblical Interpretation.
Clarke's Hebrew criticism and poetry.
Christian Examiner. 1:201. 2:210. 22:170.
Christian Review. 1:597. 6:66. 13:545.
Collyer's Sacred Interpreter.
Conybeare's Lectures on Bible. doctrines.
Cook's Inquiry into the Books of the N. T.
Davidson's (Sam.) Lectures on Bib. Crit.
Dedier's Dissertations on the Old Test.
Dibden's Introduction. (An account of Bibles, Polyglots, and Testaments.)
Dimock's Critical and explan. notes, &c.
Dodd's Dissertations on the Old Test.
——— Dissertations on the Gospels.
Doddridge's Lectures. Lect. 92 and 97.
Dove's Vindic. of the Hebrew Scriptures.
Eclectic Review. 4th Series. 8:270.
Edinburgh Review. 72:69. 94:1.
Edwards' (Thomas) Dissertations.

Biblical Criticism—*continued.*

Ernest's Inst. of Bib. Crit. Tr. by M. Stuart.
——— ——— ——— Tr. by Terrot.
Fife's Critica Sacræ.
Forbes' Principles of interpretation.
Geddes' Prospectus of a new translation.
——— Critical remarks on the Heb. Script.
Gerard's Institutes of Biblical criticism. (A very good elementary work.)
Gray's Key to the Old Test. and Apocrypha.
Gray's Connexion between the sacred writings, and the literature of Jewish and Heathen authors.
Henderson's Elements of Bib. Criticism.
——— Biblical Researches.
Holston on the Word Σάρξ in the N. T.
Horseley's Biblical Criticism.
Hurdis on the first Ten Chapters of Genesis.
Jebb's Sacred Literature.
Jones' Critical Lectures.
King's (Edw.) Morsels of criticism.
Kitto's Journal of Sac. Lit. 1850, onward.
——— Biblical Cyclopedia.
Lamy's Biblical apparatus.
Lawrence's Critical remarks on detached passages.
——— Reflections on important misrepresentations in the Unitarian version.
Leigh's Critica Sacra. (Observations upon all the Greek words in the N. Test.)
McGill's (Prof.) Lectures.
McKnight on the Gospels and Epistles.
Marsh's Course of Lectures.
——— Letter to Archdeacon Travis.
Methodist Quarterly Review. 3 : 34.
Middleton's Doct. of the Greek article.
New York Rev. 2:133. (On Germ. Criticism.)
Nolan's Integrity of the Greek Vulgate. (Classifies the manuscripts, and vindicates the received text.)
Owens (H.) Observations on the Gospels.
——— Critica Sacra.
——— Critical Disquisitions.
——— Introduction to Heb. Criticism.
Platt's Ethiopic biblical manuscripts.
Pococke's Miscellanies.
Preston's Phraseological notes on the Hebrew text of Genesis.
Princeton Review. 9 : 266.
Quarterly Review. 1 : 473.
Roberts' Clavis Bibliorum.
Sargeant's Compend of biblical criticism.
Scrivener's Introd. to the Crit. of the N. T.
——— Collation of 20 Greek manuscripts of the four gospels.
Simpson's (D.) Sacred Literature. (A condensation, into 4 vols., of a great amount of criticisms by the early Fathers.)
Stuart's Elements of Bib. Crit. from the Latin of Ernest, Keil, Beck, Morus, &c.
Tregelles' Account of the printed text of the New Testament.
——— Edition of the Greek Test. 1861.
Van Mildert's Bampton Lectures.
Whiston's Essay toward restoring the true text of the Old Testament.
Yong's Crit. Dissertations on the N. Test.

See other authors on this subject, cited in Bp. MARSH'S *Lectures*, HORNE'S *Introduction*, ORME'S *Bibliotheca Sacra*, and CALMET'S *Dictionary*.

Biblical Geography. See GEOGRAPHY.

Biblical History.
See JEWISH ANTIQUITIES.

Alexandri Historia Eccles. Vet. Test.
Alliolis Biblischen Alterthumskunde.
Andilly, Histoire de l'ancien Testament.
Bassnage, Histoire du vieux Testament.
Bercherodius Lumen Hist. Sac. V. et N. T.
Berruyer, Histoire du peuple de Dieu.
Buddæi Historia Ecclesiastica V. T.
Capelli Historia Sacra et Exotica.
Carpzovii Apparatus Historiæ Criticus.
Eusebii Chronicon.
Heideggeri Historia Patriarcharum.
Hornii Historia Ecclesiastica.
Josephi Opera.
Kurtz's Biblische Geschichte.
Langii Historia Ecclesiastica Vet. Test.
Leydecker, Historia Eccles. Vet. et N. Test.
Markii Historia Paradisi.
Nichol, Hist. Sacra. (Acta erud. 1712.)
Robinson, Annales Mundi, sacri et secularis.
Saurin, Discours historiques, critiques, &c.
Schmidii Compendium. (Acta erud. 1708.)
Selden de Diis Syriis.
Simon, Hist. Critique du Vieux Test.
Spanheim, Introd. ad. Hist. et antiq. Sac.
Spondanii Annales Sacri a creatione.
Usseri Annales Veteris et Novi Test.
Venema, Institutiones Hist. V. et N. Test.
Vitringæ Hypotyposis.
Vosii Historia de Idolatria.
Witsii Miscellanea Sacra.

Bassnage's History of the Jews.
Bedford's Scripture chronology demonstrated by astronomical calculation.
Bell's Mission of St. John.
Biscoe's Hist. of the Acts of the Apostles confirmed from other authors.
Blome's Hist. of the O. and N. Testaments.
Bryant on the Plagues of Egypt.
Calmet's History of the Old and New Test.
Clarke's Bible History. (Malachi to Christ.)
Craddock's Hist. of the O. Test. methodized.
——— Apostolical History methodized.
Ellwood's Sacred Hist. of the O. and N. T.
Fleury's History of the Israelites.
Gales' Court of the Gentiles.
Geneste's Parallel histories of Judah and Israel. (Valuable matter.)
Gleig's (G. R.) Hist. of the Bible. (Maps.)
Hall's (Bp.) Contemplations.
Hawker's (Robt.) Extracts and Notes.
Hawkins' Objects and uses of the Historical Scriptures of the O. T.
Howard's Scripture History of the Earth.
Howell's History of the Bible. (Plates.)
Jamieson's Use of Sacred History.

Biblical History—*continued.*

Jones' (Jos.) Chronol. and analysis of Sc.
Kimpton's History of the Bible.
Kurtz's History of the Old Covenant. Trans. by J. Martin.
Kurtz's (John H.) Manual of Sacred history. (Learned and interesting.)
Palfrey's (J. G.) Academical Lectures.
Parker's (S.) Old Test. illustrated.
Shuckford's Connexion of Sac. and Prof. Hist.
Simon's Critical History of the Old Test.
Smith's History of the Old Testament.
——— History of the New Testament.
Stackhouse's Hist. of the Bible. (Poor.)
Stillingfleet's Origines Sacræ.
Stukeley's Palæographia Sacra.
Thompson's (And.) Scripture History.
Trimmer's Sacred History.
Watts' (Isaac) Scripture History.
Wheeler's (J. S.) Analysis of N. Test. hist. (Very valuable.)
Winder's History of knowledge.

There exists a vast multitude of Bible histories, but few are as lucid and interesting as the Bible itself. Some, however, are useful as school books, and some as works of general reference.

Biblical Interpretation.
See HERMENEUTICS.

Bibliography. See PRINTED EDITIONS.

Assemani Bibliotheca Orientalis. (Great.)
Bailly, Notices historiques sur les Bibliotheques anciennes et modernes; suivi d'un tableau comparatif des produits de la presse, de 1812 à 1825.
Balæi Scriptorum illustrium majoris Angliæ et Scotiæ Catalogus. 1615.
Bellarmin, de Scriptoribus Ecclesiast. 1617.
Bengel's (E. G.) Archiv fur die Theologie und ihre neuste Litteratur.
Brunet, Manuel du libraire, 1865. (Very complete.)
Cave, Scriptorum ecclesiasticorum Historia literaria a Christo nato, usque ad seculum XIV. 1517.
Ceillier, Hist. generale des auteurs sacres et ecclesiastiques, contient leur vie, la critiq., la demonologie, l'analyse, &c. 24 vols. 4to. 1729.
Doederlein's Theologische Bibliothek. 1710.
Doering's Gelehrte theologen in Teutschland in 18 and 19 Jahrhunderten.
Dowling, Notitia Script. Patrum aliorumque.
Du Pin, Nouvelles Bibliotheques. 43 vols. 1688. (Gives the lives of authors, and a sketch of the contents of every book.)
Ebert's Allgem. bibliographisches Lexicon. 1821–30.
Eichhorn's Bibliothek der biblisch. litteratur. 1801.
Ersch's Litteratur der Theologie. 1810.
Fabricii (Jo.) Historia Bibliothecæ. 1788. 6 vols., 4to. (Gives the various editions, with an epitome, biographic sketch, and much other information.)

Bibliography—*continued.*

Fabricii (J. A.) Bibl. Ecclesiastica. (A selection from twelve authors, who, from the 4th to the 17th centuries, composed notices of ecclesiastical writers.)
Fluegge's Ges. d. theolog. Wissenschaften.
Fuerst Bibliotheca Judaica.
Fuhrman's Theologischen Litteratur.
——— Neusten theol. Litteratur.
Godwin de Praesulibus Angliæ. 1616. (Enlarged and continued to 1743, by Richardson.)
Halloix, Illustrium ecclesiæ Orientalis scriptorum. 1648.
Hardt, Hist. litter. Reformationis. 1717.
Josephi (Octav. M.) Bibliographia critica. (Contains a great amount of information not elsewhere concentrated. His analysis of the *Acta Bollandiana*, occupies 100 columns; of the *Decretals*, 60 columns. 1740. 4 vols., folio.)
Le Long, Bibliotheca Sacra. 1720.
Lippenii Bibl. realis theologica. 1685.
Noeselt's Anweisung. zur Kentniss der besten algemeinern Bücher, &c. 1808.
Olearii Bibl. scriptorum eccles. 1711.
Peignot, Repertoire Bibliog. universel.
Petzholdt's Anzeiger für Bibliographie. Periodical, begun 1840.
Photii Myriobiblion. 1620. (A vast treasury of extracts from writers of the first nine centuries. Of many of these there is nothing now extant but these selections.)
Sabbathier, Dict. pour l'intelligence des auteurs. 1815. 37 vols.
Schmidt's (J. A. F.) Handbuch der Bibliothek wissenschaft. 1840.
Stäudlin's Archiv fur kirchengeschichte.
——— Litteratur der kirchen Geschichte.
Ugolini Thesaurus antiq. sacrorum. 1744.
Walchii Bibliotheca Theologica. 1757.
Wolfii Bibliotheca Hebræa. 1600.

Bickersteth's Christian Student. 1829.
Bury's Philobiblion. Trans. in 1832.
Cave's Lives of the Fathers. 1677.
Clarke's (A.) Succession of sac. lit. To 1300.
Clarke's (Wm.) Repertorium. 1819.
Darling's Encycl. Bibliographica. 1854.
Dibdon's Acc. of polyglott Bibles, &c.
——— Bibliomania.
Dodwell's Extant works of the Christian writers of the first three centuries.
Edwards' (Edw.) Memoirs of libraries. 1859. (A work which, though not theological, is of great use to every scholar, and the best of its kind in the English language.)
Guild's Librarian's Manual. 1858.
Hoffmann's Lexicon bibliographicum. 1836.
Horne's (T. H.) Biblical bibliography. 1839.
Kemp's Biblioth. of English theol. writers.
Leigh's Religious and learned men. 1656.
Lowndes' Bibliographers' Manual. (Not entirely theological.)
Marsh's (Bp.) Lectures.
Orme's Bibliotheca Biblica.

Platt's Cat. of Ethiopic biblical manuscripts.
Rhees' Manual of libraries in Amer. 1861.

The above list comprises more than any student will desire to consult. "A complete collection of bibliographical works would exceed 20,000 volumes."—NORTON. NAMUR, above cited, gives *a list* of 10,236 separate works, some of them comprising numerous volumes; comparatively few, however, of these are theological. Under more than 150 of the heads in this work, the reader is referred to the Bibliography of those particular subjects.

Bigotry. See TOLERATION.

Chandler's (H.) Effort against Bigotry.
Eaton's Familiar Dialogues.
Edwards' (Thomas) Dissertations.
Enfield's (William) Sermons.
Falkland's Essay on bigotry.
Fuller's Calvinistic and Socin. systems.
Investigator. 7:243.
Roble's (M.) Bigotry worse than Atheism.
Wesley's (John) Sermons.

Biography, Christian.

Acta Sanctorum, quotquot toto orbe colunter. (A stupendous work, issued from time to time, since 1643, till it has reached 59 folio volumes, and is still continued. It furnishes a history of Europe, and of the so-called church, in all ages.)
Adamus (M.) de Vitis Theologorum. 1620.
Bates, Vitæ selectorum. (Lives of Budeus, Scaliger, Bucer, Grotius, Savonarola, &c.)
Böhringer's Kirche Christi, u. ihre Zeugen.
Brucker's Ehren-tempel der Deutchen Gelehrsamkeit. (Has 50 fine portraits of Buxtorf, Fagius, &c.)
Dupin, Bibliotheque des auteurs. 1688.
Pippingii Sacer decadum septenarius. 1707. (Lives of seventy Lutheran ministers.)
Schaffer's Galerie der Reformators.
Schröck's Lebensbeschreibungen berühmter. (Luther, Zuingle, Eck, Brent, Bucer, &c.)
Smith, Vita quorundam illustrium. (Usher, Briggs, Dee, Bainbridge, &c.)
Wendlerus de Præcipuorum, &c. (Luther, Melancthon, Chemnitz, Tarnow, Gerard.)
Wittonii Memoriæ Theologorum.

Allen's Biographia Eccles. (1st four cent.)
Brooks' Lives of eminent Puritans. (Gives memoirs of nearly 500 persons.)
Brown's Practical piety exemplified.
Burder's Pious women of Britton. 1815. (78 memoirs.)
Burnham's Pious Memorials.
Caves' Lives of the Fathers.
Chalmer's (Alex.) Biographical Dictionary. 32 vols. 1812.
Clarke's Lives of Puritan divines. 1683.
Cox's Fathers of the first three cent. 1833.
Evans' Biog. of the early Church. 1837.
Fuller's Worthies of England. 1662.
Gibbons' Eminently pious women. 1760.
Gilpin's Lives of the Reformers. 1800.

Biography, Christian—*continued.*

Granger's Biographical Dictionary. 1760. (Continued by Noble to 1806.)
Hone's Eminent Christians. 1834. (Vol. 1. Usher, Hammond, Evelyn, Wilson. Vol. 2. Bernard, Gilpin, Philip de Morney, Bedell, Horneck. Vol. 3. Ridley, Hall, Boyle. Vol. 4. Bradford, Grindale, Sir Matthew Hale.)
Hook's Ancient and modern divines. 1852.
Howie's Scots Worthies. 1781.
Innes' Select Christian Biography. 1820.
Jones' Christian Biography. 1829.
Kippis' Biographia Brittanica. 1778.
Le Clerc's Lives of eminent fathers. 1696.
Library of Chris. Biog. Period. 1837 et seq.
Livingston's Divines of Scotland. 1660.
Middleton's Biographia Evangelica. 1779.
Palmer's Non-conformist's memorial. 1770.
Sprague's Annals of the Amer. pulpit. 1865.
Stephens' Ecclesiastical biography.
Strype's Annals. 1700.
Tullock's Leaders of the Reformation.
Walton's Lives. 1680. (Donne, Wotton, Hooker, Herbert, and Sanderson.)
Waterhouse's Piety and policy of elder times.
Wood's Athenæ Oxoniensis. (Memoirs of the writers and bishops educated at Oxford, from 1500 to 1690.)
Wordsworth's Ecc. biog. (Wholly English.)

The numbers following indicate the time of decease.

Alexander, Archib.; by J. W. Alexander. 1851.
Alleine's Life and letters. 1672.
Anderson, Chris.; by H. Anderson. 1851.
Atterbury, Bp. F.; by Stackhouse. 1732.
Baxter's Narrative of his life. 1691.
Baxter's Life; by Orme.
Bedel, Bp.; by Burnett. 1692.
Bedell, Gregory T.; by Tyng. 1834.
Belfrage's Life and correspondence. 1835.
Boardman, Geo. D.; by King. 1831.
Bœhmen, Jacob; by O'Kelly. 1674.
Bonnell, James; by Hamilton. 1699.
Boyle, Robert; by Birch. 1691.
Bradford, John; by Stephens. 1555.
Brainard, James; by Styles. 1747.
——— ——— by Pres. Edwards.
——— ——— by Pratt.
——— ——— by Peabody.
Buchanan, Claudius; by Pearson. 1718.
Buck, Charles; by Styles. 1815.
Budd, Henry; by himself. 1852.
Bull, Bp.; by Nelson. 1710.
Bunyan, 1688. See BUNYAN.
Burder, George; by F. Burder. 1832.
Bury, Mrs. E.; by Dr. Watts. 1720.
Calvin, 1564. See CALVIN.
Carey, Wm. D. D.; by John C. Marshman. 1834.
Carson, Alex.; by Moore.
Cecil, Richard; by Newlin. 1810.
Chalmers, Thomas; by Hanna. 1847.
Chamberlain, Missionary; by Yates.

Biography, Christian—*continued.*

Chrysostom, 407. See CHRYSOSTOM.
Colet, John; by Knight. 1519.
Cornelius, Elias; by B. B. Edwards. 1832.
Cranmer, 1556. See CRANMER.
De Foe, Daniel; by Wilson. 1731.
De Renty, Cardinal; by St. Jure. 1649.
Doddridge, Philip; by Orton. 1751.
——— ——— by Stoughton.
Duncan, Mary L.; by M. G. L. Duncan. 1840.
Durant's Mem. of an only son. 1822.
Edwards, John; by Hawkesley. 1716.
Elliott, John; by C. Mather. 1690.
Erasmus, 1536. See ERASMUS.
Erskine, Ebenezer; by Wellwood. 1754.
Evans, Christmas; by Jos. Cross. 1791.
——— ——— by D. Phillips.
——— ——— by D. R. Stephens.
Ewing, Greville; by his daughter. 1841.
Fenelon, Abp.; by C. Butler. 1715.
Fiske, Pliny; by Bond. 1825.
Fletcher, John W.; by Benson. 1785.
Fletcher, Mrs.; by H. Moore.
Foster, John; by Ryland. 1843.
Fry, Elizabeth; by Timson. 1844.
Fuller, Andrew; by Morris. 1815.
Gardner, Col.; by Doddridge. 1741.
Gilpin, Bernard; by Carleton. 1583.
Good, John M.; by O. Gregory. 1827.
Graham, Isabella; by Mason. 1814.
Guyon, Madame; by herself. 1717.
Haldane, James; by Alex. Haldane. 1851.
Haldane, Robt.; by Alex. Haldane. 1842.
Hale, Matthew; by Bp. Burnett. 1676.
Hall, Bp.; by Jones. 1656.
Hall, Robert; by O. Gregory. 1831.
Halyburton, Thos.; by Dr. Watts. 1712.
Hawkes, Mrs.; by Cath. Cecil.
Heber, Bp.; by Taylor. 1826.
——— ——— by his widow.
Henry, Matthew; by Williams. 1714.
Henry, Philip; by M. Henry. 1696.
Hervey, James; by Ryland. 1758. (A very singular book.)
——— ——— by Brown.
Hewitson, W. H.; by Baillie. 1850.
Howard, John; by Aikens. 1790.
——— ——— by Dixon.
——— ——— by Brown.
——— ——— by Field.
Howels, William; by Morgan. 1832.
Huntingdon, Lady; by A. H. New. 1791.
Huntingdon, Susan; by Wisner. 1824.
Hutchinson, Col.; by Mrs. Hutchinson.
Janeway, John; by J. A. Janeway. 1670.
Jebb, Bp. John; by Forster. 1833.
Jewell, Bp. John; by Le Bas. 1751.
——— ——— by Humphreys.
Judson, Adoniram; by Wayland. 1850.
Judson, Mrs. Anne; by Knowles. 1826.
Judson, Mrs. S. B.; by Mrs. Emily Judson. 1845.
Jukes, Mrs. H. M.; by Mrs. Gilbert. 1854.
Justin Martyr, 166. See JUSTIN MARTYR.
Kiffin, William; by himself. Edited with notes, by Orme. 1823.

Biography, Christian—*continued.*

Kitto, John; by J. A. Ryland.
Knox, 1572. See KNOX.
Latimer; by Gilpin. 1555.
——— by Watkins. (And others.)
Luther, 1546. See LUTHER.
Martyn, Henry; by Sargeant. 1821.
Mather, Cotton; by Sam. Mather. 1728.
Melancthon, 1568. See MELANCTHON.
Mills, Samuel; by Spring.
Mores, Henry; by Ward. 1687.
Neff, Felix; by Bost. 1840. (Of several this is the best.)
Newell, Harriet; by Woods. 1812.
Newton, John; by Cecil. 1807.
Oberlin, John F.; Anonymous. 1826.
Owen, John; by Orme. 1683.
Payson, Edward; by Cummings. 1827.
Pearce, Samuel; by Fuller.
Richmond, Leigh; by Grimshaw. 1827.
Riddle, Bp.; by G. Riddle. 1555.
Romaine, William; by Haweis. 1795.
Rutherford, Sam.; by Murray. 1661.
Ryland, John; by Newman. 1825.
Savage, Mrs.; by Williams.
Scott, Thomas; by J. Scott. 1821.
Schwartz, C. F.; by Pearson. 1798.
Spencer, Thomas; by Raffles. 1811.
Sharp, Granville; by Hoare. 1813.
Staughton, Will.; by Lynd. 1829.
Summerfield, John; by Holland. 1825.
Taylor, Jeremy; by Bp. Heber. 1667.
Tillotson, Abp.; by Burch. 1694.
——— ——— by Bp. Burnett.
Urquhart, John; by Orme. 1827.
Usher, Bp.; by Parr. 1656.
Waldo, Peter. 1179.
Walton, Bp. Bryan; by Todd. 1660.
Watts, Isaac; by Gibbon. 1748.
Wesley, 1791. See WESLEY.
Wesley, Cha.; by Jackson. 1788.
——— ——— by Whitehead.
Whitefield, George. See WHITFIELD.
Wickliff, 1384. See WICKLIFF.
Williams, Roger; by Elton. 1683.
Winter, Richard; by Jay. 1799.
Woolsey, Card., 1531. See WOOLSEY.
Xavier, 1617. See XAVIER.
Ximenes, 1517. See XIMENES.
Zinzendorf, 1760. See ZINZENDORF.
Zuingle, 1531. See ZUINGLE.

There is scarcely a limit to to this class of books, and to make a selection generally satisfactory is impossible. The above are among the most precious.

Biography, Scripture. See under individual heads, such as ABRAHAM, ANDREW, &c.

Capelli (Lud.) Historia Apostolica.
Coquerell, Biographie Sacrée.
Dorotheus de Vita prophetarum, apostolorum, et septuaginta discipulorum.
Genoude, Biographie Catholique.
Grube's Characterbilder aus der H. S. (So arranged as to constitute a hist. of relig.)

Biography, Scripture—*continued.*

Heideggeri Historia Patriarcharum.
Peronius de Rebus gestis, vitisque Apost.
Aguilar's Women of Israel.
Bloomfield's (E.) Lives of Christ and the most eminent persons mentioned in the New Testament.
Candlish's Scripture characters.
Copley's Scripture Biography. (Comprises all the names recorded.)
Cox's Female Scripture Biography.
Craddock's Apostolical History.
Crossman's Old Testament characters.
Enfield's Biographical Sermons.
Evans' (R. W.) Scripture Biography.
Farr's Bible Biography. (In Bible words.)
Fleming's Sacred Biography.
Fountain's Old Test. saints.
Hall's (Bp.) Contemplations.
Hifferman's Characters of Scripture history. (Precious.)
Hughes' Female characters of Holy Writ.
Hunter's Sacred Biography.
Jowett's (Wm.) Characters of the New Test.
——— Characters of the Old Test.
King's Female Scripture characters.
McDuff's Sunsets on the Heb. mountains.
Mearns' Lectures on Scrip. characters.
Morris' Sacred Biography. (Plates.)
Roberts' (G.) Sacred Biography.
Robinson's (Tho.) Scrip. characters.
Smith's (S.) Sacred Biography.
Stevenson's Scripture Portraits.
Thompson's (F. E.) Lent Lectures.
Trench's (F.) Scripture Biography.
Watkins' (Isaac) Scripture Biography.
Watkins' (John) Scrip. Biography for youth.
Wordsworth's Scripture Biography.

Birth of Christ. See CHRISTMAS, INCARNATION, JESUS CHRIST, NATIVITY.

Black Friars. See DOMINICANS.

Black Jews.

Gregoire, Hist. des sectes religieuses.

Buchanan's Researches in Asia.
Wolf's Missionary Journal.

Blasphemy. See UNPARDONABLE SIN.

Witsii Ægyptica. Lib. 1, cap. 5.

Barrow's (Isaac) Works.
Campbell's (Geo.) Preliminary Dissert.
Foster's (James) Sermons.
Robinson's Scripture plea.
Trial of Elwell.

Blessedness of God. See ATTRIBUTES.

Colliber's (Sam.) Theological Treatises.
Doddridge's Lectures. Pt. 2, propos. 38.
Howe's (John) Works.
Price's Four Dissertations.
Tillotson's (Abp.) Sermons.
Watts' Scale of blessedness.

Blessedness of the Righteous. See BEATITUDES, HEAVEN, PLEASURES OF PIETY, WISDOM OF BEING RELIGIOUS.

Harding's (John) Sermons.
Howe's Blessedness of the righteous.
Langhorne's (William) Sermons.
Manton's (Tho.) Sermons.
Robinson's (D.) Privileges of the righteous.
Tillotson's (Abp.) Sermons.

Blessedness of the Persecuted.

Bragge's (Francis) Practical Discourses.
Collings' (Dr. John) Sermons.
Powell's (Samuel) Sermons.

Blood. See PROHIBITION.

Bloody Sweat. See SUFFERINGS OF CHRIST.

Bartholini Hypomnematum.
Calmeti (Augustin.) Dissertationes.
Clotzii (Stephan.) Dissertationes.
Koenigii (Georg.) Dissertationes.
Mayeri (Joann. Frider.) Dissertationes.
Widelii (Geo. W.) Exercitationes philol.

Boasting.

Irving's (Edw.) Sermons.

Body of Moses.

Bachmani (Fridem.) Dissertationes.
Calmeti (Augustin.) Dissertationes.
Deylingii Observationes Sacræ.
Frischmuthii (Joann.) Dissertationes.
Gerard de Sepultura Mosis.
Hornii (Conrad.) Dissertationes.
Nierembergii Dissertationes.

Bœhmen.

Franckenburgii Vita Bœhmii.
Lüdeken (Th.) Nachricht von J. Böhme.
Rumpæi Diss. de Iacob Bœhmio.
Wullen's J. Böhme's Leben und Lehre.
Bœhmen's Works. Trans. by Sparrow.
Hotham's Life of Jacob Bœhmen.
Oakley's Memoirs of Jacob Bœhmen.

Bœhmenists. See BOURIGNONISTS, MYSTICISM, PIETISTS, QUIETESTS.

Pro.

Bœhmenis Opera. (The best edition is said to be that of Franckenberg. 1730.)
Calo, Hist. Jacobi Bœminis.
Franckenbergii Opera. (Numerous.)
Kuhlman's Neubegeisterter Bœhm. (Adelung gives a list of forty-two works by this author, who was burnt for his opinions in Russia, 1689. All his writings have a holy tendency.)
Richter's Bericht von B.'s Leben und Schrift.
Tschech's Vertheidigung Bœhmens.
Zimmermani Orthodoxia theosoph. Teuton.

Con.

Arnold's (G.) Kirchen u. Ketzerhistorie, &c.
Bücher's Systematis anti-fanatici.

Calovii Anti-Bœminum.
Carpzovii Disputationes Academicæ.
Fabricii (Joann) Dissertationes.
Gilberti Admonitio adv. scripta B.
Harenburg, de Quirino Kulmanno.
Holzhausen's Anmerkungen über auroram.
Mori Censura philosophiæ Teutonicæ.
Wirnsdorfii (Gottl.) Dissertationes.

Dublin University Mag. 33 : 90.

Bohemian Brethren. See MORAVIANS.

Bogomiles.

Andreæ (Samuel.) Dissertationes.
Commeria Alexiados.
Engehardt's Kirchengeschichte.
Fabricii (Joann. Albert.) Dissertationes.
Heumanni (Chris. August.) Dissertationes.
Wolfii Historia Bogomilorum.

Boodhism. See BUDHISM.

Book of Common Prayer.

Anderson's Manner of Garrick in reading the book of common prayer. 1797.
Bayley's Parallel of the liturgy and mass book. 1789.
Bennet's Paraph. and Annotations. 1708.
Berens' Offices of the Church. 1830.
——— Hist. of the Prayer book. 1832.
Biddulph's (Thomas T.) Lectures. 1815.
Bisse's Sermons at the Rolls chapel. 1716.
Blakeney's Hist. of the book of C. P. 1865.
Bosworth on the Book of Common Prayer.
Boyd's Sermons on the Church. 1840.
Boyse's Exp. of all the Scriptures used in the English liturgy. 1622.
Brogden's Ritual of the Ch. of Engl. 1842.
Brownel's Introd. to the book of C. P. 1815.
Bulley's Tabular view of the variations in the communion and baptismal offices, from 1549 to 1662.
Burrows' (R.) Sermons on the lessons. 1817.
Burrows' (E. J.) Summary of faith. 1822.
Calvin's Judgment concerning the English book of common prayer. 1554.
Campion's Book of C. P. With historical and critical explanations.
Cardwell's Two books of Common Prayer, set forth under Edward VI.
Clay's (W. R) Hist. of the book of C. P.
Comber's Companion to the temple. 1701.
——— Discourses. 1668.
Close's Sermons on the Liturgy. 1840.
Cobden's (Edward) Sermons. 1755.
Downes' Lives of the compilers and revisers, &c. 1722.
Draper's (H.) Lectures. 1806.
Eclectic Review. 4th Series. 8 : 489.
Harwood's Illustrations of the C. P. 1826.
Hole's (Matt.) Practical discourses. 1714. (Extensive and judicious, but not evangelical.)

Book of Common Prayer—*continued.*

Howlett's Instructions as to reading the Liturgy. 1826.
Hutchin's Lectures. 1729 to 1763. (By Mangey, Watson, Stebbing, Cobden, Shuckford, Asheton, Ridley, and others.)
Keeling's Liturgiæ Brittannicæ. (The six liturgies, from the time of Edward VI. to Charles II., arranged in parallel columns.)
Ketley & Clay's Liturgies, private prayers, &c. Put forth by authority.
Lathbury's Hist. of the book of C. Prayer, with the state of religion and religious parties, from 1640 to 1660.
Mant's Selected notes. (Valuable.)
Marbeke on the Book of Common Prayer.
Markell's Ecclesiæ Anglicæ monumenta. (The fullest account of English liturgies. Enumerates 91 old "Service books.")
Nichols' Book of Common Prayer. 1712. (Notes by Bp. Andrews, Bp. Cosin, &c.)
Palmer's Antiquities of the English ritual.
Powell's (Vavassor) The Common prayer book no divine service.
Proctor's Hist. of the book of com. prayer.
Pruen's Illustrations; with a history. 1815.
Reeves' Bk. of C. P.; with preface and notes.
Rogers' (Tho.) Lectures on the Liturgy.
Sharpe (Archdeacon) on the Rubric.
Shepherd's Crit. and prac. elucidat. 1817.
Sparrow's Rationale of the C. P. 1647.
Stoddart's Hist. of the book of C. P. 1864.
Tyrrell's Ritual of the Ch. of England.
Veneer's Proof-texts, explanations, &c. 1727.
Waldo's (Peter) Commentary. 1772.
Warner's Illustrations. 1754. (Gives the observations of numerous eminent divines.)
Wheatley on the Book of C. P. 1710. (The substance of every thing liturgical in Sparrow, L'Estrange, Comber, Nichols, and others.)

For lists of the early editions of the Book of Common Prayer, see LOWNDES' *Brit. Librarian;* KEELING'S *Liturgiæ Brittanicæ,* 1851; and CARDWELL'S *History of the book of common prayer.*

Books of Prayers.
See PRAYER BOOKS.

Borrowing of the Egyptians.

Danville Review. September, 1864.
Edwards' (Bp.) Critical Exercitations.
Holbrook on Israel's borrowing, &c.
Jennings' Jewish Antiquities.
Patrick's Commentary in loc.
Shuckford's Connexion of O. and N. Test.
Waterland's Scripture vindicated.

Botany of the Bible.
See NATURAL HISTORY.

Bounty to the Poor.
See ALMSGIVING.

Bourignonists.

Pro.

De Cordt, l'Innocence reconnue.
Œuvres de Mad. Antoinette Bourignon. 18 vols., 8vo. The following works of this eminent lady have been translated into English:
Light of the World.
On solid virtue.
Light risen in darkness.
The Gospel spirit.
Warnings against the Quakers.
Academy of the learned divines.
Poiret de Auctoribus Mysticis.
——— Cogitationes Rationales.
——— Sainte Bible avec des explicat.
——— (Opera alia.)

De la Combe on Christian Perfection.

Con.

Arnold, Historia Eccles. et Hæretica.
Baieri (Joann. Guill.) Dissertationes.
Berkendal's Wahre Abbildung Bourignon.
Burchard's Anmerkungen über die groben Irthumer, &c.
Jurien, Traité Historique.
Molleri Cimbria Litterata.
Neumanni Dissertationes.
Pungelerus de rerum possibilium ideis.
Wolfgang, Examen theologiæ novæ.

Blackwell's Reasonableness of rev. religion.
Cockburn's Bourignonism detected.
Honeyman's Bourignonism displayed.

Brahminism. See HINDUISM.

Brazen Serpent. See SERPENT WORSHIP.

Cyril (Alex.), Glaphyra.
Buxtorfii Exercitationes.
Deylingii Observationes Sacræ.
Hottingeri (Joann. Henric.) Exercitationes.
Krafftii (Jo. Melch.) Observationes Sacræ.

Anderson's (M.) Life of Moses.
Berriman's (William) Sermons.
Cooper's (Edward) Sermons.
Dimock's Critical notes on Genesis.
Erskine's (Thomas) Life through death.
Forsyth's (J. G.) Sermons.
Gilpin's (William) Sermons.
Milner's (Joseph) Sermons.
Tait's (Wm.) Serpent in the wilderness.

Bread of Life.

Arnold's (Thomas) Sermons.
Whately's (Abp.) Sermons.

Brethren of Christ.

Bloomii (A. H.) Disputationes.

Brevity of Life. See FRAILTY.

Adey's (William) Sermons.
Amory's (Dr. Thomas) Sermons.
Benson's (George) Sermons.
Chalmer's (Thomas) Congregation sermons.
Dorrington's (Theophilus) Sermons.
Edwards' (Bp.) Theological discourses.
Green's (Samuel) Sermons.
Noel's (Gerard T.) Sermons.
Pearce's (Thomas) Sermons.
Sterne's (Lawrence) Sermons.

Bribery. See SIMONY.

Downame's (John) Treaties on various subj.
Reeves' (William) Sermons.

Brotherly Love. See FELLOWSHIP.

Abernethy's (John) Sermons.
Berriman's (William) Sermons.
Blencoe's (Edward) Sermons.
Carmichael's (Frederick) Sermons.
Darnell's (W. N.) Sermons.
Gatty's (Alfred) Sermons.
Gearing's Philadelphia Sermons.
Gisbourne's (Thomas) Sermons.
Gresley's (William) Sermons.
Hall's (Robt.) Works. Notes of sermons.
Haynes' Illustrations of faith and practice.
Hill's Apology for brotherly love.
Horsely's (Bp.) Sermons.
Hussey's (Robert) Sermons.
James' Sermons on brotherly love.
Milner's Practical Sermons.
Owen on Evangelical love.
Thomas' (Bp.) Sermons.
Thompson (J. R.) on the Christian graces.
Tillotson's (Abp.) Sermons.
Ward's (Richard) Sermons.
Wilkes' (Samuel) Sermons.
Worthington's (John) Discourses.

Brownists.

Pro.

Brown (R.) on Church Government.
——— Life and manners of true Christians.
——— Description of the visible church.
——— (Various other works.)
Ainsworth's (Henry) Works.
Barrow's (H.) Discovery of the false Church.
——— Prelatism. (For these books the author was executed at Tyburn.)
Canne's (John) Works.
Clifton's Reply to Lawrence.
Davenport's (John) Letter to the Dutch.
Greenwood's Answer to Gyffard.
Jacobs' (H.) Divine institution of the Chur.
Johnson (F.) on the Ministry of England.
——— (Several other treatises.)
Robinson's Justification of separation.
Smyth's (John) Parallels and censures.
——— Difference of the Churches.

Con.

Maimbourg, Histoire du Calvinisme.

Abbot's (Abp.) Trial of Church forsakers.
Baillie's Dissuasives from the errors of the times.
Bell (Tho.) on Church Government.
Bernard's Separatist's Schism.
Bredwell's Foundation of Brownism.
Cawdwell on the Ordained ministry.
Crashaw's Sermons at the Cross.

Brownists—*continued.*

Con.

Fellowes' Anti-calvinist.
Gyffard's Plain declaration that our Brownists be full Donatists.
——— Reply to Greenwood and Barrow.
Hall's (Bp.) Polemic Works.
Kipling on the XXXIX. Articles.
Lawne's Schism of the Brownists.
Paget's Reply to Ainsworth.
——— Reply to Davenport.
Rathband's Grave and modest Confutation.
Scarlet's Plain Confutation.

Brutes. See CRUELTY, SOULS OF BRUTES.

Budhism.

Bochinger, La Vie contemplative.
Bournouf, Hist. du Budhism Indien.
——— Essai sur le Veda.
Callery, Le Liki. Tr. from the Chinese.
Riganvet, Memoire sur les Ponghies.
Spiegel (F. R.), Kammavakya.
St. Hilaire, Histoire du Budhism.
Vassilief, le B. ses dogmes, son histoire, et sa literature.
Weber's Indische Studien.

Adelung's Sanscrit literature. Tr. by Talboys. (A full epitome, and much superior to the German original.)
Bird's (Jas.) Historical Researches.
Calcutta Review. (Many articles.)
Cunningham's Bhilsa topes. 1854.
Dublin University Magazine. 33:612, 681. 34:61.
Edkin's Notices of Chinese Budhism.
Elphinstone's History of India.
Franklin's Tenets of the Budhists.
Hardy's Eastern Monachism. (Very full.)
——— B. in its modern developments.
——— B. compared with hist. and science. 1850.
Hodgson's Literature and religion of the Budhists.
Joinville's Religion of Ceylon.
Journal of Amer. Oriental Society. 1850 to 1856. Especially 1:1, and 2:1.
Legge's Chinese Classics. (Contains the works of Confucius, Mencius, &c. With English translation and notes.
London Quart. Review. 10:513.
Mahony on Ceylon. (Also in Asiatic Researches.)
Malcom's (Howard) Travels in Southeastern Asia. 1837.
Mason's (Francis) The Buddhist Genesis.
Maurice's Boyle Lectures. 1847.
Monthly Review. 118:577.
Muir's Origin and progress of the religions of India.
New Englander. 3:182.
Newman's Catechism of the Shamans. Tr. from the Chinese. With notes.
Stevenson's Trans. of the Sanhita.
Tennent's Christianity in Ceylon. 1850.
Upham's (Edw.) Sacred books of Ceylon. Trans. from the Cingalese. (So comprehensive as to be sufficient for most persons in itself.)
——— Hist. and doctrines of Budhism. (43 curious plates.)
Westminster Review. 43:162.

Bulgari. See ALBIGENSES, CATHARI.

Bullaria. See PAPAL BULLS.

Burial of Moses. See BODY OF MOSES.

Burial of the Dead.

Christian Examiner. 31:137, 281.
Westminster Review. 37:201.

Bunyan.

Bunyan's Works. 8 vols., 8vo.
Baptist Family Magazine. 1851.
Christian Review. 4:394.
Dublin University Magazine. 37:435.
Eclectic Magazine. 23:318.
Eclectic Review. 4th Series. 3:263. 6:468. 19:129.
Frazier's Mag. 3:54. 20:115. 31:308.
Life of John Bunyan; by Condor.
——— ——— by Ivemy.
——— ——— by Montgomery.
——— ——— by Philip.
——— ——— by Southey.
——— ——— by Nelson.
——— ——— by Offir.
Littell's Living Age. 5:107.
Macauley's Miscellanies.
North American Review. 36:449.
Quarterly Review. 43:469.
Tulloch's English Puritanism.
Westminster Review. 17:103.

Burghers. See ASSOCIATE CHURCH.

Business Religion. See RELIGION.

Cabala. See RABBINICAL LITERATURE.

Buddæi Introd. ad hist. philos. Hebræorum.
Despeire, Dissertations.
Eisenmenger's Entdecktes Judenthum.
Franck's Religion's philosophie der Hebr.
Hottingeri Thesaurus. Lib. I., cap. 3.
Joel's Religion's philasophie des Sohar.
Knorr, Kabàla denudata.
Molitor's Tradition des Juden.
Monk, Philosophie des Juifs.
Morini Exercitationes.
Rosenroth, Cabala denudata.
Senstius de Kabala Judæorum.
Simonis Historia Critica.
Waltoni Prolegomena.
Wolfii Bibliotheca Hebraica.

Butler's Horæ Biblicæ.
Eclectic Review. New Series. 11:141.
Etheridge's Jerusalem and Tiberias.
Joel's Religious Philos. of the Sohar.
More on interpreting Moses according to the Cabala.

Munk's Philosophical Jewish writers.
Oxlee's Doctrine of the Trinity.

Cabiri. See IDOLATRY, MYTHOLOGY.
Astorii (J. A.) Dissertationes.
Heumanni Comment. de secta C.
Relandi (H.) Dissertationes.
St. Croix, sur les Mystéries du Paganism.
Edinburg Review. 3:313.
Faber's (Geo. S.) Mysteries of the Cabiri.

Cainites.
Heumannus Com. de secta Cainorum.

Call. See VOCATION.

Call to the Ministry. See MINISTRY.
Sadelii Vocatio pastorum.
Sanchii Dissertationes.
Tossanus de Vocatione pastorum.
Vireti (Pet.) Opera.

Amer. Quarterly Register. 1:145. 7:157.
Christian Review. 10:7.
Manual of Ministerial education.
Perkins (W.) on the Call to the ministry.
Taylor's (Jer.) Office ministerial.

Callixtines. See SYNCRETISTS.

Calumny. See CENSORIOUSNESS, DETRACTION, EVIL SPEAKING, SLANDER.

Calvin.
Calvini Opera.
Audin, la Vie, des ecrits, le devot., &c., de C.
Beza, Vie de Calvin.
Bolsec Vie, mœurs, actes, doctrine, &c., de C.
Henry's (Paul) Leben d. J. Calvin.
Lettres Francaise, de J. C. par Bonnet.

Amer. Biblical Repository. 2:541.
Analytical Magazine. 4:153.
Audin's Life of C. Trans. by J. McGill.
Biblioth. Sacra. 2:329, 489, 710. 14:125.
Bonnet's Letters of Calvin.
Bungener's Life and writings of Calvin.
Christian Examiner. 69:73.
Christ. Monthly Spectator. 3:408. 10:239.
Christian Observer. 16:435.
Cunningham's Reformers and theology of the Reformation.
Dyer's (T. H.) Life and times of C. (Repeats refuted calumnies, and paints C. in odious colors.)
Eclectic Review. 4th Series. 27:251. New Series. 3:1.
Exeter Hall Lectures to young men.
Henry's Life of C. Trans. by Dr. Stebbing. (Not only a superior memoir, but an excellent selection from his works.)
Jones' Christian Biography.
Literary and Theological Review. 6:325.
Littell's Living Age. 25:571.
McKensie's Life of Calvin.
North British Review. 13:46.
Presbyterian Review. 3:391.
Princeton Review. 9:29. 11:339. 20:279.
Quarterly Review. 88:277.
Scott's (J.) C. and the Swiss Reformation.
Smyth's (Tho. H.) Life and character of C.
Spirit of the Pilgrims. 3:559, 615.
Stebbing's (H.) Life and times of C.
Tulloch's Leaders of the Reformation.
Waterman's Life of Calvin.

Calvinism.

Pro.

Calvini Opera omnia. 9 vols., folio.
Bayle, Refutatio de Maimbourg.
Benoit, Hist. de l'edit de Nantes.
Bezæ (Theod.) Opera.
Heideggeri Historia Papatus.
Jurieu, Histoire du Calvinisme. (Reply to Maimbourg.)
Turretini Institutiones Theologicæ.
Ursini Catechismus.
Zanchii Theses.
——— Compend. Doctrinæ christianæ.
——— de Natura Dei.

Alleine's Vindiciæ pietatis.
Biblical Repository. (Various pieces.)
Bledsoe's Theodicy. (A very able discussion of the points controverted by Armenians.)
Crisp's (Tobias) Works. Notes by Dr. Gill.
Drelincourt's Defence of Calvin.
Dutton's Letters to John Wesley.
Edwards' (Prest.) Works.
Ely's (Ezra S.) Contrast between Calvinism and Hopkinsianism.
Fisher's (Edw.) Marrow of mod. divinity.
Frazier's (James) Critical Expos. of Rom. vi. and vii. (Controverts with great ability Hammond, Locke, Grotius, &c.)
Fuller's (Andrew) Works.
Gill's Cause of God and truth. (A noble work.)
——— Defence of Calvinism.
Hussey's (Jos.) Glory of Christ. (Answer to Hunt.)
Lime Street Lectures.
Mandeville's Horæ Hebraicæ. (Learned.)
Princeton Review. (Many articles.)
Scott's (Tho.) Reply to Bp. Tomline.
Smyth's (T.) Calvin and his enemies.
Twisse's Works. (Powerful, but somewhat ultra.)
Vaughn's Doctrines of Calvin.
Williams' (Dan.) Def. of modern Calvinism.
——— Gospel truth stated.

Con.

Arminii Opera Theologica.
Becani Disputationes.
Eckhardi Fasciculus controv. theologicarum.
Finckii Controversiæ Theologicæ.
Gerlach's Einheimischer Kreig.
Heilbrunner's Sammarischer Begrif, &c.
Himmelii Controversiæ Theologicæ.
Kellisoni Examen Reformationis.
Maimbourg, Histoire du Calvinisme.
Mentzeri Elenchus Errororum.
Osiandri Enchiridion Controversiarum.
Reginald, Calvini-Turcissimus.

Calvinism—*continued.*

Con.

Romæi Calvini Effigies.
Schallingii Synopsis Doctrinæ.
Schmid's (Sebast.) Glauben der Reformirten.
Selnecceri Calvinus redivivus.
Wandalin, von der Calvinischen Lehre.
Winkelmanni Errores Calviniorum.

Fellows' Anti-calvinist.
Fisk's (Wilbur) Calvinistic controversy.
Graves' (Rich.) Discourses.
Houghton (W.) on Calvinism.
Hunt on the Doct. of eternal decrees.
Jones' (of Nayland) Theological works.
Kipling on the XXXIX. Articles.
Lawrence's (Abp.) Bampton Lectures. 1804. (Argues that the articles of the Church of England are not Calvinistic.)
Nichols' Calvinism and Armin. compared.
Pearson's Calv. and Arminian controversy.
Thorn's Assurance of faith. (Identifies Calvinism with Universalism.)
Tomline's (Bp.) Refutation of Calvinism.
Wesley's (John) Works.

This article might be extended indefinitely. The reader is referred to kindred heads, such as *Creeds, Decrees, Effectual calling, Election, Hist. of Doctrines, Human depravity, Human responsibility, Moral ability, Perseverance, Reprobation, Synod of Dort, Will,* &c. &c.

Calvinism, History of. See CALVIN, HISTORY OF DOCTRINES.

Bassnage, Hist. de la religion.
Bayle, Histoire du Calvinisme.
Bretschneider's Bildung und Geist Calvin's.
Gerdesii Introduc. ad hist. evangelii.
Heideggeri Historia Papatus.
Henry's Leben Calvin's.
Polenz's Ges. d. französichen Calvinismus.
Schieksal's Protestisten in Frankreisch.
Schulteti Annales Evangelici.
Souliere, Hist. du C. contenant sa naissance, son progress, sa decadence, et sa fin, en France.

Laval's Hist. of the Reformation in France.
Toplady's History of Calvinism.

Camaldolites.

Heylot, Histoire des ordres.
Mabillonii Annales Benedictini.
Manriques, Annales.

Cameronians. See CHURCH OF SCOTLAND, REFORMED PRESBYTERIANS, SECTS.

Blackwood's Magazine. 6:169, 513, 663. 7:48, 157, 277, 374, 482, 508.

Campbellites. See DISCIPLES.

Camp Meetings.

Porter's Hist. philosophy, and importance of camp meetings.

Candor. See SINCERITY.

Barret's (Joseph) Sermons.
Bell's (William) Sermons.
Eaton's Conversations on bigotry.
Fuller's Calv. and Socin. systems compared.
Goddard's Bampton Lectures. 1824. (C. necessary to a right enquiry into religious evidence.)
Hall's (Robt.) Notes of sermons.
Hey's (John) Lectures. Bk. 1, ch. 1.
Howson's (John S.) Sermons.
Jortin's Six dissertations. Diss. 3.
Van Mildert's Theological works.
Watts on Truth and sincerity.

Canon of Scripture. See APOCRYPHA.

Cochlæus de Canonica S. S.
Credner's Geschichte des Canons.
Frick de Cura vet. ecc. circa canonem S. S.
Kortholtus de Canone.
Millii Prolegomena ad Nov. Test.
Morus de Canone Scripturæ.
Planck, de Signif. canonis in ecc. antiq.
Reuss, Histoire du Canon, &c.
Schmidii Vindicatio canonis, V. et N. T.
Strosch, Hist. critica de librorum N. T.
Van Mastricht, Commentatio de canone, &c.
Weber's Gesch. des Neutestamentl. Kanons.
Wolfius de Integritate codicis sacri.

Alexander (A.) on the Canon of S. S.
Amer. Quart. Church Review. 17:583.
Blair (John) on the Canon of Scripture.
Bryant's (Jac.) Authent. of the Chris. relig.
Christian Quart. Spect. 10:69.
Cosin's Scholastic hist. of the Canon.
Dupin's Complete hist. of the Canon, &c.
Finlay's Vindication.
Gaussen on the Canon of Scripture.
General Repository. 4:1.
Giles' (J. A.) Hebrew Records.
Jenkins' Reasonableness of Christianity.
Jones' (Jer.) Method of settling the Canon. (Best short treatise.)
Kitto's Journal. 7:174.
Lardner's Credibility of the Gospel hist.
——— Antiquities.
Nye on the Canon.
Owen's Introd. to Comment. on Hebrews.
Prideaux's Connexion of O. and N. Test.
Richardson's Vindication. (Reply to Toland's Amyntor.)
Stuart's (Moses) Defence of the O. T. Canon.
Townley's Illustrations of biblical literature.
United States Literary Gazette. 5:327.
Westcott's Hist. of the Canon of the N. T., during the first 4 centuries.
Wadsworth's Hulsean Lectures. 1847.

Canonization.

Buddei (J. F.) Dissertationes et Orationes.
Powell's (H. T.) Roman fallacies.

Canon Law. See COUNCILS, DECRETALS.

Balthasar Jus ecclesiasticum pastorale.
Barbosæ Opera omnia.

Canon Law—*continued.*

Berardi Commentaria. (1780. Reprinted 1846.)
Beveridgii (Bp.) Synodicon. (Contains the canons of all the early councils, with learned notes.)
——— Adnotationes ad canones apostolicos.
Boehmer, Jus ecclesiasticum Protestantium.
Calderwood, Altare Damascenum.
Cosini Ecclesiæ Anglicanæ politia.
Du Moulin, Definitions du droit canon.
Eichhorn's Grundsätze des Kirchrechts.
Feraris, Bibliotheca Canonica.
Gibson, Codex juris eccl. Anglicanæ.
Harduini Concordia discors canonum.
Hericourt, Les loies eccl. de France.
Justelli Bibliotheca canonum, &c.
Lancellotti Institutiones juris canonici. (Alphabetical arrangement.)
Lucet, Principes du droit canonique.
Meermanni (G.) Novus thesaurus jurus.
Permaneder's Handbuch des Kirchenrechts.
Phillips' Kirchenrecht.
Prompsault, Dictionaire de droit.
Reiffenstueli Jus canonicum.
Richter, Corpus juris, &c.
Schilling's Canonischen Rechte.
Schmalzgrueber Diss. generalis, Index, &c.
Schmidt, Thesaurus juris eccles.
Schmitz, Medulla Juris canonici.
——— Diss. prelectæ in jus eccles. (Containing 126 Diss., by eminent authors, on special points of Eccles. jurisprudence.)
Van Espen, Jus ecclesiasticum. ("There is nothing better, on universal Canon Law, than Van Espen."—DUPIN.)
Voelli Bibliotheca juris canonici veteris.
Walter's (F.) Lehrbuch des Kirchenrechts.
Weiss' (C. E.) Kirchenrechtswissenschaft.
Zallweinii Jus ecclesiasticum.
Zoesii Com. in Jus canonicum.
Zullingeri Instit. Juris Nat. et Eccles.

Baker's Reflections on learning. Ch. 13.
Bingham's Origines ecclesiasticæ.
Bohun on Ecclesiastical jurisdiction.
Buckley's Canons of the Council of Trent.
Butler's (Cha.) Horæ Juridicæ. (Notes on all the chief codes.)
Cranmer's (Abp.) Works. (Parker Society publications.)
Degge's Parson's counsellor.
Gibson's Codex juris ecc. Anglicanæ. ("The most valuable work on the subject."—BP. WATSON.)
Hammond's (W. A.) Canons of the early Ch.
Johnson's (John) Collections of all the canons, rescripts, &c., of the Church of England, published in Latin.
Waterworth's Essays.

See many other writers on this subject in DOUJAT, *Praemonitiones canonicae*, which names the various collections of canons, from A. D. 1200 to 1762; and LIPPENII, *Biblioth. Juridica, cum supplimento* SCHOTTII, 5 vols., folio. 1823.

Capital Punishment.

Pro.

Bierling (F. W.), Dissertationes.
Grotius de Jure civilis.
Michaelis de Judiciis pœnisque in S. S.
Stockius de Pœnis Hebræorum.

Amer. Biblical Repository. 5:9.
Beccaria on Crimes and punishments.
Bibliotheca Sacra. 4:270.
Blackstone's Commentaries.
Blackwood's Magazine. 58:129.
Cheever on Capital punishment.
Christian Examiner. 12:1. 14:298. 43:355.
Christian Review. 14:365.
Doddridge's Lectures. Part 3, prop. 71.
Dwight's Discourses. Disc. 115.
Eclectic Review. 4th Series. 10:554. 23:339. 24:129. 26:98. 27:33. 28:317.
Foreign Quarterly Review. 25:394.
Frazier's Magazine. 69:753.
Godwin's Political Justice.
Haynes' Letter to Hall.
Hutchinson's Moses' Principia.
Lewis' (Taylor) Grounds of capital pun.
Montesquieu's Spirit of Laws.
New Englander. 1:128. 3:562. 4:563.
Paley's Political Economy.
Patton's Capital Punishment sustained by Reason and Scripture.
Princeton Review. 13:307. 14:307.
Puffendorf's Law of Nature.
Quarterly Review. 7:159.
Schmucker's Popular Theology.

Con.

Blackwood's Edin. Mag. 27:865.
Carey's Museum. 4:78. 5:47. 7:7, 69. 20:71. 204:300.
Democratic Review. 10:272. 12:227, 409. 19:90.
Dodd (Wm.) on the 6th Commandment.
Eclectic Review. 7:
Fleetwood (Sir P. H.) on Capital Punishm.
Livingston (L.) on Capital Punishment.
Mandeville on Executions.
Montagu on the Punishment of Death.
North American Review. 62:40.
O'Sullivan's Lectures in New York City.
Pamphleteer. 3:115. 8:281. 12:287.
Polodori (John W.) on the Death penalty.
Rippon (John) on Capital punishment.

Capucins. See FRANCISCANS.

Aremberg, Flores Seraphici.
Bernardi Opera.
Bibliotheca Scriptorum Capucinorum.
Bononiæ Biblioth. Scrip. Ord. minorum, &c.
Bouchier, de Martyrio F. F. Minorum.
Boveri Annales Capucinorum. To 1612.
Bullarium Ordinis Capucinorum a P. F. Michaelis. (A coll. of bulls, briefs, decrees, rescripts, &c., with notes.)
Genvæ Biblioth. Script. Ord. minorum, &c.
Johannis, de Terra Nova, Narratio de origine fratrum Capucinorum Sancti Francisci.

Du Moulin's (P.) Lives of the Capucins.

See a great list of Capucin writers in GENVA and BONONIA, cited above.

Caraites. See KARAITES.

Cardinals.

Fabricii Bibliographia Antiquarum.
Muratori de Origine Cardinalatas.
Sagittarii Introd. ad Hist. Ecclesiast.
Thomassini Disciplina Eccles. Vet. et Nov.

Care. See ANXIETY.

Carmelites. See FRANCISCANS.

Annales Ordinis Præmonstratensis.
Grossus de Viris illustribus et sanctis.
Jean, Histoire de l'ordre des Carmes.
Lezana, Annales sacri prophetici, &c.
Lucii Carmelitana Bibliotheca.
Martiali Bibliotheca Script. Carmelitani.
Riboti Speculum ordinis Carmelitani.
Thomæ (a Jesu) Opera. Ed. J. S. Brewer.
Trithemii de Ortu, progressu, laudibus, &c.

Carnal Mind. See HEAVENLY MINDEDNESS, HUMAN DEPRAVITY, SENSUALITY.

Brady's (N.) Sermons.
Cooper's (G.) Sermons.
Hurd's (Bp.) Sermons.
Jones' (Wm., of Nayland) Sermons.
Leighton's (Abp.) Sermons.
Mant's (Bp.) Sermons.
Powell's (Sam.) Sermons.
Rose's (H. J.) Sermons.
Skelton's (P.) Sermons.
Spurgeon's (Cha. H.) Sermons. 1st Series.
Whewell's (W.) Sermons.
Wilson's (Bp.) Sermons.

Carpocratians. See HERESIES.

Clemens' (Alex.) Stromata.
Hebenstreitii (Jo. Frid.) Dissertationes.
Gesenius de Inscriptione Phœnicio-græca in Cyrenaica nuper repertâ.

Cartesians.

Pro.

Bekker's Besauberte Welt.
Cartesii Meditationes metaphysicæ.
——— Principiæ philosophiæ.
Rohaultii Physica.
Schrodellii (Phil. Dan.) Commentatio.
Velthusius de Existentia Dei.
——— (Various other works.)
Willichii Adnotationes. (Agt. Maresius.)

Con.

Andalæ Syntagma theologico-physico.
Hennischii Demonstratio.
Huetii Censura philosophiæ Cartesianæ.
Maresius de Abusu philosophiæ.
——— Adnotationes. (Reply to Willichius.)
Revii Method. Cartes. theol. consideratio.
Roellius de Religione rationali.

Cartesians—*continued.*

Con.

Rohaultii Physica. (Edited by Dr. S. Clark, in which the notes quietly refute the text.)
Van Mastrecht, Gangrena.
Voetius de Atheismo.

Baker's Reflections on Learning.
Boyle on Final causes.
——— on the Vulgar notion of Nature.
Cudworth's Intellectual System.
Eclectic Review. New Series. 2:1.
Ray on the Creation.
Rohault's Physics. (Trans. by Dr. John Clark. With all the notes from Dr. S. Clark's Edition.)

The writers for and against Cartesianism, previous to A. D. 1700, are diligently described by FABRICIUS, *Syllab. scriptor. de religion.* Cap. X.

Carthusians.

Corbin, Hist. de l'ordre Chartreux.
Dorlandi Chronicon Carthusiense.
Guidon (in "Bibliotheca manuscriptorum").
Mabilloni Annales Benedictini.
Miræi Origines Carthusianorum.
Morotii Theatrum chron. Carthus. ordinis.
Nova Collectio statutorum ordinis C. 1736.
Petreii Bibliotheca Carthusiana.

Casuistry. See CONSCIENCE.

Amesius de Conscientia et ejus jure.
Baldwin, de Casibus conscientiæ.
Clavasius de Casibus conscientiæ.
Dannhaveri Liber cons. apertus.
Dicsoni Therapeutica Sacra.
Encyclopedie Theologique.
Fagundez (Steph.), Questiones.
Gilotte, le Directeur des consciences.
Lessius de Jure et Justitia.
Misleri Opus questionum theologicarum.
Osiandri Theologia casualis.
Pontas, Dictionaire des cases de consc.
Toleti Instructio sacerdotum.

Alleine's Alarm to the unconverted.
Ames' Power of conscience.
Barlow's (Bp.) Cases of cons. resolved.
Baxter's (Richard) Cause and cure of a wounded conscience.
——— Christian Directory. (Often reprint.)
Christian Magazine. Vol. 1.
Feltham's Resolves: divine, moral, and political. ("A cabinet full of precious ornaments."—BP. WRANGHAM.)
Fuller's (Dr. Thomas) Cure of a wounded conscience.
Gillespie's Miscellaneous Questions.
Hall's (Bp.) Resolutions of divers cases.
Hamilton's Mourner in Zion comforted.
Hammond's Resolution to six queries.
Hog's Casuist. Essay on the Lord's Prayer.
Jessey's Storehouse of provision to resolve cases, &c.
Kennett's Christian Casuist.

Casuistry—*continued.*

Morning Exercises at Cripplegate.
Norman's Cases of conscience.
Perkins' (Wm.) cases of conscience.
Phillips' Christian experience.
Pike & Hayward's Cases of conscience.
Placette's Christian Casuist. Tr. by Kennet.
Ponta's Dictionary of cases of conscience. (The original, in 3 vols., fol., is abridged by Collet into 2 vols., 4to.)
Saunderson's Obligatio Conscientiæ.
——— Nine cases of conscience.
Saurin's Christian Casuistry.
Scott's (J.) Cases of conscience.
Sharp's (Abp.) Sixteen casuistical sermons.
Shephard's Select cases resolved.
Stubbe's (Henry) Sermons. (3 on this subj.)
Taylor's (Jer.) Ductor dubitantium.

Cataphrygians. See MONTANISTS.

Catechising.

Augustin de Catechizandis Rudibus.
Busch's Anleit. zur mittheilung der Religion.
Febiger's Vorles. über d. kunst zu katech.
Harnisch's Anweisen zur Unter. in christen.
Ludewig's Anweisen zur rel. Katech.
Plutarch de Liberis educandis.
Schmerbach's Hist. u. Doctrinellen Religions unterricht.
Thierbach's Niedern und höhern Schulen.
Weinkopf's Wissenschaftlichen katechetik.

Addison's Antiq. and benefits of catechising.
Amer. Journal of Education. 9:367.
Athill's Way of catechising.
Bather (Edw.) on the Art of catechising.
Best (Samuel) on Catechising.
Evangelical Review. 1:221.
Gilley's Advantage and duty of catechising.
Henry (Matt.) on the Catechising of youth.
New Englander. 2:180.
Princeton Review. 21:59.
Quarterly Review. 71:184.
Watts (I.) on Instruction by catechisms.
Willison's Example of catechising.

Catechisms.

Augustin, de Catechizandis rudibus.
Chrysostom, Catechesis ad illuminandos.
Cyrill (Hierosol.), Cat. ad competens.
Gregory (Nys.) Orationes.

Bellarmini Catechismus.
Boeckel's Bekentniss-schriften. (Gives the Catechisms of various national churches.)
Calvini Cat. Ecclesiæ Genevensis.
Capel, la Doctrine des eglises reformès.
Catechismus ex decreto concilii Trident.
Dieterici Institutiones Catecheticæ.
Dinter's Unterredungen. (13 vols., 8vo.!)
Drelincourt, Catechisme.
Ernesti's Katechismus-literatur.
John A Lasco, Catechismus.
Langemackii Historia Catechetica.
Luther's Catechismus.

Catechisms—*continued.*

Melancthonis Catechismus puerilis.
Niemeyeri Collectio conf. fidei Eccles. Reformatæ. (Gives the catechisms of Geneva, Belgium, Bohemia, &c.)
Norvelli Christianæ pietatis institutio.
Ostervald, Instruc. de la rel. chrètienne.
Pictet, C. familiar pour les enfans.
Saurin, Abregè de la theologie, et de morale, en forme de catechisme.
Streitwolf, Dibri symbolici Ecc. Cathol.
Waldensii Explic. orationis Dominicæ, Symboli apostolici, ac Decalogi.

Abercrombie's Lectures on the Church C.
Adams' Lectures on the Church Catechism.
Assembly's Catechism.
Baxter's (Isaac) Catechism.
Beddome on the Baptist Catechism.
Bellfrage on the Assembly's Catechism.
Beveridge's (Bp.) Exposition of the C.
Brown's Explication of the Assembly's C.
Buckley's Trans. of the C. of the Council of Trent. With notes.
Bundy's Lectures on the C.
Burnett's (Bp.) Exposition of the Church C.
Cartwright's Catechism.
Clarke on the Church C.
Crossman's Church C. explained.
Dickson's Church C. explained.
Ellis' Scripture catechist.
Fleetwood's Exposition of the Church C.
Gordon's (A.) 52 Lectures on the Church C.
Girdlestone's Lectures on the Church C.
Halton's Exposition of the Church C.
Hammond's Practical Catechism.
Hazelius' Materials for Catechization.
Hewey's Scripture Catechism.
Hole's Exposition of the Church C.
Law (E.) on Catechising.
Lowth's Catechism.
Nowell's Catechism. (Puritan.)
Perkins' Catechism. (Puritan.)
Prideaux's Commentary on the C. of the Ch. of England.
Princeton Review. 2:50.
Purdy's Lectures on the Church C.
Quarterly Review. 71:332.
Ridgeley's Body of Divinity. (On the Assembly's Catechism.)
Rogers' Grounds of the Christian religion.
Secker (Abp.) on the Church of Eng. C.
Sherlock's Principles of the Christian relig.
Vincent's Exposition of the Shorter C.
Wake's Comm. on the Church C.
Waterland's Works.
Wesley's (Cha.) Short commentary, &c.

To enumerate all catechisms and their commentators would require a volume. WALCH'S *Bibliotheca Theologica* gives a great list, divided into—1. Lutheran. 2. Papal. 3. Reformed. 4. Arminian. 5. Socinian. 6. Bohemian Brethren. 7. Fanatics. 8. Greek. 9. Jews. Of expositions of the Church of England catechism, there are at least 250.

Catenæ Patrum.
See USE OF THE FATHERS.

Aquinatis (Tho.) in Lucam et Joannen Cat.
Comitioli C. P P. Græcorum xxiv. in Jobum.
Corderii C. P P. Græc. in Jobum.
——— ——— ——— Psalmos.
——— ——— ——— Lucam.
——— ——— ——— Johannen.
Ittigii Biblioth. et Caten. Patrum.
Lipomani Catena in Genesin.
——— ——— Psalmos.
Nicetæ Catena in Jobum.
——— ——— Lucam.
Possini Catena in Matthæum.
——— ——— Marcum.
Roxas, Catena in Evangelia vi.
Theodoki Catena in libros Mosis.

The Catenas are very numerous, and, for the most part, very worthless. The above are given merely as specimens. Others are named in various places under the head Commentators. A very extensive list is given by WALCH, *Bibliotheca patristica*.

Cathari. See ALBIGENSES, WALDENSES.

Chatel, Histoire de Languedoc.
Codex Inquisitionis Tolosanæ.
Ecberti Sermones adversus Catharos.
Launoy de Scholis celebrioribus Caroli Mag.
Limborchii Historia Inquisitionis.
Moneta contra Catharos et Valdenses.
Muratori Antiquitates Ital. medii ævi.
Richini Dissertationes.
Schmidt (C.), Hist. et doctrine des Cathares.
Hurter's Hist. of Pope Innocent III.
Universalist Quart. Review. 7:363.

Causation. See MOTIVES.

American Biblical Repository. 2d Series. 2:381. 3:174. 4:217, 467. 5:153.
Boyle's (Hon. Robt.) Works.
Brown's Philosophy of the mind.
Buchanan's Modern Atheism.
Christian Monthly Spectator. 3:583.
Frazier's Magazine. 16:254. (Final causes.)
Hume's (David) Essays.
Irons' Doct. of final causes. (Admirable.)
Mills' Exam. of Sir W. Hamilton's philos.
——— Philosophy of necessity.
Miller's Old red sand stone. (Final causes.)
Müller's Christian doct. of sin.
New Englander. 8:160.
North Amer. Review. 12:395.
North British Rev. 7:1. (Final causes.)
Scott's Limits of metaphysical science.
Travis (Henry) on Moral freedom.
Whish on the First cause.
Woods (Dr.) on Cause and effect.

Caution. See PRUDENCE.

Celibacy of the Clergy.

Chrysostom de Virginitate.
Gregory (Nys.) de Virginitate.

Celibacy of the Clergy—*continued.*

Bugenhagius de Conjugio Episcoporum.
Calixtus (Geor.) de Conjugio clericorum.
Campegius de Cœlebatu sacerdotum.
Carove's Coelibatz gesetze d. Rom. clerus.
Erasmus (Rot.), Gedanken die Priesterehe.
Espencæus de Continentia.
Gaudin (l'Abbe) Les inconvéniens du célebat des prêtres.
Gusman de sacris ministris.
Hosii (Stanisl.) Opera.
Hubrici Defensio conjugii sacerdotum.
Mayeri Dissertationes.
Melancthonis Defensio conjugi sacerdotum.
Orichovii Orationes contra Syricium.
Osiandri Dissertationes.
P. Martyr de Cœlibatu sacerdotum.
Sasii Œcumenicum. (Extracts from Councils, Fathers, &c.)
Schmidii (J. A.) Dissertationes.
Smith de Cœlibatu sacerdotum.
Trefurt's Cölibat aus d. gesichtspunkte.
Wicellii Via Regia.

Beaver's Doct. of the Scripture.
Billingsley's (John) Sermons.
Hall's (Bp.) Polemic Works.
Hall's (J.) Honor of the married clergy.
Hey's Lectures on theology. Bk. 4.
Martin's Traictise declaryng and provyng that the pretended marriage of priestes is no marrige.
Merrick's Marriage a Divine institution.
Morning Exercises at Cripplegate.
Payne's Exam. of the texts which Papists cite, &c.
Tullie's (George) Sermons.
Wharton's Rise and progress of the celibacy of the clergy. (Reprinted in Gibson's Preservative.)

Cellites. See LOLLARDS.

Censoriousness. See EVIL SPEAKING.

Benson's (Joseph) Sermons.
Blair's (James) Sermons.
Bourne's (Samuel) Sermons.
Brady's (Nicolas) Sermons.
Christian Examiner. 35:311.
Evans' (Dr. John) Christian temper.
Faulkner's (Will.) Essays. Ess. 1.
Jeter's (J. B.) Sermons.
Kendall (I.) on Eccentricity.
Mason's (Richard) Sermons.
Parry's (Joshua) Sermons.

Ceremonial Law. See ABROGATION.

Creizenach's Schulchan Aruch.
Dassovii Dissertationes.
Maimonides Opera.
Spencer de Legibus Hebræorum ritualibus ("Of infinite use."—WARBURTON.)
Witsii Theocratia Israelitarum.
Calmet's Dictionary of the Bible.
Doddridge's Lectures. Part 6.

Ceremonial Law—*continued.*

Greswell's Discourses. (Comparison of the Hebrew ritual with Christianity.)
Jones on the Mosaic distinct. of animals.
Lightfoot's Horæ Hebraicæ.
Lowman's Ritual of Hebrew worship.
Maimonides' Reasons for the law of Moses. Trans. with notes, by Townley.
Michaelis' Laws of Moses. Tr. by Dr. Smith.
Stanhope's Boyle Lectures.
Sykes on Christianity.
Tappan's Lectures.
Warburton's Julian.
Weems' Expos. of the ceremonial law.
Wines on the Ceremonial law.
Witsii Egyptiaca.

Ceremonies. See CHURCH GOVERNMENT, RELIGIONS, RITES, WORSHIP.

Cerinthians. See GNOSTICS.

Alexandri (Natalis) Dissertationes.
Bassnage, Annales polit. eccles.
Buddeus de Ecclesia apostolica. (Opposes Bassnage and Faydit in some points.)
Edzardi (Esdræ Henr.) Disputationes.
Faydit, Eeclaircisemens sur l'Eglise.
Pauli (H. E. G.) Historia Cerinthi.

Chaldee Language.

Bagsteri Lexicon Analyticum.
Beelen, Chrestomathia Chaldaica.
Buddei Historia Ecclesiastica.
Calmeti Dissertationes.
Danzii (Jo. And.) Dissertationes.
Fuerst, Concordantia Chaldaica.
Langius de Charactere primævo bibliorum.
Pfeifferi Critica Sacra.
Reineccii Lexicon Hebræo-Chaldaicum.
Renferdus de Antiquitate lit. Chaldaicarum.
Scheid, Lexicon Hebræo-Chaldaicum.
Winer's Chaldaischer Lesebuch.
Wolfii Bibliotheca.

Chaldee Paraphrase.

Beckii Paraph. C. I. lib. Chronicorum.
Clarke (S.), Variæ lectiones et obs. in C. P.
Danzii Interpretes Ebræo-Chaldæus, omnes utriusque linguæ idiotismos dextere expl.
Fagii Paraphrasis.
Hottingeri Thesaurus philologicus.
Josephi Paraph. C. cum versione Latina.
Lusatto, Philoxenus.
Onkelos, P. Chald. in sacra biblia.
Peterman de Duabus Pent. paraph. Chald.
Simonis, Historia Critica Vet. Test.
Smith (Tho.) Diatriba de C. paraphrastis.
Winer de Onkeloso ejusque paraph.
——— de Jonathanis in Pent. paraphras.
Zunz's Gottesdienstliche Vorträge der Juden.

Etheridge's Targums of Onkelos and Jonathan; with the fragments of the Jerusalem Targum. Translated from the Chaldee. 1865. (The first English translation.)

5

Hey's (Dr. J.) Lect. on Divinity. Bk. 1, ch. 9.

The Targums are given in the Bibles of BUXTORF, BOMBERG, and others.

Chance. See ATHEISM, CAUSATION, FATE, NECESSITY, PROVIDENCE.

Buchanan's Modern Atheism. Chap. 6.
Bentley's Boyle Lectures. 1693.
Clarke (Dr. Sam.) on the Laws of chance.
Hoyle's Essay on the doctrine of chances.
Howe's (Charles) Meditations.
Watts' Ontology.

Change of Sabbath. See SABBATARIANS.

Liebetrut d. Tag des Herrn.

Agnew on the Sabbath.
Amer. Bibl. Repository. 3d Series. 1:366.
Amner's Weekly festival of the Church.
Barclay's Apology for the true divinity.
Burnett on the 39 Articles.
Chandler's (Sam.) Discourses.
Doddridge's Lectures.
Edwards' (Pres.) Sermons.
Glen (John) on the Sabbath. (A valuable historical treatise.)
Glenworth on the Sabbath.
Hallet's (Jos.) Notes on Scripture.
Holmes' Essays on the Sabbath.
Jennings' Jewish Antiquities.
Kennedy's Chronology on the Heb. text.
Kennicott on the Sabbath.
Lenfant on the New Testament.
Malcom's Bible Dictionary. Art. "Sabbath."
Mede on Ezekiel.
Morer on the Sabbath.
Orton's (Job) Discourses.
Sharp's (Abp.) Sermons.
Wallis on the Sabbath.
Warren's (Edm.) Jews' Sabbath antiquated.
Watts' (Isaac) Works.
Wells' Practical Sabbatarian.
Wilson's (Bp.) Obligation of the Lord's day.

Chanting. See PSALMODY.

Charity. See ALMS, LOVE.

Abernethy's (John) Sermons.
Atterbury's (Lewis) Sermons.
Barrow's (Bp.) Works.
Beattie's Elements of moral science.
Beveridge's (Bp.) Sermons.
Blair's (James) Sermons.
Blundell's (Thomas) Sermons.
Calamy's (Benjamin) Sermons.
Chalmer's (Thomas) Sermons.
Conybeare's (Bp.) Sermons.
Crosinge on Charity.
Dwight's (Tim.) Discourses. Dis. 96, 99, 130.
Enfield's (William) Sermons.
Evans (Dr. John) on Christian Temper.
Fenelon's (Abp.) Character of true charity.
Foster's (Dr. James) Sermons.
Girdlestone's (Charles) Sermons.
Hawkins on the Nature extent, &c.
Haynes' Illustrations of faith.

Charity—*continued.*

Hole's (Matt.) Practical Discourses.
Hurd's (Bp.) Sermons.
Limborch's Christian theology.
Milner's (Joseph) Sermons.
Newman's (J. H.) Sermons.
Oakley's (Frederick) Sermons.
Owen on the Ep. to the Hebrews. Chap. 6.
Paley's Moral Philosophy.
Porter's (Ebenezer) Sermons.
Riddle's (J. E.) Sermons.
Salsbury's (Bp.) Nature and extent of C.
Scott's (Tho.) Sermons.
Secker's (Abp.) Sermons.
Seed's (Jeremiah) Sermons.
Smith's (Samuel S.) Discourses.
Spring's (Gardner) Essays.
Sumner (Bp.) on Christian charity.
Taylor's (Jeremy) Discourses.
Thompson (J. P.) on the Christian Graces.
Tillotson's (Abp.) Sermons.
Topping's Christian love.
Tucker's Light of Nature. Ch. 19.
Watts' (Isaac) Sermons.
Whitefield's (George) Sermons.
Witherspoon's Enquiry, &c. (Works.)
Yonge's (James) Sermons. 2d Series.

Chartreuse. See CARTHUSIANS.

Chastisement. See AFFLICTION, BEREAVEMENT, DESPONDENCY, MOURNERS, SUBMISSION.

Chastity. See UNCLEANNESS.

Brown's Philosophy of the mind.
Cave's Primitive Christianity.
Dwight's (Timothy) Discourses.
Ogden's (Samuel) Sermons.
Ovington's Christian chastity.
Paley's (William) Sermons.
Rush on the Diseases of the mind.
Ryan's (Dr. S.) Prostitution in London, Paris, and New York; the most fertile source of personal and social misery.
Scott (Tho.) on Female prostitution.
Tait's Magdalenism. (Extent, causes, and consequences of prostitution.)
Watts' (Isaac) Sermons.
Wayland's Moral Science.

Cheerfulness. See DESPONDENCY.

Bridges' Religion without gloom.
Carter's (N.) Sermons.
Fuller's Calvinistic and Socinian systems.
Horne's (Bp.) Discourses.

Cherethites.

Lakemacheri Observationes Philologicæ.

Cherubim. See ARK OF THE COVENANT.

Dorien de Cherubinis.
Grosmanni Philonis Judæi anecdoton.
Markii Fascicula Dissertationes.
Spencer de Legibus Hebræorum. Diss. 4.

Cherubim—*continued.*

Thalemani (C. W.) Tractationes.
Velthusen, von den Cherubinen, &c.
Zollig's Cherubim-wagen.

Christian Quart. Spect. 3:247. 8:368.
Christian Review. 14:592.
Hodge's Strictures on Sharp's Examination.
Hutchinson's (John) Works.
Killen's Our companions in glory.
McLeod's Cherubim and the Apocalypse.
Sharp's Exam. of Hutchinson's hypothesis.
Simpson on the Language of Scripture.
Smith's (G.) Doctrine of the Cherubim.
Whitby's Scheme of Prophecy. (Appendix.)

Chief End of Man. See END OF MAN.

Chiliasm. See MILLENARIANS.

Chivalry. See KNIGHTS.

Belloy, de l'Origine des divers ordres.
Bonani Ordinum Equestrium.
Cabany, Hist. des ordres de chevalerie.
Clement, Bibliotheca curieuse historique.
Favini, Theater d'honeur.
Gruteri Chron. chronicorum ecclesiæ. Lib. 2.
Hermant, Histoire des ordres militaire.
Honoré, Dissertations historiques et critique. (Extensive and complete.)
Lagerloefii Dissertationes.
Zentegravii Dissertationes.

James' (G. P. R.) History of chivalry.
Mills' (C.) History of chivalry.
Oxford Prize Essays. 1798.

Choice of Company. See COMPANY.

Christian Antiquities. See ARCHÆOLOGY.

Alt's Kirchenlehre in ihrer hist. Entwickel.
Ammon's (C. F.) Fortbildung d. Christenthums zur Weltreligion.
Augusti's Christlichen Archæology.
Baehr's Lehre der Kirche, in den ersten 3 Jahrh.
Bebelii Hist. 4 prioribus sæculis.
Bingham, Origines Sac. antiq. eccles.
Böhmer's Christliche-Kirchliche Alterthums Wissenschaft.
Callixti Historia eccl. Occidentalis. Sec. viii., ix., x.
Caroli Memorabilia Ecclesiastica.
Dodwellii Dissertationes Cyprianicæ.
Gfrorer, Gesch. des Urchristenthums.
Guerikė's Lehrbuch der Christlich-kirchlich. Archæologie.
Hagerup de Catechumenis ecc. Africanæ in sæc. v.
Langhornii Elenchus Antiquitatem, &c.
Locherer's Lehrbuch der Christlich-kirchlichen Archæologie.
Mammachii Origines Christianæ.
Martigny, Dict. de Antiq. Chrétienne.
Mosheimii Commentarius de rebus Christianorum ante Constantinum.

Christian Antiquities—*continued.*

Nicolai de Moribus Christianorum vet.
Pearsoni Opera posthuma.
Rauscher's Gesch. der christlichen kirche.
Rheinwald's Kirchliche Archæologie.
Schone's Geschichtforschungen.
Semleri Com. de antiq. christianorum.
Siegel's Handbuch der chris. kirchl. alterthümer in alphabet. ordnung, mit steter Beziehung, &c.
Staudenmaier's Geist des christenthums.

Archæological Journal. Lond. Begun 1844.
Bates' (Wm.) Lectures. (Very useful.)
Bingham's Antiq. of the Christian Church. (Makes one of the best of church histories, but is not always impartial.)
Blackmore's Christian Antiquities.
Burton's Theological Works.
Coleman's Christian Antiquities. (Chiefly trans. from Augusti, with additions from Rheinwald, Siegel, and others.)
Cooper's Church of ancient Christendom.
Dalrymple's (Lord Hales) Disquisitions.
Guericke's Manual of Chris. antiq. Trans. by Morrison.
Henry's Compendium of Christian Antiq.
King's Constitution, discipline, unity, and worship of the primitive church.
Ketts' Bampton Lectures. 1792.
Lingard's Antiq. of the Anglo-Saxon church. (Papal.)
Parker's Gov. of the Church for the first 600 years.
Princeton Review. 24:1.
Riddle's Manual of Christian antiquities. (Compiled chiefly from Augusti.)
Semler's State of the church in the first centuries.
Strutt's Ecclesiastical Antiquities.
Whateley's Rise, propagation, and corruption of Christianity.
Whittington's Eccles. antiquities of France.

Christian Conflict. See FIGHT OF FAITH.

Christian Deportment. See DEPORTMENT.

Christian Experience. See CONVICTION, CONVERSION.

Christian Intercourse.

Christian Observer. 24:678.
Goodman's Winter-evening conferences.
Lucas' (Richard) Sermons.
Miller's (John) Sermons.
Sprague's Hints on the intercourse of Chris.

Christian Liberty. See LIBERTY.

Buddei Prolegomena de theol. polem. studio.
Vassor, de la Manniere d'examiner les differens de religion.

Abernethy's Sermons.
Balguy's (Thomas) Sermons.
Berriman's (William) Sermons.
Bolton's Bounds of Christian liberty.

Christian Liberty—*continued.*

Brackenbury's (Edward) Discourses.
Brooks' Hist. of religious liberty in England. (To the death of George III.)
Butler (Dr. S.) on Christian liberty.
Christian Examiner. 10:87. 34:100.
Christian Observer. 11:41.
Clarke's (Tho.) History of Intolerance.
Deane's (S.) Sermons.
Downame (Bp.) on Christian freedom.
Fellows' (Robt.) Religion without Cant.
Foster's (John) Sermons.
Girdlestone's (Cha.) 20 parochial sermons.
Hall's (Bp.) Sermons.
Hodgkin's Progress of religious liberty.
Jackson's Defence of human liberty.
Lothrop on Christian liberty.
Mainwaring's (John) Sermons.
Priestley's Essays on Government.
Princeton Review. 31:664.
Robinson's (Robt.) Miscellaneous works.
Stuart (Moses) on Religious liberty.
Taylor's (W.) Sermons.
Thomson's (Thos.) Sermons.
Universalist Quarterly. 6:371.
Westminster Review. 13:188.
Zollikoffer's (Geo. J.) Sermons.

Christian Race.

Arnold's (Thos.) Miscellaneous Works.
Baddelly's (George) Discourses.
Beveridge's (Bp.) Sermons.
Collison's (M. A.) Sermons.
Haverfield's (Tho. T.) Sermons.
Hoadly's (Bp.) Sermons.
Horne's (Bp.) Discourses.
New Englander. 7:369.
Scott's (Benjamin) Sermons.
Scott's (John) Christian life.
Seabury's (Bp.) Sermons.
Summerfield's (John) Sermons.
Summer's (Samuel) Sermons.
Sylvester's Christian race and patience.
Williams' (Roger) Bloody Tenet.
——— (Other works.)

Christian Temper. See EMOTIONS, GODLINESS, PRACTICAL PIETY.

Christian Union. See BROTHERLY LOVE, SCHISM, SECTARIANISM.

Cyprian, Epistolæ.
Acontii Strategematum Satanæ.
Bullingeri Decades.
Duten (L.), de l'Eglise.
Glanzow's Wiederherstellung des ächten Protest.
Hus (Joan.) de Unitate Ecclesiæ.
Koch, der Evangelisch Verein.
Kocher's Abildung einer Freidens-theologie.
Prætorii (M.) Tuba pacis.
Schuberth über Allgemein. Union der chris. Bekenntnisse.
Starck, Entretiens philologique.
Steudel's Religionsvereinigung.

Christian Union—*continued.*

Tabaraud, de la Reunion des communions.
Tittman's Vereinigung d. evang. Kirchen.
Turrettini (J. A.) Nubes testium.

Adams (J.) on Christian Union.
Amer. Bibl. Repository. 11:86, 363.
Barrow's (Isaac) Sermons.
Bather's (Edward) Sermons.
Baxter's (Rich.) Only way of concord.
Berriman's (William) Sermons.
Bowes (J.) on Christian Union.
Butler's Account of confessions of faith.
Bullinger's Decades. (Parker Soc. pub.)
Christian Examiner. 16:24. 39:53. 40:56.
Christian Quart. Spectator. 9:65, 289.
Christian Rev. 3:109. 7:342. 12:155, 477.
Dalrymple on Christian Unity.
Eclectic Review. 4th Series. 17:664.
Fawcett's (John) Sermons.
Gale's (John) Sermons.
Greenfield's (Edmund) Works.
Harris' Divided church made one.
Hall's (Peter) Harm. of Prot. confessions.
Howe's (John) Sermons.
Innis (Will.) on Christian Union.
Jamieson's Sermons on brotherly love.
Johnson's (Dr. Samuel) Sermons.
Jones' (Will. of Nayland) Sermons.
Le Messurier's Bampton Lectures. 1808.
Literary and Theol. Rev. 2:507. 3:140, 311.
McCrie on the Unity of the church.
Mather's (Cotton) Sermons.
New Englander. 4:132, 532.
North British Review. 1:412. 2:565.
Princeton Review. 8:11. 20:104.
Ridgeley's (Bp.) Way of Peace.
Schmucker's Appeal to the Amer. churches.
Spirit of the Pilgrims. 4:245.
Spry's Bampton Lectures. 1816. (The subject historically considered.)
Starck's (Baron de) Philosophical dialogue.
Trench's (Francis) Sermons.
Van Mildert's (William) Sermons.
Whateley's Bampton Lectures. 1822. (Use and abuse of party feeling.)
Wilson's Bampton Lectures. 1851.

Christian Warfare. See FIGHT OF FAITH.

Christians of St. John. See HEMEROBAPTISTS.

Christians of St. Thomas. See NESTORIANS.

Christ's Limited Public Appearance after his Resurrection.

Atterbury's (Bp.) Sermons.
Blackwell's Boyle Lectures.
Burnett's (Bp.) Discourses.
Ditton on the Resurrection of Christ.
Fleming's Christology.
Superville's Sermons.
Sykes on Christianity. Ch. 10.

Christ's Personal Reign. See MILLENARIANS, SECOND ADVENT.

Christianity.

The Fathers here cited are arranged in chronological order.

Hermas, Philosophi philosophorum irrisio.
Justin Martyr, Parænesis ad Græcos.
——— Oratio ad Græcos.
——— Apologia pro christianis.
——— Apologia secunda pro christianis.
——— de Monarchia Dei.
——— Dialogus cum Tryphone.
——— Epistola ad Diognetum.
Tertullian, Apologeticus adversus Gentes.
——— ad Nationes.
——— de Testimonio animæ.
——— ad Scapulam.
——— adversus Judæos.
——— Oratio ad Catechumenos.
Athenagoras, Legatio pro christianis.
——— Atheniensis Apologia.
——— de Mortuorum resurrectione
Theophilus, contra Calumniatores.
Clemens (Alex.), Protrepticon ad Gentes.
Minutius Felix, Octavius.
Origen, contra Celsum.
Cyprian, de Idololatrium vanitate.
——— Testimonia ad Quirinum.
Lactantius, de Mortibus persecutorum.
Athanasius, Oratio contra Gentes.
Cyril (Alex.), contra Julianum.
Eusebius, Preparatio Evangelica.
——— Demonstratio Evangelica.
Chrysostom, adversus Judæos.
——— contra Gentiles.
Ambrose, Responsio relationi Symmachi.
Theodoret, de curandis affectionibus Græcor.
Augustine, de Vera religione.
——— de moribus Ecclesiæ Catholicæ.
——— adversus Judæos.
——— de civitate Dei.
——— adversus Paganos.
Arnobius, adversus Gentes.

Arndtius de vero Christianismo.
Bergier, Preuves du Christianisme.
Bernard, de l'Excellence de la Rel. chrét.
Boesnier, Preservatif contre l'irreligion.
Bretschneider's Systematische Entwickelung.
Buddei Miscellanea Sacrorum. Part I.
Cartwright, Certamen Religionum.
Chateaubriand, de genere du Christianisme.
Curcellii (Steph.) Opera.
Du Plessis de veritate relig. christianæ.
Edemus de Veritate relig. christianæ.
Fabricius de Veritate relig. christianæ.
Gotti de Veritate, &c. (Acta erud.)
Grotius de Veritate relig. chris. ("Equally approved by Catholics and Protestants." —C. Butler. A fine edit., with English notes and illustrations by Middleton. Printed 1855.)
Hornbeckii Summa controversiarum relig.
Houtville la Religion chrétienne prové par les faits. (Highly esteemed. It is preceded by an acc. of the methods taken by writers for and against Christianity.)

Christianity—*continued.*

Huetii Demonstratio Evangelica.
Kortholti Grundlichen Beweis, &c.
Lamy, Preuves evidentes de la verité, &c.
Le Clerc, Bibliotheque ancienne et moderne.
Limborch, de Veritate, &c.
Malebranche, Conversations chrétiénne.
Pascal, Pensées sur la religion. ("Contains the germ of all that can be said, for or against the Chris. relig."—VENTOUILLAC.)
Picteti Dissertationes Theologicæ.
Sagittarii Intro. in Hist. Ecclesiasticæ.
Schuberti de Veritate, &c.
Stattleri Demonstratio Evangelica.
Tappen, Wahreit der christlichen Religion.
Tollner's Gœttl. Eingeb. der heiligen Schrift.
Turretini Dissertationes.

Abbadie's Truth of Chris. Trans. by Booth.
Addison's Evidences, &c. (Many editions.)
Alexander's (Archib.) Evidences of Chris.
Alexander's (W. L.) Christ and Christianity.
Alley's Vindiciæ Christianæ. (Comparison of the Greek, Roman, Hindu, Mahometan, and Christian religions.)
Allix's Reflections on the Holy Scriptures.
Apology of Ben Mordecai. (Powerful; with valuable notes by Henry Taylor.)
Appleton's Works. Lectures 18 to 25.
Apthorp's Obser. on Gibbon's Decl. and fall.
Arndt's True Christianity.
Bampton Lectures. (Particularly for 1780, '84, '86, '87, '88, '92, '94, '97, '98, 1803, '08, '11, '12, '23, '25, '31.)
Bassett's Reasonableness of revelation.
Bates' (William) Works. Chap. 5.
Baxter's (Rich.) Reasons of the Christian religion. (Dr. S. JOHNSON pronounced it the best work on the subject.)
Bean's Evidences, &c.
Beattie's Evidences, &c. (Popular.)
——— Nature and immutability of truth.
Benson's Hulsean Lectures. 1820.
Biscoe's Acts of the Apostles confirmed from other authors.
Bolton's Evidences. (Prize essay. 1852.)
Bonnet's Philosoph. and critical enquiries. (Refutes modern French philosophy.)
Boyle (Robt.) Lectures. (Commenced 1692.)
Broadley's Christianity a divine revelation.
Brown's Essay on the characteristics.
Burgess' (Bp.) Easter catechism.
Butler's Analogy of Relig. and Nat. Part 2.
Butler's (Alban) Meditations and Discourses.
Carey's (P. M.) Evid. and corruptions of C.
Chalmer's Evidences, &c.
Channing's (W. E.) Dudleian lecture.
Chelsum' Remarks on Gibbon's Rome.
Chichester on Deism.
Clarke's (Dr. Sam.) Reflections on Amyntor.
——— Truth and certainty of the Chr. rel.
——— Sermons.
Cook's Historical view of Christianity.
Croley's Three cycles of revelation. (Argues the parallelism of the Patriarchal, Jewish, and Christian dispensations.) ("More fanciful than sound."—BRIT. CRITIC.)

Christianity—*continued.*

Crosskey's Defence of Religion.
Dalrymple on the Causes which Gibbon assigns for the progress of Christianity.
Davies' Exam. of the 15th and 16th chapters of Gibbon.
Doddridge's (P.) Evid. (Many editions.)
Duchall's Presumptive evidence, &c. ("Singular merit."—KIPPIS.)
Duguet's Principles of relig. Tr. by Lalby.
Durham's Christianity the friend of man.
Dwight's (Prest.) Discourses.
Edwards (Dr. John) on the Authority, &c.
Fawcett's (James) Sermons.
Fell's (John) Lectures.
Foote's Leading aspects of Christianity.
Fuller's Gospel its own witness.
Gastrel's Necessity and certainty of religion.
Gerard on the Genius of Christianity.
Gisbourne's Survey of Relig. (Admired.)
Goddard on the Mental condition necessary to a due enquiry into religious evidence.
Gray's (Robt.) Ten discourses.
Green's (Robt.) Demonstration of the truth of Christianity.
——— Nine discourses.
——— Norrisean prize essay. 1796.
Greenfield's Evid. by inductive philosophy.
Grew's Cosmologia Sacra.
Grotius on the Truth of the Ch. religion.
Gurney's Evidences, &c.
Hale's Influence of Gibbon's five causes.
Hammond's Reasonableness of the C. relig.
Hampden's Essay on the evidences, &c. (A worthy companion to Butler's Analogy.)
Harness' Connection of C. and happiness.
Hey's Lectures on Divinity. Vol. 1.
Hodge's Summary of corroborative evid.
Hulsean Lectures. 1820, 1821, 1831, 1837.
Hunter's (Henry) Evidences, &c.
Inglis' Vindic. of the Christian faith.
Ireland's (J.) Chr. and Paganism compared.
Jenkins' Reasonableness and certainty, &c.
Jortin's Truth of the Christian religion.
Knox's (Vicessimus) Christian philosophy.
Lardner's Credibility of the Gospel history.
Leslie's Short method with the Jews.
——— Short method with the Deists.
——— Truth of C. demonstrated.
Less' (G.) Demonstration of the truth of the Christian religion.
Littleton's Conversion of St. Paul.
Locke's Reasonableness of Christianity.
McIlvaine's Evid. (A brief compilation.)
Maltby's Illustrations. (8 good dissertat.)
Marsh's Evid. and nature of the C. religion.
Middleton's Miscellaneous Works.
Moore's (D.) Chr. vindicated. (Cambridge prize essay.)
Nare's Evidences, &c. (Able and original.)
Osterwald's Grounds and principles, &c.
Paley's Evidences, &c.
——— Horæ Paulinæ.
Parker's Demonstration of the Divine authority, &c.

Christianity—*continued.*

Penrose's Evidences, &c., from its wisdom.
Porteus' Summary of the evidences, &c. (Good for young people.)
Price's (Rich.) Dissertations. Diss. 4.
Priestley's Letters to a philosoph. unbeliever.
Roberts' Vindication, &c. (Reply to Volney's ruins.)
Robinson's (Tho.) Nature and Evidence, &c.
Rosse's (Earl of) Proof of the C. religion.
Ryland's (John) Essays.
Salsbury's Strictures on Gibbon's Rome.
Scott's (Tho.) Works.
Seiler's Reasonableness of belief.
Sharp's (Gregory) Defence of C.
Sheppard's Divine origin, &c. (Deduced from evidences which are not founded on the authenticity of Scripture.)
Sherlock on the Resurrection of Christ.
Simmes' Nature and reception of Chr.
Smith's (J. Pye) Testimony to the Messiah.
——— Sacrifice and priesthood of Christ.
Sprague's Contrast between Christianity and other systems.
Steele's (J.) Philosophy of the evidences.
Stephens' Comparison of C. with other sys.
Stillingfleet's Origines sacræ.
Sumner's (Bp.) Nature and reception of C.
Sykes' (A. A.) Truth of Christianity.
Thompson's Types, Prophecies, and Miracles.
Tillotson's Sermons.
Tunstell's Academica.
——— Lectures.
Warburton's Divine legation of Moses.
Watson's (Bp.) Apology. (Reply to Gibbon.)
——— Tracts.
Wellwood's Authority of the N. Testament.
West's Defence of Revelation.
Whitby's Necessity, Usefulness, &c.
Wilson's (J.) Reasonableness of C. (An able development of the principles of Butler's Analogy.)

The above are but a fraction of the writers on this subject, but are abundantly sufficient for the purposes of this work. See a full list of writers for and against Christianity, up to the 14th century, in CAVE'S *Hist. Litteraria.*

Christianity Adapted to Man.

Pluguet, Memoires pour servir a l'histoire des egaremens de l'esprit humain par rapport a la relig. chretienne. ("Excellent ouvrage."—BRUNET.)
Titman's Verhaeltniss des Christenthums zur Entwickelung des Menchengeschlechts.

American Bibl. Repository. 3:229. 5:403. 2d Series. 1:180.
American Eclectic Mag. January, 1858.
Barton's Divine wisdom in the natural, moral, and physical world.
Bunsen's (C. C. J.) Christ'y and mankind.
Butler's (Piers E.) Rationality of revealed religion.
Butler's Analogy of Religion and Nature.

Christianity Adapted to Man—*cont.*

Chalmers on the Power and wisdom of God.
Christian Examiner. 45:194.
Christian Quart. Spectator. 9:573.
Christian Review. 2:74, 495. 13:572.
Fry's (Edw.) Essays on the Accordance of Christianity with the nature of man.
Hampden's Philosophical evidences of C.
Harness' Christianity adapted to man, and therefore true.
Jones on the Claims of Religion.
Kitto's Journal of Sacred Literature. 4:34.
Literary and Theol. Review. 1:632.
Methodist Quart. Review. 1:39.
Miller's Bampton Lectures. 1817.
Morehead's (Robt.) Sermons.
New Englander. 5:433.
Norman's Necessity of Revelation.
Redford's Holy Scriptures verified by science, history, and human consciousness.
Reid's (Tho.) Works. Essay 1, ch. 1.
Spence's Religion for mankind.
Trench's Hulsean Lectures. 1845.
Universalist Quarterly. 7:156.
Williamson's Boyle Lectures. 1778.
Woodgate's Bampton Lectures. 1838.

Christianity Applied to Business. See RELIGION AND BUSINESS.

Christians. See DISCIPLES, FREE-WILL BAPTISTS.

Christmas. See FESTIVALS, JESUS CHRIST, BIRTH OF, NATIVITY.

Andrews' (Bp.) Sermons.
Barrow's (Isaac) Sermons.
Berriman's (William) Sermons.
Blomfield's (George B.) Sermons.
Brownrig's (R.) Sermons.
Clerke's (Richard) Sermons.
Cooper's (Edward) Sermons.
Conybeare's (Bp.) Sermons.
Davies' (Prest.) Sermons.
Dehon's (Bp.) Sermons.
Donne's (John) Sermons.
Faringdon's (Anthony) Sermons.
Girdlestone's (Charles) Sermons.
Gordon's (Adam) Sermons.
Heber's (Bp.) Sermons.
Horne's (Bp.) Sermons.
Horseley's (Bp.) Sermons.
Jones' (Will. of Nayland) Sermons.
Lake's (Bp.) Sermons.
Latimer's (Bp.) Sermons.
Marshall's (Nathan) Sermons.
Newman's (John H.) Sermons.
Pott's (J. H.) Sermons.
Smallridge's (Bp.) Sermons.
Townsend's (George) Sermons.
Whateley's (Richard) Sermons.

Christology. See FAITH OF THE PATRIARCHS, MESSIANIC PSALMS.

Bertholdt, Christologia Judæorum.
Coquerell, Essai sur la person de J. C.

Christology—*continued.*

Dorner's Lehre von der person Christus.
——— Geschichte der christologie.
Fabricii Chris. Noachica et Abrahamica.
Frischmuthii (J.) XXIII Dissertationes.
Glassii Opuscula (Explic. Ps. cx.)
——— Christologia Mosaica.
Guers, le Campe et le tabernacle du desert.
Gutleri Dissertationes.
Hengstenberg's Christologie des A. Test.
Leibner's Chris. Einheit des dogm. Systems.
Meignan, les Prophetics messianique.
Redepenning's Com. in locos Vet. Test.
Stegmanni Christognosia. (A storehouse of thought.)
Steinwenderi Christus Deus in Vet. Test.
Umbreit, der Knecht Gottes.
Weber de Natura Christi.

Abbott on the 110th Psalm.
Bloomfield's Traditional Knowledge of a promised Redeemer.
Brown's Norrisean prize essay. 1835.
Burgh's (Wm. D.) Donellian lecture. 1862.
——— ——— ——— ——— 1863.
Fleming's Christology.
——— Loganthropos.
Franck's Sum and substance of Scripture.
Gill's (John) Prophecy resp. Messiah. (A reply to Collins' scheme of literal proph.)
Gordon's (Robt.) Christ as made known to the ancient church.
Guild's (Wm.) Moses unveiled.
——— Harmony of all the prophets.
Hale's (W.) Dissertations.
Harpur's Christ in the Psalms.
Harris' (Dr. W.) Practical Discourses.
Hengstenberg's Christology of the Old Test. Trans. by Dr. Keith.
——— ——— Abridged by T. K. Arnold.
Howson's Norrisean prize essay. 1841.
Hussey's Glory of Christ.
Kidd's Christophany. (Able and learned.)
Literary and Theol. Rev. 4:71.
Owen's (John) Glorious majesty of Christ.
Pierce (Sam. E.) on the Pentateuch.
Polhill's View of some divine truths.
Princeton Review. 31:1, 38. 32:101.
Reynolds' (Bp.) Com. on the 110th Psalm.
Robinson's (Tho.) Proph. of the Messiah.
Sartorius on the Person of Christ.
Stephenson's Christology of the O. and N. T.
Williams' Psalms interpreted of Christ.
Wilson's Early opinions of Jews and Chris.

See writers named by DORNER, *in his Gesch. der Christologie.*

Chronology. See CHRONOLOGICAL ARRANGEMENT OF SCRIPTURE, PERIOD OF 1260 YEARS, SEPTUAGINT CHRONOLOGY, SEVENTY WEEKS.

Assemani Kalendaria Ecc. Universæ. (An investigation of the origin of churches in all nations.)
Barnard, Chronologia Samaritanarum.
Baronii Annales.

Chronology—*continued.*

Bassnage, Annales.
Bengelii Ordo Temporum.
Bucholstzeri Index chronol. utriusque Test.
Buhle, Calendarium Palestinæ Œconomicon.
Camprian, Chronologia universalis.
Capelli Historia Apostolica illustrata.
Clemencet et Durand, Art du verifier les dates des faits historique. (An immense and valuable work.)
Corsini Dissertationes.
Eusebii Thesaurus temporum.
——— Chronicon. cum notis J. Scaliger.
Frankii Systema chron. fundamentalis.
Frenoy, Tablettes chronologique.
Gaultheri Tabula chron. status ecclesiæ.
Gauz, Chronologia, sacra et profana.
Genebrardi Chronologia ecclesiastica.
Gregory (John), de Æris et Epochis.
Harduini Chron. V. T. ad Vulgatum exacta ex nummis antiquis illustrata.
Hoffman's Ægyptische und Israelitische Zeitrechnung.
Hornii Dissertationes. (On the true age of the world, against J. Vossius.)
Hottingeri Diss. Biblic. chronologicæ.
Ideler's Handbuch der mathematischen Chronologie.
Kepler, de Jesu Christi vero anno natali.
Kochii Strict. theol. in Harduini opera.
Labbæi Chronologia technica.
Longchamps, les Fastes universel.
Longuevue, Dissertations.
La Combe, Chronolog. de l'hist. ancienne.
La Croze, Vind. vet. script. (Ag. Harduin.)
Lamy, Apparatus chronologicus.
Marshami Chronon canonicus. (Confined to the difficulties of the O. T. "Learned and accurate."—HALE.)
——— Ægyptiarum antiq. investigatio.
Martian, Defence du texte Hebr. (Against Pezron.)
Mover's Kritische Untersuchungen.
Noldii Historia Idumeæ.
Page, Critique sur Baronius.
Parei Chronologia Sacra.
Petavii Rationarium temporum. (For a long period the favorite text-book, and often reprinted with improvements.)
Petiti Eclogæ chronologicæ.
Pezron, Antiquité des temps defendu.
Polock, Principes de chronologie.
Reus' Beweis das die Zeitrechnung, &c.
Riccioli Dissert. de annis patriarcharum.
Scaliger, de Emendatione temporum.
——— Thesaurus temporum.
Selden de Anno civile veterum.
Seyffarth's Entdeckungen in der biblischen Zeitrechnung.
Spanheimii Chronologia et Historia sacra. (Comes down to the reformation.)
Tholuck's C. des alten Testaments.
Tournemin, Conjecture sur l'origine de la difference du texte Hebreu, de l'edition Samaritan, et de la version des Septante.

Chronology—*continued.*

Usseri Annales utriusque Testamenti.
Vater's Synchronistische Tafeln der kirchen Geschichte.
Vignole, Chron. de l'hist. sainte, et des hist. etrangeres. (From the Exodus from Egypt to the captivity in Babylon.)
Vitringa Hypotyposis. (An elegant compendium.)
Vossii (G.) Chronologia sacra Isagoge.
——— de LXX. Interpretibus.
Vossii (I.) Vera ætate mundi.
——— Castigationes ad scripta Hornii.
Walchii Calendarium Palestinæ.
Wieseler's Chron. u. Abfassungszeit d. apostelgeschichte u. d. Paulin Briefe.

Allen's Chain of Scrip. C. (Convenient tables.)
Amer. Biblical Repos. 2d Series. 6 : 114.
Amer. Quart. Rev. 2 : 509. (Egyptian chron.)
Amphlet's Key to Script. eras. (Very convenient.)
Ancient Universal History. (Last vol.)
Andrews' (J.) Key to Scripture chronology.
Bedford's Scripture chronology demonstrated by astronomical calculation.
Bennett's Temple of Ezekiel. (Reconciling the Jewish and Christian chronologies.)
Benson's Chronology of our Saviour's life.
Bentley's Critical observations.
Bibliotheca Sacra. 15 : 289.
Bickmore's Tables of comparative chronol.
——— Chronological Instruction.
Blackadder's (R. B.) Chron. of the New Test.
Blair's Chronology. (With useful tables.)
Bosanquet's Chron. of the times of Daniel, Ezra, and Nehemiah.
Boyle's (H.) Chronicle of the 18th and 19th centuries.
Brett's General history of the world.
Broughton's (Hugh) Concent of Scriptures.
Burton's Chron. of the Acts of the Apostles.
Browne's (Henry) Ordo seculorum. (Very condensed.)
Carpenter's Calendarium Palestinæ.
Carr's Jewish calendar explained.
Christian Monthly Spect. 1 : 339.
Christian Quart. Spect. 9 : 193. 10 : 656.
Clayton's Hebrew chronology vindicated. (Defence of Usher.)
Craddock's Hist. of the O. Test. methodized.
Crosthwaite's Synchronology. (Showing the harmony of Egyptian, Greek, and Phœnician C., with that of the Scriptures.)
Cunningham's Chronology of Israel and the Jews.
——— Synopsis of chronology.
——— Septuagint and Hebrew chronology tested by their internal scientific evidence.
Downe's Ordo Seculorum. (Contains a valuable compend of the principal chronologies, an exam. of Greswell, &c.)
Drake's Sacred chronology.
Ethnological Journal. 1 : 9, 91, 266.
Eyton's (E. T.) Dates in Daniel and Revelations.

Chronology—*continued.*

Fysh's Historical chronology.
Greswell's Greek calendar.
Hale's Analysis of Sacred hist., chronology, geography, and prophecy. (Harmonizes and explains. An invaluable work.)
Holmes' (W. A.) Prophetical chronology.
Idler's Handbook of chronology.
Jackson's Chronology of the most ancient kingdoms.
Jarvis' Chron. Introd. to the history of the Church.
Jennings' Application of Astronomy to C.
Jones' Chronological and analytical view of the Bible.
Kennedy's (John) Scripture chronology.
King's (Robt.) Chron. of Sacred history.
Kitto's Journal. 5 : 60. (C. of Josephus.)
Knott's New aid to memory. 147 engrav.
Lardner's Cabinet Encyclopedia. (Chronol. of the Chinese.)
Lewin's Early Chris. C. (B. C. 70 to A. D. 70.)
Lloyd's System of Chronology.
McDougal's Chronology of the Bible.
Macfarlane's Scripture Chronology.
Mann on the true years of Christ's birth and death.
Manchester's Times of Daniel examined.
Marsham's Canons of Chronology.
Marshall's Chron. tables of Sacred history.
Monthly Review. 105 : 10. (Hindu chron.)
Neil's Dictionary of dates. (20,000 historical facts, to 1857.)
Newton's Chron. of ancient kingdoms. (Sir Isaac spent thirty years on this work, and wrote it over sixteen times.)
Nolan's Egyptian Chronology analyzed.
Parker's (Frank) Chronology.
Pearson's Annales Paulina.
Peckson's Chart of the Patriarchs.
Playfair's System of Chronology.
Priestley's Chart of universal history.
Riddle's Eccles. chronology. (Gives a list of councils, and is otherwise a convenient book of reference.)
Skene's Chronology of the O. Test. compared with profane history.
Skinner's Dissertations. (The chronological difficulties of the Mosaic history.)
Sponde's Annals; from the Creation to Christ.
Tallant's Chronological Tables.
Wallace on the True age of the world.
Warburton's Divine legation of Moses.
Westminster Review. 16 : 327.
Yeates' (T.) Bible chronology reconciled with the histories of Eastern nations.

Chron. Arrangement of Scripture.

Calovii Chronicon Biblicum.
Capelli Chronologia Sacra.
Harduini Chronicon Vet. Test.
Hottingeri Dissertationes.
Lightfoot's Harmony, order, chronology, &c., of the O. Test. and Evangelists.

Marshami Chron. can. ("Accurate."—HALE.)
Torshell's Design of a harmony, &c.
Townsend's Harmony of the O. and N. Test. (On the basis of Lightfoot. Highly commended by Archdeacon Nares.)
Usher's Annals of the O. and N. Testaments.
Whiston's Chronology, harmony, &c.

Chrysostom. See FATHERS.

Chrysostomi Opera. (Many editions.)
Albert, Chrys. considére comme orateur.
Assemanni Bibliotheca Orientalis.
Bergier, Hist. de St. Chrysostome.
Bœhringer, die Kirche Christi.
Erasmi Vita Chrysostomi.
Georgii Vita Chrysostomi.
Hermance, Vie de St. Jean Chrysostome.
Johan. Damasceni Oratio in laudem C.
Laval, Instructions tirèes de St. C.
Leonis Oratio Encomiastica.
Matthæi Animadv. in homiliæ Chrysostomi.
Mayeri Chrysostomus Lutheranus.
——— Apologeticus pro Lutheranismo.
Montfaucon, Vita Chrysostomi.
Neander's C. und die Kirche.
Palladi Vita Chrysostomi.
Tillemont, Vie de St. Chrysostom.
Trombelli Commentarius.
Vollandi Dissertationes quinque.

Bayle's Dictionary. Art. ACACIUS.
Bibliotheca Sacra. 1:669. 4:605.
Boyd's Select passages from Chrysostom.
Bunce's Trans. of C. on the priesthood.
Christian Review. 12:512.
Chrysostom on the Epist. of Galatians and Ephesians.
Chrysostom on the Priesthood. Trans. by Cowper.
Eclectic Review. New Series. 3:21.
Evangelical Review. 1:84.
Hollier's Trans. of C. on the priesthood.
Kitto's Journal of Sacred Litera. 1:193.
Neander's Life of C. Trans. by Stapleton.
North Amer. Review. 62:23.
Perthes' Life of C., based on the investigations of Neander, Boehringer, and others. Trans. by A. Hovey.

Church Architecture.

Caumont, Hist. de l'architecture religieuse au moyen âge.
Ciampini Hist. de sacris Ædificiis a Constantino Constructis.
Garnaud, Etudes d'architecture chrétiene.
Kallenbach's Kirchen-baukunst des Abendl.
Le Roy, Hist. de la disposition et des formes différent qui le chrétiens ont donneès á leur temples, depuis Constantin, jusque á nous. (1764.)
Kreutz, das Ideal des christl. Kirchenbaues.
Lützow's Meisterwerke der Kirchenbaukunst.
Mandelgren, Monumens Scandinaviques du moyen âge.
Minutoli, der Dom. zu Drontheim, &c.
Quast's Form, Einrichtung, und Ausschmückung der altesten kirchen.

Church Architecture—*continued.*

Anderson's Ancient models in eccl. archit.
Bardwell's Temples, anc. and modern. 1837.
Barr's Anglican church architecture.
Bloxham's Gothic church architecture.
Bowman & Hatfield's Ecclesias. architecture of Great Britain. From the Conquest to the Reformation.
Brandon's Church architecture. (Plates.)
British and Foreign Review. 7:1.
Britton's Chronological, historical, and graphic illustrations of English church architecture.
——— Cathedral antiquities.
Brown's Sacred Architecture. (Embraces the Babylonian, Indian, Egyptian, Greek, Roman, &c. 63 plates.)
Christian Examiner. 31:60. 44:316.
Church Review. 3:372.
Close's Early church architecture.
Coney's Ecc. edifices of olden time.
Democratic Review. 20:139.
Dennison's Lectures on Ch. Architecture.
Dublin University Mag. 21:614.
Dublin Review. 7:250.
Hamilton's Designs for rural churches.
Hart's Designs for churches.
Hope's Historical Essay on Church Archit.
Knight's Eccles. architecture of Italy, from Constantine to the 15th century. (Plates.)
Milner's Arch. antiquities of Great Britain.
New Englander. 6:1.
Pettit's Church Architecture. (Plates.)
Plans for Churches. Pub. by the General Congregational Convention. 1852.
Pocock's Designs for churches.
Poole's History of English Church Architec.
Princeton Review. 25:121. 27:625.
Pugin's Revival of Christian A. in England.
Quarterly Review. 6:62. 26:37. 75:179. 76:193.
Sharp's Architectural parallels.
Trimmer's Chapel and Church A.
Whewell's Notes on German churches.

Church Discipline. See DISCIPLINE OF PRIMITIVE CHURCHES, OFFENCES.

Junius de Natura et administrationibus ecclesiæ Dei.
Koopman de Disciplina Theologia.
Burgess' Directory for Church officers.
Christian Review. 9:416.
Christian Observer. 19:497.
Christmas' Discipline of the Anglican Chur.
Dwight's (Tim.) Sermons.

Church Government.

Amyrald, du Gouvernement de l'Eglise.
Buddeus de Ecclesia.
Hase (C. A.) de Jure Ecclesiastica.
Pfaffius de Originibus juris ecclesiastici. (Against the interference of the State.)
Royard, de hominum varietate, in Christianæ societatus historia observanda.
Walchii (J. G.) Miscellanea Sacra.
Zanchius de Religione Christiana.

Church Government—*continued.*

Bibliotheca Sacra. 1:591. 8:378.
Bohmer's Protestant ecclesiastical code.
Brokesby's Government of the Church for the first three centuries.
Bunsen's Hippolytus and his age.
Cartwright's Directory of Church governm.
Christian Examiner. 12:125.
Christian Monthly Spectator. 3:462.
Christian Review. 11:64. 12:529. 17:48.
Clarendon's Religion and Policy.
Colman's Apostolic church.
Davidson's (Sam.) Congregational Lectures.
Gillespie's Aaron's rod blossoming.
Hiscox's Baptist Church directory. (Doctrines, ordinances, discipline, and practices.)
Kaye's (Bp.) External gov. of the Church in the first three centuries.
Keufel's Ecclesiastical jurisprudence.
Lloyd's Histor. account of church government in England.
Methodist Quarterly Review. 11:429.
Milton's Prose works. (Various able treatises.)
Mudge's Nat. and extent of Ch. authority.
Parker's Church gov. of the first 600 years.
Planck's Government of the Church.
Stillingfleet's Irenicum.
Stovel (Cha.) on the Regulation of Churches.
Thorndike on the Forms of Ch. government.
Woodgate's Bampton Lectures. 1838.

Church History, General.

Ammon's Fortbildung des Christenthums.
Africani Fragmenta Chronographia.
Alberi Institutiones hist. ecclesiasticæ.
Alexandri Hist. Eccles. (To 1600. Deemed the best of the Papal historians. Often reprinted.)
Anastasii Historia Ecclesiæ.
Antonini Summa Historialis. (To 1459. Very respectable, but superseded by better works. Many editions.)
Arnoldi Hist. Eccl. (Shows that in all ages, the clergy, as a whole, have been the enemies of vital religion; and that the sufferers for "heresy" have been those of whom the world was not worthy.)
Assemani Kalendaria Eccl. universæ.
Augusti Gesch. und Statistik der Kirche.
Bahrdt, Entwurf einer Kirchenhistorie.
Baronii Annales ecclesiastici. (Comprises 12 centuries. The supplements of Raynold and Spondanus bring the narrative to 1697, and that of Theiner to 1856. B. spent thirty years on this work. He everywhere labors to defend Popery from the Magdeburg centuriators. 34 vols., folio.)
Bassnage (J.), Hist. de l'Eglise. (A powerful reply to Bossuet's variations of Protestantism.)
Bassnage, Annales Ecclesiastici.
Baumgarten, Breviarium Hist. Christianæ.

Church History, General.

Bebellii Antiquitates Ecclesiæ.
——— Memorabilia. (From the Reformation to 1680.)
Benzelii Breviarum hist. ecclesiæ.
Berniera, Hist. eccl. (From Zuingle to 1702.)
Berruyer, Hist. du peuple de Dieu. (To A. D. 40.)
Beugnot, Hist. de la destruc. du Paganisme en occident. (Great.)
Beza de Viris et viribilis eccles. notis.
Biermann's Gesch. der evangel. Kirche.
Bost, Hist. de l'etablissement du Christianisme dans toutes les contrées, &c.
Buddei Ecclesia Apostolica.
Busch's (W.) Gesch. d. Christl. Kirche.
Callixti Hist. de eccles. Occident. (8th, 9th, and 10th centuries.)
Capelli Hist. Eccles. (First 5 centuries.)
Caroli Memorabilia. (Acta eruditor.)
Casauboni Exercitationes. (Criticises Baronius.)
Casiodori Historia. (A trans. of Socrates, Zosomen, and Theodoret.)
Cave, Script. Eccles. hist. literaria.
——— Dissertationes de scriptoribus eccl. incertæ ætatis.
Centuriæ Magdeburgenses. (Invaluable.)
Choisy, Histoire de l'Eglise.
Clerici Hist. Eccles. (First 2 centuries.)
Cotta's Kirchen Historie.
Crevier, Hist. des empereurs Romains.
Darras, Histoire de l'Eglise. To 1854.
Dannenmayer's Leitfaden in d. Kirchenges.
Danz's Lehrbuch der Kirchengeschichte.
D'Aubigné, sur l'etude de l'hist. Chris. et son utilité pour l'epoque actuelle. 1832.
Diezii Succincta Hist. ecclesiastica.
Dolling's Kirche und Kirchen.
Döllinger's Gesch. der Kirche, am J. 680.
Dupin, Bibliotheque des auteurs eccles.
Engelhardt's Handbuch der Kirchengesch.
Epiphanii (Scholasticus) Hist. Eccles. (A Latin translat. of Socrates, Sozomen, and Theodoret.)
Eusebii Hist. Ecclesiæ. (The first regular church history. Many editions and translations.)
Evagrii Hist. Eccles. (From 431 to 594.)
Fabricii (J. A.) Lux salutaris evangelii.
——— Dissertationes.
Fleury, Histoire Eccles. jusqu'en 1414.
——— Continuation par Fabre " 1726.
——— " par Lacroix " 1776.
(78 volumes in all.)
Flugge's Gesch. d. Rel. und Theologie.
Franz's Zustande der Kirche in d. ersten sechs Jahrhunderts.
Gfrörer's Allgemeine Kirchengeschichte.
——— Gesch. des Urchristenthums.
Gieseler's Kirchengeschichte. To 1848.
Gronovii Observ. in scriptoribus eccles.
Gruner's Kirchengeschichte.
Gudii Disputationes et Observationes.
Guerike's Handbuch der Kirchenges.

Church History, General.

Hafels' (J. K.) Kirchengeschichte.
Hagenbach's Kirchenges. des 18 u. 19 Jahrh.
——— Kirchenges. der drei ersten Jahrh.
Hase's Kirchengeschichte.
Haymo, Hist. eccl. usque ad temp. Theodos.
Henichii Hist. Eccl. (First 5 centuries.)
Henke's Gesch. der Kirche.
Henrion, Hist. Ecclesiastica. (To Pius IX.)
Heppe's Ursprung u. Gesch. der Bezeichnung Reform. &c.)
Hoffmann's Christenthum in ersten Jahrh.
Holzhausen de Fontibus quibus Socrates, Sozomenus, et Theodoretus, in scribenda hist. sac., usi sunt.
Hornii Hist. Eccles. (To Constantine.)
Hottingeri Hist. Ecclesias. (Stops at the Council of Trent.)
Hubneri Cent. quatuor, hist. sacra.
Illyrici Catalogus testium veritatis.
Ittigii Schediasma de auctoribus, &c.
——— Hist. Eccles. (1st and 2d centuries.)
Jablonski Institutiones hist. eccl. ("Great merit."—Bp. Walton.)
Jageri Historia Ecclesiast. cum parallelismo profanæ.
Klein, Hist. Eccles. christianæ.
Koethe vom Einfluss des Kirchen historisch. studium, auf die bildung des gemuths und das Leben.
Kortholti Historia Ecclesiæ N. Test.
Kranzii Hist. Eccl. (To 1736. Acta erud.)
Kurtz's Allgemein Kirchengeschichte.
Lampii Synopsis Historiæ Ecclesiæ.
Lange's Geschichte der Kirche.
Langii Instit. studii theol. littera.
La Placette Observationes hist. eccles.
Laroque, Adversaria Sacra. (Acta erud.)
Leo's Gesch. der christlichen religion.
Le Seur, Histoire de l'Eglise.
Limborchii Epistolæ. (By Arminius, Vorst, Grotius, &c. "A precious book."—Dr. Parr.)
Linder's Lehrbuch der Kirchengeschte.
Marcæ Opuscula. (Acta eruditorum.)
Marheinecke's Universal Kirchenhistorie.
Matter, Histoire de l'Eglise. (To 1835.)
Matthes' Kirchliche Chronik. (To 1858.)
Meiner's Gesch. der Religionen. (To 1806.)
Montrond, Tableau historique de la decadence du Paganisme en occident.
Mosheimii Institutiones hist. chris.
——— de Rebus christianorum ante Constantinum. (Replete with references to original sources.)
Natalis (Alex.), Ordinis F F. Prædicatorum. (Many editions. That of Bingen, 1790, 20 vols., 4to, is generally preferred. Said to be the best church history written by a Romanist.)
Neander's Kirchen Geschichte. (To 1834.)
Nicephori Historia Ecclesiæ. (To 610.)
Nicolai Antiquitates Ecclesiasticæ.
Olshausen, Hist. Eccl. veteris monumenta.
——— Gesch. d. zwei ersten Jahrh.

Church History, General.

Orsi Hist. Eccl. (To 1587. 50 vols., 4to.)
Osiandri Hist. Eccl. (An admirable epitome of the Magdeburg centuriators, and continued to 1600.)
Parei Medulla historia eccles.
Peterson's Religions geschichte vom Standpunkte d. Offenbarung.
Pfaffii Inst. Hist. Eccl. (Acta eruditor.)
Philo, Historia Ecclesiastica.
Philostorgii Hist. Eccl. (From 300 to 425.)
Picot, Hist. Eccl. pendant le 18e siécle.
Picteti Hist. Eccl. et civilis; sec. xi.
Raynaldi Annales Eccles. (A continuation of Baronius to 1534. Violently Papal.)
Rechenbergii Summarium Hist. Eccles.
Reffelt's Hauptsachlichste d. Gesc. d. Relig.
Rheinwaldi Acta historico-eccl. Sec. 19.
Rivet, Histoire de l'Eglise.
Ruffini Historia Ecclesiastica.
Sackreuter's Kirchengeschichte.
Sagittarii Introd. ad hist. ecc. (Furnishes a good account of the Councils of the 16th century.)
Sandii Nucleus hist. ecc. (Strongly Arian.)
Schaff's Gesch. der Apostolischen Kirche, nebst einer allgem. Einleit. in d. Kirchengeschichte.
Schelhornii Amenitates.
Schleiermacher's Evangelischen Kirche.
Schmidii (And.) Compendium hist. eccl.
Schmidii (Seb.) Sagittarianæ.
Schmid's (H.) Lehrb. d. Kirchengeschichte.
Schmidt (J. E. C.), Handbuch d. christlichen Geschichte.
Schoene, Tabula Hist. ecclesiasticæ.
Schröck's Kirchenges. 45 vols., 4to. (What Fleury is to France, Schrock is to Germany.)
Schrœderi Hypomnemeta Hist. eccles.
Semleri Hist. Eccles. (Neologist.)
Sigonii Hist. Ecclesiast. (To 211. Papal.)
Sleidani (J.) de Statu relig. et reipub. Carolo V. Cæsare; Commentarii.
Socrates, Historia Ecclesiastica.
Sozomeni Hist. Eccles. (A good edition of Socrates and Sozomen is that of Reading, 3 vols., folio.)
Spanheimii (F.) Institutiones Hist. eccles. (Very polemic. "No better church history."—Cotton Mather.)
Spittler's Grund. d. Gesch. der Kirche.
Spondani Annales Eccles. (An abridgment and continuation of Baronius.)
Starck's (J. A.) Ges. d. Kirche d. ersten Jahrh.
Stäudlin's Gesch. u. literatur der Kircheng.
Stubneri Tabulæ synopticæ.
Sueur, Hist. de l'Eglise. (To the end of the 10th cent. Continued by Pictet to 1700.)
Suiceri Thesaurus Ecclesiasticus.
Theodoreti Historia Ecclesiastica.
Thiersch's Geschichte der Christl. Kirche in Alterthum.
Thiele's Gesch. der christl. Kirche.

Church History, General.

Tillemont, Memoires, &c. (A vast magazine of facts.)
Troutman's Gesch. der christlichen Kirche.
Turretini Comp. Hist. eccl. (To 1700.)
Tzschirner's Fortsetzung der Schröck.
Usseri Historia Ecclesiastica. (To 1600. Written in the polemic spirit.)
Vater's Kirchengeschichte.
Venemæ Institutiones Hist. Eccl. (To 1700.)
Vitringæ Historia ecclesiastica.
Voetii Disputationes.
Walch's (C. G. F.) Grundsätze der Kirchen.
——— Historie der Kezereien, Spaltungen, und Religionstreitigkeiten. ("The German Tillemont."—DOWLING.)
Walchii (Jo. G.) Hist. eccles. ("Opus eximium."—WEISMAN.)
——— Miscellanea Sacra.
Weisman (C. E.), Hist. Eccl. (One of the Pietists. "As accurate as Mosheim, and as pious as Milner."—CONYBEARE.)
Zimmermann's (Dr. W.) Gesch. der Kirche.

Bates' (Wm.) Lectures on eccles. history.
Baumgarten's (M.) Hist. of the Apos. chur.
Bede's Church History. To 1700.
Bilson's Church of Christ.
Blunt's History of the first 2 cent. (Drawn entirely from the Fathers.)
Bright's History of the church. From 313 to 431.
British and For. Review. 12:336.
British Quarterly Review. 2:72.
Burgess' Hist. of the first 5 cent. (Extracted from the Fathers in their words.)
Burnap's Lectures.
Burton's Church Hist. (To the 4th cent.)
Campbell's (Geo.) Lectures. (Admirable.)
Carwithen & Lyall's History of the Church. From the 4th to the 12th cent.
Cave's Lives of the Apostles and primitive Fathers. (Embraces the first 4 centuries. Nothing better to this day.)
Christian Examiner. 22:27. 29:174. 33:1. 48:411.
Christian Quarterly Spectator. 3:433.
Christian Review. 1:417.
Clarke's Marrow of Eccl. history.
Comber's Ch. hist. cleared from the Roman forgeries of Councils and Baronius.
Cunningham's Tables of Eccl. history.
Dollinger's Church Hist. Tr. by E. Cox.
——— ——— ——— Tr. by N. Darnell.
Dowling's Introd. to the study of Ch. Hist.
Dublin University Magazine. 16:252.
Dupin's Hist. of ecclesiastical writers.
Echard's Ecclesiastical History. (To 400.)
Eclectic Review. 8:166. 16:402, 706. 30:192.
Edinburg Review. 8:272. 62:132.
Erskine's Sketches and Hints.
Eusebius' Ch. Hist. (Various translations.)
Eusebius, Socrates, and Evagrius. Trans. by Hanmer.
Eusebius, Socrates, Sozomen, and Theodoret. Trans. by S. Parker.

Church History, General.

Fleury's Church History. Trans. by J. H. Newman. (To 1414. Continued by Fabre and Goujet.)
Formey's Eccl. History. (With a particular acc. of the Methodists. Superficial.)
Foulke's Manual of Church history. (To the 12th century.)
Fox's Acts and Monuments of the Church.
——— Book of Martyrs.
Fuller's (Tho.) Ch. History of Great Britain. (To 1648.)
Gieseler's Church Hist. Tr. by Cunningham.
——— ——— ——— Tr. by Davidson.
("I prefer Gieseler's to any other church history."—Prof. STUART.)
Gillies' Historical Collections. (Describes the remarkable periods of the success of the gospel, and the eminent instruments of it.)
Hardwick's Hist. of the Church. (To 1520.)
——— Hist. of the Church during the Reformation.
Hase's Church hist. Trans. by Blumenthal.
Haweis' Church History.
Hinds' Rise and progress of Christianity.
Howell's (Wm.) Ecclesiastical History.
Jeremie's Hist of the 2d and 3d centuries.
Johns' Eccles. Hist. of the 2d and 3d cent.
Jones' (John) Ecclesiastical Researches.
——— Sequel to " "
Jones' (Wm.) Hist. of the Church. (Full as to Waldenses.)
Jortin's Remarks on eccl. history.
Kaye's Eccl. hist. of the 2d and 3d centuries. (Taken from various writ. of Tertullian.)
King's (Peter) Constitution, discipline, worship, &c., of the primitive church.
Kurtz's Text-book of Church history. Tr. by C. T. Schaeffer. (A convenient condensation.)
Marsden's Hist. of Churches and sects.
Maurice's Lectures. (1st and 2d centuries.)
Merivale's Boyle Lectures. 1865.
Millar's Propagation of Christianity.
Milman's Hist. of Latin Church.
Milner's (Jos.) Hist. of the Church.
Monthly Review. 84:140.
Mosheim's Eccles. Hist. (Tr. by McLaine; continued by Coote to 1819; improved with notes by Dr. Murdock; and since edited, with additions, by H. Soames.)
——— On the affairs of Christians during the first 3 centuries. Trans. by Vidall.
Neander's General history of the Church.
Peterson's History of the Church. (A good compilation for ready reference.)
Povah's Course of historical sermons.
Pridden's (W.) Early Christians.
Priestley's Church History.
Prince's Success of the gospel.
Princeton Review. 5:47. 13:237.
Reeves' Hist. of the Christian Church.
Riddle's Eccl. chron. of the Ch. (To 1840.)
Robertson's Hist. of the Church. (To 1122.)

Church History, General.

Robinson's (Robt.) Eccles. Researches.
Rose's (Hugh J.) Works. (Study of Church history recommended.)
Schaff's Apostolic Church. Tr. by Yeoman.
Soper's Hist. of the Chur. (To Constantine.)
Sozomen's Eccl. Hist. Tr. by Walford.
Spanheim's Church Hist. Tr. by Wright.
Steane's Religious condition of Christendom. 1852.
Stebbings' Hist. of the Church, from 1530 to the 18th century. (Designed as a continuation of Milner.)
Stevens' Lectures on Church history.
Stoughton's Ages of Christendom before the Reformation.
Taylor's History of Christianity.
Theodoret's Hist. of the Church. (From 322 to 427.)
Thiersch's History of the Church.
Timson's Ecclesiastical history.
Townley's Essays on various subjects of ecclesiastical history.
Townsend's Eccles. and civil hist. (To the death of Wickliff.)
Welch's External hist., &c. (First 3 cent.)
Whitaker's (Wm.) Lectures. (Arian.)
Woodrow's Church history.

The above, on general church history, are all that the largest library need contain. The remainder of this article will consist of the church histories of particular countries; and at the end will be found a bibliographical note, for the use of the curious.

Church History, Local.

AFRICA. See COPTS, JACOBITES.

Almeydæ Litteræ ex Æthiopia.
Bassnage, Hist. de patriarchat de Alexandr.
Boniouri Ægyptiaca Bibliotheca.
Capelli (M. A.) Dissertationes.
Danhaveri Dissertationes.
Dresserius de Statu religionis, &c.
Eutychius de Origine eccl. Alexandrinæ.
Fabricii Bibliotheca Ecclesiastica.
Goes, Religio moresque Æthiopum.
Guerické de Schola Alexandrina.
Hoffman's Schilderung der Missionen in Lande Joriba. 1859.
La Croze, Hist. du christianisme d'Ethiopie.
Leydekker, Hist. Ecclesiæ Africanæ.
Lobo, Iter in Abyssiniam. 1650.
Loescherus de Patrum Africanorum.
Luderi Quinque Disputationes.
Ludolphi Historia Æthiopica.
Morcelli Africana Christiana.
Munteri Primordia eccles. Africanæ.
Oertelii Theologia Æthiopum.
Sanchez, Historia Ecclesiæ Africanæ.
Schelstraten Ecc. Af. sub Primatu Carthag.
Sollerii Tractatus Historico-theologicus.
Titelmannus de Fide, &c., Æthiopum.
Ureta, Hist. ecclesiastica do Æthiopia.
Wanselbe, Hist. de l'eglise d'Alexandrie.

Church History, Local.

Geddes' History of the Ethiopian church. (Gives a full account of the Papal missions in that country.)
Leydekker's African Church.
Ludolph's Ethiopia.

FABRICIUS, in his *Bibliotheca Ecclesiast.*, names many other writers on the African church; but of no use now.

AMERICA, NORTH.

Avilla, Theatro Eccles. de las Inglesias.
Biselii Argonauticon.
Chalmer, Nouveau Monde.
Crantz's Historie von Greenland.
Le Clerc, Premier etablissement de la foi dans la nouvelle France.
Loskiel's Mission d. Evang. Bruder.
Mœbii Dissert. an Evangelium ab apostolis etiam Americanis fuerit adnunciatum?
Oldenthorp's Missionen d. evang. Bruder.
Urlsperger's Ausfuhrl. Nachrichten von der Salzburg. 1738.
Velthusen's Nachr. v. d. Kirchenverfassung in Nord Carolina. 1786.
Witsii Exercitationes Academicæ. (Discusses the same topic as Mœbius.)
Amer. Quarterly Church Review. 2:219.
Backus' Church History of New England. 1766 to 1804.
Baird's Religion in America. Map. 1842.
Clay's Annals of the Swedes on the Delaware.
Coleman's New England colonies.
Dwight's Travels in New England. 1820.
Elliot's Christian Commonwealth.
Episcopal Magazine. 1:15, 121, 345.
Felt's Ecc. hist. of N. Eng. 1845. (A valuable collection of materials.)
Foote's Histor. sketches of Virginia. 1855.
Greenleaf's Hist. of all the churches in New York, from its first settlement to 1850.
——— Ecclesiastical History of Maine.
Halket's Indians of North America. 1825.
Hawkes' Contributions to the eccles. history of the United States.
Higginson's Plantation of New England.
Hobart (Bp.), Life of; by McVicar. (The preface, by Dr. Hook, gives the early history of the Episc. Ch. in America.)
Holmes' Annals of America. 1492 to 1826.
Hubbard's History of New England.
Mather's (Cotton) Ecclesiastical history of New England. To 1688.
Mather's (Increase) Missions to the Indians.
Morton's New England's Memorial. 1721.
Peck (Rev. John M.), Memoir of; by Dr. Babcock. 1860.
Neal's (D.) History of New England.
Phillippo's Past and pres. of Jamaica. 1840.
Prime's Eccle. history of Long Island, N.Y. To 1845.
Reed & Mattison's Visit to America. 1836.
Uden's New England Theocracy.
Waylen's Eccles. reminis. of the U. S. 1846.
Winslow's Planting of New England.

Winthrop's Hist. of N. England. 1630–1649.
Young's Chronicle of the Pilgrims.

AMERICA, SOUTH.

Bollusii Hist. rerum in Peruana. 1604.
Bourgoing, Vertus et bienfaits des mission.
Fernandez, Tuba Evangelii.
James' Religious state of South Amer. 1827.
Murator's Missions to Paraguay.

ASIA. See ARMENIANS, EUTYCHIANS, JACOBITES, MARONITES, MISSIONS, MONOPHYSITES, NESTORIANS, SEVEN CHURCHES.

BELGIUM.

Augusti (J. C. W.) Betrachtungen über den gegenwärtigen Zustand, &c. 1837.
Baselii Historia religionis instauratæ, corruptæ, reformatæ, &c.
Bertolett, Hist. ecclesiast. du Luxembourg.
Bucellini Gallo-Flandria.
Castelloni Sacra Belgii chronologia.
Heussenii Batavia Sacra.
Le Roy, Theater sacré du Brabant.
Lobetti Lodiensis Ecclesia.
Miræi Opera Historica.
Mudzoerti Historiæ ecclesiæ Belgicæ.
Revii Hist. Belgicarum Ecclesiasticarum.
Rosweidi Historia ecclesiæ Belgicæ.
Sanderi Brabantia Sacra.

Brandt's Reformation in the Netherlands.
Heugh's State of rel. in Belgium. 1844.
Rosweide's History of the Belgic church.
Vernlay's Propagation of religion in B.

CHINA. See JESUIT MISSIONS.

Huc, Christianisme en Chine.
Kircheri China monumentis, &c.
Leibnitz, Novissima sacra.
Lettres Edifiantes. (Periodical, Rome.)
Mosheim, Erzehlung der neuesten Chinesisch. kirchengeschichte.

Dean's Hist. of Missions to China. 1860.
Gusman's History of China.
Gutzlaff's Travels. 1835.
Huc's Christianity in China.
Medhurt's China: its state and progress. 1838.
Yeates' (Tho.) Indian Church history.

DENMARK.

Alsace, Hist. de la Reformation en D.
Christiani Gesch. d. Glaubens. u. d. Schleswig und Holsteins.
Erici Pontoppidani annales. (Acta erud.)
Hansen's Wesen u. Bedeutung d. Grundtvigianismus in der Dänischen kirche.
Huelfeldii Historia eccles. Daniæ.
Krafftii Narratio de Ansgario.
Kranzii Chronicon.
Lukbert's Kirchl. Statistik Holsteins. 1837.
Matthiæ Introductio Chris. en Denmark.
Münter's Kirchengeschichte v. Danemark u. Norwegen. To 1823.

Pontoppidan's Kurtzgefaste reformat. Hist.
——— Annales eccl. Danicæ.
Slangendorfii Orationes.
Wormii Oratio de corruptissimo eccl. Danicæ ante Reformationem.

Numerous other ancient Latin historians of the Danish church are given by SIBBERN in his *Bibliotheca histor. Dano-Norwegica.*

ENGLAND. See DISSENT, NON-CONFORMITY.

Alfordi Fides Regia Brittanica. (First 5 centuries.)
Bedæ Hist. eccles. Anglorum. (From the invasion of Julius Cæsar to A. D. 731. This is the first historical work which employs the calculation of the year of our Lord.)
Camdeni Collectio.
Duchesne, Hist. Eccl. Angl. (838 to 1220.)
Durelli Historia Eccles. Anglicana.
Gibsoni Chronicon Saxonicum.
Goodwin, de Conversione Britt. ad Chris.
Harpsfeldi Hist. Anglicana ecclesiastica.
Hemming, Chartularium eccl. Wigornensis.
Mürdter's Reformatoren u. Martyrer in Eng.
Reggius de Statu eccl. Brit. hodierno. 1647.
Sanderus de Origine et progressu schismatis, &c. (Trans. into English, French, and Spanish.)
Sparkii Scriptores rerum Anglicarum.
Staudlin's Kirchengesch. von G. Brittan.
Usseri Antiq. Brittannicarum. (First 7 cent.)
Weber's Ges. der Kirchen Reforma. in G. B.
Weismanni Memorabilia Ecclesiastica.
Whartoni Anglia Sacra. (To 1550.)

Alford's Church in G. B. under the Romans.
Amer. Bibl. Repository. 2d Series. 4:147. 5:126.
Anderson's History of the Church of England in her colonies. (To 1845.)
Baxter's (J. A.) Church History.
Bede's Eccl. Hist. Trans. by Stevens.
Bennet's Brit. deliverance from Popery.
Blunt's Hist. of the reformation in England.
Brewster's Ecc. hist. of E. in the 18th cent.
Broughton's Eccl. Hist. of Great Britain.
Burnett's Reformation in England.
——— Hist. of his own times.
Burns' Hist. of the Walloon Churches.
Butler's English, Irish, and Scotch Cathol.
Cardwell's Documentary annals of the Reformed C. of Eng. (From 1546 to 1716.)
Carwithen's Hist. of the C. of E. (To 1660.)
Churton's Early English Church.
Clarendon's Hist. of the rebellion.
Coit's Early hist. of Christianity in Engl.
Collins' Ecclesiastical history of Gr. Britain. (To the reign of Charles II. Edited with valuable improvements, in 1852, by T. Lathbury.)
Crosby's Hist. of the English Baptists.
Daniels' Ecc. hist. of the Britons and Saxons.

Dod's Church Hist. of Engl. 1500 to 1688.
Dugdale's Abbeys, monasteries, churches, &c.
Durell's Hist. of the English church.
Fitzherbert's Antiquities of the Eng. Ch.
Fox's Acts and monuments. (Huge.)
Fuller's (Tho.) Church history of England.
Gibson's Hist. of Convocation. 1357 to 1689.
Giles' Patres Eccles. Anglicanæ. 35 vols.
Gillies' Historical Collections.
Gilpin's Life of Cranmer.
Grant's English Church, and the sects which have dissented; with an answer to each. 1811.
Hale's Origin of the Ch. in the British isles.
Hart's Ecclesiastical records. (From the 5th century to the Reformation.)
Heylin's (Peter) Ecclesia Restaurata.
Hody's Eng. Councils and Convocations.
Innet's Origines Anglicanæ. (Continuation of Stillingfleet, to the death of King John.)
Ivemy's History of the English Baptists.
Kennett's Parochial Antiquities.
——— Synods and Councils of England.
Lathbury's History of English episcopacy. (From the Long Parliament to the Act of Uniformity. Reviewed in the British Critic, 20:329; and in Edinburg Review, 64:93.)
Murch's Hist. of Presbyterian and Baptist Churches in the West of England.
Murray's English and Scotch Churches.
Palin's History of the Church of England. (1688 to 1717.)
Parker's Antiquities of the British Church.
Parsons' Three conversions of England.
Perry's Church of England, from Elizabeth to the present time. 1861.
Price's Prot. non-conformity in England.
Richards' Welch Non-conformist's memorial, or Cambo-British Biography. 1820.
Ridley (Bp.), Life of.
Robinson's Original letters relative to the English reformation.
Russel's Anglican Church.
Salmon's Lives of the Eng. bishops. (From the restoration to the revolution.)
Short's Hist. of the Ch. of Eng. (To 1683.)
Soame's Hist. of the Reform. in England.
——— History of the Anglo-Saxon Church. (A great repository of facts.)
——— Elizabethian religious history.
Southern Quart. Review. 12:170.
Stillingfleet's Antiq. of the English Church.
Strype's Annals. (Superior.)
——— Memorials relating to religion.
——— Life of Tho. Cranmer.
——— Life of Matt. Parker.
——— Life of Edmund Grindall.
——— Life of John Whitgift.
Tayler's Hippolytus. (Hist. of the 3d cent.)
Thackaray's Ecclesiastical state of Britain under the Roman emperors.
Tholuch's Church history. Tr. by Torrey.
Timson's British Ecclesiastical History.

Church History, Local.

Tillemont's Memoirs. (Several translations.)
Trapp's England's conversion and reformat.
Tyrrel's General history of England.
Uhden's Ch. of Eng. in the 19th century.
Usher's Antiquities of British churches.
Wake's Church and Clergy of England. (From the conversion of the Saxons to the present. 1703.)
Walker's History of Independence.
——— Sufferings of the clergy in the rebellion.
Warner's History of the English Ch. ("Deserves the highest applause."—Mosheim.)
Wharton's Anglia Sacra.
Willis' Cathedral churches.
Wilson's Dissenting Churches in and near London.
Williams' Antiquit. of the Cymry. (Wales.)
Woodward's Rise and progress of religious societies in England.
Wordsworth's Eccl. Biography. (English.)

Nearly every Cathedral Church in England has its own history published—often in very costly style. They relate chiefly to the ecclesiastical edifices. The history of the English Church in America is given under *"Church History, America."*

FRANCE. See REVOCATION.

Abadie, le Temps auquel la religion Chret. a été établie en Gaul.
Aignan, l'Etat des Protestants en F. depuis le 16e siécle, jusq. nos jour. 1818.
Alexandri Dissertationes.
Barruel, l'Etat du Clergé pendant la revolut.
Beza, Hist. des Eglises reform. de France.
Bossuet, Histoire Ecclesiastique.
Calmet, Histoire de Lorraine.
Carron's Gallikan Kirche am ende des 18 Jahrh.
Carrové's Rel. u. Philos. in Frankreich.
Corbiére Hist. de l'eglise reform. (To 1861.)
De Fraissé, l'Origine des Eglisses de F.
Du Bois, Historia eccles. Parisiensis.
Du Pleix, Hist. generale, &c., avec l'etat de l'eglise. (To the death of Louis XIII.)
Felice, les Protestants de France. (To 1851.)
Gregory (Turonensis), Hist. eccl. Francorum.
Gerettè, Hist. de l'Eglise de Fr. (To 1856.)
Gersoni Epistola ad Sirmondum.
Haag, La France protestant. (To 1850. 10 vols.)
Imberdis, les Guerres rel. en Auvergne.
Köhler's Darstellung vom Gallikan Klerus im 1682.
Labat, Conciliorum Galliæ Collectio.
Labenazie, Defensio antiquit. eccles. G.
Le Boeff, Dissertationes. Confined to Paris.
Le Cointe, Annales Ecclesiastici Francorum. (To 680. "Opus vastum."—Walch.)
Longueville, Hist. de l'Eglise Gallicane. (A stupendous work; to which is added a Martyrology.)

Church History, Local.

Launoy de tempore quo primum in Galliis suscepta est fides.
Marcæ Dissertationes. (On the time of the introduction of Christianity.)
Menardi Disputationes. (Contra Launoy.)
Polenz's Gesch. d. Franz. Calvinismus.
Rollin, l'Etat des Prot. jusq. Louis XVIII.
Saucliere, Hist. du Protestantisme en F.
Scavolæ et Ludovici Gallia Christiana.
Sirmondi Dissertationes.
——— Concilia Galliæ.
Soldan's Protestantismus in Frankreich.
Soulier, Hist. du Calvinisme en France.
Urban, l'Introd. du chris. dans les Gaules.
Vincent, Protestantisme en F. (As in 1829.)
Vinet, Hist. de la predication parmi les Reformés de France, au XVIIe siècle.
Wolf's Geschichte d. Kirche in F.

Amer. Biblical Repos. 2d Series. 4:449.
Blackwood's Mag. 40:772. 48:252.
Browning's Hist. of the Huguenots.
Christian Examiner. 10:272.
Dublin University Mag. 12:64.
Eclectic Review. 4th Series. 16:535.
Edinburg Review. 16:473.
Felice's Protestants of F. Tr. by P. E. Barnes.
Geeve's Eccles. Hist. of France. (To 1670.)
Lavall's Hist. of the Reformation in F.
London Quart. Review. 83:109.
Lorimer's Hist. of the Protest. church in F.
Marolle's Persecution of the Protest. in F.
Quick's Synodicon. 1682.
Smedley's Reformed Ch. of Fr. (To 1832.)
Whittington's Eccles. antiquities of France.

GERMANY. See REFORMATION.

Altingii Historia Ecclesiæ Palatinæ.
Bertholdi Austria Sancta.
Bottger's Einfuhrung d. christenthums in Sachsen.
Broweri Antiquitatum Fuldensium.
Calles, Annales. (Vast labor and research.)
Eichhoff's Kirchenreform. in Nassau.
Francké's Halle-schen Reformation.
Frege's Reform. in der Mark Brandenburg.
Eckerman's Lehrbuch der Religion.
Hansizii Germania Sacra.
Hartnoock's Prussiche Kirchen.
——— Dissertationes.
Hassencamp's Hessiche Kir-Ges. seit d. Ref.
Hechtii Germania Sacra.
Henke's Allgem. Geschichte der Kirche.
Heppe's Deutsch. Protestantismus.
Hermann's Evang. luther. Friedenskirche.
Hiemer's Einfuhrung d. chris. in Deut. land.
Keim's Schwabische reform. Gesch. bis zum Augsburger Reichstag.
Krafft's Kircheng. d. Germanischen Volker.
Krantz (Albert), Metropolis.
Latzel's Evang-lutherische Kirche in Preussen. 1852.
Müller's Kirche in Konigreich Wurtemberg.
Muquart de Statu relig. in Germania.
Paulus' Kirche in Pfalz.

Church History, Local.

Pezii Scriptores rerum Austriacarum.
Raderi Bavaria Sancta.
Regenvolschii Hist. eccles. Sclavoniæ.
Reschii Monumenta vet. ecclesiæ.
Rettberg's Kircheng. Deutschland's.
Richter's Evang. kirchenverfassung.
Ruckerts' Culturgesch. d. Deutschen Volkes.
Sanger's Geistliche d. Chris. kirche Deutsch. nation. (To 1857.)
Schamati Corpus traditionum Fuldensium.
——— Hist. episcop. Wormatiensis.
Schlegel's (J. K. F.) Kirchen und Reform. Gesch.
Schoenleben Carniola, antiqua et nova.
Schopper's Chronographie u. Historie, &c.
Schottii, Prusia Christiana.
Schröck's Christliche Kirchengeschichte.
Spangenbergii Bonifacius.
Straus, Einfuhrung d. chr. in Schwaben.
Theobaldii Chronologia eccles. Bohemicæ.
Ursinus de Ecclesiarum Germanicarum.
Wanisch's Statistik aller Seelsorger-bezirke, &c. 1835.
Wiggers' Kirchenschte Mecklenberg.
Wingelsii Hist. ecclesiæ Sclavoniæ.

Amer. Biblical Repos. 1:1, 201, 409, 613.
Bibliotheca Sacra. 4:236. (By Tholuck.)
Bruschius' Ecclesiastical Hist. of Germany.
Christian Rev. 10:544. (Introd. of Chris.)
Cottrell's Religious movements in G. in the 19th cent. (Gives an account of the Rationalist school.)
Eclectic Review. 4th Series. 2:217.
Evanson's (W. A.) Apology for the modern theol. of Prot. Germany. 1827.
Hollii Statis. eccl. Germanicæ. (As in 1779.)
Hartcock's Ecc. history of Prussia.
Kahnis' Hist. of German Protestantism.
Lowenberg's Persecution of the Luth. Ch. in Prussia. (From 1831 to the pres. 1840.)
Pescheck's Hist. of the Reformat. and anti-reformation in Bohemia. Tr. by Benham. (Mr. B. has added particulars as to the Moravians.)
Princeton Review. 18:514. 22:347.
Pusey's (E. B.) Causes of Rationalism in Germany. 1828.
Rose's Present state of relig. in G. 1825.
——— Reply to Pusey's "Causes," &c. 1829.
Spirit of the Pilgrims. 1:96. 3:57.

GREECE. See SEVEN CHURCHES.

Croix, Etat present des eglises Gr. 1695.
Elssner's Griech. Christen in der Turckei.
Schmidt's Gesch. der Neugriechischen Kir.
Stroschius de Ecclesia Thyatirena.
Usseri Dissertationes.
Wenger's Kenntniss des gegenwartigen Geistes, &c. 1839.

Jowett's Researches in the Mediterranean.
Ricaut's Present state of the Ch., &c. 1692.
Wadington & Harbury's Condition and prospects, &c. 1829.

Church History, Local.

GREENLAND. See MORAVIANS.

HOLLAND.

Benthem's hollandische Kirch. u. schulen.
Brandt's Historie der Reformation.
Flugge's Gesch. des deutschen Kirchen.
Frigland, Kirchelücke Historie.
Gazete, Histoire eccl. du Pays Bas.
Hildebrand's Urkunden und Nachricht, &c.
Huessenii Batavia Sacra.
Müller's (H. A.) Kirchengebäude.
Seubert's Prot. Kirche in Deutschland.
Spieker's Gesch. d. Reformation in D.
Uytenbogard, Kircheltücke Historie.

Brandt's Reformation in the Low countries. (To the end of the Synod of Dort.)

HUNGARY.

Batthyani Leges eccl. regni Hungariæ.
Berceviczy, Nachrichten über den jetzig Zustand, &c. 1822.
Debrezeni Hist. Eccles. Reform. in H.
Farlatti Historia Ecclesiastica.
Friederich Lage der Kirche in Ung. 1825.
Hornadi Initia religionis chris. in H.
Inchoferi Annales eccles. regni H.
Klein's Lebensumständen u. Shicksalen prediger, &c. 1789.
Lehman's Zustande der Protestanten in U.
Mailath's Geschichte der Magyaren.
Peterffy, Concilia eccles. Hung. (To 1715.)
Ribini Memorabilia Augsb. confess. in H.
Rimaud's Presburger Kirchen.
Sigismundi Comment. de rebus Hung.

Craig's Protestant Church of H. (To 1850.)
D'Aubigné's Hist. of the Prot. church in H.

INDIA. See NESTORIANS, MISSIONS.

Allatius de Eccles. Orientalis.
Costa, de Promulg. Evang. apud Barbaros.
D'Avila, Theatro Ecclesiastico.
Gabrielis Fides Ecclesiæ Orientalis.
Hoffman's Epochen der Kirchenges. Indiens.
Hoornbeckius de Conversione Gentilium.
Jarrici Thesaurus rerum Indicarum.
La Croze, Hist. du Chris. des Indes. (To 1720.)
Le Quien, Oriens Christianus.
Ludovicus de Missionibus in India.
Morini Antiquitates Eccles. Orient.
Raulini Hist. Ecclesiæ Malabariæ.
Vennent's Christenthum in Ceylon. (A survey of the Portuguese, Dutch, English, and American missions.)

Christian Disciple. 5:295.
Christian Examiner. 1:301. 2:149, 313.
Christian Monthly Spectator. 3:20.
Dwight's (H. G. O.) Christianity in the East.
Geddes' Hist. of the Church of Malabar.
Guzman's History of India.
Heber's Journey thro. the Provinces. 1829.
Hough's History of Chris. in India, from the Christian era. (A work of great research.)
Kay's (J. W.) Christianity in India. 1859.

Church History, Local.

Littell's Living Age. 3:420.
Malcom's (H.) Travels in Southeastern Asia.
Monthly Review. 105:94.
Neale's History of the Eastern church.
North British Review. 13:313.
Quarterly Review. 33:445.
Pearson's Memoir of Schwartz.
Periodical Account of Baptist missions.
Pettit's Tinnevelly mission. (To 1851.)
Tennent's Hist. and present state of Christianity in Ceylon. 1850.
Trevor's Historical sketch of India. 1858.
Ward's (Wm.) Letters. (Serampore missions.)
Yeates' (Tho.) Indian Ch. history. (Planting of Chr. in Syria, Mesopotamia, &c.)

IRELAND.

O'Sullivani Historia eccles. Iberniæ.
Porteri Annalium ecclesiastic. Iberniæ.
Waraei Comment. de præsulibus Hiberniæ.

Brenan's Eccles. history of I. (To 1829.)
Campbell's Ecc. and liter. hist. of Ireland.
Foye's Early Irish church.
Hart's (R.) Ecclesiastical records. (Plates.)
King's (Abp.) State of the Protestants in I. under James II. ("Truly and finely written."—Bp. Burnett.)
Lanigan's Hist. of the Ch. in I. (To 1300.)
Lifford's Ireland and the Irish. 1842.
Mant's Chur. of I. (From the Reformation.)
Mason's Primitive Chris. in Ireland.
Murray's Hist. of the Ch. of I. (Shows that it was not papal in the beginning.)
O'Sullivan's Irish church history.
Porter's Catholic church of Ireland.
Reid's Presbyterian Ch. in I. (To 1833.)
Sibthorp's Comm. on Usher's relig. of the I.
Todd's Ancient Irish church.
Usher's Ancient religion of the Irish.
Ware's Hibernia Sacra.
Witherow's Hist. of the Presb. church in I.

ITALY.

Carriacoli Napoli Sacra.
Corradini Opuscula.
Georgius de Antiquis Ital. metropolibus.
Gradonici Brixia Sacra.
Lubini Italia Ecclesiastica.
Lucentii Italia Sacra.
Martenella Roma.
Matthæi Sardinia Sacra.
Monachi Sanctuarium Capuanum.
Neander (A.), Marco Antonio Flaminio. (An account of the rise of the Reformation in Italy.)
Neigebaur's Italienischen evang. Kirche.
Rubei Monumenta Ecclesia.
Ughelii Italia Sacra. (10 folios.)

Baird's Protest. in I., past and pres. 1844.
Foreign Quarterly Review. 10:335.
McCrie's Rise and suppression of the Reformation in Italy.
North Amer. Review. 44:153.

Church History, Local.

Quarterly Review. 37:50.
Savonarola's Life and times. (15th cent.)
Steele's History of Rome.

JAPAN.

Aloysii Descriptio Japoniæ. 1595.
Charlevoix, l'Établisement et decadence du Christianisme dans le Japon.
Kempfer, Beschreibung des Japan. Reichs.
Solier, Hist. eccles. des Iles de J. 1548 to 1624.
Sotelus de Statu Eccles. Japoniæ. 1673.
Trigaut, Rei chris. apud. J. Comm. 1610.

Gusman's History of Japan.
Gutlaff's Voyages. 1835.

NORWAY.

Kranzii Norwegiæ Chronicon.
Massenii Chronologia de rebus Scondiæ. (*i. e.*, Danes, Norwegians, and Swedes. "Tres savant."—LENGLET DU FRESNOY.)
Maurer die Bekehrung d. Norweg. Stammes.

POLAND.

Fischer's Reformation in Polen.
Herbinii Status Eccles. in Polonia. 1671.
Jablonski Hist. consensus Sendomirensis.
Krasinski's Reformation in Polen.
Lengnichii (Godofr.) Dissertationes.
Lubienicii Hist. reform. in Polonia.
Thom's Zustand der Lutherischen kirchen im Polen. 1750.
Tricesii Hist. Sacrosancti evang. in P. 1556.

Krasinski's Rise, progress, and decline of the Reformation in Poland.

PORTUGAL.

Cardosi Hagiologium Lusitanum.
Fernandez, Hist. de neustros tiempos. 1611.
Guerre, Corunna regni Lusitaniæ.
Murr's Gesch. der Jesuiten in Portugal.

Geddes' Miscellaneous Tracts.

RUSSIA. See GREEK CHURCH.

Bellerman's Abriss d R. kirche. 1788.
Benzelius de Sectis eccl. Orient. nostri temporis. XVII. cent.
Busching's Evang. Luth. Gemeinden in R.
Dobrowsky, Cyrill u. Method, d. Slaven apost.
Elsner's Neueste Beschreibung, &c.
Grot's Religionsfreiheit der Auslander. 1798.
Helladii Status præsens, &c. 1714.
King's Gebräuche d. kirche in R.
Kohlii Eccles. Græca Lutheranizans.
Krasinski's Gesch. d. Ursprungs, Fortsch, &c.
Le Quien, Oriens Christianus. (Splendid.)
Maimbourg, Hist. du schisme des Grecs.
Mosheim, Hist. Tartarorum ecclesiastica.
Mouravieff, Hist. de l'eglise en Russe.
Murawijew's Gesch. d. Russischen kirche.

Church History, Local.

Philaret, Hist. de l'eglise Russe. (To 1847.)
Picteti brevis Collatio, &c.
Regenvolsc, Hist. chron. eccl. Sclavonic.
Schmid's Ges. d. griechischen kirche. 1840.
Simon, Histoire critique, &c., du Levant.
Strahl's Gesch. d. Russland. kirche.
Wahrmund's Religion der Muscoviter.
Zialowsky, Delineatio eccl. Orient.

Constet's Present state of the Ch. of R. 1729.
Heineck's Hist. of the Greek church.
Jowett's Researches in the Mediterranean.
Mouravieff's Hist. of the Russian Church.
Pinkerton's State of the Gr. Ch. in R. 1816.
Stanley's History of the Eastern Church.

SICILY.

Cajetani Historia Sicilia.
Carrera, Pantheon.
Pirri Sicilia Sacra. (A standard author.)
Rocchi Sicilia Sacra.

SCOTLAND. See CHURCH OF SCOTLAND.

Buchanan, Historia ecclesiæ Scoti. 1570.
Camerarius de Scotorum pietate, &c.
Conæus de Duplici statu rel. apud Scotos.
Dempsteri Hist. ecclesiastica Scotorum.
Gemberg's Schottische national Kirche.
Sack's Kirche von Schottland.
Thompson, de Antiquitate rel. apud S.

Aikman's Annals of persecution in S.
——— Hist. of the national Covenant.
Annals of the General Assembly; from the Secession, in 1739, to the origin of the Relief, in 1752.
Balfour's Annals. (To 1652.)
Beattie's C. of S. during the Commonwealth.
Bower's Hist. of the Church of S. (To the disruption, 1843.)
Bryson's (James) Ten years of the Ch. of S. (1833 to 1843.)
Buchanan's (Geo.) Ten years' conflict. (Hist. of the rupture.)
Buchanan's Hist. of Scotland. (To 1565.)
Calderwood's Hist. of the Ch. of S. (From the Ref. to the end of the reign of James VI.)
Church of S. (From the secession, in 1739.)
Collier's Eccles. history. (To the origin of the Relief, in 1752.)
Cook's History of the Church of Scotland. (1567 to 1693.)
Cruikshank's Hist. of the Ch. of S. (From the Restoration to the Revolution. Chiefly abridged from Wodrow.)
Cunningham's Hist. of the Ref. in S.
Eclectic Review. 4th Series. 25:584.
Frazier's Magazine. 12:651.
Fyfe's Ch. of Scotland. (1560 to 1836.)
Henderson's (Alex.) Life and Times.
Hetherington's History, &c. (To 1843.)
Hill's (Rowland) State of the S. Ch. 1799.
Jamieson's Hist. of the ancient Culdees.

Church History, Local.

Jubilee Memorial of the Scottish Congregational Churches. 1849.
[Keith's] Planting of Christianity in S.
——— Affairs of the Church, from the beginning of the Reformation to 1568.
Kirkton's Hist. of the Ch. of S. (To 1678.)
Knox's (Jno.) Reformation in Scotland.
Laing's Hist. of the eccles. divisions in S.; with suggestions for reunion. 1852.
Lawson's Episcopal Ch. of Scotland.
Lee's Lectures on the Chursh history of S.
McCrie's Lives of Knox and Melville.
——— Sketches of Scottish Ch. hist.
McLaughlin's Early Scottish Church.
Middleton's Appendix to Spottiswood.
Miscellany of the Wodrow Society.
Morren's Annals of the Church of Scotland. (From 1739 to 1776.)
Murray's Eng. and Scotch Ch. (To 1771.)
North British Review. 11:234.
Quarterly Review. 7:107.
Row's Hist. of Church of S. (1538 to 1639.)
Russell's Church of S. Portraits. 1834.
Scott's (W.) Kirk of S. since the Ref. 1846.
Simpson's Banner of the Covenant.
Skinner's Eccles. history of Sc. (To 1788. Strongly Episcopal.)
——— Annals of Scottish Episcopacy.
Smith's (Tho.) Hist. of the free Church of S.
Soames' Elizabethian religious history.
——— Anglo-Saxon Church.
Spalding's Transactions of the reign of Charles I.
Spottiswood's Church and State of Scotland. (Excellent.)
Stephens' Church of S., from the Reformation to the present. 1843. 24 portraits.
Stevenson's Church and State of Scotland. (From Charles I. to 1649.)
Stuart's (Gilbert) Estab. of the Ref. in S.
The Spottiswood Miscellany. (A valuable collection of papers and pamphlets touching Scottish Church history.)
Watson's (Rich.) Historical collection.
Wilson's Early hist. of Christianity in S.
Wodrow's Sufferings of the Church in Scotl., from the restoration to the revolution.
Wodrow Society's publications. (Reprints of the writings of the fathers of the Reformed Church of Scotland. Not the same as the Wodrow Society's Miscellany.)

SPAIN.

Aguirre, Conciliorum Hisp. Collectio.
Cennii Antiquitates Eccl. Hispaniæ.
Florensii Hispania Sacra. (Ample of itself, forming 46 vols., 4to; the last of which was printed in 1836.)
Heffele, le Cardinal Ximenes.
Moralis Annales.
Perezii Dissertationes Ecclesiasticæ.
Segoviæ Dissertationes Ecclesiasticæ.
Villanuno, Summa Conciliorum Hispaniæ.

Geddes' Miscellaneous tracts.

Church History, Local.

McCrie's Progress and suppression of the Ref. in Spain.
Weiss' Hist. of the Refugees, from the revocation of the edict of Nantz.

SWEDEN.

Arhenii Hist. eccl. Sueorum, Gothorum, &c.
Alander de Chris. in Vestrogothiam introd.
Baazii Inventarium Sue-gothorum.
Bangii Hist. Ecclesiæ Sueorum.
Benzelii Monumenta.
Henningii (Jacob.) Dissertationes.
Krummacher's St. Ansgar. die alte u. neue Zeit. zur Gesch. der K. To 1828.
Münter's Magazin f. Kirchengesch. u Kirchenrecht des Nordens.
Neumanni Historia Reformationis, &c.
Oernhjalms, Hist. Gothorum Ecclesiæ.
Tegner's Kirche und Schule Schwedens.

Anjou's Hist. of the Ref. in S. Tr. by Mason.
Bang's Ecclesiastical history of S.
Steane & Hinton's Tour in Sweden. 1858.

SWITZERLAND.

Bucelini Rhætia Ethnica.
Fischer's Gesch. der Reform. in Bern.
Fusslin's Kirchenreform. gesch. des S.
Hagenbach's Kirchl. Denkwurdigkeiten, &c.
Haller's Gesch. d. Reform. des Bern.
Hennigii (Jacob.) Dissertationes.
Hottingeri Acta Ecclesiæ Helvetiæ.
Kuhn's Reformatoren Berns.
Leger, l'Eglises des Valleés de Piedmont.
——— die Evangelische Schweiz.
Malan, Procès du Methodisme de Genève. 1835.
Mignet, Mem. sur l'estab. de la Réforme, &c.
Mureri Helvetia Sancta.
Ruchat, Ref. de la Suisse. (Copious and accurate.)
——— Hist. eccl. du pays de Vaud.
Scherer's Verhaltniss Zwischen Kir. 1854.
Simler (J. J.), Urkunden zur beleucht der kircheng. vornehm der S.
Spanheimii Historia religionis Christianæ restituæ apud Genevensis.
Urstisii Historia Basileensis.
Wirz's Helvetische Kirchengeschichte.

Alexander's (W. L.) Switzerland and the Swiss churches. 1846.
Allix's Ancient Churches of Piedmont.
Christian Quart. Spectator. 2:99.
Eclectic Mag. 9:556. 13:258, 296.
Eclectic Review. 4th Series. 20:713.
Mercier's Church history of Geneva.

SYRIA. See ARMINIANS, COPTS, MARONITES, MONOTHELITES, NESTORIANS, &c.

Abul Pharagii Chronicon Syriacum.
Assemani Bibliotheca Orientalis.
Bessoni Syria Sancta.
La Croix, l'Etat present des eglises Greque.
Tirzi, Syria Sancta.

Church History, Local.

Etheridge's Syrian Churches. (To 1846.)
Jowett's Researches in the Mediterranean. 1820.
Yeates' (Tho.) Indian Church history.

TARTARY.

Haythoni Historia Tartarorum.
Mosheimii Hist. Tart. (The true author of this excellent book is H. C. Paulson.)

TURKEY. See GREEK CHURCH.

For notices of many hundred other church histories, see Boss, *Introd. in notitiam scrip. eccles.*; CAVE, *Hist. literaria*; DUPIN, *Bibliotheque des auteurs eccles.*; CEILLIER, *Hist. des auteurs*; BELLARMIN, *Script. eccles.*; SIENNA, *Bibliotheca Sancta*; SLUTERI, *Prophylaeum hist. Christianae*; GOUGET, *Biblioth. des auteurs ecc. du* 18ᵉ *siecle*; J. G. DOWLING'S *Introd. to eccl. hist.*; WALCH, *Biblioth. Theologica*; TRITHEM, or TRITTENHEM, *Collecteana de script. eccles.* The student will, however, find them to be, for the most part, works which never were important, or are now entirely superseded by those given above.

Church Music. See HYMNOLOGY, INSTRUMENTAL MUSIC, PSALMODY.

Church of England.

The symbolical books of the Church of England are: The Articles of Henry VIII. and of Edward VI.; The 39 Articles; The Canons; Book of Common Prayer; and the Book of Homilies.

Articuli Eccles. Cath. Angliæ et Hiberniæ. (A collection of tracts—many of them in the English language—published between 1547 and 1588; reprinted 1846.)
Crackenthorpii Defensio Eccles. Anglic.
Durelli Hist. rituum sanctæ eccl. Anglicanæ.
——— Eccl. Anglicanæ Vindiciæ.
Fennell, sur les Ordinations des Anglois.
Giles, Bibliotheca patrum Anglic. 36 vols.
Jewelli Apologia Ecclesiæ Anglicanæ.
Nicholsii Defensio Ecclesiæ Anglicanæ.
Sack's Ansichten und Beobachtungen, &c.
Spelmanni Concilia, decreta, leges, &c.
Sydow's Beitrage zur characteristik, &c.
Uhden's Zustande d. Anglican. Kirche. 1833.

Allen's (S. J.) Lectures on the Church of E.
Alsop's Melius Inquirendum.
Anderson's Hist. of the church in the colonies of England. (To 1855.)
Bates' Ritual of the church.
Bayle's Institutions of the Church of Engl.
Bingham's Apology for the Church of E.
Blackwood's Magazine. 4:341. 16:395, 548. 17:20. 19:36. 28:273, 794. 31:181. 55:221.
Boyse's (Archdeacon) Sermons.
Bramhall's Church of England defended.
Brett's Government of the C. of E. apostolic.

Church of England—*continued.*

Bristed's Anglican and Anglo-American Ch.
British and Foreign Review. 1:172.
British Anti-State-Church Assoc. Reports.
British Reformers. (A choice collection, published by the London Tract Society.)
Burnet on the XXXIX. Articles.
——— Apology for the Church of England.
Carey's Testimony of the fathers of the first 4 centuries. (May be classed with Pearson and Bull.)
Carleton's (Bp.) Examination of those points wherein the Church of England is charged with being Armenian.
Christmas on the Doct. of the Eng. Church.
——— on the Discipline of the Eng. Chur.
Churchman Armed. (A collection of treatises by Brett, Bull, Burgess, Hoadley, Leslie.)
Coleridge's (Derwent) Character of the E. C.
Collins' (C. T.) Perranzabuloe.
Constance's Fundamental doctrines, &c.
Cooper's E. Church the slave of the State.
Daubeny's Vindication of the Church of E.
Draper's Lectures on the Church Catechism.
Dugdale's Councils, decrees, laws, &c.
Eclectic Review. 4th Series. 8:121. 15:448. 16:431. 17:346. 19:220. 24:740. 26:257. 27:626. 28:99. 30:513.
Edinburg Review. 44:490. 56:203. 58:498.
Falkner on the Worship of the Ch. of E.
Foley's Defence of the Church of E.
Frazier's Mag. 9:127, 379. 11:247. 18:187, 750. 19:367. 31:116.
Garbet's Bampton Lectures. 1842. (Anti-tractarian.)
Gibson's Codex juris, &c. (The statutes, canons, &c., arranged under heads; with a commentary.)
Gray's Bampton Lectures. 1796.
Grey's Vindication. (Reply to Pierce's Vindication of Dissenters.)
Grice's Vindication of the Church of E.
Hall's (Jos.) Works. (Agt. the Brownists.)
Hammond's Defence of the Church of E.
Harding's Confut. of Bp. Jewell's Apology.
Heylin's Ecclesia Vindicata.
Hicks' Bibliotheca scriptorum, &c. (A collection of choice tracts by Hoard, Bayley, Pearson, &c.)
Hill's Apology for the Church of England.
Hole on the Liturgy.
Hooker's Works. (Nothing stronger in favor of the Church of England.)
Hopkins' Primitive Church compared with the Episcopal Church.
Horne's (Tho. H.) Ministry, doctrine, &c.
Jackman's Success no rule.
Jebb's Practical Theology.
Jewell's Apology for the Church of England.
——— Defence of the Church of England.
Jones' Rome no mother of the Ch. of E.
Joyce's Hist. of all the English Councils.
Kipling's XXXIX. Articles not Calvinistic.
Lawrence's (Abp.) Sermons. (To show that the 39 Articles are not Calvinistic.)

Church of England—*continued.*

L'Estrange's Alliance of Divine offices. (Exhibits all the liturgies of the Church of England to 1659.)
Lindsey on the Church of England.
Littell's Living Age. 1:401.
Lloyd's Formularies of the Church of E. put forth in the reign of Henry VIII.
McNeile's Lectures on the Church.
Maddox's Vindication. (Reply to Neale's Puritans.)
Manning's Answer to Leslie's case stated between the Ch. of Rome and the C. of E.
Mant's The Church and her ministrations.
Marshall's Defence of the Church of E.
Maskell's Monumenta: or, Offices of the Ch. of England. With dissertations.
Mason's (Fr.) Vindication of the Church.
Melbourne's Church of England defended.
Mills' Apology for the Church of England.
Monthly Review. 115:253. 126:430. 129:207, 284.
Morton's Innocence of the three ceremonies. (Surplice, sign of the cross, and kneeling at the supper.)
——— Episcopacy of the Church of Eng.
Muscut's Church and laws of England.
New York Review. (Many able pieces.)
Nichols' Doct. and discipline of the C. of E.
Nicholson's Apol. for the discipline, &c.
——— Expos. of the Catechism.
Nixon's Lectures on the Catechism.
Overton's Portraiture of Episcopacy.
Palmer's Antiquities of the Eng. ritual.
Parker's (Abp.) Defence of the Church.
Quarterly Review. 5:252. 21:167. 48:452. 53:94. 69:256. 72:124.
Quesnel's Validity of English ordinations.
Richmond's Fathers of the Church.
Savage on the Church of England.
Saywell's Church of England vindicated.
Sinclair's (John) Dissertations.
Skinner's Primitive truth and order.
Soames' Bampton Lectures. 1830.
Southey's Book of the Church. ("The principal object of this book seems to be to keep alive rancorous feelings, already too prevalent."—Bp. Bathurst.)
Sparrow's Collection of articles, injunctions, canons, orders, ordinances, and constitutions, in the time Elizabeth, James, and Charles I.
Sykes' Ans. to the charge of schism.
Taylor's Vindication of the Church of E.
Thackary's (F.) Ecclesias.
Thelwall's Letters to a friend.
Thorn's (W.) Errors and evils of the Eng. C.
Toplady's (A.) Historical proof of the Calvinism of the Church of England.
——— Review of the rise and progress of Arminianism in England.
——— Church of England vindicated.
Tucker's Apology for the Church of Eng.
Uhden's Anglican Ch. of the 19th cent. Tr. by W. C. C. Humphreys.

Church of England—*continued.*

Vivian's Expos. of the Church Catechism.
Ward's Controversy with Ritchell: "Whether the Church of England is part of the true church." (Ward is the author of "Errata of the Protestant Bible.")
White's (Alex.) Confutation of Church-of-Englandism.
Wise's Vindication of the Church of Eng.
Wotton's Rights of the clergy.

See a great collection of Chur. of England writers, on all subjects, in Bibliotheca Patrum *Eccles. Anglicanae.*

Church of God [Winebrennarians].

The views of this class of Christians have been set forth chiefly in essays, sermons, &c.

Bolton's Church book.
Church Advocate. Periodical. 33 vols.
Harn on Feet-washing.
Schwartz's Trial of Pædobaptism.
——— History of Infant baptism.
Winebrenner's Hist. of religious denominations. Art. "*Church of God.*"
——— Sermons on Regeneration.
——— Monthly preacher.
——— Letters to Nevin.
——— The Church of God.

Church of Scotland. See Covenanters, Free Church, Reformed Presbyterians, Relief Kirk, &c.

Camerarius de Scotorum doctrinæ, &c.
——— de Scotorum infantia et virilis ætas.
Dempsteri Hist. Eccl. gentis Scotorum.
Gemberg's Schottische national Kirche. As in 1827.
Niemeyer Collectio confessionum fidei.
Thompson, Antiq. Christianæ apud Scotos.

Acts of the General Assembly. 1560 to 1618.
Acts, declarations, and testimony for the whole covenanted reformation, between 1638 and 1649.
Acts of the General Assembly. 1638 to 1860.
Aikman's Annals of the Ch. of Scotland.
American Eclectic Review. 2:100.
Anderson's Defence of the Church of S.
Annals of the General Assembly.
Bailey's Defence of the Reformation in S.
Balfour's Annals. To 1652.
Blackwood's Magazine. 5:136. 46:573, 799. 50:27. 55:221. 89:288.
British and Foreign Review. 16:175.
Calderwood's Altar of Damascus.
Canne's Snare broken.
Chalmer's (Tho.) Present prospects of the Church of Scotland. 1840.
——— (Numerous other treatises.)
Cumming's Apology for the Church of S.
Doctrine and discipline of the Church of S. (Composed by John Knox and John Erskine. Subscribed 1581.)

Church of Scotland—*continued.*

[Dunlop's] Collection of Confessions, Catechisms, Acts of Assembly, &c. To 1720.
Eclectic Magazine. 5:340.
Eclectic Review. 4th Series. 3:332, 432. 6:214. 13:121.
Edinburg Monthly Review. 1:70.
Frazier's Magazine. 23:251, 503. 27:362.
Gillispie on English Popish ceremonies.
Hill's Constitution of the Church of S.
Ker & Graham's Discovery of a conspiracy.
Lawson's (John P.) Episcopal Church of S. (Throws much light on the history of the Presbyterian Church of Scotland.)
Lee's History of the Church of S., from the reformation to the revolution.
Lorimer's Scottish Reformation. (25 plates.)
McCrie's Life of Knox.
——— ——— Veitch.
——— ——— Bryson.
Martin's Dialogue anent the new ceremonies.
Methodist Quarterly. 4:485.
Museum of Foreign Literature. 19:552.
North British Review. 11:234.
Naphthali: or, the Wrestlings of the Church of Scotland for the Kingdom of Christ. 1667. (Burnt by Parliament, and a fine of £10,000 decreed against any with whom a copy should be found.)
Peterkin's Book of the Kirk. (Acts and proceedings of the General Assembly, from 1678 to 1840.)
Princeton Rev. 10:362. 15:405. 16:86, 229.
Quarterly Review. 1:390. 18:502. 67:110.
Roberts' Hist. of the disruption of Ch. of S.
Rutherford's Peaceable and temperate plea.
——— Due right of Presbyteries.
——— (Various other tracts.)
Scott's State and government of the Kirk.
Shiel's Hind let loose.
Sibbald's Liberty of the church.
Solemn League and Covenant. (Sworn to in 1581, and in 1643; annulled in 1674. Touching this Covenant, a multitude of books and pamphlets are extant, pro and con.)
Stephens' (Tho.) Hist. of the Church of S. To 1638.
Stewart's Collections and observations. (A manual, with forms of process, &c.)
Walker's Discipline, constitution, &c.
Westminster Review. 31:98. 34:461. 40:102.
Williams' Defence of the Church of Scotland.
Wodrow Society Miscellany. (A volume of letters, &c., edited by David Laing, relating to the government and faith of the Scotch Church in the 16th and 17th centuries.)

Church Rates. See TITHES.

Pro.

Arnold's (of Rugby) Miscellaneous Works.
Blackwood's Magazine. 41:682.
Campbell on the Law of Church rates.
Denison on Church rates.

Church Rates—*continued.*

Pro.

Hale's (W. H.) Antiquity of the Church rate system considered.
Hale's (W.) Law of Church rates.
Percival's Origin of Church rates.
Report of the Select Committee on Church rates. (House of Commons. 1851.)
Trelawney's Epitome of the above.
Stanley's Church rates considered.
Swan's Principle of Church rates.

Con.

Allen (John) on Church rates.
Eclectic Review. New Series. 1:56, 325. 5:218. 9:348.

Cicero.

Cicero de Natura Deorum.
Buddæi Isagoge.
Freaneri Dissert. de theologia Tullii.
Gesneri Chistomathia Ciceroniana.
Haferingii Cicero Theologicus.
Zimmermani Dissertationes.

Forsyth's Life of Cicero.
Middleton's (Conyers) Life of Cicero.

Circumcision.

Bartolocci Dissertationes.
Deylingii (S.) Observationes Sacræ.
Grotius de Veritate relig. Christianæ.
Lossius de Epispasmo Judaico.
Philo Judeus de circumcisione.
Quandtii Dissertationes Sacræ.
Spencer, de Legibus Hebræorum. Lib. 1, Sec. 4. (Discusses the origin of circumcision, and adduces the views of Herodotus, Philo Sanconiatho, Josephus, and others.)

Bassnage's History of the Jews.
Brekel on Circumcision.
Calmet's Preface to Genesis.
——— Preface to Epistle to Romans.
Fawcett's (John) Sermons.
Goodwin's (Thomas) Sermons.
Le Clerc's 12 Dissertations. Tr. by Brown.
Marsham's Chronological Canon.
Montagu's Origines Ecclesiasticæ.
Reading's (William) Sermons.
Revelation examined with candor.
Stackhouse's History of the Bible.
Vanderhardt's Prodromus.
Whiston's (J.) Sermons.

Circumcellians.

Dietzii (S. G.) Dissertationes.
Varellas, Histoire des revolutions.

Circumspection. See PRUDENCE, WATCHFULNESS.

Cistercians.

De Visch, Biblioth. scriptorum Cist.
Gaillardin, les Trappists. To 1844.

Cistercians—*continued.*

Henrique, Regula, constitutiones, &c.
Heylot, Histoire des Ordres.
Le Nain, Histoire de l'ordre de Citaux.
Manrique, Annales Cisterciensis.
Rance, Règlemens de la Trappe.
Richardson, Prelectiones ecclesiasticæ.
Sartorii Historia Cistertium.
Tissier, Bibliotheca patrum Cister.
Vischii Biblioth. scriptorum ord. Cisterc.

See a huge list of Cistercian writers in the Bibliotheca of FABRICIUS, and in DE VISCH, or VISCHIUS, above named.

Citaux. See CISTERCIANS.

Cities.

Fregier, des Classes dangereuses, et le moyens de les rendre meilleures.

Buckley's Landmarks of civilization.
Chalmer's Christian econ. of large towns.
——— Commercial discourses. Disc. 6.
Guthrie, The City: its sins and sorrows.
Huntingdon's The Church's work in cities.
Kennaway's (Cha. E.) Sermons at Brighton.
Newcombe's Harvest and the Reapers.
Presbyterian Quart. Rev. 1:433.
Todd's Moral influence of great cities.
Vaughn's Age of great cities. (Discusses their influence on morals and religion.)

Cities of Refuge. See TYPES.

Osiandri (J. A.) Dissertationes.
Reis, Tractatus Theologicus de Asylis.

Blencoe's (Edward) Sermons.
Gouldburn's (E. M.) Parochial Sermons.
Watson's (J. W.) Sermons.

Civil Government. See DIVINE RIGHT OF KINGS, MAGISTRACY, ORIGIN OF GOVERNMENT, ORIGIN OF LAWS, PASSIVE OBEDIENCE.

Augustin, Opera.

Guizot, l'Origine du gouvernment represent.
Mably, Droits et devours du citoyen.
Matter, Influence des lois sur les mœurs et des mœurs sur les lois.
Zornii Deliniatio Theolog. patristicæ.

Acherly's British Constitution.
American Whig Review. 2:327.
Andrews' (Bp.) Sermons.
Aristotle on Government. Tr. by W. Ellis.
Atterbury's (Bp.) Sermons.
Ayliffe's Roman Law.
Bentham (J.) on Civil Government.
Bever on the Study of jurisprudence.
Blackstone's Commentaries.
Brown's Law of Christ respecting civil obedience.
Burke's Reflect. on the French revolution.
——— Nature and end of civil government.
Butler's Horæ Juridicæ.
Chalmer's (Thomas) Sermons.
Chitty on Criminal law.

Civil Government—*continued.*

Cunningham's (W.) Principles of Governm.
Danville Review. June, 1864.
Doddridge's Lectures. Part 3.
Domat on Civil law.
Donne (John) Sermons.
Edinburg Review. 49:159, 273. 50:99.
Fenelon on Civil Government.
Ferguson's History of civil society.
Filmer's (Sir R.) Patriarchal scheme.
——— Freeholder's grand inquest.
Franklin's (Benj.) Works.
Gee's Divine right of magistrates.
Gibbon's Roman Empire.
Goodrich's Observations on Price's theory.
Gresley's (William) Sermons.
Grey (W.) on Civil government.
Hall's (Robt.) Works.
Hoadley's Institution of civil government.
Hobbes' Philosophical rudiments of gov.
Horne's (Bp.) Origin of government.
——— Sermons.
Jones' (Sir Will.) Dialogue on Government.
Justinian's Institutes.
Latimer's (Bp.) Sermons.
Leland's Advant. and neces. of Revelation.
Locke (John) on Government.
Matthews' (J. M.) Bible and civil govern.
Mills' (James) Essay on Government.
Murray's (H.) Inquiries; histor. and moral.
Needham's Excellency of a free state.
New Englander. 3:525. 7:530.
Paine's (Tho.) First principles of governm.
Pothier on Obligations.
Pownall's Principles of polity.
Price's Nature of civil liberty.
Ramsay's (G.) Disquisitions on G.
Russel's (Lord J.) Hist. of the English Gov.
Ryan's Effects of revealed religion.
Schonberg's History of Roman law.
Secker's (Abp.) Sermons.
Seed's (Jer.) Sermons.
Sheraton on Subjection to civil government.
Stebbins on Civil government.
Story on the Constitution of the U. S.
Stuart on the Constitution of England.
Sydney (Algeron) on Government.
Taylor's Elements of civil law.
Temple's (Sir Will.) Works.
Tucker (Josiah) on Civil Government.
Warwick's (Sir Philip) Discourses.
Watts (Isaac) on the Civil power.
Wayland's Elements of moral science.
Westminster Review. 11:254, 526. 13:265.
Wilson's (Bp.) Sermons.
Wines' Laws of the ancient Hebrews.
Wrottesley on Government and Legislation
York's (Henry) Thoughts on Government.

Civilization. See HUMAN PROGRESS.

Guizot, Hist. de Civilization.
Jonnès, Statistique de l'antiquité.
Martin, les Civilizations primitives.
Matter, Influence des lois sur les mœurs.
Wuttke's Gesch. des Heidenthums.

Civilization—*continued.*

Amer. Whig Review. 2:80. (J. Q. Adams.) 3:611. 4:27.
Balme's Protestantism and Catholicity compared in their effects on the civilization of Europe.
Blackwood's Magazine. 52:27. 89:27.
Christian Examiner. 52:165. 64:233.
Democratic Review. 6:208. 15:62.
Dublin University Mag. 51:12.
Edinburg Review. 68:243. 69:55. 80:132.
Ferguson's History of civil society. 1767.
Fourier on the Passions. Tr. by Doherty.
Guizot's Hist. of C. in Europe, from the fall of the Roman Empire to the French Revolution.
Hall's (Cha.) Effects of C. on Europe.
Hamilton (Dr.) on the Progress of Society.
Harris' Civilization considered as a science.
McCabe's Lectures on Civilization.
McKinnon's Hist. of Civilization.
Lord's Lectures on Civ. and government.
Moreton's C. as influenced by natural laws.
Moseley's Progress of modern legislation.
Seaman on the Progress of nations.
Taylor's (Isaac) Essays. Essay 1.
Tyler (R. H.), The Bible and social reform. (The Bible as a means of civilization.)
Vaughn on Modern civilization.
Vericour's Histor. analysis of Christian C.

Clairvoyance. See MESMERISM.

Ashburner on Clairvoyance.
Cahagnet's Celestial Telegraph.
Davis' (A. J.) Principles of nature.
——— Great Harmonia.
——— Harmonial man.
——— Several other treatises.
Frazier's Magazine. 20:17.
Gregory (Prof.) on Clairvoyance.

Clean and Unclean Beasts.
See SACRIFICES.

Cleanliness.

Littell's Living Age. 20:130.

Clemens Alexandrinus.

Clementis (Tit. Flav.) Opera quæ extant. (Many editions. Some prefer that of Potter, 1715. The most recent, and probably the best, is that of Migne. 1857. 2 vols.)
Bernholdi Hypomnemeta.
Bielcke de Clemens, ejusque erroribus.
Cognat, Clément, sa doctr. et sa polemique.
Dæhne de γνωσει Clem. Alex. et de vestigiis neoplatonicis philos. in ea obviis.
De Groot, Disputationes.
Gieseleri Clement. et Origenis doctrinæ.
Ittigii Prefatio ad operum Clem. Alex.
Le Clerc, Viè de Clement,
Müller (J. H.) Idées dogmatique de C.
Tribbechovii Dissertationes.
Walchii Miscellanea Sacra.

Clemens Alexandrinus—*continued.*

British Critic. 19:100.
Conybeare's Bampton Lectures. 1839.
Kaye's Writings and opinions of Clement.
Le Clerc's Life of Clemens.
Wray's Writings and opinions of C.

The writings of this Father are not in the English language, though they deserve to be, better than some of the others.

Clemens Romanus.

Clementis Epistolæ. (Many editions. The most esteemed by some is that of Schwegler. 1847.)
Assemani Bibliotheca Orientalis.
Buddei Syntagma Dissertationum theol.
Cyprian (E. S.) de Clement. Rom. evangel.
Ephraimi Homiliæ.
Freudenbergeri Historia controversiæ de Clem. Rom. epistolis.
Grabii Commentatio de Clementis scriptis, genuinis et supposititiis.
Goltz, Gesch. aus d. apostol. Zeitalter.
Herzog des Clem. von R. Brief.
Kesleri Philosophemata potiora recognition. Clem. R. falso attributur.
Nerreter de Fragmentis Clem. R. quod sub nomine epistolæ habetur.
Oudini Com. de scriptis S. Clementis.
Randinus de St. Clemente martyre. (Collects what has been said of Clement by credible writers.)
Bibliotheca Sacra. 22:353.
Burton on the Ep. of C. to the Corinthians.
Cave's Lives of the Fathers.
Chevalier's Translation of the Epistles of Clement, Polycarp, and Ignatius; with introduction, &c.
Lardner's Dissert. on the two epistles of C., published by Mr. Wetstein. (Shows them not to be genuine.)
——— Credibility of the Gospel history. (Touching the two epistles generally received.)

A list of the various editions of this Father is given by FABRICIUS in his *Bibliotheca.* The most esteemed is that of SCHWEGLER. 1847.

Clerical Habits.

Miller (Prof.) on Clerical Habits.
Moody's Hints to young clergymen.
North Amer. Review. 28:503.
Smith on Public Worship. (Treats only on the proprieties of the Sanctuary.)
Stillingfleet's Amusements of a clergyman.
United States Lit. Gazette. 6:377.

Close Communion.

Pro.

Arnold's Scriptural terms of admission to the Lord's Supper.

Close Communion—*continued.*

Pro.

Baldwin (Thomas) on Baptism.
Bayne's Strict communion vindicated.
Bibliotheca Sacra. 19:133.
Birt's Vindication of the Baptists.
Booth's Apology for the Baptists.
Braidwood's Purity of Christian comm.
Butterfield's Free C. an innovation. 1776. (Reply to John Brown.)
Christian Review. 16:210. 23:364.
Curtis (T. F.) on Communion.
Dagg's (J. L.) Letters on communion.
Davis' (G. F.) Peter and Benjamin.
Foster's (James) Sermons.
Fuller's (Andrew) Works.
Fuller's (Richard) Terms of communion.
Gale's Reflections on Wall on Baptism.
Hickes' (Dr. Geo.) on Occasional communion. (Reasons why Churchmen should not commune with dissenters.)
Howell on Sacramental communion.
Ivemy's Baptism necessary to communion.
Keene's (Henry) Free address to Pacificus.
Kiffin (Wm.) on Church communion.
Killingworth's Reply to Robt. Hall.
——— ——— Foster.
——— ——— Bulkeley.
Kinghorn's Baptism a term of communion. (Reply to Robt. Hall.)
——— (Other pieces.)
Knapp on Close communion.
Merriam on the Terms of communion.
Morgan's Principles of Christian comm.
Newman's Bapt. an indispens. prerequisite.
Pressly (J. T.) on Communion.
Remington (S.) on Baptism.
——— Defence of restricted communion.
Ripley's Reply to Griffin's letters.
Strictures on Dr. Mason on Communion.
Taylor (J. B.) on Restricted communion.
Thomas (D. E.) on Christian Baptism.

Con.

Brown's (of Haddington) House of God opened.
Bulkeley's Plea for Catholic communion.
Bunyan's Reasons for my practice.
——— Peaceable principles.
Foster (John) on Catholic communion.
Griffin's (Edward Dorr) Letters.
Hall's (Robt.) Terms of communion.
Horner's Popery and close communion identified.
Mason's (John) Terms of communion.
Noel (B. W.) on Baptism. Ch. 5.
Pressly (J. T.) on Ecclesiastical communion. (Presbyterian.)
[Ryland's (Sen.)] Plea for free communion.
Sawtelle's The Lord's supper for the Lord's people.
Spirit of the Pilgrims. 6:103.
Towgood's Address to the opposers of free C.
Watts on Communion.
Worcester (N.) on Close communion.

Clugni.

Balusii Miscellanea. Tom. v. and vi.
Mabillonii Annales Benedictini. Tom. v.

Coat of Treves.

Smith's (H.) Apostolical Christians. (Authentic documents.)

Cocceians.

Coccei Opera.
Alberti Διπλουν καππα.
Burmanni Synopsis Theologiæ.
Kromayeri Scrutinium Religionum.
Leydeckeri Fax veritatis.
Spanheimii (F.) Epistolæ.
Van Till, Antidotum.
Voetii Opera. (The chief opponent of C.)
Witsii Œconomia fœderum Dei cum homin.

Coincidences of Scripture.

See INTERNAL EVIDENCES.

Burke's Horæ Evangelicæ.
——— Horæ Apostolicæ.
Blunt's Undesigned coincidences. (Excel'nt.)
Graves on the Pentateuch.
Grotius' Truth of Christianity.
Faber's (G. S.) Horæ Mosaicæ. (Coincidences of the Mosaic record with profane antiq.)

Coins.

Augustini (Ant.) Opera. Vol. VIII. Plates.
Bayer de Nummis Hebræorum. (Controverts Cumberland.)
Bergeri Numismata Pontificum Roman.
Biragi Numismata. (Many engravings.)
Brerewood de Ponderibus et Pretiis, &c.
Bunting, de Monetis et Mensuris S. Scrip.
Buxtorfii Dissertationes. (Anc. Hebrews.)
Camerarii (J.) Dissertationes.
Cavedoni (G.) Biblische numismatik.
Coringii (H.) Dissertationes.
Deylingii Observationes. (Anc. Hebrews.)
Eckhel, Doctrina nummorum vet. (9 v. fol.)
Foy-Vaillant, Numismata Ærea Imperator.
Gagnier, de Nummis Samaritanis.
Gesneri Opera Numismatica. 300 plates.
Goltzii Opera numismat. (6 great folios.)
Grasse's Handbuch der alten Numismatik.
Harduini Chronologia Vet. Test.
Hottinger, de Nummis Orientalium inscript. Samaritanis.
Kock, de Nummorum Hebraicorum.
Kœhler, Remarques Historiques.
Lavy, Museum Numismaticum. (The most complete work of the kind. It names 4879 Greek coins, and 5747 Roman; with engravings.)
Lingen de Origine et inventoribus pecuniæ et numismatum.
Margraaf, Observationes.
Occo Imperatorum Roman. numismata.
Otii (J. B.) Epistolæ. (Samaritan coins.)
Patin (C.) Dissertationes.
Petavii (P.) Dissertationes.

Coins—*continued.*

Rayheri (Sam.) Dissertationes.
Rechenberghii Biblioth. nummaria.
Reland de Nummis Vet. Hebræorum.
Scaligeri Opuscula varia.
Schmidt de Drachmis a Christo solutis.
Seldeni Opera.
Semleri Vocabularia rei nummariæ Gr., Lat., Hebr., Arab, &c., ex diversis auctoribus.
Spanheim (Ezek.) de Præstantia numis.
Thottii Thesaurus Numismatum.
Tresor de Numismatique et de glyptique. (1851. Very complete. Price $250.)
Wachteri Archæologia Nummaria.
Waltoni Biblia Polyglotta. (Prolegomena.)
Waser (or Vaser) de Ant. num. Hebr. et Syr.
Wedelii Exercitationes.
Werholf's Bibliotheca Numismatica.
Widmannus ad Matt. xxii. 19.
Wilde, Selecta Numismata antiqua.

Akerman's Illustrations of the N. T. Cuts.
Arbuthnot's Tables of ancient coins.
Calmet's Dissertations. Tr. by N. Tindal.
Cardwell's (E.) Lectures. (Greek and Rom. coins.)
Cumberland on Jewish coins, weights, &c.
Eclectic Review. 4th Series. 22:215.
Ede's Gold and silver coins of all nations.
Madden's Hist. of Jewish coinage. 254 cuts.
Monthly Review. 114:457.
Murray's (John) Truth of Revelation demonstrat. by an appeal to gems, coins, &c.
Numismatic Chronicle. Periodical. London. From 1844. 32 vols.
Pelletier on Coins, Weights, &c.
Princeton Review. 2:131. 28:238.
Till's Essay on the Roman Denarius.
Walch's (R.) Ancient coins and medals. Many plates. (Intended to illustrate the progress of Christianity in the early ages.)
Walker (O.) on Coins and Medals.

Lipsius *Biblioth. Numaria*, gives a catalogue of all the authors who have written upon money and coins, up to the close of the 18th century. John Hearne, bookseller, London, in his catalogue for 1859, offers for sale about 700 works on this subject.

Collegiants. See socinians.

Colonization, African. See negroes.

African Repository. Monthly. Washington, United States. Since 1825.
Alexander's Hist. of C. on the West coast.
American Monthly Review. 2:151. 4:282.
Amer. Quart. Review. 4:395. 12:213. 18:245.
Ashmun, J., Life of; by Gurley.
Bacon's Plea for Africa.
Bibliotheca Sacra. 14:622.
Cary, Lott, Life of; by J. B. Taylor.
Christian Examiner. 13:96, 200, 287.
Christian Monthly Spectator. 5:485, 540. 10:358, 493.

Colonization, African—*continued.*

Christian Quarterly Spectator. 2:459. 4:311. 5:145, 631. 6:332, 445. 7:330, 503, 521.
Colonization Herald. Monthly. Philada. Since 1835.
Eclectic Review. New Series. 3:282.
Foreign Quarterly Review. 26:213.
Frazier's Magazine. 2:334. 3:114.
Jay's (Will.) Character and tendency of the Colonization Society.
Liberia Herald. Monrovia.
Literary and Theol. Review. 1:62. 2:429.
Maryland Colonization Journal. Periodical. Baltimore. Since 1841.
Methodist Quarterly Review. 12:361.
New York Colonization Journal. Period. Since 1850.
Niles' Weekly Register. 13:164. 15 Sup. 42. 16:165, 233. 17:201. 23:39, 138. 24:333. 25:175, 381. 26:270, 282, 373. 27:29. 29:329. 47:208.
North Am. Review. 18:40. 21:462. 35:118. 41:265. 63:269.
Oxford Prize Essays. 1815. (Tho. Arnold.)
Princeton Rev. 5:257, 281. 12:169. 13:266. 16:57.
Reese's (David M.) Letters to the Hon. Wm. Jay. (Reply to his book.)
Southern Review. 1:219.
Spirit of the Pilgrims. 6:322, 396, 539.
Torrey on the Slave trade.
United States Literary Gazette. 3:20.
Wadstorm on Colonization particularly as applied to the West coast of Africa. 1794. (Describes also the then condition of Sierra Leone and Bulama.)

Colporter System.

Anneau, le Necessaire.
Amer. Biblical Repos. 2d Series. 12:214.
American Messenger. Period. New York. (Many fine articles on this subject.)
Annual Reports of Amer. Tract Society.
——— ——— Am. Tract Soc. Boston.
——— ——— Am. Bapt. Publica. Society.
Colportage as conducted by the Amer. Tract Society. (A tract. 1859.)
Cook (R. S.) on Home Evangelization.
Fison's History of Colportage. (An English abridgment of Cook's work.)

Comfort. See affliction, consolation.

Bolton's (Robt.) C. for afflicted consciences.
Colquhoun (John) on Spiritual comfort.
Durant's (Puritan) Comfort for the dejected.
Gerard's Divine Meditations.
Hall's (Robt.) Notes of sermons.
Reyner's Sermons.
Russell's Letters, practical and consolatory. Letter 6.
Sharp's (Dr. J.) Sermons.
Sherlock's (Bp.) Sermons.
Sibbs' Saints' comfort.
——— Letter to an afflicted conscience.

Sibbs' Heavenly conference between Christ and Mary.
Stebbing's (Henry) Sermons.
Taylor's (Jer.) Christian consolation.

Commandments. See MORAL LAW.

Dannhaveri de Collegio Decalogo.
Grotius (H.) in Decalogam.
Philo-Judæus de Decalogo.
Selnecceri Pædagoga Christiana.
Thummii Opera.
Turrettini Institutiones.
Zanchii Opera Theologica.

Anderson's (Bp.) Exposition of the C.
Andrews' (Bp.) Pattern of doctrine.
Babington's (Bp. G.) Works.
Barker's (Peter) Exposition of the ten C.
Barrow's (Bp.) Exposition of the ten C.
Bird's (C. S.) Exposition of the ten C.
Boyse's Exposition of the ten C.
Blackall's (Bp.) Sermons.
Brady's (N.) Sermons.
Bradford's Godly Meditations.
Brougham's (John) Sermons.
Bullinger's Decades. (Pub. of the Parker Society.)
Bunne's Guide to Godliness.
Burgess' Vind. of the moral law. (Against Papists, Arminians, Antinomians, and Socinians.)
Burton's Exposition of the Decalogue.
Candlish's Two great commandments.
Clay's (John) Twenty-five sermons.
Cleaver's (Robt.) Sermons.
Clowes' (J.) Sermons.
Chaffer's (Rich.) Exposition of the C.
Cudworth's (Ralph) Sermons.
Dod's (John) Plain and familiar expos.
Durham's (Jas.) Law unsealed.
Dwight's Discourses. Disc. 100–132.
Edwards' (John) Body of Divinity. (Excellent.)
Elton on the Ten commandments.
Fidde's (Rich.) Body of Divinity.
Graham's (John) Practical Sermons on the ten commandments.
Glass' (S.) Sermons. (Plain and valuable.)
Granger's Tree of good and evil.
Hall's (Bp.) Works.
Harrison's (Wm.) Sermons on the C.
Hill's (G. D.) Practical sermons on the C.
Hooper's (Bp.) Declaration of the ten C.
Hopkins' (Bp. E.) Exposition of the ten C.
Jefferson's (J.) Lectures.
Jones' (Robt.) Sermons.
Jortin's (J.) Sermons.
Knewstub's Lectures on Exod. xx.
Larkin's (E. R.) Sermons on the C.
Laurie's (Dr. Thomas) Sermons.
Leighton's (Abp.) Sermons.
McCaul's (J. R.) The ten Commandments the Christian's rule.
Marsh's (E. G.) Sermons on the C.
Nance's (J.) Sermons on the C.

Commandments—*continued.*

Oakley's (J.) Christian aspect and application of the Decalogue.
Ogden's (Sam.) Sermons.
Piggot on the Decalogue.
Plumer's (Wm. S.) Law of God.
Powell on the Decalogue.
Robinson's (Disney) Law and Gospel.
Russell's Hulsean Lectures.
Ross' (John L.) Lectures.
Scott's (Tho.) Essays.
Secker (Abp.) on the Catechism.
Stackhouse's Works.
Stowel's (W.) Lectures on the ten C.
Thornton's (H.) Lectures.
Tudor's The Decalogue the Christian's law.
Wadsworth (Benj.) on the Decalogue.
Weems' (John) Expos. of the Decalogue.
Whately's Exp. of the Decalogue.

Commentators.

ON THE WHOLE BIBLE.

Augustine, Jerome, Origen.

Brenii (Dan.) Notæ in V. et N. Test. 1660.
Brentii Opera. 1575. (Lauded by LUTHER.)
Alberi Interpretatio. 1804.
Calmet, Commentaire litterale. 1707.
——— Dissertations preliminaires. (Exceedingly valuable. Horne used it largely in his introduction.)
Calovii Biblia Illustrata. 1672. (An immense storehouse of information, touching versions, expositions, and other Biblical subjects. Strong against Papists and Socinians.)
Calvini Prelectiones et Comm. 1578
Capelli Com. et notæ criticæ. 1600.
Cartwright, Melificium Hebraicum. 1627.
Castellionis, Annotationes. 1510.
Clerici (or Le Clerc) Translatio cum commentario, et Dissertationes. 1693. (Not so much a commentary as a series of criticisms. Armenian.)
Coccei (or Le Coq.) Versio et Comm. 1701. ("Spiritualizes too much.")
Critici Sacri in Biblia. 1698.
De Dieu Animadversiones. 1631.
Drusii Annotationes. 1612.
Grotii Annotationes. 1631. (An unsafe guide; but DODDRIDGE thinks "he has done more to illustrate Scripture by profane learning, than all other commentators put together.")
Heideggeri Enchiridion Biblicum. 1700.
Houbigantii Notæ crit. cum Proleg. 1753
Hugonis (Victor), Adnotationes. 1526.
Hugonis (St. Caro) Postillæ. 1487.
Junii et Tremelii Biblia cum notis. 1600.
Lapide, Commentarii. 1664. (12 vols., fol. Highly prized by Romanists.)
Lightfoot, Commentaria Historica. 1659.
Lutheri Commentaria. 1510.

Commentators.

Marlorati Thesaurus in locos communes. 1600. (An abridgment of the best remarks of the Reformers.)
Martyris (Petri), Commentaria. 1579.
Mauri (Rabanni) Com. grammatico-criticus. 1534. (Verbal criticisms on the plan of Schaufelberger's *Clavis Homerica.*)
Melancthonis Commentaria. 1543.
Menochii (Soc. Jesu) Comment. ex optimis auctoribus collecti. 1719.
Olearius' Biblische Erklärung. 1681.
Parei Commentaria. 1620.
Pellicani Commentaria. 1532.
Piscatoris, Commentaria. 1638. (Armenian.)
Poli Synopsis Criticorum. 1674. (Gives whatever is useful in the Critici Sacri, and is more convenient and valuable, on account of its admirable arrangement, and additional matter.)
Quistorpii Commentaria. 1648.
Raphelii Annotationes. 1700. (From Zenophon, Polybius, Arrian, and Herodotus.)
Ravanelli Thesaurus Scripturæ. 1660. ("One of the most useful books to a preacher, in the world."—C. MATHER.)
Schidii (Sebastian.) Commentaria. 1740. ("Erudite, accurate, and perspicuous."—WALCH.)
Schoetgenii Horæ Hebraicæ. 1733.
Storr (G. C.), Opuscula Academica. 1796.
Tarnovii Exercitationes Biblicæ. 1632.
Thilonis, Medulla. 1683. (An epitome of Poole's Synopsis.)
Tirini (Soc. Jesu) Commentaria. 1630.
Tossani Paraphrasii et Annotationes. 1606.
Tostati Commentaria. 1491. (24 volumes, folio.)
Tremelii. (See Junii.)
Venemæ Dissertationes. 1747.

Allen's (Jno.) Exposition. 1765.
Assembly of Divines' Annotations. 1651.
Benson's Bible; with notes. 1811. (Chiefly a compilation from Wesley.)
Boothroyd's Improved vers. and notes. 1818.
Brown's Self-interpreting Bible. 1777.
Burder's (S.) Scripture Expositor. 1809.
Calvin's Com. Trans. by various persons. ("Calvin's Commentaries remain, after three centuries, unparalleled for force of mind, justness of expression, and practical views of Christianity."—BP. WILSON, of Calcutta.)
Clarke's (J.) Annotations. 1743.
Clarke's (Adam) Commentary. 1810.
Clarke's (Sam.) Analysis of the S. S. 1700.
Clarke's (Sam., Junr.) Annotations. 1760.
Clarke's (Samuel) Annotation and parallel passages. 1690.
Cobbins' Comm. 1837. (A family book.)
Coke's Commen. 1803. (Plagiarized from Dodd.)
Cornwallis' Observations. 1820.
Davidson's Pocket Commentary. 1836.
Diodati's Annotations. 1651.

Commentators.

D'Oyly and Mants' Bible. 1814.
Dodd's Commentary. 1770.
Dutch Annotations. Ordered by the Synod of Dort. Tr. by T. Haak. 1657.
Fawcett's Family Bible. 1811.
Gill's Exposition. 1748. (A great treasury of Rabbinical and Oriental literature; with criticisms. "In Rabbinical literature Dr. Gill had no equal."—HORNE.)
Girdlestone's Comm. 1835. (Short reflections for family use.)
Hawker's Poor man's comm. 1822. (Family book.)
Henry's Expos. 1731. (Pious and practical.)
Holden's (Geo.) Christian Expositor. 1834.
Kalisch's Historical and critical commentary; with new translation. 1858.
Knatchbull's Animadversions. 1659.
Lange's Comm. Tr. by Dr. Schaff. 1866.
Le Clerc's Commentary. 1710. (Critical.)
Mayer's Com. 1653. (A synopsis of preceding writers.)
O'Neill's Biblical Gleanings. 1854. (About 3000 selected comments and criticisms.)
Ostervald's Bible. 1722. (Wholly superseded by better works.)
Patrick, Lowth, Whitby, Arnold, & Lowman combined. 1769.
Piscator's Commentary. 1638.
Poole's Annotations. 1683. (Universally commended.)
Roberts' Clavis Biblicum. (Some account of each writer, and the occasion, scope, and analysis of each book.)
Scott's Commentary. 1792. (Superficial.)
Sharp's (Sam.) Historic notes. 1854.
Shitler's Domestic Commentary. 1854.
Sutcliffe's (Jos.) Commentary. 1840.
Trapp's Comm. 1662. (Very valuable.)
Wall's Critical notes. 1730. (With amendments to the Hebrew text.)
Wells' (Ed.) Paraphrase. 1708. (With a revised translation.)
Wesley's (John) Notes. 1764. (Those on the New Test. are best.)
Williams' Cottage Bible. 1825.
Wilson's (Bp.) Bible. 1785. (Chiefly useful for its collation of the present with former English versions.)

ON THE OLD TESTAMENT.

Athanasius, Cyril Alex., Theodoret.

Jewish.—Aben Ezra, Abraham Scholom, Jos. Carpi, Abarbanel, Kimchi, Medraschim, Levy, Gerson, Moseh ben Nachman, Solomon Jarchi, Ben Malek, Alscheich, Simeon, Maimonides, &c.

Amama, Collatio Biblica. 1620.
Baumgarten's Theologischer z. A. T. 1844.
Bibliandri Commentaria. 1543.
Boetii Commentaria. 1644.
Capelli (L. & J.) Com. et notæ criticæ. 1575.
Dathii Vet. Test. Latine versio. 1773.

Commentators.

Diodati Explicationes. 1635.
Grynæi Explicatio et Exegesis. 1584.
Hackspanii Notæ philologico-theolog. 1640.
Leusdeni Clavis Hebræica. 1686.
Maureri Commentarii. (One of the best for mere Historico-Grammatical Exegesis.)
Parei Opera Theologica. 1614.
Pfeifferi Clavis. 1690. (Philological.)
Rosenmulleri (E. F. C.) Scholia. 1821. (23 volumes of unsurpassed criticism.)
Scholz, die heilige Schrift des A. Test.
Schotani Commentaria. 1628.
Schultenii Animadversiones. 1760.
Schulzii Scholia. 1783.
Starkii Synopsis Exegetica. 1741.
Stephani Biblia. 1590. (Philological.)
Zanchii Commentaria. 1600.

Barrett's Synopsis of Criticisms on passages in which Commentators differ from King James' version. 1855. (The Hebrew, Septuagint, and English, are given in juxtaposition; and the opinions of Commentators, on disputed passages, quoted and considered.)
Hill's Lectures on portions of the O. T. 1810.
Keil & Delitzsch's C. Trans. by J. Martin. 1864.
Orton's Exposition. 1791. (For families.)
Patrick's Commentary. 1695.
Pyle's Paraphrase and notes. 1725.
Richardson's Observations. 1655.

PENTATEUCH. See PENTATEUCH, SAMARITAN PENTATEUCH.

Isidore, Ambrose, Gregory N.

Alcuini Interrogat. et Responsiones. 800.
Altingii Opera. 1670.
Aretii Commentaria. 1602.
Bedæ Expositio. 725.
Borrhai Commentarii. 1555.
Burmanni Commentaria. 1670.
Catena Græcorum patrum in P. 1547.
Chrytræi Commentarius. 1557.
Drusii Annotat. ad loca difficil. 1588.
Fabricii (Geo.) Commentarius. 1584.
Fagii Paraphrasis. 1540.
Gesneri Disputationes XXXVIII. 1604.
Hammelmani Adnotationes. 1600.
Hartman's (H. C.) Historisch-kritische Forschungen.
Herrheimer, תורה d. Funfbuchs Moses. 1854.
Junii Explicationes Analyticæ. 1639.
Koolhaus, Observationes Exegeticæ. 1751.
Leusdeni Precepta Mosaica. 1686.
Lyseri Commentarius. 1604.
Marbachii Hypomnemeta. 1597.
Marckii Commentaria. 1734.
Meklenburgii Scriptura ac traditio. 1839.
Merceri Prelectiones. 1570.
Osiandri Commentaria. 1676. ("Princeps." —WALCH.)

Commentators.

Selnecceri Commentaria. 1559.
Varenii Decades Mosaicæ. 1659.
Vater's Commentar. 1805.
Von der Hardt's Ephemeridem Philolog. 1696.

Ainsworth's Annot. 1616. (Makes constant reference to the Greek and Chaldee versions.)
Alexander's (W.) The P. illuminated from history, geography, &c. 1828.
Allix's Reflections on the P. 1650.
Babington's (Bp.) Comfortable Notes. 1622
Blunt's Family Exposition. 1841.
Brightwell's Notes. 1840. (Selected from Poole, Rosenmuller, Le Clerc, Schrank, Dathe, &c.)
Clapham's Books of Moses. 1818. (Family book.)
Delgado's New translation and notes. 1789.
Faber's (G. S.) Horæ Mosaicæ. 1818.
Gerlach's Com. Tr. by H. Downing. 1859.
Graves' (Richard) Lectures. 1807.
Hamilton's (W. T.) P. and its assailants. 1850.
Havernick's Historico-critical introduction to the P. Trans. by A. Thompson. 1850.
Hengstenberg's P. illustrated by the monuments of Egypt. Tr. by Ryland. 1847. (A noble refutation of such writers as Bohr and Van Bolen.)
Howard (Henry E.) on the Pentat. 1856. (Learned.)
Jameson's (A.) Crit. and pract. Exposition. 1748. (A compilation from the best interpreters, ancient and modern.)
Jamieson's (Robt.) Critical and explanatory Commentary. 1858.
Kidder's Commentary, Dissertations, &c. 1694. (Refutes Le Clerc and others.)
Lowman's Ritual of Hebrew worship. 1740.
Marsh's (W.) Lectures on the Pentat. 1822. (Dwells mainly on the authenticity.)
McDonald's (D.) Introduction to the P.
Morison' Key to the first 4 books. 1810.
Parker's Bibliotheca Biblica. 1720. (A convement compilation from writers previous to the year A. D. 451.)
Penrose's Lectures on the Pentateuch.
Pierce's (Sam. E.) Discourses on the Pent. 1815.
Popham's Extracts from the P. compared with similar passages from Greek and Latin authors. With notes.
Robertson's Clavis Pentateuchi. 1770. (An analysis of each word in its order.)
Smith's (Geo.) Lectures on the Pentat., with special reference to recent objections. 1863.
Stewart's Bible Gems. 1839.
Thompson's Guide to the study of the Pent. (A series of questions, with references to works in which answers may be found.)
Thistlewaite's Expository Sermons. 1837.

Commentators.

Townsend's Spiritual communion with God. 1849. (The P. and Job arranged in one connected history, in chronological order, with notes.)
Tyndale's Introduction to the P. 1573.
Wilson's Notes; crit. and devotional. 1854.
Wolfe's (J. R.) Messiah in the Pentateuch. 1850.
Wright's Exposition. 1688.

GENESIS. See COSMOLOGIES, CREATION, THEORIES OF THE EARTH.

Chrysostom.

Bleek (F.) Observationes. 1836.
Bohlen, Histor. Introductio. 1854.
Buttman's Mythos der Sündfluth.
Cartwright, Electa Targumico. 1648.
Casmanni Cosmopœia et Ouranographia.
Chemnitii Collegium Theologicum. 1665.
Clerici Dissertationes. 1684.
Gerhardi Com. in G. 1637. (On the embarrassing passages.)
Grambergii Liber G. secundum fontes rite dignoscendus.
Hackmanni Præcidanea sacra. 1700.
Lipomani Catena patrum in G. 1546.
Marlorati G. cum catholica expos. 1562. (A collection of the best expositions of the Reformers.)
Merceri Comm. 1598. (Preface by Beza.)
Musculi Commentaria. 1554.
Œcolampadii Annotationes. 1523. (Chiefly translations from Chrysostom.)
P. Martyris Commentaria. 1572.
Riveti Exercitationes. 1634.
Schmidii (Sebast.) Commentarius. 1597.
Schwenke's Bibelstunden u. d. erste Buch Mose.
Venemæ Dissertationes. 1747.
Von Sanden, Questiones Biblicæ. 1716.
Zuinglii Farrago adnotationum. 1527.

Bassett's (Wm.) Sermons on G. 1690.
Beke's Researches in primæval hist. 1834.
Burrough's (W. K.) Lectures on G. 1848.
Bush's (Geo.) Notes on Gen. 1832. (Small value.)
Bohlen's Introduction and Comment. 1855.
Candlish's Contrib. toward an Exposition, &c. 1852.
Close's (Francis) Historical Discourses. 1826.
Coghan's Scripture Commentary on G. 1832.
Dawson's New translation and notes. 1763.
Delitzch's Comm. on Genesis. 1860. (See Keil and Delitch, under "Old Testament.")
Dimock's Critical and explan. notes. 1804.
Foster's (John) Critical Essays. 1840. (A strong rebuff to late German critics—especially Simon.)
Frank's (James) Sacred Literature. 1802. (A compilation from eminent authors.)
Fuller's (And.) Expository Lectures. 1806.
Gibbin's Questions and disputations on G. 1601.

Commentators.

Greenfield's Interlinear tr. and notes. 1831.
Groves' (H. C.) Commentary. 1861.
Harwood's (T.) Annotations. 1789. (Practical.)
Hopkins' Corrected trans. and Notes. 1784.
Hughes' (Geo.) Analytical Expos. 1672.
Jacobus' Crit. and explan. Notes. 1865.
Jervis' (J. J. W.) Genesis illustrated. 1853.
——— Discourses on subjects contained in Genesis. 1845.
Johnson's Vindic. of the book of G. 1838.
Kennedy's Philosophy of the Mosaic record. 1827.
Le Clerc's Dissertations. 1731.
Lee's Diss. on difficult passages. 1710.
Lightfoot's Observations on G. 1670.
Lookup's Berashith. (Hutchinsonian.)
McGregor's Notes on Genesis. 1854. (For students.)
Murphy's (J. G.) Commentary. 1865. (Very valuable.)
Osborn's Genesis and Exodus illustrated by existing monuments. 1854.
Parker's (S.) Bibliotheca Biblica. 1720. (Observations gathered from the Fathers.)
Paul's (Wm.) Analysis and Interpretation.
Pratt's Genealogy of creation. 1861. (Translates from the unpointed text.)
Priaulx's Questiones Mosaicæ. 1842. (Compares the Mosaic record with ancient religions, from the Creation to Abraham.)
Preston's (T.) Notes on the Hebrew text. 1853.
Putnam's (C. H.) Gospel by Moses. 1854.
Quarry's Genesis and its authorship. 1866.
Rudge's (James) Lectures. 1823.
Sibthorp's (R. W.) Observations on G. 1835.
Turner's Companion to the book of G. 1840.
Van Bohlen's Introd. to the book of G. 1855.
Warner's Specimens of Biblical Exp. 1842.
Whately's (Wm.) Prototypus. 1640.
Willet's Hexapla, or Sixfold Com. 1608.

ON SELECT PORTIONS.

Bates (Julius) on the 3d ch. (A refutation of Warburton's 3d proposition.)
Scott on the 3d ch. 1753.
White (John) on the first 3 ch. 1656.
Wright (T. W.) on the first 5 ch. 1788.
Hurdis on the first 10 ch.
McGregor (C.) on the first 11 ch. 1853.
Ross on the first 14 ch.
Shute (Josiah) on the 10th ch. 1649.
Foster's (C.) Crit. essays on 20th ch. 1826.

EXODUS. See COMMANDMENTS.

Tertullian, Epiphanius.

Cartwright, Electa Targumico-Rabbinica. 1648.
Hackmanni Præcidanea Sacra. 1735.
Riveti Commentarium. 1634.
Rungii Prelectiones. 1614.

Commentators.

Simleri Commentarius. 1584.
Zuinglii Farrago Adnotationes. 1527.

Buddicom's Christian Exodus. 1826.
Bush's (Geo.) Commentary. 1842.
Cockburn's Credibility of the Jewish Exod. (Reply to Gibbon.)
Dimock's Critical Remarks. 1804.
Hopkins' New translation and notes. 1785. (Valuable for giving the additions and variations of the Samaritan and Septuagint versions.)
Lightfoot's Handful of gleanings. 1670.
Murphy's Commentary. 1865.
Murray's (M.) Practical remarks. 1830. (Adapted to family worship.)
Willet's Hexapla. 1608.

LEVITICUS.

Ambrose.

Dassovii Scholia Criticorum. 1707.
Franzii Commentaria. 1696.
Hackmanni Præcidanea Sacra. 1735.
Phrygii Explicatio. 1543.
Wolfgangii Scholia sacrificialis.

Bonar's Commentary. 1851. (Critical and practical.)
Bush's (Prof. Geo.) Commentary. 1843.
Murray's Practical remarks on L. 1845. (For family worship.)
Princeton Review. 15:164.
Spanheim's Observations. 1700.
Willet's Hexapla. 1622.

NUMBERS.

Ambrose.

Attersol's Commentary, wherein the whole body of divinity is handled. 1618. (But with small profit.)
Babington's (Bp.) Comfortable Notes. 1615.
Cumming's Sabb. morning readings. 1855.
Howard's (Dean) Translation from the LXX. With notes. 1857.

DEUTERONOMY.

Altingii Commentaria. 1688.
Bugenhagii Comment. 1824. (Able criticism.)
Gerardi Commentaria. 1657.
Maccabeus (or McBee) Commentaria. 1563.

Babington's (Bp.) Comfortable notes. 1615.
Cumming's (J.) Sabbath morning readings.

HISTORICAL BOOKS.

Arthur on the Historical Books.
Horsely's Criticisms. 1820.
Jackson's (Arthur) Annotations. 1643.
Jamieson on the O. T. Hist. books. 1860.
Lindsay's Practical Lectures. 1828.
Mayer on the Historical books. 1650.

Commentators.

JOSHUA.

Burmanni Explicatio. 1669.
Hannekenii Adnotata Philologica. 1665.
Herwerdeni Disputatio de libro J. 1826.
Isingii Exercitationes. 1683.
Keil's Commentar. über Joshua. 1847.
Lavateri Commentaria. 1576.
Masii Explicatio. 1574. (Papal. Valuable for giving the readings of the Syriac and Hexaplar versions.)
Osiandri Comment. 1681. (Gives various readings.)

Jamieson on J. (Condensed and valuable.)
Keil's Com. Tr. by J. Martin. 1849.

JUDGES.

Bertheau, Richter und Ruth Erklart. 1845.
Buceri Commentarius. 1563.
Burmanni Explicationes. 1670.
Chytræi Comm. cum chronologia. 1589.
Osiandri Commentarius. 1682.
Schmidii (Sebas.) Com. 1684. ("Præclarum opus."—Walch.)
Strigelii Argumenta et Scholia. 1575.

Coleridge (John) on the 17th and 18th chap. 1768. (A new trans. and learned notes.)
Noble's (Sam.) Sermons on the first 11 chap.
Rogers' Commentary. 1650. (Rich and practical.)
Rose's (Henry J.) Hulsean Lectures. 1833.

RUTH.

Isidore.

Burmanni Explicationes. 1671.
Carpzovii Collegium Rabbinico-biblicum. 1703. (Gives the text, Massora, four Rabbinical commentators, and many learned notes.)
Drusii Hist. Ruth, ex Ebræo Lat. conversa et explicata. 1617.
Merceri Commentaria. 1580. (Rabbinical.)
Metzger's Liber Ruth illustratus. 1856.
Rambachii Notæ uberiores. 1719.
Ringler das Buch Ruth. 1812.
Stöckicht's Auslegung. 1856.
Strigelii Illustratio. 1571.
Werneri Illustrationes. 1740.

Cadogan's Book of R. illust. 1850. Plates.
Fuller's (Thomas) Commentary. 1650.
Lawson's (G.) Expository Discourses. 1805.
McCartney's Observations. 1842.
McGowan's Discourses on Ruth. 1781.
Toller's Discourses on the book of R. 1848.

SAMUEL.

Ambrose, Gregory N.

Bugenhagii Adnotationes. 1525.
Burmanni Explicationes. 1669.
Osiandri Commentarius. 1681.
Sarceri (Sebast.) Commentarius. 1559.

Commentators.

Schmidii (Seb.) Com. 1684. ("Princeps." —WALCH.)
Strigelii Commentaria. 1572.
Guild's (Wm.) Throne of David. 1660.
Steel's (Robt.) Life and times of S. 1860.
Willet's (And.) Expos. and Harmony. 1605.

KINGS.

Ambrose, Gregory Naz.

Bugenhagii Adnotationes. 1525.
Keil's (C. F.) Commentar. 1847.
Welleri Commentaria. 1557.
Keil's Com. Trans. by J. Murphy. 1857.

CHRONICLES.

Beckii Paraphrasis Chaldaica.
Keil's (C. F.) Apologetischer Versüch. 1833.
Loenhart Hypomnemata. 1608.
Michaelis et Rambachii Adnot. 1745.
Sarceri Commentarius. 1559.
Keil's Com. Trans. by Murphy. 1857.

EZRA.

Keil's Versüch ueber de integritat, &c. 1834.
Strigelii Argumenta et Scholiæ. 1572.
Wandalini Questiones Philolog., &c. 1654.
Lee on the Books of Ezra; spurious, and genuine. 1722.
Pemble's (Wm.). Works. 1659. (Remarks on various passages.)

NEHEMIAH.

Strigelii Illustrationes. 1572.
Wolfii Neh. Instaurata Hierosolyma. 1733.
Pilkington's Commentary. 1560. (Published by Parker Society. 1842.)
Stowell's (Hugh) Character of N. 1855.
Woodward's Hist. and character of N. 1849.

ESTHER.

Adami Observ. Theologico-philolog. 1710.
Baumgarten (M.) de Fide libri Estheræ. 1839.
Burmanni Explicationes. 1671.
Rambachii Notæ uberiores. 1720.
Rossi Specimen Var. Lect. sac. textus, &c.
Brent on Esther. Transl. by Stockwood.
Carson (Alex.) on the Book of E. 1833.
Davidson's Lectures on the book of E. 1859.
Hughes' Esther and her people. 1842.
Lawson's (Geo.) Discourses on E. 1804.
Lowrie's (John M.) Lectures on E. 1858.
McCrie's (Thomas) Lectures. 1838.

HAGIOGRAPHA.

Doderlini Scholia. 1779.
Ewald's (H.) Erklärung. 1836.
Köster, über den Strophischen character, &c. 1831.
Merceri (J.) Commentaria. 1651.

Commentators.

Meyer's Poetischen Bucher des alt. T.
Michaelis (J. H. et C. B.) Annotationes. 1720.
Michaelis et Rambachii Notæ uberiores. 1745.
Strakii Davidis aliarumque poetarum Heb. carmina. 1673.
Durell's (David) Critical remarks. 1770. See Monthly Review. 47:119.
Green's New trans. and notes. 1771.
Holden's (Lawrence) Paraphrase and notes. 1763.
Isham's (Z.) Divine philosophy. 1706.
Leigh's Poetical books of the O. T. 1657.
Lowth's Lectures on Heb. poetry. 1787.
Monthly Review. 68:1.

JOB. See HAGIOGRAPHA.

Gregory Th., Ambrose, Theodoret.

Bahrdt's Paraphrastische Erklärung. 1764.
Bezæ Commentaria. 1583.
Bockel's Uebersetzung und Erläutert. 1821.
Boullier, Observationes Miscellaneæ. 1758. (The author reproves Schultens for depending so much on the Arabic to explain Hebrew words and idioms.)
Blumenfeld's Uebersetzung u. Commentar. 1826.
Bridell, Job traduis d'apres l'original non punctue, avec un commentaire. 1818.
Buceri Commentarius. 1526.
Corderii Jobus elucidatus. 1646. (A catena of the Fathers.)
Drusii Nova versio et scholia. 1636. (Separate from his Com. on the whole Bible.)
Ebrard's Buch Hiob. überset. und Erläutert. 1858.
Eckerman, Observat. 1779. (Philological and critical.)
Grey, Liber J. in versiculos metrice divisus. 1740.
Hahn's Commentar. 1850.
Hardtii Commentarius. 1728.
Hengstenberg über das buch Hiob. 1835.
Heiligstedt, Commen. grammatico-historico-criticus. 1847.
Herbart's Gedankin über Buch Hiob. 1760.
Hirzel's Hiob Erklärt. 1852.
Hottingeri Analysis. 1689.
Justi's Hiob neu übersetzt und erläutert.
Kemmler's (G.) Weisheit der Urzeit. 1853.
Koster (F. B.) das Buch Hiob. 1831.
Krehlii Observationes. 1834.
Melsheimer's Buch Hiob Anmerkung. 1823.
Œcolampadii Exegemata. 1531.
Pineda, Comment. 1600. (The best Papal commentary on this book; and serves to complete the work of Lapide.)
Schärer's Grundtext, metrisch, &c., Erläutert. 1818.
Scheuchzeri Jobi physica Sacra. 1721.
Schmidii (Sebas.) Comm. 1670. (A coherent collection of the best observations.)

Commentators.

Schlottman's Verdeutscht, &c. 1851.
Schulteni (Albert) Nova versio, et commen. 1737. (A famous work; of which an abridgment has been published by Prof. VOGEL.)
Strigelii Scholia. 1570.
Terenti liber Jobi. (Gives the Chaldee, Greek, and Latin texts, and various readings.)
Titelmanni Elucidatio, cum adnot. 1547.
Umbreit's Uebersetz. u. Auslegung. 1824.
Vavasoris Commentaria. 1679.

Barnes' (Albert) New Tran. and notes. 1844.
Bellamy's (D.) Discourses. 1748.
Beza's Exposition. 1600. (Paraphrastic.)
Blackmore's Paraphrase. 1700.
Broughton's (H.) Translation with notes. 1610.
Carey's (C. P.) Translation with notes and preliminary dissertations. 1858.
Caryll's Exposition. 1676. ("Elaborate, learned, judicious, and pious."—WILLIAMS.)
——— Abridged by John Berrie. 1836.
Chappelow's New trans. and comm. 1752. (Curious.)
Conant's (Prof.) New Translation. 1858.
Costard on various parts of Job. 1747.
Croley's (Geo.) Book of Job. 1863.
Davidson's (A. B.) Com. with new translat. 1862.
Delitzsch's Commentary. Trans. by Bolton. 1866.
Evans' (Alfred R.) Lectures on Job. 1857.
Ewing's (W.) Observations. 1844. (Critical.)
Fry's (John) New translation and notes. 1827.
Garden's Improved vers. and notes. 1796.
Garnet's Nature, arguments, age, author, &c. 1749.
Hulbert's (C. A.) Thirty lectures on Job. 1853.
Heath's New version and comment. 1756.
Hodge's Elihu. 1750. (In no estimation.)
Hutchinson's 316 Discourses on Job. 1669.
Isham's Divine philosophy. 1706.
Kempe's Course of lectures on Job. 1855.
Lee's New translation and notes. 1837.
Lowth's (Wm.) Design, argument, style, &c. 1730.
Michaelis on Lowth's 32d lecture.
Noyes' (G. R.) New Trans. and notes. 1827.
Peters' Critical Dissertations. 1751. ("Valuable."—ORME. Refutes some of Warburton's positions.)
Princeton Review. 29:281.
Umbreit's Comment. (In Biblical Cabinet.)
Warburton's Div. Legation of Moses. 1766.
Wemyss' Job and his times. 1849.
Wesley's (Sam.) Dissertations and conjectures. 1736.
Worthington's (Wm.) Dissertations. 1743. (On the design of the book.)

Commentators.

Many of these writers on Job treat on the question whether a future state was the popular belief of the ancient Jews. See further, on that subject, *Faith of the Patriarchs*.

PSALMS. See HAGIOGRAPHA, IMPRECATIONS, MESSIANIC PSALMS.

Ambrose, Athanasius, Gregory Nys., Hilary, Augustine, Theophilact.
Amyraldi Paraph. cum annotationibus. 1762.
Berlini Psal. ex recentione textus Heb. 1805. (An excellent Latin translat., with useful notes.)
Berthier, les P. avec reflections. 1785.
Bezæ, Argumentis et Paraphrasis. 1566.
Bossuet, Dissertatio in Psalmos. 1693.
Buceri Enarrationes. 1526.
Bugenhagii Adnotat. 1535. (Preface by Luther.)
Bullingeri Consciones. 1570.
Burkii Gnomon. 1760.
Bythneri Lyra prophetica. 1650. (Of great use to a student of the Heb. language.)
Clauss Beiträge zur Exegese der P. 1831.
Dathii Ps. ex rescensione textus Heb. 1787.
Delitzsch's Commentar. 1860.
De Wette, Commentar.
Duport Metaphrasis; cum vers. Lat. 1666.
Fisher's Auslegung. 1590.
Geieri Com. adductis locis parallelis. 1709.
Gomari Davidis Lyra. 1637.
Hengstenberg's Commentar. 1842.
Hesusii Commentarius. 1586.
Hitzig's Historisch-Kritischer Com. 1835.
Hupfeld's Uebersetzt. und Augelegt. 1854.
Johnston, Paraphrasis poetica. 1741.
Lampii Commentarius. 1738.
——— Meditationes Exegeticæ. 1741.
Marini Annotationes cum nova vers. 1748.
Muis Commentarius. ("One of the best."—FELLER.)
Musculi Comm. 1550. (Many editions.)
Opitii Exercitationes. 1700. (Divisions, chronology, use, and abuse of the Psalms.)
Paulus' (H. E. G.) Clavis. 1815.
Reinhard's Ueberset. u. Erläuterung. 1818.
Riveti Opera. 1651.
Tholuck (A.) Ueberset. u. Auslegung. 1843.
Titelmanni Elucidatio. 1572.
Venemæ Commen. 1781. ("Excellent."—CLARKE.)
Vicars' Decapla. 1639. (A curious and useful work, drawn from ten languages.)
Westhemeri Explicatio. 1566. (Wholly from the Fathers.)
Zuingli Farrago Annotationum. 1528.
——— Translatio nova in ling. Latinam.

Alexander's (Jos. A.) New translation and Exposition. 1850.
Ainsworth's Annotations. 1612.
Allix's (Peter) Notes of interpretation. 1687.
Augustin's Homilies on the Psalms.

Commentators.

Baker's (Richard) Psalms evangelized in a continued explanation. 1811.
Bernard's (John) Short notes agreeably to the sense applied in the N. T. 1816.
Bonar's Christ and his ch. in the book of P. 1815.
Bouchier's Manna in the heart. 1855.
Boys' Key. (Dwells on the parallels.)
Buxtorf's Lyre of David.
Bythner's Lyre of David.
Champney's Textual commentary. 1852.
Cole's (Wm.) Key. 1788. (A concise and convenient explanation of words and allusions, selected from the best authors.)
Cope's Meditations on 20 selected psalms. 1547.
Dickson on the Psalms. 1645. (Old Scotch piety.)
Edwards' (Jos.) Devotional Expos. 1850.
Ewart's (John) Lectures on the P. 1822.
Exton's Sixty lectures on the P. 1847.
Fenwick on the Psalms. 1747. (Unique; the lines are the same as the Hebrew.)
Gesner's Use, dignity, and connection of the Psalms. 1630.
Gillie's Notes: devotional and practical. 1796.
Gower's Exposition of the difficult passages. 1709.
Hammond's Paraphrase and notes. 1649.
Hengstenberg on the Psalms. Translated by Fairbairn. 1848.
Hibbard's Chronological arrangement; with historical introductions. 1857.
Johnson's Holy David and his English translators. 1710.
Luther's Commentary. Trans. by H. Cole. 1837.
McGavin's Copious Index, and notes.
Maclin's Pastor's gift. 1835. (For families.)
Mant's Notes; critical and illustrative. 1824.
Merrick's New trans. Paraph. and notes. 1765.
Morrison (John) on the Psalms. 1828.
Neale's Com. from primitive and mediæval office books, of Gallican, Greek, Syriac, and Armenian rites. 1860.
Nicholson's David's harp tuned. 1662.
Phillips' Chrit. and philological Com. 1846.
Plummer's Studies on the book of P. 1867.
Pridham's (A.) Notes and Reflections. 1852.
Reeves' Collation of the Hebrew and Greek texts. 1800.
Ryland's Psalms restored to Messiah. 1853.
Stoddard's Imagery and ornaments of the P., and the mode of using them; from the earliest times. (Compiled from Jebb, Horsley, Patrick, &c.)
Tholuck's Commen. Trans. by J. Mombert. 1856.
Thompson's (And.) Lectures on the Psalms. 1826.
Thompson's (Mrs.) Prac. Illustration. 1826.
Thrupp's Study and use of the Ps. 1860.

Commentators.

Warner's Psalms illustrated and explained; with Dissertations and Notes. 1828.
Wilson's Evangelical and prophetical Expos. 1860.

ON PARTICULAR PSALMS.

Smith's David's blessed man.	Ps. 1.	1617.
Stoneham (Matthew) on	" 1.	1610.
Hildorp's Commentary on	" 2.	1742.
Custard's Commentary on	" 2.	1747.
Pitcairn's Zion's King.	" 2.	1851.
Smith's Garment of praise.	" 3.	1850.
Horton (Thomas) on	" 4.	1670.
Leighton (Abp.) on Ps. 4, 130, 132, 135.		1664.
——— Lectures on	Ps. 39.	1670.
Schroederi Com. philologicus.	" 10.	1605.
Cartwright's Polemic Comm.	" 15.	1658.
Downame's (Geo.) Lectures on	" 15.	1603.
Dale's Golden psalm.	" 16.	1847.
Frame's Christ in Gethsemane.	" 16.	1858.
Greenham's Commentary.	" 16.	1585.
Harper's Expo. of the 2d, 45th, 110th.		1862.
Agricola's Commentary.	Ps. 19.	1730.
Stevenson's Christ on the cross.	" 22.	1842.
Stevenson's The Lord our Shep.	" 23.	1846.
Sedgwick's Shepherd of Israel.	" 23.	1658.
Stoughton's Song of C.'s flock.	" 23.	1860.
Dale's (Tho.) Good shepherd.	" 23.	1845.
Newton's Pastoral char. of God.	" 23.	1857.
Harrison's Shep. and his sheep.	" 23.	1845.
Mossom's Preacher's tripartite.	" 25.	1657.
Halket's (Lady) Meditations on	" 25.	1778.
Owen (John) on	" 30.	1669.
Bingham's Lectures on	" 32.	
Reeves' (J. W.) Lectures on	" 32.	1859.
Taylor's (T.) David's Learning.	" 32.	1618.
Horton's Ten sermons on	" 42.	1674.
McDuff's Hart and the water brooks.	" 42.	1860.
Sibbs' Soul's conflict and vict.	" 42.	
Kennicott, Notæ Criticæ. Ps. 42, 43, 44, 48, 49.		
Vansittart's Trans. and notes.	Ps. 49.	1810.
Horton's Twenty Sermons on	" 51.	1675.
De Coetlogon's Chris. Penitent.	" 51.	1775.
Hildersham's 152 Lectures.	" 51.	1630.
Cowper's Good news fr. Canaan.	" 51.	1612.
Alexander's Penitent's prayer.	" 51.	1860.
Biddulph (T. T.) on	" 51.	1830.
Buck's (J.) Sermons on	" 51.	
Bull's (J. S.) Sermons on	" 51.	1824.
Hieron's Thirty Lectures on	" 51.	1614.
Smith's David's Repentance.	" 51.	
Pearson on Psalms 27, 84, 85, 87.		1660.
Horton's Seven sermons on	Ps. 63.	1675.
Sharp (Granville) on	" 68.	1805.
Clarke's (Rich.) Commentary.	" 68.	1763.
Dixon's New Interpretation.	" 68.	1811.
Parry's David restored.	" 73.	1660.
Pierson's Exercise under afflict.	" 85.	1647.
Reynolds (Bp.) on	" 90.	1632.
Stevenson (J.) on Gratitude.	" 103.	
Romaine's Nine sermons on	" 107.	1770.
Bergami's Commentary on	" 110.	1819.

Commentators.

Reynolds' (Bp. E.) Explica. Ps. 110. 1633.
Gouge's Saint's Sacrifice. " 116. 1635.
Chapman's (R.) Hallelujah. " 117. 1709.
Calvin's 22 Sermons on " 119.
Greenham (Richard) on " 119. 1660.
Manton's (Tho.) 190 Sermons. " 119. 1585. (Often reprinted. Full of solid criticism and devout remarks.)
Bridges (Charles) on Ps. 119. 1841.
Stephens' Lectures on " 119. 1861.
Cowper's (Bp.) Holy alphabet. " 119. 1623.
Pierce's Incarnat. of Jehovah. " 121. 1833.
Hutchinson's 45 Sermons on " 130. 1691.
Bethune's Hist. of a Pentinent. " 130. 1848.

PROVERBS. See HAGIOGRAPHA.

Ambrose, Theophilus, Gregory Naz., Basil.

Bezæ Expositio. (Died 735.)
Cartwright, Commentaria. 1618.
Danæi Commentarius. 1590.
Fabricii Carmen. in Proverb. Solom.
Hitzig's Uebersetz. und Ausgelegt. 1856.
Jaegeri Observationes. 1721.
Lavater, Commentaria. 1576.
Merceri Com. liter. crit. et gram. 1573.
Pettani Catena aurea Græcorum. 1576.
Schleusneri Commentaria. 1794.
Schulteni Versio cum Com. 1748.
Strigelii Scholia cum Argumentis. 1570.
Umbreit's (F. W. K.) Commentar. 1826.

Arnot's Laws from heaven for life on earth. 1858.
Brooks' New arrangement of the P. Notes. 1860.
Bridges' (C.) Exposition. 1847.
Case's (R. J.) Commentary. 1822.
Cleaver's (Robt.) Brief Explanation. 1615.
Cope's (M., of Geneva,) Commentary. 1580.
Day's (Wm.) Notes and dissertations. 1862. ("Deep and striking thoughts."—BICKERSTETH.)
Dimock's Crit. and explan. notes. 1791.
Gauntlett's (H.) Observations. 1813.
Grey's Hebrew Grammar. 1738. (With book of Proverbs annexed, divided according to the meter, with Massoretic readings, Pagnin's Latin version, Notes, Analysis, &c.)
Hunt's Observations. 1775. (Proposes emendations of the trans. "Important." —ORME.)
——— Dissert. on Prov. vii. 22, 23.
Jermin's Meditations. 1638.
Lawson's (Geo.) Exposition. 1821. (Practical.)
Nichols' (B. E.) Proverbs explained. 1842.
Stuart's (Moses) Commentary. 1852.
Taylor (Francis) on Proverbs. 1655.
Wardlaw's (Ralph) Lectures on Proverbs. 1862.
Wilcock's (Puritan) Sound Commentary. 1589.

Commentators.

ECCLESIASTES.

Gregory Nys., Gregory Thaum., Hippolytus, Theophilus A.

Bezæ Paraphrasis. 1588.
Buceri Commentarius. 1532.
Desvoux, Essai philosophique. 1760.
Du Viel, Explicatio literalis. 1681.
Elster's (E.) Commentar. 1854.
Fagii Versio cum notis. 1540.
Frankii Systema ethicis divina. 1724.
Guieri Comm. 1730. ("Inter optimas."—WALCH.)
Hahn Ueber den Predigerbuch Salomos. 1860.
Pineda Commentaria. 1609.
Rambachii Uberiores Adnotationes. 1720.
Schmidii (Seb.) Commentatio. 1691.
Strigelii Ecc. ad Ebraicam recognitus. 1573.
Varenii Gemmæ Salomonis. 1659.

Amer. Biblical Repository. 12:197.
Bernard's (Rich.) 86 Sermons. 1620.
Beza's Solomon's Sermon to the people. 1595.
Bridges' (Cha.) Exposition. 1848.
Buchanan's Eccl.: its meaning and lessons. 1859.
Christian Monthly Spectator. 4:524.
Desvoux's Philosophical and critical Essay. 1760. (With new version, old version, and paraphrase, in parallel columns.)
Du Viel's Commentary. 1679. (Superior.)
Granger's (Tho.) Commentary. 1621.
Greenway's New trans. and notes. 1781.
Hamilton's (Jas.) Lectures on E. 1851.
Hengstenberg's Com. Tr. by D. W. Simon. 1859.
Hodgson's New Trans. and notes. 1791.
Holden's (G.) Attempt to illustrate the Eccl. 1822. ("The best."—HORNE.)
Jermin's (M.) Commentary. 1639.
McDonald's (James) Exposition. 1793.
Methodist Quarterly Review. 9:173, 417.
Milne's Christian's daily walk. 1859.
Nisbit's Expos. and practical observ. 1694.
Preston's Hebrew text, with Latin version. 1845.
Princeton Review. 29:419.
Reynolds' (Bp.) Commentary. 1669. (Prized for its practical observations.)
——— Revised by Washburn. 1811.
Stuart's (Moses) Commentary. 1840.
Wardlaw's (R.) Lectures on Eccles. 1821.
Weis' New trans. and Exposition. 1857.
Young's (L.) Commentary. 1865.

SOLOMON'S SONG.

Cyprian, Gregory Nys., Ambrose.

Bauermeisteri Commentarius. 1828.
Bezæ Adnotationes. 1600.
Blaubach's Uebersetzt. u Erläuterung. 1855.
Bossuet, Canticum canticorum. 1695.

Commentators.

Brightmanni Analysis et Scholia. 1614.
Delitzsch's Untersücht und Ausgelegt. 1851.
Du Viel, Explicatio literalis: ex ipsis scripturam fontibus, Ebræorum ritibus, et idiomatis, veterum et recentiorum monumentis eruta. 1679.
Gerson (John.), Opusculum. 1420.
Hahn's Uebersetzt. und Erklärt. 1852.
Hengstenberg, Hohelied Sal. Ausgel. 1853.
Keri Cantici Salom. paraph. gemina. 1727.
Kistemakeri Illustratio. 1818.
Lowth, Prelectiones.
McPherson's Cant. Canticorum structura architectonica. 1857.
Magnus' Bearbeitung und Erklärung. 1842.
Markii Analysis et Comm. 1703.
Meinhold's Hohe Lied Salomo's. 1855.
Michaelis (J. H.) Adnotationes. 1720.
Paul, Etude sur le Cantique des Cantiques.
Sanchez, Annotationes criticæ. 1619.
Scheidii Diss. philologico-exegetica. 1670.
Sennerti Notæ philologicæ. 1671.
Thomæ Aquinatis Commentarium. 1520.
Titmanni Meletemata Sacra. 1816.
Uhlemanni Versio Latina et Com. 1821.
Weseneri (or Gebhard) Explicatio. 1624.
Weissbach's Erklärt, Uebersetzung. u. Dargestellung. 1858.

Brown's (Alex. W.) Discourses on Solomon's Song. 1848.
Burrowes' (George) Commentary. 1850.
Cole (J. W.) on the Prophecies. 1830.
Collings on the Intercourse of divine love between Christ and his Church. 1652.
Cotton's (Jno.) Explication. 1645. (Makes it describe the condition of the Church in all ages.)
Dathe's Philological and crit. notes. 1750.
Davidson's (Will.) Examination. 1817.
Durham's (James) Clavis Cantica. 1668. (Preface by John Owen.)
Gill's (John) Lectures on Sol. Song. 1728.
Good's (J. M.) Sacred Idyls. 1803. (Elegant.)
Guild's Lamb and his Bride. 1658.
Hall's (Joseph) Paraphrase. 1600.
Hammond's (Henry) Paraphrase. 1653.
Harmer's New commentary. 1768. (Drawn from accounts of Eastern nations.)
Hildersham's Paraphrase. 1672.
James' Exposition. (Extracts from the Fathers.)
Knolly's (Hansard) Exposition. 1656.
Krummacher's Solomon and the Shulamite. 1838.
Leigh's Annotations. 1657.
Lowth's Prelections. 1770.
Neale's (J. M.) Sermons on the Canticles. 1857.
Princeton Review. 21:503. 26:1.
Sibbs' (Rich.) Twenty sermons. 1641.
Stuart's (A. Moody) Exposition. 1857.
Taylor's (Charles) Holy Minstrel. 1820.
Whiston's Essay for restoring the canon. 1745. (Appendix.)

Commentators.

Williams' Translat., Commentary, and notes. 1800.
Withington's Commentary. 1860.

THE PROPHETS.

Hamakeri Commentaria. 1833. (Dwells at length on the birthplace, life, &c., of each prophet.)
Hitzig's Prophetisch. Bücher d. Alten Test. 1835.
Œcolampadii Commentaria. 1538.
Tossarii Paraphrases. (The author's real name was J. Sartorius. Other Reformed writers used assumed names to escape persecution.)
Van Till, Commentaria. 1744.
Venemæ (Hermann.) Lectiones Academicæ.

Guild's Harmony of all the prophets. 1649.
Horsley's First 9 prophetical books. 1800.
Lowth's (Wm.) Commentary. 1730.
Mayer's (Jno.) Commen. on all the prophets. 1652. (Examines divers translations and criticisms; ancient and modern.)
Noyes' Translation and chron. arrangement. 1831.
Smith's (John) Summary View. 1787. (A very convenient abstract from Lowth, Newcombe, Newton, Kennicott, and Blaney.)

ISAIAH.

Ambrose, Bazil.

Bossuet, Explication. 1704.
Bullingeri Homiliæ. 1570.
Caspar's Einleitung in I. 1848.
Doderlini Esaias; ex recensione textus Heb. 1789. ("Profound and elegant."—Rosenmuller.)
Drechler's Uebersetzung u. Erklärt. 1856.
Gesenius' Uebersetzt. mit comm. 1821.
Glassii Onomatologia Messiæ proph. 1648.
Gualtheri Sermones. 1583.
Heilbrunneri Commentaria. 1590.
Hendewerk, des Proph. I. chronol. geordnet übersetzung und Erklärung. 1838.
Heshusii Commentarius. 1617.
Hitzig's Uebersetzung und Ausgelegt. 1830.
Leighii Commentarius. 1727.
Markii Analysis Exegetica. 1720.
Meier's I. Erklärt. 1850.
Montani (Ariæ) Commentaria. 1599.
Œcolampadii Hypomnemeta. 1525.
Rambach's Gründliche Erklärung. 1741.
Sanctii Comm. cum Paraph. 1615.
Schellingii Animadversiones. 1799. (Only on the difficult passages.)
Varenii Comm. ex Concilio fontum; contra Judæos, Hæreticos, et Exorbitantes. 1708.
Vitringa (C.) Com. cum Prolegomenis. 1720. ("He has left all other interpreters of Isaiah far behind."—Rosenmuller.)
Zuinglii Explanatio cum Apologia. 1529.

Commentators.

Alexander's (J. A.) New Trans. and Expos. 1850.
Amer. Biblical Repos. 1:700.
Barnes' (Albert) Notes. 1855.
Calvin's Com. on I. Tr. by Cotton. 1609.
Dimock's Crit. and explan. notes. 1804.
Dodson's Tr. and notes. 1790. (Unitarian.)
Eclectic Review. 4th Series. 9:285. (Review of Henderson.)
Frazier's Paraphrase and notes. 1800.
Gataker's Annotations. 1630. (All his writings are of eminent value.)
Govett's Expos. with new version. 1841.
Henderson's New Trans. and Comm. 1840.
Holden's (L.) Notes; critical, historical, and practical. 1776.
Jackson's Annotations. 1682.
Kitto's Journal of Sacred Literature. 6:346. (On Jewish Commentators.)
Lowth's New translation and notes. 1730.
McCulloch's Lectures. 1791. (An Epitome of Vitringa.)
Princeton Review. 2:153. (On the genuineness.)
Stock's Isaiah; with the Hebrew, new translation, and notes. 1803.
Strache's Hebrew politics in the times of Sargon and Sennacherib, &c. 1853.
Theological and Literary Journal. 1:544. 2:1, 222, 402, 633. 3:60, 287, 384, 595.
White's Commentary. 1709. (Valuable notes on geography, history, &c.)
Williams' (Wm.) Commentary on I. 1858.
Durham's (Jas.) 72 Sermons on Ch. 53. 1650.
Hambleton's (John) Sermons. " " 1831.
Harris' (S.) Com. (Curious.) " " 1739.
McDonough's 24 Lectures. " " 1858.
Margoliouth's Lectures. " " 1846.
Milman's Devotional Expos. " " 1853.
Storr's Lectures. " "
Stewart's (J. H.) Lectures. " 55. 1846.

JEREMIAH.

Ambrose.

Altingii Commentaria. 1688.
Broughtoni Commentarius. 1606.
Bullengeri Conciones. 1575.
Catena Patrum Græcorum et Latinorum, Chislerii. 1623.
Erdmanni Curæ Exigeticæ. 1818.
Gaab's (J. F.) Erklärung, &c. 1824.
Kueper Interpretatio atque vindicatio. 1838.
Movers, de utriusque recensionis Vaticinior. Jeremiæ, Græcæ, Alexandrinæ, et Hebraicæ, Masoreticæ, indole, et origine, Com. Crit.
Œcolampadii Commentarius. 1533.
Schleusneri Dissertationes tres. 1800.
Schmidii (Sebastian.) Commentarius. 1685. ("The best of all the Expositions of this book"—WALCH.)
Spohn, Jeremias Vates. 1833.
Wiedenfeld's Jeremiah's Klagelieder. 1820.
Zuinglii Complanatio. 1531.

Commentators.

Bullinger's Twenty-six Sermons on J. 1575.
Dimock's Critical Notes. 1804.
Gataker's Annotations. 1630.
Lowth's Commentary. 1718.

LAMENTATIONS.

Bugenhagii Adnotationes. 1546.
Kalkari Illustrationes crit. et exeget. 1836.
Lessingii Observationes. 1770.
Œcolampadii Ennarrationes. 1533.
Schnurreri Diss. philol. critica. 1795.

Gataker's Annotations. 1633.
Henderson's (E.) New translat., with critical and exegetical notes. 1850.
Hull's Exposition by way of Lectures. 1618.
Lowth's Commentary. 1718.
Jewell's (Jos.) Contemplative Glance, &c. 1823.
Topsel's Commentary. 1615.
Udall's Commentary. 1637.

EZEKIEL.

Gregory Naz.

Greenhill, Expositio. 1660. (Doctrinal. One of the most celebrated of the Puritan divines.)
Havernick's Commentar. 1843.
Heilbrunneri Ezech. proph. in locos communes theologicos digesta. 1587.
Polani Analysis et Comment. 1608.
Pradi et Villipandi Explicatio. 1596. ("The best comment. on Ezekiel ever written."—HORNE.)
Starkii Commentarius. 1731.
Strigelii Ezech. ad Ebraicam veritatem recognitus. 1572.
Venema (H.) Lectiones Academicæ. 1790.

Dimock's Critical notes. 1804.
Fairbairn's (Patrick) Exposition. 1851.
Greenhill's (W.) Exposition. 1645.
——— ——— Revised by J. Sherman. 1846.
Guthrie's (Tho.) Discourses on Ezek. 1855.
Henderson's Critical and exegetical comm. 1855.
McFarlan on the Prophecies of Ezek. 1845.
Newcombe's Improved version, metrical arrangement, and exposition. 1788.
Bennett's Temple of Ezek. (Com. on chap. 40, 41, 42.) 1824.
Mead's (Matt.) Vision of the wheels. 1689.

MINOR PROPHETS. See PROPHETS.

Cyril Alex.

Abarbanel, Commentarius. (Jewish.) 1480.
Ackermani Proph. minores illustrati. 1830.
Bahrdt, Apparatus criticus. 1775. (Makes great use of the Septuagint, and Oriental versions.)
Burkii Gnomon. 1753.
Cocceii Commentarius. 1701.

Commentators.

Credneri Comment. Proph. minor. versionis Syriacæ indole.
Dahl (J. C. G.) Observationes philologicæ., 1798.
Danæi Commentarius. 1586.
Du Viel, Explicat. literalis ex scriptor. ipsis fontibus. 1680. (Lauded by CALMET.)
Fabricii (Steph.) Sacræ Conciones. 1641.
Heilbrunneri Loci communes. 1603.
Kalinsky, Illustratio. 1748. (Recommended by BP. WATSON.)
Lively, Adnot. 1587. (Extolled by POOLE.)
Lyseri Prelectiones Academicæ. 1709.
Marckii Annot. et Analysis exegetica. 1704.
Merceri Commentarii. 1573. (A work of vast erudition in regard to Hebrew usages, idioms, &c. It recites the comments of Kimchi, Aben Ezra, Jarchi, and other Rabbis.)
Schmidii (Joan.) Commentaria. 1585.
Schroeder, die Kleinen propheten. 1829.
Strigelii Argumenta et Scholia. 1572.
Thuani Exp. 1604. (Approved by ROSENMULLER.)
Croft's (G.) Sermons on the Minor P. 1811.
Danæus' (or Daneau) Commentary. Trans. by Stockwood. 1594.
Dimock's Critical and explanatory remarks. 1804.
Du Viel's Literal Exposition. 1680.
Henderson's New Trans. and Comm. 1845.
Hutcheson's (Geo.) Exposition. 1654. Preface by Calamy. (Strongly commended by ORME and WILLIAMS.)
Lowth on the Minor prophets. 1726.
Pocock's Commentary. 1659.
Pusey's (E. B.) Commentary. 1861.
Stokes on the Minor Prophets. 1659.
Wells' Help to the understanding, &c. 1723.

DANIEL. See DANIEL, PERIOD OF 1260 YEARS, SEVENTY WEEKS.

Ambrose, Cyril.

Alstedii Trifolium propheticum. 1640.
Bertholdt's Einleitung mit Einigen, Hist. und exeget. Excursen. 1808.
Brightmani Exp. partis difficilimæ. 1640.
Bullengeri Commentaria. 1575.
Geieri Prelectiones Academicæ. 1608.
Gesneri Dissertationes, et prefatio Chronol. 1601.
Havernich Ueber das Buch Daniel. 1836.
Heilbrunneri Loci communes. 1587.
Lengerke's Verdeutscht u. Ausgelegt. 1835.
Mendelii Commentaria. 1805.
Michaelis (J. D.) Epistolæ. 1773.
Michaelis (J. H.) Adnotationes philologicæ-exegeticæ. 1745.
Schröder (J. F.) Die kleineren Propheten. 1829.
Suaningii Commentaria. 1554.
Venemæ Dissertationes. 1754.
Wigandi Explicatio. 1564.

Commentators.

Auberlen's Mutual relation of Daniel and John. Tr. by A. Saphir. 1856.
Barnes' (Albert) Notes, &c. 1855.
Birks' Four prophetic Empires. 1845.
Brightman's Disquisitions. 1644.
Broughton's Daniel's visions. 1619.
Chandler's Antiquity, authority, &c. 1728.
Chauncey's (Isaac) Essay on D. prophecy. 1699.
Christian Review. 7:1.
Cox's (F. A.) Lectures on Daniel. 1833.
Crosthwaite's Lectures on Daniel. 1863.
Cumming's (John) Lectures on D. 1854.
Darby's Studies on the book of D. 1848.
Desprez's Apocalypse of the O. Test. 1865.
Dublin University Mag. 25:612. 27:497.
Eclectic Review. 4th Series. 15:53.
Folsom's Crit. and histor. interpret. 1842.
Frere's Combined view of Esdras, Daniel, and John. 1815.
Gaussen on the Book of Daniel. 1850.
Girdlestone's Observations. 1820.
Havernick's Critical Commentary. 1833.
Hengstenberg on Daniel and Zachariah. Translated by J. E. Ryland. 1847.
Holmes on the Apocalypse and Daniel. 1819.
Huit's Commen., Analysis, and Paraphrase. 1643.
Irving's (Edward) Babylon and infidelity doomed. 1826.
Joy's Exposition. 1855. (Gathered out of Melancthon, Œcolampadius, Pellican, and others.)
Literary and Theological Journal. 3:352.
Miles' (C. P.) Lectures on Daniel. 1841.
More's (Henry) Plain Exposition. 1681.
New Englander. 1:231.
Newton's (Sir I.) Observations on D. 1723.
Parker's (T.) Visions and prophecies of D. 1646.
Parker's (F.) Light thrown upon Thucydides. 1866.
Pemble's Remarks on difficult passages in Ezra, Nehemiah, and Daniel. 1659.
Pusey's Lectures on Daniel. 1864.
Roos' (M. F.) Exp. of such of the prophecies of D. as received their accomplishment under the New Testament.
Stephens' Proph. of Dan. and John. 1861.
Stuart's (Moses) Commentary. 1850
Tregelles's Visions of Daniel. 1840.
Tyro's Exp. of D. and the Revelation. 1838.
Venema's Diss. on various portions. 1768.
Walter's Genuineness of the bk. of D. 1863.
Wells' Help for the understanding of Daniel. 1716. (Gr. text, trans. paraph. and notes.)
Willet's Hexapla. 1610. (Much praised.)
Wilson's Dissertations on Daniel. 1824.
Brightman (Tho.) on the 12th ch.
Downame's (John) Lectures. 1630. (On the first 4 ch.)
Hawkins' (John) on the 2d chapter. 1833.
Wodrow on the 8th and following ch. 1844.

Commentators.

HOSEA.

Cyril Alex.
Abarbanel, Commentaria. 1687.
Burmanni Commentaria. 1718.
Goldwitzer's Anmerkungen. 1828.
Krackewitzii Commentarius. 1619.
Kuinoel, Hosea; Hebr. et Latin. 1792.
Meisneri Commentaria. 1620.
Merceri Commentaria. 1575. (Gives the com. of Kimchi, Aben Ezra, and Salomon Jarchi.)
Œcolampadii Adnotationes. 1529.
Shroeder's (J. G.) Anmerkungen, &c. 1782.
Stuckii Hoseas Propheta. 1828.
Vonderhardt, Comm. 1702. (Drawn from the Chaldee version, and distinguished Rabbins.)

Burrough's (Jer.) Exposition. 1643.
Drake's Notes; critical and exposit. 1853.
Neale's (W. H.) Commen. on Hosea. 1850.
Neale's (James) New translation and Comment. 1771. (A much improved edition. 1850.)
Princeton Review. 31:74.

ON SELECT PORTIONS.

Lightfoot on the first 4 chapters. 1684.
Downame on the first 4 chapters. 1608.
Reynolds (Bp.) on the 14th chapter. 1649.
Pierce (S. E.) " " " " 1822.
Sibbs (Rich.) " " " " 1639.
Margulïouth " " " " 1854.

JOEL.

Baueri Interpretatio. 1742.
Burmanni Commentaria. 1671.
Credner's Uebersetzt. und Erklärt. 1831.
Draconitis Comm. 1565. (With the Chaldee, Greek, and German versions.)
Grimm, Notæ Philologicæ. 1805.
Meyer's (E.) Uebersetzt. u. Erklärt. 1841.
Olshausen's die Weissagung. des J. 1829.
Pocockii Commentaria. 1705.
Rutger's (A.) Annotationes. 1830.
Svanborgii Versio Lat. cum notis, &c. 1806.
Chandler's (Sam.) Paraph. and critical com. 1735.
Pocock's Commentary on Joel. 1691.
Topsel's Commentary. 1613.

AMOS.

Dahl's Uebersetzt und Erläutert. 1795.
Gerhardi Adnotationes. 1663.
Harenburgii Amos Expositus. 1763.
Juynboll, Disputationes Academicæ. 1828.

Chandler's (Sam.) Paraph. and notes. 1735.
Drake's (W.) Sermons. 1853.
Goodman's Commentary. 1560.
Ryan's (Bp.) Expository Lectures. 1850.
Benefield's 21 Sermons on Chap. 1. 1613.
——— 21 Sermons on " 2. 1620.
——— Commentary on " 3. 1629.
Hall's (Tho.) Exposit. of chap. 4 to 9. 1661.

Commentators.

OBADIAH.

Crocii Specimen philologicum. (Hebrew, Chaldee, Syriac, and Arabic.)
Gesneri Commentarius. 1618.
Grynæi Commentarius. 1584.
Hendewerkii Com. et transl. Latina. 1835.
Jäger über das Zeitalter Obadias. 1837.
Kœnigii Dissertationes Theologicæ. 1647.
Leighii Commentaria. 1697.
Leusdeni Obadias; Ebraice et Chaldaice. 1656.
Pfeifferi Comment. cum versione Latina, et examen com. Aberbanelis. 1670.

Ellis' Commentary. 1660.
Marbury's Commentary. 1649.
Pilkington's (Jas.) Commentary. 1558.
Raynold's (John) Commentary. 1613.

JONAH. See JONAH.

Bircherodii Expos. liter. et exegetica. 1686.
Bugenhagii Expositio. 1561.
Forbigeri Prolusio de Lycophr. Cassandra cum epinetro de Jona. 1827.
Grimm, Jonas Oracula Syriaca, cum notis philolog. et crit. 1805.
Jäger's Sittlichreligiosen Endzweck. 1840.
Lavater's Predigten ueber d. Buch. J. 1775.
Mylii Com. grammatico-critica. 1640.
Pfeifferi Prelectiones. 1670.
Ursini Com. ex optimis interpretibus. 1580.

Abbott's (Abp.) Expos. 1600. Reprinted 1845.
Broad's (John) Lectures on Jonah. 1860.
Cunningham's (J. W.) Lectures on J. 1815.
Desprez's Book of Jonah; illustrated by discoveries at Nineveh. 1859.
Drake's Notes; critical and explan. 1853.
Eclectic Review. 4th Series. 20:217.
Edwards' (Henry) Exposition. 1837.
Fairbairn on Jonah. 1855.
Harding's Expos. lectures on Jonah. 1855.
Hooper's Ouersighte and deliberacion vppon Jonas. 1550. (Pub. by the Parker Soc.)
King's (John) Lectures on Jonah. 1600.
Macpherson's Lectures on Jonah. 1849.
Peddie's Practical Exposition. 1842.
Preston's (M. M.) Lectures on Jonah. 1840.
Sibthorp's (R. W.) Pulpit Recollections. 1835.
Southern Quart. Review. 22:505.
Young's (G.) Lectures on Jonah. 1819.

MICAH.

Chytræi Commentarius. 1565.
Draconitis Explicatio—cum translationibus Chaldaica, Græca, Latina, et Germanica. 1565.
Graveri Explicatio. 1664.
Hartman's neu Ueberset. und Erläut. 1800.
Justi's Uebersetzung u. Erläuterung. 1799.

Gilby on the Prophecy of Micah. 1591.
Pocock's (Edward) Works. 1680.

Commentators.

NAHUM.

Abarbanel, in Nahum. 1703.
Bibliandri Translatio et Exegesis. 1534.
Capelli (Lud.) Observationes. 1689.
Chytræi Commentarius. 1565.
Hafenrefferi Commentarius. 1663.
Kalinsky, Vaticinia N. illustrata. 1748.
Kreeneri Expos. 1808. (Able criticism.)
Middledorpf's Uebersetz. u. Anmerk. 1808.
Ursini Hypomnemeta. 1652.
Van Hœke, Explicatio. 1709.
Wildii Meditationes. 1712.

HABAKKUK.

Abichtii (Joann. Geo.) Adnotationes. 1732.
Capitonis Enarrationes. 1526.
Garthii (Helvici) Commentarius. 1605.
Haenlein Symbolæ Criticæ. 1795.
Kalinsky, Vaticinia Chabacuci illus. 1748.
Ranitzii Introductio. 1808.
Scheltingi Com. philol.-theologica. 1747.
Stickel Prolusio ad interpret. tertii capitis. 1827.
Van Hœke, Explicatio analytica. 1709.
Wolf's (A. A.) Uebersetz. u. krit. com. 1822.

Attersoll on Habakkuk. 1614.
Marbury's Commentary. 1650. ("Full of matter."—BICKERSTETH.)

ZEPHANIAH.

Buceri Commentarius. 1528.
Gebhardi Z. a Abarbanel. et al. vind. 1701.
Lareni Tuba Tsephaniæ. 1653.
Nolteni Com. cum Prolegomenis. 1724.
Selnecceri Ausleg. üb. d. Sophoniam. 1566.
Van Hœke, Explicatio Analytica. 1709.

HAGGAI.

Draconitis Versio Latina et explic. 1549.
Grynæi (Jo. Jacob.) Commentarius. 1580.
Merceri Scholia et Versio. 1551.
Reinbeckii Exercitationes. 1692.
Scheibelii Observ. crit. et exeget. 1822.
Tarnovii Commentaria. 1624.
Uhlandi Dissertatio exegetica. 1784.
Varenii Trifolium propheticum. 1662.
Wokenii Adnotationes exegeticæ. 1719.

Grynæus' Com. Tr. by Featherstone. 1600.
Moore's Prophets of the Restoration. 1855.
Pemble's Exposition. 1640.
Pilkington's Exp. 1560. (Parker Soc. 1842.)
Rainolds' Prophecy of Haggai. 1649.

ZECHARIAH.

Andalæ Dissertationes in præcipua Zachariæ dicta. 1720.
Balduini Commentarius. 1610.
Bieamani Commentatio. 1699.
Burges, Etudes exegetiques et crit. 1841.
Dorschæi Synopsis Theol. Zach. 1637.

Commentators.

Draconitis Zacharias, cum translationibus Chaldaica, Græca, Latina, ac Germanica. 1564.
Forbergii Com. critica et exegetica. 1824.
Koesteri Meletemata crit. et exeget. 1818.
Reinbeckii Exercitationes. 1694.
Tarnovii Commentaria. 1636.
Van Hœke, Explicatio Analytica. 1711.
Varenii Trifolium propheticum. 1664.
Vitringæ Commentarius. 1734.

Blaney's New translation and notes. 1797.
Hengstenberg's Com. Tr. by Ryland. 1847.
Kimchi's Com. Trans. by McCaul. 1837.
Moore's Prophets of the restoration. 1855.
Park's Controv. with a Jewish Rabbi. 1832.
Raynolds on Zachariah. 1640.
Stonard's Com. and corrected trans. 1824.
Venn's Mistakes in religion exposed. 1807.
Wardlaw's (Ralph) Lectures on Z. 1861.

MALACHI.

Balduini Commentarius. 1610.
Bohlii Disputationes et Explicationes; cum commentariis Rabbinorum. 1637.
Draconitis Explic. cum Vers. Chaldæa. 1564.
Reinke's Einleitung, Grundtext, u. Ueberset.
Tarnovii Commentaria. 1624.
Ursini Hypomnemeta. 1670.
Van Hœke, Explicatio Analytica. 1709.
Van Till, Commentaria analytica. 1701.
Varenii Trifolium propheticum. 1663.
Venemæ (H.) Commentarius. 1759.
Vitringæ Observationes sac. Lib. iv. 1734.

Moore's Prophets of the Restoration. 1855.
Pocock's Works. 1667.
Schlatter's Exposition and notes. 1650.
Stock's (Richard) Commentary. 1641.
Torshell's Exercitationes. 1641.

New Testament. See ANALYSES, HERMENEUTICS, INTRODUCTIONS.

Alberti Observ. philologicæ. 1725. (Illustrates the style and meaning of New Test. writers, from the Greek classics.)
Altmani Observ. philol.-criticæ. 1753.
Baumgarten Crusii, Commentar. 1817.
Beausobre, Remarques historiques, critiques, et philologiques. 1742.
Bedæ Catenena Græca. 1520.
Bengel's Gnomon. 1734. (Invaluable.)
Bezæ Annotationes. 1565.
Bibliotheca Fratrum Polonorum. 1656. (Socinian. Abounds in good criticisms.)
Bos, Observationes. 1710. (Excellent.)
Bullingeri Commentaria. 1554.
Calvini Comm. 1670? Curavit et prefatus est a Tholuck. 1834. ("Of expositors, I know none to be compared with Calvin." —WOTTON.)
Cameronis Myrothecium. 1632. (Observations on select passages.)
Carpzovii Commentaria critica. 1758.

Commentators.

Cartwright, Commentaria practica. 1630.
Cassauboni Adnotationes. 1660.
Castelii Adnotationes. 1667.
Crameri Catenæ Græc. patrum in N. Test. 1844.
Crellii Opera Exegetica. 1656. (Socinian.)
Crome's Beiträge zur Erklärung. 1828.
Doughty, Analecta Sacra. 1658.
Du Viel, Explicatio literalis. 1672. (In actis eruditor. Du V. was a learned Baptist convert from Popery. His comm. is eminently valuable, and is reprinted by the Hansard Knollys Society.)
Elsneri Observationes sacræ. 1720.
Erasmi Paraph. et Annotationes. 1516. (In 1546, the clergy of England were enjoined to procure the New Testament, and the paraphrase of Erasmus, "for their better instruction;" and in 1550, the work was ordered to be set up in all the churches, "that the common people might read it.")
Ernesti Institutio Interpretis. 1780.
Fabricii Observationes Selectæ. 1712.
Flaccii Glossa compendaria. 1580.
Fritzche's Commentar. 1830. (Prolix.)
Gebseri Explicatio e Zend-Avesta. 1824.
Griesbachii Com. critica in textum. 1798.
Gualtperi Sylloge vocum exoticarum.
Heinsii Exercitationes Sacræ. 1639.
Hengelii Annotationes. 1824.
Heuman's Erklärung. 1750.
Hunnii Thesaurus Evangelicus. 1600.
Keuchenii Adnotat. 1755. (Philological.)
Knatchbul, Animadversiones. 1693.
Koppii Annotationes. 1738. (Reprinted 1818 and 1832, in 10 vols., 8vo.)
Krebsii Observationes ex Flav. Josepho. 1755.
Kypke, Observationes. 1755. ("Nothing of the kind superior."—MICHAELIS.)
Lightfoot, Horæ Hebraicæ et Talmudicæ. 1684. ("Held in the highest esteem."—HORNE.)
Loesneri Observationes. 1777. (Useful collection of parallel passages.)
Lyræ Glossa ordinaria. 1507. (A book regarded as having no small part in bringing on the Reformation. "Lyra's lyre woke Luther's dance.")
Marlorati Expositio Catholica. 1605. (Contains the Latin version of Erasmus, and a synopsis of the expositions of numerous great Protestants.)
Meuschen, N. Test. ex Talmude, et antiquit. Hebr. illustrat. 1736. (Highly esteemed.)
Meyer's (H. A. W.) Critisch exegetischer Com. 1856. (The Greek text, new German translation, and Commentary.)
Michælis Notæ Criticæ. 1706.
Montani (Bened. A.) Elucidationes. 1575.
Mori Prelectiones. 1661. (Philological.)
Olshausen's Commentar fur prediger. 1833.
Ottii Spicelegium ex F. Josepho. 1741.
Palairet Obs. philologico-criticæ. 1752.

Commentators.

Priscæi Comm. 1660. (From the Fathers.)
Quesnel, le N. T. avec Reflexions. 1693.
Reiche, Com. crit. 1856. (On the difficult passages.)
Rosenmulleri (J. G.) Scholia. 1805.
Scaligeri (Jos.) Notæ. 1545.
Schmidii (Seb.) Animadversiones; cum versione nova. 1658. ("Greatest of all biblical commentators."—WALCH.)
Schoetgenii Horæ Ebraicæ et Talmudicæ. 1742.
Schottii Isagoge historico-critica. 1830. (A very valuable supplement to Lightfoot.)
Schulteti Paraph. et Annot. grammaticæ, historicæ, logicæ, et theologicæ. 1720.
Simon, Hist. crit. et principaux Comment. 1689.
Slichtingii Commentaria. 1656.
Spangenbergii Tabulæ Concionaturis. 1560.
Storr (G. C.), Dissertationes exegeticæ. 1790.
——— Notitiæ historicæ. 1788.
Tholuck, Expositio. 1831.
Valckenarii Scholia. 1780.
Valpy, Notæ theologicæ et philol. 1816.
Walchii (J. G.) Observationes. 1727.
Wetsteinii Prolegomena. 1751.
Winkleri (J. D.) Hypomnemeta. 1745.
Wolfii Curæ criticæ. 1741.
Zwinglii Adnotationes. 1526.

Ainsworth's Commentary. 1600.
Alford's Greek Testam. (Revised version, various readings, prolegomena, references, and comment. A very important work.)
Ash's Notes and comments. 1849.
Ashton's Christian Expositor. 1774.
Barnes' (A.) Notes. 1855. (For Youth.)
Baxter's Paraphrase and notes. 1685.
Bengel's Gnomon. 1747. Tr. by Badinel.
Bliss' (Geo.) Explanatory notes. 1832.
Bloomfield's Greek text, with English notes. 1841.
——— Synoptica. 1826. (A critical digest of numerous eminent works, especially Wetstein's exegetical remarks. Almost necessary to a Bible student.)
Bowyer's Critical conjectures and observations. 1782. (Selected from Barrington, Gosset, Shultz, Markland, and others. "The best that can be said of these observations is that they are often ingenious."—ORME. The work was edited, with notes, by Bp. Barrington. 1815.)
Boyse's Expos. 1827. (For family use.)
Bruce's (Wm.) Commentary. 1838.
Cartwright's (Thomas) Annotations. 1618. (Confutes the Rhemish translation.)
Chapman's Critical and explanatory notes.
Churton & Jones' Expos. (Plates.) 1865.
Crosby's (Howard) Notes and Scholia. 1862. (On the surface difficulties of the text.)
Dalton's (Wm.) Commentary. 1838.
Davidson's Pocket Commentary. 1834.

Commentators.

Doddridge's Family Expos. 1738. ("Doddridge is my favorite among divines."—ROBT. HALL.)
Gillie's N. Test., with devotional reflections. 1790. (For family use.)
Gilpin's (W.) Exposition. 1804.
Girdlestone's (Charles) Commentary. 1836.
Guyse's.Paraphrase. 1745. (Unimportant.)
Hammond's Paraphrase and Notes. 1659.
Heylin's Lectures. 1760.
Hinchcliff's Studies of the N. T. 1843.
Kenrick's Exposition. 1807. (Unitarian.)
Keyworth's Expositor. 1825. (For family worship. Commended by Dr. WAUGH.)
Knatchbull's Annotations. 1693.
Leigh's Annotations. 1650. (Translated into Latin and German.)
Lindsey's N. T. compared with the original, and the several English translations. 1736.
Longhurst's Companion to the N. T.
Mayer's (John) Comm. 1631. (Formerly thought to be the best, next to Trapp.)
Moody's Exposition; with notes and translations. 1846.
Olshausen's Com. 1851. Trans. by Brown.
——— ——— Tr. by Loewe; with notes.
Penn's (Granville) New translation; with preface and notes. 1838.
Perrin's Book of the New Covenant. (Revision of the Greek text, and new transl.)
Platt's Self-interpreting N. Testam. 1827. (Thousands of various readings, and parallel passages; collected from approved critics.)
Quesnell's Reflections on each verse. 1720.
Scott's (Wm.) N. T. illustrated. (Corrections of the text, and notes, from various authors.)
Sharp's (Sam.) Critical notes. 1856.
Simon's Crit. Hist. of the principal commentators. 1695. Trans. by Webster.
Stanhope's Paraphrase and Comm. 1751.
Sumner's (Abp.) Practical Expos. 1837.
Tholuck's Com. Trans. by Kaufman. 1837.
Townsend's Chronological arrangement and notes. 1838.
Trollope's Analecta. 1834. (Critical and philological; digested from the best authors.)
Turnbull's (Joseph) Notes, &c. 1854.
Valpy's Gr. Test. with Eng. notes. 1810.
Wesley's (John) Explanatory notes. 1764.
Weston's (W.) Critical Conjectures. 1748.
Whitby's Paraphrase and Comment. 1703.
Wilson's Explan. of the New Testam. by the early Fathers, &c. 1797. (New edition, 1838.)
Wynne's New Testament collated with the Greek; with notes. 1764.

FOUR EVANGELISTS. See DURATION OF OUR LORD'S MINISTRY, HARMONIES, MONOTESSARON.

Basil, Theophylact.

Commentators.

Alexandri Expos. literalis et moralis. 1707.
Baumgarten's (L. F. O.) Commentar. 1846.
Boisii Veteris interpretatio cum Beza, aliis, collatio. 1855. ("Exquisite criticism."—TODD.)
Buceri Interpretatio. 1554.
Catena aurea: Thomæ Aquinatis. 1474.
Chemnitii Harmonia Evangelica. 1600. (A commentary as well as Harmony. "I am beholden every way to Chemnitius."—LEIGH.)
Crameri Catena Græcorum patrum. 1838.
Dorchæi Com., Analysis, &c. 1706.
Ewald's (H.) Uebersetzt. u. Erklärt. 1850.
Gualtheri Archetypi Homiliarum. 1600.
Himmelii Postilla in Evang. 1650.
Hoffmani Demonstratio Evangelium. 1773. ("Learned and judicious."—ORME.)
Lucæ (De Bruges) Commentaria. 1606.
Lyseri Paraph. et Commentaria. 1590.
Olearii Observationes Sacræ. 1743.
Russworm's Untersuchung über den Ursprung, &c. 1797.
Saa (or De Sas) Scholia. 1596. (Often reprinted.)
Sandii Interp. paradoxæ IV. Evang. 1670.
Sarcerii Scholia. 1538. (Many editions.)
Schulteti Exercit. 1624. (Philological.)
Thomæ (Aquin.) Glossa continua. 1260.
Tischendorfii Synopsis, ordine chronologico, cum commentario.
Wallæi Com. ex antiq. illustrata. 1653.
Wichelhaus' Kommentar. 1855.

Adams' (Tho.) Exposition. 1805 and 1837. ("Holy and solid."—BP. WILSON.)
Bickersteth's Practical reflections on the plan of a harmony. 1841. (Selections from various expositors.)
Birk's (T. R.) Horæ Evangelicæ. 1852. (Structure, design, &c., of the gospels.)
Bland's (M.) Annotations. 1829. (A compilation from the best old authors.)
Boucher's Manna in the house. 1853. (Daily meditations.)
Calvin's Com. 1584. Tr. by E. Paget.
Campbell's (Geo.) Trans. and lectures. 1789.
Clarke's (Sam.) Paraphrase and notes. 1741.
Cotton's (Archdeacon) Notes. 1857.
Ebrard's Gospel History.
Elsley's Annotations. 1812. (Vehemently praised in the British Critic. Revised and reprinted by Walker. 1844.)
Ford's Gospels illustrated from ancient and modern authors.
Gillies' Spirit of the Gospels. 1818. (Pious.)
Harcourt's 193 Lectures on the Gospels harmonized. 1851.
Jacobus' Critical and explan. notes. 1849.
Jones' (John) Illustrat. 1808. (Unitarian.)
Jowett's Christian Visitor. 1838.
Juke's Characteristic differences of the four gospels. 1853.
Kenrick's Hist. writings of the N. T. 1807.

Commentators.

Lardner's Credibility of the Gospel history. 1730.
Lightfoot's Horæ Hebraicæ. 1675.
Livermore's (A. H.) Commentary. 1841.
Longking's Crit. and explan. notes. 1853.
Lyttleton's Explanatory notes. 1856.
Macknight's Harmony and Commen. 1763.
Mann's (Bp.) Notes. 1780. (A family book.)
Marlorati's Catena. Tr. by Timme. 1750.
Marsh's Dissertations on the Composition of the Gospels. 1800.
Meyer's Commentary. 1855.
Mempriss' Harmony and Exposition. (An extensive mass of introductions, illustrations, notes, indexes, maps, &c., from the best authors.)
Newman's (J. H.) Catena aurea. 1842.
Pearce's (Bp.) Comm. 1772.
Riddle's British Com. on the Gospels. 1843. (A respectable compilation.)
Ripley's (H. J.) Notes. 1850.
Robinson's Evangelists and the Mishna. 1859.
Smith's (James) Dissertations, and Synopsis of parallel passages. 1853.
Stabback's Annotations. 1809.
Stier's Words of Jesus. Tr. by Pope. 1859.
Strong's (James) Harmony and exposition; with analytical dissertations. 1852.
Sumner's (Abp.) Practical Expos. 1838.
Thomas Aq. Catena aurea. Trans. 1845.
Thompson's (And.) Practical Lectures. 1816.
Thompson's (Robt.) Crit. and explan. Notes. 1811.
Townson's (Tho.) Discourses. (Chiefly discusses the design of each gospel, and the time and place of writing. "A capital performance."—LOWTH.)
Trapp (Joseph) on Difficult passages. 1743.
Westboy's Exposition. 1837. (Experimental.)
Westcott's Histor. and explan. notes. 1861.
Wheedon's Commentary. 1862.
Williams (Isaac) on the Study of the Gospels. 1842.
Wilson's (John) Key to the critical reading of the Gospels.

MATTHEW. See MATTHEW.

Ambrose, Athanasius, Chrysostom, Cyprian, Hilary.

Crucigeri Enarrationes. 1540.
Gomari Selectorum loc. explicatio. 1631.
Gratz's Krit.-historischer Com. 1823.
Hegendorfii Enarrationes. 1624.
Kirstenii Notæ; ex collatione textum Arabicorum, Ægyptiacum, Syriac., Ebraicum, Græc., Lat., &c. 1620.
Meisneri (J.) Exercitationes. 1654.
Melancthon's Annotationes.
Munsteri (Seb.) Adnotationes. 1540.
Olearii Observationes. 1675.
Pelargi Questiones et Responsiones. 1612.
Pfaffii Notæ Exigeticæ. 1721.
Sauberti Variæ lectiones textus. 1660.

Commentators.

Van Till, Analysis, Notæ, &c. 1687. (Agt. Deists, and nominal Christians.)

Alexander's (J. A.) Exposition. 1860.
Blackmore's Paraphrase and notes. 1705.
Chrysostom's Homilies on M., with notes.
Coglan's Comm. and marginal ref. 1832.
Dunster's Synopsis. 1812.
Ford's Gospel of M. illustrated from ancient and modern authors. 1859.
Goodwin's (H.) Commentary. 1857.
Harte's (W. M.) Lectures on M. 1834.
Jones' (Wm.) Vindication of the former part of M.'s gospel, from Whiston's charge of dislocation. 1719.
Knowles (J. Sheridan) on Matthew. 1855.
Langes' Commentary. 1861.
Lodge's (O.) Lectures on M. 1818.
Nast's Com., critical and doctrinal. 1864.
Overton's (C.) Expository preacher. 1850.
Owen's (John J.) Commentary. 1857.
Penrose's (John) Explan. Lectures. 1832.
Percival's (C. G.) Plain Lectures. 1845.
Porteus' (Bp.) Lectures. 1802.
Scott's (Dan.) New version and notes. 1741. (Corrects some errors of Mill.)
Scrivener's (F. H.) Notes on Matt. 1845. (Critical remarks on the more difficult passages; from the Syriac, Latin, and early English versions.)
Wasse's (W.) Annotations. 1832.
Watson's (Rich.) Exposition. 1799.

ON SELECT PORTIONS.

Williams (J.) on the authenticity of ch. 1, 2.
Blakeley's lectures on the first 4 ch. 1842.
White's (Tho.) lectures on ch. 4 to 7. 1654.
Blackwood (Chris.) on the first 10 ch. 1659.
Leighton (Abp.) on the first 9 chap. 1660.
Vaughn's Sermons on 11th ch.
Manton on the 25th chapter.

MARK. See MARK.

Danæi Questiones et Scholia. 1594.
Gomari Selectorum loc. illustratio. 1633.
Knobel de Evang. Marci origine. 1831.
Myconii Commentarius. 1538.

Alexander's (Joseph A.) Exposition. 1861.
Bouchier's Manna in the house. 1852.
Bland's (Dr. M.) Annotations. 1828.
Dunster's Synopsis. 1812.
Forshall's Mark arranged in parts; with notes, preface, summaries, &c. 1862.
Owen's (John J.) Commentary. 1857.
Percival's (C. C.) Lectures on M.
Petter's Commentary. 1661. (Spiritual, but spread over 2 vols., folio.)
Watson's (Rich.) Commentary. 1800

LUKE. See LUKE.

Ambrose, Athanasius, Cyril, Gregory Naz., Epiphanius, Theodoret.

Agricolæ (Fran.) Commentarius. 1599.

Commentators.

Bornemanni Scholia. 1700. (Philological.)
Corderii Catena Græcorum patrum. 1628.
Lamberti Commentationes. 1524.
Lücke's (F.) Kommentar. 1820.
Oosterzee's Kommentar. 1861.
Planck, Observ. de Lucæ evang. a Schleiermacero proposita. 1819.
Weberi Authentia, &c. 1823.

Cyril's Com. on Luke. Tr. by R. P. Smith. 1859.
Dunster's (C.) Synopsis. 1812. (Date, &c.)
Foote's (J.) Lectures. 1839. ("Very useful." —BICKERSTETH.)
Major's Interlineary translation and notes. 1826. (A very convenient book.)
Oosterzee's Com. Trans. by Sophia Taylor. 1863.
Ryle's (J. C.) Exposition. 1859.
Schleiermacker's Critical Essay, &c. 1825. (Neological.)
Starck's Commentary. 1866.
Sumner's (Abp.) Exposition. 1839. (Practical.)
Thompson's (James) Lectures on L. 1849. (Highly commended by KITTO.)
Trollope's (W.) Commentary. 1848.

JOHN. See JOHN.

Basil, Chrysostom, Cyril Alex.

Astié, Explication. 1864.
Baumgarten Crusius, Auslegung. 1843.
Bugenhagii Commentarius. 1550.
Casiodori Annotationes. 1525. (Chiefly an argument for the Divinity of Christ.)
Chrytæi Commentaria et Scholia. 1556.
Corderi Catena LXX. Patrum. 1628.
Cromii Probabilia haud probabilia. 1819. (Review of Bretschneider.)
Gomari Explic. loc. selectiorum. 1640.
Lampe, Comm. analytico-exigeticus. 1724. (The most extensive commentary on this gospel ever published; and one not excelled.)
——— Dissertationes Philologicæ. 1737. (A necessary supplement to the commentary.)
Lücke's Commentar. 1840–1856.
Lyseri Disputationes Exigeticæ. 1620.
Meyer's Krit. exeget. Handbuch über d. J. 1818.
Matthäi (G.) Auslegung, &c. 1837.
Munteri Symbolæ ad interpret. evang. J. ex marmoribus et nummis. 1828.
Nefanii Com. 1684. (Against Grotius and others.)
Rolloci Com. cum Harmonia. 1599.
Schmidii (Seb.) Resolutio brevis. 1685.
Steinii Authentia evangel. J. contra Bretschneideri objectiones. 1830.
Storr über d. Zweck der evang. Geschichte. 1810.
Stronck de Doctrina et dictione J. 1797.

Commentators.

Tarnovii Comment. quo verba et phrases ex Græca, Hellenistica, Ebraica, et cognatis orientalibus linguis, explicantur. 1629.
Tholuck (A.), Com. zu d. Evang. J. 1827.
Titmanni Meletemeta Sacra. 1816.
Usteri Commentatio Critica. 1833.
Virginii Selectissimæ Notæ. 1647.
Weberi Authentia capitis ultimi, &c. 1823.
Wegscheider's Einleitung. 1806.

Anderson's (Robt.) Practical Expos. 1841.
Beith's (A.) Christ our life. 1857.
Bloomfield's (Bp.) Lectures on J. 1823.
Bosanquet's Fourth seal. 1856. (Homilies.)
Brown's (G. J.) Lectures on John. 1862.
Clagget's Paraphrase and notes. 1693.
Chrysostom's Homilies on John.
Clowes' (J.) Translation and notes. 1819. (Swedenborgian.)
Foote's (James) Lectures on J. 1858.
Heberden's Reflections on John. 1830.
Hengstenberg's Commentary. 1855.
Hutchinson's (George) Exposition. 1657. (Practical.)
Jacobus' (M. W.) Notes, critical and expository. 1864.
McIntyre's Philosophical Comment. 1833. (Against Atheists and Infidels.)
Marloratus' Expos. Trans. by Timme. 1575.
Merrick's Crit. and grammat. Notes. 1764.
Moysey's Lectures on John. 1823.
Patterson's (J. B.) Lectures on John.
Pollock's Commentary on the Gospel of J.
Rhees' (Louis) Annotations. 1846.
Shephard's (Archdeacon) Notes. 1796 and 1844. (Critical.)
Sumner's (Bp.) Exposition. 1835.
Tholuck's Comm. Trans. by C. P. Krauth. 1859. (Very valuable to scholars.)
Titman's Comm. Trans. by Young. 1845. (Notes from Tholuck, Lücke, Kuinoel, &c.)
Turner's (S. H.) Commentary. 1854.
Wade's (T.) Notes on the Gospel of John, as translated by five clergymen. 1857.

ON SELECT PORTIONS.

Arrowsmith's God-man. 1660. On ch. 1.
Bibliotheca Sacra. (On ch. i. 1–18.)
Hildersham's 180 Lectures on ch. 4. 1629.
Clagget's (W.) Paraph. and notes " 6. 1693.
Bryson on " 8.
Pitman on first 10 chapters. 1846.
Bonnet's Family of Bethany. ch. 11. 1855.
Watson's Lazarus of Bethany. " 11. 1853.
Beausobre's Resurrection of Lazarus. 1822.
Drummond's Last scenes in the life of Christ. 1856.
Jones' (John B.) Lectures on chap. 14, 15, 16. 1840.
Jones' (Joseph) Sermons on chap. 13 to 17. 1839.
Cogswell's 26 Sermons on chap. 17. 1839.
Burgess' (Ant.) 145 Sermons on " 17. 1656.
Manton on " 17.

Commentators.

Newton's (Geo.) Exposition of ch. 17. 1660.
Scobel's (Edw.) Christ's intercessory prayer. 1848.
Jefferson's (John) Sermons on ch. 17. 1828.
Burgess' (Ant.) Exposition of " 19. 1656.

ACTS OF THE APOSTLES. See APOSTLES, PLANTING OF CHRISTIANITY.

Chrysostom.

Amyraldi Commentarius. 1654.
Baumgarten's (M.) Apostelgeschichte. 1852.
Bugenhagii Commentarius. 1524.
Callixti Com. literalis. 1663.
Capelli Historia Apostol. illustrata ex epistolis Paulinis. 1683.
Casaubon (J.), Exercitationes. 1615.
Crameri Catena Græcorum patrum. 1620.
Heinrichii Annotationes. 1792.
Hildebrand's Gesch. d. Apost. Exeget. 1824.
Kistemaker's Anmerkungen. 1822.
Langii Isagoge generalis. 1730.
Limborchii Commentaria. 1711.
Malcomi Comment. et Analysis. 1615.
Œcumenii Comment. Græco-latina. 1631. (Chiefly an abridgment of Chrysostom.)
Pearsoni Annales Paulini. 1688.
Rinkii Lucrubratio Critica. 1830.
Walchii (J. E.) Dissertationes in Acta apos. 1756. (Explains many important facts, in both sacred and profane history.)

Alexander's (Jos. A.) Exposition. 1857.
Barrington's (J. S.) Miscellanea sacra. 1725.
Baumgarten's (M.) Apostolical history. Tr. by Morrison & Meyer. 1854.
Bennet's (James) Lectures on the Acts. 1847.
Bentham's (Jos.) Exposition. 1636.
Bevan's (J. G.) Life of Paul, with the epistles inserted in their proper place; with notes. 1807.
Biscoe's History of the Acts confirmed from other authors. 1739. (The Boyle lectures for 1736, '7, '8.)
Bloomfield's (Bp.) 12 Lectures on the Acts. 1828.
Bouchier's Manna in the house. 1858. (For daily family worship.)
Brewster's (J.) Lectures on A. 1807. (Many illustrations from the Fathers.)
Burton's Chronology of the Acts. 1836.
Calvin on Acts. Tr. by Featherstone. 1585.
Cook's Prac. and devotional Comm. 1850.
Dick's (J.) Lectures on the Acts. 1805.
Downing's (Henry) Short notes. 1860.
Du Viel's Com. 1674. Tr. from the Latin by the Author. (Very valuable.)
Eadie's Paul the preacher. 1859. (A commentary on Paul's discourses.)
Eclectic Review. 21:183.
Ellesley's Annot. 1812. (Highly esteemed.)
Hacket's Com. on the original text. 1853.
Hodgson's (R.) Lectures on Acts. 1845.
Humphrey's (W. G.) Commentary. 1847.

Commentators.

Jacobus' Notes. 1849.
Lechler & Gerok's Homiletical Commentary. Trans. by Gloag. 1864.
Livermore's (A.) Commentary. 1844.
McBride's Lectures on the Acts. 1858.
McKenzie's Commentary. 1847.
Mant's (Bp.) Primitive Christianity. 1842.
Maskew's (T. R.) Annotations. 1847.
Neander's Planting and training of the Church. Trans. by J. E. Ryland. 1851. Also by E. Robinson.
Pemberton's Introd. to the Acts. 1842.
Pierce's Commentary and Notes. ("Beyond all praise."—A. CLARKE.)
Ripley's (H. J.) Notes. 1840. (Excellent.)
Robinson's (Hastings) Notes. 1839.
Schaff's Apostolic Church. Tr. by Yeomans. 1854.
Stack's Lectures on A. 1805. (Worthless.)
Sumner's (Bp.) Lectures on the A. 1838.
Thompson's (James) Lectures. 1822. (Dwells chiefly on the prophecies which were fulfilled in the Apostolic times.)
Wheeler's Analysis, Summary, &c. 1852.

Alford's (H.) Homilies on the first 10 chap. 1858.
Krummacher's (F. A.) Cornelius; or, Meditations on the 10th chapter. 1840.
Hodgson's (R.) Lectures on the 17th chap. 1845.

THE EPISTLES.

Chrysostom, Theophylact.

Augusti's Excursen und Einleitung. 1808.
Buddei Ecclesia Apostolica. 1730.
Calixti Expositiones literales. 1663.
Chemnitii Commentariolus. 1676.
Crameri Catena Patrum.
Dicksoni Expositio Analytica. 1645.
Estius in Omnes Epistolas. 1709. (A Papal work of great merit.)
Gualtheri Homiliæ. 1599.
Œcumenii Expositio. 1610.
Schottii Commentarius. 1839.
Zanchii Commentaria. 1600.

Belsham's (Tho.) Notes. 1822. (Unitarian.)
Benson's (Geo.) Paraph. and notes. 1752. (Not on all the epistles; but, published with Locke & Pierce, makes it complete.)
Christian Observer. 1807.
Collet on the 7 Catholic Epistles. 1734.
Dale's Analysis of all the Epistles. 1850.
Dickson's (David) Analytical Expos. 1659.
Heberden's (Wm.) Literal trans. and comm. 1839.
McBride's Lectures on the Epistles. 1858.
McKnight's New translat. and notes. 1795. (Great.)
Mendham's Clavis Apostolica. 1821.
Peiles' (Tho.) Annotations. 1852. (For students of the Greek text.)
Pyles' Paraph. and annotations. 1725.

Commentators.

Roberts' Harmony of the Epistles. (Very convenient, both for reference, and as a commentary.)
Shuttleworth's New trans. and Notes. 1829.
Slade's Annotations. 1816.
Sumner's (Bp.) Apostolical preaching. 1815.
Trower's (W. J.) Exposition.

EPISTLES OF PAUL.

Alphenti Specimena analytica. 1734.
Anselmi Enarrationes. 1533.
Balduini Com. cum Indice. 1644.
Burgess Initia Paulina. 1659.
Capelli Historia apostolica. 1655.
Heydenreich's Erläuterung. (Learned, copious, and pious.)
Langii Commentaria Historico-hermeneutica. 1718. (A learned Pietist.)
Laurentii Explic. locor. difficil. 1630.
Michaelis (Jo. David.) Paraphrasis. 1750.
Picquigny, Explic. par une analyse. 1838.
Stenersenii Com. perpetua. 1829.
Storr, Opuscula Academica. 1789.
Van Till, Commentarius. 1726.
Weingart, Commentarius. 1816.

Addington's Discourses of Paul. 1784.
Bevan's (Joseph G.) Life of Paul; with the Epistles inserted in their order, with crit. and explanatory notes. 1807.
Burgess' (Tho.) Introd. to P. epistles. 1822.
Conybeare's (W. J.) Life and epistles of Paul. 1852. Plates and maps.
Davies' Pauline Epistles. 1866.
Eyre's New trans. and notes. 1832.
Ellicott's Critical Commentary. 1865. ("The best of its kind."—Prof. G. R. BLISS.)
Ferguson's (James) Exposition. 1661.
Hey's General observ. on P.'s writings. 1811.
Jowett's Epistles of Paul. 1849. (Unsafe critic.)
Linton's Paraphrase and notes. 1857.
Newland's New catena on P.'s epistles. 1861.
Paley's Horæ Paulinæ. 1800.
Pierce's New transl., paraphrase, and notes. 1747. ("Exceeds, on the whole, any English commentator I have read."—Prof. M. STUART.)
Wells' (Edw.) Help for the understanding of Paul. 1720.
Whately's Essays on some of the difficulties in the writings of Paul. 1833.

ROMANS.

Altingii Com. theoretico-practicus.
Amyraldi Paraphrasis cum notis. 1656.
Baumgarten's (S. J.) Auslegung. 1749.
Beneke's Brief P. an die Römer. 1831.
Brais [or De Brais], Analysis, Paraph., &c. 1720.
Buceri Metaphrasis et enarratio. 1562.
Chytræi Dispositio, ac notæ criticæ. 1599.
Crucigeri Commentarius. 1567.
Cundisii (G.) Exercitationes XVI. 1646.

Commentators.

Danhaveri Collegium disputatoricum. 1708.
Ferme, Analysis logica. 1651. ("Excellent." —ORME.)
Fritzschii Commentaria. 1839.
Glocker's Brief an die Römer. 1834.
Hengelii (W. A.) Interpretatio. 1853.
Klee's (H.) Commentar. 1830.
Kolner's Commentar. 1836. (With special reference to Tholuck and Rüchert.)
Leydekker de Mente Pauli in Ep. ad Rom. 1707.
Lossius (F.), Uebersetzt. und Erklärt. 1836.
Martyr (Pet.) Commentarius. 1558. ("That great man."—BEZA.)
Meyer's Kritisch-exegetisch Handbuch.
Mosheim's (J. L.) Erklärung, &c. 1770.
Œcolampadii Adnotationes. 1526.
Oleviani Notæ. 1579.
Phillippi's Commentar. 1854.
Rambachii Introd. historico-theol. 1727.
Reiche's Ausfuhlich. Erklärung. 1834.
Rückert's Commentar. 1831.
Rungii Disputationes ex Ep. ad R. 1603.
Schomeri Exegesis. 1699.
Semlerus de Tempore quo scripta fuit Ep. ad R. 1550.
Spener's (P. J.) Auslegung. 1695.
Turretini (J. A.) Prelectiones criticæ. 1741.
Varenii (A.) Analysis et Exegesis. 1696.
Welleri (J.) Adnotationes. 1654. (A convenient collation of versions.)
Winzeri Adnot. ad loca quædam. 1835.

Allie's Sermons on the Ep. to the R. 1844.
Anderson's (Robt.) Practical Expos. 1833.
Beneke's (Wm.) Exposition. 1854.
Bosanquet's (Edwin) Paraphrase and notes. 1840.
Bowles' Paulus Parochialis. 1826.
Brown's (David) Commentary. 1860.
Brown's (Dr. John) Expos. discourses on R. 1765.
Brown's (John) Analysis and Expos. 1857.
Brown's (John) Explanation. 1679.
Chalmers' (Tho.) Lectures on R. 1837.
Colenso's (Bp.) New trans. and Expos. 1861. ("From a missionary standpoint.")
Cox's (Robt.) Horæ Romanæ. 1824.
Edwards' (Tim.) Paraph. and notes. 1752.
Ewbank's Trans. and commentary. 1850.
Ferme's Logical analysis. Tr. by Skae. 1850.
Fry's (John) Pract. Lectures on R. 1816.
Haldane's (Robt.) Exposition; with critical remarks on MacKnight, Tholuck, and M. Stuart. 1835. (A treasure of sound theology, and able criticism.)
Hinton's (J. H.) Exposition on the principles of parallelism, with introd. and appendix. 1863.
Hodge's (Prof. Cha.) Commentary. 1835.
Jones' (John) Analysis: developed from the circumstances of the Church of Rome by which it was occasioned. 1801.
Knight's (Rob.) Critical Commentary. 1854.

Commentators.

Livermore's (A. A.) Commentary. 1853.
Locke's (John) Paraphrase and notes.
Marriot's (Cha.) Lectures on R. 1859.
Moysey's Lectures on R. 1830.
Parr's (Elnathan) Expos. 1633. (Puritan.)
Parry's (Bp.) Lectures on R. 1857.
Prichard's Pract. and critical Comm. 1862.
Pridman's Notes and Reflections. 1852.
Purdue's New trans. and com. 1855.
Ritchie's (David) Lectures on R. 1831.
Ruckert's Exposition. 1840.
Shepherd's The argument illustrated. 1862.
Schlater's (Wm.) Exposition and notes. 1629.
Stanhope's (Dean) Paraph. and notes. 1705.
Stuart's (Moses) New trans. and com. 1832.
Taylor's (John) Paraphrase and notes. 1745.
Terrot's Gr. text, Introd., and Notes. 1828.
Tholuck's Expos. Trans. by Menzies. 1833.
Turner's Notes for students of theology. 1824.
——— Ep. to the R. in Greek and English; with analysis, and exegetical com. 1852.
Vaughn's (C. J.) Notes. 1860.
Walford's New translation and notes. 1846.
Warner's (Rich.) Sermons.
Whitwell's New trans. and notes. 1848.
Willet's Hexapla on R. 1611.
Wilson's (Puritan) Commentary. 1614.

ON SELECT PORTIONS.

Adams (Thomas) on the first 11 chap. 1780.
Newton (B. W.) on the Greek of ch. 1. 1856.
Käuffer's Examinatur novissima Bretschneideri. Ch. 5.
Frazier's Crit. Exposition of ch. 6, 7. 1813.
Kohlbrugge's (H. F.) Expos. of ch. 7. 1854.
McKidd's (Alex.) " " 7. 1854.
Stafford's (John) " " 7. 1772.
Elton's (Edw.) Exposit. of ch. 7, 8, 9. 1630.
Ashley's Victory of the Spirit. Ch. 8. 1865.
Bryson's (T.) Sermons on " 8. 1795.
Jacomb's (Tho.) Exposition of " 8. 1762.
Binning's (Hugh) " " " 8. 1650.
Maitland's Fifteen discourses on " 8. 1831.
Horton's Forty-six sermons on " 8. 1664.
Winslow's No condemnation in Christ. " 8. 1852.
Goodwin's (John) Exposition of " 9. 1640. ("Great learning and good sense."—JOB ORTON.)
Jarrom's (J.) Discourses on " 9. 1827.
Sutton's Lectures on " 11. 1632.
Scott's (John) Lectures on ch. 8 to 12. 1847.

CORINTHIANS.

Chrysostomi Homiliæ XXX. in Ep. poster.
Clementis Romani Epistolæ ad Cor.

Bierman's (Jo.) Verkläringe. 1795.
Bilroth's (G.) Commentar. 1833.
Emerlingii Commentatio perpetua. 1823.
Flatts' Vörlesung.: Heraus. von Hoffman. 1827.
Gualtheri Homiliæ in spir. ad C. 1588.
Heydenreichii Com. in priorem epis. 1827.

Commentators.

Krousii Annotationes. 1792.
Martyris (P.) Commentarius. 1551.
Mosheimii (J. L.) Erklärung des ersten Brief. 1741.
Peile's Annot. 1848. (For Greek scholars.)
Pott (D. J.), Annotationes. 1834.
Royardi Disputatio, &c. 1818.
Ruckert's Briefe Pauli, &c. 1836.
Scharlingii Adnotationes. 1840.
Schlatteri Explicatio et Scholia. 1835.

Biblical Cabinet. Vols. 21 and 22.
Bilroth's Comm. Tr. by W. L. Alexander. 1836.
Bramston's (J.) Exposition. 1700.
Burgess' (Ant.) Com. 1661. (Huge bulk.)
Chrysostom's Homilies on C.; with notes.
Eclectic Review. 4th Series. 19:513.
Hodge's (Cha.) Com. 1859. (Critical and sound.)
Lightfoot's Horæ Ebraicæ et Talmudicæ. 1670.
Lothain's (W.) Expository Lectures. 1828.
Olshausen's Com. Tr. with notes by J. E. Cox.
Pridham's Commentary. 1864.
Robertson's (F. W.) Sermons on C. 1859.
Sibb's Commentary.
Stanley's (A. P.) Commentary. 1854.
Thorn's Revised trans. and com. 1852.
Tolley's Paraph. of the first Ep. 1825.

ON SELECT PORTIONS.

Burgess' (Ant.) Directory for church officers. Com. on 1 Cor. 3. 1659.
Bramston's (John) Charity. Exp. of 1 Cor. 13. 1835.
Fuller's (Tho.) Joseph's coat. On 1 Cor. 2. 1640.
Verschoyle's Bond of perfectness. On 1 Cor. 13. 1849.
Alexander's (John) Paraphrase, Notes, and Dissertations on 1 Cor. 15. 1766.
Coleman's (Tho.) The Redeemer's final triumph. 1 Cor. 15. 1855.
Greenwood's (Wm.) Exposition of 1 Cor. 15.
Sibbs' (Rich.) Comment. on 2 Cor. 1. 1655.
——— " " " 4. 1656.
Watson's (Jonathan) Preparing for home. Expos. of 2 Cor. 5. 1859.

GALATIANS.

Chrysostom.

Feurbornii Expositio. 1653.
Hoffmanni (Chr.) Introductio. 1750. (Great.)
Koppei Annotations. 1791.
Leydekker, de Mente Pauli in ep. ad Gal. 1694.
Lyseri Analysis theol. et scholastica. 1616.
Matthies' (C. S.) Erklärung. 1833.
Meyers' (H. A. W.) Krit. exeget. Handbuch. 1820.
Müller's Erklärt in Bibel-stunden. 1850.
Ruckert's Commentar. 1833.

Commentators.

Sardinoux, Commentaire. 1837.
Spener's Erklärung. 1697.
Storr de Consensu Epis. ad Heb. et Gal. 1812.
Vitringæ (Campeg.) Exercitationes. 1784.
Wieseler's Commentar. 1859.
Winer, Versio Lat. et Comm. 1829.

Bagg's Revised text, and com. 1856.
Brown's (Dr. John) Exposition. 1853.
Calvin on Gal. Tr. by Golding. 1574.
——— ——— Tr. by W. Pringle. 1854.
Chandler's (S.) Paraph. and notes. 1777.
Chrysostom on Galatians.
Edwards' (Tim.) Paraph. and crit. notes. 1752.
Ellicott's Critical and grammat. Com. 1854.
Furguson's (James) Exposition. 1659.
Gwynne's New trans. and Com. 1863.
Haldane's (J. A.) Exp. 1848. (Precious.)
Headland & Swete's Notes, &c. 1866.
Jowett's Crit. notes and Dissertations. 1850.
Lightfoot's Commentary. 1865.
Luther's Com. 1540. (An able discussion of justification by faith.)
Perkins on the first 5 chapters. 1617. (Finished by Ralph Cudworth.)
Ricaulton's Notes and Observations. 1671.
Ruckerts' Commentary. 1840.
Turner's (S. H.) Epistle to G. in Greek and English; with analysis. 1856.
Winer's Com. Tr. by Cunningham. 1840. (With additions from Koppe, Borger, &c.)

EPHESIANS.

Chrysostom.

Alpen, Specimen analyticum. 1742.
Amyraldi Paraphrasis cum notis. 1654.
Battii Disputationes XXI. 1519.
Bemmelini Diss. exeget. critica. 1803.
Buceri Prelectiones. 1562.
Dinantii Com. et Prolegomena. 1722.
Gerbaden's Het. Heiligdom. 1707.
Harless' Commentar. 1834.
Hoelemanni Commentarius. 1839.
Koppei Annotationes. 1791.
Matthies (C. S.) Erklärung, &c. 1835.
Oleviani Notæ. 1580.
Passavant's Auslegung, &c. 1836.
Roeli Explicatio et Analysis. 1715.
Ruckerts' Erläuterung.
Sarceri Adnotationes. 1541.
Van Till, Commentarius. 1726.
Welleri (Hieron.) Commentarius. 1559.

Bayne's (Paul) Commentary. 1647.
Chandler's Paraph. and Notes. 1767.
Chrysostom's Homilies on E. 1581 and 1845.
Eadie's Commentary on the Gr. text. 1853.
Eastburn's Lectures on E. 1832.
Ellicott's Trans. and grammat. Com. 1855.
Ferguson's (James) Exposition. 1659.
Hodge's (Cha.) Commentary. 1856.
Lathrop's Expos. 1864. (Fifty sermons.)

Commentators.

Leyburn's Soldier of the Cross.
Lillie's (John) Lectures on E. 1860.
McGhee's (R. J.) Expository lectures. 1846.
Newland's Catena. 1860. (Collects criticisms from the earliest times.)
Pattison's (R. E.) Doct. and prac. Com. 1859.
Percival's (A. P.) Lectures on E. 1846.
Pounden's (P.) Ephesus; or, the Church precedent. 1846.
Prichard's Com. on Ephesians, Philippians, and Colossians; for Eng. readers. 1865.
Pridman's Exposition and notes. 1854.
Sincoe's Expos.: with texts, parallel, expository, and illustrative; gathered from all parts of the word of God. 1833.
Turner's Analysis and exegetical Com. 1856.

ON SELECT PORTIONS.

Bayne's (Paul) Comm. on chapter 1. 1628.
Goodwin's (Tho.) Expos. of " 1, 2, 3. 1681.

PHILIPPIANS.

Batti Com. cum XVII. Disputationibus. 1627.
Breighthauptii Animadversiones. 1693.
Dallæi Sermones in Epis. ad P. 1644.
Flatt's Vörlesungen über d. P.
Hoelemann's (H. G.) Interpretatio. 1834.
Hoog, Specimen academicum inaugur. 1825.
Krause's Uebersetz. mit Anmerkung. 1790.
Matthies' (C. S.) Erklärung. 1835.
Meier's Comment. 1834. New edition. 1865.
Schotani Analysis cum Observat. 1737.
Weis (B.), Ausgelegt und die Gesch. seiner Auslegung Kritisch Dargestellt. 1859.
Wiesinger's Commentar. 1850.

Acaster's Expository Lectures. 1827.
Airay's Lectures on P. 1648. New ed. 1864.
Bayne's Church at Philippi. 1834.
Daille's Sermons on P. Tr. by J. Sherman. 1841.
Eadie's Critical Commentary. 1852.
Eastburn's Practical Lectures on P. 1833.
Ellicott's Crit. and grammatical Com. 1857.
Hall's (Robt.) 12 Lectures on P. 1833.
Neal's (C.) Discourses on P. 1841.
Neander's Pract. Com. Tr. by Mrs. Conant. 1851.
Neat's (C.) Sermons on Epis. to P.
Newland's (H.) Commentary. 1860. (A collection of the most learned criticisms in every age.)
Robertson's (J. S.) Practical Exposit. 1849.
Sibbs' Exposition of chapter 3. 1639.
Weisinger's Comm. Tr. by Fulton. 1851.

COLOSSIANS.

Altingii Analysis exegetica. 1680.
Baehr, über den Brief P. an de K. 1833.
Daillæi Sermones XLIX. in Col. 1659.
Davenantii Expositio. 1630. (Highly praised by POOLE.)
Flatt's (D. J.) Vörlesungen, &c. 1829.

Commentators.

Gerardi Adnotationes. 1560. (Pious)
Hoffmanni Introductio. 1750.
Junker's Histor.-krit. und phil. Com. 1715.
Quenstedii Disputationes. 1664.
Rambach's (J. J.) Erklärung, &c. 1740.
Rappolti (F.) Observationes. 1680.
Schleiermacheri Expositio. 1823.
Schmidii (Seb.) Paraphrasis, &c.
Spener's Erklärung. 1730.
Steiger's (Wilhelm) Commentar. 1835.
Suiceri Com. critico-exegeticus. 1699.

Byfield's (N.) Exposition. 1615.
Cartwright's Com. 1612. New edition. 1864.
Daillæ's Forty-nine sermons on C. 1662.
Davenant's (Bp.) Expos. Tr. by Alport. 1831.
Eadie's (J.) Com. on the Gr. text. 1855.
Eclectic Review. 4th Series. 17:296.
Ellicott's Critical and grammat. Com. 1859.
Furguson's (James) Exposition. 1656.
Gisbourne's (Tho.) Familiar Expos. 1816.
Kitto's Journal of Sacred Literature. 3:349.
Milner's (Jos.) Sermons on C. 1841.
Pierce's Paraph. and Notes. 1727. (Arian.)
Tolley's Paraphrase and Commentary. 1825.
Watson's (Tho.) Discourses on C. 1833.
Wilson's (Dan.) Expos. Lectures on C. 1845. (An attempt to apply the Apostle's argument to the present circumstances of the Church.)
Bayne on Chapters 1 and 2. 1634.

THESSALONIANS.

Burgerhoudt, Specimen Academicum. 1830. (A useful introd. to the 1st Epistle.)
Flatt's (D. J. F.) Vörlesungen, &c.
Koch's (D. A.) Commentar. 1850. (1st Ep.)
Krause's Uebersetzt. mit Anmerkung. 1790.
Musculi Commentaria. 1565.
Peltii Expositio. 1830. ("Learned and judicious."—BLOOMFIELD.)
Reichii Authent. epist. posterioris. 1829.
Rückert's Briefe Pauli T. 1836. (1st Ep.)
Schleiermacheri Commentationes. 1807.
Schottii Commentaria. 1834.
Turrettini (J. A.) Commentaria. 1739.

Chandler's Crit. and practical Com. 1760.
Edmunds' (John) Practical Com. 1853.
Ellicott's Trans. and critical Com. 1858.
Furguson's (James) Exposition. 1674.
Jewell's (Bp.) Works. 1560.
Jowett's Notes and Dissertations. 1855.
Lillie's Lectures on Thess. 1860.
Martin's Analysis of the 1st Epistle.
Patterson's (Alex.) Expos. 1st Epis. 1854.
Philips' Theological, critical, and philological notes. 1751.
Schleiermacker's Exposition. 1823.

TIMOTHY. See MINISTRY.

BOTH EPISTLES.

Chrysostom.

Alesii Disputationes. 1550.

Commentators.

Gerhardi (Jo.) Adnotationes. 1643.
Mosheim's (J. L.) Erklärung. 1755.
Planck's Bemerkungen. 1808.
Schmidii (Seb.) Paraphrasis, &c. 1694.

Benson's (Geo.) Paraphrase and notes. 1750.
Ellicott's New trans. and critical Com. 1856.
Slade's Lectures at Hampton. 1837.

FIRST TIMOTHY.

Beckhaus' Observationes crit.-exeget. 1810.
Chytræi Enarratio et Scholia. 1643.
Crucigeri Commentarius. 1540.
Curtii Disquisitio. 1828. (Pref. by Neander.)
Hagenbach's Interpretatio. 1829.
Planck's Bemerkungen, &c. 1808.
Wegscheider's Erste Briefe, &c. 1810.
Weisenger's Commentar. 1849.

Berriman's Critical Dissertation. 1741.
Pindar's Candidate for the ministry. 1837.
Weisinger's Com. Trans. by Fulton. 1851.

SECOND TIMOTHY.

Barlow's (J.) Exposition. 1625.

TITUS. See MINISTRY.

Chrysostom.

Alesii Commentaria. 1550.
Breithaupti Exercit. Exegetica. 1703.
Cramer, Hypomnemeta. 1758.
Fechtii Idea veri eccl. ministri. 1692.
Gebhardi Paraphrasis cum notis. 1714.
Schrammii Commentarius. 1763.
Von Haven, Comment. analytica. 1742.
Zentegravii, Analysis, et Exegesis. 1706.

Taylor's (Tho.) Commentary. 1612. ("Laude omnino dignum."—WALCH.)
Wallis' Exposition. 1657.

PHILEMON.

Chrysostom.

Danæi Commentarium. 1579.
Hagenbachii Interpretatio. 1829.
Himmelii Interpret. 1641. Several editions.
Kock's Commentar. 1586.
Kuhne's Bibelstunden zur Erbauung. 1855.
Schmidii (Seb.) Paraphrasis, &c. 1698.

Attersol's (Wm.) Commentary. 1612.
Dyke's Exposition. 1618.
Jones' (Wm.) Exposition. 1635.
Parry's Paul, Philem., and Onesimus. 1834.
Parry's (Bp.) Lectures on P. 1857.
Taylor's (Tho.) Commentary. 1625.

HEBREWS.

Alresch Paraph. et Annotationes. 1789.
Amthor, Com. exegetico-dogmaticæ. 1828.
Baumgarten (S. J.), Erklauterung. 1763.
Baumgarten Crusius, Conjecturæ de origine Epist. ad H. 1829.
Bleek's Erläutert durch Einleitung. 1828.

Commentators.

Boehme, Lat. vers. atque Comment. 1825.
Braunii Com. cum tabulis, &c. 1705.
Brentii (Junioris) Commentaria. 1571.
Carpzovii Exercit. sacræ, ex Philone Alex. 1750. ("Of singular utility."—HORNE.)
Cellarii Verklärter Jesus. 1731.
De Grootii Disputatio. 1826. (To prove Paul to be the author.)
Delitzsch's Commentar. 1858.
Dorschei Comm. pluribus hypomnematibus apodicto analytico-exegeticus. 1718.
Ernesti (J. A.) Lectiones Academicæ. 1795.
Gelpke, Vindiciæ originis Paulinæ ad Heb. Epist. nova ratione tentatæ. 1832.
Gerhardi Commentarius. 1641.
Hornei Explanatio literalis. 1655.
Junii Enarratio. 1610.
Klee's Auslegung. 1833.
La Harpe, Essai critique.
Lyseri (Junioris) Commentarius. 1616.
Megandri Farrago Adnotationum. 1539.
Mestrezat, Sermons sur l'Ep. aux Hébreux. 1689. ("Sublime."—COBBIN.)
Moll's Theologisch-Homiletisch Bearbeitet. 1861.
Œcolampadii Explanationes. 1534.
Rambach's Grundliche Erklärung. 1742.
Schomeri Exegesis. 1710.
Spanheim (F.), Exercitationes.
Starkii (H. B.) Notæ selectæ. 1710.
Steir's Ausgelegt.
Storr, de Consensu Epistolæ ad Hebr. et Galatas. 1809.
Spanheim, de Authore, &c. 1680.
Ziegler's Einleitung. 1678.

Brown's (John) Exposition. 1861.
Collet's (Samuel) Exposition. 1734.
Dickson's (David) Explanation. 1649.
Downame's Commentary. 1646.
Duncan's (R.) Exposition. 1731. (A mere abridgment of Owen, but scarcely less valuable than the original, and much more convenient.)
Ebrard's Biblical Com. Tr. by Felton. 1851.
Forster's Apostolical authority, &c. 1838. (Refutes Michaelis and others.)
Gouge's Commentary. 1655. (The substance of 33 years' labor in lectures, and very able. 2 vols., folio.)
Haldane's (J. A.) Exposition. 1860.
Jones' (Wm.) Lectures on H. 1635.
Knox's (J. S.) Sermons on the sacrificial character of Christ. 1835.
Knowles' (E. H.) Notes; with analysis and paraphrase. 1861.
Lawson's Exposition. 1662.
Lushington's Comm. 1646. (Socinian.)
Maclean's (Archib.) Paraph. and Com. 1819. ("The best of its size."—ORME.)
Maurice's Lectures on H. 1846. (The preface renews Newman's theory of development.)
Miller's (J. A.) Expos. and notes. 1851.

Commentators.

Owen's Expos. and preliminary dissertations. 1674. (Particularly strong in relation to Judaism.)
Parry's (Bp.) Lectures on Hebrews. 1834.
Patterson's (A. S.) Commentary. 1856.
Peirce's (James) Paraph. and notes. (With a very learned essay on the authorship, and original language of the epistle.)
Peile's Annotations for students of the Greek text. 1851.
Sampson's Trans. and critical Com. 1828.
Stuart's (Moses) Commentary. 1827.
Sykes' Paraphrase and notes. 1755.
Tait's (Wm.) Meditationes Hebraicæ. 1845.
Tholuck's Com. Tr. by Hamilton. 1842.
Turner's Ep. to H. in Greek and English, with analysis and Com. 1852.

ON SELECT PORTIONS.

Deering's 26 Lectures on chap. 1 to 6. 1576.
Anderson's Cloud of witnesses. On ch. 11. 1839.
Binney's Power of faith. On ch. 11. 1830.
Sylvester's Christian race. On ch. 12.

JAMES.

Clemens Alex.

Baumgarten's (S. J.) Auslegung. 1750.
Bensoni Notæ philol, et exegeticæ. 1746.
Gebser's Uebersetzt. und Erklärt. 1828.
Heisen, Hypotheses interpretandæ felicius. 1739. (Highly esteemed.)
Hottingeri Com. cum vers. Germana. 1815.
Kern's Untersuchtung und Erklärt. 1838.
Mori Prelectiones. 1794.
Stier's Brief Jacobi Ausgelegt. 1859.
Schreckenburgeri Annotationes. 1822.
Theile, Commentaria. 1833.
Turnemanni Medulla meditationum. 1625.

Benson's (Geo.) Paraph. and notes. 1738.
Calvin's Com. Trans. by C. Cotton. 1605.
Gataker's (Charles) Annotations. 1660.
Hemminge's (Nich.) Commentary. 1577.
Jacobi's Expository Lectures. 1838.
Manton's (T.) Practical Exposition. 1656.
Neander's Com. Tr. by Mrs. Conant. 1851.
Patterson's (Alex.) Commentary. 1851.
Steir's Com. Trans. by W. B. Pope. 1860.
Turnbull's (R.) 28 Lectures on James. 1592.

PETER.

BOTH EPISTLES.

Amesii Expositio Analytica. 1635.
Augusti's Excursen und Einleitung. 1801.
Bibliandri Commentarium. 1536.
Eisenschmid's Uebersetzung, &c. 1824.
Gerhardi Commen. in quo textus declaratur, questiones solvuntur, et loca in speciem pugnantia, conciliantur. 1660.
Goltz's Schriftmatige Verkläringe. 1689.
Laurenti Com. perpetua. 1640.

Commentators.

Turnemanni Meditationes. 1625.
Van Alphen's Sendbrief. 1734.

Adams' (T.) Exp. 1624. (Odd and happy.)
Ames' Analytical Exposition. 1700.
Benson's Paraphrase and notes. 1742.
Demarest's Exposition. 1851.
Luther's Expos. Trans. by Tho. Newton.
Nisbit's Brief Exposition. 1658.
Simpson's Commentary. 1632.
Steiger's Expos. Tr. by Fairbairn. 1836.
Whitaker's Doctrine, argument, &c. 1751.

FIRST PETER.

Clemens Alex.

Hottingeri Com. cum vers. Germana. 1815.
Klemmii Anacrisis. 1837.
Schotani Comm. et Analysis. 1637.
Watther's Kurzgefasste Erklärung. 1750. (Copious preface by J. L. Mosheim.)

Alley's Poore man's librarie. 1565.
Brown's (John) Expos. discourses. 1849.
Demarest's Trans. and Exposition. 1851.
Fairbairn's (Patrick) Exposition. 1836.
Leighton's Lectures on 1 Pet. 1648. (One of the most precious books ever printed.)
——— ——— Abridged by Bradley. 1821.
Kohlbrugge on 1 Pet. Tr. by O. Winslow. 1856.
Byfield on first 3 chapters. 1620.

SECOND PETER.

Dahl, de authentia Ep. posterior. 1807.
Nietzche, Ep. posterior vindicata. 1785.
Ullmann's Kritisch Untersucht. 1821.
Zeigleri Animadversiones. 1804.

Demarest's Exposition. 1865.
Love's Sixteen sermons. 1653.
Mede (Jos.) on Peter's prophecy of Christ's second coming.

JOHN.

ALL HIS EPISTLES.

Dusterdieck, die Drie Joh. Briefe. 1854.
Eckhardi Disputationes XVI. 1609.
Egard's Guldenes Christenthum. 1628.
Japsis Versio Latina, et Annotat. 1821.
Langii Explicatio, Analysis, &c. 1713.
Marperger's Grundliche Auslegung. 1710.
Mori Prelectiones Exegeticæ. 1797.

Benson's Paraphrase and notes. 1749.
Bickersteth's Family Exposition. 1846.
Ebrard's Commentary. Tr. by Pope. 1860.
Hawkins on J.'s canonical epistles. 1808.
Eclectic Review. New series. 3:348.
Lückes' Com. 1837. (Biblical Cabinet.)
Shephard's Notes, crit. and explan. 1841.

FIRST JOHN. See GENUINENESS OF 1 JOHN V. 7.

Clemens Alex., Augustine.

Commentators.

Episcopii Lectiones sacræ. 1705.
Frelinghausen's Erklärung. 1741. (A series of pious meditations.)
Hornii Explicatio literalis. 1654.
Jaspis, Versio Latina, et com. 1821.
Mori Prelectiones. 1800.
Rappolti Theologia Aphoristica. 1688.
Schmidii (Seb.) Commentarius. 1687.
Spener's Paraph. und erklärt. 1699. (All Spener's works are highly valued.)
Sarkani Analytica exegesis. 1757.
Wolf's (K. A.) Prakt. Com. über d. 1 Brief J. 1850.

Binney's Sermons on 1 John.
Cotton's (John) Practical Com. 1656.
Graham's Spirit of love. 1857.
Hancock's (W. J.) Commentary. 1861.
Hurdy's Com. 1656. New edition. 1865.
Morgan's (James) Exposition. 1865.
Neander's Pract. Com. 1850. Tr. by Mrs. Conant.
Pierce's (Bradford) Sermons on 1 John. 1855.
Stock's (John) Exposition. 1865.
Tindall's (William) Exposition. 1531.

SECOND JOHN

Carpzovii (Junioris) Explicatio. 1790.
Dorschei ζητηματα. 1697.
Mori Prelectiones. 1800.
Rambonnet, Specimen academicum. 1819.

Cawdrey on the 2d Ep. of John. 1640.
Cotton's (John) Practical com. 1658.
Jones' (Wm.) Explanation. 1635.
Pococke's New trans. and notes. 1660.

THIRD JOHN.

Mori Prelectiones. 1800.

Pococke's New trans. and notes. 1660.

JUDE.

Clemens Alex., Ambrose.

Arnaud, Recherches critiques.
Creightoni Commentar. 1719.
Dorschei Fragmentum commentarior. 1700.
Gerhardi Adnotationes posthumæ. 1650.
Haenleinii Comm. critica. 1799.
Jessein de Αυθεντια Ep. J. 1820. (Masterly.)
Lauermanni Collectanea. 1818.
Martini Commentarius. 1727.
Rappolti Observationes philologicæ. 1675.
Steir's der Brief Judä auslegung.
Titelmanni (or Schenck) Commentar. 1693. (Highly commended.)
Witsii Commentarius. 1703.

Bickersteth's (Ed.) Family exposition. 1846.
Gardner's (Frederick) Commentary. 1848.
Gardner's Last of the Epistles. 1857.
Jenkins' (W.) Exposition. 1634. (Often reprinted. Revised by J. Sherman. 1839.)
Lauerman's Dissertations on J. 1820.
McGilvary's Expository lectures. 1855.

Commentators.

Manton's Practical Com. and notes. 1650.
Muir's Discourses on Jude. 1822.
Oates' Explanation. 1633. (41 sermons.)
Perkins' Godly and learned Expos. 1606.
Pococke's New trans. and notes. 1662.
Ridley's (Launcelot) Commentary.
Turnbull's (Rich.) 36 Sermons on J. 1606. (With an analysis, &c.)
Willet's Commentary. 1603.

APOCALYPSE. See NUMBER 666, ANTICHRIST, MILLENNIUM, PERIOD OF 1260 YEARS, MILLENARIANS, PROPHECY, SEVEN CHURCHES.

Irenæus, Epiphanius, Cyril, Basil, Ambrose.

Abbadie, l'Ouverture des sept sceaux. 1723.
Andalæ Exegesis illustrium locorum. 1718.
Auberlen's Prophet Daniel, u. die Offenbarung J. in ihrem gegenseitigen Verhältniss, &c.
Bassett, Explication raisonée. 1833.
Bengel's (Albert) Erklärte. 1746. (Strongly praised, and no less strongly censured.)
Bengel's (M. E.) Erklärende Umschreibung. 1772.
Bibliandri Commentarius. 1549.
Blicke in die Apocalypse. 1858.
Brandt's Offenbarung Johannes. 1847.
Brightmani Analysis et scholia. 1600.
Bullingeri Consciones in Apoc. 1557.
Chytræi Commentarius. 1563.
Cocceii Cogitationes de Apocalyp. 1659.
Dressel's Offenbarung d. Johannes. 1851.
Dressenii Meditationes. 1717. (Analytical.)
Dupin, Analysé de l'Apocalypse. 1690.
Ebrard's Offenbarung Johannes. 1853.
Eichhorn, Comm. 1791. (Regards the book as a prophetic drama, exhibiting the *spiritual* victories of the Church.)
Ewaldi Com. exegeticus et criticus. 1828.
Fehr's Anleitung zum rechten verstand, &c. 1761. (The author in the main follows Bengel, but largely notices other writers.)
Graber's Hist. Erklärung d. Offenbarung m. Berücksicht der Auslegungen v. Bengel, Hengstenberg, u. Ebrard. 1857.
Gravii Tabulæ apocalypticæ. 1657.
Hales, Comment. in Apoc. Johannis. 1647.
Harenburg's Erklärung. 1749.
Heideggeri Comment. 1687. (Eminent.)
Heinrich Annotationes. 1821. (Adopts the theory of Eichhorn.)
Hengstenberg's Offenbarung, &c. 1849.
Hennischii Synopsis chrono taxeos. 1578.
Hoe (Matt.) Commentarius. 1640. (Powerful against Romanism.)
Honerti Dissertationes Apocalypticæ. 1736.
Junii Analysis methodica, cum notis. 1590.
Kolthoffii Apocalypsis vindicata. 1829.
Langii Commentarius. 1730.
Lauermanni Dissertationes. 1822.
Lisco's Einleitung in die Offenb. J. 1852.
Lücke's (F.) Einleitung. 1832.
Luthardt's (C. E.) Uebersetzt. u. Erklärung. 1861.

Commentators.

Lyon's (J. C.) Erklärung, &c. 1859.
Marckii Commentarius. 1680.
Mede Clavis apocalyptica. 1627.
Reinhardi Chronotaxis nova. 1741.
Rettig's Achtheit der im Kanon, &c. 1829.
Rinck's Apokalyptische Forschungen. 1852.
Schmid (C. F.) Untersuch. ob die Offenbarung, &c. 1771.
Storr's Neue Apologie. 1800.
Stoschii Dissertationes. 1757.
Tinius' Einleitung, und Erklärung. 1839.
Van Honert, Dissertationes. 1736. (Able.)
Vitringæ Ανακρισις apocalypseos. 1705.
Vogelii Comm. de apos. Joannis. 1811.
Weyeri Initium disputationis de lib. Apoc. 1828. (Reviews the hypotheses of Grotius, Herder, Eichhorn, Heinrich, &c.)
Züllig's Erklarung. 1840.

Allwood's Key to the Revelations. 1829.
American Bib. Repos. 3d Series. 3:272, 385.
Amphlett on the Revelations. 1855.
Arnold's (T. K.) Remarks on Elliot. 1845.
Arthur's (M.) Expos., doct. and pract. 1789.
Ashe's Compendious notes. 1834.
Auberlen's Proph. of Daniel and John compared. Tr. by A. Saphir. 1856.
Bachman's (John J.) Historical Explanation. 1778.
Baillie's (John) Lectures on the Rev. 1798.
Bale's (Bp.) Image of both Churches. 1560. (Repub. by the Parker Society.)
Bengelius' Exp. Tr. by Robertson. 1757.
Bernard's Key to the mysteries, &c. 1647.
Bibliotheca Sacra. 21:319.
Bland's Apocalyptic history solved. 1858.
Bowdler's Practical Observations. 1800.
British Critic. 1827. (Compares the merits of various writers.)
Broughton's (H.) Expos. 1610. (Strongly against the Roman Church.)
Brown's (J. A.) Eventide. 1823.
Bullinger's Sermons vpo ye Apocalips. 1561.
Burder's (H. F.) Notes. 1849.
Burgh's (W.) Apocalypse unfulfilled. 1834. (Discards all previous theories.)
Christian Disciple. 4:65.
Christian Examiner. 2:75. 8:146. 37:192. 40:161. 44:368. 65:60.
Christian Quart. Spectator. 9:570. 10:408.
Clark's (B. S.) Interpret. of the Apoc. 1864.
Clarke's (J.) Dragon of the Apoc. 1814.
Clay's (Edmund) Practical Expos. 1864.
Condor's Harmony of hist. and proph. 1849.
Cooke's Tr. and Explan.; with Introd., &c. 1789.
Cooper's (R. B.) Commentary. 1833.
Cowper's (Bp.) Commentary. 1623.
Craddock's (Sam.) Exposition. 1695.
Cressener's Protestant application of the Apocalypse. 1699.
Croley's (G.) New Interpretation. 1827.
Crone's (R.) Glossarial Interp. 1826.
Cuthbertson's Pract. and Expos. lectures. 1826.

Commentators.

Daubuz' Comm. 1720. (A useful symbolical dictionary is appended.)
Dent's Ruin of Rome. 1603.
Desprez' Apoc. fulfilled. 1854. (Disputes Cummings.)
Durham's (Jas.) Comm. 1658. (Often reprinted.)
Eclectic Magazine. 7:66.
Eclectic Review. 4th Series. 19:156.
Elliott's (E. B.) Critical and historical Com. 1844. (Numerous engrav. of medals, &c.)
Eyton's Dates in Daniel and the Rev. 1855.
Faber's (G. S.) Calendar of prophecy. 1828. (See British Critic. April, 1833.)
Fleming's Apoc. Key. 1793. (Curious.)
Foster's (J. W.) A. its own interpreter. 1853.
Fox's Prelections and meditations. 1722.
Frazier's Magazine. 16:477.
Fuller's (And.) Expos. discourses. 1815.
Fysh's Divine hist. of the Church. 1839.
Galloway's (Joseph) Commentary. 1802.
Galloway's (W. B.) Gate of prophecy. 1846.
Galton's (J. L.) Lectures on the A. 1859.
Gascoyne's Solution of the symbols. 1815.
Gauntlett's (H.) Exposition, in 44 lectures. 1820. (Praised by T. H. Horne.)
Gell's (P.) Histor. and crit. interp. 1854.
Girdlestone's (H.) Notes on the A. 1833.
Goodwin's (Tho.) Sermons on the A. 1690.
Govet's Rev. of J. literal and future. 1841.
Habershon's Historical Expos. 1841.
Head's (H. E.) Dialogues. 1747.
Hengstenberg on the A. Trans. by P. Fairbairn. 1852.
Hoare's Harmony of the Apoc. with other prophecies. 1848.
Holmes' (J. I.) Elucidation. 1815. (Opposes Faber, Cunningham, and Pastorini.)
Hooper's (F. B.) Exposition. 1861.
Hote (or L'Hote), A. expl. by history. 1855.
Huntingford's Voice of the last prophet. 1858.
Hutcheson's Guide to the study of A. 1857.
Irving's (Edw.) Exposition. 1831. (A series of lectures.)
Jenour's Expos. 1852. (Contains an analysis of the principal commentaries.)
Johnston's (Bryce) Commentary. 1794.
Jones' (Tho.) Interpreter. 1836. (Based on Gauntlett.)
Jones' (W.) Lectures on the A. 1830.
Keith's (Alex.) Harmony of prophecy. 1823.
Kelly's (Wm.) Lectures on the A. 1861.
Kershaw on the Principal passages. 1780.
Kitto's Jour. of Sacred Literature. 6:107.
Kollock's (S. K.) Sermons.
Knight's (John C.) Genuineness, authority, &c. 1842.
Lee (Prof.) On the study of Sc. 1840.
——— Events and times of the visions of John. 1851.
Lord's (D. N.) Exposition. 1847.
——— Theol. and Liter. Journal. (Many articles.)

Commentators.

Lovett's Revel. of John explained. 1831.
Lowman's (M.) Paraphrase and notes. 1737.
McCausland's Latter-days of the Jewish Church. 1841.
McLeod's Lectures on y[e] prophecies of the Revelations. 1841.
Macdonald's (J. M.) Key to the Apoc. 1849.
Maurice's Lectures on the Apoc. 1860.
Mede's (Jos.) Key to the A. Tr. by R. More. 1643. And again by B. B. Cooper. 1835.
Methodist Quart. Review. 7:5.
Milner's (Jos.) Sermons on the A. 1790.
Mill's (John) Thoughts on the A. 1860.
Mitchell's (Jno.) New trans. and notes. 1805.
Morell's Connected Elucidation.
Murray's (Rich.) Study of the A. 1826.
Museum of For. Lit. 4:458. 7:157. 22:517.
Napier's (Lord John) Essay. 1593.
New Englander. 4:139. 5:585.
Newton (Sir I.) on the Apoc. 1728.
Overton (John) Chronology of the A. 1822.
Parks' (J. R.) Exposition. 1825.
Pearson's Prophetic char. of the A. 1783.
Pollock's (Robt.) Lectures on the A. 1858.
Porter's (S. T.) Christian prophecy. 1858.
Presbyterian Review. 1:529.
Princeton Review. 19:141.
Purves' Prophetic times. 1793.
Pyles' Preservative against Popery. 1735.
Robertson's (J.) Perpetual Comment. 1730. (Discusses the whole Millennary controv.)
Robertson's (D.) Structure and unity of the Apocalypse. 1815.
Roe's (R.) Analytical arrangement. 1834.
Rogers' (G.) Lectures on the A. 1844.
Roy's Exposition. 1848. (Numerous citations from the Talmud and ancient histories.)
Ryland (Robt.) on the A. 1850.
Sanderson's (R. B.) Essays. 1838.
Schmucker (S. S.) on the Revelat. 1852.
Scott's (W. H.) Interpretation of the A. 1853.
Skeen's 23 lectures on the A. 1857.
Snodgrass' Comm. and notes. 1799.
Stuart's (Moses) Comm. 1845.
Sutcliffe's (J. K.) Lectures on the A. 1850.
Taylor (L.) on Important passages. 1770.
Tillock's Introd. to the study of the A. 1819.
——— Opening of the sealed book.
Todd's (J. H.) Lectures on the A. 1846.
Vaughn's (Cha. J.) Lectures on the A. 1863.
Ward's (W.) Fulfilment of Revelation.
Whitaker's (E. W.) Com. 1802. ("A book of reference and authority."—Brit. Crit.)
Whitaker's (J.) Review of Gibbon's Rome. (Compels Gibbon to give testimony to the fulfilment of prophecy.)
Whitgift's Works. (Parker Society's pub.)
Wickes' (Thomas) Discourses. 1851. (With a chart.)
Winslow's (G. E.) Israel in the Apoc. 1857. (Finds the interpretation in the Hebrew people, and their enemies.)

Commentators.

Woodhouse's New trans. and notes. 1806. (Controverts Mede. "The best book of the kind I have seen."—HURD.)
The same, abridged. 1828. (The symbols are all understood in a spiritual, not literal sense.)
Wordsworth's Hulsean lectures. 1848.
——— Greek text, with MS. collations, Eng. trans. and notes. 1849.

ON SELECT PORTIONS.

Hoare's Christ in glory. On chap. 1. 1848.
Perkins' Expos. of first 3 chapters. 1607.
Phelps' Com. on first 5 chapters.
Moule's Lectures. Chap. 4-7. 1853.
Birk's Myst. of providence. " 8, 9. 1848.
Burton on " 10, 11. 1640.
Biley on " 12. 1848.
(Makes it the hist. of Arianism.)
James' (Horatio) Lectures on ch. 17, 18. 1850.

The preceding list, extended as it is, comprises but a minor portion of extant commentaries, though it probably omits few which are not either obsolete or unimportant. Those who choose to seek further for old writers, are referred to DORCHÆUS, *Historia interpretationibus.* 1674. SIMON, *Hist. crit. des principeaux com. du N. Test.* WALCH, *Bibliotheca.* 1693. These specify more than 1500 commentators who are not named here.

Commonplace Books. See ANALYSES.

Common Prayer. See BOOK OF C. P.

Common Sense. See MIND.

Turrettini (Jo. Alph.) Cogitationes.
Baxter's (Richard) Works. Vol. 2.
Beattie's Immutability of truth.
Buffier's First Truths.
Locke on the Understanding.
Oswald's Appeal in behalf of religion.
Reid's (Thomas) Works.
Sale's Preface to his trans. of the Koran.
Stewart's Philosophy of the mind.
University Quarterly. 2:85.
Watts' Essays. Ess. 4.
Wilson's (D.) Oxford Prize Essay. 1805.

Communion of Saints. See CHRISTIAN UNION, FELLOWSHIP, UNITY.

Ainsworth on the Communion of saints.
Arndt's Meditations.
Arnold's (Dr. Thomas) Sermons.
Behmen's (Jacob) Works.
Bennet on the Communion of saints.
Beveridge's (Bp.) Sermons.
Gerhard's Fifty sacred meditations.
Grant's (Johnson) Sermons.
Hill's (G. D.) Practical Sermons.
Newman's (J. H.) Sermons.
Nicholson's (Will.) Sermons.
Ryan's (Vincent) Sermons.
Secker (Abp.) on the Catechism.
Spurgeon's (Charles H.) Sermons.
Venn's (John) Sermons.
Wilson's Bampton lectures. 1851.

Communion with God. See DEVOTION.

Bennett's (W. J. E.) Sermons.
Charnock's Works.
Christian Quart. Spectator. 9:345.
Henry's (Matt.) Miscellaneous works.
Hussey's (Robt.) Sermons.
Moody on Communion with God.
Owen's (John) Sermons.
Phelps' (A.) Still Hour.
Pike's Guide to the Devotional.
Rutherford's Letters.
Ryan's (V. W.) Sermons.
Sandford's (John) Lectures.
Wilkes' (Sam. C.) Sermons.

Community of Goods. See SOCIALISM.

Company. See EVIL COMPANY, EXAMPLE, SOCIAL INTERCOURSE, YOUTH.

Brady's (Nicholas) Sermons.
Bridges' (William) Sermons.
Calamy's (Benjamin) Sermons.
Cecil's Remains.
Clark's (John) Sermons to Youth.
Cooper's (Edward) Sermons.
Enfield's (William) Sermons.
Franklin's (Thomas) Sermons.
Henry's (Matt.) Miscellaneous Works.
Jones' (Will., of Nayland,) Sermons.
Milner's (Joseph) Sermons.
Pott's (J. H.) Sermons.
Rees' (Abraham) Practical sermons. (Exct.)
Rogers' (John) Sermons.
Stennet's (Jos.) Discourses.
Trebeck's (Andrew) Sermons.
Tyerman's Evils of bad company.
Wake's (Abp.) Sermons.
Wright's (Samuel) Sermons.

Compassion. See SYMPATHY.

Abercrombie's Moral feelings. Part 1, sec. 2.
Butler's (Bp.) Sermons.
Enfield's (Will.) Sermons.
Gibson's (David) Sermons.
Mason's (William) Sermons.
Vincent's (William) Sermons.

Compulsion in Religion. See CHRISTIAN LIBERTY, LIBERTY OF CONSCIENCE, PERSECUTION, TOLERATION.

Conceit. See PRIDE, SELF-CONFIDENCE.

Barrow's (Isaac) Sermons.
Bourne's (Samuel) Sermons.
Cooper's (Edward) Sermons.
Delany's (Patrick) Sermons.
Erskine's (Ralph) Sermons.
Francklin's (Thomas) Sermons.
Hall's (Bp.) Practical works.

Hunt's (Thomas) Dissertations.
Johnson's (Dr. Samuel) Sermons.
Le Bas' (Cha. W.) Sermons.
Munkhouse's (Richard) Practical Sermons.
Taylor's (John) Sermons.
Young's (Dr. John) Sermons.

Concordances. See PARALLELS.

HEBREW.

Bombergii Concordentiæ Ebrææ. 1523. (This is the concordance of Rabbi Nathan, edited by Bomberg.)
Buxtorfii Concordantiæ Ebrææ. 1632.
Calasii Conc. Sac. bibliorum Ebræicorum. 1621. (An invaluable work, serving not only as a Concordance, but as a Lexicon. By the side of the Hebrew words is the Latin translation of them; and in the margin, the differences between the Septuagint and Vulgate versions. The work is in four large folios, printed at the expense of the Pope. The edition of London, 1747, is the most esteemed.)
Fuerstii Conc. Vet. Test. Heb. atque Chaldaiæ. 1840. (An improved edition of Buxtorf, with indexes, tables, &c.)
Lanckischi Conc. Bib. Germanico-Ebraico-Græcæ Deutsche.
Nathan (Rabbi) Concord. Hebraica. 1523.
Noldii Conc. partic. Ebræo-chaldaicarum. 1675. (The edition of 1734 is the best.)
Ravii Fons Zionis. 1677. (An abridgment of Buxtorf.)
Reuchlini Conc. Ebraicarum capita. 1556. (A Latin trans. of Rabbi Nathan.)
Stephani (Henrici) C. Græco-Latinæ N. T.
Stephani (R.) Concord. utriusque Testam.
Tympii Concord. pronominum separatorum Ebræic. et Chaldaicorum.

Englishman's Concordance, Heb. and Chald.
Taylor's Heb. Conc. adapted to the English Bible. 1754. (A huge work.)

OF THE SEPTUAGINT.

Kircheri Concord. Vet. Test. Græcæ; Ebræis Vocibus respondentes. 1607.
Tromii Conc. Græcæ versionis. 1718. (Better than Kircherer for daily use; being, in fact, a good Hebrew concordance also. "Indispensable." — MICHAELIS. "The best concordance published in any language."—DR. HALES.)

OF THE LATIN VULGATE.

Dutripon, Conc. Bibliæ sacræ. 1838. (The latest and most complete.)
Frobenii Conc. majores; cum declinabilium tum indeclinabilium, utriusque Test. dictionum. 1500.
Hugo, Sac. Bib. Concord. 1479. (The edition of Beugens, 1606, is most esteemed.)
Stephani C. cum adnotationibus. 1555.
Tossani Concordantia. 1687.

Concordances—*continued.*

Various other Latin Concordances are extant among curious book collectors; obsolete, because better are to be had.

OF THE GREEK TESTAMENT.

Arnauld, Histoire et Concorde des quatre evangelistes.
Betulii C. N. Test. 1546. (The earliest.)
Bruderi Concordantia. 1842.
Buchner's Real und verbal C. 1858.
Schaffii Lex. Syriacum et Conc. N. T. 1720.
Schmidii C. Græca N. T. 1717. (The best.)
Stephani (H.) Conc. Græco Latinæ. 1816.

Englishman's Greek Concordance.
Gall's Interpreting C. of the N. Test. 1863. (Gives the Greek original of every word; with a glossary of all the words, and their varied renderings in the authorized English version.)
Symson's Alphabetical Concordance.
Williams' Concordance. (Gives the corresponding Hebrew root of every word, and the rendering in the authorized English version.)

ENGLISH.

Gibson's Concordance. 1536. (Of the New Testament only.)
Marbecke's Concordance; that is to saie, a worke wherein by the Ordre of the letters A B C, ye maie redely find any worde conteigned in the whole Bible, so often as it is there mencioned. 1550. (The *first* Concordance to the English Bible. J. Fox, in his Martyrology, first edition, states that it was the chief cause of the Author's martyrdom.)

Knight's Concordance.	1st Edition.		1610.
Cotton's (C.)	"	"	1630.
Bernard's	"	"	1644.
Wickens'	"	"	1655.
Newman's	"	"	1658.
Downame's	"	"	1671.
Powell's	"	"	1680.
Cambridge's	"	"	1689.
Clarke's	"	"	1696.
Pilkington's	"	"	1749.
Butterworth's	"	"	1767.
Fisher's	"	"	1786.
Taylor's	"	"	1801.
Bellamy's	"	"	1819.
Hawker's	"	"	1820.

None of these will compare in value with Cruden's Concordance. 1st Edition. 1737.

Concordat.

Arnoldi Historia Eccles. Lib. XVI.
De Boulay, Historia Academ. Paris.
Du Closs, Histoire de Louis XI.
Grevii Memoria.
Hainault, Histoire de France.
Horix, Concordata nationis German.
Musæi Prelectiones.

Munch's Vollständ. samlung aller alt. und neu Koncordät.
Salig, Historia Augsb. confessionis.

Burnet's History of the Reformation.

Concubinage. See LEWDNESS.

Breithauptii (J. J.) Dissertationes.
Encratitæ (P.) Epistolæ.
Gaji Institutiones. Lib. I.
Grotius de Jure. Lib. II.
Justiniani Institutiones. Lib. I.
Puffendorf de Jure. Lib. VI.
Stoltzii Questio. an concubinatus sit tolerabilior polygamia?
Thomasii (Christian.) Dissertationes. (*Pro.*)

Doddridge's Lectures. Part 3.
Salmon on Marriage.

Concupiscence. See CHASTITY.

Chemnitii Examen Concilii Tridentini.

Abernethy's (Bp.) Sermons.
Brackenbury's (Edward) Sermons.
Jenkins' (Joseph) Sermons.
Newcombe's Sermons.
Piggot on the Commandments.

Condescension. See HUMILITY, MEEKNESS.

Brady's (Nicolas) Sermons.
Enfield's (William) Sermons.
Faringdon's (Anthony) Sermons.
Marriott's (Hervey) Sermons.
Rees' (Abraham) Sermons.
Waterland's (Dean) Sermons.

Confessing Christ. See PROFESSION.

Confession of Sin. See AURICULAR C.

Baxter's (Rich.) Christian directory.
Bishop's (William) Sermons.
Bradford's (The Martyr) Works.
Bramhall's (Abp.) Sermons.
Bright's (George) Sermons.
Butler's (Alban) Sermons.
Faringdon's (Anthony) Sermons.
Gouldburn's (Edward M.) Sermons.
Greenham's (Richard) Sermons.
Hole's (Matthew) Sermons.
Knowles' (Thomas) Sermons.
Sharp's (Abp.) Sermons.
Sherlock's (Bp.) Sermons.
Spurgeon's (C. H.) Sermons.
Summerfield's (John) Sermons.
Tillotson's (Abp.) Sermons.
Yonge's (James) Sermons.

Confessional. See AURICULAR CONFESSION.

Confessions of Faith. See CREEDS.

Confirmation. See IMPOSITION OF HANDS.

Bodeker (H. W.) ueber Confirmation.
Dallæi (Joann.) Disputationes.
Drieri (Christian.) Dissertationes.

Confirmation—*continued.*

Gau, de Valore manum impositionis.
Geuzken's Bibelsprüchen.
Hammond (H.) de Confirmatione.
Henhofer's Konfirmanden-Unterricht.
Morini Opera Posthuma.
Munchmeyer's Gedenkbuch fur Konfirm.
Musæus de Conversione hominis.
Orsi Dissertationes historico-theol.
Tombes' (A Baptist) Refutatio, &c.
Tournelii (H.) Prælectiones Theologiæ.

Allen (James) on Apostolical confirmation.
Baxter on Confirmation.
Beren's (Edw.) Lent lectures.
Bingham's Origines Ecclesiasticæ.
Bradford's (Samuel) Sermons.
Canfield on Confirmation.
Christian Observer. 22:753.
Clark's (Dr. Sam.) Exp. of the Church Cat.
Cranmer's (Abp.) Works.
Comber's Companion to the temple.
Creswell's (Daniel) Sermons.
Dehon's (Bp.) Sermons.
Ellison's (L.) Sermons.
Frere's Doctrine of Confirmation.
Griffith's (Thomas) Lectures.
Hale's Method of preparation.
Hanmer (J.) on Confirmation.
Hare's (A. W.) Sermons.
Harmer's Exercitations.
Haverfield on Confirmation.
Henshaw on Confirmation.
Hopgood on Confirmation.
Knowles' (Thomas) Sermons.
Lancaster on Confirmation.
Morris' Testimony of Presbyterians, Baptists, and Methodists, to Confirmation.
Myers' Christian Guide.
Newton's (Bp.) Dissertations.
Patrick's Aqua genitalis.
Priaulx's (John) Sermons.
Robinson's Parochial Addresses.
Scott's (John) Sermons.
Secker's (Abp.) Works.
Skelton's (P.) Sermons.
Smyth's (Tho.) Rite of C. examined.
Southgate's (Richard) Sermons.
Stebbing's Defence of the order of conf.
Stubb's Sermons. Ser. on Heb. vi. 2.
Taylor (Jer.) on Episcopacy. Sect. 8.
Tyng (S. H.) on Confirmation.
Vaughn's (Cha. J.) Lectures.
Watson's Lectures on Confirmation.
Wilson on Confirmation.
Wood (Basil) on Confirmation.
Wordsworth's Instruc. for first communion.
Yardley on Confirmation.

Conflagration of the World. See CONSUMMATION.

Conformity to the World. See WORLDLINESS.

Confucius. See BUDHISM.

Acta Eruditorum. 1700.

Buddei (Jo. F.) Historia philosophicorum.
Pritii (J. G.) Controversia circa cultum C.

Legge's Chinese Classics. (The original text of Confucius, with Eng. trans. and notes.)

Confusion of Tongues.
See TOWER OF BABEL.

Abrami Pharus Vet. Testamenti. Lib. IV.
Buxtorf de Confusione linguarum.
Casaubon Diatribe de lingua Heb.
Cellarii Philologia Sacra.
Crinesius de Confusione linguarum.
Dieterici Antiquitates Biblicæ.
Meisner, de Conf. linguarum Babylonica.
Morini Exercitationes.
Quenstedtius de Confusione linguarum.
Scaligeri Exercitationes.
Simonis Hist. Crit. de V. Test. Lib. I.
Vitringæ Observationes. Diss. I.
Waltoni Prolegomena ad Bib. Polyglot.
Wotton de Confusione linguarum.
Zeiger de Confusione linguarum.

Abbott (Abp.) on the Conf. of tongues.
Bedford's Chronology. (Appendix.)
Berrington's (Simon) Dissertations.
Brerewood on the Diversity of languages.
Brett's Essay on the Conf. of tongues.
Calmet's Dissertations.
Charles' Dispersion of men at Babel, and the cause.
Christian Review. 13:510.
Close's (Francis) Sermons.
Doddridge's Lectures. Part 6. Prop. 119.
Fuller's (And.) Discourses on Genesis.
——— Revelation examined.
Hutchinson's (John) Works.
Jenkins' (Joseph) Sermons.
Jones' (J.) Tower of Babel.
Law's Theory of religion.
Le Clerc's Dissertations. Diss. 6.
Newton's (Bp.) Dissertations.
Parkhurst's Essay on the Conf. of tongues.
Patrick's Commentary. *In loco.*
Shuckford's Connec. of Sac. and Prof. hist.
Smith's (C. S.) Lectures.
Stackhouse's History of the Bible.
Stillingfleet's Origines Sacræ. Bk. 2, ch. 15.
Ward's Dissertations. Diss. 2.
Wotton on the Conf. at Babel.

Congregationalists. See BROWNISTS.

Pro.

Stahl's Kirchenverfassung nach Lehre und Recht der Protestantismus.
Vinet, Memoire en faveur de la liberté des cultes.

Amer. Quart. Register. 1:159. 2:153. 4:307.
Bibliotheca Sacra. 15:661. 22:284.
Brett on Church government.
Bridge's (Wm.) Works.
Brokesby's Church of the first 3 centuries.
Brown's (Robt.) Works.
Burrough's (Jer.) Sermons.

Congregationalists—*continued.*

Pro.

Cambridge Platform. 1648.
Canne's (John) Zion's prerogative.
Chauncy's Ministry and Ordinances, &c.
Christian Disciple. 2:257. 5:236.
Chris. Examiner. 8:85. 17:177. 41:230, 427.
Christian Review. 6:246.
Clap's Doct. of N. Eng. churches. 1755.
Coleman's (L.) Ancient Christianity.
——— Apostolic church.
Confession of Faith, by the messengers of the churches assembled in Boston. 1680.
Congregational Magazine. London. 1818 to the present.
Cotton's (John) Keys of the kingdom.
——— Way of the churches in N. Eng.
Cummings' Dictionary of C. usages.
Davenport's Power of churches.
Davidson's (S.) Eccles. polity of the N. T.
Declaration of faith and order agreed upon at Savoy. 1658.
Declaration of the New England churches agreed upon at Saybrook. 1708.
Declaration of the National Council convened at Boston. 1865.
Dexter (H. M.) on Congregationalism. 1865.
Eaton & Taylor's C. way justified.
Eclectic Review. 4th Series. 23:649.
Fuller's (And.) Discipline of the primitive churches.
Gill's Body of Divinity.
Godwin's Government of the church.
Glas' (John) Works.
Innis on Church government.
Jacobs' (Henry) Divine institution of Christ's true church.
Johnson's (G. B.) Our principles.
Johnson's (Francis) Works.
Le Bosquet's Congregation manual.
Mather's (Rich.) Reply to Herle on Cong.
——— Reply to Rutherford.
Mather's (S.) Ratio disciplina.
——— Apology for the New Eng. churches.
Mather's (Increase) Order of New England churches.
Mitchell's Guide to the principles of the New England churches.
Moulin's (Lewis) Discipline and government of the primitive Christians.
New Englander. 1:586. 2:39, 180. 4:173, 182. 7:109.
Nye (Philip) on Church Government.
Owen's (John) Nature, power, &c., of the church.
——— True nature of Schism.
Payne's Manual of Cong. principles.
Pearsall (J. S.) on Congregationalism.
Sawyer's (L. A.) Organic Christianity.
Spirit of the Pilgrims. 1:57, 113. 2:128, 370. 3:539.
Upham's (C. W.) Principles of C.
Upham's (Tho.) Ratio Disciplina.
Vaughn's Causes of the corruption of Christianity.

Congregationalists—*continued.*

Pro.

Vaughn's Congregationalism viewed in relation to the State and tendency of modern society. 1842.
Watt's Foundation of a church.
——— Sermons.
Wise's Church's quarrel espoused.
——— Gov. of New England churches.
Wisner's Hist. of Old South Church, Boston.
Wood's (L.) Lectures on Ch. government.

Con. See EPISCOPACY, ESTABLISHMENTS, PRESBYTERIANISM.

Allen (Wm.) on Catholicism.
Ayton on Church government.
Bastwick's Independency not of God.
Cawdrey's Independence a great schism. (Reply to Owen.)
——— Survey of Owen's rejoinder.
——— Inconsistencies of the Indep. way.
Edwards (Thos.) on Independ. government.
——— Gangrena.
——— Antapologia. (Against Godwin, Burroughs, &c.)
Herle on Congregationalism.
Lamb's Fresh suit against Independency.
Paget's Defence of Church government.
Porter's Ecc. system of the Independents.
Princeton Review. 27:239.
Rutherford's Government of the church.
Stillingfleet's Irenicum.
Taylor's (Jer.) Ductor Dubitantium.
Vickars' (John) Picture of Independence.
[Walker's] History of Independence.
——— Anarchia Anglicana.
——— Cromwell's slaughter-house. (These books were published about 1661, under the assumed name of VERAX, and are very bitter.)

Congregationalists, Hist. of.

Bohn's Englische reformations-Historie.
Uden's Geschichte d. Congregationalisten in New-England.

Burnet's Hist. of his own times.
Clarendon's Hist. of the rebellion. (Unfair.)
Coleman's Indep. in Northampton. 1853.
Felt's Eccles. hist. of New England.
Fletcher's Revival of Independency in England since the Reformation.
Hanbury's Historical memorials.
Neale's History of the Puritans.
Punchard's Hist. of Congreg'm. To 1865.
Rapin's History of England. (An enormous misrepresentation.)
Taylor's (Rich.) Hist. of the union between the Presbyt. and Cong. churches in and about London. 1698.
Uden's New England theocracy.
Vaughn's (Robt.) Essays on history, &c.
Waddington's Cong. church history.
Walker's Hist. of Independency. To 1651.
Whiston, Memoirs of.

Congress of Nations. See WAR, PEACE.

Amer. Whig Review. 5:341.
Amer. Quart. Observer. 2:50.
Beckwith's Prize Essay.
Bolles on a Congress of nations.
Christian Examiner. 29:83.
Ladd's (Wm.) Essay on a Cong. of Nations.
Meth. Quart. Review. 2:220.
North Brit. Review. 16:1.
Reports of Amer. Peace Society.
Reports of London Peace Society.

Conjugal Duties. See MARRIAGE, HUSBANDS, WIVES.

Grantham's (Tho.) Sermons on conj. duties.

Connection of Body and Mind. See RECIPROCAL INFLUENCE.

Connection of O. and N. Testam.

Alexander's Congregational Lecture. 1853.
Daubeney's (Archdeacon) Discourses.
Faber's Horæ Mosaicæ.
Jones' (Wm., of Nayland,) Lectures.
Prideaux's Connection of O. and N. Test.

Connection of Sac. and Prof. Hist. See TESTIMONY OF PROFANE AUTHORS.

Diodorus Siculus, Historia.
Jægeri Hist. ecclesiastica, cum parallelismo profanæ.
Jurieu, Histoire critique.
Tornielli Annales, ab orbe condito. (Explains numerous difficulties in Scripture chronology, geography, &c.)

Blakie's (W. G.) Bible history.
Davidson's Connection of sac. and prof. hist.
Gray's Connect. between the Scriptures and heathen authors; particularly in the classical ages. ("Profound and elegant."—ORME.)
Nary's New history of the world. 1720.
Russel's Con. of sac. and prof. history, from the death of Joshua to the decline of the kingdom of Judah. (Completes the work of Shuckford.)
Scaliger's Works.
Shuckford's Con. of sac. and prof. history.
Smith's (Geo.) Sacred annals.
Thompson's (And.) Scripture History.
Whiston's (Wm.) Sacred History; from the creation to Constantine.

Consanguinity, Degrees of, Forbidden in Marriage. See COUSINS, INCEST.

Anselm, de Nuptis consanguineorum.
Brower, de Jure Connubiali. Lib. XI.
Butler's (C.) Syngenia.
Fleury, Institutiones.
Hericourt, des Lois Eccles. Part 2.
Puffendorf, de Jure naturæ, &c.

Alleyne's Degrees of consang. considered.
Cummings on Marriages between kindred.

Consanguinity—*continued.*

Doddridge's Lectures. Part 3, prop. 60.
Foster's Review of the law prohibiting, &c.
Fry on Marriages between kindred.
Marshall on Marriages between parties related; with a history of opinions on this subject, and the action of ecclesiastical bodies. 1843.
Taylor's Civil Law touching marriage.
Turner's Defence of the marriage of an Uncle with the daughter of his half-brother.
Wynne's Miscellany. (Argues for the unlimited extension of collateral consang.)

Conscience. See GOOD CONSCIENCE, LIBERTY OF CONSCIENCE.

Danhaveri Dissertationes.
Drexellii Trismegistus Christianus.
Gisberti Antiprobalismus.
Hermes' grosse Lehre vom Gewissen.
Sanderson, de Obligatione conscientiæ.

Abercrombie's Moral feelings. Part 3.
Allestree's (Rich.) Sermons.
Anderson's (J. S. M.) Sermons.
Appleton's Works.
Barcroft's Rule of Conscience.
Basnage's Treatise on Conscience.
Bolton's Intructions for afflicted consciences.
Bradshawe's (John) Discourses.
Brady's (Nicholas) Sermons.
Brown's Philosophy of the mind.
Butler's (Bp.) Sermons.
Carr's (Geo.) Sermons.
Charnock's Works.
Christian Examiner. 13:69.
Christian Monthly Spectator. 2:337, 393.
Christian Quart. Spectator. 7:629.
Christian Review. 12:369.
Colston's (Alex.) Essays.
Emmon's (Nathaniel) Sermons.
Fidde's (Richard) Sermons.
Foster's (James) Sermons.
Fuller's Cause and cure of a wounded C.
Hall's (Bp.) Practical works.
Harris' (Robert) Sermons.
Hurd's (Bp.) Sermons.
King's C. considered as to obligation.
Lowth's (Bp.) Sermons.
Methodist Quart. Review. '3:5.
Paley's Moral Philosophy.
Palmer on the Doctrine of the development of conscience.
Placette on Conscience.
Princeton Review. 12:299.
Sanderson's (Bp.) Works.
Sharp's (Abp.) Sermons.
Shephard on Conscience.
Smith's (Sam. S.) Sermons.
South's (Robert) Sermons.
Taylor's (Jer.) Ductor Dubitantium.
Tillotson's Sermons.
Trapp's (Joseph) Sermons.
Universalist Quarterly. 2:90. 6:168.
Vincent's (John) Sermons.
Walker's (Dr. James) Sermons.
Wayland's Limits of Human Responsibility.
Whewell's (W.) Sermons.
Woodhouse's (G. W.) Sermons. (Hardening conscience.)

Consideration.

Atterbury's (Francis) Sermons.
Bourne's (Samuel) Sermons.
Bromley's (R. A.) Sermons. (On our latter end.)
Carr's (Geo.) Sermons.
Fawcett's (J.) Sermons.
Gale's (Dr. John) Sermons.
Grove's (Henry) Sermons.
Horneck's Great law of consideration.
Lardner's (Nath.) Sermons.
Secker's (Abp.) Sermons.
Tillotson's (Abp.) Sermons
Westcott's Sermons.
Woodhouse's (G. W.) Sermons.
Wroughton's (Charles) Sermons.
Zollikoffer on Festivals and Fasts.

Consistency of Reason and Revel. See HARMONY OF REASON AND FAITH.

Consistency of Conduct.

Baxter's (R.) Christian Directory.
Cox's (R. C.) Sermons.
Fawcett's (John) Sermons.
Fisk's (Geo.) Sermons.
Heurtley's (Cha. A.) Sermons.
Hewlett's (J. P.) Sermons.
Jeter's (J. B.) Sermons.
Lewis (J.) on Christian duties.
Mannering on Christian consistency.
Taylor's (Daniel) Sermons.
Thornwell's (J. H.) Discourses on Truth.
Titcomb on Inconsistency of conduct.

Consolation. See AFFLICTION, CHEERFULNESS, COMFORT, DESPONDENCY.

Alexander's (J. W.) Discourses.
Bateman's (Josiah) Sermons.
Becon's (Thomas) Works.
Collings' Cordial for the fainting.
Colquhoun on Spiritual comfort.
Downame's (Bp.) Sermons.
East on Affliction and desertion.
Fuller's (Andrew) Sermons.
Hall's Help to Zion's travellers.
Kempis' Imitation of Christ.

Constancy. See STEADFASTNESS.

Seneca, Opera moralia.

Bloomfield's (C. J.) Sermons.
Bradford's (The Martyr) Declarations.
Cook's (Shadrach) Sermons.
Cunningham's (J. W.) Sermons.
Evans on Christian Temper.
Gerard's (Alexander) Sermons.
Grove's (Henry) Sermons.
Mason's (John) Sermons.

Paterson's (James) Sermons.
Sullivan's (Henry W.) Sermons.
Tillotson's (Abp.) Sermons.
Vaughn's (Charles) Sermons.

Constantine.

Cellarii Dissertationes.
Dalhusii (Enewaldi) Dissertationes.
Gualtheri Diatriba Elenchtica.
Nicolai (Jo.) de Constantini baptismo.
Polli (Reginald) Dissertationes.
Sandini (Antonii) Dissertationes Historicæ.
Schwezfleishii Disputationes.

Constantine's Vision.

Baringii (Nicol.) Dissertationes.
Cellarii (Chris.) Dissertationes Academicæ.
Fabricii (Jo. Albert.) Exercitationes Criticæ.
Granville, sur la verité de la vision, &c.
Koeberi (Jo. Frider.) Dissertationes.
Molinet, Dissertation Historique.
Schmidii (And.) Dissertationes.
Wolfii Dissertationes.

Consubstantiation.

Pro.

Andreæ (Abrah.) Opera.
Baumgarten (S. I.) Theses Theologicæ.
Callixti Epitome theologia moralis.
Chemnitius, Fundamenta doctrinæ, &c.
Ernesti Opuscula Theologica.
Heshusii Defensio, &c. (Violent.)
Kapp's liturgische Grundsätze.
Lutheri Opera.
Melancthon, de Controv. cœnæ Domini.
Musæi Introductio ad theologiam.
Sartor's Abendmahlslehre.
Scheibel's Abendmahl des Herrn.
Schrœderus de Vero corpore et sang., &c.
Zeibichii Disputationes quatuor.

Con.

Bezæ Opera.
Danæus contra Chemnitium.
Hoffmanni Errores XVII. Jac. Andreæ.
Œcolampadii Dialogus de Cœna.
Rung's Nothwendigen Unterricht.
Sturmii Epistola Apologetica.

Consummation of the World. See DURATION OF THE WORLD.

Origen contra Celsus.
Cyprian de Casu stellarum in fine mundi.

Balduin de Fine seculi.
Benner de Exaustione mundi.
Benzelii Syntagma dissertationum.
Grotius de Veritate.
Hippolyti Orationes.
Klemmius de Orbe hoc interito, sed non annihilando.
Landius de Excidio universi totali.
Osiandri (Adam) Dissertationes.
Osiandri (Andr.) Conjecturæ.
Wagneri Tractationes theologicæ.
Christian Examiner. 29:207. 34:75.
Fleming on the Millennium.
Ibbot's Dissolution of the world by fire.
Joye's Conjectures on the end of the world.
Knight's (J.) Sermons.
More's (H.) Theological works.
Ray's Miscellaneous works.
——— Three discourses.

Contempt of the World. See OVERCOMING THE WORLD, WEANEDNESS, WORLDLINESS.

Contending for the Faith.

Gregory Naz., de Moderatione in disputat.
Jaegerus de Moderatione in controv. theol.

Beattie on Faith.
Benson's (C.) Sermons.
Bishop's (Tho.) Moyer lectures. 1724, 1725.
Dehon's (Bp.) Sermons.
Dickinson's (D.) Truth's victory over error.
Hey's Lectures. (Rules for conduct. contr.)
Hoadley's (Bp.) Sermons.
Hook's (W. F.) Sermons.
Horne's (Bp.) Sermons.
Howe's (John) Sermons.
Howarth's Hulsean lectures. 1836.
Lancaster's (Tho. W.) Sermons.
Ogden's (Sam.) Sermons.
Robinson's Claude on the comp. of a sermon.
Smith (Rich.) on Religious controversy.
Taylor's (John) Sermons.
Toulmin's (Josh.) Sermons.
Wake's (Abp.) Sermons.
Watts on the Improvement of the mind.
Wrangham's (Francis) Sermons.

Contention. See PEACEABLENESS.

Contentment. See PEACE OF MIND, RESIGNATION.

Du Moulin, de la Paix de l'ame.

Amory's (Tho.) Sermons. 5 on this subj.
Barrow's (Isaac) Sermons.
Barrow's (S.) Sermons.
Bell's (W.) Sermons.
Berriman's (W.) Sermons.
Brougham's (John) Sermons.
Brownrig's (Bp.) Sermons.
Burroughs' (Jer.) Sermons.
Burrows' (E. J.) Sermons.
Carr's (Geo.) Sermons.
Carrington's (James) Sermons.
Claggett's (Wm.) Sermons.
Cooper's (Edward) Sermons.
Delany's (Pat.) Sermons.
D'Oyley's (Geo.) Sermons.
Du Moulin on Peace of soul. Trans. by J. Scrape.
Enfield's (Wm.) Sermons.
Evans on Christian temper.
Fletcher's (Jos.) Posthumous sermons.
Gataker's (Tho.) Sermons.
Hales' (Sir I.) Contemplations.
Harwood's Duty and delight of contentment.

Contentment—*continued.*

Haynes' Illustrations of faith and practice.
Hunt's (Jer.) Sermons.
Jortin's (John) Sermons.
Katterus' (Dan.) Sermons.
Knagg's (Tho.) Sermons.
Knowles' (Tho.) Sermons.
Mason's Christian morals.
Mede's (Jos.) Works.
Milner's (Jos.) Sermons.
Morning Exercises at Cripplegate.
Pakington's Art of C.
Paley's (Wm.) Sermons.
Patrick's (Bp.) Sermons.
Price's (Rich.) Sermons.
Sanderson's (Bp.) Sermons.
Secker's (Abp.) Sermons.
Sibbs' (Rich.) Sermons.
Smith's (Henry) Sermons.
Taylor's (Jer.) Holy living.
Tucker's Light of nature. Chap. 34.
Vaughn's (Henry) Sermons.
Watson's Art of Divine contentment.
Williams' (Alfred) Sermons.
Zollikoffer's Fasts and festivals.

Controversy. See CONTENDING FOR THE FAITH, PEACEABLENESS, POLEMICS.

Contradictions of Scripture. See APPARENT CONTRADICTIONS.

Conversation. See SOCIAL INTERCOURSE.

Contingency. See NECESSITY, SCIENTIA MEDIA.

Abernethy's (John) Sermons.
Clark's (Sam.) Boyle lectures.
Grove on Human liberty.
——— on Wisdom.
Hutchinson's Metaphysics.
Jackson on Human liberty.
Limborch's Theology.
Locke's Essays.
More's Enchiridion. Bk. 3, ch. 2.
Ridgeley's Body of divinity.
Watt's Ontology.

Conversion. See CONVICTION.

Fechtius de Ordine et modo gratiæ.
Koenigii Tractationes theologicæ.
Musæi Tractatio de conversione.

Ambrose's (I.) Looking to Jesus.
Bellamy's (Joseph) Discourses.
Berens' (Edward) Sermons.
Bibliotheca Sacra. 23:48.
Bisland's Preaching the Cross.
Charnock's (Stephen) Sermons.
Close's (F.) Sermons.
Cooper's (James) Sermons.
Craig's Cases recorded in the N. Testament, defective, doubtful. and real.
Doddridge's Rise and progress of religion in the soul.
Du Bose's (P. T.) Sermons.

Conversion—*continued.*

Fuller's (And.) Sermons.
Gale's (John) Sermons.
Hall's (Robt.) Works.
Hickman's (Bp.) Sermons.
Leifchild (John) on Christian experience.
Sibbs' Soul's conflict and victory.
——— Bruised reed, and smoking flax.
Spencer (Theod.) on Conversion.
Stewart's (J. H.) Sermons.
Stovel's Pastoral appeals.
Summerfield's (John) Sermons.
Thayer's (Elihu) Sermons.
Tillotson's (Abp.) Sermons.
Whichcott's (Bp.) Sermons.
Wright's Discourses.
Zanchius' How a man may know he is a child of God.

Conversion of Paul. See PAUL.

Augustin, Sermones.
Adami Exercitationes exegeticæ.
Kuckleri Dissertationes. (One is on the *date* of Paul's conversion.)
Spanheimii Dissertationes. (On the epoch of Paul's conversion; and on the name Paul.)

Bather's (Edw.) Sermons.
Burder's (Geo.) Village sermons.
Cennick's (John) Discourses.
Cooper's (E.) Sermons.
Dehon's (Bp.) Sermons.
Donne's (John) Sermons.
Glasse's (Dr. Sam.) Lectures.
Hall's (Robt.) Notes of sermons. (Superb.)
Heber's (Bp.) Sermons at Hodnet.
Lyttleton on the Conversion of Paul.
Marshall's (N.) Sermons.
Neve's (Timothy) Sermons.
Newman's (J. H.) Sermons.
Townsend's (Geo.) Sermons.
Van Mildert's (Bp.) Sermons.
Whitefield's (Geo.) Sermons.

Conversion of the Jews.

Altingii Spes Israelis.
Diefenbach's Verschiedene Urtheile, &c.
Hoorneck de Convincendis Judæis.
Hosmann's Schwehr zu Bekehrenden Juden-hertz.
Raw's Bekehrung d. Juden zu befœrdern.
Spanheim (Fred.) Elenchus controversiarum. (On the causes of the unbelief of the J.)
Wasmuth's Besten mitteln, die Juden zu bekehren.
Zeltner, de Impedimentis et adjumentis conv. Judæorum præcipuis.

Atkin's Christians bound to diffuse Christ'y.
Bicheno's Crisis of all nations.
Blaney on Jeremiah. Chap. 30 and 31.
Calvert's Naphtali.
Clarke (Sam.) on the Promises.
Clayton's (Bp.) Dissertations.

Conversion of the Jews—*continued.*

Collyer's Glory of Israel.
Cooper's (C.) Sermons at the Jews' chapel. London.
Deluc's Letters to Jews.
Durell's Paral. proph. of Jacob and Moses.
Eyre's Observations on prophecy.
Faber's Gen. view of the prophecies relating to the restoration of the Jews.
Fletcher's Israel redux.
Girdlestone's (Cha.) Sermons.
Gregoire on the Physical, moral, and political reformation of the Jews.
Israel's Advocate. Periodical.
Jerram's (Cha.) Theological treatises.
Jewish Expositor. Periodical. London.
Lardner's Circumstances of the Jews.
Mather's (Increase) Mystery of Israel's salvation.
Priestley's Evidences of revealed religion.
Scott's Answer to Rabbi Crool.
Sermons before the London Society for the conv. of the Jews. (By Cooper, Cunningham, Graves, Gillies, Noel, &c.)
Thelwall's Scripture encouragement.

Conversion of the World. See MILLENNIUM, MISSIONS.

Conviction of Sin. See INQUIRERS.

Arnold's (Tho.) Sermons.
Atterbury's (Bp.) Sermons.
Bateman's (Josiah) Sermons.
Charnock's (Steph.) Sermons.
Cooper's (Edw.) Sermons.
Halyburton's Great concern.
Henry's Letters to an anxious inquirer.
James' Anxious Enquirer.
Joles' Word to afflicted consciences.
Noel's (G. T.) Family sermons.
Oxenden's Pathway of safety.
Spencer's (J. S.) Pastoral sketches.
Spring's (Gardner) Essays. Ess. 4.
Trench's (Richard) Sermons.
Wilcox's Letters of instruction and comfort.

Copts. See EGYPT, JACOBITES.

Bonjour, Monumenta Coptica.
Gerhardi (Ernest.) Dissertationes.
Kircheri Prodomus Coptus.
Makrizii Hist. Coptorum christianorum.
Sollerus de Erroribus et institutis Coptojacobiticis.
——— de Patriarchis Alexandrinis.
Tromler's Abbildung der Copt-kirche. (As in 1749.)

Butler's Horæ Biblicæ. Ch. 13.
Stanley's Hist. of the Eastern Church.

Corban.

Capelli (L.) Corban.
Meinhardtii Dissertationes Philolog.

Cordeliers. See FRANCISCANS.

Corporation and Test Acts. See DISSENT, SUBSCRIPTION TO CREEDS.

Pro.

Crofts' (Dr.) Sermons.
Ellis on the Sacramental test.
Fox's Speech in the House of Commons, on the repeal, &c.
Pitt's Speech in the House of Commons, on the repeal, &c. 1790. (And other speeches on that occasion.)
Sherlock's (Bp.) Hist. of the test act.
——— Vindication of the test act.
Warburton (Bp.) on the Alliance between Church and State.

Con.

Bogue on the C. and T. acts.
Bristow's Cursory reflections.
Chandler's (Sam.) Works.
Heathcote on the C. and T. acts.
Loft's Hist. of the C. and T. acts.
——— Defence of the History.
Pearce's Nat. and tendency of the, &c.
Pierce's Reflections on Sherlock's vind.
——— (Other treatises.)
Priestley's Letter to Pitt, occasioned by his speech, &c.
Robinson (Robt.) on Sacramental tests.

Many books contain discussions of this subject, some of which are named elsewhere under "Dissent," "Establishments," and "Toleration;" but the controversy has subsided. "An arranged catalogue of the publications relating to the repeal of the corp. and test acts, from 1772 to 1790, containing a list of 165 pamphlets, mostly anonymous," was printed by J. JOHNSON, London, 1790. The full titles and date of publication are given in each case. There is also a list of tracts for and against the repeal in Kippis' Edition of Doddridge's lectures.

Corruption of Antediluvians.

Hall's (Robt.) Notes of sermons.

Cosmology. See CREATION.

De Serres, la Cosmogone de Moise.
Grotius de Veritate.
Johann, Kosmogonische Ansichten der Jud.
Kurtz's Bibel und Astronomie.
Moeller's Kosmologie in d. griechischen Kirche. (Compared with the Gnostic system.)
Shultz's Astron. Copernicum instaurata rel.

Bibliotheca Sacra. Jan., 1854.
Chevalier's Hulsean lectures. 1827.
Christian Examiner. 59:379.
Dawson's (J. W.) Archaia.
Hamilton's Pentateuch and its assailants.
Hoare's Veracity of the book of Genesis.
Howard's Scrip. hist. of the earth, compared with Oriental traditions.
Huxtable's (E.) Sacred record of Creation.
Kurtz's Bible and astron. Tr. by Simonton.

Lewis' (Taylor) Six days of creation.
Lord's Theol. and Literary Journal. 8:271. (Review of Lewis.)
Mitchell's Astronomy of the Bible.
Rhinds' Six days of creation.
Robinson's (N.) Christian Philosopher.

Councils. See CANONS, SYNODS.

Aguirre, Collectio Concil. Hispanæ, &c., cum notis et dissertationibus, &c.
——— Cura et labore Catalini.
Amyraldi Disputationes Theologicæ.
André, Hist. chron. et dogmat. des C. to 1851.
Annati Apparatus ad positivam theol. meth.
Augustini Epitome Juris Pontificii.
Aymon, Synodes Nationaux d'Eglisses Reformees en France.
Bail, Summa conc. omnium.
Balusii Nova Collect. Conciliorum.
Beveridgii Pandectæ, Canon. S. S. Apostolorum et conciliorum ab. eccl. Græca receptorum.
Biancini et Nerri, Hist. Ecclesiasticæ.
Binii Concilia General. et Provinc. Græca et Latina. (9 vols., fol.)
Binterim's Pragmatische Gesch., &c. (From 400 to 1400.)
Cabassutii Notitia Conc. ecclesiæ.
Camerarii Enumeratio œcumenicar. Synod.
Cappeli Thesaurus disputat. theologicæ.
Carranze Summa Conciliorum.
Catalini C. Œcumenicæ Prolegomenis.
Cave, Notitia Historica omnium concil.
Cellier, Hist. generale des Auteurs sacrès.
Chowanetz's Handbuch aller Concilien.
Chytræi Catalogus Conciliorum.
Coleti Sacro-Sancta Concilia. (A collection filling 30 folios.)
Collection Universelle et Complète des conciles generaux, nationaux, provinceaux, et synodeaux. (80 vols. 1858.)
Cossartii S S. concilia.
Cupii Dissertationes.
De Rives, Epitome Canonum C.
Fabricii Bibliotheca Ecclesiastica.
Filsjeau Dictionaire des Conciles.
Harduini Collectio max. conciliorum.
Hardt, Historia Œcumen. concilii.
Hefele's Concilien Geschichte.
Hermant, Hist. de C. depuis la naissance de l'eglise jusq. present. 1704.
Hildebrandi Hist. Concil. a nato Christi.
Labbei S. S. Concil. collectio. (The latest and perhaps the most complete edition of the councils. 1759–1798. 31 vols., folio.)
Leandri Historia et Harmonia Conciliorum.
Longi (F.) Summa concilior. omnium.
Lupi Notæ et dissertationes.
Luther de Conciliis.
Maire, Le promptuaire des Conciles.
Mansi Conciliorum collectio nova. (A supplement to Coletus.)
Merlinus de Conciliis Generalibus.
Pons, Dictionaire des Concils.

Councils.

Potter, l'Esprit de l'Eglise. (Equivalent to a full ecclesiastical history.)
Pratioli Narratio historica C. omnium.
Prideaux (J.), Opera. (Synopsis of all C.)
Richard, Analyse des conciles généraux et particuliers.
——— Analysis C. generalium et particular.
Salmon, Etude des Conciles.
Schannat Concilia Germaniæ. (An immense collection.)
Selnecceri Catalogus brevis præcip. C.
Stumpff's Grossen gemeinen conciliums.
Surii Concilia Omnia.
Sutlivius de Conciliis et eorum auctoritate. (Against Bellarmin.)
Tregarii Paradoxa de Conc. auctoritate.
Wessenberg's Kirchenversammlungen.
Wilkins' Concilia Brittaniæ et Hiberniæ. (A. D. 1346 to A. D. 1717.)

Baxter's (Rich.) True history of Councils.
Cave's Gov't of the ancient church.
Christian Monthly Spectator. 6:520.
Comber's Roman forgeries in the councils of the first 4 centuries, and in the annals of Baronius.
Dupin's Dissertations and History of eccles. writers. (To the end of the 12th century. "Distinguished for integrity and moderation."—HALLAM.)
Eclectic Magazine. 12:357.
Grier's General Councils. (From the Council of Nice, 325, to the end of that of Trent, 1563.)
Hammond's Definitions of faith.
Hey's (Dr. J.) Lectures. Bk. 4.
Hilarius on Synods.
James on the Councils and Fathers.
Jenkins' Authority of general councils. (Showing their false dealings.)
Prideaux's Synopsis of Councils.
Pusey's Councils of the Church. (To 381.)
Richer's History of General Councils.
Spelman's Roman Forgeries.

PARTICULAR COUNCILS.

Writers differ as to the number of Councils called "General," or embracing the whole Church. Romanists reckon 18, Beveridge 8, Prideaux 7, Bullinger 6. They are usually reckoned to be 10. As named here, they stand in alphabetical order.

ANTIOCH. A. D. 345. See PHOTINIANS.

Schelstrate, Sacrum Antiochenum C.

BASLE. A. D. 1431.

Ferrier, Concil. Basiliense.
Gratii Fasciculus rerum expectandarum et fugiendarum.
L'Enfant Hist. de la guerre des Hussites.

Councils.

Martene, Thesaurus anecdotorum. (Fourteen folios of documents, now of small value. See list of contents in DOWLING'S Notitia.)
Sylvius de Concilio Basiliensi.

CARTHAGE. A. D. 252.

Balduini Disputationes de ecclesia.
Massonii Gesta Collationis C. habitæ.
Pontius' Life of Cyprian.

CHALCEDON. A. D. 451. 4th General Council. See EUTYCHIANS, NESTORIANS.

Francisci, Chalcedonensi Concilia.
Pelasgi Schola fidei.
Rumpæi Commentatio de symbolis.

CONSTANCE. A. D. 1414–1418.

Chastanet, Nouvelle hist. du C. du Const.
Ferrier, Conc. Constantiense.
Hardt [or Von Der Hardt] Hist. Œcumenicum Concilium Constantiensis. (Fine portraits of all the leading members, and views of remarkable places. 7 volumes, folio.)
L'Enfant, Hist. du C. de Constance.
Marmor's Konzil zu Konstanz.
Müller's (F. D.) Kampf um d. Autoritat, &c.
Vries, Historia Concilii Constantinensis.
Wissenberg's Kirchenversammlungen.

L'Enfant's Conc. of C. Tr. by S. Whateley. ("I cannot recommend it too highly."—BP. BURNETT.)

I. CONSTANTINOPLE. A. D. 381. 2d General Council. See MACEDONIANS, SABELLIANS.

Cowper's (B. H.) Syriac miscellanies.

II. CONSTANTINOPLE. A. D. 553. 5th General Council. See ARIANS, ORIGEN.

Verpoortenii Hist. Conc. 2d Constant.
Crackenthorp's 5th General Council. (Refutes Baronius. Preface by D. Featley.)

III. CONSTANTINOPLE. A. D. 680. 6th General Council. See IMAGE WORSHIP, MONOTHELITES.

IV. CONSTANTINOPLE. A. D. 754.

Some call this the 7th General Council, but it is generally rejected, and the 2d C. of Nice called the 7th.

V. CONSTANTINOPLE. A. D. 869. 8th General Council.

Raderi Acta Concilii octavi.
Crackenthorp's Fift Generall Covncel at Constantinople.

Councils.

EPHESUS. A. D. 431. 3d General Council. See EUTYCHIANS, NESTORIANS.

Allatii (Leo) Vindicat. Syn. Ephesinæ.
[Hermannus Pacificus, seu Herdesiani,] de Synod. Ephesina, cum adjunctis thesibus.
Lucii Doct. et certamina Synodi Ephesinæ.
Lupi Opera.
Pelargi Schola Fidei.
Rumpæi Commentarius de Symbolis.
Tabberti Dissertationes.

Christian Examiner. 54:49.

FLORENCE. A. D. 1439.

Abrami Acta Synodi Florentini.
Allatius de Ecclesia.
Creightoni Historia Conc. Florentini.
Justiniani Conc. Florentini acta.
Purmanni (J. G.) Narratio, &c.
Syropuli Vera Hist. unionis non veræ inter Græcos et Latinos.

FRANKFORT. A. D. 1794.

Curtius de C. Francofurtensis.
Dorschii Collatio ad Conc. Francofurtensim.
Struvii Historia Conc. Franc.

I. JERUSALEM.

Danhaveri Disputationes Theologicæ.
Heidegger de Libertate Christianorum.
Ittigius de Hæreses ævi apostolici.
Leonhardi Diatribe de decreto C. Hierosol.
Schelvigii Exercitatio de C. Hierosol.
Stigzelii Diss. de Conc. Apostolico.

II. JERUSALEM. A. D. 1672.

Aymon, Memoires de la relig. des Grecs.
Bassnage, Hist. des Eglises Reformees.
Gisberti Cuperi epistolæ.

Crowell's State of the Greek church.

I. LATERAN. A. D. 1123. 9th General Council. See CELIBACY OF THE CLERGY.

Evans' Statutes of the C. of Lateran.

II. LATERAN. A. D. 1139. 10th General Council. See IMAGE WORSHIP, WALDENSES.

Buddei Miscellanea sacra.
Cennii Conc. Lateranensis.
Hannius de C. Lateranensis.
Raymondi Decretalium Gregorii IX.
Walchii Commentarius de Conc. L.

There were several other Lateran Councils. That of 1512 (5th) annulled decrees of the Council of Pisa.

MENTZ.

Sagittarii Introd. ad Hist. ecclesiasticum.
Schmidius (Jo. And.) Dissertationes.

Councils.

NICE. A. D. 325. 1st General Council. See ARIANISM, CREED NICENE.

Assemanni Bibliotheca Orientalis.
Baieri Disputationes Theologicæ.
Beausobre, Histoire de Manicheisme.
Benzelii Vindiciæ Conc. Nicenæ.
Camerari Hist. synodi Nicenæ.
Danhaveri Disputationes Theologicæ.
Dorschei Exercitationes.
Eisenschmid, über de Unfehlbark, &c.
Fichtii Dissertationes. (*Acta erud.*)
Gelasii Acta N. conc. cum corrollario.
Ittigii Hist. Synodorum in Gallia.
Le Clerc, Bibliotheque Universelle.
Mentzeri Exercit. historico-theologica.
Pisani Acta Consilii Nicæni.
Renaudot, Hist. Patriarch. Alexandrinorum.
Sandii Hist. Concilii N.

Boyle's Trans. of Eusebius. (Introd.)
Cowper's Syriac Miscellanies.
Cruce's Histor. view of the C. of Nice.
Kaye's (Bp.) Acc. of the Council of Nice.
Tillemont's History of the C. of Nice.

II. NICE. A. D. 786. 7th General Council. See IMAGE WORSHIP.

Danhaveri Disputationes Theologicæ.
Baieri Disputationes.
Gelasii Commentarius actorum Con. N.
Ittigii Hist. Synodorum in Gallia.
Mentzeri Bibliotheca.

Comber (T.) on the 2d C. of Nice.

PISA. A. D. 1409.

Acta Concilii Pisani.
Hieronymus de Croaria Conc. Pisani.
Lenfant, Histoire de C. de Pise.

SIRMIUM.

Dorschei Collatio hist. C. Sirmienses.
Mansi Collectio nov. Conciliorum.
Petavii Theologia Dogmatica.
Sirmondi (R.) C. Antiqua Galliæ.

TRENT. A. D. 1545-1563. 10th General Council.

Aymon, Lettres et memoires du Nonce Visconti.
Baumgarten (S. I.), Observ. de C. Trident.
Bungener, Histoire du C. de Trent.
Calvini Acta Synodi Tridentini.
Canones et Decreta C. Trid. (Many editions: that of Richter, 1853, is very complete.)
Cellarii Disputationes. Disp. XVII.
Chemnitii Examen concilii T. (In this immortal work, not only are the doctrines of this celebrated council ably refuted, but the truth happily inculcated.)
Danzii Libri symbolici eccl. Catholicæ.
Dupin, Hist. du C. de T. et des choses qui se sont passees en Europe touchant la relig.
Ebelingi Examen C. Tridentini.
Gentilleti Examen C. Tridentini.
Gentillet, le Bureau du C. de Trent. (To prove that its decisions are contrary to those of the ancient councils.)
Heideggeri C. Trident. Anatomia.
——— Tumulus C. Trid. (Reply to Reding.)
Hottingeri Dissertationes.
Jurieu, Abregé de l'hist. du C. de T. avec reflexions.
Köllner, de Actis C. Tridentini.
Labbæ C. Trid. Canones et decreta, cum aliis in concilio gestis.
Le Plat, Monumentorum ad hist. C. Trident. (Embraces 1400 treatises, protests, &c., in 8 volumes, quarto.)
Lettres, Anecdotes, et Memoires. (Acta erud. 1719.)
Meincii Christus a C. Trid. excommunicat.
Mendham, Acta Conc. Tridentini.
Mollinæus de C. Tridentini.
Paliotto, Acta Conc. Tridentini.
Pauli (Sarpi, sive Polani, "Father Paul,") Conc. du Trente. (Translated into many languages. Exposes the intrigues with which it was conducted.)
Reding's Concilia Tridentini.
Salig's Historie des Tridentischen C.
Thuani Historia C. Tridentini.
Vargas, Lettres et Memoires.

Buckley's Canons and decrees of the C. of T.
——— Catechism of the C. of T.
——— History of the C. of Trent.
Bungener's Hist. of the C. of Trent. Tr. by Scott.
Calvin's Tracts. (Pub. of Parker Society.)
Cramp's (J. M.) Text Book of Popery. (A fair and convenient abridgment.)
Fysh's (Fred.) Beast and his image.
Geddes' C. of T. no free assembly.
——— Miscellaneous tracts.
Jurieu's Hist. of the C. of Trent. (An epitome of Father Paul.)
Luzancy's Reflections on the C. of T.
Matthias' Hist. of the C. of T. (Brief.)
Mendham's Hist., &c., from MSS. and unpublished records.
Paul's Hist., &c. Trans. by N. Brent.
Ranchin's Review of the C. of Trent.
Stillingfleet's C. of T. exam. and disproved.
Watermouth's Trans. of the canons and decrees, &c., with the external and internal history of the council.

It is of no consequence what general councils have done, except as part of the history of mankind. They have not contributed either to the peace or the purity of the church. Those who would search further, will find plenty of books named by BRUNET, *Manuale du libraire;* CAVE, *Hist. literaria scriptorum conciliorum;* SALMON, *Etude des conciles.* The catalogue of a single London bookseller, DAVID NUTT, 1851, offers several hundred on this subject, besides those given above.

Courage. See FORTITUDE.

Bloomfield's (C. J.) Sermons.
Davies' (S.) Sermons. (Curse of cowardice.)
Dowling's (J. G.) Sermons.
Evans' (Arthur B.) Sermons.
Foster's (James) Sermons.
Hogg's Supports for the timorous.
Hutchinson's (A.) Sermons.
Lloyd's (Pearson) Sermons.
Roe's (James) Sermons.
Webb's (Francis) Sermons.
Williams' (Alfred) Sermons.

Courtesy. See CLERICAL HABITS, POLITENESS.

Blair's (Hugh) Sermons.
Christian Monthly Spectator. 5:57.
Christian Observer. 3:83.
Davis' Discourses on Courtesy.
Franklin's (Thomas) Sermons.
Gresley's (William) Sermons.
Hervey's (Geo. W.) Principles of courtesy.
Hurd's (Bp.) Sermons.
Mason's (William) Sermons.
Stebbing's (Henry) Sermons.
Summerfield's (John) Sermons.
Warter's (John W.) Sermons.

Cousins, Marriage of. See CONSANGUINITY.

Covenant of Grace.

Burmanni Œconomia Fœderum Dei.
Cappelus de religione Christiana.
Cloppenburgii Disputationes.
Cocceii Summa doctrinæ de fœdere Dei.
Fabricii Christus unicum et perpetuum fundament. ecclesiæ.
Glassii Christologia Mosaica.
Hulsemannus de Pacto Dei.
Leydekkeri Synop. Controv. (Agt. Cocceius.)
Martinus de Fœderus naturæ. et gratiæ.
Michaelis Dissertationes.
Musæus de Pactis Dei cum hominibus.
Oliviani Substantia fœderis inter Deum et electos.
Rambachii Christus in Mose.
Witsius de Œconomia fœderum. ("All his works have a sweet savor of holiness."—HERVEY.)

Alleine's (R.) Heaven opened.
Allen's Nature, ends, and difference of the two covenants.
Ball on the Covenant of Grace.
Bell's (Thos.) Cov. of Grace and of Works.
Berry Street Lectures.
Blake on the Covenants.
Bostock on the Covenant of Grace.
Boston's (Thos.) Sermons.
Brown's Natural and revealed religion.
Calvin's Discourses.
Cave's Apparatus. (Prefixed to his "Lives.")

Covenant of Grace—*continued.*

Charnock's Works.
Colquhoun on the Covenant of Grace.
Cotton (John) on the Covenant of Grace.
Dickinson's Nature of the New Testament.
Doddridge's Rise and Progress. Ch. 17.
——— Lectures. Part 8.
Dwight's Theology. Sermon 43.
Edwards' Hist. of all the Dispensations.
Erskine's (John) Dissertations. Diss. I.
Forbes' (Duncan) Thoughts on religion.
Gibb's Sacred Contemplations.
Gillespie's Ark of the Covenant opened.
Kelly (John) on the Divine Covenants.
Mede on the difference between the Old and the New Covenant.
Moor's Mystery of Godliness.
Petto's Diff. between the Old and New C.
Potts' Consideration of the Covenants.
Pratt's Doctrine of the two covenants.
Steward on Mediatorial dignity.
Strong (Wm.) on the two C.'s. ("Precious as the wedge of Ophir."—COT. MATHER.)
Taylor's (H.) Beauty of the Div. Economy.
Taylor's (John) Scripture Divinity.
Taylor (Tho.) on the Covenant of Grace.
Thorndike on the Covenant of Grace.
Truman's Grand Propitiation.
Watt's Harm. of Divine Dispensation.
Watson's Tracts.
Wells' Help to the understanding of the Divine laws. ("Admirable."—LOWNDES.)
Williams' Gospel Truth.
Witsius on the Covenants between God and Man. ("The finest combination of genius, eloquence, true divinity, and ardent devotion, that perhaps ever appeared."—RYLAND.)

Covenant of Works.

Gerhardi Dissertationes.
Jaegerus de Fœdere legali.
Kromayerus de Pacto legali et evangelico.
Mulderus de Pacto legali et evangelico.

Alford's O. and N. T. dispensat. compared.
Berry Street Lectures.
Boston's View of the Cov. of Works.
Colquhoun on the Covenant of Works.
Dixon's Nature of the two Covenants.
Hopkins (Ezek.) on Original Sin.
Kelly's (John) The Divine Covenants.
Strong on the Covenants.

Most writers on the preceding subject treat also this.

Covenanters.

Anderson's Letters on the Overtures.
Bailey's Historical Vindication.
Biographia Presbyteriana. (Lives of Peden, Wellwood, Cameron, Cargill, Renwick, &c.)
Biographies edited for the Wodrow Society, by W. K. Tweedie.

Covenanters—*continued.*

Blackwood's Magazine. 6:169.
Bramhall's Fair Warning.
British Quart. Review. 4:325.
Covenanter, The. Periodical. Belfast.
Fealtey's League illegal.
Henderson's (Alex.) Life and times.
Hetherington's Church of Scotland.
Napier's Montrose and the Covenanters: from original documents hitherto unpublished. 1838.
Nye's Exhortation to take the covenant.
Rule's Good old way defended.
——— Vindication.
Sage's Letters. (Against the Cov't.)
Shiel's Hind let loose.
Simpson's Traditions of the Covenanters.
Wilson's Defence of the Ch. of Scotland.
Womock's League and Cov. condemned.

Covetousness. See LIBERALITY.

Augustine, Sermones.

Abernethy's (Bp.) Discourses.
Baxter's (Rich.) Christian Ethics.
Bourn's (Samuel) Sermons.
Christian Examiner. 22:218.
Chalmer's (Thos.) Commercial discourses.
Copley's (Esther) Evils and cure of C.
Crouch's (Wm.) Sin of C. detected: with its branches—fraud, oppression, lying, &c.
Delany's (Patrick) Sermons.
Dick's (Thomas) Works.
Dowling's (J. G.) Sermons.
Dwight's Discourses.
Ellaby's (Thelwell) Anti-Mammon: an exposure of the unscriptural statements of "Mammon," and a statement of the true doctrine.
Enfield's (William) Sermons.
Foster's (Dr. James) Sermons.
Foster's (John) Lectures at Broadmead.
Frazier's Magazine. 15:161.
Fuller's (A.) Works.
Gisborne's (Thomas) Sermons.
Glassford's Enquiry into Covetousness.
Harris' (Robert) Sermons.
Harris' Mammon: or, Covetousness the sin of the Christian Church.
Haynes' Illustration of faith and practice.
Hopkins' (Bp.) Sermons.
Hume's (David) Essays.
Hunt's (Thomas) Dissertations.
Jeter's (J. B.) Sermons.
Jones' (William) Essay on Covetousness.
Lamont's (D.) Sermons on Prevalent Vices.
Latimer's (Bp.) Sermons.
Lavington's (Samuel) Sermons.
Mardley's Instruc. for covetous riche men to beholde and learne what perel and danger they be brovght unto, yf they have their consolation in miserable mammon.
Monod's (Adolphe) Sermons. Tr. by H. C. Fish.
Panoplist. 9:256.
Robertson's Moral Exercises.
Saurin's (James) Sermons.
Scott's (Thomas) Theological Essays.
South's (Robert) Sermons.
Stoughton's Arraignment of C.
Tillotson's (Abp.) Sermons.
Tindale's (Wm., the Martyr,) Sermons.
Treffry on Covetousness.
Verschoyle's (Hamilton) Sermons.
Whitaker's (Edw. W.) Sermons.

Cowardice. See COURAGE.

Cranmer. See MARTYROLOGY.

Cranmer's Works. (Pub. by Parker Soc.)
——— Remains; by H. Jenkins.
——— Life of; by Le Bas.
——— ——— by Todd.
Christian Examiner. 55:63.
Christian Magazine. 1:9.
Edinburg Review. 54:312.
Gilpin's Lives of the Reformers.
Strype's Memorials.
Todd's Vindication of Abp. Cranmer against Lingard, Milner, and Butler.

Creation. See COSMOLOGY, GEOLOGY, HARMONY OF REVELATION AND SCIENCE, THEORIES OF THE EARTH.

Basil, Hexameron. (Homiliæ.)
Gregory Nys., Hexameron. (The best of his works.)
Ambrose, de Opere sex dierum.

Abrami Pharus Vet. Testamenti.
Aberlen's Gottliche Offenbarung.
Affelmanni Exercitationes Academicæ.
Balthasari Historia Creationis.
Beausobre, Histoire de Manicheisme. Lib. V., ch. 3, 4, 5.
Burnett's Doctrina antiqua de rerum originibus. (Gives the sentiments of the philosophers of all nations.)
Danhaveri (Joann. C.) Exercitationes.
Fabricii Hexameron Dei opus explicatum.
Fenelon, l'Existence de Dieu demontrée.
Graverolii Vindicatio Mosæ. (Agt. Burnet.)
Honerti Dissertationes Historicæ.
Hottingeri Hist. creationis Examen.
Junii Disputationes.
Keil's (C. F.) Apologia Mosaicæ.
Kippingii Exercitationes Sacræ.
Leibnitz, Essais de Theodicée.
Leydekkeri Archæologia Sacra.
Martinii Commentatio de Creatione.
Reynoldi Dissertationes Philosophicæ.
Rougemont, du Monde dans ses rapport avec la Bible et les philosophes.
Seldeni Exercitationes.
Serres' Kosmogonie d. Moses im vergleiche mit d. geologie.
Sigwart's Problem des Bosen.
Silberschlag's Geogenie der heilig-Schrift.
Teller's (W. A.) Alteste Theodicee.

Creation—*continued.*

Vossii (G. J.) Theses Theologicæ.
Zanchius de Operibus Dei.
Zorni Theologia Patristica.

Arnold's (Thomas) Sermons.
Barrow's (Isaac) Sermons.
Berrington's (Simon) Dissertations.
Bibliotheca Sacra. 13:83, 743. 14:61, 388. 15:314.
Binning's (Hugh) Sermons.
Birks on the Difficulties of belief.
Blackmore's Creation. (A philosophical poem, greatly praised by DR. JOHNSON.)
Bloomfield's (Cha. J.) Sermons.
Boston's (Thomas) Discourses.
Bowden's (J. W.) Thoughts on the work of Creation.
Bridgewater Treatises. (On the power, wisdom, and goodness of God in creation; by Chalmers, Kidd, Buckland, Prout, Bell, Kirby, Roget, Whewell, &c.)
Burton's View of the Creation.
Challis' Creation; in plan and in progress.
Charnock's Works.
Chevalier's Hulsean Lectures. 1827.
Clarke's (Dr. Adam) Discourses.
Cudworth's Confutation of Atheism.
Cumberland's Sanchoniathon.
De Bow's Review. 4:177.
Donne's (John) Sermons.
Dublin University Mag. 47:580.
Edwards' (Pres.) Sermons. (God's object in Creation.)
Essenius on the first 3 ch. of Genesis.
Foster's (Cha.) Critical Essays.
Garbett's Book of God vindicated.
Gilfillan's Alpha and Omega. Ch. 3.
Got's Genesis of the world.
Gray's Antiquity of the earth in harmony with the Mosaic record.
Grew's Cosmologia Sacra.
Hale's (Sir M.) Origin of mankind.
Hall's (Bp.) Contemplations.
Hamilton's Pentateuch and its assailants.
Hartwig's Harmony of Nature.
Hasting's (H. J.) Parochial sermons.
Hervey's (Jas.) Meditations.
Hoare's Veracity of the book of Genesis.
Horne's (Bp.) Sermons.
Hutchinson's Moses' Principia.
Kendrick on the Primæval History.
Kennedy's Donnellan Lectures. 1824.
King's Morsels of Criticism.
Kirwan's Critical notes on Genesis. Ch. 1.
Kirwan's (Rich.) Geological Essays.
Kitto's Journal of Sacred Lit. 3:159. 5:186.
Knapp's Christian Theology.
Lewis' (Taylor) Six days of creation.
Literary and Theol. Review. 4:526.
McCosh's Typical forms, and special ends in creation.
McCullock's (John) System of Geology.
McDonald's Defence of the first 3 chapters of Genesis.

Creation—*continued.*

Mason (T. M.) on the Creation. (Reply to "Vestiges of Creation.")
Meade's (Bp.) The Bible and the Classics.
Methodist Quart. Review. 12:497.
Milne's Physico-theological Lectures.
Murray's (Jas.) Design of the Mosaic Hist.
New Englander. 9:510.
North American Review. 6:264. 60:426.
Parker's (Benj.) Survey of the six days.
Pirie's Posthumous Works.
Poole's Genesis of the earth and man. (A critical examination of passages of Scripture.)
Powell's (Baden) Inductive philosophy.
Pratt's Genealogy of Creation.
Pye's Moses and Bolingbroke.
Quarterly Review. 16:37.
Ragg's Creation's Testimony to its God.
Rawlinson's Bampton Lectures. 1859.
Ray's Physico-theology.
Repton's Boyle lectures. 1808.
Rhind's (G. W.) Letters.
Ryland's Contemplations.
Shuckford's Dissertations.
Sligo's (A.) Essays.
South's (Robt.) Sermons.
Stillingfleet's Origines Sacræ.
Sturm's Reflections on the works of God.
Thayer's (Elihu) Sermons.
Tottie's (John) Sermons.
Townsend's Moses as a historian.
Vincent's (Will.) Sermons.
Walker's (J. B.) God revealed in the process of creation.
Witty's Vindic. of the Mosaic history.
Wood's Mosaic account of the Creation, illustrated by modern discoveries. 1811.
Wright's Mosaic creation viewed in the light of modern Geology. 1847.

(See Councils)

Creeds. See HISTORY OF DOCTRINES, SUBSCRIPTION TO CREEDS, USE OF CREEDS.

Augusti, Corpus librorum symbolicorum. (The most complete collection of Protestant creeds extant.)
Baier's Symbolik d. christlichen Confess.
Boeckel's Bekenntniss-Scriften der Evang. Reform. Kirche. 1847.
Bohmer's Glaubenswissenschaft.
Creuzer's Symbolik.
Danzii Lib. symb. eccl. Romano-catholicæ.
Feldmann, der Symbolzwang.
Guerikè's Allgemeine Christl. Symbolik.
Hahn's (C. U.) Symbolischen Bücher d. Evang. Prot. Kirche.
Hase, Libr. symb. ecclesiæ evangelicæ concordia.
Heppe's Bekenntniss schriften d. altprotest. kirche.
Hosii Confessio fidei. (H. was President of the Council of Trent, and his work is a standard among Papists.)
Kimmelii Libri symbol. eccl. Orientalis.
Koecheri Bibliotheca. (Praised by WALCH.)

Creeds—*continued.*

Köllner's Symbolik aller chris. Confess.
Lillienthalii Theologica Bibliotheca.
Lindbergii Libri symb. Eccles. Danicæ.
Matthes' Comparative Symbolik aller christlichen Confessionen.
Mess' Symbol. Bücher d. reformirten Kirche.
Möhler's Darstellung der Dogm. gegensätze der Katholiken und Protestanten. (Papal.)
Müller's Symbolische Bücher.
Niemeyer (H. A.) Collectio. (Gives the principal creeds—twenty-eight in all.)
Ritschl, über das Verhältniss d. Bekenntnisses zur kirche.
Semleri Symbolici Lutherani.
Suiceri Thesaurus.
Titmanni Libri symb. eccl. evangelicæ.
Vossii (G. J.) Theses Theologicæ.
Walchii (C. G. F.) Biblioth. symbolica vetus. (First 5 centuries.)
Walchii (J. E. J.) Antiquitates Symbolicæ.
Winer's Darstellung des lehrbegriffs. (Gives over 60 creeds of sects previous to the 12th century.)
Zornii Opuscula Sacra. (60 ancient creeds.)

Bingham's Antiquities of the Church.
Blackburn's Confessional. ("Scarcely any age has produced a more keen and nervous reasoner."—TOPLADY.)
Butler's Historical and critical account of Roman, Greek, and Protestant creeds.
Dunlop's Collection of Confessions of F.
Hall's (Peter) Harmony of Prot. confessions. (A useful manual, bringing into a single volume the decisions of almost every sect in Europe; showing a unity of Christian sentiment most impressive. Of each confession a brief historical account is given, and the Scripture references.)
Harvey's Hist. and theol. of the 3 creeds.
Heurtley's (C. A.) Harmonia Symbolica.
Moehler's (J. A.) Symbolism. (Differences between Papists and Protestants.)
Nares' Discourses on the three Creeds.
Swainson's Hulsean Lectures. 1857. (The relation of creeds to Scripture and to conscience.)
Toplady's History of the Creeds.

Out of the thousand books on this subject, the above are all sufficient: but a great list of others may be found in LOWNDES' *British Librarian.*

CREED, APOSTLES.

Ambrose, de Fide Orthodoxa.
Athanasius, in Symbolum Apostolicum.
Augustine, de Fide et Symbolo.
Cyril Alex., Expositio Orthodoxæ fidei.

Amyraldi Exercitationes in Symbolum.
Ashwell, Fides Catholica.
Bassnage, Exercitationes Historicæ.
Beckell's Bekenntniss Schriften, &c.

Creeds—*continued.*

Bellarmin, Explication du Symb. Apôtres.
Bemboldi Commentatio.
Borneri Institutiones Symbolicæ.
Buddæi Isagoge.
Callixti Disputationes.
Callovii Dissertationes.
Carpzovii Isagoge.
Chytræi Artic. de filio Dei.
Cockburn in Symbolum Apostolicum.
Danæi Explicatio symboli Apostolici.
Erasmi Explanatio symboli quod Apostolorum dicitur.
Eusebii Dissertationes.
Fortunati Expos. Symboli Apostolici.
Gernlerus de Origine Symbole Apos.
Heideggeri Dissertationes Selectæ.
Lyseri Disputationes.
Marheineckii Institutiones Symbolicæ.
Meyerus de Titulo, Origine, &c.
Neumannus de Conditoribus symb. Apos.
Oliviani Expositio symb. Apostolici.
Selnecceri Exegesis symbol. Apostolici.
Sennerti Symbolum Apostolicum.
Strauchii Historia symboli Apostolici.
Streitwolf, et Klener Libri Symbolici.
Tentzelii Exercitationes.
Ulmeri Symboli precipua Synodorum.
Usseri Diatriba de Romana Eccles.
Voetii (Gisbert.) Dissertationes.
Witsii Exercitationes Sacræ.

Amer. Bibl. Repos. 3d Series. 1:577.
Barrow's Exposition of the Apos. Creed.
Baylie's Sermons on the Apos. Creed.
Beza's Confession of Faith, with a computation of Papistical errors.
Bullinger's Decades. (Pub. by Parker Soc.)
Burgess' Canons of the Apostles.
Cave's Lives of the Fathers.
Church Review. 1:352.
Edwards' Body of Divinity.
Gill's (Alex.) Sacred Philosophy.
Griffith (Tho.) on the Apostles' creed.
Heylin's Sum of Ancient Theology.
Hey's (Dr. J.) Lectures. Bk. 4.
Hooper's Confession of the Christian Faith.
Hutchings on the Apostolic Creed.
Jackson's (Tho.) Commentaries on the A. C.
Ken's (Bp.) Exposition.
Kennet's Paraphrase and Annotations.
Kettlewell's Practical Believer.
King's History of the A. Creed. (Valuable, especially for the quotations.)
Lardner's Credibility of the Gospels.
Law's Catechetical Exposition.
Lightfoot's Works.
Mercersburg Review. Vol. I.
Moore's Mystery of Godliness.
Pearson's Exposition of the A. C.
Perkins on the Apostolic Creed.
Poole's (George A.) Sermons.
Princeton Review. 24:602.
Secker's (Abp.) Lectures on the Catechism.
Stackhouse's Exposition.

Creeds—*continued.*

Stephens' (Robt.) Discourses on the A. C.
Toplady's Hist. of the Apostolic Creed.
Towerson on the Creed.
Viret's Dialogues.
Witsius' Diss. on what is called the A. C.
Yates' Model of Divinity.

CREED, ATHANASIAN. See ARIANISM, GENUINENESS OF 1 TIM. 3:16, TRINITY.

Acta Eruditorum.
Anthelmii Disquisitiones.
Benzelii Dissertationes.
Brunoni Commentarius.
Comeri Symbolum Athanasii.
Fortunati Expositio fidei Catholicæ.
Genebrardi Explicatio.
Heideggeri Dissertationes Selectæ.
Laurentii Explicatio.
Parei Notæ.
Rixneri Disputatio Theologica.
Tentzellii Judicia Eruditorum.

Ashwell's Fides Apostolica. (*Appendix.*)
Bloomfield's (Bp.) Sermons.
Burgess' (Bp.) Doctrine of the Trinity.
Card's Uses of the Athanasian creed.
Dennis (John) on the A. creed.
Dodwell on the Athanasian Creed.
Harwood's (Dr. Edw.) Dissertations.
Hey's (Dr. John) Thoughts on the A. C.
Hook (W. F.) on the Use of the A. Creed.
Horne's (T. H.) Doctrine of the Trinity.
——— Vindication of the A. Creed.
——— Hist. and Analysis of A. C.
Horbery's Defence and Explanation.
Hull's Disuse of the A. Creed advisable at the present time. 1831.
Jenyn's (Soame) Tracts.
Lloyd's Vindication.
Miller's (Dr. G.) Doctrines of Christianity.
Myers' Vindication of the A. Creed.
Quesnell's Dissertations.
Prattent's Notes on the A. creed.
Radcliffe's Creed of A., illustrated by parallel passages from the Bible, by quotations from Greek and Latin writers of the first 5 centuries, and by the Apostles' and Nicene creeds.
Rotherham's Apology for the A. Creed.
Seed's (Jeremiah) Sermons.
Waterland's Critical Hist. of the A. Creed.
Wheatley's (Charles) Lady Moyer's lecture. 1733. 1734

CREED, NICENE.

Athanasii εκδοσις πιστεως.

Baieri Disputationes Theologicæ.
Benzelii Dissertationes Academicæ.
Bulli Defensio fidei Nicenæ. ("We need no better help."—KNOWLES.)
Heideggeri Disputationes Selectæ.
Ittigii Hist. Concilii Nicæni.
Melancthonis Explicatio.

Creeds—*continued.*

Selnecceri Exegesis Symboli Nicæni.
Waltheri Dissertationes Theologicæ.
Whitby, Disquisitiones Modestæ in Bulli defensionem.

Ashwell's Fides Apostolica. (*Appendix.*)
Forbes' Explanation of the Nicene C.
Gregorie's (John) Works.
Waterland's Crit. Hist. of the Nicene C.
Wheatley's N. Creed expl. by Scripture.
Whitby's Remarks on Bull's Defence.

For the creeds of particular churches or sects, see under their several names.

Cromwell.

Guizot, Vie de Cromwell.
Villemain, Histoire de Cromwell.

Cromwell, Life of; by Carrington.
——— ——— by O. Cromwell.
——— ——— by T. Cromwell.
——— ——— by D'Aubigné.
——— ——— by Harris.
——— ——— by Headley.
——— ——— by Guizot.
——— ——— by Herbert.
——— ——— by Noble.
——— ——— by Russel.
——— ——— by Jos. D. Smith.
——— ——— by Southey.
——— ——— by Wilson.
Blackwood's Magazine. 61:391.
Burton's Hist. of the Lord Protector.
Carlyle's Letters and speeches of C.
Christian Observer. 19:811.
Christian Quart. Spectator. 1:385.
Eclectic Review. New Series. 1:224.
Edinburg Review. 61:393.
Noble's Memoirs of the Cromwells.
Princeton Review. 17:1.
Quarterly Review. 25:279.
Tullock's English Puritanism.
Vaughn's (Robert) Essays on history and philosophy.

Crosses. See AFFLICTION, SELF-DENIAL.

Ambrose's Looking to Jesus.
Atterbury's (Lewis) Sermons.
Candlish's (Robt.) Sermons.
Christian Review. 11:500.
Daniels' (M.) Sermons.
Hall's (Bp.) Practical works
Hambleton on the Cross of Christ.
Holland's (John) Sermons.
Hook's (W. F.) Sermons.
Penn's (Wm.) No cross no crown.
Princeton Review. 18:158.

Crucifixion. See SUFFERINGS OF CHRIST.

Cruelty to Brutes.

Barrow's (S.) Sermons.
Benson's (Joseph) Sermons.

Cruelty to Brutes—*continued.*

Booker's (Dr. Luke) Sermons.
Chalmers' (Dr.) Sermons.
Creswell's (Dan.) Serm. on domestic duties.
Crowe's Zorphilos; or, Considerations on the treatment of animals.
Dauběney's (Archdeacon) Sermons.
Drummond on Humanity to animals.
Erskine (Lord) on Wanton Cruelty.
Fletcher's Inadequacy of penal law.
Foster's Sermons.
Graham's Apology for the Brute Creation.
Granger's (Jas.) Sermons.
Guardian. No. 61.
Hall's Contemplations.
Hawtry's (Charles) Sermons.
Macauley on Cruelty to animals.
Mant's Reflections on the Sinfulness, &c.
Moore's (Tho.) Sermons.
Mushet's Wrongs of the animal world.
Oliver's (Benj.) Essays. Ess. 6.
Primatt on Mercy to animals.
Puffendorf's Law of Nature.
Rawlinson (John) on Mercy to brutes.
Reports of the London Society for suppressing cruelty, &c.
Richmond's (Leigh) Sermons.
Squires' (Bp.) Sermons.
Styles' (John) Sermons.
Toplady's Works.
Wayland's Elements of Mor. Science. Bk. II.
Youatt on Humanity to Brutes.
Young on Humanity to Animals.

Crusades.

Accolitis de Bello a Christianis contra Barbaros, &c.
Aubert, Histoire des Guerres contre les Turcs, sous la Conduite de Godefroi.
Benzelii Dissertationes.
Bongarsii Gesta Dei per Francos. (This great work [1611] contains histories of the Crusades, by fourteen different authors, all of them contemporary with the events they describe. Most subsequent histories of the Crusades draw largely on this book for their materials.)
Buddæi Selectæ juris Naturæ et Gentium.
Fabricii Salut. lux Evangelii. Cap. XXX.
Funk's Gemälde aus dem Zeitalter der K.
Gulielmi Belli Sacri Historia. (Valuable, as written by an eye-witness.)
Joinville, Histoire de St. Louis. (The best account of the *last* Crusade.)
Maimbourg, Histoire des Crusades.
Matthæi Veteris Ævi Analecta.
Michaud, Bibliothéque des Croisades.
Nouvelle, Encyclopédie Theologique.
Perault, Hist. de Godefroi de Bouillon.
Rechenburgii (Adam.) Dissertationes.
Reineccii Chronica Hierosolymitana.
Schoepflini Commentatio. (Act. Erud. 1727.)
Schulze die Kreuzzüge.
Sybel's Gesch. des ersten Kreuzzüges.
Voltaire, (F. M.) Hist. des Croisades.

Crusades—*continued.*

Wilkins' Geschichte der Kreuzzüge nach Morgenlændischen und Abend-lændischen Berichten.

Amer. Eclectic Review. 3:340.
Analytic Magazine. 3:411.
Blackwood's Mag. 4:303. 59:475.
Buddeus on the Morality of the Crusades.
Christian Examiner. 55:97.
Eclectic Magazine. 4:471.
Edinburg Monthly Review. 4:509.
Encyclopedia Brittanica.
Foreign Quart. Rev. 5:623. 28:12.
Fuller's (Tho.) Hist. of the Holy Wars.
Herder on Man. Book II., chap. 3.
Hume's History of England.
James' History of Chivalry.
Joinville's Chronicles of the Crusades.
Maimbourg's History of the Crusades.
Michaud's Hist. of the C. Tr. by Robson.
Mills' (Chas.) History of the Crusades.
Monthly Review. 87:519. 97:389. 99:533. 121:65.
North British Review. 1:114.
Oakley's Oxford prize essay. 1827.
Proctor's Rise, Progress, Results, &c.
Sismondi's History of the Crusades.
Sybel's History of the first Crusades.

Curiosity.

Charnock's (Steph.) Discourses.
Coppleston's (Edward) Sermons.
Hewlett's (John) Sermons.
Hurd's (Bp.) Sermons.
Leighton's (Abp.) Works.
Newton (W.) on Curiosity in religion.
Seed's (Jer.) Posthumous works.
Stanhope's (George) Sermons.

Custom. See FASHION, WORLDLINESS.

Grindal's (Abp.) Remains. (Published by the Parker Society.)
Stanhope's (Geo.) Sermons.

Cyprian.

Cyprian, Opera omnia quæ extant.
Gregory Naz., Orationes.

Dodwelli Dissertationes Cyprianæ.
Gervaise, Vie de St. C. (With an abridgment of his works, and able notes.)
Huther's Cyprian's Lehre von der Kirche.
Le Clerc, Vie de St. Cyprian.
Marani Vita Cyprianæ.
Rathmanni Priscorum Patrum Theosophia.

Cave's Primitive Christianity.
Conybeare's Bampton lectures. 1839.
Cyprian's Works. Trans. by J. Pearson.
Elyot's Tr. of C.'s sermon on Mortality.
Husenbeth's Cyprian vindicated.
James' Cyprian revived.
Jamieson's Confutation of J. Sage.

Marshall's Genuine Works of St. C., with his life. ("Sometimes makes the translation serve a purpose remote from the mind of the author."—Dr. A. CLARKE.)
Newman's (J. H.) Trans. of C.'s treatises.
Poole's (G. A.) Life and times of C.
Read's (J. B.) Tracts of C. condensed.
Sage's (J.) Vindication of principles.
Whiston's Sermons and Essays.

Cyril of Alexandria.

Cyril (Alex.), Argumenta cont. Nestorianos.
——— Commentarius in Pentateuchum.
Cyrilli Opera. Edit. Migne.
Benzelii Vindicia Cyrilli Alex.
Oudini Dissertationes.

Bibliotheca Sacra. 23:452.
Lardner's Cred. of the gosp. hist. Part 2.
Smith's (R. P.) Trans. of C.'s com. on Luke.

Cyril of Jerusalem.

Cyrilli Opera, Gr. et Lat. recens. et illust. Petavius. 1631.
Cyrilli Opera, Gr. et Lat. recens. et illust. Reischl. 1847.
Plitt de C. Hier. orationibus quæ extant.
Touttæi (Ant. August.) Dissertationes.

Cyril's Com. on Luke. Tr. by R. P. Smith.

Dagon.

Roseri (T.) Diss. de Philistæorum idolo.

Damianists. See TRINITY.

Assemanni Bibliotheca Orientalis.

Dancing. See AMUSEMENTS.

Boiseul, Contre les danses.
Daneau, Traitè des danses.

Brooks' (John T.) Sermons.
Christian Monthly Spectator. 1:185.
Christian Observer. 12:434.
Davis' (M.) Thoughts on dancing.
Dunn on Private and ball-room dancing.
Southern Literary Messenger. 1:512.
Theleur's (E. A.) Letters on dancing.

Daniel. See PERIOD OF 1260 YEARS, SEVENTY WEEKS.

Frederici (Dowen.) Disputationes.
Hengstenberg's Authentie des Daniel.

Brown's Eventide: or, the last triumph.
Girdlestone's (Charles) Sermons.
Horne's (Bp.) Sermons.
Ken's (Bp.) Sermons.
Manchester's "Times" of Daniel.
Pearson's (Hugh) Sermons.
Presbyterian Quart. Review. 1:32, 208.
Thompson's (F. E.) Lent lectures. Lec. 9.

Dark Ages. See MIDDLE AGES.

David. See BIOGRAPHY.

Choisy, Histoire de la Vie de David.
Hasii Regni Davidici descriptio geographica historica. (Acta erud. 1740.)

Andrews' (Bp.) Sermons.
Bayle's Dictionary. Art. David.
Chandler's (Saml.) Critical Hist. of the life of David. (Examines and refutes the objections of Bayle and others. "A book above all praise."—HORNE.)
Christian Monthly Spect. 5:595. 6:23.
Delany's Life and reign of David; interspersed with Conjectures, Digressions, and Disquisitions.
Harris' (Robert) Sermons.
Holdsworth's (R.) Sermons.
Kitto's Journal of Sac. Lit. 2:59. 4:335.
Laurie's (Dr. Tho.) Sermons.
Lawson's Discourses on the hist. of D.
Macduff's Sunsets on the Heb. mountains.
Milner's (Jos.) Practical Sermons.
Newman's (J. H.) Sermons.
Patten's (Tho.) King D. vindicated.
Porter's Character of David considered.
Secker's (Abp.) Sermons.
Thompson's (F. E.) Lent lectures. Lect. 18.
Thompson's (H.) Davidica. (12 Sermons on the life and character of David.)

Davidists.

David's (Geo.) Wunderbuch.
——— Erklarung der schœpfung. (And 16 other books in German, now forgotten.)
Ancronii Epistolæ de vita et secta Davidis Georgii.
Emmius' Grundlicher Unterricht.
Jessenii Larva D. G. detracta.
Stolterforth's Hist. von David Georgen.
Zeidleri (C. G.) Dissertationes.

Day of Grace. See DEATHBED REPENTANCE.

Alleine's Alarm.
Baxter's Call to the Unconverted.
Sherlock on Death.
Snower's (Jno.) Sermons.

Day of Judgment. See JUDGMENT.

Deacons. See CHURCH GOVERNMENT.

Limborchii Theologia Christiana.
Maydorn's Diakonie und der Diakonat.
Ziegler, de Diaconis et diaconisses vet. eccl.

Christian Monthly Spectator. 9:281, 482.
Howell (R. B. C.) on the Deaconship. (Judicious and full.)
Lorrimer on the Office of Deacon.
Newman's (Dr. William) Sermons.
Smith's (Tho. H.) Functions of Deacons.
Watt's (Isaac) Works.
Whitgift's (Abp.) Works. (Parker Society publications.)

Deaconesses.

Basnagii Annales Polit.-Ecclesiasticæ.
Beck, Quelque mots sur l'œuvres des Diac.
Bingham's Origines Ecclesiasticæ. Lib. II.
Fleidner und Disselhoff, der Armen und Krankenfreund.
Odelemii (J. Ph.) Dissertationes Theologicæ.
Pinii Tractatus de ecclesiæ diaconessis.
Ziegler, de D. Vet. Ecclesiæum. Cap. XIX.

Edinburg Review. 87:223,430.
Hayne on the Revival of Deaconesses.
Howson's Deaconesses; or, woman's help in parochial work.
Ludlow's Women's work in the church.
Mosheim's Ecclesiastical History.
Quarterly Review. 54:179.
Twining's Deaconesses of the Chur. of Eng.

Deadly Sins. See SINS OF IGNORANCE, SINS OF INFIRMITY, VENIAL SINS.

Godeschalcus, Confessionale.

Benson's (Geo.) Dissertations on the Catholic epistles.
Gahan's (William) Sermons.
Gregory's (Thomas) Sermons.
Hey's (Dr. John) Lectures.
Kidder on Wilful sins.
Taylor's (Jer.) Polemic discourses.

Dead Sea. See GEOGRAPHY.

Amer. Bibl. Repository. 6:112.
Bibliotheca Sacra. 5:764. 7:393. 12:528.
Kitto's Journal. 7:334.
Littell's Living Age. 22:157. 23:1. 31:307.
Lord's Theol. and Lit. Journal. 2:288.
Lynch's Expedition to the Dead Sea.
Methodist Quart. Review. 9:633.
New Englander. 7:443.
North Brit. Review. 11:265.
Taylor's Vestiges of Divine Vengeance.

Death. See DEATHBED REPENTANCE, FEAR OF DEATH, SLEEP OF THE SOUL, SUDDEN DEATH.

Augustine, Opera.
Cyprian, de Præsagiis mortis.

Baerus de Agone mortis.
Carpzovius de Genuina notione mortis.
Chytæus de Morte, et vita æterna.
Erasmus de Preparatione mortis.
Klencke, der Sterbend u. sine Zukunft.
Man (H. A.), vom Tode.
Mayerus de Morte.
Maywahlen der Tod: Zustand d. von hier abgeschiedenen Seelen.
Muret, Ceremonies funebres de tout les nat.
Ritmeierus de Nomenclaturis mortis emphat.
Schmidtius de Morte fidelium corporali.
Titius de Morte ac preparatione ad mortem.
Zornii Delineatio Theologiæ Patristicæ.
[Zschokkes] Stunden der Andacht.

Death—*continued.*

Anderson's (William) Sermons.
Arnold's (Fred.) Sermons.
Atterbury's (Francis) Sermons.
Bates' (William) Sermons.
——— Four Last Things.
Baxter's Dying Thoughts.
Beachcroft's (R. P.) Sermons.
Bellarmin's Art of dying well. Tr. by J. Ball.
Beren's (Edward) Sermons.
Berry's Death improved.
Beveridge's Thesaurus Theologicus.
Bolton's Discourses.
——— Four Last Things. (Excellent.)
Bossuet's Funeral Orations.
Bradbury on Christian joy.
Bradley's (Charles) Sermons.
Bromley's Consideration of our latter end.
Buckland's Inquiry concerning death.
Burnhame's Pious memorials.
Burrows on Preparing for Death.
Calamy's (Benjamin) Sermons.
Cappe's Practical Discourses.
Carr's (George) Sermons.
Carter's (N.) Sermons.
Charnock's Works.
Christian Examiner. 2:178. 9:161.
Christian Monthly Spectator. 2:454. (False resignation.)
Clerke's (Richard) Sermons.
Clissold's Last hours of eminent Christians.
Cobbin's Dying sayings of eminent Chris.
Cole's True Description of Death.
Cooper's (Edward) Sermons.
Coverdale's (Miles) Remains.
Cox's (R. C.) Death disarmed.
Crawford's (Wm.) Dying Thoughts.
Davies' (Pres. Sam.) Sermons.
Dehon's (Bp.) Sermons.
Dodd's Reflections on death.
Donne's (John) Sermons.
Dwight's Sermons.
Eccles' (Samuel) Sermons.
Emlyn's Funeral Consolations.
Erasmus on Prepar. for D. Tr. by Berthelet.
Farmer's (John) Sermons.
Featley's Hexatexium.
Fellows on Death. (The philosophical view.)
Francklin's (Thomas) Sermons.
Gerson's (John) Lityll tretise, spekyng of the arte to know well to dye.
Green's (Bp.) Discourses.
Grove's (Henry) Sermons.
Hale's (Sir Matt.) Contemplations.
Hall's (Bp.) Practical works.
Hall's (Robert) Sermons. (Death of the Princess Charlotte. Nothing in the language is more eloquent.)
Hambleton on Preparation for death.
Harris' (Robert) Sermons.
Harwood on Paul's description of death and its consequences.
Hawker's Dying pillow made easy.
Hodge's Cordial against the fear of death.
Hopkins' Death Disarmed.

Death—*continued.*

Horneck's (Anthony) Sermons.
Horseley's (Bp.) Sermons.
Janeway's Death Unstrung.
Jellinger's Living way of Dying.
Jones' (William, of Nayland,) Sermons.
Jortin's (John) Dissertations. Dissert. 6. (The state of the dead, as described by Homer and Virgil.)
Ken's (Bp.) Sermons.
Kettlewell's Death made comfortable.
Kitto's Journal of Sacred Lit. 1:167.
Le Bas' (Cha. W.) Sermons.
Leifchild's (John) Discourses.
Logan's (John) Sermons.
Mandell's (Wm.) Sermons.
Mant's (Bp.) Sermons.
Massilon's Sermons.
Memoirs of Mrs. Graham.
Milner's (J.) Sermons.
Morony's (Joseph) Sermons.
Mortimer's Sermons on death.
Müller's Christian doctrine of sin.
Oliver's (Ben. L.) Essays. Ess. 5.
Pearce's (Edw.) Great Concern.
Pierce's (John) Sermons.
Placette's Death of the Righteous.
Pyle's (Thomas) Sermons.
Reid's Philosophy of Death.
Reynolds' (Bp.) Sermons.
Scattergood's (Samuel) Sermons.
Sherlock (Bp.) on Death.
——— Sermons.
Smallridge's (Bp.) Sermons.
Smith's (Sydney) Sermons.
Spurgeon's (Cha. H.) Sermons.
Stebbin's (Henry) Discourses.
Styles' (John) Sermons.
Sutton's (Chris.) Disce mori.
Taylor's (Jer.) Discourses.
——— Holy living and dying.
Taylor's (Z.) Sermons.
Thompson (H.) on Death and Eternity.
Tillotson's Sermons.
Tucker's Light of Nature. Chap. 37.
Wake's Preparation for Death.
Warton's Deathbed scenes.
Watson's (Jonathan) Preparing for home.
Watt's Works. (Various pieces.)
Westminster Review. 56:168.
Wilson's (Bp. Daniel) Sermons.
Wood's Funeral Sermons, by emin't divines.
Wrangham's (Francis) Sermons.
Zschoke's Meditations on D. Tr. by Rowan.

Deathbed Repentance. See PROCRASTINATION.

Bernard, Traité de la repentance tardif.
Hegelmaieri (Tho. G.) Dissertationes.

Asheton's (Dr. W.) Works.
Burnett's (Gilbert) Sermons.
Carr's (George) Sermons.
Clagget's (William) Sermons.
Dorrington's (Theoph.) Sermons.

Deathbed Repentance—*continued.*

D'Oyly's (Dr. George) Sermons.
Dunton's Danger of living in known sin.
Fenner's Caveat against late repentance.
Fiddes' (Richard) Sermons.
Graves' (Dean) Sermons.
Hammond's (Henry) Practical discourses.
Harwood's Reflections on the unacceptableness of deathbed repentance.
Hayward's Horrors of the hour of death.
McGill's (Stephen) Sermons.
Morning Exercises at Cripplegate. (Sermon by Edw. Veal.)
Newman's Case of the thief on the cross.
Payne (Dr. W.) on Repentance. (Argues the entire invalidity of deathbed repent.)
Scott's (John) Sermons.
Sherlock on Death.
——— Sermons.
Smallridge's (Bp.) Sermons.
Taylor's (Jer.) Sermons.

Deborah. See SONG OF DEBORAH.

Decalogue. See COMMANDMENTS.

Deceit. See SINCERITY.

Hampden's (R. D.) Sermons.
Skelton's (Philip) Sermons.
Smallridge's (George) Sermons.
Taylor's (Bp.) Sermons.
Wilson's (Bp.) Sermons.

Deceitfulness of Sin. See TEMPTATION, WATCHFULNESS.

Laget. Sermons sur divers sujets.

Caswall's (E.) Sermons.
Christian Observer. 1802 and 1803.
Craig's (William) Sermons.
Edwards' (Pres.) Sermons.
Evans' (Caleb) Sermons.
Hook's (W. F.) Four treatises.
Knowles' (Tho.) Discourses for families.
Lloyd's (Pearson) Sermons.
Lucas' (Dr. Richard) Sermons.
Ryan's (Vincent W.) Sermons.
Stebbings' (Henry) Sermons.
Stillingfleet's Sermons.
Tillotson's Sermons.
Whichcott's (Bp.) Sermons.
Witherspoon's (Pres.) Works.
Wright on the Deceitfulness of sin. ("Great simplicity, and awful solemnity."—DODDRIDGE.)
Zollikoffer on the Fasts and festivals.

Deceitfulness of the Heart. See GOVERNMENT OF THE HEART, SECRET FAULTS, SELF-DECEPTION.

Black's (David) Sermons.
Blencoe's (Edward) Sermons.
Calamy's (Benjamin) Sermons.

Deceitfulness of the Heart—*continued.*

Dyke's Mystery of self-deceiving.
Girdlestone's (Charles) Sermons.
Hall's (Bp.) Sermons.
Haweis' (Thomas) Sermons at Oxford.
Jackson's (Miles) Sermons.
Jamieson's (Dr. John) Sermons. (Two volumes of excellent discourses on this topic.)
Jortin's (John) Sermons.
Martyn's (Henry) Twenty sermons.
Mayhew's (Jonathan) Sermons
Newton's (John) Sermons.
Sharp's (Abp.) Sermons.
Styles' (John) Sermons.
Taylor's (Jer.) Sermons. (2 on this subject.)

Decencies of Public Worship. See PROPRIETIES.

Decision. See INDECISION, INDIFFERENCE, PROCRASTINATION.

Appleton's (Pres.) Works.
Burroughs' (James) Sermons.
Clarke's Nature and curse of irresolution.
Coleman's (Tho.) History of Daniel and his friends.
Cook's (John) Sermons.
Cooper's (Edward) Sermons.
Dorrington's (Theoph.) Sermons.
Foster's (John) Essays.
Gerard's (Alexander) Sermons.
Heber's (Bp.) Sermons at Hodnet.
Jeter's (J. B.) Sermons.
Jortin's (John) Sermons.
Mace's (Daniel) Sermons.
McGill's (Stephen) Sermons.
Nichols' (Benj. E.) Sermons.
Pyle's (Thomas) Sermons.
Rhees' (Abraham) Sermons.
Ryan's (Vincent W.) Sermons.
Summers' (Samuel) Sermons.
Tennison's (Abp.) Sermons.
Thomas' (David) The Crisis of Being.
Tillotson's Sermons.
Verschoyle's (Hamilton) Sermons.
Wayland's (Samuel) Sermons.

Decrease of Mankind. See POPULATION.

Godwin's Power of increase of the number of mankind.
Hume's Essays. (Pop. of ancient nations.)
Malthus on Population.
Wallace's Dissertations.

Decrees of God. See ELECTION, GODESCHALCIANS, REPROBATION.

Pro.

Affelmanni (Joann.) Dissertationes.
Amyraldus de la Predestination.
Beausobre, Defence de la doct. de la Reform.
Bucer, de Predestinatione.
Calovii Systema locorum theologicum.

Decrees of God—*continued.*

Deylingii Observationes Sacræ.
Erasmi Opera.
Gomarus de Predestinatione.
Hottingeri (Joann. Jacob.) Dissertationes.
Hulsemanni (Joann.) Breviarium.
Kortholti (Christian.) Dissertationes.
Kunadi (Andr.) Loci Theologici.
Musæi (Pet.) Dissertationes.
Perkensii (Guilielm.) Dissertationes.
Polani (Amand.) Didascalia.
Rheinhard's Vorlesung. über die Dogmatik.
Scharfii (Joann.) Dissertationes.
Schelvigii (Sam.) Dissertationes.
Spanheimii (Fred.) Dissertationes.
Turrettini (Jo. Alphonsi) Cogitationes.
Twisse, Dissertatio de Scientia Media.
Zanchii Miscellanea Sacra.

Amer. Biblic. Repository. 2d Series. 9:285. (Hist. of the doctrine.)
Bagshaw's Practical Discourses.
Berry Street Lectures.
Bibliotheca Sacra. 4:77. 19:400.
Bradford's (The Martyr) Five Dissertations.
Bradwardine's (Thomas) Works.
Brown's Natural and Revealed religion.
Butterworth on Moral government. Part 4.
Charnock's (Stephen) Works.
Christian Monthly Spectator. 1:115.
Christian Quart. Spectator. 5:597.
Coles on Divine Sovereignty.
Cooper (W.) on Predestination.
Dwight's (Tim.) Discourses. Disc. 14, 15.
Edwards' Veritas Redux.
Fawcett's Critical Expos. of Romans ix.
Fuller's (Andrew) Essays.
Gale's Court of the Gentiles. Part 4.
Grimes' Doctrine of Predestination according to the Church of England.
Hammond's Works.
Helwys' Cause of man's condemnation.
Howe (John) on Predestination.
Hunt (John) on God's Eternal Decrees.
King on Predestination and Foreknowledge.
Knight's (Robt.) Doct. of predestination.
Knox's (John) Works.
Lambert (The Martyr) on Election.
Leighton's Lectures.
Lime Street Lectures.
Matthews' (John) Divine purposes.
Morton's Divine purpose explained.
Musgrave's Doct. of the divine decrees.
Polhill (E.) on the Divine will.
Princeton Review. 12:225. (Controversy in the 9th century.)
Pryme's Anti-Arminianism.
Rice's God sovereign, and man free.
Scott's Reply to Tomline.
Sumner's Apostolical Preaching.
Theological Essays, reprinted from Princeton Review.
Toplady's Christian and philosophical necessity asserted. (Against Wesley.)
——— Doct. of Predestination stated.

Decrees of God—*continued.*

Pro.

Twisse's Clearing of John Cotton's doubts.
——— Riches of God's love.
——— Scientia Media.
Weeks (W. R.) on the Decrees of God.
Whitfield (Thomas) on God's decrees.
Williston's Sermons.
——— Vindication of the doctrines of the Reformation.
Wilson's (Thos.) God's eternal purpose.
Witsius on the Covenants. Book 3.
Zanchius on Predestination.

Con. See ARMINIANISM, PELAGIANISM, &c.

Decretals. See CANON LAW, PAPAL BULLS.

Augustini (Ant.) Collectio Decretorum.
Burchardi Decretorum libri XX.
Decretalia Gratiani, Gregorii IX., et Clementis V.
Harduini Collectio regia maxima.
Joseph (Octav.), Bibliographia Critica.
Panoramitanus in Decretales.
Schambogen, Commentaria in D.
Schmitz, Medulla juris Canonici.
Schonemanni Pontificum Epistolæ.
Steinbergii Notæ ad Decretum.
Theineri Com. de Pontificum Epistolis.
Van Aspen, Opera.
Wagnereck, Expositio Decretalium.

For a great list of writers on these epistles, see NUTT'S *Catalogue.* A full account of the various collections of ancient decretals and canons is given by DOUJAT, *Praenotionum Canonicarum.*

Dedication of Churches. See PLACES OF WORSHIP, PUBLIC WORSHIP.

Hospinian, de Templis.
Siberi Schediasma.

Andrews' (J.) Sermons.
Benson's (Joseph) Sermons.
Beveridge's (William) Sermons.
Brown's (John) Sermons.
Bull's (Robert) Sermons.
Burd's (Richard) Sermons.
Burnett's (Gilbert) Discourses.
Channing's (W. E.) Sermons.
Everett's (Edward) Sermons.
Gill's (John) Sermons and tracts.
Goddard's (Peter) Discourses.
Grey's (Richard) Discourses.
Harrington's Antiquity of the rite of consecration of churches, as shown by the Holy Scriptures and the Fathers.
Jones' (T.) Sermons.
Kennitt's (Dr. B.) Sermons.
Leng's (John) Sermons.
Lyng's (William) Sermons.
Marshall's (Nath.) Discourses.
Pearce's (Zachary) Discourses.
Shepherd's (John) Sermons.
Smith's (John) Sermons.
South's (Robert) Sermons.
Taylor's (John) Sermons.
Watt's Holiness of Times and Places.
Wesley's Sermons.

Definite Atonement.
See SUBSTITUTION, &c.

Pro.

Bellamy's Works.
Brine's Efficacy of Christ's death.
Calvin's Institutes.
Coles on the Sovereignty of God.
Finley's Extent of Christ's purchase.
Gilbert on the Atonement.
Gill's Body of Divinity.
Hurrion's Scrip. doctrine of redemption.
Jenkins on the Atonement.
Malcom's (H.) Extent and efficacy of the Atonement.
Marshall (A.) on the Atonement.
Owen's Salus Electorum.
Rushton on Particular redemption.
Spaulding on Universalism.
Symington on the Atonement. Sec. 11.
Toplady's Works.
Twisse's Riches of God's love.
Usher (Abp.) on the Extent of Christ's death.
Witsius on the Covenants. Lib. 2, cap. 9.

Con.

Amer. Biblical Repos. 2d Series. 10:110.
Barnes (Albert) on the Atonement.
Bellamy's True religion delineated.
Bernard's Reply to Abp. Usher.
Bibliotheca Sacra. 15:132.
Dwight's System. Ser. 56.
Griffin on the Atonement.
——— Discourses.
Hamilton's (William) Sermons.
Huntingdon's Calvinism improved.
Richards (Dr. James) on the Atonement.
Strong on Benevolence and Misery.
Treffry's Letters.
Wardlaw's (Ralph) Sermons.
Watson (R.) on Atonement.
Wert on Atonement. Chap. 10.
Whitby's Discourses.

Degrees in Glory.

Pro.

Cotta (J. F.) Dissertationes.
Danhaveri (J. C.) Dissertationes.
Mülleri Gradus vitæ eternæ.
Neumanni Dissertationes.

Balguy's (John) Sermons.
Barrow's (William) Sermons.
Boyse's Four last things.
Bull's (Bp.) Sermons.
Clarke's (G. W.) The Righteous Dead.
Conybeare's (Bp.) Sermons.
Edwards' Body of Divinity.
Fuller's (And.) Works.

Degrees in Glory—*continued.*

Pro.

Howe's Blessedness of the Righteous.
Kollock's (S. K.) Sermons.
Mant's (Rich.) Happiness of the Blessed.
Mede on the Reward in the life to come.
Ridgely's Body of Divinity. Quest. 90.
Russel's Letters, Practical and Consolatory. Letter 13.
Thompson's (Edward) Sermons.
Toplady's Works.
Universalist Quart. Mag. 14:129.
Watt's World to Come.
Williiams' (Alfred) Sermons.
Woodward's (Henry) Essays and Reflections.

Con.

Spanheimii Opera.

Degrees of Guilt in Sin. See DEADLY SIN, UNPARDONABLE SIN, VENIAL SIN.

Baumgarten, de Gradibus peccatorum.
Multerus de Diversis peccati gradibus.
Tellerus de Inæqualitate peccatorum.

Deism. See HARMONY OF REASON AND FAITH, NECESSITY OF REVELATION, PROVINCE OF REASON.

Pro.

Barthius (Jo. Henr.) de Vera Religione.
Bodini (Joann.) Colloquium.
Celsii Opera.
Chawin, de Naturali Religione.
Connor, Evangelium Medici.
Constant (B.), Religion considérées dans ses sources, ses formes, &c.
De La Serre, Examen. de la Religione.
Diderot, Pensèes philosophiques.
Gebhard, Cogitationes rationales.
Gundlingii Observationes Selectæ.
Herbert de Veritate. (The first to make Deism a science. 1624.)
——— de Causis Errorum.
——— de Religione Gentilium.
Hobbesii Opera Philosophica.
Holbach, Christianisme dévoilé.
Langsdorf's Gott und die Natur.
Liebnitz, Opera Theologica.
Machiavellii Discursis in Livium.
Meyeri Philosophia.
Mirabaud, Systéme de la nature.
Muralt, sur la Religion Essentielle.
Parizot, la Foi devoilée par la Raison.
Peyrerii Preadamitæ.
Roell, de Religione Naturali.
Rosseau, Confessions, &c.
——— Emile.
——— Various other works.
Sué, Lettres sur la Religion.
Vanini Amphitheatrum.
Voltaire, Epitre a Urane.
——— Lettres Philosophique.
——— Various other works.

Deism—*continued.*

Pro.

Blount's Anima Musedi.
——— Life of Apollonius Tyaneus.
——— Oracles of Reason.
Bolingbroke's Letters on History.
——— Philosophical Religion.
——— Various other works.
Brown's Religio Medici.
Chubb's Discourse on Miracles.
——— Foundation of the Chris. religion.
——— Subjects of the Old Testament.
——— True Gospel of Christ asserted.
——— On Redemption.
——— Four Dissertations.
——— Collection of Tracts.
——— Previous Question.
Collins' Enquiry into human liberty.
——— Grounds of the Christian religion.
——— On Free Thinking.
——— Scheme of Literal Prophecy.
——— Man's other voices.
——— Vind. of the Divine Attributes.
Elwell on the Incarnation.
English's Grounds of Chris. examined.
Evanson's Doctrine of the Trinity.
——— Dissonance of the Evangelists.
——— Letter to Dr. Hurd.
——— Letter to Dr. Priestly.
Hartley on the Human Mind.
Hobbes' Historical Narration of Heresy.
——— Human Nature.
——— Letter on Liberty and Necessity.
——— Letter to the Duke of Newcastle.
——— Leviathan.
Hume's Essay on Miracles.
——— Treatise on Human Nature.
——— Dialogues.
Kame's (Lord) Essays.
Lyon's Infallibility of Human Judgment.
Morgan's Moral Philosopher.
——— Deism fairly stated.
——— Conceptions of the Jews considered
——— Defence of the Moral Philosopher.
——— Physico-theology.
——— Reply to Chandler.
——— Sacerdotism displayed.
New Harmony Gazette. Pub. from 1825 1834, by R. Dale Owen.
Newman's (F. W.) Theism.
Paine's Age of Reason. (Numerous replie viz., by Disney, Drew, Estlin, McNeill Scott, Simpson, Watson, &c.)
Palmer's Principles of Nature.
Shaftesbury's Charact. of men, manners, &
Syke's Innocency of Error.
Taylor's Translation of the arguments Celsus, Porphyry, and Julian.
Tindall's Christianity as old as Creation.
Toland's Amyntor.
——— Pantheisticon.
——— Christianity not mysterious.
Volney's Works.
Woolston's Discourses on Miracles.
——— Defence of Do.

Deism—*continued.*

Pro.

Woolston's Moderator.
——— Supplement to Moderator.
——— Second Supplement to Moderator.

A multitude of other Deistical writers might be cited, especially in the German language, but the arguments are the same in all.

Con.

Origen, contra Celsus.

Abbadie, Verité de la Relig. Chrétien.
Baumgarten, Opera.
Bergier, Deisme refuté par lui meme.
Bullet, Responses Critique. (Refutes many cavils of the infidels of the 18th century.)
Carpzovii Apparatus Historico-criticus.
Crouzas, Examen du Pyrronisme, ancienne, et moderne.
Deylingii Observationes Sacræ.
Diecanni Schediasma de Naturalismo.
Fabricii Delectus argumentorum veritat. relig. Christ. versus Atheos, Deistas, Judæos, &c.
Grotius de Veritate Relig. Christianæ.
[Guenèe] Lettres de quelques Juifs.
Houtteville, le Christianisme prouvé par les faits.
Huetii Demonstratio.
Jacquelot, Defence de la Religion.
Kortholtus de Tribus impostoribus. (Herbert, Hobbes, and Spinoza.
Langii Causa Dei et Religionis.
Le Clerc, de l'Incredulité.
Lemper Vorbericht der Nachricht.
Less' Wahrheit der Christl. Religion.
Limborch de Veritate rel. Christianæ.
Loescheri Prenotiones Theologicæ.
Mersen, Impieté des Deistes.
Musæi (Jo.) Dissertatio. (*Contra Herbert.*)
Musæi Examen Methodi Herberti de investigatione veritatis.
Noesselt's Wahrheit und Gottlichkeit, &c.
Olearii Synopsis Controversiarum.
Pfafiii (Chr.) Dissertationes.
Picteti (Benedict.) Dissertationes.
Placette, Réponse à M. Bayle.
Rosemond, Défense de la Rel. Christienne.
Stein's Apologetik der Offenbarung.
Titius de Insufficientia rel. naturalis.
Tribbechovii Historia Naturalismi.
Trin's Freydencker Lexicon.
Turretin, de Veritate et Divinitate, &c.
Wolfii Manichæismus ante manichæos.
Wollii Oratio in Collinum.

Allix's Reflections on the Old Testament.
Applegarth on the Human Understanding.
Apthorp's (East) Prevalence of Christianity before its civil establishment. (Gives a very useful account of civil and ecclesiastical historians.)
Asgill's (J.) Reply to Woolston on miracles.

Deism—*continued.*

Con.

Atkinson on Christianity. (Rep. to Tindall.)
——— Remarks on a late work. (Reply to Morgan.)
Atkey's Examination of "Christianity as old as Creation."
Ayscough on Gospel Obedience.
Balguy's Letters to a Deist.
Bates' Infidelity scourged. (Rep. to Chubb.)
Beard's Christian Relig. defended from the assaults of Owenism.
Belknap's Dissertation. (Ans. to Paine.)
Benson's Answer to Morgan.
Bentley's Remarks on a late discourse, &c. (A powerful answer to Collins.)
Bergier's Deism self-confuted.
Berkley's Minute Philosopher.
Berriman's Boyle Lectures. 1730.
Bidlack's Bampton Lectures. 1811.
Bliss' Observations. (Reply to Chubb.)
Bolton's Hulsean prize essay. 1852.
Boyle Lectures. (Annual since 1692.)
Boyle on Things above Reason.
——— on the Resurrection.
Bradley's Impartial View. (Ans. to Blount.)
Bramhall against Hobbes.
Broadley on the Evidences, internal and external, of the religion of Moses.
Broughton's Answer to Tyndall.
Brown (Bp.) on the Human Understanding.
Brown's Essay on the "Characteristics."
Burnett's Scriptural doctrine of Redemption. (Reply to Morgan.)
Butler's Analogy of Religion and Nature.
Calamy's Sermons.
Campbell on Miracles.
Cary's (S.) Review of English's "Grounds of Christianity."
Chalmers' Evidences of Christianity.
Chandler (Edw.) on the Prophecies of the O. Testament. (Reply to Collins.)
——— Vindications of the same.
Chandler's (S.) Vind. of the Chris. religion.
——— on the Conduct of modern Deists.
——— Antiquity and authority of the prophecies of Daniel.
——— Reasons for being a Christian.
——— On the History of the Old and New Testaments. (Reply to Morgan.)
Chichester's Deism and Christianity.
Chapman's Eusebius.
——— Reply to Morgan and Tindall.
——— Remarks on the Prophecies of Daniel. (Reply to Collins.)
Clarke's (Dr.) Reflections on that part of the book called *Amyntor*, which relates to the writings of the Primitive Fathers.
Clayton's Vindication of Scripture. (Reply to Bolingbroke.)
Collyer's Lectures.
Conybeare's Defence of Religion. (Reply to Tindall. "The best reasoned book in the world."—Warburton.)
——— on Miracles.

Deism—*continued.*

Con.

Curtis' Folly and danger of infidelity.
Dalrymple's Inquiry into the secondary causes which Mr. Gibbon assigns for the rapid progress of Christianity.
Delany's Revel. examined with candor.
Ditton on Christ's Resurrection.
Doddridge's Lectures. Part 6.
——— Answer to Chubb.
Dwight's Discourses. (Infidel Philosophy.)
Earbury's Deism Refuted.
Eclectic Review. New Series. 3:253.
Edinburg Review. 2:661.
Ellis on Hume's Essay on Miracles.
Entick's Evidences. (Reply to Woolston.)
Everett's (E.) Defence of Christianity.
Fenton's Lady Moyer's lectures. 1728.
Fleming's (Caleb) Truth and Deism at variance.
Forbes (D.) on Incredulity.
Foster's (James) Usefulness and Truth of Christianity. (Answer to Tindall.)
Frothingham (N. L.) on Deism.
Fuller's Gospel its own witness.
Gassendi's Answer to Herbert's De Veritate.
Gastrell's Certainty of Christianity.
Gibson's Pastoral Letters.
Gilderdale on Nat. and revealed religion.
Giles' (Rev. Dr.) Christian Records.
Girdlestone's Anatomy of Scepticism.
Grave's Lectures on the Pentateuch.
——— Evidences of Christ's Resurrection. (Reply to Woolston.)
Gurdon's Boyle Lectures. 1721 and 1722.
Gregory's (Olynthus) Evidences, &c.
Grove (H.) on Christ's Resurrection.
Haldane (Robt.) on Divine Revelation.
Hallet on Providence. (Powerful.)
Hall's (Robt.) Infidelity considered with respect to its influence on society.
Halyburton's Inquiry. (Reply to Herbert.)
Hamilton's Pentateuch and its assailants.
Harris' Reasonableness of Believing.
Horne's (Geo.) Letters on Infidelity.
Horne's (T. H.) D. refuted. (Many editions.)
Hulsean Lectures. Commenced 1820. (The lectures by Benson, 1820, Franks, 1821, Wordsworth, 1848, Curry, 1852, and others, are very able, and are printed separately.)
Ibbot's (Benj.) Boyle Lectures. 1721, 1722.
Jackson's (J.) Examination. (Ans. to Chubb.)
——— Plea for Reason. (Rep. to Tindall.)
——— Address to Deists.
Jeffry's True grounds and reasons.
Jenkins' (R.) Certainty of Christianity.
Jew's Letters to Voltaire. (By Guinnée.)
Johnston's Chris. older than Creation.
Jones on the Canon. (Reply to Toland.)
Jortin's (J.) Discourses.
Kidder's Demonstration of the Messiah.
King's Origin of Evil.
La Crosse's Animad. on "Oracles of Reason."
Lardner's Credibility of the Gospel History.
——— Circumstances of the Jews.

Deism—*continued.*

Con.

Lavington on the Types. (Reply to Collins.)
Law's Case of Reason. (Reply to Tindall.)
Lawson's Exam. of Hobbes' "Leviathan."
Le Clerc's Causes of Incredulity.
Leek's Interpretation of the Law and Prophets. (Reply to Woolston.)
Leland's Advantage and Necessity of Revel.
——— Defence of the Christian Religion.
——— Divine authority of the Sacred Scriptures asserted. (Reply to Morgan.)
——— Answer to late book, &c. (Tindall.)
——— View of Deistical writers.
Leslie's Short Method with Deists.
Less' Authority, Preservation, and Credi-ibility, &c. Trans. by Kingdon.
Lindsay (H.) on Infidelity.
Lobb's Defence of Relig. (Ans. to Collins.)
London Quart. Review. 3:1.
Lowman's Hebrew Government.
——— on Prophecy. (Reply to Collins.)
Lyttleton on the Conversion of St. Paul. ("A treatise to which Infidelity has never been able to fabricate a specious answer."—Dr. Johnson.)
Maltby's (E.) Illustrations.
Mangey's Reply to Toland's Nazarenus.
Markland on Miracles. (Ans. to Woolston.)
Marshall on the 70 Weeks. (Ans. to Collins.)
McKnight's Truth of the Gospel History.
Middleton's Case of Abraham defended.
Moss (Bp.) on the Resurrection.
Moyne on Miracles. (Reply to Chubb.)
Nares' Bampton Lectures. 1805.
Nash's Standard of Truth. (Ans. to Paine.)
Newcombe on the Character of the Saviour.
——— Sure Word of Prophecy.
Newton (Bp.) on the Prophecies.
Nichols' Conference with a Theist.
Nisbet's Triumphs of Christianity.
Norrison on Reason and Faith.
Ogilvie on the Cause of Scepticism. (Remarks on Herbert, Shaftsbury, Bolingbroke, Hume, and Gibbon.)
Paley's Evidences.
——— Horæ Paulinæ.
Patton's (Will.) Christianity the true theology. (Reply to Paine.)
Pearson's (Geo.) Hulsean Lectures. 1834.
Penrose's Bampton Lectures.
Porteus' Summary of Evidence.
Potter's Authority of the O. and N. Testam.
Prideaux's Letter to Deists.
Pye's Moses and Bolingbroke.
Reynolds' Letter to a Deist.
Richardson's Hist. and Def. of the Canon.
Riddle's Bampton lectures. 1852.
Roberts' Christianity Vindicated. (Reply to Volney.)
Robinson's Usefulness of Revelation.
——— Distinguishing Char. of the Gospel.
Rogers' Reply to Collins.
——— Eight Sermons.
Ross' Reply to Hobbes' Leviathan.

Deism—*continued.*

Con.

Rotheram's Truth of Christianity.
Rust's Discourse on the use of reason.
Ryland (J.) on Infidelity.
Schmucker's Modern Infidelity. 1848.
Scott on Inspiration. (Reply to Paine.)
Seaton's Compendious View. (Reply to Woolston.
Sherlock's Use of Prophecy. (Agt. Collins.)
Shuttleworth's Consistency of the Scheme of Prov. with itself and with human reason.
Skelton's Works. (Reviews all the principal Deistical writers.)
Smith's (Elisha) Cure of Deism.
Smith's (Sam. Stanhope) Lectures.
Squier's Christianity founded on reason.
Stackhouse's State of the Controversy.
Staples' Polemic Theology.
Stebbings' Defence of Scripture History.
——— Advantage of Revelation.
——— Boyle Lectures. 1747.
——— Charge to the Clergy.
Stephens (W.) on the Growth of Deism.
Stephenson on the Miracles of Christ.
Stillingfleet's Letter to a Deist.
Sykes (Ashley) on the Christian Religion. (Answer to Collins.)
——— on Phlagon's eclipse.
[Taylor's (H.)] Ben Mordecai's Apology.
Taylor's (Nath.) Preserv. against Deism.
Tennison's Creed of Hobbes, examined.
Thompson's (H.) Infidelity confuted on its own grounds.
Tillotson's Sermons.
Toulmin's (J.) Dissertations.
Walpole's (R.) Misrepresentations, ignorance, and plagiarism of infidel writers.
Warburton's View of Bolingbroke's Philos.
——— Divine Legation of Moses.
Waterland's Scripture Vindicated. (Reply to Tindall.)
Watson's Apology for Christianity. (Reply to Gibbon.)
——— Apology for the Bible. (Reply to Paine.)
Webster on the Jewish Dispensation. (Reply to Morgan.)
West on the Resurrection of Christ.
Whately's Historic doubts relative to Napoleon Buonaparte.
Whiston's Account of Scrip. Prophecies.
——— Examination of late discourses. (Reply to Collins.)
——— Reason and Philosophy no enemies.
Whitby's Necessity and Use of Revelation.
Wilson's (John) Dissertation on Christianity. (A powerful work, built on Butler's Analogy.)
Witherspoon's Works. (Lectures. Lect. 8.)
Witty's First principles of Deism.

See large lists of writers on the Deistical controversy, in LELAND on *Deistical Writers*, and VAN MILDERT'S *Boyle Lectures*.

Deism, History of.

Baumgarten's (M.) Geschichte der Religions parteien.
Dieckmanni Schediasma de naturalismo.
Gregoire, Hist. des Sectes religieuses.
Grundig's Geschichte der heutigen Deisten und Freydenker.
Henke's Kirchengeschichte.
Kortholtus de tribus Impostoribus. (Herbert, Hobbes, and Spinoza.)
Lechler's Gesch. des Englischen Deismus.
Lemker Vorbericht der Nachricht von Wollaston.
Lerminier, de l'Influence de la philosophie du 18e siecle.
Saintes, Hist. Critique du rationalisme en Allemagne.
Schlosser's Gesch. des 18 Jahrhunderts.
Stäudlin's Gesch. des Rationalismus.
——— Gesch. des Scepticismus.
Villemain, Cours de litterature Francaise.

Amer. Bibl. Repository. April, 1840.
Riddle's Natural history of Infidelity.

See HOUTTEVILLE'S *Principal authors for and against Christianity, from the beginning, and their methods.* 1739.

Deity of Christ. See JESUS CHRIST.

Dejection. See CONTENTMENT, DESPONDENCY, PATIENCE, RESIGNATION.

Delay. See PROCRASTINATION.

Delivery. See ELOQUENCE.

Deluge. See GEOLOGY.

Alexandri (F.) Dissertationes. Diss. I.
Burnet (Th.), de Diluvio.
Capelli Historia Diluvii illustrata.
Heideggeri Historia Patriarcharum.
Kircheri (Athanas.) Dissertationes.
Marchii Scripta in selecta Scripturæ.
Neve, l'Origine de la tradition Indienne.
Strauchii Dissertationes. (The year of its occurrence.)
Vossius de Ætate Mundi. (Makes the deluge partial.)

Amer. Bibl. Repos. 9:78. 10:328. 11:1.
Ancient Universal History.
Berington's (S.) Dissertations. Dissert. 2. (Opposes the conjectures of several distinguished writers.)
Bloomfield's (Cha. J.) Sermons.
Bonjour's Select Dissertations.
Brown's Geology of Scripture.
Bryant's Analysis of Ancient Mythology.
Buckland's Reliquæ Diluvianæ.
Burnett's Theory of the Earth. (Much fuller in some parts, and in others less so, than the Latin edition. Of no value now.)
Burton's (Charles) Lectures.

Deluge—*continued.*

Catcoll's Proof of a Deluge. (Gives the principal Heathen accounts.)
Chambers' Dictionary. "Ark."
Clayton's Vind. of Scripture. Part 2.
Close's (Francis) Sermons.
Cockburn's Inquiry into the truth and certainty, &c. ("One of the most valuable books on the subject."—DARLING.)
Delany's Revelation exam. with candor.
Faber's Mysteries of the Cabiri.
Fairbairn's Demonst. of the fact and time of the Deluge. (Highly approved.)
Fuller's Discourses on Genesis.
Gilfillan's Alpha and Omega. Ch. 7.
Gisbourne's Natural Theology.
Grove's (Henry) Discourses.
Hall's (Bp.) Contemplations.
Hamilton's Pentateuch and its assailants.
Howard's Sacred History compared with the cosmogonies and traditions of ancient nations.
Jackson's (Thomas) Works.
Jones' (Sir Wm.) Asiatic Researches.
King's (Edw.) Attempt to account for the D.
Le Clerc's Dissertations. Diss. 5.
Littell's Living Age. 11:109.
Maurice's Indian Antiquities.
Meade's The Bible and the Classics.
Nichols' Conference with a Theist.
Panoplist. 4:345, 436, 529.
Ray's Physico-theology.
Royal Transactions. Vol. 75, No. 4.
Saurin's (James) Dissertations.
Silliman's Journal of Science.
Stillingfleet's Origines Sacræ. (Holds to a partial deluge.)
Townsend's Character of Moses.
Warter's (John W.) Sermons.
Whiston's Cause of the Deluge.
Woodward's Natural history of the earth.
Young (J. R.) on Modern Scepticism. 1865.

Demoniacal Possession.

Aderi Enarr. de Ægrotis et Morbidis in N. T.
Lecanu, Histoire de Satan: son culte, ses manifestations, ses œuvres, &c.
Meyeri Historia Diaboli.
Nanz, die Besessenen im N. Test.
Semlerus de Dæmoniacis. de N. Test.
Thyræi (Soc. Jesu.) de Demoniacis.
Zimmerman de Demoniacis Evangeliorum.

Appleton's (Pres.) Works. Lect. 50, 51, 52.
Arnold's (Dr. Tho.) Sermons.
Barker's Nature and circumstances of the D.
Burgh's Crito; or Essays on various subj.
Calmet's Dissertations.
Dalton's Relation of Joyce Dovey.
Darrel's True Narrative of the grievous vexation of seven persons in Lancashire.
Deyling's Sacred Observations.
Doddridge's Lectures. Lect. 214.
D'Oyly's (Dr. George) Sermons.
Encyclopedia Brittanica.

Demoniacal Possession—*continued.*

Farmer on the Demoniacs of the N. T.
——— Remarks on Ward's Dissertations.
Fell on Demoniacs. (Reply to Farmer.)
Girdlestone's (Charles) Sermons.
Kitto's Journal. 4:1. 7:394.
Lardner's (Nath.) Discourses.
Mather's (C.) Magnalia. (Salem witches.)
Mede's Works. (Holds the same views as Farmer and Lardner.)
Methodist Quart. Review. 10:213.
Newton's (Bp.) Dissertations.
Pegge on Demoniacal Possession.
Porteus' (Bp.) Dissertation on Demoniacs.
Seed's (Jeremiah) Sermons.
Sharp's (Granville) Case of Saul.
Sharp's (Gregory) Review of the Controv.
Sykes on Demoniacal Possession.
——— Further enquiry.
Townsend's (George) Sermons.
Twells on the Demoniacs. (Reply to Sykes.)
Van Mildert's (Bp.) Serm. at Lincoln's Inn.
Vincent's (William) Sermons.
Warburton's Sermons.
Ward's Dissertations on passages of Scrip.
Whiston's Account of the Demoniacs.
Worthington's Inquiry in the cases, &c.
——— Further Inquiry. (Rep. to Farmer.)
Young on the Gospel Demoniacs.

Demonolatry. See WORSHIP OF SPIRITS.

Demons. See EVIL SPIRITS.

Apuleus de deo Socratis. (Gives a clear view of the ancient doctrine of Demons.)
Beausobre, Hist. de Manichæisme. Lib. V.
Ditmar de Dæmonibus.
Hundeshagen (J.) Dissertationes.
Jacobi I. (Britt. regis) Demonologia.
Jamblicus de Mysteriis.
Plutarch, Opera quæ extant.
Senecæ Opera.
Thomasii Dissertationes.
Winzeri Dæmonologia in N. T. proposita.

Bekker's World bewitched. ("The best account of the power of Devils."—LOWNDES.)
Berg's Abaddon and Mahanaim.
Bibliotheca Sacra. 1:117. 16:119.
British Quart. Review. No. 9. 1847.
Burgh's Crito; or Essays on var. subjects.
Doddridge's Lectures. Part 10.
Donaldson's Chr. orthodoxy reconciled with modern learning. Ch. 4.
Fell's Heathen doctrine of Demons.
Foreign Quarterly Review. 6:1.
Frazier's Magazine. 2:507.
Gilpin on Temptation.
Glanvil's Sadducismus triumphatus.
Sharp's (Granville) Influence of D.
Toplady's (Augustus M.) Sermons.
Townsend's (George) Sermons.
Whewell's Good and evil angels.

Denarius. See COINS.

Dependence of the Mind on the Body. See RECIPROCAL INFLUENCE.

Deportment. See CONSISTENCY, COURTESY, EXAMPLE OF CHRIST, RELIGION AND BUSINESS, SOBRIETY, SOCIAL INTERCOURSE.

Arnold's (Thomas) Sermons.
Berens' (Edward) Sermons.
Blackall's (Offspring) Sermons.
Colet's Order of a Christian life.
Cooper's (Edward) Sermons.
Evans' (A. B.) Sermons.
Farringdon's (Anthony) Sermons.
Findlater's (R.) Sermons.
Girdlestone's Christian life.
Gresley's (William) Sermons.
Gurnall's Christian armor.
Hickman's (B.) Sermons.
Hinton's Active Christian.
Hoare's Sermons on Christian character.
Holdsworth's (R.) Sermons.
Jackson's (J.) Sermons on Chris. character.
Jewell's (John) Sermons.
Law's Serious call.
MacLean's (Archibald) Sermons.
Melville's (Henry) Sermons.
Neale's (E.) Sermons.
Scudder's Christian's daily walk.
Secker's Non-such Professor.
Skelton's (Philip) Sermons.
Smallridge's (George) Sermons.
Whichcott's (B.) Sermons.
Whole duty of man. (The author of this inestimable work, of which millions have been printed, is unknown!)
Wilson's (Bp. Thomas) Sermons.
Woolton's Christian manual.
Wynyard's (M. J.) Sermons.

Dervishes. See RELIGIONS.

Thornbury's Turkish life and character.
Wolf's Missionary Journal.

Descent into Hell.

Pro.

Clemens Alex., Stromata.
Cyril Alex., Opera.
Origen, contra Celsum.
Justin M., Dialogus cum Tryphone.

Classen, de Descensu J. C. ad inferos.
Dietelmair, Historia Dogmatis, &c.
Dietelmayer, Hist. dogmatis de descensu.
Dummer, de Christi ad infernos descensu.
Eckhard de Descensu Christi ad inferos.
Harenbergii Theologia Dogmatica.
Hacker (J. G. A.) Dissertationes.
Ittigii (Thomas) Dissertationes.
Lavateri Καταβασις εις Αδου.
Zezschwitzii Dissert. Exegetica dogmatica.

Ballou's Histor. sketch of the interpretations of 1 Peter iii. 18–20, and iv. 6.
Bilson's Survey of Christ's sufferings.

Descent into Hell—*continued.*

Pro.

Bingham's (Richard) Immanuel.
Hey's (Dr. John) Lectures. Bk. 4.
Hill (Adam) on the Apostles' creed.
Hobart's (Bp.) Sermons on Redemption.
Horsely's (Bp.) Sermons.
Hottinger's Dissertations.
Newman's (John H.) Sermons.
Parke's Apology. (Ans. to Limbomastix.)
Smith on Christ's descent into hell.

Con.

Augustini Epist. 57 ad Dardanum.
Bezæ Tractationes Theologicæ.
Calovii Dissertationes.
Chemnitii Dissertationes.
Clausenii Observationes crit.-philologicæ.
Hacker (J. G. A.) Dissertationes.
Holtzfusii Dissertationes.
Limbomastix. [Anonymous.]
Thummii (Theodor.) Dissertationes.
Volborth, Quantum error Apollinaris contulerit, &c.
Witsii Exercitationes. Exer. 18.

Allen on the Thirty-nine articles.
Barrington on the Divine dispensations.
Barrow on the Apostles' Creed.
Benson's Paraph. and Notes. (1 Pet. iii. 19.)
Bibliotheca Sacra. 16:309.
Broughton (Hugh) on Christ's descent, &c.
Burnet on the Thirty-nine articles.
Christian Examiner. 50:401.
Clarke's (Dr. Samuel) Sermons.
Cox's (John Redman) Considerations.
Doddridge's Exposition. (1 Pet. iii. 19.)
Edwards' History of Redemption.
Frazier's Magazine. 1:341.
Gill's Commentary. (1 Pet. iii. 19.)
Hammond's Reply to Smith.
Harwood's Five Dissertations.
Jacobs' Sufferings and victory of Christ. (Reply to Bilson.)
Lightfoot's (John) Dissertations.
More's (H.) Theological Works.
Muencher on the Descent into hell.
Pearson on the Creed.
Peters on Job.
Seabury's (Samuel) Discourses.
Secker (Abp.) on the Catechism.
Sturmy's (Daniel) Discourses.
Willet's (Andrew) Loidoromastix.

See a long list of other writers on this subject in ALGER'S *Doct. of a future life*—Appendix.

Desertion.

East (J.) on Affliction and Desertion.
Flavel's Works.
Gibb's (John) Sermons.
Godwin's Child of light walking in darkness.
Hervey's Theoron and Aspasio.

Hill's (Bryant) Sermons.
Lambert's Sermons.
Lavington's (John) Sermons on the 77th Ps.
Sharp's (Archbishop) Sermons.
Watts' Meditations on Job.

Despondency. See MELANCHOLY, RESIGNATION, TRUST.

Barry's (J.) Reviving Cordial.
Baxter on Religious Melancholy.
Bolton's Comfort of afflicted conscience.
Buddicom's (Robert) Sermons.
Claude on the Composition of Sermons.
Christian Observer. 20:332, 401, 469.
East on Affliction and Desertion. (A collection of treatises by Sibbs, Manton, Reynolds, Flavel, Bates, Collins, Charnock, Godwin, Jay, &c.)
Fowler's (Bp.) Discourses.
Fuller's (Andrew) Sermons.
Gisbourne's (Thomas) Sermons.
Gordon's Collection of curious Tracts.
Hackett's (Bp.) Christian Consolations.
Hall's (Bp.) Balm of Gilead.
Hall's (R.) Discouragements of pious men.
Jowett's (Jos.) Fifty-two sermons.
Knight's (Samuel) Sermons.
Lucas' (Dr. Richard) Sermons.
Mannering's Christian Consolations.
Rogers on Trouble of Mind.
Sherlock's (Bp.) Sermons.
Toplady on the fears of God's people.
Waterland's (Daniel) Sermons.

Destructionists. See ETERNITY OF HELL TORMENTS, RESTORATIONISTS.

Pro.

Barlow (J. W.) on Eternal punishment.
Blain's (Jacob) Death not life.
Bourne's (Samuel) Sermons.
Clarke's (Geo.) Vind. of the honor of God.
Coombe's (John) Teachings of the Old and New Testament.
Davis (Tho.) on Endless suffering.
Dobney (H. H.) on Future punishment.
Edwards on the Salvation of all men.
Ellis' (Aaron) Bible versus tradition.
Hobbes' Leviathan.
Hudson's (C. F.) Debt and Grace. (Regarded as the ablest work on this side.)
Marsom's (John) Works.
Mitchel's (Tho.) The gospel crown of life.
Scott's (J. N.) Sermons.
Sellon's (J.) Sermons.
[Storr's (Geo.)] Unity of man.
——— Other treatises.
Taylor's (John) Scripture doctrine of original sin.
——— Paraphrase and notes on Romans.

Con. See IMMORTALITY OF THE SOUL.

Martin, la Vie future.

Amer. Theolog. Review. 3:215.
Bagnall on the Intermediate state.

Destructionists—*continued.*

Con.

Barrows' (E. J.) Doctrine of a future state.
Bartlett's Life and death eternal.
Bibliotheca Sacra. 15:625. 17:111.
Blair's Sermons.
Burton on the Annihilation of the wicked.
Campbell's (Alex.) Life and Death.
Hinton's (J. H.) Athanasia.
Hovey's State of the impenitent dead.
Landis on the Immortality of the soul, and final condition of the wicked.
Lee's (L.) Immortality of the soul.
Massilon's Sermons.
Methodist Quart. Review. 40:404.
New Englander. 11:362. 21:248.
Presbyterian Quart. Review. 8:594.
Stearne's (J. G.) Immortality of the soul.
Strong's (James) Review of Hudson.
The Guardian. No. 129.
Theological and Lit. Review. 3:395.
Warren's (J. P.) Sadduceeism.

Destruction of Canaanites.

Doddridge's Lectures. Part 6, prop. 120.
Leland's Authority of Scripture.
——— Answer to Tindall's "Christianity as old as Creation."
Lowman's Hebrew Government.
Paley's (William) Sermons.
Shuckford's Connec. of Sac. and prof. hist.
Sykes' Connec. of Nat. and Rev. Religion.

Destruction of Jerusalem.

Burrows' (E. J.) Hours of devotion.
Christian Disciple. 4:206.
Churton's Bampton Lectures. 1785.
Collyer's (Will. B.) Lectures on prophecy.
Ely's (John) Winter Lectures.
Josephus' History of the Jews.

Destruction of Sodom and Gomorrah.

Amer. Bibl. Repository. April, 1840.
Le Clerc's Dissertations.
Robinson (E.) on the Dead Sea.

Detraction. See SLANDER.

Barrow's (Isaac) Sermons.
Burrows' Hours of devotion.
Butler's (Alban) Sermons.
Johnson's (Dr. Samuel) Sermons.
Leighton's (Abp.) Works.
Mercier's Works.
Morning Exercises at Cripplegate. (Sermon by Matt. Poole.)
Opie's (Miss) Detraction Displayed.
Vaughn's Spirit of detraction convicted. (Very curious and amusing, but of no theological value.)

Development, Physical. See CREATION, EQUIVOCAL GENERATION, GEOLOGY.

Pro.

Brongniart, Tableau des genres de végétaux, fossiles, &c.
Lamarck, Hist. des Animaux sans vertébres.
Maillet, Philosophie.

Atkinson's (H. G.) Letters.
Darwin's Zoonomia.
Huxley's (Prof. T. H.) Works.
Spencer's (Herbert) Illustrations of universal progress.
Vestiges of the Natural History of the creation.
——— Sequel to the same.
Westminster Review. 44:242.

Con.

Agassiz's Study of Natural History.
Amer. Quart. Church Review. 17:505.
Brodie's (Sir Benj.) Lectures.
Buchanan's (Jas.) Modern Atheism. 1855.
Christian Examiner. New Series. 1:60.
[Fontenelle's] Plurality of worlds.
Lubbock's Lectures on the Origin of man.
Lyell's Antiquity of Man.
Miller's (Hugh) Law versus Miracle.
——— Testimony of the Rocks.
Oken's Physico-philosophy.
Presbyterian Review. 1:106. 24:275.
Stillingfleet's Origines sacra.
Walker's (Jas. B.) Sacred Philosophy.

Development of Doctrine.

Pro.

Bauer. (Many articles in the "Theologische Jahrbücher.")
Moehler's Symbolik.
——— Neue Untersuchungen der Lehr gegensätze, &c. (A defence of the Symbolik.)

Dorner's Doct. of the person of Christ.
Foxton's (F. F.) Popular Christianity.
Moehler's Symbolik. Tr. by J. B. Robinson.
Newman's (John H.) Essays.
Newman's (F. W.) Phases of Faith.
Schaff's What is Church History?

Con.

Amer. Biblic. Reposit. 3d Series. 3:193.
Brownson's Quart. Review. 1:43.
Buchanan's Modern Atheism. Chap. 2.
Butler's (W. A.) Letters on Romanism.
——— ——— Revised by A. P. Moor.
——— Letters on Chris. doctrine.
——— ——— Revised by C. Hardwick.
——— ——— " by T. Woodward.
Dublin University Mag. 27:405. 37:276.
Edinburg Magazine. 86:397.
Frazier's Magazine. 33:253.
Greenfield on Doctrinal development.
Irons' (W. J.) Sermons.

Development of Doctrine—*continued.*

Con.

Maurice's Warburton Lecture. 1846. Preface.
Mithridates; or Mr. Newman's Essay its own confutation.
Moberly's Exam. of Newman's Development.
North British Review. 5:418.
O'Sullivan's (M.) Theory of development.
Palmer's Doct. of D. considered in reference to the evidences of Christianity.
Phillipsohn's Devel. of the religious idea.
Presbyterian Quart. Review. 1:106.
Quarterly Review. 77:404.
Townsend's (Dr. Geo.) Sermons and charges.

Devils. See DEMONS.

Devotion. See FORMS OF PRAYER, MANUALS, PRAYER, RETIREMENT.

Adams' (T.) Posthumous Works. (Precious.)
Addison's Daily Sacrifice.
Andrews' Manual of private devotion.
Augustin's Confessions and Meditations.
Batty's (Adam) Sermons.
Baxter's Dying Thoughts.
——— Saint's Rest. Chap. 12.
Bellamy's True religion delineated. Sec. 7.
Bennet's Christian Oratory.
Beren's (Edward) Devotions.
Beveridge's Private Thoughts.
Bridges on the 119th Psalm. (Excellent.)
Bragge's (Francis) Sermons.
Bull (J.) on Early Devotion.
Cave's Primitive Christianity.
Christian Examiner. 4:281.
Christian Quart. Spectator. 5:41.
Christian Review. 6:477.
Corbet's Self-Employment.
Davis' (M.) Helps to devotion.
Dorney's Divine Contemplations.
Evans on the value of religious feeling.
Fenelon's Private Thoughts.
Griffiith (Tho.) on the Lord's prayer.
Hall's (Bp.) Contemplations.
——— Walking with God.
Hopkins' (Benj.) Parochial Sermons.
Huntingdon's (Prof.) Sermons.
Inet's Guide to the devout Christian.
Jay's (W.) Exercises for the Closet.
Jenks' Offices of devotion.
Kempis' Imitation of Christ. *Malcom's Ed.*
Ken's Retired Christian exercised.
Law's Serious Call. *Malcom's Ed.*
Lee's (R.) Handbook of devotion.
Milner's Sanctuary and Oratory.
Munkhouse's (Rich.) Sermons.
Nelson's Practice of devotion.
Norris' Scriptural Counsel.
Owen (John) on the Work of the Spirit.
Pascall's Thoughts.
Patrick's (Bp.) Devout Christian.
Pott's (J. H.) Sermons.
Rambach on the Sufferings of Christ.
Rogers' (H.) Helps to devotion.

Devotion—*continued.*

Romaine's Life of faith.
Rowe's (Mrs.) Devout Exercises.
Sales' Introduction to a devout life.
Sharpe's (William) Sermons.
Sheppard's Private thoughts.
Sherlock's (Bp.) Sermons.
Sherlock's (of Winnick) Practical Christian.
Smith's (Sam. Stanhope) Sermons.
Sterry's Kingdom of God in the soul of man.
Still's (J.) Horæ Privatæ.
Taylor's (Jer.) Golden Grove.
Waterhouse's Piety, character, and policy of early Christians.
Westoby's Helps to devotion.
Wettenhall's Enter into the closet.
Wilson's (Dan.) Meditations and Prayers.
Wilson's (Thos.) Sacra Privata. (Many ed.)
Zollikoffer's (Geo. J.) Sermons.

Dialect of the New Testament. See BIBLICAL CRITICISM, IDIOMS, STYLE.

Ahrens (H. L.), de Græcæ linguæ dialectis.
De Rossi, de Lingua Palestinæ.
Georgii Vindicia N. T. ab Hebraismis.
Leusden, de Dialectis N. Test. singulatim.
Rhenferdi (Jacob.) Dissertationes.
Salmasius de Lingua Hellenistica.
Vorstius de Hebraismis Nov. Test.
Wyes, Dialectologia Sacra.

Beckhaus' Lang. of the N. T. Tr. by Tertot.
Blackwall's Sacred Classics.
De Rossi & Pfannkuche on the Language of Palestine in the age of Christ. Tr. by Repp.
Green's Grammar of the N. Test. dialect.
Planck's Greek diction of the N. T.
Tholuck's Study of the O. T. Tr. by Patton.

Dialectics. See LOGIC.

Diatesseron. See MONOTESSARON.

Dictionaries of the Bible.

Bost (J. A.), Concordance Raisonée. 1849.
Calmet, Dict. Historique, Chron., &c. 1730.
Herzog, Theolog. real Encyklopädie. (20 volumes. Very complete and valuable.)
Hoffman's Volks-Bibellexikon.
Illyrici Clavis Scripturæ Sacræ. 1764. (Besides the explanation of principal words, it contains treatises on the study of Scripture, quotes the opinions of others, &c. &c.)
James, Dict. de l'Ecriture sainte. 1853.
Krehl's Neutestament. Hand-woerterbuch.
Sauley, Dict. des antiquités Bibliq. 1859.
Simon, Grand Dictionaire de la Bible.

Alexander's Dictionary of the Bible. 1835.
Arrowsmith's Geog. Dict. of the B. 1807.
Ayre's Treasury of Bible knowledge. 1866.
Beard's Household Bibl. Cyclopædia. 1848.
Bibliotheca Sacra. Edinburg. 1806.

Dictionaries of the Bible—*continued.*

British Critic. New Series. 8:445. (What a good Bible Dictionary should be.)
Brown's Dictionary. 1769. (Superseded.)
Calmet's Dict. 1722. Tr. by D'Oyly & Colson.
Cobbin's (Ingram) Bible Dictionary. 1850.
Creighton's Dictionary of Scripture proper names. 1808.
Eadie's Biblical Cyclopedia. 1849.
Herzog's Real Encyclop. Tr. by Bomberger.
Hird's Dict. of Scrip. proper names. 1851.
Jones' Biblical Cyclopedia. 1816.
Kitto's Biblical Cyclopedia. 1845.
Malcom's Dictionary of the Bible. Cuts. 1829. Enlarged, 1855.
McBean's Dict. of the Bible. 1779.
Oliver's Scripture Lexicon. 1792. (Limited to proper names, of which it gives 4,000.)
Robinson's (Edw.) Dict. of the Bible. 1833.
Robinson's (John) Theological, Biblical, and Ecclesiastical Dictionary. 1815.
Smith's (Will.) Dict. of the Bible. 1860.
Timson's Key to the Bible. 1845.
Wall's (Geo.) Domestic D. of the Bib. 1826.
Watson's Biblical and Theolog. Dict. ("A compilation from compilations, strongly anti-Calvinistic."—LOWNDES.)
Wilson's Christian Dict. 1648. (The signification of all Bible words.)

Difficulties of Scripture. See APPARENT CONTRADICTIONS, BIBLICAL CRITICISM, HERMENEUTICS, ILLUSTRATIONS, PHILOLOGY.

Originis Philocalia.

Adami (Corn.) Observ. Theologicæ.
——— Exercitationes Exegeticæ.
Altmanni Meletemata philol.-critica.
Arnoldi Lux in tenebris. (Discusses several thousand controvert. passages.)
Bertrami Expositio in difficiliora utriusque Testamenti Loca.
Bootii Animadversiones Sacræ.
Bos (Lambert.) Exercitationes.
Clerici (D.) Questiones Sacræ.
De Dieu, Critica Sacra, sive Animadversiones, &c. ("Inter præstantissimos."—WALCH.)
Deylingii Observ. Sacræ. (Fine index.)
Drusius, ad Loca Difficiliora Vet. et Novum Test. (Not surpassed by any critic of the 17th eent. His notes were much used by the translators of our version of the Bible.)
Elsneri Observationes.
Ernest, de Difficultatibus Nov. Test.
Estii in Difficiliora loca Commentaria. ("One of the best Papal expositors."—ORME.)
Fesselii Adversaria Sacra.
Frankii Observationes Biblicæ.
Gatakeri Adversaria Miscellanea.
Hackspanii Notæ theologico-philologicæ.
Hasæi et Ikenii Thesaurus novus. (A great collection, similar to that of Menthenius.)
Hengelii Annot. in loca nonnulla N. Test.
Hoffmanni Observationes.

Difficulties of Scripture—*continued.*

Hottingeri Opuscula.
Ikenii (Conrad.) Dissertationes.
Jablonski (Paull. Ernest.) Opuscula.
Knatchbull, Animad. paradoxiæ orthodoxæ.
Kœnigii Centuria Vindiciarum Sacrarum.
Langii Observationes Sacræ.
Laurentii Explicatio locorum difficilium.
Marckii (J.) Exercitationes.
Martin, Explications de plusieurs textes. (In the style of Harmer's observations, with plates.)
Mel, Antiquarius Sacer.
Menthenii Thesaurus. (A great collection of dissertations by eminent German divines of the 17th century.)
Michaelis Introductio ad Novum Test.
——— Observationes Sacræ.
Noeselt, Exercitationes.
Obenheim, de N. Test. locis pugnantibus.
Oderi Observationes Sacræ.
Ott, Excerpta ex. Flav. Josepho.
Pfeifferi Dubia Vexata. S. S.
Rosenmuller, Theologicæ Commentationes.
Schelling (J. E.) Animad. philol. crit.
Schroederi Nova Janua.
Schulteti Exercitationes Evangelicæ.
Simonis, Nov. Test. (Critical remarks.)
Spanheimii Dubia Evangelica.
Starkii (H. B.) Notæ selectæ, crit., exeget.
Storr, Exercit. exeget. ad selecta, etc.
Surenhusii Βιβλος καταλλαγης.
Tarnovii Exercitationum Biblicarum.
Venemæ Dissertationes Selectæ.
Vitringæ Exercit. in Epist. Pauli ad Corin.
Vitringæ (Filii) Dissertationes Sacræ.
Vogtii Miscellanea Biblica.
Waltheri Exercitationes Biblicæ.
Waltoni Biblia polyglotta Prolegomena. (The Edition of 1827, with Wrangham's notes, is best.)
Wesselii Dissertationes Leidensis.
Winkleri Disquisitiones.
Witsii Miscellanea Sacra.
Wolfii Curæ Philologicæ.
Zornii Opuscula Sacra.

Beausobre & L'Enfant on the Difficult passages in Matthew.
Benson's (C.) Hulsean Lectures. 1822.
Biblical Cabinet. Periodical. Edinburg and London. 1832. 35 vols.
Biblical Repertory. 1825 to 1861.
Blackmore on Four select passages.
Bowyer's Critical conjectures and observat.
Bryant's Observations on Passages of Scrip. obnoxious to enemies of religion. (700 passages.)
Bloomfield's Critical digest of the New Test. (A great storehouse of erudition.)
Carpenter (Wm.) on Scripture Difficulties.
Cochran on Some of the most difficult texts.
Conybeare's (Bp.) Discourses.
Cooper's (E.) Sermons.
Dimock's Notes on Genesis, &c. (Appendix.)

Difficulties of Scripture—*continued.*

Doddridge's Lectures. Part 6, prop. 51.
Edwards' (John) Exercitations; critical, philosophical, and historical.
——— Enquiry into some difficult texts.
Falconer's Bampton Lectures. 1810.
Featly's Clavis Mystica. (Seventy sermons on hard texts.)
Godwin's Moses and Aaron.
Goodwin's Hulsean Lectures. 1856.
Gregory's (John) Observations and notes.
Gurdon's Boyle Lectures. 1721.
Hallet's (Jos.) Notes on Scripture.
Hall's (Bp.) Explication of all the hard texts of the whole Scriptures.
Harmer's Observations.
Hawkins' Bampton Lectures. 1787.
Heath's Hulsean Lectures. (The advantages of difficult texts.)
Hewlett's Bible difficulties explained.
Hume's (M. C.) 12 obscure texts illustrated.
Jeane's Mixture of scholastic and practical divinity.
Kennicott's State of the printed text.
——— Remarks on select passages.
Kentish's Notes on passages of Scripture.
Kidder's Remarks on certain passages.
King's Morsels of Criticism.
Knatchbull on Diff. texts in the New Test. (An English trans. by the author himself, and more complete than the orginal.)
Lightfoot's Horæ Hebraicæ.
——— Explanation of difficult passages.
Longhurst's Commonplace Book.
Mann's Crit. Notes. (Comparing some passages with the ancient versions.)
Mayer's Treasury of Expositions, collected out of the most eminent interpreters.)
Moody's (N. J.) Helps to Bible readers.
Newton's (Thos.) Dissertations.
Nisbett's True Key to the more difficult passages in the New Testament.
Pilkington's Remarks on several passages.
Popham (Edw.) on Various texts.
Pott's (J. H.) Sermons.
Prescott's Every-day Scrip. difficulties.
Scragg's Ques. in Divinity, Hist. and Biog. (Expounds over 400 difficult texts.)
Scrivner's Supplement to the authorized version of the N. T. (Uses the Syriac, Latin, and earlier English versions.)
Secker's (Abp.) Sermons.
Sharp's (Abp.) Sermons.
Sherlock's (Bp.) Sermons.
Skelton's (Philip) Sermons.
Theological Reposit. (Many fine papers.)
Thompson's (Sam.) Exercitations.
Tomlinson's Attempt to rescue the Holy Scriptures from ridicule by a new translation of controverted passages, illustrated with critical notes.
Wake's (R.) Rationale upon some texts, &c.
Ward's (Dr. John) Dissertations.
Waterland's Scripture vindicated.
Weston on Diff. pass. in the Song of Deborah.

Whately (Abp.) on Some of the difficulties in the writings of Paul, and other parts of the New Testament.
Wratislaw's Difficulties of the N. Test.

Diligence, Christian. See INDUSTRY, REDEEMING TIME.

Dionysius Alexandrinus.

Dionysii Opera quæ extant.
Eusebius, Historia Ecclesiastica.
Lardner's Credibility of the Gospel.

Dionysius Areopagus.

Dionysii Areopagitici Opera.
Assemanni Bibliotheca Orientalis,
Bebellii Antiquitates Eccles. Sæc. IV.
Buddæi Isagoge ad Theologiam. Lib. II.
Dallæus de Scriptis quæ Dion. et Ignatii nominibus circumferunter.
Fabricii (Alb.) Bibliotheca.
Ittigius de Patribus.
Lanselii Dissertatio Apologetica.
Mayeri (Frid.) Dissertationes.
Meieri (G. A.) Dion. A. et Mysticorum, sæc. xiv.; doctrinæ inter se comparatæ.
Oudinus de Scriptoribus Ecclesiasticis.
Pachymeræ Paraph. in omnia D. opera.
Riveti (And.) Opera Theologica.
Usseri Dissertationes.

Buddeus, cited above, names many authors who have written about the impostor of this name.

Discerning of Spirits.

Benson's Planting of Christianity.
Chandler's Commentary on Joel.
Foster's (John) Letters.
Stebbing against Foster.

Discerning the Lord's Body. See LORD'S SUPPER.

Brett's (Tho.) Discourses.

Disciples of Christ, or Christians. COMMONLY CALLED "CAMPBELLITES."

Pro.

Campbell's (Alex.) Christian Baptism.
——— Christian System.
——— Debate with Purcell.
——— ——— Rice.
——— ——— Walker.
——— ——— McCalla.
Christian Baptist. Periodical, from August, 1823, to August, 1829.
Lord's Review of Jeter on Campbellism.
Millennial Harbinger. Periodical, from January, 1830, to the present time.
Richardson's Principles and objects of the religious reformation.
Scott's (Rev. Walter) Death of Christ.
——— Gospel Restored.

Disciples of Christ—*continued.*

Pro.

Scott's (Rev. Walter) Messiah.
——— Union of Christians.
Stone's (Barton) Letters.

Con.

Campbell's (J. P.) Strictures on B. Stone.
Cleland's Unitarianism unmasked.
Jeter's (J. B.) Campbellism examined.
Landis' Rabbah taken.
Stile's Reply to articles in the Millennial Harbinger.

The "Debates" mentioned above, show both sides of the questions discussed.

Discipline of Primitive Churches. See CHURCH DISCIPLINE, PENANCE.

Bebelli (Balthas.) Dissertationes.
Beyeri Vet. eccl. circa penitentiæ rigorem.
Crucigeri Observationes Selectæ.
Dupin, Dissertationes Historicæ.
Hottingeri Exercitationes.
Orsi (Joseph. Aug.) Dissertationes.
Pelliccia, de Chris. eccl. primæ polititia.
Strauchii (Ægid.) Dissertat. (Acta erud.)

Brokesby's Government of the Church for the first 3 centuries.
Bryson's Compendious View.
Fuller's Discipline of the Primitive Churches.
Hall's View of the Gospel Church.
King's Enquiry into the Constitution, &c.

Discretion. See PRUDENCE.

Bateman's (Edward) Sermons.
Claggett's (William) Sermons.
Fiddes' (Richard) Sermons.
Jortin's (John) Sermons.
Lucas' (Dr. Richard) Sermons.
Van Mildert's Sermons at Lincoln's Inn.

Disinterested Benevolence. See HOPKINSIANISM.

Pro.

Doddridge's Lectures. Part 3, prop. 51.
Fawcett's (Joseph) Sermons at old Jewry.
Godwin on Political Justice. Bk. 4, ch. 8.
Hopkins' (Dr. Sam.) Works.
Hume's Principles of Morals.
Hutchinson on the Passions.

Con. (That there is no such thing.)

Brown's Essays on Shaftsbury. Ess. 2.
Rutherford's Essay on Moral Virtue.
Wardlaw's Christian Ethics.
Woodward's (Henry) Essays.

Dispersion at Babel. See CONFUSION OF TONGUES.

Dissenters. See ESTABLISHMENTS, NONCONFORMITY, SUBSCRIPTION TO CREEDS.

Pro.

Barker's (T.) Vindication of Dissenters.

Dissenters—*continued.*

Pro.

Barrowe's (Henry) Reply to Giffard.
Best's (Tho.) Answer to Foley's Discourses.
Beverly's Letters to the Abp. of York. (This bold and powerful attack called forth many replies.)
Binny's (D.) Dissent not Schism.
Bourne's Principles and practice of D.
Bradbury's Dissenting ministers defended.
Calamy's (Edmund) Tracts. (Admirable.)
Choate's (J.) Reasons of Dissent, &c.
Conder on Protestant Nonconformity.
De Foe's Test of Loyalty.
Disney's Reasons for resigning the rectory of Panton.
Eclectic Review. (Many articles.)
Ely's Address at Parade Chapel.
Foster's (Dr. J.) Answer to Stebbings.
Fownes on the Principles of toleration.
Hinton's (Jas.) Vindication of Dissenters. (Answer to Tatham.)
Hurh's Reasons for secession from the Chur. of England.
James' (John A.) Protestant Nonconformity.
Johnson's Reasons for Dissent.
Jones' (Wm.) Dissenter's Plea.
Kippis' Vindication of Dissenters.
Manning on Dissent from the Ch. of Engl.
Mauduit's Case of dissenting ministers.
Newman's Dissenter's Catechism.
Palmer's Review of England's Hierarchy.
——— Vind. of modern Dissenters.
Parry (Will.) on the Penal statutes affecting Protestant Dissenters.
Pearson's (Edw.) Three plain reasons.
Pierce's Vindication of Dissenters.
Priestley's Letters to the inhabitants of Birmingham.
Robinson's Separation from the Ch. of Eng.
——— (Other treatises.)
Scale's Principles of Dissent.
Scragg's Reasons for dissenting.
Smectymnus. (A work of prodigious ability.)
Smith's (J. Pye) Dissent vindicated.
——— Reply to Dr. Lee.
Sturgess on the State of the Church.
Swaine's Shield of Dissent.
Tasker's Reasons for separation.
Theological Repository. Birmingham. Edited by Dr. Priestley.
Thomas' (Benj.) Works.
Thompson's Comparative view of English and Scotch Dissenters. (Has a valuable preliminary dissertation on the views and duties of Dissenters.)
Tiptaft's Fourteen reasons for Dissent.
Toulmin's State of Dissenters.
——— Sermons.
Towgood's Answer to White's letters.
——— Answer to the Editor of Dr. Warren's sermons.
——— on Dissent from the Ch. of England.
——— Tracts on important subjects.
Vaughn's (Robt.) Essays.

Dissenters—*continued.*

Welch Nonconformist's Memorial. Period.
Withers' (John) Vindication of Dissenters.
Wood & Bulstrode's Letters.

Con.

Nicholsii Defensio Ecclesiæ Angl.

Barker's Defence of the English Church.
——— (Other treatises.)
Barry's (Edward) Theological essays.
Bennett's Abridgment of the London cases.
Boyd on Episcopacy, Ordination, &c.
Bramhall's (Abp.) Works.
Cock's Church of England secured.
Coleridge's Script. character of the Church of England.
Courtenay on the Revolution in France.
Crackenthorp's Defensio fidei.
Evans' (A. B.) Inconsistencies of Dissent.
Fausset's Bampton lectures. 1820.
Foley's (R.) Discourses on the Ch. of Eng.
Frazier's Magazine. 13:523.
Giffard's Donatists of England.
Grey's Vindication of the Chur. of England. (Reply to Pierce.)
Grove's Persuasives to communion.
Hall's Apology for the Ch. of England.
Hicks' (Dr. George) Works.
Hoadly's (Benj.) Works.
Hull's Pulpit guarded.
Hungerford's Call for Union.
Jessie's Defence of the Church.
Jewell's (Bp.) Apology for the Church.
Johnes' Causes of Dissent. (Received the royal medal of the Cambrian Institute. 1831.)
King's (Abp.) Admonition to Dissenters.
Langley's Tracts for priest and people.
Lee's Dissent unscriptural.
Lowth's (Wm.) Sermons. (On Acts ii. 42.)
Madan's Charges against Dissenters.
Maddox's Gov. and worship of the church.
——— Vindic. of the Church. (Reply to Neale and Pierce.)
Masheder's Dissent and Democracy.
Mason on the Lawful Ministry.
Pool's Lectures on Ely's address.
Potter on Church government.
Pruen's Popular view of the church.
Robertson's Dissenters self-condemned. (Reply to Delaune.)
Rogers' Persuasion to Conformity.
Rose's Ans. to the case of Dissenters.
Scarlet's Confutation of Brownism.
Sherlock's (Bp.) Discourses.
Stebbing's Polemic tracts.
Tatham's (Edw.) University sermons.
Thelwall's Letters to a friend.
The Independent Whig. Periodical.
Tucker's Reply to Kippis' vindication.
Vaughn's (Robert) Essays.
Ware's Foxes and Firebrands.
Wells' Ceremonies of the Eng. Church.
——— (Various other tracts.)
Wilberforce's Parochial system.

Dissenters, History of.

Bogue & Bennett's Hist. of Dissenters. From 1689 to 1808. Continued by Bennett to 1838.
Calamy's Life of Baxter.
Fletcher's History of Independency.
Hall's (Robert) Works.
Hunter's (J.) Life of Oliver Heywood.
Ivemy's (Jos.) Hist. of Dissenters. To 1810.
Neale's History of the Puritans.
Orton's Memoir of P. Doddridge.
Palmer's Dissenter's Catechism.
Rees' Hist. of Dissent in Wales. To 1861.
Sanders' Origin and progress of Dissent.
Thomson's Comparison of English and Scotch Dissenters.
Toulmin's (Josh.) State of Dissenters.
Uden's Anglican Church of the 19th century. Trans. by Humphries.
Walker's Hist. of Eng. Independence. To 1651.
Wilson's History of dissenting churches in London. To 1806. (Extensive and authentic; includes memoirs of many ministers.)

Dissolution of the World.
See CONSUMMATION.

Distinctions in Society.
See INEQUALITIES.

Distractions. See WANDERING THOUGHTS.

Diversity of Languages.
See CONFUSION.

Diversity of Races. See UNITY.

Divination. See ASTROLOGY.

Cattan, la Geomance.
Cocles, Compendium de Chiromancie.
Hartlieb's Kunst chyromantia.
Jurieu, Hist. Critique des dogmes, &c.
Lisle, des Talismans.
Peucer, les Devins.
Placet, la Superstition du temps.
Van Dale, de Origine et progressu idolitræ et superstitionum.
Zanchii Opera Theologica. Tom. VIII.

[Phillips'] English fortune-tellers.

Divine Government.
See GOVERNMENT OF GOD.

Divine Right of Kings.
See PASSIVE OBEDIENCE.

Pro.

Puffendorf de Jure. Lib. VII., C. 3.

Delany on Religious duties.
Filmer's Patriarchal scheme.
Heylin's (Peter) Miscellaneous tracts.
Usher's Power communicated from God.

Divine Right of Kings—*continued.*

Pro.

Weldon's Origin of Dominion.
Williams' Jura Magistrata.

Con.

Mehliss, Comparatio Platonis doctrinæ de sua republica, cum christiana doctrina de regno divino.

Buchanan (Geo.), de Jure Regni.
Edinburg Review. 1:456.
Hoadly (Bp.) on Government.
——— on the Rights of subjects.
Kettlewell's Measures of Chris. obedience.
Monthly Review. 93:144.
Paley's Political Economy.
Rutherford's Lex Rex. (Famous.)
Sidney on Government.

Divorce. See MARRIAGE.

Tertullian, contra Marcion. Lib. IV., cap. 34.
Basil, Epistolæ.
Chrysostom, Homiliæ. Hom. XVII.
Epiphanius, Pannarium.

Bezæ Tractationes Theologicæ.
Buxtorf de Nuptiis et Divortiis Hebrorum.
Dassovii (T.) Vidua Hebræa.
Erasmi Opera.
Hotman, de la Dissolution du marriage par l'impuissance.
Housonus (J.), de Uxore dimissa.
Miltoni Tetrachordon.
Peleus de Dissolutione matrimonii ex causa frigoris.
Puffendorf de Jure, &c.
Seldeni Uxor Hebraica ex Talmudico.
Tagereau, sur l'Impuissance.
Ugolini Uxor Hebræa.

Amer. Quart. Review. 2:70.
Bibliotheca Sacra. 23:384.
Blackall's (Dr. Offspring) Discourses.
Blackwood's Magazine. 26:756.
Blair's (James) Sermons.
British and Foreign Review. 7:269.
Bucer on Divorce. Trans. by John Milton. (In the preface, Milton defends his own treatise on this subject.)
Bunney (E.) on Divorce.
Calmet's Preface to Deuteronomy.
De Bow's Commercial Review. 2:155.
Doddridge's Lectures. Part 3, prop. 61.
Dwight's Sermons.
Erasmus' Judgement whyther divorsement betwene man and wyfe standeth with the law of God.
Greswell's (Edward) Dissertations.
Gilbert's Exp. of the 39 Articles. Art. 25.
International Magazine. 5:198.
Investigator. 2:146.
Milton's Doctrine and Discipline of D.
Necker's (Madam) Reflections.
Ochinus' Dialogues. Trans. by Osborn.
Paley's Moral Philosophy. Book 3.

Pamphleteer. 18:153.
Pye on Hebrew Divorces.
Reynolds on Divorce for Adultery.
Trumbull's Appeal to the public.
Westminster Review. 42:187.
Wolseley on Divorce and Marriage.

Docetæ. See SUFFERINGS OF CHRIST.

Clemens Alex., Stromata.
Ignatius, Epistolæ.
Irenæus, adversus Hæreses.
Tertullian, de Carne Christi.

Giesleri Com. de corpore Christi.
Neander's Gnostische Systeme.
Niemeyer de D. comment. histor. theol.

Burton's Bampton Lectures. 1829.

Dogmatic Theology. See THEOLOGY.

Doing Good. See GOOD WORKS.

Doing as we would be done by.

Atterbury's (Bp.) Sermons.
Beveridge's (Bp.) Sermons.
Carter's (N.) Sermons.
Conybeare's (Bp.) Sermons.
Secker's (Abp.) Sermons.

Domestic Economy. See FAMILY GOVERNMENT, FAMILY RELIGION.

Abbot's Mother at home. (Excellent.)
Anderson's Domestic Constitution. (Deserves the widest circulation.)
Babington on Christian Education in its early stages.
Bailey (R. W.) on Domestic Duties.
Bamford on the Discipline of Children.
Belfrage's Monitor to Families.
Biber's (G. E.) Lectures.
Christian Quart. Spect. 5:363. 7:185. 8:43.
Cleaver's Godlie forme of hovsehold govt.
Creswell's (D.) Sermons on domestic duties.
De Foe's Family Instructor. (Excellent.)
Dick's Christian Philosopher.
Dyke's (Oswald) Sermons.
Eclectic Magazine. 13:126.
Gouge's (William) Eight treatises. (All on this subject.)
Grant (Mrs.) on Intell. and dom. education.
Hamilton (Eliza) on the Formation of moral and religious principles.
Harris' Patriarchy.
Huntingdon's (Prof.) Sermons.
Kruger on the Educ. of Children. (Medical.)
Mother's Magazine.
Mother's Monthly Journal.
Munton's (Thomas) Sermons.
Nelson on the Government of Children.
Parke's Duties of Married life.
Payson's Sermons to Christian families.
Pickard on Family Government.
Stennett's (Sam.) Domestic Duties.
Tickell's Bottomless pit smoking. (Commended by BP. LAW.)
Tyerman's Importance of dom. discipline.
Witherspoon's Lectures.

Domestic Happiness.

Boardman's (H. A.) Bible in the family.
Enfield's (William) Sermons.
James' Family Monitor.
Jay's Lectures.
Malcom's Christian rule of Marriage. (Contends against the marriage of believers to unbelievers.)
Mason's Christian Morality.
Taylor (J.) on the Importance of children.
——— on Home Education.

Dominicans.

Albertus de Viris illust. ordinis prædicat.
Altimura Bibliotheca Dominica.
Annales Ordinis prædicatorum.
Antonii Biblioth. ord. frat. prædicatorum.
Bareille, Hist. de St. Thomas d'Aquin.
Echardi, Scriptores ordinis Prædicatorum.
Gerard et Liblin, Annales, &c. To 1854.
Gozzei Catalogus virorum prædicatorum.
Heylot, Hist. des Ordres Monastique.
Mamachio, Annales Prædicatorum.
Ripoll, Bullarium ord. Prædicatorum.
Rovetta, Biblioth. illustrium virorum.
Senensis, Chronicon Fratrum Prædicator.
Sovege et Teuillet, L'année Dominicaine.
Touron, Hist. des hommes illustre, &c.
——— Vie de St. Thomas d'Aquin.

Echard, cited above, gives a huge list of Dominican writers; professedly complete.

Donatists. See COUNCIL OF CARTHAGE.

Augustine, contra Donatistas de baptismo. (Falsely attributed to A.)
——— contra Parmenianum.
——— de Baptismo.
Jerome, de Scriptoribus Ecclesias.

Alexandri (Natalis.) Dissertationes.
Balduini Historia Collationis Carthagensis.
——— de Schismate Donatistarum.
Danhaveri (Jo. Conradi) Disputatio ad collationem Carthaginiensem.
Dupin, Historia Donatistarum.
Ittigii Hæreses ævi apostolici.
Leydekkeri (Melchoiris) Dissertationes.
Milevetanus de Schismate Donatistarum.
Mosheimii Dissertationes Hist. Eccl.
Noris Historia Donistarum.
Optatas de Schismate D. ("Handsomely written."—MOSHEIM. But very bitter, and often unjust, which does not displease Dr. M., who calls them "a troublesome sect.")
Ottii Delineatio Schismate Donatistarum.
Rhenferdi Dissertationes.
Ribbeck's (F.) Donatus und Augustinus.
Tillemont, Memoires Ecclesiastiq. Tom. VI.
Valesii (Henr.) Dissertatio de schismate D.
Witsii (H.) Miscellanea Sacra.

Donatists—*continued.*

Barrow (Henry) on the Donatists of Eng.
Benedict's Hist. of the Baptists. (Introd.)
Burton's Eccles. hist. of the 2d and 3d cent.
Gregory's (Pope) Epistles.
Lardner's Credibility, &c. Part 2.
Long's History of the Donatists.
Lowth's (Simon) Excerpts from Eccl. Hist.
Princeton Review. 36:385.

Dort, Synod of.

Acta Synodi Dordrechti.
Benthem's dem holländischen Kirchen.
Brandt's Hist. d. Ref. de Nederlanden.
Gomari Opera.
Halesii Hist. Concilii Dordraceni.
Langii Gloria Christi.
Leydecker's nationale Synod von Dordregt. (Reply to Brandt.)
Masii (Hect. G.) Dissertationes Academ.
Peltii Harmonia Remonstrantium et Socinianorum.

Brandt's History of the Reformation.
Christian Observer. 18:761, 790.
Hale's (John) History of the Synod of D.
Leydecker's National Synod of Dort.
Nichols' Calvinism and Socin'm compared.
Scott's (Tho.) Articles of the Synod of D.
Spirit of the Pilgrims. 4:256.

Doublemindedness. See INDECISION.

Double Sense of Prophecy.

Pro.

Amer. Presbyterian Review. 4:214.
Barrow's (Isaac) Works.
Chalmers' (Tho.) Lectures on Paley's Evidences. Part 2, Ch. 1.
——— Notes on Hill's Lectures in Divinity. Book 1, Ch. 7.
Claggett's Truth defended.
Doddridge's Lectures. Lect. 132.
Haberson on the Prophetic Scriptures.
Hey's (Dr. J.) Lectures. Bk. 1, Ch. 17.
Hurd (Bp.) on the Prophecies.
Jenour's Trans. of Isaiah; with notes.
Johnson's (Rev. Sam.) Exp. of prophecies.
Jortin's Remarks on Eccles. history.
Lowth's Sacred poetry of the Hebrews.
Mudge's Preface to the Psalms.
Turner's (S. H.) Interp. of Scrip. prophecy.
Warburton's (Bp.) Divine legation. Bk. 6.
——— Hist. of double prophecies.
Whiston's Boyle Lectures.

Con.

Benson's Critical Dissertations.
Stuart (Moses) on the Interp. of Prophecy.
Sykes' Truth of the Christian religion.
——— Principles and connection of natural and revealed religion.

Doubt. See CASUISTRY, INDECISION.

Hewlett's (C. A.) Sermons
Lewis' (W. S.) Landmarks of Faith.
Muston's (C. R.) Sermons.
Orton's (Job) Discourses. (Sinfulness of doubtful actions.)
Sharp's (Abp.) Sermons.
Taylor's (Jer.) Ductor Dubitantium.
Zollikoffer's Sermons on prevalent errors and vices.

Dreams.

Tertullian de Anima.

Boisment, des Hallucinations.
Cicero de Divinatione. Cap. 46.
Francastorius de Intellectu.
Jamblicus de Mysteriis.
Witsii Miscellanea Sacra.

Amyrald on the D. mentioned in Scripture.
Atterbury's (Lewis) Sermons.
Baxter (And.) on the Nature of the soul.
Binns' (E. E.) Anatomy of sleep.
Blackwood's Mag. 21:549. 22:173. 48:194.
Boismont on Hallucination. Translated by Mrs. Gent.
Branch on Dreaming.
Bulstrode's (W.) Essays. Ess. 2.
Christian Observer. 1:473.
Cook's True relation of a wonderful dream.
Delany's (Patrick) Dissertations.
Dendy's (W. C.) Philosophy of Dreams.
Diodati on Dreams.
Edwards (John) on the Creed.
Elwin on the Operations of the mind in sleep.
Ennemoser's History of Magic.
Goodwin's Mystery of D. (Historical.)
Jackson (Tho.) on the Apostles' Creed.
Macnish's Philosophy of sleep.
Mirror, The. Nos. 73, 74.
Newton's (Bp.) Dissertations.
Phillips' (A.) Nature of sleep and death.
Smith's (John) Select Discourses.
Turner's Hist. of remarkable providences.
Wotton, Life of.

Dress. See FASHION, SELF-DENIAL.

Gregory Naz., Adv. mulieres ambitiosas.

Matensii Sermones de Exorno.

Allsop's Sinfulness of strange apparel.
Blackwood's Magazine. 53:230.
Buck's Cautions.
Collier's (Jer.) Essays on moral subjects.
Cooper's (Edward) Sermons.
Delany's (Patrick) Sermons.
Hall's (Thos.) Loathsomeness of painting, patches, naked backs and breasts, &c. 1654.
Hammond's (Henry) Sermons.
Judson's Letter to American females. (An admirable tract.)

Morning Exercises at Cripplegate. Vol. 3.
Newton's (John) Miscellaneous Papers.
North Amer. Review. 47:148.
Taylor's (Jer.) Sermons. (Auxiliary beauty.)
Wesley's (John) Sermons.
—— Advice to Methodists with regard to dress.

Drinking Healths. See TEMPERANCE.

Matensii Opera.

Brown's (Bp. Peter) Works. Last vol.

Druids. See ETHNOLOGY.

Barth, Ueber die Druiden der Kelten.
Frickii Com: de D. Occidentalium.
Hartlieb (J. F.), de Druidis.
Julius Cæsar, de Bello Gallic. Lib. V.
Pictet, les Bardes de l'Ile de Bretagne.
Suetonii Historia.
Tacitus de M. Germanorum. Cap. 7.

Borlase's Antiquities of Cornwall.
Bowles' Hermes Brittanicus.
Cook on the Patriarchal and Druidical relig.
Davies' (Edward) British Druids; with their poems, rites, &c.
Duke's Druidical temples of Wiltshire.
Duncan's Religions of profane antiquity.
Eclectic Magazine. 17:320.
Edinburg Review. 4:391.
Higgins' Celtic Druids. Plates.
Jones' History of the Druids.
Knickerbocker Magazine. 2:90.
Moulin's Hist. of the ancient Druids.
Nash's (D. W.) Taliesen.
North's Religion of the first inhabitants of Great Britain.
Richards' (W.) Nonconformist's Memorial.
—— Essay on Druidism. (Published first in the Welch Nonconformist's Memorial.)
Rowland's Mona Antiqua.
Short's Druidical remains in England.
Smith's (Dr. John) Gaelic Antiquities.
Southern Review. 3:207. 4:1.
Stukeley's Stonehenge and Abury. Plates.
Timson's British Ecclesiastical History.
Toland's History of the Druids.
Tressan's Heathen Mythology. (Appendix.)
Williams' (Eliezer) English works. (Contain an Essay on the taste and literature of the Druids.)

Drunkenness. See TEMPERANCE.

Abernethy's (Bp.) Sermons.
Backer's Sermons.
Buck's (Rev. Charles) Anecdotes.
Burnet's (Gilbert) Sermons.
Dwight's Discourses. Disc. 118.
Flavel's Works.
Garbent's Sober Testimony.
Gibson on Intemperance.
Guthrie's Plea in behalf of drunkenness.
Hornby's (Wm.) Scovrge of drvnkenness. 1618.

Drunkenness—*continued.*

Junius' (R.) Drvnkard's character. 1638.
Lamont's (David) Sermons.
McGowan's (John) Works.
McNish's Anatomy of Drunkenness.
Paley's Moral Philosophy. Bk. 4.
—— Sermons.
Parsons' (B.) Anti-Bacchus.
Rush's (Judge, of Philadelphia,) Charges. (Powerful.)
Trotter on Drunkenness.
Walker's (Samuel) Essays.
Ware (Henry) on Intemperance.
Whitefield's Sermons.
Worcester (Samuel) on Intemperance.

Druzes.

Adleri Museum cuficum Borgianum. 1800. ("The best account of the Druzes."—MILLS.)
Aucapitaine, Etude sur les Druzes.
Bock, Œuvres diversée.
De Sacy, Exposé de la rel. des D. 1838.
—— Chrestomathie Arabe.
Eichhorn's Religion der Drusen. 1820.
Mariti, Voyages dans la Syrie, &c. 1791.
Niebuhr's (C.) Reisebesehreibung nach Arabien. 1830.
Sandys, Travailes, &c. 1615.
Silvestre, la Religion des Druzes.
St. Pierre, Histoire des Druzes. 1763.
Volney (C. O.), Voyage en Syrie. 1790.
Wolf's Drusen und ihre Vorläufer.
Worbs' Gesch. u. Beschreibung d. D. 1799.

Bibliotheca Sacra. 1:205.
Burkhardt's Travels in Syria. 1822.
Carnarvon's (Earl of) D. of Lebanon. 1860.
Chassaud's D. of Lebanon. 1855. (Mr. C. was born and brought up at Beyrut.)
Christian Examiner. 57:362.
Churchill's Ten years in Mt. Lebanon. 1852.
—— Druzes and Maronites. 1862.
Conner's Journal in Syria. 1822.
Foreign Quart. Review. 29:92, 168.
Missionary Herald. Boston. (Almost every volume since 1827.)
Tudella's Voyages. Tr. by A. Asher. 1840.
Venture's Druzes of Mt. Lebanon. 1785.
Wortabet's Religions of Syria.

Dualism. See MANICHÆISM.

Duelling.

Boemeri Jus eccles. Protestantium.
Carafa de Monomachia.

Chalmers' Discourses. (2 on this subject.)
Christian Quarterly Spectator. 10:353.
Cockburn's Hist. and examination of duels.
Collier's (Jer.) Moral Essays. Ess. 3.
Comber (Dr. Tho.) on Duels.
Delany's (Patrick) Discourses.
Democratic Review. 11:311, 415.

Duelling—*continued.*

Dwight's Theology. Discourse 116.
Edinburg Review. 75:228.
Espagne's Anatomie of Duels.
Foster's (Dr. James) Sermons.
Frazier's Magazine. 21:498.
Godwin's Political Justice.
Hale's (John) Golden Remains.
Hey's Dissertation on Duelling.
Holbrook's (Anthony) Sermons.
Ingram's (Rowland) Reflections on D.
Jones' (Thomas) Sermons.
Lucas' "Duellists." (A good tale.)
Millingen's History of Duelling, from the earliest period to the present. 1841.
Montesquieu's Spirit of laws. Bk. 28.
Moore's Essays. Ess. 2.
Mosheim's Eccles. History. Cent. 9.
Museum of Foreign Literature. 7:317. 14:59. 26:498. 35:18.
Paley's Moral Philosophy.
Pamphleteer. 12:79.
Princeton Review. 20:542.
Rush's (Judge) Charges.
Sabine (L.) on Duelling.
Segas' (James) Means to suppress D.
Selden's (John) Works.
Sharp (Granv.) on Manslaughter and Murd.
Spectator. No. 97.
Watts (Dr. Isaac) on Self-murder.
Westminster Review. 4:20.

Dunkers. See GERMAN BAPTISTS.

Duration of our Lord's Ministry. See MONOTESSARON.

Buddei Miscellanea Sacra.
Clerici Harmonia Evangelica. (Appendix.)
Frisius de Tempore ministerii Christi.
Weberi Questiones historico-theologicæ.
Witsii Meletemata Leidensia. Diss. IX.

Benson's (C.) Chron. of our Saviour's life.
Carpenter's (L.) Dissertations.
——— Harmony. (Makes it embrace but two passovers, or a little over one year.)
Jarvis' (S. F.) Introduction to the history of the church.
[Mann (Nic.)] on the True years of the birth and death of Christ.
Newcombe's (W.) Duration of our Lord's ministry. (Makes it embrace four passovers.)
Priestley's Greek Harmony of the Gospels.
——— Letters to Dr. Newcombe. (Makes our Lord's ministry to have lasted a little more than a year.)
Tichendorf's Harmony. (Makes it embrace three passovers, or two years.)
Williams' Hist. of Christ's ministry.

Duration of the World. See THEORIES OF THE EARTH.

Allix's Reflections.
Cheyne's Philosophical Principles.
Doddridge's Lectures. Part 2, prop. 21.
Jenkins on Christianity.
Patrick (Bp.) on Genesis.
Stillingfleet's Origines Sacræ.
Toulmin's Eternity of the Universe.
Watts' (Isaac) Essays. Ess. 10.

Duties of Church Members.

Crowell's Church member's manual.
Jay's Church member's guide.
Treffrey's Church member's catechism.

Duty of Parents. See PARENTAL DUTIES.

Early Piety. See YOUTH.

Bellamy's True religion delineated.
Bourne's (S.) Sermons.
Cecil's Sermons on early piety.
Chandler's (Sam.) Sermons.
Chearn's Instructions for youth.
Clarke's (John A.) Young Disciple.
Clarke's (Tho.) Motives to early piety.
Dodd's (William) Sermons.
Drysdale's (John) Sermons.
Durant's Mem. of an only Son. (Beautiful.)
Edwards' (Pres.) Works. (On revivals.)
Fawcett's (J.) Sermons.
Fletcher's (Joseph) Sermons.
Fuller's (And.) Sermons.
Gilpin's Monument of Parental affection.
Head's (Mrs.) Pious Mother.
Henry's Pleasantness of a religious life.
Hooper's Advantages of early piety.
Janeway's Token for Children.
Jenning's Beauty and benefit of Early P.
Jerment's Early piety recommended.
Jessy's Narrative of some children, &c.
Kippis' Example of Jesus in his youth.
Kyther's Morning Seeker.
Logan's (John) Sermons.
Nott's (Sam.) Sermons to Children.
Richards' Hints for religious conversation.
Robinson's Nat. and necess. of early piety.
Ryther's (John) Sermons.
Summerfield's (John) Sermons.
Taprell's Discourses for Children.
Thirwall's Child Jesus.
Tillotson's Sermons.
Whitefield's Sermons.

Earnest of the Spirit. See WITNESS.

Easter. See FESTIVALS.

Mosheim, de Rebus ante Constantinum.

Christian Examiner. 38:41.
London Quart. Review. 18:496.

Easter Sermons.

Andrewes' (Bp.) Sermons.
Barrow's (Isaac) Sermons.
Cunningham's (J. W.) Sermons.
Dealtry's (William) Sermons.

Easter Sermons—*continued.*

Faringdon's (Anthony) Sermons.
Hare's (A. W.) Sermons.
Heber's (Bp.) Sermons.
Lake's (Bp.) Sermons.
Secker's (Abp.) Sermons.
Sherlock's (Bp.) Sermons.
Skelton's (Philip) Sermons.
Townsend's (George) Sermons.
Whately's (Richard) Sermons.

Eating Blood. See PROHIBITION.

Ebionites.

Epiphanius de Hæresibus.

Ittigius de Hæresibus ævi Apostolica.
Fabricius ad Philostr. de Hæresibus.
——— Codex Apocryph. Nov. Test.
Le Quien, Adnotationes ad Damascenum.
Mosheimii Dissertationes.
——— Observationes Sacræ.
——— Meditationes de Ebione.
Rhenferdi (Jacobi) Dissertationes.
Schelgvigii (Sam.) Dissertationes.
Schliemann's Clementinen nebst d. verwandten Schriften.
Schmidt's Bibliothek fur Exegetik.
Sirici Ασκημα historico-theologicum.
Vogtii [or Voight] Dissertationes.

Burton's Bampton Lectures. 1829.
——— Eccl. Hist. of the first 3 centuries.
Hey's Lectures. Vol. 1. (Appendix.)
Jones on the Canon of the New Test.

Ecclesiology. See CANONS, CREEDS, LITURGIES, RELIGIONS, RITES, &c.

Eden. See GEOGRAPHY.

Abrami Pharus Veteris Testamenti.
Bertheau's Beschreibung der lage des P.
Bocharti Phaleg et Canaan.
——— Delineatio Paradisi terrestris.
Burnet (T.), Telluris Theoria Sacra.
Corschii (Martin) Dissertationes.
Fabricii (Joann.) Dissertationes.
Honerti Dissertationes Historicæ.
Hopkinsoni Descriptio Paradisi.
Hottingeri Dissertationes Theologicæ.
Huet, de Situ Paradisi. (In UGOLINUS, and in the Critica Sacra. "An amazing range of learning."—C. BUTLER. The work is also extant in French.)
Kirkherdere de Situ P. terrestris.
Korthulti (Chris.) Dissertationes.
Malvendæ de Paradiso Commentatio.
Marckii Historia Paradisi.
Michaelis (H.), Dissertationes.
Moses bar Cephæ Comment. de Paradiso.
Olearii (Joann.) Dissertationes.
Relandi (Adriani) Dissertationes.
Schulthess' das Paradies.
Seldenus de Horto Hedenis.
Spanheimii (Fred.) Dissertationes.

Eden—*continued.*

Vantilli [or Van Till] Dissertationes. (At the end of his Commentary on Malachi. Opposes Huet.)
Varenii Trifolium historicum sacrum, &c.

Amer. Biblical Repos. 9:180.
Bedford's Chronology of Scripture.
Bridges' Testimony of profane antiquity.
Burnet's Theory of the earth.
Campbell's History of the Bible.
Carver's Situation of Paradise.
Horne's (Bp.) Sermons.
Hopkinson's Description of Paradise.
Meade's The Bible and the Classics.
Reland's Miscell. Dissertations. Diss. 1.
Salkeld's Treatise on Paradise.
Shuckford's Connect. of sac. and prof. hist.

Edict of Nantes. See REVOCATION.

Editions of the Sacred Text. See PRINTED EDITIONS.

Education. See DOMESTIC ECONOMY, EDUCATION SOCIETIES, FEMALE EDUCATION, MATERNAL DUTIES, PARENTAL DUTIES, RELATIVE DUTIES, &c.

Biedermann's Wissenschaft u. Universitaten.
Huber's Englischen Universitaten.
Kock, die Preussischen Universitaten.
Niemeyer's Grundsatze der Erziehung, &c.
Nieuhoff, de Ratione studii.
Pestalozzi, meine Lebensschicksale, &c.

Ainsworth on Domestic Education.
Alison's (Archib.) Sermons.
American Annals of Education. 1831–1840.
American Institute of Instruction Reports. (For 1830, by Pres. Wayland; 1831, Pres. Walker; 1834, Caleb Cushing; 1835, Dr. Furness; 1839, Robt. Rantoul. The whole series is very valuable.)
American Quart. Review. 6:165. 9:283.
Amer. Presbyt. and Theol. Rev. 3:408.
Amer. Journal of Education.
Antrobus' Philos. and social bearings of E.
Appleton (Miss) on Early Education.
Arnold's (Matt.) Middle Class Education.
Arnold's (Tho.) Sermons at Rugby.
Ash's (Dr. John) Sentiments on Education.
Babington's Views of Christian Education.
Badger's Friendly Admonitions.
Barrow's (Wm.) Essay on Education.
Barwell's Letters from Hofwyl. 1842. (Very useful for practical hints.)
Bentham's (Jer.) Chrestomathia.
Biber's Lectures. (Religious Education. Describes and advocates the system of Pestalozzi.)
Blackwood's Mag. 45:275. 55:541.
Boswell's (J.) Method of study.
Bowden on Religious Education.
Brook's (Mrs.) Dialogues.
Brougham on Popular Education.
Buckminster's (Jos. S.) Sermons.

Education—*continued.*

Burgh's Dignity of Human nature.
——— Thoughts on Education.
Burns' Pastoral hints.
Caldwell's Thoughts on physical education.
Campbell's (John) Antichristian tendency of modern education.
Carey's Amer. Museum. 4:25, 108, 217, 310.
Carpenter's (Lant) Principles of Education.
Chapman's (E.) Treatise on Education.
Christian Disciple. 1:444. 5:161.
Christian Exam. 8:293. 9:223. 10:1. 26:163.
Christian Museum. 4:25, 108, 217, 310.
Christian Observer. 2:37. 10:686. 12:508, 569, 637, 699, 767, 825.
Christian Month. Spect. 2:349. 4:393. 7:169.
Christian Quar. Spect. 4:557. 5:363. 8:43. 9:1.
Christian Review. 16:275.
Church's Rise and progress of Ed. in Engl.
Clark on Study, and the collec. of a Library.
Comber on Popular Education.
Cousin's Education in Holland.
——— Education in Prussia.
Davis on a Religious Education.
De Foe's Family Instructor.
Denham's (J. F.) Letters to a Mother.
Doddridge's Lectures. Lec. 74.
——— on the Education of Children.
Dwight's Discourses. Disc. 147, 148.
Eclectic Review. 4th Series. 7:241.
Edgeworth (Miss) on Practical Education.
——— on Professional Education.
Edinburg Review. 38:437.
Evans (J.) on the Education of Youth.
Foote (W.) on Education.
Fordyce's Dialogues on Education.
Foster's (Dr. James) Discourses.
Foster (T.) on the Prevention of crime.
Francis' (C.) Errors in Education.
Frazier's Magaz. 69:655. 70:319.
Gaillard's Directions for the Ed. of youth.
Gibbon on the Study of Literature.
Giles' Strictures on Education.
Girard's Practical Lectures.
Goodacre's (Robert) Essays.
Hamilton (R. W.) on Institutions of popular education. (Manchester prize essay. 1846.)
Hamilton's (Sir W.) Works. (Several diss.)
Heberden on Education. (After the manner of Cicero's Philosophical Disquisitions.)
Heinroth's Physical, intellectual, moral, and religious education.
Helvetius on the Intellectual Faculty.
Hill's National Education: its present state and prospects. 1836.
Hunt's Merchant's Magazine. 9:53.
Hurd's (Bp.) Moral and religious Dialogues.
Jacques' (W.) Essays on Education.
Jardine's Outlines of philosophical E.
Jarrold's Instinct and reason philosophically investigated.
Kay's Social condition of the people of England. 1850.
Knox's (Vicessimus) Methods of acquiring useful learning.

Education—*continued.*

Lancaster on Education for the industrious classes.
——— Many other tracts.
Langford on Religion and education.
Lee's Sunday Lecturer.
Locke on Education.
London Review. 12:462.
Lowe's Critique on Education.
McCombie's (Wm.) Essays and Reviews.
Mackenzie's (Wm. L.) Principles of Educ.
Mayhern's Means and end of universal E.
Milton's (John) Tractate on Education.
Morice on the System of teaching.
Newnham's Principles of Education.
North Am. Review. 27:67. 30:323. 48:380.
North British Review. 41:55.
Norton on Religious Education.
Pestalozzi's Letters on Early education.
——— Various other important tracts.
——— Life and writings; by Biber.
Poole on Educating children, criminals, the aged, &c.
Potter's Moralist.
Potts' (Archdeacon) Charges.
Priestley's Observations on education.
Quarterly Review. 116:177.
Selections from Edinburg Review. 2:554.
Shepherd's Education of the common people.
Sheridan's (Tho.) Source of the disorders of Great Britain.
Siljistrom's Educational institutions of the United States. Trans. by F. Rowan. (As in 1852.)
Simpson's Necessity of popular education.
——— Philosophy of Do.
Smith's (Prof. H. J.) History of Education; ancient and modern.
Smith's (Sydney) Sermons.
Southern Literary Messenger. 1:432.
Southey's Life of And. Bell; with the history of the rise and progress of the system of mutual instruction.
Spencer (Herbert) on Education.
Spirit of the Pilgrims. 1:561.
Spurzheim's Education founded on nature.
Taylor's (Mrs.) Practical Hints.
Taylor (Isaac) on Home Education.
Thornley's True ends of Education.
Thring's Education and School.
Tucker's Light of nature pursued.
Turnbull (J.) on Liberal Education.
Turner's Hints on religious education.
Tyler's (W. S.) Prayer for Colleges.
Vincent's Defence of public education.
Watts' (Isaac) Works. (Several pieces.)
Wayland on the Collegiate system of the U. States. (As in 1842.)
Wells' (Edward) Sermon
Westminster Review. 2:1. 3:492.
Whewell on the Principles of Eng. university education. (As in 1837.)
Whitaker's (William) Sermons.
Winter's Obstacles to success in religious E.
Witherspoon's Letters on Education.

Education—*continued.*

Witherspoon's Sermons.
Woodward (E.) on Education. (Recommended by GOUGE, CALAMY, and others.)
Wordsworth on Public Education. (A comprehensive survey of the subject, in a series of sermons.)
Wotton's (W.) Advice to a student.
Wyse (Tho.) on Educational Reform.
Zollikoffer's Sermons on Education.

Education Societies. See MINISTERIAL EDUCATION, STUDY OF THEOLOGY.

Amer. Quarterly Register. 1:118, 220. 6:34. 10:31. 14:27.
Amer. Inst. of Instruction. Periodical.
American Bibl. Repository. 9:474. 11:187. 2d Series. 8:444. 10:462.
Christian Month. Spect. 9:92, 241. 10:81.
Christian Review. 3:343.
"Reports" of the various Ed. Societies.
Spirit of the Pilgrims. 3:301.
Woodbridge's Annals of Education.

Effects of Christianity. See INFLUENCE.

Effectual Calling. See VOCATION.

Basil, Homilia in Psal. xxviii.
Clemens Alex., Stromata.
Cyprian, Epistolæ. Ep. LIX.
Irenæus, contra Heresios.
Justin Martyr, de Resurrectione.
Jerome, Com. in Epist. ad Ephesianos.

Breithauptii Vocatio primaria et secondaria.
Meisneri Fasciculus Disput. Theolog.
Wagnerus de Gratiosa Dei vocatione.

Balmer's Academic Lectures.
Firmin's Real Christian.
Foote (Jas.) on Effectual calling.
Gough's (Strickland) Sermons.
Hall's Help to Zion's travellers.
Kendall's Theopatia. (A precious treatise.)
Love's 16 Sermons on II. Peter i. 10.
Morning Exercises at Cripplegate.
Neal's Berry Street Sermon.
Skeppe's Divine Energy. ("I heartily recommend this work."—JOHN GILL.)

Efficacy of Prayer. See ANSWERS.

Efficacy of Sacraments. See BAPTISMAL REGENERATION, EXTREME UNCTION, INFANT BAPTISM, INFANT COMMUNION, LAY BAPTISM.

Alasco, de Sacramentis eccl. Christi.
Dallæi Dissertationes.
Gerdesii Disputationes Theologicæ.
Selneccer, de Vera doct. de cœna Domini.
Socinus de Usu et fine cœnæ Domini
Vossii Dissertationes.
Whitakeri Prelectiones.

Bell (Wm.) on the Doctrine of John vi.

Efficacy of Sacraments—*continued.*

Biddulph on Baptism. (Reply to Mant.)
Bradford (Bp.) on Baptismal Regeneration.
Clarke's (Samuel) Essays.
D'Aubeny (C.) on Regeneration.
Finch's True church views, in contrast with modern High-churchism. 1841.
Hoadly (Bp.) on the Lord's Supper.
Hook (R.) on the Sacraments.
Jewell's (Bp.) Works.
Jolly (Alex.) on the Christian Sacrifice.
Knox (Vicessimus) on the Lord's Supper.
Lawrence's (Rich.) Doct. of the Ch. of Eng.
Mant's (Richard) Tracts.
Potts (J. H.) on Baptism.
Scott (John) on the Effects of baptism.
——— Appendix to Do.
Vaux on Baptism and the Lord's Supper.
Waterland on the Christian sacraments.
Wilson's Doctrine of regeneration.
——— Address to the Society for promoting Christian knowledge.
Yardley on Baptism and confession.

Egypt. See HIEROGLYPHICS.

Bauer's Gesch. der Hebraischen nation.
Biot, Recherches Egyptiene.
Bockh's Manetho, u. d. hundsstern Periode.
Boehlen's Alte India und Egypt.
Bunsen's Ægypten's Stelle in der Weltgesch.
Cailliaud, Recherches sur les usages, &c.
Champollion, l'Egypte sous les Pharions.
——— Monumens.
Combes, Egypte et Nubia. 1846
Denon, Voyage en Egypte. 1802.
Jablonski Opuscula.
Jamesoni Spicelegia antiq. Egyptiorum.
Meiners' Religionsgesch. der Egypter.
Norden, Voyage d'Egypte. 1755.
Perizonii Ægyptiarum originum, et temporum antiquissimorum Investigatio.
Quenstedii Antiquitates Biblicæ.
Savary, Lettres sur l'Egypte. 1798.
Schwartze's Alte Ægypten.
Sonnini Egypte. 1800.
Strabo, Rerum Geographicarum libri.
Vogel's Religion der alten Egypter.
Wagenseilii Dissertationes.
Witsii Ægyptiaca.

Belzoni's Discoveries in Egypt. 1822.
Bibliotheca Sacra. 21:425, 666. 22:684.
Boaz's Egypt. 1861. (Popular.)
Bunsen's E.'s place in hist. Tr. by Cottrell.
Christian Examiner. 52:51.
Denon's Travels in E. (Time of Buonaparte.)
Eclectic Review. 1:384.
Edinburg Review. 83:391.
Edmonstone's Upper Egypt. 1822.
Egmont's (J. A.) Travels. 1759.
Gosse's Monuments of Ancient Egypt, and their relation to the worship of God.
Hawkes' E. a witness to the Bible. 1850.
Hengstenberg's E. and the books of Moses. Tr. by R. D. C. Robbins.

Egypt—*continued.*

Jones' Egypt in its Biblical relations.
Kendrick's (John) E. under the Pharaohs.
Lane's (Ed. W.) Modern Egyptians. 1836.
Legh's Journey in Egypt. 1816.
Millard's Travels in E. and Arabia. 1853.
Montalembert's Monks of the West.
Morris' (Edw. J.) Travels in Egypt. 1842.
Osborne's Monumental hist of Egypt.
Palmer's Harmony of Sacred and Ægyptian chronology.
Pococke's (Rich.) Travels. 1743.
Prichard's Analysis of historic records.
Princeton Review. 28:715.
Russel's Ancient and modern Egypt. 1831.
Sandys' Egypt and the Holy land. 1632.
Sharp's (Sam.) Early history of Egypt, from Manetho, Herodotus, &c.
——— Hist. of E. under the Ptolemies.
Spencer's Egypt and the Holy land.
Stephens' Egypt and the Holy land.
Taylor's Illustrations of the Bible, from the monuments of Egypt.
Thomas' Travels in Egypt. 1853.
Thompson's E., past and present. 1854.
Tolowic's Bibliotheca Ægyptiaca.
Trevor's Ancient Egypt. (To the close of the Old Testament period.)
Vansleb's Present state of Egypt. 1678.
Volney's Travels. 1780.
Vyse's Upper Egypt. 1842.
Warburton's Div. legation of Moses. Bk. 4.
Wilkinson's Ancient Egyptians. 600 plates.
——— ——— ——— 2d Series. 88 plates, and index.
Whaten's Ancient Egyptians.
Wotton on Ancient and modern learning.
Yates' Hist. and Condition of E. 1848.

TOLOWIC'S *Bibliotheca Ægyptiaca*, is a classified catalogue, in two large volumes, of works on the language, history, and antiquities of Egypt, brought down to 1861.

Eighth Commandment. See COMMANDMENTS, FRAUD, INTEGRITY, THEFT.

Ejaculatory Prayer.

Cook's Exhortation to ejaculatory prayer.
Polwheile (Theod.) on Ejaculatory prayer.
Townsend's (John) Discourses.

Elcesaites.

Kruftii Bibliotheca Theol. Vol. IV.
Schwarz, de Elcesaitis, et eorum erroribus.
Seidel, Abhandlung v. d. Sect. d. Elcesaiten.

Election. See REPROBATION.

Pro. See SOVEREIGNTY OF GOD.

Augustine, de Predestinatione.
——— de Natura et Gratia.

Election—*continued.*

Pro.

Battus de Æterna Predestinatione.
Bezæ Tractationes Theologicæ.
Crameri Dissertationes.
Davenantii Dissertationes. Diss. II.
Fulgentius de Veritate predestinationis.
Hutteri (Elias) Dissertationes.
Lyseri (Polycarp.) Disputationes.
Matthæi (Ioann.) Explicationes.
Pfaffii Historia Dogmaticæ.
Piscatori Tractationes.
Sigwarti Tractatus de libro vitæ.
Tossanus de Predestinatione.
Twisse, Animadv. ad J. Arminii collationem cum F. Junio.
——— de Potestate et Providentia Dei.
——— Vindiciæ Gratiæ.
Velthusius de Gratia.

Appleton's (Pres.) Works. Lectures 44, 45.
Atkinson (John) on Election.
Backus (Isaac) on E. and perseverance.
Barby's Doct. of particular election.
Barry on Unconditional election.
Beza on Predestination.
Boardman (H. A.) on Election.
Bradwardine's (Thomas) Sermons.
Calvin's Institutes.
——— Sermons.
Chalmer's (Thomas) Sermons.
Charnock's Works.
Christian Month. Spect. 10:273.
Coles (Elisha) on Divine Sovereignty.
Cooper's (Wm.) Four sermons on Election.
Cotton (John) on the Covenant of Grace.
Cudworth's Free thoughts on the doct. of E.
——— Defence of Theoron and Aspasio.
Edwards' (Dr. John) Veritas Redux.
Edwards' (Jonathan) Works.
Erskine (Tho.) on the Doctrine of E.
Hall's (Robt.) Help to Zion's travellers.
Hill's Logica Wesliensis.
——— Strictures on Fletcher.
Horne's (Will. W.) Sermons.
Kendall (Geo.) on the Doctrine of special grace. (Answer to Goodwin.)
King's (Abp.) Discourses.
——— Origin of Evil.
Jortin's Dissertations. Diss. 2.
Literary and Theological Review. 2:307. 4:250, 326.
McCheyne's (Robt. M.) Sermons.
McClelland (Geo.) on Predestination.
Malkin's (W.) Dissertations.
Manser on Election and Predestination.
Mell on Predestination and Perseverance.
Owen's (John) Works.
Park Street Lectures. Lec. 9.
Prynne's (Will.) God no impostor.
Saurin's (James) Sermons.
Spurgeon's (C. H.) Sermons. 8th Series.
Toplady on Absolute predestination.
——— Letter to John Wesley.
——— Other treatises.

Election—*continued.*

Pro.

Tucker's Light of nature pursued.
Twisse on the Scientia Media.
Watts' (Isaac) Works.
Williston's Sermons.
Wisheart's (W.) Sermons.
Witsius on the Covenants.

Con. See ARMINIANISM.

Arminii Opera.
Brennii (Daniel.) Opera.
Clerici Delineatio christianæ relig.
Curcellius de Ecclesia Christi.
Dieberge's Samlung von alten und neuen theol. Sachen.
Episcopii Opera.
Herberti Brevem ad Structionem, &c.
Loescheri Palladio.
Mollinæus de Religio Christianæ.
Socini Opera.
Thummii Μισανθρωπια.
Vorstii Opera.
Winkelmanni Dissertationes.

Benson's (John) Revival and Rejection of an old traditional heresy.
Berriman's (William) Sermons.
Bird (E.) on Absolute Election.
Brocas' Calvinism unmasked.
Coppleston on the Doctrine of Necessity.
Faber's (Geo. S.) Primitive doctrine of E.
Fearon on Universal Redemption.
Goodwin's (John) Redemption redeemed.
——— Expos. of the 9th ch. of Romans.
Graves (Richard) on Predestination.
Heylin's Judgment of the Western churches.
Hoard's (J.) Love of God to mankind.
Hussey's (John) Glories of Christ.
Kipling's Articles of the Church of England proved to be not Calvinistic.
Lindsay on Universal love and grace.
Marshall's (Nath.) Sermons.
Pierce's (Tho.) Christian's rescue from the grand error of the Heathen.
Sellon's (Walter) Works. (Replies to Coles.)
Sherlock's (Bp.) Sermons.
Whitby's (Daniel) Works.

It is not needful to give numerous references under this head, as they are given abundantly under *Arminianism, Calvinism, Remonstrants, Socinians, Universalists,* &c. See HOTTINGERI *Fata doct. de predestinatione et gratia.*

Eleusinian Mysteries.

Gesneri Dogma de perenni animor. Natura.
Le Clerc, Bibliothèque Universel.
Lobeck's (C. A.) Aglaophamus.
Meursius de Mysteriis Eleusiniis.
Nägelsbach's Griechischen Volksglaubens.
Ouvaroff, Essai sur les Mystères, &c.
Sainte-Croix, Recherches historiques.
Welcker's Griechische Götteslehre.
Winiewskii (Franz.) Dissertationes.

Eleusinian Mysteries—*continued.*

Apthorpe's (East) Letters. Let. 4.
Christie on the Painted Greek vases.
Leland's Adv. and nec. of Revelation. Part 1, Ch. 8. (Dissents from Warburton.)
Ouvaroff's Mysteries of Eleusis. Tr. by Rice.
Pamphleteer. 8:33, 455.
Rollins' Ancient History.
[Taylor's] Eleusinian and Bacchic mysteries.
Warburton's Divine legation of Moses.
Woolsey's Ancient Mysteries.

Elijah.

Camarti Elias Thesbites.
Danielis Speculum Carmelitanum.
Frischmuthi (Ioann.) Dissertationes.
Markii Scripta in selectæ Scripturæ.

Anderson's (J. S. M.) Discourses.
Harte's (W. M.) Practical Sermons.
Krummacker's Elijah the Tishbite.
Simpson's Sixteen Lectures.
Stanley's Lectures on the Jewish Church.

Elisha. See BIOGRAPHY.

Blunt's (Henry) Lectures.
Glynn's (George) Sermons.

Elohim. See NAME OF GOD.

Eloquence. See PREACHING.

Belin, Hist. critique de l'Eloquence.
Causinus de Eloquentia Sacra.
Cicero de Oratore.
Fabricii Orator Sacer.
Gisbert, l'Eloquence chrétienne.
Gregorii Pastoralis. Pars III.
Henry (A.), Histoire de l'Eloquence.
Landie, Hist. morale de l'Eloquence.
Quinctillian de Corruptione Eloquentiæ.
——— Institutiones.
Volsii Rhetorica.

Amer. Bibl. Repos. 10:169. 2d Series. 1:22. 4:571. 7:69.
Austin's Chironomia.
Barber's Lectures on Elocution.
Biblioth. Sacra. 2:683. 4:96.
Blackmore's Accomplished Preacher.
Blackwood's Mag. 2:131, 318. (Chalmers.)
British and For. Review. 10:608.
Bungener's Preacher and the King. (A view of pulpit eloquence in the time of Louis XIV.)
Burgh on Pronunciation and Gesture.
Campbell (Dr. Geo.) on Pulpit Eloquence.
Chris. Examiner. 41:49. 42:425.
Chris. Monthly Spect. 1:341. 9:337. 10:635
Eclectic Rev. 4th Series. 13:189. 28:539.
Edinburg Rev. 6:521. 45:147.
Episcopal Magazine. 2:201, 341.
Fenelon's Ancient and Modern Orators.
——— on Pulpit Eloquence.
——— Letter to the French Academy.

Eloquence—*continued.*

Fordyce's Eloquence of the pulpit.
Frazier's Mag. 30:287. (E. of the 19th cent.)
Gardner's (John) Eloquence of the pulpit.
Hartley's Principles of Elocution.
Henley on Speaking and Action in Preach.
Holwell's Trans. of Aristotle's Rhetoric.
Hume's (David) Essays. Ess. 12.
Knickerbocker Mag. 4:413.
Knox's Hints to public speakers.
Langhorne's (John) Letters.
Lawson's Lectures on Oratory.
Leland's (Thos.) Principles of Eloquence. (Relates to the style of the New Testam.)
London Quart. Review. 29:283.
Maury's Principles of Eloquence.
North American Review. 10:204.
Porter's (Ebenezer) Lectures on Eloquence.
Princeton Review. 7:177.
Quarterly Review. 29:283.
Rapin's Eloquence of the Bar and Pulpit.
Rush's Philosophy of the Human voice.
Russel's Pulpit Eloquence. Introd. by Park.
Sharp's (Thomas) Discourses.
Sheridan on Elocution.
Smart's Theory of Elocution.
Spirit of the Pilgrims. 2:488.
Ward's (John) System of Oratory.
Watts' Miscellaneous Thoughts. No. 26.
Wilson's (John) Principles of Elocution.
Witherspoon's Lectures.
Wright's Philosophy of Elocution exemplified by readings from the Liturgy.

Emotions. See MIND.

Bain's, The Emotions and the Will.
Chalmers' Moral Philosophy.
Dawes' Duties of the closet.
Edwards (Pres.) on the Affections.
Hodge's (Cha.) Essays and Reviews.
Ken's (Bp.) Retired Christian.
Kennaway's (Cha. E.) Sermons.
Maclaurin's Essays.
Natural History of Enthusiasm.
Newman's (J. H.) Sermons.
Ramsay's Analogy and theory of E.
Spaulding's Value of feelings in religion.
Spring's (Gardner) Essays.
Wilberforce's Practical View.
Yonge's (James) Sermons.

Employments of Heaven.
See HEAVEN.

Blackmore's Felicity of the Just.
Davies' Glimpses of our eternal home.
Fern's (Robt.) Celestial Work.
Fuller's Nature of the heavenly glory.
Harbaugh's Heavenly Home.
Horneck's Glory of the other world.
Landor's Last fruits off an old tree.
Mant's (Bp.) Happiness of the blessed.
Sherlock's (Bp.) Sermons.
Thompson's (Edward) Sermons.

Emulation.

Abercrombie's Phil. of moral feelings.
American Bibl. Repository. 5:393.
American Quart. Register. 5:65.
Christian Observer. 13:81, 151, 230, 493.
Hamilton's (Sir Wm.) Dissertations.
New England Magazine. 2:107.
North Amer. Review. 43:496.
Oxford Prize Essays. 5:89.
Religious Magazine. 2:5.

Encratites. See GNOSTICS, HERESIES.

Clemens Alex., Stromata. Lib. III.
Origen, de Oratione. Cap. XIII.

Longuerue, Dissertatio de Tatiano.
Vogtii Bibliotheca histor. hæresiolog.

End of Man's Existence.
See SELF-DEDICATION.

Baxter's (Arthur G.) Sermons.
Dwight's Theology. Sermon 25.
Hall's (Robt.) Notes of sermons.

End of the World. See CONSUMMATION.

Endowments.

Chalmers' (Tho.) Use and abuse of literary and Ecclesiastical endowments.
Edinburg Review. 1:578.
Princeton Review. 25:545.
Pusey (E. B.) on Cathedral Institutions.
Skinner's Scottish endowment question; ecclesiastical and educational.
Westminster Review. 22:119.

English Bible. See REVISION.

Ainsworth's Tr. of Pentateuch. Notes. 1627.
——— —— Psalms. 1630.
——— —— Solomon's Song. 1632.
Aislabie's Tr. of Matthew and John. 1819.
Alexander's (Jos. A.) Translation and Exposition of Psalms. 1850.
——— ——— ——— of Isaiah. 1851.
Amer. Bible Union. Trans. of Job. 1863.
——— Revised version of New Test. 1865.
Amer. Quart. Rev. 22:313. Canticles. 1837.
Anderson's Annals of the Eng. Bible. 1845.
The same. Continued by Prime. 1852.
Anglo-Rhemish New Testament. 1582.
Baber's History of the Saxon and English versions, previous to the 15th century. 1810. (Prefixed to his edition of Wickliff's New Testament.)
Bagge's Translation of Galatians. 1855.
Baldwin's Ballads of Solomon, in English meter. 1549.
Barham's Corrected tr. of the Bible. 1850.
Barlee's Free transl. of the Epistles. 1837. (*Very* free!)
——— ——— Minor prophets. 1839.
Barnard's Version of the Psalms. 1752.

English Bible.

Barnes' Notes on Job; with new trans. 1844.
——— ——— Isaiah; " " 1838.
Barrett's Synopsis of criticisms on the Old Testam., in which modern commentators differ from the common version. With an explanation of the difficulties in the Hebrew and English texts. 1847. (In this learned work, the Hebrew, Greek, and English are given side by side; and the opinions of the most eminent critics stated at length, and commented on.)
Barton's Errors and absurdities of the old English metrical translat. of the Psalms; and other late translations. 1655.
Bates' (Julius) Trans. of the O. Test., as far as Chronicles; with notes. 1773. (A curious attempt to be entirely literal; but many renderings are improved.)
Bellamy's Translation of the Bible. 1819.
——— Examination of objections. 1820. (The improprieties of this translation are exhibited in the LOND. QUART. REVIEW, 19:250, 446, and 23:287; ECLECTIC REV., New Series, 10:1, 130, 280; ANTI-JACOBIN REVIEW, 54:97, 193, 305.)
Belsham's Tr. of the N. Test. 1808. (Learned and scorching reviews are in the LONDON QUART. REVIEW, 30:79; ECLECTIC REV., 1823; EDINBURG REVIEW, Vol. 4; BRIT. CRITIC, Vol. 22, &c. Mr. B. published several vindications of his work.)
Benjoin's Tr. of Jonah; with notes. 1796. ("A failure."—ORME.)
Bennett's Specimen of a new translation of the Old Testament. 1836.
Bennett's Translation of Acts. 1847.
Bentham's Trans. of the Psalms. 1560.
——— ——— Ezekiel and Daniel. 1565.
Bernard's Amended tr. of the Bible. 1842.
Bernard & Aaron on faithful transl. 1842.
Bible: according to the received version, except the substitution of the original Hebrew names, instead of the words "Lord," "God," &c. 1830.
Bishop's Bible. 1568. (A revision of Cranmer's.)
Byble, trans. out of the avthentical Latin, by ye Englishe College at Douay. 1609. (A fine ed. was printed at Edinburg, 1796.)
Blackwall on the Wrong divisions of chapters and verses; and faulty translations. 1731. (Appended to his "Sac. Classics.")
Bland's Song of Sol., in blank verse. 1750.
——— Genesis translated according to the vowel points. 1746.
Blaney's Trans. of Jer. and Lament. 1784.
——— ——— Zechariah. 1787.
Boothroyd's Improved version of the Bible, from corrected texts; with introduction and notes. 1818.
Bowring's Literal tr. into Eng. verse. 1858.
Brameld's Gospels translated, spurious passages expunged, doubtful ones bracketted, and the text revised. 1863.

English Bible.

Brenton's Translation of the LXX. according to the Vatican.
Brett on the Ancient Eng. versions. 1713.
Broughton's Trans. of Daniel. 1596.
——— ——— Jer. and Job. 1610.
Buchanan's Trans. of the Psalms. 1772.
Bulkley's Answer to ten foolish reasons of the Rhemish Papists for translating from the Latin, instead of the originals. 1588.
Burrow's (G.) Tr. of Solomon's Song. 1853.
Burton's Phraseology, manners, religion, &c., of Eastern nations; and an enquiry into the accuracy of the Eng. translation. 1805.
Bush's Literal tr. of Psalms. Notes. 1838.
Butler's Horæ Biblicæ. Chap. 15.
Calender's Literal version of the New Test. 1779. (Follows exactly the order of the Greek words, and of course makes curious English sometimes.)
Caldecot's Tr. of the N. Test. Notes. 1834.
Campbell's (Alex.) New Testament, as tran. by Geo. Campbell, Macknight, and Doddridge. 1826.
Campbell's (Geo.) Tr. of the Gospels. 1790.
Carey's Tr. of Job; with illustrations, various readings, notes, maps, and plates. 1858. (Many valuable extracts in relation to customs, geography, &c.)
Carson (Alex.) on Prof. Lee's incompetency to translate the Scriptures. 1829.
Cartwright's Confutation of the Rhemish version. 1618.
Challoner's Translat. of the Vulgate. 1823.
Chappelow's Translation of Job, and Commentary. 1752.
Cheke's New Test. 1550. Reprinted 1843.
Christian Disciple. 2:1. (On Wakefield's translation.)
Christian Review. 3:34.
Clarke's Translation of Job. 1685.
Clay's Translation of the Psalms. 1864.
Clowes' Tr. of the Gospels; with notes. 1769. (Swedenborgian.)
——— Translation of the Psalms. 1771.
Coleman's Tr. of the Psalms. Notes. 1863.
Coleridge's Tr. and Notes on Judges, 17th and 18th chapters.
Conant's (Mrs.) Popular hist. of the various English translations. 1858.
Congleton's Version of the Psalms. 1860.
Conquest's Holy Bible, with 20,000 emendations. 1843.
Colenso's Tr. of Romans. 1861. ("From a missionary point of view.")
Colton's Translation of the five books of Maccabees. 1832.
Cook's Tr. of the Revelations. Notes. 1789.
Cooper's Tr. of the Ep. to the Romans. 1844.
Cottle's Version of the Psalms. 1802.
Cotton's History of editions of the English Bible, and parts thereof; from 1505 to 1820. (Intended as an appendix to Lewis At the end are specimens of the early versions.)

English Bible.

Coverdale's O. and N. Test., with Apocrypha. 1535. (The first English translation of the whole Bible, and the first Protestant version in any language.)
Cowherd's Authentic facts, in science and religion; designed to illustrate a new tr. of the Bible. 1820. (Over 6,000 extracts.)
Cox's (Robt.) Horæ Romanæ: an original translation, with notes. 1824.
Cranmer's Byble in Englishe; trulye translated after the veryte of ye Hebrve and Greke textes; by ye dylygent studye of diuerse excellent men, expert in ye forsayde tongues. 1539.
Crawford's Ep. to the Romans. Tr. from the editio septima of Tichendorf. 1860.
Darling's Poetical tr. of the Gospels. 1801.
Daubuz's Tr. of Revelat., with Com. 1720.
Davies' Epistles to the Eph., Col., and Philemon. Introduction and notes. 1866.
Davidson's Tr. of Job, and Com. 1862.
Day's Fower Evangelistes, trans. in ye olde Saxon's tyme, out of Latin into ye vulgare toung; newly collected. 1571.
Delgado's Tr. of the Pentateuch. 1789.
Demarest's Tr. of 1 Peter; with Exp. 1851.
Dennis' Psalms, in blank verse. 1808.
Denvers' Trans. of the Latin Vulgate.
Desvoeux's Tr. of Ecclesiastes. 1760. (The common version in parallel columns.)
De Sola, Lindenthal, and Raphael's translation of Genesis. 1844.
Dewees' Tr. of the Epis. to Romans. 1866.
Dickinson's Tr. of ye New Testament. 1833. (Trifling.)
Doddridge's Tr. and paraph. of N. T. 1760.
Doderline's Trans. of Sol. Song. 1780.
Dodson's Tr. of Isaiah; with notes. 1790.
Douay's Version from the Vulgate. 1600.
Drake's Metrical tr. of the Psalms. 1837.
Du Jion's Tr. and Expos. of Revelat. 1596.
Dupont's Three books of Solomon in English verse. 1666.
Durell's Prophecy of Jacob and Moses: a new translation and notes. 1764.
Eden's Psalms, in blank verse. 1841.
Edwards' (Tho.) Trans. of the Psalms; with notes. (Unimportant.) 1755.
Ellicott's Tr. of Ephesians. 1855.
——— —— Timothy and Titus. 1856.
——— —— Thessalonians. 1858.
——— —— Galatians. 1859.
——— —— Philippians, Coloss. 1862.
——— —— Philemon. 1865.
Essay for a new tr. of the Bible; showing from reason, and the best commentators, the necessity of revision. *Anon.* 1763.
Etheridge's Literal tr. of the N. Testament, from the Peschito. 1846.
Ewbank's Tr. of Ep. to the Romans. 1850.
Eyre's Trans. of Paul's Epistles. 1832.
Farr's Version of the Psalms. 1846.
Ferme's Transl. of the Vulgate. Edited by W. L. Alexander. 1850.

English Bible.

Francis' (Ann) Poetical trans. of Solomon's Song and Psalms. Notes. 1781.
French & Skinner's Tr. of Psalms. 1830.
——— —— Proverbs. 1831. (See British Critic. 9:404.)
Fry's (John) Tr. of Sol. Song. Notes. 1811.
—— —— —— Psalms. 1819.
—— —— —— Job. 1827.
—— —— —— Romans. 1830.
Fulke's Text of the New Testam., translated out of the Vulgate by the Papists at Rheims; with the trans. out of the original Greek; with a confutation of false glosses, &c. 1580. (The Papal and the English translations in parallel columns.)
——— Defence of the translation of ye holie Scriptures into the Englische tong against ye manifold cauils, friuolous qvarrels, and impvdent slaunders of *Gregory Marten*, one of ye readers in ye trayterous seminarie of Rheimes. 1617. (Republished by the Parker Society. 1843.)
Fuller (Tho.) on the English transl. 1810.
Fysh's Lyrical literal version of Ps. 1851.
Garden's Improved tr. of Job. 1796.
Geddes (Alex.) on the queries and difficulties relating to an English version. 1787.
——— New tr. of the Bible [as far as Ezra]. from corrected texts and various readings. 1800. (The unscholarly and erroneous character of this work, is shown in the British Critic, Vol. 4, et seq. Geddes, though a professed Roman Catholic, was evidently an infidel.)
Gell's Amendment to the last Eng. tr. 1659. (Many quaint and cabalistic renderings, but of small value.)
Genevan Nevve Testament. 1557.
Genevan Byble. 1560. "The H. Scriptures conteyned in ye olde and nevve Test., with profitable annotations vpon all ye hard places." (The united work of Coverdale, Gilby, Whittingham, Woodman, Sampson, Cole, Knox, Bodley, and Pullein.)
Gifford's Poetical trans. of Sol. Song. 1598.
Giles' New Testament construed literally, word for word. 1859.
Ginsbury's Tr. of Solomon's Song. 1861.
Godwin's Tr. of Matthew. Notes. 1863.
Good's (J. M.) Tr. of the Psalms. Metrical.
——— ——— —— Sol. Song. 1803.
——— ——— —— Job. 1812. ("The most valuable work on Job in the Eng. language."—Orme. Severely criticized in the Eclectic Review, of 1816.)
Goode's (Will.) Tr. of Ps. Crit. notes. 1811.
Goodwin's Tr. of the Apocalypse. 1855.
Govett's Tr. and Expos. of Isaiah. 1841.
Green's (T. S.) Tr. of the N. Test. 1858.
——— Developed criticisms on passages of the N. T., affected by various readings.
——— Tr. of the Psalms; with notes. 1762.
Green's (W.) Tr. of the poetical books of the Old Testament. Notes. 1771.

English Bible.

Green's (W.) Tr. of parts of Isaiah. 1776.
Greenaway's Tr. of Ecclesiastes. 1781.
Greenfield's (W.) Genesis; with interlinear translation and notes. 1831.
Grier's Answer to Ward's Errata. 1812.
Gwynne's Tr. and Exp. of Galatians. 1863.
Hale's Tr. of the New Test. 1830. (The common version altered to correspond with Griesbach's altered text.)
Hall's Emendations of our N. Test. 1857.
Hamilton's Observations on the Engl. Papal version; showing that all the censures of Ward's Errata are as applicable to it as to the Protestant Bible. 1825. (A letter to Dr. Murray.)
——— Second letter to Dr. Murray. 1826.
Hardy's Tr. of the Ep. to the Hebrews. 1783.
Hare's Metrical tr. of the Ps. Notes. 1755.
[Harmer's] New tr. of Sol. Song. 1768.
Harness' State of the English Bible. 1859.
Harwood's Liberal tr. of the N. Testament. 1768. (Arian.)
Haweis' (Tho.) Trans. of the N. Test. 1795.
Haydock's Tr. of the Vulgate. 1811.
Heath's New version of Job. 1756.
Heberden's Literal trans. of the Epistles and Revelation. 1839.
Heinfetter's Literal tr. of the N. T. 1854.
Henderson's Tr. of Isaiah. 1840.
——— ——— Minor prophets. 1845.
——— ——— Jerem. and Ezek. 1851.
Henry VIIIth. Byble. 1539.
Hexepla: or the Six important English tr. of the N. Test. (Viz., Wickliff's, Tyndall's, Cranmer's, Genevan, Rhemish, and Authorized.)
Highton's Revised tr. of the N. T., with the various readings of the Greek text. 1862.
Hodgson's Trans. of Solomon's Song. 1785.
——— ——— Proverbs. 1788.
——— ——— Ecclesiastes. 1791.
Holden's Tr. of Proverbs. 1819. ("The best help to the critical understanding of the book."—Horne.)
Hollybush's Tr. of the N. Test. 1538. (This is Coverdale's translat. from the Vulgate, published under an assumed name.)
Holmes' (A.) Historical sketch of the English translations. 1815.
Hopkins' (Wm.) Tr. of Genesis and Exodus. 1784. (Notices all the variations of the Samaritan Pentateuch.)
Horsely's Trans. of Hosea. Notes. 1800.
——— ——— Psalms. " 1815.
Howard's (Henry) Tr. of Ecclesiasticus from the Vulgate. 1827.
——— Tr. of the Pentateuch from the LXX.; with notes on important misrepresentations. 1857.
Hunt's Translation of Job. 1775.
Hussey's Revised tr. of the Bible and Apocrypha; with Com. 1844. (The received version and the revised in parallel columns, with important marginal readings.)

English Bible.

Improved version of the N. Test., upon the basis of Newcombe's translation. 1808. (By eminent Unitarians.)
Jebb's Literal trans. of the Psalms. 1840.
Jenour's Trans. of Isaiah. 1831.
——— ——— Job. 1841.
Jervis' Trans. of Genesis, from the Hebrew; collated with the Samaritan Pentateuch, and with the Septuagint and Syriac versions. Notes. 1852.
Johnson's (John) Holy David and his English translators. 1716.
Johnson's (Ant.) Hist. of the several English translations. 1730. (Reprinted in "Watson's Tracts," 1791.)
Jones' (John) Tr. of Isaiah, from the text of Vanderhoot. 1830.
Jones' (John, LL. D.,) Tr. of Col., Thess., Tim., Titus, and James. 1819. (Unitarian.)
——— Tr. of first 3 ch. of Genesis. 1820.
Joy's (G.) Trans. of Isaiah. 1531.
——— ——— Jeremiah. 1534.
Kalisch's Tr. of the O. T.; with Com. 1856.
——— ——— N. T., and Com. 1858.
Kay's Tr. of the Psalms. Notes. 1864.
Kelly's (Wm.) Greek text, and new tr. 1860.
Kenrick's Translat. of the Gospels, from the Vulgate. 1849.
——— Tr. of the Ep. and Apocalypse. 1851.
Kilburn's Errors in lately printed Bibles. 1659.
King James' Version. 1611.
Lawrence's Crit. reflections on the misrepresentations of the Unitarian version. 1811.
Le Cene's Essay for a new French translation. 1727. Trans. and applied to the English version by Hugh Ross.
Lee's Letter to J. Bellamy, on his new trans. of the Bible. 1821.
——— Tr. of Job, with critical Com. 1837.
Leeser's Holy Scriptures, tr. according to the Masoretic text; on the basis of the Engl. version. A.M. 5614. (1853. Jewish.)
Leusden's Tr. of the Psalms. 1688. (Contains the Hebrew text, and is dedicated to "the Rev. and pious John Elliot, the Apostle of the Indians in N. America, and the 24 red Indian ministers, lately Gentiles.")
Lewis' Complete history of the several Eng. translations of the whole Bible, both in MS. and print, and the various editions. Plates. 1739. (The 3d ed. brings down the list of Eng. translations to 1818.)
Lindsey's List of false readings in the English Bible.
Lingard's Tr. of the N. T.; with notes. 1836.
Literal tr. of the Prophets, by Lowth, Blaney, Newcombe, Wintle, Horsely, &c. 1836.
Livermore's Tr. of Romans; with Com. 1854.
Llewellyn's History of the British and Welch translations. 1768.
Lookup's Erroneous translations in the common version. 1739.

English Bible.

Lookup's Berashith; a new translation of Genesis. 1740.
Lowth's (Bp.) Tr. of Isaiah. Notes. 1770.
Mace's N. Test.; a corrected text, and new version; with notes, and various readings.
McCloskey's N. T., from the Vulgate. 1864.
McCrie's Revised translation, after the Eastern manner. 1799. (Worthless.)
McKnight's Trans. of the Epistles; with the text, common version, new translation and paraphrase, in parallel columns; with notes. 1795.
McLean's Tr. of Hebrews; with Com. 1819.
Major's Interlineary translation and notes on Luke. 1826.
Malan's (S. C.) Vind. of the authorized version from recent charges. 1826.
Mann's (Nic.) Crit. notes on some passages. 1747. (Corrects many renderings.)
Mant's Metrical tr. of the Ps. Notes. 1824.
Marcus' (B.) Mistranslations of the O. Test. corrected. 1846. (Jewish.)
Mardon's Tr. of the Epistles of John. 1853.
Marsh's (H.) Hist. of our Eng. vers. 1812.
Marsh's (E. G.) Psalms in English verse. Notes. 1832.
Marsh's (Wilmot) Biblical versions, &c. 1845. (Gives specimens of the various versions since Wickliffe.)
Martin's Manifold corruptions of the Holy Scriptures by the English sectaries. 1852. (See Fulke.)
Mather's (Cotton) Trans. of Psalms. 1718. (Blank verse.)
Matthews' [or Rogers'] Olde and Nevve Test. trvelye and pvrelye translated. 1537.
Maule's (J.) Trans. of the N. Test. Notes.
Merrick's Metrical tr. of Psalms. 1765.
Mitchell's Tr. of the Revelations. 1800.
Modern and close tr. of the Bible, arranged in order of time. "By the authors of the Christian Code." 1812.
Montague's Metrical vers. of the Ps. 1851.
Moore's (T. V.) Translation and Expos. of Haggai, Zechariah, and Malachi. 1855.
Mortimer's Trans. of the Gospels and Acts, from the text of Mills. 1761.
Mudge's Trans. of the Psalms. 1744.
Murphy's Tr. of Genesis, and Com. 1863.
Murdock's N. T. tr. from the Peschito. 1852.
Musgrave's Tr. of Ps. in blank verse. 1833.
Nares on the Unitarian version. 1808.
Nary's N. Test., from the Vulgate. 1719.
Neale's (Jas.) Tr. of Hosea. Notes. 1771.
——— ——— With additions, by W. H. Neale. 1850.
Newcombe's Tr. of the min. Prophets. 1785.
——— —— Ezekiel. 1788 and 1836.
——— —— N. T.; with notes. 1796.
——— Historical view of the English translation. 1792.
Newman's (F. W.) Tr. of Sol. Song. 1839.
Newman's (W.) Emendations of the authorized version. 1839.

English Bible.

Nevv. Testament of Jesvs Christ, tr. out of the avthentic Latin; vvith argvmentes, bookes, chapters, annotations, and other necessary helpes; by the College at Rhemes. 1582.
Norton's (And.) Tr. of the Gospels. Notes. 1855.
Noyes' Tr. of Job. 1827.
——— —— Psalms. 1831.
——— —— the Prophets. 1843.
——— —— Prov., Eccles., and Cant. 1846.
O'Callaghan's List of editions of the English Bible, and parts thereof, printed in America, previous to 1860.
Oliver's Trans. of Psalms from the Syriac-Peschito version. 1861.
Pardue's Trans. of Romans. 1855.
Parker's Bible. 1568, 1570, 1572, &c. (Commonly called the *"Bishop's Bible.)*
Parkhurst's Literal vers. of Psalms. 1825.
Pearce's Tr. of 1 Corinthians. Notes. 1772.
Penn's (Granville) Critical revision of the text, and new tr. of the N. Test. 1836.
——— The same, with Annotations and Supplement. 1841.
Percy's Tr. of Solomon's Song. 1764.
Perowne's Tr. of the Psalms. Notes. 1864.
Perrin's Revised text, and new tr. of N. T.
Philalethes' [John Jones] Tr. of Colossians, Thessalonians, Titus, and James. 1819. (Socinian.)
Pick's Tr. of the Minor prophets; with notes from various Rabbis. 1833. (Jewish.)
Pierce's Trans. of Epistles of Paul. 1747.
Pococke's Tr. of 2 Peter. Notes. 1660.
Pratt's (H.) Genealogy of creation. 1861. (Tr. of Genesis from the unpointed Hebrew text.)
Purver's Literal tr. of the Bible. 1764.
Rae's Trans. of Isaiah. Notes. 1858.
Rainhold's Refutation of sundry reprehensions and cavils by which Mr. Whitaker labors to deface the Eng. translation and Catholic notes of the Rhemish Testament.
Ray's Tr. of the Sacred Scripture after the Eastern manner. 1815.
Rick's Tr. of the Minor prophets.
Reichardt's Psalms, Heb. and Eng. 1841.
Reid's Literal tr. of the Psalms. 1821. (Has the original, without points, with a grammar and lexicon.)
Rennel on the Unitarian version.
Rhemish Bible; from the Vulgate. 1582.
Roberts' (W. H.) Corrections of the English translation of the O. Test. 1794. ("Very valuable."—British Critic.)
Rodwell's Translation of Job. 1864.
Rogers' Collation of the principal English translations; with a historical account of ancient MSS. and editions. 1778. (Many fac-similes. Reprinted 1847.)
Role's Trans. of the Psalms. 1840.
Ryan's Analysis of Ward's "Errata." 1808.
Sampson's Tr. of Hebrews. Notes. 1828.

English Bible.

Sawyer's Tr. of the O. and N. Test., with chronological arrangement of the books, and a new division of chapters and verses. 1858–1862.
Scarlet's Tr. of the N. Test. 1798. (Conforms to the sentiments of the Universalists.)
Scott's (Dan.) New tr. of Matthew. 1741.
Scott's (Tho.) Tr. of Job. 1771. (Poetical.)
Scott's (Wm.) Tr. of the New Test. Notes. 1775.
Shadwell's Tr. of Matthew. Notes. 1859.
Sharp's Tr. of the N. Test., from the text of Griesbach. 1840. (All quotations from the Old Test. are given in Italics.)
——— ——— Hebrew Scriptures. 1864.
Shuttleworth's Tr. of the Epistles. 1829.
Sibthorp's Trans. of Jonah. Notes. 1835.
Sidney's Psalms of D. in verse. 1810.
Skinner's Tr. of the Psalms. Notes. 1830.
Smart's Metrical tr. of the Psalms. 1765.
Smith's (Eliza) Tr. of Job. 1810. (Regarded by Abp. Magee as then the best.)
Stather's Job in English verse. Notes.
Stennett's Tr. of Sol. Song. Notes.
Stewart's (C. E.) The New Testament and its translations. 1855.
Stock's Metrical tr. of Job. 1803. ("An entire congeries of precipitancies, mistakes, and mutilations."—Magee.)
——— Metrical tr. of Isaiah. ("Close, nervous, and manly."—Brit. Critic, 28:466.)
Stonard's Tr. of Zechariah. Notes. 1824.
Street's Literal tr. of the Psalms; with preface and notes. 1790.
Stuart's Tr. of Rom. and Excursus. 1832.
Sturges' Remarks on Dodson's Isaiah. 1791.
Swedenborg's Tr. of the Psalms. 1760.
Sylvester's Tr. of the Psalms. Notes. 1754.
Tatham's Tr. of Job from the Coptic. 1846.
Taverner's Moste sacred Byble; recognized wyth great dylygence, after the moste faythful exemplars. 1539.
Thomson's (Cha.) Tr. of the LXX. 1808. (The only English translation, and highly approved.)
——— Tr. of the New Covenant. 1810.
Thompson's (John S.) Monotessaron: a new trans. and notes. 1826.
Thompson's (Lawrence) Tr. of the N. Test. from the Latin of Beza. 1575.
Thompson's (W.) Tr. of the N. Test.; with critical notes. 1816. (In small estimation.)
Thomson's (W. A.) Hist. of the translation and circulation of the Scriptures. 1815.
Thorn's Revised tr. of Corinthians. 1852.
Todd's (H. J.) Memoir of Bp. Walton. (Bp. W. was engaged on a revised translation of the English Bible in 1658.)
——— Vind. of our authorized vers. 1819.
——— Observations on the metrical versions of the Psalms, by Sternhold, Hopkins, and others. 1822.

English Bible.

Todd's Account of our authorized version. 1834.
Tomline's (Bp.) Account of the English translations. 1820.
Tomlinson's (R.) Tr. of incorrect passages in the common version. With notes. 1803.
Torshell & Madden's Bible and Apocrypha; according to the earliest English versions. 1850.
Trappe's Commentary. 1670. (Many excellent retranslations.)
Tregelle's Tr. of the Apocalypse. 1844.
Tunstell & Heath's Bible. 1541.
Turnbull (Jos.) Tr. of the N. Test. 1856.
Turner's Poetical tr. of the Psalms. 1824.
Twell's Critical exam. of the late new version. (Mace's work, both as to the text and version, is here severely handled.)
Tye's (Doctor in mvsyke) Actes of the Apos. in Englishe meter, wyth notes to eche chapter to synge; and also to play vpon the lvte. 1553.
Tyndale's Tr. of the N. Test. 1526.
——— ——— Pentateuch. 1530.
——— ——— Jonah. 1531.
——— ——— N. Testament, with the essential variations of Coverdale's, Matthew's, Genevan, and Bishop's Bible, as marginal readings. By J. P. Dabney. 1837.
Umbreight's Tr. of Job; with notes. Translated by J. Gray. 1836.
Vansittart's Tr. of the 49th Psalm. 1810.
Wake's Liberal tr. of the Psalms. 1793.
Wakefield's Tr. of the N. Test. 1790. (Unitarian. Examined by Nares, Magee, Lawrence, and the Eclectic Review.)
Walford's Tr. of the N. Test. Notes. 1837.
——— ——— Psalms. 1838.
Walter's Letter to Bp. Marsh. 1823. (To show that Tyndale's version was not framed upon that of Luther.)
Ward's Errata of the Protest. Bible. 1706.
Webster's (Noah) Bible; with emendations of language. 1833.
Webster's (Will.) New Testament from the ancient Latin; with notes from the French of Father Simon. 1730.
Wier's Tr. of Ps., and chron. arrang. 1830.
Weiss' Tr. of Ps.; with crit. notes. 1852.
——— ——— Ecclesiastes. " " 1857.
Wellbeloved's Trans. of the N. Testament; with notes. 1833. (Unitarian.)
Wellbeloved, Smith & Porter's Holy Scriptures of the Old Testament. 1859.
Wells' (Edw.) Help to the understanding of the Scriptures. 1708. (A revised translation of the O. and N. Testament, with prefaces, Greek text, notes, &c.)
Wemys' Biblical Gleanings. 1816. (A collection of proposed emendations, with important various readings; compiled from over fifty distinguished critics.)
——— Tr. of Job; with notes. 1839.
Wesley's (John) New Testament revised.

English Bible.

Whiston's Primitive New Testament. 1745. (Important, as translating from the Codex Bezæ, the Clermont MS., and the Alexandrine MS., as collated by Mill.)
Whitaker's Histor. and critical Inquiry into the right interpretation of the Hebrew Scriptures; with remarks on Mr. Bellamy's translation. 1819.
——— Answer to Wm. Rainhold.
Whitwell's Tr. of Romans; with introduction and notes. 1848.
Wickliffe's New Testament from the Vulgate. 1387. (Not printed till 1731, when it was published by John Lewis, with a history of the various English translations. A reprint was issued in 1810, with a good memoir of W., and a continuation of the history of English versions. A beautiful edition was published in 1850, by Torshall & Madden, who spent several years on the work, and compared about two hundred manuscripts.)
Williams' (Benj.) Book of Psalms, as translated, paraphrased, and imitated, by the most eminent English poets. 1781.
Williams' (Rowland) Transl. of the Hebrew Prophets. 1866.
Williams' (Tho.) Lit. tr. of Sol. Song. 1800.
——— ——— N. Test. 1812.
Willis' Tr. of Acts. 1789. (Not esteemed.)
Wilson's Emphatic Diaglot, notes, and new tr. of the New Testament. 1866.
Wilson's (Bp.) Bible, with notes. 1785. (Collates the received version, with preceding and subsequent versions.)
Winthrop's (J.) Tr. of the Apocalypse into familiar language. 1794.
Wintle's Tr. of Daniel; with notes. 1792.
Witham's N. Test. from the Vulgate. 1730.
Wolfe's (J. R.) Messiah in the Psalms, and Pentateuch.
Woodhouse's Tr. of the Apocalypse. 1806. (Answers the objections of Michaelis.)
Wordsworth's Tr. of the Apocalypse. 1829. (The Greek text, MSS. collations, and learned notes.)
Worseley's Trans. of the New Test. Notes. 1770. (Pays special attention to the particles.)
Wrangham's Tr. of the Psalms.
Wynne's New Test. collated with the Greek. 1764. (Chiefly follows Doddridge.)
Young's (Robt.) Tr. of the Bible. 1862.

THE FIRST ENGLISH VERSIONS.
(In the order of time.)

A. D. 706. Adhelm's Saxon Psalms.
721. Egbert's Four Gospels.
734. Bede's Gospel of John.
880. Alfred's Psalms.
1340. Roles' [or Hampole's] Psalms.
1387. Wickliffe's Bible.
1526. Tyndale's New Testament.
1530. ——— Pentateuch.

English Bible.

A. D. 1531. Tyndale's Jonah.
1531. Joyce's Isaiah.
1534. ——— Jeremiah, Psalms, and Songs of Moses.
1535. Coverdale's Bible.
1537. Matthews' [or Rogers'] Bible.
1538. Cranmer's Bible.
1539. Taverner's Bible.
1541. Tunstell & Heath's Bible.
1550. Cheke's New Testament.
1557. Geneva Bible.
1568. Bishop's Bible.
1582. Rhemish Testament.
1600. Douay Bible.
1611. King James' Version.

Some of these dates are disputed, but nearly all of them are certain.

Enmity of the Heart.
See CARNAL MIND.

Barnes' (Albert) Sermons.
Cooper's (G.) Sermons.
Cooper's (James) Sermons.
Sherlock's (Bp.) Sermons.
Wayland's (Dr. Samuel) Sermons.
Weston's (Bp.) Sermons.

Enmity of the World.

Hall's Help to Zion's travellers.
Leighton's (Abp.) Comm. on 1 Peter iii:16.
Ray's Persuasives to a holy life.
Stennett's (Samuel) Sermons.
Wayland's (Samuel) Sermons.

Enoch.

Libri Enoch, Versio Ethiopica.
Heinii (J. P.) Dissertationes.
Hoffman's Ueberset. mit Commentar. 1838.

Amer. Biblical Repository. 3:
Ewald's Origin, meaning, &c., of the book of Enoch.
Hoffman's Trans. and commentary.
Lawrence's Translation, and preliminary Dissertations.
Murray's Enoch restitutus. (An attempt to separate from the book of Enoch the book quoted by Jude.)
Stuart's Christology of the book of Enoch.

Enquirers. See CONVICTION.

Enthusiasm.

Baieri (Joan. Guil.) Dissertationes.
Bebellii (Balthas.) Dissertationes.
Casauboni Commentarius de Enthusiasmo.
Chladenii Introversio in se ipsum.
Colberg's dem Platonisch-Hermetischen.
Corbini Enthusiasticum Pantheon.
Gerdesii (Hen. Joann.) Schediasma.
Himmelii Collegio Anti-enthusiasticum.
Hoornbeckii (Joann.) Dissertationes.

Enthusiasm—*continued.*

Jæger de Enthusiasmo moderno. 1709.
Kahler de Hæresi Enthus. abominibili.
Krohn's Gesch. der Enthusiastischen.
Mori Enthusiasmus Triumphatus.
Schrammius de Enthusiastis.
Teustkingii Gynæcium hæretico-sanitico.
Turretin, Preservatif, &c.
Zeltneri Breviarium controversiarum adhuc agitarum. 1724.
Zentgravii Dissertationes. (Divine and Diabolical Enthusiasm.)

Barclay's Apology.
Bellamy's True religion delineated.
Bidlake's Bampton Lectures. 1811.
Casaubon on Enthusiasm as mistaken for divine inspiration.
Christian Observer. 19:800.
Christian Quart. Spectator. 4:118.
Edinburg Review. 71:124.
Evans' (F.) Hist. of Modern Enthusiasm.
Evans' (John) Sermons. (Effects of E.)
Evans' (Theophilus) History of E., from the Reformation to the present time. 1752.
Foster's Essays. (On the epithet Romantic.)
Frazier's Magazine. 9:159.
Green (Bp.) on Enthusiasm.
Hawkins' (Robt.) Works.
Hunter's Letter on Enthusiasm.
Lavington's E. of Methodists and Papists.
Locke on the Understanding.
Monthly Review. 119:159.
More's (Henry) Philosophical works.
Notts' Bampton Lectures. 1802.
Pickets' Academician.
Scholar Armed against error. Vol. 2.
Scott's Force of Truth.
Southern Literary Messenger. 2:321.
Spectator. No. 201.
Spirit of the Pilgrims. 3:256, 330.
Stephens' Essays in eccles. biography.
Sterne's (Lawrence) Sermons.
Taylor's (Isaac) Natural history of E.
Wesley's (John) Sermons.
Wilson on Warrantable and unwarrantable inspirations.
Zollikoffer's (Geo. J.) Sermons.

Envy.

Abernethy's (Bp.) Sermons.
Berens' (Edward) Village Sermons.
Blair's (Hugh) Sermons.
Burton's (Hezekiah) Sermons.
Carrington's (J.) Sermons.
Delany's (Patrick) Sermons.
Fawcett's (John) Sermons.
Hey's (Dr. John) Sermons.
Johnson's (Dr. Samuel) Sermons.
Jones' (Walter) Sermons.
Knox's (Vicessimus) Sermons.
Lloyd's (Pearson) Sermons.
South's (Robert) Sermons.
Zollikoffer's Sermons on prevalent vices.

Ephraem, Syrus.

Ephraimi Opera; Assemanno editis. (Only complete edition. Six vols., folio.)
Gregory Nys., Vita atque encomium Ephr.

Assemani Bibliotheca Orientalis. (Has many extracts from E.'s works.)
Augusti (J. C. G.) Quest. Patristicarum, &c.
Coleri (Chr.) Disquisitiones Criticæ.
Hoyeri (Guil. Ernest.) Dissertationes.
Lengerke, Com. crit. de Ephræmo interprete.
Oudini (Casimer.) Dissertationes.
Tentzelii (Guil. Ernest.) Dissertationes.
Tischendorf, Codex Ephræmi rescriptus.
Vossii Sancta Ephræmi narratio.

Burgess' Hymns and homilies of Ephræm. (The introduction gives an account of Syriac metrical church literature, &c.)
St. Ephraim's Select works. Trans. by J. B. Morris.
——— Repentance of Nineveh. Translated by H. Burgess.

Epicureanism.

Origen, contra Celsus.

Epicuri Vita, per Diogenem Laertium.
Cicero de Natura deorum.
——— de Fato et de finibus.
Du Rondel, Vie d'Epicure.
Gassendi Vita Epicuri.
Lucretii Opera. Lib. II.
Plutarch, de Placitis philosophiæ. Lib. I., Cap. II.
Rapin, Reflexions sur la Philosophie.

American Quart. Review. 1:357.
Brucker's History of Philosophy.
Christian Examiner. 71:1.
Cudworth's Intellectual System.
Hume's (David) Essays. Ess. 15.
Ray on the Creation. Part 1.
Stanley's Lives of the Philosophers.
Stillingfleet's Origines Sacræ. Bk. 3.
Taylor's (Jeremy) Sermons.
Tenniman's History of Philosophy.

Epiphanius.

Epiphanii Opera quæ extant. (Several editions, the best of which is said to be that of PETAVIUS, 1682. That of MIGNE, 1858, in three volumes, is much approved.)
Assemanni Bibliotheca Orientalis.
Gervasse, Vie de St. Epiphane.
Oudini (Casimer.) Dissertationes.
Papebrochii Commentarius de St. E.
Whiston's Essays.

Epiphany.

Gregorii Naz., Orationes sex.

Arzbergeri (J. Seb.) Dissertationes.
Blumenbachii Antiquit. Epiphaniorum.

Dehon's (Bp.) Sermons.

Hare's (A. W.) Sermons.
Horne's (Bp.) Sermons.
Newman's (J. H.) Sermons.
Russel's (Alex. R.) Sermons.

Episcopacy. See APOSTOLICAL SUCCESSION, CONFIRMATION, ORDINATION.

Pro.

Beveridge, Canon. vet. eccl. Vindicatio.
Cosini Religio et Gubernatio.
Downamii Diss. de gubernatione Ecclesiæ.
Hammond (H.), Dissertationes quatuor.
Juellæ Apologia Ecclesiæ Anglicanæ.
Saravia de Diversis gradibus, &c.
Usserus, de Origine Episcop. et Metropol.

Ainsworth (T.) on Ordination.
Bancroft's (Abp.) Works.
Barwick on Church Government.
Beaulieu's Extremes of Popery and Presbytery.
Bilson's Government of Christ's Church. (One of the ablest on this side.)
Bingham's Origines Ecclesiasticæ.
Bisse's (Thomas) Sermons.
Bowden on Episcopacy.
Boyd's (Archibald) Episcopacy and Presbytery.
Bramhall's (John) Works.
Brett on Church Government.
Bridges on the Christian ministry.
Brokesby's Hierarchy of the 3 first cent.
Burnett on the 39 Articles.
Chandler's (T. B.) Appeal on behalf of E. in America. 1768.
——— Defence of the same.
Chapin's Organiz. of the primitive church.
Chillingworth on Episcopacy.
Christian Observer. (Many articles.)
Church of Eng. Magaz. 1836 to the present.
Church of E. Quar. Rev. 1837 " "
Church Review. 1848 to 1858.
Churton's Defence of the Church of England.
Colton on Episcopacy.
Cook's Instability of Presb. ordination.
Dodwell on Episcopacy.
Dyer's Testimonies of early Chris. writers.
Earbery's Principles of Church unity.
Edwards (Tho.) on Diocesan Episcopacy.
Faber's Episcopal ordination necessary.
Fields' Book of the Church. (The best edition of this important work is that of J. S. Brewer, 1842, which gives the quotations in full.)
Gauden's Hieraspistes.
Gray's Ministry of Dissenters null and void.
——— Vindication of the Church of Engl.
——— Schismatics delineated.
Good's (Wm.) Vind. of the Ch. of England.
Hall's (Bp.) Polemic Works.
——— Answer to Smyctemnus.
——— Epis. by Divine right asserted.
Hammond on E. (Replies to Blondell.)
Hawk's Constitution and Canons of the E. Church in America.

Episcopacy—*continued.*

Pro.

Heylin's History of Episcopacy.
Hicks (Geo.) on the Episcopal Order.
Hoadley's Defence of Epis. ordination.
——— Other treatises.
Hobart's Apology for Apostolical order.
Hooker's Laws of Ecclesiastical polity.
Horton on Episcopacy.
How's Letter to the Rev. Dr. Miller.
Ingraham's Double witness of the Church.
Jackman's Success no rule. (Rep. to Pierce.)
King's (Peter) Primitive Church.
Leaming (Jer.) on Episc. Government.
Lowth's Character of the Apostol. Church.
Manning on the Unity of the Church.
Marshall's Notes on Episcopacy.
Mason (F.) on Episcopacy.
Maurice on Diocesan Episcopacy.
Mills' Christian Priesthood.
[Mines' (F. S.)] A Presbyterian clergyman looking for a church.
Newman's (J. H.) Sermons.
Ogilvie's Lectures on the Church.
Onderdonk's E. tested by Scripture.
Overall's Convocation Book.
Overton's True Churchman.
Parker's Ecclesiastical Polity.
Pearson on the Creed.
Potter on Church Government.
Prettyman's Elements.
Pruen's View of the Church of God.
Rogers' Visible and invisible Church.
Sage's Principles of the Cyprianic age.
——— Vindication of Do. (Reply to Rule.)
Saravia on Ministerial grades.
Sclater's Draft of the primitive church.
Sinclair's Diss. on polity and doctrine.
Skinner's Primitive truth and order.
Stillingfleet's Origines Sacræ.
——— Irenicum.
Sparks' (J.) Letters on the Prot. Episc. Ch.
Spencer's Christian Instructed.
Taylor's (Jer.) E. a Divine institution.
——— Collection of polemic Discourses.
The Churchman. Periodical. Lond. (High Church.)
Thorndyke's Early Church.
Tracts for the Times. Tr. 33, and others.
Usher's Opuscula. (Origin of Bishops.)
——— Apostolical institution of E.
——— Reduction of Episcopacy.
Wainwright's No church without a bishop.
Wharton's Concise View, &c.
Whitby's Preface to the Ep. of Titus.
Whitgift's (Abp.) Answer to an admonition.
——— Defence of the same.
Woodhead's Ancient Church Government.

Con.

Baur's Ursprung des Episcopats in der Christlich Kirche.
Blondel, de Episcopis et Presbyteris.
——— Apologia pro sententia Hieronymi de Episcopis et Presbyteris.

Episcopacy—*continued.*

Con.

Buddæi Dissertationes.
Cameron, de Ecclesia.
Capelli Theses Theologicæ.
Frenkelii Schediasma de origine Episc.
Goetzii (Geo. H.) Dissertationes.
Grenzii (Adam.) Commentationes.
Maresius de Episcoporum Origine.
Odelemi (Joan. Philip.) Dissertationes.
Salmasii (Claud.) Dissertationes.
Zeiglerus de Diaconis vet. eccles.
Zimmerman de Presbyteris in eccles. vet.

Abbot's History of the Roman and English hierarchies, and the abuses, &c.
Alexander's (W. L.) Anglo-catholicism not apostolical.
Amer. Biblical Repos. 3d Series. 1:315.
Austin's (Sam.) View of the church.
Ayton's Const. of the Primitive Church.
Barnes' Inquiry into the organization, &c. (Reply to Onderdonk.)
——— Argument for E. examined.
Bedford's Ch. of Eng. indefensible; a reply to several recent defences. 1834.
Baxter on Church gov. and discipline.
Benson's (Christopher) Discourses on E.
Benson's (Geo.) Primitive Church.
Beza's (Theod.) Reply to Saravia.
Boardman (H. A.) on High Church E.
Boyd on Episcopal ordination.
Boyse's (J.) Ancient Episcopacy.
Bradshaw's Reply to Bilson.
Bristed on the Anglican Church. (Reply to Wilkes.)
Brown (Dr. John) on the Divine right of E.
Calderwood's Altare Damascenum. (KING JAMES, it is said, was provoked at this attack on Episcopacy; but when one of his prelates proposed to reply, he said, "Toot, mon! what would you say? Here is nothing but Scripture, Reason, and the Fathers.")
Campbell's (Geo.) Lectures on Eccles. Hist.
Cartwright's Admonition.
Chauncey's (C.) View of Episcopacy. (Reply to Chandler.)
——— Divine institution of Cong. churches.
——— Reply to Dr. Chandler's Appeal defended.
Christian Examiner. 25:190.
Christian Quart. Spectator. 8:591.
Christian Review. 1:552.
Christian Quart. Review. 6:1.
Clarkson's (D.) Primitive Episc. stated.
——— No evidence of Diocesan Episc. (A learned answer to Stillingfleet.)
Coleman's Church without a Bishop.
Collins' Priestcraft in perfection.
Collings' Ordinance of the ministry.
Dickinson (J.) on Ordination.
Davidson's (S.) Eccl. polity of the N. Test.
Delaune's Theological treatises.
Doddridge's Lectures. Part 9.

Episcopacy—*continued.*

Con.

Drummond's (D. K.) Episc. in Scotland.
Duffield's Claims of Episcopal Bishops.
Dury's Model of Church government.
Eclectic Review. 4th Series. 1:305. 18:621.
Fenner's Reply to Bridges.
Forrester's Hierarchical bishop's claim.
Hall's Constitution, Order, Discipline, &c.
Harding's Confutation of Jewel's Apology.
Hildersham's Ministry of the Ch. of Eng.
Hooker's Sum of Christian discipline.
Hopkins' Body of Divinity.
Jamieson's Sum of the E. controversy.
Jenkyns' Celeugma.
Gillespie's Aaron's rod blossoming.
Glass' Testimony of the King of Martyrs.
King's (David) Const., Discipline, &c. of the primitive chur. (Profound and powerful.)
Leighton's (Alex.) Appeal to Parliament, or Sion's plea. (For this book, the author was whipped and pilloried, his ears cut off, his nose slit, his cheek branded S. S. [Sower of sedition], and imprisoned 11 years in London, at the end of which he died insane. 1644.)
Maddox's Vindication.
Martin mar Prelate's Tracts. (Treatises attributed to Penry, Throgmorton, Udal, & Fenner, of whom see interesting notices in FULLER's Church History, and BELOE's Anecdotes of Literature.)
Mason's (J. M.) Essays on Episcopacy.
Mather's (Increase) Order of the Churches.
Miller's Letters on the Christian Ministry.
Milton's Prose Works.
New Englander. 1:390, 545, 586. 2:143, 309, 440. 3:333.
Norman's Apostolical Church.
Owen's (John) Plea for Scrip. ordination.
——— Origin, &c., of evangel. churches.
——— Nature of the Gospel church.
——— Sundry other treatises.
Paget on Church Government.
Palfrey's (J. G.) Review of Sparks on E.
Palmer's Dissenter's Catechism.
Payne's Eccles. polity of the New Test.
Pierce's Vindication of Dissenters.
Presbyterian Review. 3:28.
Princeton Review. 5:333. 7:239, 573. 8:390. 13:129. 21:116, 355, 534.
Prynne's Unbishoping of Tim. and Titus.
——— Looking-glass for lordly bishops.
——— Questions touching Church Gov.
Robinson's Christian System.
Rogers' Tabernacle of the Sun.
Rule's Cyprianic bishop examined.
Rutherford's Lex Rex.
Sage's Principles of the Cyprianic age.
Shimeal's End of Prelacy.
Smectymnus' Ans. to Bp. Hall. (The word is formed from the initials of the writers' names, viz.: S. Marshall, Ed. Calamy, T. Young, M. Newcomen, W. Spurstow.)
Smyth's Presbytery not Prelacy.

Smyth's Ecclesiastical Republicanism.
Toulmin's Historical Review.
Towgood's Letters.
Traver's Holy discipline of the Church.
Welles (N.) on Presbyterian ordination.
Willson's (James) Apostolical Government.
Wood's (Dr. L.) Objections to Episcopacy.

Episcopius.

Limborch, Vita S. Episcopii.

Calder's Memoirs of Episcopius. (With an account of the Synod of Dort.)

Equality of Mankind. See CIVIL GOVERNMENT, NEGROES, RACES, UNITY.

Crass' (H. C.) Disputationes de principiis doctrinæ morum.

Brown's (Dr. W. Lawrence) Essays.

Equivocal Generation.
See DEVELOPMENT.

Pro.

Aristotle, Opera.
Cicero, Epistolæ ad familiares.
Lamarck, Histoire des Animaux.
Mela, de Situ Orbis. (Edit. Gronovii.)
Ovidii Metamorphoses.
Pouchet, Hetérogénie.
Wolfii (C. T.) Theoria Generationis.

Ælian's History of Animals.
Lowthorp's Abridg. of Philos. transactions.
Pliny's Natural History.
Plott's History of Staffordshire.

Con.

Boerhaave, Elementa Chemica.
Buddei Philosophia Theoretica. Part I.
Etmulleri Institutiones Medicæ. Cap. 23.
Halleri Elementa Physiologiæ.
Harvei Exercitationes. Exer. 49, 50.
Lister de Insectibus.
Rhedi (Francisc.) Experimenta.
——— de Generatione Insectorum.
Straus-Durckheim, Theologie de la Nature.

Bentley's Boyle Lectures. 1693. Ser. 4.
Blackwood's Magazine. 89:165.
British Quarterly Review. 33:107.
Bulstrode's Essays. Ess. 3.
Durham's Philosophical letters.
——— Physico-theology. Book 4, ch. 15.
Hale's Origin of Mankind. Sect. 3.
Harris' Lexicon. (*"Generation."*)
Hooker's Flora of Australia.
Lyell's Geological evidences of the antiquity of man.
Müller's Elements of Physiology.
Nieuentyt's Religious Philosopher.
Ray's Wisdom of God in Creation.
Watts' Philosophical Essays.

Erasmus.

Burigné, Vie d'Erasme.
Fabricii Opusculorum Sylloge.
Hess' Erasmus nach seinen Leben und Schriften.
Lieberkuhn, de E. ingenio et doctrina.
Müller's Leben des E. von Rotterdam.

Erasmus, Life of; by Butler.
——— ——— by Jortin.
——— ——— by Knight.

Erastians. See ESTABLISHMENTS.

Erastii Explicationes.
Beckhaus' Ueber den Heidelberger Kat.
Beza de Vera Excommunicatione.

Bruce on the Supremacy of civil powers.
Erastus' Works.
Hall (A.) on the Government of the church.
Lawson's Power of the civil magistrate.
Middleton's True powers of the church.
Prettyman's Ch. of Engl. and Erastianism.
Urquehart's (David) Reflections.
Wilberforce's (Rob. I.) Hist. of Erastianism.

Esau. See BIOGRAPHY.

Benson's (C.) Lectures. Lec. 16 and 17.
Cooper's (Edward) Sermons.
Van Mildert's (Bp.) Sermons.

Eschatology. See DEATH, JUDGMENT, HEAVEN, HELL.

Essenes.

Athanagoræ Πρεσβεια περι χριστιανων.
Bellermann's Gesch. d. Essäer u. Therap.
Gravius de Pythagoreorem, &c., disciplina.
Herodoti Historia. Lib. II.
Josephus, Historia. Lib. II., cap. 7.
Monblet, Description de l'Egypt.
Schulze (B. W.), Conjecturæ hist. criticæ.

Biblical Repository. 3d Series. 3:162.
De Quincey, Theological Essays.
Gerard's Institutes of Criticism.
Holstein's Notes on the life of Pythagoras.
Lardner's Credibility. Part 1, book 1.
Marsh's Michaelis. Chap. 15.
Mosheim's Observations on Cudworth's true notion of the Lord's Supper.

Essentials. See FUNDAMENTALS.

Establishment of Christianity.
See PLANTING OF CHRISTIANITY.

Establishments.

Pro. See ERASTIANS.

Stahl's Christliche Staat.

Addis' Theory of Prophecy
Arnold's (of Rugby) Miscellaneous Works.
Birks on State Religion.
Blackburn's Duty of Ministers.
Boys' Word for the Church. (Ans. to Noel.)
British Quarterly Magaz. (Many articles.)
Brown (C. J.) on Church Establishments.
Buchanan on a Colonial establishment.

Establishments—*continued.*

Pro.

Burnet's (Bp.) Rights of Princes.
Cator (C.) on the Union of Church and State.
Chalmer's Lectures on National Churches.
Christie's Essay on Establishments.
Clarendon's (Earl) Religion and Policy; the countenance each should give the other.
Curzon on Eccles. Estab. and Jurisdiction.
Dodwell's Separation schismatical.
Eclectic Review. 4th Series. 3:1. 16:317.
Edinburg Review. 69:231.
Faussett's Bampton Lectures. 1820.
Frazier's Mag. 13:521. 17:742. 18:396. 20:619.
Gilmor on Establish. (Ans. to B. W. Noel.)
Gordon's Independent Whig.
Gregg's Protestant ascendancy vindicated.
Grice's Const. of the Church of England.
Healy (J.) On an established church.
Hey's (Dr. John) Lectures. Bk. 3.
Hoadly's (Bp., of Bangor) Works.
Hobson's (S.) Claims of the Church.
Holden on Church Establishments.
Holmes' Duty of a Christian state.
Hooker's Ecclesiastical polity.
Hook's (Wm. F.) Sermons.
Hull (Wm.) on Eccles. Establishments.
Inglis (John) on Eccles. Establishments.
Jenyns' (Soame) Disquisitions. Disq. 8.
Kemp's A Church not Episcopal, not Scriptural; and the support of the Church the duty of Government.
Law's Theory of Religion.
Lorimer (J. G.) on Church Establishments.
Marsh's (W. T.) The Church and the State. (Reply to Baptist W. Noel.)
Milner (Jos.) on Eccles. Establishments.
Nichols' Defence of the Church of England.
North British Review. 4:255.
Osler's Church and King.
Paley's Mor. and Polit. Philosophy. Bk. 6.
Parker's (Bp.) Ecclesiastical Politie.
Potter (Bp.) on Ch. Government. (Puts the argument for the supremacy of the prince in its strongest light.)
Rankin's Ecclesiastical Polity.
Ritchie on Establishments. (Presbyterian.)
Robinson (J.) on Church Establishments.
Rogers (John) on Civil estab. of religion.
——— on Church Government.
Ross' Obligations of the civil power.
Rotherham on Church Establishments.
Sherlock on the Corporation and Test acts.
Shuttleworth's The Church and the Clergy.
Sinclair's (J.) Dissertations.
Stebbings on Civil Government.
Taswell on National Establishments.
Taylor's (Bp.) Episcopacy asserted.
Thorndike's (Herbert) Rights of the Church.
Towers' Illustrations of prophecy.
Usher's Gov. and discipline of the Church.
Vint on Prophecy.
Warburton's Alliance of Church and State.
Westminster Review. 5:504. 26:244. 36:308.

Establishments—*continued.*

Pro.

Whalley on the Estab. of religion by law.
Wilks (Cha.) on Correlative claims and duties.
Wilks (S. C.) on Church Establishments in a Christian country.
Wrangham's (Francis) Sermons.

Con. See DISSENT.

Jottrand, Les Eglises d'Etat.
Pfaffii de Originibus juris ecclesiastici.
Vinet, sur la Manifestation des convictions religieuses, &c.
Vossii Theses Theologicæ.

Allen (Jno.) on Religious Establishments.
American Biblical Repository. 6:207.
Angus (J.) on the Voluntary System.
——— The Christian Church the noblest form of social life.
Baird's (Robt.) Religion in America.
Baker (W. R.) on our State Church.
Barnes' (A.) Episcopacy examined.
——— Government of the Apostol. Church.
Benlow on Religious Establishments.
Blackburn's (Francis) Confessional.
Blackwood's Magazine. 40:787.
Brett's Independence of the Church.
British "Anti State-Church Assoc." Reports.
British Critic. (Many able articles.)
Candlish's Question respecting the Church of Scotland.
Christian Disciple. 3:27. 31:209.
Christian Examiner. 28:171.
Cock's (Cha. G.) Household of God.
Condor's Why are we Dissenters?
Davies (J. J.) on Eccles. Establishments.
De Foe's Interests of England.
——— Fox unmasked.
——— on English Liberty.
——— Various other tracts.
Dick (A. C.) on Church polity.
Eclectic Review. New Series. 9:105, 348.
Erskine's (Ebenezer) Works.
Frazier's Magazine. 12:464, 575.
Graham's European eccles. establishments.
Griswold's (S.) Church and State.
——— Advantages and disadvantages, &c.
Hinton's (John H.) Test of experience. ("Approaches as near to demonstration as the nature of the case permits."—ECLECTIC REVIEW.)
Jones' (Wm.) Millennial Harbinger.
Lord's Theolog. and Lit. Journal. 2:153.
Maitland (S. R.) on the Voluntary System.
Methodist Quart. Rev. (Various articles.)
Miall's View of the voluntary principle.
Milton on Civil power in eccles. matters.
Noel's (B. W.) Union of Church and State.
North Amer. Rev. 15:431. (Edw. Everett.)
North British Review. 10:188. 27:224.
Princeton Review. 9:101. 35:679. 36:1.
Publications of the "Society for the liberation of religion."

Establishments—*continued.*

Con.

Robinson's (Robt., of Cambridge) Reflections on Christian Liberty.
Schaff's (P.) Germany. (As in 19th cent.)
Sykes' Answer to John Rogers.
Thorn on the Union of Church and State.
Toulmin's Letter to Dr. Sturgess.
Vinet on a Profession of religion.
Ward's (W. G.) Ideal of a Christian Church.
——— on the Anglican Establishment.
Wardlaw on Church E. (Rep. to Chalmers.)
——— on Congregational Independency.
Watts on Civil power in things sacred.
[Whately's] Christianity independent of civil government.

Eternal Generation of Christ.

Pro.

Bossuet, Œuvres.
Braunii Com. in Ep. ad Hebr. (Appendix.)
Bullii Defensio Fidei Nicenæ.
Dorchæi Dissertationes Theologicæ.
Fechtii (Ioan.) Dissertationes.
Frismuthii (Ioann.) Dissertationes.
Grappii (Zach.) Disputationes.
Lampii (Frid. Adolph.) Dissertationes.
Maurocenus de Æterna Christi generatione.
Semlerus de Æterno Dei Filio.
Wesselii (Joan.) Dissertationes Academicæ.

Bull on the Nicene creed. (Quotes largely from the Fathers.)
Gill's Body of Divinity.
Hawtrey's Appeal to the New Testament.
Hodson on the Filiation of the Son.
Hopkins' System of Divinity.
Kidd's Dissertation on the Messiah.
Lawrence's Apology for Dr. Clarke.
Owen on the Person of Christ.
Pearson on the Creed.
Sherlock's Vindication.

Con.

Bibliotheca Fratrum Polonorum.
Theophilus ad Autolycum.

Clarke's (Dr. S.) Scripture doctrine of the Trinity. (Gives copious quotations from the Fathers.)
Priestley's History of early opinions.
South on the Generation of the Son.
Stuart's Letters to Dr. Miller, of Princeton.
Sykes Truth of the Christian Religion.
Taylor's (H.) Letters.
Tucker's (Sam.) Triumph of Scripture truth.

This dispute seems so useless, that a mere tithe of the writers upon it are here adduced.

Eternal Existence of Matter.

Pro. See MATERIALISM.

Athanagoras, de Resurrectione mortuorum.
Aristotle, de Cœlo. Lib. I., cap. x.
Spinoza, Opera posthum. Pars. I., prop. 3.
Blount's Oracles of reason.

Eternal Existence of Matter—*cont.*

Con.

Burnet, Archæologia. Lib. II., cap. 1.
Fabricius de Veritate rel. Christianæ.
Mori Opera Philosophica. Part I., cap. 10.
Mosheim de Rebus Christianorum.
——— Institutiones seculi primi.
Parkeri Disputationes. Disp. IV.

Baxter (And.) on the Nature of the soul.
Bentley's Boyle Lectures. 1693.
Burnet's Theory of the Earth.
Campbell's Necessity of Revelation.
Cheyne's Philosophical Principles. Ch. 4.
Clarke's (Sam.) Being and attrib. of God.
Colliber's (Samuel) Inquiry.
Doddridge's Lectures. Part 2, prop. 21–23.
Dwight's (Timothy) Discourses.
Gastrell's Boyle Lectures. 1697.
Good's Book of Nature.
Hale's Origin of Mankind.
Harris' Refutation of infidel objections.
Howe's Living Temple.
Law's Notes to King's Origin of Evil.
McCaul's Philosophy of mind and matter.
Nichols' Conference with a Deist.
Stillingfleet's Conference with a Deist.
Stoddard's Guide to Christ.
Tillotson's Sermons.
Wilkins' Natural Religion. Bk. 1, ch. 5.

Eternity.

Brent on the Nature of Eternity.
Charnock's Works.
Davies' (Pres.) Sermons.
Drexel's Considerations on Eternity. Trans. by Dunster. (A work of great merit.)
Heylin's (Dr. John) Sermons.
Law (Edm.) On the ideas of space, time, &c.
Orton (Job) on Eternity.
Pike's Guide to the thoughtful.
Saurin's (James) Sermons.
Shower on Eternity.
Tillotson's Sermons.

Eternity of God.

Doderlini Theologia.
Feverlinus de Eternitate Dei.
Gerhardi Loci Theologici.
Winckleri (J. D.) Dissertationes.

Abernethy (John) Discourses.
Atterbury's (Lewis) Sermons.
Burnet on the 39 Articles.
Clarke (Sam.) on the Divine attributes.
——— Sermons at the Boyle Lectures.
Doddridge's Lectures. Part 2.
Dwight's (Tim.) Sermons.
Hall's (Robt.) Notes of Sermons.
Jenyns' (Soame) Disquisitions.
Leland's (Dr. Thomas) Sermons.
Paley's Natural Theology.
Pearson on the Creed.
Saurin's Sermons.
Tillotson's Sermons.

Watts' Ontology.
Wilkins' Natural Religion.
Williams' (Alfred) Sermons.
Wisheart's (W.) Sermons.

Eternity of Hell Torments.

Pro.

Burthogge's (Rich.) Apology for God.
Delany's (Patrick) Sermons.
Dodwell on Future punishment. (Answer to Whiston.)
Edwards' Salvation of all men examined. (Against Chauncy. Very strong.)
Horberry on Future Punishments.
Lampe's Theological Dissertations.
Lewis' Nature of Hell.
Sherlock's (Bp.) Discourses.
Simpson on Fut. rewards and punishments.
Strong (N.) on the Doctrine of Eternal Misery.
Thompson's (Jos. P.) Love and Penalty. (Dwells much on the absolute immortality of the soul.)
Vaughn's (Cha. John) Sermons.
Whitby on Eternal Punishment.
Whitefield's (George) Sermons.
Wisheart's (W.) Sermons.

Con. See DESTRUCTIONISTS, RESTORATIONISTS.

Ethics. See MORAL PHILOSOPHY.

Ethnicism. See PAGANISM.

Ethnology. See MAN, NATURAL HISTORY OF, NEGROES, ORIGIN OF NATIONS, UNITY OF THE HUMAN RACE, &c.

Beke, Origines Biblicæ.
Blumenbach, de Generis humani varietate.
Brec, Essai sur les races humaines.
Camper, sur les Differences du visage, &c.
De Pauw, Recherches Philosophique.
De Sales, Hist. des races humaines.
Dubois, Mœurs, Institutions, &c., des peuples de l'Inde.
Dumbeckii Tabulæ ab rerum primordiis, ad annum 1820.
Duprat, Essai Historique sur les races de l'Afrique.
Edwards, Influence réciproque des races sur le caractére national.
Eichtha, l'Hist. primitive des races.
Gobineau, sur l'Inegalité des races.
Halloy, des Races humaines.
Hornii de Originibus Americanis.
Klaproth, Tableaux historiques de l'Asie depuis Cyrus jusqu'a nos jours. 1826.
Klemm's Cultur-Geschichte der Menchheit. (9 vols., with many plates. 1851.)
Longchamps, des Fastes universels. (With copious chronological tables, notices of great men and their writings, &c. &c.)
Meinicke's Sudseevolker.
Memoirs de la Soc. Ethnol. de Paris.
Vivien, Hist. de Anthropologie.
Walkenaer, Hist. de l'Epèce humaine.
Zeuss, die Deutsch. und die Nachbarstämme.

Ethnology—*continued.*

American Whig Review. 9:385.
American Ethnological Society transactions. (Since 1844.)
Archæologia Americana. (Transactions of the American Antiquarian Society. 1820 to the present.)
Baillier's Ethnographical Library.
Balby's Ethnographical Atlas.
Bartlett's Progress of Ethnology. (To 1847.)
Bradford's Origin and Hist. of the red race.
Brownell's Indian races of America.
Cass' History, traditions, languages, manners, &c., of the Indians in the U. States.
Catlin's Manners, customs, and condition of Amer. Indians. (A noble work, with over 300 superior engravings.)
Christian Review. 16:226.
Dallas' History of the Maroons.
De Bow's Review. 10:113.
Democratic Review. 17:50. 11:603.
Donaldson's Varronianus.
Drake's Indians of North America.
Dublin University Magazine. 51:293.
Earle's Races of the Indian Archipelago.
Eclectic Magaz. 1:419. 14:31. 16:55. 19:500.
Eclectic Review. 4th Series. 12:660. 30:318. New Series. 1:586. 7:35.
Edinburg Review. 88:223.
Ellis' Saxon and Celtic races.
Ethnological Journal. Periodical. London.
Ethnological Societies' Reports. (London, Paris, &c.)
Foreign Quart. Rev. 1:377. 24:351. 32:424.
Gallatin's Semi-civilized nations of Mexico.
Glass' History of the Canary Islands.
Gobineau's Divinity of races. Tr. by Holtz.
Hale's (Hor.) Ethnography and philology.
Herder's Philosophic hist. of the races, &c.
Huxley's Lectures on Ethnology.
Latham's Ethnology of Europe.
——— ——— of British Islands.
——— ——— of British Colonies.
——— ——— of Russian Empire.
——— Germania of Tacitus. With Notes and Dissertations.
Lawton's (Edward) Lectures.
Logan's Ethnology of the Indian Pacific.
McCausland's Adam and the Adamite. (The harmony of Scripture Ethnology.)
MacCulloch's Researches in America.
Mallet's Northern Antiquities.
Massey's Analytical Ethnology. (Confined to Great Britain and Ireland.)
Monthly Review. 119:18.
Moritz's Diss. on the Gypsies.
Morton's Crania Egyptiaca.
Müller's Antiq. of the Doric race. (Maps.)
Niebuhr's Ancient Ethnog. Tr. by Schmitz.
Niles' Weekly Register. 14:105.
Norris' Ethnological Library.
North American Review. 73:163.
North British Review. 4:177.
Nott's (Dr. Eliphalet) Lectures.
Pickering's Races of men.

Ethnology—*continued.*

Princeton Review. 22:313, 603. 27:193.
Pritchard's Ethnological Maps.
——— Infl. of physical and moral agencies.
Rafinesque's Annals of Kentucky.
Roberts' Origin, &c., of the Gypsies.
Robertson's History of South America.
Schoolcraft's (H. R.) Works. (A superb set of books, containing all his papers laid before the Congress of the U. States, in relation to the red men of America.)
Smith's (Sam. S.) Causes of the variety of complexion, figure, &c.
Theological and Literary Journal. 3:424.
Troost's Ancient Remains in Tennessee.

Eunomians. See ARIANS.

Athanasius, Dialogi V.
Basil, adversus Impium Eunomium.
Gregory Naz., Orationes de Theologia.
Gregory Nys., Opera. Lib. XIII.

Eunomii Απολογιας απολογιαν.
Bassnage, Diss. in Canesii lectiones.
——— Diss. de Economio.
Bezæ Athanasii Dialogi.
Klose's Gesch. und Lehre der Eunomius.
Zeibichii (C. H.) Dissertationes.

See a full list of writers against the Eunomians, in FABRICIUS, *Biblioth.*, Lib. VIII., and in VOGTIUS, *Hist. Haeresiolog.*

Eusebius Pamphilius.

Eusebii Opera. (There are many editions. Those of Stroth, 1779, Zimmerman, 1822, and Heinichen, 1830, are preferred.)
Baur, Comparatur Eusebius historia eccles. parens cum parente historiar. Herodoto.
Ernestus de Eusebio.
Kestner, de Eusebii auctoritate.
Le Clerc, Vie de Eusebie.
Moller de Fide E. in rebus enarrandis.
Reuterdahl, de Fontibus hist. eccl. Eusebii.
Rienstra, de Fontib. ex quibus hist. eccles. opus hausit, et de ratione qua iis usus est Eusebius.

Eutychians. See COUNCIL OF CHALCEDON, AND FOURTH COUNCIL OF EPHESUS, HYPOSTATIC UNION, JACOBITES, MONOTHELYTES.

Cyril (Alex.), adversus Nestorii.
Theodoret, Homiliæ.

Bassnage, Hist. de Eutychianes.
Chrysologi (Petr.) Epistolæ.
Ecchellensi Eutychius vindicatus.
Jablonsky, Exercitationes.
Le Quien, Oriens Christianus.
Leontii Dubitat. hypotheticæ et definientes, contra eos qui negant esse in christo duas naturas.
Liberati Hist. controv. Eutychianæ.
Rustici Disputationes adv. Acephalos.
Salig, de Eutychianismo ante Eutychen.
Schroder (Ioan.), de Eutychismo.
Schroder (Nic.) de Eutyc. et ejus sectis.
Simleri Scripta veter. de una persona J. C.
Ursini Tractationes Theologicæ.
Vogtii Historia Hæresiologicæ.
——— de Recentissimis Nestorii defensor.

Evangelical Lutheran Church.

Marten's Symbol-bücher d. Evang. Luth. Kirche.

Evidences of Christianity. See AUTHENTICITY, DEISM, INSPIRATION, INTERNAL EVIDENCE, MIRACLES, PROPHECY, REVELATION.

Evidences of Regeneration.

Appleton's (Pres.) Lectures.
Backus on Regeneration.
Baxter's Saint's Everlasting Rest.
Bellamy's (Joseph) Tracts.
Dwight's Discourses. Disc. 88 to 90.
Doddridge's (Philip) Sermons.
Ecking's (Sam.) Essays on Grace, &c.
Edwards on the Affections.
——— on the Revival in New England.
Spring's (Gardner) Essays.
Toffin's Marks of the children of God.
Wood's (of Andover) Works.

Evil. See EXISTENCE OF EVIL, ORIGIN OF OF EVIL, SIN.

Alison's (Arch.) Sermons. (Evils of life.)
Christian Examiner. 33:197. 47:227. 59:116.
Christian Observer. 20:105.
Cudworth on Eternal and immut. morality.
Dale's (Thomas) Sermons.
Foster's (James) Sermons.
Gisborne (Thomas) on the Divine love.
James (Henry) on the Nature of evil.
Müller's Christian doctrine of Sin.
Oakley's (Fred.) Sermons.
Shuttleworth's (P. N.) Sermons.
South's (Robt.) Sermons.
Universalist Quarterly. 3:167. (Uses of evil.)
Van Mildert's (Bp.) Sermons.
Young (John) on the Uses of evil.

Evil Company. See COMPANY.

Abernethy's (John) Sermons.
Alison's (Archibald) Sermons.
Batty's (Adam) Sermons.
Blair's (James) Sermons.
Bolton's (Robt.) Letters and tracts.
Butler's (Alban) Sermons.
Cooper's (Archdeacon) Sermons.
Dodd's (William) Sermons.
Doddridge's (Philip) Sermons.
Edwards' (John) Sermons.
Enfield's (William) Sermons.
Farmer's (John) Sermons.
Guyse's (John) Six annual sermons.
Hall's (Robt.) Sermons.
Jortin's (John) Sermons.

Lawson's (Dr. John) Sermons.
Parry's (Joshua) Sermons.
Priest's (Isaac) Sermons.
Thompson's Christian Theism.

Evil Speaking. See DETRACTION, SCANDAL, SLANDER, TONGUE.

Barrow's (Isaac) Sermons.
Berens' (Edward) Village sermons.
Blencoe's (Edward) Sermons.
Carr's (George) Sermons.
Enfield's (William) Sermons.
Fiddes' (Richard) Practical discourses.
Francklin's (Thomas) Sermons.
Jack on Evil speaking.
Jortin's (John) Sermons.
Lamont's (David) Sermons on prevalent vices.
Seed's (Jeremiah) Sermons.
Shuttleworth's (Wm.) Essays.
Smith's (Sydney) Sermons.
Sterne's (Lawrence) Sermons.
Tillotson's Sermons.
Wesley's (John) Sermons.
Zollikoffer's Festivals and Fasts.

Evil Spirits. See DEMONS.

Jacobi I. (Britt. rex) Demonologia.
Gottermasius de Exist. demonorum, e naturæ lumine innotescit.
Heideggeri Disputationes Theologicæ.
Heinii Dissertationes Sacræ.
Mayer, de Malorum spirituum existentia.
Pfaffius de Operationibus diabolicis.
Platinæ Prelectiones Theologicæ.
Stengelii Dissertationes.
Winzeri Demonologia in N. T. proposita.

Beaumont's Historical, physiological, and theological treatise on spirits.
Bekker's World bewitched. ("The best account of the power of devils."—LOWNDES.)
Berg's Abaddon and Mahanaim.
Bullinger's Decades.
Burgh's (James) Crito.
Casaubon's True relation of what passed for many years, between John Dee and some spirits.
Christian Monthly Spect. 5:293. 10:650.
Doddridge's Lectures. Part 10.
Donaldson's Christian orthodoxy reconciled with the conclusions of modern biblical learning. Chap. 4.
Draper's Doctrine of Scripture relating to evil spirits.
Eclectic Review. 4th Series. 16:35.
Edwards' Body of divinity. (On the Creed.)
Foreign Quarterly Review. 6:1.
Frazier's Magazine. 5:207.
Gilpin on Temptation.
Girdlestone's (Charles) Sermons.
Glanvil's Sadduceism silenced.
Heber's (Bp.) Parish Sermons.
Howe's (John) Works.
Hutchinson's (Francis) Works.

Evil Spirits—*continued.*

Mede's (Joseph) Sermons.
Scott's (Walter) Existence of Evil Spirits.
Seed's (Jer.) Sermons.
Sharp on the Influence of Demons.
Shepherd on Angels.
Spirit of the Pilgrims. 2:491.
Toplady's (Augustus M.) Sermons.
Townsend's (Geo.) Sermons.
Whately's View of the future state.
Whewell on Good and evil Angels.
Wilson's (Bp.) Sermons.

Evil Thoughts. See THOUGHTS.

Chilcott's Treatise on evil thoughts.
Gilpin's (William) Sermons.
Goodwin's (Tho.) Vanity of thoughts discovered.

Exaltation of Christ.

Limborchii Theologia Christiana.
Markii Hist. exaltationis J. C.
Martinii Demonstrationes.
Sohnii Disputationes de filio Dei.
Varenii (August.) Dissertationes.

Bennett's Christian Oratory.
Berriman's (William) Sermons.
Burton's (Edward) Sermons.
Russel's Letters, practical and consolatory.
Watts' (Isaac) Glory of Christ.

Example. See APPEARANCE OF EVIL, COMPANY, DEPORTMENT.

Alison's (Archibald) Sermons.
Allestree's (Bp.) Sermons.
Blackall's (Bp.) Sermons.
Fawcett's (James) Sermons.
Hickman's (B.) Sermons.
Lamont's (David) Sermons.
Latimer's (Bp.) Sermons.
Melvill's (Henry) Sermons.
Potts' (J. H.) Sermons.
Secker's (Abp.) Sermons.
Skelton's (P.) Sermons.
Smallridge's (George) Sermons.
Steadman's (R.) Sober Singularity.
Van Mildert's (Bp.) Sermons.

Example of Christ.

Alison's (Archibald) Sermons.
Arnold's (Tho.) Sermons. (4 on this subj.)
Barrow's (Isaac) Sermons.
Barrow's (William) Sermons.
Bennett's (W. J. E.) Sermons.
Bickersteth's (J.) Sermons.
Bisset's (Tho.) Sermons. (4 on this subject.)
Bradford's Boyle Lectures. 1699.
Calamy's (Benj.) Sermons.
Channing's (W. E.) Sermons.
Durand's (J. F.) Sermons.
Fisk's (George) Sermons.
Frey (C.) on the Example of Christ.
Fuller's (Thomas) Sermons.

Example of Christ—*continued.*

Hastings' (H.) Parochial Sermons.
Horne's (Bp.) Sermons.
Hubbard's (J.) Berry Street Lectures.
Kempis' Imitation of Christ. (Malcom's Edition omits the sentiments objectionable to Protestants.)
Markby's The Man Christ Jesus.
Marshall's (Nathaniel) Sermons.
Mason (John) on the Christian Virtues.
Richardson's (William) Sermons.
Riddock's (James) Sermons.
Scott's (Tho.) Jesus a pattern. (20 good sermons.)
Serle's Horæ Solitariæ.
Tillotson's (Abp.) Sermons.
Townsend's (George) Sermons.
Van Mildert's (Bp.) Sermons.
Ward's (Richard) Sermons.
Waters' (Edward) Sermons.
Watson's (Alex.) Sermons.
Whately's (Rich.) Sermons.
Wilks' (Sam. C.) Sermons.
Williams' Private life of Christ.
Wilson's (Bp.) Sermons.
Zimmerman on the Knowledge of Christ.

Excellence of Christianity. See CHRISTIANITY, DEISM, INFLUENCE OF RELIGION, LIGHT OF NATURE, PLEASURES OF PIETY.

Morgues, Parall. de la monde chret. avec celles des anciens philosophes.

Gerard's Genius of Christianity.
Hall's (Robt.) Works.
Knox's Evidence and Excellence, &c.
Paynton's Evidence and Character of C.
Watson's Tracts.

Excitement. See EMOTIONS, PASSIONS, PEACE OF MIND, REVIVALS.

Excommunication. See CH. DISCIPLINE.

Augustini Opera.

Beza de Vera Excommunicatione.
Bindrin de Gradibus excom. Judæis.
Erastus (T.) de Excommunicatione.
Godeschalci Dissertationes.
Krackewitzii (Berthold.) Dissertationes.
Meisneri (Ioann.) Dissertationes.
Morinus de Disciplina. Lib. IX.
Opitii Disp. de Excom. ritu apud Judæos.
Orsi (J. A.) Dissertationes.
Sirmondus Hist. pœnitentiæ publicæ.

Eclectic Review. New Series. 5:229.
Edwards' (Pres.) Works.
Hey's (Dr. John) Lectures. Bk. 4.
Hopkins' (Bp.) Sermons.
Pirie's (Alex.) Miscellaneous Works.
Prynne's Four serious Questions.

Exegesis. See HERMENEUTICS, PHILOLOGY, RULES OF INTERPRETATION, &c.

Exhortation. See ADMONITION.

Sturmey's Discourses.
Witherspoon's Works.

Existence of Evil. See EVIL, OPTIMISM, ORIGIN OF EVIL.

Bretschneider's Handbuch der Dogmatik.
Maimonides, More Nevochim. Par. III., c. 12.
Rheinard's Vorlesüngen über die Dogmatik.

Abernethy's (John) Sermons.
Balguy's Divine benevolence asserted.
Baxter's (Richard) Works.
Bonet's Contemplations of Nature.
Butterworth on Moral Government.
Dwight's Discourses. Disc. 15.
Foster's (Dr. James) Sermons.
Hallet's Notes on Scripture.
Hopkins' System of Divinity. Ch. 4.
Mandeville's Free Thoughts.
Pope's Ethical Epistles. No. 1.
West on Free-agency. Part 2.

Existence of God. See ATHEISM, LIGHT OF NATURE, NATURAL THEOLOGY.

Basil, de Providentia: Conscio 22.
——— Epistolæ.
Chrysostom, Orationes.
Gregory Naz., Orationes. Orat. XXXIV.
Gregory Nys., Orationes. Orat. II.
Lactantius, Opificium Dei.

Abbadie, la Religion chretienne. Sec. 1.
Baumgarten's Glaubenslehre.
Bunsen's (C. C. J.) Gott in der Geschichte.
Callixti Dissertationes.
Cicero, de Natura Deorum.
Fenelon, Demonst. de l'existence de Dieu.
Hennichii Demonstratio existentiæ Dei.
King, de Origine Mali. (With Law's notes.)
Meiner, Hist. doctrinæ de vero Deo. (Highly praised by Dr. Parr.)
Melchoris (J. A.) Dissertationes.
Mendelssohn's Morgenstunden.
Parkeri Disputationes de Deo.
Paschal, Œuvres. Tom. 2.
Ruckeri Demonst., methodo mathematica.
Schrœdelii Demonstratio ex idea a priori.
Schwarzii Demonstrationes Dei.
Stapferi Theologia. Cap. III.
Vossius de Origine et progressu Idolatria.

Abernethy's (John) Sermons.
Allen's Oracles of Reason. Sect. 2, Ch. 1.
American Biblical Repository. 9:421. 2d Series. 5:273. 6:350.
American Presbyterian Review. 4:357.
American Quarterly Observer. 1:299.
Appleton's (Jesse) Works. Lect. 1.
Arrowsmith's (John) Discourses.
Atterbury's (Bp.) Sermons.
Barrow's (Bp.) Discourses.
Bates' Considerations of the exist. of God.
Bennet's Philosophical Researches.
Bentley's Boyle Lectures. 1693.
Berkeley's Minute Philosopher. (Beautiful.)

Existence of God—*continued.*

Bibliotheca Sacra. 7:326. 12:338.
Boyle Lectures. (Most of the series.)
Boyle (Robt.) on Final causes.
Bridgewater Treatises.
Brown (Wm. Lawrence) on the Existence, power, and wisdom of God. (Received the Burnet prize of $6,000, at Aberdeen, August, 1815.)
Brown (Tho.) on Cause and Effect.
Brownson's Quart. Rev. 2d Series. 6:141.
Bryant's Authenticity of Scripture.
Bullet's Existence of God demonstrated.
Burnet on the 39 Articles.
Charnock's (Stephen) Works.
Christian Monthly Spectator. 1:414, 586.
Clapham on the Argument *a priori.*
Clarke's (Sam.) Demonstration.
Clark (Jos.) Exam. of Dr. Clark's notions.
Clark (John) Def. of Clark's demonstration.
Clark (Geo.) on the Existence of God. (Intended as a supplement to Paley's Evidences.)
Collibeare's Existence and nature of God.
Crombie's Natural Theology. Ess. 1.
Crouza's Art of Logic.
Democratic Review. 21:102, 253.
Doddridge's Lectures. Part 2, prop. 27, 28.
Drew's (Sam.) Attempt to demonstrate, &c.
Durham's Physico-Theology.
——— Astro-Theology.
Dwight's (T.) Sermons.
Eclectic Review. 4th Series. 18:720. New Series. 1:68.
Edwards (J.) on the Existence and providence of God.
Emmons' (Nath.) Sermons.
Evangelical Review. 1:348.
Fenelon's Demonstration of the existence of God.
Foster's (Dr. James) Discourses.
Fuller's Part of a Body of Divinity. Let. 4.
Gastrell on Natural Religion.
Gillespie's Necessary existence of God.
Glover's (P.) The argument *a priori.*
Hall's Modern Infidelity.
Hamilton's Existence of God demonstrated.
Heath's (Benj.) Demonstration *a priori.*
Hodgson's Existence of God.
Jack's Existence of God geometrically demonstrated.
Jackson on the Div. essence and attributes.
Jamieson's Use of Sacred History.
Jaquelot's Existence of God.
Kiel's Astronomy. Lect. 21.
Knight (H.) on the Argument *a priori.*
Knowles' (Thomas) Discourses.
Law's Enquiry into the ideas of space, immensity, and eternity.
Le Clerc's Ontology. (End of the Book.)
Leibnitz's Mathematical principles of Theol.
Leighton's (Abp.) Lectures. Lect. 7.
Lowman's Tracts.
Macworth's Christian meditations.
Marshall's (N.) Discourses.
Millar's Propagation of Christianity.
Moore's Divine Dialogues.
More's Antidote against Atheism.
Neuentyt's Religious Philosopher.
Nicholson's (Bp.) Discourses.
Paley's Natural Theology.
Pearce's Study of Nature.
Pearson on the Creed.
Pillings on the Existence of God.
Price's Principal questions in morals.
Saurin's (James) Sermons.
Shaftesbury's Letter to a Clergyman.
Sillery on the Existence of God.
Smith's (S. S.) Sermons.
Squier's Irreligion indefensible.
Stillingfleet's Origines Sacræ. Bk. 3, Ch. 1.
Sturm's Reflections.
Sumner's (John B.) Records of Creation.
Taylor's (J.) Summary of the evidence.
Thompson's (R. A.) Christian Theism. (Received the first Burnet prize, of $9,000.)
Tillotson's Sermons.
Tulluck's (John) Theism.
Vaughn's (J.) Lectures.
Warburton's Divine Legation. Part 1.
Waterland on the Argument *a priori.*
Watts' Ontology.
Whish (J. C.) on the First Cause.
Whiston's Principles of Religion.
Wilkins on Natural Religion.
Williams' (R.) Dialogue of the knowledge of the Supreme Lord; in which are compared the claims of Christianity and Hinduism. (A prize essay. 1856.)
Wood's (Prof.) Works.

Existence of Matter.

Metaphysicians and philosophers generally touch upon this subject, taking the reality of the visible world for granted. The following do something more.

Pro.

Bayle's Histor. and Crit. Dict. Art. "Zeno."
Grand's Institutes of Philos. Part 4, Ch. 2.
Green's Principles of Philos. Bk. 1, Ch. 1.
Hamilton's (Sir Wm.) Dissertations.
——— Notes on Reid.
Locke's Essays. Bk. 4, Ch. 2, Sect. 14.
Norris' Ideal World. Part 1, Ch. 4.
Regnault's Philosophical Conversations.
Reid on the Intellectual powers.

Con.

Berkeley's Principles of human knowledge.
——— Dialog. between Hylas & Philolonous.
——— Minute Philosopher. Dialogue 2.
——— New theory of vision. Sect. 43.
Collier's Clavis Universali.

Exodus of the Jews.

Ayroli Dissertationes.
Dunn, de Perigrinatione in Ægypt.

Lightfoot, Opera Posthuma.
Ockelii Iter Israelitarum ex Ægypto.
Strauchii (Ægid.) Disputationes.

American Biblical Repository. 2:743.
Cockburn's Jewish Exodus. (Agt. Gibbon.)
Frazier's Magazine. 14:461.
London Quarterly Review. 1:80.
Stuart's Course of Heb. study. Excursus 4.

Exorcism.

Hoffmanni Orthodoxa doctrina de Exorcismo in administratione baptismi.
Alberi Bericht von der Kinder Taufe.
Calovii (Abrah.) Dissertationes.
Meisneri (Balthas.) Dissertationes.
Musæi (Pet.) Dissertationes.
Mylii (Georg.) Disputationes.
Sigfredi Commentatio an exorcismus de essentia religionis sit?

Expediency, Doctrine of.
See MORALITY.

Bibliotheca Sacra. 1:301.
Sanderson's (Bp.) Sermons.
Van Mildert's Sermons.

Experience. See CONVERSION.

Alexander (Archib.) on Relig. Experience.
Armstrong's Theology of Christian Exp.
Barrow's Works.
Booth's Reign of Grace.
Buck on Religious Experience.
Bunyan's Pilgrim's Progress.
——— Holy War.
Bridges' Exposition of the 119th Psalm. (Highly devotional.)
Crossman's (F. G.) Sermons.
Dorney's Contemplations.
Eckings' (Rev. Samuel) Essays.
Edwards on the Religious Affections.
Gurnall's Christian Armour.
Jackson's (Miles) Sermons.
Kempis' Imitation of Christ.
Leifchild's (John) Discourses.
Owen on the 130th Psalm.
Philip (R.) on Christian Experience.
Reade's Life and writings of Paul.
Scott's Christian Life.
Scougal's Life of God in the soul of man.
Secker's Nonsuch Professor.
Shepherd's Sincere Convert.
Tweedie's Lights and Shadows in the Christian life.
Wallin's (Benj.) Sermons. (Very valuable.)
Watson's Hints on Christian Experience.
Zollikoffer's (Geo. J.) Sermons.

Expository Preaching.
See PREACHING.

American Biblical Repos. 5:317, 384. 10:33.
Brodbelt's (Geo.) Original Essays.
Princeton Review. 10:33.

Extempore Prayer. See FORMS.

Extempore Preaching.
See ELOQUENCE, PREACHING.

Fritsch (J. H.), über d. extemporiren Predigten.
Kastner's Schnellen u. sichern memoriren d. Predigten.
Kottmeyer über d. extemp. Redekunst.
Thierbach's Entscheidenden Beautwort. der frage.

Bautain on Extemp. preaching. (Excellent.)
Brodbelt's (Geo.) Original Essays.
Christian Monthly Spectator. 6:131.
Christian Observer. 3:343.
Newton on Ext. preaching and recitation.
North American Review. 19:297. (Prof. Upham.)
Presbyterian Review. January, 1867. (Prof. Shedd.)
Princeton Review. 21:453. 26:145.
Rippingham's Art of public speaking.
Southern Literary Messenger. 1:7.
Ware (Henry) on Extempore preaching.
Warne (Jos. A.) on Reading sermons.
Wayland's (F.) Letters on the Christian ministry.

Extent of the Atonement.
See DEFINITE ATONEMENT.

Extravagance. See DRESS, FASHION, FRUGALITY, LOVE OF PLEASURE, LUXURY, MODERATION, PLEASURE, SELF-DENIAL.

Extreme Unction.

Andreæ Comment. de extremo unctione.
Dallæi (Io.) Disputationes.
Faber, Disputationes Theologicæ.
Krackewitzii (Barthol.) Examen libri controversiæ.
Victorellus de Ext. unct. sacramento.

Burnet on the 39 Articles.
Calvin's Sermons.
Princeton Review. 37:188.
Secker's (Abp.) Sermons.
Stephenson's (Geo.) Romish Church.
Whiston (William), Life of.

Extremes. See ENTHUSIASM, FANATICISM, MODERATION.

Exucontians. See EUNOMIANS.

Ezekiel. See BIOGRAPHY.

Frederici Disputationes.
Verpoorteni Fasciculus dissertationum.

Faith. See HARMONY OF REASON AND FAITH, JUSTIFICATION, PAUL AND JAMES, PROVINCE OF REASON, WALK OF FAITH.

Abichtius de Fidei difficultate.
Antonius de Harmonia fidei.
Arndtii Tract. de una fide ad salutem.
Carpzovii Disputationes Academicæ.
Chemnitii Examen Conc. Tridentini.

Faith—*continued.*

Clauswitzii Syntagma doct. de fide.
Cramer's Abbildung des wahren Glaubens.
Dassovius de Fide sine operibus.
Gerardus de Discrimine fidei Divinæ et humanæ.
Holdeni Fidei Analysis. (A summary of the whole gospel.)
Le Blanc, Thesis prima de fide.
Martin, 20 Sermons sur Heb. xi.
Musæi de Certitudine salutis.
Neumannus de Fide aliena.
Schmidtius (Sab.) de Fide προσκαιρω.
——— de Fide miraculosa.
——— de Fide viva et mortua.
Schelvigii Dissertationes.
Tarnovii Synopsis veræ doctrinæ.
Weidneri Fides salvivifica.

Abernethy's (John) Sermons.
Allen's (William) Works.
Allestree's (Richard) Sermons.
American Biblical Repository. 3:189. 3d Series. 1:391. 4:315,644.
Anderson's (J. S. M.) Cloud of Witnesses.
Appleton's Works. Lect. 42.
Arnold's (Thomas) Works.
Backus' (Isaac) Discourses.
Ball (John) on Faith.
Barrow's (Isaac) Works.
Bates' (Will.) Works.
Bellamy's Letters and Dialogues.
Besley's (J.) Doctrinal discourses.
Beveridge's Thesaurus Theologicus.
——— Sermons.
Bickersteth on the Romish Controversy.
Binney's (P.) Power of faith.
Blackall's (Bp.) Sermons.
Booth's (Abraham) Glad tidings.
Brady's (Nicholas) Sermons.
Bridges' (Will.) Sermons on faith.
Brougham's (John) Sermons.
Bullinger's Decades.
Burton's Truth's triumph over Trent.
——— Christian's Bulwark.
Butler's (Alban) Sermons.
Capp's Devotional Discourses.
Carr's (George) Sermons.
Chalmers' (Thomas) Sermons.
Charnock's (Stephen) Sermons.
Christian Examiner. 13:239. (Faith a moral act.)
Christian Review. 1:511.
Christian Monthly Spectator. 1:109, 591.
Cobb's Bampton Lectures. 1783.
Cooper's (Edward) Sermons.
Clagget's (Will.) Sermons.
Colquhoun's View of Saving faith.
Cranmer's (Abp.) Homilies.
Cudworth's (Will.) Aphorisms.
Dickinson's (Jonathan) Letters.
Doddridge on Salvation by grace.
Dore's (James) Letters.
Eaton's Honeycombe of Justification.
——— Danger of dead faith.
Ecking's (Samuel) Essays.

Faith—*continued.*

Eclectic Magazine. 19:289.
Edinburg Review. 90:115.
Edwards' (Pres.) Works.
Erskine's (John) Theological Dissertations.
Erskine's (Ralph) Sermons on faith.
Erskine's (Thos.) Essays on faith. (Caused a great controversy, an account of which is in the Eclectic Review for July, 1830.)
Evans on Christian Temper.
Fowles' (F. W.) Sermons.
Glasse's (G. H.) Sermons.
Goodwin's (John) Works.
Grew's (Obadiah) Christ our righteousness.
Griffith's (Tho.) Sermons.
Grove on Saving faith.
Haldane's (J. A.) Works.
Hale's (Sir M.) Contemplations.
Hall's (A.) Faith of the Gospel.
Hall's (Robt.) Works. (Increase of faith.)
Hall's Help to Zion's travellers. (Nature.)
Hammond's (Henry) Practical Catechism.
——— Sermons.
Hampden's (R. D.) Sermons.
Hare's (J. C.) Sermons.
Harding's (John) Sermons.
Hawkins' Bampton Lectures. 1841.
Hayne's Illustrations of faith and practice.
Hayward's (Roger) Sermons.
Hervey's Theoron and Aspasi
Jackson (A.) on Faith. (Is faith a *duty?*)
Jelf's Bampton Lectures. 1857.
Johnson's (John) Faith of God's elect. (Reply to Jackson.)
Kollock's (S. K.) Sermons.
Lambert's (George) Sermons.
Laurence's Use and practice of faith.
Lavington's Nature of the Gospel offer.
Lee's The family and its duties.
Lunt's Dudleian Lecture. 1855.
Maitland's Lent Lectures.
Malkin's Sermons and Dissertations.
Manton's (Dr. Thomas) Works.
McLean's (Archibald) Sermons.
Methodist Quarterly Magazine. 12:9,169.
Milner's (Joseph) Practical Sermons.
Morehead's (R.) Sermons.
Morren's Biblical Theology. Vol. 1.
Morris' Bampton Lectures. 1791.
Nares' (R.) Sermons on Faith.
Newman's University Sermons.
Owen's (John) Sermons.
Packman's (R. C.) Sermons.
Pemble (W.) on Faith.
Pike's (Samuel) Sermons.
Polhill on Precious Faith.
Potts' (J. H.) Sermons.
Powell s (Vavasor) Dialogues.
Princeton Review. 18:53. 35:403.
Raffle's Lectures on faith and practice.
Robinson's Christian System. Ess. 41–51.
Rogers (John) on the Doctrine of faith.
Romaine's Walk and triumph of faith.
Rotherham's Connexion of faith and good works. (Recom. by Van Mildert.)

Faith—*continued.*

Saurin's (James) Sermons.
Scott's (Tho.) Theolog. Works. Essay 6.
Secker's Lectures on the Catechism.
——— Sermons.
Seed's (Jer.) Sermons.
Sherlock's (Bp.) Sermons.
Short's (T. V.) Sermons.
Sibb's Soul's conflict with itself.
Skelton's (P.) Sermons.
Smith's (Theyre) Sermons.
Spring's (Gardner) Essays. Ess. 8.
Spurgeon's (Cha. H.) Sermons. 7th Series.
Stebbings on Justifying faith.
Sumner's (J. Bird) Sermons.
Taylor's (Jer.) Discourses. (Nature of F.)
——— Life of Christ.
Taylor's (N.) Nature and necessity of faith.
Taylor's (T.) Necessity of faith in prayers.
Theological and Literary Review. 5:473.
Tillotson's Sermons.
Tottie's (John) Sermons.
Trail's (Will.) Christian Graces.
Tucker's Light of Nature pursued.
Waterland's Works.
Watts' Degree and foundation of faith.
Watson's (Thomas) Sermons.
Wayland's (Samuel) Sermons.
Wesley's (John) Sermons.
Westminster Review. 56:64. 52:379.
Whitaker's (Will.) Sermons.
Witherspoon's Works. (Nature of faith.)
Witsius on the Covenants. Bk. 3, Chap. 7.
Young's (T.) Sermons on faith.

Faith of Devils.

Chemnitii (C.) Dissertationes.
Zulichii Theologia dæmonum.

Ecking's Essays on Grace, faith, &c.

Faith of Infants. See INFANT BAPTISM, INFANT COMMUNION.

Affelmanni (Joan.) Dissertationes.
Balthasaris (Jac. Henr.) Dissertationes de fide presumpta.
Boerner de fide Iacobi in utero.
——— de fide Infantum in utero.
Buttstett's Vernunstmæsigen Gedancken von dem Glauben der ungetaüften Christenkinder.
Deutschmanni (Ioan.) Dissertationes.
Hecht's Versuch eines Beweises, &c.
Hulsemanni (Ioan.) de Fide infant. actuale.
Muller's Gedancken von Glauben der Kinder in mutterleibe.
Nifanii (Christiani) Exercitationes.
Osiandri (Ioann.) Dissertationes.
Quistorpii (Ioann.) Dissertationes.
Scherzeri (Io. Adam) Dissertationes.
Voigtii Commentatio de fide infantum.
Waltheri (Mich.) Dissertationes.
Weinmanni (Ioan.) Dissertationes.

Faithfulness. See INTEGRITY.

Faithfulness of God. See ATTRIBUTES.

Charnock's (Stephen) Works.
Enfield's (William) Sermons.
Robinson's Christian System.
Tillotson's (Abp.) Sermons.
Wisheart's (W.) Sermons.

Faith of the Patriarchs.

Carpzovii (Jo.) Theologia Judæorum.
Fabricius de Fide Patriarchum.
Gramberg's Krit. Gesch. d. Religionsideen.
Hahn, de Spe immortalitatis sub V. Test.
Heideggeri Patriarchum Historia.
Iohannsenii Veterum Hebr. notiones de rebus post mortem.
Mamachius de Animabus Justorum.
Oehler's Prologomena zur Theologie.
Pareau de Spe Immortalitatis.
Ritangelii Libra Veritatis.
Wigandi Corpus doctrinæ Dei.
Zornii Theologia Patristica.

Addington's Relig. knowl. of the anc. Jews.
Bauer's Theology of the Old Testament.
Berriman's (Wm.) Boyle Lectures. 1733.
Bibliotheca Sacra. 14:166.
Biddulph's Theology of the early P.
Bloomfield's Traditional knowledge of a Redeemer.
Christian Examiner. 60:1, 169.
Christian Observer. 18:1, 158. 20:142.
Cook (John) on the Patriarchal religion.
Cook's (Wm.) Patriarchal and Druidical faith.
Craven's Jewish and Christian dispensations compared.
Faber's Genius of the several dispensations.
Fenton's Scrip. doct. of the resurrection.
Hulbert's Gospel revealed to Job.
Jackson's Belief of a future state among the early Jews. (Disputes some of Warburton's statements.)
Peters' Critical Dissertations on Job.
Pierce (S. E.) on the Pentateuch.
Putnam's Gospel by Moses.
Smith's (Eli) Patriarchal Age.
Stephens' Rel. knowledge of the anc. Jews.
Town's Opinions of ancient philosophers.
Warburton's Divine legation of Moses.
Wemyss' (Tho.) Job and his Times.

Fall of Man. See IMAGE OF GOD, ORIGIN OF EVIL, ORIGINAL SIN, SERPENT, STATE OF INNOCENCE, TREE OF KNOWLEDGE.

Abichtius de Sapientia et bonitate Dei.
Balthasaris (Jac. Henr.) Dissertationes.
Cloppenburgii Opera Theologica.
Faustus de Serpente seductore.
Frischmuthii (Ioan.) Dissertationes.
Gerhardi (Ioan.) Disputationes.
Hulsemanni (Ioan.) Disputationes.
Junius de Peccato primo Adami.
Kahlerus de Innocentia Dei circa lapsum.
Klemmius de Serpiente Seductore.
Placet, sur le Peché d'Adam.

Fall of Man—*continued.*

Selden, de Jure naturali et Gentium.
Spanheimii Disputationes.
Stapferi Institutiones.

Adams' (William) Sermons.
Barrington (Shute) on Divine dispensations.
Barry's Introd. to the Old Testament.
Bates' Harmony of the Divine attributes.
Bellamy's Works.
Berry Street Lectures. Vol. 1.
Besly's (John) Doctrinal Discourses.
Birk's Difficulties of Belief.
Boston's Fourfold State.
Bridges' Testimony of Profane Antiquity.
Burnet's Archæology.
Calcott on the Fall, Incarnation, &c.
Chandler's Posthumous Sermons.
Charnock's Works.
Chauncey's Dissertations.
Christian Observer. 2:522.
Clarke's (Sam.) Sermons.
Collier's Sacred Interpreter.
Craig's (William) Sermons.
D'Oyley's (Dr. Geo.) Dissertations. Diss. 1.
——— Sermons.
Doddridge's Lectures. Part 8.
Dwight's Sermons. Ser. 27 and 28.
Emmon's (Nathaniel) Sermons.
Felton's (Henry) Sermons.
Fletcher's Appeal to facts.
Foster's (Dr. James) Sermons.
Fuller (And.) on Genesis. Diss. 4, 5, 6.
Gilfillan's Alpha and Omega. Ch. 4.
Goodman's Fall and corruption of man, proved from reason.
Green's (John) Sermons.
Guyse's (John) Sermons.
Holden (Geo.) on the Fall. (Able and full.)
Holden's (Lawrence) Sermons.
Howe's (John) Sermons.
Hubbard's Berry Street Lectures.
Hunt on the Divine dispensations.
Hutchinson's Moses, sine Principio.
Jeffrey's (John) Sermons.
Jenkins' (Joseph) Sermons.
Jones' (Will., of Nayland,) Sermons.
Kennicott's Dissertations.
King's (Abp.) Sermons.
Le Clerc's Dissertations.
Manton's (Thomas) Sermons.
Mede's Works.
Middleton's Examination of Sherlock.
Müller's Christian doctrine of sin.
Panoplist. 3:446. 4:5.
Pearson on the Creed.
Potts' (J. H.) Sermons.
Scott's Reply to Bp. Tomline.
Sherlock on Prophecy.
Shuckford on the Creation and Fall.
South's (Robert) Sermons.
Tennis on Idolatry.
Toplady's Works.
Turner's Introduction of Sin.
Waterland's Scripture Vindicated.
Watts' Ruin and recovery of man.
Witherspoon's Works. Lect. 14.
Witsius on the Covenants. Book 1, Ch. 8.
Witty's Mosaic history of the Fall.
Worthington's Mosaic account vindicated.

Fallen Angels. See EVIL SPIRITS.

Busmanni (Io. E.) Dissertationes.
Dorscheus de Satanæ obsessione.
Fabricius de Lapsorum Angelorum peccato.
Hannekenius de Lapsu Angelorum.
Olearii Dissertationes.
Seldenus de Lapsu Angelorum.

Baumgarten's Supp. to universal history.
Boyse's (Joseph) Works.
Gisborne on the Divine attribute of love.
Henley's Dissertations on the controverted passages in Peter and Jude, &c.
Hunt's Historical Essay toward explaining divine Revelation.
Hutchinson on Witchcraft.
Reynolds on Angels.
Scott's (Walter) Existence of Evil Spirits.
Spirit of the Pilgrims. 2:491.

Falling from Grace. See FIVE POINTS, PERSEVERANCE.

False Christs.

Christian Observer. 22:687.
Fuller on the True Messiah.
Jortin's Remarks on Ecclesiastical History.
Kidder's Demonstration of the Messias.
Lent's History of False Christs.
McLaurin on the Prophecies.
Simpson's Key to the Prophecies.

False Confidence. See SELF-DECEPTION.

Falsehood. See LYING, TRUTH.

False Miracles. See APOLLONIUS, MIRACLES OF THE CHURCH OF ROME.

Alberti Observationes Philologicæ.
Bosii (Lambert.) Exercitationes.
Brusson, Relation des mervielles que Dieu fait en France. 1694.
Chamieri Panstratiæ Catholicæ.
Helvetius, de M. quæ Pythag. Apoll. Tyan., Loyolæ, &c., tribuunter.
Raphaeli Annotationes.
Stephans (H.), Apologie pour Herodote.
[Zimmerman] de Miraculis quæ Pythagoræ, Loyolæ, &c., tribuunter.

Chapman's Eusebius.
Christian Observer. 14:565. 16:783.
Clarke's Boyle Lectures. 1704–1706.
Douglas' Criterion of miracles.
Edinburg Review. 39:55. 52:388. 53:261.
Edwards' (John) Theologia Reformata.
Farmer on Christ's Temptation.
Fleetwood on Miracles.
Hill's Lectures on the Old Test. (Egyptian Magi.)

Jortin's Remarks on Ecclesiastical history.
Limborch's Theology.
Middleton's Free Inquiry into the miraculous powers, &c.
——— Vindication of the Free Inquiry.
Richardson's Choice Observations.

False Prophets. See NEW PROPHETS.

Caroli Memorabilia Ecclesiæ.
Grapii Comment. theol. de Neoprophetis.
Groteste, Caractére des nouvelles prophecies.
Van Dale, Dissertationes.

Andrews on Divine Grace.
Arnold's History of Heresies.
Atterbury's (Lewis) Sermons.
Blackall's (Dr. Offspring) Sermons.
Blair's (James) Sermons.
Ellis' Pseudo-christus.
Kingston's Enthus. impostors no prophets.
Lacy's Cry from the Desert. (Lacy was a prominent English prophet.)
Marion's Prophetical Warnings. (A famous French prophet.)
Stampe on Spiritual Infatuation.
Vernon's Preservative against false prophets.
——— Remarks on the impostor Hermas.
Warburton (Bp.) on the prophecies of Arise Evans.

False Shame.

Benson's (Joseph) Sermons.
Cookman's (Dr. Tho.) Theolog. Discourses.
Zollikoffer on the Fasts and Festivals.

Fame. See AMBITION, HONOR.

Buckminster's (J.) Sermons.
Christian Observer. 1:218.
Fuller on Commendation.
Mason on Self-knowledge.
Smith's (S. S.) Sermons.
Venn's (Richard) Sermons.
Oxford Prize Essays. 1806. Marsh.

Familists.

Arnold's Kirchen und Ketzer-Historie. Part II., Lib. 16.
Bailieus' (R.) Wiedertæuferey, &c.
Bourn's Beschreibung u. Wiederlegung.
Grevinchovius (Casp.) Dissertationes.
Hoornbeckii Summa controversiæ relig.
Martini Disputationes.
Nicolai (Hen.) Revelatio Dei. (Pastor at Leyden, regarded as the founder of the "Family of Love." He wrote many treatises, some of which are translated into English.)

Ainsworth's Refutation of H. Nicholas.
Bourne's Description of the Familists.
George's (David) Works.
Knewstubs' Confutation of the horrible heresies taught by H. Nichols.
Micron's Confut. of D. George & H. Nichols.
Rogers' Display of a horrible Sect.
Rutherford's (Sam.) Spiritual Antichrist. A very curious book. Three of the chapters are on "the Familists of New England." Antinomians are severely handled.)

Family Government. See DOMESTIC ECONOMY, PARENTAL DUTIES.

Family Religion. See FAMILY WORSHIP.

Abbot's (Jacob) Fireside.
Abbot's (J. S. C.) Child at home.
Anderson's Domestic Constitution.
Baxter's Teacher of Householders.
Bell's (William) Sermons.
Berriman's (William) Sermons.
Buckminster's (J.) Sermons.
Christian Disciple. 1:9.
Clayton (H.) on Family Religion.
Collier's (J. A.) Christian Home.
Cooper's (Edward) Sermons.
Dale's (Thomas) Sermons.
Davies' (Samuel) Sermons.
Dewar on Family Religion.
Fisk's (Geo.) Sermons.
Fletcher's Guide to family devotion.
Garnier's (Tho.) Sermons.
Gilfillan's Domestic piety.
Gouge's Christian Householder.
Halyburton's Great concern.
Henry's (Matt.) Miscellaneous Works.
Howe's (John) Sermons.
Humphreys on Domestic Education.
Hunter's (A.) Sermons.
Innes on Domestic Religion.
Jacobson's Family Instructor.
James' Family Monitor.
Jortin's (J.) Sermons.
Kingsbury's Recommendation of fam. relig.
Lewis' (T.) Discourses on Christian duties.
Lucas' (Richard) Sermons.
Mayo on the Religious care of families.
Milnes' Practical Sermons.
Molesworth's (J. E. N.) Sermons.
Moore's (Dan.) Lectures on family duties.
Morehead's (R.) Discourses.
Nicholson's (Bp.) Sermons.
Orton's Religious Exercises.
Panoplist. 10:393.
Parker's Domestic Duties.
Parkhurst's Sermons.
Richmond's (Leigh) Domestic Portraiture.
Risley on Family Religion.
Ryan's (V. W.) Sermons.
Scamp on Family Religion.
Sharp's (Abp.) Sermons.
Sherlock's Sermons.
Slater's Earnest call to family religion.
Smith (B. M.) on Family Religion.
Stennet's Domestic Duties.
Trapp's Duties of domestic devotion.
Venn's Complete duty of man.
Walker's (Robt.) Sermons.
Whitaker's (Edw. W.) Sermons.
Whitfield's Sermons.
Willison's Works.

Wroughton on Religious Education.
——— on Domestic Religion.

Family Worship. See PRAYER BOOKS.

Alexander (Jas. W.) on Family Worship.
Baxter's (Rich.) Christian Directory.
Bishop's (Wm.) Sermons.
Bogatsky's Golden Treasury.
Brewster's Restoration of family worship.
Bridges (C.) on Family Prayer.
Burrows' (E. J.) Hours of devotion.
Cecil's (Rich.) Sermons.
Christian Examiner. 28:199. 61:182.
Christian Disciple. 4:1.
Christian Observer. 11:486. 19:145.
Cockrane's Manual. (Preferred by Dr. Chalmers.)
Collins' Necessity of family prayer.
Colman's (Benj.) Sermons.
Cooper's (E.) Sermons.
Dale's (T.) Sermons.
Dalton's Family Altar.
Dehon's (Bp. T.) Sermons.
Dewar's Nature and obligation of fam. wor.
Field on Household worship.
Gibson (J.) on Family worship.
Gilfillan's Duty of family worship.
Hall's (Robt.) Notes of Sermons.
Hammond on Family worship.
Hastings' (H. J.) Parochial sermons.
Jay's (Wm.) Domestic minister's assistant.
Morris' (Jos.) Sermons.
Nelson's (Robt.) Exhortation to fam. wor.
Orton's (Job) Discourses.
Princeton Review. 20:57.
Seed's (Jer.) Sermons.
Sladen (J.) on Family prayer.
Warter's (John) Sermons.

Fanaticism.

Arnold's Kirchen und Ketzerhistorie.
Calixti Disputationes.
Catron, Histoire du Fanatisme.
Colberg's Platonish-hermet. Christenthum.
Corvini Enthusiasticum-Pantheon.
De Brueys, Hist. du F. de notre tems. 1737.
Duttenhofer's Geschichte d. Religions Schwaermereien.
Fuestkingii Gynæceum heretico-fanaticum.
Hottingeri Disquisitiones.
Krug's (F. W.) Gesch. der protestantisch rel. Schwaermerien.
Sontagii Animadversiones.
Stinstra's Wärnung von dem Fanaticismus.
Turrettin, Preservatif contre le Fanaticisme.
Wernsdoorfii Hylotheismus.
Wideburgius de Fanaticorum caracteribus.
Zeltneri Prolegomena controversiarum.

Amer. Quarterly Review. 8:227.
Bidlake's Bampton Lectures. 1811.
Cecil's 60 Curious and authentic narratives.
Christian Quarterly Spectator. 6:118
Collinne's Spirit of Fanatics.
Eclectic Review. 1836.

Fanaticism—*continued.*

Edinburg Review. 59:30.
Ellis' Pseudo-Christus. (Against W. Franklin and Mary Gladbury.)
Fellows' Religion without cant.
Frazier's Mag. 9:159. 37:312, 441, 549.
Gray's Looking-glass for Fanatics.
Henderson's Modern Fanat. unveiled. 1831.
Mackay's Extraordinary popular delusions. 1852. Plates.
Madden's (R. R.) Phantasmata. 1857.
Owen's (Cha. G.) Scene of delusion.
Stillingfleet's Fanat. of the Church of Rome.
Stintra's Essay on Fanaticism.
——— Letters to the Mennonists.
Stone's Matthias and his impostures.
Taylor's (Isaac) History of Fanaticism.
Vole's Sources and Influence of Fanaticism. (Gives an account of the impostor Matthias, of New York. 1825.)
Zollikoffer's (Geo. J.) Sermons.

Farnovians. See SOCINIANS.

Fashion. See AMUSEMENTS, DRESS.

Schrœderi Commentaria philolog. de vestitu mulierum; ad Jesuiæ 3:16–23.

Burnside's Religion of mankind. Essay 23. (The influence of fashion on religion.).
Carr's (George) Sermons.
Foster's (James) Sermons.
Hall's (Bp.) Sermons.
Hill's Warning to professors.
More's (Hannah) Relig. of the fashionable.
Overbury's (Sir Tho.) Serious Queries.
Owen's Fashionable world displayed.
Stone's (Mrs.) Chronicles of fashion. (From the time of Elizabeth to 1840.)
Tucker's Light of Nature pursued.

Fasting. See LENT.

Ambrose, de Elia et Jejunio.
Chrysostom, de Jejunio.
Tertullian, de Jejuniis.
Bazil, Sermones.

Beveridge, de Jejunio quadragesimali.
Marheineke, Theologia Moralis.

Abernethy's (John) Sermons.
Alison's (Archibald) Sermons.
Andrews' (Bp.) Sermons.
Arnold's (of Rugby) Sermons.
Atterbury's (Bp.) Sermons.
Becon's (Tho.) Works. (Parker Soc. pub.)
Bennet's Christian Oratory.
Berriman's (W.) Sermons.
Beveridge's (Bp.) Sermons.
Bingham's Origines Ecclesiasticæ. (Fasts of the ancient church.)
Brome's Use, measure, and manner of F.
Brown's (W. L.) Sermons.
Cave's Primitive Christianity.
Christian Observer. 2:75.
Cowper's Expostulation.

Fasting—*continued.*

Delany's (Patrick) Sermons.
Francklin's (Bp.) Sermons.
Gardner's Causes of the inefficacy of Fasts.
Gordon's (Adam) Sermons.
Gregory's (Thomas) Sermons.
Gresley's (W.) Parochial Sermons.
Grosvernor's (Benjamin) Sermons.
Harris' Lawfulness and use of public F.
Harvey's (J.) Fast Sermons.
Kirk's (Ed. N.) Sermons.
Leland's (Thomas) Sermons.
Lloyd on Religious fastings.
Marshall on Sanctification.
Mason's (Henry) Treatise on fasting.
Methodist Quarterly Review. 9:205.
Milner's Practical Sermons.
Morning Exercises at Cripplegate.
Nelson's Fasts and Feasts of the church.
Potts' (Archdeacon) Sermons.
Reynolds' (Bp.) Sermons.
Robinson's Hist. and myst. of Good Friday.
Sancroft's (Bp.) Sermons.
Secker's (Abp.) Sermons.
Simpson's Essay on Fasting.
Skelton's (P.) Sermons.
Stillingfleet's (Bp.) Sermons.
Taylor's (Jer.) Discourses. (Life of Christ.)
Tillotson's (Abp.) Sermons.
Warburton's (Bp.) Sermons.
Waterland's (Daniel) Sermons.
Whitby's Appendix to Com. on Matt. ch. 6.
Woodward's (Henry) Essays and Sermons. (On the question whether literal fasting is a duty.)
Zollikoffer's (G. J.) Sermons. ("They discover a talent seldom possessed—a knowledge of the human heart."—CHALMERS.)

Fast-Day Sermons.

Adams' (William) Sermons.
Allen's (John) Sermons.
Amory's (Thomas) Sermons.
Appleton's (Nath.) Sermons.
Benson's (George) Sermons.
Blackall's (Bp.) Sermons.
Burgess' (Anthony) Sermons.
Burton's (Dr. John) Sermons.
Calamy's (Edmund) Sermons.
Carrington's (James) Sermons.
Chandler's (Samuel) Sermons.
Chillingworth's (W.) Sermons.
Disney's (John) Sermons.
Evans' (John) Sermons.
Gastrell's (Bp.) Sermons.
Herring's (Abp.) Sermons.
Hughes' (Obadiah) Sermons.
Kirkland's (J. T.) Sermons.
Porter's (Ebenezer) Sermons.
Priestley's (J.) Sermons.
Scott's (Thomas) Sermons.
Talbot's (Bp.) Sermons.
Tennison's (Abp.) Sermons.
Wayland's (Francis) Sermons.

Fate. See CHANCE, DECREES, FREE AGENCY, NECESSITY.

Arpe, Theatro Fati.

Buchanan's Modern Atheism.
Compte's Positive philosophy.
——— Positive politics.
——— Positive catechism.
Cudworth's Intellectual system. Ch. 1.
Toplady on the "Fate" of the ancients.

See a great list of foreign writers in ARPE, above named.

Fathers. See CATENÆ, LIVES OF THE FATHERS, USE OF THE FATHERS.

Acta Sanctorum.
Augusti, Christomathia Patristica.
Baltus, Defense des Pères.
Bellarmin, de Scriptoribus Eccles.
Bigne, Bibliotheca S. S. Patrum.
Bonæ Notitia Auctorum et Librorum.
Callixti Adparatus Theologicus.
Canisii (H.) Thesaurus.
Cave, Hist. literaria scriptorum eccles.
Cellier, Hist. generale des auteurs sacrés et ecclesiastiques.
Cotellerii Eccles. Græcæ monumenta.
——— Animadv. in Pat. apostolicis.
Danzii Initia doctrinæ patristicæ.
Despont, Bibliotheca vet. P. (30 v., fol.)
Dowling, Notitia scriptor. S. S. patrum.
Dupin, Bibliothéque des auteurs eccles.
Fabricii Bibliotheca Ecclesiastica.
——— Biblioth. Græca. (Contains an account of *all* known Greek writers, and of all their editions, and commentators.)
Flaccii Catalogus Testium veritatis.
Gallandii Bibliotheca Vet. patrum.
Grabæi Spicelegium patrum et hereticorum.
Grynæi Monumenta patrum orthodoxograp.
Goldwitzer's Bibliog. der kirchenväter.
Guillon, Bibliothèque Choisie.
Hefele Patrum Apostolicorum Opera. (Describes the best editions of each, and adds valuable notes, prefaces, and index.)
Hennischii Ætates patrum principuorum.
Hilgenfeld's Apostolischen Väter.
Huber's Philosophie der Kirchenvaeter.
Hulsemanni Patrologia.
Ittigii Biblioth. et Catenis patrum.
Locherer's (J. N.) Lehrbuch der Patrologie.
Lumperi Hist. de vitis, scriptis, &c.
Maii Biblioth. patrum sanctorum.
Martene, Thesaurus Anecdotorum.
Migne, Patrologiæ cursus. (220 vols.)
Miræi Bibliotheca Ecclesiastica.
Moehler's Patrologie.
Montfaucon, Collectio Nova.
Nourry Adparatus ad bibl. max. Patrum.
Oberthuri Opera patrum cont. Gentiles et Judæos.
Olearii Abaccus Patrologicus.
Oudini Dissertationes. (Gives an account of each early writer, and an analysis of his work.)

Fathers—*continued.*

Rheinwaldi Patrist. Homiliarum collectio.
——— Reliquæ sacræ. (Consists of very scarce fragments.)
Rössler's Bibliothek der Kirchenväter.
Sandius de Veteris scriptoribus eccles.
Schleichert, Institutiones Patrologiæ. (Designates interpolations and spurious works.)
Schonemanni Biblioth. Patzum Latinorum.
Schopfii Academia Jesu Christi.
Schulteti Medulla theologiæ patrum.
Suiceri Thesaurus Eccles. (A magnificent work, illustrating the Greek Fathers, historians, rites, ceremonies, language, &c. It answers as a complete index to those Fathers, and illustrates many obscure passages of Scripture.)
Tentzelii Exercitationes.
Varenii Rationarium Theologicum.
Walchii Bibliotheca Patristica. (An account of the books, editions, commentators, &c. With chapters on their lives, learning, errors, &c.)
Whitby (Dan.), Diss. de Scripturarum interpretatione. (Quotes the conflicting opinions of the Fathers.)

Bennet's Theology of the early church. (Consists of quotations from the Fathers.)
Beveridge's Apostolical Fathers.
Bickersteth's Fathers of the 1st and 2d centuries. (Extracts from their writings.)
Blunt's Cambridge Lectures. 1840.
Boyd's Fathers not Papists. (A translation of discourses by Chrysostom, Gregory Naz., Basil, &c.)
Cary's Fathers of the first 4 centuries.
Chevalier's Trans. of the Epistles of Clement, Polycarp, and Ignatius; and the apologies of Justin M. and Tertullian.
Clarke's Succession of sacred literature. (A conspectus of the topics written upon by the fathers, the best editions, translations, &c.)
Collingson's Bampton Lectures. 1813.
Conybeare's Bampton Lectures. 1839.
Cox's (R.) Fathers of the first 3 centuries.
Crofts' Bampton Lectures. 1786.
Dodwell's Catalogue of the Christian writers of the first 3 centuries.
Dupin's History of ecclesiastical writers. (Gives the topics of each writer, and his opinion of the work.)
Exeter Hall Lectures to young men.
Gill's Cause of God and Truth.
Hills' (S.) Vindication of the primitive fathers against Bp. Burnet.
Jortin's (John) Works.
Keary's Commonplace book to the Fathers.
Kett's Bampton Lectures. 1790.
Lardner's Credibility of the Gospel history.
Law's Theory of Religion.
Library of the Fathers anterior to the division of the East and West. (Translated by Dr. Pusey and others, with the text. 50 vols.)

Fathers—*continued.*

Lupton's Glory of early times.
Middleton's Free Enquiry.
Osborn's Doctrinal errors of the early F.
Parker's Bibliotheca Biblica. (A comm. on the Pentateuch, from the writings of the Fathers of the first 5 centuries.)
Riddle's Manual of Christian Antiquities. (The prefix gives an analysis of the writings of the ante-Nicene fathers.)
Shuttleworth's Translation of the Apostolical epistles; with notes.
Simpson on Religious opinions.
Wake's Epistles of the Apostolical Fathers.
Warburton's Julian.
Whiston's Primitive Christianity.

Collections of the Patristic writings, and editions of the separate fathers, are exceedingly numerous. Those of DUPIN, WALCH, OUDIN, and HEFELE, are either of them sufficient. NUTT, in his sale catalogue for 1857, offers no less than 923 works, or editions, of the Fathers. The most splendid, as well as most recent, is the uniform edition of MIGNE, begun in 1839, and completed 1861.

The following list of the early fathers, in the order of time, will be convenient for reference.

1st Century.—Barnabas, Clemens Romanus.
2d Century.—Hermas, Ignatius, Polycarp, Papias, Justin Martyr, Irenæus, Athanagoras, Theophilus, Theodosian, Clemens Alexandrinus.
3d Century.—Tertullian, Minutius Felix, Hippolytus, Origen, Gregory Thaumaturgus, Dionysius, Cyprian.
4th Century.—Lactantius, Athanasius, Cyril, Isidore, Eusebius, Chrysostom, Hilary, Epiphanius, Gregory Naz., Basil, Ambrose, Jerome, Theodoret, Gregory Nys.
5th Century.—Augustin, Arnobius.

Fear of Death. See DEATH.

Barrow's (Wm.) Sermons. (2 on this subj.)
Bowers' (Dean) Sermons.
Bradford's (The Martyr) Works.
Burnside's Religion of mankind. Last essay.
Coxe's (R. C.) Course of Lent sermons.
Drelincourt on Death.
East's (T.) Christian Companion.
Eaton's (Sam.) Sermons.
Enfield's (William) Sermons.
Erskine's (Eben.) Sermons.
Grove's (Henry) Sermons.
Heber's (Bp.) Sermons.
Hogg's Scriptural supports for the timorous Christian.
Lucas' (Rich.) Sermons.
Mason's (John) Dialogues on death.
Pierce's (Sam. E.) Sermons.
Rees' (Abraham) Sermons.
Sherman on Death and Heaven, and the Christian's desire for both.

Fear of God.

Alleine's Nature and necessity of godly fear.
Bates' Works. Discourse 17.
Boyle on the Veneration of the Deity.
Burroughs on Gospel fear.
Butcher's (Wm.) Sermons.
Carr's (George) Sermons.
Christian Observer. 18:345. 22:685.
Clarke's (S.) Sermons.
Cooper's (Edward) Sermons.
Dale's (Tho.) Sermons.
Dwight's Discourses. Disc. 93.
Hale's (Sir M.) Contemplations.
Hall's (Bp.) Practical works.
Hurd's (Bp.) Sermons.
Johnson's (John) Sermons.
Johnson's (Sam.) Sermons.
Jortin's (John) Sermons.
Kollock's (Shepard K.) Sermons.
Packman's (R. C.) Sermons.
Paley's (Wm.) Sermons.
Potts' (J. H.) Sermons.
Reading's (Wm.) Sermons.
Secker's (Abp.) Sermons.
Sherlock (Bp.) on Religious Fear.
Sherlock's (Wm.) Sermons.
Smallridge's (Bp.) Sermons.
Tothes' (J.) Sermons.
Trapp's Nature and infl. of the Fear of God.
Young's (Dr. Edw.) Sermons.

Fear of Man. See MAN-PLEASING.

Brown's (Francis) Sermons.
Christian Observer. 16:133.
Enfield's (William) Sermons.
Foster's (Jas.) Sermons.
Frank's (Mark) Nicodemus.
Hunt's (Jer.) Sermons.
May's (Wm.) Sermons.
Smith's (James) Sermons.
Smith's (Sam. Stanhope) Sermons.
Wood's (Wm.) Sermons.
Zollikoffer's (Geo. J.) Sermons on prevalent vices.

Feasting. See FESTIVALS.

Stuckii Antiquitates Conviviales. (A curious and learned treatise on ancient feasts, both Jewish and Pagan.)
Garnet's (Bp.) Sermons.
Horton's (Thomas) Sermons.
Sheridan's (Bp.) Sermons.
Wheatley's (Richard) Sermons.

Feet Washing. See WASHING FEET.

Felicians. See ADOPTIANS.

Fellowship. See BROTHERLY LOVE, CHRISTIAN INTERCOURSE, CHRISTIAN UNION, COMMUNION OF SAINTS.

Christian Quarterly Spectator. 8:292.
Christian Monthly Spectator. 4:504.
James' Church-member's guide.
Literary and Theological Review. 2:194.
Owen's Guide to Christian fellowship.
Sutcliff's Mutual communion of Saints.
Tate's Cure of contention.
Torshell's Help to Christian fellowship.
Watts' Invitation to Church fellowship.
——— Berry Street Lectures.
Wheatley's (Richard) Sermons.

Female Communion.

I know of no book on this subject; but it is often introduced into works in defence of Infant baptism. See PETER EDWARDS, DORE, &c.

Female Education. See EDUCATION.

Babbington on Education.
Beaumont on the Instruct. of young ladies.
Burton's Lectures on fem. ed. and manners.
Christian Examiner. 22:90. 28:44.
East's Memoir of Miss Humphrey.
Edinburg Review. 15:273. (Sydney Smith.)
Fenelon on the Education of daughters.
Frazier's Magazine. 31:703.
Genlis (Madam de) on Education.
Gray (Maria) on Self-culture.
Hervey on the Religious educ. of daughters.
Jerment on Education.
Lectures to Ladies. (A collection of Tracts, by Maurice, Kingsly, &c. &c.)
Monthly Review. 112:502.
More's (Hannah) Strictures on Education.
Museum of Foreign Lit. 4:118. 32:139.
New England Magazine. 3:278.
Pendered on Female education. (A practical treatise on school management.)
Southern Lit. Messenger. 1:169. 5:597. 6:451.
Williams' (Anna) Hints from a Mother.

Female Sex. See WOMAN'S RIGHTS.

Tertullian, de cultu Feminarum.

Agrippa (H. C.) Opera.
Goguet, l'Origine des lois, des artes, &c.
Hoffman's Erziehung geschl. in Indien.
Junckeri Ephemerides eruditarum fœminar.

Alexander's (Wm.) History of woman of all nations, from the earliest times to the present. 1730.
American Institute of Instruction. 1845.
American Quarterly Review. 5:438.
Beattie's Lectures on the format. of charac.
Blackwood's Magazine. 33:124, 391.
Buckminster's (J. S.) Sermons.
Burder's Memoirs of pious women.
Cary's (Mrs. V.) Letters to a young lady.
Child's (Mrs.) Cond. of women in var. ages.
Clarke's World-noted women in all ages.
Clayton's (E.) Notable women.
Clement's Noble deeds of women.
Cobb on the Pursuits of women.
——— Theory of Morals.
Conant's (W. C.) The great revival in 1847.
Cox's (F. A.) Female Biography.
De Witt's Woman: her excellence and usefulness.

Female Sex—*continued.*

Dublin University Mag. 52:1, 623, 696.
Ellis' Women of England.
——— Wives of England.
——— Daughters of England.
Farnham's (Mrs.) Woman and her Era.
Frazier's Magazine. 7:591.
Fuller's (S. M.) Woman in the 19th century.
Fullom's Hist. of woman, and her connection with religion and civilization. (To 1850.)
Garnett's Lectures.
Gibbon's Mem. of eminently pious women.
Gisbourne's Duties of the female sex.
Grave's Woman in America: her moral and intellectual condition. (As in 1844.)
Gray (Mrs.) on Self-culture.
Hale's (Mrs.) Woman's Record. (Sketches of distinguished women in all ages.)
Heywood's Exemplary lives. (Curious. 1624.)
Houston's Man a creation of woman.
Huntingdon's (Prof.) Sermons.
Jameson's Characteristics of women.
Jay's (Wm.) Lectures.
Kavenaugh's Woman in France in the 18th century.
Landell's Woman's sphere in the light of Scripture.
Lawrence's History of Woman in England.
Lectures to Ladies. (A collection of valuable treatises.)
Letheredge's Woman the glory of Man.
McIntosh's (Maria) Woman in America.
Mariot's (H.) Sermons.
Marshall's (Emily) Woman in America.
Meiner's Influence of W. in all nations.
Memoirs of Isabella Graham.
" Martha Dunn.
" Mrs. Fletcher.
" Madame Guion.
" Lady Huntingdon.
" Mrs. Lydia M. Malcom.
" Mrs. Ramsay.
Monod's (Adolph) Sermons.
——— Woman and her mission.
Montesquieu's Spirit of Laws.
Newton's (John) Letters to a wife.
North American Review. 42:849.
Parke's Essays on Woman's work.
Parsons' Mental and moral dignity of W.
Phillips' The Lydias.
Reid's (Mrs.) Plea for Woman.
Robinson's (Edw. J.) Daughters of India. (Their social and religious condition in 1860.)
Sanford's Woman in her social and domestic character.
Segur's (J. A.) Condition and influence of W.
Sprague's (W. B.) Excellent Woman.
——— Letters to a daughter.
Starling's Noble deeds of Woman.
Taylor's (D.) Practical hints to young ladies.
Tonno's Wrongs of Woman.
Toplady's Sketch of mod. female character.
Wade's (John) Women: past and present. 1859.
Walker's (Alex.) W. considered as to mind, morals, marriage, and divorce.
West's (Mrs.) Letters to a young lady.
Westminster Review. 8:378. 34:254. 35:13. 84:166.

Festivals.

Alt's (J. C. W.) Predigten.
Dresserus de Festis Christianorum.
Hildebrandi Enchiridion.
Hospinian de Festis Judæorum, Ethnicorum, et Christianorum.
Mayer de Origine et causis festorum.
Nork's Deutung der Geheimlehren, &c.
Schmidii Hist. festorum et dominicarum.

Armstrong's (John) Sermons.
Bachman's Law of the Pentateuch relating to Festivals.
Cave's Primitive Christianity. Pt. 1, Ch. 7.
Christian Examiner. 38:35.
Cowper's (Dean) Sermons on the great festivals of the English Church.
Glasses' Lectures on the Holy Festivals. (Give an account of the person who is the subject of the day's celebration.)
Hobart's Fest. and Fasts of the Episc. Ch.
Mant's (H.) Holidays of the Church.
Marsden's Festivals of the Ch. of England.
Mossman's (T. W.) Sermons.
Nelson's Fasts and Feasts.
Povah's (R.) Sermons.
Russel's (A. T.) Sermons.
Stevens' Fest. and Fasts of the church.
Sumner's (Abp.) Sermons.
Whitgift's (Abp.) Works. (Parker Soc. pub.)
Zollikoffer's Festivals and Fasts.

Fetichism.

De Brosses, du culte des dieux Fétiches. (The first work which gave general use to the term. 1760.)
Krugg's Allgemeines Handwörterbuch der philosophischen Wissenschaften.
——— System der praktischen Philosophie.

This form of idolatry is more or less described by all travellers in Africa.

Fiction.

Amer. Biblical Repos. 2d Series. 9:362.
Amer. Quarterly Observer. 1:25.
Butler's (Piers E.) Rationality of revealed religion. (Appendix.)
Brownson's Quart. Rev. 2d Series. 1:116.
Christian Examiner. 42:101.
Christian Observer. 14:512. 16:298, 371, 425.
Christian Quart. Spect. 1:247. (Religious novels.)
Dehon's (Bp. T.) Sermons.
Dunlop's (John) History of fiction.
Episcopal Magazine. 2:373.
Frazier's Magazine. 1:318.
Murray's (H.) Tendency of fictitious narrative.

Museum of Foreign Literature. 4:40.
N. Amer. Review. 56:271. 57:128. 65:348.
Quarterly Review. 72:25. ("Evangelical novels.")

Fifth Commandment.
See FILIAL DUTIES.

Fifth Monarchy. See FOUR KINGDOMS, MILLENARIANS.

Burnet's History of his own times.
Falkner's Reproach and Censure. (Append.)
Goodwin's (Thomas) Sermons.
Hartley's Paradise Restored.
Maton on Christ's personal reign.
Ranew's Glory of the saints.
Sherwin on the Prophecies.
Tillinghast's (John) Works.
Tombes' (John) Saints no Smiters. (Very able.)

Fight of Faith. See ARMOR OF GOD.

Alleine's (R.) The World conquered.
Ambrose's (Isaac) Works.
Becon's (Tho.) Works. (Parker Soc. pub.)
Boston's (Thomas) Sermons.
Breckell's (J.) Christian Warfare.
Butcher's (J.) Sermons.
Christian Examiner. 1:102.
Christian Observer. 14:75.
Christopher's (Henry) Sermons. (The entire volume is on this subject.)
Downame's Christian Warfare. ("One of the best pieces of practical divinity extant."—HERVEY.)
Fuller's (Tho.) Works. (Too little known.)
Gray (Andrew) on Spiritual warfare.
Greenham's (Richard) Sermons.
Hall's (Robt.) Works. Ser. 20.
Hawker's (Robert) Sermons.
Hayward's (Roger) Sermons.
Hooker's The Christian life a fight of faith.
Lardner's Works.
Latimer's (Bp.) Works.
Leifchild's (John) Discourses.
Leyburn's Soldier of the Cross.
Love's Combat between the flesh and the spirit.
McKay on the Christian Warfare.
Scott's (Tho.) Essays on important subjects.
Sibbs' (Rich.) Sermons. ("The soul's conflict with itself.")
Steele's (Sir Rich.) Christian Hero.
Vance's (W. F.) Sermons.
Vaughn's Christian Warfare illustrated.
Watts' Contest between flesh and spirit.
Wiseman's (Sir Wm.) Christian Knight.

Figurative Language of Scripture.

Gebelin, Monde primitif. (Includes Oriental allegories, sacred and profane.)
Gerdesii Dissertationes.
Hugonis (a St. Victoire) Opera.
Lowth, Prelectiones de Sac. Poes. Prelec. 4.
Philonis Judæi Legis allegoriarum.

Figurative Language—*continued.*

Rambach, de Sensus mystici criteriis.
Rudebach de Symbolis Sac. Scripturæ.
Spanneri Polyanthea Sacra.
Vitringæ Observationes Sacræ. Lib. VI.
——— Prefatio ad comment. in Jesaiam.

Bechaus on Biblical Interpretation.
Bibliotheca Sacra. 13:314.
Bloomfield's (G. B.) Serm. (5 on the subj.)
Brown's (John) Sacred Tropology.
Carson's (Alex.) Principles of Biblical Crit.
Christian Disciple. 5:178.
Christian Examiner. 48:390. 68:390.
Christian Review. 5:321. 10:113.
Claude on the Composition of a sermon.
Collyer on Scripture comparisons.
Conybeare's Bampton Lectures. 1824.
Foreign Quarterly Review. 23:62.
Fuller's Abuse of allegory in preaching.
Gray on Parables and allegorical writings.
Hall's (Tho.) Centuria Sacra, &c.
Horne's (Bp.) Preface to his Comm. on Ps.
Hurd's Introd. to the study of prophecy.
Jones (Wm.) on the Fig. language of Scrip.
Lord's (D. N.) Characteristics of Fig. lang.
——— Theological and Literary Journal. (In nearly every number.)
Lowth's Preface to commentary on Isaiah.
Ludlam on Scripture metaphors.
Mather's (Sam.) Figures of the Old Test.
Mills' (J.) Sacred Symbology.
Norwood on Scripture figures.
Paschall's Thoughts. Sec. 10–14.
Taylor's Moses and Aaron. (Oft. reprinted.)
Waterland's Preface to "Scrip. vindicated."
Wemyss' Symbolical language of Scripture.
West's (J. R.) Figures and types of the O. T.
Williams on the Song of Solomon. (Introd.)
Wood's (J.) Nature and use of figures.

Filial Duties. See YOUTH.

Belfrage's (Henry) Sermons.
Cleaver on the 5th Commandment.
Davis' (William) Sermons.
Doddridge's Lectures.
Dwight's Discourses. Disc. 110.
Edwards' Theologia Reformata.
Fleetwood's (Bp.) Sermons.
Hole on the Catechism.
Hopkins' (Bp.) Sermons.
Lightfoot's Sermons.
Paley's Moral Philosophy.
——— Sermons.
Parsons on the Catechism.
Pyle's (Philip) Sermons.
Secker (Abp.) on the Catechism.
Scott on the Fifth commandment.
Smith's (Sydney) Sermons.
Wesley's (John) Sermons.
Wright (R.) on the Duty of children.

Filled with the Spirit.
See OPERATIONS.

Goodwin (John) on Being filled with the Spirit.

Hall's (Silas) Sermons.
Howe's (Samuel) Sermons.

Final Causes. See CAUSATION.

First Commandment. See COMMANDMENTS, CATECHISMS, IDOLATRY, UNITY OF GOD.

First Resurrection. See MILLENARIANS.

Burnet's Theory of the Earth.
Campbell's Necessity of Revelation.
Fleming on the First resurrection.
Glanvil's Lux Orientalis.
Newton (Bp.) on the Prophecies.

Five Points. See under each of the points, viz.: ELECTION, DEFINITE ATONEMENT, GRACE, FREE AGENCY, PERSEVERANCE.

Cloppenburgii (Ioann.) Disputationes.
Heidanni Examen Catech. Remonstrantium.
Heylini Historia Quinquarticularis.
Hickmanni Historia quinque articularis. (A reply to Heylin, and strongly Calvinistic.)
Mollinæi Enucleatio Controversiarum.
Pœlenburgii Disputat. (Reply to Spanheim.)
Schlichtingii (Ionas) Dissertationes.
Spanheimii (Frid.) Disputationes.

Bates on the Controversy between Arminians and Calvinists.
Dickinson (J.) on the Five points.
Edwards' Veritas Redux.
Gill's Cause of God and truth.
Heylin's (Peter) Historical declaration of the judgment of the Western churches.
Ness' Antidote against Arminianism.
Parks' (Wm.) Sermons on the five points.
Whitby on the Five points.
Williams' (Dr. Edw.) Equity of the Divine government. (Reply to Whitby.)

Flagellantes.

Boileau Historia Flagellantium.
Cyprian (Ernest) de Ecclesia subterranea.
Delolme Historia Flaggellantium.
Forstman die Christlichen Geisslergesellschaften.
Kortholtus de Ecclesiis suburbicariis, &c.
Martene, Voyages literaire.
Muratori Antiq. Ital. Medii ævi.
Schneegans, le Grand pelerinage des F. a Strassburg en 1348.
Schoetgenii Commentatio de secta F.
Thiers (J. B.), Critique de l'histoire Flag. (A Justification.)
Winzeti Flagellum sectariorum Historia.
Wolschoendorfii Disquisitiones Historicæ.
Zornius de Usu sacri cordicicis.

Boileau's Hist. of the F. Tr. by De Lolme.
[De Lolme's] Hist. of religious flagellations among different nations, and especially among Christians. (A paraph. and com. on the Hist. of Boileau. Curious engravings. Reprinted under the title, "Memorials of Superstition.")

Flattery.

Coney's (Dr. Thomas) Sermons.
Hust's (Henry) Sermons.
Newton's (Bp.) Dissertations.
Rees' (Abraham) Sermons.
South's (Robert) Sermons.
Taylor's (Jeremy) Sermons.
Wells' (Francis) Sermons.

Flemingians. See ANABAPTISTS.

Folly of Sin.

Brady's (Nicolas) Sermons.
Waples' (Edward) Sermons.

Forbearance.

Baxter's (Arthur G.) Sermons.
Christian Observer. 16:291.
Haldane's (James) Works.
Hewlett's (John) Sermons.
Hook's (W. F.) Sermons.
McCann's (G.) Lectures.

Forbearance of God. See PATIENCE.

Foreknowledge of God. See ATTRIBUTES, DECREES, HUMAN RESPONSIBILITY, SCIENTIA MEDIA.

Crellius de Deo.
Kromayer de Prescientia rerum contingent.

Bromley's Divine prescience viewed in connection with human liberty.
Charnock's Works.
Clarke's (S.) Boyle Lectures. 1705, 1706.
Edwards' (Pres.) Works.
Haggar's Order of Causes.
Howe's (John) Letter to Sir Robt. Boyle.
——— Defence of the Letter.
Jackson on Human liberty.
Killingsworth's (Grantham) Tracts.
——— Essay on free agency and exposition of John i. 1, 2.
King's Sermons on the Divine prescience.
Tillotson's (Abp.) Sermons.

Forerunners of the Reformation.

Flathe's Gesch. d. Vörlaufer d. Ref.
Ulmann's Reformatoren vor d. Ref.
Wessel's Vörgänger Luther's.

Gilpin's Lives of Jerome, Zisca, &c.
Perrin's Luther's Forerunners.
Rolt's Lives of the principal Reformers.
Sharley's Lives of the Fathers and Reform.
Ulman's Reformers before the Reformation. Trans. by Menzie.

Forgiveness of Injuries. See PEACEABLENESS, RESENTMENT.

Baxter's (Richard) Christian Politics.
Bell's (William) Sermons.
Berens' (Edward) Village sermons.
Blair's (James) Sermons.
Bourdaloue's Sunday sermons.

Forgiveness of Injuries—*continued.*

Brackenbury's (Edward) Discourses.
Brady's (Nicolas) Sermons.
Brett's (Thomas) Sermons.
Butts' (Thomas) Sermons.
Clarke's (Dr. Samuel) Sermons.
Cosens' (John) Sermons.
Davies' (Thomas) Sermons.
Faringdon's (Anthony) Sermons.
Fawcett's (John) Sermons.
Fiddes' (Richard) Sermons.
Franklin's (Thomas) Sermons.
Fuller's (Andrew) Sermons.
Gatty's (Alfred) Sermons.
Gilpin's (William) Sermons.
Girdlestone's (Charles) Sermons.
Gordon's (Sir A.) Sermons.
Green's (Samuel) Sermons.
Henry's (Matthew) Miscellaneous works.
Hill's (Bryan) Sermons.
Kennaway's (Charles E.) Sermons.
Mason's (John) Sermons on the human virtues.
Morony's (Joseph) Sermons.
Newlin's (Thomas) Sermons.
Paley's (William) Sermons.
Pott's (J. H.) Sermons.
Skelton's (Philip) Sermons.
Smith's (Sydney) Sermons.
Southgate's (Richard) Sermons.
Sterne's (Lawrence) Sermons.
Tillotson's (Abp.) Sermons.
Tilly's (William) Sermons.
Weston's (Bp.) Sermons.

Forgiveness of Sin.

Augustine, Sermones.

Danæus de Peccatorum remissione.
Du Bosc (Pierre), Sermonnaire.
Goezius de Remissione peccatorum.
Loescherus de Deletione peccatorum.
Reuss' Lehre von der Rechtfertigung.

Allen's (James) Sermons.
Bates' (William) Sermons.
Baxter's (Arthur) Sermons.
Beachcroft's (Robert) Sermons.
Beveridge's (Bp.) Sermons.
Bull's Harmonia Apostolica.
Charnock's (Stephen) Sermons.
Collibeare on Natural and Rev. Religion.
East on Forgiveness and Assurance.
Foster on Natural Religion.
Gilpin's (William) Sermons.
Gleig's (G. R.) Sermons for plain people.
Henry's (Philip) Sermons.
Hervey's (James) Works.
Hopkins' (Ezekiel) Discourses on sin.
Hughes' (Henry) Sermons.
Jenyn's Evidences of the Christian religion.
Maclean's Apostolical commission. (Exc.)
Magee on the Atonement.
Massillon's Sermons.
Morning Exercises at Cripplegate. (Sermon by T. Vincent.)

13

Forgiveness of Sin—*continued.*

Owen (John) on the 130th Psalm.
Schobel's (Edw.) Sermons on the Lord's prayer.
Secker's (Abp.) Lectures on the Catechism.
Tillotson's Sermons.
Trench's (Francis) Sermons.
Truman's Prevailing errors in the Church of England.
Watts' Strength and weakness of human reason.
Williams' (John) Sermons.
Witsius on the Covenants.
Yonge's (James) Sermons.

Formality. See RITES.

Beveridge's (Bp.) Sermons.
Blackall's (Bp.) Sermons.
Blackley's (Thomas) Practical Sermons.
Bradford's Unprofitableness of external rel.
Bragge's (Francis) Sermons on undissembled religion.
Bull's (Bp.) Sermons.
Clagget's (William) Sermons.
Fawcett's (John) Family Sermons.
Fernie's (John) Sermons.
Hall's (Bp.) Sermons.
Horneck's (Anthony) Sermons.
Milner's (Joseph) Sermons.
Newman's (J. H.) Sermons.
Scattergood's (Samuel) Sermons.
Secker's (Abp.) Sermons.
Tillotson's Sermons.
Weston's (Bp.) Sermons.
Whitby's (Daniel) Sermons.
Wilson's (Bp.) Sermons.
Yonge's (James) Sermons.

Forms of Prayer. See LITURGIES, PRAYER, PRAYER BOOKS.

Pro.

Annand's Panem quotidianum.
Bennet's History of the ancient methods of prayer.
Bull's (Bp.) Sermons.
Burrows' Christian faith and practice.
Butler's (C.) Hist. of formularies in Papal, Greek, and Protestant churches.
Calder (Robt.) on Set forms of prayer.
Comber's Scholastic history of Liturgies.
Edwards' Theologia Reformata.
Falkner (D. W.) on Liturgies.
Gorham on Public Worship. (Prize essay.)
Jackson (E. D.) on the Lord's prayer.
Mede's (Joseph) Sermons.
Paley's Moral and Political Economy.
Prideaux's (H.) Connection of O. and N. T.
Prideaux's (John) Doctrine of prayer.
Secker's (Abp.) Sermons.
Sharp's (Abp.) Sermons.
Smallridge's (Bp.) Sermons.
South's (Robert) Sermons.
Stebbing's (Henry) Lectures.
Taylor's (H.) Account of prayer.
Taylor (Jer.) on Extempore prayer.

Forms of Prayer—*continued.*

Con.

Addington on the Necessity and expediency of forms.
Brekell on Forms of Prayer.
Calderwood's Altare Damascenum.
Clarkson (David) on Liturgies.
[Collings] on Prescribed forms of prayer.
Doddridge's Lectures. Part 3, lect. 86.
Dwight's Sermons. Ser. 144.
Fleming's (Caleb) Theophilus to Gaius.
Haldane on Worship and Ordinances.
Owen's (John) Discourses concerning Litur.
Peirce's Vindication of Dissenters. Bk. 3.
Princeton Review. 18:487.
Robinson (Benj.) on Forms of prayer.
Taylor's (John) Scripture act of prayer.
Waltford's Manner of public prayer.
Watts' (Isaac) Guide to prayer.
——— Miscellany.

Formula Concordiæ. See CONSUBSTANTIATION.

Pro.

Andre's Fünf predigten.
Anton's Gesch. der Concordienformel.
Augusti Corpus librorum symbolicum.
Chytræus' Bedencken über die Apologie, &c.
Deutshmanni (Ioann.) Disputationes.
Elsvichii Disquisitiones Historicæ.
Francke, Libri symbolici Lutheranæ.
Graumundi Opera.
Hutteri Concordia Concors.
Hulsemanni Prælectiones Publicæ.
Kirchneri (Timoth.) Apologia.
Kuess, La formule de concorde dans ses rapports avec le N. Test.
Laurentius de Disput. et Controversis.
Müller's Lutherisches Concordienbuch.
Osiandri (Andr.) Disputationes XIII.
Petri Responsio ad scriptum, &c.
Piscatori Com. in Formulam Conc.
Quistorpii (Ioan.) Exercitationes.
Schilbe's Bekentnisstand d. Sog. reform.
Schilteri Defensio libri concordiæ.

Con.

Alhantiner's Bedencken über die Vörrede des Concordienbuch.
Balthasar's Hist. des torgischen Buchs.
Bremensii Defensio negatæ subscriptionis.
Gerdesii Scrinium Antiquarium.
Hermanni Disquisitio Historica.
Hospiniani Concordia Discors.
Irenæi Examen Form. Concordiæ.
Muhlii Dissertationes Historicæ.
Neostadiensii Admonitio Christiana.
Palmerii Protestatio.
Reinhardii (Mich. H.) Dissertationes.
Sturmii (Io.) Opera. (Many replies.)
Velerii Epistola Apologetica.
Wolfius de Ubiquitate atque adeo de corporali presentia corporis Christi.

See an account of many books on this subject, explanatory, polemic, and historical, in KOECKER, *Bibliotheca Symbolicae.*

Fornication. See UNCLEANNESS.

Acton's Prostitution considered in its moral, social, and sanitary aspects.
Foster's (Fr.) Thoughts on the Times. 1779.
Hanger's Life and Opinions.
Hanway's Causes of dissoluteness among the lower classes. 1780.
Hurd's (Bp.) Sermons.
Nourse's (P.) Homilies.
Paley's (Wm.) Sermons.
Stebbing's (Henry) Sermons.
Turner (J.) on Fornication.
Wardlaw on Female prostitution.
Wilson's (Thomas) Sermons.
Wilson's (Bp.) Sermons.

Fortitude. See DESPONDENCY.

Limborchii Theologia Christianæ.

Abernethy's (John) Sermons.
Baddelly's (George) Sermons.
Blair's (Hugh) Sermons.
Cappe's Practical discourses.
Duchall's (James) Sermons.
Evans on Christian Temper. Ser. 19.
Fawcett's (John) Sermons.
Foster's (Dr. James) Sermons.
Glass' (Samuel) Sermons.
Hewlett's (John) Sermons.
Hunt's (Jer.) Sermons.
Kennicott's (Benj.) Sermons.
Kidder's (Bp.) Grounds of Christian F.
Leechman's Excellency of Christianity.
Mason's (John) Christian Morals.
Rees' (Abraham) Practical Sermons.
Steel's Christian Hero.
Tucker's Light of nature pursued. Ch. 31.
Watts' Sermons.
Zollikoffer's (Geo. J.) Sermons.

Fortune. See CHANCE, FATE.

Four Kingdoms. See FIFTH MONARCHY.

Deylingii (Salom.) Observationes Sacræ.
Dieterici Antiquitates Sacræ.
Goldast, Monarchia sancti Romani imperii.
Hardt (Herman.) Dissertationes.

Allix's Advent of Christ.
Beroald's View of the Persian Monarchy.
Birk's Four prophetic Empires.
Brown's (J. A.) Eventide.
Heling's Chronology of the four monarchies.
Helvic's Chronology of the four monarchies.

Fourierism. See SOCIALISM.

Fourth Commandmnent. See COMMANDMENTS, CHANGE OF SABBATH LORD'S DAY, SABBATH.

Fox, George.

Fox's (George) Journal.
——— Works.
Life of George Fox; by Janney.
——— ——— by Marsh.
——— ——— by Watson.

Frailty of Life.

Amory's (Thomas) Sermons.
Breckenridge's (John) Sermons.
Bull's (Bp.) Sermons.
Cook's (George) Sermons.
Crowe's (William) Sermons.
Dubois' (Peter) Sermons.
Duchall's (James) Sermons.
Henchman's (Richard) Sermons.
Hodge's (John) Sermons.
Kennett's (Basil) Sermons.
Langhorn's (William) Sermons.
Leighton's (Abp.) Lectures on Psalm 39.
Mason's (John M.) Sermons.
Mayhew's (Jonathan) Sermons.
Miller's (Joseph) Sermons.
Morris' (Joseph) Sermons.
Owen's (John) Sermons.
Quincy's (Samuel) Sermons.
Reeves' (William) Sermons.
Wallis' (Benjamin) Sermons.
Warren's (Robert) Sermons.
Whichcote's (Dr. Benjamin) Sermons.
Williams' (Bp.) Sermons.
Wilson's (William C.) Sermons.

Franciscans.

Albicii Liber Conformitatum.
Antonio Bibliotheca Franciscana.
Aremberg, Flores Seraphici.
Benonia Biblioth. scrip. ord. minorum.
Bouchier, de Martyrio fratrum sub Henrico VIII.
Boverii Flores seraphici. (A vast collection of lives, with 190 plates of miracles done by these friars during the 16th century.)
Bullarium Ordinis fratrum Minorum.
Chalippe, Vie de St. Francois.
Corneii Chronica Seraphica.
Dionysii Genuensis Biblioth. scrip. ordinis Minorum.
Ferot, Hist. des saints et saintes des tres ordres de St. Francois.
Gonzaga de Origine relig. Franciscanæ, ejusque progressu. (Embraces not only the old world, but Mexico, Peru, Yucatan, Chili, &c.)
Gubernati Orbis Seraphicus.
Kresslingeri Ortus et Progressus, &c.
Lanovii Chronicon generale.
Matutensi Bullarium Fratrum Minorum.
Sedulii Historia Franciscana.
Thuellier, Diarium patrum, fratrum et sororum ord. Minorum.
Waddingii Annales ordinis Minorum. ("A work of vast labor, but often fabulous."—WALCH.)
Willeti Athenæ orthodoxorum sodalitii, &c.
Hearne's Hist. of the English Franciscans.

For full lists of Franciscan writers, see SEDULIUS and WADDINGIUS, named above. Waddingius gives the nation of each writer, his topics, number of volumes, &c. His work has several "continuations," bringing it down to 1700, in 25 volumes, folio.

Fraud. See INTEGRITY.

Enfield's (William) Sermons.
Foster's (Dr. James) Sermons.
Whitaker's (Edw. W.) Sermons.

Free Agency.

Augustine, de Gratia et libero arbitrii.
Basil, Opera.

Alvarezii de Auxiliis Div. gratiæ et humani arbitrii libertate.
Amyraldi (Moses) Dissertationes.
Andala (Ruard.) Disputationes.
Chemnitii Examen Concilii Tridentini.
Cochlæus de Libero arbitrio hominis.
Dittes' (F.) Ueber die Sittliche Freiheit. (Revises the systems of Spinoza, Leibnitz, and Kant.)
Erasmi Opera. (His Diatribe on this subject occasioned many publications, pro and con.)
Fischer, Freiheit des mensch. Willens.
Frankii Commentationes.
Haberkornii Vindicatio Lutheri.
Hunnii (Nicol.) Disputationes.
Krafftius de Servo et libero arbitrii.
Luther de Servo arbitrio.
Lyseri (Guil.) Dissertationes.
Märtens' Eleutheros.
Molinæ Liberi arbitrii cum gratiæ donis, providentia, et predestinatione, concordia.
Mori Victoria Gratiæ.
Pennoti Propugnaculum.
Petavius de Libero arbitrio.
Placæi (Iosua) Opera.
Quenstedii (Ioann.) Dissertationes.
Quistorpius de Viribus liberi arbitrii.
Suarez de Divina Gratia.
Thummii (Theod.) Dissertationes.

Barnes' (Robt., the Martyr) Works.
Ball (John) on the Covenant of grace.
Berriman's (William) Sermons.
Bibliotheca Sacra. 4:77.
Brown's (Tho.) Philosophy of the mind.
Buffier's First Truths.
Butler's (Bp.) Sermons.
——— Analogy. Part 1, Ch. 6.
Butterworth on Moral Government.
Cairns (W.) on Moral Freedom.
Cole on Divine Sovereignty.
Crisp's Christ alone exalted.
Crybbace's (T. T.) Essays.
Edwards' (Dr. John) Veritas Redux.
Edwards (Pres.) on the Will.
——— Liberty and necessity.
Emmons' (Nathaniel) Sermons.
Flavel's Method of Grace.
Fuller's (And.) Essays.
Gibbs' Contemplations.
Goodwin's (John) Triumviri.
Hey's (John) Lectures.
Hussey on God's operations of grace.
Investigator. 1:35.
Jackson's Defence of human liberty.

Free Agency—*continued.*

Jortin's Six Dissertations.
Locke on the Human Understanding.
Macombie (W.) on Moral Agency.
Müller's Christian doctrine of sin.
Park Street Lectures. Lect. 10.
Princeton Review. 29:101.
Robinson's Christian System. Essay 14.
Sanderson's (Bp.) Sermons.
Smith's Theory of moral sentiments.
Skelton's (P.) Sermons.
Spring's Dialogues and Disquisitions.
Stebbings' Operations of the Holy Spirit.
Theological Essays reprinted from the Princeton Review.
Tindall's (Wm., the Martyr) Works.
Toplady's Works. (Sermons.)
Townsend's (Geo.) Sermons.
West on Moral Agency. Part 1.
Whedon's Freedom of the will, as a basis of human responsibility.

Free Church of Scotland.

Blackwood's Magazine. 53:352. 55:221.
British Quarterly Review. 1:390.
Bryson's Ten years of the Church of Scotland. (1833 to 1843.)
Buchanan's (Geo.) Ten years' conflict.
Eclectic Museum. 3:305.
Frazier's Magazine. 23:503. 24:112. 28:1.
Princeton Review. 21:82.

Freedom of the Press.

Hall's (Robt.) Works. (Splendid.)
Hunt's (F. K.) History of newspapers. (To 1850.)

Freedom of Opinion. See LIBERTY OF CONSCIENCE, OPINION, PRIVATE JUDGMENT, TOLERATION.

Buddæus de Libertate cogitandi.
Crouza, Examen de traité de la liberté de penser.
Pfaffius de Libertate cogitandi.

Alison's (Archibald) Sermons.
Dupree's (Dr. John) Sermons.
Edinburg Review. 76:198.
Ibbot's Boyle Lectures. 1713, '14.
Princeton Review. 24:312.
Tombs' Saints no Smiters. (Powerful.)

Freemasonry.

Pro.

Acerrello's Freimaurers in ihrem Zusammenhang mit d. Rel. d. Ægypter, der Juden, u. d. Christen.
Encyclopedie Maconique. 1825.
Kloss' Geschichte der Freimaurer.

Ash's Masonic Manual.
Bagnal (Tho.) on Freemasonry.
Calcott's Principles and practices, &c.
Carlisle's Manual of Masonry.

Freemasonry—*continued.*

Pro.

Chandler's Masonic Discourses.
Creigh's Masonry and Antimasonry.
Cross' True Masonic Chart.
——— Masonic text book.
——— Templar's chart.
Davis' Freemason's Monitor.
Entick's Constitutions, Regulations, &c.
Fellowes' Defence of F. (Wood cuts.)
Free Mason's Quarterly Review. London. 1834 to the present.
Harris' (T. M.) Principles, Tendency, &c.
——— Discourses on public occasions.
Hutchinson's Spirit of Masonry.
Hyneman's Masonic Record.
——— Origin of Freemasonry.
Knapp's Genius of Masonry.
Laurie's History of Freemasonry.
Leslie's (C. S.) Principles of Freemasonry.
McCoy's True Masonic guide.
Masonic Library. (A series of 30 volumes, of approved Masonic literature.)
Moore's Ancient Regulations of Masonry.
Morris' Code of Masonic laws.
Oliver's (Rev. J.) Account of the schism among free and accepted Masons in England, in the 18th century.
Oliver's (Geo.) Masonic History.
——— Theocratical philosophy.
——— (Sundry other treatises.)
Preston's Illustrations of Masonry.
Sandys' History of Masonry.

Con.

Adams' (J. Quincy) Letters on Masonry.
Alger's Ritual of Masonry. Plates.
Antimasonic Review. N. York. 1828–1836.
Baruel's History of Jacobinism.
Bernard's Light on Masonry.
Brown's Narrative of the Anti-masonic excitement in 1829.
Carwithen's Antichristian character of M.
Dublin Review. 6:137.
Dublin University Magazine. 52:271.
Fellowes' Mysteries of Masonry.
Freemasonry Exposed; in extracts from its standard authors.
Jones' (H.) Letters on Masonry.
"Master Mason" on Masonry. (Extracts from Masonic authors.)
Morgan's Illustrations of Masonry.
New England Antimasonic Almanac, from 1829 to 1835. (Contains the oaths, signs, grips, &c.)
O'Brien's Round towers of Ireland.
Odiorne's Origin, nature, tendency, &c.
Perkins' Downfall of Masonry.
Preston's Illustrations of Masonry.
Prichard's Masonry detected. 1776.
Proceedings of Anti-Masonic Convention at Albany. 1829, 1830.
——— Boston. 1830, '1, '2, '3, '4.
——— Philadelphia. 1831, '2, '3.
——— Middlebury, Vermont. 1830.

Freemasonry—*continued.*

Con.

Proceedings of Anti-Masonic Convention at Baltimore. 1831, 1832.
And many others.
Robinson's Proofs of a conspiracy, &c.
Rush (Rich.) on Freemasonry.
Spencer's Report to the Senate of N. York, 1830, on the abduction of Morgan.
Stearne's (J. G.) Nature, Tendency, &c.
Stone's (W. L.) Letters on Masonry.
[Ward's (H. D.)] Pretensions of Masonry by a Master Mason.
Whittlesey's Report on the abduction of Morgan.

GOWAN'S *Catalogue*, 1866, embraces 550 treatises on this subject. BARTHELMES' *Catalogue of American books on Freemasonry*, 1856, cites 450.

Free Thinkers. See INFIDELITY.

French Prophets.
See FALSE PROPHETS.

Frequent Communion.

Arnauld, Œuvres. (Gives the sentiments of the Fathers, and decisions of Councils.)
Baker's (D. B.) Sermons.
Beveridge's (Bp.) Advantages of frequent C.
Brown's (John) Apology for more frequent administration.
Duncan (Prof.) on the Lord's Supper.
Erskine's (Dr. John) Theolog. Dissertations.
Girdlestone's Sermons on the Lord's Supper.
Hesketh's Exhortation to frequent C.
Mason's (John M.) Letters.
Patrick (Simon) on the Lord's Supper.
Tillotson's (John) Sermons.
Tracts for the Times. Tract 26.
Wilson's (Thomas) Sermons.
Wordsworth's (Charles) Sermons.

Free Will. See FREE AGENCY.

Free-Will Baptists.

Pro.

The Free-Will Baptist Manual.
The Doctrine.
The Church Member's Book.
History of the Free-Will Baptists.
Memoir of John Colby.
" " Daniel Marks.
" " Benjamin Randall.
Minutes of the General Conference.
Morning Star. Period. Dover, N. Hamp.

Friends ["Hicksite"].

Pro.

Advocate of Truth. Periodical.
Belanger, James, Life of.
Berean, The. Periodical.
Christian Examiner. 51:321.

Friends ["Hicksite"]—*continued.*

Pro.

Cockburn's Review of the late divisions, &c. 1829.
Comly, John, Life of.
Friend's Intelligencer. Periodical. 1844 to present.
Friend's Miscellany. A compilation of 11 volumes.
Gibbon's Review of the causes of the separation.
Hicks, Elias, Life of; by himself.
——— ——— by M. T. C. Gould.
——— Journal and letters.
——— Extemporaneous Discourses.
——— Letters and Essays.
Jackson on the Christian ministry.
Janney's Conversations on religious subjects.
Michener's Annals of "Quakerism."
Paul & Amicus. (A forcible polemic work.)
Report of the trial of Shotwell and others.
Story's Conversations and anecdotes.
The Quaker. Periodical.
Witherald's (Thomas) Sermons.

Con.

Burnap's Elias Hicks and the Hicksites.
Senneff's (George) Bible Advocate.
View of the sentiments of E. Hicks respecting future rewards and punishments.

Numerous pamphlets, *pro* and *con*, were published on this controversy in Pennsylvania and New York, about A. D. 1820–1840.

Friends ["Orthodox"].

Pro.

Benezet, sur les Quakers.
Caton, Alarm, geblasen zu allen Nationen.
Crisp, Klang des Alarms.
Green's Zeugnis an alle Nationen.
Keith (Geo.) Responsio ad Bajeri dissertationem.
Kolhausii Dilucidationes.
Lawson, Antwort auf ein Buch gennant, der Unflat der Quaker.

Abell's Deceit made manifest.
Adams' Exhortation to all who desire to know the truth.
Alexander on Worship and the Ministry.
Anderson's Visitation in love to the people called Baptists.
Armistead's Principles and sufferings of Friends.
Arscott's State of the Chris. religion. 1730.
Ash's (E.) Essays.
——— Christian Doctrine and Practice.
Ashley's Scripture Teachings.
——— Christian Counsel.
——— True light vindicated.
Atkinson's Standard of the Lord.
Aynsloe's Besom of Truth.
Baker's (Daniel) Thundering voice out of Zion.
——— (Many other treatises.

Friends ["Orthodox"]—*continued.*

Pro.

Barclay's Truth cleared of calumny.
——— Theses Theologicæ.
——— Quakerism confirmed.
——— Anarchy of the Ranters.
——— Apology for Christian divinity.
——— Universal love.
——— Inward revelations of the Spirit.
——— Truth triumphant.
——— Many other tracts.
Bates' (Elisha) Doctrines of the Friends.
Bathhurst's (Eliz.) Truth vindicated.
Bayley on the State of man before and after the Fall.
——— Government of the Lamb.
——— Warning to all Papists.
——— Warning to Reformed churches.
Besse's Defence of Quakerism. (Answer to Smith's Preservative.)
Bevan's (John) Salutation to the Baptists.
——— Defence of Quaker doctrines.
Bevan's (Tho.) Reply to Plymton.
Burroughs' (Edw.) Works. 1672. (A very voluminous collection of the writings of Fox and others.)
Camm's Truth prevailing against Clamor.
Caton's (Wm.) Enquirer resolved. 1660.
Chalkely's (Thomas) Works. 1751.
Chandler's Apology for Quakers. 1714.
Claridge's (Richard) Works. 1723.
Clarkson's Portraiture of Quakerism. 1806.
Crisp's (Stephen) Scripture Truths. 1693.
——— Charitable Advice.
——— Declarations.
Crouch's Posthuma Christiana. 1712.
Crook's (John) Works.
Dewsberry's Works.
Ellwood's Forgery no Christianity.
——— Other Treatises.
Epistles of Yearly and Monthly Meetings. (Contain a great amount of wisdom and piety.)
Evans' Exp. of the faith of Friends. 1828.
Farnsworth's Light rising out of darkness.
Field's Defence of the people called Q.
——— Light and truth.
Fisher's (Samuel) Works. 1679.
Forster's Quakers defended. 1732.
Fothergill's Life, travels, and letters. 1780.
——— Reply to Owen on Baptism.
Fox's (Geo.) Journal. (A deeply interesting book.)
——— Various works.
Friend's Intelligencer. Phil. 1838, et seq.
Friend's Review. Phil. 1847 to the present.
Fuce's Fall of the visible idol.
Fuller's (Sam.) Reply to Joseph Boyle.
Grattan on Baptism and the Lord's supper.
Grubb's Life and religious labors.
Gurney's (J. J.) Distinguishing views, &c. 1825.
——— Peculiarities of the Society of Friends. 1840.
Gutton's Remarks on Quaker principles.

Friends ["Orthodox"]—*continued.*

Pro.

Hancock's (Tho.) Reply to Crewdson.
——— Several other treatises.
Haydock's Writings, labors, and sufferings.
Helton's (John) Reasons for quitting the Methodists.
Hodden's One good way of God.
Holme's Serious call to all people.
Howgill's (Francis) Works.
Hubbertson's Works. (Voluminous.)
Keese's The Church and the People.
Lawson's (Tho.) Baptismalogia. 1703.
Marshall's Way of life revealed.
——— Various other treatises.
Naylor's Old serpent's voice.
——— Discovery of the Man of sin.
——— Answer to Baxter's Q. catechism.
——— Satan's designs discovered.
——— Wickedness weighed.
——— Blindness of Babel's builders.
Pemberton's (John) Life and Travels.
Penn's (Wm.) Primitive Christ'y revived.
——— Innocency with open face.
——— Defence of Gospel truths.
——— Complete works. 2 thick folios. 1756.
Pennington's (Isaac) Works. 1761.
Phillip's Vindiciæ Veritatis.
Phipps' (Joseph) Works.
Pike on Baptism and the Lord's supper.
Pugh's (Ellis) Salutation to Brittons.
Rogers' (Wm.) Christian Quaker.
Russel's Quakerism no Paganism.
Rutty on Women's preaching.
——— on Christian discipline.
Salthouse's Works.
Savery's Discourses.
Stephenson's Call from death. 1667.
Tuke's Principles of the Quakers.
White's (Dorothy) Works.
Whitehead's Antidote to the venom of the snake in the grass.
——— Christian Quaker.
——— Apology for the Quakers.
——— Truth prevalent.
——— Other works.
Whitehouse's Doct. of perfection vindicated.
Whiting's (John) Life and writings. 1708.
Woolrich's Declaration to the Baptists.
Woolman's (J.) Works. 1794.

Con.

Arnoldi Exercitatio de Quakerismo.
Baieri Collatio Doct. Quakerorum et Protestantium.
Berkendal's der Quacker geist entdecket.
Colberg, Platonisch-hermetischen Christen.
Croesii Historia Quakeriana.
Danhaveri Disputationes Theologicæ.
Loeber's Quaker Greuels.
Morgenbesser's Prüfung d. Quaker-pulvers.
Müller (J.) Quaker-quakeln.
Neumanni Synopsis errorum fanaticorum quos Tremuli fovent.

Friends ["**Orthodox**"]—*continued.*

Con.

Paul's Augensalbe vor die welche sagen, &c.
——— Quaker Glaube und Dienst.
Rhayii Confusa confessio tremulantium.
Rieseri Anti-Barclaius.
Schelvigii Quakerismus confutatus.
Schroederus de Spiritu.

Adamson's Quaker principles quaking.
Alexander's Jesuitico-Quakerism.
Allen's Danger of Enthusiasm.
American Quarterly Review. 15:380.
Andrews' Expostulation with the Quakers.
Audland's Spirit of Quakerism.
Ball's Holy Scripture the test of truth.
Bartlett's Soveraigne balsame applied.
Bates' Quakero-Methodism.
Baxter's (R.) Quaker's Catechism.
Bennett's (Thos.) Necessity of Revelation.
——— Confutation of Quakerism.
Bewick's Answer to Quakerism.
Bristed (John) on the Society of Friends.
Brown's Quakerism the road to Paganism.
Brownlee (Will. C.) on Quakerism.
Bugg's (Francis) Picture of Quakerism.
——— Sober expostulations.
——— Pilgrim's Progress from Quakerism to Christianity.
——— Quaker principles exposed. 1699.
——— Various other bitter treatises.
Burrough's Generation of the Quakers.
Byne's Scornful Quakers answered.
Christian Monthly Spectator. 6:530.
Christian Observer. 13:95.
Cockson's Quaker dissected.
Cox's Quakerism not Christianity.
Dove on Inspiration. (Internal light.)
Eaton's Quaker confuted.
Faldo's Quakerism no Christianity.
Grey's True picture of Quakerism.
Hale's Quaker principles quaking.
Hancock's (John) Reason for withdrawing from the Society.
——— The Peculium.
Haworth's Quaker confuted.
Hicke's Q. condemned out of his own mouth.
Jenner's Quakerism anatomized.
Kay's Answer to 18 queries. (Reply to Whitehead.)
Keach's Quaker doctrine weighed.
Keith's (Geo.) Deism of Wm. Penn exposed.
——— Doctrine of the Apostles.
——— Magic of Quakerism. (Against Barclay.)
——— Serious call to the Quakers.
——— Many other treatises.
Leslie's Snake in the grass.
——— Defence of the same.
——— Primitive heresy revived.
——— Other tracts.
Maurice's (F. D.) Kingdom of Christ.
Moore & Horne's Dangerous principles of the Quakers. (Especially against George and John Whitehead and George Fox.)

Friends ["**Orthodox**"]—*continued.*

Con.

Newton's Sentiments of the Quakers.
Norris' Works.
Pilkington's Address to Quakers.
Plimpton's Charges against the Quakers.
Princeton Review. 5:417. 20:353.
Pryne's Quaker unmasked.
Roswell's Answer to 30 queries.
Russell's Quakerism is Paganism. (Reply to Luddington.)
Scaudrell's Antidote against Quakerism.
Scotton's Becoldus redivivus.
Sharp's (Granville) Principles of the Q.
Sherlock's Quaker's questions answered.
Smith's (Pat.) Preservative against Q.
Stalham's Reviler rebuked.
Stebbing's Conference with Middleton.
Stillingfleet's Advice concerning Quakerism.
Taswell's Antichrist revealed.
Thompson's Letter to Wm. Penn.
Thornley's Doctrines of Barclay's Apology.
Underhill's (T.) Hell broke loose.
Weld's Perfect Pharisee.
Wilkinson's Quakerism examined. (Reply to Tuke.)

After this article was written I expunged about half the citations as superfluous. For a list of over three thousand works, controversial and practical, see JOHN WHITING'S "*Catalogue of Friends' books,* from the first appearance of said people." 1708.

Friends, History of.

See FOX, PENN, RELIGIONS.

Alberti's Nachrict von der Relig. d. Quäker.
Arnold's (G.) Kirchen und Ketzerhistorie. 1688.
Croesii Hist. Quakeriana. 1695. (The first history of this people.)
Danhaveri Disputationes Theologicæ.
Gregoire, Histoire des Sects. (History of the French Quakers.)
Histoire abregée de la Naissance et du progres du Quakerisme. (Acta erudit.)
Lassen's Historie der Quakerischen Secte.
[Naudé] Histoire de la naissance, &c.

Allen, Wm., Life of. Died 1843.
Backhouse, Edw., Life of. 1854.
Barclay's (John) Memoirs of the Friends in the North of Scotland.
Benezet's Origin of the religious society of Friends. 1780.
Besse's Sufferings of the Quakers. (From 1650 to 1689. 2 vols., folio.)
Bishop's New England judged. (An acc. of the persecution of Quakers. 1656 to 1660.)
Bowden's History of Friends in America. To 1845.
Chris. Exam. 2:252. 30:237. 40:145. 51:322.
Clark's Portraiture of Quakerism. (See Edinburg Review. 10:85.)

Friends, History of—*continued.*

Clark's Memoirs of the private and public life of Wm. Penn. (See Edinb. Rev. 21:444.)
Crisp, Stephen, Life of. 1695.
Croese's General History of the Quakers.
Crouch's (W.) Collection of papers, &c. 1712.
Davis' Digest of legislative enactments relating to the Quakers in England. 1849.
Davies' (Rich.) Travels in North Wales.
De Thou's (Madame) History of the Q.
Eclec. Rev. 4th Series. 1:280. N. S. 5:225.
Edinburg Review. 10:85. 87:503.
Edmundson's Journal of his life.
Fox's (Geo.) Journal. 1694.
Fox's (Jos. John) Inquiry into the causes of the weakness, &c. 1860.
Fothergill's Essay on the Society of Friends. (Causes of its decline. 1860.)
Gough's History of the Quakers. To 1790.
Hancock's Peculium. (Causes of the decline.) 1859.
Holmes' Travels in Europe and America. 1753.
Jaffray's Rise and prog. of Q. in Scotland.
Ketty's Memoirs of the primitive Quakers.
Littell's Living Age. 17:390.
Macnair's Causes of the moral and numerical decline of the Society of Friends. 1860.
Mather's (Cotton) History of New England.
Minutes of Quarterly and yearly meetings.
Mosheim's Eccles. History. (Supplement.)
Naylor, James, Life of.
Nile's Register. 24:303. 45:11.
North British Review. 27:180.
Penn's Rise and progress, &c.
Ree's Cyclopedia. (Art. "Quaker.")
Rountree's Quakerism, past and pres. 1859.
Rutty's History of Irish Quakers. 1750.
Sewell's History of the rise, increase, &c.
Tuke's Biographical notices of eminent members of the Society.
Wagstaff's History of the Quakers. 1845.
Westminster Review. 1:593.
Wight's Rise and progress of the Quakers in Ireland. 1653 to 1700. Continued by Rutty.
Yearly Meeting Minutes.

Friendship.

Abercrombie's Moral feelings. Part 1, sec. 2.
Arnold's (Thomas) Sermons.
Blair's (Hugh) Sermons.
Burton's (Edward) Sermons at Oxford.
Case's (Charles) Sermons.
Coney's (Thomas) Sermons.
Darnell's (W. N.) Sermons.
Dodwell's (William) Sermons.
Enfield's (William) Sermons. (Caution in forming.)
Franklin's (Thomas) Sermons.
Holland's (John) Sermons.
Hopkins' (Dr. Sam.) System of Divinity.
Lawton's (Edward) Lectures.
Lochier's (Nicolas) Sermons.
McCrie's (Dr. Thomas) Sermons.
Mann's (Bp.) Sermons.
Pierce's (John) Sermons.
Porteus' (Bp.) Sermons.
Short's (T. V.) Sermons.
Short's (William) Sermons.
Taylor's Nature and offices of friendship.
Wilkins' (Bp.) Sermons.

Frivolity. See DISCRETION, SOBRIETY.

Frugality. See PRODIGALITY.

Buckminster's (Joseph) Sermons.
Burgh's Dignity of Hum. nature. Bk. 1. pt. 2.
McKenzie's Moral history of frugality and its opposite vices.

Fruits of the Spirit. See SPIRITUALITY.

Bethune's (Geo. W.) The Fruits of the Sp.
Haweis' (Thomas) Sermons.
Hooper's (Bp.) Sermons.
Mant's (Bp.) Sermons.
Potts' (J. H.) Sermons.
Sanderson's (Bp.) Sermons.
Secker's (Abp.) Sermons.
Thornton's Fruits of the Spirit.
Vaughn's (Henry) Sermons.
Yonge's (James) Sermons.

Fulness of Time. See SEVENTY WEEKS.

Frischmuthii Prosographia Messiæ.

Amer. Presbyterian Review. 4:375.
Berriman's Boyle Lectures. 1730.
Cunninghame on the Chron. of the LXX.
Clarke's (Dr. Samuel) Sermons.
Clayton's Time of the coming of Christ.
Collinson's (J.) Observations.
Delany's (Patrick) Sermons.
Fiddes' (Richard) Discourses.
Foster's (Dr. James) Sermons.
Hall's Bampton Lectures. 1798.
Hartes' (W. M.) Sermons.
Hoare's (Cha. J.) Course of Div. judgments.
Hetherington's (W. M.) Fulness of time.
Horne's (Bp.) Discourses.
Jenkins' Reasonableness of Christianity.
Le Bas' (Cha. W.) Sermons.
Lord's Theo. and Lit. Journal. 4:447. 5:469.
Maclaurin's Essays.
Marshall's (Nathan) Sermons.
Robinson's Proph. of the Messiah.
Secker's (Abp.) Sermons.
White's Fitness of the time when Christ came.

Fundamentals.

Aymé, les Fondemens de la foi.
Bergii Disputationes Theologicæ.
Curtius de Articulis fundamentalibus.
Graverolius de Artic. fundamentalibus.
Holdeni Divinæ fidei Analysis.
Hulsemanni (Ioann.) Disputationes.
Meisneri (J.) Irenicum Duræanum.
Pfaffius de Fidei Christi articulis, ejusque analogia.

Fundamentals—*continued.*

Schmidtii (Seb.) Dissertationes.
Sennertus de Articulis fidei fundamental.
Spanheimii Disputationes.
Turrettini (J. A.) Disquisitiones.
Walch's Geschichte der Glaubenslehre.
Wandalinus Dissertationes.
Zeltneri (Gustav.) Dissertationes. ("Cur articuli fidei fundamentales non sint in scrip. sacra pressus definiti?")

Baxter's Saint's Rest. Ch. 3.
Bennet on Scripture.
Burder's (Henry F.) Lectures.
Burton's (Dr. John) Concio ad clerum.
Byfield's Principles: or, Wholesome words.
Chillingworth's Safe way to salvation.
Clarke's (Samuel) Sermons.
Craddock's Knowledge and practice.
Douglass' (James) Truths of Religion.
Foster's (James) Essay on fundamentals.
Hammond's (Henry) Works.
Holden's Analysis of faith.
Locke's Reasonableness of Christianity.
MacCosh on Fundamentals.
Milner's (Jos.) Essentials of Christianity.
Moore on Fundamentals. (The genuine marks of a fundamental.)
Pollock's (Wm.) Essays on fund. truths.
Rymer on Revelation.
Short's (Tho. V.) Sermons.
Taylor's (Dan.) Fund. of faith and practice.
Waterland's Discourses and Charges.
Whowell's Essentials of faith.

Funeral Sermons.

Alden, T., on Gen. Washington.
Appleton, N. Several.
Ashworth, C., on Isaac Watts.
Baldwin, Tho., on Gov. Phillips.
Bentley, W., on B. Hodges.
——— on Gen Fiske.
Buckminster, J., on S. Haven and wife.
Calamy, Edm., on Mrs. Williams.
Chandler, S., on T. Hadfield.
——— on G. Smith.
——— on M. Lowman.
Dana, D., on Gen. Washington.
Doddridge, P., on I. Norris.
——— on a Child.
Edwards, Jon., on D. Brainerd.
Everett, Edw., on J. L. Abbot.
Featley, Dan. Several.
Fleetwood, Bp., on Duke of Gloucester.
Fleming, C., on J. Foster.
Forbes', Bp., Funeral sermons.
Foster, J., on T. Emlyn.
Furman, Rich., on Gen. Washington.
Gadsden, C., on Bp. Dehon.
Gano, John, on Gen. Washington.
Hall, Robt., on Princess Charlotte.
Harris', W., Funeral discourses.
Hitchcock, E., on Gen. Washington.
Knaggs, T., on Princess Sophia.
Lardner, N., on W. Harris.

Funeral Sermons—*continued.*

Mather, Cotton. Many.
Mayhew, J., on S. Sewall.
Mellen, J., on I. Dunster.
Norton, J., on his Wife.
Nott, Eliphalet, on Alex. Hamilton.
Orton, J., on P. Doddridge.
Parsons, J., on Geo. Whitefield.
Patrick, Bp., on I. Smith.
Pemberton on Geo. Whitefield.
Phillips, S., on a Suicide.
Priestley, J., on Dr. Price.
Reeves, W., on the Queen.
Ridgeley, T., on murder of N. Hall.
Sherlock, W., on Rev. Edm. Calamy.
Showers', J., Funeral discourses.
Skinner, I., on his Wife.
Stennett, J., on J. Piggott.
Stillman, Sam., on S. Ward.

See a list of over 200 funeral sermons in HORNE'S "*Catalogue of Queen's library.*" Also an extensive list in PEIRCE'S "*Systematic Index to the Catalogue of the library of Harvard College.*"

Future Punishment.
See ANNIHILATION, DESTRUCTION, ETERNITY OF HELL TORMENTS, HELL, RESTORATIONISTS, UNIVERSALISM.

Future State.
See FAITH OF THE PATRIARCHS.

Gerardi Loci Theologici.
Kiesselbachii Dogma de rebus post mortem futuris e vet. test. illustratum.

Alger's Critical history of the doctrine of a future life.
Amer. Bibl. Repository. 3d Series. 2:686.
Amory's (Tho.) Sermons.
Amyrald's State of the soul after death.
Bakewell's Evidences of a future life from the properties of matter.
Balguy's (Thomas) Six Sermons.
Barrow's (Isaac) Works.
Baxter's Reasonableness of Christianity.
Beattie's Elements of Moral science.
Belsham's Essays. Ess. 11 and 12.
Beveridge's (Bp.) Sermons.
Bibliotheca Sacra. 15:381,625,753.
Blair's (James) Sermons. (Degrees of punishment.)
Boston's Fourfold state.
Broughton's (Thomas) Dissertations.
Bull's (Bp.) Sermons.
Butler's Analogy of Religion and Nature.
Campbell's Notes on Matthew's Gospel.
Christian Examiner. 7:390. 8:115,265.
Clarke's (Samuel) Boyle Lectures. 1706.
Copland's Mortal life. ("Gives all that can be known on the subject."—LOWNDES.)
Craven's Jewish and Christian dispensation compared.
Crombie's Natural Theology.
Dick's Philosophy of a future state.

Future State—*continued.*

Doddridge's Lectures.
Ferns on Human bodies in their state of glorification.
Fiddes' (Rich.) Doctrine of a future state.
Franklin's (Thomas) Sermons.
Furguson's Princ. of moral science. Ch. 3.
Gastrel's Boyle Lectures. 1737.
Griffin's Scriptural account, &c.
Grove's Proofs of a future state.
Hall's (Bp.) Devotional Works.
Hallet's Notes on Scripture.
Hooker's (Herman) Portion of the Soul.
Howe's Vanity of Man.
Humphrey's Hulsean Lectures. 1849.
Lancaster's Harmony of law and gospel.
Lounsdale's Testimonies of Nature, Reason, and Revelation.
Mant's (Bp.) Happiness of the Blessed.
Masillon's Sermons.
Mercier (L. P.) on a Future State.
Mills' Belief of the Jew and Gentile philos.
Nicolson's Conferences between the soul and the body.
Panoplist. Vol. 11.
Parker's Law of Nature.
Physical Theory of another life.
Porteus' (Bp.) Sermons.
Protestant Layman's [Alex. Copland] State of the soul after death. (Very comprehensive.)
Price's Evidences of a future state.
——— on Morals.
Reader's Views and Reflections.
Romaine's (William) Sermons.
Sherlock on the Happiness and misery of the next world.
Shuttleworth's (P. N.) Sermons.
Spectator. No. 111.
Stuart's (Moses) Essays.
Sturges' (Dr. John) Discourses.
Talbot (Mrs.) on a Future state.
Thompson (E.) on Future Happiness.
Tillotson's Sermons.
Tottie's (John) Sermons.
Warburton's Divine legation of Moses.
Watson's Intimations and Evidences.
[Whately's] Scripture Revelations.
Young's Night-Thoughts. No. 7.

ALGER'S *Critical history*, cited above, gives a complete bibliography of the subject, presenting the views of all nations and creeds, ancient and modern.

Galenists. See MENNONITES.

Commelini Descriptio urbis Amstelodami.
Schyn, Deductio plenior historia Mennonit. Cap. 15–18.
Stoupa's Religion der Hollander.

Gaming. See LOTS.

Atterbury's (Lewis) Sermons.
Balmford (James) on Games of chance.

Gaming—*continued.*

Brown's (Dr. John) Sermons. (This powerful sermon is said to have caused the suppression of public gambling houses of Bath, in 1750.)
Collier's (Jer.) Works. (Essay on Gaming.)
Delany's (Patrick) Sermons.
Denham's (Sir John) Timely Advice.
Dorrington's (Theophilus) Sermons.
Dwight's (Tim.) Sermons. Ser. 124.
Green's Gambling unmasked.
——— The Gambler's life.
——— Secret band of brothers.
——— Reformed Gambler: an autobiogr.
Hey's Pernicious effects of gaming.
Holloway's Letter to Sir Richard Ford.
Moore's (C.) Essays. Ess. 3.
Rennel's (Thomas) Sermons.
Ridgeley's Body of Divinity.
Rush's (Judge) Charges.
Wilcox's Glass for Gamesters.
Zollikoffer's Sermons on prevalent vices.

Gaudama. See BUDHISM.

Gaurs. See MAGI.

Gehenna. See HELL.

Benzelii Dissertationes.

Balfour's Import of Hades, Gehenna, &c.
——— Reply to J. Sabine.
——— Reply to Prof. Stuart.
——— Other treatises.
Campbell's (Geo.) Preliminary Dissertations.
Fair (J.), The Elegchios. (Rep. to Balfour.)
Livermore's Bible doctrine of Hell.
Palmer's (John E.) Essays.
Scott's (Russel) Lectures.
Stuart's (Moses) Exegetical Essays.

Gemara. See TALMUD.

Genealogies.

Felsdorf's Völkertafel der Genesis.

Burrington's Genealogies of the Old Testam. and Apocrypha; and also certain Kings of Egypt, Syria, &c.
Leigh's (Sam.) Scripture Genealogies from Adam to Christ. (Exhibits the nation, tribe, family, and posterity of every person mentioned in the Bible.)
Morris' G. of every family in Sacred Script.
Palfrey's (J. G.) Academical Lectures.

Genealogy of Christ.

Benzelii Dissertationes.
Braselmann's Messianische Stammbaum.
Calmeti (Aug.) Dissertationes.
Calovii (Abr.) Dissertationes.
Chemnitii (M.) Dissertationes.
Eusebii Historia Ecclesiastica.
Flinsbachii Genealogia Christi.
Kockii Disquisitio exegetico-historica de utraque geneal. Christi.

Genealogy of Christ—*continued.*

Lagorce, l'Arbre généalogique.
Langii (Ioann. Mich.) Dissertationes.
Lentzii (Salom.) Dissertationes.
Meigius de Stemmate Davidico-Christi.
Michaelis (I.) de Temporalibus, &c.
Rabani (Mauri) Opera.
Richardson, Prælectiones Ecclesiasticæ.
Vossii (G. J.) Dissertatio Gemina.

Barrington's Genealogies of the Old Test.
Beeston's Genealogies of Matt. and Luke.
Berry's Scripture Tables.
Bibliotheca Sacra. 18:410.
Blair's Chronological Tables.
Broughton's (Hugh) Works.
Christian Observer. 11:72.
Cochrane's (James) Discourses. (The two genealogies compared.)
Green's Genealogy of Jesus Christ.
Greswell's (Edward) Dissertations.
Hervey's (Lord Arthur) G. of our Lord.
Kitto's Journal of Sacred Literature. 3:197.
Luther's (Martin) Sermons.
Methodist Quarterly Review. 11:593.
Morris' Scripture Genealogies.
Speed's Cloud of Witnesses.
Sympson's Explication of Christ's G.
Vilvain's Theses of Divinity.
Watson's Genealogy of Christ.
Whiston's Harmony of the Evangelists.
Yardley's Genealogies of C. reconciled.

General Baptists.

Baptist Repository. Periodical. London.
Blackwood's Storming of Antichrist.
Braidwood's Letters on Church order.
Fisher's Baby baptism meer Babism.
Foster's (Dr. James) Works.
Gale's (Dr. John) Works.
Haldane's (J. A.) View of Social Worship.
Killingworth's (G.) Letter to Rev. Mr. Whiston. (A full account of their principles, &c. 1757.)
McLean's Apostolical Commission.
Taylor (Dan.), Life of; by Adam Taylor.
——— Principal parts of religion.
Taylor (Adam) Hist. of the Gen. Baptists.

Many of the writers under Baptists, pro., are General Baptists. The name implies only that they are not Calvinistic on the subject of the Atonement.

Generation. See TRADUCTION.

Gentiles. See PAGANISM.

Gentleness. See COURTESY, FORBEARANCE, PEACEABLENESS, POLITENESS.

Gentoos. See BRAHMINISM.

Genuineness of 1 John v. 7.

Pro.

Bengelii Apparatus Criticus.

Genuineness of 1 John v. 7—*continued.*

Pro.

Gerhardus de Tribus testibus in Cœlo.
Ketneri Hist. dicti Joannei de S. S. Trinitate.
Wagneri (J. E.) Integritas 1 Joan. v. 7.

Bull's Judgment of the Catholic Church.
Burgess' Three letters to Dr. Scholz.
——— Selection of Tracts.
——— on 1 John v. 7. (Rep. to Griesbach.)
——— Reply to the Quarterly Review.
Butler's (C.) Horæ Biblicæ. (States the evidences on both sides.)
Calamy's (Ed.) Sermons on the Trinity.
Delany's (Pat.) Sermons and Dissertations.
Edwards' (Bp.) Body of divinity.
Emlyn's Enquiry into the authenticity, &c.
Gill's Commentary: *in loco.*
Hammond's Commentary: *in loco.*
Henderson's Mystery of godliness. (Refutation of Sir Isaac Newton.)
Hey's Lectures in Divinity.
Huysch's Examination of Porson's 4th letter to Travis.
——— Examination of Wiseman's letters.
Jones' (John) Letters to the Quart. Review.
Knittel's New criticisms on 1 John v. 7.
Martin's (D.) Critical Diss. on 1 John v. 7.
——— Examination of Emlyn's reply.
Mills' New Testament. (Giving the evidence of all antiquity, for and against, and his own judgment.)
Selection of tracts on 1 John v. 7, by Bp. Barlow, Bp. Smallbrook, Dr. Bentley, and others.
Sloss on the Doctrine of the Trinity.
Smith's (Tho.) Miscellanea.
Stillingfleet (Bp.) on the Trinity.
Travis' Letters to Gibbon. (Replies to Benson, Newton, Griesbach, Wetstein, &c.)
Wheatley's Lady Moyer's Lecture. 1734.
Wiseman's (Nic.) Two letters on some parts of the controversy.
Worcester's (Bp.) Vindication of the Trinity.

Con.

Griesbachii Diss. (At the end of his N. T.)
Scholtz, Diatribe brevis, in loc. 1 Joh. v. 7.
Semleri Introductio ad Nov. Testamentum.
Simon, Critique du passage St. Jean v. 7.
Smithii (Thomas) Dissertationes.

Benson (Geo.) on the Epistles. *In loco.*
Dobbins' (O. T.) Codex of Montford collated.
Eclectic Review. 3d Series. 3:181.
Emlyn's Inquiry into the authority, &c.
——— Answer to Martin's Dissertation.
——— Reply to Martin's Answer.
——— Collection of Tracts.
Le Clerc's Art of Criticism.
Marsh's Letters to Dr. Travis.
Michaelis' Introduction to the N. Testament. Tr. by Marsh, with notes.
Newton's (Sir I.) Historical account of two notable corruptions of the Scripture.
Oxlee's Letters to Rev. Mr. Nolan.

Genuineness of 1 John v. 7—*continued.*

Con.

Oxlee's Letters to the Bishop of Salisbury.
Porson's Letters to Archdeacon Travis.
Smith on the Socinian controversy.
Turton's Vindication of the literary character of Porson. (Reply to Burgess.)
Westminster Review. 6:523.
Wetstein on 1 John v. 7.

MILLS, who is cited above, gives the evidence of all antiquity, for and against, and his own judgment. For a full account of the writers on this controversy, see BUTLER, and CRITICUS, as above; also HORNE'S *Introduction*, Vol. 2. But the works of TRAVIS, PORSON, and MARSH, named above, exhaust the controversy, which, indeed, is considered settled. Rev. W. ORME published, in 1830, a *Memoir of the controversy respecting the three heavenly witnesses.*

Genuineness of 1 Tim. iii. 16.

Pro.

Baumgarten, Vind. vocis Θεος 1 Tim. iii. 16.
Weber, Crisis loci Paulini 1 Tim. iii. 16.

Berriman's Crit. Dissertation. (Gives the readings of 100 MSS.)
Biblical Repository. 1:777.
Henderson's Great mystery of godliness.
Stuart's Various readings of 1 Tim. iii. 16.
Velthuysen's True reading of 1 Tim. iii. 16.

Geography of Scripture. See DEAD SEA, ILLUSTRATIONS, JERUSALEM, JORDAN, PALESTINE.

Abarbanelis Dissertationes. 1495.
Adrichomii Theatrum Terræ sanctæ. 1590.
Beda (Venerab.) de Locis Sanctis. 1563.
Bernardi Commentatio de causis quibus effectum sit, ut regnum Judæ diutius persisteret quam Israel. 1825. (Prize essay.)
Bocharti Phaleg et Canaan. 1660.
——— Geographia Sacra. 1690.
Bonfrerii Onomasticon Urbium, &c. 1631.
Buntingii Itinerarium Biblicum. 1606.
Buxtorfii (Filii) Dissertationes. 1620.
Cellarii Geog. antiqua, juxta, et nova. 1701.
Clerici Onomasticon. 1715.
Cloden's Landeskunde von Palästina. 1817.
Crome, des Landes Syrien. 1834.
Deylingii Observationes Sacræ. 1735.
Dicel's Beshreibung der Welt, &c. 1704.
Dufour, Geog. Sacrée. (Describes the holy land as in the period between the Patriarchs and the Apostles.)
Eusebius de Locis Hebræicis. (The best edition is that of 1720.)
Hottinger, Geog. terræ Chanaan. 1650.
Lightfoot (Jos.), Chronographia. 1684.
Michaelis (J. D.) Geographia Hebræorum. 1751.
Raumer's Palestina. 1835.

Geography of Scripture—*continued.*

Relandi Palestina: ex monumentis vet illustrata. 1714. ("The most valuable work on Biblical geography ever printed."—ORME.)
Ritter's (Carl) Erdkunde. B. XV, XVI, XVII.
Rosenmuller's Handbuch der biblischen Alterthumskunde.
Sansonis Geographia Sacra. 1665.
Spanheimii Introd. ad G. antiquam. 1679.
Vitringa Geog. Sacra. 1723. (6 vols., 4to.)
Wagnerus de Ur Chaldæorum. 1681.
Wiltsch, Atlas Sacer, inde ab antiquissimis relig. chr. propagatæ temporibus, usque ad sec. XVI. 1843.

Alexander's Geography of the Bible. 1830.
Allen's Ancient Geography.
Arrowsmith's Geog. Dict. of Script. 1855.
Beker's Origines Biblicæ. 1834.
Bogue's (D.) Lectures. 1810.
Carpenter's Geog. of N. Test. (Small.)
Cheever's Sacred Streams. 50 plates. 1804.
Coleman's Bible G. and Atlas. 1850.
Condor's (Josiah) Modern traveller. 1835. (33 useful volumes, embracing as many subjects.)
Cooper's Scripture Gazetteer. 1855.
Cox's Geography, Topography, &c. 1852.
D'Anville's Complete body of ancient Geog.
Fairbairn's Biblical Geography.
Flemming's Gazetteer of O. and N. T. 1838.
Foster's Histor. Geog. of Arabia. 1844.
Gosse's Rivers of the Bible. 1850.
Hemings' Scripture G. 1818. (Very full.)
Hughes' (E.) Scripture Geography. 1850.
Journal of the Royal Geographical Society. London. 1830 to the present.
Keith's Land of Israel. 1844. Maps and plates.
Kitto's Biblical Cyclopedia. 1841.
——— Physical G. of the Holy land.
Laurent's (P. E.) Ancient Geography.
McFarlane's Mountains of the Bible. 1849.
Mansford's Scripture Gazetteer.
Mayo's View of Ancient Georgraphy.
Middleton's New System of Geography.
Miles' Dict. of Scripture Geog. (Gives hist. population, custom, produce, and present condition. 1838.)
Parish's Gazetteer of the Bible.
Phillips' (J. S.) Approximations of proph.
Ransom's Biblical Topography. Maps.
Robinson's Physical G. of Palestine. 1865.
——— Biblical Researches in Palestine, Mt. Sinai, and Arabia Petræa. 1852.
Rosenmuller's Biblical Geography of Central Asia. Trans. by N. Morren. 1841.
Sansom's Geographia Sacra.
Simes' Sacred Geography in the form of a Dictionary. 1835.
Stanley's Sinai and Palestine.
Toy's Dict. of the Scripture Geography.
Tullidge's (Henry) Triumphs of the Bible.

Walton's Prolegomena. 1650.
Wells' Ancient Geography. 1711.
Wigram's G. of the Holy land. Maps. 1836.
Wilton's Negel; or the "South Country" of Sacred Scripture.

Geology. See HARMONY OF SCIENCE AND REVELATION.

Amer. Biblical Repository. 5:439. 6:46,261. 7:210,448. 9:78. 10:328. 11:1. 12:1.
Amer. Eclectic Review. 2:87. 3:576.
Amer. Journal of Science. Many articles.
Amer. Quarterly Review. 6:73. 7:361.
Anderson's (John) Course of Creation.
Anderson's (Robt.) Introd. to Geology.
Ansted's Great Stone-book of Nature.
Bailey's Genesis of the world.
Bakewell's (Robt.) Introd. to Geology.
Beke's Researches into primæval history. (The first attempt [1834] to reconstruct history on the principles of modern G.)
Bibliotheca Sacra. 15:300.
Brande's Outline of Geology.
Brown's Geology of Scripture.
Buckland's Bridgewater Treatise.
Bugge's Scripture G (Reply to Cuvier.)
Bush (Prof. Geo.) on Genesis.
Candlish (R. S.) on Genesis.
Christian Examiner. 29:335. 53:51.
Christian Review. 2:552. 15:380.
Coles' Popular G. subversive of Scripture. (Reply to Sedwick.)
Crofton's Genesis and Geology. (A fine introduction by Dr. Hitchcock.)
Cuvier's Theory of the Earth.
Dana's (D.) Geology. 21 plates.
De Luc's Physical history of the earth.
——— Geology.
Eclectic Magazine. 1:187.
Eclectic Review. 4th Series. 1:23. 3:185. 7:426. 11:216. 13:558. 35:468. New Series. 1:672.
Evangelical Review. 1:363.
Fairholme's General view of Scripture G.
——— New Demonstrations. 1840.
Fowler's Remarks on Genesis. (Reply to Buckland.)
Gillespie's Theology of Geologists.
Gisborne's Consistency of modern Geology with Scripture.
Gloag's Primitive World.
Gosse's (Henry) Omphalos.
Gray's (James) Harmony of Scrip. and G.
Harcourt's Doctrine of the Deluge.
Harris' (John) Pre-adamite Earth.
Higgins' Mosaic and mineral G. compared.
Hitchcock's (Edw.) Religion of Geology.
Johnsone's Defence of the word of God. (Answers Buckland.)
King's G. in relation to Religion.
Kirwan's (Rich.) Geological Essays.
Kitto's Journal. 2:115. 6:261.
Littell's Living Age. 4:597. 6:597.
Lord's (David) Geognosy.
Lord's (E.) Epoch of creation.

Geology—*continued.*

Lord's Theol. and Lit. Journal. 5:1. 8:445.
Mantell's Medals of Creation.
McCausland's Sermons in stones.
McClelland's Kemaon.
Methodist Quarterly Review. 5:198.
Miller's (Hugh) Works.
Monthly Review. 126:133.
New York Review. 5:457.
Nimshi's Scriptural Geology.
Penn's (G.) Mineral and Mosaic Geologies.
Pratt's Genealogy of creation.
Presbyterian Review. 1:83.
Princeton Review. 11:271 (on Bush). 13:368.
Quarterly Journal of the London Geological Society. (1844 to the present.)
Robinson's (Edw.) Bible Researches.
Sedwick's (Adam) Commencement Sermons.
Silliman's Consistency of modern Geology with Sacred History.
Smith's (J. Pye) Relation of Scripture to G.
Southern Quarterly Review. 21:48.
Sutcliffe's Geological Essays.
Taylor's (Geo.) Indications of the Creator.
Taylor's (W. E.) Facts and fictions of G.
Townsend's Character of Moses established.
Ure's System of Geology.
Wallace on the True age of the world.
Westminster Review. New Series. 2:67.
Wight's Geology and Genesis.
Young's (Dr. Geo.) Essays on Scripture G.

These treat of geology with reference to Scripture. Works on the subject, which have no such reference, need not be mentioned here.

German Baptists [Tunkers].

Pro.

Christian Family Companion. Periodical. 1865 to the present.
Gospel Visitor. Period. 1851 to the present.
Mack's View of the ordinances of God.
Nead's (Peter) Theology.

German Reformed Church. See HEIDELBURG CATECHISM.

Braunii Theologia didactica et elenctica.
Collectio Confessionum in Eccles. Reform. publicatorum. Leipsic. 1840.
Ebrard's Christliche Dogmatik.
Finsler's Kirch. Statistik d. ref. Schweis-Zurich. 1856.
Hagenbach's Vorlesungen ü. d. Gesch. d. Prot. Reformation. 1856.
Heppe's Evang. Reform. Kirche.
Ursini Opera.

Acts and Proceedings of the G. R. Church.
Berg's Ancient Landmarks.
——— Old Paths.
Bibliotheca Sacra. January, 1863.
Bomberger's Old Race St. Church, Philad.
Craig's Hungarian Reformed Church.
Fisher's Constitutional hist. of the R. D. Ch.

Gerhard's German Reformed Church.
Harbaugh's Fathers of the Reformed Ch.
Memorial Volume of Essays read at the tercentenary celebration, &c.
Mercersburg Review.
Nevin's Mystical presence.
Schaff's Churches in Europe and America.

Ghosts. See APPARITIONS.

Giants.

Bangii Exercitationes. (Affirms the existence.)
Boulduc, de Eccles. ante legem.
Goropii Dissertationes. (Affirms.)
Heideggeri Historia Patriarcharum.
Kircheri (Athan.) Dissertationes. (Affirms.)
Rachneri Dissertationes. (Affirms.)
Sangutelli Disquisitiones histor. et crit.

Calmet's Dissertations.
Hamilton (W. T.) on the Pentateuch.
Parker's State of the antediluvian world.
Smith's (C. H.) Natural History of the human species.

Gibeonites.

Fechtii (Ioann.) Disputationes.
Pfeiffenger de Gibeonitorum.

Gift of Tongues.

Gregory Naz., Orationes sex.
Augustine, Opera.

Schulthesius de Ratione et utilitate dotis linguarum.

Barrow's (William) Sermons.
Benson's Plantation of Christianity.
Bibliotheca Sacra. 22:99.
Chandler's Vind. of the Christian religion.
——— on Joel.
Christian Observer. 1861. P. 501.
D'Oyly's (Robt.) Dissertations. Diss. 2.
Hale's (Sir M.) Dissertations.
Hawker's (Robert) Sermons.
Irving's (Edw.) Works. (Various pieces.)
Jones' Jewish Antiquities.
Jortin's Remarks on Eccles. History.
Leland's Answer to Morgan.
Middleton's (Conyers) Essays.
——— Free enquiry into the miracles, &c.
Reickert's Essays.
Warburton's (Bp.) Sermons.

Glassites. See SANDEMANIANS.

Glory of Christ. See EXALTATION.

Glory of God. See ATTRIBUTES.

Dick's Philosophy of Religion.
Edwards' (Pres.) Works.
Venn's (John) Sermons.
Wisheart's Sermons.

Gnostics.

Polycarp, Fragmenta.
——— Epistola ad Philippenses.
Justin M., Hermiæ irrisio gentilium phil.
Irenæus, Detectio, et Eversio falso, &c.
Clemens (Alex.), Stromatum. Lib. 3, cap. 5.
Tertullian, Apologeticus.
——— adversus Marcionem.

Bauer's Christliche Gnosis.
Bruckeri Historia de Ideis.
Burckhardt, les Chrétiens de St. Jean Bapt.
Erdmann de Notionibus ethicis Gnosticorum.
Heideggeri (Io. H.) Dissertationes.
Hildebrandi Diss. historico-philosophica.
Ittigius de Hæresiarchis ævi Apostolici.
Keifer de Gnosticis in N. T. tactis.
Lewald de Doctrina Gnostica.
Maresii (Sam.) Disputationes Selectæ.
Mater, Hist. critique du Gnosticisme, et de son influence sur les sectes; des six premiers siecles.
Michaelis Introd. ad Nov. Test. Sect. 125.
Möhler Versuche über des Gnostikers.
Mosheimii Dissertationes.
Münter's Kirchl. alterthümer der G.
Neander's Gnostischen Systeme.
Nieuwland de Gnosticorum theologia.
Schram de Prophetis Gnosticorum.
Thomas, Hist. philos. et ecclesiæ.
Tillemont, Memoires pour servir a l'hist., &c.
Tittman, de Vestigiis Gnosticorum in N. T.
Vitringæ Observationes Sacræ.

Amer. Bib. Repos. 2d Series. 3:353. 6:253.
Beaven's Life and writings of Ireneus. (Contains a full account of their doctrine, discipline, and history.)
Burton's Bampton Lectures. 1829.
Cheever's Philosophy of the Gnostics.
Christian Examiner. 24:112.
Conybeare's Bampton Lectures. 1839.
Foreign Quarterly Review. 5:569.
King's (C. W.) G. and their remains. Plates.
Lardner's Works.
Macknight on the Epistles. (Pref. to 1 John.)
Mosheim's Eccles. History. Century 1.
Norton's Genuineness of the Gospel.
Tenniman's History of Philosophy.
Tittman's History of Philosophy.

For a large account of writers on this subject, see MATER, named above.

Godeschalcians. See DECREES, ELECTION, HISTORY OF DOCTRINES.

Alexandri (Natalis.) Dissertationes.
Boullay, Histoire Academ. Paris.
Cellotii Hist. Gotteschalci, &c. (A great work.)
Erigenus contra Godeschalcum.
Fabricii Biblioth. Latina medii ævi.
Godeschalci Opera.
Hottingeri, Diatriba historico-theologica.
Mabilloni Præf. ad acta Benidictorum.
Norrisii Synopsis hist. Godeschalcanæ.

Rabanus Maurus de Predestinatione.
Ruckeri Disputationes.
Usseri Hist. prædestinatione controv.
Vossii Historia Pelagianna.

Godliness. See PRACTICAL PIETY.

Abernethy's (John) Sermons.
Ayres' Mystery of G. (Sound and sensible.)
Barrow's (Isaac) Sermons.
Berens' (Edward) Sixteen sermons.
Bloomfield's (C. J.) Sermons.
Brook's Crown and glory of Christianity.
Burton's (Hezekiah) Sermons.
Chandler's (Samuel) Sermons.
Christian Observer. 25:279.
Colet's Order of a Christian life.
Cooper's (Edward) Sermons.
Corbett's Self-improvement in secret.
Downame's Guide to godliness.
Evans on Christian Temper. Disc. 8.
Faringdon's (Anthony) Sermons.
Girdlestone's (Cha.) Course of a Chris. life.
Griffith's (William) Sermons.
Hammond's (Henry) Sermons.
Hare's (A. W.) Sermons.
Horneck's (Anth.) Happy Ascetic.
Holdsworth's (R.) Sermons.
Jewell's (Bp.) Sermons.
Johnson's (Dr. Sam.) Sermons.
Jortin's (John) Sermons.
Kettlewell on the Christian life.
Law's Serious Call to Christians.
Liefchild's (John) Christian temper; or lectures on the Beatitudes.
Mason on Christian Morals.
Mather's (Cotton) Walking with God.
——— Essays to do good.
Milner's (Jos.) Practical Sermons.
Moore's (Henry) Mystery of godliness.
Scott's (Thomas) Christian life.
Sherlock's (Bp.) Sermons.
Skelton's (Philip) Sermons.
Snowden's (W.) Sermons.
Stillingfleet's (Bp.) Sermons.
Stowell (Hugh) Lectures on Nehemiah.
Sumner's (Bp.) Sermons.
Taylor's (Jer.) Holy living.
Thompson (J. P.) on the Christian graces.
Venn's (John) Sermons.
Warburton's (Bp.) Sermons.
Whichcot's (B.) Sermons.
Wilson's (Bp.) Sermons.
Wrangham's (Francis) Sermons.

Gog and Magog.

Buckenroder's Gog und Magog.
Calmet, Dissertationes.
Danderstat de Antichristo Orientali.
Gebhardi (J. H.) Dissertationes.
Gerardi Chiliasmus.
Musculi (Andr.) Dissertationes.
Prideaux (J.) Orationes Inaugurales.

Christian Observer. 14:141,365.
Jackson's Credibility of Scripture.
Maton on the Millennium.
Patrick's Commentary: *in loco.*
Penn's (Granville) Proph. of Ezekiel, concerning the last tyrant of the Church.
Pyle on the Apocalypse.
Stuart (Moses) on the Apocalypse.
Worthington's Extent of Redemption.

Gomarists. See CALVINISM, HISTORY OF.

Good Conscience. See CONSCIENCE.

Allestree's (Richard) Sermons.
Anderson's (J. S. M.) Sermons.
Beveridge's (Bp.) Sermons.
Harris' (Robert) Sermons.
Lake's (Bp.) Sermons.
South's (Robert) Sermons.
Tillotson's (Abp.) Sermons.
Whewell's (W.) Sermons.

Good Friday. See FASTS.

Robinson's Hist. and mystery of Good Frid.

Good Shepherd.

Bloomfield's (Bp.) Sermons.
Cooper's (E.) Sermons.
Potts' (J. H.) Sermons.

Good Works. See ANTINOMIANISM, PAUL AND JAMES, SYNERGISTS.

Gregory Nys., de Opificio hominis.

Alesius de Necess. bonorum operum.
Bullii Harmonia Apostolica.
Chemnitii Exam. Concilii Tridentini.
Cocceii (Ioann.) Disputationes.
Graverii (J.) Dissertationes.
Heilbrunneri Flagellatio Jesuitica.
Holdeni Divinæ fidei Analysis.
Placette, de la Foi Divine.
Thummii (Theod.) Dissertationes.
Voetii (Gisbert) Disputationes.
Vossii (G. J.) Theses Theologicæ.

Allen's (James) Sermons.
Allix's Merit of good works.
Amer. Biblical Repos. 3d Series. 4:325.
Arnold's (Fred.) Sermons.
Atterbury's (Lewis) Sermons.
Backus' (Isaac) Discourses. (The one on "True faith productive of good works," is often printed separately.)
Baxter's (Arthur G.) Sermons.
Beveridge's (Bp.) Sermons.
Bickersteth's (Edward) Sermons.
Billingsley's (John) Sermons.
Blackall's (Bp.) Sermons.
Bloomfield's (G. B.) Sermons.
Booth's Glad tidings to perishing sinners.
Burgh's (Wm.) Discourses. (Superior.)
Burton's Truth triumphant over Trent.
Church Review. 3:169.
Close's (Francis) Sermons on the Liturgy.
Colquhoun on Law and Gospel.
Cooper's (E.) Sermons.
Cranmer's (Abp.) Works.

Good Works—*continued.*

Edwards' Theologia Reformata.
Erskine's (Eben.) Sermons.
Erskine's (Tho.) Freeness of the Gospel.
Faber's (G. S.) Primitive doct. of truth.
Gale's (Dr. John) Sermons.
Gill's (Dr. John) Miscellaneous Works.
Hooker's (Richard) Discourses.
Law (William) on Faith and Works.
McCausland's Evangelical Ethics.
Malkins' Sermons and Dissertations.
Mather's Essays to do good.
Miller's (James) Sermons.
Norris' Mystery of Christianity.
O'Brien's Sermons before the Univ. of Camb.
Parry's (John) Sermons.
Placette on Good Works.
Reynolds' (Bp.) Sermons.
Riddle's (J. E.) Sermons.
Rogers' (John) Sermons.
Romaine's (Wm.) Works.
Rotherham's Connection of faith and works.
Scattergood's (Samuel) Sermons.
Smallridge's (George) Sermons. (Rewards proportioned to works.)
Smith's (William) Sermons.
Smith's (Theyre) Sermons.
Sumner's (Bp.) Sermons.
Tottie's (John) Sermons.
Trail's Vind. of Protestant doctrine.
Troughton's Luther Redivivus.
Venn's (John) Sermons.
Waterland's (Daniel) Sermons.
Watson's (J. W.) Sermons.
Whitaker's (William) Sermons.
Williams' (Alfred) Sermons.
Witherspoon's Works.

Goodness of God. See BENEVOLENCE.

Goshen. See GEOGRAPHY.

Bellerman's Biblische Archäologie.
Iablonski (P. E.) Dissertationes.
Michaelis, Supplem. ad Lexicon Hebraic.

Amer. Bibl. Repos. Years 1832 and 1840.

Government. See CIVIL GOVERNMENT.

Government of God. See PROVIDENCE.

Alford's Hulsean Lectures. 1842.
Beecher's (Lyman) Sermons.
Bledsoe's (A. T.) Theodicy.
Christian Observer. 16:767.
Christian Review. 17:183.
Cornthwaite's Divine conduct justified.
Emmon's (Nathaniel) Sermons.
Hare's Conduct of God to the human species.
Hinton (J. H.) on God's government of man.
Hunt's (Jeremiah) Sermons.
Kern's Moral government of God.
Leland's (Dr. Thomas) Sermons.
McCosh on Divine government.
Methodist Quarterly Review. 34:458.
North British Review. 13:275.
Porteus' (Bp.) Sermons.
Princeton Review. 23:598.
Smith's (T. S.) Illustrations of the Div. gov.
Smith's (Southwood) Goverment of God.
Taylor (N. W.) on the Moral govt. of God.
Weaver's Harmony and glory of the Divine government.

Government of the Heart. See DECEITFULNESS, PURITY, SELF-GOVERNMENT.

Alleine's Instructions about heart-work.
Atterbury's (Lewis) Sermons.
Barrow's (Isaac) Sermons.
Bather's (Edward) Sermons.
Beveridge's (Bp.) Sermons.
Blair's (Hugh) Sermons.
Calthrop's (John) Sermons.
Carr's (George) Sermons.
Chandler's (Samuel) Sermons.
Dawes' (Abp.) Sermons.
Doddridge's (Philip) Sermons.
Drysdale's (John) Sermons.
Duchall's (James) Sermons.
Flavel on Keeping the heart.
Hussey's (Christopher) Sermons.
Jelf's (R. W.) Sermons.
Lardner's (Nathaniel) Sermons.
Latham's (Ebenezer) Sermons.
Lloyd's (Pearson) Sermons.
Mace's (Daniel) Sermons.
Marshall's (Nathan) Sermons.
Mede's (Joseph) Sermons.
Newlin's (Thomas) Sermons.
Orr's (John) Sermons.
Porteus' (Beilby) Sermons.
Seed's (Jeremiah) Sermons.
Sharp's (Abp.) Sermons.
Smallridge's (Bp.) Sermons.
Smith's (Sydney) Sermons.
Smith's (Benj.) Vice-Royalty.
Stone's (Edward) Sermons.
Sumner's (Bp.) Sermons.
Trapp's (Joseph) Sermons.
Waterland's (Daniel) Sermons.
Watson's (Thomas) Sermons.

Government of the Passions. See PASSIONS.

Government of the Thoughts. See THOUGHTS.

Government of the Tongue. See TONGUE.

Grace. See COVENANT, GROWTH.

Beausobre, Defence de la doct. d. Réformé.
Ferrii Scholastici Orthodoxi specimen.
Friglandus de trina Dei gratia.
Haberti Theologia Grecorum patrum.
Harenbergii Theol. prim. Christianorum.
Hennichius de Gratia et Predestinatione.
Honerti (T. H.) Dissertationes.
Hottingerus de Prædestinatione.
Mori Dissertationes septem.
Pfaffii Specimen Historiæ Dogmaticæ.

Grace—*continued.*

Piscator de Gratia Dei.
Pœlenburgii Exam. disp. theol. Spanheimii.
Spanheimii (F.) Disputationes Theologicæ.
Strimesii Chartologia Sacra.
Velthusius de Gratia et predestinatione.
Vita Apologia pro Synode Dordracena.

Abbot on Divine grace and perseverance.
Andrews (John) on Divine grace.
Backus' (Isaac) Discourses.
Barclay's Apology.
Beveridge's (Bp.) Sermons.
Booth's Reign of grace.
Bradley's (Charles) Sermons.
Buckminster's (Joseph) Sermons.
Burch's (Tho.) Free grace displayed.
Charnock's Works.
Cooper's (Edward) Sermons.
Ecking's (Samuel) Essays.
Edwards (Pres.) on Efficacious grace.
Edwards' (Thomas) Doctrine of grace.
Gill's Cause of God and truth.
Horberry's (Matthew) Sermons.
Isaacs' (Jacob) Doctrine of free grace.
Johnson's (John) 12 Discourses.
Lime Street Lectures.
Newman's (J. H.) Sermons.
Pike's (Sam.) Free grace indeed.
Rutherford's Apologetical Exercises.
Sanderson's (Bp.) Sermons.
Saurin's (James) Sermons.
Sharpe's (Abp.) Sermons.
Shuttleworth's (P. N.) Sermons.
Stafford's Scriptural doct. of sin and grace.
Thompson on Divine grace.
Usher's (Abp.) Sermons.
Wales' Mount Ebal leveled.
Warburton's Doctrine of grace.

Gratitude. See THANKSGIVING.

Adams' (Thomas) Sermons.
Arnold's (Dr. Thomas) Sermons.
Bourne's (Samuel) Sermons.
Brady's (N.) Sermons.
Chalmers' (Tho.) Congregation sermons.
Christian Observer. 12:681.
Davies' (Pres.) Sermons.
Deverell's (Mary) Sermons.
Eaton's (Bp. S.) Sermons.
Edwards' (Pres.) Works.
Girdlestone's (Charles) Sermons.
Graves' (Richard) Sermons.
Hancock's Great duty of Thankfulness.
Hills' (G. D.) Practical Sermons.
Hills' (John) Lectures and Reflections.
Keating's (W.) Sermons.
Leechman's (Dr. W.) Sermons.
Sanderson's (Bp.) Sermons.
Stevenson's Exposition of the 103d Psalm.
Ward's (Bp.) Sermons.
Warren's (Robert) Sermons.
Whitefield's (George) Sermons.

Gradual Revelation of the Gospel.

Berriman's Boyle Lectures. 1730–32.

Gravity. See DEPORTMEMT, JESTING, LAUGHTER, SOBRIETY.

Gray Friars. See FRANCISCANS.

Greek Antiquities.

Christian Review. 2:515. 10:530.
Dalzel on the Ancient Greeks.
Edinburg Rev. 56:350. (Greek banquets.)
Finlay's Greece under the Romans.
Foreign Quarterly Review. 7:33.
Frazier's Magazine. 30:450.
New Englander. 9:161.
Potter's Greek Antiquities.
Rouse's Greek Antiquities.
Smith's Dict. of G. and Roman Antiquities.
Southern Literary Messenger. 14:129.
Southern Quarterly Review. 11:273.
Southern Review. 6:32,385.

Greek Church.

Allatii (Leo.) Dissertationes.
——— de Eccles. Occident. consensione.
Angeli Enchiridion de statu hodiernorum Græcorum. 1665. (Much esteemed.)
Baronius de Ruthenorum origine, &c.
Bergius de Statu eccl. Muscovitæ. 1709.
Beveridgii Pandectæ canonum, &c.
Chytræi Status eccl. hoc tempore. 1569.
Confessio Orthodoxa Ecc. Orientalis.
Cottelerii Ecc. Græca monumenta.
Crusii (M.) Turco-Græciæ. ("Egregius."—WALCH.)
Cyrilli (Lucaris) Confessio fidei Græc.
Fabricii Bibliotheca Græca.
Feverlinus de Religione Ruthenorum.
Frischii Liber de Symbolis Russorum.
Galitzin, l'Eglise Græco Russe.
Girardin, La Syrie en 1861.
Goar Ευχολογιον.
Haberti Αρχιερατικον
Heineccius' Abildung d. alten u. neuen G. Kirche. (Sufficient of itself for most persons.)
Hoffmanni Orthod. confessio Ecc. Orient.
La Croix, Etat present, &c. 1695.
Lucaris. See Cyril, above.
Mogilla, Confessio ecclesiæ G.
Renaudotii Liturg. Orient. collectio.
Ricaut, l'Etat present, &c. 1692.
Schlosser's Morganlandische Kirche. 1845.
Schwabe, de Religione Ritibus, &c. 1710.
Simon, Histoire critique des dogmes, et des controversies des chretiens Orientaux.
Smith (Tho.), Miscellanea. (Greek Church as in 1670.)
Strahl's Russischen Kirchengesch. 1827.
Zeltneri Dissertationes.

Amer. Quart. Church Review. 15:169.
Bibliotheca Sacra. 15:501.
Blackmore's Doct. of the Russian Church. (A translat. of its creed, catechisms, &c.)
British and Foreign Review. 9:319.
Christian Examiner. 59:57.
Consett's State of the Greek Church. 1729.
Covell's State of the Greek Church. 1722.

Greek Church—*continued.*

Elsner's Present state, &c. 1737.
Goar's Notes on the Greek ritual.
Heineccius' Account of the G. Church. 1712.
King's Doctrines, rites, &c. 1772.
Mouravief's Church of Russia. Trans. by Blackmore.
Palmer's (William) Dissertations.
Pinkerton's State of the Greek Chur. 1814.
Platon's Present state of the G. Ch. 1815.
Ricaut's Present state, &c. 1678.
Smith's (Tho.) Doctrines of the G. Church.
Tournefort's Voyage in the Levant. 1718.
Waddington's Condition, prospects, &c. 1829.

Gregory Nazianzen.

Gregorii Opera. (Edit. Benedictinæ. 1842.)
Assemani Bibliotheca Orientalis.
Baronii Annales.
Bohringer's Kirche und ihre Zeugen.
Grenier, Vie de St. Gregoire.
Hermance, Vie de St. Gregoire.
Le Clerc, Vie de St. Gregoire.
Maximi Explicatio loc. difficil. Greg. N.
Melancthonis Orationes.
Oudini Dissertationes.
Ulman's G. von Naz. der Theologie, &c.

Boyd's Select poems of Gregory.
Christian Review. 3:467.
Collier's Trans. of Gregory's panegyric on the Maccabees.
Drant's Epigrams, &c., of Gregory.
Le Clerc's Life of Gregory.
Ulman's Contributions to Church History. Translated by G. V. Cox.
Westminster Review. 56:101.

Gregory Nyssen.

Gregorii Nys., Opera.
Assemanni Bibliotheca Orientalis.
Boehringer die Kirche Christi.
Boye (Ludov.), Dissert. de G. Neocæs.
Frontomi Vita et Opera G. N.
Moeller's G. doctr. de hominis natura.
Oudini (Casimir.) Dissertationes.
Papebrochii Commentarius Historicus.
Rupp's Leben und Meinungen, &c.

Gregory's Exp. of the faith. Tr. by Cave.

"There is hardly one error of the Romish Church which Gregory Nyssen does not defend strongly."—Clarke.

Gregory Thaumaturgus.

Gregorii Neocæsareensis Opera.
Boye (Io. Ludov.) Dissertationes.
Canisii Thesaurus monumentorum ecclesiasticæ et historiæ.
Pallavicina Vita Gregorii Thaumatur.

Christian Observer. 25:407.
Gregory's Expos. of the faith. Tr. by Cave. (In his lives of the fathers.)

Grieving the Spirit.

Bloomfield's (G. B.) Sermons.
Burder's (Henry F.) Sermons.
Chalmers' (Tho.) Congregational sermons.
Close's (Francis) Miscellaneous sermons.
Cooper's (Edward) Sermons.
Dale's (Thomas) Sermons.
Dutton's (T.) Warnings of the Spirit.
Evans' (R. W.) Sermons.
Girdlestone's (Charles) Sermons.
Graves' (Richard) Sermons.
Howe's (Dr. John) Sermons.
Scattergood's (Samuel) Sermons.
Slade's (James) Sermons.
Tilly's (William) Sermons.
Watson's (Alexander) Sermons.
Wesley's (John) Sermons.
Wilks' (Sam. C.) Sermons.
Wilson's (Thomas) Sermons.

Groningenists. See ANABAPTISTS.

Growth in Grace. See GRACE.

Bather's (Edward) Sermons.
Batty's (Adam) Sermons.
Boardman's (W. G.) Higher Christian life.
Brameld's (G. W.) Sermons.
Brine's (John) Sermons. (Excellent.)
Charnock's (Stephen) Works.
Cooper's (Edward) Sermons.
Dwight's (Timothy) Discourses. Disc. 86.
Edwards' (Bp.) Theologia Reformata.
Goodwin (Tho.) on Growth in grace.
Johnston's (John) Way of life.
Jones' (Wm., of Nayland) Sermons.
Lavington's (Samuel) Sermons
Marshall's (Nath.) Sermons.
Neves' (Timothy) Sermons.
Owen on the Mediation of Christ.
Pierce (J.) on Growth in grace.
Princeton Review. 32:608.
Scott's (Tho.) Theological Works.
Slater's (Sam.) Sermons. (Several on this subject.)
Spring's (Gardner) Essays. Ess. 14.
Spurgeon's (C. H.) Sermons. Sixth Series.
Taylor's (Jeremy) Sermons.
Yonge's (James) Sermons. Second Series.

Guardian Angels.

Chrysostom, Epistola ad Colos. Hom. III.
——— ——— ad Hebr. Hom. XIV.
Basil, contra Eunomius. Lib. III.

Ambrey's Miscellanies.
Amer. Biblical Repository. Vol. 12.
Berg's (J. F.) Abaddon and Mahanaim.
Bibliotheca Sacra. 1:107.
Dingley's Deputation of Angels. (Adduces Scripture, and many ancient writers.)
Edwards (Bp.) on the Apostles' Creed.
Gould's (Sarah) The guardian angels.
Kennaway's (Cha. E.) Sermons.
——— Sermons to the young.
Kitto's Journal. New Series. Vol. 1.
More's Antidote against Atheism.

Guebres. See PARSEES.

Gymnosophists.

Augustine, de Civitate Dei. Lib. XIV.
Clemens Alex., Stromata. Lib. I, III.

Diodorus Siculus, Hist. Lib. II.
Lucian, Opuscula Selecta.
Pliny, Historia Naturalis. Lib. VII.
Plutarch, Alexand. LXIV.
Porphyry, de Abstinentia. Lib. IV.
Strabo, Historia. Lib. XV.

Hardy's Eastern Monachism.
Ruffner's Fathers of the desert.

Habit. See MIND.

Abernethy's (John) Sermons.
Amory's Sermons on habitual religion.
Brown's (Tho.) Philos. of the mind. Lect. 43.
Buckminster's (Joseph S.) Sermons.
Butcher's (E.) Sermons.
Carmichael on Habit considered in conjunction with the love of novelty.
Carr's (George) Sermons.
Christian Observer. 1:576,718.
Cogan on the Passions.
Collison's (M. A.) Sermons.
Doddsley's Preceptor.
Edwards' (Bp.) Body of Divinity.
Emmons' (Nathaniel) Sermons.
Fawcett's (Joseph) Sermons.
Ferguson's Principles of Moral Science.
Grove's Moral Philosophy.
Gurney's (J. J.) Thoughts on habit and discipline.
Howson's (J. S.) Sermons. (3 on this subj.)
Jortin's (J.) Sermons. (On bad habits.)
Kames' Elements of Criticism.
Knight's (Samuel) Sermons.
Le Bas' (Cha. W.) Sermons.
Locke's Essay on the Understanding.
Maltby's (Edw.) Sermons at Lincoln's Inn.
Mouseley on Moral strength.
Paley's Moral Philosophy.
Reid on the Active powers.
Richardson's (William) Sermons.
Skelton's (Philip) Sermons.
Spectator. No. 447.
Spencer's (Aubrey G.) Sermons.
Tillotson's (Abp.) Sermons.
Tucker's Light of Nature pursued. Ch. 31.
Zollikoffer's Sermons on prevalent vices.

Hades. See DESCENT INTO HELL, INTERMEDIATE STATE, PURGATORY.

Bibliotheca Sacra. 13:153.
Campbell's (George) Dissertations.
Church Review. 5:232.
Edwards' (Bp.) Body of Divinity.
Gilfillan's (George) Discourses.
Hammond's Annotat. (On Matt. xi. 23.)
Huidekoper's Belief of the first 3 centuries.
Pearson's (Bp.) Exposition of the Creed.
Scott's (Russell) Lectures.
Sturmy's (Daniel) Discourses.
Wake on the Church Catechism.
Wheatley's (Charles) Sermons.
Williams' (Bp.) Exposition of the Creed.

Hagiographa. See COMMENTATORS, POETRY OF THE HEBREWS.

Halfway Covenant. See PURITANS.

Pro.

Allen's (John) Animadversions on the Antisynodalia.
Cotton (John) on Baptism.
——— on the Covenant of grace.
Mather's (Richard) Visible Church in covenant with God.
——— Vindic. of the New Eng. Churches.
Scripturista on Infant Baptism.

Con.

Bellamy's One Covenant.
——— Reply to Mather's Vindication.
——— Letter to Scripturista.
——— Dialogues.
Chauncey's (Pres.) Antisynodalia.
Davenport's (John) Allegations of Scripture against the baptizing of certain kinds of infants.

Most of this controversy was carried on in pamphlets. Much may be gathered concerning the history of it from BACON'S *Historical Discourses*, and UDEN'S *New England Theocracy*.

Happiness. See BEATITUDES, PLEASURE.

Augustin, Sermones.
Buddei Miscellanea Sacra.
Dassovius de Initio Beatitudinis.
Pfaffii (Christoph. Matt.) Dissertationes.
Senstius de Beatitudine, nunc et tunc.

Adderly's Essay on Human happiness.
Bell's (William) Sermons.
Bigland's Essays. Ess. 1.
Bolton's (R.) Works. ("Most useful."—DODDRIDGE.)
Chandler's (Samuel) Sermons.
Charnock's Works.
Christian Review. 2:161. 5:354.
Clark's (Dr. Samuel) Sermons.
Cobb's Bampton Lectures. 1783.
Ferguson's Moral and political science.
Foster's (James) Sermons.
Francklin's (Thomas) Sermons.
Fuller's Calvinistic and Socinian systems compared. Let. 13.
Genlis' Religion the only basis, &c.
Glanhill's Different ways to happiness.
Graves' (Richard) Sermons.
Hale's (Matthew) Contemplations.
Harness' Boyle Lectures. 1821–2. (Connection of Christianity and happiness.)
Harris' Dialogue on Happiness.
Hussey's (Christopher) Sermons.
Lucas' Inquiry after H. (Many editions.)

Happiness—*continued.*

Maclaurin's Essays.
Marshall's (Nathaniel) Sermons.
Milner's (Joseph) Sermons.
Monthly Review. 131:85.
More's (Hannah) Search after happiness.
Morehead's Principles of religious belief.
Nettleton (Dr. Tho.) on Virtue and H.
Newman on Happiness.
North American Review. 27:115.
Oliver's (Benj. L.) Essays.
Orr's (John) Sermons.
Paley's Moral Philosophy.
Pierce's (John) Sermons.
Ramsay's Principles of human happiness.
Ray's Persuasive to a holy life.
Reading's (William) Sermons.
Seed's (Jeremiah) Sermons.
Spencer's (H.) Social Statics. (Elaborate.)
Sterne's (Lawrence) Sermons.
Stewart's (J. H.) Lectures on Isaiah 55.
Stoughton's (John) Sermons.
Tucker's Light of Nature pursued.
Webb's Enquiry after happiness.
Zollikoffer's (Geo. J.) Sermons on the dignity of man. (Five of these admirable discourses are on this subject.)
——— Sermons on Education.

Hardness of Heart.

Buys, de Induratione peccatoris.

Abernethy's (Bp.) Sermons.
Bather's (Edw.) Sermons. (Gospel sinners more guilty than Heathen.)
Bradbury's (Thomas) Sermons.
Christian Monthly Spectator. 3:617.
Fenner's (W.) Works. (Sermons.)
Gouldburn's (Edward M.) Sermons.
Haverfield's (Tho. T.) Sermons.
Johnson's (Dr. Sam.) Sermons.
Saurin's Sermons. Trans. by R. Robinson.
Wilson's (Thomas) Sermons.

Harmonies. See ANALYSES, APPARENT CONTRADICTIONS, CHRONOLOGICAL ARRANGEMENT OF SCRIPTURE, DURATION OF OUR LORD'S MINISTRY, MONOTESSARON.

Augustin, de Consensu Evangelistarum.

Angeri Synopsis Evangelicorum. 1852.
Bengel's Harm. d. 4 Evangelisten. 1736.
Bunting, Harm. Evangelistarum. 1712.
Burmanni Harm. Evangelistarum. 1713.
Calixti Quatuor Evang. Concordia. 1624.
Calovii Harm. Evang. Monotessaron. 1672.
Calvini Harmonia et Comment. 1553.
Cartwright, Harmonia Evangelica. 1630.
Chemnitii, Harmonia Evangelica. 1593.
Clausenii Tabulæ synopticæ. 1829.
Clerici Harmonia Evangelica. 1699. ("Aureum."—RIEMANN. "All critics unite in commendation of Le Clerc's Harmony." —HORNE.)
Claveri Harmonia Evangelistarum. 1628.

Harmonies—*continued.*

De Wette et Lücke Synopsis Evangel. 1818.
Eusebii (Cæsarensis) Canones. 300.
Fabri Syntagma histor. Evang. 1652.
Gerardi Harmonia Evangelica. 1646.
Greswelli Harm. Evang. 1830. (In Greek, with valuable dissertations.)
Griesbachii Synopsis. 1776.
Grynæi Historia Sacra. 1569.
Gürtleri Harmonia Evangelica. 1700.
Lamy, Concordia, &c. 1689. ("Peculiarly valuable."—HORNE.)
Le Clerc. See Clerici.
Lightfoot, Harm. Evang. inter se, et cum Vet. Test. 1655.
Lyseri Harm. Evangelistarum. 1590.
Natalis Concordantia Evangeliorum. 1595.
Newcombe, Harmonia Evangeliorum. 1778.
Osiandri Harm. Grece et Latine. 1537.
Rus (Jo. R.), Harmonia Evangeliorum. 1727.
Stephani Harmonia Græca. 1553.
Tischendorfii Synopsis Evangelica. 1851.
Toinardi Harm. Græco-Latina. 1707.
Vossii Harmonia Evangelica. 1656.
Walch's (E. I.) Einleitung in d. evang. 1749.
Ziegleri Concordia Evangelica.

Bickersteth's Harmony of the Gospels. 1832.
Calvin's ——— ——— 1553.
Carpenter's ——— ——— 1835.
Cartwright's ——— ——— 1630.
Chapman's ——— ——— 1836. (Incorporates the arrangements of Newcombe, Townsend, and Greswell.)
Chambers' (John) Harmony. 1813.
Christian Examiner. 10:358. 13:87. 22:43.
Craddock's Harmony of the Gospels. 1668.
Cranfield's ——— ——— 1795.
Da Costa's Four witnesses. 1851.
Doddridge's Family Expositor. 1762.
Douglas' Harmony of the Gospels. 1859.
Drax's ——— ——— 1616. (Against Calvin's.)
Eclectic Review. 4th Series. 6:505. 19:732.
Greenwood's (W.) Harmony. 1766.
Greswell's Harmony. 1830. See Chapman.
——— Dissertations on the principles of a Harmony. 1830.
Jacobus' Notes on the Gospels. 1856.
Le Clerc's Harm. and Dissertations. 1699.
Lewin's Early Christian chronology.
Lightfoot's Harmony of the Evang. among themselves and with the Old Test. 1644.
Lloyd's (Bp.) Harmony. 1710.
McKnight's H. and paraphrase. 1756.
Mimpris' (R.) Harm. of the Gospels. 1833.
Newcombe's ——— ——— 1780.
Newton's (Sir I.) Harmony. 1717.
Paley's Horæ Paulinæ. 1800. (A comparison of the Acts and Epistles.)
Peddie's Gospel narrative. 1857.
Phillips' Harmony. (Very convenient.)
Pilkington's Evangelical History. 1747.
Priestley's Greek Harmony. 1777. (Critical notes in English.)

Harmonies—*continued.*

Roberts' Harmony of the Epistles. 1800.
Robinson's (Edw.) H. of the Gosp. Greek.
——— *The Same.* English. 1834.
Strong's Greek H. of the Gospels. 1854.
Stroud's Greek H. of the Gospels. 1853.
(Elaborate introduction, with notes, tables, indexes, &c.)
Thompson's Gospel History. 1829.
Townson's Evangelical History. 1793.
(See Chapman, above.)
Warner's Harmony of the Gospels. 1803.
Wells' Harmony and new translation. 1724.
Westcott's Gospel Harmony. 1850.
Wheeler's (H. M.) Popular Harmony, &c.
Whiston's Harmony of the Gospels. 1702.
Williams' (Isaac) H. of the Gospels. 1850.

Harmony of Christianity with Man's Nature. See ANALOGY OF RELIGION AND NATURE, INFLUENCE OF RELIGION.

Legge's (George) Lectures.

Harmony of Reason and Faith. See DEISM, MYSTERY, PROVINCE OF REASON.

Ackermann's Christliche im Plato.
Engel's Religion nach Vernunft u. Schrift.
Fuerbach's Philosophie u. Christenthum.
Haferungii Mysteria neque comprehendi posse, neque tamen ratione adversari.
Huetii Alnetanæ Questiones. ("Beautiful.")
Iacquеot, l'Conformité de la foi avec la raison. (Reply to Bayle.)
Kirchmeyeri Theses Theologicæ.
Lamy, sur l'Alliance de la raison avec la foi.
Maius de Ratione in rebus fidei.
Matter, Hist. de la philos. dans ses rapport avec la religion.
Mentzerus de Consensu rationis humanæ cum mysteriis divini.
Murator über der Rechten Gebrauch der Vernunft in sachen d. Religion.
Nahmmacher de Syncretismo phil. et theol.

Boyle's Reconciliation of R. and faith.
Candlish's (R. S.) Reason and Revelation.
Edwards (John) on Truth and Error.
Galloway's Mutual bearings of phil. and rel.
Hedge's (F. H.) Reason and Religion.
Hinton's (J. H.) Harm. of truth and reason.
Mailler's Philosophy of the Bible.
Mansel's Limits of Religious Thought.
Mial's Bases of belief.
Mortlock's Christianity agreeable to reason.
Ragg's Creation's testimony to its God.
Shuttleworth's Consistency of Revelation with itself, and with human reason. (Powerful.)
Tournour's (E. J.) Twenty-four sermons.

Harmony of Character. See CONSISTENCY.

Appleton's (Pres.) Works.
Foster's (John) Essays.

Harmony of the Law and Gospel.

Scharpii Symphonia Prophetarum et Apostolorum.

Addie's Harmony of the Divine will.
Alexander's (Wm. L.) Congregational Lecture. 1841.
Alford's Hulsean Lectures. 1841 and 1842.
Arnot's Method of grace.
Bradford's (The Martyr) Works.
Brown's Bampton Lectures. 1806.
Colquhoun's Treatise on law and gospel.
Gill's (John) Occasional sermons.
Hamilton's Estab. of the law by the gospel.
Lancaster's (Wm.) Doct. of a future state.
Maclean's Unity of God's moral law.
Mainard's Law ratified by the Gospel.
Mainwaring's (John) Sermons.
Smith's (G.) Har. of the Div. dispensations.

Harmony of Revelation and Science.

Bonar, Concordia scientiæ cum fide. 1665. (Curious.)
Bouterwick's Religion und Vernunft.
D'Aubigné, Foi et Science.
Erdman's Vörlesung. zu Glauben u. Wissen.
Kuhn's Glauben und Wissen.
Pauvert, Harmonie de la religion, et de l'intelligence humaine.
Wiseman (Nic.), sur le Rapport entre la science et la religion.

American Eclectic Review. 2:186.
American Quarterly Observer. 2:24.
Bibliotheca Sacra. 13:80,631. 14:338,461.
Blackwood's Magazine. 6:35.
Bridgewater Treatises.
Brougham's Advant. and pleas. of science.
Buckland's Reliquiæ Diluvianæ.
Combe's Relation bet. science and religion.
Dick's Christian Philosopher.
Dingle's Harm. of Revelation and Science.
D'Oyly's (George) Sermons.
Exley on the First chapter of Genesis.
Farrar's (Adam) Sermons at Oxford.
Forbes' Progress of Science.
Hampden's Philosoph. evid. of Christianity.
Harcourt's Doctrine of the Deluge.
Harris' Pre-adamite earth. (Popular.)
Hitchcock's Relig. truth illust. from science.
Kurtz's The Bible and Astronomy.
Lewis' (Taylor) The Bible and Science.
London Quarterly Review. 79:49.
Mailler's Philosophy of the Bible.
Melville's (Henry) Sermons.
Morell's History of Philosophy and Science.
Nares' Bampton Lectures. 1805.
Nolan's Bampton Lectures. 1833.
North American Review. 30:293.
Pendleton's Science a witness for the Scrip.
Pratt's Scrip. and Science not at variance.
Ragg's Creation's Testimony to its God.
Scott's (R. E.) Limits of Physical Science.
Silliman's Consistency of the discoveries of modern geology with sacred history.

Harm. of Revel. and Science—*cont.*

[Taylor's] Nat. History of Enthusiasm.
Troup's (George) Art and Faith.
Tullidge's Triumphs of the Bible.
Walker's (James) Sermons.
Warburton's (Bp.) Sermons.
Wiseman's (Nic.) Connect. bet. Sci. and Rel.
Williams' (Cha.) First week of time.
Wood's Mosaic creation illustrated by discoveries and experiments in the present age. 1811.
Worgan's Divine Week.
Wright's Creation and Geology. 1847.

Hatred. See FORGIVENESS, LOVE.

Abernethy's (Bp.) Sermons.
Dick's Philosophy of Religion.
Hey's (John) Sermons.
Limborch's Theology.
Smith's (Sydney) Sermons.

Haughtiness. See CONDESCENSION, HUMILITY, MEEKNESS, PRIDE.

Hearing. See PARABLE OF THE SOWER.

Andrews' (Bp.) Sermons.
Atterbury's (Lewis) Sermons.
Baxter's (Richard) Practical Works.
Beveridge's (Bp.) Sermons.
Bickersteth's Christian Hearer.
Bloomfield's (Bp.) Sermons.
Clapperton's (J.) Duty of hearing.
Clarkson's (David) Sermons.
Close's (Francis) Sermons.
Collins' (W. B.) Sermons.
Cunningham's (J. W.) Sermons.
Davis' Profitable attendance on an evangelical ministry.
Downe's (John) Sermons.
Dupre's (John) Sermons.
Dwight's (Tim.) Sermons. Ser. 138.
Eastcheap's Lectures. (Six excellent ones on this subject.)
Fiddes' (Richard) Sermons.
Fleetwood's (Bp.) Sermons.
Girdlestone's (Charles) Sermons.
Gisbourne's (Thomas) Sermons.
Hampden's (R. D.) Sermons.
Hewlett's (C. A.) Sermons.
Hurd's (Bp.) Sermons.
Jortin's (John) Sermons.
Knowles' (Thomas) Sermons.
Leighton's (Abp.) Sermons.
Lewis' (T.) Christian Duties.
McGill's (Stephen) Sermons.
Mant's (Bp.) Sermons.
Scattergood's (Samuel) Sermons.
Skelton's (Philip) Sermons.
Seabury's (B.) Sermons.
Secker's (Abp.) Sermons.
Smallridge's (George) Sermons.
Summerfield's (John) Sermons.
Wilson's (Bp.) Sermons.
Yonge's (James) Sermons.

Heaven. See DEGREES IN GLORY, EMPLOYMENTS OF HEAVEN, PLACE OF HEAVEN, RECOGNITION.

Augustin, Opera.
Chrysostom, de premiis Sanctorum.
Lactantius, Institutiones. Lib. VII.

Callixtus de Bono perfecte summo.
Chytræus de Morte, et vita eterna.
Engel, wir Werden uns Wiedersehen.
Grävell's der Mench.
Gretzer (Jac.) Disputationes.
Hildebrandus de Vita eterna.
Lessii (Leonardi) Opuscula.
Musæus de Eterna beatitudine.
Nicolai Theoria vitæ eternæ.
Nonnenius de Aucta beatorum gloria, post consummationem mediatoris.
Olshausen, Opuscula Theologica.
Storr (Gottl. C.) Opuscula Academica.

Ambrose's (Isaac) Sermons.
Arnold's (Thomas) Sermons.
Bates' Four last things.
Beveridge's (Bp.) Sermons.
Bonar's Morning of joy.
——— Eternal day.
Bradley's (Charles) Sermons.
Bradford's (John) Fruitful treatise, &c.
Broughton's (Thomas) Sermons.
Bull's (Bp.) Sermons.
Butler's (Alban) Sermons.
Case's Mount Pisgah.
Chalmers' (Thomas) Sermons.
Channing's (W. E.) Sermons.
Charnock's Works.
Christian Observer. 17:360.
Clarke's (R. W.) Heaven and its emblems.
Clerke's (Richard) Sermons.
Close's (Francis) Sermons.
Davies' Glimpses of our heavenly home.
Davis' (W.) The beautiful city.
Dell's (Robt.) The blessed hope.
Donald's My father's house.
Dorrington's (Theophilus) Sermons.
D'Oyly's (George) Sermons.
Dunlop's (William) Sermons.
Dwight's (Tim.) Discourses. Disc. 17.
Edmondson's Heavenly world.
Faber's (Geo. S.) Many mansions.
Freeman's Heaven entered.
Gahan's (William) Sermons.
Garden's (Francis) Discourses.
Gataker's (Thomas) Sermons.
Goodwin's State of future glory.
Green's (Bp.) Discourses.
Hill's (H. F.) Saint's Inheritance.
Hincks' (John) Sermons.
Horneck's Glory of the other world.
Jenks' Ouranography.
Killing's (J. M.) Our companions in glory.
King's Morsels of criticism.
Kollock's (S. K.) Sermons.
Leifchild's (John) Discourses.
Mant's Happiness of the blessed.
Mather's (Increase) Glory of heaven.
Meek's (Robt.) Heavenly things.

Heaven—*continued.*

Melville's (Henry) Sermons.
Merry's Phil. of a happy futurity.
Milner's (Joseph) Sermons.
Orton's Religious Exercises.
Pierce's (S. A.) Riches of divine grace.
Pirie's (Alexander) Sermons.
Pott's (J. H.) Sermons.
Powell's (Vav.) Three-fold state of the elect.
Princeton Review. 27:269.
Roberts' Nature, locality, &c.
Salkeld's Paradise and its contents.
Saurin's (James) Sermons.
Seed's (Jeremiah) Sermons.
Sharp's (Abp.) Sermons.
Short's (T. V.) Sermons.
Taylor's Contemplations on the state of man.
Thompson's (A. C.) The better land.
Tillotson's (Abp.) Sermons.
Toplady's (A. M.) Works.
Van Mildert's (Bp.) Sermons.
Venn's (Henry) Sermons.
Wake's (Abp.) Sermons.
Watts' (Isaac) Death and Heaven.
——— Scale of happiness.
Whitley's The life everlasting.
Witherspoon's (John) Works.

Heavenly Mindedness. See DEVOTION, GODLINESS, WALK OF FAITH, WORLDLINESS.

Allestree's (Richard) Sermons.
Arnold's (Thomas) Sermons.
Baker's (Arthur) Sermons.
Blunt's (Henry) Sermons.
Bowdler's (John) Theological Essays.
Brady's (Nicholas) Sermons.
Burroughes (J.) on Conversing in heaven.
Cecil's (Richard) Sermons.
Christian Observer. 12:213.
Cooper's (Edward) Sermons.
Durham's (James) Sermons.
Evans' Sermons on Christian temper.
Evans' (R. W.) Parochial sermons.
Flavel's Husbandry spiritualized.
——— Navigation spiritualized.
Fothergill's (George) Sermons.
Goodwin on being Filled with the Spirit.
Graves' (Richard) Sermons.
Hervey's Meditations.
Horton's (Thomas) Sermons.
Jones' (Wm., of Nayland) Sermons.
Milner's (Joseph) Sermons.
Owen's Grace and duty of being sp. minded.
Paley's (William) Sermons.
Powell's (Samuel) Sermons.
Price's (James) Sermons.
Riddock's (James) Sermons.
Rowe (John) on Heavenly-mindedness.
Sherlock's (Bp.) Sermons.
Skelton's (Philip) Sermons.
Tillotson's Sermons.
Venn's (John) Sermons.
Watts on the Christian graces.
Weston's (Bp.) Sermons.
Whitefield's (George) Sermons.

Hebraisms of the New Testament. See IDIOMS.

The grammars and Lexicons of Bretschneider, Wahl, Tittman, Gersdorf, Winer, and Gesenius, throw all the light on this wearisome controversy which is now possible.

Hebrew Commonwealth. See JEWISH ANTIQUITIES.

Hebrew Language. See VOWEL POINTS.

Chrysostom, de Ebræa lingua.
Augustine, de Civitate Dei.
Origen, Homiliæ.

Avianus de Ebræa Lingua.
Bartolocci Dissertationes.
Bellarmini Gramatica Hebræica.
Berndii (Adam.) Disquisitiones.
Bianconi, de Antiquis litteris Hebr.
Bocharti Phaleg et Canaan. Lib. I.
Buxtorfii (Sen.) Thesaurus Grammaticus.
——— de Abbreviaturis.
Buxtorfii (Jun.) Dissertationes Philol.
Capellus (Ludov.) de Ebræorum literis.
Celsius de Variis fatis ling. Ebrææ.
Clerici (David.) Dissertationes.
Diecmanus de Ebr. ling. primigenia.
Dobrowsky de Antiquis Heb. caracteribus.
Dolingii Hist. cum Theoria ling. Ebrææ.
Elias Levita, Dissertationes.
Ewald, Heb. Grammatik.
Gesenii Historia linguæ Ebrææ.
——— Thesaurus philologicus.
Guarin, Grammatica Hebr. (A noble work.)
Hardtii (Herman.) Dissertationes.
Hartmann, Einleitung in des Bucher A. T.
Hauptmanni Elementa Ebræa.
Hezel's Gesch. der Heb. Sprache.
Hottingeri (Ioann.) Dissertationes.
Hulsius de Linguæ Ebraicæ origine.
Iunius de Præstantia, et Antiquitate, &c.
Leusdeni Dissertationes.
Loescherus de Causis linguæ Ebraicæ.
Martinet's Hebräische Sprache.
Michaelis de Ebr. et affinibus linguis.
Morini (Steph.) Exercitationes.
Reineccii Ling. Hebrææ Vet. Test. Janua.
Robertsoni (G.) Thesaurus ling. sanctæ.
Schroederi Fundamenta linguæ Hebrææ.
Schultens (A.) Oratio de lingua Hebraica.
Selden de Synedris. Lib. 2, cap. 9.
Sennertus de Idiotismus ling. orientalium.
Simon, Hist. critique de Vieux Test.
Waltoni Prolegomena.

American Biblical Repository. 1:491. 8:44 11:131,482. 12:113.
American Quarterly Register. 1:193.
Bennet's Primogeniture and integrity of the holy language.
Brekell's (John) Essay on the Heb. tongue.

Hebrew Language—*continued.*

Burgess' Elements of Hebrew. (A most valuable primer, especially for such as have no living teacher.)
Christian Monthly Spectator. 3:236.
Craik's History and characteristics, &c.
Fitzgerald's Originality and permanency of biblical Heb. (Applies to Deism.)
Forbes on the Study of the Heb. language.
Gerard's Biblical Criticism.
Gesenius' Hist. of the Heb. lang. and letters.
Holden's Guide to the Hebrew language.
Jennings' (David) Dissertations.
Journal of Science. 24:87.
Kitto's Journal of Sacred Literature. (Many good articles.)
Le Clerc's (John) Dissertations.
Leigh's (Edw.) Critica Sacra. (Observations on all the Hebrew roots.)
Princeton Review. 2:293. 13:250.
Rhenfred's Antiquity of the Hebrew letters.
Wahl's Oriental languages and literature.
Wall's Ancient Heb. orthography, and the original state of the text of the Old Test.

Hebrew Poetry. See POETRY.

Heidelburg Catechism.

Altingii Historia Ecclesiæ Palatinæ.
Augusti Versuch einer Hist.-Kritischen Einleitung, &c.
Klemme's Entstehung d. H. Katechismus.
Köcker's Gesch. der Reformirten kirche, sonderlich d. Schicksale d. Heid. Cat.
Le Boucq, Succincta et dilucida explic.
Meieri Explicatio et Commentatio.
Mylii Meletemeta catechetica.
Paul's Unterricht christlicher Lehre.
Piscatoris, Explicatio.
Plack's Gesch. d. prot. Lehrbegriff.
Seissen's Gesch. der Ref. zu Heidelberg.
Struve's Pfalzische Kirchenhistorie.
Sudhoff's Handb. zur Auslegung d. H. C.
Thelemann's Gesch. d. H. C. u. seiner verfas.
Van Alpen's Gesch. und literatur des H. C.
Vierordt's Gesch. d. Reformation in Baden.
Ursini Corpus doctrinæ orthodoxæ.
Zohn, zur 300 Jahr. Gedachtniss fier d. H. K.

Amer. Presb. and Theol. Review. 1:369.
Basting on the H. Catechism.
Bethune's (Geo. W.) Lectures on the H. C.
De Witte on the H. Catechism.
Nevins' (J. W.) Hist. and genius of the H. C.
Ursinus on the H. C. Tr. by G. W. Willard.
——— ——— Tr. by H. Parrie.

Hell. See DESCENT INTO HELL, GEHENNA, HADES, PLACE OF THE DAMNED.

Augustine, Opera.
Cyril (Alex.), Orationes.
Boullier, Considerations sur la certitude, et la grandeur des recompenses du monde a venir.
Crocii Conversationes prutenicæ.

Hell—*continued.*

Drieburg de Statu hominis futuro.
Fabricius (Jo.) Predigten über die Augspurgische Conf.
Fechtius Consideratio status damnatorum.
Feverlini Novissimorum novissima.
Loescheri Exercitationes. Ex. VIII.
Mosheim's (J. L.) Lehre vom ende der Höllenstrafen.
Schottel's Beschreibung u. Vorstellung der Hœlle.
Theiss' Meinung von d. Ewigkeit der Höllens.
Adams' (John) Sermons.
Adams' (Neh.) Truths for the times.
Adey's (William) Sermons.
Ambrose's (Isaac) Sermons.
Amer. Biblical Repository. 2d Series. 3:1.
Barrow's (Dr. F.) Dissertations.
Bates' Four last things.
Benson's (Joseph) Sermons.
Berry Street Lectures.
Beveridge's (Bp.) Sermons.
Boyse's (Joseph) Sermons.
British Quarterly Review. 7:105.
Boston's Fourfold State.
Brine's (J.) Vindic. of Divine justice.
Brooks' Golden Key.
Bunyan's Sighs from hell.
Burgess on Original sin.
Burnett's Theory of the earth.
Campbell's (Geo.) Prelim. Dissertations.
Christian Examiner. 8:392.
Christian Quarterly Review. 1:598.
Christian Monthly Spectator. 3:505.
Church Review. 2:359. (Review of John Foster.)
Cudworth's Intellectual System.
Dawes' (Abp.) Sermons.
Dobney on Future punishment.
Doddridge's (P.) Lectures.
Drexel on Hell.
Dwight's Sermons. Ser. 167 and 168.
Eclectic Review. 4th Series. 18:153. (Review of Dobney.) 22:389.
Edwards' (Pres.) Sermons.
Foster (James) on Natural Religion.
Foster's (John) Letters.
Frith's (John, the Martyr) Works.
Fuller's Gospel its own witness.
Gill (John) on the Hebrew language.
Goodwin's Works. Book 13.
Green's (Bp.) Discourses.
Gregory on Moral liberty. Bk. 14.
Hammond's (Dr. H.) Works.
Horberry's (Dr. M.) Works.
Horsley's (Bp.) Sermons.
Jenkins' Reasonableness of Christianity.
Jewell's (Bp.) Sermons.
Lewis on the Nature of Hell.
Lord's Theological and Literary Journal. 3:395. (Review of Dobney.)
Loring's (I.) Sermons.
Morony's (Joseph) Sermons.
Morse's Grand mystery of godliness.
New Englander. 9:168.

Hell—*continued.*

Ray on the Dissolution of the world.
Rogers' (Dr. John) Sermons.
Saurin's (J.) Sermons.
Seed's (Jeremiah) Sermons.
Sherlock's (Dean) Sermons.
Simpson on Scripture language.
Skelton's (Philip) Sermons.
Smallridge's (Bp.) Sermons.
Spirit of the Pilgrims. Vol. 2.
Stuart's (Moses) Exegetical Essays.
Swinden on Hell. (Many editions.)
Tillotson's Sermons.
Van Mildert's (Bp.) Sermons.
Watts' World to come.
Wesley's (John) Sermons.
Whiston on Hell.
Whitby's (Dan.) Discourses.
Whitefield's Sermons.

Hellenists.

Hertzog's Real Encyclop. Tr. by Bomberger.
Lardner's Remarks on Ward's Dissertations.
Ward's (Dr.) Dissertations.

Helvetic Confession.

Confessio et Expositio simplex orthodoxæ fidei auctore Frederico, electore Palatino. (This is the confession of faith commonly called the Helvetic, composed in 1566, by Bullinger, and differs little from that of Zuingle before it was remodeled by Calvin.)
Heideggeri Formula consensus Ecclesiarum Helveticarum.
Hottingeri Formulæ cons. Helv. historia.
Koecheri Biblioth. theolog. symbolic.
Pfaffius de Formula consensus Helvetica.

Hemerobaptists.

Epiphanius de Hæresiis.
Mosheim, de rebus christianorum ante Constantinum.

Robinson's History of Baptism.

Henricians. See WALDENSES.

Ganfredi Epistolæ. Lib. VI.
Gesta Episcoporum Cenomanens.
Hecker's (Henr. Conrad.) Dissertationes.
Mabilloni Analecta ad historiam eccles.
Meisneri (Ioan.) Dissertationes.

Heracleonites.

Rhenferdi (Io.) Dissertationes.
Vogtii (Ioan.) Dissertationes.
——— Biblioth. hist. hæresiologic.

Hereditary Depravity. See FALL, HUMAN DEPRAVITY, IMPUTATION OF ADAM'S SIN, ORIGINAL SIN.

Heresy. See HISTORY OF DOCTRINES.

Clemens Alex., Stromata.
Epiphanius, Παναριος Αιρεσεων LXXX.
Tertullian, Prescriptiones adversus Heretic.
Athanasius, Orationes.
Theodoret, de Hæresibus.
Augustine, Opuscula polemica.
Irenæus, contra Hæreses omnes.

Arnoldi Historia Hereticos.
——— Kirchen und Ketzer-historie. (A new edition of the above, with improvements, and a supplement.)
Assemanni Bibliotheca Orientalis.
Baaz Λεξιδιον.
Baur's Christl. Lehre von der Dreieinigkeit.
Beckmani Hæresiographia.
Bellarmin de Controversiis fidei.
Breithauptii Observationes Theologicæ.
Buddeus de Ecclesia apostolica.
Callixtus de Schismate et Hæretic. pœnis.
Callovii (Abrah.) Dissertationes.
Castro, adversus omnes Hæreses. (Partly polemic, and partly historical.)
Colbergius de Origine et progressu errorum.
Crameri Arbor Hæreticæ consanguinitatis.
Damascenus (Jo.) de Hæresibus.
Danæi Elenchi Hereticorum.
Echard, de Fonte Hæresium.
Epiphanius contra Octoginti Hæreses.
Fabricii Lux Evangelii salutaris, &c. C. 8.
——— Bibliotheca Greca.
Heickmanus de Origine erroris.
Hippolyti Refutatio omnium Hæresium.
Horbius de Hæresii in genere.
Hoornbeckii Summa Controversiarum.
Ittigii Dissertationes. (Heresies of the apostolic age. "The best modern work on the subject."—BP. TOMLINE.)
Iocherus de Philos. hæresium obici.
Leontii Sectarum Historia.
Loescheri Premonitiones Theologicæ.
Lutzenburgeri Catal. Hæretic. To 1528.
Marckii Exercitationes miscellaneæ. Par. I.
Mayii Dissertationes Selectæ.
Mori Enthusiasmus Triumphatus.
Mosheimii Dictionaire de Heresiis.
Œhleri Corpus H., Græce et Latine. (Vast.)
Olearii Synopsis Controversiarum.
Perodil, Diction. des hérésies. 1845.
Schenkel's Wesen des Protestantismus.
Schrœderi Disp. an Hæresis sit crimen?
Steren [or Stieren], de Irenæi adv. Hæreses.
Stockman, Lexicon Hæresium.
Thomasii Disp. an Hæresis sit crimen?
Vitringa, Observationes Sacræ.
Vogtii Bibliotheca historiæ hæresiologicæ.
Wolfii Manichæismus ante Manichæos.
Wolderi Hæresiologiæ Synopsis.
Zigadeni Panoplia dogmatica fidei.
Zwinglius de Vera et falsa religione.

Baxter's (Rich.) Works.
Bayle's Crit. and hist. Dictionary. (Under the several names.)
Burton's Bampton Lectures. 1829. (Heresies of the apostolic age.)
Campbell's (Geo.) Preliminary Dissertations.
Commentators generally, on Titus iii. 10.
Evans' Scripture Standard.

Heresy—*continued.*

Finch's Bampton Lectures. 1797.
Foster's (James) Sermons.
Lardner's Heretics of the first 2 centuries.
Leslie's History of Heresy.
Osterwald's Corruptions of Religion.
Powell on Subscription to Creeds.
Rawlins on Heretical opinions.
Rogers' (John) Sermons.
Spirit of the Pilgrims. 3:354.
Stebbings (Henry) on Heresy.
Trapp's Preservative against unsettled opinions.
Turner's History of heretical opinions.
Varilla's History of Heresies.
White (Blanco) on Heresy and Orthodoxy.

Hermas.

Hermas, Opera.
Anger u. Dindorf's Nachträgliche Bemerkungen zu H.
Cotelerii Vitæ Patrum Apostolicæ.
Jackman's Hirte des Hermas.
Nourrii Bibliotheca max. patrum.
Lardner's Credibility. Part 2.
Pringle's Trans. of the three books of H.
Spirit of the Pilgrims. 5:485.
Stuart's Commentary on the Apocalypse.

Hermeneutics. See BIBLICAL CRITICISM, STUDY OF SCRIPTURE.

Ambrose, Clavis ad sacram scripturam.
Jerome, Prolegomena.
Alberi Institutiones Hermeneuticæ.
Arigleri Herm. Biblico-generalis.
Bahrdt Apparatus criticus Vet. Test.
Baumgarten (S. J.), Unterricht von Auslegung d. H. S.
Beckii Monogrammata Hermeneutices N. T.
Danhaveri Hermeneutica Sacra.
Ernesti Institutio interpret. Nov. Test.
——— Opuscula philologica critica.
Flaccius de Sermone sacrar. literarum.
——— Clavis Scripturæ Sacræ.
Franckii Prelectiones hermeneuticæ.
——— Com. de scopo librorum S. Sc.
Franzii Tractatus Theologicus. (A work of immense labor, and always useful.)
Glassii Hermen. Sacra. (Of great value.)
Griesbach's Vörlesungen über d. H. d. N. T.
Hederick, H. analytica et synthetica.
Hilleri Syntagma Hermeneutica.
Hoffmanni Institutiones Theologiæ.
Huet de Interpretatione, &c.
Iahn, Enchiridion Herm. generalis.
Ianssenii Hermeneutica Sacra.
Kaizer's Grundrisseines systems der H.
Keilii Opuscula Academica.
——— Elementa Hermeneutices N. T.
Klausen's (H. N.) Hermeneutik des N. Test.
Langii Hermeneutica Sacra.
Loescheri Breviarium theol. exegeticæ.
Lucke's Grundriss der H. und ihrer Gesch.
Meyer's Geschichte d. Exegese. (To 1802.)

Hermeneutics—*continued.*

Mori Hermeneutica N. Test.
Pareau, Institutio interpretis Vet. Test.
Pfeifferi Hermeneutica Sacra.
Planck's Einleitung in d. theol. Wissensch.
Rambackii Hermeneutica Sacra.
Schottii Opuscula.
Seiler's Biblische Hermeneutik. (Praised by J. PYE SMITH.)
Semleri Preparatio Hermeneutica.
Senensi Ars interpretandi scripturas.
Spitzner de Parenthesi libris sacris.
St. Victoire (Hugo) de Erudit. didascalica.
Turretin de S. Scrip. interpretandæ modo.
Winer de Hypallage et hendiadyi in N. T.
Wolfius de Agnitione ellipseos.
Wollii Examen regularum a Calmeti.
——— Com. de parenthesi sacra.
Wyttenbachii Elementa proposita.

American Biblical Repository. 1:111,139. 3:684. 5:92. 7:241. Second Series. 5:9.
Apthorpe's (East) Canons of interpretation.
Arnold (T.) on the Interp. of Scripture.
Biblical Cabinet. (Many excellent articles on this subject.)
Carson's (Alex.) Exam. of the principles of interpretation, as laid down by Ammon, Ernesti, Stuart, and others. (Masterly.)
Christian Month. Spect. 2:9. (The principles.) 3:169. 8:169. (The history.)
Christian Observer. 11:11.
Christian Review. 4:481. 5:211,321. 10:411.
Conybeare's Bampton Lectures. 1824. (The limits to secondary and spiritual interpretations.)
Davidson's Sacred Hermeneutics. (Includes a history of Bib. interpr. from the earliest fathers, to the Reformation.)
Ernest's Princ. of Interp. Tr. by M. Stuart.
——————— Tr. by C. H. Terrot.
Fairbairne's Hermeneutical Manual.
Griesbach's Lectures.
Kaiser's System of N. Test. Hermeneutics.
Lee's (Prof.) Six sermons on the study of Sacred Scripture.
Lucke's Elements of Hermeneutics.
McLelland's Manual of sac. interpretation.
North American Review. 14:391.
Pareau's Princip. of interp. Tr. by Forbes.
Planck's Sacred philol. and interp. Trans. and enlarged, with notes, by Turner.
Princeton Review. 1:128. 3:90. 17:409.
Sawyer's Elements of Bib. interpretation.
Seiler's Biblical H. Trans. by W. Wright.
Stuart's (Moses) Elements of interpretation.
Theol. and Literary Journal. 3:80,235.
Toelner's Outlines of sacred Hermeneutics.
Universalist Quarterly. 7:138.
Van Mildert's Bampton Lectures. 1814.
Whitby's (Dan.) Dissertations.

For other works on interpretation, see TERROT'S *Trans. of Ernesti's Institutes*, and DAVIDSON'S *Sacred Hermeneutics.*

Hermits. See MONASTICISM.

Arrhenii Dissertatio de Eremitis.
Ballerini (Ioann.) Dissertationes.
Deylingius de Ascetis veterum.
Fontanini Historia literaria.
Mabillonii Prefatio ad Acta Sanctorum.
Muratori Antiquitates Italiæ medii ævi.
Palladii Historia Eremitarum. (To 421.)

Palladius' Lausiac history.
Rosweide's Acc. of the hermits of Palestine.

Hernhutters. See MORAVIANS.

Herodians. See JEWISH ANTIQUITIES, SECTS.

Ellis' (Sir R.) Fortuita Sacra.

Herod the Great.

Altemanus in Tempe Helvetica.
Bergeri (Paul.) Dissertationes.
Cellarii (Balthaz.) Dissertationes Academ.
D'Artigney, de l'Origine d'Herode.
Deylingii Observationes Sacræ. Pars II.
Hambergii (Geo. Albert.) Dissertationes.
Josephi (Flav.) Opera.
Noldii Historia Idumeæ.
Spanheimii (Ez.) Stemma de prosapia Her.

Atterbury's (Bp.) Sermons.
Brownrig's (Bp.) Sermons.
Sherlock's (Bp.) Sermons.

Hicksites. See FRIENDS.

Hieroglyphics. See EGYPT.

Bailey, Hieroglyphicorum origo et natura.
Champollion, Systeme Hieroglyphique.
Goulianof, sur les H. d'Horapollon.
Kircheri Œdipus Ægyptiacus.
Klaproth, Examen des travaux de Champol.
Langlois, Hiéroglyphes Egyptiens.
Lenoir, Nouvelle explication des H.
Pahlin, Lettres sur les Hieroglyphes.
——— Analyse de l'inscription du monument trouve a Rosette.
Roblano, Etudes sur les Hieroglyphe.

American Quarterly Review. 1:438. 9:339.
Bunsen's Egypt's place in history.
Deverell's Discoveries in H. 1813.
Grappe [or Greppo] on the Hierogl. system of Champollion, and the advantages it offers to sacred criticism.
Hinks on the Powers of Hieroglyphics.
Landseer's Sabean Researches.
Salts' Essay on Young's Phonetic system.
Sharp's Vocabulary of Egyptian hieroglyphics. (Gives 1,300 hieroglyphics, with explanations.)
Spineto's Egyptian Antiquities.
Spohn on the Lang. of ancient Egypt.
Wathen's Antiq. and chronol. of anc. Egypt.
Young's Recent discoveries in Egyptian antiquities. 1823.

High Church. See APOSTOLICAL SUCCESSION, EFFICACY OF SACRAMENTS, ORDINATION, OXFORD DIVINITY.

Hilary.

Hilarii Opera, quotquot extant.
Bollandi Acta Sanctorum.
Constanti Vita Hilarii.
Erasmi Prefatio ad Hilarii opera.
Grynæi Vita H. præmissa Hilarii operibus.
Oudini (Cassimer.) Dissertationes.

Lardner's Credibility.

Hinduism.

Bartholomæi Systema Brahm. liturgicum.
Bohlen, Das alte Indien.
Bournouf, Yadjnadattabada: traduction, avec la texte.
Bruckeri Historia critica philosophiæ.
Franck's Mythologie der Hindus.
Kleuker's Braminische Religions system.
Lord, Hist. de la religion de Banians.
Nork's Brahminen und Rabbinen.
Paulini Systema Bràhminicum.
Poley, Devi Mahatmyam.
Raspe's Gesetzbuch d. Gentoos.
Rhodes, Mythol. und philos. der Hindus.
Tassy, Hist. de la literatur Hindui.

Asiatic Researches. Periodical since 1790. (Many valuable articles.)
Belno's Daily prayers of the Brahmins. (Plates, showing the attitudes.)
Bjornstjerna's Theogony of the Hindus.
Blackwood's Magaz. March, 1859. (Creeds and castes.)
Butler's (Arthur) Lectures on philosophy.
Carey & Marshman's tr. of the Ramayuna.
Carwithen's Bampton Lectures. 1809.
Christian Examiner. 63:174.
Colebrook's (H. T.) Essays.
Coleman's Mythology of the Hindus. Plates. (A comprehensive and convenient work.)
Cole's Mythology of the Hindoos.
Crawford's Religion and learning of the H.
Duff's (Alex.) India and Indian missions.
Duperon's Oupnek hat.
Forbes' Oriental Memoirs.
Grose's Voyage to the East Indies.
Halded's Code of Gentoo laws.
Jones' (Sir W.) Works. (In the highest esteem.)
Journal of the American Oriental Society. New Haven. (1853 to the present.)
Malcom's Travels in S.-Eeastern Asia. 1839.
Malcolm's (Sir J.) Central India.
Massie's Continental India. 1840.
Maurice's Boyle Lectures. 1847.
Maurice's Indian antiquities. (Noble.)
Mills' History of the British empire.
Moore's Hindu Pantheon. 100 plates.
Mullen's History of Sanscrit literature.
——— Aspects of H. philosophy. 1860.
North British Review. 1:366.
Oriental Translation Society Publications.
Ousley's (Sir Wm.) Oriental Collections.
Rammohun Roy's translation of the principal sacred books, &c.
Ritter's History of philosophy.

Hinduism—*continued.*

Roberts' Illustrations of the Hindu Sacred Scriptures.
Stephenson's Trans. of the Sanhita.
——— ——— Kalpha Sutra.
Upham's Trans. of the Mahavansi, &c. (The sacred books of Ceylon.)
Ward's Hist. liter. mythology, &c., of the H.
Williams on the Knowl. of the supreme Lord.
Wilson's (H. H.) Tr. of the Vishna Puranna.
——— " Rig Veda Sanhita.
Wilson's (John) Exposure of H. religion.
Wrighton's Sanscrit Hagiographa.

Many translations of Brahminical books are extant. A long list may be found in ABBOT'S *Literature of the doctrine of a future life.*

Hippolytus.

Hippolyti Opera. (Ed. Fabricio. 1716.)
Bassnage de Vita, morte, et scriptis H.
Bunsen's H. und seine zeit.
Cellier, Hist. generale des auteurs sacrés.
Cottelerii Monumenta eccl. Græcæ.
Haenell de H. tertii sæculi scriptore.
Hermanni (Ernest.) Dissertationes.
Histoire literaire de France. (By the Benedictine monks.)
Moyne, Prolegomena ad varia sacra.
Ruggeri de Portuensi H. Dissertatio.
Ruinarti Acta primorum martyrum.

Bunsen's Hippolytus and his age.
London Quarterly Review. 4:142.
North British Review. 19:85.
Tayler's (W. E.) H. and the Church. (Translates the newly discovered manuscripts.)
Wordsworth's H. and the Ch. of the 3d cent.

Historic Form of Conveying Christianity.

Charlesworth's Sermons. Pref. to Vol. 2.
Simpson on the Superiority of the historic form, &c.

History of Doctrines.

Epiphanius, adversus LXXX hæreses.
Irenæus, contra omnes Hæreses.

Altingii Theologia Historica.
Arnold's (G.) Kirchen und Ketzerhistorie. (To 1699.)
Augusti Chrestomathia Patristica.
——— Lehrbuch d. christl. Dogmenges.
Baieri (F. C.) Theologia Historica.
Bartholmès, Hist. crit. des doct. religieuses.
Basnage, Hist. des principaux dogmes de l'eglise Romain.
Baumgarten Cru., Evangel. glaubens lehre.
——— Christlichen Dogmengeschichte.
Becani Opuscula.
——— Manuale Controversiarum.
Beck's Christliche Dogmengeschichte.
Benzelii Syntagma.
Bergier, Dictionaire Thèologique.

History of Doctrines—*continued.*

Berthold's Handbuch der Dogmengesch.
Blumröder's Religion nach ihre Idee.
Bretschneider's Hist.-dogmat. Auslegung.
Bruckeri Historia critica Philosophiæ.
Buddei Eccles. Apostolica. (Minute.)
Daub's Christlichen Dogmengesch.
De Wette's Dogmatik d. Ev. Lutherisch. K.
Dorner's Entwickelungsgeschichte d. Lehre von der Person Christi.
Dupin, Biblioth. des auteurs ecclesiast.
Ebrard's Handbuch der Kirchen.
Elster, Medii ævi Theologia Exegetica.
Engelhardt's Dogmengeschichte.
Flaccii Illyrici Clavis scripturæ sacræ. ("An admirable work."—CONYBEARE.)
——— Catalogus testium veritatis.
Flügg's Gesch. d. theolog. Wiesenschaften.
Forbesii Instructiones historico-theologicæ. (A history of the controversies, with the writers fairly quoted. "The most valuable book of the kind."—WOTTON.)
Fourquevaux, Catechisme Historique.
Frank's (G.) Gesch. d. protestant. Theol.
Gass' Gesch. des protestant. Dogmatik.
Giesler's Lehrbuch der Kirchenges. Vol. 6.
——— Clement. Alex. et Origenis doct.
Ginoulhiac, Hist. du dogme, pendant les trois premier siécles de l'eglise.
Grimmii Inst. theol. dogmaticæ evangelicæ.
Hagenbach's Dogmengeschichte.
Harenbergii Theol. prim. Christianorum.
Hasei Hutterus redivivus.
Heppe's Dogmatik d. Deutschen Protestantismus im 16 Jahrh.
Hermann's Gesch. d. protestantischen Dogmatik, v. Melancthon bis Schleiermacker.
Hottingeri Fata doctrinæ de predestinatione ad hæc usque tempora, ab ortu Christ. in annales digesta. 1727.
Ittigius de Hæresiarchis ævi apostolici.
Jurieu, Hist. critique des dogmes et cultes depuis Adam jusqu'a Jésus Christ.
Kargii (A. F. F.) Opera.
Klein's Darstellung des Systems, &c.
Lange's Ausfuhr. Gesch. der Dogmengesch.
Lentz's Gesch. d. Christlichen Dogmen.
Maffei Hist. dogmatum et opinionum.
Maguini Vet. doct. qui IX. seculo scripserunt collectio.
Marheineke's Theologische Vörlesungen.
Neander's (A.) Antignosticus. (Faith and morals of the first Christians.)
Paffei Specimen Hist. Dogmaticæ.
Petavii Dogmata Theologica.
Philonis Judæi Opera.
[Planck's] Gesch. d. protestant. Theologie, v. d. Konkordienformel bis in d. mitte d. 18 Jahrh.
——— Darstellung d. dogmat. systeme d. Christl. Hauptparteien.
Reinard's Hist. præcip. dogmatum.
Reuss, Hist. de la theologie au siécle apostol.
Sack, Com. quæ ad theol. histor. pertinet.
Schwaz, Gesch. d. neuesten Theologie. 1856.

History of Doctrines—*continued.*

Schweizer's Centraldogmen in ihrer Entwickelung innerhalt.
——— Theologisch-ethischen zustande d. 17 Jahrh. in d. Zwicherischen Kirche.
Schroeck's Christliche Kirchengeschichte.
Seileri Theologia dogmatico-polemica.
Simon, Hist. critique des dogmes.
Stäudlin's Gesch. d. theol. Wissenschaften.
Suiceri Thesaurus Ecclesiasticus.
Tholuck's Glaubwurdigkeit der kirche.
Titmann's Gesch. d. Theologie in d. protestant kirche.
Ulman's Beitrag zur kirchen und Dogmengesch. des IV. Jahrh.
Vossii (G. J.) Theses, theol. et historicæ.
——— Historia de Controversiis.
Walch's (C. W. F.) Entwurf einer vollsstaendigen hist. der ketzerein.
Walch's (J. G.) Einleitung in d. Religionsstreitigkeiten d. Luther. Kirchen.
Wallenburch de Controversiis de fide.
Wetzer und Welte's Kirchen Lexicon. 1856.

Allen's (Rich.) Lives of the Fathers.
American Biblical Repository. 3:143.
Bennett's (James) Theol. of the early church. (Quotations from the Fathers.)
Berriman's Moyer Lectures. 1723, 1724. (A historical account of the controversies on the doctrine of the Trinity.)
Bibliotheca Sacra. 4:552.
Boone's Book of Churches and Sects.
Bull's Opinions of the Church for the first three centuries.
Bunsen's Hippolytus and his age. (A comparison of ancient with modern theology.)
Burton's Ante-Nicene Fathers.
——— Bampton Lectures. 1829. (Heresies of the apostolic age.)
Casaubon's Origin of heresies.
Cave's Primitive Christianity.
Christian Examiner. 9:182.
Christian Monthly Spectator. 9:27,249.
Christian Quart. Spectator. 4:291.
Christian Review. 7:586.
Cunningham's Review of the principal doctrinal discussions, since the Apostles. 1863.
Dewar's Hist. of German theology, from the Reformation to the present. 1844.
Donaldson's Hist. of Chr. doctrine. To 1866.
Eclectic Review. 4th Series. 22:257. 26:428.
Ellis' First half century of the Unitarian controversy. 1857.
Erskine's (John) Sketches of history.
Foulke's Christendom's divisions.
Giesler's Church History.
Giles' Writings of the 2d century.
Hagenbach's History of doctrines.
Horseley's (Bp.) Tracts.
Jurieu's Crit. hist. of doctrine and worship. (Includes an account of all the ancient idolatries, so far as they affected Judaism.)
Kahnis' Internal history of German Protestantism. Tr. by Meyer. 1856.

History of Doctrines—*continued.*

Ketts' Bampton Lectures. 1790.
Killen's Ancient Church.
Morgan's Infl. of Plato and Philo Judæus.
Muenscher's Dogmatic hist. Tr. by Murdock.
Murray's Hist. of religion. (Convenient.)
Neander's Lectures. Tr. by Ryland.
Newton's Review of Church history so far as concerns the progress, declensions, and revivals of evangelical doctrine.
Osborne's Errors of the Apostolic Church.
Priestley's History of early opinions.
Princeton Review. 4:14,167. 19:91. 24:250.
Schwarz's Hist. of the most recent theology. Since 1830.
Shedd's (W. G. T.) Hist. of Christian doct.
Sismondi's Relig. opinions of the 19th cent.
Stackhouse's Origin and design of Creeds.
Vaughn's Hours with the Mystics.
Wallace's Theology of New England. 1857.
Waterland's Critical history of the Athanasian Creed.
Whitaker's Origin of Arianism.
Wilson's (Will.) Illustrations of the method of explaining the New Test. by the early opinions of Jews and Christians. (A virtual refutation of Priestley.)
Wood's (Jas.) Old and New Theology. (Exhibition of the controversy between new and old school Presbyterians in the U. S.)

History of the Bible. See BIBLICAL HISTORY.

Holiness. See GODLINESS, IMITATION OF CHRIST, MORTIFICATION OF SIN, PERFECTION, PRACTICAL PIETY, RELIGION AND BUSINESS, SANCTIFICATION, SELF-DENIAL, &c.

Holiness of God. See ATTRIBUTES.

Balguy on Divine Rectitude.*
Bays on Divine Benevolence.*
Charnock's (Stephen) Works.
Foster's (Dr. James) Discourses.
Grove's (Henry) Works.*
Mole's (Thomas) Sermons.
Peabody's (A. P.) Lectures before the Lowell Institute. 1864.
Tillotson's (Abp.) Sermons.
Wisheart's (George) Sermons.
Wright's Answer to Mole.

* A controversy exciting much attention at the time (1730), but now forgotten, was carried on by these authors. Balguy refers the Divine actions to *rectitude*, Bays to *benevolence*, and Grove to his *wisdom*. Balguy and Grove are still valuable on general accounts.

Holydays. See FESTIVALS.

Holy Spirit. See OPERATIONS, PERSONALITY, PROCESSION, TRINITY.

Ambrose, de Spiritu Sancto.
Basil, Homiliæ.
Cyrill Hieros., Catacheses.
Arnold, contra Socinianos.

Holy Spirit—*continued.*

Cloppenburg, de Deitate Sp. Sancti.
Fritzche, de Spiritu Sancto.
Gerdin de Martyribus.
Gerhardi Loci Theologici.
Hackspanii Disputationes Theologicæ.
Hasselbach's Studien und Critiken.
Jahn (Alb.), Diss. ad quosnam pertineat promissio Spiritus.
Lampe de Spiritu Sancto.
Pfeifferus de Divinitate Sp. Sanc.
Rungius de Æternitate Spiritus Sanc.
Sandii (Christ.) Disputationes.
Storr, Doctrina Christiana.
Wernrichii Controv. contra Photinianos.
Wittichii Dissertationes Academicæ.

Barrow's (Bp.) Sermons on the Creed.
Berry Street Lectures.
Biddle on the Divinity of the Spirit.
Biddulph's Lectures on divine influence.
Booth's Reign of grace.
Buchanan's (James) Office and work of the Holy Spirit.
Bullinger's Decades. (Parker Society pub.)
Burnet on the Thirty-nine articles.
Burton's Testim. of the ante-Nicene Fathers.
Calamy's (Edm.) Sermons on the Trinity.
Carsdale on the Worship of the Holy Spirit.
Christian Quarterly Spect. 9:345.
Clagget (W.) on the Holy Spirit.
Edmondson's (Jonathan) Sermons.
Edwards' Mission of the Holy Ghost.
Estwick's Pneumatologia.
Gilfillan's (Sam.) Discourses on the H. S.
Guyse's Divinity of the Holy Spirit.
Hawker (Robt.) on the Person, Ministry, &c.
Heber's Bampton Lectures. 1815.
Howe's (John) Works.
Hurrion's 16 Sermons on the Spirit. (Great.)
Middleton on the Greek article.
Muir's (Will.) Sermons.
Nolan's (F.) Sermons.
Owen (Dr. John) on the Holy Spirit.
Poole's (Matt.) Blasphemer slain.
Ridley's Moyer Lectures. 1740. ("Incomparable."—Bp. Horne.)
Scott's (Tho.) Theological Essays.
Serle's Horæ Solitariæ.
——— Charis.
Simeon's Four sermons at Cambridge.
Smith's (John Pye) Sermons.
Watts' (Isaac) Works.
Whateley's Essays. Ess. 9.
Whitby's Last Thoughts.
Wilson's (Jos.) Sacred Pneumatology.
Witherspoon's Works.

Holy Water. See POPERY.

Baieri (Ioan. Guil.) Dissertationes.
Siberii Comm. de aquæ benedictæ potu.

Home Missions. See MISSIONS.

Amer. Biblical Repos. 3d Series. 4:252.
American Messenger. Periodical. N. York.
Home Evangelist. Period. N. Y.
Home Missionary. Period. Boston.
Home Mission Record. Periodical. N. Y.
Hutcheson (W.) on Home Evangelization.
Jethro; or an Essay on lay agency.
Matheson's Our Country.
Reports of the various H. M. Societies.
Sandford's Bampton Lectures. 1861.

Homiletics. See PREACHING.

Honesty. See INTEGRITY

Honor. See LOVE OF PRAISE, FAME.

Foster's (Dr. J.) Discourses.
Heber's (Bp.) Oxford Prize Essay. 1805.
Hall's (Bp.) Practical Works.
Markland's (Abraham) Sermons.
Paley's Moral Philosophy.
Tucker's Light of Nature pursued. Ch. 24.
Zollikoffer's (Geo. J.) Sermons.

Hope. See PASSIONS.

Zöckler de Vi et notione vocabuli ελπις in N. T.

Allestree's (Richard) Sermons.
Arnold's (Thomas) Sermons.
Bateman's (Josiah) Sermons.
Bowdler's Theological Essays.
Brougham's (John) Sermons.
Chalmers' (Thomas) Sermons.
Clark's (Adam) Sermons.
Cooper's (Edward) Sermons.
Craig's (Edward) Sermons.
Dehon's (Bp.) Sermons.
Fuller's Circular letter to the Northamptonshire Baptist Association.
Glasse's (G. H.) Sermons.
Greenwell's Patience of hope.
Grove's Moral Philosophy.
Haverfield's (Tho. T.) Sermons.
Howe's (John) Sermons. (None better.)
James' (J. A.) Christian hope.
Jay's (William) Sermons.
Lamb's (Robert) Sermons.
Lamont's (David) Sermons.
Lee's The family and its duties.
Rees' (Abraham) Practical Sermons.
Styles' (John) Sermons.
Summerfield's (John) Sermons.
Tappan's (D.) Sermons.
Taylor's (Jer.) Christian Consolation.
Tilly's (William) Sermons.
Tucker's Light of Nature pursued.
Tyerman (D.) on Evangelical Hope.
Venn's (John) Sermons.
Vidal's (Bp.) Sermons.
Walker's (James, D.D.) Sermons.
Wilks' (S. C.) Christian Essays.
Woodhouse's Practical Sermons.

Hopkinsianism.

Pro.

Hopkins' System of Doctrines.
——— Memoirs of himself.
Bellamy's Works.
Christian Spectator. 7:566. 10:530.
Emmons' (N.) Sermons.

Hopkinsianism—*continued.*

Pro.

Hopkinsian Magazine.
Perine's Letters on the Plan of Salvation.
Spring's (Rev. S.) Strictures on the Rev. D. Tappan.
Strong's (Dr. N.) Sermons.
Triangle. (A series of numbers.)
West (Dr. Stephen) on Moral agency.
Williams' (Thomas) Sermons.

Con.

Amer. Bibl. Repos. 2d Series. 8:314. 10:352.
Bangs' Errors of Hopkinsianism.
Biblioth. Sacra. 19:635.
Channing, W. E., Life of.
Christian Examiner. 33:169.
Ely's (E. S.) Contrast between Calvinism and Hopkinsianism.
——— Quarterly Theological Review.
Princeton Review. 14:530. 25:1.
Scott's (Tho.) Theological detached papers.
Tappan's (D.) Sermons.
Wilson's (J.) Letters.
Wilson's (J. R.) Historical sketch of opinions on the Atonement. (Containing Ely's Contrast, a translation of Turretin on the Atonement, &c.)

Hospitalers. See KNIGHTS OF MALTA.

Hospitality.

Leighton's Lectures on 1 Peter iv. 9.
Peronet's Sermons. (Serm. on Romans xii: 13. True and false hospitality.)
Stennett's Discourses on domestic duties.

Host. See TRANSUBSTANTIATION.

Huguenots. See REVOCATION.

Androque, Histoire du Languedoc.
Bouthillier, Reponse a l'avertisement des Catholiques. (Advising the killing of all the Huguenots.)
D'Aubigné (T. A.), der Hugenott von altem schrot u. Korn.
Histoire des Eglises reformées en France. (Supposed to be written by Beza.)

Browning's Hist. of the H. during the 16th century. (A new edition carries the history to 1842.)
Bungener's The Priest and the Huguenot. (Persecution under Louis XV.)
Christian Examiner. 36:74.
Eclectic Magazine. 16:21.
Lee's Huguenots in France.
Littell's Living Age. 20:145.
London Quart. Review. 20:21.
Marsh's (Mrs.) History of the Huguenots. (A work of intense interest.)
Martin's History of the Huguenots.
Methodist Quart. Review. 4:383.
Peyrat's Pastors in the Wilderness. (A valuable history, extending from the revocation of the Edict of Nantes, to the death of Louis XIV.)
Princeton Review. 12:71.
Smedley's Reformed religion in France.
Weis' History of the French Protestant Refugees. To 1854.
Wilk's (M.) Protest. of the South of France.

Human Depravity. See ORIGINAL SIN.

Prideaux, de Relig. capitib. controversis.
Stapferi Institutiones theol. polem.
Zanchius de Religione Christiana.

Appleton's (Pres.) Works. Vol. 1.
Bellamy's Nature and glory of the gospel.
Boston's Fourfold State.
Burgess on Original sin.
Calvin's Institutes.
Chalmers' (Dr.) 17 Sermons on Depravity.
Charnock's Works.
Clarkson's (David) Sermons.
Close's (Francis) Sermons on the Liturgy.
Cooper's (James) Sermons.
Delaune's (William) Sermons.
Dick's Philosophy of religion. Chapter 4. (Deals in facts.)
Doddridge's Lectures.
Dwight's Theology. Ser. 29–33.
Emmons' (Nathaniel) Sermons.
Fuller's (And.) Dialogues.
——— Essays.
Goodwin's (Thomas) Sermons.
Gray's Answer to Pierce's Vindication.
Griffin's Park Street Lectures.
Halyburton's Great Concern. Part 1.
Jamison's Use of Sacred history.
Leigh on the Depravity of the heart.
Leland's Advant. and necess. of revelation.
Lime Street Lectures.
McCheyne's (Robt. M.) Sermons.
Magee on Atonement. Diss. 12.
More (Hannah) on Female Education.
Müller's Christian doctrine of sin.
Panoplist. 3:561. 4:150,206,302.
Park Street Lectures. Lect. 1 and 2.
Princeton Review. 7:546.
Robinson's Christian System. Essays 13–18.
Scott's (Thomas) Essays. Ess. 5.
Seed's Sermons at the Moyer lecture.
Sewall on Human depravity.
Thorn's Three grand exhibitions.
Truman's Natural and moral impotence.
Venn's (John) Sermons.
West on Moral Agency.
Wilberforce's Practical View.
Wilcox's (Daniel) Sermons.
Williams' Vanity of childhood and youth.
Williams' (Thomas) Sermons.
Yonge's (James) Sermons.

Human Progress. See CIVILIZATION.

Buisson, Homme, la famile et la société; dans les rapports avec le progrès moral.

Amer. Bibl. Repos. 3d Series. 3:193.
Arnold's (of Rugby) Miscellaneous Works.
Baird's Christian Retrospect.
Bigland's Effects of physical and moral causes on the character of nations.

Human Progress—*continued.*

Chandler's Bampton Lectures. 1825. (Connection of Revelation with the improvement of Society.)
Christian Examiner. 42:46,345. 52:344.
Christian Review. 2:102.
Dick's (Dr. John) Works.
Dimmick's Moral influence of railroads.
Douglass' Advancement of society.
Draper's History of the intellectual development of Europe. 1864.
Eclectic Review. New Series. 1:389.
Eclectic Mag. 19:1. 29:389.
Edinburg Review. 21:8.
Foxton's (Fred. J.) Popular Christianity.
Frazier's Magazine. 1:147.
Hamilton (Robt.) on the Progress of society.
Home's (Lord Kames) History of man.
Huntingdon's Div. aspects of hum. society.
Kitto's Journal. 7:126.
Lord (J. C.) on Civilization and governm't.
Macintosh's Prog. of Ethical philosophy.
Mackay's Progress of the intellect as exemplified in the religious development of the Greeks and Hebrews.
Murray on the Character of nations.
Princeton Review. 18:1.
Seaman on the Progress of nations.
Selections from Edinb. Rev. 3:214.
Southey's (Robt.) Progress and prospects of society.
Stewart's Mental Philosophy.
Stuart's (G.) Soc. in Europe in its progress from rudeness to refinement.
Trusler's Progress of Society.
Westminster Review. 52:1.
Zollikoffer's Festivals and Fasts.

Human Responsibility. See FREE AGENCY, MORAL ABILITY, NECESSITY, OPINION.

Amer. Month. Review. 1:69. 4:152.
Amer. Quart. Register. 8:117.
Barrow's (Isaac) Sermons.
Christian Examiner. 24:277.
Dublin University Mag. 52:155.
Edwards (Pres.) on the Will.
Fuller's (Andrew) Essays.
Gibson's (James) Truths in Theology.
Haldane's (J. A.) Essays.
Hinton (C. J. H.) on Man's responsibility.
Jones (Jos.) on Human responsibility.
Leechman's (W.) Sermons. (R. for opinions.)
Lit. and Theol. Journal. 5:553. 6:23,151.
Meek's (E.) Responsibility of man.
New York Review. 3:378.
Percival's (A. P.) Sermons. ("Proportional responsibility.")
Smith's Hulsean Lectures. 1840. (Responsibility for religious belief.)
Spurgeon's (Cha. H.) Sermons. 6th Series.
Taylor's (Isaac) Man responsible for his dispositions.
Wardlaw's Man's accountab. for his belief.
Wayland's Limits of human responsibility.
West on Moral agency.
Wood's (Leonard) Works.

Human Sacrifices. See SACRIFICE.

Ghillany, die Menschenopfer d. alt. Hebräer.
Selden de Jure. Lib. IV., C. 6, 7.
Jennings' Jewish Antiquities.
Leland's Answer to Tyndall.
Magee on the Atonement. Vol. 1.
Sykes' Connection of Nat. and Rev. religion.

Humanity. See BENEVOLENCE, CRUELTY

Kames' Elements of criticism.
Pratt's Poem on Humanity.
Robinson's Christianity a humane system.

Humanity of Christ. See APOLLINARIANS, HYPOSTATIC UNION, INCARNATION.

Bullii Defensio fidei Nicenæ.
Calovii (Abr.) Dissertationes.
Haberkornii Christologia.
Harenburgii Theologia dogmatica.
Scherzeri Dissertationes.
Bradbury's Mystery of godliness.
Vaughn's (J.) Lectures. Lect. 6.
Wood's (Leonard) Works.

Humiliation of Christ.

Bodenmeyer's Lehre der Kenosis.
Hulseman, de Jesu Christi exinanitione.
Kirchmieri Exercitationes Academicæ.
Koeppenius de Jesu Christi exinanitione.
Kunardi Exinanitio et exaltatio Christi.
Polani Prelectiones.
Sohnii Dissertationes Theologicæ.
Straubel von der Entæusserung Christi.
Clarke's (Dr. Samuel) Sermons.
Edwards (Bp.) on the Apostles' Creed.
Hall's (Robt.) Works. (Notes of sermons.)
Jenkins' Reasonableness of Christianity.
Jortin's (John) Discourses.
Witherspoon's Sermons.

Humility. See BEATITUDES.

Allen's (William) Works.
Arnold's (Thomas) Sermons.
Bather's (Edward) Sermons.
Baxter's Christian Directory.
Bellamy's True religion delineated.
Berens' (Edward) Village sermons.
Beattie's Moral science.
Binning's (Hugh) Miscellaneous Sermons.
Bloomfield's (C. J.) Sermons.
Bowdler's (John) Theological Essays.
Brady's (Nicolas) Sermons.
Butler's (Alban) Sermons.
Carr's (George) Sermons.
Cave's Primitive Christianity. Pt. 2, ch. 1.
Charnock's (S.) Works.
Christian Disciple. 1:89,118.
Clarke's (Dr. Samuel) Sermons.
Dehon's (Bp.) Sermons.
Donne's (John) Sermons.
Dowling's (J. G.) Sermons.

Humility—*continued*

Drysdale's (Dr. John) Sermons.
Dwight's (T.) Theology. Ser. 94.
Edwards (H.) on Christian Humility.
Edwards (Pres.) on the Affections.
Emmon's (Nathaniel) Sermons.
Enfield's (William) Sermons.
Evans on the Christian Temper.
Faringdon's (Anthony) Sermons.
Fawcett's (John) Sermons.
Fuller's Calvinistic and Socinian systems. Letter 119.
Gregory's (George) Sermons.
Grove's Moral Philosophy.
Hale's (Sir M.) Contemplations.
Hall's (Bp.) Contemplations. (Precious.)
Hinck's (John) Sermons.
Holmes (Robt.) on Humility.
Hurd's (Bp.) Sermons.
Jennings' (D.) Berry Street Sermons.
Jewell's (Bp.) Works.
Jortin's (John) Sermons.
Keating's (Wm.) Sermons.
Law's (W.) Serious Call. Chapters 17-19.
Leechman's (Wm.) Sermons.
Lucas' (Richard) Sermons.
Mason on Self-knowledge.
——— Christian morals.
Milner's (Jos.) Practical Discourses.
Morony's (Jos.) Sermons.
Muston's (C. R.) Sermons.
Newton's (John) Sermons.
Norris' (John) Practical Treatise on H.
Panoplist. 9:353.
Potts' (J. H.) Sermons.
Price's (Richard) Morals.
Roderigue's Virtue of Humility.
Rogers' (John) Sermons.
Scattergood's (Samuel) Sermons.
Scott's (Tho.) Theological Works.
Scott's (John) Christian life.
Short's (T. V.) Sermons.
Spencer's (Bp.) Sermons.
Spring's (Gardner) Essays. Ess. 9.
Sumner's (Samuel) Sermons.
Taylor's (Jeremy) Holy living.
Thayer's (Elihu) Sermons.
Walker's (Robt.) Sermons. (Model sermons.)
Watts' Character of St. Paul.
——— on Humility.
Wright's Great Concern.
Wynyard's (J. M.) Sermons on Chris. duties.
Young's (Dr. Edward) Sermons.
Zollikoffer's Fasts and Festivals.

Hunger, Spiritual. See BEATITUDES.

Boston's (Thomas) Communion sermons.
Cooper's (Edward) Sermons.
Innes' (Dr. Alexander) Sermons.
Mace's (Daniel) Sermons.
Secker's (Abp.) Sermons.
Sumner's (Bp.) Sermons.
Webster's Sermons.
White's (Hugh) Sermons.
Woodhouse's (G. W.) Parochial sermons.

Husbands. See FAMILY GOVERNMENT.

Anderson's Domestic Constitution. (Exc't.)
Foster's (Dr. James) Discourses.
Gill's Body of Practical Divinity
Leighton's Lectures on 1 Peter.

Huss. See COUNCIL OF CONSTANCE, FORERUNNERS.

Hussii Anatomia Antichristi.
——— Unitas Ecclesiæ.
——— Epistolæ.

There are several editions of his whole works. That of 1558 is reputed the best. A translation of several of his writings is given in Fox's Martyrology.

Becker's Böhmischen Reformatoren.
Horzovini Hussius et Lutherus.
Hussii et Hieronymi Historia et monumenta.
Jeep, Wiclefus et H. inter se comparati.
Martini Hussius et Lutherus.
Mayeri Concordia H. et Lutheri.
Rudigeri Vita et mors Jo. Hussi.
Seigfreidi Dissertationes de H. Vita. (Has a valuable preface by Hallbaur, and notes by Mylius.)
Spondani Annales. (Justifies his burning.)
Troutmansdorf's H.'s Martyrtod. Juli 1415.
Ulmann's Reformatoren vör d. Reformation.
Van der Horst, Hussi vita, præsertim illius condemnati causis.
Werneri J. Hus historice descriptus.
Winklemann's Gerson, Wiclefus, Hussus, comparati.
Zürn's (J. H.) Concile zu Costnitz.
Zitte's Lebenschreibung.

Bonnechose's Reformers before the Reform.
Gilpin's Lives of the Reformers.
Huss, Life of; by Gillett.
—— ——— by Myles.
—— ——— by Seigfreid.
Huss' Letters in exile and imprisonment.
L'Enfant's Reflections on Seigfreid's Life of Huss.

Hussites. See MORAVIANS, WALDENSES.

Beausobre, Supplement a l'histoire de la guerre de Hussites, de L'Enfant.
Byzinii Diarium Hussittici Belli.
Camerarii Narratio Historica.
Cochlæi Hist. Hussitarum. (Very bitter.)
Comenii Hist. fratrum Bohemorum.
Confessio Fidei nobilum Bohemiæ.
Flaccii Confessio Taboritarum.
Kœcheri Historia de variis confessionibus fratrum Bohemorum.
Langermani Polemographi Hussitica.
Lasittius de Origine, rebus gestis, &c.
L'Enfant, Hist. des Concils.
——— Guerres des Hussites.
Lydii Waldensia.
Martinii Hussius et Lutherus.
Paletz, Anti-Hussum.
Rechenburgii (Adam.) Dissertationes.
Rieger, die alte und neue Böhmiche Brüder. (Praised by WALCH.)

15

Hussites—*continued.*

Rudigeri Narratiuncula de fratr. Bohemor.
Schubert's Gesch. der Hussiten-krieges.
Segfreidi (Guil.) Dissertationes.
Slavatæ Origo ecclesiarum Bohemicarum.
Stephani Anti Hussus.
Theobald's Hussitenkrieg. (Much esteemed.)
——— Bellum Hussiticum.
Varellasii Hist. bellorum in Bohemia.
Walpurgeri Hussus Redivivus.

Hutchinsonians.

Pro.

Hutchinson's Philosophical and Theological Works. 12 vols.
Bamfield's All in one.
——— House of wisdom.
Bates' Attempt to demonstrate that the Hebrew language is founded upon natural ideas.
——— on the Types.
——— Expos. of the 3d chap. of Genesis.
——— Meaning of Aleim and Berith.
——— Reply to Sharp on Aleim and Berith.
——— Integrity of the Hebrew text.
——— Philosophical principles of Moses.
Biddulph's Theol. of the ancient patriarchs.
Catcott on the Deluge.
——— Reply to the Bp. of Clogher.
——— True Philosophy.
Clarke's (Dr. Samuel) Works.
Dore's (Jas.) Works.
Fenwick on the Heb. titles of the Psalms.
Forbes' (Duncan) Letters to a Bishop.
Hodge's (Walter) Elihu.
——— Christian plan.
——— Strictures on Dr. Sharp.
Holloway's Remarks on Sharp's Dissertat.
——— Letter and Spirit.
Horne's (Bp.) Apology for certain gentlemen.
——— Abstract of Hutchinson's writings.
——— Candid and impartial statement.
——— Somnium Scipionis explained.
Horsely's (Bp.) Works.
Jones' (of Nayland) Principles of nat. phil.
——— Disquisitions on select subjects.
——— Mosaic distinction of animals.
——— Memoirs of Bp. Horne.
——— Figurative language of Scripture.
Moody's Evidences of Christianity.
Parkhurst's Hebrew Dictionary.
Pike's Philosophia Sacra.
Romaine's (W.) Hebrew Concordance.
——— Works.
Scott's Observations on Genesis.
Spearman's Enq. after philos. and theology.

Con.

Berrington's (Simon) Dissertations.
Douglass' Apology for the Clergy.
Heathcote's Use of Reason in religion.
Kennicott's Word to Hutchinsonians.
Sharp's (J.) Dissertations.
——— Defence of do.

Hydroparastates. See ENCRATITES.

Hymnology. See PSALMODY.

Augusti, de Antiquissimis hymnis et carminibus christianorum.
Bjorn, Hymni vet. christianorum.
Bona de Divina Psalmodia.
Bunsen's (C. J.) Versuch eines allgemeine Gesangbuchs.
Curze's Gesch. des Kirchengesangs.
Daniel, Thesaurus Hymnologicus. (A great collection, in five volumes, of hymns in common use in the 16th century.)
Gebseri Bibliotheca Lat. veterum poetarum christianorum.
Gerbert, de Cantu et musica sacra, a prima eccles. ætate, usque ad presens tempus. 1774.
Kock's Gesch. d. Kirchenlieds und Kirchengesangs. 1847.
Konigsfeld's Hymnen u. Gesänge aus dem Mittelalter.
Laurenein's Gesch. der Kirchenmusic. 1856.
Moni Hymni Latini medii ævi.
Schurzfleischeri Disputationes. (Hymns of the early Christians.)
Walchii (J. G.) Miscellanea Sacra.
Wetzel's Hymnopolographia.

Belcher's (Jos.) History of hymns.
Bibliotheca Sacra. 17:134. 21:284.
Busby's History of church music.
Christian Examiner. 69:402.
Christian Observer. 1861. P. 588.
Eclectic Review. New Series. 10:535.
Evans' Day in the sanctuary. (Introd.)
Gadsby's Memoirs of the principal hymn writers of the 17th and 18th centuries.
Holland's Psalmists of Great Britain. (Sketches of 150 hymn writers, previous to 1843.)
Kennedy on the Words and Music of Psalmody.
Kreamer's Methodist Hymnology.
Littell's Living Age. 2d Series. 14:129.
London Review. 16:189.
Marsh (Wilmot) on Versions of the Psalms. (From 1250 to 1820. Curious and valuable.)
Mason's (Will.) Historical and crit. Essay.
Miller's Our hymns and their authors.
Neale's (J. M.) Mediæval hymns.
Phelps & Park's Hymns and Choirs. 1845.
Princeton Review. 6:605. 30:52.
Quarterly Review. 38:40.
Stevenson's Hymns and Hymn writers of Germany.
Todd on the Vers. of Sternhold & Hopkins.
Toplady on Sacred poetry.

The curious are referred to SEDGWICK'S *"Index to the names of authors and translators of hymns and psalms, with dates;"* and also his *Catalogue of sixteen hundred Psalm and Hymn Books.* London. 1861.

Hypnotism. See MESMERISM.

Hypocrisy. See CANDOR.

Abernethy's (Bp.) Sermons.

Hypocrisy—*continued.*

Abernethy's (John) Sermons on Self-deceit.
Bellamy's True religion delineated.
Clarke's (David) Sermons.
Clarke's (Dr. Samuel) Sermons.
Clarkson's (David) Sermons.
Crook's (Sam.) Divine characters.
Decoegleton's (C. E.) Sermons.
Duchall's (James) Sermons.
Edwards' (Pres.) Works.
Fawcett's (John) Sermons.
Flavel's Touchstone of sincerity.
Francklin's (Thomas) Sermons.
Gregory's (George) Sermons.
Grove's (Henry) Moral Philosophy.
Hall's (Bp.) Sermons.
Hammond's (Henry) Sermons.
Hill's (John) Lectures and Reflections.
Hooker's Four Treatises.
Littleton's (Edward) Sermons.
Morning Exercises at Cripplegate.
Moss' (Robert) Sermons.
Parry's (Joshua) Sermons.
Sanderson's (Bp.) Sermons.
Sheffield's Hypocrite's Looking-glass.
South's (Robert) Sermons.
Spurgeon's (C. H.) Sermons. 6th series.
Thayer's (Elihu) Sermons.
Torshell's Hypocrite discovered and cured.
Verschoyle's (H.) Sermons.
Weedon's (James) Sermons.
Welton's (Richard) Sermons.
Whately's (Wm.) God's Husbandry.
Wilcox's (Daniel) Sermons.
Wilson's (Will. C.) Sermons.

Hypostatic Union.
See ARIANS, SABELLIANS.

Bezæ Tractationes Theologicæ.
Boethius de Trinitate.
Botsacci Gymnasium Christologicum.
Bullingeri Adsertis Orthodoxæ.
Cambachius de Persona Christi.
Chemnitii (M.) de Duabus naturis in C.
Gerhardi (Ioann.) Dissertationes.
Hutteri (Leonard.) Dissertationes.
Jageri (Ioan. Wolfgang.) Dissertationes.
Lampe, Diss. philologico-theologicæ.
Martini (Matt.) Dissertationes.
Matthæus de Unione personali, &c.
Meisneri (Balthas.) Dissertationes.
Schrœderi (Ioan.) Problema Theologica.
Semleri Adsertio orthod. doctrinæ.
Zanchii (Hieron.) Theses.

Bull's (Bp.) Sermons.
Fawcett's Reflections on the Trinity.
Fleming's (Robert) Christology.
Howe's (John) Works.
Owen's Mystery of the person of Christ.
Wallis' Letter on the Trinity.

Hyssop. See NAT. HISTORY OF THE BIBLE.

Iconoclasts. See COUNCILS—2d OF NICE, AND 4th OF CONSTANTINOPLE—IMAGE WORSHIP.

Danhaveri Iconothetes Chris. Adiaphorus.

Iconoclasts—*continued.*

Iohannes (Damasc.) Opera.
La Fevre, Histoire des Iconoclastes.
Mabilloni Annales Benedictini.
Maimbourg, Histoire des Iconoclastes. ("Full of absurd and malignant fictions."—MOSHEIM.)
Mollani Theses Theologicæ.
Muratori Annali d'Italia.
Spanheimii (Fred.) Hist. imaginum restituta. (A powerful defence, rather than a history.)
Thummii Schultetus Iconoclastes.
Walch's Historie der Kezereien.

Anderson's History of the Iconoclasts.

Iconomachi. See ICONOCLASTS.

Ideas. See BERKELEY'S THEORY, MIND.

Blackwood's Magazine. 51:812. 53:762.
Brown's Procedure of the Understanding.
Cudworth's Intellectual System.
Des Cartes on the Passions.
Dublin University Mag. 7:437,534.
Le Clerc's Logic.
Malebranche's Researches after Truth.
Monboddo's Orig. and prog. of lang. (Queer.)
More's (Henry) Philosophical Works.
Price's Review of Morals.
Stillingfleet's Answer to Locke. (To prove his doct. of ideas to be inconsistent with itself, and with Christianity.)
Taylor's (Tho.) Metaphysics of Aristotle. (Analyses also the doctrine of Plato and Pythagoras, concerning ideas.)

Identity. See PERSONAL IDENTITY.

Identity of the Body in the Resurrection.

Pro.

Canzii (J. G.) Dissertationes.
Cloppenburgii (Ioan.) Dissertationes.
Fechtii Schediasmata Sacra.
Kunadi (And.) Dissertationes.
Opitius de Statu resurgentium.
Wolfii (I.) Dissertationes.

Doddridge's Lectures. Part 10.
Locke on Romans viii. 11.
Moore's Theology.
Watts' (Isaac) Philosophical Essays.

Con.

Alexander's Preliminary Diss. to his paraphrase on 1 Cor. 15.
Felton's (Henry) Sermons.
Newton's (Bp.) Works.
Sykes' Inquiry when the resur. of the body was first inserted in the creed.

Idioms of the New Testament.
See BIBLICAL CRITICISM, DIALECTS, PHILOLOGY, STYLE OF NEW TESTAMENT.

Bockelius de Hebraismis N. T.
Cocceji Stricturæ in Pfochen Diatribe.
Gataker de Stylo Nov. Test. (Vindicates the purity of the Greek text from Pfochen's charge of Hebraisms.)

Idioms of the New Test.—*continued.*

Georgius de Latinismis Nov. Test.
——— Vindic. N. Test. ab Hebraismis.
Glassii Philologia Sacra.
Hermann, de Emendenda ratione gram. Gr.
Hombergii Parerga Sacra.
Leusden de Dialectis N. T. singulatum de ejus Hebraismis.
Pasoris Grammatica Sacra Nov. Test.
Pfocheni Diatriba de ling. N. T. puritate.
Porschebergeri Sententiæ a poetis Græcis, ad illustranda sacræ codicis oracula.
Schultzii (Laurent.) Opera.
Sturtz de Dialecto Alexandrina.
Vorst, de Hebraismis N. Test. comment.
Wachleri Annales Theologicæ.
Wahl, Clavis Nov. Test. philologica.
Wolfii Curæ Philologicæ.

Blackwall's Sacred Classics.
Green's Grammar of the New Testament.
Stuart's Grammar of the N. T. dialect.
Viger's Greek idioms. Translated and abridged by Seager; with notes.
Winer's Greek idioms of the New Testament. Translated by Agnew & Ebbeke.

Idleness. See INDUSTRY.

Berriman's (William) Sermons.
Milner's (Joseph) Sermons.

Idle Words. See TONGUE.

Christian Examiner. 3:277.
Flavel's Works.
Gale's (Dr. John) Sermons.
Gouldburn's (Edw. M.) Religious Essays.
Lardner's (Nathaniel) Sermons.
Littleton's (Edward) Sermons.
Secker's (Abp.) Sermons.
Sherlock's (Bp.) Sermons.
Vaughn's (Cha. John) Sermons.

Idolatry. See COMMANDMENTS, MYTHOLOGY, PAGANISM, RELIGIONS, SALVATION OF THE HEATHEN.

Basil, Homiliæ.
Chrysostom, Opera.
Cyril Alex., Opera.
Lactantius, Divinæ Institutiones.
Augustine, de Civitate Dei.
Tertullian, Apologeticus adv. Gentes.
——— de Gentium diis.
Cyprian, de Idolorum vanitate.

Aberbanel de Idolatriæ speciebus.
Adami (J. C.) Exercitationes.
Brogami Theologia Gentium.
Buddeus (Guil.) de transitu Hellenismi ad Christianismum.
Bynckershoeck, de Cultu apud Romanos.
Carpzovii (Ioann. Bened.) Dissertationes.
Constant (Benj.), Polytheisme Romaine.
Doret, Histoire de la philosophie payenne.
Dulaure, des Cultes qui ont precédé l'Idol.
Ficini Theologia Platonica.
Herbert (Ed.) de Relig. Gentilium, errorumque causis.

Idolatry—*continued.*

Jurieu, Dogmes et cultes, bon et mauvais.
Maimonides de Idolatria.
Maury, Religion primatif de la Greece.
Mayeri (I. F.) Dissertationes Selectæ.
Millii (D.) Dissertationes.
Mori Inquisitio in mysterium iniquitatis.
Mourques, Theol. du Pythagorisme.
Pfanneri Syst. theol. Gentilis purioris.
Pici Examen vanitatis Gentium.
Plutarch, de Iside et Oside.
Rogers' der Offen Thur zu dem Vorborgenen Heidenthum.
Saubertus de Sacrificiis veterum.
Schmidt's Religionssystemen des Orients.
Schmitt (H. J.), Grundidee des Mythus.
Seldenus de diis Syriis. (Truly great.)
Steuchi (Aug.) Opera.
Turretini Institutiones Theologiæ.
Van Dale, de Origine et progressu idol.
Viret, de Origine vet. et nov. idolatriæ. (A strong plea against Popery.)
Voetii Disputationes Selectæ.
Vossius (E. J.) de Idolatriæ origine ac progressu. (A work which can never be obsolete.)
Wichmanshausenii Dissertationes. (gods of Babylon.)
Zend-avista. *Which see.*

Ainsworth's Arrow against Idolatry.
Apthorpe (East) on the Prevalence, &c.
Arnold's (Thomas) Sermons.
Barker's (John) Sermons.
Bellamy's True religion delineated.
Beveridge's (Bp.) Sermons.
Buchanan's Asiatic Researches.
Calmet's Idolatry of the Jews in the wilderness.
Calvin's (John) Sermons.
Casaubon's Origin of Idolat. and Heresies.
Cherburg's Religion of the Gentiles.
Christie on the Worship of the elements.
Cudworth's Intellectual System.
Cunningham's Christianity in Judea.
Doddridge's Lectures.
Erskine's (Eben.) Discourses.
Faber's Origin of Pagan Idolatry.
——— on the Mysteries of the Cabiri.
Farmer's Worship of human spirits.
Fell's Idolatry of Greece and Rome.
Gale's Court of the Gentiles.
Grove's Moral Philosophy.
Hall's (Robert) Sermons.
Johnson's (John) Sermons.
Jones' (Sir William) Works.
Jortin's (John) Sermons.
Jurieu's Doctrine and Worship from Adam to Christ. (Gives an account of all the Idolatries which affected Jewish worship.)
Kames' History of man.
Law's (Bp.) Theory of Religion.
Leland's Advant. and necess. of Revelation.
Lindsey on Christian idolatry.
Marshman's Confucius.
Mehegan's Origin and progress of Idolatry.

Idolatry—*continued.*

Millar's Overthrow of Paganism.
Moore's Hindu Pantheon.
Moore's (Dr. Henry) Philosophical works.
Newton's Messiah.
Prideaux's Connection of the O. and N. T.
Saurin's Sermons.
Shuckford's Connect. of sac. and prof. hist.
Tennison's Nature, cause, commencement, and progress of idolatry, and its distinction from superstition. (Reviews its practice by Gentiles, Jews, Mahometans, Socinians, and Romanists.)
Tertullian's Defence of Christians. Translated by H. Brown.
Tennant's Thoughts on British Government in India. (Valuable for facts.)
Tholuck's Nature and moral influence of I.
Wake's (Abp.) Discourses.
Warburton's Divine Legation. Book 4.
Watts' Strength and weakness of human reason.
Wisheart's (George) Sermons.
Young's Idolatrous corruptions of religion, and the method of Providence in reforming them, from the beginning of the world.

Idolatry of the Church of Rome. See IMAGE WORSHIP, INVOCATION OF SAINTS.

Balduini (Frider.) Speculum idolat. papalis.
Dallæi (Ioan.) Disputationes.
Heerbrandi (Iacob.) Dissertationes.
Hœpfnerus de Idolatria Antichristi.
Lyserus de Pudenda pontificior. idolatria.
Mayeri (Io. Frider.) Dissertationes.
Rainoldus de Romanæ Ecclesiæ idolatria.
Rechenberg de Idolatria in Rom. eccl.
Sirici Ostensio abominat. papatus.
——— Idolum papale.
Thummii (Theod.) Disputationes.
Viret, Idolatria vet. et nova.

Mayhew's (Dr. Jonathan) Sermons.
Mede's (Jos.) Gentile theology revived.
More's (Henry) Disc. on Papal Idolatry.
Princeton Review. 26:147.
Stillingfleet's Idolatry of the Ch. of Rome.
——— Defence of Do.
Thelwall's Idolatry of the Church of Rome.
Wake's (Abp.) Discourses.

Ignatius. See LOYOLA.

Ignatii Epistolæ. (Edition of Cureton, 1849, is most esteemed.)
Arndt's Studien und Critiken.
Cottelerii Syntagma dissert. theologic.
Crucigeri Acta Martyrum.
Fabricii Biblioth. Græca. (Gives an account of the controversy touching the genuineness of the Epistles.)
Grabii Spicilegium S. S. patrum.
Oudini (Casimer.) Dissertationes.
Pearsoni (Io.) Dissertationes.
Ruinarti Actæ primorum martyrum.
Surii Vitæ sanctorum.

Ignatius—*continued.*

Tillemont, Memoires pour servir a l'histoire de l'eglise.
Usseri Dissertationes.

Bennet's (Benjamin) Discourses.
Bonhour's Life of Ignatius.
Bunsen's Ignatius and his times.
Burton's Eccl. hist. of the 2d and 3d cent.
Calder's Epistles of Ignatius.
Chevalier's Trans. of the Epistles of I.
Christian Month. Spect. 5:393.
Christian Observer. 2:129,526.
Clementson's Trans. of the Epistles of I.
Cockburn on the Epistles of Ignatius.
Cureton's Complete collection of the Ignatian epistles, genuine, interpolated, and spurious; with quotations from them by eccles. writers, Syriac, Greek, Ethiopic, and Latin; with English translation, notes, introductions, &c.
Edinburg Review. 90:82,155.
Hammond on the Epistles of Ignatius.
Killen's Hist., Doct., worship, and const. of the ancient church. (Regards the Epistles as spurious.)
Kitto's Journal. 5:339.
Lardner's Credibility of the gospel history.
New Englander. 7:501.
New York Review. 1:367.
Princeton Review. 21:379.
Quart. Review. 88:69.
Smith's Epistles of Ignatius.
Tracts for the Times. ("Records of the Church.")
Wake's Epistles of the Fathers.
Whiston's Primitive Christianity revived. (Contains the Epistles of Ignatius, and the Apostolical constitutions; and an essay on each.)

See a list of all the editions of the Epistles of Ignatius in DUPIN, *Bibliotheque des auteurs ecclesiastiques.*

Ignorance. See SINS OF IGNORANCE.

Butler's (Bp.) Sermons.
Doddridge's Lectures. Proposition 10.
Foster's (John) Essays.
Hall's (Robert) Sermons.
Rennel's (Thomas) Sermons.
Reynerd's Sermons. (Secret faults.)

Illustrations of Scripture. See COINS, GEOGRAPHY, JEWISH ANTIQUITIES, NATURAL HISTORY OF THE BIBLE.

Calovii Biblia illustrata.
Celsii (Olaus.) Dissertationes.
Dieterici Illustramentum N. Test.
Goerii Antiquitates Mosaicæ.
Hartmann's Aufklärungen über Asien.
Hilleri Hierophyticon.
Lamy, Apparatus Biblicus.
Martin, Explications de textes difficile.
Mey, Physiologia Sacra.
Millii Dissertationes Selectæ.

Illustrations of Scripture—*continued.*

Perezonii Origines Babylonicæ et Egypt.
Rosenmüller's Morgenland.
Schæchi Sacrorum Ebræochrismaton.
Tohren (Konrad) Dissertationes.
Valesius de Philosophia Sacra.
Warlitz de Moribus Biblicis.
Witsii Miscellanea Sacra.

Burder's (Sam.) Oriental customs.
Bush's (Geo.) Illustrations, &c.
Callaway's Oriental collection.
Calmet's Dictionary of the Bible.
Carpenter's Scripture difficulties examined.
Chateaubriand's Travels in Greece, &c.
Christian Disciple. 1:13,53,80. 2:13,229,291, 235. 3:39,78,100,163,207,262,324. 6:356.
Clarke's Travels in Europe, Asia, &c.
Corbett's Oriental Key to the Scriptures.
Fowler's Eastern Mirror. (A compilation from Harmer and others.)
Fuller's (T.) Pisgah sight of Palestine.
Goadby's Illus. of S. S. Plates. 6 v., folio.
Goodell's Old and New; or 30 years in the East.
Guilford's Oriental and Jewish Antiquities.
Hacket's Illustrations of Scripture, suggested by a tour through the Holy land. 1853.
Harmer's Observations.
Jamieson's (Robt.) Eastern Manners.
Jones' Scripture Antiquities.
King's (Edward) Morsels of Criticism.
Kitto's Bible illustrations.
——— Journ. of Sac. Lit. 2:101. 3:309. 4:46.
Latrobe's Scripture Illustrations.
Lobo's Voyages to Abyssinia. 1670.
Malcom's Travels in S. Eastern Asia. 1839.
Maundrel's Journey to Jerusalem, &c. 1697.
Methodist Quarterly Review. 3:325.
Morier's Journey through Persia, &c. 1816.
Murray's (John) Truth of S. S. demonstrated from monuments, gems, coins, &c. Plates.
Niebuhr's Travels in Arabia. 1767.
Norden's Travels in Egypt & Nubia. 1735.
Paxton's Illustrations of Holy Scripture.
Pococke's Observations in Egypt, Palestine, Syria, and Mesopotamia. 1743.
Roberts' (Jos.) Illustrations of Scr. (From customs, traditions, &c., of the Hindus.)
Robinson's Biblical Researches.
Shaw's Travels in the Levant. 1740.
Taylor's Illustrations and Confirmations of the Bible, from the monuments of Egypt. Plates.
Thompson's The Land and the Book.
Thrup's Ancient Jerusalem. A new investigation into the history, topography, and plan of the city, environs, and temple. 1845.
Vansittart's Observations on the O. T.
Wait's Jewish and Oriental antiquities.
Wemyss' Job and his times.
——— Symbolical Dictionary.
——— Biblical Gleanings.
West's Dissertations on the Olympic games.
Westminster Review. 37:358. (Egyptian Anaglyphs.)
Wylie's (J.) Ancient prophecy. (Modern Judea compared with ancient prophecy.)

Image of God in Man.

Chemnitii (Martin.) Dissertationes.
Himmelii (Io.) Dissertationes.
Hoepfneri (Henric.) Dissertationes.
Langii (Io. M.) Dissertationes.
Misleri (Io. Nicol.) Dissertationes.
Osiandri (Io. Adam.) Dissertationes.
Schess de Imagine Dei in homine.
Schmidius de Imag. Dei in homine.
Van Velsen de Hominis cum Deo similitud.
Zanchius de Operibus Dei. Cap. III.
Zemannus de Controversia difficilima.

Atterbury's (Lewis) Sermons.
Barrow's (William) Sermons.
Bibliotheca Sacra. 7:409.
Bowdler's (Thomas) Sermons.
Foster's (Dr. James) Sermons.
Girdlestone's (E.) Reflected truth.
Glas' (John) Notes on Scripture texts.
Grinfield's (E. W.) Nature and import of the image of God in man. (A Universalist work.)
Marriot's (Charles) Sermons.
Ogden's (Dr. Samuel) Sermons.
Vidal's (Bp.) Sermons.
Weemes' Works. Dissert. 2.

Image Worship. See COUNCILS, II. NICE, ICONOCLASTS, IDOLATRY OF ROMISH CHURCH.

Alexandri Historia Ecclesiastica.
Allatius de octavâ Synodo Photiana. (This Council ended the controversy, by confirming the new custom.)
Ansaldi Dissert. de Cultu. (One of the latest defences of the custom. 1753.)
Baldwin's Bericht von Bildern Gottes.
Baronii (Jos.) Dissertationes.
Carolus Magnus de impio imaginum cultu.
Chappuzeau, Icones Historicæ Vet. Test. (360 cuts.)
Crellii Ethica.
Daillé de la Creance des Peres.
——— de Cultus Religiosi.
Damasceni Orationes Apologeticæ.
Fechtii Examen Conciliationis inter Lutheranos et Pontificos, &c.
Goldasti Imperialia Decreta, &c.
Hottinger, de Ecc. Orient. et Occ. dissensu.
Hus, de Mysterio Antichristi.
L'Enfant, Preservatif contre la re-union avec la Siege de Rome.
Molinæii Iconomachus.
Pfafii Dissertationes. ("Very able.")
Rivaldi Dissertationes Historicæ.
Schrœderi Apodixis Theologicus.
Schultetus de Imaginibus Idololatricis.
Seligmanni Exercitationes Academicæ.
Spanheimii (Fred.) Exercitationes.
——— Historia Imaginum.
Thummei Schultetus Iconoclastes.
Voetii Disputationes Theolog. selectæ.

Image Worship—*continued.*

Council of Constantinople. *Against.*
Council of Nice (2d). *For.*
Dick's Philosophy of Religion.
Edwards' (Bp.) Body of Divinity.
Evans' (B.) Modern Popery. 1855.
Fletcher's Lectures on the Romish religion.
Geddes' (M.) Miscellaneous Tracts.
Hole on the Catechism.
Hopkins on Do.
Jewell's (Bp.) Works. (Parker Soc. publ.)
King's Inventions in the worship of God.
Limborch's Theology. Bk. 5, Chap. 33.
Marshall's (Nathaniel) Sermons.
More on the Epistles to the seven churches.
Moyle's Posthumous Works.
Owen's (James) Hist. of Image Worship.
Piggott's (Edw.) Sermons.
Powell's (H. T.) Roman fallacies.
Richardson on Pilgrimages in Ireland.
Ridley's (Bp.) Works.
Sarcon's God only to be worshipped.
Soames' Latin Ch. during Anglo-Sax. times.
Stillingfleet's Works.
Tyler (J. E.) on Image Worship.
Wake's (William) Discourses.
Whitby's (Daniel) Works.

See a very large list of writers on this subject in VOGTIUS, *Catal. libr. med. aetat.* Few of them, however, are now to be found.

Imagination. See MIND.

Démangeon, de l'Imag. considerée dans ses effets sur l'homme et les animaux.

Atkinside's Pleasures of Imagination.
Burke on the Sublime and Beautiful.
Christian Examiner. 52:329.
Hogarth's Analysis of Beauty.
Mason's English Garden.
Price on the Picturesque.
Sortain's (Joseph) Sermons. (Province of imagination in religion.)
Spectator. No. 411, et seq.
Wayland's (Francis) Occasional Discourses.

Imitation of Christ. See EXAMPLE OF CHRIST.

Corneille, l'Imitation de Jesus Christ.
Keil, de Examplo Christi recte imitando.
Kempis, de Imitatione Christi.
Schulze's Bewegungsgründe d. Chr. Moral.

Bennet's Lectures on the history of C.
Carter's (T. T.) Series of Lent lectures.
Channing's (William E.) Discourses.
De Burgh's (William) Discourses.
Hill's Wayfarings in Christ.
Kempis' Imitation of Christ.
Law's (E.) Reflections on the life of Chris .
Mason's (John) Sermons.
Taylor's (Jer.) Great Exemplar.
Williams' Private life of Christ.
Zollikoffer's (Geo. J.) Sermons.

Immaculate Conception of the Virgin Mary.

Pro.

Astorga Armamentarium.
Ballerini Sylloge Monumentorum, &c.
Bullarium Magnum Romanorum. (Especially the bulls of Sextus IV., Urban VIII., Clement XI., and Pius IX.)
Codur, de la St. Vierge.
Gousset (Cardinal) Opera.
Lanois, Prescriptiones touchant, &c.
Lezana, Apologia pro imm. conc. Virginis.
Maldonadi Armamentaria Seraphica.
Montalben de Immaculata conceptione.
Passaglia de Immaculata conceptione.
Serranus de Immaculata conceptione.

Con. See DOMINICANS.

Albertus Magnus, super Evangelium.
Alffius de Maria, peccato immuni.
Anselm, Dissertationes.
Bonaventuræ Carmina.
Callixti Im. conceptionis Historia.
Chemnitii Examen Concilii Tridentini.
Echard, Scriptores ord. Prædicatorum.
Kieslingii Testes sistit antiq. eccles.
Laborde, Memoire des Opposants, &c.
Munscher's Kirchen Geschichte.
Passagli de Immaculato conceptu.
Rosenmülleri Observ. ad hist. dogmatis.
Strossa de Conceptione V. Mariæ.
Thomæ Aquinatatis Opuscula.
Waddingii Scriptores ordinis Minorum.
Laborde's (Abbe) Impossibility of the immaculate conception as an article of faith. Translated by Coxe.
Tyler on Image worship.

A small volume would be requisite to enumerate the extant works on this useless subject.

Immateriality of the Soul. See MATERIALISM.

Immensity of God. See ATTRIBUTES.

Limborch, Theol. Christiana. Lib. II., c. 6.
Turretini Theologia Elenctica.

Doddridge's (Philip) Lectures.
Foster's (James) Discourses.
Howe's Works.
Locke on the Understanding.
Watts' Ontology.

Immortality of the Soul. See SOUL.

Ambrose, de Dignitate humane conditioni.
Augustine, de Anima.

Bengelii (E. G.) Dissertationes.
Blasche's Unsterblichkeitslehre.
Brocke's Materie und Geist.
Bruno (Ant.), Entelechia.
Camphoræ Dialogus. (This Genoese book is rare, but is said to be worthy to be printed in letters of gold.)
Cottæ Hist. dogmatis de vita æterna.
Digbæi (Ken.) Demonst. immort. animæ.

Immortality of the Soul—*continued.*

Fichté (I. H.), Idee der Persönlichkeit.
Horn's (G.) Ewigkeit der Seele.
Houppelande, de Anima. (A collection of extracts from ancient philosophers, poets, and Christian Fathers.)
Iohannsenii Veterum Hebr. notiones de rebus post mortem.
Kant's Kritik der praktischen Vernunft.
Kiesselbach, de Rebus post mortem.
Lange (J. J.), Dissertationes.
Mendelssohn's Phaedon.
Naumann's Unsterblichkeit der Seele.
Olearii (J. G.) Dissertationes.
Osiandri (J. A.) Dissertationes.
Paulus' (C. H. E.) Unsterbl. der Seele.
Pomponatus de Immort. animi. (Denies.)
Sismondi Demonstratio de immort., &c.
Strauss' Dogmatik.
Turrettini Dissertationes. Diss. XII.
Wall (A. R.) Psychotheologia.
Wielandi Euthanasia.

Alling's (Tho.) Folly of modern Atheism.
Amer. Bib. Repos. 2d Series. 10:411. 12:294.
Amory's (Thomas) Sermons.
Appleton's Works. Lectures 9 and 10.
Ashton (W.) on the Soul and a future state.
Bakewell's Evidence of a future state from the properties of matter.
Balguy's (John) Sermons.
Bates' (William) Works.
Baxter (Andrew) on the Nature of the Soul. (Profound and clear.)
Bayle's Histor. Dictionary. Art. "Pereira."
Blackmore's (Sir Richard) Essays.
Boyle Lectures.
Boyle's Physico-theological considerations about the reconcileableness of reason and religion.
Broughton's (John) Psychology.
Brown's Philos. of the mind. Lect. 96.
Bryant's Attractions of the world to come.
Burlemaqui on the Soul.
Butler's Analogy of religion and nature.
Calvin (John) on the Soul.
Charleton's Immortality of the soul proved by the light of nature.
Chishull's Heresy of Mr. Dodwell.
Christian Examiner. 3:365. 40:349.
Christian Quart. Spectator. 8:556.
Cicero on the Imm. of the soul. (A trans. by Chace of all the allusions to this subject, in Cicero's writings.)
Clark's (S.) Letters to Dodwell.
Collier (Jer.) on the Human soul.
Craven's (Wm.) Sermons.
Crombie's Natural Theology.
Davis' True dignity of human nature.
Democratic Review. 22:59,124,225.
Digby (Sir K.) on Man's soul.
Dod's Immortality triumphant.
Dodwell's Proof from Scripture and the first Fathers that the soul is naturally mortal, but that immortality is the gift of the Holy Spirit.

Immortality of the Soul—*continued.*

Doddridge's Lectures. Part 4.
Drew on the Immortality of the soul.
Drysdale's (Dr. John) Sermons.
Duncan's (John) Evidences from reason, independent of abstruse enquiries into the nature of matter and spirit.
Eclectic Review. 4th Series. 26:338.
Fiddes' Doctrine of a future state.
Flavel on the Soul.
Flügge's Hist. of the belief of the imm., &c.
Foster's (John) Works.
Franzen's Critical history of the doctrine.
Frazier's Magazine. 13:694.
Gale's (Dr. John) Sermons. (5 on this subj.)
Gill's (Dr. John) Sermons.
Gray on the Immortality, &c.
Groves' Essay toward a demonstration, &c.
Hallet's (Joseph) Works. (A learned Arian, who takes the same view as Dodwell on this subject.)
Hartly on Man.
Hinton's (J. Howard) Euthanasia.
Jackson on Matter and Spirit.
Keach's (Benj.) French impostor detected.
Kuhnhardt's Comm. on the Phædo of Plato.
Layton's (H.) Search after souls. (Gives the opinions of many writers, ancient and modern.)
Leighton's (Abp.) Lectures. Lect. 5.
Locke on the Understanding.
Mattison (H.) on the I. of the soul.
Mede's Apology of the latter times.
Miller's (T.) Immortality of the soul.
Mills' Natural immortality of the soul.
Moore's (Bp.) Sermons.
Morehead's (Robert) Discourses.
New Englander. 11:362.
Nichols' Conference with a Theist.
Norris on the Soul. (Reply to Dodwell.)
Parker's (Benj.) Philos. Dissertations.
Pitt's Defence of Mr. Chishull.
Plato's Phædo. Trans. by C. S. Stanford.
Porteus' (Bp.) Sermons.
Reynolds (Bp.) on the Soul.
Sherlock's (Dean) Discourses.
Smith's (Sydney) Sermons.
Spectator. No. 111.
Tenneman's Doct. of the Socratic School.
Tillotson's (Abp.) Sermons.
Towns' Opinions of the ancient philosophers. (Preface by Warburton.)
Turner's Justice done to human souls. (Reply to Dodwell.)
Vaughn's (J.) Lectures. Lect. 10.
Vizard's Principles in philos. and religion.
Wadsworth's Immortality of the soul.
Watts' (I.) Ontology.
Whitby's Reflections on some opinions of Mr. Dodwell.

For other such books see WM. GOWAN'S *Cat. of books on the immortality of the soul*, FLUGGE'S *Himmel der Zukunft*, and DORING'S *Euthanasia*.

Immutability of God.

Gerardi Loci Theologici.
Sherzeri Systema Theologiæ.

Abernethy's (John) Discourses.
Atterbury's (Lewis) Sermons.
Backiller's Select. from Mornay and others.
Charnock's (Stephen) Works.
Dwight's Theology. Disc. 5.
Jortin's (John) Sermons.
Price on Providence.
Saurin's Sermons.
Stackhouse's Body of Divinity.
Tillotson's Sermons.
Watts' Ontology.
Wilkins on Natural religion.

Impenitence. See HARDNESS OF HEART.

Imposition of Hands.
See CONFIRMATION, ORDINATION.

Spanheimii (Frider.) Miscellanea.

Clarke's (Sam.) Annot. (On Matt. xix. 15.)
Firmin's Weighty questions discussed.
Frere's Doct. of the imposition of hands.
Fuller's (Andrew) Works.
Haldane (J. A.) on Social worship.
Hall's (Bp.) Polemic Works.
Hammond's (Henry) Works.
King's Primitive Church.
Maurice on Social Religion.
Turner on Church Government.
Watts' Rational foundation of a church.
Woolton (Bp.) on the Soul.

Imprecations in the Psalms.

Bibliotheca Sacra. 1:97. 13:551. 19:165.
Christian Monthly Spect. 8:630.
Colman's (Benj.) Sermons.
Doddridge's Lectures. Part 6, Prop. 120.
Jackson's Truth of Scripture.
Jenkins' Reasonableness of Christianity.
Lowth on Inspiration.
Peters' (Cha.) Sermons. (On the 109th Ps.)

Improvement of Mankind.
See CIVILIZATION, HUMAN PROGRESS, PERFECTABILITY OF MAN.

Imputation of Adam's Sin.
See FALL, ORIGINAL SIN.

Carpzovii (Iacob.) de Imputatione. (Against Whitby.)
Garisolii Defensio Synodi Carentoniensis.
Kahleri (Wigand.) Disputationes.
Musæi (Ioann.) Dissertationes.
Pfaffii (C. M.) Dissertationes.
Placæus de Statu hominis ante gratiam.

Edwards on Orig. Sin. (Reply to Whitby.)
Glas' (John) Notes on Scripture texts.
Sandeman's Letters.
Watts' Ruin and recovery.
Whitby on the Imputation of Adam's sin.

Imputation of Christ's Righteousness. See JUSTIFICATION, SUBSTITUTION.

Allix (P.) de Justitiæ Christi imputatione.

Imputation—*continued.*

Bernholdus de Justitiæ Christi imputatione.
Bullii Harmonia Apostolica.
Hoepfneri Disputationes duodecim.
Holdeni Divinæ fidei Analysis.
Schmidtius (Iacob.) de Justificatione.

Baxter's End of the controversy.
——— Various pieces on this subject.
Bibliotheca Sacra. 8:594.
Bull's Harmony of the Apostles.
Burgess' True doctrine of Justification.
Burnet's (Tho.) Boyle Lectures. 1724, 1725.
Burton's Christian Bulwark.
Chandler's (Sam.) Posthumous sermons.
Cole (Tho.) on Imputed Righteousness.
Edwards' (Pres.) on Original sin.
Erskine's (Ebenezer) Sermons.
Fuller (And.) on Sandemanianism.
——— Dial. bet. Peter, James, and John.
Gataker's Way of Truth and Peace.
Goodwin's (T.) Restoration of Man.
Grove's Posthumous works.
Hall's (Robt., Sen.) Help to Zion's travellers. (Small, but very precious.)
Hall's (Robt.) Sermons.
Hervey's Theoron and Aspasio.
Knight's (Titus) Sermons.
Malcom (Howard) on the Extent of the Atonement.
Nelson's Review of Bp. Bull.
Owen (Jno.) on Justification by faith.
——— Meditations and Discourses.
Princeton Review. 11:553.
Ricoulton on the Spirit and tendency of Theoron and Aspasio.
Romaine's (W.) Works.
Sandeman's Letters on Theoron and Aspas.
Saurin's (James) Sermons.
Taylor's (Jeremy) Sermons. (Supplement.)
Theol. Essays reprinted from the Princeton Review.
Tyson (Wm.) on Imputed righteousness.
Venn's (Henry) Sermons.
Watts' Ruin and Recovery.
Wesley (John) on Imputed righteousness.
Whateley's (Richard) Essays. Ess. 6.
Witherspoon's Essays.

A controversy, prolific in books, has existed on this subject for two centuries. A fair account of it is in NELSON's *Life of Bull.*

Incantations. See MAGIC.

Incarnation of Christ.
See GENUINENESS OF 1 JOHN V. 7.

Cyrill Alex., de Incarnatione.
Cyrill Hieros., Catecheses.
Gregory Naz., Oratio in nativitatem Christi.
Gregory Nys., Oratio de deitate filii.

Baumgarten, Vind. vocis Θεος, 1 Tim. iii. 16.
Calmeti Diss. (Prefixed to Com. on Isaiah.)
Danæi Confirmatio orthodoxæ doctrinæ.
Gaillardi Specimen Questionum.
Hackspanii (Theod.) Disputat. Theologicæ.

Incarnation of Christ—*continued.*

Martinus de Natura Jesu Christi.
Schmidtii (Sebast.) Dissertationes.
Schomeri (I. C.) Dissertationes.
Spanheimii (Fred.) Dissertationes.
Zanchius de Incarnatione filii Dei.
Zornii Delineatio Theol. Patristicæ.

Atterbury's (Bp.) Sermons.
Balmer's (Robt.) Academic Lectures.
Bedford's Moyer Lectures. 1739.
Benson's (Joseph) Sermons.
Berriman's Critical Dissertations.
Beveridge's (Bp.) Sermons.
Biblical Repository. Jan., 1832.
Bradbury's Mystery of Godliness.
Brownson's Quarterly Review. 2d Series. 4:136. 5:137. 6:287.
Bull's Defence of the Nicene creed.
Butler's (William A.) Sermons.
Casaubon's Dissertations.
Caswall's (E.) Sermons.
Church Review. 4:428.
Dimock's (Henry) Eight Sermons.
Dow's (William) Sermons.
Dwight's Theology. Ser. 42.
Eaton's Mystery of God incarnate.
Edwards (Pres.) on Redemption.
Foster's (John) Sermons.
Hacket's (Bp.) Sermons. (15 on this subj.)
Hall's (Bp.) Polemic Works.
——— Contemplations.
Harris' (Dr. John) Critical Dissertations.
Hewitt's Points of Christian Doctrine.
Hodgson's Summary of corroborating evid.
Hopkins' (Bp.) Works.
Hooper's (Bp.) Works. (Parker Soc. publ.)
Horseley's Sermons and Tracts.
Irving's (Edward) Sermons.
Jamieson's Sacred History.
Kidder on the Messiah.
Kollock's (Shepard K.) Sermons.
Lardner's Works.
Law's (Wm.) Theory of Religion.
Le Bas' (Cha. W.) Sermons.
Magee on the Atonement.
Mandell's (William) Sermons.
Meldrum's Illustration of the Incarnation.
Methodist Quart. Rev. 11:114.
Moyer Lectures. 1737 and 1738.
Neal's Berry Street Sermons.
Owen on the Person of Christ.
Pearson on the Creed.
Sherlock's (Bp.) Sermons.
Smith's (Sam. Stanhope) Sermons.
Sumner's (Bp.) Sermons.
[Taylor's] Apology of Ben Mordecai.
Tillotson's (Abp.) Sermons.
Trench's (Francis) Sermons.
Usher's Mystery of the Incarnation.
Velthusen's True reading of 1 Tim. iii. 16.
Watson's (Bp.) Collection of tracts.
Watts' (Isaac) Works.
Wilberforce (R. I.) on the Incarnation.
Williams' (Griffith) Sermons.
Witsius on the Covenants.

Incest. See CONSANGUINITY, MARRIAGE TO A WIFE'S SISTER.

Hottingeri (J. H.) Discursus Gemaricus.

Amer. Bibl. Repository. 8:423.
Fry on Marriage between kindred.
Glas' (John) Works.
Livingston on Incestuous marriages.
Paley's Moral Philosophy.
Ryan's Philosophy of marriage.

Incomprehensibility of God.

Abernethy's (John) Sermons.
[Brown's] Things divine and supernatural.
Caryll on Job. Ch. 27., v. 25.
Doddridge's Lectures. Part 3, prop. 46.
Fiddes' (Richard) Sermons.
Grove's (Henry) Sermons.
Hussey's (Christopher) Sermons.
King (Abp.) on Predestination.
Law's Notes on King's Origin of evil.
Lucas' (Richard) Sermons.
Tillotson's (Abp.) Sermons.
Wisheart's (George) Sermons.

Inconstancy. See CONSTANCY.

Incredulity. See INFIDELITY, UNBELIEF.

Indecision. See DECISION, INSTABILITY, PROCRASTINATION.

Atterbury's (Bp.) Sermons.
Barnes' (Albert) Practical sermons.
Cecil's (Richard) Sermons.
Chishul On Being almost a Christian.
Clarke's Nature and cause of irresolution.
Cunningham's (J. W.) Sermons.
Dealtry's (William) Sermons.
Denham's (John E.) Sermons.
Doddridge's (Philip) Sermons.
Edwards' (Pres.) Sermons. (Lot's wife.)
Fuller's (And.) Sermons.
Hickman's (Bp.) Sermons.
Hopkins' (Bp.) Sermons.
Horberry's (M.) Sermons.
Knowles' (Thomas) Discourses.
Milner's (Joseph) Sermons.
Seed's (Jeremiah) Sermons.
Smith's (Sydney) Sermons.
Smith's (Henry) Sermons.
Tillotson's (Abp.) Sermons.
Townsend's (George) Sermons.
Trapp's Preservative agt. unsettled notions.
Venn's (John) Sermons.
Wilson's (Bp.) Sermons.
Yonge's (James) Sermons. Second Series.

Independence of God.

Abernethy's (John) Sermons.
Burnet on the 39 Articles.
Clarke's (Sam.) Boyle Lectures. 1704.
Collibeare's Theological Treatises.
Doddridge's Lectures. Part 2, prop. 37.
Dwight's (Tim.) Discourses.
Edwards' (Pres.) Works.
Emmons' (Nathaniel) Sermons.
Grotius' Truth of the Christian religion.

Independents. See CONGREGATIONALISM.

Indexes Expurgatory and Prohibitory.

Brasichelleni Index libri expurgandorum. (Mendham's description of this remarkable book occupies 16 pages.)
France, de Papistorum indicibus libr. prohib. et expurgandorum. (Gives the author, occasion, contents, &c., and is all sufficient up to the date of its publication. 1684.)
Hannot, Index des princip. livres, &c. 1714.
Mendhami Index libri prohibitorum.
Peignot, Dict. critique et bibliographique, des livres condamné au feu, supprimés ou censurés. 1806.
Quirogæ Index libr. expurgandorum. 1583.
Soto-majoris Index libr. prohib. et expurg. ("As valuable as any."—MENDHAM.)

Gibbings' Exact reprint of the Vatican Index, &c. 1837.
Mendham's Account of the various Indexes; with extracts, anecdotes, and remarks. 1826.
——— Touching books since Sextus V. 1835.
Taylor's (Jer.) Polemic Discourses.

Books of this class are numerous, and of some of them there are various editions. The above are sufficient. The Papal church circulates its "indexes" with much reserve; and they are not generally obtainable by Protestants. They furnish a ready and complete reference to every book, chapter, or page, where anti-Papal sentiments may be found; a knowledge which no opponent could otherwise obtain. An original and complete enumeration of the Indexes previous to 1560, is given by VERGERIUS, *Catalogus Haereticorum*. The work of MENDHAM, however, is amply sufficient for most purposes.

Indexes to the Bible. See ANALYSES.

Indifference.

Amyraldi Traité des religions.
Haberkornii Admonitio.
Lamennais [or Mennais], sur l'Indifference en matiére de religion.
Pictet, contre l'Indifference, &c.

Foster's (John) Essays.
Froude's (Rich. H.) Sermons.
Gerard on Indifference to religious truth.
Gray on Indifference to religion.
Horneck's Antidote against Indifference.
Squier's Indif. to religion inexcusable.
Young's (Dr. Edward, Sen.) Sermons.

Indifferentists.

Arnold's Kirchen und Ketzer Historie.
Calovii Syntagma.
Fechtii Examen novæ theologiæ.
Flacii (Matt.) Opuscula.
Gerdes' Beschæmter Indifferentist.
Grevii Memoria.
Koch's Abgewiesener Indifferentist.
Loescheri Antilatitudinius.
Melancthonis Opera.
Musæi Prelectiones.
Quistorpii (Ioann.) Dissertationes.
Voetii Dissertationes Selectæ.

Indolence. See SLOTH

Individual Effort.
See LAY PREACHING.

Allen's Our Home population.
[Campbell's (J.)] Jethro. Prize essay. 1839. (Treats the subject historically and Scripturally.)
Crompton's Agency of the Church.
Fish's Primitive piety revived. Ch. 6.
Hinton's (John Howard) Works.
Malcom's (H.) Evangelism the individual and universal duty of Christians.
Presbyterian Magazine. 1:137.

Indulgences. See COUNCIL OF TRENT.

Amortius de Origine, progressu, ac valore indulgentium.
Bertling's Unterricht v. Päbstisch Jubeljahr.
Capetis (J.) de Indulgentiis.
Hirscher's Ansichten von dem Jubiläum. (Papal.)
Hunnii (A.) Dissertationes.
Hussius de Indulgentiis.
Lutheri Opera.
Lyseri (Polycarp.) Dissertationes.
Sutlivius de Indulgentiis.
Thiers (J. B.) Traité des indulg. (Papal.)
Thummii (Theod.) Dissertationes.

Bennett's (W. J. E.) Lecture Sermous.
Billingsley's (John) Sermons.
Geddes' (M.) Miscellaneous Tracts.
Jerram's (Charles) Lectures.
Mendham's Venality of Rome.
Morning Exercises at Cripplegate. Vol. 6.
Protestant Advocate. Periodical.
Protestant Herald. Periodical.
Reading on the Principal points, &c.
Staveley's Horseleech.
Stevenson's Discourses on the Catholic Ch. (A compilation from Secker and others.)

Innumerable treatises on this subject were published in the first stages of the Reformation, and many since. See lists of them in ALLEGAMBE, *Biblioth. Scriptor. Soc. Jes.*; LILLIANTHAL, *der Theolog. Biblioth.*; and VOGTIUS, *Catal. libror. varior.*

Industry. See REDEEMING TIME.

Balguy's (John) Sermons.
Barrow's (Isaac) Sermons.
Banfield's (T. C.) Sermons.
Barnard's (Thomas) Sermons.
Berriman's (William) Sermons.
Bisset's (Thomas) Sermons.
Butcher's (Edward) Sermons.
Calthrop's (John) Parochial Sermons.

Industry—*continued.*

Delany's (Patrick) Sermons.
Dodd's (William) Sermons.
Dwight's (Timothy) Discourses. Disc. 122.
Dyke's (Oswald) Sermons.
Edwards' (John) Sermons.
Enfield's (W.) Sermons.
Fothergill's (George) Sermons.
Franklin's (Bp.) Sermons.
Froude's (Richard) Sermons.
Granger's (James) Sermons.
Guise's (John) Sermons.
Hill's (John) Sermons.
Humphreys' (John) Sermons.
Jay's (William) Sermons.
Jortin's (John) Sermons.
Knowles' (Thomas) Family Sermons.
Manton's (Thomas) Sermons.
Markland's (Abraham) Sermons.
Marriot's (Harvey) Sermons.
Morning Exercises at Cripplegate.
Oakley's (Fred.) Sermons.
Patterson's (Dr. James) Sermons.
Ridgeley's Body of Divinity. (On the 8th commandment.)
Stebbings' (Henry) Sermons.
Thompson's (Thomas) Sermons.
Tillotson's (Abp.) Sermons.
Tucker's Light of Nature pursued.
Waples' (Edward) Sermons.
Waters' (Edward) Sermons.
Watts' (Isaac) Sermons.
Zollikoffer's Evils that are in the world.

Indwelling Sin. See SECRET FAULTS.

Baxter's (Richard) Practical Works.
Edwards' (Dr. J., of Oxford) Doctrine of sin.
Owen's (John) Works.
Taylor's (Jeremy) Works.
Whitby's Full answer to Dr. Edwards.

Inequalities of Human Condition.

Abernethy's (John) Sermons.
Balle's (Nic. E.) Select sermons.
Butler's Analogy of religion and nature.
Byllsby's Sources of unequal wealth.
Conant's (John) Sermons.
Conybeare's (Bp.) Sermons.
Doddridge's Lectures. Lect. 89.
Foster's (James) Sermons.
Grove's (Henry) Sermons.
Hall's (Robert) Sermons.
Heywood on Distinctions in Society under the Anglo-Saxon government.
Jortin's (John) Sermons.
Lawson's (John) Sermons.
Miller's Distinction of ranks in society.
Moss' (Robert) Sermons.
Newton's (Benjamin) Sermons.
Pyle's (Thomas) Sermons.
Rees' (Abraham) Sermons.
Rosseau's Origin of the inequality, &c.
Saurin's Sermons.
Scott's Christian life.
Skeeler's (Thomas) Sermons.
White's (Thomas) Sermons.
Wilkins' Nature of religion.
Young's (Bp.) Sermons.

Infallibility of the Pope.

Brochmandus de Pontifice Romano.
Cranmer, contra Primatum Papæ.
Gaultheri Problemata.
Illyrici Opera.
Lubberti Opera.
Newmani (Io. Georg.) Dissertationes.
Stillingfleet, Opera varia.
Van Till, de Petro non Pontifice.

Billingsley's Sermons.
Bray on Papal usurpation.
James' (King) Pope's supremacy confuted.
James' (Tho.) Bellum Papale. (A tremendous blow. He adduces over 2,000 variations between the "infallible" editions of the Vulgate of Sextus V., and that of Clement VIII.)
Keary's Hist. Review of Papal infallibility.
Luther's Works.
Mathias' Popery not Catholicism.
Robins' (S.) Services of the Roman Church.
Sermons at Cripplegate.
Stillingfleet's Protestant grounds of faith.
Todd's (Jas.) Search after infallibility.

This topic is amply discussed in some of the works named under Popery. It is not likely to be renewed.

Infant Baptism. See ABRAHAMIC COVENANT, BAPTISMAL REGENERATION, FAITH OF INFANTS, INFANT CHURCH MEMBERSHIP.

Pro.

Augustine, de Baptismo.
Bucer (Mart,), de Baptismate infantium.
Cassander de Baptismo infantium.
Edzard's Nothwehr für die kindertaufe.
Grotii Baptizatorum Pueror. Institutio.
Harduin de Baptismo.
Hoornbeckii (Ioann.) Disputationes.
Hulsemanni Fides salvifica infantum.
——— de Fide infantum actualli.
Lange's Kindertaufe in d. evang. Kirche.
Melancthonis Refutatio erroris Serveti.
Plitt's Kindertaufe in der H. Scripturen und in ersten Kirche.
Salmasius Dissertatio de pædobaptismo.
Savage, Questiones Theologicæ.
——— Defensio, &c. (Contra J. Tombes.)
Scarella, de Baptism. infantium in utero.
Slotanus da Baptismo parvulorum.
Stier's Taufe und Kindertaufe.
Van Mastricht, de Susceptoribus infantium ex baptismo.
Voralei de Abortivorum baptismo.
Vossii (Gerard.) Disputationes.
Walchii Diss. de fide infantum in utero.
——— Hist. pædobap. quatuor priorum sæculorum.
Wallis, de Pædobaptismo.
Wardumus de Vi et Efficacia, etc.
Winkler's Beweis der Kindertaufe.

Infant Baptism—*continued.*

Pro.

Adams' (Wm.) Mercy to babes.
Addington's Reasons for baptizing infants.
Armstrong's (G. D.) Doctrine of baptisms.
Arnauld's Subversion of morality.
Asheton's Conference with an Anabaptist.
Bailey's Antidote against Anabaptism.
Bakewell's Defence of infant baptism.
Barlow's (Bp.) Letter to Mr. Tombes.
Baxter's State of Christian infants.
——— Infant baptism and church membership. (Against Tombes.)
Bibliotheca Sacra. 14:54.
Bickersteth on Baptism.
Biddulph's (Tho.) Seal of the Covenant.
Bingham's Antiquities of the Church.
Blake on the Covenants.
Bostwick on the Right of infants, &c.
Bottomly's Short plea for infant baptism.
Bowden's Covenant right of infants.
Breckel's Pædobaptism examined.
——— Defence of Do.
Brinsley's (William) Discourses.
Brownlee on the Mode and Subjects.
Budd's Infant baptism the means of national reformation.
Bullinger on the Baptism of Children.
Carter's Strictures on Infant baptism.
——— Reviewer reviewed. Ans. to Richards.
Cassel's (J.) Lectures.
Chapman (W.) on Infant baptism.
Christian Observer. 28:323.
Clarke's (P.) Divine right of infant baptism.
Clarke's (Dr. Sam.) Exp. of the catechism.
Cleaveland's Infant baptism from heaven.
Cotton's (John) The end of the baptism of the children of the faithful.
Cook's Answer to a treatise entitled "The vanity of childish baptism."
Craig's Arraignment of Anabaptism.
Cummings' (Dr. John) Baptismal font.
D'Assigney's Antidote against Errors.
——— Anabaptism unmasked.
Davis' Right of infants to baptism.
Dehon's (Dr. T.) Sermons.
Dodwell's Soul naturally mortal, but immortalized by the baptismal spirit which none but Bishops can impart.
Donaldson on Baptism.
Dorrington's Vind. of the Christian Church.
Douglass (R.) on Infant baptism.
Edwards' (Peter) Candid reasons, &c.
Exall's (Joshua) Serious Enquiry.
Finley's Plea for the speechless.
——— Vindication of Do.
Firmint's Weighty questions discussed.
Fish (Elisha) on Infant baptism.
Fleming's (Caleb) Plea for infants.
——— Appendix to Do.
Floyd's Essays to restore the dipping of infants.
Ford's (S.) Practical use of infant baptism.
Frith's Declaration of baptism.
Fuller's Infant's Advocate.

Infant Baptism—*continued.*

Pro.

Garner's Primitive Baptism.
Gerrie's Vindication of infant baptism.
Goode's Doctrine of the Church of England as to the effect of infant baptism.
Graves' (Rich.) Infant baptism vindicated.
Hall's (Thomas) Font guarded.
——— Words to T. Collier and J. Tombes.
Halley's Congregational Lectures.
——— Bap. the designation of catechumens.
Hammond on Infant baptism.
Harrison (Michael) on Infant baptism.
Hewerdine's Plain letters on baptism.
Hibbard (F. G.) on Infant baptism.
Hicks' Case of infant baptism.
Hitchins' Infant's cause pleaded.
Hoare on the Baptism of infants.
Hodges' Infant baptism tested by Scripture.
Holmes' Animadversions on Mr. Tombes.
Horne (John) on Infant baptism.
Horsey on Infant baptism.
Hussey's Examination. (Ans. to Tombes.)
Inglis' (Cha.) Essay on infant baptism.
Irving (Edw.) on the Sacrament of Baptism.
Jerram's Conversations on Baptism.
Kidd on Infant baptism.
Kurtz's Necessity of Infant Baptism.
Lewis' Defence of inf. bapt. (Agt. Tombes.)
Littleton's (Lord) Thoughts on inf. baptism.
Lord's (Joseph) Reasons why not Anabaptists plunging, but Infant-believer's baptism should be approved.
Luke's (J. N.) Sermons.
Mareschall's Defence of infant baptism. (Against Tombes.)
Mason's (J. M.) Essays on the Church.
Mather's (Increase) Div. right of inf. bapt.
Menge's Vindiciæ fœderis.
Middleton's (J.) Vindic. of the ord. of Bapt.
——— Second Vindication.
Miller's (Sam.) Infant baptism scriptural and reasonable.
Milligan's Plea for infant baptism.
Mills' Vindication.
Nash's Circumcision and Baptism.
Osgood (David) on Baptism.
Owen's (Rich.) Lawfulness of inf. baptism.
——— Practice of the primitive church.
Pearson's Three plain reasons, &c.
Petto on Inf. bapt. (Reply to Grantham.)
Pierre on Infant baptism.
Priestley's Letter to an Antipædobaptist.
Princeton Review. 29:1,73. 35:622.
Ram on the Baptizing of infants.
Reed's (John) Apology for infant baptism.
Rellie on Baptism.
Robertson's (D.) Parent's Guide.
[Rothwell's] Pædobaptismus vindicatus.
Saltmarsh's Smoke in the temple.
Schaffer on Infant baptism.
Shrewsbury's Infant baptism scriptural.
Stephens' Precepts out of the New Testament for Infant baptism.
Stewart (A.) on Infant baptism.

Infant Baptism—*continued.*

Pro.

Stokes on Infant baptism.
Sydenham's Exercitation on infant baptism.
Taylor's (Cha.) Facts and evidences on B.
Taylor's (Jno.) Covenant of grace.
Taylor (Nath.) on the Baptism of infants.
Towerson's Fourth part of the Catechism.
Towgood's Reasonable service.
Turner's Vindication of infant baptism.
Tyerman on Infant sprinkling.
Walford's Holiness of a Christian child, &c.
Walker's Modest plea for infant baptism.
Wall's History of Infant baptism.
——— Defence of Do.
Wardlaw's (R.) 6 Dissertations.
Webster (S.) on Infant baptism.
Whiston's Prac. of the first 2 centuries.
——— Address to the Baptists.
Whitby's Comm. (Appendix to Mark ii.)
Wills' (O.) Appeal to the Baptists.
——— Infant baptism asserted.
Williams (E.) on Antipædobaptism.
Wilson (Robt.) on Inf. bapt. and immersion.
Woods (James) on Infant baptism.
Woods' (Leonard) Lectures on Inf. baptism.
Wynell's Covenant of free grace.

Con.

Tertullian de Baptismo.

Mehring's Heilige Tauf historie.
Mennonis' (Simon) Opera Theologica.
Montanus (H.) de Vanitate pædobaptismi.
Munzer's Protestation und Entheitung.
Smith (Rich.) de Infantium baptismo.
Tombes' (Io.) Refut. positionis H. Savage.
——— Dissertationes.
Van Dale, Historia Baptismorum.

Anderson's Baptists Justified by Jer. Taylor.
Ashdowne's (Wm.) Theological works.
Baldwin (Thomas) on Baptism.
Blackwood's Storming of Antichrist.
——— Apostolical baptism.
Booth's Pædobaptism examined.
Braidwood's Letters on the grace of God.
Burroughs (Jos.) on Positive Institutions.
Carson's Mode and subjects of baptism.
Chapin's Letters on baptism.
Christian Repository. 1:561.
Collier's Font-guard routed.
Collins (Hercules) on Baptism.
——— Sandy foundation shaken.
Cornwell's Vindication of the commission. (Matthew 28:18,19.)
Cox's (F. A.) Strictures on Greville Ewing, Pres. Dwight, and Ralph Wardlaw.
Crap's (John) Infant baptism.
Dagg (J. L.) on Infant baptism.
Danvers (Henry) on Infant baptism.
Davids' Reply to Priestley.
Dobell on the Baptism and salv. of infants.
Dore's Antipædobaptism and female communion consistent. (Reply to P. Edwards.)
Ellison's (Seacome) Truth Defended.
——— Baptism as instituted of God.

Infant Baptism—*continued.*

Con.

Ewer's (Sam.) Answer to Hitchin.
Exall's Spirit of enquiry assisted.
Fleming (Caleb) on Baptism.
Foote's Letters to Bp. Hoadly.
Gale's Reflections on Wall's hist. of inf. bapt.
Gibbs' Defence of the Baptists.
Gill's Infant B. a part and pillar of popery.
——— Divine right of inf. bapt. examined.
——— Infant baptism an innovation.
——— Apostolic tradition.
——— Reply to Dr. Clarke.
Grantham on Infant baptism.
Hall (Robt.) on Infant baptism.
Hall (Jos.) on the Practice of inf. baptism.
Hobson's Fallacy of infant baptism.
Hoskin on Inf. bapt. (Reply to Brownlee.)
Howell's Evils of infant baptism.
Ives on Infant baptism. (Reply to Rellie.)
Jackson on Infant baptism.
Jenkins' (Jos.) Defence of the Baptists.
——— Inconsistency of infant sprinkling.
——— Reply to De Courcey.
Keach's Infant baptism unlawful.
——— Axe laid to the root. (Reply to Flavel and others.)
——— Rector rectified. (Ans. to Burket.)
——— Counter-antidote. (Ans. to Shute.)
Killingworth's Answer to Towgood.
——— Supplement to the sermons at Salter's Hall.
——— Exam. of the Apostol. constitutions.
Kinghorn's Defence of Infant Baptism its best refutation.
——— Sermons.
Knolly's (Hansard) Flaming fire in Zion. (Reply to Saltmarsh.)
Knott's Principles of the Baptists.
Law on the Abrahamic covenant.
Lay's Light for smoke. (Rep. to Saltmarsh.)
McGregor on Inf. B. (Rep. to Addington.)
McLean's Nature and import of baptism.
Martin's Letters to Rev. John Horsey.
May's Technobaptist.
Morgan's (Abel) Antipedorantism.
——— Antipædorantism defended.
Rees (David) on Infant baptism.
Richards' (W.) Review of Carter's strictures.
——— Serious discourse on baptism.
Richardson's Reply to Featley's "Dipper dipt."
Robinson's (Robt.) History of baptism.
Russell's Vindication of baptized churches.
——— Portsmouth Disputation. 1699.
——— Infant baptism is will-worship. (Answer to Berault.)
Spillman's God's ordinance the saint's privilege.
Stennett on Inf. bapt. (Reply to Russen.)
——— Answer to Addington.
Stovel on Christian Discipleship. (Reply to Halley.)
Tasker's Examination of Stokes' argument.
Taylor's (Dan.) Principal parts of religion.

Infant Baptism—*continued.*

Con.

Taylor's (D.) Strict. on Addington's reasons.
Tombes' (Jno.) Antipædobaptism.
——— Precursor.
——— Various other pieces. (Tombes was a B. D., and a prominent member of the Westminster Assembly. "There were few better disputants."—Wood.)
Wilson's Scripture Manual.

A large list of ancient Latin and German authors on this subject is given by Pfaffius, *Introd. ad hist. theolog. litter.* Part II.

Infant Church-Membership.

Pro.

Baxter (Rich.) on Inf. church-membership.
Biddulph's Seal of the Covenant.
Croly's (G.) Regeneration of infants.
Gregg on Infant church-membership.
Hitchins' Covenant interest of infants.

Though there are scarcely any books on this express point, yet many writers in support of infant baptism take this ground.

Infant Communion.

Pro.

The Fathers generally.

Augusti Archæologia.
Harenbergii Theologia Dogmatica. (Quotes the Fathers largely.)
Meyer de Eucharistia Infantum.
Zornii Hist. Eucharistiæ Infantum.

Chillingworth's (Wm.) Additional discourses.
Peirce (Jas.) on the Ancient practice of giving the Lord's supper to infants.
Priestley's Address to Protestant Dissenters.
Taylor's (Jer.) Worthy communicant.
Waterland's Antiquity of infant communion.

Infant Schools.

Bethune (Mrs. D.) on Infant Schools.
Currie's Principles and pract. of Inf. schools.
Russell (Wm.) on Infant education.

Infants, Salvation of. See BAPTISMAL REGENERATION, FAITH OF INFANTS.

Augustine, de Pœnis parvulorum qui sine baptismo decederunt.
Beaucaire, Traité des enfans mort dans le sein.
Cassander de Baptismo infantium.
——— contra Anabaptismum.
Cœlius, von der Kindertaufe.
Conrius [or Conroy] de fato parvulorum sine baptismo, decedentium.
Florentini Disputationes.
Gueroud, de l'Efficace du baptisme.
Hulsemanni Calvinismus in agone.
——— Fides salvifica infantum.
Sartorii Hist. opinionum de sorte infantum sine baptismate mortuorum.

Beecher's (Lyman) Letters to the editors of the Christian Examiner.

Infants, Salvation of—*continued.*

Bethune's Early lost, early saved.
Bibliotheca Sacra. 18:383.
Bomberger (J. H. A.) on Infant salvation.
Brown's (R.) By-ways of the Bible.
Bruce's (John) Cypress wreath.
Christian Examiner. 4:431. 5:229,310.
Christian Review. 13:334.
Croly's Regeneration of Infants.
Cumming (John) on Infant salvation.
Doddridge's Lectures.
Edwards (Pres.) on Original sin.
Gentleman's Magazine. 9:177.
Gillard on the Salvation of infants.
Grantham's Infant's Advocate.
Harris' (Dr. Wm.) Ground of hope.
Kollock's (S. K.) Sermons.
Prime (Sam. I.) on the Death of children.
Robinson's Claude on the comp. of a sermon.
Rowlatt (David) on the Salvation of infants.
Russell's (David) Works.
Smyth's (Tho.) Solace to bereaved parents.
Spirit of the Pilgrims. 1:149.
Toplady on the Scheme of necessity. (Intr.)
Watts' Ruin and Recovery of man.
Williams on the Salvation of infants.

Infidelity. See DEISM.

Callenbergii Comment. de Scepticismo.
Frantz, Briefe an einen Zweifler.
Holwerda, de Veterum Scepticor. sententia.
Meisneri Historia doctrinæ de vero Deo.
Merault, les Apologistes involontaires. (Christianity proved by the observations of Infidels.)
Seligmani Exercitationes Academicæ.
Voetii (Gisbert.) Dissertationes.
Vries, Exercitationes Rationales.

Amer. Biblical Repos. 10:89.
Anderson's Remonstrance. Ag. Bolingbroke.
Auchincloss' Sophistries of Tho. Paine.
Barnes' Certainty of the Christian religion.
Barrow's (Isaac) Sermons on the Creed.
Baxter's Unreasonableness of Infidelity.
Beecher's (Ly.) Lectures on Scepticism.
Berkeley's Principles of human knowledge.
Bibliotheca Sacra. 15:693.
Bidlake's Bampton Lectures. 1811.
Birk's Difficulties of belief in the creation and fall. (Profound.)
Blake's Infidelity inexcusable.
Bradford's (Sam.) Discourses.
Broughton's Christianity distinct from the religion of nature.
——— Common doctrine of the soul.
Brown's System of Natural and Revealed religion.
Chrichton's Converts from Infidelity.
Christian Disciple. 3:332.
Christian Examiner. 17:23,332.
Christian Month. Spect. 6:75.
Christian Observer. 18:215.
Christian Quart. Spect. 5:469.
Christian Review. 2:271. 3:134. 6:191.

Infidelity—*continued.*

Davies' Two Antichrists, Infidelity and Romanism, viewed in their relative bearings. (As in 1856.)
Disney's (John) Sermons.
Dove's Logic of the Christian faith.
Duncan's Libertine led to reflection.
Dwight's (Tim.) Nature and danger of I.
Eclectic Rev. New Series. 6:740.
Edinburg Monthly Review. 3:60.
Estlin's (John P.) Sermons.
Evans' (John) Sermons.
Evans' (J. H.) Checks to Infidelity.
Faber's Difficulties of Infidelity.
Farrer's Bampton Lectures. 1862.
Finch's Bampton Lectures. 1797.
Forbes (D.) on the Sources of incredulity.
Foster's (James) Sermons.
Gale's Anatomy of Infidelity.
Girdlestone's Progress of Scepticism in England. 1863.
Grant's Foes of our Faith, and how to defeat them.
Grisenthwaite's Refutation of Tho. Paine.
Hall's (Robert) Sermons.
Hallet's Consistent Christian.
Hennel's (Miss) Christianity and Infidelity.
Hodge's (Cha.) Essays and Reviews.
Hooker's Popular Infidelity.
Horberry's (Matthew) Sermons.
Hurd's (Bp.) Sermons.
Jamieson on the Causes of Infidelity.
Law's Appeal to all who doubt the gospel.
Leng's Boyle Lectures. 1719.
Mansel's Limits of religious thought.
McBurnie's Errors of Infidelity. ("An armory, hung all over with keen weapons." —EVANG. MAG.)
Michaelis' Introd. to the New Testament.
Moore's Christian system vindicated.
Morgan's Christianity and modern I. comp.
Neale's (Erskine) Christianity and infidelity contrasted. (An account of the deaths of many prominent persons.)
Nelson's Cause and cure of Infidelity.
New York Review. 2:483.
Nichols' Conference with a Theist.
North British Rev. 15:18.
Ogilvie on the Causes of Infidelity.
Pearson's (Geo.) Charac. and tendency of I.
Pearson's (Thos.) Aspects, causes, &c., of I.
Post's Skeptical era in modern history.
Princeton Review. 12:31.
Quarterly Review. 28:493.
Ragg's Creation's testimony to its God.
Rennel's (Tho.) Remarks on Scepticism. (An answer to Bichat, Morgan, &c., on questions touching organization and life.)
Ripley's (Geo.) Latest form of infidelity. (Viz., German theology.)
Schmucker's (S. S.) Errors of modern I.
Seed's (Jeremiah) Sermons.
Simpson's (David) Plea for religion.
Smith's (Sam. Stanhope) Sermons.
Smith's (Sydney) Sermons.

Infidelity—*continued.*

Smith's (Cha.) Shadow of Death. (Prize Essay.)
Spear's Creed of Despair. (Prize Essay.)
Spirit of the Pilgrims. 6:204. 8:1,447.
Stanhope's Truth of the Christian religion.
Stebbings' Christianity justified.
Stillingfleet's (Bp.) Sermons.
Thompson's French Philosophy.
Treffrey's Infidel's own book.
Turner's Boyle Lectures. 1709.
Valpy on the Course of Nature.
Van Mildert's Boyle Lectures. 1802. (A historical view of the rise and progress of infidelity, with able reasonings.)
Warburton's View of Bolingbroke's Philos.
Wilberforce's Practical View of Christianity.
Young's (Edw.) Centaur not fabulous.
Young's (J. R.) Modern scepticism viewed in relation to modern science. 1865. (Specially notices Colenso, Huxley, Lyell, and Darwin.)

In FABER'S *Difficulties of Infidelity*, New York edition, 1853, is given a list of all the books known to have been written on the evidence of revealed religion.

Infinity of God. See ATTRIBUTES.

Christian Review. 14:23.
Clarke's (Sam.) Boyle Lectures. 1705.
Gurdon's Boyle Lectures. 1721, 1722.
Howe's Works. Vol. 1.
——— Living Temple. Part 1, Ch. 4.
Locke's Essays.
Scott's Christian Life.

Infirmity. See PRESUMPTION, SINS OF IGNORANCE, SINS OF INFIRMITY.

Influence of Body on Mind. See RECIPROCAL INFLUENCE.

Influence of Christianity on Temporal Affairs. See CHRISTIANITY ADAPTED TO MAN, HAPPINESS, PLEASURES OF PIETY.

Balme, le Protestantisme comparé au cathol.
Carrèire's Religion in ihrem Begriff ihrem Weltgeschichtlichen entwickelung und Vollendung.
Dreolle, de l'Influence du principe religieux sur l'homme.
Gregoire, de l'influence du Christianisme sur la condition des femmes.
Laget, Sermons sur divers sujets.
Meyer's Verdienst des Chris. um den Staat.
Neubig's Christenthum als Weltreligion.
Pister, Inf. du Christianisme sur le droit.
Reinhard's Geist des Christenthums.
Rothe's Wirkungen des Christenthums.
Senac, Chris. consideré dans ses rapports avec civilization.
Tittmann's Verhältniss d. Christen. zur Entwickelung des menschl. Geschlechts.
Troplong, l'Infl. du. Chris. sur le droit civile des Romaines.

Influence of Christianity—*continued.*

Arnold's (Thomas) Sermons.
Blakey's Temporal benefits of Christianity.
Boyle's Basis of National security.
Bryant's Mutual influence of Christianity and the Stoic school.
Campbell's (George) Sermons.
Chandler's Bampton Lectures. 1825.
Channing's (W. E.) Miscellaneous Essays.
Cook's Historical view of Christianity.
Delany's (Patrick) Sermons.
Douglass' (James) Discourses.
Durham's (J. E.) Sermons.
Erskine's (Dr. John) Sermons.
Fawcett's (James) Sermons.
Fothergill's (George) Sermons.
Gresley's (William) Sermons.
Hall's (Robt.) Sermons.
Hampden's (R. D.) Sermons.
Hare's (Thomas) Sermons.
Harness' Boyle Lectures. 1821.
Haverfield's (Tho. T.) Sermons.
Hoare's Fitness of Chris. to improve the social condition of the nations which overthrew the Roman empire.
Horseley's (Bp.) Sermons.
Kennedy's Hulsean prize essay. 1856.
Krasinski's Reformation in Poland.
Lancaster's (Tho. W.) Sermons.
Lupton's (Dr. W.) Sermons.
Mackensie's Inf. of the Christian Clergy of the first 10 cent. on European progress.
Meyer's Inf. of Prot. missions on the moral and physical condition of man.
Monsell's (C. H.) Sermons.
Morehead's (R.) Discourses.
Porteus' (Bp.) Sermons.
Rogers' (John) Sermons.
Ryan's Hist. of the influence of religion on ancient and modern nations. 1788.
Scobel's (Edward) Sermons.
Sterne's (Lawrence) Sermons.
Stillingfleet's (Bp.) Sermons.
Tillotson's (Abp.) Sermons.
Westminster Review. New Series. 1:182.
White's The gospel promotive of happiness.

Influences of the Spirit.
See OPERATIONS.

Innate Ideas. See IDEAS, PLATONISM.

Pro.

Ciceronis Tusc. Disputat. Lib. I. c. 24.
Herbert de Veritate.
Le Grande, Institutiones philos. Pars IX.
Platonis Phædo.
Sanderson, de Conscientia.

Beattie's Immutability of truth.
Buffier on the Origin of opinions.
Cudworth's Intellectual System. Ch. 4.
King on the Origin of evil.
Oswald's Appeal to common sense.
Sherlock on a Future state.
Taylor's (Tho.) Edition of Plato.

Innate Ideas—*continued.*

Con.

Aristotle's Ethics.
Crouza's System of Logic.
Doddridge's Lectures. Part 1. Lect. 7.
Locke on the Human understanding.
Pearson on the Creed.
Stewart's Philosophy of the mind.

Inquirers. See CONVICTION.

Baxter's Saint's Everlasting Rest.
Bethune's History of a penitent.
Carleton's Letters to an anxious friend.
Henry's Letters to an anxious Inquirer.
James' Anxious Inquirer.
Matheson's Advice to religious Inquirers.
Russel's Letters. Letter 16.
Spencer's (Ichabod) Pastor's Sketches.
Spurgeon's (Cha. H.) Sermons. 3d Series.
Winslow's (Octavius) Inquirer directed.

Inquisition.

Arnoldus de Tractandis Hæreticis.
Assemanni Acta sanc. martyrum. (Vast.)
Baker's Vollstændige Historie.
Bebellius de Inquisitione Hispanica.
Benthem de Causis conservati Papatus.
Comensis Lucerna Inquisitorum.
Dillon, Relation de l'Inquisition de Goa.
Erasmus contra Monachos Hispanos.
Fabricius, Histoire de l'Inquisition.
Fereal, Mysteres de l'I. 200 plates.
Lamothe, Hist. de l'Inq. en France.
Leger, Hist. des Eglises evang. de Piemont.
Limborchii Historia Inquisitionis. (The only work containing the acts of the Toulouse Inquisition agt. the Waldenses.)
Llorente, Hist. de la Inq. d'Espana.
Loescher's Romischen Huren Regiment.
[Marsollier (J.)] Hist. de l'I. et son origine.
Montani Inquisitionis Hispanicæ.
Pignatelli, Consultationes Novissimæ.
Sarpii Historia Inquisitionis.
Servita, Historia Inquisitionis.
Thuani Historia. Lib. III.
Usserus de Eccles. successione. Cap. IV.

Achilli's Papal Rome.
——— Dealings with the Inquisition.
Amer. Quart. Review. 18:142.
Baker's History of the I. in Portugal, Spain, Italy, East Indies, and West Indies. 1736.
Blackwood's Mag. 20:70,332.
Cousta's Unparalleled sufferings at Lisbon.
Davies' Hist. of I. to the present time. 1850.
Dellon's History of the Inquisition at Goa. (Himself a prisoner there.)
Dugdale's Spanish Inquisition.
Garin's Mysteries of Popery.
Gavin's Detestable Inquisition.
Geddes' View of the I. in Portugal.
Gibbings' Record of the Roman Inquisition.
——— Were heretics ever burnt at Rome?
Gould's History of the Reformation.
Lavalle's Treatise on the Inquisition.

Inquisition—*continued.*

Limborch's Hist. of the I. Translated by Chandler; with a valuable introduction.
Llorentes' Hist. of the I. in Spain. (To the reign of Ferdinand VII. This truly great work obtained for its author the cognomen of the Suetonius of the Inquisition.)
Marchant's Bloody tribunal. (Historical.)
Monthly Rev. 91:396,535. 92:473.
Mora's Inq. revived. (A narrative of his sufferings and escape.)
Museum of Foreign Lit. 2:110. 10:328.
Niles' Register. 21:329.
Paul's [Sarpi] History of the Inquisition.
Piaza's (H. B.) Inquisition in Italy.
Princeton Review. 21:174.
Puigblanch's Inquisition unmasked.
Quart. Review. 6:313. 10:203.
Servita's Hist. of the I. Tr. by Gentilis.
Simes' History of the Inquisition.
Stockdale's History of the I. Plates.
Taylor's (Matt.) England's bloody tribunal.
Timson's Origin, policy, &c. (With memoirs of its victims, and plates.)

Insabbates. See WALDENSES.

Inscription on the Cross.

Altmanni Meletemata critica.

Insolvency, Morality of.

Hunt's Merchant's Magazine. 7:352. 8:294.

Inspiration. See CANON.

Carpzovius de Divina inspiratione.
Credner de Librorum N. T. inspiratione.
Dupin, Prolegomena.
Gaussen, Théopneustie.
Grotius de Veritate relig. Christianæ.
Henrici Lucubrationes.
Huetii Demonstratio Evangelica.
Potter, Prelectiones Theologicæ.
Quenstedtius de Divina inspiratione.
Sontagii de Inspiratione, ejusque ratio.
Waltheri (Mich.) Dissertationes.

Appleton's (Pres.) Works. Lect. 26, 27.
Bailey's (Benj.) Essay on Inspiration.
Bannerman on Inspiration.
Bateman (Josiah) on the Inspiration, &c.
Baylie's (J.) Authority and Inspiration, &c.
Bennett's (Benj.) Sermons. (14 on this subj.)
Bibliotheca Sacra. 12:217. 15:29,314.
Bingham (W. A.) on the Insp. of Scripture.
Bogue's (David) Essays.
Burgon's Bible and modern thought.
Burnet on the 39 Articles. Art. 6.
Butler's Anal. of relig. and nature. Part 2.
Butler's (W.) Testimony of history.
Calamy's (Edmund) Sermons.
Calmet's Dissertations.
Campbell (Geo.) on the Four gospels.
Carlyle's Origin and authority of the S. Scr.
Carson's (A.) Refutation of Henderson.
——— Review of Wilson, Smith, and Dick.
Cellerier's Divine origin of the Old Testam.

Inspiration—*continued.*

Chalmer's Evidences of Christianity.
Chris. Examiner. 8:362. 32:119,204. 35:340.
Christian Review. 9:1. 12:219.
Davidson's (Sam.) Text of O. T. considered.
Davies' (S.) Nature of the Divine agency as to inspiration.
Dick (John) on Inspiration.
Doddridge's Dissertations on the New Test.
Dyer on the Inspiration of Sacred Scripture.
Eclectic Review. 4th Series. 1:91. 11:365.
Emmons' (Nathaniel) Sermons.
Findlay's Vindic. of the sacred books and Josephus. (Reply to Voltaire.)
Fuller's Part of a Body of divinity.
Gasparin on Plenary inspiration.
Gaussen's Theopneustia. Tr. by E. N. Kirk.
Gerard's Institutes of Criticism.
Haldane (Robt.) on Inspiration.
Hawker's Evidence of plenary inspiration.
Henderson (E.) on Divine inspiration.
Hervey's (A.) Five Sermons.
Hinds on the Inspiration and authority, &c.
Howarth on Revealed religion.
Jenkins' Reasonableness of Christianity.
Kelly's Exam. of Davidson's statement.
Kitto's Journal. 5:437. 7:315.
La Mothe on Inspiration.
Le Clerc's Letters.
Lee's Nature and proofs of inspiration.
Leslie's Easy method with Deists.
Lond. Quart. Rev. 10:286.
Lowe's I. a reality. (Reply to Macnaught.)
Lowth's (W.) Authority and insp. of S. Scr.
Lowth's (S.) Insp. of the Holy Scriptures.
McCaul's Testimonies to the authority, &c.
Macleod's View of inspiration.
Macnaught on Inspiration.
Marston's Manual on the inspiration, &c.
Methodist Quart. Rev. 5:594.
Michaelis' Introd. to the New Test. Ch. 3.
Middleton's Miscellaneous works.
Morel's Philosophy of Religion.
Morris' (A. J.) The Bible, what is it?
New Englander. 7:515.
Newton (Bp.) on the Prophecies.
Noble on Plenary inspiration.
Paley's Evidences of Christianity.
Parry on the Insp. of the Apostles.
Powell's Nature and extent of inspiration.
Prettyman's Elements of Christian theology.
Princeton Review. 29:598,660.
Redford's Holy Scriptures verified by science, history, and human consciousness.
Scott's (Thomas) Essays.
Secker's (Abp.) Sermons.
Seed's Sermons at the Moyer Lecture. 1747.
Simpson's Plea for the sacred writings. (A masterly refutation of Deism.)
Spirit of the Pilgrims. 1:402,474,624. 2:9,70, 185,237,289. 3:369,420.
Stennet's Authority and use of Scripture.
Storr on the Historical sense.
Stuart's (Moses) Critical history and defence of the Old Testament Canon.

Inspiration—*continued.*

Taylor's (D.) Truth and insp. of Scripture.
Thomson's (Alex.) Lectures.
Tillotson's Sermons.
Tomlin's Introd. to the study of Scripture.
Townsend's (George) Works.
Van Mildert's (William) Sermons.
Vaughn's (J.) Lectures. Lect. 9.
Wardlaw's (Ralph) Discourses.
Watson's (Rich.) Theological Tracts.
——— Apology for the Bible.
Westcott's Elements of Gospel harmony.
Wettenhall's Div. authority of Sac. Script.
Whitehead's (Robt.) Warrant of faith.
Whitby's Preface to Commentary on N. T.
Whittington's Inspiration of the Old Test.
Wilkinson's (T.) Inspiration of Scripture.
Williams' (Bp.) Boyle Lectures. 1695, 1696.
Wilson (Bp.) on Plenary inspiration.
Wilson's (John) Essay on enthusiasm.
Wood's (Leonard) Works.
Wordsworth's Five lectures in Westminster Abbey. 1861.

Inspired Psalmody.

Pro.

Jack, Onomasticon Poeticum: sive propriorum, &c., descriptio.
Claybaugh's Ordinance of Praise.
Dodd's (Robt. J.) Reply to Morton.
Houston's Divine Ps. agt. human hymns.
MacLaren's Psalms of Holy Scripture the only songs of Zion.
MacMaster's Apology for the bk. of Psalms.
Martin's Psalms of David. (Preface.)
Pressly's The true Psalmody.
——— Review of Ralston.
——— Strictures on Annan's Letters.
Somerville's Exclusive claims of David's Ps.
The True Psalmody. A compilation.
Wickersham's Excellence of Scripture Ps.

The above maintain the impropriety of using, in public worship, hymns of human composition.

Con.

Annan's (Wm.) Letters on Psalmody.
——— Vindication of Do.
Johnson's (Wm.) The Ps. and paraphrases.
Morton's Review of Pressly.
Ralston on the Use of evangelical Psalms.

Instability. See INDECISION.

Alison's (Archibald) Sermons.
Atterbury's (Francis) Sermons.
Caswall's (E.) Sermons.
Dehon's (Dr. T.) Sermons.
Jowett's (Joseph) Fifty-two sermons.
Venn's (John) Sermons.
Verschoyle's (H.) Sermons.

Installation Sermons.

Allen (Thomas)	at	his own.
Bacon (John)	"	his own.
Beecher (Lyman)	"	A. J. Keyse's.

Installation Sermons—*continued.*

Belknap (Jeremy)	at	J. Morse's.
Chauncy (C.)	"	J. Bowman's.
Cummings (Alex.)	"	his own.
Dana (James)	"	A. Holmes'.
Dana (Joseph)	"	D. Dana's.
Eckley (Joseph)	"	H. Holley's.
Emmons (Nath.)	"	J. Emerson's.
——— ———	"	H. Weeks'.
Knowles (Jas. D.)	"	Howard Malcom's.
Lord (B.)	"	N. Whitaker's.
Macarty (T.)	"	his own.
Marsh (J.)	"	W. Lockwood's.
McKean (J.)	"	E. Richmond's.
Osgood (David)	"	P. Thatcher's.
Phillips (S.)	"	S. Chandler's.
Ripley (E.)	"	W. Frothingham's.
Tappan (David)	"	H. Packard's.
Thayer (N.)	"	W. Emerson's.

Such sermons, though very numerous, are almost always pamphlets.

Instinct.

Antoine, les Animaux célèbres.
Cambray, sur l'Existence de Dieu.
Chesnel, les Animaux raisonment.
Chiaverini, Analyse comparative sur les caractères de l'intelligence et de l'instinct.
Dugès, Physiologie comparé de l'homme et des animaux.
Fée (A. L. A.) Etudes Philosophiques.
Flourens, de l'Intelligence des animaux.
Gabillot, Etude Physiologique.
Posner's Seelenleben der Thiere.
Rouse, Mœurs et sagacite des animaux.

Amer. Biblical Repos. 11:74.
Baxter's (Rich.) Practical works.
Bingley's Animal Biography.
Brougham's (Lord) Dissertations.
Brown's Biog. sketches of quadrupeds.
Buffon's Natural History.
Bushnan's Philosophy of Instinct.
Couch's Illustrations of instinct.
Democratic Review. 15:408.
Derham's Physico-theology.
Eclectic Rev. 4th Series. 2:402. New Series. 6:649.
Edwards' (George) Works.
Edwards' (Pres.) Works.
Ferguson's Being and perfections of God.
French's True nature of Instinct.
Garratt's Marvels and mysteries of instinct.
Good's (J. M.) Book of nature.
Goulburn's (E. M.) Parochial sermons.
Guardian, The. Nos. 156 and 157.
Hancock's Phys. and moral relations of I.
Hutcheson on the Origin of our ideas of beauty and virtue.
Jarrold on Instinct and Reason.
Kemp (T. L.) on Instinct.
Kirby's Bridgewater Treatise. (The 7th.)
Knickerbocker Magaz. 22:404,507.
Law (T.) on Instinctive Impulses.
——— Second thoughts on Do.
Littell's Living Age. 16:345. 17:595.

Instinct—*continued.*

Morris' Records of animal sagacity.
Mower on the Nature of instinct.
North Amer. Review. 63:91.
Paine's (Dr.) Soul distinct from matter.
Paley's Natural Theology.
Pennant's Arctic Zoology.
Pope's Ethical Epistles.
Proceedings of the American Academy of Arts and Sciences. December, 1860.
Ramsay (Sir Geo.) on Instinct and reason.
Ray's Wisdom of God in creation.
Rumball on Instinct and reason.
Scott's (John) Christian Life.
Swainson's Habits of animals.
Wakefield's Instinct displayed.
Ware's Philosophy of natural history.
Westminster Review. 48:352.

Instrumental Music in Churches.

Pro.

Apthorp on Sacred poetry and music.
Battel's (Ralph) Sermons.
Beveridge's Thesaurus Theologicus.
Bromley's (Robt. A.) Sermons.
Christian Observer. (Numerous articles.)
Cromar's Vindication of the Organ.
Dodwell on the Lawfulness of instrumental music in holy offices.
Fleming's (Alex.) Letters and Answers. (On the first attempt to introduce organs into Scotch Presbyterian Churches. 1808.
Hickman's (C.) Sermons.
Horne's (Bp.) Antiquity of church music.
Mason's (Will.) Essays on church music.
Oliver's Sermons.
Organs and Presbyterians. (Anonymous. Edinburg. 1829.)
Taswell on Church music.
Stillingfleet's (H.) Sermons.

Con.

Justin M., Questiones.
Augustine, Confessiones. Lib. X., cap. 33.
Isidore, Epistolæ.
Jerome, Comm. in Eph. 5:19.
Chrysostom, in Psalm. 144 and 150.
Theodoret, in Psalm. 33 and 150.
Basil, Commentaria in Isa. v.
Constitutiones Apostolici. Lib. VIII., c. 32.
Aquinas (Tho.) Questiones. Ques. 91.
Bona de Divina Psalmodia.
Cajetan (Card.) ad Tho. Aquin.
Erasmus, Comm. in 1 Cor. 14:19.
Candlish's The Organ Question.
Edwards' (John) Theologia Reformata.
Hickman's (Henry) Apology for Nonconformists.
Panoplist. Periodical. (Various pieces.)
Pierce's Vindication of Dissenters.
Poole (Matthew) on Evangelical worship. (Reply to Oliver.)
Ridgeley's Body of Divinity. Quest. 154.
Taylor's (Jer.) Ductor Dubitantium.
The Organ Cause. (Anon.)

Insufficiency of Human Reason. See LIGHT OF NATURE, NECESSITY OF REVELATION, PROVINCE OF REASON, WEAKNESS OF HUMAN REASON.

Integrity. See FRAUD.

Berens' (Edward) Village sermons.
Brady's (Nicholas) Sermons.
Burgess' (Anthony) Sermons.
Cave's Primitive Christianity. Part 3, ch. 1
Chalmers' Commercial discourses.
Paley's (William) Sermons.
Smith's (Dr. H.) Sermons.
Steele's (John) Sermons.
Thornwell's (J. H.) Discourses on Truth.
Watts' (Isaac) Sermons.
Wheatland's Sermons.

Intemperance. See DRUNKENNESS, MODERATION, TEMPERANCE.

Intercessory Prayer.

Close's (Francis) Sermons on the Liturgy.
Foster's (Dr. James) Sermons.
Hall's (Robert) Works.
Henry (Matthew) on Prayer.
Hordern's (Joseph) Sermons.
Mylne (G. W.) on Intercessory Prayer.
Newman's (J. H.) Sermons.
Nichols' (Benj. E.) Practical sermons.
Ogden's (Samuel) Sermons.
Romaine's (William) Sermons.
Venn's (John) Sermons.
Whitefield's Sermons.
Williams' (Isaac) Sermons.

Intercession of Christ. See MEDIATION.

Intercession of the Spirit. See ADVOCACY.

Interim. See ADIAPHORISTS.

Arnold's Kirchen und Ketzer Historie.
Bieck's Dreyfaches Interim.
Calvin, L'Interim, ou provision, &c.
Clingius de Securitate conscientiæ.
Epini Epistola ad Illyricum.
Epistola Concionatorum Hambergensium ad Melancthonem: et responsio.
Flacii (Matt.) Opera.
Frege, das Interim.
Grossman's Verdienste der chürfürsten von sachsen um abschluss d. Augsburger Religionsfreidens.
Hirsch's Gesch. des Interim zur Nurnberg.
Illyricus de Veris et falsi Adiaphoris.
——— Apologia.
——— Epistola ad Melancth. (An able and bitter oppenent of M. on several subjects.)
Joachim, Brevis comprehensio argumentorum, de ceremoniis a Papistis impositis.
Kahnis Vindiciæ pacis relig. Augustanæ.
Melancthonis Opera.
Rinks Erinnerungen zur dritten Jubelfeier.
Schmidti (C. F.) Observ. ad naturam peccati.
Schmidii (J. A.) Historia Interimistica.

Interim—*continued.*

Schmid's (K. C. E.) Untersüchung philos. theol.
Strigelii (V.) Confessio προιρετική.
Wigandt, de Neutralibus et mediis.

Calvin's Tracts.
Melancthon's Weighing of the Interim.
Planck's History of Protestant theology.
Rank's History of the Reformation.
Wirth's System of speculative Ethics.

A full account of the writers on both sides is given in DIE DANISCHE BIBLIOTH. Pt. 5.

Intermediate Place of Existence. See PURGATORY, SLEEP OF THE SOUL.

Pro.

Ambrose, de Bono Mortuis.
Chrysostom, Opuscula varia.
Jerome, Opera.
Origen, Homiliæ.

Capelli (Lud.) Dissertationes.
Wiedenfeld, der Unmittlebare Zustand.

Bennet's (Geo.) Olam Haneshemoth.
Blakeman's State of the soul after death.
Brown's (Dr. John) Dead in Christ.
Campbell's (Geo.) Dissertations. (Claimed by both parties, and not very consistent with himself.)
Campbell's (Archib.) Doct. of a middle state.
Cockrane's (J.) World to come.
Coleman's (J. N.) Sermons.
Cook's Examination of Balfour.
Doddridge's Lectures. (Claimed on this side, but not decisive.)
Dorrington's Family Devotion.
Dwight's (Tim.) Discourses. Disc. 164.
Fisher's Doct. of an intermed. state consid.
Fuller's (Andrew) Letters.
Goddard's (Peter S.) Sermons.
Goddard's (Thomas) Sermons.
Govet on the Place of departed spirits.
Harbaugh's Abode of the sainted dead.
Heath's Man's heaven to be this earth.
Hobart's (Bp.) Sermons.
Hodge's (Walter) Place of departed souls.
Horsley's (Bp.) Sermons.
Hovey's State of the impenitent dead.
Hudson's Letters to Balfour.
Huntingford's Testimonies in proof, &c. (An able reply to Whately. Selected from the writings of Beveridge, Butler, Calvin, Grotius, &c.)
Irving's (Ed.) Judgment to come.
Jortin's (John) Sermons.
Leifchild's (John) Discourses.
McCullough's Dead in Christ. Ch. 2 and 3.
McCausland's Truths for the times.
Methodist Quarterly Rev. 12:240.
Murdock's History of Dogmatic Theology.
Newman's (John Henry) Sermons.
Panoplist. 11:393.
Peters on Job.
Rickett's Condition of the soul after death.
Ridgeley's Body of Divinity. Quest. 86.

Intermediate Place, &c.—*continued.*

Pro.

Seabury's (Bp.) Sermons.
Sherlock's Practical Discourses.
Sherwood on the Intermediate state.
Smallridge's (Bp.) Sermons.
Smalley's Sermons.
Smith's (S.) Sacred Biography.
Stuart's Evangelical Essays.
Taylor's (Jer.) Sermons.
Thompson (Edw.) on the Future state.
Watson's Theological Institutes.
Watts' (Dr. Isaac) Essays.
——— World to come.
Whiston's Tr. of Josephus. (Appendix.)
Whitby's Commentary. (On 2 Tim. 4:8.)
White (Tho.) on the Intermediate state.
Wightman's The undying soul. (Superior.)

Con.

Amer. Bibl. Repos. 2d Series. 5:464.
Balfour's Essays.
Bibliotheca Sacra. 13:153.
Crookshank's No Intermediate state.
Dawson on the State of departed souls.
——— Further remarks on Do.
Edwards' (Bp.) Body of Divinity.
Pearson on the Creed.
Peckard's Obs. on the doct. of an int. state.
——— Further Observations.
Polwheel's Evidence from Scripture.
Pond (Enoch) on the Intermediate state.
Priestley's Works.
Princeton Review. Oct., 1839.
Wheatly on the Book of Common Prayer.

It is impossible to separate with precision the writers on an intermediate *place* from those on an intermediate *state*. They often confound the two subjects. All Papal writers, and most Protestant, hold the latter doctrine. The books here cited are, for the most part, not controversial, nor wholly on the subject, but discuss it among other doctrines. See a list of over a hundred Latin and German writers on this subject in ALGER'S *Doctrine of a future life.* Appendix.

Intermediate State. See DESCENT INTO HELL, HADES, PURGATORY.

Baumgarteni (S. J.) Hist. doct. de statu, &c.
Bretschneider's Handbuch der Dogmatik.
Burnett (Tho.) de Statu mortuorum.
Capellus de Statu animi post mortem.
Cotta, Hist. dogmat. de pœnarum duratione.
Ebrard (J. H. A.), Christ. Dogmatik. Th. III., Ab. 3.
Ernest de Vet. patrum opinione, &c.
Güder, die Lehre von der Erscheinung J. Ch. unter den Todten.
Hahn, Christliche Glaubenslehre.
Socini Epistolæ. Epis. ad Valkel.
Vossii (G. J.) Theses Theologicæ.
White, de Medium animarum statu.

Baylee (Jos.) on the Intermediate state.
Belsham's Essays. Ess. 11 and 12.

Intermediate State—*continued.*

Bennet's (G.) View of the Intermed. state.
Blackburne's Historical view of the controversy from the Reformation to the present time. 1772.
Broughton's Doctrine of the human soul.
Bryant's Attractions of the world to come.
Bull's (Bp.) Works. (Vol. 1. Sermons.)
Burton's (Edward) Sermons at Oxford.
Burton's (Hezekiah) Sermons.
Christian Review. 20:381.
Cockburn's (Alex.) Philosophical Essays.
Copland's Mortal life. (A good compilation from Protestant authors.)
Dawson's Lady Moyer's Lectures. 1764, '5.
Ditton on the Resurrection.
D'Oyly's (G.) Sermons.
Earberry's (Mathias) Reply to Tho. Burnett.
Faber's (Geo. S.) Many mansions.
Holden's (Lawrence) Sermons.
Hopkins' System of Divinity.
Humphreys' Trans. of Athanagoras on the state of the dead.
——— Hulsean Lectures. 1849.
Jones' Diss. on Paul's wishing to depart.
Lucas' (Richard) Sermons.
McLeod's Cherubim and the Apocalypse.
Mant's (Bp.) Happiness of the Blessed.
Maywahlen's (Ulr.) Christ among the dead.
Moore's Theological Works.
Newton's (Bp.) Dissertations.
Partridge's (Samuel) Discourses.
Peers on the State of the departed.
Presbyterian Quart. Review. 10:241.
Regis on the Intermediate state.
Scott's (Tho.) Theological Essays.
Secker on the Catechism.
Sheppard's Autumn Dream.
Steffe's State of the soul after death.
Sturm's (D.) 19 Discourses on the state, &c.
Tillotson's (Abp.) Sermons.
Tournour's (E. J.) Sermons.
Townson's (Tho.) Practical Discourses.
Wadsworth on the Soul. ("Contains satisfactory evidences of the Intermediate state."—BICKERSTETH.)
Walker (Geo.) on the Separate state.
Williams' (Alfred) Sermons.
Wood's Believer's Guide.

See BLACKBURNE'S *Historical view of the controversy, from the beginning of the Reformation, to* 1772. DODGSON, in note C. to his translation of Tertullian, has given many passages from the Fathers on this subject.

Internal Evidences of S. Script.

Callixtus de Sacra Scriptura.
Borgeri Com. de Evangelio Joannis; cum Matt. Marc. et Lucæ comparato. ("A work of deep research."—HORNE.)
Edwardus de Stylo Sacræ Scripturæ.
Huettii (P. D.) Demonstratio Evangelica.
Hutteri (Leonard.) Disputationes.
Kuckler de Simplicitate Scriptorum.
Meisneri (Ioan.) Disputationes.

Internal Evidences, &c.—*continued.*

Thummii (Theod.) Disquisitiones.
Alison's (Archibald) Sermons.
Bennet's (Benj.) Discourses on 2 Tim. 3:16.
Bennett's (Jas.) Internal evidence of S. S.
Biscoe's Acts of the Apostles confirmed from other authors.
Bolton's Hulsean prize Essay. 1852.
Broadley's (Thomas) Essays.
Campbell (Arch.) on the Gospel history.
Carlyle's (Jas.) Letters. (Exc. for the young.)
Clayton's Vind. of the Scripture histories.
Dewar on the Design of Christianity.
Doddridge's Lectures. Parts 5 and 6.
Epp's Evidences from Phrenology.
Erskine's Evidences. (Often reprinted.)
Frank's Hulsean Lectures. 1821.
Graves' (R.) Character of the Apostles.
Jackson's Eternal truth of S. Scripture.
Jenyn's (Soame) Internal evidence. (Popular and effective.)
Keith's Lectures. (Very useful.)
Knox's (Vicess.) Christian Philosophy.
Lancaster's (Tho. W.) Sermons.
Lardner's Credibility of the gospel history.
McKnight's Truth of gospel history.
Maclean's (Archib.) Letters to S. Jenyns.
Marsh's (E. G.) Seventeen sermons.
Nares on the Evangelists.
Owen's (J.) Authority of the Holy Script.
Paley's Horæ Paulinæ.
Powlett's Reasons for being a Christian.
Rawlinson's Contrast of Christianity with Heathen and Jewish systems.
Seed's (Jeremiah) Sermons.
Shepherd's Divine origin of Christianity.
Shuttleworth's Consistency of revelation with itself.
Simpson's Internal Evidence.
Sinker on the New Testament literature.
Stephens' Christianity compared with other religions, and systems of philosophy.
Sumner's (Bp.) Evidences, &c.
Thompson (Ed.) on Prophecy. (Very able.)
Toulmin's (Joshua) Dissertations.

International Law.
See LAW OF NATIONS.

Intolerance. See TOLERATION.

Introductions to Scripture.
See STUDY OF SCRIPTURE.

TO THE WHOLE BIBLE.

Abichtii Ars distincte legendi, &c.
Berger's Einleitung.
Boetneri Isagoge. ("Elegant."—WALCH.)
Buddei Isagoge historico-literaria.
Calmeti Prolegomena et Dissertationes.
Calovii Prolegomena.
Carpzovii Apparatus historico-criticus.
Du Hamel, Institutiones Biblicæ.
Dupin, Dissertations préliminaires.
Eichhorn's (J. G.) Einleitung. (Deistical.)
Frankii Manductio ad lectionem S. S.
Frassenii Disquisitiones Biblicæ.

Introductions—*continued.*

Glaire, Introd. historique et critique.
Heideggeri Enchiridion Biblicum.
Hottingeri Clavis Scripturæ.
Houbiganti Prolegomena in S. S.
Ianssen's (J. H.) Hermeneutica Sacra. (Has an introduction to each book.)
Lamy, Biblicus Apparatus.
Marheineke's Theologische Vörlesungen.
Michaelis' Prolegomena ad S. S.
Moldenhaverii Introd. in omnes libros, &c.
Noack's Biblische Theologie, ein Handbuch zum Selbstunterricht.
Prittii Introductio ad omnes libros, &c. ("Nothing superior to it."—Bp. Watson.)
Ravii Exercitationes. (Refutes some rash principles of Houbigant.)
Riveti (And.) Isagoge.
Schumann's Einleitung, &c.
Titmanni Bibliotheca.
Van Till, Opus analyticum.
Waltheri Officina Biblica.
Waltoni Biblicus Apparatus.
——— in Biblia polyglotta prolegomena.
Whitby de S. S. Interpretatione.
Angus' Bible Hand-book. (A wonderful condensation of facts.)
Bickersteth's Scrip. Help. (Useful to youth.)
Brown's Introduction to the Bible.
Collyer's (David) Sacred Interpreter.
Frank's Guide to the study, &c. Trans. by W. Jaques.
Hamilton's (G.) Introduction to the S. S.
Havernick's Historico-critical Introduction. Trans. by W. L. Alexander.
Hayne's General view, &c. (Times, places, and persons.)
Horne's Introd. to the critical study, &c.
——— ——— Edited and improved by Davidson.
Jones' Analytical view of the Bible.
Lamy's Introduction. (Much improved by notes, &c., of the translator, R. Bundy.)
Liefchild's Help to the reading of the S. S. (A convenient little manual.)
Lukins' Introduction to the S. Scriptures.
Michaelis' Introduction, &c. Translated by Marsh. With valuable notes.
Roberts' Clavis Bibliorum.
Schumann's Introduction. Trans. by Beard.
Simon's Crit. history of the O. and N. Test.
Simpson's Sacred Literature. (Contains proofs of the authority of Scripture, directions for reading it, extracts from early writers, &c.)
Stowe's (C. E.) Int. to the interpretation, &c.
Tomline's Introd. (Small, but convenient.)
Townley's Literary history of the Bible.

TO THE OLD TESTAMENT.

Ackermanni Introd. in libros fœderis.
Augusti's Grundriss einer Einleitung, &c.
Berger's Einleitung ins alte Test.
Hartmann's Linguistische Einleitung, &c.
Hävernick's Handb. d. histor. kritischen, &c.
Hengstenberg's Beiträge zur Einleitung.

Introductions—*continued.*

Herbert's Einleitung.
Herbst's Historisch-kritische Einleitung.
Hottingeri Thesaurus philologicus, &c.
Jahn, Introd. ad libros V. Test.
Keil's Einleitung in die Schriften, &c.
Simon, Histoire critique du Vieux Test.

Barry's Introd. to the study of the O. Test.
Coverdale's Prologues to his translation of the Bible.
Davidson's Horne's Introd. to the O. Test.
Gray's Key to the O. Test. and Apocrypha.
Hamilton's (G.) Introd. to the Heb. Script.
Jahn's Introd., &c. Trans. by Turner and Whittingham. (With consid. improvem.)
Lyall's Propædia Prophetica. (Use and design of the Old Testament.)
Maurice on the Old Testament.
Morrison's Key to the first four books.
Planck on Theological Science.
Turner's Introd. (Chiefly a trans. of Jahn.)
Tyndale's Prologues to the five books.
Winer's Theological Literature.

TO THE NEW TESTAMENT.

Beausobre & L'Enfant, Introduction.
Bengelii Apparatus criticus.
——— Gnomon Nov. Test. (Highly prized.)
Credner's Einleitung.
Ellenberg's Einleitung.
Griesbach's Vörlesung. über Hermeneutic.
Guerikė Historisch-kritische Einleitung, &c.
Haenlein's Handbuch der Einleitung, &c.
Hug's Einleitung.
Kuinoel, Prolegomena.
Millii Prolegomena.
Rumpæus de libris N. Testamenti.
Russii Introductio ad N. Testamentum.
Schottii Isagoge historico-critica.
Wetstein, Prolegomena ad Nov. Test.

Amer. Bibl. Repos. 12:133. (Matthew.)
Beausobre & L'Enfant's Introduction.
Bengel's Gnomon. Tr. by Faussett.
Biblioth. Sacra. 5:97. (Galatians.)
Chris. Disciple. 3:626. (John.) 5:435. (Eph.)
Christian Review. 12:192. (John.)
Davidson's Introd. to N. Test. (One of the latest, and very convenient. 1851.)
Harwood's Introd. to the New Testament.
Horne's Introduction.
Hug's (Dr. J. L.) Introd. Tr. by D. Fosdick.
——— ——— Tr. by D. G. Wait.
Lardner's Works.
McWhorter's (G. C.) History of the N. Test. (Authorship, preservation, translat., &c.)
Michaelis' Introduction. Translated by Marsh; with notes.
Percy's Key to the New Testament.
Princeton Review. 21:144.
Roberts' (Fr.) Clavis Bibliorum.
Taylor's (John) Key to the Apost. writings.
Townson's Discourses on the Four gospels.
Tregelle's Introd. to the New Testament.
Tyndale's Prologues to the several books.
Westcott's Introduction to the Gospels.

Investitures. See SIMONY.

Dithmari Historia belli inter Imperium et Sacerdotium.
Lohenschioldii (O. Ch.) Dissert. Historicæ.
Lupi (Christian.) Dissertationes.
Mascovius de Rebus imperii Germanici.
Meibonius de Jure investituræ episcopalis.
Noris Historia Investitutarum.
Thomasii Hist. contentionis inter Imperium et Sacerdotium.

Mosheim's Eccl. History. Cent. XI., Part 2.

Invocation of Saints. See MARIOLATRY.

Abichtus de Honore Sanctorum.
Affelmanni Syntagma exercitat. theolog.
Agricola (F.) de Cultu Sanctorum.
Basnage, Histoire du culte des saintes.
Bernard (Jac.) de Invocatione Sanctorum.
Brentii Opera Polemica.
Callixti (Geo.) Dissertationes.
Gerhardi Εθελοθρησκεια.
Heissii Dissertationes.
Mabilloni Opera posthuma.
Mollinæi (Petr.) Disputationes.
Schrœderi (Jo.) Disputationes.
Seligmanni (G. F.) Exercitationes Academ.
Trombellii (J. C.) Dissertationes.
Voetii Disputationes Theologicæ.
Vossii (G. J.) Theses Theologicæ.

Barlow (T.) on the Invocation of Saints.
Bradford's (The Martyr) Works.
Claggett's (Dr. William) Discourses.
Coverdale's (Miles) Remains.
Fletcher's (Jos.) Lectures on the Rom. relig.
Freeman's (Bp.) Discourses.
Geddes' Miscellaneous Tracts.
Mede's Apostacy of latter times.
Montagu on the Invocation of Saints.
Morning Exercises at Cripplegate. Vol. 6.
Powell's (H. T.) Roman fallacies.
Princeton Review. 14:407.
Salter's Hall Sermons.
Stephenson's Romish Church.
Tyler's (J. E.) Primitive Christian worship.
Wharton's Enthusiasm of the Ch. of Rome.

Irenæus. See FATHERS.

Irenæi Opera. (The last edition is that of STIEREN. 1853.)
Deylingii Observationes Miscellanea.
Dodwelli (H.) Dissertationes.
Fevardentii Vita Irenæi.
Gervaise, Vie de St. Irenée.
Grabii Prolegomena ad Irenæi opera.
Massueti Dissertat. in Irenæi libros.
Sterenii (A.) Irenæi Opera. (Contains such dissertations, by previous editors, as seemed worthy of republication.)

Beavan's Life and writings of Ireneus.
Conybeare's Bampton Lectures. 1839.

Irony. See RIDICULE.

Grulich, üb. d. Ironien in den reden Jesu.

Irresistible Grace. See EFFECTUAL CALLING, FIVE POINTS, MORAL SUASION.

Brandt's History of the Reformation.
Edwards' (Thomas) Doctrine of irresistible grace without foundation.
Emmons' (Nathaniel) Sermons.
Foster's (James) Sermons.
Jortin's (John) Dissertations.
Ludlam's Essay on Justification.
Saurin's Sermons.
Tillotson's Sermons.

Irresolution. See INDECISION.

Irvingites.

Pro.

Irving's (Edw.) Orations. (This was his first publication, and does not indicate his subsequent peculiarities.)
——— Judgment to come.
——— Babylon and infidelity foredoomed.
——— Sermons and Lectures.
——— On the Sacraments.
——— Exposition of Revelations.
Baxter's (Robt.) Narrative. (Mr. B. afterwards recanted, and declared himself to have been under the influence of the Devil.)
Morning Watch. Periodical. Lond. Edited by Irving. 1829 to 1833.
Norton's Life of Edw. Irving.
Oliphant's ——— ———
Story's (R. H.) Life of Rev. Robt. Story.

Con.

Haldane's (J. A.) Refutation of the doctrines of Edw. Irving.

Irvingites, History of.

Memoir of Ed. Irving; by Wm. Jones.
——— ——— by Wash. Wilkes.
Blackwood's Magazine. 14:145,346.
Frazier's Magazine. 11:99.
Gentleman's Magazine. 1832.
Methodist Quarterly. 9:109.

Isaac. See OFFERING OF ISAAC.

Scobel's (Edward) Sermons.
Thompson's (F. E.) Lent Lectures. Lect. 3.

Isaiah.

Hahnii Introductio ad Iesam.
Michaelis' Dissertationes.

Kitto's Bible Illustrations.

Isidore [Pelusiota].

Henschenius de Scriptoribus ecclesiasticus.
Heumanni Diss. de I. et ejus epistolis.

Islamism. See MAHOMETANISM.

Jacob. See BIOGRAPHY, PATRIARCHS.

Benson's (George) Lectures.
Blunt's Eight lectures on the history of J.
Craig's Patriarchal Piety.
Gataker's (Thomas) Sermons.
Gilfillan's Alpha and Omega. Ch. 21.

Macduff's Sunsets on the Hebrew mountains.
Melville's (Henry) Sermons.
Milner's (Joseph) Sermons.
Puckle's Parochial Sermons.
Thompson's (F. E.) Lent Lectures. Lect. 4.

Jacobites. See EUTYCHIANS, MONOPHYSITES, NESTORIANS.

Abudeni Hist. Jacobitarum.
Eutychii Annales, ab orbe condito. To 940.
Naironi Fides Cathol. ex Syrorum monumentis. Pars I.
Renaudotti Historia Patriarcharum Alexandrinorum. (To the end of the 13th cent.)
Simon, Hist. de chrètiens Orientaux.
Tromler's Abbildung der Jacobitisch. kirche.

Badger's Nestorians. (With notices of the Syrian Jacobites.)
Southgate's Syrian Churches.

Jains. See BUDHISM, HINDUISM.

Bird's (Jas.) Historical Researches.
Francklin's (W.) Jeynes and Boodhists.
Stephenson's Kalpa sutra, and Nava tatra. Tr. from the Magadhi into English.
Winslow's Trans. of Vishnu Paráua.

James the Greater.

Caraciola (Anton.) Opera.
Cuperi (Guil.) Acta S. Jacobi majoris.
Koessingius de Anno quo mortem obierit J.
Mülleri (August.) Dissertationes. (Whether there were 3 Jameses among the Apostles.)
Sanctii (Caspar.) Com. in Acta Apostolorum.

Princeton Review. 37:1.

Jansenists. See PORT ROYAL.

Abelii Medulla Theologia.
Arnauld. (Wrote 100 different works.)
Bernard, Nouvelles de la Republique les lettres.
[Colonne] Bibliotheque Jansenistes. (With a supplement by Patouillet.)
[Gerberon] Hist. de Jansenisme.
Hase's Kirchengeschichte.
Iansenii Augustinus. (Every sentence in the voluminous works of Augustine, relating to the Pelagian controversy, is here collected and arranged, with fairness and perspicuity.)
Kleinius de J. origine, doctrina, et historia.
Labbé, Bibliotheca anti-Jansenismi.
Launcelot, Memoires de l'Abbe de St. Cyran.
Leydekkeri Historia Jansenismi.
Luschesimii Hist. polemica Jansenismi.
——— Jansenis hæres. Enchiridion.
Masii Hist. propositionum Jansenii.
Moraines, Anti-Jansenius.
Nouvelles Ecclesiastiques. (Periodical from 1723 to 1782.)
Ottius de Causa Jansenistica.
Pascal, Lettres Provinciales: precedèes d'un précis historique sur le Jansenisme, par Louandre.

Jansenists—*continued.*

[Patouillet], Dictionaire des livres Jansenistes, ou qui favorissent le Jansenisme.
Quesnell, Novum Testamentum.
Sauvage (Soc. Jesu) la Realité du project de Bourgfontaine. (The origin of Jansenism.)
Walchii Bibliotheca Theologica.
Amer. Bibl. Repos. 3d Series. 3:689.
Bayle's Universal Dictionary.
Beard's (Charles) Contrib. to the history of religion. (A history of this order.)
Gale's True idea of Jansenism.
Kitto's Journal. 7:34.
Leydekker's History of Jansenism.
Neale's Jansenist Church of Holland; with an account of the "Brothers of the common life."
Princeton Review. 28:132.
St. Amour, Journal of.
The Papal Bull "Unigenitus."
Tregelles' Jansenists: their rise, persecution by the Jesuits, and existing remnant. 1851.

Jansenists are comprehended, by most writers, under the term "Messieurs de Port Royal." But strictly, that appellation is applicable only to certain distinguished Jansenists who lived in a community at Port Royal, a short distance from Paris. See a vast list of Jansenist writers in DUPIN, *Cat. des livres Jansenistes, ou suspect de ces erreurs;* COLONNE, *Bibliotheque Janseniste;* and OTTIUS, *de Causa Jansenistica.* And of the opponents of Jansenism, in LABBE, *Biblioth. anti Jansenismi.*

Japhet. See ETHNOLOGY.

Gorres' Völkertafel des Pentateuch.
Perkins' Expos. of the 10th ch. of Genesis.

Jasher, Book of.

Alcuin's Trans. of the book of Jasher. (A literary forgery by one Ilive; first published in 1751.)
Donaldsoni Fragmenta archetypa carminum Hebræicorum. (Defends this bold imposture with zeal; laboring, under this cover, to undermine the proofs of inspiration.)
British Critic. Jan., 1834.
Donaldson's Jasher. (With dissertations.)
Eclectic Review. 4th Series. 12:630. New Series. 9:320.
Frazier's Magaz. 5:643.
Horne's Introd. to the Holy Scriptures.
Methodist Quart. Review. 7:82.
Monthly Review. 5:250.
Noah's (M. M.) Trans. of the book of J.

See "Bibliographical notes on the book of Jasher," by THO. H. HORNE.

Jehovah. See NAME OF GOD.

Jephthah's Vow.

Bartolocci de Sacrificio Jephthæ.
Benzelii Dissertationes Academicæ.

Jephthah's Vow—*continued.*

Calmeti Dissertationes.
Capelli (Ludov.) Spicelegium, &c.
Danhaveri (Ioann. C.) Disputationes.
Pfeifferi Exercitationes. Exerc. VII.
Schotani (Ioann.) Dissertationes.
Sennerti (Andr.) Dissertationes.
Spanheimii (Fred.) Miscellanea Sacra.
Zeidleri (Carol. G.) Dissertationes.

Amer. Bibl. Repos. 2d Series. 9:143.
Church Review. 4:415.
Dodwell (Wm.) on Jephthah's vow.
Dublin Univ. Mag. 12:273.
Edwards' (Dr. J.) Sermons.
Holbrook on Jephthah's vow.
Houghton's (Pendlebury) Sermons.
Kennicott's Dissertations.
Osgood's (David) Sermons.
Randolph's (Tho.) Sermons.
Reddel's (J. S.) Dissertations.
Romaine's (Wm.) Sermons.
Smallridge's (George) Sermons.
Smith's (James) Sermons.

Jerome.

Hieronymi Opera. (Edited by Valesius in 1734. 11 vols., 4to.)
Cinelii Vita Hieronymi.
Clerici Questiones Hieronymiæ.
Collombet, Hist. de St. Jerome.
Vita Hieronymi. Dolci.
—— —— Erasmi.
—— —— Genadi.
—— —— Guadalupi.
—— —— Mabillonii.
—— —— Melancthonis.

Bibliotheca Sacra. 5:117.
Jerome's Select Epistles.
—— Epistle to Nepotian.
Lardner's Credibility of the gospel history.
Princeton Review. 36:364.

Jerome of Prague. See FORERUNNERS.

Bibliotheca Sacra. 2:636.
Gilpin's Lives of the Reformers.
Kidder's Martyrs of Bohemia.

Jerusalem. See DESTRUCTION OF JERUSALEM, GEOGRAPHY.

Altmüller's Jerusalem nach seiner örtlichen Lage, &c.
Borculoo, Descriptio civitatis. 1538.
Capelli (L.) Iconographia. 1650.
D'Anville, l'Entendue de l'anc. J. 1747.
Dubliolii Peregrinationes. 1599.
Krafft's Topographie Jerusalems. 1847.
Lamy (B.) de Sancta Civitate. 1725.
Montani (Arii) Nehemias. 1572. (Often printed.)
Olshausen's Topographie des alten J. 1838.
Reisneri Jerusalem. 1563. (Curious cuts.)
Waltoni Prolegomena. 1673.
Witsii Exercit. Academic. (History of J.)
Zimpel's Beleuchtung der Jerusalem. 1852. (With particular reference to the times of Christ.)

Jerusalem—*continued.*

Barclay's City of the great King. 1859.
Bartlett's City and environs of J. 1844.
—— Jerusalem revisited. 1855. Plates.
Bibliotheca Sacra. 1:1.
Dupuy's Two years in Jerusalem. 1856.
Fergusson's Topography of Jerusalem. 1847.
Fisk's (G.) Memorial of Jerusalem. 1847.
Jessey's Descrip. of 268 places in J. as they stood in the time of Christ.
Lewin's J. from the earliest times, to the siege by Titus.
Lowthain's Visit to Jerusalem. 1843.
Maundrel's Journey from Aleppo. 1697.
Odenheimer on Sacred localities. 1855.
Robinson's (Ed.) Biblical Researches. 1841.
Sandie's Horeb and Jerusalem. 1864.
Sepp's J. and the Holy land. 400 cuts. 1864.
Thrupp's Anc. Jerusalem. (Useful both as to history and prophecy. Maps, plans, &c.)
Williams' (Geo.) Holy city. (Topographical and antiquarian notices, with an account of its condition in 1845.)

Jesting. See LEVITY, SOBRIETY.

Schelhornii (Ioann. Geo.) Observationes.

Barrow's (Isaac) Sermons.
Burgess (Dan.) on Foolish talking.

Jesuits. See JESUIT MISSIONS, LOYOLA, SUPPRESSION.

Acta Sanctorum. 50 folios.
Alegambe, Biblioth. Scriptorum Soc Jesu.
Annales de la Societé des Jesuites.
Arnauld, Œuvres. (A powerful opponent.)
Backer, Biblioth. de la Soc. J. To 1854.
Bartol, Histoire de l'Origine, &c.
—— Asiaticæ Historicæ. Par. III., IV.
Boucher, Histoire des J. To 1846.
[Boyer], Parallele de la doct. des Payens avec celles de Jésuites.
Chemnitii Theol. J. præcipua capita.
Claudii (Soc. Jesu) Opera.
[Coudrette], Hist. generale de la naissance, et des progrés de la Comp. de Jésus. (This book had a large share in producing the suppression of the order in France.)
Crastovi Bellum Jesuiticum.
Crétineau, Hist. de la Comp. de Jésus: composé sur les documens inedits et authentique. (Embraces the religious, political, and literary history.)
Damiani Synopsis primi seculi Soc. Jesu.
D'Aubigny (J. B. L.) Histoire des Jésuites.
Echavarre, Histoire de Paraguay.
Ellendorf's Moral und politik der J.
Engelschalli Fides Jesu, et Jesuitarum.
Flaccii Ethnica.
Fletcheri Locustæ. (A keen satire.)
Forest, Les J. ennemis de l'ordre social, et de la religion.
Gazaignes, Annales des Jésuites.
Gratiosi Michaevelus—mus Jesuiticus.
Graveri (Albert.) Dissertationes.
Harenburg's Pragmatische Geschichte.

Jesuits—*continued.*

Hassenmulleri Hist. J. ordinis. (Great.)
Heideggeri Commentationes.
Hospiniani Historia Jesuitica. (The origin, regulations, privileges, increase, frauds, impostures, &c. "Liber prohibitus." Romæ, 1625. "Opus luculentum."—WALCH.)
Imago Primi sæculi Soc. Jesu. 1640. (This book, though written by Jesuits, did much to put them down. It is full of absurd and blasphemous pretensions.)
Institutum Soc. Jesu in ordinem digestum. (A complete body of all that regards the government and practice of the order, printed for the use of their establishments exclusively. 1705.)
Jarrige, les J. mis sur l'eschafaut.
Jordan's Jesuiten und Jesuitismus.
Jouvence, Histoire des Jésuites.
Julius' Ges. der Grundung, Ausbreitung, &c.
Keller's Aushebung und Ausweisung des J.
Kortüm's Entstehungs Geschichte der J.
Laurentii Vulpina Jesuitica.
——— Conscientia Jesuitica cauteriata.
Leu's Würdigung des Jesuiten-ordens.
Linguet, Histoire des Jésuites.
Loescherus de Peccato philosophico.
Long's Jesuiterische Pratiken.
Lucii Historia Jesuitica.
Marcett de la Roche, les J. modernes. 1826.
Marmontel, Régence du duc d'Orleans.
Michelet (J.), die Jesuiten.
Misleri Speculum Anti-jesuiticum.
Montlosier, Système rel. et polit. tendant a renverser la société.
Olearius de Peccato philosophico.
Orlandini Historia Soc. Jesu. (To 1556—that is, during the lifetime of the founder. 7 vols., folio.)
[Pascal] Lettres Provincialles.
Pelargi Paradoxa.
Perrault, Morale des Jésuites.
Platel, Mémoires Historiques des J.
[Quesnel], Histoire de la Comp. de Jésus.
Rainoldi Theses de Scriptura, &c.
Reifenbergii Historia Soc. Jesu.
Relation des Jésuits. (Their own missionary labors. (A huge repository of facts.)
Ribadeneiræ Biblioth. scriptorum J. 1643.
Rodingius contra impias scholas J.
Sacchini (Soc. Jes.) Hist. Soc. J. To 1620.
Salaceti Elixir Jesuiticum.
Schmidii Historia Soc. Jesu Bohemiæ.
Schwarzius de Meth. divigendæ intentionis.
Sciopii (Casp.) Opera.
Spittler's Geschichte der Jesuiten.
Ulmer's Neuer Jesuiten Speigel.
Vargas de Stratagismatis, &c., Soc. Jesu.
Wild, der Moderne Jesuitismus. 1843.
Wiskemann's Lehre u. Praxis der Jesuiten in Religioser, Moralischer, u. Politissher, Beziehung.

Arnauld's Modern Jesuitism.
Brewer's (William) Jesuitism.

Jesuits—*continued.*

Bryson's Jesuitism delineated.
Carr's Jesuits as they were and are. 1845.
Chretineau-Joly, History of the Jesuits.
Christian Examiner. 42:360.
Christian Observer. 14:166.
Christian Review. 8:161,346.
Church Review. 1:575.
Compton's Secrets of the Jesuits.
Dallas' (R. C.) Hist. of the J. (Defends.,
Dalton's (J.) Principles and acts.
Daubeny's Protestant's Companion.
Foreign Review. 3:309.
Frazier's Magazine. 19:667.
Freake's Doctrine and practice of the J.
Geddes' Monks and nuns of the Rom. Chur.
Gosselin's Mysteries of the Jesuits.
Grinfield's Jesuits; a historical sketch, from the earliest periods to 1850.
Hassenmuller's History of the Jesuits.
Jarridge's Jesuits displayed.
Kitto's Journal. 8:38.
Lathbury's Popery in England. (From the Reformation to 1829.)
Leoné's J. conspiracy. Pref. by Considerant.
London Quart. Review. 5:363.
Michelson's Modern Jesuitism. 1855.
Monthly Review. 83:267.
Nicolini's History of the Jesuits. 1854.
North Amer. Review. 5:26,309. 6:129,465. 7:112. 8:200. 59:412.
North British Review. 2:589.
Pamphleteer. 6:99.
Paroessiens' Principles of the Jesuits. (Consists of extracts from their own writers.)
[Pascal's] Letters of a Provincial. (A withering exposure of Jesuit morality.)
Penrose's Bampton Lectures. 1808. Append.
[Poynder's] History of the Jesuits. (Reply to Dallas.)
Princeton Review. 6:559. 17:239. 26:647.
Retrospective Review. 9:370.
Robertson's (Prof.) History of the Jesuits.
Spindler's Jesuit. (An illustration of their practices in the 18th century.)
Steinmitz's Hist. of the Jesuits. (From the origin of the order, to its suppression by Clement XIV. Portraits. A new edition continues the history to 1848.)
Stephens' (J.) Essays in Eccl. biography.
Taylor's (I.) Jesuitism in its rudiments.
Tonge's J.'s morals: from their own books.
Usher's (Abp.) Answer to a Jesuit.
Wharton's Enthusiasm of the Ch. of Rome.
Whately's (Stephen) Parallel of the doctrine of Pagans with the doctrine of Jesuits, and the Constitution Unigenitus.
Wiskeman's Doctrine and practice of the Jesuits. (As in 1858.)

For a full list of Jesuit authors see ALEGAMBE, BACKER, CRETINEAU, and RIBADENEIRE, above cited. NUTT, a London publisher, offers in his catalogue for 1837, over 300 works of this sort.

Jesuit Missions. See MISSIONS.

Acostæ Rerum a Soc. Jesu gestarum in Oriente. To 1571.
Assemani Bibliotheca Orientalis.
Bayeri Museum Sinicum. (Preface.)
Bouvet (La Pére) Mémoires.
D'Halycarnasse, de la Cochin Chine.
Hay, de Missionibus Orientalibus.
Historia Cultus Sinensum.
Jarric (P.), Choses les plus memorable, &c.
Kircheri China Illustrata.
La Crose, Hist. du Christianisme des Indes.
Lettres Edifiantes et Curieuses. Periodical. (A vast collection of letters from missionaries in all parts of the world.)
Maffei Hist. Indicarum. (Narratives of the missions in India and Japan, to 1600.)
Nicolai de Christ. expeditione apud Sinas ex P. M. Riccii. ("The most satisfactory acct. of China by the J."—PINKERTON.)
Pelleprat, M. dans l'Amerique meridionale.
Relations des Jésuites du missions dans la Nouvelle France.
Renaldi Annales Ecclesiastici.
Renaudot, Relations anciennes des Indes et de la Chine.
Ricci de Expeditione apud Sinas.
Rougemont, Historia Tartaro-Sinica.
Schall, Narratio de initio et progressu fidei orthodoxæ in regno Chinensi. (To 1660.)
Voyages et travaux des missionaires. 1858.

Boquine's Defence of old Christianity.
Ingraham's Early J. missions in N. America.

Jesus Christ.

DEITY OF. See ETERNAL GENERATION, GENUINENESS OF 1 JOHN V. 7, HYPOSTATIC UNION.

Baumgarten, Vind. vocis Θεος. 1 Tim. 3:16.
Bos (Lambert.) Exercitationes.
Bullii Defensio fidei Nicænæ. Sec. 3.
——— Primitiva apostolica traditio.
Calixti (Fred. U.) Dissertationes.
Calovii (Abraham.) Dissertationes.
Chemnitii (Mart.) Dissertationes.
Cloppenburgii Defensio deitatis Christi
Danæi Confirmatio veræ Doctrinæ, &c.
Dannhaveri (Io. C.) Christosophia.
Gerhardi Loci Theologici.
Gomari Opera Theologica.
Haberkornii Christologia.
Meisneri Disputationes quinquaginta.
Schœttgenii (C.) Horæ Hebraicæ.
Wagneri (Io. C.) Dissertationes.

Abbadie's Divinity of Christ. Tr. by Booth.
Alexander's (Caleb) Primitive Christianity.
Allen's (Joshua) Sermons.
Allestree's (Richard) Sermons.
Alsop's Anti-Sozzo. ("Unanswerable."—HERVEY.)
Amer. Bibl. Repository. 3:652.
Arrowsmith's God-man.
Balguy's (Thomas) Sermons.
Balmer's Academic Lectures.

Jesus Christ.

DEITY OF—*continued.*

Barnard's Demonstration. (The first Dudleian lecture. 1756.)
Beatson's (John) Dialogues.
Benson's (C.) Lectures. Lect. 5.
Berryman's Critical Dissert. on 1 Tim. 3:16. (Gives the readings from 100 MSS.)
Beveridge's (Bp.) Sermons.
Bickersteth's (E. H.) Rock of ages.
Blencoe's (Edward) Sermons.
Bloomfield's Lectures on the Gospel of John.
Bowdler's (Thomas) Sermons.
Boyse on the true Deity of Jesus Christ.
Bradbury's Myst. of Godliness. (Excellent.)
Brett's Mediatorial character of Christ.
Brooks' Golden Key.
Burgess' (Bp.) Tracts.
Burgh's Scriptural confutation of the arguments against, &c.
——— Belief of the Christians of the first three centuries.
Burnet on the 39 Articles.
Burton's Test. of the anti-Nicene Fathers.
Bull's Judgment of the Catholic Church of the first three centuries.
Charnock's (Stephen) Works.
Christian Monthly Spectator. 2:224.
Clagget on the Divinity of Christ.
Clayton (Bp.) on the Spirit.
Courayer on the Divinity of Christ.
Coxe's (R. C.) Symmetry of revelation.
Dale's (Thomas) Sermons.
Denyer on the Div. of Christ. (Prize essay.)
Dwight's Theology. Ser. 25 to 41.
East's (Timothy) Discourses.
Eclectic Review. New Series. 1:221.
Emmons' (Nathaniel) Sermons.
Evans' (Caleb) Sermons.
Fairbairn's Theological Essays.
Geddes' Letter to Dr. Priestley.
Goode on the Names and titles of Christ.
Gordon's Supreme Godhead of Christ.
Grinfield's Hulsean Lectures. 1856.
Guyse's Jesus Christ God-man.
Hall's Help to Zion's travellers.
Harris on the Messiah.
Hawker's Sermons on the Div. of Christ.
Hervey's (James) Sermons.
Hey's (Wm.) Tracts and Essays.
Hodson's Jesus Christ the true God.
Holden's Trinity in Unity.
——— Scripture Testimonies collected.
Horne's (Bp.) Sermons.
Horseley's (Bp.) Tracts. (Powerful on the Historical question. Agt. Dr. Priestley.)
Hughes' Evidences of the Div. of Christ.
Jamieson's Vind. of the primitive faith. (An ans. to Priestley's Hist. of early opinions.)
Kelburn's Sermons on the Div. of Christ.
Knowles' Primitive Christianity.
McWhorter's Yahveh Christ; or the memorial name.
Mant's (Bp.) Sermons.
Marsden's Hulsean Lectures. 1843, 1844.

Jesus Christ.

DEITY OF—*continued.*

Massillon's Sermons.
Matthews' (E. W.) Lectures.
Mayer's Crit. exam. of our Saviour's disc.
Melville's (Henry) Sermons.
Moyer's (Lady) Lectures in defence of the Divinity of Christ. (They extend from 1719 to 1774. The following are among the most important, and are also printed separately.)
Waterland, 1719. Knight, 1720. Berriman, Wm., 1723. Bishop, 1724. Felton, 1728. Trapp, 1729. Brown, 1730. Seed, 1732. Wheatley, 1734. Berriman, John, 1737. Twells, 1738. Bedford, 1739. Ridley, 1740. Clements, 1757. Dawson, 1764.
Owen's Mystery of the person of Christ.
Parkhurst's Divinity and Pre-existence, &c.
Pearson on the Creed.
Pirie's Posthumous Works.
Quaife on the Divinity of Christ.
Quarterly Review. 6:391.
Robinson's Plea for the Div. of our Lord J. C.
Saurin's Sermons.
Serles' Horæ Solitariæ.
Sharp on the Definite Greek Article.
Sherlock's Scripture Proof, &c.
Simpson's Plea for the Divinity of Christ.
Skelton's (P.) Sermons.
Smith's (John Pye) Scripture Testimony to the Messiah. (A very precious book.)
——— Discourses.
Stackhouse's Life of Christ.
Stephens' Celestial Filiation.
Stuart's (Prof.) Letters to Channing.
——— on the various readings of 1 Tim. 3:16.
Talbot's Divinity of Christ.
Taylor's Ben Mordecai.
Tillotson's Sermons.
Tucker's (Dean) Sermons.
Turnbull's Claims of Jesus.
Urwick's (Tho.) Saviour's right to Divine worship.
Van Mildert's (Bp.) Sermons.
Velthusen on the True reading of 1 Tim. 3:16.
Wardlaw's Discourses. (Grand.)
Waterland's Vindic. of Christ's divinity.
——— Second Vindication.
Witsius on the Covenants.
Wright (Rich.) on the Divinity of Christ.
Wynperse's Demonstration, &c. (Small, but powerful.)
Young's (John) The Christ of history. (Very original.)

BIRTH OF. See CHRISTMAS, GENEALOGY, INCARNATION, NATIVITY, SIBYLLINE ORACLES.

LIFE OF. See DURATION OF MINISTRY, HARMONIES, MONOTESSARON.

Becilli Evangeliorum Connexio. (A life of Christ in the order of events, in the language of the Evangelists, with marginal references, tables, &c.)

Jesus Christ.

LIFE OF—*continued*

Ewald's Geschichte Jesus.
Fabricii Historia filii Dei.
Franke's (A.) Leben Jesu.
Freppel, Examen critique de la vie de J. de Renan.
Fritzsche Αναμαρτησια.
Genoude, La vie de J. C. et des apôtres.
Hase's Leben Jesu.
Hess' Lebengeschichte Jesu.
Hoffman's Leben Jesn nach apocryphen.
Hug's Gutachten über das leben J. (Cont. Strauss.)
Krabbe's Vörlesungen ueber das leben Jesu.
Lange (J. P.), das leben Jesu.
Lichtenstein's Lebengeschichte d. Jesu.
Ludolphi Vita Jesu Christi.
Neander's Leben Jesu in seinem Geschichtlichen Zusammenhange.
Neander, Vie de Jésus: trade par P. Goy.
Offerhausii Dissertationes historico-philolog.
Pianello, Portrait de J. C. par lui-même.
Strauss' Leben Jesu. (Infidel.)

American Bibl. Repos. 8:1.
Andrews' Life of C. considered in its histor., chronolog., and geographical connections.
Barton's (Bernard) History of Christ.
Beard's Voices of the Church. (Reply to Strauss.)
Benson's Chronology of our Saviour's life.
Biblioth. Sacra. 3:166,653. 22:177.
Blunt's (Henry) Lectures.
Bradford's History of Christ.
British Quarterly Review. 5:206.
Cappe's Life of Jesus; with notes.
Cave's Life and death of Christ.
Craig's Essay on the life of Christ.
D'Oyly's Life and death of our Saviour.
Dublin Univ. Mag. 28:268.
Dupin's Evangelical History.
Ellicot's Histor. lectures on the life of C.
Fellowes' Guide to Immortality.
Fleetwood's Life of Christ. (Popular.)
Foote's Incidents in the life of Christ.
Foreign Quarterly Review. 22:101.
Gillispie's Truth of Evangelical History. (Reply to Strauss.)
Hare's Divine Mission of Christ.
Harwood's (Edward) Dissertations.
Hind's Rise and progress of Christianity.
Hunter's History of Jesus Christ.
Hutman's Life of Christ.
James on the Sign of the Prophet Jonah.
Lit. and Theol. Journal. 1:256.
Mant's (Bp.) Life of Christ.
March's (H.) Life of Christ.
Methodist Quarterly Review. 8:248. 9:18.
Milner's Life of Christ. (Adds also the lives of John the Baptist, Mary, and the Apostles.)
Neander's Life of Christ in its historical connection and development.
Newcombe on our Lord as an instructor.
Norris' (Wm.) History of our Lord.

Jesus Christ.

LIFE OF—*continued.*

Pressensé's Life and work of Christ.
Randolph's View of our Saviour's ministry.
Reading's Life of Christ.
Stevens' (Tho.) Gospel history of our Lord.
Taylor's (Jer.) Life of Christ.
Ulman's Sinless Character of Christ.
Wait's Comparison of certain traditions with circumstances.
Ware's (H.) Life of Christ. (Unitarian.)
Wesley's (S.) Life of Christ.
Williams' (Tho.) Private life of Christ, as a demonstration of his mission.
Young's (John) the Christ of history.

CHARACTER OF. See EXAMPLE OF C.

Coquerel, Christologie. (On the person and acts of Christ, with a view to harmonizing Christian Churches.)
Baillie's Tenor of the N. T. regarding J. C. (A collection of all the passages of the N. T. which relate to the subject.)
Bowdler's (Thomas) Sermons.
Christian Examiner. 26:373. 39:236.
Christian Month. Spect. 8:199.
Christian Review. 12:475.
Farrar's Bampton Lectures. 1803.
Fellowes' Guide to immortality. ("Beyond all praise."—DR. PARR.)
Goode's Scriptural names of Christ. ("A most valuable work."—LOWNDES.)
Hale's (William) Dissertations.
Knox's (J. L.) Sermons.
Law's Reflections on the Character of Christ.
Maitland's (C. D.) Discourses.
Meredith's Prophet of Nazareth.
Newcombe on our Lord's conduct and char.
Ogilvie's Bampton Lectures. 1836. (Christ's demeanor towards his chosen companions.)
Sartorius on the Person of Christ.
Sumner's Ministerial character of Christ.
Universalist Quarterly. 7:391.
Ware on the Character of Christ.
Wray (G.) on Our Lord's Character.
——— Sermons.

DEATH OF. See CRUCIFIXION, SUFFERINGS.

Bahrdt, de Morte Jesu Christi.
Eberhardt [or Ebrard], Wissenschaftliche Kritik der evangelischen Geschichte.
Gerhardi Loci Theologicæ.
Huyseri Specimen exegetico-theologicum.
Mulleri Historia passionis, crucifixionis, et sepulturæ. ("Learned and pious." —WALCH.)
Sagittarii Hist. Harmonia passionis.
Witsii Meletemata.
Zeigleri Hist. dogmatis et Redemptione.
Amer. Bibl. Repos. 3d Series. 2:381,660
Barrow on the Apostles' Creed.
Berriman's (William) Sermons.
Bradford's (The Martyr) Works.
Bibliotheca Sacra. 7:205.
Charnock's (Stephen) Works.

Jesus Christ.

DEATH OF—*continued.*

Christian Review. 11:584. 13:422.
Eclectic Review. 4th Series. 23:738.
Methodist Quart. Rev. 1:212. 6:227. 9:185.
New Englander. 5:415.
Owen's Death of Death in the death of C.
Pearson (Bp.) on the Apostles' Creed.
Secker's (Abp.) Sermons.

OBEDIENCE OF.

Hartmanni Obed. Christi activa, vicaria.
Tittmann, de Obedientia Christi.
Walchius de Obedientia Christi activa.
Winzer de Obedientia Christi activa.
Amer. Biblical Repository. 8:1.
Christian Spectator. Vol. 2.
Fuller's (Andrew) Essays.
Spaulding's Universalism destroys itself.
Wilkes' (S. C.) Christian Essays.
Witsius on the Covenants. Bk. 2, ch. 6.

OFFICES OF. See MEDIATION, TITLES.

Gesneri Orthodoxa Confessio de off. Christi.
Hunnii (Ægid.) Disputationes.
Jaegeri (Ioan. Wolf.) Disputationes.
Lyseri (Guil.) Disputationes.
Mentzeri (Balth.) Disputationes.
Mulleri (Ioan. Ernest.) Disputationes.
Winkelmanni (Ioan.) Disputationes.
Bowdler's (Tho.) Sermons.
Crombie's Character and offices of Christ.
Dwight's Theology. Ser. 44 to 63.
Jerram on the Doctrine of the Atonement.
Stevenson's (G.) Offices of Christ.
Urwick on the Atonement.

SONSHIP OF. See SONSHIP.

A PROPHET.

Frischmuthii (Ioan.) Exercitationes.
Koeppenii Disputatio de Messia prophetico.
Reuchlini (Chris.) Dissertationes.
Sanden (Bern.) Exercitationes.
Stiers, Reden des Herrn Jesu.
Bennett's Lectures on the preaching of C.
Cappe's Ministry of Christ.
Charnock's (Stephen) Works.
Goodwin's (John) Works.
Kirk's (Edward N.) Sermons.
Newcombe on our Lord as an instructor.
Sumner's (Bp.) Ministry of Christ.
Vaughn's (Henry) Sermons.
Willan's Hist. of the ministry of Christ.
Williams' (H. W.) Ministry of the Redeemer.

A PRIEST. See INTERCESSION.

Baierus de J. C. solo et unico sacerdote.
Callixti (Geo.) Dissertationes.
Calovius de Officio Christi sacerdotali.
Danhaveri Christosophia.
Fabricii de Sacerdotio Christi. (Dwells on the Old Test. teachings on this point.)
Hulsemanni (Ioann.) Dissertationes.

Jesus Christ.

A PRIEST—*continued.*

Mallet's (F.) Priesterthum des Herrn.
Mayerus de Officio Christi sacerdotali.

Arnold's (Thomas) Sermons.
Berry Street Lectures. No. 18.
Brown's Nat. and Revealed Relig. Book 4.
Charnock on Christ's Intercession.
Flavel's Works.
Grey (James) on the Priesthoods of Christ and Melchisedec.
Jackson on the Priesthood of Jesus Christ.
Le Bas' (C. W.) Sermons.
Lessey's (T.) Sermons.
Moore (T.) on the Priesthood of Christ.
Parry's Apostleship and Priesthood of C.
Randolph's (Bp.) Mission of Christ.
Smith's (J. Pye) Scrip. test. to the Messiah.
Tholuck's Diss. on Sacrifices. (At the end of his Commentary on Hebrews.
Tomkins' Christ the Mediator.
Vaughn's (Henry) Sermons.
Wilson on the Priesthood of Christ.
Witsius on the Covenants.

A KING.

Alphen (Hier. Sim.) Dissertationes.
Calovii (Abraham.) Dissertationes.
Fabricii (Franc.) Diss. philol.-theologicæ.
Frischmuthii (Ioann.) Disseriationes.
Nonnen de Summo domino Θεανθρωπου.
Schmidtii (Io. Andr.) Dissertationes.

Amer. Biblical Repos. 3:748. 2d Ser. 2:439.
Blundell's (Thomas) Sermons.
Charnock's (Stephen) Works.
Christian Review. 14:568.
Lit. and Theol. Review. 5:193.
Maurice (F.) on the Kingdom of Christ.
Owen's Meditations on the glory of Christ.
Ryland's Life of Rev. James Hervey.
Sabin's (J. E.) Kingship of Christ.
Vaughn's (Henry) Sermons.
Whately (Abp.) on the Kingdom of Christ.

Jewish Antiquities. See BIBLICAL HISTORY, COINS, FESTIVALS, ILLUSTRATIONS OF SCRIPTURE, JEWS, HIST. OF, REPUBLIC OF THE JEWS, WEIGHTS, &c.

Abicht, de Servorum Heb. acquisitione, &c.
Altingii de Servis Hebræorum.
——— de Conscionibus Judæorum.
Antonii Antiquitates Hebræicæ.
Aster, Eleemosynæ Judæorum.
Babelii Antiquit. Judaicæ et Evangelicæ.
Babor's Alterthümer der Hebræer.
Bartolocci Bibliotheca Rabbinica. (Vast.)
——— de Judæorum Sectis.
——— Ritus studendi in Academiis.
——— de Musicis instrumentis Hebræor.
Bauer's Handbuch der Geschichte der Hebräischen Nation. ("The best on the subject."—HEEREN.)
——— Kurzgef. Hdbh. d. Heb. Alterthümer.
Bertramus de Republica Hebræorum.
——— de Politia Judaica.

Jewish Antiquities—*continued.*

Blume, Lex Dei. (Written to show how extensively the Roman law was based on that of Moses.)
Brannii Selecta Sacra.
Bucheri Antiquitates Biblicæ.
Buxtorfii Synagoga Judaica, &c.
——— (Opera varia.)
Calmet, Dictionaire Historiques.
Carpzovii (J. G.) Apparatus hist. crit. antiquit. sacr. (There is, perhaps, nothing better on this subject.)
Cunæus de Republica Hebræorum. (Formerly the general text-book on this subj.)
Danhaveri Politia Hebræorum.
Dassovii Antiquitates Hebræicæ.
——— Dissertationes.
De Rossi de Heb. typographiæ origine.
De Wette's Lehrbuch der Heb. Archæologie.
Deylingii Dissertationes.
Dieterici Antiquitates Biblicæ.
Drusius de Sectis Judaicis.
Eisenmenger's Entdecktes Judenthum. (Wonderful! 193 Rabbinical writers procured, consulted, digested, and every quotation given at length in the original, with an exact translation.)
Eusebii Onomasticon.
Faber's (J. E.) Horæ Mosaicæ.
Fabricii (J.) Bibliographia antiquaria.
Fuerst's Cultur Geschichte der Juden.
Gatakeri Adversaria Miscellanea.
Gessenius' Verschiedene Werke.
Geyer, de Luctu Hebræorum.
Godwini Synopsis Antiquitarum Heb.
——— Moses et Aaron.
Hecht de Secta Scriborum.
Herbelot, Bibliothéque Orientale.
Hildebrandi Antiquitates Sacræ.
Hospinianus de Templis et festis Jud.
Hostius de Hydriarum capacitate.
Hottinger de Decimis Judæorum.
——— Cippi Hebraici.
——— Juris Hebræorum leges.
Ikenii Antiq. Hebr. delineatæ.
Iohannsen's Kosmogonische Ansichten.
Josephi (Flav.) Opera.
Keil's Handbuch d. biblischen Archæologie.
Lamii Apparatus Biblicus.
——— de Tabernaculo, templo, &c.
Le Long, Bibliotheca.
Leydekkeri Republica Hebr. (Immense.)
Lightfoot, Horæ Hebraicæ.
Lund's Alte Judische Heiligthümer.
Maimonides, Opera varia.
Meyer, de Temporibus sacris, et festis, &c., cum animadversiones in Spencer. de legibus Heb.
Miegii Constitutiones servi Hebræi.
Millii (D.) Dissertationes Selectæ.
Montani (Ben. A.) Antiquitum Judaicarum.
Muller, de Sepulchris Hebræorum.
Pareau, Antiq. Heb. breviter descripta.
Pfeifferi Delineatio antiq. Hebræorum.
——— Sciographia.

Jewish Antiquities—*continued.*

Quenstedtii Antiquitates Biblicæ.
Reckenbergeri Judæorum ritus antiqui.
Reimar ——— ———
Relandi Antiquitates Sacræ.
——— Other works. (All valuable.)
Rhenferdi Ethnarca Judæorum.
Rosenmuller's Biblische Alterthumskunde.
Scaliger de tribus Sectis Judæorum.
Schachtii Animad. ad Ikenii Antiq. Heb.
Scholz's Handbuch d. bibl. Archäologie.
Schrœderi Com. philologico-critica de vestitu mulierum Hebræorum.
Schulze Compendium Archæologia Hebraicæ. (A book never finished. The above treats of the polit. and eccles. state of the Jews.)
Selden de Synedriis juridicis.
——— de Successione in Pontificat. Heb.
——— Uxor Heb. sive de nuptiis, &c.
——— de Anno civili et Kalendario.
Simonis Onomasticon.
Spencer, de Legibus Hebræorum ritualibus. (Learned, but considered unsound.)
Trigland de Tribus Jud. sectis.
Ugolini Thesaurus Antiq. Sacrarum. (Contains, in 35 folios, a republication of nearly 500 treatises on this subject, by the most eminent writers previous to 1768. With ample indexes.)
Ursini Antiquitates Hebræorum.
Van Dale, Dissertationes.
Van Till, de Musica vet. Hebræorum.
Vitringa de Syagoga vetere.
——— Observationes Sacræ.
Vorstius de Synedriis Hebræorum.
Witsii Egyptiaca.
——— (Opera varia.)
Wolfii Bibliotheca Hebraica.
Wormius de Corruptis antiquit. Hebræorum apud Tacitum et Martialum vestigiis.
Zornii Bibliotheca Antiquaria.

Addington's (Steph.) Dissertations.
Amer. Bib. Repos. 2d Series. 2:174. 6:154.
Arndt's Key to Jewish Antiquities.
Bogue's (David) Lectures.
Brooke's History of the Jews. To 1840.
Brown's (W.) Antiquities of the Jews illustrated from recent travels. 1820.
Burder's Oriental Customs.
Calmet's Dictionary.
——— Antiquities, sacred and profane.
——— Pref. to the various books of S. S.
Croxall's Scripture Politics.
Fleury's Ancient Israelites.
Frazier's Magazine. 13:579,682.
Godwin's Moses and Aaron. ("The most elaborate system of Jewish Antiquities extant."—Horne.)
Gray's Connection between Jewish and Heathen Literature.
Harmer's Observations.
Horne's (Jas.) Jews and their Republic.
Isaacs' Ceremonies, Customs, Rites, and Traditions of the Jews.
Jahn's Archæologia Biblica. Tr. by Upham.

Jewish Antiquities—*continued.*

James' Office of Judge among Hebrews.
Jenning's Jewish Antiquities. (A course of Lectures on Godwin's Moses and Aaron. Universally esteemed.)
Jones' (Prof.) Scriptural Antiquities. (A good compend.)
Josephus' Jewish Antiquities.
Kitto's Journal. 3:50. (Fine arts.)
Lewis' (Tho.) Origines Hebrææ. (An admirable compilation for private libraries.)
Lightfoot's Horæ Hebræicæ.
——— Miscellaneous Works.
Lowman's Civil government of the Hebrews.
——— Rationale of the Hebrew worship.
Mede's (Joseph) Works.
Michaelis' Commentaries on the laws of Moses. Trans. by Alex. Smith. (A fair specimen of reckless modern German conjecture and criticism.)
Mills' (Abp.) The Ancient Hebrews.
Museum of Foreign Lit. 15:157.
North British Review. 13:141.
Palfrey's (J. G.) Academical lectures.
Reland's Dissertations. (Ancient medals.)
Rose's (John) Hulsean Lectures. 1853.
Saurin's (James) Dissertations.
Shaw's History and philosophy of Judea.
Tappan's (David) Lectures on Jewish Antiq.
Weems' Ceremonial law of Moses.

See a great number of authors, who wrote before 1700, in Wolfii *Bib. Hebraica;* and in Imbonati *Biblioth. Latino-Hebraica.*

Jewish Controversy.

See JUDAISM, MESSIAH.

Pro.

Abarbanelis Commentaria in Vet. Test.
——— Rosch Amanah.
——— Predicator salutis.
Aben Ezra Commentaria in Vet. Test.
Albonis Fundamenta fidei.
Gaon, Liber de fide.
Isaac ben Abraham, Chizzouk Emounah.
Jarchi Commentaria in Vet. Test.
Maimonides, Jad Chazakak.
——— More Nevochim.
——— Sepher Hammizooth.
——— Many other treatises.
Manasseh Ben Israel, Concionator.

Abendanna's Polity of the Jews
Aguilar's (Grace) Jewish Faith.
——— Spirit of Judaism.
Crool's Restoration of Israel.
Fernandes' (Benj. D.) Dias' letters.
Leeser on the Jewish Religion.
Moccalta's (Moses) Faith strengthened.
Raphall's Almuth.

Con.

Augustine, Tractatus adversus Judæos.
Basil, Demonstratio contra Judæos.
Chrysostom, Homiliæ quinque.
Cyprian, Testimonia contra Judæos.
Cyril Alexandrinus, adversus Judæos.

Jewish Controversy—*continued.*

Con.

Eusebius, Demonstratio Evangelica.
Gregory Naz., Delecta testimonia ex V. T.
Hippolytus, Demonstsatio adv. Judæos.
Justin Martyr, Dialogus cum Tryphone.
Origen, contra Celsum.
Tertullian, adversus Judæos.

Allix (Pet.), Dissertationes.
Bibliandri Consideratio de Jud. et Christ.
Buxtorfii Liber Cosri.
Calovii (Abraham.) Dissertationes.
Danzii Inauguratio Christi ad docendum.
Eisemenger's Entdeckter Judenthum.
Frischmuthii (Ioan.) Dissertationes.
Gatica de Adventu Messiæ.
Gussetii Jesu Christi veritas salutifera. (Reply to Chizzouk.)
Hackspanii (Theod.) Disputationes.
Helvici Elenchi Judaici.
Hoornbeckii Disputationes anti-judaicæ.
Hulsii Disputatio cum Iacobo Abendana.
Langii Causa Dei.
Limborchii Collatio amica cum Orobio.
Martini Pugio fidei Christianæ.
Mulleri (Ioan.) Judaismus.
Munsteri (Sebast.) Disputationes.
Perezonii Dissertationes.
Pfeifferi Matæologia.
Placæi (Iosua) Disputationes.
Plesner's Jüdisch Mosaiche Religion.
——— Test-reden fur Israeliten.
Porchet, adversus Impios Hebræos.
Schöttgen's Jesus der wahre Messias.
Spanheimii (Fred.) Dubia Evangelica.
Turretini Theologiæ Institutiones.
Widmari (Abdias.) Disputationes.

Allix's (P.) Observat. on the sacred books.
Alphonsus' Dial. bet. a Christian and a Jew.
Barrow on the Creed.
Calman's Errors of modern Judaism. 1846.
Chandler's Prophecies of the Messiah.
Clayton's Enq. into the coming of Messiah.
Crawford's Letter to the Hebrew nation.
De Luc's Letter to the Jews.
Frey's (J. C. F.) Works. (A converted Jew.)
Hawtrey's Knowl. of Messiah the only hope.
Isaiah's Messias of the Christian and Jew.
Kidder's Demonstration of the Messiah.
Lardner's Works. ("Testimonies.")
Leslie's Short method with Jews.
Marcus' Motives for leaving the Jew. faith.
Sharp's Concessions of Jews and Heathen.
Simeon's Answer to Jewish objections.
Stanhope's Truth of the Christian religion.
Turner's Disc. concerning the Messias.
Warburton's Address to the Jews.
Ward's Philosophical Essay.

The curious will find a multitude of now-forgotten opponents of Judaism, chiefly Jews who became Christians, in IMBONATUS, *Biblioth. Lat. Hebraica;* FABRICIUS, *Syllabus script. de veritate Relig. Christi;* and WALCH, *Bibliotheca*, Cap. V. Sec. 8.

Jewish Proselytes. See PROSELYTES.

Jews, Civil Disabilities of.

Blackwood's Magazine. 68:73.
Edinburg Review. 52:363. 86:73.
Foreign Quart. Review. 11:441.
Frazier's Magazine. 1:541. 36:623,738.
Herschell's Present state of the Jews. 1837.
Monthly Review. 122:106.
Pellat's Civil disabilities of the Jews.
Quarterly Review. 8:282.
Westminster Review. 10:435. 19:215.

Jews, Conversion of. See CONVERSION.

Jews, History of. See BIBLICAL HISTORY, JEWS, CONDITION AND PROSPECTS, TEN TRIBES.

Bassnage, Histoire des Juifs depuis Jésus Christ jusqu'a present. 1700.
Baur's Handbuch d. Gesch. d. Hebraischen nations. ("The best on the subject."—HEEREN.)
Berruyér, Hist. du peuple de Dieu.
Calmet, Hist. de la Bible, et des Juifs.
Conringius de Republica Hebræorum.
Engelstoftii Historia populi J. biblica.
Halevy, Histoire des Juifs moderns.
Hegisippi Hist. J. a temp. Maccabæorum.
Herzfeld, Chron. Judic. et primorum Regum.
Holbergi Historia Judaica.
Josephi Opera.
Jost's Gesch. der Juden seit der Maccabeer bis auf ünsere Tage. 1846.
——— Gesch. d. Juden. u. seiner Secten.
Lamy, Hist. de l'Ancienne paque des Juifs.
Leo's (H.) Geschichte d. Jüdischen staates.
Maizonnet, Histoire du peuple d'Israel. (To the return from Babylon.)
Münter's Jud. Krieg unter Trajan u. Hadr.
Prideaux, Hist. des J. (To the death of Chr.)
Usseri Annales Vet. Testamenti.
Venemæ Institutiones Historicæ.

Adams' Hist. of the Jews, from the dest. of Jerusalem to the present time. 1818.
Alexander's Hist. of Israel. (To the destruction of Jerusalem. An accurate compend.)
Amer. Quart. Register. 4:109. (Poland.)
Bassnage's Hist. of the Jews. To 1708.
Beausobre & L'Enfant's Introd. to the N. T.
Berk's Hist. of the Jews. (From the destruction of Jerusalem to 1842.)
Blunt's Establishment and residence of the Jews in England.
——— Hulsean Lectures. 1832. (Against Milman.)
Brooks' History of the Jews. To 1841.
Bruce's History of the Jews in all ages.
Calmet's History of the Old and New Test.
Chris. Examiner. 9:290. 45:48.
Cockayne's Civil history of the Jews, from Joshua to Hadrian.
Craddock's Hist. of the O. Test. methodized.
Da Costa's Israel and the Gentiles.
Edersheim's History of the Jewish nation. (From the destruction of Jerusalem.)

Jews, History of—*continued.*

Elliott's Jews in America.
Evans' Jews in England, from the Norman conquest to the present time. 1848.
Fausett's Sermons before the University of Oxford. 1839. (Attacks Milman.)
Fleury's History of the Ancient Israelites.
Geneste's Parallel hist. of Judah and Israel.
Green's Jews since the death of Christ.
Hale's (Archdeacon) History of the Jews. (From the time of Alexander to the destruction of Jerusalem.)
Hegissippus on the Jewish war. (In 5 bks.)
Hewlett's History of the Jews. (From Nehemiah to the destruction of Jerusalem.)
Horne's (Jas.) Scripture hist. of the Jews.
Huie's Hist. of the Jews, from the destruct. of Jerusalem to the pres nt time. 1841.
Jahn's Hist. of the Hebrew Commonwealth.
Jenks' History of the Jews.
Josephus' History of the Jews.
Jost's History of Judaism and its Sects.
Lewis Origines Hebrææ.
Lincoln's Elements of Christian Theology.
Lindo's History of the Jews in Spain and Portugal, from the earliest times. (With translations of all the laws respecting them.)
Mayer's Hist. of the J., to their dispersion.
Methodist Quarterly Review. 2:192.
Mier's Chronicles. (Very full in describing the state of the J. during the Crusades.)
Mitchell's Records of events connected, &c.
Neal's History of the Jews.
Newman's (F. W.) Hist. of the Heb. monar.
North American Review. 32:234.
Parsons' (Ed.) Hist. of the Jews in all ages.
Prideaux's Connection of the O. and N. T.
Raphall's Post-biblical history of the Jews. (From B. C. 420, to A. D. 70.)
Riddle's (J. E.) History of the Jews.
Russell's Connection of Sac. and Prof. Hist. (Designed as a supplement to Shuckford.)
Saurin's Historical Discourses.
Shuckford's Connect. of Sac. and Prof. Hist.
Smith's (Geo.) The Hebrew people. (To the time of Christ.)
Spirit of the Pilgrims. 3:480.
Stackhouse's History of the Bible.
Stanley's History of the Jewish Church.
Stephens' (W.) Kings of Judah and Israel.
Tomlin's Hist. of the Jews and Jewish Sects.
Tovey's History of the Jews in England.
Trimmer's History of the Jews, from Nehemiah to the destruction of Jerusalem.

Jews, Present Condition and Prospects.

Archives Israelites. Periodical. Paris.
Bédarride, les Juifs en France, et Italie, et en Espagne. 1860.
Beugnot, les Juifs d'Occident.
Cohen's Darstellung des Gottesdienstes, &c.
Gaussen, les Juifs evangelisés.
Gregoire, Histoire des Sectes. 1828.
John a lent, de Moderna theol. Judaica.

Jews, Present Condition—*continued.*

Kirchner's Jüdisches Ceremoniel.
Montbron, Littérature des Hébreux.
Addison's State of the Jews, particularly in Barbary. 1672.
Amer. Bibl. Repos. 2d Series. 3:398. 4:176.
American Quart. Register. 4:109.
Asmonean, The. A Jewish Periodical.
Ayerst's Jews of the 19th century.
Bodenschatzan's Ceremonies, &c. 1748.
British and For. Rev. 5:402. (Poland.)
Brooks' Hist. of the Jews. Chap. 13. 1841.
Calman's State of the J. religion. 1839.
Christian Examiner. 54:1.
Christian Observer. 1861.
Dallas' (A.) Look at Jerusalem. 1841.
De Castro's Jews in Spain.
Eclectic Review. New Series. 2:342.
Etheridge's Jerusalem. 1856. (A survey of the religious learning of the Jews.)
Finn's Jews in China. 1840.
——— Jews in Spain and Portugal. 1841.
Foreign Quart. Review. 24:511. (Egypt.) 27:241. (Poland.)
Hall's (Robt.) Miscellaneous Pieces. 1828.
Harold's Modern Judaism.
Hennert's State the Jews. 1821.
Herschell's Present State, &c. 1833.
Isaacs' Forms, Customs, &c. 1834.
Jewish Chronicle. Periodical.
Jewish Intelligencer. Periodical.
Jewish Repository. Periodical.
Kitto's Journal. 8:172.
Levis' Spanish and Portuguese Jews.
——— Jews in their dispersions. 1783.
Littell's Living Age. 24:511. (Egypt.) 31:298. (England.)
McCaul's The old paths. (Modern Judaism compared with the relig. of Moses. 1838.)
McCausland's Latter days of the J. nation.
McCheyne's Travels as a Deputation from the Church of Scotland. 1839.
McNeil's Lectures on the prophecies.
Margoliouth's Modern Judaism. 1843.
——— Jews of Great Britain.
Mayer's Present condition of the J. 1700.
——— On the Prophecies.
Mills' British Jews. 1852.
Modena's Rites and mode of life of the present Jews throughout the world. 1650.
Monthly Review. 122:251.
Museum of For. Lit. 9:470. 32:50.
Niles' Register. Vol. 15. Supplement. (Maryland.)
Ockley's History of the present Jews. 1707.
Princeton Review. 19:378.
Reports of the Lond. Society for promoting Christianity among the Jews. Since 1811.
Schmucker's Modern Judaism. 1860.
Steinschneider's Jewish literature, from the 8th to the 18th century.

Jews, Lost Tribes. See TEN TRIBES.

Jews, Restoration. See RESTORATION.

Jeynes. See JAINS.

Job. See FAITH OF THE PATRIARCHS.

Calmet's Dissertationes.
Chemnitii (Chris.) Dissertationes.
Deylingii (Salom.) Disputationes.
Feri Jobi historiæ explicatio.
Müllerus de terra Jobi.
Spanheimii (Fred.) Historia Jobi.

Amer. Bib. Repos. 2d Series. 3:163. 11:163.
Bibliotheca Sacra. 7:144.
Christian Examiner. 4:309. 23:29.
Clerke's (Richard) Sermons.
Eclectic Review. New Series. 3:29.
Garnett on the Argument, age, author, &c. (Regards the book as an allegory, written by Ezekiel!)
Halbert's Gospel revealed to Job.
Hickman's (Bp.) Sermons.
Hodge's Elihu. (Design of the book.)
Kitto's Bible Illustrations.
Kollock's (Shepard K.) Sermons.
Lamont's (David) Sermons.
Magee on the Atonement. No. 59.
N. York Review. 4:457.
North American Review. 26:40.
Palfrey's (J. G.) Academical Lectures.
Peters' (Cha.) Critical Dissertations on Job.
Shuckford's Connec. of Sac. and Prof. Hist.
Southern Literary Messenger. 6:563.
Trench's (Francis) Sermons.
Wemyss' Job and his times. (State of religion, morality, arts, sciences, manners, customs, &c.)

John the Baptist. See BIOGRAPHY.

Beckmanni (Frideman.) Disputationes.
Butneri (Jo. E.) Historia Joannis.
Bythneri Inquisitio in historiam J.
Cellarii (Balthas.) Dissertationes.
Du Bosc (Pierre) Sermones. (Very fine.)
Hammerschmid, de Vita et morte Johannis.
Herzog's Theol. Real-encyclopädie. B. VI.
Hottingeri (Ioan. H.) Dissertationes.
Konneman's Johannes der Taufer: ein Fortbild für unsern zuchen, &c.
Krummacher's Johannes der Täufer.
Lisco's (J. G.) Biblische Betrachtungen.
Rabius de Victu Ioannis.
Rhoden's J. der täufer in sein leben, &c.
Winer's Realwörterbuch.
Witsii Observationes Historicæ.

Allestree's (Richard) Sermons.
Anderson's (J. S. M.) Discourses.
Belfrage's Portrait of John the Baptist.
Dehon's (Bp.) Sermons.
Duncan's (W. C.) Life and character of John.
Faringdon's Anthony) Sermons.
Hewlett's (John) Sermons.
Holmes' Bampton Lectures. 1782.
Horne's (Bp.) Life and death of John.
Horseley's (Bp.) Sermons.
Krummacher's Life and character of John.
Le Bas' (Cha. W.) Sermons.
Macduff's Sunsets on the Hebrew mountains.
Mede's (Joseph) Sermons.
Potts' (J. H.) Sermons.
Stebbings' (Henry) Sermons.
Weston's (Bp.) Sermons.

John the Evangelist. See BIOGRAPHY.

Calmeti Dissertationes. (Prolegom.)
Callenbergii (Ioan. Henr.) Dissertationes.
Cellarii (Balthas.) Dissertationes.
Cromii Probabilia haud probabilia.
Flovini Exercit. historico-philologiæ.
Koster's (C. M. L.) Enstehung, Fortbild., &c.
Lampii Prologomena in Evang. J.
Mosheimii Dissertationes.
Parei (David) Dissertationes.
Stein de Evang. J. (Cont. Bretschneider.)
Amer. Bibl. Repos. 7:440. 3:299.
Bishop's (Charles) Discourses.
Dehon's (Theodore) Sermons.
Horne's (Bp.) Sermons.
Lee's (Bp.) Practical Discourses.
Macfarlane's Disciple whom Jesus loved.
Princeton Review. 3:569.
Trench's Life and character of John.
Westcott's Introduction to the study of the Gospels. Chap. 5.

Jonah. See BIOGRAPHY.

Bryant's (Jacob) Dissertations.
Close's Typical persons of the Old Test.
Fairbairn's Life, charac., and mission of J.
Foster's Lectures at Broadmead Chapel.
Jones' (Thomas) Jonah's Portrait.
Methodist Quart. Rev. 5:382.
Preston's Parochial Lectures.
Sibthorp's Pulpit Recollections.
Simpson's (James) Evening Exercises.
Southern Quart. Review. 22:505.
Townsend's (George) Sermons.
Young's Lectures on the book of Jonah.

Jordan. See GEOGRAPHY, PALESTINE.

Amer. Bibl. Repos. 2d Series. 3:265.
Bibliotheca Sacra. 3:184. (Sources.)
Lord's Lit. and Theol. Journal. 2:288.
Lynch's Expedition to the Dead Sea.

Joseph, Father of Christ.

Calmet, Prologomena et Dissertationes.
De Soto, Vita et excellentia Josephi.
Goetzii (Geo. Henr.) Meletemata.
Larom's Dissertations on the history of J.

Joseph, Son of Jacob.

Adamson's (John L.) Jos. and his brethren.
Bitaube's Life of Joseph.
Bullock's (Wm.) Practical Lectures.
Close's Typical persons of the Old Test.
Collier's (W. B.) Lectures on Scripture facts.
Cummings' (John) Last of the Patriarchs.
Davie's Lectures on the history of Joseph.
D'Oyly's (George) Sermons.
Edelman's Sermons on the history of J.
Gibson's (Timothy) Lectures.
Gordon on Particular providences.

Joseph, Son of Jacob—*continued.*

Howard's (H. L.) Joseph and his brethren.
Larom's Bow in strength.
Lawson's (Dr. Geo.) Lectures.
Lincoln's (W.) Joseph and Jesus.
McGowan's (Dr. John) Works.
Mason's Hist. of J. spiritually improved.
May's (Nath.) History of Joseph.
Smith's (Thornley) History of Joseph in connection with the customs of the time.
Sprague's Letters to young men.
Wardlaw's (R.) Lectures on the life of J.
Winslow's (Octav.) Fulness of Christ.

Josephus. See TESTIMONY OF JOSEPHUS.

Josephi Opera omnia. (The edition generally preferred is that of Hudson, 1720, on account of the accuracy of the text, and the admirable indexes.)
Eichstadt, Testimonia de J. C.
Krebsii Observationes in Nov. Test.
Ottii Excerpta ex J. ad N. T. illustrationem.
Schmidii (C. F.) Enarratio sententiæ J.
Trendelenburgii Christomathia.

Findlay's Vindication of the sacred books.
Frazier's Magazine. 25:115.
Jones' (John) Ecclesiastical Researches.
Kitto's Journal. 6:292.
Lodge's (Tho.) Transl. of the works of J.
Trail's Translation of "The Jewish War."
Whiston's Translation of the works of J.; with notes, and eight dissertations.

Joshua. See BIOGRAPHY.

Close's (Fr.) Sermons on typical persons.
Potts' (J. H.) Sermons.
Smith's (Thornley) Hist. of J. in connection with the customs of his time.
Thompson's (F. F.) Lent Lectures. Lect. 6.
Williams' (Bp.) Sermons.

Joy.

Abernethy's (Bp.) Sermons.
American Biblical Repository. 9:267.
Barrow's (Isaac) Sermons.
Bather's (Edward) Sermons.
Blair's (Hugh) Sermons.
Bradbury on Christian joy.
Christian Observer. 25:673.
Christian Quarterly Spectator. 4:513.
Cooper's (Edward) Sermons.
Craddock's (Walter) Sermons.
Dodson's (Joseph) Twelve Discourses.
Donne's (John) Sermons.
Dwight's (T.) Sermons.
Evans on Christian Temper.
Gale's (Dr. John) Sermons.
Gilpin's (William) Sermons.
Grove's (Henry) Sermons and Tracts.
Hervey's (James) Sermons.
Howe (John) Delighting in God. ("One of the finest pieces of practical theology in the English language."—BOGUE & BENNETT.)
Lamont's (David) Sermons.

Joy—*continued.*

Limborch's Christian Theology.
Morris' (Joseph) Sermons.
Muston's (C. R.) Sermons.
Oakley's (Fred.) Sermons.
Reynolds' (Bp.) Sermons.
Ryan's (Vincent W.) Sermons.
Scattergood's (Samuel) Sermons.
Slade's (James) Sermons.
Smallridge's (George) Sermons.
Tappan's (David) Sermons.
Vaughn (Henry) on the Fruits of the Spirit.
Whichcot's (B.) Sermons.

Jubilee.

Gerhardi (Ioan.) Exercitationes.
Kranold de Anno Hebræorum jubilæo.
Maimonides de Jubilæo Hebræorum.
Voisin, de Jubileo secundum Hebræos.
Wagenseilii (Ioan. Chr.) Disputationes.
Woldius de Anno Hebræorum Jubilæo.

Godwin's Moses and Aaron.
Rose's Law of Moses.

Judaism. See CABALLA, CEREMONIAL LAW, JEWISH CONTROVERSY, RABBINICAL LITERATURE, TALMUD.

Altingii Republica Hebræorum.
Ascher, ארבעה טורים.
Badenschartz' Kirchliche Verfassung, &c. (A great work.)
Bähr's Symbolik des Mosaichen Cultus.
Bartolocci Bibliotheca magna Rabbinica. (A synopsis of Heb. literature. It contains an account of the lives, as well as writings, of Jewish authors; and copious extracts, with a Latin translation.)
Beer's Geschichte Lehren und Meinungen.
Benjamini Itinerarium. 12th century.
Bindrim de Excom. apud Hebræos.
Bretschneideri Capita Theologiæ Judæorum Dogmaticæ.
Buddæi Historia Philosophiæ Hebræorum.
Buxtorf de Synagoga Judaica.
Cameri Theologia Israelis.
Coringius de Politia Hebræorum.
Danhaveri Politia Hebræorum.
Dassovius de Lustratione Judæorum.
Drusius de tribus Sectis Judæorum.
Eisenmenger's Entdecktes Judenthum.
Goremburgii Synagoga Judaica.
Gramberg's Gesch. d. religionsideen d. A. T.
Heideggeri Dissertatio de articulis fundamentis Judaicæ religionis.
Hemberg de Politia Hebræorum.
Hottingeri Juris Hebræorum Leges. CCLXI.
——— Compendium Theologiæ Judaicæ.
Joseph Zarphati יד יוסף.
Koecheri (H. F.) Nova Bibliotheca Hebraica. (Necessary to complete Wolfius.)
Lent, Moderna Theologica Judaica. (Acta erud.)
Levi (Simon) Hist. religionis Judæorum.
Lightfoot, Opera omnia.
Maii Synopsis Theol. Jud. veteris et novæ.

Judaism—*continued.*

Meieri Judaica: seu vet. scriptorum profanorum de rebus Judaicis fragmenta.
Meyer de Origine et causa festorum Jud.
Mordechai Japhe, לבוש האורה.
Nicolas, des Doct. relig. des Juifs pendant les deux siècles anterieurs a l'ere chrét.
Pinchas, מדרש פנחס.
Relandi Dissertationes Miscellaneæ.
Salvador, Hist. des Institutions de Moïse.
Schelomo, עבודת הקדש.
Schoettgenii Horæ Hebraicæ.
Schrœder's Satzungen und Gebräuche, &c.
Selden de Synedriis vet. Hebræorum.
Selemon b. Melech, מכלל יופי.
Spencer de Legibus Hebr. ritualibus et eorum rationibus. (It attempts to show that the Mosaic ritual was borrowed from the Egyptians.)
Stein's Koheleth.
Surenhusii Theologia Hebræorum.
Thummius de festis Judæorum.
Tillemont, Ruine des Juifs.
Tissard de Hebræorum ritibus.
Tolandi (J.) Dissertationes.
Triglandius de Judæorum sectis.
Ugolini Thesaurus. (A collec. of the works of eminent writers on the laws, customs, rites, &c., of the anc. Heb. 34 vols., folio.)
Vendii Dissertationes.
Vitringa de Synagoga vetere.
Voisin, Theologia Judæorum.
——— de lege Divina.
Vorstius de Synedriis Hebræorum.
Winer, Chrestomathia Talmud. et Rabbin.
Witsius de Theocratia Israelitarum.
Wolfii Bibliotheca Hebræa. (Not confined to Jewish writers. Gives an account of Old Testament Scriptures, Editions, Lexicons, and writers against the Jews.)

Abendana's Ecc. and civil polity of the Jews.
Addington's Relig. knowl. of the anc. Jews.
Aguilar's (G.) Spirit of Judaism.
——— The Jewish faith.
Allen's (John) Modern Judaism. 1816. (The best modern English work. Seueral editions since.)
Alexander's (L.) Hebrew ritual and doctrine; oral and traditional.
Asher's Itinerary of Rabbi Benjamin.
Asmonean, The. Periodical. N. York.
Bernard's Creed and ethics of the Jews.
Berry Street Lectures.
Calmet's Preface to Exodus and Deuteron.
——— Dissertations prefixed to Comment. on Exodus.
Cappe's Critical Remarks.
Chandler on the Prophecies.
Christian Examiner. 54:1.
Christian Month. Spectator. 1:125.
Croxall's Scripture Politics.
D'Israeli's Genius of Judaism.
Durell on the Mosaic Institutions.
Eisenmenger's Traditions of the Jews.

Judaism—*continued.*

Etheridge's (J. W.) Religious and scholastic learning of the Jews. 1856.
Ewing's (G.) Essays.
Fergus' Laws and Institutions of Moses.
Fleury's Manners of the Jews.
Fuller's Sermon on the Messiah.
Godwin's Moses and Aaron. (Many editions.)
Helon's Pilgrimage to Jerusalem, by Strauss.
Henry's (H. A.) Religious belief of Israel.
Home's (Jas.) Jews and their republic.
Hoppus' Hist. and polity of the Hebrews.
Isaacs' Ceremonies, customs, traditions, &c.
Jahn's Heb. Commonwealth. Tr. by Stow.
Jewish Advocate. Periodical. London.
Jewish Herald. " "
Jewish Repository. Period. Lond. 1813–1815. Continued as J. Expositor 1816–1829, and as J. Intelligencer 1830 to the present.
Johnston's Israel after the flesh. (To show that Judaism was purely national and territorial, and not a system for individual salvation.)
Jurieu's History of doctrines and worship.
Kidder's Demonstration of the Messias.
Knickerbocker Magaz. 22:168.
Law's Theory of Religion.
Leeser (Isaac) on the Jewish religion.
Leo's Ceremonies and customs of the Jews.
Lewis' Origines Ebraicæ. (Explains every branch of the Levitical law, and all the Jewish usages.)
Lightfoot's Jewish Miscellanies.
——— Temple service in the time of Christ.
——— Works. Ed. by Putnam. (13 v., 8vo.)
London Eclectic Rev. 4th Series. 27:315.
Lowe's Annual festivals of the Jews.
Lowman's Rationale of the Heb. ritual.
——— Civil government of the Jews.
McCaul's Sketches of Judaism. 1838.
Maimonides' Creed and Ethics of the Jews.
Mede's Works.
Mendelssohn's Jerusalem. Tr. by Samuels.
Michaelis' Com. on the Laws of Moses.
Moccalta's Faith strengthened.
Monthly Review. 84:18. 131:117.
Pendahzur's Book of Religion.
Priestley's (Jos.) Letters to the Jews.
Raphall's Tr. of 18 treatises from the Mishna.
Ross' View of the Jewish religion.
Salomon's Sermons. Trans. by Goldsmid.
Saurin on the Conception of Christ.
Scott's (Dr.) Controv. with a learned Jew.
Selden's Tracts.
Shaw's Hist. and philos. of Judaism. (An admirable defence of the Mosaic system. Against Hume.)
Smith's Hebrew people.
Spectator. No. 495.
Stanhope's Boyle Lectures.
Stehelen's Traditions of the Jews.
Tama's Transactions of the Sanhedrim convoked at Paris. 1806.
Tomlin's Account of the Jewish Sects.
Townley's Reasons for the law of Moses.

Judaism—*continued.*

Warburton's Divine legation of Moses.
——— Address to the Jews.
Watson's (Alex.) Miscellaneous Discourses.
Weemes on the Ceremonial law.
Wotton's Usages of the Scribes in the time of Christ and Pharisees.

The curious will find every work against the Jews, up to 1694, in IMBONATUS; and every work in their favor in BARTOLOCCI. FUERST, in his *Bibliotheca* notices *all* the books relating to Jews in alphabetical order, down to 1863.

Judas Iscariot.

Buddei Meditationes Sacræ.
Goetzius de Judæ proditoris cultu.
Gronovii (Iacob.) Exercitationes Academ.
Krackewitzii (Alb. Iochim.) Dissertationes.
Raymondi Metamorphosis latronis in Apos.
Rusmeyeri (M. C.) Dissertationes duæ.
Schollmeyer's Jesus und Judas.
Seldeni Opera Theologica.
Serrarii (Nicol.) Opera.
Woergeri Symbolæ Theolog. et historicæ.

Bonar's Observations on Judas Iscariot.
Bradley's (Charles) Sermons.
Christian Review. 5:328.
Girdlestone's (Charles) Sermons.
Harris' (Robert) Sermons.
Smith's (Henry) Sermons.
Spirit of the Pilgrims. 6:215,226,427.

Judas, or Jude. See APOSTLES.

Bibliotheca Bremensis.
Biel (Io. Chris.) Observationes.
Quade, Commentatio de vita Judæ.

Judea. See PALESTINE.

Judgment. See RASH JUDGMENT.

Judgment Day. See SAINTS JUDGING THE WORLD.

Altingii Dissertationes Theologicæ.
Amyraldi Dissertationes Theologicæ.
Franzii (Wolfgang) Disputationes.
Schottii Comment. exegetico-dogmaticus in Christi sermones.
Vossii Disputationes theol. Disp.14,15,16.
Willeti Tuba monitoria.
Zornii Delineatio Theologiæ patristicæ.

Amory's (Tho.) Sermons. (8 on this subj.)
Barrow's (Bp.) Works.
Bates' Four last things.
Baxter (R.) on the Judgment day.
Berens' (Edward) Sermons.
Bibliotheca Sacra. 8:471.
Bolton on Death, Judgm., Heaven, and Hell.
Boston's Fourfold state.
Brooks' Golden Key.
Brownrig's (Bp.) Sermons.
Carr's (George) Sermons.
Christian Observer. 18:137.
Clarke's (Samuel) Sermons.

Judgment Day—*continued.*

Cooper's (Edward) Sermons.
Davies' (Samuel) Sermons.
Doddridge's (Philip) Lectures.
Dwight's (Timothy) Discourses. Disc. 156.
Edwards' (Pres.) Sermons.
Fiddes' (Richard) Sermons.
Foster's (Dr. James) Natural Religion.
Fuller's (And.) Gospel its own witness.
Girdlestone's (Charles) Sermons.
Greenham on the Universal Judgment.
Green's (Bp.) Discourses.
Greenwood's Day of Judgment.
Hale's (Sir Matthew) Contemplations.
Hampden's (R. D.) Sermons.
Hervey's Theoron and Aspasio.
——— Sermons.
Hopkins' (Bp.) Works.
Horne's (Bp.) Sermons.
Horneck's Prospect of the day of judgment.
Howe's Blessedness of the righteous.
Irving's (Edward) Orations.
Jenkins' Reasonableness of Christianity.
Jephson's Certainty of a future judgment.
Jortin's (John) Sermons.
King's Morsels of Criticism.
Latimer's (Bp.) Sermons.
Lonsdale's Test. of nature, reason, and Rev.
Lucas' (Richard) Sermons.
McCaul's (Alexander) Sermons.
Massillon's Sermons.
Melville's (Henry) Sermons.
Monthly Review. 68:417.
Scattergood's (Samuel) Sermons.
Seabury's (Bp.) Sermons.
Sherlock's Practical treatise on the J.
Simpson on the Language of Scripture.
Smith on the Great day of Judgment.
Stoddard on the Day of Judgment.
Summerfield's (John) Sermons.
Thayer's (Elihu) Sermons.
Trench's (R. C.) Sermons.
Venn's (Henry) Sermons.
Walker's (James) Sermons.
Watts' World to come.
Whiteley's (Jos.) Advantages of Revelation.
Wilson's (Bp.) Sermons.
Yonge's (James) Sermons.

Judgments of God. See JUSTICE OF GOD, NATIONAL RETRIBUTIONS, PROVIDENCE.

Arnold's (Dr. Thomas) Sermons.
Beard's Theatre of God's judgments. (A curious collection of narratives.)
Brown's (W. L.) Sermons.
Charnock's Works.
Fowle's (F. W.) Plain sermons.
Hoare's (C. J.) Lectures.
Hooper's (Bp.) Works. (Pestilence.)
Taylor's Life of Christ.
Tillotson's (Abp.) Sermons.
Turner's Hist. of remarkable providences.

Julian the Apostate.

Juliani (Imp.) Opera. Many editions.

Julian the Apostate—*continued.*

Gregory Naz., Invectivæ.
Augustine, contra Julianum.
Cyril Alex., contra Julianum.

Abichtii (Joann. Geo.) Dissertationes.
Bassnage, Histoire des Juifs.
[Bletterie], Vie de l'Empereur Julien.
Fabricii Lux Evang. toti orbis. (Gives all the testimony as to the attempt to rebuild the temple.)
Korner's Kaiser Julian d. Abtrünnige.
Neander's Kaiser J. und sein Zeitalter.
Rabbaneri Amenitatum quinque decades.
Schulz, de Philosoph. et moribus Juliani.
Wiggers, de J. apostata et chris. persecutore.

[Bletterie's] Life of the Emperor Julian.
Duncombe's Select works of the Emperor J.
Gregory's (Naz.) Declarat. of condemnation.
Hicks' (Geo.) Jovian. (Ans. to Johnson.)
Methodist Quart. Review. 9:387.
Moyle's Posthumous Works.
Neander's Emp. Julian and his generation.
Taylor's Orations of Julian against the Christians. Trans. from the Greek.
Warburton's Julian. (Defends the reality of the miracle of the fiery eruption.)

Justice. See MORALS.

Abercrombie's Moral Feelings. Part 1, sec. 2.
Dyke's (Oswald) Sermons.
Jortin's (John) Sermons.
Watts' (Isaac) Works.

Justice of God.

Abernethy's (John) Sermons.
Amer. Bibl. Repository. 3d Series. 4:586.
Bellamy's (Joseph) Essays.
Bourne's (Samuel) Sermons.
Brakenridge's (William) Sermons.
Butler's Analogy of Religion and Nature.
Charnock's (Stephen) Works.
Clarke's Demonstration of the Exist. of God.
Clarke's (Dr. Samuel) Sermons.
Cole on the Righteousness of God.
Dwight's (Timothy) Theology. Disc. 10.
Foster's Natural Religion.
Griffin (Edw. D.) on the Atonement.
Grindal's (Abp.) Remains.
Jamieson's Use of Sacred History.
Jefferson (J.) on Divine Justice.
Ludlam's Essays. Essay 2.
McCaul's (Alexander) Sermons.
Magee on the Atonement. No. 24.
Owen on Divine Justice.
Robinson's Christian System. Ess. 8.
Ryland's Contemplations.
Saurin's Sermons.
Scott's Christian life.
Tillotson's (Abp.) Sermons.
Venn's (Henry) Sermons.
Wishcart's (William) Sermons.
Witsius on the Covenants. Book 12, Ch. 8.

Justification. See FAITH, GOOD WORKS, IMPUTATION, PAUL AND JAMES, UNION WITH CHRIST.

Ignatius, Epistola ad Magnesianos.
Irenæus, adversus Hæresis.

Battus adversus Pontificos.
Beckmannus de foro Dei absolutorii.
Bezæ Apologia de Justificatione.
Bulli Harmonia Apostolica.
Bullinger de Gratia Dei. (Much esteemed.)
Burmanni (Francisc.) Disputationes.
Calvini Institutiones Theologicæ.
Chemnitii Examen concilii Tridentini.
Crocius de Justif. peccatoris coram Deo.
Cundisius de Lege et Evangelio.
Fechtii Examen Conciliationis.
Fox (Joseph.) de Christo gratis, &c.
Frisius de Norma Justificationis.
Gerardi Loci Theologici.
Gerlachus de Justif. hominis coram Deo.
Gisenii Diascepsis.
Grynæi (Io. Iacob.) Dissertationes.
Hagenbachii Historia Doctrinæ. Sec. 251.
Heshusius de Justificatione hominis. (Agt. the decree of the Council of Trent.)
Hoepfneri Disputationes duodecim.
Le Blanc, Thesis de Justificatione Christi.
Loescherus de Effectibus Justificationis.
Musæus de Ratione formali Justificatione.
Noesselti Opuscula.
Paræus de Justificatione impii.
Piscator de Causa meritoria nostra.
Placette, Traite de la Justification.
Prideaux, Lectiones de capitibus Controv.
Redman de Justificatione. ("The most learned man of his time." [1515.] BP. BURNET.)
Riveti Vindiciæ Evangelii.
Scharpius de Justificatione coram Deo.
Schelvigius de Just. fidelium veteris test.
Schwartz, de Disputatione inter Melancthonem et Lutherum.
Selneccerus de Just. hominis coram Deo.
Spener's Glaubens-Gerechtigkeit.
Storr, Doctrina Christiana.
Teuberi Meletemata et Problemata.
Thummii Explicatio terminorum et distinctionum in arduo articulo Justificationis.
——— Justitia Christi; activa, et passiva.
Witsii Economia Fœderis.
——— Miscellanea Sacra.

Abernethy's (John) Sermons.
Adam (Tho.) on the first 11 ch. of Romans.
Allen's (W.) Christian Justification stated.
Appleton's Works. Lecture 43.
Barrow's (Bp.) Works. (Two sermons on Romans 5:1.)
Bates' Sermons on forgiveness of sin.
——— Harmony of the Divine Attributes.
Baxter's (Rich.) Aphorisms of Justification.
——— on Saving faith.
——— Reply to Eyre, Kendall, and others.
Bennett's (J.) Justificat. revealed in Script.
Bennett's (William) Sermons.
Berriman's (William) Sermons.

Justification—*continued.*

Black's (David) Sermons.
Booth's Reign of Grace.
Boyse's Theological Works. (Collects the passages from the New Testament, and gives a paraphrase.)
Bradshaw on Justification. (Puritan. Translated into several languages.)
Bull's (Bp.) Defence of the Nicene Creed.
Bullinger's Decades. (Parker Society pub.)
Bunyan's Defence of the doctrine of J.
Burgess' (Anthony Lectures.
Burgh's (William) Discourses.
Burton's (H.) Truth's triumph over Trent.
Charnock's (Stephen) Works.
Chris. Monthly Spectator. 8:334.
Christian Observer. 19:360.
Cloag on Justification by faith.
Comber's Roman forgeries in the Councils of the first four centuries.
Cooper's (Edward) Sermons on Doctrines.
Crandon's J. by Grace. (Severe on Baxter.)
Davenant's (Dr. John) Lectures.
Davies' (Samuel) Sermons.
Dickinson's (Jonathan) Letters.
Downham on Justification.
Dwight's Theology. Sermon 34.
Eaton's Honeycomb of Justification.
Eclectic Review. July, 1830.
Edwards' (Pres.) Discourses.
Elliott's Sin destroyed. and sinners saved.
Enfield's (William) Sermons.
Erskine's (Ralph) Faith no Fancy.
Erskine's (Tho.) Essay on Faith. (Exc't.)
Erskine's (Ebenezer) Sermons on Heb. 10:22.
Eyer's (W.) Justification without conditions.
Faber (Geo. S.) on Primitive Doctrine. (Gives the several definitions of the Roman and Anglican Churches.)
Flavel's Method of grace in the gospel.
Fox's Grace of Christ in Justification.
Fuller's (Andrew) Sermons.
Gill's Doct. of J. stated and maintained.
Gisbourne's (Thomas) Sermons.
Goodwin's (J.) Exp. of the 9th ch. of Rom.
Grew's (Obadiah) Sermons on Jer. 2:6.
Guyse's Pref. to the Epistle to the Romans.
Hampden's (R. D.) Sermons.
Hawker's (Robert) Sermons.
Hayward's (Roger) Sermons.
Hervey's Theoron and Aspasio.
Heurtley's Bampton Lectures. 1845.
Hewitt's Points of Christian doctrine.
Hey's Lectures on Divinity.
Hill's (G. D.) Wayfarings in Christ.
Holloway's Analogy of faith. (Beautiful.)
Hooker's (Rich.) Discourses on Justification.
Junkin (George) on Justification.
Kollock's (Shepard K.) Sermons.
Lawrence's Use and practice of faith.
Lime Street Lectures.
Lond. Eclectic Rev. 4th Series. 8:312.
Maitland on the 8th chapter of Romans.
Melancthon's J. of man by faith alone.
Meth. Quart. Rev. 4:5. 5:5.

Justification—*continued.*

Norris on Reason and Faith.
O'Brien's Ten Sermons at Trinity College.
Owen (John) on Justif. by faith. (Precious.)
Pemble on Justification by faith.
Polhill's Precious faith considered.
Prideaux's Heads of the Controversy.
Princeton Rev. 12:268,561.
Rawlin on J. by Christ's Righteousness.
Rogers' Doctrine of Faith.
Romaine's (William) Sermons.
Russell's (D. M.) Discourses.
Salter's Hall Sermons. Ser. by J. Newman.
Scharp (John) on the J. of men before God.
Sim's (W. F.) Sermons.
Smith's (Theyre) Sermons.
Smith's (W.) Sermons. (Unworking faith.)
Taylor's Scripture Doctrine of Justification.
Toplady's Free will and Merit examined.
Trail's (Robt.) Works. (Several editions.)
Troughton's Lutherus redivivus.
Usher's (Abp.) Sermons.
Ward on Special justification.
Whitfield's (George) Sermons.
Wilson's Selections on the Atonement.
Witherspoon's (John) Works.
Yonge's (James) Sermons.

Justin Martyr. See FATHERS.

Justini Opera. (Ed. Otto. Prefatus est Baumgarten-Crusius. 1850.)
——— ——— (With corrected text, English introd. and notes, by W. Trollope. 1845.)
Baronii Anales.
Fabricii Interp. locorum quorundam St. J.
Grabii Spicelegium.
Halloixii Acta et documenta Justini.
Kromii Authentia dialogi cum Tryphone.
Langii (S. G.) Dissertationes.
Le Clerc, Vie de Justin Martyr.
Oudinus de Scriptoribus Ecclesiasticis.
Tentzelii Exercitationes. Par. 1.
Volkmar's Justin der Martyrer.

Brown's Tr. of J. M.'s "Dialogue." Notes.
Cave's Primitive Christianity.
Chevalier's Trans. of the "Apology" of J. M.
Christian's Magazine. 3:291.
Conybeare's Bampton Lectures. 1839.
Kay's Account of the writings of Justin.
Lardner's Credibility of the Gospel. Pt. 2.
Moses' Trans. of the "Exhortation to the Gentiles."
Reeves' Apologies of Justin, Tertullian, and Minutius. Translation and notes.
Semisch's Life and writings of Justin M. Translated by Ryland.
Tomline's (Bp.) Writings and opinions of J.
Universalist Quarterly. 3:272.

Kabbala. See CABALA.

Kantism. See TRANSCENDENTALISM.

Karaites. See JUDAISM.

Drusius de Sectis Judaicis.
Hechtii Antiquitates Karæorum.

Karaites—*continued.*

Fürst's Gesch. d. Karäerthums bis 900.
Held (J. M.) de Secta Karæorum.
Scaligeri Opuscula.
Schupartus de Secta Karæorum.
Simonis (Rich.) Dissertationes.
Triglandi (Iacob.) Diatribe.
Ugolini Thesaurus Antiquitat. Sacræ.
Warneri (L.) Dissertationes.
Wolfii Notitia Karæorum.

Beausobre's Introd. to Sacred Scripture.
Bibliotheca Sacra. 21:39.
Henderson's Biblical Researches.
Ockley's Hist. of the Jews. (Appendix.)

Keeping the Heart. See GOVERNMENT.

Keri and Ketib.
See VARIOUS READINGS.

Keys of the Church. See POPERY.

Botsaccus de Clavibus Petri.
Carpzovii (Ioan. Bened.) Disputationes.
Danhaveri (Ioan. Conrad.) Disputationes.
Hulsemanni Potestas clavium.
Mullerus de Clavibus regni cœlorum.
Newmannus de Auctorit. clavis ligantis, &c.
Olearii (Ioan.) Dissertationes.
Pfaffii (Christoph. Matt.) Dissertationes.
Wagnerus de Efficacia clavium.
Waltheri (Mich.) Dissertationes.
Wigandi (Ioan.) Dissertationes.

Hammond's (Henry) Power of the Keys.

Kingdom of God. See MILLENARIANS.

Augustine, de Civitate Dei.
Dorperi Dissertationes exeget. theologiæ.

Allestree's (Richard) Sermons.
Baxter's (Arthur G.) Sermons.
Beveridge's (Bp.) Sermons.
Blunt's (Henry) Sermons.
Burton's (Hezek.) Sermons.
Campbell's (George) Dissertations.
Chalmers' (Thomas) Sermons.
Dehon's (Bp.) Sermons.
Erskine's (Ebenezer) Sermons.
Heber's (Bp.) Sermons.
Jebb's (Bp.) Sermons.
Milner's (Joseph) Sermons.
Pring's (John) Sermons.
Storr's (Prof.) Dissertations.
Tracts for the Times. No. 49.
Wilson's (Will.) Kingdom of our Lord.

Knights. See CHIVALRY, MILITARY ORDERS.

Knights of St. John of Jerusalem, or Knights of Malta.

Caoursini Stabilimenta militum Hieros.
Clozeaux, Priviléges des Papes, Empereurs, Roys, et Princes, en faveur, &c.
Dienemann's Nachricht vom Johanniterord.
Fabricii Biblioth. Græc. et Lat. antiquar.
Goussancourt, le Martyrologie des Chevaliers de Malte.

Knights of St. John—*continued.*

Honore, Diss. historiques et critiques.
Nicolai's Beschuldigungen, &c.
Sibert, Hist. des ordres royaux.
Vertot, Hist. des Chevaliers Hospitaliers.
Wedekind's Ritterlichen St. Johan. Ordens.
Zentgravii Dissertationes.

Boisgelins' Ancient and modern Malta.
Dublin Univ. Mag. 57:60.
Porter's (W.) Hist. of the Knights of Malta.
Southern Literary Messenger. 7:830. 8:41, 139,186. 9:86,163.
Tauffe's Hist. of the sovereign order, &c.
Vertot's Hist. of the Knights Hospitallers.

CLOZEAUX and FABRICIUS, quoted above, each give a large list of works relating to this order.

Knights Templar.
See MILITARY ORDERS.

Dupuy, de l'ordre militaire des Templiers.
Falkenstein's Gesch. des Tempelhemordens.
Gurtleri Historia templariorum militum
Maillard, Règles secret des Templiers.
Mansuet, Hist. critique et apologetique.
Michelet, Procés des Templars.
Putean, Hist. de l'ordre des Templiers.
Raynouard, Monumens histor. relatifs a la condemnations des Chevaliers du temple.
Strauchii Disputationes Historicæ.
Thomasii (Christiani) Dissertationes.

Addison's (C. G.) Hist. of the Knights Tem.
Burnes' (Dr. J.) Hist. of the Knights Temp.
Dublin University Mag. 20:197.
Eclectic Rev. 4th Series. 12:189. N. S. 2:1.
Edinburg Review. 9:196.
Foreign Quar. Rev. 4:608.
Museum of For. Lit. 2:243. 15:385.
Southern Quar. Rev. 9:457.

Knowledge.

Abernethy's (John) Sermons.
Balguy's (Thomas) Sermons.
Baxter on Knowledge and Love.
Boys on Christian Knowledge.
Brown's Philosophy of the human mind.
Buckminster's (Joseph S.) Sermons.
Burgess' (Bp.) Sermons.
Burgh's Dignity of Human nature.
Chalmers' (Dr.) Sermons. (Distinction between Knowledge and Consideration.)
Clagget's (William) Sermons.
Cooper's (Edward) Sermons.
Enfield's (William) Sermons.
Fiddes' (Richard) Sermons.
Hall's (Robt.) Advantage of knowledge to the lower classes.
Nugent's Origin of human knowledge.
Thompson (J. P.) on the Christian graces.
Winder's Rise, progress, &c., of knowledge.

Knowledge of God. See ACQUAINTANCE.

Knox, John.

Krummacher's J. Knox u. die König. Maria.

Knox's Works. Edited by D. Laing. 1846.
McCrie's Life of John Knox.
Quarterly Review. 9:418.
Tulloch's Leaders of the Reformation.

Koran. See MAHOMETANISM.

Alcoran de Mahomet: trans. par Sieur de Ryer.
Acoluthi ττpaπλa Alcoranica. (Arabic, Persian, Turkish, and Latin; valuable notes.)
Beidhawii Commentarius in Koranum.
Caschii Commentarius in Koranum.
Chinchon, Anti-koranum.
Elberkevi, La foi Musselmane.
Hinkelmanni Alcoranus.
Kasimirski Traduction nouvelles.
Leuchteri Alcoranus Mahometicus.
Maracii Alcoran, cum vita Mahometi.
Nöldeke, Histoire de Koran.
Savary, Le Koran traduit de l'Arabe. Notes.
Turpin, Histoire de l'Alcoran.
Vertot, Discours sur l'Alcoran. (Often appended to Vol. 5 of his History of the Knights of Malta.)
Wagner's Turkenbüchlein.
Weil's Historisch-krit. Einleitung in d. K.

Butler's (C.) Horæ Biblicæ. (Appendix.)
——— Notes on the Koran.
Cureton's Book of Religions.
Du Ryer's Translation of the Koran.
Eclectic Rev. 4th Series. 19:375.
Foreign Quart. Rev. 24:1.
Lane's Selections from the Koran.
Museum of For. Literature. 2:13.
Retrospective Review. 3:1.
Sales' Tr. of the Koran; with preliminary dissertations, notes, &c. (All sufficient.)
Savary's Trans. of the Koran, &c.

Labadists.

Pro.

L'Abadié, Introduction a la pieté.
——— Odes Sacrées.
——— (Thirty other publications.)
Labadianorum Declaratio. 1571.
Lignon (Petrus du), Catechismus.
Schurmanniæ (Annæ Mariæ) ευκληριαν.
Sluter (H.) de Regeneratione.
Yvon (Pet.) Essentia relig. patefacta.
——— (Other works in German and Latin.)
Veritas sui Vindex; seu solemnis Fidei declaratio J. de Labadie, P. Yvon, P. de Lignon, &c. 1672.

Con.

Arnold, Lettre d'un docteur en theologie.
Brownii Causa Dei cont. Antisabbatarios.
——— Epistolæ.
Calovii (Abr.) Theses Theologicæ.
Colberg's Platonisch-hermetisches Christen.
Jaegeri (Ioan. Wolfgang.) Dissertationes.
Maresii Propemticon ad Ioan. Labadium.
Mayeri (Ioan. Frid.) Dissertationes.
Nifanii (Chris.) Matæologia Labadiana.
Pauli Examen errorum de Labadie.
Scheibler, Probe der Labadistischen Relig.
Wolzogenii (Ludov.) Opera.

Labadists, History of.

Arnold, Relation touchant Labadie.
——— Histoire Eccles. P. II. lib. 17.
Gregoire, Histoire des Sectes.
Hackenbergii Epistola de J. Labadie.
Histoire curieuse, de la vie, les vrais sentiments, &c.
Weismanni Hist. Ecclesiastica. P. II. sec. 17.

Lactantius.

Lactantii Opera.
Ammon, Lactantii opiniones de religione.
Cellarii Excerpta de vita Lactantii.
Falsteri Conspectus errorum Lactantii.
Fresnoy, Lactantii Vita.
Gereti (Georg.) Dissertationes.
Goldneri Vita Lactantii.
Kortholti Diss. de Cicerone Christiano.
Krebsii (J. A.) Dissertationes.
Merlin, Apologie de Lactance. (Written to refute what he regarded as calumnies in Bayle Dictionary.)
Nourrii (Nicol.) Dissertationes.
Rau, Diatribe de philosophia Lactantii.
Walchii Diatribe de L. ejusdemque stilo.
Winckleri Philologemata Lanctantiana.

Dalrymple's Trans. of L. on the death of persecutors.
Hailes' Trans. of Do.
Lardner's Credibility, &c. Part 2.
Mountain's Summary of the works of L.

Lamb of God. See SACRIFICE.

Jones' (Will., of Nayland) Sermons.

Lamaism.

Dinters, Diss. de religione Lamaica.
Edinburg Review. 93:206.
Littell's Living Age. 30:1.

Lamech.

Vansittart's Cain and Lamech: or a comparative view of the numbers seven and seventy times seven.

Language. See AFFILIATION, CONFUSION OF TONGUES, ORIGIN OF LANGUAGE.

Lapsed Christians.

Cyprian, Epistolæ.

Albaspinæi Observationes.
Dalœlus de Pœnis et satisfactionibus.
Rechenbergius de Iterata regeneratione.
Zentgravius de Conversione secunda.

The Church histories of EUSEBIUS, MOSHEIM, and SPANHEIM, are full on this subject; but the whole history of the controversy may be gathered from the Epistles of CYPRIAN, and MARINUS, *Vita Cyprianae.*

Latitudinarians.

The term is used by MOSHEIM as including

what some call *Low-Church men.* He enumerates as Latitudinarians, Chillingworth, Cudworth, Hales, Whichcot, Tillotson, &c. WALCH uses the term as nearly equivalent to Deists. See INDIFFERENTISTS.

Laughter. See GRAVITY, JESTING.

Law of God. See COMMANDMENTS, LAW OF MOSES.

Law of Nations. See ORIGIN OF LAWS.

Azuni, Origine et progrés du droit.
Burlemaqui, Droit naturel.
Cumberland, de Legibus naturæ.
Demangeat, Droit international privé.
Dufour, Droit maratime.
Grotius de Jure belli et pacis.
Hautefeuille, Droits et devoirs des nations neutres.
——— Droit maratime.
Heinecii Jus naturæ et gentium.
Klubner, Droit des gens modérne. 1861.
Leibnitz, Codex juris gentium.
Mably (G. B.), Œuvres.
Marten (Cha.), Manuel diplomatique.
Marten (G. F.), Droit des gens moderne.
Montesquieu, Esprit du lois.
Nau's Grundsätze des Volkerseerecht.
Ortolan, Régles internationales.
Petrushavecz, Droit international.
Pouget, Principes de droit maratime.
Proudhon, La guerre et la paix.
Puffendorf de Jure nat. et gentium.
Rayneval, Institutions du droit.
Vattel, le Droit des gens.
Villefort, Droit international.

Amer. Advocate of Peace. 1:64,333.
Amer. Biblical Repos. 5:1.
Bailey's International policy of the great Powers. In 1861.
Beller's Delineation of universal law.
Brit. and Foreign Review. 9:144.
Burlemaque on Natural law. Tr. by Nugent.
Bynkershoeck's Laws of war.
Chitty on the Law of nations.
Cobbet's (Wm.) Laws of nations.
Democratic Review. 21:23.
Doddridge's Lectures. Part 3, prop. 72.
Duane's Law of N. popularly considered.
Eden's Historical sketch of the international policy of Europe. 1823.
Edinburg Review. 71:161.
Fergus' (Henry) History of the Hebrews.
Flanders on Maritime law.
Godwin's Political Justice.
Grotius' Law of war and peace. (The edition of 1738, with the learned notes of Barbeyrac, is generally preferred.)
Grove's Moral Philosophy.
Heineccius' System of universal Law.
Hobbes' Moral and political Law.
Hunt's Merchants' Mag. 12:255.
Jenkins on Admiralty jurisdiction.
Kennedy's Hulsean Prize Essay. 1856. (The influence of Christianity on internat. law.)

Law of Nations—*continued.*

Mackintosh's (Sir J.) Law of nature and nat.
Macqueen's Chief points in the laws of war, neutrality, search, and blockade.
Marten's Law of Nature. Tr. by W. Cobbett.
Montesquieu's Spirit of Laws.
Museum of Foreign Literature. 37:289.
North Amer. Review. 6:310. 41:287. 44:16.
Polson's Principles of the law of nations.
Puffendorf's Laws, &c. Tr. by Kennett.
Rutherforth's Institutes of Natural law.
Sharp's (Granville) Law of nature.
Vattel's Law of nations.
Ward's History of the law of nations in Europe, from the time of the Greeks.
Wheaton's Elements of the law of nations.
Woolsey on International law.

Law of Nature. See LIGHT OF NATURE.

Ambrose, de Officiis.
Alberti Compendium Juris Naturæ.
Cicero, de Officiis.
——— de Legibus.
Crellii Ethica Aristotelica et Christiana.
Cumberland, de Legibus Naturæ.
Grotius (G.) de Principiis juris naturalis.
Grotius (H.) de Jure belli et pacis.
Heydenreich, über die Philosophie, &c.
Plato, de Legibus.
Puffendorf, de Jure naturæ.
——— de Officio hominis et civis.
Selden de Jure naturæ et gentium.
Sharrock de Officiis secundum naturæ jus.
Turrettini Dissertationes. Diss. viii—xi.

Buchanan's (James) Lectures.
Clark's (Sam.) Obligations of Nat. Religion.
Cobb's Bampton Lectures. 1783.
Conybeare's Reply to Tindall.
Cumberland's Law of N. Trans. by Towers. (A powerful refutation of Hobbes.)
——— ——— Translated by J. Maxwell. With Introduction, notes, &c.
Dawson's Origin and obligation of Law.
Erskine's (J.) Theol. Dissertations. Diss. 4.
Foster's (Dr. James) Discourses.
Hodge's (Walter) Elihu. Preface.
Mackintosh's (Sir J.) Law of N. and nations.
Morehead's (Robert) Sermons.
Parker's Divine authority of the law of nature. (Highly praised by LARDNER, who makes great use of it in the 39th chapter of his "*Testimonies.*")
Taylor's (Jer.) Ductor Dubitantium. Bk. 2.

Laws of Honor. See DUELLING.

Bluett's Laws of honor condemned.
Paley's (William) Sermons.

Laws of Moses. See CEREMONIAL LAW.

Arndtii Manuale legum Mosaicarum.
Baumgarten-Crusius de Lege morali Mosaica.
Bialoblotzky de Lege Mosaica.
Blume, Lex Dei. (A comparison of Roman and Mosaic law.)

Laws of Moses—*continued.*

Cunæi Republica Hebræorum.
Maimonides, More Nevochim.
Michaelis de Lege Mosaica.
Pastoret, Histoire de la legislation.

Barrow's (Isaac) Sermons.
Blackall's (Bp.) Sermons.
Bull's (Bp.) Discourses.
Dwight's Theology. Disc. 91.
Fergus' (H.) Institutions of Moses.
Howarth's Abiding obligation of the law.
Jones' (Wm., of Nayland) Sermons.
Lewis' Origines Hebraicæ.
Litton's Mosaic dispensation introductory to Christianity.
Lowman's Dissertations.
Maimonides' Reasons for the law of Moses. Tr. by Townley. Notes and dissertations.
Michaelis on the Law of Moses.
Rose's (Hugh) Hulsean Lectures. 1833.
Stanhope's Boyle Lectures. 1701.
Tilly's (William) Sermons.
Townley's (James) Reasons for the law of Moses. (From the More Nevochim; with notes and dissertations.)
Van Mildert's (Bp.) Sermons.

Lay Agency. See INDIVIDUAL EFFORT.

Lay Baptism.

Pro.

Tertulliani Opera (de Baptismo).
Thomas Aquinas, Summa Theologiæ.
Zanchii (Hieron.) Miscellanea.

Bingham's Hist. of the practice of the Chur.
Episcopal Magazine. 1:171.
Fleetwood's (Bp.) Judgment of the Church of England.
Hooker's Ecclesiastical Polity.
Whitgift's (Abp.) Works.

Con.

Brett's Doctrine of lay baptism.
——— Reply to Bingham's history.
Cosin's (Bp.) Letter to Mr. Cordell.
Dodwell on the Soul.
Hickes (G.) on Lay baptism.
Lawrence (R.) on Lay baptism.

Lay Preaching.

Campbell's (John) Jethro. (Prize Ess. 1839.)
Martin's Preacher sent.
——— Vindication of Do.
Mills' Local ministry of the Methodists.
Pearson's (Ed.) Admonition agt. Lay Pr'ng.
Poole's (Matt.) Quo warranto.
Presbyterian Review. 1:137.

Laying on of Hands. See CONFIRMATION.

Pro.

Keach's (Benj.) Works.

Con.

Danvers [or D'Anvers] on Baptism.
——— Treatise on laying on of hands.

Legends.

Acta Sanctorum. (60 volumes, folio.)
Baillet, les Vies des Saints.
Bonini Sanctuarium.
Giry, Vies des Saints. Continued by Guérin to 1862. (Immense.)
Haræi Vitæ Sanctorum.
Lipomani Vitæ Sanctorum.
Majoris Magnum speculum exemplorum.
Marigot, Vie des Saints.
Martene, Thesaurus Anecdotorum.
Mombritii Sanctuarium.
Ribadeneiræ Flos Sanctorum.
Roswidi Vitæ Patrum.
Ruinarti Acta primorum martyrum.
Salazari Anamnesis. (Immense.)
Surii Vitæ Sanctorum. (Next to the first named work, this is the most extensive.)
Voragini Legenda aurea.
Wicellii Hagiologium.

Villegas' Lives of the Saints.
Wright's L. current in the middle ages.

These worthless books are innumerable.

Lent Sermons. See FASTING.

Allestree's, Richard, Sermons.
Andrewes' Bp., "
Beveridge's, Bp., "
Bird's, Charles S., "
Blackall's, Offspring, "
Brownrig's, Bp., "
Burnett's, Gilbert, "
Cotes', Henry, "
Donne's, John, "
Fleetwood's, Bp., "
Gunnings', Bp., "
Hankinson's, Thomas E., "
Hare's, A. W., "
Hooper's, Bp., "
Horne's, Bp., "
Ken's, Bp., "
Neve's, Timothy, "
Oxford Lent Sermons. By eminent divines.
Patrick's, Bp., Sermons.
Porteus', Bp., Lent Lectures.
Secker's, Abp., Sermons.
Shuttleworth's, P. N., "
Smallridge's, George, "

Leonistæ. See CATHARI, WALDENSES.

Leprosy.

Altingii (Henric.) Dissertationes.
Clerici (J.) Dissertationes.
Maimonides, More Nevochim.
Wedelii (Geo. Wolfg.) Exercitationes.
Withofii (F. T.) Opuscula.
Calmet's Dissertations.
Maimonides' Law of Moses. Translated by Townley.

Leviathan. See BEHEMOTH, NATURAL HISTORY.

Baieri (Io. Guil.) Dissertationes.

Hasei (Theod.) Disquisitiones. Wood cuts. (Curious.)
Woergeri (Francisc.) Dissertationes.
Vansittart's Remarks, critical and philological, on Job, ch. 41. (Sometimes appended to his new translation of Psalm 49.)

Levitical Law. See CEREMONIAL LAW.

Levity. See CONSIDERATION, DEPORTMENT, GRAVITY, SOCIAL INTERCOURSE, SOBRIETY, THOUGHTFULNESS, WATCHFULNESS.

Lewdness. See CHASTITY.

Liberality. See ALMS, BENEVOLENCE.

Allen on Christian Beneficence.
Barrow on Bounty to the poor.
Boase's Tithes and offerings.
Dowling's (John G.) Sermons.
Gough's (Tho.) Surest way of thriving.
Pike (J.) on Christian liberality.
Porteus' (Bp.) Sermons.
Wells' Rich man's duty.
Woodhouse's (G. W.) Practical sermons.

Libertines.

Deylingii Observationes Sacræ.
Hardouin de Synagoga Libertinorum.

Liberty of Conscience. See CHRISTIAN LIBERTY, ESTABLISHMENTS, TOLERATION.

D'Aubigné, die religiöse Freiheit v. christlichen Standpunkte.
Jurieu, Maximes de Morales.
Saurin, sur les Droits de la conscience.
Simon (Jules) la Liberté de conscience.
Vinet's Freheit des religiosen Cultus.

American Quart. Review. 17:319.
Bayle's (P.) Commentary on Luke 14:23.
Beatson's Divine right to religious freedom.
Blackburn's Confessional.
Brook's History of religious liberty.
Brook & Steane's Results of an investigation of Protest. intolerance in Germany. 1854.
Brown's Rebuke to a ludicrous infidel. (The preface is a noble defence of liberty of conscience.)
Bunsen's Signs of the times. 1856.
Christian Disciple. 4:91.
Christian Examiner. 10:87,385.
Christian Review. 14:305.
Clarke's History of Intolerance.
Colebrook's (Geo.) Letters on Intolerance.
Eclectic Review. New Series. 10:337.
Edinburg Review. 21:293.
Fish's (Henry C.) Price of soul liberty, and who paid it.
Foster's (James) Sermons.
Fowler's (Bp.) Libertas Evangelicus.
Ibbot's Boyle Lectures. 1727.
Montesquieu's Spirit of laws.
Moyle's Doctrinal Works.
New Englander. 3:392. 6:194.

Liberty of Conscience—*continued.*

Niles' Register. 16:226. 23:261.
Pett (Sir P.) on Liberty of conscience.
Pickard's Discourses.
Piper's (Henry H.) Sermons.
Spirit of the Pilgrims. 4:117,326.
The Old Whig. Nos. 5,6,8,9,10.
Underhill's (E. B.) Tracts.
——— Struggles and triumphs of religious liberty.
Westminster Review. 2:1.
Whiteman on Religious liberty.
Williamson's (David) Lectures.

Life of Christ. See JESUS CHRIST.

Licentiousness. See CHASTITY, FORNICATION, PURITY, UNCLEANNESS.

Life of Faith. See WALK.

Light of Nature. See DEISM, EXISTENCE OF GOD, IDOLATRY, NATURAL THEOLOGY, NECESSITY OF REVELATION.

Chauvin, de Religione Naturali.
Creutzer, de Leibnitii doctrina.
Diogenes Laertius, de Vitis Philosophorum.
Fortlage's Darstellung und Kritik der Beweiss fur das Dasein Gottes.
Grotius de Veritate.
Hammii Scrutatio principii primi.
Hansennii (Petr.) Meditationes.
Mori (Henr.) Demonstrationes.
——— Enchiridion Ethicum.
Pfhänner, Systema Theologiæ Gentilis.
Platonis Opera. (De rebus divinis, &c.)
Plutarchi Moralia.
Poiretus de Deo.
Proclus de Theologia Platonica.
Puffendorf, de Officiis hominis et civis.
Reimar's (H. S.) Naturalische Religion.
Simon (Jules), Religion Naturelle.
Velthusii de Cultu naturali.
Vossius de Philosophia et Philosoph. Sectis.
——— de Theologia Gentili.
Walch's (C. W. F.) Natürlichen Gottesgelehrtheit.
Wolfii Theologia naturalis.

Abernethy's (John) Sermons.
Barr's Summary of Natural Religion.
Bates' (William) Works.
Baxter's (Andrew) Matho.
Blackwell's (Thos.) Sacred Scheme.
Bourne's (Samuel) Sermons.
Boyle Lectures for 1692,1695,1704,1713,1717, 1721,1747,1766,1778,1808,1847.
Boyle (Robt.) on the Veneration due to God.
Bridgewater Treatises.
Broughton's Christianity distinct from the religion of nature.
Brown's Natural and revealed relig. Bk. 1.
Bulkley (C.) on Natural Religion.
Bushman's Introd. to the study of nature.
Butler's Analogy of religion to nature.
Calamy on the Light of nature.
Charnock (Stephen) on Providence.

Light of Nature—*continued.*

Cheyne's Philos. principles of religion.
Christian Examiner. 52:117.
Chris. Month. Spectator. 4:249. 3:85.
Clarke's (S.) Boyle Lectures. 1704.
Conybeare's Defence of Revealed Religion.
Culverwell on the Light of Nature.
Cumberland's Laws of Nature.
Dick's Philosophy of Religion.
Dryden (J.) on Natural Religion.
Duncan's (J. S.) Botano-theology.
Duncan's (H.) Sacred Philosophy.
Durham's Astro-theology.
——— Physico-theology.
Edwards on the Causes of Atheism.
Ellis on the Knowledge of Divine things.
Erbury's Confutation of Deism.
Fiddes' Theologia Speculativa.
Foster's (James) Discourses on social virtue.
Gardner's (James) Sermons.
Gastrell on Natural religion.
Gerard's Evidences of nat. and rev. religion.
Glover's (P.) Tracts.
Greenfield's Connexion of nat. and rev. relig.
Hale's (Chief Justice) Knowledge of God.
Hall's (Robt.) Modern Infidelity.
Hallet's Future state not proved by the Light of Nature.
Halyburton's Insufficiency of natural relig.
Harris' Eight Sermons on the being of God.
Hey's (Dr. John) Lectures.
Hume's Dialogues on natural religion.
Jack's Mathematical Theology.
Kames (Lord) on Natural Religion.
Law's (W.) Theory of Religion.
——— Argument *a priori.*
——— Case of Reason fairly delineated.
Mackay's Progress of the intellect.
Mole's Obligations of Natural religion.
Morehead's Dialogues.
Nye on Natural and revealed religion.
Orr's (J.) Theory of religion.
Parker's Defence of natural and revealed religion.
Peabody's (A. P.) Lowell Institute Lectures. 1864.
Ramsay's Principles of religion.
Ray's Physico-theology.
Scott's Christian Life. Part 2.
Search. *See Tucker.*
Sherlock on Providence.
Simon on Nat. Religion. Trans. by Marsden.
Squier's Natural and revealed religion.
Stanley's Lives of the Philosophers.
Stillingfleet's Origines Sacræ.
Stuynoe's Salvation by Christ alone.
Sturm's Reflections on the works of God.
Sykes' Connection of nat. and rev. religion.
Taylor's (Jer.) Ductor dubitantium.
——— Necessity of faith in Christ.
Tennison against Hobbes.
Totham's Scale of truth.
Tucker's Light of nature pursued. (Profound and clear. First published under the name of Edward Search.)

Light of Nature—*continued.*

Tunstell's Natural and revealed religion.
Twells' Vindic. of the Gospel of Matthew.
Tytler's Essays on important subjects.
Wakefield on Public worship.
Warburton's Sermons at Lincoln Inn.
Watson's Popular evidences of nat. religion.
Watts' (Isaac) Berry Street Sermons.
Wayland's Elements of moral science. Ch. 7.
Whiston's Astronomical principles of relig.
Wilkes' (S. C.) Christian Essays.
Wilkins' Principles and duties of nat. relig.
Willatts on the Religion of nature.
Wilson's (Jos.) Letters on religion. (A good introduction to Butler's Analogy.)

Life a Pilgrimage.

Blunt's, Henry, Sermons.
Boyd's, John, Sermons.
Bradley's, Charles, Sermons.
Bull's, Bp., Sermons.
Bryant's, Matthew, Sermons.
Conybeare's, John, Sermons.
Dehon's, Bp., Sermons.
Duché's, Jacob, Sermons.
Girdlestone's, Charles, Sermons.
Hare's, J. C., Sermons.
Horne's, Bp., Sermons.
Potts', J. H., Sermons.
Skelton's, Philip, Sermons.
Walker's, Robert, Sermons.

Limits of Human Knowledge.
See PROVINCE OF REASON.

Little Sins. See VENIAL.

Liturgies. See BOOK OF COMMON PRAYER, FORMS OF PRAYER, REVISION OF LIT.

Pro.

Brometii (C. H.) Dissertationes
Friderici Liturgia vetus et nova. (Lutheran.)
Krehl's Evangelische Gebete.
Lorrain, l'Ancienne manière de prier.

Ashton's (Thomas) Sermons.
Barclay's (P.) Persuasive to the people of Scotland to overcome their prejudices.
Bennett's History of precomposed forms.
——— Letter to Robinson.
Bingham's Origines Sacræ.
Blackwood's Mag. 18:573.
Bowdler's (T.) Discourses on the Liturgy.
Bull's (Bp.) Works.
Christian Observer. 11:501.
Clagget's Answer to objections.
Croft's Bampton Lectures. 1786.
Durell on the Public worship of God.
Edwards' Theologia Reformata.
Faulkner on the Lawfulness of Liturgies.
Fisher s Defence of the English Liturgy.
Freeman's Principles of Divine Service.
Gorham on Public Worship. (Prize Essay.)
Hall's (Bp.) Polemic Works.
Hammond's Practical Discourses.
——— Defence of the L. of the Ch. of Engl.

Liturgies—*continued.*

Pro.

Hooker's Ecclesiastical Polity.
Jewell's (Bp.) Apology.
Lindsey's Vind. of the Church of England.
Mangey's (Thomas) Sermons.
Mant's Sermons before the Univ. of Oxford.
Maskell's Offices of the Church.
New York Review. 4:109.
Quarterly Review. 50:509.
Shuckford's (Samuel) Sermons.
Stebbings' (Henry) Sermons.
Taylor's (Jer.) Polemic discourses.
Watson's (Thomas) Sermons.
Wheatley on the Common Prayer.

Con.

Amer. Presbyt. Rev. 4:230.
Boyse's (Jos.) Theological works.
——— Remarks on Liturgies.
Brekell on the use of forms in public prayer.
Christian Exam. 49:258. 54:23.
Clarkson (David) on Liturgies.
Doddridge's Lectures. Parts 3d and 9th.
Dwight's Theology. Ser. 144.
Eclectic Rev. N. Series. 1:412.
Haldane (J. A.) on Social Worship. (Able.)
Harding's Reply to Jewell's Apology.
Jones' Essay on Public Worship.
King's Inventions of men in worship.
Orton's (Job) Lectures.
Owen (John) on Liturgies.
——— on Church Peace.
Pierce's Vindication of Dissenters.
Powell's (Vavassor) The Common Prayer book no divine service.
Robinson's (B.) Case of Liturgies.
——— Letter to Wm. Bennet.
Taylor on Public Worship.
——— Account of prayer.

Liturgies, History of. See CHRISTIAN ANTIQUITIES, RITES AND CEREMONIES.

Allatius de Libris eccles. Græcorum.
Assemanni Codex liturg. Orientalium.
Augusti's Christlichen Kunstgeschichte.
Bonæ Rerum Liturgicarum, etc.
Boquilot, Histoire de la liturgie.
Brandt's Homiletisch-liturgisches correspondenz-blatt.
Cave, de Officiis eccles. Græcorum.
De Vert, Explicatio hist. de ceremonies.
Eisenschmid's Einige Gebräuche.
——— Kirchengebräuche d. Protestanten.
Friderici Liturgia, vetus et nova.
Gavantii Thesaurus Rituum.
Gerberti Monumenta vet. liturgiæ.
Grancolas, Lit. d'Occident et d'Orient.
Hoffmanni Collectio rariss. et inedit, &c.
Koecheri Bibliotheca Liturgica.
Koehleri Principia theologiæ liturg.
Krazer de Apostolocis necnon antiquis eccles. occid. liturgiis. (Very complete.)
Lienhart de Antiquis liturgiis.
Lindani Libri ecclesiastici Latini.

Liturgies, History of—*continued.*

Mabillonii Antiqui libri rituales.
Martene, de Antiquis ecclesiæ ritibus.
Muller's Lexicon des Kirchenrechts.
Muratori Liturgia Romana vetus.
Renaudoti Lit. Orientalium collectio. (Contains fifty liturgies, some of them declared to be 1,400 years old; with learned dissertations and notes.)
Zaccariæ Bibliotheca Ritualis.

Bennet's Use of preconceived forms.
Bingham's Christian antiquities. Ch. 13–15.
Bray's Bibliotheca Parochialis.
Brerewood on Languages and religions.
Brett's Collection of liturgies.
Bunsen's Hippolytus and his age.
Clay's L. of Edward VI. and Elizabeth.
Comber's Rise and use of Liturgies.
Down's History of the Lit. and its revisions.
Eclectic Review. 95:236.
Frazier's Magazine. 23:33.
Hall's Reliquæ Liturgicæ. (12 liturgies, including the Middleburg, Saxon, Scotch, and American.)
Heylin's Miscellaneous Tracts.
Keeling's Liturgiæ Brittanicæ. (The six liturgies from the time of Edward VI. to Charles II., in parallel columns.)
Neale's History of the Eastern Church.
——— Translation of the liturgies of Mark, James, Clement, and Chrysostom.
Neale & Forbes' Ancient liturgies of the Gallican church; with introd., notes, &c.
New Englander. 1:469.
Schaff's Ancient Catholic liturgies.

In BRAY'S *Bibliotheca* is a list of the chief liturgies, of all ages. L'ESTRANGE, in his *Alliance of divine offices*, exhibits all the English Protestant liturgies; with various readings, and a running commentary. PAESINI *Liturg. orient. collectio*, gives those of the East. DANIEL, *Codex liturgicus*, gives those of the Papal, Lutheran, Oriental, and Reformed churches; with valuable notes. BRUNET gives those of various nations.

Lives of the Apostles. See APOSTLES.

Lives of the Fathers. See FATHERS.

Barbeyrac, de la Morale des Peres.
Gerhardi Patrologia.
Ildefonsus de Illustribus eccles. scriptores.
Martene, Thesaurus Anecdotorum.

Allen's Fathers of the first 5 centuries.
Blakey's (R.) Primitive fathers.
Butler's (Alban) Fathers and Martyrs. (Endeavors to exculpate them from the sharp censures of Barbeyrac.)
Cave's Lives of the F. of the first 3 cent.
——— Eminent F. of the 4th century.
Evans' Biography of the early church.
Le Clerc's Lives of the primitive Fathers.
Lupton's Glory of their times.
Wayne's Religious biography.

Lives of the Saints. See LEGENDS.

Locusts. See NATURAL HISTORY.

Bornemanni (Olaus.) Dissertationes.
Cellarii (Chris.) Schediasma historicum, &c.
Gleichius de Victu Ioannis.
Oldius in Domicilio, et victu Ioannis.
Rabii Exercitationes Philologicæ.
Stolbergius de Amictu et victu Ioannis.

Elsner's Com. on the New Testament.
Paxton's Illustrations of Scripture.
Sandys' (George) Travels.
Shaw's (Thomas) Travels.

Logic. See MIND.

Abicht's Philos. d. Erkenntnisse. 1791.
Albertus Magnus. 1494. (Several treatises in his "works.")
Aristotelis Ars Rhetoricæ.
——— Demonstratio Log. veræ.
Baumgarteni Acroasis Logica. 1761.
Berg's Epikritik der philosophie. 1805.
Caseii Summa vet. interpretum in universam logicam Aristotelis.
Campenellæ Philosophia rationalis. 1638.
Crousaz, Systéme de logique. 1725.
Degerando, de l'Art de pensèr. 1800.
Destutt, Elemens d'Idéologie. 1818.
Engel's Methode d. Vernunftlehre. 1780.
Ernsthausen's Inhalt der logischen Wahrheit. 1804.
Euler, Lettres a une princess. 1810.
Feverlini (J. G.) Dissertationes. 1712.
Fichté, Begriff d. Wissenschaftslehre. 1798.
Hegel (C. W. F.) Wissenschaft der Logic. 1816.
Hillegeri Institutiones logicæ eclecticæ.
Kant's Logik. 1800.
Krug's Denklehre, oder Logik. 1806.
Laromiguière, Leçons de Philosophie. 1815.
Leibnitzii Opera. 1768.
Malebranche, Recherche de la Vérité. 1700.
Ramus (P.), Institutiones Dialecticæ. 1545.
Reinhold's (K. L.) Kritik der Logic. 1789.
Rosenkreutz, Modifications de Logique.
Sluteri Anatomia logicæ Aristotelicæ.
Twesten's (A. D.) Logik. 1825.

Aristotle's Logic.
Bacon's (Sir Francis) Works.
Barron's Lectures on Belles lettres.
Belsham's Compendium of Logic.
Bentham's (Jer.) New system of Logic.
Blakey's (Robt.) Essay on Logic.
Bohour's Logic. (Examples from ancient and modern authors.)
Bosanquet's System of Logic.
Brown's (Francis) Logic.
Campbell's Philosophy of Rhetoric.
Christian Examiner. 40:263.
Christian Quart. Spectator. 7:322.
Coleridge on True and false reasoning.
Collard's Essentials of Logic.
De Morgan's First Notions.
Gambier on Moral evidence.
Glassford's Principles of evidence.

Logic—*continued.*

Hamilton's (Sir W.) Lectures on Logic.
Hill's System of Logic.
Houghton's Prodromus.
Kett's Logic. (Analysis of Aristotle.)
Latham's L. in its application to language.
Le Clerc's Art of reasoning.
Locke on the Human understanding.
Mansell's Prolegomena Logica. (The psychological character of logical processes.)
Mills' System of Logic.
Milton's (J.) Ars logica.
Moberly's Lectures on Logic.
Newman's (F. W.) Lectures.
Reid's Analysis of Aristotle's Logic.
Solly's (Tho.) Syllabus of Logic.
Tappan's (H. P.) Logic.
Tatham's Scale and chart of truth.
Thompson on the Laws of thought.
Waddington's Life of Ramus.
Walker (J.) on Logic.
Watts' Right use of reason.
Wesley's (C.) Guide to Syllogism.
Whately's Elements of Logic.
Whewell's History of inductive sciences.
——— Philosophy of Do.
——— Logic for the million.

See, at the end of ROBT. BLAKEY'S *Essay on Logic*, London, 1848, an alphabetical list of more than a thousand writers on this subject. Few of those here cited are named in that list. The author of *Reflections upon learning*, an able work of the last century, attributed to Mr. BAKER, states that between Albertus Magnus, and the time of the Reformation, "there have been twelve thousand authors that have commented on the books of Aristotle."

Logos. See CHRISTOLOGY.

Carpzovius de λογω Philonis non Johanneo adversaria.
Dorner's Entwickelung-Geschichte der Christologie.
Eusebii Preparatio Evangelica.
Kostlin's Lehrbegriff des Evangilium.
Lampe de Λογω υποστατικω, &c.
Meier, die Lehre von der Trinitat.
Misleri Theognosia.
Winzer, num quid discriminis inter τον λογον et το πνευμα intercedat.

Bryant's Sentiments of Philo Judæus.
Burton's Bampton Lectures. 1829.
Dawson's Moyer Lectures. 1773. (On the Texts in which the word occurs.)
Elmlicht's Theophania; or, pre-existent Messiah.
Howe's Critical Observations.
Kitto's Journal. 3:107.
Lady Moyer's Lectures. (Waterland, 1720; Felton, 1728; Seed, 1733; Dawson, 1764; and others.)
Lardner on the Logos.
Lowman's Tracts. Tract 3.

Logos—*continued.*

Lawrence's (Rich.) Dissertation on the Logos. (Often appended to his reflections on the Unitarian version.)
Luck's Dissertations.
Methodist Quar. Review. 11:377,536.
Pearson on the Creed.
Smith's (J. Pye) Scrip. test. to the Messiah.
Tucker's Light of nature pursued.
Upham's Letters on the Logos.
Watts' Dissertations. Diss. 4.
Whitaker's Origin of Arianism.
Whitby's Exposition of John Chap. 1.

Lollards. See WICKLIFFITES.

Gellenius de Admiranda sacra et civili, &c.
Gramaye, Antiquitates Belgicæ.
Sanderus Brabantia et Flandria illustratæ.
Walchii (J. G.) Miscellanea Sacra.

Apology for Lollard Doctrines. (Attributed to Wickliffe. Edited by Todd. 1842.)
Knox's (John) Works. (L. of Scotland.)
Mosheim's Ecclesiastical History.
Walch's Dissertation on the Lollards.

Lombards. See ALBIGENSES.

Long Life. See LOVE OF LIFE, OLD AGE.

Longsuffering of God. See PATIENCE.

Loquacity. See TONGUE.

Cooper's (Archdeacon) Sermons.
Dawes' (Abp.) Sermons.
Fell's (Bp.) The Ladies' calling.
Gouldburn's The idle tongue.
Morning Exercises at Cripplegate.
Reyner's Rules for the govt. of the tongue.
Richardson's (William) Sermons.

Lord's Day. See SABBATH.

Franke, de Diei dominici apud vet. Christianos.
Hartman, de Rebus gestis Christianorum.
Hengstenberg, Ueber den Tag des Herrn.
Liebetrut's Tag des Herrn.

Agnew (J. H.) on the Christian Sabbath.
Arnold's (Thomas) Sermons.
Barnes' (Albert) Practical Sermons.
Baxter's Chris. Sabb. (Reply to Whately.)
Baylee's Statistics and facts on the L.'s day.
Benson's (Charles) Lectures.
Bloomfield's Letters to the Inhabitants of London.
Brooks' Div. and moral oblig. of the L. day.
Brown's Sunday Thoughts.
Brown & Taylor's Discussion on the obligation of the Sabbath.
Bryan's (Matthew) Discourses.
Bulkley's (John) Discourses.
Burder's (H. F.) Lectures.
Burnet on the 39 Articles.
Burnside on the different sentiments entertained in Christendom in relation to the weekly Sabbath.

Lord's Day—*continued.*

Burton's Proper observance of the L.'s day.
Caudrey's Christian Sabbath.
Chalmers on the Christian Sabbath.
Christian Examiner. 30:92. 50:55.
Christian Monthly Spectator. 8:449,571. 9:225,393. 10:225.
Christian Observer. 16:315. 26:358.
Christian Quarterly Spectator. 4:334. 6:580.
Christian Sabbath, The. A series of discourses by
Dr. Rice, Origin and history.
Dr. Hague, Authority and perpetuity.
Dr. Ganse, Duties.
Dr. Adams, Benefits.
Dr. Vinton, Civil relations.

Close's (F.) Sermons.
Cooper's (Edward) Sermons.
Croly's (Dr. George) Sermons.
Dealtry's (Wm.) Sermons.
Dehon's (Bp.) Sermons.
Doddridge's Lectures. Part 9.
Dorrington's (Theoph.) Discourses.
Dwight's Sermons. Ser. 105.
Eclectic Review. 4th Series. 22:697.
Edwards' (Justin) Sabbath Manual.
Edwards' (John) Discourses.
Edwards' (Pres.) Works.
Estlin's Apology for the Sabbath.
Fairbairn's Theological Essays.
Farquhar's Torch of time. (To show the advant. of Sunday to the working classes.)
Fisher's History of the Sabbath day. (Its uses and abuses, with notices of the Puritans, Quakers, &c.)
Foster's (James) Discourses.
Gilfillan's (James) The Sabbath viewed in the light of reason, revelation, and history.)
Gilfillan's (S.) Essay. (Practical.)
Gilpin's (Wm.) Sermons.
Glasse's (G. H.) Sermons.
Guild on the Profanation, &c.
Hacket's (Bp.) Sermons.
Hakewell's Institution, End, Dignity, &c.
Hambleton's (John) Sermons.
Hengstenberg on the Sabb. Tr. by Martin.
Hessey's Bampton Lectures. 1860.
Heylin's (Peter) Hist. of the Sabbath, from the Apostles to the present. 1636.
Hill's (Robert) Discourses.
Hill's (M.) The Sabbath made for man. (Origin, history, principles, &c.)
Holden's (George) Christian Sabbath.
Hole's (Matthew) Discourses.
Hopkins' (Bp.) Discourses.
Horseley's (Bp.) Sermons.
Howlitt's (John) Sermons.
Hughes (Joseph) on the Christian Sabbath.
Humphrey on the Sabbath.
Ives' Sunday no Sabbath.
Jebb's (Bp.) Sermons.
Jenkins' (George) Sabbatismos.
Jepson on the Proper observance, &c.
Jones' (Wm., of Nayland) Sermons.
Kingdon's History, Obligation, &c.

Lord's Day—*continued.*

Knowles' (Thomas) Sermons.
Mant's (Bp.) Christian Sabbath.
McFarlane on the Authority, &c. (Discusses the question of civil enforcement.)
Mede's (Joseph) Sermons.
Miller's Physiology in harm. with the Bible.
Milner's (Isaac) Sermons.
North British Rev. 18:393.
Ollerenshaw's Sabbath labor is seventh day slavery. (Prize essay.)
Orton's (Job) Six Discourses on the Sabbath.
Owen's (John) Sermons.
Owen's (J. B.) Six Sermons on the Sabbath.
Parsons' (Joseph) Discourses.
Piret's (David) Ethics of the Sabbath.
Pocklington's (John) Sermons. (Sunday no Sabbath.)
Porteus' (Bp.) Sermons.
Princeton Review. 35:537.
Quinton's Antidote to the curse of labor.
Rush's (Judge) Charges.
Sharp's (Abp.) Discourses.
Sherman's Plea for the Sabbath.
Singleton's Duty of keeping holy the Sabb.
Skeeler's (Thomas) Discourses.
Skelton's (P.) Sermons.
Spirit of the Pilgrims. 2:142,198,331. 5:39,89.
Stopford's Scripture account of the Sabbath.
Symond's (J.) Enquiry into the design, &c.
Thorn's Lectures on the Christian Sabbath.
Treffrey's Christian Sabbath.
Turner's (J. M.) Sermons on the Lord's day.
Twisse's Christian Sabbath defended.
Umfreville's (Charles) Discourses.
Veale's (W.) Prize Essay on the Sunday question. 1854.
Venn's (Henry) Sermons.
Walker's (Robt.) Sermons.
Wardlaw's (Ralph) Discourses on the Sabb.
Webster's Sermons on the Sabbath.
Wells' Practical Sabbatarian.
Whately's Thoughts on the Sabbath. (Elicited replies from Baxter, Foster, Stopford, and others. He maintains thet the Sabbath is not a New Testament ordinance.)
White's Def. of the doct. of the Ch. of Engl.
Willison on the Sanctification of the Sabb.
Wilson's (Bp., of Calcutta) Discourses.
Wright on the Christian Sabbath.
Wroughton's (Charles) Discourses.
Wyman (R.) on the Lord's day.
Younger's Light of the week. (Prize essay.)

So many writers on the *Lord's day* call it the Sabbath, that it is impossible to separate, accurately, the references under these heads.

Lord's Prayer.

Cyprian, in Orationem Dominicam.
Origen, Περι ευχης.
Chrysostom, Homiliæ in Matt. Hom. XIX.
Tertullian, Opera.
Gregory Nyssen, in Orationem Dominicam.
Augustine, de Oratione Domini.

Lord's Prayer—*continued.*

Amyraldi (Moses) Exercitationes.
Arndt's (F.) Vaterunser.
Bonnet (L.), Sermons sur la prière, etc.
Brunner de Oratione Domini.
Chemnitii Harmonia evangelica.
Danæi Explicatio.
Harms' Vaterunser in 11 Predigten.
Marheineke's (Ph.) 13 Predigten.
Matthai's Auslegung des Vaterunser.
Noesseltii Exercitationes.
Olearii Observationes Sacræ.
Posner's (A. S.) Eilf Predigten.
Suiceri Observationes Sacræ. Cap. vii—xi.
Vitringa de Synagoge vetere.
Weber, Eclogæ Exeget. Loc. II, III.
Wernsdorfii Vindicia orationis Dominicæ.

Alison's (Archib.) Sermons.
Amer. Bibl. Repos. 5:190. 6:187.
Anderson's (Robert) The Lord's prayer a manual of religious knowledge.
Andrewes' (Bp.) Sermons. (19 on this subj.)
Atmore's Discourses on the Lord's prayer.
Baker's (Sir R.) Meditations.
Barrow's (Isaac) Sermons.
Baxter on the Lord's prayer.
Benson's Hulsean Lectures. 1820.
Berens' (Edward) Lent lectures.
Bevan on the Lord's prayer.
Bisse's (Tho.) Course of Sermons on L. P.
Blackall's (Bp.) Eight Sermons.
Booker's (L.) Lectures on the Lord's prayer.
Bradshaw on the Lord's prayer.
Busfield's (J. A.) Sermons on the Lord's Pr.
Cappe's Remarks upon important passages.
Clowe's (J.) Sermons.
Dallas' Ten practical Sermons.
Dalton's Expository discourses on the L. P.
Daniels' (W. B.) Sermons.
Denton on the Lord's prayer.
D'Espinassous' Law of life. Translated by Wilkinson.
Downame's Doctrine of practical praying.
Edwards' (E.) Lectures on the Lord's Prayer.
Edwards' (Bp.) Theologia Reformata.
Elton on the Lord's prayer.
Faringdon's (Anthony) Sermons.
Fenner on the Lord's prayer.
Fuller's (Andrew) Works.
Gouge's (William) Guide to God.
Griffith (T.) on the Lord's prayer.
Hale's (Sir Matt.) Contemplations.
Hebden's Dissertation on the Lord's prayer.
Hill's (G. D.) Sermons on the Lord's prayer.
Hole's Exposition of the Catechism.
Hooker on the Lord's prayer.
Hopkins' (Ezek.) Expos. of the Lord's Pr.
Horlock's (H. D.) Sermons on the Lord's P.
Howell's (William) Eleven Sermons on the Lord's prayer. ("One of his paragraphs would have been another man's sermon. His ideas were great ideas, and struggled forth in their naked and unadorned grandeur."—H. Melvill.)
Hugo's (Tho.) Sermons on the Lord's prayer.

Lord's Prayer—*continued.*

Jackson on the Lord's prayer.
Jones' (Joseph) Sermons.
Jortin's (John) Sermons.
Karslake's Expos., devotional and practical.
King's Exposition of the Lord's prayer.
Latimer's (Bp.) Sermons.
Leighton's (Abp.) Works.
Lloyd (J. C.) on the Lord's prayer.
Loraine's (N.) Lectures on the Lord's prayer.
Manton (Thomas) on the Lord's prayer.
Mangey's (Thos.) Practical Discourses.
Marriot's (Harvey) 8 sermons on the L.'s P.
Maurice's (F. D.) Sermons.
Mendham's Exposition and critical notes.
Nance (J.) on the L. P. and ten command'ts.
Nicholson on the Lord's prayer.
Packer's (J. G.) Ten sermons on the L.'s P.
Page on the Lord's prayer.
Perowne's Sermons on the Lord's prayer.
Pigott's (Edward) Discourses.
Rowsell's (T.) Sermons.
Saunders' (S.) Discourses on the Lord's Pr.
Scobell's (E.) Sermons on the Lord's prayer.
Scudder's Key of Heaven.
Sharp (G.) on the Lord's prayer.
Shepherd's Critical and practical elucidation.
Tapprel on the Lord's prayer.
Tholuck's Com. on the Serm. on the Mount.
Towerson on the Lord's prayer.
Trail's (Robert) Sermons.
Verschoyle's (Hamilton) Sermons.
West's Nature, design, and importance of prayer. (Contains several dissertations on the Lord's prayer.)
Williams' (W. R.) Lectures on the L. prayer.
Witsius on the Lord's prayer. Tr. by Pringle.
Wix's Sermons on the Lord's prayer.
Yates' Modell of Divinitie.

Lord's Supper. See FREQUENT COMMUNION, INFANT COMMUNION, CLOSE COMMUNION, PRIVATE COMMUNION, WEEKLY COMMUNION.

Augustine, Sermones.
Chrysostom, Homiliæ.
Gregory Nyssen, Opera.

Albertin, de Eucharistia. ("Against the Papal view, and the best treatise on this side of the question."—WIESMAN.)
Baxtorfii Dissertationes.
Bezæ Summa Doct. de re sacramentaria.
Blondell de Eucharistia veteris ecclesiæ.
Bullinger de forma, &c., Cœnæ Domini.
Burmanni Disputat. XVIII, de cœna.
Calvin de Cœna Domini.
Dorschei (Ioann. Geo.) Considerationes.
Du Moulin, Abrégé des Controverses.
Hammelii Collegium Testamentarium.
Harenbergii Theol. Dogm. ex monumentis Patrum.
Hildebrandi rituale Eucharistiæ vet. eccles.
Hoepfneri Isagoge ad salutarem usum cœna.
Hospiniani Historia Sacramentaria.
Hottingeri Dissertatio philologico-theolog.

Lord's Supper—*continued.*

Laroque, Histoire de l'Eucharistie.
Melancthonis Sententia de cœna Domini.
Mylii Tract. de Sacramento eucharistico.
Pfaffii Syntagma Dissert. Theologicarum.
Quenstedii Disputationes.
Rückert d. Abendmahl in d. alten Kirche.
Vorstii (Conrad.) Dissertationes.

Adams' (Neh.) The communion Sabbath.
Addison on the Lord's Supper.
Alexander's (J. W.) Young Communicant.
Allix's Preparation for the Lord's Supper.
——— Examination of the scruples of those who refuse to partake.
Am. Bibl. Repos. 2d Series. 2:1.
Arnold's (Thomas) Sermons.
Barrow's (Isaac) Discourses.
Bayard's Letters on the Lord's Supper.
Beachcroft's (Robert) Sermons.
Bell's (Wm.) Authority, nature, &c.
Belfrage's Sacramental addresses and meditations. (Excellent for young ministers.)
Bennett's (W. J. E.) History, doctrine, &c.
Beza's Discourses. (Chiefly agt. Papists.)
Bibliotheca Sacra. 1:499. 19:384.
Bickersteth's Guide and Compan. (Popular.)
Blair's Essays on important subjects.
Bloomfield's (Bp.) Sermons.
Bonnet's Meditations on the Lord's Supper.
Boston's Communion Sermons.
Bowyer (T.) on the Nature, end, &c.
Bradley's (Charles) Sermons at the Celebration, &c.
Brett's Nature and benefits of the Eucharist.
Brevant's Sacrament and Sacrifice. (Able.)
Brown's (J.) Communion Sermons.
Bullinger's Decades.
Calamy's (Benjamin) Sermons.
Campbell's Sacramental Meditations.
Card's (R.) Dissertat. on the Lord's Supper.
Cave's Primitive Christianity. Part 1, ch. 11.
Chaplin's (J.) The memorial hour.
Charlesworth on the Supper of our Lord.
Chris. Exam. 11:203. 13:261.
Chris. Monthly Spect. 4:66,476. 10:203.
Clarke (Adam) on the Eucharist.
Clarke's (Dr. S.) Sermons.
Cleaver's (Bp.) Sermons.
Clowe's Design of the Lord's Supper.
Comber's Companion to the Altar.
Cooper's (Edward) Sermons.
Cotton's (R. L.) Lectures.
Cranmer's (Abp.) Def. of the true doctrine.
Cudworth's True notion of the L.'s Supper.
Dehon's (Dr. T.) Sermons.
Dodsworth's (William) Sermons.
Doolittle's Treatise on the Lord's Supper.
D'Oyly's (George) Sermons.
Drum on the Lord's Supper.
Duncan's Communicant's assistant.
Dwight's Theology. Ser. 160 and 161.
Dyke's Worthy Communicant.
Earle's Sacramental Exercises.
Edwards' (Pres.) Works.
Enfield's (William) Sermons.

Lord's Supper—*continued.*

Erskine's (R.) Sermons on sacram. occasions.
Erskine's (Ebenez.) Sacramental sermons.
Erskine's (J.) Theological Dissert. Diss. 5.
Falconer's Devotions.
Faringdon's (Anthony) Sermons.
Featley's Grand sacrilege of the Ch. of Rome.
Flavel's Sacramental Meditations.
Fleetwood's Reasonable Communicant.
Ford's (Jas.) Devotional Communicant.
Francklin's (Thomas) Sermons.
Frith's (John, the Martyr) Works.
Gardner's (Dr. John) Sermons.
Gibson on the Lord's S. (Often reprinted.)
Girdlestone's (Charles) Seven Sermons.
Gleig's Guide to the Lord's Supper.
Goode's Nature of Christ's presence, &c.
Goodwin's Evangelical Communicant.
Gordon's (Adam) Sermons.
Gray's Communion Sermons.
Grierson's Doct. and practical Treatise, &c.
Grotius' Treatise on the Lord's Supper.
Grove on the Lord's Supper.
Halley (Robt.) on Symbolic institutions.
Halyburton's 10 Sermons before and after.
Haweis' Communicant's companion.
Hawker's (Robt.) Sacramental Meditations.
Henry's Communicant's companion. (Among the best known.)
Hesketh on Eating and drinking unworthily.
Hewlett's Manual of Instruction, &c.
Hildersham on the Lord's Supper.
Hoadley's Nature and end of the Supper. (Gave rise to much controversy. A list of numerous writers who engaged in it, is given in HORNE'S *Catalogue of Queen's College library*.)
Horneck's Crucified Jesus. (Excellent.)
Hunter's (Dr. Henry) Sermons.
Hutchinson's (R.) Works. (Parker Soc. pub.)
Ibbetson's Plain and affectionate discourses.
Immen's Pious communicant encouraged.
Jackson on the Lord's Supper.
Jefferys' (Dr. John) Sermons and tracts. (Collects and paraphrases all the passages in the New Testament where the subject is mentioned.)
Johnson's (J.) Unbloody sacrifice. (Gives the sentiments of the first four centuries.)
Kidder's Convivium Celeste.
King's Sacramental devotions.
——— Morsels of Criticism.
Kittlewell's Help to worthy communicants.
Knox's (Vicessimus) Nature, Efficacy, &c.
Lake's Guide to the Lord's Supper.
Larroque's History of the Eucharist. (Collects passages from writers in every century, and upon every question connected with the Lord's Supper.)
Law's Demonstrations of gross errors, &c. (Reply to Hoadley.)
Lisle's Testimony of Antiquity.
Maclear's Witness of the Eucharist. (Norrisian prize essay. 1863.)
Masillon on the Proper dispositions, &c.

Lord's Supper—*continued.*

Mason's First ripe fruits.
Mede's (Joseph) Sermons.
Morice (W.) on the Lord's Supper.
Morning Exercises at Cripplegate.
Morrison's Counsels for the Communion Table. (Against Hoadley.)
Oakley's (Frederick) Sermons.
Ogden's (Samuel) Sermons.
Orme's Ordinance of the L. S. illustrated.
Orton's Sacramental Meditations.
Osterwald's Duties of communicants.
Owen's (John) 25 Sacramental discourses.
Patrick's Necessity, end, and manner, &c.
Pierce's (S. E.) Twenty-two discourses. (Much esteemed.)
——— Essay on the Eucharist.
Pilling's Discourses on the Sacraments.
Princeton Rev. 12:14. 20:227.
Proudfit's Sacramental Sermons.
Prynne's Vindic. of the free admission both of regenerate and unregenerate.
Randall's 23 Sermons on the Lord's Supper.
Rawlett on the Lord's Supper.
——— on Covenanting with Christ.
Reynolds' (Bp.) Meditations on the Lord's Supper. ("Displays stupendous erudition."—BRITISH CRITIC.)
Ridley's (Bp.) Christian Passover.
Roberts' Communicant instructed.
Robertson's Letters and Dialogues.
Sellers' Week's preparation for the Lord's S.
Sharpe's (Thomas) Sermons.
Shower's Sacramental Discourses.
Skelton's (P.) Sermons.
Smith's (Samuel S.) Sermons.
Smithie's Non-Communicant.
South's (Robert) Sermons.
Spalding's Synaxis Sacra.
Stoughton's Trew Judgemente of a *Chyrstyan*, agreeing with Scripture, and moost Catholycke and trew dyffinicyon of the Doctours.
Sykes' Rational Communicant. (Many editions. Suited to humble capacities.)
Taylor's (Jer.) Christian consolation.
——— Life of Christ. Disc. 19.
——— Worthy Communicant.
Taylor's (J.) True doctrine of the Eucharist. (Replies to Archdeacon Wilberforce, and most ably.)
Temple on the Lord's Supper.
Thayer's (Elihu) Sermons.
Thompson's (Henry) Forty addresses.
Trott on the Lord's Supper.
Tyndale's Works. (Pub. by the Parker Soc.)
Vaux's Bampton Lectures. 1826.
Vides on the Lord's Supper.
Walters' Discourses on Isaiah, Ch. 55.
Warburton's Rational account of the nature, end, &c.
Warren on the Supper. (Reply to Hoadley.)
Waterland's Doctrine of the Eucharist. (Against Hoadley.)
Watson on the Lord's Supper.
Watts' (Isaac) Works.

Lord's Supper—*continued.*

Whiston on the L. S. (Against Hoadley.)
White (Alex.) on the Lord's Supper.
Wilberforce's Doct. of the Eucharist. (High Church.)
Willet on the Supper.
Williams (W. R.) on the Lord's Supper.
Willison's Meditations and Sermons.
——— Catechism for Communicants.
Wilson's Introduction to the Lord's Supper.
Wilson's (Dan.) Addresses to young persons.
Wrangham's (Francis) Sermons.

The books on this theme amount to thousands. A large number of them belong to the Popish controversy.

Lost Tribes. See TEN TRIBES.

Lots. See GAMING.

Atterbury's (Lewis) Sermons. (On games of chance.)
Balmford's (James) Reply to Gataker on L.
Down's Defence of lots in light matters.
Gataker's (Tho.) Historical and theological treatise on the use of lots. (Eminent in all he undertook.)
——— Defence of the treatise on lots against J. B.
Hall's (J. V.) Nature and use of lots. (Strong against playing cards.)
Mason's (J. M.) Christian Magazine.

Lot's Wife.

Baumanni (M.) Thesaurus.
Clerici (Ioann.) Dissertationes.
Fischeri Statua Salina.
Grammii Exercitationes.
Tieroff de sacris Judæorum vinculis.
Witsii Exercitationes Academicæ.

Fiske's (George) Sermons.
Le Clerc's Dissertations. Tr. by Brown.
Philman's Dissertations.

Lotteries.

[Coudrette] Dissertation Theologique.
Amer. Quart. Review. 21:355.
Christian Monthly Spect. 8:196.
Christian Observer. 1:579.
Doyle's Five years in a lottery office.
Meikle's Solitude sweetened.
More's (J. C.) Six years in a lottery office. (A vivid exposure.)
North Amer. Review. 37:494.
Ridgeley's Body of divinity.
Tyson's (J. R.) L. system of the U. States.

Love of Country.

Dietz's Versuch über d. Patriotismus.
Müller (J. F.), Ueber Patriotismus.

Abercrombie's Philos. of the moral feelings.
Adams' (William) Sermons.
Barker's (John) Sermons.
Barrow's (William) Sermons.
Berkley's (Bp.) Sermons.

Love of Country—*continued.*

Bolingbroke's (Lord) Letters.
Brougham's (John) Sermons.
Bulkley's (Benjamin) Sermons.
Burney's (C. P.) Oxford prize Essay. 1809.
Burnside's Religion of mankind.
Cecil's Serm. before the St. Andrew's Assoc.
Conybeare's (John) Sermons.
Cook's (John) Sermons.
Davies' (Pres.) Sermons.
Fawcett's (Jos.) Sermons. (Why Christ did not inculcate patriotism.)
Foster's (James) Sermons. (Same subject.)
Fuller's (Andrew) Sermons.
Hewlett's (John) Sermons. (The Christian hero.)
Hutton's (F. H.) Discourses.
Jortin's (John) Sermons.
Leland's (Thomas) Sermons.
Mason's (William) Sermons.
Milne's Christian Patriot.
Munkhouse's Occasional discourses.
Nance's (John) Sermons.
New England Magazine. 6:318.
Price's (Richard) Sermons.
Smith's (Sam. Stanhope) Sermons.
Smith's (Sydney) Sermons.
Southern Literary Messenger. 8:600.

Love of God.

Jurieu (P.), de L'Amour divin.
Rechenbergii (Adam.) Dissertationes.
Saurin (E.) de l'Amour de Dieu.
Scharf's (G. B.) Entheiligtes Gotteshaus.

Alford's (Dean) Sermons.
Barnes' (Albert) Practical Sermons.
Butler's (Bp. Joseph) Sermons. (Profound.)
Clarke's (Dr. Samuel) Sermons.
Clarkson's (David) Sermons.
Cruso's (Timothy) Sermons.
Eadie (Dr. John) on Divine love. (Noble.)
Gisbourne's (Tho.) Enquiry respecting love as one of God's attributes.
Hall's (Robt. Sen.) Help to Zion's travellers.
Hastings' (Henry J.) Sermons.
Kirk's (Edward N.) Sermons.
Le Bas' (Cha. W.) Sermons.
Muston's (C. R.) Sermons.
Peabody's (A. P.) Lectures before the Lowell Institute.
Stanhope's Augustin on the love of God.
Tindall's (The Martyr) Works.
Watts' (Isaac) Sermons.
Whitby's (Daniel) Sermons.

Love of Life.

Abernethy's (John) Sermons.
Barnes' (D.) Sermons.
Chevallier's (Temple) Discourses.
Hall's (Robert) Sermons.

Love of Novelty.

Cawood's (John) Sermons.
Newton's (Bp.) Dissertations.

Love of Pleasure. See PARABLE OF THE PRODIGAL SON, PLEASURE.

De Joux, Predication du Christianisme.

Barker's (John) Sermons.
Capp's Devotional discourses.
Chandler's (Samuel) Sermons.
Dorrington's (Theophilus) Sermons.
Hoole's (Joseph) Sermons.
Ibbot's (Benjamin) Sermons.
Irving's (Edward) Sermons.
Pearson's (Hugh) Sermons.
Secker's (Abp.) Sermons.
Tucker's Light of nature pursued.
Van Mildert's (William) Sermons.

Love of Praise. See FAME.

Appleton's Works. (Addresses at Commencement.)
Blackall's (Offspring) Sermons.
Blair's (Hugh) Sermons.
Hurd's (Bp.) Sermons.
Jortin's (John) Dissertations. Diss. 4.
Mason on Self-knowledge.
Montgomery's (Robt.) God and man. (Able.)
Morning Exercises at Cripplegate. (Hurst's.)
Noel's (Gerard T.) Sermons.
Oliver on the Pursuit of happiness.
Rose's (Hugh) Sermons.
Smith's (Sam. Stanhope) Sermons.
Thompson's (J. P.) Lectures to young men.
Trapp's (Joseph) Sermons.
Van Mildert's Sermons at Lincoln's Inn.
Venn's (John) Sermons.
Wayland's (D. S.) Sermons.

Love of the World. See WORLDLINESS.

Love of our Neighbor.

Bourdaloue, Sermons.
Feverlin's (C.) der Schuldigen Liebe, etc.
Franckius' Bewegungsgründen zu Beoebachtung, etc.

Barrow's (Isaac) Sermons.
Bather's (Edward) Sermons.
Berens' (Edward) Sermons.
Boyse's (Joseph) Sermons.
Butler's (Bp.) Sermons.
——— Sermons on public occasions.
Candlish's Two great commandments.
Caryl's (Joseph) Sermons.
Clarke's (Dr. Samuel) Sermons.
Dick's Philosophy of religion.
Evans (Dr. John) on Christian temper.
Gresley's (William) Sermons.
Hastings' (H. J.) Parochial sermons.
Horsely's (Bp.) Sermons.
Kirwan's (W. B.) Sermons.
Milner's (Joseph) Sermons.
Morning Exercises at Cripplegate. (Sermon by Milward.)
Morony's (Joseph) Sermons.
Neal's (D.) Berry Street Sermons.
Secker's (Abp.) Sermons.
Sherlock's (Bp.) Sermons.
Smith's (Theyre) Sermons.
Thompson's (Edward) Sermons.
Tillotson's (Abp.) Sermons.
Whichcot's (Bp.) Sermons.
Whitaker's (Edw. W.) Sermons.
Wilson's (Thomas) Sermons.

Love to Christ.

Blundel's (Thomas) Sermons.
South's (Robert) Sermons.
Vaughn (Henry) on the Fruits of the Spirit.

Love to Enemies. See FORGIVENESS.

Allestree's (Richard) Sermons.
Balguy's (John) Discourses.
Blackall's (Bp.) Sermons.
Blair's (James) Sermons.
Burton's (Hezekiah) Sermons.
Butts' (Thomas) Sermons.
Fawcett's (Joseph) Sermons.
Fuller's (Andrew) Works.
Jortin's (John) Sermons.
Scholefield's (Radcliffe) Sermons.
Scougal's (Henry) Discourses.
Seed's (Jeremiah) Sermons.
Skelton's (P.) Sermons.
South's (Robert) Sermons.
Stock's (Gabriel) Sermons.
Tillotson's (Bp.) Sermons.
Waterland's (Bp.) Sermons.
Waters' (Edward) Sermons.
Zollikoffer's (Geo.) Sermons.

Love to God.

Saurin de l'Amour de Dieu.

Abernethy's (John) Sermons.
Amory's Dialogues on Devotion.
Atterbury's (Lewis) Sermons.
Barrow's (Isaac) Sermons.
Bather's (Edward) Sermons.
Baxter's (Arthur G.) Sermons.
Beattie's Elements of moral science.
Beveridge's (Bp.) Sermons.
Binnings' (Hugh) Sermons.
Boyle's (Hon. Robt.) Seraphic love.
Burnet's (Gilbert) Sermons.
Butler's (Joseph) Sermons.
Candlish's (R. S.) Two great commandm'ts.
Cappe's (N.) Devotional Discourses.
Christian Observer. 11:685.
Clarke's (Dr. S.) Sermons.
Davies' (Pres. Samuel) Sermons.
Dick's Philosophy of Religion. Ch. 1.
Donne's (John) Sermons.
Dwight's Theology. Disc. 92.
Erskine's (Ebenezer) Sermons.
Evans' Sermons on Christian temper.
Fuller's Calvinistic and Socinian syst. comp.
Grove's Ethics.
Hall's (Bp.) Devotional works.
Hall's (Robert) Sermons.
Heber's (Bp.) Sermons.
Jortin's (John) Sermons.
Joyce's Love to God the perfection of Christian morals.
Kollock's (S. K.) Sermons.

Love to God—*continued.*

Lake's (Bp.) Nine sermons.
Le Bas' (C. W.) Sermons.
Moberly's Law of the Love of God.
Morning Exercises at Cripplegate. Vol. 1. (Sermon by Annesley.)
Neve's (Timothy) Sermons.
Paley's Principles of Moral Philosophy.
——— Sermons.
Porteus' (Bp.) Sermons.
Romaine's (William) Sermons.
Scott's Christian Life.
Secker's (Abp.) Sermons.
Seed's (Jeremiah) Sermons.
Sherlock's (Bp.) Sermons.
Shuttleworth's (P. N.) Sermons.
Spring's Essays on Chris. character. Ess. 6.
Van Mildert's Sermons at Lincoln's Inn.
Watts on the Passions.
Weston's (Bp.) Sermons.
Wilson's (Thomas) Sermons.
Wright's Great Concern.
Zollikoffer on the Evils in the world.

Love to Men. See LOVE OF NEIGHBOR.

Love-Feasts.

Henchelii de Agapis vet. Christianorum.
Kestner Geheime Weltbund der Christen.
Quistorpius de Agapis nascentis ecclesiæ.
Schenckii Dissertationes.
Schlegelii (Christoph.) Dissertationes.
Schurzfleischius de veteri Agaparum ritu.
Stolbergii (Balthas.) Dissertationes.

Council of Carthage.
Council of Laodicea.
Edinburg Encyclopedia. Art. Agapæ.
Hallet's Notes on Scripture texts.
Jones' Biblical Cyclopedia. Art. Agapæ.

Loyola. See JESUITS.

Allegambe, Bibliotheca.
Bartoli, Histoire de St. Ignace.
Beavais, Vie de St. Ignace.
Bohours, " "
Bussier, " "
De Silva, Hist. de Dom. Inigo de Guipuscoa chevalier de la vierge. (Satirical history of Loyola.)
Hane's Leben und Thaten Ig. Loyolä.
Maffæi Vita et mors St. Loyola.
Orlandini Hist. Soc. Jesu. Pars I.
Pasquier, Cat. des Jesuites. Chap. 17.
Possino de Vita et morte Ignatii.
Ribadeneire, Vie de Loyola.

Amer. Eclectic Review. 4:351.
Bonhours' Life of Ignatius.
Eclectic Rev. 4th Series. 26:84.
Edinburg Review. 75:161.
Foreign Review. 5:271.
Museum of For. Lit. 4:319.
N. Amer. Review. 59:412.
Princeton Review. 26:647.
Retrospective Review. 9:39.

Stillingfleet's Works.
Taylor's (Isaac) L. and the early Jesuits.
Taylor (W. E.) on Popery.
Wharton's Enthusiasm of the Ch. of Rome.

Luciferians.

Luciferi Opera omnia quæ extant.
Hieronymi Dialogus adv. Luciferianos.

Luke. See LIVES OF THE APOSTLES.

Clauswitzii Diss. de Luca evang. medico.
Frischii Dissertationes.
Kirstenii Vitæ Evangelistarum quatuor.
Kochleri Sanctus Lucas Evangelista.
Schlichteri Ecloga Historica.
Spanheimii Exercitationes Academicæ.
Winkleri (Ioann. Dieter.) Dissertationes.

Dunster (C.) on McKnight's hypothesis of the date of Luke's Gospel.

Lukewarmness. See BACKSLIDING.

Bramston's (Dr. William) Sermons.
Burrow's (E. J.) Hours of devotion.
Christian Examiner. 1:13.
Collison's (M. A.) Sermons.
Cooper's (Edward) Sermons.
Davies' (Samuel) Sermons.
Erskine's (John) Sermons. (2 on this subj.)
Fellowes' (Robt.) Religion without Cant.
Fuller on Spiritual declension and the means of revival.
Gardner's (John) Sermons.
Gatty's (Alfred) Sermons.
Jackson's (Miles) Sermons.
Masillon's Sermons.
Mason (John) on the Human virtues.
Monsell's (C. H.) Sermons.
Morning Exercises at Cripplegate. (Sermon by Matt. Sylvester.)
Oakley's (Frederick) Sermons.
Pictet on Religious Indifference.
Skelton's (Philip) Sermons.
Taylor's (Jeremiah) Sermons.
Winslow's Personal declension and revival.
Zollikoffer's Sermons on prevalent vices.

Lusts of the Flesh. See CONCUPISCENCE, LEWDNESS, LOVE OF PLEASURE, SENSUALITY, &c.

Luther. See REFORMATION.

Audin, Hist. de la vie de Luther.
Becker's M. Luther in den Hauptzugen seines Lebens geschildert.
Buchholtz's Aufenthalt in Worms. April, 1521.
Cochlæi Commentatio de actis et scriptis M. L. (Papal.)
Danhaveri Memoria thaumasiandri L.
Effner's Luther's Lebengeschichte.
Fabricii Centifolium Lutheranum.
Forstmanni Vita Lutheri.
Hennige's Lebenslauf Luther.
Hennegii Sanctus thaumasiander Lutherus.
Hernschmidii Vita Mart. Lutheri.

Luther—*continued.*

Junckneri Vita L. et successorum.
Keil's M. Luther's Lebens Umstände.
Kies' (Ludwig) Luther's Leben und Tod.
Kirchmayeri Disquisitio historica de M. L.
Klein (C.), L. consideré comme predicateur.
Konig's M. Luther d. Deutsche reformator.
Kock, Ehrengedächtnis.
Ledderhose's M. Luther, nach seinem äussern u. innern Leben Dargestellt.
Mattherii Historia Martini Lutheri.
Melanchthonis Hist. vitæ Lutheri.
Meurer's L.'s letzte Lebenstage, Tod, und Begräbniss.
Michelet, Hist. de la vie de Luther.
Niemeyer's M. L.: sein Leben und Wirken.
Pfizer's Leben Luther's.
Schoepffer's Anverbrandter Luther.
Selnecceri Vita Lutheri.
Spieker's Geschichte Dr. M. Luthers.
Spangenberg's Predigten von Luther.
Stang's Luther: sein Leben und Wirken.
Ukert's Luther's Leben.
Vogel, Bibliotheca Lutherana.
Zeibichii Electa hist. vitæ et mortis, etc.

Adams' (C.) Words that shook the world; or Luther his own biographer.
Amer. Bibl. Repos. 3d Series. 1:130. 2:191. 3:553,594.
Atterbury (F.) on the Spirit of Luther.
Bell's Colloquia Mensalia.
Blackwood's Mag. 25:26,200.
Christian Examiner. 27:402. 30:148. 32:19. 43:98. 45:170.
Eclectic Mag. 6:1.
Edinb. Rev. 7:354. 68:145. 82:50.
Fox's (John) Acts and monuments.
Hare's Vindic. of L. from his recent English assailants. 1855. (Wm. Hamilton, Hallam, Ward, Newman, &c.)
Life of Martin Luther; by Bowers.
——— ——— by Burkhardt.
——— ——— by Croley. 50 plates.
——— ——— by Cubitt.
——— ——— by D'Aubignè.
——— ——— by Gelzer.
——— ——— by Haynes.
——— ——— by Hazelin.
——— ——— by Konig.
——— ——— by Martyn.
——— ——— by Meurèe.
——— ——— by Michelet.
——— ——— by Riddle.
——— ——— by Sears.
——— ——— by Stork.
——— ——— by Tischer.
——— ——— by Worsley.
London Quart. Review. 3:201.
Museum of For. Lit. 28:271. 29:446. 35:321.
North Amer. Review. 63:433.
Scott's (J.) Luther, and the L. reformation.
Southern Lit. Messenger. 4:596.
Stephens' (Sir James) Essays.
Tulloch's Leaders of the Reformation.

See a notice of "all the extant works referring to the labors of Martin Luther," in VOGEL, *Bibliotheca Biographica.*

Lutheranism. See AUGSBURG CONFESSION, CONSUBSTANTIATION.

Pro.

Lutheri Opera. (Many editions; that of Halle, 1740–1750, in 24 volumes, is deemed as good, on the whole, as any.)
Albert's die Gründliche Widerlegung eines pæbstlichen Buchs.
Augusti's Syst. der Christlichen Dogmatik.
Bahrd, Systema Theologiæ.
Balduini Apologia pro Augustana confess.
Bretschneider's Handbuch der Dogmatik.
Chemnitzii Loci Theologici.
Confessio Doctrinæ Saxonicarum ecclesiarum. (The famous confession drawn up by Melancthon, Bugenhagen, &c.)
Fabricii Harmonia confess. Augustanæ.
Francke, Libri symbolici Ecc. Lutheranæ.
Franzii Disputationes.
Gerhardi Loci Theologici. ("The Coryphæus of Lutheranism."—LOWNDES.)
Hardtii Historia Reformationis.
Heinrich, Lutheri Theologia sincera.
Heppe, Confess. fidei Eccl. reformatæ.
Hoffkuntz's Lehr und Wehrcatechismus.
Hulsemani Conf. August. vindicans.
Hunnii Opera. (Very bitter agt. Calvinists.)
Koecheri Opera.
Krackewitzii Theses Theologicæ.
Loescher's Reformationsacten.
Masius, Défence de la rel. Luthérienne.
Melancthonis Opera. (Often reprinted. His "Loci Communes" passed through fifty editions in his lifetime.)
Mueller der Anti-Bretschneider.
Phillippi, Kirchliche Glaubenslehre.
Schrœder's Unterricht.
Seckendorf, Commentarius historicus et apologeticus de Lutheranismo. (Reviews all Luther's writings, and gives copious extracts.)
Strigelii Loci Theologici.
Twesten's Vörlesungen über d. Dogmatik.
Waltheri Demonstratio.
Zeitschrift für die Lutherische Theologie.

Bretschneider's Manual of doct. theology.
Buddeus' Exhibition of religion, as professed in the Lutheran Church.
Calixtus' Adjudication of theolog. controv.
De Wette's Doctrinal System.
Gerhard's Catholic Confessions.
Hunn's Doctrines of the Lutheran Church.
Luther's Works. Trans. by H. Cole. 10 vols.
Schmidt's Dogmatic of the Lutheran Church.
Schmucker's Lutheran Manual. (Illustrates the Augsburg Confession, and gives the forms of govern't and discipline in the L. Churches of the U. States, as in 1855.)
——— Popular Theology.
——— Vindic. of American Lutheranism.
——— Church of the Redeemer.

Lutheranism—*continued.*

Con.

Abbadie, Verité de la relig. reformé.
Andreæ (Jacob.) Widerlegung d. pezelichen Berichts.
Andreæ (Conrad) Zwolff underschiedliche Tractatlein aus Luther's Schrifften Zusammen getragen. (Satirical.)
Arcudii Libri vii de Concordia Ecc. Occid. et Orient. in Septem sacramentum administratione.
Botsacci Παρα Βαλλεταιρος.
——— Reformatum pseudo-Augustanum.
Cancerin's Rettung der Augspurgischen Confession.
Corvin's Richtige Antwort aufein gedrucktes Bittschreiben eines Calvinisten.
Eckhardi Fasciculus Controv. theologicarum. (Contains the opinions of Zuingle, Calvin, Beza, Piscator, and many others, arranged under the various controverted heads.)
Fischeri Assertionis Lutheranæ confutatio.
Gabillon, la Verité de la relig. reformée.
Hutteri Calvinista auto-politicus.
Lintrupii Specimen Calumniæ.
Mentzeri Collatio Augustanæ Confessionis cum doctrina Zuinglii, Calvini, Bezæ, et sociorum.
Mueleni Veritas relig. Christ. reformatæ.
Reiser's Wiederhotter Beweis.
Saluti Recens Lutheranarum Assertionum oppugnatio.
Treug, Calvinisches Todbett.
Vervesii Disputationes Viginti.
Vorstii Apologia pro ecclesiis orthodoxis.
Wernsdorfii (Gottl.) Demonstratio.

Brett on Lutheranism.

Lutheranism, History of.

Augusti, Gesch. und Statistik d. evangelischen kirche. (To 1837.)
Feverlini Bibliotheca Symbolica. (A learned account of the various confessions of faith, with the editions, versions, &c., to 1766.)
Harnack's Lutherische kirche in Lichte der Geschichte.
Langemackii Historia Catechetica.
Lentz's Gesch. der Christlichen Homiletik.
Maimbourg, Histoire du Lutheranisme.
Osiandri Enchiridion controversiarum inter Lutheranos et Calvinianos.
Planck's Entwickelung des protestantischen Lehrbegriffs.
Scheibel's Archiv für hist. Entwickelung, &c.
Seckendorfii Commentarius historicus et apologeticus. (A great standard work, which gives Papal as well as Protestant statements, reviews Luther's writings, and spreads out the original documents.)
Seelenii Stromata Lutherana.
Walchii (J. G.) Introductio in libros eccles. Lutheranæ symbolicos.
——— Einleitung in die Religions-streitigkeiten der Evang. Lutherischen Kirche, bis auf jetzige Zeiten. 1739.

Lutheranism, History of—*continued.*

Amer. Biblical Repos. 3d Series. 1:130.
Amer. Quarterly Register. 13:162. 15:378.
Christian Examiner. 27:402.
Edinburg Review. 68:145.
Hazelius' L. Church in America. To 1846.
Lives of Luther. (See LUTHER.)
Lockman's History, doctrine, &c., of the L.
Marheinecke's Hist. of the Ref. in Germany.
Planck's Origin, changes, &c., of L.
Robertson's History of Charles V.
Schaeffer's Early history of the L. Church.
Schmucker's American Lutheran Church.
Scott's History of the Church from the Diet of Augsburg (1530), to the death of Luther (1546).
Seckendorf's History of Lutheranism.

Luxury. See LOVE OF PLEASURE.

Brown's Essay on the Characteristics.
Burgh's Importance of manners to a State.
Carrington's (James) Sermons.
Cole's (T.) Discourses.
Dennis' (J.) Vice and luxury public mischiefs. (Reply to Mandeville's fable of the bees.)
Ferguson on Civil Society.
Innes on Virtue.
Law's Theory of Religion.
Newton's (Bp.) Dissertations.
Pinto's Essay on Luxury.
Robinson's Claude on the composition of a sermon.
Stockdale's Three discourses on luxury.
Zollikoffer's Sermons on prevalent vices.

Lying. See FALSEHOOD, TRUTH.

Kierkegard, de Notione atque turpitudine mendacii.
Nabe (F. A.), Dissertationes.
Rostii Mendac. non necessaria.

Beddome on the Catechism.
Brady's (Nicholas) Sermons.
Brent's Nature and guilt of lying.
Brown on the Catechism.
Clarke on the Catechism.
Clarke's (Samuel) Sermons.
Clerke's (Richard) Sermons.
Doddridge's Lectures. Lect. 68.
Downame's (John) Treatise against lying.
Dwight's Theology. Ser. 125 to 127.
Dymond's (Jonath.) Essays. (Superior.)
Enfield's (William) Sermons.
Grove's Moral Philosophy.
Hole on the Catechism.
Hopkins' (Bp.) Sermons.
Lamont's (D.) Sermons on prevalent vices.
Museum of For. Literature. 7:61.
New Englander. 1:184.
New England Mag. 7:302.
(These two discuss the question, "Is it ever justifiable?")
Owen's (Edward) Sermons.
Paley's Moral Philosophy. Bk. 3, ch. 15.

Lying—*continued.*

Parsons on the Catechism.
Ridgeley on the Catechism.
Secker (Abp.) on the Catechism.
——— Sermons.
Smallridge's (George) Sermons.
South's (Robert) Sermons.
Taylor's (John) Sermons.
Vaughn's (Charles J.) Sermons.
Vincent on the Catechism.
Watts' (Isaac) Sermons.

Maccabees. See APOCRYPHA.

Macedonians.
See I. COUNCIL OF CONSTANTINOPLE.

Athanasius, Epistolæ ad Serapianum.
Bazil, de Spiritu sancto ad Amphilochium.
Theodoret, Dialogi.

Alexandri Dissertationes.
Amphilochius de Spiritu sancto.
Didymus (Alex.) de Spiritu sancto.
Goetzii (Geo. Henrici) Dissertationes.
Paschasius de Spiritu sancto.

See ample list of writers in VOIGTII *Bibliotheca Historiae haeresiologicae.*

Magi. See RELIGIONS, PARSEES.

Allix, de anno et mense natali J. C.
Anquetil du Perron, Systèmes des Mages.
Beausobre, Hist. de Manichæisme. L. I, c. 5.
Bodinus de Magorum Dæmonomania.
Hyde, Hist. vet. Persarum, Magorum, &c.
Schmidtii (G. F.) Magi advenientes.

Adams' (H.) Dict. of Religions. Art. *Gaurs.*
Amer. Biblical Repos. 3d Series. 2:517.
Frank's (J. C.) Hulsean prize Essay. 1814.
Gibbon's Decline and Fall of Rome.

Magic. See WITCHCRAFT.

Bekker, le Monde enchanté.
Giraldo, Hist. curieuse des sorciérs, magiciens, &c., jusq'a nos jours. 1846.
Horst's (G. C.) Zauber-bibliothek.
Le Brun, Histoire des superstitions.
Levi, Histoire de la Magic.
Masse, l'Imposture des devins.
Maury, la Magic.
Résie, Hist. des sciences occultes.
Salverte, des Sciences occultes.

Analytical Magazine. 13:470.
Barrett's Celestial Intelligencer.
Bigland's Essays. Ess. 8.
Blackwood's Mag. 69:450.
Brewster on Natural Magic.
Colquhoun's History of Magic.
Cox's (Francis) Detestable wickedness of magical sciences. 1561.
De Foe's History of the Black Art.
——— History of the Devil.
Dublin Univ. Magaz. 29:28.
Eclectic Mag. 5:433.
Ennemoser's Hist. of Magic. Tr. by Howitte.
For. Quar. Review. 6:417.
Frazier's Mag. 22:1.

Magic—*continued.*

Gaule's Magical Diviner pozed and puzzled.
Godwin's (Will.) Lives of the Necromancers. (A very interesting and convenient book.)
Littell's Living Age. 5:567.
Mason's Anatomy of Sorcery and charms.
North Brit. Review. 3:1,165.
Salverte's Philosophy of magic and apparent miracles. Trans. by Thompson.
Southern Lit. Messenger. 6:629.
Wilkins' Wonders of Geometry.
Wright's Narratives of Sorcery and Magic.

Writers on Satanic agency and magic have been diligently enumerated and reviewed by THOMASIUS, *de Origine et progressu processus inquisitorii contra sagas.*

Magistracy. See BANGORIAN CONTROVERSY, CIVIL GOVERNMENT.

Dentchmanni (Ioan.) Dissertationes.
Echardi Opus de ordine eccles. et polit.
Habichorstius de Magistratus et suppliciorum capitalium Constitutione Divina.
Hennichii (Ioan.) Dissertationes.
Niehenckii (Geo. F.) Dissertationes.
Scharfii (Ioann.) Dissertationes.

Abernethy's (John) Tracts.
Amer. Quart. Rev. 8:58.
Atterbury's (Bp.) Sermons.
Berkeley's (Bp.) Works.
Butler's (Bp.) Occasional Sermons.
Collyer's (W. B.) Scripture duties. Lect. 8.
Donne's (John) Sermons.
Dublin Univ. Mag. 16:530.
Dwight's Theology. Ser. 114.
Faringdon's (Anthony) Sermons.
Gee's Divine right of the civil magistrate.
Goodman's Obedience to civil powers.
Graves' (Richard) Sermons.
Green's Conscientious obed. to Governors.
Gresley's (William) Sermons.
Griffith's (Thomas) Sermons.
Hopkins' (Bp.) Works. (Submission to rulers.)
Ibbot's (Benjamin) Sermons.
Johnson's (Dr. Sam.) Sermons.
Latimer's (Bp.) Sermons.
Leighton's (Abp.) Sermons.
Lightfoot's (Dr. J.) Sermons.
Neves' (Timothy) Sermons.
Owen on the Power of magistrates.
Reynolds' (Bp.) Sermons.
Scott's (John) Sermons.
Seed's (Jeremiah) Sermons.
Sherlock's (Bp.) Sermons.
Skelton's (Philip) Sermons.
Taylor's Ductor Dubitantium.
Tombes' Saints no smiters. (A lucid argument against the interference of magistrates with religion.)
Tottie on Subjection to civil powers.
Tucker's Light of Nature.
Usher's Power of the Prince.
Warburton's (Bp.) Sermons. (Appendix.)
Wilson's Duty of Magistrates.

Magnanimity.

Butcher's (William) Sermons.
Witherspoon's (John) Sermons.

Mahomet.

Abulfeda, de Vita et rebus gestis Moham.
Boulanvilliers, la Vie de Mohamed. ("A prolix fable."—MOSHEIM.)
Gagnier, Vie de Mahomet.
Savary, la Vie de Mahomet. ("Of all the lives of M., this is the best."—MILLS.)
Turpin, Histoire de la vie de Mahomet.

Chr. Examiner. 9:360. 49:184.
Chr. Quart. Spect. 3:169,176.
Church Review. 3:401.
Eclectic Magaz. 21:36.
For. Quart. Rev. 24:1.
Life of Mahomet; by Abulfeda.
——— ——— by Addison.
——— ——— by Boulanvilliers.
——— ——— by Bush.
——— ——— by Hawkins.
——— ——— by Wash. Irving.
——— ——— by Merrick.
——— ——— by Miles.
——— ——— by Muir.
——— ——— by Prideaux.
——— ——— by Savary.
——— ——— by Springer.
N. Amer. Review. 63:496. 71:273.
North Brit. Rev. 13:101.
Southern Quart. Review. 18:375. 20:173.

Mahometanism. See KORAN.

Al Koran: Lex Islamitica. (Many editions.)
Andreæ Confusio sectæ Mahomedanæ.
Bibliandri M. Saracenorum principis, ejusque successorum, doctrinæ, &c.
Brentii Homiliæ. Hom. XXII.
Butner's Beschreibung d. turkischen Relig.
Callixti (Fred.) Dissertationes.
Chardin, Voyage aux Indes Orientales.
Danhaveri Disputationes Theologicæ.
Doederlin, de Fundamentis theologiæ M.
D'Herbelot, Bibliotheca Orientalis.
Döllinger's Mohammed's Religion.
Erhardus de Erroribus præcipuis de historiis Mahometi.
Fabricii (J.) Delectus argumentorum, &c.
Frischmuthii (Ioan.) Dissertationes.
Garsin, Exposition de la foi Musselmann.
Geropoldi Arcana Muhammedanismi.
Hackspanii Fides et leges Mahomedis.
Henningii Muhammedanus precans.
Holmii Theologiæ Muham. consideratio.
Hoornbeckii Summa Controversiarum.
Hottingeri Historia Orientalis.
Kortholti (Chris.) Dissertationes.
Langii (Ioann. M.) Dissertationes.
Michaelis de Muham. laxitate morali.
Millii (D.) Dissertationes Selectæ.
Moebius de Causis et mediis quæ Muhametanam relig. introduxerunt.
Nerriter's Mahometanische Moschea.

Mahometanism—*continued.*

Œlsner, des Effets de la rel. de M. pendant la trois premier siècles, sur l'esprit, les mœurs, &c., des peuples.
Pastoret, Zoroastre, Confucius, et Mahomet comparés.
Reland de Relig. Mohammed. (Acta erud.)
Schneider's Theologie Turckenspiegel.
Schrœderi M. testis veritatis contra seipsum.
Schuberti Institutiones Theolog. Polemicæ.
Systema Religionis Muhamed. (Acta erud.)
Tassy, Expos. de la foi Musselmane.
Tholuck's Vermischte Schriften, &c.
Voetii Select. Disputat. Theolog. Par. II.
Wallich, der Turcken Religion.
Warneri Compendium eorum quæ Mohammedani de Christo aliisque capitibus rel. Christ. tradiderunt.

Addison's First state of Mahometanism.
——— Present " " 1798.
Amer. Eclectic Rev. 4:97,268.
Amer. Quart. Rev. 7:64.
Amer. Quart. Obs. 1:103.
Analyt. Mag. 1:178. 16:235.
Arnold's (J. M.) Islamism, and its relation to Christianity.
Bibliotheca Sacra. 23:406.
Bryant's Truth of the Christian Religion.
Butler's (E.) Horæ Biblicæ.
Christian Examiner. 65:95.
Chris. Review. 5:372.
Chris. Month. Spectator. 1:509.
Controversial Tracts on Mahometanism, with preface by Prof. Lee.
Dublin Review. 7:98.
Eclectic Rev. 4th Series. 2:171.
Edinb. Monthly Rev. 4:323.
For. Quart. Review. 12:192.
Forster's (Chas.) Mahometanism unveiled. (See British Critic. 7:1.)
Gibbon's Decl. and Fall of the Rom. Empire.
Hamilton's Trans. of the Hedaya. (The code of Mahometan Law.)
Lane's Selections from the Koran; with commentary.
Macbride's Mahometan religion explained, with suggestions for its confutation.
Martyn's (Henry) Controversial Tracts. Trans. by Prof. Lee.
——— Memoirs.
Matthews' Mishcat-al-masabih. (A translation of M. traditions; held sacred next to the Koran. The only work of the kind in English.)
Maurice's (F. D.) Boyle Lectures. 1847.
Mede's Works. (Diss. on Rev. 9th chap.)
Merrick's Life and religion of Mahomet.
Millar's Propagation of Christianity.
Mills' History and present state of M. 1816.
Modern Universal History.
Monthly Review. 91:199. 119:362,475
Mosheim's Ecclesiastical History.
Muehleisen's Koran and the Bible.
Museum of Foreign Lit. 15:168,289.
Neale's (W. H.) M. contrasted with Christ'y.

Mahometanism—*continued.*

Neale's (F. A.) Rise and progress of M., and the present condition of the Turks. 1854.
Newton (Bp.) on the Prophecies.
Niebuhr's Travels.
Pitt's Religion and manners of Mahometans.
Rabadan's M. Tr. by Morgan. (Curious pl.)
Reland's Mahomedisa.
Ricaut's History of the Turks.
Simpson's Key to the Prophecies.
Southern Quart. Review. 20:173.
Stanley's History of the Eastern Church.
Taylor's (W. C.) Hist. of M. and its sects.
Van Mildert's Boyle Lectures. 1806.
White's Bampton Lecture. 1784. (Christianity and M. compared in the history, effects, &c.)

For numerous other works on Mahometan doctrine and customs, consult DE SACY, *Bibliotheque*, 1830; and ELLIOTT'S *Bibliographical index to Mahometan history*. 1849.

Malice. See HATRED, RESENTMENT.

Dehon's (Bp. T.) Sermons.
Hey's (Dr. John) Discourses on the malevolent sentiments.

Mammon. See COVETOUSNESS, PARABLE OF THE POLITIC STEWARD, RICHES.

Man, Natural History of. See ETHNOLOGY, ORIGIN OF NATIONS, UNITY.

Du Moulin, Hist. des races humaine.
Edward, des Caractères physiologique des races humaine.
La Cépède, Histoire naturelle de l'homme.
——— Les ages de la nature.
Pauw, Œuvres Philosophique.
Virey, Hist. naturelle du genre humain.

Amer. Biblical Repos. 2d Series. 11:274.
Brit. Quarterly Rev. 1:337.
Democratic Rev. 26:227. 27:41,133.
Dunbar's History of mankind in rude and in cultivated ages.
Frazier's Magaz. 30:537. 44:651.
Guyot's Earth and man. Tr. by Felton.
Home's (Lord Kames) Sketches.
Jones' Origin of differences of color, &c.
Latham's Nat. Hist. of the varieties of man.
——— Man and his migrations.
Lawrence's Lectures. (Able.)
Littell's Living Age. 24:490. 29:323.
Lond. Quart. Review. 1:328. 86:1.
Methodist Quart. Rev. 4:255. 10:531.
Mudie's (Robt.) Works. Vol. 3.
Murray's (Jas.) Creation, and the design of the Mosaic history.
Princeton Review. 21:159. 22:603,313.
Prichard's Physical History of Mankind. (Modifying inf. of physical and moral causes, &c. 1836. Greatly improved in 1855. 162 engravings.)
Schoolcraft's Notes on the Iroquois.
Smith's (Sam. S.) Causes of difference in color.

Man, Natural History of—*continued.*

Smith's (C. H.) Natural hist. of the species. (With an introduction, containing the views of Blumenbach, Prichard, Bachman, Agassiz, &c.)
Van Amrige's Natural History of Man. (Reviews Lawrence, Prichard, and others.)
Ward's (S. H.) Nat. history of man. Plates.
Westminster Review. 14:17. 20:186. 55:83.
Young (J. R.) on Modern Scepticism. 1865. (Reviews Lyell, Huxley, Colenso, &c.)

Man, Perfectability of.
See HUMAN PROGRESS.

Man-Pleasing. See FEAR OF MAN.

Adams' (Wm.) Sermons bef. the University.
Faringdon's (Anthony) Sermons.
Marshall's (Nathan) Sermons.
Smallridge's (George) Sermons.
Wesley's (John) Sermons.
Williams' (Geo.) Sermons. (Two discourses on this subject—one showing it as a snare, and the other as a duty.)

Manichees.

Augustine, contra Adimantum.
——— ——— Fortunatum.
——— ——— Faustum.
——— ——— Secundinum.
——— de Natura boni.
——— de Fide.
Gregory Nys., Opera.
Alexander, Προς τας Μανιχαιουδοξας.
Alticotii Dissertatio histor. critica.
Arnold, Histoire des heresies.
Baur's Manichæisches Religionssystem.
Beausobre, Hist. critique de. M. ("Calculated to mislead."—DOWLING.)
Colditz's Entstehen des M. Religionssystem.
Didymus adversus Manichæos.
Heilmanus de Auctoritate librorum N. Test.
Horbii Historia Manichæorum.
Hyde, Vet. Persarum et Medorum religio.
Mosheim, de Rebus Christ. ante Constantin.
Petri Historia Manichæorum.
Photii Historia Manichæorum.
——— Bibliotheca.
Serapion, adversus Manichæos.
Spangenbergii Historia Manichæorum.
Strauchii recensio Historica.
Tillemont, Memoires Ecclesiastique, etc.
Victorinus contra Duo principia, &c.
Vossii (G. J.) Theses Theologicæ.
Wegneri (A. F. V.) Disputationes.
Wolfii Manichæismus ante Manichæos.

Burton's Bampton Lectures. 1829.
Lardner's Credibility, &c. Part 2.
Mosheim's Observ. on Cudworth's Intel. sys.
Toplady on the Scheme of necessity. Ch. 7.

Manna. See NATURAL HIST. OF THE BIBLE.

Bocharti Opera. (Different kinds of Manna.)
Buxtorfii Exercitationes.
Calovii (Abrah.) Disputationes.

Imbonati (Jos.) Dissertationes.
Salmasius De manna et saccharo. (Two volumes, folio !)
Stapelii Thesaurus diss. philologicarum.

Manners. See CLERICAL HABITS.

Manuals of Devotion. See DEVOTION, PRAYER BOOKS.

Andrews' Manual of Devotions.
Arndt's Garden of Paradise.
Bogatzky's Golden Treasury.
Churchman's Manual of Devotion.
Cochrane's Manual of Devotion. ("Nothing better."—CHALMERS.)
Cosin's (Bp.) Private Devotion.
Dewar's (D.) Manual of Devotion.
Grinfield's Devotional Exercises.
Hawkins' (L.) Devotional Exercises.
Hele's Select offices of private devotion.
Holderne's Manual of Devotion.
Hutchinson's Devotional Exercises.
Hutton's Private Devotions.
Hutton's (J.) Devotional Exercises.
Ken's Retired Christian's Exercises.
Mason's (William) Spiritual Treasury.
Quarle's (Francis) Manual of Devotion.
Shephard on Private Devotion.
Spinkes' Manual of Devotion.
Strutt's (J.) Manual of Devotion.
Sturm's Evening Devotions.
——— Morning Devotions.
Taylor's Golden Grove.
Timson's Devout Musings.
Wellbeloved's Devotional Extracts.
Wilson's Sacra Privata.

Manuscripts of S. S. See BIB. CRITICISM, PHILOLOGY, VARIOUS READINGS.

Assemani Bibliotheca Orientalis. (Enumerates and compares an immense collection of MSS.; Turkish, Syriac, Persian, Hebr., Armenian, Samaritan, and Ethiopic.)
De Rossi, Var. Lectiones. (Prolegomena.)
Dupin, Dissertations Preliminaire.
Houbiganti Prolegomena.
Montfaucon, Bibliotheca Bibliothecarum.
Pfaffii (C. M.) Dissertationes.
Tischendorf, Anecdota, sacra et profana. (Gives a catalogue of the manuscripts obtained by Prof. T., and also those of the British Museum, and Bodleian Library.)
Waltoni Prolegomena.

Bibliotheca Sacra. 1:254.
Butler's Horæ Biblicæ.
Curzon's Visit to monasteries in Lebanon.
Dupin's Preliminary Dissertations.
Kennicott's (Benjamin) Dissertations.
Lawrence on the Systematic classification of MSS. adopted by Griesbach. (An able disproof of some of G.'s decisions.)
Marsh's Michaelis. (Introduction.)
Mills' Prolegomena.
Pettigrew's Bibliotheca Sussexiana. (A descriptive catalogue of 295 ancient MSS., and 1,543 different editions of printed Bibles, collected by the Duke of Sussex.)
Platt's Catalogue of Ethiopic Biblical MSS.
Simons' Critical history of the Old Test.
Walton's (Bryan) Prolegomena.
Westwood's Paleographia Sacra. (50 beautiful illustrations.)
Wetstein's (John James) Prolegomena.

Marcellians.

Augustini Epist. ad Marcellinum.
Alexandri Dissertationes.
Irgens de Marcello, Ancyræ episcopo.
Montfaucon, Bibliotheca Manuscriptorum.

Marcionites.

Epiphanius, de Hæresibus.
Irenæus, contra Hæreses.
Origen, contra Marcionitas.
Tertullian, contra Marcionitas.

Alexandri (Natalis.) Dissertationes.
Beausobre, Hist. de Manichæisme. Lib. 4.
Leschnerti Diss. de baptismate vicario.
Strumii Historia Bardesanii.
Tillemont, Memoires pour servir a l'histoire de l'Eglise.

Lardner's Credibility of the gospel history.

Mariners. See SEAMEN.

Mariolatry.

Baillè, de la Devotion a la Saint vierge. (This book produced a strong sensation at the time of its publication, in 1696.)
Basnage, Histoire du culte de la Vierge.
Callixti (Frider. Ulric.) Dissertationes.
Catharini (Ambr.) Opuscula.
Costeri (Francisc.) Meditationes.
Marraccii Bibliotheca Mariana.
Memoires de Trevoux.
Sandii Horologium Mysticum.
Voetii (G.) Disputationes Selectæ. Pt. III.

Bull's (Bp. Geo.) Sermons.
Evans' (B.) Modern Popery. 1855.
Fleetwood's Life and death of the virgin M.
Gibson's Preservative against Popery.
Hall's (John) The Virgin Mary.
Horne's (T. H.) Mariolatry.
North British Review. 8:182.
Patrick's (Bp.) Mary misrepresented by the Roman church.
Powell's (H. T.) Roman forgeries.
Seymour's Mornings among the Jesuits.
Tayler's (W. F.) Char. and crimes of Popery.
Taylor's (Jer.) Wholesome advice from the Virgin to her indiscreet worshippers.
Tyler's Worship of the Virgin contrary to the Scriptures, and to the practice of the first five centuries.

Mark.

Bibliandri Protevangelion.
Dorschei (Ioan. Geo.) Dissertationes.
Justiniani Marci Evangelist. vita.
Kirsteni Vita Evangelistarum.
Knobel, de Evang. Marci origine.

Molleri (Ioann.) Disputationes.
Saunier's Quellen des Marcus.
Schneringii (Godf.) Disputationes.
Spanheimii (Frid.) Exercitationes.

Maronites. See MONOTHELITES.

Assemanni Bibliotheca Orientalis.
De la Croix, Etat present, &c. 1695.
Ecchellensis Constitut. Ecc. Maronitarum.
Gerhardi (Ioann. Ernest.) Dissertationes.
Lacroix, Etat present des eglise M. 1715.
La Roque, Voyage de Syrie et de Montliban.
Le Brun, Explication de la Messe.
Le Quien, Oriens Christianus.
Naironi Diss. de origine, nomine, &c. (A strong defence of the sect.)
Renaudot, Hist. Patriarcharum Alexandrin.
——— Collectio Liturgiarum Orient.
Schnurrer, de Eccl. Maronitica. As in 1810.
Simon, Histoire critique de Chrétiens Orientaux. Ch. 12.
Sionata (a Maronite), de Maronitar. vitibus.

Churchill's Ten years' residence on Mount Lebanon. 1842 to 1852.
——— Druses and Maronites. To 1862.
Clayton's Journey to Damascus. 1736.
Green's Journey to Damascus. 1725.

Marriage.

Augustin, de Nuptiis.
Tertullian, Apologeticus adv. Gentes.
——— ad Uxorem.
——— de Monogamia.

Amyraut, Considerationes sur marriage.
Bourdaloue (Comp. de Jésus), Sermons.
Brehmii Sex conciones nuptiales.
Calmeti Dissertatio. (Prefixed to Commentary on Canticles.)
Carpzovii Schediasma. (On the question, "Should persons of different religions intermarry?")
Chaussée, l'Excellence du marriage.
De Jonghe, de M. ejusque impedimentis.
Erasmi Christiani Mat. institutio.
Fabricii Bibliographia Antiquaria.
Haferungius de Jure matrimoniali.
Hotomanus de Veteri ritu nuptiarum.
Kerner's Köstliche Hockzeitperlen.
Klee (H.), Die Ehe: eine dogmatisch-archæologische Abhandlung.
Kochii Dissertatio. (To prove that Paul was married.)
Melancthonis Opera. Tom. 1.
Neubour, Diss. in 1 Tim. 4:7,8.
Puffendorf de Jure. Lib. VI, c. 1.
Sanchez, Disp. de matrimonio. 2 vols., fol.!
Seldeni Uxor Hebræica.
Sontagius de Connubiali paradiso.
Spangenburg's Ehespiekel.
Twiskii Disputationes sacræ.

Adair's Plan of Platonic matrimony.
Amer. Biblical Repos. 2:70.
Archer's Sermons on matrimonial duties.
Astell's Reflections on marriage.
Baily's Marriage as it should be.

Marriage—*continued.*

Barr's (E.) Theolog. and philos. Essays.
Baxter's (Rich.) Christian Directory.
Bean's Advice to a new-married couple.
Broadbelt's (Geo.) Original Essays.
Bullinger's Christian state of matrimony. Trans. by Miles Coverdale.
——— on the Cohabitacion of ye faythfull with ye unfaythfull.
Butler's (Alban) Sermons.
Carey's Amer. Museum. 4:21,105,213.
Cecil's Remains. (Marriage of ministers.)
Christian Month. Spect. 1:514.
Cockburn's Dignity of married life.
Coe's Christian Duties and Cautions.
Creswell's (Daniel) Sermons.
Davis' (James M.) Pastor's Offering.
Defoe's Religious courtship. (Admirable.)
——— Family Instructor.
Doddridge's Lectures. Lec. 225,234,265.
Dodwell's Obligation to marry in the true communion.
Dwight's Theology. Disc. 119.
Elliot's Wedding Sermon.
Ellison's (H. J.) Way of holiness.
Foster's Duties of the married state.
Gahan's (William) Sermons.
Gataker (Tho.) on Conjugal Duties.
Gawden's Sanctity and solemnity of M.
Gilly on Clandestine marriages.
Gilson's (David) Sermons.
Grant's (James) Essays.
Grantham's (Tho.) Discourses on conj. duty.
Hall's (Bp.) Cases of Conscience.
Hill's Letters and Reflections.
Hole's (Matt.) Sermons.
Hooker's Ecclesiastical Polity.
Hooper's Seconde booke of Tertullian unto his wyf; wherein is conteyned most godly counsel how ye unmarried may choose companyons, and soe live quietly.
Jay's (Will.) Essay on marriage.
Johnson's (J.) Advantages and disadv. of M.
Johnson's (Dr. Samuel) Sermons.
Kendall's Address to young women.
Lawrence's (William) Marriage vindicated. (The free love doctrine of 2 centuries ago.)
Lawton's (Edward) Lectures.
Leslie's (Charles) Theological Works.
Luther's Fruitful sermon on marriage.
Malcom's (Howard) Christian rule of marriage. (Against the marriage of believers with unbelievers.)
Milton's Paradise lost. Bk. 4, line 750, et seq.
Morison's Counsels to a newly wedded pair.
North Brit. Review. 12:532.
O'Donahue on Social happiness.
Ovington's Duties, advant., and sorrows of M.
Owen's (Charles) Sermons.
Pamphleteer. 17:347. 18:553.
Petrie's Marriage gift. (Admirable.)
Ryan's Philosophy of Marriage.
Salmon's Essay on M. (The M. ceremonies of all nations, and other curious matter.)
Secker's (William) Wedding ring.

Marriage—*continued.*

Skelton's (Philip) Sermons.
Stennet on Domestic Duties.
Stoughton's (John) Sermons.
Strachy on Holy Matrimony.
Summerfield's (John) Sermons.
Taylor's (Jer.) Sermons.
——— Wedding ring.
Taylor's (Dr. John) Sermons.
Tunstell's Considerations on government.
West's (Moses) Unlawfulness of mixed M.
Wheatley's Rationale of the Book of common prayer.
——— Bride-bush. (Duties of M.)
——— Cure-cloth. (Troubles of M.)
Witherspoon's (John) Letters.

Many old German and Latin books on marriage are mentioned by WALCH, *Biblioth.*

Marriage with a Wife's Sister.
See CONSANGUINITY.

Pro.

Harpprecht, Com. in iv. libros Institutionem Justiniani.
Bibliotheca Sacra. 1:283.
Coppleston's (Bp.) Tracts.
Cook's (Parsons) The marriage question.
Denham (J. F.) on M. with a wife's sister.
Denman (Lord) on Do.
Eclectic Review. 4th Series. 3:735.
Foster's Review of the laws prohibiting certain marriages.
Frazier's Magaz. 41:112.
Fry's Case of marriage between relations.
Jenkinson (J. S.) on M. with a wife's sister.
London Quart. Review. 10:545.
McIlvaine's (Bp. C. P.) Letters on marriage.
Quarterly Review. 85:84.
Sleigh on Marriage with a wife's sister.
Westhead's Marriage code of Israel.
Whately's (Abp.) Tracts and Discourses.

Con.

Bucer (Martin), Commentaria. (Matt. xix.)
Chemnitii (Chris.) Dissertationes.
Perizonii (Ioachim.) Dissertationes.
Sanchez (Soc. Jesu) Disputationes.
Selden de Jure naturale et gentium.
Spengleri Instructio parochialis. Pars IV.
Wagenseil's Belehrung d. Jüdisch-teutschen.
Zanchius de Sponsalibus.

Ainsworth's Commentary. (Levit. 18.)
Andrews (Bp.) on the Moral law.
Assembly of Divines, London: *Voted* that "A man may not marry any of his wife's kindred nearer in blood than he may marry of his own."
Babington's (Bp.) Notes on the five books of Moses.
Berriman's (William) Sermons.
Beza on Polygamy and Divorce.
Butler's (Charles) Propinquity an impediment to Marriage.
Calvin's Commentary. (Levit. 18.)

Marriage, &c.—*continued.*

Con.

Dwight's (S. E.) Hebrew wife.
Edwards' (Bp.) Body of Divinity. (On the 7th commandment.)
Hammond's (Henry) Works.
Hayward's British laws relating to the marriage of a wife's sister. 1846.
Hope's Report on the laws, &c. 1850.
Janeway (J. J.) on Unlawful marriages.
Keble's (John) Address to Eng. churchmen.
Lee's History of the Church of Scotland. (Appendix.)
Livingston (J. H.) on Incestuous marriages.
North British Review. 12:286,532.
Perkins' Christian Economy.
Princeton Review. 15:182,420.
Proctor (W.) on M. with a wife's sister.
Pusey (E. B.) on Do.
Tindall's (Translator of the N. T.) Practice of Prelates.
Weemse's Exposition of the moral law.

Martyrology.

Chrysostom, Homiliæ.
——— Sermones panegyrici.
Ignatius, Martyrii acta.
Origen, Exhortatio ad martyrium.
Lactantius, Opera.
Tertullian, Apologeticus adv. Gentes.
——— ad Martyras.
Augustine, Sermones.

Arnoldi Historia Christianorum ad metalla damnatorum.
Assemanni Acta martyrum. (A noble work.)
Bedæ (Venerab.) Martyrologium.
Bernard, les Héros du Christianisme. (From Christ, to 1858.)
Bohemicæ Eccles. persecutionum synopsis hist. (A valuable supplement to Fox's Book of Martyrs.)
Buchta de Numero cruentorum.
Calovii (Abr.) Confessio Martyrum.
Crispini Actiones et monumenta martyrum. (From the time of Wickliffe and Huss, to 1560.)
Crocius' Gross Martyrbuch. (The martyrology of Germany, France, England, Italy.)
Dodwelli Dissertationes Cyprianæ.
Fleidner's Buch der Martyrer, und andrer Glaubenszeugen der evangel. kirche.
Galonius de Cruciatibus sanct. martyrum.
Geddes de Mart. protestantibus Hispanis.
Goebel's Marter Chrönik.
Hast's Gesch. der Wiedertaufer.
Heckel, die Martyrer der evang. Kirche in den ersten zeiten, nach der Reformation.
Histoire des Martyrs, depuis le temp des apotres, jusq'a present. 1619. (The first Protestant general martyrology.)
Ittigius Selecta hist. ecclesiastica.
Kortholtus de Vita et moribus Christianis primævis.
Loescheri Dissertations. (Early Martyrs.)

Martyrology—*continued.*

Luykin, Théatre des martyres. (Has 104 curious old engravings of martyrdoms, of Apostles, early Christians, Waldenses, &c. It is little more than extracts from Van Braght.)
Marangoni Thesaurus Parochorum. (English, Scotch, and Irish martyrs.)
Martelaers Spiegel der Werclose christenen.
Metius de Persecutione Pliniana.
Muhlii Commentaria de Martyribus.
Niemanni (Sebast.) Dissertationes.
Ortlobii (Christoph.) Dissertationes.
Ostii Diss. de hymnis martyrum.
Reuchlinus de Studio M. in eccl. primativa.
Ries' (Hans de) Hist. de Martelaaren. (A great treasure, embracing the period from 1524 to 1600. Often reprint. and enlarged.)
Ruinarti Selecta et sincera martyrum acta. (Lauded by WALCH and WEISMAN. He collects about all the authentic accounts of the sayings and doings of the early martyrs.)
Saligius de Diptychis veterum.
Sausay, Martyrologium Gallicanum.
Schmidtii (Sebast.) Dissertationes.
Sebastiaenzoon's Het offer des Heeren. Events in 1599.
Tillemont, Memoires pour servir, &c.
Van Braght's Bloedigh toonel der Doopsgesinde en weereloose Christenen.
Walchii (Geo.) Dissertationes.
Wandelberti Martyrologium.
Weinrichii Martyrologium sanctorum.
Zornii (P.) Acta Martyrum.

Bilson's Martyrs of the reign of Mary.
Bloomfield's History of the martyrs. Plates.
Bonar's Last days of martyrs.
Boyle's Martyrd. of Theodore and Didymus.
Bray's Papal dominion.
Brown's (J. Newton) Baptist martyrs.
Cave's Lives of the Apostles.
Challoner's Modern British martyrology.
Clarke's (Sam.) General martyrology. (A very useful work, extending from the beginning to 1560.)
Comber's History of the French massacre.
Coverdale's Letters of the martyrs who gave their lyves in the late bloodye persecution. 1564.
Crookshank's Martyrology. (Modern M.)
Dodwell's Primitive martyrs.
Fox's Martyrology. (A complete edition, with plates, was published in 1841. An edition in 3 vols., folio, 1861, has an immense number of curious wood-cuts. But that of Mendham & Pratt, in 1855, is preferred. 8 vols., 8vo.)
Geddes' Miscellaneous Tracts.
Haile's (Lord) Remains of Chris. antiquity.
Harper's (T.) Lives and sufferings of the M.
Hook's (Ellis) Spirit of the martyrs.
Kirkman's Lives and sufferings of the M.
Mall's History of the Martyrs.

Martyrology—*continued.*

Moore's (Henry) Persecutions of the Church of Rome. (A full Protestant martyrology, with lives of Reformers and Popes, history of the Inquisition, &c. Many plates.)
Reece's Martyrology. (A valuable compend.)
Rey's Persecutions by the French clergy.
Stamp's (J. S.) Martyrologia. Plates. (Comprehensive.)
Stephens' Martyrological Biography.
Taylor's (B.) England's bloody tribunal.
Van Braght's Martyrology of the Baptists. Trans. by Underhill.
Watson's (John) English Martyrology.

A multitude of other martyrologies are extant, chiefly Papal. BOLLAND, in his general preface to the *Acta Sanctorum*, treats at length on the subject of Martyrologies and Menologies. A list of Latin martyrologies is given by FABRICIUS, *Biblioth. Graec.* Vol. 9.

Mary Magdalen.

Anquetin, Dissertation. (To prove that Mary Magdalen, Mary, sister of Martha, and Mary the sinner, were three different persons.)
Bossuet, Œuvres Complètes. Vol. 27. ("The three Magdalens.")
Bourdaloue, Sermons.
Calmeti Dissertationes. (Pref. to Com. on Luke.)
Casauboni Exercitationes. Exerc. XIV.
Lamii Apparatus Biblicus. (Maintains that there was but one Mary Magdalen.)
Masson, La femme pecherisse de l'Evangile: son unitè avec Marie Madeleine, et Marie de Bethanie.
Pezroni Historia Evangelica.
Sorii Apologetica. (Same opinion as Lamy.)
Newlin's (Thomas) Sermons.
Smith's (Sydney) Sermons.
Tillemont's Ecclesiastical History.
Townley's Essays on var. subjects. Ess. 5.
Williams' (William) Sermons.

Mary, Mother of Christ.

Lipinii (Martin.) Disputationes.
Meisneri (Ioann.) Dissertationes.
Montagu (R.), Analecta.
——— Apparatus.
Riamboldi testis veritatis in historiæ Mariæ; adv. Baronium et alios.
Schmidii (Jo. Andr.) Prolusiones.

Masonry. See FREEMASONRY.

Masora. See VOWEL POINTS.

Mass.

Albertin (Valen.) de Eucharistia.
Arcularii (Ioan. Dan.) Disputationes.
Balduini (Frider.) Disputationes.
Bauer, Prüfung der Gründe.
Bochart, Traité de sacrifice de la messe.

Mass—*continued.*

Buddei Miscellanea Sacra.
Callixti (Frider.) Dissertationes.
Carlstadt's Auslegung der Worte Christi.
Dassovii (Theodor.) Disputationes.
Derodon [or Rodon], le Tombeau de la messe.
Du Moulin, Pratique des ceremonies de la M.
Fechtius de Orig. et superstitione Missarum.
Fuerleini Dissertationes histor. theol.
Gerhardi (Ernest.) Dissertationes.
Haberkorn, d. Grundlichen Widerlegung.
Gesner de Ritibus quas Rom. eccl. a majoribus suis Gentilibus in sacra transtulit.
Jaegeri Suppositio missæ sacrificio.
Kiliani Tract. de sacrificio missatico.
Le Brun, Explication des prières, &c.
Lutheri Opera.
Molinæi Anatome Missæ.
Mornay, de doct. de l'Euchariste, quand, et par quels degres, la messe s'est introduite à sa place.
Osiandri (J. A.) Dissertationes.
Pfaffius de Falsitate, vanitate, etc.
Scheibel's Abendmahl des Herrn.
Schmidtii (And.) Exercitationes.
Schulthess' Lehre von h. Abendmahl.
Sohnii (Georg.) Opera.
Sutlivius de Variis erroribus Romanæ Eccl.
Thummii (Theodor.) Disputationes.
Zornii (Pet.) Dissertationes.
Zwinglii Expositio eucharistiæ.

Anderson's (Dr. W.) The Mass.
Becon's (Tho.) Relics of Rome.
——— (Various other tracts.)
Bradford's (The Martyr) Works.
Brevint's (D.) Missale Romanum. (Strong.)
Cotter's Trans. of the M. and rubrics. Notes.
Cranmer's (Abp.) Works.
Dering (Sir Ed.) on Proper Sacrifice.
Derodon's Funeral of the Mass.
Du Moulin's Anatomy of the Mass.
Hicks' Controversial Letters.
Lee's The Family and its duties.
Maguire's One hundred defects of the Mass.
Meager's Popish Mass celebrated by heathen priests, for the living and the dead, for ages before Christ.
Retrospective Review. 12:70.
Whitby's Absurdity and Idolatry of the M.

See ancient books and pamphlets on this subject, in WALCH'S *Biblioth.*, and LOWNDES' *British Librarian.* At the time of the Reformation, most of the productions of the press had reference to some part of the Popish controversy.

Massacre of St. Bartholomew.

Brizzard's Bartholemäus nacht.

Cockburn's Massacre of St. Bartholomew.
Comber's Hist. of the Mass. of St. B. Plates.
Dublin Univ. Magazine. 33:298.
Waddington's Black Bartholomew.
Wilkes' Persecut. of Protestants in France.

Masters. See RELATIVE DUTIES.

Materialism. See IMMORTALITY, NECESSITY, SOUL, SPINOCISM.

Pro.

Büchner (Louis) Kraft und Stoff.
Cabanis, Rapports du physique et du moral de l'homme.
Camper (Pierre), Œuvres.
Ezalbe's Neue Darstellung d. Sensualismus.
Feurbach's Wesen d. Christenthum.
Hobbes' Elementa Philosophiæ.
Holbach's (P. T.) Systeme de la Nature.
La Mettrie, L'Homme machine.
——— Œuvres Philosophique.
Pallas, Elenchus Zoophytorum.
——— Spicilegia Zoologica.
Spinoza, Opera posthuma.
Voigt's Bildern aus d. Thierleben.

Atkinson (Henry G.) on Materialism.
Broussais on Irritability and insanity.
Compte's Positive Philosophy.
Cooper's (Dr. Tho.) Philosophical Essays on Materialism and association of ideas.
Coward's (Dr. W.) Thoughts on the Soul.
——— Second Thoughts.
——— Further Thoughts upon Second Thoughts. (Reply to Turner.)
Fearon's (H. B.) Thoughts on Materialism.
Hartley on Man.
Hegel's Encyclopedia of philos. sciences.
Hobbes' Elements of philosophy. Sec. 1.
——— Human Nature.
——— Leviathan.
Holmes (Ed.) on the Materiality of the soul.
Holyoake's Works. (Various articles.)
Lawrence's Lectures on Physiology.
Martineau's (J.) Rationale of relig. enquiry.
Martineau's (Miss) Laws of man's nature.
Mirabaud's System of Nature.
Morgan on the Philosophy of life.
Parker (T.) on Matters in relation to religion.
Priestley (Jos.) on Matter and Spirit.
——— Essay on Hartley's Theory.
Tattersall on the Anatomical argument.
Toland's Pantheisticon.
Vestiges of the Nat. history of creation.

Con.

Bacon, de Augmentis Scientiarum.
Bergier, Examen du Matérialisme.
Cicero, de Senectute.
Fabri, Briefe gegen d. Materialismus.
Fichté (J. H.), Anthropologie.
Frauenstadt's Materialismus sein Wahrh.
Frohschammer's Menschenseele u. Physiol.
Plato, de Legibus.
Schaller (Julius) Leib und Seele.
Scholten, M. modérne, et ses causes. 1859
Tittman (F. W.), Ueber Leben u. Stoff.
Vitringæ Observationes. Lib. III.
Weber, die neuste Vergotterung d. Stoff.

Abernethy's Physiological Lectures.
Allen on the Immortality of the soul.
Baxter (And.) on the Soul. ("Just, precise, and finished."—WARBURTON.)

Materialism—*continued.*

Con.

Barrow's (Isaac) Works.
Beattie on Truth.
Belsham's Essays. Vol. 2.
Benson's Reply to Dr. Priestley.
Bentley's Boyle Lectures. 1691,1692.
Berington's Letters on Materialism.
Berkeley's Minute Philosopher.
Bibliotheca Sacra. 17:201.
Bold (Sam.) on the Resurrection.
Boyle's (Robert) Free Enquiry.
——— Essay on final causes.
Broughton's Psychologia. (Masterly.)
Brown's Philosophy of the human mind.
Buchanan's Modern Atheism. Ch. 4. 1855.
Cheyne's Principles of Natural Religion.
Christian Review. 27:289.
Clarke's (S.) Boyle Lectures. 1704,1705.
——— Against H. Dodwell on the Soul.
Ditton on the Resurrection.
Doddridge's Lectures. Part 2, prop. 24.
Drew (Sam.) on the Soul. ("Wonderful. Nothing like it was ever published."—PROF. KIDD.)
Dudley's (John) Anti-materialist.
Dwight's Sermons. Ser. 23.
Eclectic Rev. New Series. 2:410.
Fearon's Thoughts on Materialism.
Ferriar on the Doctrine of Materialism.
Fleming's Survey of Coward on the Soul.
Frazier's Mag. 43:418.
Gifford's Outline of an Answer to Priestley.
Grove's (Henry) Thoughts on a future state.
——— Essay on the soul's immateriality.
Gurdon's Boyle Lectures. 1721,1722,1723.
Hallet's Notes on Scripture.
Hart's Materialism tested by reason.
[Hole's, (Matt.)] Antidote to Infidelity.
Horseley's Tracts.
How's Living Temple.
Hunter's Physiology.
Jackson on Matter and Spirit.
Jaeger's Examination of Spinoza.
Jenkins' Reasonableness of Christ'y. (Pref.)
Keach's (Benj.) Impostor detected.
Kenrick's Essay on primæval history.
Langston on the Rational Soul.
Lee's (Arthur) Immortality of the soul.
Lee's (Samuel) Eschatology.
Littell's Living Age. 29:323,373.
Locke's Essays. Book 4, chap. 3.
Memoirs of Manchester Philos. Society. 4:20.
Monboddo's (Lord) Ancient Metaphysics.
Monthly Review. 2:382. (Rev. of Holmes.)
More's Immortality of the Soul.
Nichols' Conference with a Theist.
Paine's Soul and Instinct, physiologically considered.
Price's Dissertations.
Princeton Review. 37:243.
Purves' Observations on Dr. Priestley.
Ramsay's Principles of Nat. and Rev. Relig.
Reid's (Thomas) Essays.
Roe's Bible versus Materialism.

Materialism—*continued.*

Con.

Rotherham on the Distinc. bet. soul and body.
Stewart's Philosophy of the mind.
Stillingfleet's Origines Sacræ.
Tarrier on the Brain.
Tillotson's (Abp.) Sermons.
Tucker's Light of Nature pursued.
Turner on the Separate existence of the soul. (Reply to Coward.)
Urwin (Joseph) on Materialism.
Watts' Ontology.
——— Essays. Essay 3.
Wilkinson's Connect. of the body with man.

Clarke, Baxter, Law, Pickard, and others, give the principal arguments on both sides.

Maternal Duties. See FAMILY GOVERNMENT, FEMALE SEX, RELATIVE DUTIES, WIVES.

Aime-Martin, Education des méres: ou de la civilization du genre humaine par les femmes.
Abbot's (John S.) Mother at home.
Anderson's (Christ.) Domestic Constitution. (Has scarcely an equal on this subject.)
Bakewell's (Mrs.) Mother's Guide.
British Mother's Journal. Period. London.
Christian Review. 2:20.
De Foe's Family Instructor.
Denham's (J. F.) Letters to a mother.
Duncan's Cottage Fireside.
Ellis' (Mrs.) Mothers of England.
Englishwoman's Magaz. Lond., from 1846.
Fry's Scripture principles of education.
Garnett's Lectures.
Hall on the Education of children.
Hamilton's (Mrs.) Letters.
Helme's Maternal Instruction.
James' Family Monitor.
Kendall on Parental Education.
Marshall's (Emily) Woman's Worth.
Martin on the Education of mothers.
Memoir of Mrs. Isabella Graham.
Memoir of Mrs. Susan Huntingdon.
Milner's (Mrs.) Christian Mother. (Exemplifications from Bible narratives.)
Mother's Magazine. Period. N. York.
Mother's Journal. Period. N. York.
Mother's Friend. Period. London.
Payson's Sermons for Christian families.
Phillips' The Hannahs. (The influence of mothers over sons.)
Reed's Mother's Manual.
Sigourney's (Mrs.) Letters to mothers.
——— Letters to young ladies.
Sprague's Letters to a daughter.
Spring (Gard.) on the Relig. Ed. of children.
Spurr (Mrs.) on the Educ. of infant children.
Taylor's (of Ongar) Advice to Mothers.
Taylor's (Mrs.) Maternal solicitude.
Wall's (C.) Mother's Book.

Matter not Self-Existent.
See ATHEISM, ETERNAL EXISTENCE OF MATTER, GNOSTICS.

Matthew. See APOSTLES.

Buslavii Dissertationes. (On the original language of his gospel.)
Ferf, de Auctor. Matt. in referendo C. v–vii.
Florini Exercitationes Philologicæ.
Frischii Dissertationes. (Matthew not to be confounded with Levi.)
Michaelis Prolegomena ad N. Testamentum.
Olshausen, Apostol. evang. M. origo defend.
Schuberti (Ioann.) Dissertationes.

Arnold's (Thomas) Sermons.
Dehon's (Bp.) Sermons.
Jones' (Jer.) Reply to Mr. Whiston's charge of dislocation.
Marsh's Michaelis.
Milner's (Joseph) Sermons.

Means of Grace. See HEARING.

Charnock's (Stephen) Works.
Darnell's (W. N.) Sermons.
Dehon's Sermons on the means of grace.
Dwight's Theology. Ser. 135,137.
Foster's Essays. (On the epithet Romantic.)
Fuller's (Andrew) Works.
Griffin's Park St. Lectures. Lec. 7 and 8.
Jelf's Bampton Lectures. 1844.
Kettlewell on Christian Obedience.
Lawson's (Charles) Sermons.
Martin's (Henry) Sermons.
Morning Exercises at Cripplegate. (Sermon by W. Greenhill.)
Scott's (Dr. John) Christian Life. ("Wanting in Evangelical views." BICKERSTETH.)
Wesley's (John) Sermons.
White's (Hugh) Profession and practice.

Mediation of Christ. See ATONEMENT, MESSIAH, REDEMPTION, &c.

Haueisenii Dissert. de loco Gal. iii. 20.
Osiandri Theologia Positiva.
Schotanus de Jesu Christo mediatore.

Balmer's (Robert) Academic Lectures.
Bateman's (Josiah) Sermons.
Bennet's (W. J. E.) Sermons.
Berriman's (William) Sermons.
Charnock's (Stephen) Sermons.
Clarke's (David) Sermons.
Clarkson's (David) Sermons.
Flavel's Fountain of life.
Foster's (James) Sermons.
Hopkins' (Ezekiel) Sermons.
Hurrion's Knowledge of Christ.
Jones on the Mediation of Christ.
Knox's (J. S.) Sermons.
McLauchlan's Way to God.
Meikle's Nat. of the mediator. dispensation.
Ogden's (Samuel) Sermons.
Owen on Redemption.
Pearson's Nat. and benefit of Christianity.
Symington on the Atonement.
Thompkins' Christ the Mediator.
Townsend's (John) Discourses on Prayer.
Townsend's (George) Sermons.
Vaughn's (Charles J.) Sermons.
Whiston's Sermons and Essays.

Meditation. See CONTEMPLATION, DEVOTION, SOLITUDE.

Augustine, Meditationes.
Gerardi (Ioann.) Meditationes.
Gromatensis de Oratione et Meditatione.
Riccius de mode recte Meditandi de rebus Divinis.
Sturm, Betrachtungen über d. worke Gottes.

Anthony's (John) Comfort of the soul.
Augustine's Meditations. Tr. by T. Rogers.
Bateman's (Josiah) Sermons.
Bates' (Wm.) Works. Disc. 16.
Bennet's Christian Oratory.
Berkley's (Earl of) Historical Applications.
Bogan's Mirth of a Christian life.
Brown's Natural and Revealed religion.
Brownrig's (Bp.) Sermons.
Bryson's (James) Sermons.
Bullar's (John) Lay lectures. Lect. 6.
Burroughs' (James) Sermons.
Butcher's (Wiliam) Sermons.
Calamy's (Edm.) Art of Divine meditation.
Capel's Daily Observations.
Cawood's (John) Sermons.
Chalmers' Sermons. (Difference between knowledge and consideration.)
Charnock's Works.
Corbet's Self-employment in secret.
Davies' (Thomas) Sermons.
Dwight's Theology. Ser. 146.
Edwards' (Bp.) Theologia Reformata.
Fuller's (Andrew) Sermons.
Gerard's (J.) Meditations. Tr. by Winterton.
Hall's (Bp.) Practical Works.
Horneck's Great law of Consideration.
Howe's (Charles) Devout Meditations.
Jones' Book of the Heart.
Kennaway's (Charles E.) Sermons.
Melville's (Henry) Sermons.
Morehead's (Robert) Discourses.
Paley's (William) Sermons.
Pearsall's (Richard) Contemplations.
Quarle's Spare Hours.
Sibbs' Divine Meditations.
Skelton's (Philip) Sermons.
Taylor's (Jer.) Life of Christ.
Thomas' (Bp.) Sermons.
Townson's (John) Sermons.
Usher's (Abp.) Manual of divine duties.
Verschoyle's (Hamilton) Sermons.
Waple's (Edward) Sermons.
Warwick's Spare Minutes. (Excellent.)
White's Divine Meditations.
Wilson's Sacra Privata.
Young's (Edward) Sermons.

Meekness. See BEATITUDES, PRIDE.

Bundy's (Richard) Sermons.
Chalmers' (Tho.) Posthumous Works.
Cock's (John) Sermons.
Coite's (Thomas W.) Sermons.
Cook's (John) Sermons.
Cooper's (E.) Sermons.
Cooper's (James) Sermons.
Cox's (Robert) Sermons.

Meekness—*continued.*

Dunlop's (Will.) Sermons.
Edwards on the Affections.
Enfield's (William) Sermons.
Evans on Christian Temper.
Faringdon's (Anthony) Sermons.
Henry (Matt.) on Quietness of spirit.
Hunt's (Jeremiah) Sermons.
Jones' (Will. of Nayland) Sermons.
Jortin's (John) Sermons.
Knight's (Samuel) Sermons.
Le Bas' (Cha. W.) Sermons.
Logan's (John) Sermons.
Scougal's (Henry) Sermons.
Smith's (Sydney) Sermons.
Spring's (Gardner) Essays.
Sumner's (John Bird) Sermons.
Tillotson's (Abp.) Sermons.
Vaughn (Henry) on the Fruits of the Spirit.
Vincent's (Will.) Sermons.
Whichcot's (Bp.) Sermons.
Whitaker's (Edw. W.) Sermons.
Wilkins' (Bp.) Sermons.

Meeting Houses. See CHURCH ARCHITECTURE, PLACES OF WORSHIP.

Melancholy. See DESPONDENCY.

Baxter's (Rich.) Cure of Melancholy.
Brady's (Nicholas) Sermons.
Burton's Anatomy of Melancholy. (Kinds, causes, symptoms, and cures.)
Clarke's (Samuel) Sermons.
Clifford's Signs and causes of Melancholy.
Fawcet's (Benjamin) Sermons.
Kollock's (Shepard K.) Sermons.
Marshall's (Nathaniel) Sermons.
Moss' (Robert) Sermons.
Rogers (Timothy) on Trouble of mind.
Smith's (Dr. William) Sermons.
Trebeck's (Andrew) Sermons.
Whitefield's (George) Sermons.

Melancthon.

Melancthonis Opera Omnia. (Many editions. The last is by Bretschneider. 24 vols., 4to. 1856.)
Melancthonis Werke. Herausg. von Koethe. 1830.
Camerarii Melancthonis vitæ narratio.
Dresler's Melancthon's Leben und Wirken.
Hildebrandt's Melancthon.
Knauth's (F.) Philipp Melancthon
Kuhlmen's P. Melancthon.
Ledderhose's Christliche Biographien.
Matthes' Melancthon's Leben und Wirken.
Meurer's P. Melancthon's Leben.
Neubert's (H. M.) M. und die stadt Dresden.
Strobel, Melancthoniana.
——— Apologie Melancthons.
Wohlfarth's Philip Melancthon.

Melancthon, Life of; by F. A. Cox.
——— ——— by Heppe.
——— ——— by Ledderhose.
——— ——— by Planck.

Melancthon—*continued.*

Am. Quart. Reg. 15:306.
Biblioth. Sacra. 3:301.
Brit. Quart. Rev. 3:191.
Chris. Examiner. 20:273.
Eclectic Magazine. 8:27.
Princeton Rev. 10:1.
Quarterly Review. 14:236.

There are various other lives of Melancthon. Several appeared in 1860, the tercentenary of his death.

Melchisedec.

Benzelii Dissertationes Academicæ.
Borgesii Hist. Critica Melchisedechi.
Calmet, Commentaire. (Dissertation prefixed to the Epistles.)
Deylingii Observationes Sacræ.
Fabricii de Sacerdotio Christi.
Gaillardi Melchesidecus Christus unus.
Heideggeri Historia patriarcharum.
Hottingeri Diss. philologico-theologicarum.
Koerburgii Dissertationes Philologicæ.
Kraftii Observationes Sacræ.
Van Rein, Dissertationes Philologicæ.

Amer. Bibl. Repos. 3d Series. 4:495.
Bibliotheca Sacra. 16:528.
Broughton's (H.) Works. (Affirms him to be Shem.)
Calvin's (John) Sermons.
Chevallier's Hulsean Lectures. 1826.
Close's (Francis) Historical Sermons.
Foster's (Dr. James) Discourses.
Gill's (Dr. John) Sermons and Tracts.
Glas' (John) Notes on Scripture texts.
Gray on the Priesthood of Jesus Christ.
James on the Priesthood of Christ.
Jerome's Epistles to Evangelus.
Kollock's (Shepard K.) Sermons.
Owen's (John) Dissertations.
Page (Thomas) on the Types.
Ridgeley's Body of Divinity.
Sharp's (Granville) Melchisedec.

Memory. See MNEMONICS.

Des Cartes de Passionibus.
Helvetius de L'Esprit.
Tafel's Unsterblichkeit und Wiedererinnerungskraft, &c., der Seele.

Doddridge's Lectures. Prop. 8.
Durham's Physico-Theology. Book 5, ch. 1.
Knott's New aid to memory. 1841.
Locke's Essays. Bk. 3.
Reid on the Intellectual powers. (Gives the different theories concerning memory.)
Stewart's Philosophy of the mind.
Universalist Quarterly. 5:221.
Watts' Essays. Essay 3.

Memory after Death.

Alstrin, de Anima.
Fabricii (J. A.) Exercitationes.
Guntheri (Ioann.) Dissertationes.
Olearii (B. C.) Dissertationes.

Scholand, Das ewige Leben.
Schubert's Seelen nacht dem Tode.
More's (Henry) Philosophical poems.

Mendæans. See HEMEROBAPTISTS.

Menno Simon.

Mennonis Opera theologica.
Cramer, Het leven en de verrigtingen von Menno Simons.
Harder, das Leben Menno Simons.
Roosen, M. S. den evangelischen Mennotitengemeinden.
Brown's (J. N.) Life and times of Menno.

Mennonites.

Pro.

Confessio brevis præcipuorum Chris. fidei articulorum. 1580.
Confession des Christlichen Glaubens. Dordrecht. 1632.
Confessio Fidei illorum Mennonistarum qui vulgo clarici vocantur. 1678.
Abrahami Apologia pro Protestantibus.
——— Introd. in scientiam cultus Divini.
Bekentnis des Glaubens nach Gotteswort wie Dasselbe von vielen Jahren, etc. 1618.
Bekentnissen der vereinigten Flamischen, Friesischen, und Hochdeutschen Taufgesinten Gemeinengottes. 1665.
Braghtii Theatrum Martyrum.
Centz [or Centson], Confession des Glaubens und vornehmsten Stucken der Christlichen Lehre. 1630.
Dooregeestii Apologia pro Mennot. doctrina.
——— Catechesis.
——— Epistolæ ad F. Spanheim.
Eeghemi Theologia Christiana.
Frederici (Douwen.) Catechesmus.
——— Orthodoxa Doctrina.
——— Indicatio in aphorismos fundament.
Gerberi Confessio fidei Christianæ.
Handlung der Vereinigten flamischen. 1649.
Huyzen (Cornel.) Catechismus.
Knuyt, Brevis confessio fidei.
Linder's (J.) Vaterlandes fall u. des V. Trost.
Mennonis Opera Theologica.
Munzer's Ordnung d. deutsch. Amts zu Alsted.
——— Protestation und Entbietung.
——— Deutsche evangelische Messe.
——— Several other treatises.
Nicolai Præcip. dogmatum fidei confessio.
——— Quod sit Ecclesia Dei.
Outerman das Bekæntnis, etc.
Petri (Pet.) Dissertationes.
Phillippi Enchiridion Christ. doctrinæ.
Reiswitz's Glaubensbekentniss d. M.
Riesius de Recto linguæ usu.
Roosen, Disquisitio Historica.
Schabælii Paradismus Animarum.
Togeri (Frid.) Christianæ Theolog. Systema.
Twiske, de Religionis Libertate.
——— (Other works.)
Van Gent's Aufang und Fortgang der Uneinigkeiten.
Van Huyzen, Epitome doct. Mennonitarum.
Wybrantii Catechesis in symbolum apostol.

Mennonites—*continued.*

Con.

Ampsingii (Io. Asueri) Disputationes.
Botsacc, Weiderlegung de weidertaufferischen Lehre.
Bullinger adversus Catabaptistarum.
Burgmann's (Io. Chris.) Dissertationes.
Cassander de Baptismo Infantum. Prefatio.
Cloppenburgii (Ioan.) Gangrena Theologiæ.
Hunnii (Nicol.) Dissertationes.
Koecheri (Ioan. Chris.) Commentationes.
Lasco (Johan. A.), Defensio veræ Doctrinæ.
Loescheri (Casp.) Dissertationes.
Luther, Von der himlischen Propheten.
Masecovii Anti-Mennone.
Melancthoni Opera. (Against Servetus.)
Mulleri (Ioann.) Anabaptismum.
Osiandri Enchiridion Controversiarum.
Rues, Gegenwärtigen Zustand d. M.
Rulich's Rettung unserer Kindertauffe, etc.
Schulteti Disputationes.
Schultz's Warnung fur gemeinschaft, &c.
Spanheimii Elenchus Controv. Theolog.
Wigandus in Dogmatibus Anabaptistarum.

Mennonites, History of.

Alenzoon's Gegenbericht; auf die Vorrede des Martyrbuchs.
Burgmanni de Hist. M. fontibus et subsidiis.
Crichton's Geschichte der Mennoniten.
Jehring's Gründliche Historie von der Begebenheiten, &c. (Describes the martyrdom of many.)
Hast's Geschichte der Wiedertäuffer.
Hunzinger's Kirchen und Schulwesen der Taufgesinnten.
Keltneri (Frider.) Disputationes.
Kieseling's Lehrgebäude der Wiedertäufer.
Kraftii Bibliotheca Theologica.
Loescheri (Caspar.) Dissertationes.
Maatschoen's Gesch. der Mennoniten.
Mennonis Opera Theologica.
Molleri Cimbria Literata.
Rose's Unschuld und Gegenbericht der evangelischen täufgesinten Christen.
Rues' Nachrichten vom Zustande der M.
Schultz's Warnung fur d. Gemeinschaft der Gottesdienstes d. Mennonisten.
Schyn, Hist. Christianorum in Belgio fœder. (Clearly distinguishes the Men. from the Anabaptists of Germany, and is every way profound and full.)
Twisckii Historia Martyrum.
Van Braght, Martyrologium Harlemense.
Van Gent, Hist. von der Begebenheiten der Mennonitarum.
Van Huyzen's Historische Erzählung von dem Ursprung und Fortgang, &c.

Brown's (J. N.) Life and times of Menno.
Van Bracht's Martyrology.

The M. are commonly called "Anabaptists" by writers of the 17th century: and much of what purports to be their history, may be drawn from the writers cited under that head.

Mental Reservation.
Placette's Christian Casuist.

Mercifulness. See BEATITUDES.
Carr's (Samuel) Sermons.
Cook's (John) Sermons.
Evans on Christian Temper.
Faringdon's (Anthony) Sermons.
Herring's (Abp.) Sermons.
Mason's (John) Christian Morality.
Norris' (John) Sermons.
Stephens' (H.) Sermons.

Mercy of God. See ATTRIBUTES.
Arnold's (Thomas) Sermons.
Bloomfield's (G. B.) Sermons.
Blunt's (Henry) Sermons.
Bradley's (Charles) Sermons.
Charnock's Works.
Cooper's (Edward) Sermons.
Dwight's Theology. Sermon 12.
Foster's (James) Discourses.
Hill's (Bryan) Sermons.
Ludlam's (W.) Essays.
Newlin's (Thomas) Sermons.
Paley's Moral Philosophy. Book 2, ch. 5.
Robinson's Christian System.
Saurin's Sermons.
Taylor's (Jeremy) Sermons.
Tillotson's (Abp.) Sermons.
Whitaker's (Edward W.) Sermons.
Wisheart's (William) Sermons.

Mercy-Seat. See SHECKINAH.

Mercy to Brutes. See CRUELTY.

Merit. See FAITH, GOOD WORKS, JUSTIFICATION.

Mesmerism. See CLAIRVOYANCE, RECIPROCAL INFLUENCE.
Chastanet, du Magnetism animal.
Chardell, de Psychologie physiologique.
Delaage, le Sommiel magnetique expliqué.
Deleuze, Defence du magnetism animal.
——— Hist. critique du magnet. animal.
Ennemoser's Magnetismus; in Verhältnisse zur Natur and Religion. 1853.
Kerner's Seherin von Prevorst.
Puisegur, Memoires pour servir a l'hist., etc.
Reichenbach, Researches.

Amer. Biblical Repos. 2d Series. 1:362.
Amer. Quart. Review. 4:1,26.
Amer. Quart. Magaz. 12:413.
Analytical Magaz. 10:34.
Bell's Principles of animal magnetism.
Blackwood's Magaz. 1:563. 57:219. 60:223. 70:70.
Boismont on Hallucination.
British Quart. Review. 2:402.
Bush's Mesmerism and Swedenborg.
Charl. Elizabeth's Letter to Miss Martineau.
Christian Quart. Spectator. 9:434,647.
Christian Examiner. 50:49. 51:395.
Colquhoun's Isis Revelata. (State of the doctrine in 1844.)

Mesmerism—*continued.*
Crowe's (Mrs.) Night-side of nature.
Deleuze's Practical animal magnetism.
Democratic Review. 9:515. 20:102.
Dod's Philosophy of electrical Psychology.
Dublin Univ. Mag. 23:37,286. 37:52. 38:383.
Dupotet on Animal magnetism.
Durant's New theory of animal mag. 1837.
Eclectic Mag. 1:71. 23:271.
Eclectic Review. 4th Series. 18:369. 30:222.
Ennemoser's History of magnetism.
Esdaile's (J.) Mesmerism in India.
Forbes' Illustrations of modern magnetism.
Foreign Quart. Rev. 5:96. 12:413.
Frazier's Mag. 1:673.
Gregory's Letters to an enquirer.
Grimes' Etherology.
Haydock's Somnolism and Psycheism.
International Mag. 5:198.
Lee on Animal magnetism.
Leger on Do.
Littell's Living Age. 17:28,595.
Mackay on Popular Delusions.
Martin's Animal magnetism examined.
Martineau's (H.) Letters on Magnetism.
Mayo on the Truth contained in popular superstitions.
Monthly Review. 131:291.
Museum of For. Literature. 23:361. 24:317.
Newnham on Human magnetism.
North British Rev. 13:1. 15:69.
Page's Psychomancy.
Phillips' Vital Electro-dynamism.
Quarterly Review. 61:151.
Reschenbach's Animal Electricity. Translated by W. Gregory.
Sandys' Mesmerism and its opponents.
Southern Lit. Messenger. 4:253. 5:319.
Southern Quart. Rev. 3:467. 11:212.
Townsend's Facts on Magnetism.
The Zoist. Periodical. Lond. 1844, onward.

Messieurs de Port Royal. See PORT ROYAL.

Messiah. See CHRISTOLOGY.
Allix, Judicium veteris Ecclesiæ.
Buxtorf, de Messiah nostro.
Calovii (Abrah.) Dissertationes.
Crameri Scholæ Propheticæ.
Deutschmanni (Ioann.) Exercitationes.
Frischmuthii (Ioan.) Dissertationes.
Jacquelot, Dissert. sur le Messie.
Kirchoffii Messias Elucidatus.
Norelli Phosphorus Orthodoxæ Fidei.
Olearii (Ioann.) Dissertationes.
Rittengelii Veritas relig. Christianæ.
Schoetgen's Jesus d. wahre Messias.
Sommeri Specimen Theologiæ Soharicæ.

Abbadie on the Christian religion.
Barnard's Dudleian Lecture. 1756.
Bassnage's History of the Jews.
Calmet on the Works of the Messiah.
Charon's Demonstration of the Gospel.
Farrar's Bampton Lectures. 1803.

Messiah—*continued.*

Galloway's Messiah.
Goodwin's Hulsean Lectures. 1857.
Haldane's (R.) Evid. and auth. of Div. Rev.
Isaiah's M. of the Christians and Jews.
Kidder's Boyle Lectures. (Chiefly to prove the Christian religion.)
Lowman's Argument from prophecy.
McLaurin's Messiah.
Noel's (Baptist W.) Five sermons on the M.
Parish on Revelation.
Smith's (J. Pye) Scrip. testimony to the M.
Stanhope's Boyle Lectures. 1701, 1702.
Sykes' True ground of the expectation, &c.
Turner on the Messiah.
Wolfe's M. as predicted in the Pent. and Ps.

Messianic Psalms.

Kanne's Christus im Alte Testament.
Kuinoel's Weissagungen der Alt. Test.
Mayer's Patriarchalischen Verheitzungen.
Reinke's Einleitung, Grundtext, etc.
Scherer's Ausführliche Erklärung, etc.
Schulze's Kritik aller mess. Psalmen.
Schmidii (Sebastian.) Resolutio brevis, cum paraph. psalmorum propheticorum.

Harpur's Christ in the Psalms.
Rosenmüller on the Messianic psalms.
Ryland's Psalms restored to the Messiah.
Williams' Psalms interpreted of Christ.
Wolf's Messiah in the Pent. and Psalms.

Metaphysics. See MIND.

Metempsychosis. See BUDHISM, SOULS OF BRUTES.

Conz, Shicksale der Seelenwanderung.
Hauberus de Transmigratione.
Heusse, de Metempsychosi.
Irhovius de Palingenesia veterum.
Krug, der Neue Pythagoras. Ag. Ritzen.
Meyers (J. B.), Idee der Seelenwanderung.
Naville (G. C.), Dissert. Psychologica.
Osiandri (Joh. A.) Dissertationes.
Ritzen, die Höchsten Angelegenheiten.
Sartorius de Metemp. Pythagorica. (Particularly explains Matt. 14:2, and 16:4; John 9:2; Wisdom of Solomon 8:19.)
Schlosser, über die Seelenwanderung.
Schubert's Wanderung der Seele.
Sedermark, de Metempsychosi veterum.
Slevogti (P.) Disputationes.
Ugolini Thesaurus antiq. sacrarum.
Wedekind's Bestimmung des Menschen.
Wernsdorfii (Gottl.) Disputationes.

Asiatic Researches. 6:163.
Bird's (James) Historical Researches.
Colebrook's Miscellaneous Essays.
Francklin's Doctrines of the Budhists.
Hodgson's Religion, &c., of Nepal.
Holwell's (John Z.) Dissertation on the M.
Kennedy on the Puranas.
Low's Budha and the Phrabat.
Stevenson's Analysis of the Puranas.
Upham's Hist. and doctrines of the Budhists.
Ward's Hist. and literature of the Hindus.
Wilson's (H. H.) Lectures on the Puranas.

Methodism. See WESLEY.

Pro.

Jacoby's Handbuch d. Methodismus.
Warren's Systematische Theologie.

Armenian Magazine. 85 vols.
Baker's (O.) Discipline of the M. church.
Bangs' Vindication of the M. E. Church.
Benson's Apology for the Methodists.
——— Com. on Old and New Testament.
——— Defence of the Methodists.
——— Further defence.
Bibliotheca Sacra. 19:241.
Broca's Refutation of Scott.
Clark's (Dr. W.) Works.
Doctrine and discipline of the M. E. Church, approved at the General Conference in Baltimore. 1792.
Emory's (Bp.) Defence of our fathers.
——— Episcopal controversy reviewed.
Grindal's Laws of Wesleyan Methodism.
Gorrie's Episcopal Methodism.
Hodgson's Ecclesiastical Polity.
——— Calvinism examined and refuted.
Inskip's M. explained and defended.
Macbriar's Apology for Methodism.
Methodist Magazine. London.
Methodist Quart. Review. N. York.
Pierce's Principles and polity of M.
Porter's Compendium of Methodism.
Riggs' Principles of Methodism.
Rule's Wesleyan Methodism as a system.
Stevens' (Abel) Centenary Reflections.
Tefft's Methodism successful, and the internal causes of its success.
Turner's Constitution and discipline of M.
Ward's Miniature of Methodism.
Warren's Laws of the Wesleyans.
Watson's Theological Institutes.
Wesley's (John) Works.
Wesleyan Banner. Periodical.
Wesleyan Christian Library. 43 vols.
Wesleyan Vindicator. Periodical.

Con.

Annan's Difficulties of Arminian M. (Strictures on Wesley, Clark, Fisk, Bangs, &c.)
Boucher's Christian religion made plain.
Brown's (A. M.) Arminian inconsistencies. (To show that all the distinctive doctrines of Presbyterians are taught by standard Methodist writers.)
Burns' (Wm.) Moral tendency of Methodism.
Christian Review. 6:45.
Cook's (J.) M. condemned by M. preachers.
Croft's Thoughts concerning the Methodists.
Downes' Methodism Examined.
Frees' Rules for discovery of false prophets.
——— Tracts.
Graves' Great Iron Wheel.
Green's (Bp.) Dissertation on Enthusiasm.
——— Principles and practices of M.
Hale's Methodism inspected.
Hill on the Pastoral function.

Methodism—*continued.*

Con.

Hunt's Folly and danger of Methodism.
Ingram's (R. A.) Causes of dissension.
Jackson's The Church and the Methodist.
Lavington's Enthusiasm of Methodists and Papists compared. Notes by Polwhele.
McMichael's Government of the M. church.
Morris on Methodist church polity.
Musgrave's Polity of the Methodist Church.
Nightingale's Portraiture of M. 1807.
Norris' Methodism and the church fundamentally opposed.
Nott on Religious Enthusiasm.
Owen's (T. E.) Methodism unmasked.
Pelton's Absurdities of Methodism.
Russell's Hints to Methodists.
——— Reply to Benson's defence.
Taylor's (Isaac) Wesley and Methodism.
Whitefield's (Geo.) Remarks on Enthusiasm.
Whitehead's Pious Christian's faith and hope.

See DECANVER'S *Cat. of works in refutation of M., from its origin, in* 1729, *to the present,* 1846. Spécifies 227 Anti-Methodist publications.

Methodists, History of.

Baum's Methodismus; gekronte Preisschrift.
Burckhard, Gesch. d. Methodisten in Engl.
Atmore's Methodist Memorial. (A history of the introduction of M. into America.)
Bangs' History of the M. E. Church, from its origin in 1776. 1840.
Boehm's (Henry) Reminiscences.
Bogue & Bennet's History of Dissenters.
Clarke's Life and times of Bp. Hedding. (Contains much general information.)
Coke's (Thomas) Journal.
Crowther's Portraiture of Methodism. 1814.
Dixon's Methodism in America. 1849.
——— Origin, economy, and present condition of Methodism. 1843.
Dunn's Wesleyan M. in Nottingham. 1847.
Elliot's History of the great secession [1845] eventuating in the organization of the Methodist Church, South.
——— Life of Bp. Roberts.
Finley's Sketches of Western M. 1857.
Garret's Digest of Minutes of Conferences. From 1744 to 1826.
Gorrie's History of the Meth. Church in the United States and Canada. 1849.
Goss' Statistical history of the first century of American Methodism. 1866.
Hampson's History of Methodism. 1791.
Henkle's Life of Bp. Jackson.
Investigator. 1:367.
Jackson's (Tho.) Life of C. Wesley.
——— Centenary of Wesleyism. 1839.
——— Lives of early Methodists.
Jobson's American Methodism. 1857.
Lee's Hist. of M. Ch. in the U. S. 1776 to 1809.
London Review. 14:111. (A valuable sketch of the action of American Methodists on the subject of slavery, since 1780.)

Methodism, History of—*continued.*

Minutes of the General Conferences.
Myles' Hist. of the Methodists. 1729 to 1802.
Nightingale's Rise, progress, doct., &c. 1807.
North British Review. 27:90.
Peck's Early M. in New York and Penna.
Raybold's Methodism in West Jersey.
Quarterly Review. 3:113.
Smith's (Geo.) Hist. of Wesleyan M. 1860.
Southey's Rise and progress of Methodism.
Stevens' Memorial of M. in New England.
——— ——— 2d Series.
——— History of the M. from the origin to the death of Whitefield.
——— Life and times of Nathan Bangs, D.D.
——— Centenary of Methodism. 1866.
Tucker's History of the principles of M.
Warren's Chronicles of Wesleyan M. To 1825.

Michael. See ARCHANGEL.

Middle Aged.

Lindsey's Duties of the middle aged.
Spirit of the Pilgrims. 2:105.

Middle Ages.

Achery, Spicelegium scriptorum, etc. (A vast collection of curious tracts of the middle ages; with learned notes.)
Cangii Nomenclator scriptorum, etc.
Canisii Thesaurus monumentorum ecclesiast. et historicorum.
Cave, Historia Literaria.
Cellarii Historia medii ævi.
Dewhear, Prelectiones hiemis sæculorum.
Gos' Cultus in Mittelalter.
Morhoffii Polyhistoria.
Muratori Rerum Italicarum scriptores.
——— Antiquitates Italicæ medii ævi. (These two works make 39 large folios.)
Pertz, Monumenta Germaniæ. (From A. D. 500 to 1500. A huge work.)
Pictet, l'Eglise de l'onziéme siècle.
Schmid's (H.) Mysticismus der Mittelalters.
Schmidt's (K.) Mystiques du 14 siècle.
Zaccariæ (Soc. Jes.) Anecdotorum.
Amer. Quart. Register. 6:272.
Berington's Literary hist. of the middle ages.
Blackwood's Magazine. 47:61.
Des Michael's History of the middle ages.
Dunham's Hist. of Europe in the mid. ages.
Eclectic Magazine. 6:289.
Edinburg Review. 23:229. 30:140.
Froissart's Chronicles of France, Spain, &c.
Hallam's History of the middle ages.
Koeppen's World in the middle ages. (The institutions, customs, &c., in Europe, Asia, and Africa; from the 5th to the 15th cent.)
Maitland's State of religion in 9–12th cent.
Maurice's (F. D.) Mediæval philosophy. (A conspectus of the works of Boethius, Erigena, Lanfranc, Anselm, Abelard, &c. &c.)
Monthly Review. 87:1,136.
Museum of For. Literature. 3:393.
Neander's Memorials of Christian life.
North Brit. Review. 8:68. (Italy.)

Middle Ages—*continued.*

Petrie's History of Great Britain.
Princeton Review. 27:62.
Westminster Review. 51:334.
Wright's English literature and superstitions of the middle ages.

The following list is given by EAST APTHORP, in his *"Letters."*

Collections.

Schardius, 1673. Pistorius, 1613. Reuberus, 1619. Urstisius, 1670. Goldastus, 1661. Frekerus, 1717. Lindenbregius, 1706. Meibomius, 1688. Paulinus, 1698. Leibnitz, 1700. Kulpisius, 1685. Schilterus, 1702. Reineccius, 1702. Ludewig, 1718. Echard, 1723. Canisius, 1725. Pezius, 1720.

Individual Histories.

A. D.
283– 565. Sigonii hist. de occid. imperio.
570–1286. ——— ——— regno Italiæ.
360– 570. Warnefridi F. Diaconus.
– 552. Jornandes, de rebus Geticis.
176– 628. Isidori Hist. Gothorum.
O. C.– 600. Gregorius Turonensis.
600– 735. ——— Continuatus.
714– 900. Annales Francorum fuldenses.
741– 842. Adelini Benedictini annales.
U.C.– 751. Antiq. Gauloises de C. Fauches.
755–1076. Adami Bremensis.
768– 814. Eginhardi vita Caroli Mag.
778– 840. Thegani vita Ludovici Pii.
788–1504. Alberti Crantzii de ecclesiis.
830–1370. Ioannes Trithemius.
1– 907. Regino, cum.
O. C.–1228. Conrado, et.
O. C.–1352. Lamberto Schnab.
O. C.–1100. Hermanus Contractus.
1073–1082. Brunonis Hist. belli Saxonici.
O. C.–1152. Otto Frisingensis.
1162–1237. Godefridi monachi Annales.
381–1112. Sigebertus Gemblacensis.
1113–1210. Robertus de Monte.
O. C.–1250. Vicentii Speculum.
1270–1378. Alberti Annales.
U.C.–1278. Polonus, de quo Niceron xiv. 195.
1163–1343. Continuatio.
1295–1362. Henricus de Rebdorf apud Frek.
1326–1400. Chroniques de Froissard.
1–1472. Platina de vitis Pontificum.
1–1494. Caspianus quem excipit.
1494-1540. Paulus Jovius.
1461–1500. Memoires de Philipe de Comines.

For an account of many hundred writers of the middle ages, see CANG, CAVE, DEWHEAR, and MORHOFF, mentioned above.

A most convenient *tabular* view of *all* the principal historians, with a notice of the various editions, is given in FREKER'S *Directorium historicorum medii aevum.*

The *literary* condition of the middle ages is abundantly illustrated by HODY, *de Graecis illust.;* ROSCOE, *Lorenzo de Medici;* and HALLAM, *History of Literature.*

Military Orders. See CHIVALRY.

Fabricii Bibliotheca Antiquarum, etc.
Favyne, Theatre d'Honneur.
Gregoire, Histoire des Sectes, etc.
Hermance, Histoire de Religions.
Heylot, Histoire des Ordres.
Mabillon, Annales.
Memoirs de Trevoux.
Pantaleonis Militaris ordinis rerum, etc.
Thomasii (Christian.) Dissertationes.
Vitriarius de Ordinibus Equestribus.
Burke's (B.) Orders of Knighthood.
Pamphleteer. 5:33.

Millenarians.

Pro.

Alstedius de Mille annis Apocalypsis.
Andalæ Exegesis locorum S. Scrip.
Coccei Opera exeget. didac. et polem.
Driessenii Meditationes in Apocalypsin.
Lambert, Exposition des Predictions, etc.
Petersen's Erklärung der Offenbarung. C. xx.
——— Nubes testium verit. de regno Christi.
——— Petachia.
——— Schlüssel der Offenbarung.

P. was the Ajax of this party in the 17th century, and wrote other strong treatises, between 1693 and 1718, which called forth a host of replies.

Rallii Halcyonia eccl. evangelicarum.
Riemann's Lehre der heiligen Scrift. vom taufendjahrigen Reiche.
Seitz's Melchisedeckisches Priesterthum.
Worthington, Ecclesiæ futuræ felicitas.
Alsted's Saint's reign on earth.
——— Beloved city.
Anderson (Wm.) on the Millen. doctrine.
Archer on the Personal reign of Christ.
Baxter's Louis Napoleon the destined monarch of the world.
Begg's (Jas. A.) Evid. of Christ's reign, &c.
——— Letter to a minister.
——— Scripture argument.
Bellamy (Jos.) on the Millennium.
Berg (Jos. F.) on the Second Advent.
Beverly's (Thomas) Works.
Bonar's Redemption drawing nigh.
Bryant's (Alfred) Millenarian views.
Christian Herald. Dublin. 1830–1834.
Clayton on the Time of Christ's coming.
Coleman's (J. N.) Sermons.
Cox's (John) Millenarian's answer to the hope that is in him.
Cunningham's Second coming of Christ.
——— Examination of Faber on prophecy.
——— Review of Wardlaw on the M.
——— Premillennial Advent.
Davis' (W.) Beautiful city.
Drummond's Scriptural doctrine of the M.
Duffield (G.) on the Second coming, &c.
——— Defence of Do.
Durant's Salvation of the saints.
Frere's Prophecy of Daniel and Ezra.
Fry's Glorious Epiphany of Christ.
Gill's (Philip) Second coming of Christ.

Millenarians—*continued.*

Pro.

Gregory's State of the world at the final outbreak of evil, and 2d coming of Christ.
Hartley's (Thomas) Paradise restored.
Henshaw's Lectures on the Advent.
Homes' Resurrection revealed.
Irving (Edward) on the Prophecies.
Jones' (H.) Kingdom at hand.
Jones' (Joel) Jesus and the coming glory.
McCausland's Jerusalem and Rome.
Mandeville's Exp. of the Ep. to the Hebrews.
Mansford on Millenarianism.
Maton on the Millennium.
Mede's (Joseph) Works.
Morning Watch. Periodical. Lond. 1829–33.
Newton (W.) on the first two visions of the book of Daniel.
Ogilvy on the Premillennial advent.
Pirie's French Revolution in the light of the Sacred Oracles.
Ranew's Saint's glory after the resurrection.
Roach's Imperial standard of Messiah.
Shimeal's Second coming of Christ.
Silliman's (Anna) The world's Jubilee.
Sirr's Letters to Rev. H. Gipps.
Waples on the Apocalypse.
Wattson's (Tho.) Shiloh's Sceptre.
White's (Hugh) Reflections on the 2d Adv.
Winthrop's (Edward) Lectures.
Wood's Believer's Guide.

Con.

Amyraut, de Régne de Mille ans.
Brockii Schediasma de Chiliasmo.
Calixti (F. U.) Tractatio de Chiliasmo.
Corodi's Geschichte des Chiliasmus.
Diedrich, Ueber d. Chiliasmus.
Duget, Traditions des S S. Peres.
Gebhard (V. C.) de Chiliasmo.
Koch's (Christop.) Grundliche Widerlegung d. ungegründeten tausendiährigen Reichs.
Mennlingius de Chiliasmo.
Meyeri Castigatio Petersenii.
——— Discussio circa Chiliasmum.
Neumanni (J. G.) Disputationes VIII.
Neumeister, der Kinder Gottesdienst.
Sandhagenii (C. H.) Epistolæ.
Waechtleri (Iacobus) Opera.
Wolfii (I. I.) Dialogus de Chiliasmo.
Bibliotheca Sacra. 12:470.
Brown's (David) Second coming of Christ.
Burgh's Lectures on the Second Advent.
Christian Review. 8:115. (Hist. of the doct.)
Craddock on the Apocalypse.
Crosby (Alpheus) on the Second Advent.
Eclectic Review. New Series. 1:248.
Faber's (Geo. S.) Calendar of prophecy.
Gipps on the First Resurrection.
Hall's (Tho.) Reply to Homes.
Hamilton (Wm.) on the Millennium.
Hey's (Dr. John) Lectures. Bk. 4, Art. 4.
Jefferson (John) on the Millennium.
Jones' (Wm.) Lectures on the Apocalypse.
London Quart. Review. 5:481.

Millenarians—*continued.*

Con.

Lyons' (W. P.) Millennial studies.
Maton's Israel's Redemption.
Morrison on Christ's personal reign.
Pareus' Com. on Revelations. Chap. 20.
Petrie's Chiliasto-mastix.
Princeton Rev. 19:564. 23:1. 25:66. 28:524.
Reed's (Andrew) Sermons.
Shedd's Eschatology.
Stuart's (Prof.) Strictures on Dr. Duffield.
Vint's New illustration of prophecy. (Maintains that the millennium is past.)
Waldegrave's Bampton Lectures. 1854.
Whitby (Dan.) on the Millennium.
Williamson's Letters to a Millenarian.
Young's (Cha.) Arguments about the M.

Millennial Church [Shakers].

Pro.

A Holy and Divine book, from the Lord God of Heaven; revealed in the United Society at Lebanon, New York.
Christian Secretary. Periodical.
Christ's First and second appearing.
The Day Star. Periodical.
Evans' Origin, history, principles, and rules, of the United Society of believers in Christ's second coming. 1859.
Juvenile Guide.
The Kentucky Revival.
The Millennial Church.
The Sacred Roll. (Held to be written by inspiration.)
Summary View of the Millennial Ch. 1823.
Testimony of Christ's second coming. (Contains a full statement of the faith and practice of "The Church of God in the latter day." 1808.)

Con.

Christian Month. Spectator. 6:351.
Dyer's (Mary) Sufferings among the Shakers. 1818.
Haskell's Shakerism unmasked.
Knickerbocker Magazine. 11:552. (By Horace Greeley.)
Lamson's Two years among the Shakers.
New York Theol. Magazine. 1:82.
Niles' Weekly Register. 23:37. 37:58.
Rathbone's (Valentine) Hints. (Once belonged to this people.)

Millennial Church, History of.

Brown's History of the Shakers. 1812.
Evans' Origin, History, &c.
Panoplist. 4:289.
Taylor's Account of the Shakers.
West's History of the Shakers.

Millennium. See APOCALYPSE, GOG, MILLENARIANS, SECOND ADVENT.

Justin M., Dialog. cum Tryphonte Jud.
Lactantius, Divinæ Institutiones.
Origen, de Principiis.
Irenæus, Fragmenta.

Millennium—*continued.*

Bœhmeni (Jacob.) Opera.
Corrodi Geschichte des Chiliasmus.
Daillé, de Usu Patrum.
Dupin, Analysis Apocalypsis.
Gennadius de Dogmatibus eccles. Cap. LV.
Weigelii Apparatus Literarius.

Addison's Account of the Millennium.
Allein (W.) on the Millennium.
American Monthly Rev. 3:202.
Bellamy's Works.
Biblioth. Sacra. 6:657.
Bogue's (D.) Discourses on the Millennium.
Burnett's Theory of the Earth.
Bush on the M. (Makes it to have occurred in the days of Constantine.)
Chris. Examiner. 57:1.
Chris. Monthly Spectator. 1:71,295.
Christian Observer. 27:713.
Chris. Review. 6:528. 8:115. (History of the doctrine.) 13:249. (Signs.)
Cogswell's Harbinger of the Millennium.
Edwards' (Pres.) Works.
Edwards' (Morgan) Academical Exercises.
Ellison (Seacombe) on the Millennium.
Emerson's (Jos.) Lectures on the M.
Eyre's Observations on the Prophecies.
Fleming on the First Resurrection.
Gill's (Dr. John) Sermons and Tracts.
Gorton's Scripture account of the M.
Gray's (Robert) Discourses.
Greenham on the Prophecies.
Hart's (Robert) Sermons.
Hartley's (T.) Paradise restored.
Holmes' (Nath.) Resurrection revealed.
Hopkins' (S.) System of Divinity.
——— on the Millennium. (Learned.)
Killingworth's (Grantham) Works.
Lardner's Works.
Loader's Millennium; or Joy to the World.
Mandeville's (Viscount) Horæ Hebraicæ.
Mede's (J.) Works.
Newton (Bp.) on the Prophecies. Diss. 25.
Priestley's Institutes of Religion.
Princeton Rev. 5:204.
Russel's (Dr. M.) Discourses.
Sherwin's Collection of tracts relat. to the M.
Spaulding on the Apocalypse.
Stuart on the Apocalypse.
Vint's Illustrat. of proph. (Thinks it past.)
Whitby's Diss. (At the end of his Comment.)
Winchester on the Millennium.
Woodward's (Henry) Essays and Sermons.
Worthington on Redemption.

Millerism.

Miller's Principles of prophetic chronology.
——— Evidence of the second coming of Christ about the year 1843.
——— (Other treatises.)
Christian Examiner. 41:87.
Christian Review. 9:597.
Midnight Cry. Periodical. Boston. Published from 1842 to 1847.

Mind. See COMMON SENSE, LOGIC, MOTIVES, MORAL SUASION, PROVINCE OF REASON, RECIPROCAL INFLUENCE, TRANSCENDENTALISM.

Campanella de Libris propriis, etc.
Casmanni Psychologia.
Collard, Royer. (In Jouffroy's Reid.)
Cousin, Fragmens philosophiques, etc.
——— Œuvres.
Degerando, Hist. comparée des systémes de la philosophie.
Delitzsch's Biblische Psychologie.
Destutt de Tracy, Elemens d'Ideologie.
Francastorius de Intellectu.
Helvetius, Œuvres.
Jouffroy, Œuvres.
Kant's Metaphysic der Sitten.
——— ——— der Rechtslehre.
——— Streit der Facultaten.
——— &c. &c.
Laromiguiére, Leçons de philosophie.
Leibnitzii Opera.
Maccovii Metaphysica.
Malbranche, Recherche de la verité.
Massius, sur l'Instinct, l'intelligence, etc.
Ramus, Scholæ Metaphysicæ.
Rapin, Penseès sur la nature de l'Esprit.
Rorarius de usu Rationis.
Stahlii Metaphysica.
Wallis, Institutiones Logicæ.
Zwantzigeri Kantii metaph. morum.

Abercrombie on the Intellectual powers.
——— Essays.
Amer. Institute of Instruction. Periodical.
Amer. Quart. Review. 10:291.
Appleton's (Pres.) Works. (Value of intellectual philosophy.)
Bain's (A.) The Senses and the Intellect.
Ballantyne's Examination of the hum. mind.
Beattie on Truth.
Belsham's Philosophy of the mind.
Bilfiotheca Sacra. 5:108. 8:73.
Bilfinger on Pneumatology.
Bishop's (D.) Introd. to the study of mind.
Blackwood's Mag. 4:682. 39:798. 40,122,253, 327,524,627,741. 41:258.
Blakey's History of the philosophy of mind. (Gives the opinions of all the principal writers on this subject, from the earliest period down to 1848.)
British Quart. Rev. 5:289.
Brodie's (B. C.) Psychological Inquiries.
Brown's (Peter) Procedure and limit of the understanding.
Brown's (Tho.) Lectures on the Mind.
Brucker's History of Philosophy.
Christ. Month. Review. 100:402.
Christ. Month. Spect. 7:28,66. 8:141.
Christ. Quart. Spect. 6:609. 7:89.
Christian Review. 3:418.
Clarke's (Sam.) Boyle Lectures. 1704.
Clifford (M.) on Human reason.
Colliber's Free thoughts on souls.
Corey's Metaphysical Inquiries. (Ancient and modern philosophers.)
Cousin's Elements of Psychology.

Mind—*continued.*

Crouza's Art of Thinking.
Cudworth's Intellect. system of the universe.
Davies' Cultivation of the mind.
Democratic Review. 24:24.
Des Cartes' Works.
Doddridge's Lectures.
Douglass' Philosophy of the mind.
Dublin University Mag. 1:140.
Eclectic Rev. 4th Series. 24:205.
Edinburg Review. 1:475. 27:180. 36:220. 50:194. 68:179. 70:190.
Fearns on Human consciousness.
Ferrier's Institutes of Metaphysics.
Ferrol on the Human Intellect.
Fichté's Works.
For. Quart. Review. 1:358.
Frazier's Magazine. 8:291.
Fuller's Acquirements and hist. of the mind.
Glanvill's Essays.
Gregoire's Faculties of the Negroes.
Grinfield's Evidences of Christianity, by the inductive philosophy of the mind.
Hamilton's (Sir William) Works.
Hartley on Man.
Haven's (Jos.) Mental Philosophy.
Hegel's Works.
Helvetius' Essays. Trans. by W. Mudford.
——— ——— " " W. Hooper.
Herbert's (J. F.) Philosophical works.
Hickok's Rational Psychology.
Holland's (H.) Mental Physiology.
Houghton's Prodromus. (First principles of reasoning.)
Hume's (David) Works.
Kant's Critique of pure reason.
Knickerbocker Magazine. 7:553. 11:297,435. 15:413,451. 37:525.
Le Clerc's Ontology.
Leibnitz's Philosophical works.
Literary and Theol. Review. 1:74,169,584, 614. 2:122,261,576.
Locke on the Understanding.
McCaul's Philosophy of mind and matter.
Mackey's Progress of the human mind.
Mayne's (Cha.) Philosophical works.
Mayo's Pathology of the mind.
Methodist Quarterly. 4:243.
Mills' Phenomena of the human mind.
Monboddo's (Lord) Ancient Metaphysics. ("Displays great erudition."—Lord Dalhousie.)
Monthly Review. 97:129. 118:441.
Mudie's Mental Philosophy.
Museum of For. Literature. 10:441. 11:6.
Norris' (J.) Ideal world.
North Amer. Review. 19:1. 24:56,480. 29:67. 36:488. 53:1. 85:19.
Oldfield's Improvement of Reason.
Oswald's Appeal to common sense.
Penrose on the Nature of human motives.
Pirie's (W. R.) Posthumous Works.
Priestley's Examination of Reid's Inquiry.
Princeton Review. 1:93.
Quarterly Review. 12:281. 17:39. 26:474.

Mind—*continued.*

Rauch's Psychology.
Reid's Intellectual and active powers.
Reinhold's Life and Works.
Riccalton's (Robert) Works.
Sawyer's Mental Philosophy.
Schelling's Works.
Schumacker's Mental Philosophy.
Scott's (R. E.) Elements of Intellec. Philos.
——— Limits and objects of physical and metaphysical science.
Shultzenstein's New system of Psychology.
Smart's New School of Metaphysics.
Smyth's Christian Metaphysics. (Plato, Malbranche, and Gioberti, compared with modern psychologists.)
Southern Review. 3:125.
Southern Lit. Messenger. 5:616.
Steinthall's Grammar, Logic, and Psychology: their relations to each other.
Stewart's Philosophy of the mind.
——— Essays.
Taylor's (Isaac) Elements of Thought.
——— World of mind.
Taylor's (Jer.) Sketch of Moral Philosophy.
Tenneman's History of Philosophy.
Thompson (Wm.) on the Laws of Thought.
Tucker's Light of nature pursued.
United States Lit. Gaz. 5:109. 6:161.
Upham's Mental Philosophy.
Usher's Theory of the human mind.
——— Clio.
Voltaire's Metaphysics of Newton.
Watts on the Improvement of the mind.
——— Strength and weakness of human reason.
Webb's (Prof.) Intellectualism of Locke. (Defends Locke's theory from the objections of Hamilton and others.)
Westminster Review. 54:353.
Wigan's Duality of the mind, proved by the structure, functions, and diseases of the brain.
Wolfe's Metaphysical Works. (Numerous.)

Mineralogy of the Bible.
See NATURAL HISTORY.

Ministerial Education. See CALL TO THE MINISTRY, EDUCATION SOCIETIES, ELOQUENCE, STUDY OF THEOLOGY, THEOLOGICAL SEMINARIES, THEOLOGY.

Bechmannus de Cognitu necessariis in præparando ministro.
Crocius de Ratione studii theologici.
Gerardi Methodus studii theologici.
Maresii Enchiridion candidatorum.
Strigelii Ratio discendi theologiam.

Am. Quart. Register. Periodical. (Many articles.)
Biblioth. Sacra. 8:235.
Bickersteth's Christian Student.
Bloomfield's Importance of learning, &c.
Bray's Bibliotheca Parochialis.
Bull's (Bp.) Companion for candidates.
Campbell's (Dr. George) Lectures.

Ministerial Education—*continued.*

Chris. Rev. 1:106. 2:260,579. 3:254. 7:447. 12:95.
Chris. Monthly Spect. 1:132. 4:449.
Chris. Examiner. 11:84.
Clarke's (Adam) Letter to a preacher.
Cockburn's Lectures on a ministerial education in the University of Cambridge.
Craig's (William) Sermons.
Freeston's Advice to a young minister.
Gibbon's Christian Minister.
Hall's (Robt.) Letter to Eustace Carey.
Hinton (John H.) on Min. qualifications.
Hodgson's (Chr.) Instructions to candidates.
Kentish's Importance of M. education.
Macgill's Considerations.
Marsh's (H.) Usefulness and necessity, &c.
Mason's Student and pastor.
——— Letter to a friend.
Mather's (Cotton) Directions to a candidate.
Napleton's Advice to a student.
New Englander. 1:126.
N. Amer. Review. 49:206.
Orton's (Job) Letters to students, &c. (Many notices of persons and books.)
Osterwald's Lectures.
Princeton Review. 5:55. 15:587.
Raike's Remarks on clerical education.
Secker's (Abp.) Eight charges.
Sisson's 300 questions in Divinity.
Spirit of the Pilgrims. 6:268,456.
Universalist Quarterly. 7:221.

Lists of books for small theological libraries are given in EDWARDS *on Preaching*, 1705; BRAY'S *Bibliotheca Parochialis*, 1707; CLEAVER'S *List of books for the younger clergy*, 1800; and BRIDGES *on the Ministry*, 1829.

Ministerial Habits.
See CLERICAL HABITS.

Ministerial Titles.

Christian Month. Spect. 2:297.

Ministerial Vestments.
See VESTMENTS.

Ministering Spirits. See ANGELS, GUARDIAN ANGELS.

Herara de Angelis.
Meerheimii Historia angelorum.
Victorelli Dissertationes.
Wernsdorfii Exercitationes historicæ.

Ambrose's (Isaac) Works. (Ser. on Ps. 91:11.)
Boyse on the Ministry of angels.
Bull's (Bp.) Sermons.
Camfield on Angels.
Caswal's (E.) Sermons.
Clayton's History, attributes, pursuits, &c.
Clayton's (Robt.) Vindication of the O. Test.
Copner's (James) Sermons.
Hallet's (Jos.) Notes on Scripture.
Heber's (Bp.) Parish Sermons.
Horne's (Bp.) Discourses.
Johnson's (John) Sermons.

Ministering Spirits—*continued.*

Limborch's Theology. Bk. 2, ch. 2.
Marshall's (Nathaniel) Sermons.
Mostyn's (G. T.) Ministry of angels.
Nicholson's (William) Sermons.
Patrick's (Bp.) Sermons.
Pearce's Com. on the Epis. to the Hebrews.
Reynolds on Angels.
Slade's (James) Sermons.
Stebbings' (Henry) Sermons.
Taylor's (Will.) Sermons.
Thomas' Ministry of angels in the church.
Walker's (G. R.) Ministry of angels.
Waters' (John W.) Sermons.
Wheatley's (Charles) Sermons.
White's (Thomas) Sermons.

Ministry. See CALL, CLERICAL HABITS, ELOQUENCE, LAY PREACHING, MINISTERIAL EDUCATION, PASTORAL THEOLOGY, PREACHING, STUDY OF SCRIPTURE, THEOLOGY.

Chrysostom, de Sacerdotio.
Ambrose, de Officiis Clericorum.
Jerome, de Vita Clericorum.
Augustine, de Vita Clericorum.
——— in Ezek. cap. xxxiv.

D'Aubigné, Il y a un ministère de la parole, institué de Dieu?
Eckhardi Opuscula Theologiæ.
Fechtius, de Necessitate, sanctitate, etc.
Fenelon, Traité du Ministère.
Henningii Pastor. (Mode of life.)
Maresii Enchiridion Candidatorum.
Ostervald, de l'Exercise de ministère.
Rampachii Commentatio. (Gives copious accounts of the sentiments of the Fathers.)
Sadeele de Legitima vocatione pastorum.
Zeltneri (Gustav. Geo.) Dissertationes.
Zornii Delineatio theol. patristicæ.

Addison's Primitive Institution, &c.
Anderson's (J. S. M.) Sermons.
Atterbury's (Lewis) Sermons.
American Bibl. Repos. 9:64.
American Quart. Register. (Many articles.)
Bailey's (B.) Duties of the Chris. ministry.
Balguy's (Thomas) Visitation Discourses.
Barlow's (Bp.) Remains.
Baxter's Reformed Pastor.
Bearcroft's Thirteen discourses on the M.
Berens on Pastoral Watchfulness.
Blackbourn's Duties of the clergy.
Bloomfield's (Geo. B.) Sermons.
Blundell's (Thomas) Sermons.
Blunt's Parish Priest's duties and obligat.
Boardman (H. A.) on the Chris. Ministry.
Bridge's (Chas.) Christian Ministry.
Brown's Pastor's Manual. (Contains tracts by Mason, Doddridge, Watts, Erskine, Cecil, Newton, Scott, Bostwick, A. Booth, and Jennings.)
Bulkley's Christian Minister.
Bullinger's Decades.
Cappe's (Newcombe) Practical Discourses.
Cellerier on the Ministry.

Ministry—*continued.*

Channing's (Will. E.) Discourses.
Christ. Examiner. 5:101. 15:334.
Christ. Month. Spect. 3:401. 8:441. 9:487.
Christian Observer. 14:13. 19:433. 20:533, 544. 22:329,546. 28:137,416.
Christian Quart. Spect. 4:207. 6:542. 7:353. 8:411.
Christian Review. 1:15. 3:254,576. 11:256. 13:501. 15:400.
Chrysostom on the Priesthood. Translated by Cowper.
——— ——— Trans. by Mason.
Clergyman's Instructor. (A collection of valuable treatises.)
Coetlogan's Sermons.
Condor on the Importance of the clerical character.
Cooper's (Edward) Sermons.
Crosthwaite on the Christian ministry.
Davies' (Pres. Samuel) Sermons.
Dealtry's (William) Sermons.
Donne's (John) Sermons.
Dwight's Sermons. Ser. 150–154.
Eade's Comprehensive view of the Gospel M.
Eclectic Review. 4th Series. 20:23.
Edinburg Rev. 19:360.
Edmondson on the Christian ministry.
Edwards' (John) Preacher.
Edwards' (Pres.) Works.
Enfield's Character, qualifications, &c.
Evans' Usefulness the great object, &c.
Fuller's Works. (Papers in Evangel. Mag.)
Gibbon's (Tho.) Christian Minister.
Gibson's Origin, Qualifications, &c.
Gilpin's Portrait of St. Paul.
Graves on the Clerical character.
Heber's (Bp.) Sermons.
Henry's (Matt.) Sermons and Tracts.
Hodge's (John) Sermons.
Holbrook's (A.) Duties of the ministry.
Horseley's (Bp.) Sermons.
Huntingdon's (Prof.) Sermons.
Innes' (W.) Excitement and direction. (Extracts from Baxter, Watts, Alleine, Witherspoon, Erskine, Martyn, Brainard, Cecil, and Robert Hall.)
James' (J. A.) An earnest ministry the want of the times.
Jewell's (Bp.) Works.
Johnson's Clergyman's Vade Mecum.
Jones' (William) Sermons.
Jurieu's Pastoral Letters.
Kentish's Nature and duty of the Ministry.
Latham's Difficulties and discouragem'ts, &c.
Law's (Wm.) Earnest address to the clergy.
Leechman's Temper, char., and duty of a M.
Lettuce (Dr.) on the Clerical character.
Lucas' (Richard) Sermons.
Lucy's Nature of a Minister.
Mackensie's Clergy of the first ten centuries.
McCaul's (Alexander) Sermons.
Mandell's Sermons on the Christ. Ministry.
Masillon's Charges and Conferences.
Mason's Student and Pastor.

Ministry—*continued.*

Mede's (Joseph) Sermons.
Monroe's (Edward) Sermons.
North Am. Rev. 49:206.
Orton's Letters to a young clergyman.
Osterwald's Lect. on the M. Tr. by Stevens.
Paley's (Wm.) Sermons. (Dangers of, &c.)
Pike's (J. G.) Christian M. contemplated.
Princeton Review. 26:708.
Raikes' (Henry) Ordination Sermons.
Rees on the Maintenance, &c.
Riddle's (J. E.) Sermons.
Robertson's (John) Sermons.
Rose's (H. J.) Discourses.
Ryland's (John) Sermons. (Trials of a M.)
Seabury's (Bp.) Sermons.
Secker's (Abp.) Charges to the clergy.
Shuttleworth's Speculum Sacrum.
Smith's (John Pye) Sermons.
Smith's (John) Nature, qualifications, &c.
Spirit of the Pilgrims. 6:268,456,499.
Spring's (Gardner) Power of the pulpit.
Steward on Mediatorial sovereignty.
Stillingfleet's Amusements of the clergy.
Storry's (Thomas) Sermons.
Summerfield's (John) Sermons.
Sumner's (Abp.) Sermons. (4 on this subj.)
Tappan's (David) Sermons.
Taylor's (Jer.) Sermons.
——— Institution and necessity of the M.
——— Rules and advices to the clergy.
Thompson's (Edward) Sermons.
Tilly's (William) Sermons.
Tindale's (John) Manual for young M.
Turner's (D.) Christian ministry considered.
——— Compendium of social religion.
Universalist Quart. 7:221.
Venn's (John) Sermons.
Vinet's Theory of the evangelical ministry.
Wallace's Guide to the Christian ministry.
Walker's (J.) A faithful ministry.
——— Posthumous sermons.
Watts' Foundation of a Christian church.
——— Rules for ministerial conduct.
Wayland's (Francis) Sermons.
——— Letters on the Christian ministry.
White's Letters from a father to his sons.
Wilks' Signs of conversion in ministers.
Wilkins' (Bp.) Ecclesiastes.
Wylie's Gospel ministry, and the duty of supporting it.
Wynne's The model parish. (Prize essay.)

The innumerable "charges," by Church of England Bishops, and Archdeacons, contain much valuable matter.

Ministry of Angels.
See MINISTERING SPIRITS.

Minorites. See FRANCISCANS.

Minucius Felix.

Minucii Opera. Various editions. That of Davis, Camb. 1812, is commonly preferred.
Balduini (Fred.) Dissertationes.
Bremer, Ep. crit. super aliquot M. locis.

Minucius Felix—*continued.*

Burchardi (Georg.) Dissertationes.
Heumanni (Chris. Augus.) Observationes.
Hoven, Hist. crit. de ætate, dignitate, et patria, Minucii Felex.
Lobsteini M. priscæ chris. veræ fidei testis.
Meieri (H.) Com. de Minucio Felice.
Ouselii Comm. in Minucio.
Polet's Uebersetzung und Anmerkungen.
Stieberi (F.) Observationes criticæ.

Dalrymple's Trans. of the Octavius.
Holden's —— —— With Com.
James' (Rich.) —— —— Notes.
Lorraine's (Pet.) —— —— Notes.
Reeves' (W.) —— —— Notes.

Miracles. See FALSE MIRACLES, MIRACLES OF THE FIRST AGES.

Augustine, Opera.
Justin M., Apologia.
Origen, contra Celsum.

Boniward, de la Source de l'Idolatrie.
Eck's Wundergeschichten des N. Test.
Eusebii Evangelica Demonstratio.
Gräffe, Philos. Vertheidigung, &c.
Gudii Discussio mysticæ M. Christi interp.
Helvetii Libellus de miraculis.
Hottingeri Diatribe, philos.-theologica.
Huebneri (H. L.) Dissertationes.
Koster's Immanuel.
Lilienthal's Wunderwercke Jesu
Mammachius, Orig. et Antiq. Christianorum.
Meinerhagen's Bedentung der bibl. Wunder.
Pfaffii (Christoph.) Disputationes.
Picteti Dissertationes Theologicæ.
Spencer, Notat. ad Origen contra Celsum.
Wagner's (E. F.) Thaten und Shicksale J. C.
Werenfels, Opuscula Theologica.
Witsii Meletemata. Dissertatio IV.

Adams' (Will.) Answer to Mr. Hume.
Am. Bibl. Repos. 3d Series. 3:304,423.
Arnold's (Thomas) Sermons.
Atkinson's Vindication of the literal sense.
Atterbury's (Lewis) Sermons.
Barrington on the Witness of the H. Spirit.
Bates' Works. Chap. 3 and 4.
Bibliotheca Sacra. 19:328.
Bingham's Antiquities of the Chris. church.
Bonnett's Enquiries, philosophical and critical, concerning Christianity.
Brackenridge's (John) Sermons.
Bragge on our Saviour's miracles.
Brown's Essays on the Characteristics.
Bulkley on the Miracles of Christ.
Butler's Analogy of religion and nature.
Campbell on Miracles. (Answer to Hume.)
Chapman's Eusebius.
Chapman's M. the proper credentials, &c.
Chris. Examiner. 31:348. 49:47.
Chris. Review. 12:274,408.
Clarke's Boyle Lectures. 1705.
Collyer (W. B.) on Scripture Miracles.
Conybeare's (John) Answor to Tyndall.
—— Sermons.
—— Discourse on Miracles.

Miracles—*continued.*

Cox's (R. C.) Lectures on Miracles.
Cudworth's Intellectual System. Bk. 1, ch. 5.
Cummings' (John) Foreshadows. (Poor.)
Ditton on the Resurrection of Christ.
Dodd's (William) Sermons.
Doddridge's Lectures. Part 5.
Douglass' Criterion of true miracles.
Doyle's Answer to Woolston.
Edinburg Review. 46:91. 52:388.
Edwards' (Thomas) Sermons.
Elrington's Lectures before Trinity College.
Encyclopedia Brittanica. Art. "Miracles."
Entick's Evidences of Christianity.
Episcopal Magazine. 1:202. 2:108.
Evangelical Review. 1:491.
Farmer's Dissertation on Miracles. (Great.)
Fiddes' (Richard) Sermons.
Fleetwood's Essays on Miracles.
Gardner's Short answer to a long letter.
Graves' (Richard) Sermons.
Hallett's Nature, kind, and number of Christ's Miracles.
Harris' Unreasonableness of Infidelity.
Hewlett's M. real evidences of a Div. revel.
Hook's (Walter F.) Sermons at Oxford.
Horseley's (Bp.) Sermons.
Hovey's (Alvah) The miracles of Christ.
Howarth's Hulsean Lectures. 1836.
Humphrey's (W. G.) Discourses on the M.
Hurrion on the Spirit.
James' (William) Sermons.
Jameson's Analogy between the miracles and doctrines of Scripture.
Jepton's Reality of our Saviour's miracles.
Jortin's Boyle Lectures. 1750.
Keach's Gospel mysteries revealed.
King's Morsels of Criticism.
Lardner's Credibility of the Gospel.
Laurent's Expostulation.
Lawson (Cha.) on the Miracles of Christ.
Le Bas (Cha. W.) on Miracles.
Leland's View of Deistical writers.
Le Moine's Diss. on M. (Against Chubb.)
Lit. and Theol. Review. 1:150. 4:489.
Locke on Miracles.
Mackenzie (M. J.) on Miracles.
Mant's (Bp.) Works.
Marsden's Hulsean Lectures. 1844.
Mayo on the Miracles of our Lord.
McGuire's Miracles of Christ.
McKnight's Truth of the Gospel.
Month. Review. 124:205. 126:180.
Mozley's Bampton Lectures. 1800.
Myers' Mosaic, Historic, and Prophetic M.
New Englander. 2:208.
Newton on the Prophecies.
Ogilvie's Bampton Lectures. 1836.
Owen's (H.) Boyle Lectures. 1769,1770,1771.
Paley's Evidences of Christianity. Prop. 2.
Parker's Bibliotheca Biblia. No. 28.
Patton's Two Defences. (Rep. to Heathcote.)
—— Christian Apology.
Peabody's (A. P.) Lectures before the Lowell Institute. Lect. 3.

Miracles—*continued.*

Pearce's M. of Christ. (Against Woolston.)
Penrose's Use of Scripture M. (Very able.)
Potts' (J. H.) Discourses.
Powell's (Samuel) Sermons.
Price's Dissertations. Diss. 4.
Princeton Review. 3:481. 8:348. 28:255.
Ray's Vindication of Christ's miracles.
Reeves' Apologies of Justin, Tertullian, &c.
Reinhard on Miracles.
Reynolds' (Jos. W.) on our Lord's miracles.
Rogers' (John) Sermons.
Rutherford's Credib. of M. (Much valued.)
Seaton's Compendious view of Miracles.
Sheppard's Faith and Practice illustrated.
Sherlock's Trial of the Witnesses.
Smallbrooke on Miracles.
Southern Lit. Journal. 2:442.
Stebbins' Defence of Scripture History.
Stevenson on the Miracles of Christ.
Stillingfleet's Origines Sacræ. Bk. 2, ch. 9,10.
Sutton's Christ's Miracles no Allegories.
Sykes' Credibility of Miracles.
Taylor's Apology of Ben Mordecai. (Strong.)
Thompson's (Edw.) Bulwarks of Christ'y.
Thompson's (William) Aids to faith.
Tilley's Preservative against Infidelity.
Tillotson's Sermons. Ser. 229,236,281.
Toll's Defence of Middleton's free enquiry. (Against Dodwell.)
Trench (Francis) on the M. of our Lord.
Tucker's Light of nature pursued.
Universalist Quar. 1:233. 4:346. 5:113.
Van Mildert's Boyle Lectures. 1802–1804.
Vince's Credibility of Scripture Miracles. (Masterly reply to Hume.)
Wardlaw (Ralph) on Miracles.
Watson's Tracts. Vol. 4.
West on the Resurrection.
Westcott's Characteristics of the gospel M.
Weston on the Rejection of the Christian Miracles by the Heathen.
Wescott's Elements of the Gospel Harmony.
Wood's (Leonard) Works. Vol. 4.

Miracles of the First Ages of the Church. See FALSE MIRACLES.

Pro.

Augustine, de Civitate Dei.
Justin Martyr, Apologia.
——— Dialog. cum Tryphone.
Irenæus, Opus eruditissimum. Ed. Frobenii.
Minucius Felix, Octavius.
Origen, contra Celsum.
Tertullian, ad Scapulam.

Mosheim, de Rebus ante Constantinum.
Pfannerus de Donis miraculis.
Schulz's Geistesgaben der ersten Christen.

Balmer's (Robt.) Academic Lectures.
——— Pulpit Discourses.
Barrington's (John S.) Miscellanea Sacra.
Boys' Suppressed Evidence; or proof from the records of the Fathers, Waldenses, &c.
Brook's Exam. of Middleton's free enquiry.
Burton's Eccles. hist. of the 2d and 3d cent.

Miracles of the First Ages—*continued.*

Pro.

Chapman on the Miraculous powers, &c.
——— Jesuit Cabal farther opened.
Church (Tho.) on the Miraculous powers, &c.
——— Appeal to the unprejudiced.
Dodwell's Free answer to Middleton.
Douglas' Criterion. (Exc't. Exposes Hume.)
Fleury's Eccles. Hist. (An essay at the end.)
Heathcote's Animadversions on Middleton.
Jackson's Remarks on Middleton's Inquiry.
Jenkins' (Tho.) Exam. of M.'s "Inquiry."
Newman's (J. H.) Miracles of eccl. history.
Parker's Miraculous powers of the early fathers.
Rawlinson's Bampton Lectures. 1859.
Reeves' Apologies of Justin, Tertullian, and Minucius.
Rutherford on Miracles.
Stebbins' Observations on Middleton.
Sykes' Credibility of Miracles.
——— Two questions impartially considered.
Walton's Miraculous powers of the church.
Whiston on Demoniacs.
——— on the Exact time when miraculous gifts ceased in the church.

Con.

Jenkins' Examination of Dodwell's reply to Middleton.
Middleton's Free inquiry into the miraculous powers supposed to have existed in the Church.
——— Vindication. (Reply to Dodwell and Church.)
——— Reply to Stebbins and Chapman.
——— Reply to Mr. Toll.
North British Rev. Vol. 4.
Tillotson's (Abp.) Sermons.
Toll's Defence of Middleton's Free Inquiry.
Yates' Defence of Middleton's Inquiry.

See a notice of this controversy in a note by Dr. KIPPIS, to DODDRIDGE'S *Lectures*, Part 6; and in JOSEPH CLARKE'S *Theological Treatises.*

Miracles, Pretended. See FALSE.

Miracles of the Church of Rome.

Bouchier, de Martyrio Fratrum.
Chamieri Panstraticæ Catholicæ.
Cornæi Miracula eccles. Catholicæ.
Des Vœux, Lettres sur les miracles que les Jansenistes attribuent aux reliques de l'Abbe de Paris.
Estienne, de la Conformité des marvielles anciennes avec des modern. (A keen, satirical comparison between Paganism and Popery.)
[Le Gros], Lettres Theologique.
Montgeron, la Verité des miracles de Francois de Paris.

Adams (John) on Miracles.
Brevint's Saul and Samuel at Endor.
Campbell on Miracles.

Douglass' Criterion of true miracles.
Hume's (David) Essays.
Kidder's Messiah.
Lowe on Romish Miracles.
Middleton's Free Enquiry.
Monthly Review. 124:205. 126:780.
North British Review. 4:451.
Princeton Review. 8:348.
Sykes on Miracles and Revelation.
Tillotson's (Abp.) Sermons.

Mirth. See SOBRIETY.

Colman's (Benj.) Sermons. (How to improve Mirth.)
Marriott's (John) Sermons. (Use and abuse of Mirth.)

Mishna. See RABBINICAL LITERATURE, TALMUDS.

Mishna: sive totius Hebræorum juris; cum commentariis Maimonidis et Bartenoræ. Latinitate donavit, ac notis illustravit, Surenhusius. (6 vols., folio.)
Sola & Raphall's Translation of 18 treatises from the Mishna. (The only English tr.)

Missal. See LITURGIES.

Arnaudi Epitome. (Of *Gavant.*)
Brevint, Missale Romanorum.
Cari Responsorialia et Antiphonaria.
Cochlæi Speculum antiquæ devotionis.
Gavanti Thesaurus sacrorum rituum.
Gerberti Vet. Liturgia illustrata.
Huebneri Historia Missæ. (Notices all the Papal liturgies.)
Lipenii Bibliotheca Theologica.
Mabillonii Liturgica Gallicana.
Meuschenii Ceremonialia. (Acta erud. 1732.)
Mohrenii Expos. Missæ atque Rubricarum.
Muratori Liturgia Romana vetus.
Pinii Tractatus historico-theologicus.
Pisart, Expositio Rubicarum missalis.
Piscaræ Praxis Ceremoniarum.
Rosarii Observationes.
Thomasii Codices Sacramentorum.

Lewis' Bible, Missal, and Breviary. (Contains an entire translation of the Missal, Rubrics, &c., with prefaces, and other useful matter.)

For many other works on the Missal, see LOWNDES' *British Librarian.*

Missions. See JESUIT MISSIONS, MORAVIANS, PLANTING OF CHRISTIANITY.

Annales de la Propagation de la foi. (A continuation of the "Lettres Edifiante.")
Blumhardt's Allgem. missionsgeschichte und missionsgeographie. 1828.
Callenburg's Bericht an Einige Christliche Freunde. (A truly great work.)
Cerri, L'Etat present de l'eglise Romaine. 1830.
Fabricii Lux Evang. toti orbi exoriens.
Janichii de Impedimentis circa convertandos Mohammedanos.

Missions—*continued.*

Klumpp's Evangelische Missionswesen.
Kristna Saga. (A reliable and sufficient acc. of the introduction of Christianity into Iceland in 981, and its progress till 1121.)
La Croze, Histoire du Christianisme.
Lettres Edifiantes. Periodical. (60 volumes. Embracing an account of the learning and science which the Romish missionaries discov'd or acquired in both hemispheres.)
Lücke's (G. C. F.) Missionsstunden. 1841.
Mammachii Origines Christianæ.
Mascovii Dissertationes.
Niecamp, Historia Missionis evangelicæ.
Oldenthorp's Missionsgeschichte.
Paget, Christianographie.
Schmidt's (K. C. G.) Kurzgefaste lebens Beschreibungen, &c.
Sondermann's Tabellarische Uebersicht, etc. 1846.
Steger's Protestantische Missionen.
Xavieri Epistolæ. (Full of good hints to a missionary.)
Zimmermann's Gustav.-Adolf.-Verein. 1856.
Accounts of the Society for propagating the gospel.
Aikman's Cyclopedia of Christian M. 1859.
Alder's Wesleyan missions. To 1840.
Amer. Baptist Missionary Magazine. 1803, to the present.
Amer. Biblical Repos. 3d Series. 4:453.
Amer. Quarterly Review. 3:423. 4:265. 6:77. 9:164. 10:93. 12:1.
Asiatic Researches. Periodical. Calcutta.
Baptist Missionary Magazine. London.
Barge & Strickland's American Methodist Missions.
Barth on Christian Missions.
Bibliotheca Sacra. 14:418. 15:543.
Blumhardt's Christian missions in every part of the world. Maps.
Body's (J. A.) Christian missions.
Bost's History of the Moravians.
Brown's Propagation of Christianity.
Burder's Missionary Anecdotes.
Burns' (Jabez) Sermons.
Caddel's Missions in Japan and Paraguay.
Calcutta Chris. Observer. (Many articles.)
Campbell's (J.) Philosophy of M. 1842.
——— Maritime discoveries.
Carey's Enquiry respecting missions.
Carne's Lives of eminent missionaries.
Chalmer's (Thomas) Sermons.
Chandler's (Bp.) Sermons.
Choules' History of Missions. (A revised and improved edition of Tho. Smith's.)
Christian Examiner. 1:182. 29:51. 44:416.
Chris. Monthly Spectator. 8:404.
Chris. Review. 1:325. 2:485. 6:280. 8:304. 10:566. 14:167,556.
Chris. Observer. London. (In almost every volume are valuable missionary statistics.)
Church Miss. Soc. Intelligencer. Periodical.
Clarkson's (W.) Christian Missions; or facts and principles of Evangelism.

Missions—*continued.*

Conference on M., held at Liverpool, 1860.
Cox's History of the London Baptist Missionary Society. From 1792 to 1842.
Davies' (Samuel) Sermons.
Doane's (G. W.) Sermons. (3 on this subj.)
Douglass' (James) History of Missions.
Drummond's (Abp.) Sermons.
Duff's Missions the chief end of the church.
Eclectic Review. London. (Many articles.)
Elliot's Christian Commonwealth.
Ellis' History of the London M. Soc. 1844.
Exeter Hall Lectures to young men.
Foreign Missionary. Periodical. New York. 1833–1836. (Presbyt. missions chiefly.)
Foster's (John) Sermons.
Frazier's Magazine. 4:261.
Friend of India. Calcutta. Periodical.
Fuller's (And.) Apology for Missions.
Gammel's Hist. of Amer. Baptist missions in Asia, Africa, Europe, and America.
Gillies' Historical Collections.
Grant's Bampton Lectures. 1843.
Green's (Ashbel) History of Presbyterian M.
Hall's (Robert) Sermons.
——— Address to Eustace Carey.
Hamilton (R. W.) on Missions. (An essay to which a prize of $1,000 was awarded, 1846. "One of the noblest productions of consecrated genius and learning." Prout.)
Harris' Great Commission. Prize essay.
Holmes' Missions of the United brethren. (From the beginning to 1812.)
Hoole's Year-book of Missions.
Horne's Letters on Missions.
Horsley's (Bp.) Sermons.
Hough's (James) Vindic. of Prot. missions.
Huie's Hist. of M. From the Ref. to 1842.
Humphrey's History of the Society for the propagation of the gospel. 1830.
Irving's (Edward) Orations.
Jackson's Centenary volume. (Wesleyan.)
Jenkins' Union of the Holy Spirit and the Church in the conversion of the world.
Johnson's (John) Sermons. (17 on missions.)
Kennet's History of Christianity.
——— Acct. of the Society for propagating the gospel.
Kingsmill's M. and Missionaries. To 1853.
Laughton's Progress of Christianity.
Literary and Theol. Review. 3:165.
London Review. 15:405.
Lord's History of Protestant missions.
Love's Address to the friends of missions.
——— Two hundred missionary letters.
Lowrie's For. M. of the Presbyter. Church.
——— Two years in upper India. 1848.
McBriar's Missionary travels in Egypt, Syria, &c. 1639.
McFarlane's Jubilee of the world.
McLear's History of M. in the middle ages.
Malcom's Travels in Asia. (Essays in the Appendix.)
Marshman's Thoughts on propagating Christianity among the Heathen.

Missions—*continued.*

Melsom's (J. B.) Who is my neighbor?
Merivale's Boyle Lectures. 1864.
Missionary Chronicle. Periodical. London.
——— Herald. " Boston.
——— Magazine. " London.
Mitchell on the best Means, &c. 1806.
Moffet's (R.) Missionary prize essay. 1842.
Morrison's Founders of the London M. Soc.
Newcombe's (Harvey) Cyclopedia of Miss. (Small, but accurate. 1855.)
New Englander. 9:207.
Noel's (Bapt. W.) Christian Missions. 1842.
Orme's Reply to Irving on Missions.
Paget's Christianography.
Pamphleteer. 11:471.
Pearson's Propagation of the Gospel.
Periodical accounts of Baptist M. Society. London. From 1800.
Periodical accounts of the United brethren.
Pickens' Researches of Missionaries. (The state of many missions in 1831.)
Powell's (Dr. Samuel) Sermons.
Princeton Review. 5:449. 10:535. 15:349. 17:61. 36:324.
Ramsden's Missions. *Facts and Anecdotes.*
Robinson's (C. K.) Maitland Prize Essay. 1852. (Duty and policy of missions.)
Schwartz's Life and correspondence. By Pearson.
Smith's (And.) Hist. of evangelical missions.
Smith's (Tho.) History of the M. Society.
Spurgeon's (Cha. H.) Sermons. 1st Series.
Stow's (Baron) Missionary Enterprize. (A collection of able sermons by Wayland, Griffin, Beecher, Beman, &c.)
Stowel's Miss. Church. (The spread of Christianity the true business of Christians.)
Styles' Strictures on articles in the Edinburg Review.
Swan's Letters on missions.
Thomas' (Bp.) Sermons.
Thomas (J.) on the Propagat. of the Gospel.
Thompson's Christian Missions necessary to civilization.
Townley on Missions.
Tracy's History of the American Board of Commissioners. 1840. Map.
Vormbaum's Biographical history of evangelical missions. 1845.
Walsh's (W. P.) Donnellian Lectures. 1861.
Wayland's (Francis) Moral dignity of the Missionary enterprise.
——— Sermons to the Churches.
White's (Kennet) Account of the Society for propagating the gospel.
Williams' Missionary Gazetteer. 1828.
——— Missionary enterprises in all the world to the present. 1838.
Winslow's History of Missions.
Worcester's Amer. M. to the Heathen. 1840.

Missions, Local.

ASIA.

Bouterwick's Missionars in Indien. 1852.

Missions, Local.

ASIA—*continued.*

Brouillon, l'Etat actuel, etc. *China.* 1855.
Burkhardt's Evangel. M. in Vorder Indien.
——— ——— " Hinter Indien.
——— ——— " China u. Japan.
Crasset, Histoire de l'Eglise de Japan.
Gobien, sur le Progress de la Religion.
Huc, Christ. en Chine, Tartarie, et Thibet.
Kœniglichen Dænischen Missionen.
Kulb's Reisen der Missionar. *Mongolia.*
La Croze, Hist. du Christianis. de l'Armenie.
Ludovici Exercitationes.
Niecamp, Histoire de la M. Danoise.
Norbert, Memoires Historique.
Pallu, Relation abrégée, &c. (*China, Siam,* &c. 1682.)
Paulini India Orientalis.
Rhodes, la Progrès, &c. *Cochin China.* 1652.
Schaffter, Hist. de la miss. du Tinnevelly.
Trigantii Res Chris. apud Japanios.
Zeigenbald's Ausführlicher Bericht. *Tranquebar.*

Abeel's (D.) Residence in China. 1829–1833.
"Accounts" of Danish M. in Tranquebar.
Allen's (D. O.) India: anc. and modern. 1854.
Amer. Biblical Repository. 3d Series. 3:54.
Anderson's (John) Miss. to Sumatra. 1823.
Arthur's Mission to Mysore. 1847.
Asiatic Researches. Periodical.
Bachelor's Hinduism and Christianity.
Barney's (A. M.) Star in the East. 1860.
Buchanan's (C.) Chris. Researches. 1811.
——— Christianity in India. 1813.
——— Memoir of; by Pearson. 1819.
Burns' Buckhara.
Burton's State of rel. in New S. Wales. 1840.
Buyers' Recollections of North. India. 1840.
——— Letters on Indian missions. 1848.
Calcutta Christian Observer. Periodical.
Caldwell's Tinnevelly mission. 1857.
Campbell's (J. R.) M. in upper India. 1856.
Campbell's (W.) British India. 1839. (Decline of Hinduism, and prog. of Christ'y.)
Carey, Dr., Mem. of; by Eustace Carey. 1836.
Clarkson's (W.) India and the Gospel.
——— Missionary Encouragements.
Cox's History of the Baptist Miss. Society. 1792 to 1842.
Cunningham's Introd. of Christ'y in India.
Dean's (Will.) Missions to China. 1859.
Duff's India and Indian missions. 1839.
Dwight's Christianity in the East. 1850.
Echard's Residence in Ceylon. 1844.
Eclectic Magazine. 5:382. *China.*
Edkins' Relig. condit. of the Chinese. 1859.
Fisk, Pliny, Memoir of. 1828.
For. Quart. Review. 5:485. *China.*
Foster's (John) Contributions to the Eclectic Review.
Fox's (W. H.) Missions in So. India. 1848.
——— Memoir of; by G. Fox. 1850.
Geddes' Church of Malabar. 1694.
Gillespie's Land of Sinim. 1854.
Goodell's The old and the new. 1853.

Missions, Local.

ASIA—*continued.*

Grinfield's Mission to Coromandel. 1831.
Gutzlaff's Voyages. 1839.
Hamlin, H., Memoir of. *Turkey.*
Hardy's British Governm't of Ceylon. 1844.
——— Budhism in Ceylon.
Hartley's Researches in Asia Minor.
Harvard's Wesleyan M. in Ceylon. 1822.
Hoole's Madras, Mysore, &c. 1844.
Hough's (J.) Hist. of Christianity in India. (From the Christian era to 1837.)
Jowett's Researches in Asia. 1823,1824.
Judson's (Anne H.) Burman Mission. 1855.
——— Memoir of; by Knowles.
Judson, Adon., Mem. of; by Wayland. 1853.
——— ——— by Patton. 1853.
——— ——— by Clemens.
Judson, Mrs. Sarah, Memoir of; by Emily Judson. 1850.
Kaye's Christianity in India. 1859.
Kresson's Cross and Dragon. *China.*
London Quart. Review. 10:1.
Long's Ch. of Eng. M. in Upper India. 1848.
——— ——— Bengal missions. 1858.
Lowrie's (J. C.) Two years in North India.
——— Presbyterian M. in India. 1854.
Lowrie, W., Memoir of. *China.* 1854.
McDonald, J., Memoir of; by Tweedie. 1840. *Calcutta.*
Mackie's Life of Tai-ping-wang. *China.*
Mackaye, J., Memoir of; by Culross. *Delhi.*
Malcom's Travels in S. Eastern Asia. 1835–8.
Marshman's (J. C.) Life and times of Carey, Marshman, and Ward. 1860.
——— The Serampore Mission. 1858.
Martin's British Colonies.
Martyn's (Henry) Letters and Journals.
Massie's Continental India. 1840.
——— Religion in India. 1827.
Matheson's Presbyterian M. in China. 1866.
Medhurst's State and prosp. of China. 1835.
Milne's First 10 years of the M. to China. 1820. (Contains valuable remarks on the hist., literature, and relig. of the Chinese.)
Morrison, Memoir of; by his widow. *China.*
Mosheim's Mem. of the Chur. in China. 1740.
Mullen's Results of M. in India. 1852.
Nesbit, Memoir of; by Mitchell. *Bombay.*
New Englander. 6:41.
Norbert's Memoirs of Oriental missions.
Noyes' (E.) Missions in Orissa. 1855.
Pegg's Orissa. (Contains a good history of the Baptist mission in that province.)
Perkins' 18 years' residence in Persia. 1843.
Perkins, Mrs., Memoir of. 1854.
Pettit's (Geo.) Tinnevelly mission. 1851.
Phillips' Thirty-four conferences between the Danish missionaries and the Brahmins.
Princeton Review. 12:157.
Reid, J., Mem. of; Wardlaw. 1830. *Bellary.*
Rhenius, C. T. E., Mem. of; by his son. 1841.
Schwartz's Life and correspondence. 1798.
——— Remains.
Selkirk's Recollections of Ceylon. 1844.

ASIA—*continued.*

Smith & Dwight's M. Researches. 1834.
Smith's Exploratory Tour. 1844–6. *China.*
Southgate's Visit to Mesopotamia. 1843.
Staughton's Baptist M. in India. 1820.
Stern's (H. A.) Miss. Journal. *Arabia.*
Stoddard, D. F., Memoir of; by Thompson.
Storrow's India and Chris. missions. 1859.
Sutton's Orissa, and its evangelization. 1840.
Symonds' Missions in Madras.
Temple's (D.) Life and Letters.
Tennent's Christianity in Ceylon. 1850.
Tomlin's Missionary Journal. 1840. *Siam.*
Townley's Answer to the Abbe Dubois. 1857.
Trevor's (G.) India and its missions.
Tyerman & Bennett's M. voyages. 1821–29.
Ward's (F.) India, and the Hindus. 1854.
Ward's (W.) History, literature, and religion of the Hindus. (A truly great and exhaustive work.)
——— Farewell Letters. 1821.
Warren's Miss. life in North India. 1856.
Weitbrecht's Prot. M. in Bengal. 1844.
——— Miss. Sketches. 1858. *North India.*
Wilkinson's Christianity in India. 1844.
Wilson, Bp., Life of. 1860.
Wilson's Narrative of the Greek Mission.
Winslow's Hints on missions to India.
Wolfe's (Jos.) Journal and letters. 1827–38.
Wylie's (Mrs.) Burman and Karen M. 1856.
Wylie's (Macl.) Bengal as a M. field. 1854.
Yates, Wm., Memoir of; by Hoby. 1847.
Yeates' Planting of the gospel in Syria, India, and China.

AFRICA.

Burkhardt's Kleine missions Bibliothek.
Dafalu's Lebensbild aus W. Africa.
Hoffmann's (Fr.) Missionsgeschichte.
Hoffmann's (W.) M. in lande Joruba. 1859.
La Croze, Hist. du Chr. d'Ethiopie.
Meissner's Bericht v. d. Entstehen d. Brüdermission unter den Buschnegern. 1850.
Morcalli Africa Christiana. ("A work of great extent and erudition.")

Arbousset's Tour N. E. of the Cape.
Beecham's Ashantee. 1841.
Bertram, J. M., Life of.
Bowen's (T. J.) Missionary labors. 1857.
Boyse's (W.) Notes on South Africa.
Broadbent, S., Memoir of; by Threlfall.
Calderwood's Caffres, and Caffre missions.
Campbell's Travels in Africa. 1815.
——— Second Journey. 1822.
Colenso's (Bp.) Ten weeks in Natal. 1856.
East's Western Africa, and the Baptist missions. 1844.
Ellis' Mission to Madagascar. 1858.
Fleming's (F. P.) Southern Africa. 1856.
Flud's Missionary Journal. *Abyssinia.*
Fox's M. in W. Africa. 1851. (Wesleyan.)
Freeman's (J. J.) Tour in S. Africa. 1855.
——— Persecutions in Madagascar.
Geddes' Church hist. of Ethiopia. To 1696.

Missions, Local.

AFRICA—*continued.*

Gobat's (Bp.) 3 years in Abyssinia. 1850.
Haweis' Memoir respecting a mission to Africa. 1850.
Hening's African missions of the Episcopal Church in the United States. 1850.
Isenberg's Abyssinian Missions. 1843.
Jameson's (Wm.) Gosp. labors in Afr. 1861.
Johnson, W., Memoir of.
Kraff's M. labors. 1837–55. *Eastern Africa.* (Extensive information touching the races, religions, &c.)
Latrobe's (C. J.) Visit to So. Africa. 1821.
Leydekker's History of the African Church.
Livingston's Missionary Travels. 1857.
——— Historical Sketch. 1858.
Lobo's Voyage to Abyssinia. 1670.
Merriam's Kaffir and Hottentot.
Moffat's Missionary labors.
Phillips' Missions in South Africa.
Princeton Review. 30:436.
Robertson, Mrs. H., Memoir of.
Scott's Day-dawn in Africa. 1858.
Shaw's M. in S. Eastern Africa. 1860.
Smith's (Thornley) So. Africa delineated.
Tucker's Abeokuta. 1853. (Origin and progress of the Yoruba mission.)
Walker's (S.) Missions in W. Africa. 1845.
——— Church M. at Sierra Leone. 1851.
West, Daniel, Memoir of.
Wilson's (J. L.) Western Africa.

AMERICA. See HOME MISSIONS.

Egede's Gröndlandische Mission.
Kolbing's M. in Grönland u. Labrador. 1831.
Oldendorp's Ges. d. M. auf St. Thomas. 1777.
Relations des Missions des Peres de la compagnie de Jésus, dans la Nouvelle France. 1611–1672.
Stoecklein und Keller's Reisebeschreibungen. (Nine great folios on the religious condition of the W. Indies, from 1642 to 1726.)

Baptist Miss. Mag. Boston. 1808 to present.
Bernan's M. labors in British Guiana. 1846.
Bleby's Scenes in the Carribean.
Blood's M. to the Indians of Orilla.
Brainerd's (David) Narrative. 1745.
——— Life of; by Edwards. 1765.
Brett's (W. H.) Missions in Guiana. 1851.
Buchner's Moravians in Jamaica. 1854.
Burchell, T., Life of. *West Indies.*
Christian Examiner. 42:360.
Christian Review. 12:253.
Coke's History of the West Indies.
Cornford's M. Reminiscences. 1856. *Jamaica.*
Crantz's History of Greenland. To 1767.
Democratic Review. 14:518.
Doddridge's Abridgment of Brainard. 1740.
Duncan's Wesleyan M. to Jamaica, and the state of Society in that colony. 1849.
Egede's (Hans) Journal. *Greenland.*
——— Life of.
Egede's (Paul, the son) Greenland mission.

Missions, Local.

AMERICA—*continued.*

Elliot & Mayhew's Gospel among the Indians. 1685.
Elliot's Eccl. history of Massachusetts.
Elliot, John, Memoir of. 1691.
Finley's History of the Wyandot M. *Ohio.*
Gardner, A., Mem. of; by Marsh. *Patagonia.*
Gookins' Christian Indians of N. England. 1680.
——— Historical Collections. 1674.
Gospel in America. (Bap. M. in Honduras.)
Hallet's Indians of North America.
Hawkins' Episc. M. in N. A. colonies. 1845.
Heckewelder's Missions among the Delawares and Mohegans. 1810.
Holmes' M. of the United Brethren. 1818.
Horsford's M. in the West Indies. 1856.
Humphrey's History of the "Society for the propagat. of the Gospel in Foreign parts."
Keith's Journey in America.
Kipp's Early Jesuit missions.
Knibb, Will., Memoir of. 1847.
Latrobe's Missions in N. Amer. (Moravian.)
Latter-day Luminary. Periodical. 1818–26.
Littell's Living Age. 11:276.
Loskiel's Moravian M. in N. America.
McCoy's Baptist Indian missions. 1840.
Massachusetts Histor. Soc. Collections.
Mather's Eccl. history of New England.
Mayhew's Indian converts.
Moister's Missionary labors. *West Indies.*
Muratori's Missions in Paraguay.
Oldenthorp's Hist. of M. to the Danish W. I.
Phillippo's Baptist M. in Jamaica. 1843.
Robertson's Miss. of the Secession Church in Nova Scotia. 1765 to 1847.
Samuels' Wesleyan M. in Jamaica. 1850.
Scheffer's History of Lapland.
Shea's Catholic M. in N. Amer. 1529–1854.
Slight's Researches among the North American Indians.
Smith, J., Memoir of. *Demarara.*
Southey's History of Brazil.
Stoddard's Question whether God is not angry with the country for doing so little for the Indians. 1727.
Tucker's Rainbow in the North. *Rupert's land.*
United Brethren's Retrospect of Missions in Jamaica and Antigua.
Watson's Methodist M. in the West Indies.
Winslow's Progress of the Gospel among the Indians of New England.
Wix's Newfoundland's Missionary.

EUROPE.

Henderson's Life and labors. *Denmark.*
Jowett's Researches in the Mediterranean. 1823.
Rule's Missions in Spain and Gibraltar.
Wilson's Narrative of the Greek miss. 1839.

POLYNESIA.

Kohn's (F.) Missionswesen d. Südsee. 1833.
Meinicke's Sudseevolker u. d. christenthum. 1844.

Missions, Local.

POLYNESIA—*continued.*

Michaelis' die Volker der Sudsee. 1847.
Anderson's (Rufus) Hawaian Islands.
Bamby, J., Memoir of; by Barret.
Bingham's 21 years in the Sandwich I. 1847.
Brown's New Zealand. 1845.
Campbell's Martyr of Eromanga. 1842.
Christian Quart. Spectator. 1:176.
Cross, J., Memoir of; by Hunt. *Fejee.*
Dibble's Sandwich Islands mission. 1832.
Ellis' Tour in Owyhee. 1827.
——— Polynesian Researches. 1829. Plates.
Farmer's Tonga and the Friendly I. 1855.
Gill's Gems from the Coral I. *New Hebrides.*
Hunt, Rev. J., Memoir of; by Rowe. *Fejee.*
Lawry's (W.) Missions in Tonga, &c. 1852.
Leigh, Rev. S., Mem. of; by Strachan. 1855.
Nichols & Marsden's Voyage to N. Zealand.
North Amer. Review. 55:193.
Pilmore's Labors in New South Wales.
Pritchard's Success of the gospel. 1844.
Stewart's Missions in the Sandwich Islands. 1823 to 1825.
Strachan's Life of Leigh. (With a history of the mission to Australia. To 1850.)
Tucker's Southern cross and Southern crown. *New Zealand* in 1855.
Turner's 19 years in Polynesia. 1861.
Westbrook's Religion and education in New South Wales.
Williams, J., Memoir of; by Prout. 1843.
Williams, R., Life of; by Hamilton.
——— Missionary Enterprises. 1816–1834.
Williams & Calvert's Fiji and the Fijians. 1859.
Yates' Mission to New Zealand.

Mnemonics.

Alberti (J. M.) Memoriæ libellus.
Basslé, Systéme Mnémonique.
Castilho de Mnemotechnie.
Colineus de Memoria artificiosa. 1515.
Durivau, sur la Mémoire verbale.
Feinagle, sur la Mnémonique.
Grataroli, de Memoria.
Montry, Grammaire de M.
Nauclin, Mnémonique.
Portæ Ars Reminiscendi.
Rossellii Thesaurus artif. memoriæ.

Bruin, Life of.
Fauvel's Phreno-mnemotechny.
Gray's Memoria Technica. (As good as any, being brief and easy.)
Hallworth's Rational Mnemonics.
Johnson's Memoria Technica.
Lowe's Mnemonics delineated.
Mason on Self-knowledge.
Rollin's Belles-Lettres.
Sanders' (Richard) Art of Memory.
Watts on the Improvement of memory.
Willis' (John) Mnemonica. (Has also a treatise on the *physical* improvement of memory.)

Mocking at Sin. See PRESUMPTION.

Davies' (Thomas) Sermons.
D'Oyly's (George) Sermons.
Jones' (Will. of Nayland) Sermons.
Le Bas' (Cha. W.) Sermons.
Milner's (Isaac) Sermons.
Nares' (Edward) Sermons.
Rogers' (John) Sermons.
Shuttleworth's (P. N.) Sermons.
Stillingfleet's (Bp.) Sermons.
Trapp's (Joseph) Sermons.

Modalists. See SABELLIANS.

Moderation. See LUXURY.

Bennett's (Wm.) Sermons.
Blair's (Hugh) Sermons.
Butcher's (Edmund) Sermons.
Enfield's (William) Sermons.
Glazebrook's (James) Sermons.
Hall's (Bp.) Sermons.
Hoadley's (Bp.) Sermons.
Kelsall's (Edward) Sermons.
Knox's (Vicessimus) Sermons.
Leng's (John) Sermons.
Maltby's (Edward) Sermons.
Morning Exercises at Cripplegate. Vol. 1.
Newton's (Bp.) Sermons.
Panoplist. 9:488.
Reese's (Abraham) Sermons.
Riddock's (James) Sermons.
Rogers' (John) Sermons.
Scott's (John) Sermons.
Secker's (Abp.) Sermons.
Tullie's (George) Sermons.
Watson's (John) Sermons.
Zollikoffer's (George J.) Sermons.

Modern Judaism.
See JEWS, PRESENT STATE OF.

Modes of Quotation in the N. Test.
See QUOTATIONS.

Modesty.

Limborchii Theologia Christiana.

Ball's (Nathaniel) Sermons.
Butler's (Alban) Sermons.
Dodd's (William) Sermons.
Fordyce's (James) Sermons.
Hunt's (Jeremiah) Sermons.
Taylor's (Jeremy) Holy living
Watts' (Isaac) Sermons.
Wilks' (Sam. C.) Christian Essays.

Molinists. See QUIETISTS.

Moloch. See IDOLATRY.

Calmet, Dissertatio. (Preface to Leviticus.)
Deylingii Observationes Sacræ.
Dietzschii (D.) Dissertationes.
Greissing de Immolatione facta librorum M.
Meisterlinus de Tabernaculo Molochi.
Meyeri (C. G.) Dissertationes.
Schwabii (J. G.) Dissertationes Philolog.
Selden, de Diis Syris Syntagma.
Witsii Miscellanea Sacra.
Ziegra (C. S.) Dissertationes.

Monasticism.

Altessaræ Asceticon. (Chiefly on the origin of Monasticism, which he finds in the time of Diocletian.)
Ammani Cleri totius Romanæ ecclesiæ.
Arhennius de Eremitiis.
Bavarius de Veteri Monochatu.
Biedenfeld's Mönchs-orden u. Klosterfrauen-orden.
Bochinger, la Connexion de la vie contemplative, et monastique, chez les Indous, Boudhists, et Chrètiens.
Cassianus de Institutis Cœnobiorum.
Crescellii Historia de origine, &c.
Cuyckii Speculum concubinariorum, monachorum, et clericorum.
Deylingii Observationes Sacræ.
Döring's Gesch. der Mönchsorden.
Emiliane, des Tromperies des prêtres.
Galeni Origines Monasticæ.
Hermant, Hist. des ordres religieux.
[Heylot], des ordres Monast., religieux, et militaires. (800 engravings of costumes. A library of itself, and entirely reliable.)
Holstenii Codex regularum monasticarum. (A specimen of a very large class of books which furnish authentic disclosures of the real nature of monkery.)
Hospinianus de Orig. et prog. Monachatus. (Against Bellarmin's defence of M.)
Jack's Wahres Bild der Kloster.
Jerome (Fr.) Bibliotheque Ascetique.
Leuckfeld, Monasticon Germanicum.
Mangold, de Monachatus origin. et causis.
Martene, de Antiq. Monachorum ritibus.
Michaele, Collectio scriptorum ecclesiasticorum, &c. (Describes the monastic establishments of all Europe.)
Middendorpii Historia Monastica.
Mizæi Originum Monasticorum.
Münch's Geschichte d. Mönchthums.
Paulini Dissertationes Historicæ.
Pelletier, Hist. des Ordres de religion.
Philippi Speculum monasticum. (An authentic Papal account of the canons, regulations, &c., with explanations.)
Physiophili Opuscula. (Written by Baron BORN, of Vienna. He arranges the monks according to the Linnæan system (!), and portrays their revolting vices with hideous accuracy.)
Rivii Monastica hist. occidentis scabra.
Schwan's Abbildung, &c.
Sontagius de Vanitate votorum monastic.
Sutlivius de Monachis eorumque moribus.
Weber's Mönchsthum.

Barbeyrac's Spirit of the Ecclesiastics of all ages.
Biblioth. Sacra. 1:309,464,632. 21:384.
Blackwood's Mag. 69:305.
British Critic. Feb., 1818.
Broughton's Monasticum Brittanicum.
Bunkley's (Josephine) Testimony of an escaped novice.
Christian Examiner. 19:54.

Monasticism—*continued.*

Chambers' Civil condition of the Monastic orders in France. 1860.
Christian Review. 7:73.
Curzon's M. of the Levant. (As in 1850.)
Day's Origin, progress, nature, &c., of M.
Dodworth's English Monasteries.
Dugdale's Monasticon. (A new edition enlarged by Caley and others, to 9 volumes, folio, was printed in 1846.)
Emelianne's Artifices of the Priests.
Fish's (Simon) Supplicacyon for the Beggers. (The reading of this book is said to have led Henry VIII. to suppress the monast.)
Fosbrook's British Monachism. Plates.
Geddes' Miscellaneous Tracts.
Hardy's Eastern Monachism. (An account of the Budhist priesthood.)
Knickerbocker Mag. 24:43.
Littell's Living Age. 27:17.
London Quart. Review. 11:289.
Mabillon's Posthumous works.
Monk's (Maria) Awful disclosures.
North British Review. 2:375.
Quart. Rev. 23:59. (Southey.)
Robinson's Nunnery at Lisbon.
Ruffner's Fathers of the Desert. (Origin and practice of M. among the Heathen, and its passage into the church.)
Tanner's Relig. Houses of Engl. and Wales.
Taylor's M. life in France. (As in 1866.)
Thompson on Monastic vows.
Walcott's Wykeham and his Colleges.

Papal works on Monastic history, rules, &c., are innumerable. A single bookseller's catalogue, in 1867, offers over four hundred. For a knowledge of books on the Monastic orders of particular countries, see EAST APTHORPE'S *Letters.*

Monogamy.

Athenagoras, Legatio ad Christianos.
Clemens Alex., Stromata.
Tertullian, de Monogamia.
——— Exhortatio Castitatis.
Jerome, Epistola Gerontiam.

Monophysites. See COPTS.

Assemanni Biblioth. Orientalis. (Quotes the writings of Syrian Monophysites.)
Dorner's Gesch. der Lehre der person Christ.
La Croze, Hist. d. Christianisme des Indes.
Renaudoti Hist. Patriarch. Alexandrinorum.
Severi Opera. (In Montfaucon's Biblioth.)
Simler, Scripta Latina de una persona et duabis naturis J. C.

Princeton Review. 38:567.

Monotessarons. See HARMONIES.

Ammonii Diatessaron. 1524.
Avenarii Harmonia. 1616.
Brissonii (Io.) Historia Evangelica.
Calmet, Harmonie des quatres evang. 1726.
Crellii Historia Evangeliæ. 1566.
Erythropoli Catena Aurea. 1603.

Monotessaron—*continued.*

Gersonis Monotessaron. 1700.
Hay, Hist. Evang. dispositio ipsis Evangeliorum verbis. 1607.
Krollii Monotessaron. 1700.
Lex's Leben Jesu.
Lubini Historia Christi. 1609.
Lubomlii Monotessaron Evangelicum. 1607.
Maii Concinata ut Monotes. 1707.
Perionii (Ioach.) Monotessaron. 1553.
Riccii Monotessaron. 1607.
Saxonis Vita Jesu. 1474.
Tatiani Evangelium ex IV Evang. compositum. 165.
White, Diatessaron. 1799.
Wirthii Monotessaron. 1594.

Carpenter's (R. L.) Monotessaron. 1851.
Curry's Gospel in one narrative. 1834.
Fellowes' Guide to Immortality. 1804.
Forster's Gospel narrative. 1847.
Gurthwaite's Evangelical Harmony. 1633.
Hele's Four gospels in one. 1750.
Law's Life and character of Christ. 1749.
MacBride's Lect. on the Diatessaron. 1837.
Peddie's Gospel Narrative. 1857.
Thompson's (J.) Gospel History. 1829.
Thompson's (Cha.) Synopsis of the Ev. 1815.
Warner's English Diatessaron. Notes. 1803.
Willan's Ministry of Christ. 1782.
Williams' (J.) Gospel narrative. 1848.

I cite under *Monotessarons* books which make a single narrative of the gospel history; and under *Harmonies,* such as give in parallel columns the whole of each gospel. But the words are by some writers used interchangably.

Monothelites. See MARONITES.

Assemanni Bibliotheca Orientalis.
Combefisii Hist. Monothelitarum.
Desirantii Honorius Papa vindicatus.
Dezallieri Historia Monothelitarum.
Dorner's Entwickelung Gesch. der Lehre, etc.
Fabricius (J. A.) Bibliotheca Græca.
Le Quien, Oriens Christianus.
Maximi Opera.
Schoepfii (Wolfg. David.) Dissertationes.
Strauchii (Ægidii) Dissertationes.
Suicerus in Voce Θελημα.
Tamagnani Hist. Monothelitarum.
Hey's (Dr. John) Lectures. Bk. 4.

See an account of writers on this controversy, in COMBIFISIUS, quoted above.

Montanists.

Epiphanius, de Hæresibus.
Irenæus, contra Hæreticos.
Tertullian, Præscriptiones.

Arnoldi Historia Hereticorum.
Eusebii Hist. Ecclesiæ. Lib. V, cap. 16.
Grabe, Spicelegium Hæreticorum.
Ittigius de Hæresiarchis ævi Apostolici, et Apostolico proximi.
Kirchneri de Montanistis.

Montanists—*continued.*

Mammachii Origines Christianæ.
Ruelii (Io. Ludov.) Diatribæ tres.
Schwegler d. M. und die Kirche des 2. Jahrh.
Strauchii (Ægid.) Dissertationes.
Wernsdorfii Com. de M. seculi secundi.

Hicks' (G.) Spirit of Enthusiasm exorcised.
Lardner's Heretics of the first two centuries.
Robinson's History of Baptism.
Short's Bampton Lectures. 1846.

Moral Ability. See FREE AGENCY.

Beecher's (Lyman) Views in Theology.
Bibliotheca Sacra. 22:503.
Christian Disciple. 5:256.
Christian Examiner. 75:157.
Chris. Monthly Spec. 4:512. 5:523.
Chris. Quart. Spect. 10:527.
Clarkson's (David) Sermons.
Dwight's Theology. Ser. 132.
Foster's (Dr. James) Discourses.
Fuller's (Andrew) Works.
Griffin's Park Street Lectures.
Hall's Help to Zion's travellers.
Lit. and Theological Rev. 5:206.
McCombie's Man as a moral agent.
McLean's Apostolical Commission.
Presbyterian Quarterly Rev. Oct., 1859.
Princeton Review. 25:1. 26:217.
Smalley's (J.) Inability of the sinner to comply with the Gospel.
Southern Lit. Messenger. 8:301.
Theological Essays, reprinted from the Princeton Review.
Truman on Moral and Natural impotence.
Venn's (John) Sermons.
Wood's (Prof.) Works.

Moral Fitness. See VIRTUE.

Moral Government of God.

Baieri Theologia Moralis.
Calixti Epitome Theologiæ.
Durrii (Ioann. Conrad.) Enchiridion.
Langii Œconomia Salutis.
Melancthonis Loci Theologici.
Osiandri Compendium Theologiæ.

Butler's Analogy of religion and nature.
Chris. Quart. Spectator. 10:527.
Duchall's (Dr. James) Sermons.
Literary and Theol. Rev. 5:206.
New Englander. 1:525.
Warburton's (Bp.) Sermons.

Moral Law. See ANTINOMIANS.

Bellamy's (Joseph) Works.
Booth's Death of Legal Hope.
Charnock's (Stephen) Works.
Cobbin's View of the Moral law.
Cudworth's Eternal and immutable morality.
Dick's Philosophy of Religion. Ch. 3.
Fuller's (And.) Rule of believers.
Hall's (Bp.) Contemplations.
Howarth's Abiding oblig. of the moral law.
Lamy's Demonstration of the holiness, &c.
Masillon's Sermons.
Müller's Christian doctrine of Sin.
Stanhope's Boyle Lectures. 1701,1702.
Warburton's Divine legation of Moses.
Watts' Uses of the moral law.

Moral Philosophy. See MORALITY.

Aristotle, Cebes, Cicero, Epictetus, Plato, Epicurus, Plutarch, Seneca, Xenophon.

Achterfeld de Doct. moralis Christianæ.
Baumgarten-Crusius, Lehrbuch der Christlichen Sittenlehre.
Breithauptii Dissertationes.
Buddei Institutiones Theol. moralis.
Danæi Ethices Christianæ.
Diedrich (C.), Christlichen Sittenlehre.
Dithmarsi Systema Ethicum.
Donaldson, Moralis disciplinæ summa.
——— Synopsis philosophiæ moralis.
Grabovii Ethica Christiana.
Heineccii Elementa philosophiæ moralis.
Houdry, Bibliotheca Concionatoria. (The topics alphabetically arranged, in five large folios.)
Hutchesonii Philos. moralis Compendiaria.
Kahler's Philagathos.
Klippelii Doctrina Stoicorum atque Chris. exposita et comparata.
Mably (Gabriel B.), Œuvres.
Meiner's Gesch. d. ältern u. neuern Ethik.
Michelet's System d. philos. moral.
Möller's Absolute Princip der Ethik.
Neander's Gesch. d. Christl. Ethick.
Nüsslein's Grundlinien der Ethik.
Reinhardi Introd. in Theol. moralem.
——— System der Christlichen Moral.
Rossali (Mich.) Disquisitio de Epicteto.
Schuberti Institutiones Theol. moralis.
Schwab's Vergleichung des Kant. Moralprincips mit d. Leibnitz-Wolfischen.
Stattleri Ethica Christiana. (Important.)
Staüdlin's Gesch. der Moral philosophie.
Tieftrunck's Grundriss der Sittenlehre.
Wolf (Ch.), Philos. moral, &c., pertracta.

Adams' (Will.) Christian Science.
Alden's Christian Ethics.
Alexander's Outlines of moral science.
Amer. Biblical Repos. 6:117.
Amer. Month. Review. 2:50. 4:333.
Amer. Quart. Observer. 2:247.
Amer. Quart. Review. 12:133.
Baumgarten's Practical Theology.
Beattie's Elements of Moral science.
Bell's (Will.) Sermons. (Highly esteemed.)
Beller's Delineation of universal law.
Belsham's Moral Philosophy.
Bentham's (Jer.) Dentology. (Edited with improvements by Bowring. 1834.)
Blakey's (Robt.) History of Moral scie...
Brend's Difference between the morality of Jesus and that of the Jews.
Brown's (Tho.) Lectures on Ethics.
Brown's (John) Manners and principles of the times. 1750.
Bruce's Science of Ethics.

Moral Philosophy—*continued.*

Campbell's Original of moral Virtue.
Chalmers' Moral Philosophy.
Christian Examiner. 8:265. 18:101. 19:1,25. 28:137. 29:153. 30:145. 41:97. 49:215. 52:188.
Christian Quart. Spectator. 10:527.
Christian Review. 7:321.
Clarke (J.) on Moral Obligation.
Cogan's Ethical Questions.
Cumberland's Laws of Nature.
Dewar's Christian Ethics.
Dick's (T.) Philosophy of Religion.
Doddridge's Lectures. (Superior.)
Doederlein's System of Morals.
Eclectic Review. 4th Series. 3:160: 17:579. 19:197. 21:603. 28:93.
Edinburg Review. 7:413. 61:195: 91:86.
Ensor's Principles of Morality.
Epictetus' Morals, with Simplicius' commentary. Trans. by Geo. Stanhope.
Epicurus' Morals. Trans. by W. Charleton.
Estlin's (John P.) Lectures.
Feverlein's Ethics of Christianity in its historical forms.
Fiddes on the Principles of natural reason.
Finch's Moral qualities of Man.
Fordyce's Moral P. (An elegant compend.)
Forsyth's Principles of Moral science.
Foster (J.) on Nat. relig. and social virtue.
Franklin's (Benj.) Works.
Fries' Philosophical Anthropology.
Furguson's Moral and political science.
Garve's Different principles of Moral philosophy. From Aristotle, to 1798.
Gisbourne's Principles of Moral philosophy.
Glover (P.) on Virtue and Happiness.
Glover (Henry) on Virtue and Religion.
Grant (Alex.) on the Ethics of Aristotle.
Grose's (John) Rational Ethics.
Grove's Moral Philosophy.
Hampden's (R. D.) Lectures.
Harris' Dialogue on Happiness.
Hartley's Observations on Man.
Hildreth's Theory of Morals.
Hitchcock's System of Moral science.
Hume's Principles of morals.
Hutchinson's Introd. to moral philosophy.
Innes' (A.) Examination of the notions of Hobbes, Spinoza, and Bayle.
Investigator. 4:46.
Jevon's Systematic Morality on the grounds of Natural Religion.
Johnson (Thomas) on Moral Obligation.
Jouffroy's Introd. to moral philosophy. Tr. by W. H. Channing. (Includes a critical survey of modern systems.)
Kames' Principles of Morality.
Kant's Metaphysics of Ethics.
Kortbold's Synopsis of practical Theology.
Lond. Quart. Rev. 11:494.
Mackintosh's Progress of Ethical philosophy.
Meister's Opinion of philosophers as to the fundamental principles of morality.
Merivale's Boyle Lectures. 1864.

Moral Philosophy—*continued.*

Methodist Quart. Rev. 5:220.
Monboddo's Ancient Metaphysics.
Monthly Rev. 89:130. 118:44. 123:213.
More's (Henry) Enchiridion.
Morgan's Philosophy of morals.
Muller's Ethical system of Jesus.
Nelson on Virtue and Happiness.
New England Mag. 4:208,290.
Norman's (A.) Literæ Sacræ. (Comparison of Moral Philosophy with Christianity.)
North American Rev. 60:293.
North British Rev. 14:160.
Oakeley's Remarks upon Aristotelian and Platonic Ethics.
Pearson's (Edward) Remarks on Morals. (Examines the positions of Paley.)
Paley's Moral and Political Philosophy.
Pemble's Moral Philosophy.
Pfaff's Institutes.
Price's Review of the principal questions in morals.
Priestley's Institutes of Natural Religion.
Princeton Rev. 5:33. 7:377. 18:260. 20:529.
Quarterly Review. 3:1. 6:407. 48:83.
Ready's System of Ethics.
Reinhard's System of Morals.
Salzman's Elements of M. P. for children.
Sewell's Christian Morals. (Discusses recent questions, though not with profoundness or accuracy.)
Smith (Will.) on the School of Paley.
Smith's (Adam) Theory of Morals.
Smith's (Sam. S.) Lectures on Moral philos.
Smith's (Sydney) Sketches of Philosophy.
Southern Quart. Rev. 19:242.
Spalding's Philosophy of Morals; with a review of ancient and modern theories.
Stewart's Outlines of moral philosophy.
——— Active and moral powers.
——— Progress of ethical P. in Europe.
Taylor's (J.) Exam. of Hutcheson's scheme.
——— Sketch of Moral Philosophy.
Tholuck's Christ's Sermon on the Mount.
Tieftrunk's Only possible design of Jesus.
Turnbull's (G.) Principles of moral science.
Upham's Moral Philosophy.
Wainwright's Vindic. of Paley's theory of morals from the objections of Stuart, Gisbourne, Pearson, and Tho. Brown.
Walch's Introduction to Christian Ethics.
Wardlaw's Christian Ethics.
Wayland's Elements of Moral science.
Westminster Review. 1:182. 2:254. 12:246.
Whewell's (Wm.) Lectures in Lent term.
——— Foundation of morals.
——— Systematic morality.
Wilkins' Principles of Natural Religion.
Witherspoon's Moral philosophy.

Moral Sense. See CONSCIENCE.

Pro.

Abercrombie's Philos. of the moral feelings.
Brown's (Tho.) Lectures on the Mind.
Butler's Analogy of religion and nature.

Moral Sense—*continued.*

Pro.

Hutcheson's Enquiry into beauty and virtue.
——— Essay on the passions.
McIntosh's Progress of Ethical philosophy.
Necker on Religious Opinions.
Upham's Moral and Intellectual philosophy.
Wayland's Elements of Moral science.
Witherspoon's Lectures. Lect. 4.

Con.

Bentham on Morals and Legislation.
Hume on the Principles of Morals.
Smith (Southwood) on Divine government.

Moral Suasion.

Barclay's Universal love considered and established upon the right foundation.
Burnett's Life of Rochester.
King's Origin of Evil.
Scougal's (Henry) Works.
Seed's (Jeremiah) Sermons.
Sharp's (Thomas) Sermons.
Whitby's Commentary. Vol. II. Appendix.

Morals of the Ancients.

Bautain's Moral des Evangeliums im vergleich mit den verschiedenen philosophischen Moralssystemen.
Appleton's Works. Lect. 15–17.
Barrows on the State of Pre-existence.
England's Morals of the Ancients.
Fleming's Christology.
Jenkins' Reasonableness of Christianity.
Laws' Theory of Religion. Part 2.
Leland on Revelation. Ch. 1.
Rollin's Ancient History.

Morality. See VIRTUE.

Basil, Conciones.
Chrysostom, Sermones.
Clemens Alex., Pædagogus.
Clemens Rom., Epistolæ.
Cyprian, Opera.
Ignatius, Epistolæ.
Justin M., Epistolæ.
Gregory N., de fugienda fornicatione.
——— de pauperibus amandis.
Ammon's Handbuch der Christl. Sittenlehre.
Amyrald, Morale chrétiene.
Bassnage sur les Vertus et les Vices.
Baumgarten-Crusius' Chris. Sittenlehre.
Bruch's Lehrbuch d. Sittenlehre.
Buddei Institutiones theologiæ moralis.
Callixti Epitome theologiæ moralis.
De Wette's Christlich Sittenlehre.
Flatt's Vörlesungen über christlich. Moral.
Ligori Theologia Moralis.
Merz's Christlichen Sittenlehre, in seiner Gestaltung nach den Grundsatzen des Protest. im gegensatz. zum Katholicismus.
Pictet, Morale chrétiene.
Stapferi Theologia moralis.
Staudlin's Gesch. d. Sittenlehre Jesu.
Walch's Einleitung in d. chris. Moral.
Witsii Schediasma.

Morality—*continued.*

Am. Bibl. Repos. 3d Series. 4:554.
Balguy on Moral goodness.
Baxter's Christian Directory.
Bennett's Christian morality.
Brown's Christian Morals.
Christian Exam. 17:15,283.
Chris. Monthly Spect. 2:175.
Clarke's (Dr. Samuel) Sermons.
Craddock's Knowledge and Practice.
Cudworth on Eternal and immut. morality.
De Wette's Practical Ethics.
Dymond's Essays. (Invaluable.)
Economy of Human life.
Foster's (Dr. James) Sermons.
Foster's (John) Essays on Morals.
Fox on Christian morals.
Gisbourne's (Tho.) Sixty sermons. ("We are almost at a loss for terms of approbation sufficiently strong."—ROBT. HALL.)
Hammond's Practical Catechism.
Home (Lord Kames) on Natural religion.
James' (H.) Moralism and Christianity.
Johnson's Rasselas.
Kittlewell on Christian Obedience.
Lane's Christian Morality.
Lucas' Morality of the Gospel.
More's (Hannah) Christian Morals.
North British Rev. 1:183.
Peabody's Lect. bef. the Lowell Instit. 1864.
Pictet on Christian Morality.
Placette's Essays.
Princeton Review. 11:579.
Rawlett's Christian Monitor.
Reinhard's Christian Morality.
Russell's (Lady) Letters.
Scott's (Thomas) Christ a pattern.
——— Lectures.
Smith's (Sam. Stanhope) Sermons.
Spring's (Gardner) Essays.
Taylor's (Jer.) Holy living.
Warburton's Divine legation of Moses.
Westminster Review. 20:100.
Wilkes' Essay on a moral life.

Moravians. See ZINZENDORF.

Pro.

Acta Fratrum Unitas. (A full account of the doctrines, discipline, worship, &c.)
Budingische Sammlung. Periodical, from 1740.
Der Brüderbote. Period. Bautzen, Saxony.
Der Brüder Botschafter. Periodical. Bethlehem, Pa.
Ehwald's Alte u. neue Lehre der Böhm. B.
Fressen's Bewahrte nachrichten v. Hernhut. Sachen.
——— Nöthege Prufung der Zinzendorfirchen Lehrart.
Gesänge, Lithurgische der evang. Brüder. 1791.
Graffen von Zinzendorf Erklärung.
Le Long's Gotte's Wunder mit seiner Kirche.
Müller's Nachricht von d. Gemeine zu H.
Petschœck's Unparteyische Untersuchung.

Moravians—*continued.*

Pro.

Ratio Disciplinæ Unitatis fratrum.
Seigfred's Beschiedene Beleuchtung.
Spangenbergii Opera.
Zeschwitz, Die Katechismen d. Waldenser u. Boemenischen Bruder.
Zinzindorfii Opera.
De Schweinitz's (Ed.) Morav. Manual. 1859.
Gambold's (John) Works.
——— Maxims, &c., out of Zinzendorf.
Henry's Sketches of Moravian life.
Latrobe's Doctrine of the Moravians.
Lewis' (Bp.) Sixteen Discourses.
Messenger, The. Periodical. London.
Moravian, The. Periodical. Bethlehem, Pa.
Ramftler's Select Remains.
Spangenberg's Christian Doctrine.

Con.

Baumgarten (S. J.), Theologische Bedencken.
Bengel's Abriss der sogen. Brüdergemeine.
Benneri Tirocenium Zinzendorfianorum.
Carpzow's Religions-Untersuchung, etc.
Hansen's Kann die Hernhuth. Gemeine.
Hederici Examen capitum doct. fratrum.
Kromayeri Hodomoria Zinzendorfiana.
Merling's Grundlichen Beweis, etc.
Rhoden's Schlüssel zu Hernhuth.
Schutzii Hernhuthianismus in tumore.
——— " " nuce.
——— " " dolo.
Steinmitz's Antwortschreiben.
Volkius' Bosheit der Hernhuth. Secte.
Winkler's Grafen von Zinzendorf.

Amer. Quart. Church Review. 17:231.

Moravians, History of.

Balbini Bohemia Sancta.
Berbeck's Gesch. der Brüder-Unitat.
Bost, Frères de Boheme.
Camerarii Narratio Historica. 1605.
Carpzow's Nachricht von der böhmischen B.
Comenii Fratrum Bohemorum hist. 1660.
Cranz's Alte und neue Brüderhistorie.
Crœger's Geschichte der Brüderkirche.
Gindely's Böhmen. und Währen im Zeitalter der Reformation.
Lasitii Hist. de orig. et rebus gestis, etc.
Lochner's Schicksale der Brüdergemeine.
Missions Blatt. Periodical. Hamburg.
Nitzsch's Bedentung d. Brüdergemeine.
Oldendorp's Missionsgeschichte.
Palacky's Geschichte von Böhmen. 1867.
Regenvolscii Hist. Eccl. Sclavonicæ. 1652.
Reichel's Gesch. d. alten Brüderkirche. 1856.
Rieger's Alt. u. neuen Boeh. Brüder. 1734.
Rudigeri Frat. Orthodox. in Bohemia et Moravia Eccles. 1579.
Schaaf's Brüdergem. Gesch. Dargestelt.
Schars, de Ecclesia Bohemica.
Solimanni Bohemia Exoriens. 1627.
Spangenberg's Nachricht von der Verfassung der Brüderunitat.
Stredowsky, Sacra Moraviæ historia. 1710.

Moravians, History of—*continued.*

Theobaldi Adumbratio eccles. Bohem. 1611.
Tholuck's Vermischte Schriften. Vol. I.
Verbeck's Kurzgefasste Geschichte, etc. 1857.
Wengiersky, Historia. (The second written by one of themselves.)

Amer. Quart. Church Review. 17:231.
Benham's Origin, &c., of the B. brethren.
Bost's History of the Bohemian and Moravian brethren. 1845.
Buckner's Moravians in Jamaica. 1854.
Christian Examiner. 66:1.
Comenius, John A., Life of; by Benham.
Cranz's Hist. of the M. in the remote ages, and particularly in the 18th century.
——— History of the Greenland mission.
De Schweinitz's Moravian Manual.
Eclectic Review. N. S. 5:466.
English Girl's Account of a Moravian settlement in the Black forest. 1860.
Heckwelder's Missions among Amer. Indians.
——— Life of; by Rond Thalers.
Henry's Sketches of M. life and charrcter.
Holmes' Hist. of the United brethren. 1825.
——— ——— Moravian missions. 1818.
Hutton, James, Life of; by Benham.
Koelbring's Memorial days of the Church.
Loskiel's Indian missions. 1794.
Moravian Magazine.
Moravians, The, in Jamaica. (As in 1854.)
Oldenthorpe's Hist. of the Danish mission.
——— History of the West India mission.
Periodical Accounts. (A great storehouse of facts.)
Pescheck's Reformation and anti-reformation in Bohemia.
Princeton Review. 7:77.
Presbyterian Quart. Review. July, 1858.
Reichel's M. in North Carolina. 1857.
Results of the General Synods of the Church. (Held every 10 or 12 years at Hernhut.)
Rimius' Rise and progress of the M. 1753.
Risler's Select Narratives.
Ritter's Hist. of the M. Church in Philada.
The Telescope. Periodical.

A learned and approved history of the Moravians, by John Plitt, exists in MS. in the library of the Theological Seminary at Bethlehem, Penna., written in 1828. "The Lissa folios," 14 vols. of MS., are preserved at Hernhut, containing the earliest extant accounts of the Brethren.

Mormonism.

Pro.

Book of Mormon, translated from golden plates, by Joseph Smith.
Appeal to the American people. 1840.
Pratt's (P. B.) Div. authority of the bk. of M.
——— Faith of the Latter-day saints.
Pratt's (O.) Accóunt of several remarkable visions, and of the late discovery of ancient American records.
Smith's (Jos.) Doctrines of the Church.
Times and Seasons. Periodical. Nauvoo.

Mormonism—*continued.*

Con.

Bennett's (John C.) History of the Saints.
Caswell's Prophet of the 19th cent., with an analysis of the book of Mormon.
Christian Examiner. 53:201. 64:421.
Dublin University Mag. 21:283.
Eclectic Magazine. 21:400.
Eclectic Rev. New Series. 4:669,745. 6:479.
Fuller's (Mrs.) Mormon Wives.
Geier on Irvingism and Mormonism.
Green's Fifteen years among the Mormons.
Gunnison's Valley of the Salt Lake.
Harris' Mormonism portrayed.
Howe's Mormonism unveiled.
Hyde's Mormonism and its leaders.
Kane's (T. L.) Discourse before the Pennsylvania Historical Society.
Kidder (D. T.) on Mormonism.
Law's (Cath.) Narrative of M. proceedings.
Littell's Living Age. 15:461. 30:429.
London Review. 18:351. 20:193.
Mayhew's (Horace) Latter-day Saints.
Methodist Quart. Rev. 3:111.
Smith's (Mary) Fifteen years with the M.
Southern Literary Messenger. 10:526.
Taylder's Mormon's own book.
Turner's (Prof. J. B.) M. in all ages.
Van Deusen's (A seceder) Spiritual Delusions.
Westminster Review. New Series. 3:196.

Mormonism, History of.

Olshausen's (T.) Gesch. der Mormonen.
Pichot (A.), Les Mormons.

Burton's City of the Saints. 1861.
Caswell's City of the Mormons. 1842.
Chandler's Visit to Salt Lake. 1857.
Clarke's Gleanings by the way.
Corrill's History of the Latter-day Saints.
Ferris' Utah and the Mormons. 1856.
Gunnison's History and condition, &c. 1856.
London Review. 18:351.
Mackay's Hist. of the Latter-day Saints. 1856.
Quarterly Review. 2:95.
Rémy's Journey to Salt Lake. 1861.
Schmucker's History of the Mormons. 1856.
Simpson's History of Mormonism.
Stansbury's Expedition to Salt Lake. 1852.
Ward's Sights and scenes among the M.
Westminster Rev. New Series. 3:196.

Mortal Sin. See DEADLY SIN.

Mortification of Sin. See SELF-DENIAL.

Atkinson's (Christopher) Sermons.
Bradford's (The Martyr) Works.
Brooks' Prec. remedies for Satan's devices.
Charnock's Works.
Hopkins' (Ezekiel) Sermons.
Mead's Almost Christian discovered.
Morning Exercises at Cripplegate. (Sermon by B. Needler.)
Owen (John) on Sin in believers.
Reading's (William) Sermons.
Scougal's Life of God in the soul of man.
Taylor's (Jer.) Life of Christ. Disc. 4.
Tracts for the Times. Tract 21.
Walker's (Robt.) Sermons. (These sermons are the best model a student can adopt.)
Watson's (Thomas) Sermons.

Moses. See BIOGRAPHY.

Cattenburgii Syntagma Sapientiæ Mosaicæ.
Gaulmyn, de Vita et morte Mosis.
Pastoret, Moyse considerè comme législateur, et comme moraliste.
Philonis, Vita Mosis.

Anderson's (J. S.) Life of Moses.
Anderson's (M.) Ten discourses on Moses.
Bradley's (Charles) Sermons.
Breay's Hist. of M. practically considered.
Close's (Francis) Sermons on typical persons.
Campbell's (John) Life of Moses.
Hamilton's Pentateuch and its assailants.
Heber's (Bp.) Parish Sermons.
Hengstenberg's Moses. (Biblical Cabinet.)
Hoare's Veracity of the book of Genesis.
Kitto's Bible Illustrations.
Melville's (Henry) Sermons.
Plumtree's History of Moses.
Ross' (J. L.) Twenty Lectures.
Smith's (Thornley) History of Moses.
Thompson's (F. E.) Lent Lectures.
Thornton's (T.) Life of Moses.
Townsend's Character of M. as a historian.

Mothers. See MATERNAL DUTIES.

Motives. See MORAL SUASION, WILL.

Bagshaw (W.) on Human Motives.
Christian Observer. 19:1.
Crombie (Alex.) on Philosophical Necessity.
——— Review of Gregory on motives.
Gregory's (James) Difference between motive and cause. (Replies to Crombie.)
——— Defence of Do.
Hazlitt's Principles of Human action.
McCombe on Moral Agency.
Moore's (Dr. G.) Man and his motives.
Penrose's Nature and discipline of motives.
Tucker's Light of nature. Ch. 5,15,16,17.
Walker's (James) Sermons.

Mourners. See AFFLICTION, BEATITUDES, BEREAVEMENT.

Abercrombie's Mourner Comforted.
Allestree's (Richard) Sermons.
Bragge on Undissembled Religion.
Bruce's (John) Mourners advised.
Cecil's Visits to the House of mourning.
Cook's (John) Sermons.
Dibden's (T. F.) Sermons.
Doolittle's Mourner's Directory.
Dowling's (J. Goulter) Sermons.
Faringdon's (Anthony) Sermons.
Flavel's Token for Mourners.
Francklin's (Thomas) Sermons.
Gardner (Bp.) on True obedience.
Gerard's (Alexander) Sermons.
Grosvener's Mourner Comforted.
Hincks' (John) Sermons.

Mourners—*continued.*

Lucas' (Richard) Sermons.
Manton's (T.) Works. (Advice to mourners.)
Newnham's Tribute of sympathy to M.
Patrick's Heart's Ease.
Peabody's Sermons on Consolation.
Shaw's Welcome to the plague.
Spurgeon's (Cha. H.) Sermons. 2nd Series.
Sturm's Reflections.
Universalist Quarterly. 5:36.

Muggletonians.

Pro.

Muggleton's Interp. of all the chief texts, &c.
——— Spiritual Epistles.
——— Sundry other tracts. 7 vols.
Reeves' News from Heaven.
——— Divine Looking-glass.
——— Remonstrance from the eternal God.
——— Other treatises.
Tomkinson's (Tho.) Truth's Triumph.

Con.

Taylor's Muggletonian Principles.
Williams' (Bp.) Absurd and mischievous opinions of the Muggletonians considered.

Muhammed. See MAHOMET.

Munzer.

Averbachii Dissertationes duæ.
Baleus' (J.) Bäpstliche Geschichte.
Bullinger, von der Wiedertäuffer Ursprung.
Bussiere, Histoire de Lutheranisme.
Dorp's Wahrhaftige Historie.
Hortensii Tumultuum Anabaptistic. liber.
Kerssenbroch de Bello Anabaptistico.
Loescheri (Valent. Ernest.) Stromata.
Melancthon's Hist. Thomæ Munzeris.
Menchenii Scriptor. rerum Germanicarum.
Meshovii Historia Anabaptistica.
Munzer (Tho.), oder der thuringische Bauerkrieg.
Schardii Scriptor. rerum Germanicarum.
Strobel's Leben, Schriften, und Lehren M.

Hughes' (W.) History of John a Leyden.

Very little reliance can be placed on the statements of bitter persecutors of Munzer and his doctrines, as most of these were.

Murder. See SUICIDE.

Brackenbury's (Edw.) Sermons for families.
Dwight's Theology. Ser. 115.
Forster's (Nathaniel) Sermons.
Hole (Matthew) on the Church Catechism.
Hopkins' (Bp.) Sermons.
McLean's Apostolical Commission.
Newcombe's Sermons.
Parsons on the Catechism.
Pascal's Provincial Letters. Letter 14.
Reynolds' God's revenge against Murder. (Thirty tragical histories.)
Secker (Abp.) on the Catechism.
Toogood's (Charles) Sermons.

Mystery. See PROVINCE OF REASON.

Ambrose, de Mysteriis.
Baierus de Necessitate mysteriorum in religione revelata.
Bulfinger, de Mysteriis Christianæ fidei.
Buttstett der Vernunftigen Gedancken.
Cicero, contra Verrein.
Diodorus, Bibliothecæ Historicæ.
Haferungii Mysteria neque comprehendi posse neque tamen rationi adversari.
Nouvelle Encyclopedie Theologique.

Amer. Jour. of Science. 13:217.
Bloomfield's (Bp.) Sermons.
Campbell's (Geo.) Preliminary Dissertations.
Carr's (George) Sermons.
Chris. Month. Spectator. 5:1.
Chris. Examiner. 17:202.
Chris. Disciple. 2:429.
Conybeare's Defence of revealed religion.
Cosin's (Dr. John) Sermons.
Edwards' (Pres.) Works.
Foster's (Dr. James) Sermons.
Foster's Contributions to the Eclectic Review. (The power of mystery.)
Hawkins' (Will.) Bampton Lectures. 1787.
Hone on Mysteries and religious shows.
Hurd's (Bp.) Sermons.
Leland's Advantage and necess. of Div. revel.
Littleton's (Edward) Sermons.
McKnight's Preface to Epistle to Ephesians.
Milbourn's M. of religion vindicated.
Newman's (John H.) Sermons.
Newton's (Bp. Thomas) Dissertations.
Newton's (W.) Sermons.
Randolph's Enchiridion Theologicum.
Reay's (William) Sermons.
Robinson's Claude.
Sanderson's (Bp.) Sermons.
Smith's (Thomas) Sermons.
South's (Robert) Sermons.
Southern Lit. Messenger. 6:624.
Stebbings' (Henry) Sermons.
Stillingfleet's Origines Sacræ.
——— Discourse on Scripture Mysteries.
Sumner's (Samuel) Discourses.
Warburton's Legation of Moses. Bk. 1,2.
Wheatly's (Charles) Sermons.

Mystics. See BOEHMENISTS, BOURIGNONISTS, PIETISTS, QUIETISTS.

Pro.

Abbas (Guliel.) ad Fratres Montis.
Alvarez de Perfecta contemplatione.
——— de Vita spirituali.
Arnoldi (G.) Hist. et descriptio theol. M.
——— Other works. (A wonderful man.)
Barbanson, de Amore Dei.
——— Veræ theologiæ compendium.
Bernardi Sermones.
——— de Consideratione.
Bertot, le Directeur Mystique.
Binet, Œuvres Spirituelles.
Blammevenniæ Introd. in Theologiam.
Bona, Via Compendii ad Deum.
——— Manductio ad Cœlum.

Mystics—*continued.*

Pro.

Bonaventura de Reformatione Mentis.
——— Meditationes.
——— de l'Amour Divine.
Buchon, Choix Ouvrages mystiques.
Camera, La Reine d'amour propre.
Canfield, Regula perfectionis.
Catharine de Siena, Meditat., Dialog., etc.
Corderii Isagoge.
Desmaret, Ouvrages.
Dionysius Carthusianus Opera. ("Sober, wise, and full of wholesome maxims."—DUPIN.)
Drexelii Opera. (One of the chief of the M.)
Evangelista, de Elevatione animæ supra semetipsum.
Fenelon, Œuvres Spirituelle.
Fludd, Opera Omnia. (See a full account of them in Wood's Athenæ Oxonienses.)
Galenii Summa Mysticæ Theologiæ.
Gerson [or Gessen], Considerationes.
——— de Modo vivendi.
——— Contemplations sur la passion.
——— Other works.
Guillore, Œuvres.
Harpei Mystica Theologia.
Harvengii (Philippi) Opera.
Heinroth's Geschichte und Kritik der M.
Herstentii Apparatus ad Theologiam.
Hiel, de Vita essentia, etc.
Horstii Paradisus Animæ Christianæ.
Hugo (de Palma), Opera.
John a Cruce, Ascensus Montis Carmeli.
Louvencourt, le Gâteau spirituel.
Molinos, Manductio spiritualis.
Nouet (P.), Œuvres.
Picard, Miroir du monde.
Poiret, Theologie du Cœur.
——— Cogitationes.
——— l'Economie Divine.
——— La paix des bonnes ames.
——— (Various other works. Most of his writings are translated into English.)
Pomerius de Vita contemplativa.
Pontalier, Trésor du Chrétien.
Quentin, l'Orologe de dévotion.
Richard (de St. Victoire), de Statu interioris hominis. ("The Coryphæus of the Mystics."—MOSHEIM.)
Rodriguez, Pratique de la perfection.
Rusbrochius de Ornatu nuptiar. spiritualium.
——— Deutche Theologie.
Sales (Francis de), de Amore Dei.
——— Many other tracts.
Sandæi Theologia.
Savanarola de Simplicitate Chris. vitæ.
Scherer, Preces ac Meditationes.
Schramm, Institutiones Theologiæ.
St. Angela, Theologie de la croix, etc.
Stilling's Sämmtliche Werke.
Sucquet, Via Vitæ.
Suso, Leben und Scriften.
Tauleri Institutiones.
——— Medulla Animæ.
Thomas (a Kempis) de Imitatione Christi.
Turrecremata, Meditationes.
Bromley's (Thomas) Way to rest.
——— Essay on true knowledge.
Caxton's (Wm.) Treatise on love.
Cunninghame's (Jas.) Warnings of the eternal Spirit.
Everhard's Gospel Treasury opened.
Girard's (John) Holy Meditations.
Hartley's Paradise restored. Appendix.
Hilton's (Walter) Ladder of perfection.
Law (William) on Perfection.
——— Grounds of the Teutonic philosophy.
——— Various other treatises.
Lead's (Jane) Soul's union with Christ.
Life of Madame Guion.
——— Madame Bourignon.
——— Jacob Bœhmen.
Marsay (C. A.) on the Spiritual Life.
Molino's Guide to Contemplation.
Oakley's New Creature in Christ.
——— Divine Visions.
Pavey's (John) Works.
Poiret's Divine Œconomy. (A good body of Divinity.)
Sales' Introd. to a devout life. (Edited, and purged of its Romish errors, by Nichols.)
Sherwin's Saints revealed.
Whiteford's (Rich.) Fruyte of Redempcyon.

Con.

Borgeri Disputationes.
Bossuet, Memoires sur le livre intitulé "Explication des maximes des saintes, sur le vie interieure."
——— Instruction sur les etats d'oraison.
Ewald's alte Mystik u. neu. Mysticismus.
Fritzsche's Mysticismus und Pietismus.
Gravell, der Werth der Mystik.
Haug, de Theologia Mystica.
Hofling's Mysticismus.
Jægeri Theologia.
Krause's Hist. und psychol. Bemerkungen.
Spieker's Mysticismus, dessen Begriff, Ursprung und Werth.
Weber's Myst. Tendenzen unserer Zeit. 1829.

Mysticism, History of.

Anselme (H.), le Monde païen.
Baumgarten (Crusius), Compendium.
Bausset, Hist. de la vie de Bossuet. (Contains an account of the whole controversy with Fenelon.)
Buddei Isagoge ad Theologiam.
De Wette, Christliche Sittenlehre.
Ewald's Alte und neuen Mystik.
Fontaninus Hist. litterar. Aquiliensis.
Franke's Arnold von Brescia, u. seine Zeit.
Hagenbach's Dogmengeschichte.
Helferich, die Christliche Mystik.
Heinroth's Geschichte und Kritik des M.
Muratori Antiquitates Italic. medii ævi.
Pfeiffer's Deutsche Mystiken des 14 Jahrh.

Mysticism, History of—*continued.*

Planck's Gesch. d. protestantisch. Theologie.
Poiret, Bibliotheca Mysticorum. ("I have been delighted with it."—JEBB.)
Salat's Supernaturalismus und Mysticismus.
Schmid's (H.) der M. des mittel Alters.
Schmidt (C.), les Mystiques du 14th siécle.

Christian Observer. 1861. P. 509.
Eclectic Review. N. S. 12:50.
Edinburg Review. 84:102,195.
George's (David) Writers of the XVth cent.
Knox's (Alexander) Remains.
Life of De Renty.
——— Fenelon.
——— John V. Andrea.
New Englander. 5:348.
Retrospective Review. 1:288.
Vaughn's (R. A.) Hours with the Mystics.

A complete account of the host of Mystical writers, to 1740, is given in the edition of ARNOLD's *Kirchen Historie,* published at Schaffhausen. 1742.

Mythology. See WORSHIP OF SPIRITS.

Allatius de Templis Græcorum.
Bauer's Symbolik des Alterthums.
Bergier, Dieux du Paganisme.
Bruckeri Hist. Critica philosophiæ.
Bynckershoeckii Opuscula. ("Curious and learned."—MOSHEIM.)
Choul, la Religions des anciens Romains. (300 engravings.)
Cicero de Natura Deorum.
Comes, Explicatio Fabularum, etc.
Creuzer's Symbolik der alten Völker.
Cumberland, Origines Gentium.
Dupuy, Hist. des dieux et demi-dieux.
Encyclopedie Théologique.
Galæi Opuscula Mythologica.
Gerhard's Griechische Mythologie.
Grave, de Republique de champs elisées. (A curious work, connecting the Greek mythology with that of Gaul.)
Grimm's Deutche Mythologie.
Harettii Delecta Mythologiæ Græcorum.
Heffter's Religion d. Griechen u. Römer.
Herbert de Religione Gentilium.
Hermann's Handbuch der Mythologie.
Hirt's Bildung der Ægypt. gottheiten.
Hyde, Religio vet. Persarum et Medorum.
Iamblicus de Mysteriis Ægyptorum.
Iamieson, Spicilegia Antiquitatum.
Jablonski Pantheon Ægyptiorum. (Held in the highest estimation.)
Lakemacheri Antiquitates Græcorum.
Millin, Galerie Mythologique. 190 plates.
Mover's Phœnizier. (Extensive.)
Munter's Religion der Karthagen.
Nork's (F.) Biblische Mythologie: ein neuen Theorie zur Aufhellung der Dunkelheiten u. scheinbaren Widersp. in den canon. Büchern d. Juden u. Christen.
Perizonii Origines Babylonicæ, etc.
Pfanneri Syst. theolog. gentilis purior.
Richter, Phantasien des Orients.

Mythology—*continued.*

Roack's Mythologie und Offenbarung.
Schedius de diis Germanis.
Selden de diis Syriis.
Tressan, M. comparée avec l'Histoire.
Vossii (G. J.) Theologia Gentilis.

Amer. Eclectic Rev. 2:326. (Scandinavian.)
Amer. Quart. Rev. 22:349. (Middle ages.)
Asiatic Researches.
Baldwin's Pantheon.
Banier's Mythology of the ancients.
Bassville's Elements of Mythology.
Bell's (John) Pantheon; or, Historical dictionary of gods, demigods, heroes, and fabulous personages of antiquity. Plates.
Berry's Mythological tables.
Bryant's Analysis of ancient heathen M.
Cabel's Unity of the human race.
Carr's (T. S.) Classical Mythology.
Christ. Rev. 2:515. 10:530.
Christie on the Earliest Idolatries.
Christmas' (H.) Universal Mythology.
Coleman's Mythology of the Hindus.
Cory's Mytholog. and chronolog. enquiries.
Coventry's History of false religions.
De Rougemont on the primitive people.
Dublin Univ. Mag. 12:86. (Northern.)
Faber's (G. S.) Mysteries of the Cabiri. (The gods of Phenicia, Egypt, Greece, Troas, &c.)
——— Origin of Pagan idolatry.
Farmer on the Worship of human spirits.
Foreign Quart. Rev. 7:33. (Greece.) 16:437. (Scandinavian.)
Foster's Mythol. and customs of the Hindus.
Frazier's Mag. 20:1,200,326. (Egyptian.)
Gale's Court of the Gentiles. (Showing the learning and religious knowledge of Pagans to be derived from Holy Scripture.)
Goodwin's Roman and Grecian antiquities.
Grey's Polynesian mythology.
Herbert's Ancient religion of the Gentiles.
Keightley's M. of ancient Greece and Italy.
Kennedy's Ancient and Hindu M. Plates.
Kennett's Antiquities of Rome.
King's Hist. acc. of heathen gods and heroes.
Knickerbocker Mag. 30:95. (Northern.)
Le Clerc's Religion of the ancient Greeks.
Mallet's Northern Antiquities.
Maurice's Indian Antiquities.
Mayo's M. of the Greeks and Romans.
Meade's (Bp.) The Bible and the Classics.
Monthly Review. 92:225. (Egyptian.) 128:175. (Hindu.)
Moore's Hindu Pantheon.
Müller's Scientific system of Mythology.
Mushet's Trinities of the Ancients.
North Amer. Rev. 28:18. (Scandinavian.) 41:327. (Classic.)
North's Mythology compared with History.
Pigot's Scandinavian Mythology.
Pluche's (Abbe la) History of the heavens.
Plutarch's Isis and Osiris.
Pomey's Mythology. Tr. by Tooke. Plates.
Potter's Antiquities of Greece.
Prescott's Mexico and Peru.

Mythology—*continued.*

Pococke's India in Greece; or, Truth in Mythology. (Traces the Hellenic race, the settlement of Egypt and Palestine, &c.)
Pritchard's Egyptian Mythology.
Quar. Review. 22:349. (Middle ages.)
Ramsay's Theology and M. of the Ancients.
Sheldon's History of the Heathen gods.
Smith's Dictionary of Greek and Roman M.
Spencer's Polymetis.
Thorpe's Northern Mythology. (Scandinavia, Germany, Norway, &c. Very thorough.)
Tooke's Pantheon of the Heathen gods.
Tressam's M. compared with History.
Turner's Theology of Pagans.
Ward's View of Hindu theology.
Weiderman's Essays.

The above is a mere specimen of innumerable works on this subject.

Naaman. See BIOGRAPHY.

Girdlestone's (Charles) Sermons.
Hickman's (Bp.) Sermons.
Percival's (A. P.) Sermons.
Potts' (J. H.) Sermons.
Shuttleworth's (P. N.) Sermons.

Nag's-head Consecration.

Pro.

Le Courayer's Validity of Engl. ordinations.
Le Quien's Panoplia.

Con.

Bramhall's Church of England defended.
Brett's Divine right of Episcopacy.
Brown (J.) on the Nag's-head ordination.
Harrington's Succession of English bishops.
Mason's Vindication of English bishops.

I know of no entire book written to prove the fact of such an ordination; but many writers, besides the two above named, describe it as a fact.

Names of Christ. See TITLES.

Name of God. See HUTCHINSONIANS.

Capellus de Nomine tetragramato.
Cocceii Disputationes Selectæ.
Cortici Dissertationes. (Very copious.)
Deylingii (Salamon.) Dissertationes.
Drusius de Nomine Elohim.
Falkius de Derivatione nominis Dei.
Gataker de Nomine tetragrammato.
Landauer's יהוה und אלהים.
Matani Nom. Dei juxta Hæbræos.
Michaelis (J. F.) de Nomine Dei.
Millii (D.) Dissertationes.
Osiandri (L.) Exercitationes.
Relandi Exercitationes philologicæ. (Contains extracts from Alting, Amama, Leusden, and others.)
Weberi (Ch. F.) Doctrina ævi primi.
Witsii Vindicatio argumenti desumpti a constructione nominis Elohim, cum verbo singularis numeri.
Zanchii Dissertationes.

Name of God—*continued.*

Aboab's Remarks on Sharp's Dissertation.
Bates' (Julius) Reply to Dr. Sharp.
Bayle's Dict. Articles Arnaud, Nicole, &c.
Davies' (Pres. Samuel) Sermons.
Hall's (Robert) Works.
Hodges' Christian plan exhibited.
Holloway on Elohim and Berith.
Hutchinson's Works.
Kalmar's Dissertations.
——— Reply to Holloway.
——— Reply to Aboab.
Kitto's Journal of Sac. Lit. 2:332.
Mather (S.) on the name Jehovah.
Moody's Evidences of Christianity contained in the words Aleim and Berith.
Pascall's Provincial Letters.
Sharp's (Tho.) Diss. on the etymology, &c.
——— Review and defence of the same.
Spurgeon's (C. H.) Sermons. 1st & 6th Series.
Stuart (Moses) on the Apocalypse.
Sydenham's Onomasticon.
Woodhouse's Practical sermons.

Nathaniel.

Clerke's (Richard) Sermons.
Marshall's (N.) Sermons.
Neve's (Timothy) Sermons.
Waterland's (Daniel) Sermons.

National Blessings. See THANKSGIVING.

Gerard's (Alexander) Sermons.
Gresley's (William) Sermons.
Morehead's (Robert) Sermons.
Pearson's (Hugh) Sermons before the King.
Sterne's (Lawrence) Sermons.

National Retributions.

Flower's (Benjamin) Sermons.
Fowle's (F. W.) Ten plain sermons.
Graves' (Dr. Richard) Sermons.
Huntingdon's (Prof.) Sermons.
Miller's (Joseph) Sermons.
Montgomery (Robt.) on Religious Belief.
Morning Exercises at Cripplegate. (Sermon by Williams.)
Parsons' (J.) Sermons.
Percival's (A. P.) Sermons.
Porteus' (Beilby) Sermons.
Saunders' (Erasmus) Sermons.
Sharp's (Granville) Warning to Gt. Britain.
Wesley's (John) Sermons.
Whately's (Abp.) Sermons.
Whitaker's (Edward W.) Sermons.

Nativity of Christ. See CHRISTMAS.

Augustine, Sermones.
Basil, Homiliæ.
Gregory Naz., Sermones.

Allix, Diatriba. (Memoires de Trevoux. 1715. On the month and the day.)
Cloppenburgii Diss. Chronologico-theol.
Fabricii Bibliographia antiq. Ch. 7. (Collects the opinions of the learned as to the year of Christ's birth.)

Nativity of Christ—*continued.*

Kepleri Commentatiuncula de vero anno, etc.
Kirchmeyeri Cogitationes Sacræ.
Lupus de Anno nativitatis. (*Acta erud.*)
Maii Observationes philologicæ.
Meieri Observationes chronologicæ.
Neander, Test. vet. Ebræorum de Christo.
Ravii Disputationes. (As to the time.)
Schleiermacher's Weihnachtsfeier.
Van Till, Dissertationes.

Bather's (Edward) Sermons.
Benson's (C.) Chronol. of our Saviour's life.
Christian Examiner. 38:49.
Clarke's (Dr. Samuel) Sermons.
Frazier's Magazine. 38:670.
Hastings' (H. J.) Sermons.
Hopkins' (Ezekiel) Sermons.
Jarvis' Church Chronology.
Mandell's (William) Sermons.
Mann's Dissertations. (The time.)
Pearson (Bp.) on the Birth of Christ.
Roberts' (Arthur) Sermons. (Situation of the world at the time.)
Robinson's (Ralph) Sermons.
Southern Lit. Messenger. 7:219.
Stewart's (J. H.) Discourses.
Thayer's (Elihu) Sermons.
Whitefield's (George) Sermons.

Natural Ability. See MORAL ABILITY.

Natural History of the Bible.

Aurogal de Heb. herbium, fluminum, etc.
Bocharti Hierozoicon. 1663. (Edited by Rosenmüller. 1793. A treasure.)
Celsii (Olaus.) Hiero-botanicon.
Cocquii Contemplatio plantarum, etc.
——— Exercitationes Physiologicæ.
Cyprian (Joh.) Animales Scripturæ.
Drusius de Mandragoris.
Eusebii et Hieronymi Onomasticon.
Forskal, de Animal. avi., amphib., pisc., etc.
Franzius de Animalibus sac. scripturæ.
Hilleri Hierophyticon. (As minute in regard to plants as Bochart is in regard to animals.)
Lesser's Insecto-theologia.
Maii Historia animalium Scripturæ.
Maurille, Phytologie Sacrée.
Montani Historia Naturæ, etc. (In the Antwerp Polyglott.)
Müller de Animalibus biblicis.
Relandi Palestina. (Very useful.)
Rosenmülleri Dissertationes.
Rudbeckii Icthyologia Biblica.
Scheuchzeri Physica Sacra. 1735. (8 folio volumes, with 800 engravings. Very full as to serpents and insects.)
Ursini Arboretum Biblicum.
Volger de Rebus naturalibus et medicis, etc.
Walchii Calendarium Palestinæ.

Abbot's Scripture natural history.
Balfour's Trees and shrubs of the Bible.
Biblical Cabinet. (Many articles.)
Biblical Repertory. Vol. 1. Tr. of Warnekross.
Brown on the Plants of Scripture.

Natural Hist. of the Bible—*continued.*

Buckham on the Mustard tree. (Agt. Frost.)
Carpenter's Nat. hist. of the Bible. Plates.
Catlow's Popular Scripture Zoology. Plates.
Christian Disciple. 3:49.
Copley's Scripture natural history.
Dun's Biblical natural science.
Frost on the Mustard tree of the New Test.
Harris' Natural history of the Bible. Plates. (Small, but the best in English.)
Lemnius' Scrip. Herbal. (Merely curious.)
Newton's (Thos.) Herbal of the Bible.
Osborn's Plants of the Holy land. Plates.
Princeton Review. 7:559.
Rosenmuller's Mineralogy and Botany of the Bible. (Trans. by Repp.)
Taylor's (C.) Scripture illustrated. Plates.
Williams' Bible Quadrupeds.

Natural History of Man. See MAN.

Naturalism. See RATIONALISM.

Natural Religion. See ATHEISM, LAW OF NATURE, LIGHT OF NATURE, NATURAL THEOLOGY.

Natural Theology.

Bullet, Exist. de Dieu demontré.
Curcellii Opera. Lib. I, cap. 2.
Delalle, Theologie Naturelle.
Doderleini Theologia.
Gerhardi Loci Theologici.
Lesser, Theologie des Insects.
Nahmmacher de Nat. Theol. Ciceronis.
Sabunde, Theologia Naturalis.
Siebelis, Disp. V. quib. periculum factum est ostendi in vet. Græcorum et Rom. doctrina cum Chris. consentiente.
St. Martin, Tableau des rapports qui existent entre Dieu, l'homme, et l'univers.
Vitringæ Opuscula.
Wild's Vernunftglaube.

Abbadie on the Christian Religion.
Abernethy's (John) Sermons.
Allen's Oracles of Reason.
Anderson's Course of Creation.
Atkey's Being and attributes of God.
Barker's Natural Theology.
Barrow's (Bp.) Works.
Beavan's Elements of Natural Theology.
Bellamy's (Joseph) Sermons.
Bentley's Boyle Lectures. 1692.
Berkeley's Minute Philosopher.
Biblioth. Sacra. 3:241.
Boyle on Final causes.
Bridgewater Treatises, viz.:
Bell's Mechanism of the hand.
Buckland's Geology with reference to theology. (This author expended on the 90 plates the whole of the thousand pounds received from the Bridgewater fund.)
Chalmers on the power, wisdom, and goodness of God, as seen in the adaptation of external nature to the moral and intellectual constitution of man.

Natural Theology—*continued.*

Kidd on the Adaptation of nature to the physical condition of man.
Kirby's Wisdom of God as seen in the history, habits, and instincts of animals.
Prout's Chemistry, Meteorol., & Digestion.
Roget's Animal and vegetable physiology.
Whewell's Astronomy and general physics.
Brit. Quar. Review. 7:204.
Brougham's Natural Theology.
Brown's Existence of a supreme Creator.
Burnett's (C. M.) Power, &c., as seen in the Animal Creation. (Capital.)
Bushman's Study of Nature.
Butler's Analogy of Religion and Nature.
Charnock's Works.
Chris. Exam. 30:273. 6:389. 13:187.
Christian Quar. Spect. 8:177. 10:319
Christian Review. 3:1.
Crabbe's (Geo.) System of Natural Theology.
Crombie's Natural Theology.
Dick's Christian Philosopher.
Dryden (J.) on Natural Religion.
Durham's Boyle Lectures. 1711,1712.
——— Astro-Theology.
Dublin Univ. Mag. 6:448. 7:597.
Eclectic Rev. 4th Series. 5:609.
Edinb. Review. 1:287. 64:141.
Fergus' Testimony of Nature.
Frazier's Mag. 12:375. 13:694.
Gisbourne's Test. of Nat. Theol. to religion.
Gosse's Life in its manifestations.
Gretton's Review of the argument *a priori* for the being of God.
Grew's (N.) Cosmologia Sacra.
Grinfield's Conn. of nat. and rev. theology.
Grove's (N.) Wisdom of Deity.
Hall's (Robt.) Modern Infidelity.
Hamilton on the Supreme Being.
Hampden's Philos. evid. of Christianity.
Harris' (Robert) Sermons.
Hey's (John) Lectures. Bk. 1, ch. 3 and 4.
Jones' Natural evidences of Christianity.
La Pluche on the Starry Heavens.
Laws' (E.) Theory of Religion.
Leibritz's Theodice.
Leighton's (Abp.) Lectures.
Lesser's Insecto-Theology.
Leuwenhoeck's Works. Trans. by S. Hoole.
Littell's Living Age. 19:289.
Lowman's Unity and perfections of God.
McCosh's Typical forms and special ends in Creation.
——— on Intuitions.
——— Divine Gov., physical and moral.
McCullock's Proofs and illustrations, &c.
Miller's (Hugh) Works.
Milne on the State of the old world.
Month. Rev. 88:82. 120:30.
New Eng. Mag. 4:454.
New York Rev. 1:137,298.
Nieuwentyt's Religious Philosopher.
North Am. Rev. 42:467. 54:102,256.
Ollyffe on the Origin and govt. of the world.
Paley's Natural Theology.

Natural Theology—*continued.*

Ragg's Creation's testimony to its God.
Ray's Physico-theology.
Read's (H.) Palace of the great King.
Rust's (Bp.) Use of reason.
Seaton's Grounds of religion.
Simon's (M. J.) Natural religion.
Spalding (J. J.) on Religion.
Stebbings' Defence of Dr. Clark.
Steere's (Edw.) Exist. and attributes of God.
Sykes' Foundation of religion.
——— Principles of religion.
Thompson's Christian Theism.
Towne's Actonian. (A prize essay.)
Tullock's Theism. (A prize essay.)
Tunstall's (James) Academica.
Turretin's (Francis) Dissertations. Diss. 1.
Turton's Natural Theology considered with reference to Lord Brougham's discourse.
Westminster Review. 17:413.
Wilson's (Prof.) Chemical final causes.

Nature of Virtue. See VIRTUE.

Necessity. See CONTINGENCY, HUMAN RESPONSIBILITY, MIND, SCIENTIA MEDIA, WILL.

Pro.

Belsham's Essays. Ess. 1.
Bray's Philosophy of N.; or the law of consequences, mental, moral, and social.
Chalmer's Notes on Butler's Analogy.
Clarke's (Sam.) Boyle Lectures. 1704.
Collins on Human liberty.
Crombie's Essay on Philosophical necessity.
Edwards' (Pres.) Works. (On the Will.)
Hartley's Observations on man.
Hobbes' Letter to the Duke of Newcastle.
——— Leviathan.
Hume's Essays.
Kaime's (Lord) Essays.
Leibnitz's Essay on the liberty of man.
Priestley's Essays on Hartley's theory.
——— Letter to Palmer.
——— 2d " " "
——— Letter to Bryant.
Toplady on Christian and philosophical N.

Con.

Limborchii Theologia.
Abercrombie's Intellectual Philosophy.
Amer. Bibl. Repos. 2d Series. 9:214,297.
Bates' Observations on important points.
Beattie's Works. Part 2.
Bramhall's (Abp.) Works. (Rep. to Hobbes.)
Bryant's Address to Dr. Priestley.
Burnet on the 39 Articles.
Butler's Analogy of Relig. and Nat. Ch. 6.
Butterworth on Moral government.
Christ. Examiner. 35:198.
Clarke's (S.) Remarks on Collins' Enquiry.
——— Sermons.
Colliber's Enquiry into the nature of God.
Coppleston's Enquiry into the Doct. of N.
Crybbace's Essay on Moral freedom.
Cudworth's Intellect. system of the universe.

Necessity—*continued.*

Con.

Dawson's Doctrine of Philosoph. necessity.
Doddridge's Lectures. Part 1, prop. 16.
Eclectic Rev. 12:417.
Fisher's (Jos.) Rev. of Priestley on necessity.
Fuller's Gospel worthy of all acceptation.
Gibbs' (Adam) Sacred Contemplations.
Goad on Necessity and Contingency.
Graves on Calvinistic Predestination.
——— Two Sermons in Trinity Col., Dublin.
Gregory's Essays, Philosoph. and literary.
Grove on Human Liberty.
——— Moral philosophy.
Harris' Boyle Lectures. 1698.
Horseley's (Bp.) Sermons.
Hutchinson's Metaphysics.
Jackson's Defence of human liberty.
King's Origin of evil.
Lawson's Examin. of Hobbes' Leviathan.
Lyons (J.) on the Doctrine of necessity.
Maclaurin's Newtonian philosophy.
North Am. Review. 13:384.
Palmer's Observ. on the Liberty of man.
Park Street Lectures. Lect. 10.
Price's Dissertations.
Quart. Review. 26:82. (On Coppleston.)
Reid's Essays on the mind.
Rotherham's Essay on human liberty.
Scharrock on the Law of Nature.
Tucker's (Abr.) Light of Nature.
Turner's (Prof.) Sermons. (Middle way between necessity and free will.)
Watts on Liberty.
West on Moral Agency.
Wollaston's Religion of Nature.
Wood's Works. Vol. 2.

Necessity of Divine Revelation.

Clemens Alex., Exhortatio ad Gentes.
Justin Martyr, Apologia.
——— Cohortatio ad Græcos.
——— Dialogus cum Tryphone.

Auberlen, die Göttliche Offenbarung.
Bretschneider's Systemat. Entwickelung.
Campbell, de Vanitate luminis naturæ.
Laget, Sermons sur divers sujets.
Turrettini (Jo. Alphonsi) Cogitationes.

Appleton's Works. Lect. 11,12,13.
Baker's (T.) Reflections on learning.
Barrow's Necessity of Christianity.
Brown's System of nat. and revealed religion.
Bundy's (Richard) Sermons.
Chandler's Revelation and Society.
Charnock's (S.) Works.
Christian Review. 12:186.
Conybeare on Revealed Religion.
Delany's Revelation examined with candor.
Edgecombe's Reason an insufficient guide.
Ellis' Knowledge of Divine things not from reason.
Farrer's Mission of Christ.
Foster's (Dr. James) Discourses.
Fuller's (And.) Part of a body of Divinity.

Necessity of Div. Revelat.—*continued.*

Gale's Court of the Gentiles.
Gastrell's (Francis) Boyle Lectures. 1793.
Glanville's Vanity of dogmatizing.
Halyburton's Natural Religion insufficient.
Hamilton (W. T.) on the Pentateuch.
Hey's Lectures. Bk. 1, ch. 12.
Jenkins on the Christian Religion.
Jones' Bampton Lectures. 1821.
Law's Considerations.
Leland's Advantage and necessity of Rev.
Mant on the Gospel.
Miller's Division of Scripture.
Morehead's (R.) Sermons.
Nare's Evidence versus Reason.
Norman on the Necessity of Revelation.
Penrose's Bampton Lectures. 1808.
Robinson's (Tho.) Necessity, nature, and evidence of revealed religion.
Stillingfleet's Origines Sacræ.
Tatham's Bampton Lectures. 1789.
Taylor's Apology of Ben Mordecai.
Umfreville's Excellence and necessity, &c.
Vincent's (William) Sermons.
Warburton's Divine legation of Moses.
Watson's Tracts.
Watts' Strength and weakness of hum. reason.
West's Defence of the Christian revelation.
Whiteley's Essays. (Praised by PORTEUS.)
Witherspoon's (John) Works. Vol. 2.
Woodgate's Bampton Lectures. 1838.

Necessity of Good Works.
See GOOD WORKS.

Negroes. See ETHNOLOGY, UNITY.

Duprat, Essai sur les Races d'Afrique.
Gregoire, de la Literature des Négres.

Anderson's (C. J.) Lake Ngami. 50 plates.
Armistead's Tribute to the Negro. (A vindication of his capacities.)
Ashman's Reports to the Colonization Soc.
Bacon's Plea for Africa.
Beard's Life of Toussaint L'Ouverture.
Beattie on Truth.
Benezet's (Anthony) Works.
Campbell's (John) Travels in Africa. (First journey, 1815. Second, 1822.)
Childs' (Mrs.) Appeal in favor of Africans. 1855.
Duroc's Life of Toussaint. (Valuable.)
Faber's (Geo. S.) Eight Dissertations.
Goodwin's Negro's Advocate.
Gregoire's Faculties and literature, &c.
Griffin's (Rev. Dr.) Plea for Africa.
Hodgson's Notes on Works on Africa.
Heeren's (Prof.) Politics, trade, &c., of the ancient nations in Africa.
Macauley's (T. B.) Hist. and miscel. essays.
Nesbit's Capacity of N. for improvement.
Philips' (J.) Researches in S. Africa. 1828. (Illustrating the civil, moral, and religious condition of the natives.)
Proyart's History of the Loango. 1776.
Ravenelle's Bibliotheca. (Art. Cush.)

Rees' Cyclopedia. (Art. Cush, Carthage, Ethiopia, &c.)
Sharpe's (Granville) Works.
——— Life and Memoirs.
Smith (S. S.) on the Variety of the human species.
Smith's (Adam) Wealth of nations.
——— Theory of moral sentiments.

Nehemiah.

Woodward's Character and history of N.

Neology. See RATIONALISM.

Pro.

Bahrdt's Glaubensbekentniss.
——— Briefe über die Bibel im Volkston.
——— (Other treatises, the most convenient of which for observing at one view the difference between the orthodox and the new theology, is the *Systema theologiae Lutheranae*, in which the text contains the former, and the commentary the latter.)
Bassedow, Philalethie.
Baumgarten (Jacob.) Theses Theologicæ.
Blasche, Philosophie der Offenbarung.
Bretschneideri de Evang. et epistolar. Joannis origine.
——— Handbuch der Dogmatik.
Carpovii Œconomia salutis Nov. Test.
Cranz, Compendium theologiæ puris.
——— Philosophiæ Leibnitzianæ et Wolfianæ usus in theologia.
Damm, über den historischen Glauben.
Daub, Prolegomena zur Dogmatik.
——— die Dogmat. Theologie jetziger Zeit.
——— Philos. und Theol. Vorlesungen.
Eberhard's Neue Apologie des Socrates.
Eckermanni Comp. Theologiæ Christianæ.
Ewald's (H.) Abhandlung über Entstehung.
——— Other treatises.
Fichté, die Speculative Theologie.
——— Wissenschaftslehre.
Fritsche, Com. in quatuor N. T. Evangelia.
Gruneri Institut. Theol. dogmaticæ.
Hegel's Vorrede zu Hinricks Religions Philosophie.
——— Werke, Volständige, etc.
Heinrich, Acta Apostol. cum perpetua com.
Henké, Lineamenta institutionis fidei.
——— Opuscula Theologica.
——— Gesch. der Christlichen Kirche.
Herder's Religion, Lehrmeinungen, und Gebraucher.
——— (Many other works.)
Lessing, Beiträge zur Gesch. der Literatur.
Niemayer (A. H.), Religion und Kirche.
Noesselt (J. A.) Exercitationes et Opuscula.
Paulus' Philolog, clavis über d. Alte Test.
——— Exegetisches Handbuch.
——— Commentur über das N. Test.
——— der Denkglaubige.
Reinbek's Betrachtungen.
Reuchii Introductio in Theologiam.
Ribbow, Institutiones theologiæ dogmat.
Schelling (F. W. J.), Philosophie u. Relig.
——— (Various other works.)

Neology—*continued.*

Pro.

Schmidt (J. E. C.) Litterrat. d. Kirchenges.
Schuberti Introd. in Theol. revelatam.
Semler (J. S.), Opera. (Over a hundred treatises. His principal work is the Historia Ecclesiastica.)
Senf, über die Herablassung Gottes.
Steinbart. Eudamonistisches System.
Strauss' Leben Jesu.
——— Predigten.
——— (Various other works, all of which called out answers from the more orthodox.)
Veller's Religion der Volkomnen.
Tollner's Unterschied der heiligen Schrift.
Tzschirner's Dogmatik.
Wegscheideri Institutiones.
Jowett's Commentary on the Epistles.
Maurice's (F. D.) Sermons.
——— Religions of the world.
——— Theological Essays.
——— Commentary on Hebrews.

Con.

Alberi Institutiones Hermeneuticæ.
Bagge's Princip. d. Mythus im Dienst der Christlichen Position.
Baumgarten-Crusius, Opuscula.
Baumgarten's (S. J.) Untersuchung theol. Streitigkeiten. (Rep. to Semler's History.)
Beckii Fundamenta.
Bengel's Gnomon; oder Zeiger d. N. Test.
Buddæus, Bedenken ü. Wolfe's Philosophie.
Francke, de Scopo librorum Nov. Test.
——— Prelectiones.
Fry, de Officio doctoris Christiani.
Gaussen, Theopneustie.
Gumpach's Kritik u. Antikritik. (Ag. Ewald.)
Hagenbach's Predigten.
Hengstenburg's Christologie des Alten Test.
Hugg's Gutachten über das Leben Jesu von Strauss.
Keil's Lehrbuch der historisch-kiritischen Einleitung z. A. Test.
Kratander, Anti-Straus; ernstes Zeugniss für d. Chris. Wahrheit.
Krug's Altes und neues Christenthum. (Replies to Ammon and Straus.)
Langii Causa Dei et Religionis.
Löscher's Leben und Wirken.
Michelet's Gesch. d. Philos. von Kant.
Müller's (J. N.) Anti-Bretschneider.
Pareau, Disputationes de mythica sac. codicis interp. (A masterly investigation.)
Pelts' (A. F. L.) Vier Vörlesungen.
Schmid (H.) die Theologie Semler's.
——— die Dogmatik d. evang. lutherischen Kirche.
Thiersch's Verstellung des historischen Standpunct für die Kritik der N. T.
——— Kirche in apostolischen Zeitalter.
Twesten's Dogmat. d. evang. luther. Kirche.
Ulman's Leben Jesu. (Against Strauss.)
Volkmar's Religion Jesu.
Candlish's Examin. of Maurice's Essays.

Neology—*continued.*

Con.

Christian Quart. Spectator. 6:509.
Gillespie's Truth of the evangelical history. (A powerful answer to Strauss.)
Hengstenburg's Book of Moses.
Herbert's Neol. not true, and truth not new. (Replies to Jowett and Maurice.)
Hulsean Lectures. 1833.
Lord's Theol. and Lit. Journal. 3:122.
Mansel's Bampton Lectures. 1858.
Princeton Review. 29:258.
Quarterly Review. 3:393.
Ripley's Latest form of Infidelity.
Rose's State of Protestantism in Germany.
——— Laws of Moses.
Ulman's (Karl) Works. (Replies to Strauss.)
Vaughn's (R.) Essays. (Clear and judicious.)

Neonomians.

Pro.

Edwards' Crispianism unmasked.
Williams' (Dan.) Gospel truth stated.

Con.

Chauncey's Neonomianism unmasked.
Edwards on the Will.
Hussey's Glory of Christ unveiled.

Neoplatonism.

Ammonias Saccas, Opera.
Bouillet, les Ennéades de Plotin.
Fichté, de Philosophiæ novæ Plat. origine.
Iamblicus, Commentaria.
Plotini Opera.
Porphyry, Opera.
Vogt's Neoplatonismus und Christenthum.
Biblical Repository. 1834.

Nestorians.

Pro.

Eutherii (Episc.) Sermones.

Con.

Cyril Alex., adv. Nestorii blasphemias.
Theodoret, contra Nestorium.
Buddæi Isagoge in theologiam.
Facundi Defensio Concilii Chalcedon.
Fausti Epistolæ.
Garneri (Ioann.) Dissertationes.
Leontius (Bysant.) contra Nestorianos.
Maxentius contra Nestorianos.
Mercatoris (Marii) Opera.
Mercatori Comparatio dogm. Pauli Samos. et Nestorii.
Simleri Scripta veterum Latina de una persona, etc.
Stozza de Dogmatibus Chaldæorum.
Ursini Tractationes Theologicæ.
Wolfhardi Nest. antiquum et novum.

This once great and powerful sect—about as orthodox on the whole as the Roman Church of its time—was assailed by hosts of writers, none of which were more bitter than Cyril Alexandrinus. They are now few and feeble, and only their history is interesting. BUDDEUS, in his *Isagoge,* gives a list of writers on this subject, pro and con, previous to 1700; but scarcely any of them can be found now.

Nestorians, History of.

Doucin, Hist. du Nestorianisme. (A very interesting and learned account of Nestorius and his doctrines; with observations.)
Fabricii Bibliotheca Græca. Vol. IX.
Franzius de Initiis et progressu, etc.
Govea, Histoire Orientale.
Kortholti (Chris.) Dissertationes.
La Croze, Hist. d. Christianisme des Indes.
——— ——— en Ethiopie.
Le Quien, Oriens Christianus.
Liberati Historia controv. Nestorianæ.
Raulini Hist. eccles. Malabaricæ.
Renaudoti Hist. Patriarch. Alexandri.
Schouten, Voyage aux Indes Oriental.
Schroeder, de Nestoriamismo.
Vogtius de Recentissim Nestorii defensoribus. 1727.
Am. Bib. Repos. 2d Series. 5:1. 6:454.: 7:26.
Badger's N. and their ritual. 1850.
Buchanan's Researches in Asia.
Christian Review. 2:416.
Eclectic Review. 4th Series. 10:210.
Geddes' Miscellaneous tracts.
Grant's Lost tribes of Israel. (Describes the N. as in 1840.
Hey's (Dr. John) Lectures. Bk. 4.
Jones' (Sir William) Works.
Jowett's Researches in Syria.
Kitto's Journal. July, 1853.
Lawrie's Dr. Grant and the Nestorians.
Layard's Nineveh and its remains.
Memoir of Rev. D. T. Stoddard. 1858.
North Amer. Review. 57:156.
Perkins' N. Christians. Maps, &c. 1843.
Princeton Review. 13:59.
Smith's (Ely) Researches in Armenia.
Stanley's History of the Eastern Church.

New Heavens and Earth.

See CONSUMMATION, GOG AND MAGOG, MILLENARIANS.

New Jerusalem Church [Swedenborgians].

Pro.

Swedenborgii Opera.
Hauber's Ansicht von der Heiligen Schrift.
Abbott's Desolation of the Sanctuary. (To show that the first Christian church has come to an end, and that a new church is now being established.)
Anglo-American New Church Repository. Periodical. New York.
Barrett's (B. F.) Golden reed.
——— Lectures on the new dispensation.
——— Letters on the Divine Trinity.
——— Catholicity of the Church.
——— Beauty for ashes.
——— Letters to Henry Ward Beecher.

New Jerusalem Church—*continued.*

Pro.

Beattie's Elementary View.
Bush's Reasons for embracing the doctrines of Em. Swedenborg.
Clissold's End of the church.
——— Principles of biblical interpretation.
——— Exposition of the Apocalypse.
——— Letter to the Vice Chancellor.
——— Swedenborg and his modern critics.
Clowe's (John) New Jerusalem Sermons.
——— on the Mediums.
——— Marriage of the king's son.
——— Thoughts.
——— Miracles of Christ.
Evans' New Age.
——— Celestial Dawn.
Goyder's Expos. of the Gospel of Matthew.
——— Swedenborg and his mission.
Hayden on Modern Spiritualism.
Hiller's Doctrinal Sermons.
Hindmarsh's Magazine of knowledge.
——— Letters to Dr. Priestley.
——— Dictionary of correspondencies.
——— Seal on the lips of Unitarians.
——— Vindication of Swedenborg.
Hood's Biography of Swedenborg.
Monthly Observer and Record. Periodical. London.
New Jerusalem Mag. London. 1790.
——— ——— Boston. 1827 et seq.
New Jerusalem Messenger. Weekly.
Noble's Appeal on behalf of the new church.
——— Plenary inspiration of Sac. Scripture.
——— The doctrine of a plurality of worlds.
——— on the Commandments.
Parsons' Essays.
Proud's Answer to Dr. Priestley.
——— Unitarian doctrine refuted.
——— Letters on fundamental doctrines.
Reed's Growth of the mind.
Rendell's Peculiarities of the Bible.
Silver's (Abiel) Symbolic character of S. S.
——— Holy word its own defence.
Swedenborg's Works.
Tafel's Vindication of the doctrine of S.
Turner's (Mrs. W.) Reasons for joining the New Church.
——— Points of difference between Old and New Church.
Worcester's Sermons.

Con.

Perrone, Prælectiones Theologicæ.

Amer. Monthly Rev. 1:134.
Barrouel (Abbe), Œuvres.
Bayley (Cornel.) on the doct. of the Trinity.
Christian Review. 7:423.
Democratic Rev. 20:102.
Frazier's Mag. 39:64.
Lit. and Theol. Journal. 2:478. 3:102.
New Englander. 5:495.
Pond's (Enoch) Swedenborgianism reviewed.
Priestley's Letters to members of the N. J. C.
Princeton Rev. 20:331.

New Jerusalem Church, Hist. of.

Nanz's (C. F.) Emanuel S. der nordische Seher.
Clowe, J., Memoir of.
Hindmarsh's Rise and progress of the New Jerusalem Church.
Swedenborg, Life of; by Hobart.
——— ——— by Hood.
——— ——— by White.
——— ——— by Hillers.
——— ——— by Barrett.

New Prophets. See FALSE PROPHETS.

Grappii Commentationes theologicæ.
Weplingius de Neo-prophetis.
Calamy's (Edm.) Caveat against the new prophets.
Hicks' Spirit of enthusiasm exorcised.
Nicholson's Falsehood of the new prophets.
Woodward's Remarks on modern prophets.

New Version. See ENGL. BIBLE.

New Year. See TIME.

Berriman's, William, Sermons.
Davies', Samuel, "
Dehon's, Bp., "
Dwight's, Timothy, "
Fletcher's, Joseph, "
Foster's, James, "
Foyster's, J. G., "
Francklin's, Thomas, "
Guyse's, John, "
Heber's, Bp., "
Hewlitt's, John, "
Hobart's, Bp., "
Horne's, Bp., "
Secker's, Abp., "
Shuttleworth's, P. N., "
Spurgeon's, Cha. H., " 7th Series.
Thayer's, Elihu, "
Yonge's, James, "

Nicene Creed. See CREEDS.

Nicolaitans.

Balthasseris (Augustini) Disputationes.
Hemmii (Andr.) Dissertationes.
Janii (Io. Guil.) Com. de Nicolaites.
Mosheimii Dissertationes.
Rothii (Eberh. Rudolp.) Dissertationes.
Valckenieri (Ioan.) Disputationes.
Burton's Lectures on the First century.
Neander's Planting and training of the Ch.
Stuart (Moses) on the Apocalypse.
Tillemont's Ecclesiastical Memoirs.

Nineveh.

Blackburn's Rise and ruin of Nineveh.
Fairbairn on Jonah.
Layard's Nineveh.

Ninth Commandment.
See COMMANDMENTS, FALSEHOOD, HYPOCRISY, OATHS, SLANDER, TRUTH.

Noah. See BIOGRAPHY.

Gasseri Ultima fata Noachi.
Hahnii (J. J.) Νωε αγυμνο.
Kircheri (Athanasii) Dissertationes.

Benson's (C.) Lectures. Lect. 13.
Gataker's (Tho.) Sermons.
Jones' (Wm. of Nayland) Sermons.
Horseley's (Bp.) Life and death of Noah.
Kelly's (John) Congregational Lectures.
Potts' (J. H.) Sermons.
Smith's (Henry) Sermons.

Noetians. See PATRIPASSIANS.

Nominalists and Realists.

Abelard, Opera.
Baumgarten-Crusius, de Vero scholasticor.
Biel, Collectorium ex Gulielmo Occam.
Bruckeri Historia critica Philosophiæ.
Chaldenii Hist. eccles. de vita Roscelini.
Engelhardt's Dogmengeschichte.
Koehler's Realismus u. Nomin. in ihrem Einflusse auf d. dogmatischen Systeme d. Mittelalters.
Occami Centiloquium Theologicum.
——— (Various other treatises.)
Roscellini Opera.

Berkeley's (Bp.) Works.
Brown's Lectures on mental philosophy.
Brucker's History of philosophy.
Campbell's Philosophy of Rhetoric.
Cousin's Works of Abelard.
Hobbes' Works.
Hume's Essays.
Locke on the Human Understanding.
Mosheim's Ecclesiastical History.
Reid's Intellectual and active powers.
Stewart's Philosophy of the mind.
Whateley's Logic. Bk. 4, ch. 5.

Non-Conformists. See DISSENTERS.

Pro.

Ainsworth's (Henry) Counter-poison.
Alsop's Melius inquirendum. (Witty and dexterous.)
——— Mischiefs of Imposition.
Baxter's (Rich.) Works. (Many treatises on this subject.)
——— Life of; by Orme.
Bennett (Benjamin) on Separation.
Beverly's Letter to the Abp. of York.
Binney's Conscientious non-conformity.
——— Dissent not Schism.
Brett's (Thomas) Works.
Burton's Conformity, Deformity.
Calamy's (Edmund) Works.
Canne's Necessity of Separation.
Cartwright on Ecclesiastical Discipline.
——— Answer to Whitgift.
Collier's (Jeremy) Works.
Collings' Reasons for not praying in public by prescribed forms of others.
Corbett on the Oath required of Non-conf.
De Foe's New Testament.
——— Test of Loyalty.

Non-Conformists—*continued.*

Pro.

De Foe's Shortest way with Dissenters. (For this pungent satire the honest Baptist was fined, pilloried, and imprisoned.)
De Laune's Plea for Non-conformists. (With a fine preface by De Foe.)
Dobson on Non-conformity.
Earbery on the Power of the Prince.
——— Various other pieces.
Hales (John) on Schism and Schismatics.
Heywood's Sermons and Lives.
Hickes on the Christian priesthood.
Jones' (Wm.) Lectures on Non-conformity.
——— Dissenter's plea.
Lowth's (Simon) Historical Collections.
——— on Church power.
Martin's Letters on Non-conformity.
Milton (John) on True Religion.
——— on Ref. in the Church of England.
Neale's History of the Puritans.
Owen's (Charles) Plain Dealing.
——— Vindication of Do.
——— Validity of the dissenting ministry.
Owen's (John) Nature of Schism.
Palmer's Non-conformist's Memorial.
Prynne's Practical Church.
Robinson's (Robt.) Plan of lectures on N.
[Rolle's] Answer to Bp. Patrick.
Rule's Rational defence of non-conformity.
——— Answer to Stillingfleet's Irenicum.
Shrewsbury on Conf. to the estab. church.
Strype's Annals of the Reformation.
——— Ecclesiastical Memorials.
The Non-conformist. Lond. 1841 to the pres.
Whiston's Scripture Politics.

Con.

Bascough's (Robert) Discourses.
Bennet's (Thomas) Dissenter's Plea.
Burnet's (Gilbert) Apology for the Church.
Colet on Conforming and Reforming.
Conold's (Robert) Notion of Schism.
Croft's Naked Truth.
Dodwell (Henry) on Episcopal government.
Hart's (Edward) The Bulwark stormed.
Hoadley on Conf. to the Church of England.
Kempe (E. C.) on Non-conformity.
Lucy's Apology for the Church of England.
Ollyffe on Conformity. (Reply to Calamy.)
Page on Schism. (Reply to Hales.)
Patrick's Friendly Debate.
Pearson's Three plain reasons.
Rye (George) on Non-conformity.
Sacheverell's Rights of the Church.
Stillingfleet's Unreasonableness of separation.
Warner's Church of England's principles.

Non-Conformists, History of.

Bennet's History of Dissenters.
Brown's Non-conformists of the 17th cent.
Cornish's History of Non-conformity.
Davids' Annals of Non-conformity.
James' (J.) Protestant Non-conformity.
Neale's History of the Puritans.

Non-Conformists, Hist. of—*continued.*

Non-conformity as it was stated and argued by commissioners on both sides in 1661.
Price's History of Protestant N. in England.
Rees' History of Protestant N. in Wales, from its rise to the present time. 1861.
[Reed's (And.)] Progress of Non-conf. 1825.

England, during the 17th century, produced innumerable publications on this controversy. Most of these are now obsolete, or very scarce; but the above can be had. I distinguish Non-conformists from Dissenters. The latter still exist and multiply. The former are those who were turned out of their parishes, in the 17th century, and their followers. I may not have divided all the citations accurately, as the terms are by some used interchangeably.

Non-Essentials. See FUNDAMENTALS.

Non-Jurors.

Pro.

Agonistes' Philosophical Strictures. (Ably refutes Macauley's statements.)
Ames' Suit against ceremonies.
Bisbie's (Nathan) Sermons.
Brett's (Thomas) Works.
Brokesby's Govt. of the primitive church.
Collier's Ecclesiastical History of Great Britain. (Often reprinted.)
Dodwell's Cause of Schism.
——— Vind. of the deprived bishops.
——— Defence of the Vindication.
Hickes' (Bp. George) Works.
Howel's Cause of Schism.
Kettlewell's Measures of Chris. obedience.
Lathbury's History of the Non-Jurors. (Every way sufficient.)
Smith's Principles of Non-Jurors.
Snape's Letter to the Bp. of Bangor.
Steele's Letter to the Bp. of Bangor.

Con.

Bennet's (Tho.) Rights of the clergy.
——— Non-Juror's separation examined.
Bernard's Church apostolical.
Dawson's Origin and obligation of laws.
Hoadley's (Bp.) Preservative against the principles of Non-Jurors.
Hody's Unreasonableness of separation.
Milbourne's Legacy to the Ch. of England.
Owen's (John, of Rochdale) Jacobite principles examined.
Parker's Case of the Ch. of England stated.
Perrinchief's Indulgence not justified.
Pillonier's Answer to Snape's accusation.
Rye on the Non-Juror controversy.
Sparkes' Persuasive to unity.
Stillingfleet's Unreasonableness of separation.
Sykes on Schism.
Welchman on Schism and Heresy.

Non-Resistance. See DIVINE RIGHT OF KINGS, PASSIVE OBEDIENCE TO KINGS, RETALIATION, SELF-DEFENCE, WAR.

Nostradamus.

Nostradami Opera.
Chavigny, Com. sur les centuries de N.
Couillard, les Fausses prophéties de N.
Guynaud sur les prophéties de N.
Larivey, Six centuries de predictions.
Le Clef de Nostradémus.

Novatians. See CATHARI.

Novatiani Opera. (Many editions.)
Albaspinæi Observationes.
Cornelii Epistolæ.
Dionysii (Alex.) Epistola ad Novatianum.
Kenchelii (Steph.) Disputationes.
Mayeri (Io. Ulrici) Exercitationes.
Musæi (Ioann.) Exercitationes.
Ottonis (Io. Christop.) Disputationes.
Paciani Epistolæ tres ad Symphronianum.
Schelvigii (Sam.) Dissertationes.
Socrates, Historia. Lib. I, cap. 22.
Sozomeni Historia. Lib. I, cap. 10.
Bingham's (Joseph) Dissertations.
Burton's Ecc. hist. of the 2d and 3d cent.
Lowth's (Simon) Excerpts from Eccl. hist.
Whiston's Sermons and Essays.

Novatus.*

Cyprianæ Epistolæ.
Dionysii Alex., Epistolæ de Schismate.
Paciani Epistolæ ad Sympronianum.

* Often confounded with *Novatian*, which see above.

Novels. See FICTION.

Number 666. See ANTICHRIST.

Loescherus de Numero Antichristi.
Potter, Interpretatio numeri 666.
Bibliotheca Sacra. 1:84,384.
Clarke's (Edw.) False prophet of the Apoc.
Clarke's (J. E.) Dissertations on the dragon, beast, and false prophet.
Cunningham's Chronol. of the Apocalypse.
——— Dissertation on the Seals.
Faber (Geo. S.) on the Prophecies.
——— Recapitulated Apostacy the only rationale of the concealed apocalyptic name of the Roman empire.
Frazier's Mag. 16:477.
Fysh's (Fred.) Beast and his Image. (Able.)
Habershon on the Chronological prophecies.
Holmes on Prophetical Chronology.
McDougal's Chronology of the Bible.
Park's Concise Expos. of the Apocalypse.
Potter's (Francis) Interpret. of the No. 666.
Purvess on Prophetic time.
Rabett's Lateinos.
Stevens (N.) on the Name of the Beast.
Taylor's Important passages of the Revelations of John compared with corresponding passages in Daniel.
Thorn's Number and names of the Apocalyptic beasts.
Turnbull's Duration of the Papal kingdom.
Wealth's Name and number of the Beast.

Number of the Saved.

Brown's (R.) By-ways of the Bible.
Secker's (Abp.) Sermons.
Sherlock's (Bp.) Sermons.

Numismatics. See COINS.

Oaths. See PERJURY, PROFANENESS, THIRD COMMANDMENT, VOWS.

Cicero de Officiis. Lib. I.
Grotius de Jure. Lib. II, cap. 12.
Lydii (J.) Dissertationes.
Molembecii (B. L.) Dissertationes.
Nicolai (J.) Diatribe. (Oaths of the Hebrews, Greeks, Romans, &c.)
Puffendorf, de Jure naturæ. Lib. IV, cap. 2.
——— de Officiis. Lib. I, cap. 2.
Seldeni (J.) Dissertationes.
Spenceri (J.) Dissertationes.

Alcock's Nature and obligation of an oath.
Andrews' Lawfulness and form of oaths.
Barrow's (Isaac) Sermons.
Benson's Test. concerning oaths. (Quaker.)
Bentley on the Needlessness of an oath.
Besse's Defence of Quakerism.
Blackall's (Bp.) Sermons.
Brownlee's Obligation and form of a civil O.
Calamy's (Benjamin) Sermons.
Chris. Quar. Spect. 1:438.
Clagget's (William) Sermons.
Davies' (Tho.) Faith and practice of a Chris.
Doddridge's Lectures. Part 9, prop. 146.
Edinburg Review. 59:446.
Falconer's (Tho.) Sermons.
Fox's (Geo.) Treatise against swearing.
Fuller's (And.) Works. (Papers in London Missionary Magazine.)
Gataker's Exam. of the case of Quakers.
Godwin's Enquiry into political justice.
Green's Benefit of oaths.
Gregory's (Thomas) Practical Sermons.
Gruggen's Hulsean Prize Essay. 1844.
Herepot's Essays on truths of importance.
Hey's (Dr. J.) Lectures. Bk. 4.
Hooke's Testimony against oaths.
Investigator. 4:63.
Junkin's The oath a Divine ordinance, and element of the social Constitution.
Lewis' Dissertation on oaths.
Lucas' (Robt.) Sermons.
Paley's Moral philosophy.
——— Sermons.
Phipps' Swearing prohibited by the Gospel.
Quarterly Review. 61:215,390.
Rush's (Judge) Charges.
Sanderson's Obligation of oaths.
Sharp's (Abp.) Sermons.
Tillotson's (Abp.) Sermons.
Tyler's (J. Endell) Nature, origin, &c.
Wake's (Abp.) Sermons.
Wayland's Moral Science.
Westminster Rev. 5:23. 39:80.
Whitby's Commentary. Matt. 5:33.
Whitehead's Case of the Quakers. (Answer to Gataker.)
Wynyard's (J. M.) Sermons on Chris. duties.

Obedience. See GOOD WORKS.

Allestree's (Richard) Sermons.
Anderson's (J. S. M.) Sermons.
Arnold's (Thomas, of Rugby) Sermons.
Bather's (Edward) Sermons.
Beveridge's (Bp.) Sermons.
Boone's (James) Sermons.
Chalmer's (Thomas) Sermons.
Christian Observer. 17:140.
Cooper's (Edward) Sermons.
Emmons' (Nathaniel) Sermons.
Faringdon's (Anthony) Sermons.
Haynes' Illustrations of faith and practice.
Holdsworth's (R.) Sermons.
Jewell's (Bp.) Works.
Kemp (E. C.) on Christian Obedience.
Kettlewell's (John) Five discourses. (The measures of obedience necessary to a regenerate state.)
Lamb's (Robert) Sermons.
Le Bas' (Charles W.) Sermons.
Marshall's (Nathan) Sermons.
Maul's (J.) Christian Manual.
Mede's (Jos.) Works.
Newman's (J. Henry) Sermons.
Porteus' (Bp.) Sermons.
Potts' (J. H.) Sermons.
Riddock's (James) Sermons.
Rogers' (John) Sermons.
Secker's (Abp.) Sermons.
Seed's (Jeremiah) Sermons.
Stillingfleet's (Bp.) Sermons.
Stillman's (Samuel) Sermons.
Tindall's (The Martyr) Works.
Vaughn's (Charles J.) Sermons.
Whichcote's (Benjamin) Sermons.

Obedience of Christ. See JESUS CHRIST, OBEDIENCE OF.

Obedience to Rulers. See BANGORIAN CONTROVERSY, CIVIL GOVERNMENT, MAGISTRACY, PASSIVE OBEDIENCE, &c.

Allen's Uniform obedience to rulers an indispensable duty.
Bellamy's Works.
Brougham's (Lord) Speeches.
Brown's (J.) Law of Christ respecting civil obedience.
Carr's (George) Sermons.
Carson's Review of Brown on civil obedience. (A very able book.)
Charnock's Works.
Church of Eng. Review. 4:381.
Dublin University Mag. 16:530.
Fuller's Calvinistic and Socinian systems.
——— Circular letter on obedience.
Gisbourne's (Thomas) Sermons.
Jones' (Wm. of Nayland) Sermons.
Kettlewell's Measures of Christian O.
Mede's Works. Discourse 39.
Ridgeley's Body of Divinity. Quest. 92.
Saurin's Sermons.
Spring's (Gardner) Essays. Ess. 15.
Taylor's (Jer.) Ductor Dubitantium.
Tillotson's Sermons.

Venn's (John) Sermons
Waples' (Edward) Sermons.

Obscurity of Scripture. See BIBLICAL CRITICISM, DIFFICULTIES.

Atterbury's Posthumous Works.
Bourne's (Samuel) Sermons.
Foster's Answer to Tyndall.
Jackson's (Dr. Tho.) Works. Bk. 3.
Leland's Answer to Tyndall.
Limborch's Theology.
Watts' Orthodoxy and Charity.

Occult Sciences. See ASTROLOGY, DIVINATION, MAGIC.

Offenses. See CHURCH DISCIPLINE, DISCIPLINE OF THE PRIMITIVE CHURCHES.

Bradbury's (Thomas) Sermons.
Calamy's (Benj.) Sermons. (Giving offence to weak brethren.)
Chandler's (Sam.) Sermons. (Duty towards offending brethren.)
Denison's (Edw.) Sermons. (Sin of causing offences.)
Fawcett's (John) Sermons.
Quincey's (Samuel) Sermons.
Vaughn's (C. J.) Sermons.

Offering of Isaac. See ABRAHAM.

Calvin's (John) Sermons.
Delany's Revelation examined with candor.
Favell's (James) Case of Abraham.
Francis' (Dr. John) Sermons.
Grove's (Henry) Sermons.
Jenkins' Reasonableness of Christianity.
Jortin's (J.) Sermons.
Newton's (Bp.) Dissertations.
Whiston's (William) Dissertations.

Offices of Christ. See JESUS CHRIST.

Offices of the Spirit. See HOLY SPIRIT, OPERATIONS.

Old Age. See MIDDLE AGE.

Cicero de Senectute.
Witsii Exercitationes Academicarum.

Abernethy's (John) Sermons.
Alexander's (A.) Counsels to the aged
Alexander's (J. W.) Sermons.
Bacon's (Roger) Care of old age.
Baker's (Sir Rich.) German pulpit.
Balguy's (Thomas) Sermons.
Baxter's Converse with God.
Belfrage's Duties and consolations of age.
Bernard's (Sir T.) Spurinna.
Blair's (Hugh) Sermons.
Boyse's (Joseph) Sermons.
Brewster's Meditations for the aged.
Buck (Cha.) on Religious Experience.
Burgh's Dignity of human nature.
Campbell's Hermippus revived.
Chaplin's (Jer.) Evening of life.
Christian Examiner. 57:61.
Cicero's Essay on old age. Tr. by Melmoth.
Darnell's (W. N.) Sermons. (Respect for the aged.)

Old Age—*continued.*

Davies' (James) Address to the aged; with devotions suited to their state.
Enfield's (William) Sermons.
Fawcett's (John) Sermons.
Gerard's (Alexander) Sermons.
Girdlestone (Cha.) on the Christian life.
Hare's (A. W.) Sermons.
Heygate's Evening of life.
Jerment's Religion a monitor to the middle aged, and a glory to the old.
Lavington's (Sam.) Sermons.
Lawson's Sermons to the aged.
Marriot's (Harvey) Sermons.
Mather's (Cotton) Address to old men.
Melmoth's Cicero's Cato.
Mountford's (William) Euthanasy.
Newton's (John) Sermons.
Noel's (B. W.) Meditations for the aged.
Orton's (Job) Discourses.
Pearce's (Joseph) Sermons.
Pinney's Infl. of occupation on health.
Pownall's Intellectual Physics.
Retrospective Review. 7:64.
Secker's (Abp.) Sermons.
Smith's (John) Paraph. on Eccl. 12:1–6.
Smith's (Sydney) Sermons.
Stanford's Aged Christian's companion.
Steele's (Rich.) Discourses.
Thornton's Solid Resources for old age.
Tyerman's Religion the noblest employ.
Vance's (W. F.) Sermons.

Omens. See SUPERSTITION.

Bigland's Essays. Ess. 7.

Omnipotence of God.

Abernethy's (John) Sermons.
Appleton's Works. Lect. 4.
Bradford's (The Martyr) Works.
Brakenridge's (William) Sermons.
Brown's Philosophy of the mind.
Charnock on the Attributes of God.
Chevalier's Hulsean Lectures. 1827.
Clarke's (Samuel) Sermons.
Doddridge's Lectures. Part 2.
Dwight's Theology. Sermon 7.
Fenelon's Demonstration of God.
Foster's (Dr. James) Discourses.
Lester on the Omnip. and Wisdom of God.
McCullock's (John) Sermons.
Nicholson's (Bp.) Sermons.
Saurin's Sermons.
Tillotson's Sermons.
Wilkins' Natural Religion.
Wood's (Prof.) Works. Vol. 4.

Omnipresence of God.

Abernethy's (John) Sermons.
Atterbury's (Lewis) Sermons.
Beveridge's Sermons.
Blackley's (Thomas) Sermons.
Brakenridge's (William) Sermons.
Bullinger's Decades. (Parker Society publ.)
Charnock's Works.
Dealtry's (William) Sermons.

Omnipresence of God—*continued.*

Dwight's Theology. Ser. 6.
Elliott's (E. B.) Omnip. of God. (Prize poem.)
Enfield's (William) Sermons.
Fawcett's (Joseph) Sermons.
Francis' (John) Sermons.
Gough's (Strickland) Sermons.
Heber's (Bp.) Sermons.
Hopkins' (Bp.) Sermons.
Howe's Works.
Jortin's (John) Sermons.
Knowles' (Thomas) Sermons.
Leland's (Thomas) Sermons.
Marshall's (Nathan) Sermons.
Moore's (Bp.) Sermons.
Müller's Christian doctrine of sin.
Newton's Principia.
Norris' (John) Sermons.
Pearce's (Bp.) Sermons.
Ramsay's Philosophical Principles.
Saurin's Sermons.
Smith's (S. S.) Sermons.
Spectator. Nos. 565,571.
Tillotson's Sermons.
Turner's (John) Sermons.
Walker's (Robert) Sermons.
Whitaker's (Edw. W.) Sermons.
Whitby's Sermons.
Yonge's (James) Sermons. Second series.

Omniscience of God. See ATTRIBUTES, CONTINGENCY, SCIENTIA MEDIA.

Abernethy's Sermons.
Appleton's Works. Lect. 5.
Ball's (Nathan) Sermons.
Baxter's (Arthur G.) Sermons.
Breckenridge's (Robt. J.) Knowledge of God objectively considered.
Carr's (George) Sermons.
Charnock's Works.
Clarke's (Sam.) Boyle Lectures. 1705,1706.
——— Posthumous Sermons.
Conant's (Dr. J.) Sermons.
Delaune's (W.) Sermons.
Dornan's (Wm.) Sermons.
Dwight's Theology. Ser. 6.
Edwards' (Bp.) Veritas Redux.
Fawcett's (Joseph) Sermons.
Foster's (Dr. James) Discourses.
——— Natural Religion.
Francklin's (Thomas) Discourses.
Howe's Works.
Jackson on Human Liberty.
Knight's (Sam.) Sermons.
Knowles' (Thos.) Discourses.
Leland's (Dr. Tho.) Discourses.
Miller's (James) Discourses.
Müller's Christian doctrine of sin.
Ridgeley's Body of Divinity.
Robinson's Christian System. Essay 4.
Saurin's Sermons.
South's Discourses.
Spurgeon's (Cha. H.) Sermons. 2d Series.
Tillotson's Sermons.
Wilkins' Natural Religion.

Ontology. See MIND, TRANSCENDENTALISM.

Open Air Preaching.

Christian Observer. 1861. P. 725.

Operations of the Holy Ghost. See ADVOCACY, FRUITS OF THE SPIRIT, SPIRITUAL GIFTS, WITNESS OF THE SP.

Boerneri Spiritus sancti Chrismati.
Foertschii Sp. S. ductu filiorum Dei.
Frankius de Usu et abusu officii elenct. S. S.
Frisius de Officio Sp. S. Œconomico.
Klemmii Charitosophia.
Neuman, de Unctione, omnia docente.
Perkins, de Libera Dei gratia.
Weissius de Officio Sp. S. mnemonico.
Wernsdorfii (Gottl.) Dissertationes.

Allen's (Tho.) Way of the Spirit in bringing souls to Christ.
Andrews' Doctrine of grace.
Arnold's (Thomas) Sermons.
Arthur's (Will.) Tongue of fire.
Bayley on the Person and work of the H. S.
Beachcroft's (Robt. P.) Sermons.
Benfon's (C.) Lectures. Lect. 13.
Biddulph (Tho. T.) on Divine influence.
Booth's Reign of Grace.
Boston's Covenant of Grace.
Buchanan's Office and work of the Spirit.
Burgess on Grace and Assurance.
Carter's (N.) Sermons.
Christian Observer. 20:289.
Christian Review. 11:510.
Claggett's (William) Discourses.
Close's (Francis) Sermons on the Liturgy.
Crosthwaite's (J. C.) Sermons.
Faber's Ordinary operations of the H. S.
Flavel's Method of Grace.
Gilfillin's (Sam.) Practical Discourses.
Goodwin On being filled with the Spirit.
Haldane's (James A.) Essays. (Judicious.)
Hall's (Peter) Four Sermons. (Able.)
Hawker's (Robert) Sermons.
Hewlitt (J. G.) on the Holy Spirit.
Hinton's Work of the H. S. in conversion.
Horne's (W. W.) Sermons.
Howe's (John) Office and work of the H. S.
Hurrion on the Work of the Holy Spirit.
Jameson's (J.) Reality of influence, &c.
Jenkins' Union of the H. S. and the Church in the conversion of the world.
Mant's (Bp.) Sermons.
——— Bampton Lectures.
Milner on the Holy Spirit.
Mortimer's (Tho.) Sixteen Lectures.
Muir's (William) Practical sermons.
Newstead's Offices of the H. S. in connection with the conversion of the Heathen.
Nind's (Wm.) on the Operations of the H. S.
Noel's (Gerard T.) Sermons.
Nolan's (Dr. Frederick) Sermons.
Owen's (Dr. J.) Pneumatologia. (Admirable.)
Priestley's (Tim.) Christian's looking-glass.
Riddock's (James) Sermons.
Romaine's (William) Works.
Ryan's (Vincent) Sermons.

Operations of the H. G.—*continued.*

Scott's (Tho.) Essays. (Highly commended by Dr. Gill.)
Searle's Charis.
Secker's (Abp.) Sermons.
Sherlock's (Bp.) Sermons.
Simeon's (Charles) Sermons.
Skelton's (Philip) Sermons.
Skepp's Divine Energy. (Pref. by Dr. Gill.)
South's (Robert) Sermons.
Spirit of the Pilgrims. 2:595.
Spurgeon's (Cha. H.) Sermons. 1st Series.
Stebbings on the Holy Spirit.
Stowell's (W. H.) Work of the Holy Spirit.
Sumner's (John Bird) Sermons.
Thornton's Fruits of the Spirit.
Tottie's (John) Sermons.
White's Offices of the Spirit.
Whitefield's (George) Observations on some fatal mistakes.
Wills' Historic def. of experimental religion.
Wilson's Sacred Pneumatology.
Winslow on the Work of the Holy Spirit.

Ophir. See GEOGRAPHY.

Breytenbach, Itinerar. Hierosolymitanum.
Calmeti Comm. (Diss. prefixed to Genesis.)
Cellarii Notitia orbis antiqui.
Huetius de Navigationibus Salomonis.
Lipenii (M.) Dissertationes.
Martinier, Lexique Geographique.
Oldermanus de Regione Ophir.
Ortelii Thesaurus Geographicus.
Relandi Miscellanea.
Tychsenius de Commerciis et navigationibus Hebr. ante exilium Babylon.
Varerrii (August.) Disputationes.
Wichmanshausen, Dissertationes.

Reland's Dissertations.

Ophites.

Epiphanius adversus Hæreseos.
Fuldneri Commentaria de Ophitis.
Joecherus de Ophiorum hæresi.
Kelle, Ophitarum mysteria retecta.
Mosheim's Gesch. der Schlangenbrüder.
Schumacker's Lehrtafel der Ophiten.
Vogtii (Ioan.) Bibliotheca.
Wilkii (Davidis) Dissertationes.

Opinion. See FREEDOM OF OPINION.

Necker, l'Importance des opinions relig.
Schuppii (Jo. B.) Dissertationes.

Amer. Biblical Repos. 5:114.
Bailey's (S.) Essays on the formation and publication of opinions. ("A most valuable work."—SIR J. MACINTOSH.)
Balguy's Sermons and tracts. (Opinions no ground of discord.)
Barrow's (Wm.) Bampton Lectures. 1799.
Bibliotheca Sacra. 18:246.
Bolton's Curb to wantonness of spirit.
Burnside's Religion of mankind. Essay 16. (The culpability of error.)
Christian Examiner. 39:82. 47:209.

Opinion—*continued.*

Christian Observer. 1:775. 2:526. 14:300. 19:641. 25:661,725.
Edinburg Review. 91:265,508.
Flavel (John) on Mental Errors.
Francis' (Dr. John) Sermons.
Frazier's Mag. 41:237.
Glanville's Vanity of Dogmatizing.
Hartley on Mistakes in Religion.
Hey's (Dr. John) Lectures. Book 1.
Jones' Dictionary of religious opinions.
Leechman's (William) Sermons. (Responsibility for opinions.)
Lewis' Infl. of authority in matters of O.
Michaelis' Infl. of language on opinion.
Necker's Importance of religious opinions.
Palmer on the Foundation of relig. opinion.
Powlett's (Charles) Sermons. (Danger of speculation.)
Princeton Review. 18:58.
Simpson on Religious Opinions.
Smyth's (Theyre) Hulsean Lectures. 1839.
Southern Quarterly Review. 21:341.
Taylor's (Isaac) Works. (Responsibility for opinions.)
Taylor's (J.) Liberty of prophecying. Sec. 12.
Wardlaw's (Ralph) Four sermons on man's accountability.
Westminster Review. 6:1. 24:135.
Wilks' (S. C.) Christian Essays.

Opinions of the Fathers. See HISTORY OF DOCTRINES, USE OF THE FATHERS.

Botsacci Patrologia.
Brunfelsii Confutatio sophisticæs et questionum curiosarum ex Origine, Cypriano.
Chemnitii Oratio de lectione Patrum.
Echardi Compendium theologiæ Patrum.
Eppelini Selectiones.
Flaccii Catalogus testium veritatis.
Gravinæ Synopsis theologiæ vet. Patrum.
Harenburgii Theologia primorum Christ.
Lopezii Epitome sanctorum patrum, per locos communes.
Neandri Theologia Christiana.
Noury, Apparatus ad Bibliothecam Patrum.
Petavii Dogmata Theologica.
Piscatori Bibliotheca studii theologici, ex plerisque doctorum, etc.
Schmidius de sententiis Doctorum primitivæ ecclesiæ.
Schulteti Medulla theologiæ Patrum.
Zornii Delineatio theologiæ patristicæ.

Many of the Latin writers mentioned in this work, under various heads, quote largely from the Fathers, and some of them are avowedly mere compilers of their opinions.

Oppression. See SLAVERY.

Hutchinson's (Roger) Works.
Knowles' (J. C.) Sermons.
Marriot's (George) Sermons.
Ogden's (Sam.) Sermons on the 10 comm'ts
Orton's (Job) Sermons.
Stebbings' (Henry) Sermons.

Optimism.

Pro.

Leibnitz, Essai sur la bonté de Dieu.
——— Other treatises.
——— Life of.

Godwin's (Wm.) Political Justice.
Hartley's Observations on Man.
New England Mag. 7:17.
Pope's Essay on Man.
Priestley's (Joseph) Works.
Shaftsbury's Characteristics of Men, &c.

Con.

Chalmers' Natural Theology.
McCosh on Divine Government.

Oracles. See SIBYLINE.

Justin Martyr, Oratio ad Græcos.

[Baltus], Réponse a l'Histoire des Oracles par M. de Fontenelle.
Breganii Theologia Gentium.
Bunsovius de Oraculis.
Cicero de Divinatione. Lib. I, c. 19.
Classenius de Oraculis Gentilium.
Eusebii Preparatio Evangelica.
Fontenelle, Histoire des Oracles.
Gallæi de Oraculis; Græce et Latine.
Homeri Illias. Ode. X.
Le Clerc, Remarques sur le demele que est entre M. de Fontenelle et l'auteur de la Réponse a l'histoire des oracles.
Moebii Opera. (In acta eruditorum.)
Morini (Steph.) Dissertationes. (Especially on the reason of their discontinuance.)
Ovidi Metamorphoses.
Plutarch, de Defectu Oraculoram.
——— de Pythiæ Oraculis.
Rabaneri Amœnitates hist. philolog.
Strabo, Historia.
Van Dale (Anthony), Dissertationes.
Venerii Oracula et divinat. antiquorum.
Verschuirii Opuscula Theologica.
Vossii (Isaaci) Observationes.
Zenophon, Memorabilia.

Blackwood's Mag. 51:277.
Boyse's Pantheon. (Appendix.)
Collyer's (W. B.) Lect. on prophecy. Lec. 2.
Cudworth's Intellectual System. Bk. 1, ch. 4.
Dickinson's Attempt to prove that the Greeks borrowed the story of their oracles from the Holy Scriptures.
Edwards' (Pres.) History of Redemption.
Farmer on Miracles.
Fontenelle's History of Oracles.
Gilpin on Temptation.
Hickes' Answer to Fontenelle and Van Dale.
Jackson (Tho.) on the Apostles' Creed.
Oxford Prize Essays. Ess. 5:175.
Plutarch on the Cessation of Oracles.
Potter's Greek Antiquities.
Van Dale's History of Oracles. Tr. by Behn.

Ordinances. See EFFICACY OF SACRAMENTS, POSITIVE PRECEPTS.

Brockmandi Disputat. de Sacramentis.
Carpzovius de Sacramentis in genere.
Chardon, Histoire des Sacrements. ("Opus eruditessimum."—ZACCARIA.)
Chemnitii Loci Theologici.
Danhaveri Mysteriosophia.
Dieterici Mysteriologia Sacramentorum Vet. et Nov. Test.
Hoffmanus de Sacramentis in genere.
Hunnius de Sacramentis Vet. et Nov. Test.
Lyseri Decad. I et II de Sacramentis.
Meisneri Disputationes. Disp. XX.
Niemannus de Sacramentis in genere.
Roudenii Synopsis controv. loci de baptismo et cœna Dom.

Bullinger's Decades. (Pub. of Parker Soc.)

Ordination. See APOSTOLICAL SUCCESSION, EPISCOPACY, MINISTRY.

Buddei Exercitationes.
Courayer sur la Validité des ord. Anglaise.
Koenigii Bibliotheca Agendorum.
Losii Dissertatio Inauguralis.
Melancthonis Opera.
Marinus de sacr. Ecclesiæ ordinationibus. (Contains many rituals for O., from both Oriental and Western liturgies.)
Schmidii (And.) Dissertationes.

Brewster's Reflections on ordin. services.
Brickel on Ordination.
Campbell's Ecclesiastical History.
Channing's (Will. E.) Discourses.
Chris. Examiner. 17:177.
Chris. Monthly Spect. 9:505.
Comber on the Consecration of Bishops, Priests, and Deacons.
Doddridge's Tracts.
Dorrington's Dissenting ministry condemned in Scripture.
Elrington's Validity of English ordination.
Fuller's (And.) Miscellaneous Works.
Hickman on Ordination.
Hopkins' System of Divinity.
Horseley's (Bp.) Sermons.
Ives' Confidence Encountered.
James (Dr. John) on the O. services.
Lavington's (Samuel) Sermons.
Leechman's (Dr. William) Sermons.
McCheyne's (Robt. M.) Sermons.
McKenzie's Ordination Lectures.
Neal's History of the Puritans.
Owen's (James) True Gospel Church.
Parker's (Dr. William) Sermons.
Raikes' (A.) Sermons at ordinations.
Theological Magazine. For 1802.
Watts' Christian Church.
Wright's (Sam.) Sermons.

Ordination Sermons.

Adams, Z.,	at ordination of	C. Stearns.
Balch, T.,	"	W. Patten.
Barnard, T.,	"	I. Nichols.
Beecher, Lyman,	"	Missionaries.
Bentley, W.,	"	J. Richardson.
Billingsley, S.,	"	W. Harris.
Calamy, Ed.,	"	J. Munckley.

Ordination Sermons—*continued.*

Collier, W.,	at ordinat. of	G. W. Appleton.
Conder, J.,	"	J. Stafford.
Dwight, Tim.,	"	E. Pearson.
Elliott, A.,	"	J. McKean.
Fordyce, J.,	"	Several.
Foxcroft, T.,	"	Himself.
Hale, M.,	"	J. Woodman.
Henry, Matt.,	"	M. Atkinson.
Holmes, A.,	"	D. Kendal.
————	"	W. Bascom.
————	"	H. Hildreth.
Mather, Cotton,	"	W. Waldron.
McKeen, J.,	"	A. Moore.
Porter, Eben.,	"	I. W. Putnam.
Towgood, S.,	"	D. Harson.
Wood, Leonard,	"	Missionaries.

Most ordination sermons are printed as *pamphlets*, and therefore are not here cited.

Organs. See INSTRUMENTAL MUSIC.

Origen.

Origenis Opera. (Ed. Lommatzsch. 25 vols.)

Buddei Exerc. de allegoriis Origenis.
Doucin, Hist. des mouvments dans l'eglise.
Erasmi Vita, et opera Origenis.
Ernesti Institutio interpretis N. Test.
Gaudentii Dogmatum Origenis cum philos. Platonis comparatio.
Gregorii (Thau.) in Panegyrica oratio.
Hagenbachii Observ. circa Origenis method. interpretandæ.
Halloix, O. vita, virtutes, et documenta.
Huetii Origenis commentaria cum notis.
Karstenii (J. A.) Dissertationes.
La Motte, Histoire d'Origene.
Le Clerc, Vie d'Origene.
Rosenmulleri Historia interpretat.
Ruffini Liber de depravatione libror. O.
Simon, Hist. Critique du Vieux Testament.
Tillemonte, Memoires.
Zornii Exercit. de eunuchismo Origenis.

Amer. Bibl. Repos. 4:33.
Barrow's (Capel) Theological Dissertations.
Bellamy's Trans. of O. against Celsus.
Biblioth. Sacra. 3:378.
British Quart. Rev. 2:491.
Burton's Bampton Lectures. 1829.
Chris. Exam. 10:306. 11:22.
Conybeare's (J. J.) Bampton Lectures. 1824.
Conybeare's (W. D.) " 1839.
Collinson's Bampton Lectures. 1813. (Gives a conspectus of all the numerous writings of Origen.)
Davidson's Sacred Hermeneutics.
Eclectic Mag. 7:81.
Methodist Quart. Rev. 11:645.
Quart. Rev. 89:87.
Redepenning's Life of Origen.
Rust on Origen and his chief opinions.
Vaughn's Life and writings of Origen.

Origenists.

Athanasius, Orationes.

Origenists—*continued.*

Augustin, Liber ad Orosium.
Jerome, Epistolæ.

Doucin, Histoire des mouvements, etc.
Fabricii Bibliotheca.
Fontanii Historia litterar. Aquiliensis.
Horbii Historia Origeniana.
Huet, Hist. Origenianorum.
Oudini Dissertationes.
Prato [or Jerome], Dissert. de Monachis.

Original Sin. See HUMAN DEPRAVITY, IMPUTATION OF ADAM'S SIN.

Augustin, de Peccato originali.

Bartolocci de Pec. orig. secundum Rabbinos.
Broueri (P. W.) Dissertationes Theologicæ.
Calovii (Abrah.) Dissertationes.
Chemnitii Examen Concilii Tridentini.
Chenevièrre, du Péché originel.
Hoffmann, contra Errores pontificorum.
Hulsemanni (Ioann.) Dissertationes.
Meisnerus, an Peccatum origo formaliter sit, aliquid positivi?
Osiandri (Lucas) Dissertationes.
Pfaffii (Christoph.) Dissertationes.
Quistorpius, an Peccatum originale sit mere privativum?
Rivetus de Imputatione primi peccati.
Stapferi Institutiones. Cap. 3, sec. 9.
Turner, de Primo peccati introitu.
Voetius de Propagatione peccati originalis. (Gives the Augustan, Pelagian, Semi-pelagian, and Synergistic theories.)
Walchii Hist. doctrinæ de pecc. originis.
Whitaker, de Peccato originali.
Willet, de lapsu Adami et peccato originali.

Balguy's Tracts.
Barrow's (William) Sermons.
Bates' Rationale of the doctrine of orig. sin.
Baxter on Original sin.
Beecher's (Lyman) Views in theology.
Bibliotheca Sacra. 22:494.
Boardman (H. A.) on Original sin.
Boston's Fourfold State.
Brine's True sense of atonement for orig. sin.
Burgess' (Ant.) Doc. of orig. sin vindicated.
Burnet on the 39 Articles.
Chris. Month. Spectator. 9:625. 10:16.
Chris. Disciple. 1:349. 2:183.
Chris. Observer. 20:343.
Chris. Review. 17:1.
Chris. Examiner. 52:77. 53:93.
Clarkson's (David) Sermons.
Cooper's (Edward) Sermons.
Delaune's (William) Sermons.
Edwards' (John) Armenian doct. condemned by S. Scripture. (Answer to Whitby.)
Edwards' (Pres.) Works.
Edwards (Jonathan, of Oxford) on Orig. sin.
Fairbairn's Theological Essays.
Haldane's (Jas. A.) Answer to Drummond's defence of Edw. Irving.
Hayward's (S.) Sermons.
Hey's Lectures on Divinity. Bk. 4.

Original Sin—*continued.*

Hopkins' (Bp.) Doct. of the two covenants.
Howe's Living Temple.
Lime Street Lectures.
Mede's Works.
Milner's Practical Sermons.
Owen (J.) on Original sin.
Park Street Lectures, by Dr. Griffith.
Payne's (G.) Doctrine of original sin.
Seed's (Jeremiah) Sermons.
Smith's (Robt.) Vind. and illustration, &c.
Stackhouse's Hist. of the Bible. Bk. 1, ch. 3.
Stephens' (N.) Vindiciæ fundamenta.
Taylor's (Jer.) Liberty of prophecying.
Theological Essays from the Princeton Rev.
Todd's Declarations of the Reformers.
Toplady's Essays. Essay 3.
Trapp's (Joseph) Sermons.
Ward's (Samuel) Prelections.
Watson's (Alex.) Sermons.
Watts' Ruin and recovery.
Wesley's (John) Original sin defended.
Westley's Sermons.
Whitaker, Concerning original sin.
Wilson's (Thomas) Sermons.
Witsius on the Covenants.

Origin of Evil. See EVIL, FALL, FALLEN ANGELS, PRE-ADAMITES.

Beausobre, Hist. de Manichæisme. L.V, c. 1.
Bilfinger de Origine mali præcipue moralis.
Buddei Miscellan. Sacrorum. Pars III.
Calvin, de Peccato originale.
Chenevière, du Péché originel.
Disputatio de Orig. peccato inter Flacium et Strigel. 1560.
Haberkornii (Pet.) Dissertationes.
Junii (Francisc.) Dissertationes.
King (Abp.), de Origine mali.
Leibnitz, Essais de theodicæ.
Martinus de Causa peccati.
Matthæus de Origine mali.
Scharfii Disputationes Apologeticæ.
Strangius de Voluntate Dei.
Thummii (Theod.) Dissertationes.
Tilene, la Cause et de l'origine du péché.

Am. Bibl. Repos. 2d Series. 8:314. 10:353.
Am. Quart. Register. 15:113.
Balguy on Divine Rectitude.
Bayles' Origin of evil.
Bays on Divine Benevolence.
Bellamy's (Joseph) Sermons.
Bennet on the Cause of evil.
Biblioth. Sac. 7:254,479.
Brougham's (Lord) Dissertations on subjects connected with natural theology. Diss. 3.
Butterworth on Moral Government.
Casaubon's Origin of temporal evil.
Chalmer's Natural Theology. (On the theory of Leibnitz.)
Christian Disciple. 1:300.
Christian Exam. 33:169.
Christian Rev. 7:520. 8:7.
Christmas' Sin; its causes and consequences.
Cudworth's Intellec. system of the Universe.

Origin of Evil—*continued.*

Clarke's (John) Boyle Lectures. 1719,1720. (Answers Bayle.)
D'Oyley's (George) Dissertations. Diss. 1.
Duncan's (John) Philos. of human nature.
Edwards (Pres.) on the Will. Part 4.
——— Dissert. on Liberty and necessity.
Fenelon's Philosophical works.
Ferguson's Principles of moral science.
Fleming's Necessity not the origin of evil.
Foster's (Dr. James) Sermons.
Gale's Court of the Gentiles. Part 4, bk. 3.
Gilbert's (Jos.) Reply to Bennett.
Glanvil's Lux Orientalis.
Grove on the Wisdom of God.
Hussey's (Christopher) Sermons.
Jeffrey's (John) Sermons.
Jenyn's (Soame) Enq. into the origin of evil.
Johnson's (Dr. S.) Rev. of S. J.'s Enquiry.
King's (Abp.) Origin of evil.
Law (E.) on the Origin of evil.
Lovett's Cause of evil, physical and moral.
Muller's Christian doctrine of sin.
New Englander. 1:110.
Placette's Refutation of Bayle.
Priestley's Disquisitions.
Princeton Review. 14:529.
Shepherd's Nature and origin of evil.
Smith's (John Pye) Sermons.
Squiers' Problem solved. (Not quite.)
Stillingfleet's Origines Sacræ. Bk. 3, ch. 3.
Todd's (H. J.) Declarations of the reformers.
Universalist Quarterly. 4:221.
West on Moral agency.
Williams' Hypothesis respecting, &c.
——— Vindication of Do.
Young's Evil not from God. (One of the last and best.)

A good key to the controversy on this subject may be found in CHISSOLD's *Connection of theology, psychology, and physiology.*

Origin of Government. See CIVIL GOVERNMENT, MAGISTRACY, ORIGIN OF LAWS.

Goguet, Origine des loix, etc.

Burke's Reflect. on the French Revolution.
Clark's (A.) Origin of civil government.
Delany on Relative Duties.
Fenelon (Abp.) on Government.
Filmer's Patriarchal Scheme.
Hoadly on Civil Government.
Horne's (Bp.) Discourses.
Hume's Essays. Essay 12.
Locke on Government.
Lyttleton's Persian Letters.
Paley's Moral and Polit. philosophy. Bk. 6.
Price on the Nature of civil Liberty.
Priestley's First principles of Government.
Rollin's Ancient History. (Introduction.)
Sydney on Government.
Temple's Miscellanies.
Tower's Vindication of Locke.
Tucker on Government.
Universal History. Book 1.

Origin of Languages. See AFFILIATION, CONFUSION OF TONGUES, HEBREW LANGUAGE.

Adelung's Mithridates. (A history of all known languages, and 500 specimens of the Lord's prayer.)
Ballanche, Essai sur la formation, etc.
Behnsch's Gesch. der Englischen Sprache.
Bergier, Elemens primatif des languages. (Compares the Hebrew with Greek, Latin, and French.)
Bibliandri Commentaria.
Brosses, de la Formation mechanique, etc.
Buschmann, Ueber den Naturlaut.
Buxtorfii Dissertationes.
Calmeti Dissertationes.
Celarii Sciagraphia Philologiæ Sacræ
Chevallet, Origine de la langue Francaise.
De Lara de Conventia Vocab. Rabbinicorum.
Diodorus Siculus. Lib. I.
Erpenius de Ling. Ebrææ, atque Arab. Dig.
Gebelin, Monde primatif Analysé et comparé avec la monde moderne, dans son génie allegorique. (A wonderful monument of diligence and patience.)
——— Histoire naturelle de la Parole.
Grimm's Ursprung der Sprache.
Honerti Dissertationes Historicæ.
Humbolt, Verschiedenheit d. Sprachbaues.
——— ueber die Kawisprache auf der Insel Java, etc.
Kipping de Lingua primæva.
Kircheri Œdipus Egyptiacum.
Koenig, Etymologicon Helleno-Hebræum.
Lactantius de Cultu. Lib. 10.
Morini Exercitationes.
Shulteni (A.) Excursus ad caput primum viæ veteris, etc.
Simonis Crit. Hist. Vet. Testam. Lib. I.
Vorstii Miscellanea Academica.
Banguis' Origin and Diversity of language.
Barker's Notes on Cicero de Senectute. (The appendix has some curious remarks on the affinities of language.)
Barrington's Miscellanea Sacra. Vol. 3.
Beatteau's Principles of Literature.
Beke's Origines Biblicæ.
Blair's Lectures on Rhetoric.
Boswell's Life of Johnson.
Brerewood on the Diversity of languages.
Burnet's (Jas.) Origin and progress of lang.
Cardell on the Philosophy of language.
Condellac's Origin of human knowledge.
Delany's Revel. exam. with candor. Diss. 4.
Ellis' Enquiry whence cometh wisdom.
Forster's One primeval language traced through ancient inscriptions in the four continents. Plates.
Fowler's English language; its elements, forms, origin, and development.
Gales' Court of the Gentiles.
Gerard's Instit. of Biblical criticism. Ch. 2.
Grant's (James) Essays. (Gaels, Picts, &c.)
Gregory's Essays. Ess. 6.
Harris' Hermes. (Truly great.)
Herder on the Origin of languages.

Origin of Languages—*continued.*

Higgins' (G.) Anacalypsis.
Jenour's Origin, structure, connection, &c.
Jones' (R.) Origin of languages. (Maintains that the Welch is the primæval language.)
Kavanagh's Science of language.
Kennedy's Origin and affinity of languages.
Leland's Advant. and Neces. of Revelation.
London Quarterly Review. 20:208.
Lyell's Antiquity of Man. Ch. 23.
Magee on Atonement. No. 53.
Marsh's Horæ Pelasgæ.
Maupertius' Reflections.
McKnight's Essays. Essay 8. (At the end of his Commentary on the Epistles.)
McPherson's Philological system delineated.
Monboddo's Origin and progress of lang.
Muller's (Max.) Lectures at the Royal Institution. London. 1861.
Murray's History of European languages.
Nelmes' Orig. and elements of L. and Letters.
North British Rev. 27:147.
Oxford Essays, for 1856.
Parsons' Remains of Japhet. (Origin and affinity of European languages.)
Piries' Posthumous Works. (Traces the Hebrew roots in all known languages.) *
Princeton Review. 24:405.
Richardson on the Eastern languages.
Sharp's (Gregory) Dissertations.
Smith's (Adam) Dissertations.
Squires' (Samuel) Essays.
Stuart's Philosophy of the mind.
Tiedman on the Origin of language.
Tooke's Diversions of Purley.
Townsend's Etymological Researches. (Many lang. traced in their affiinities, indicating that all are radically one.)
Transactions of the Ethnological Society.
Universal History. Book 1, ch. 2.
Warburton's Divine Legation. Bk. 4, sec. 4.
Welsford's Origin of the English language.
Westminster Review. 85:40.
Williams on the Song of Solomon. (Introd.)
Winder's History of knowledge. Chap. 112.

Origin of Laws. See CIVIL GOVERNMENT.

Aristotle de Legibus.
Cumberland de Juræ Naturæ.
Goguet, Origine des lois, etc.
Grotius (Gul.) de principiis Juris Nat.
Grotius de Jure Belli et Pacis.
Puffendorf de Jure Naturæ et Gentium.
Selden de Jure. (Critic. Sacr. Tom. 8.)
Suares de Legibus.
Dawson's (George) Origo Legum.
Goguet's Origin of laws, arts, and sciences. (Interesting, but not profound.)
Hale's (Sir Matthew) Works.
Lowd on the Nature of Man.
More's Ethics.
Parker's Demonstration.
Spence's (George) Inquiry into the origin of laws.
Waters' (Edward) Sermons.

Origin of Nations. See ETHNOLOGY, MAN, UNITY OF THE HUMAN RACE.

Bedecovichii Natale solum magni St. Hieronymi. (Very little of the book is indicated by the title. It is a vast storehouse of authentic history of the rise of the Goths, Vandals, Dalmatians, Sclavonians, &c. &c.)
Blumenbach de Generis humani veritate.
Cumberland, Origines Gentium antiquiss.
De Pauw, Recherches Philosophique.
Desroches, Monde primatif.
Fourmont, Reflexions sur la succession des anciens peuples. (Vast erudition.)
Gebelin, Monde primitif.
Gorres' Volkertafel des Pentateuch.
Grotius de Origine gentium American.
Gruber's Gesch. d. mensch. Geschlechts.
Grynæi Synopsis historiæ hominis.
Guignes, les Chinois sont une colonie Egyp.
Hornius de Originibus Americanis.
Kapp's Ursprung der Menschen und Volker.
Kosegarten's Alterthumskunde.
Laet, Responsio ad dissertatio Grotii, de origine gentium Americanarum.
Lazii Opera Politica.
Michælis, Spicelegium Geograph. Hebraic.
Salles, Hist. générale des races humaines.
Sheringhamus de Anglorum origine.

Allix's Reflections.
Barton's (Benj. S.) New view of the origin of the North American tribes.
Beke's Origines Biblicæ.
Betham's The Gael and Cymbri.
Bibliotheca Sacra. 22:395.
Bosworth's Origin of the Dutch.
Boudinot's Star in the West.
Brace's Races of the old world.
Bradford's (A. W.) American Antiquities.
Bryant's Mythology.
Buchanan's Star in the East.
Bunsen's (C. J.) Christianity and mankind.
Carpenter's Varieties of mankind.
Cumberland's Origines Gentium.
Davies' Origin and language of the Britons.
Doddridge's Lectures. Part 6, propos. 119. (Origin of the Blacks.)
Drummond's Origin of Empires.
Ethnological Journal. Periodical. London.
Ferguson's History of Civil Society.
Frazier's Magazine. 44:654.
Grant's Essays. (Origin of the Gaels, Picts, Scots, &c.)
Hale's (Sir Matt.) Origin of man.
Hale's (Wm.) New analysis of chronology.
Hemming's (S.) Colonization of the earth.
Heming's Scripture Geography.
Higgins' Anacalypsis. (Valuable only for its vast mass of citations.)
Jenkins on Christianity. (Preface.)
Jones' (Geo.) History of ancient America. (The identity of the people with those of Tyre and Israel.)
Jones' (R.) Origin of Lang. and nations.
Jones' (A. J.) Origin of the human race.
Jones' (Sir Wm.) Dissertations.

Origin of Nations—*continued.*

Kames' Origin and diversity of mankind.
Knox's (Robert) Races of men.
Lang's Origin of the Polynesian nations.
Latham's Man and his migrations.
McIntosh's Origin of the N. Amer. Indians.
McKenney's Indian tribes of N. America.
McPherson's Origin of the Caledonians.
Millar's Propagation of Christianity.
Newton's Chronology.
Patrick on Genesis.
Pearson on the Creed. Art. 1.
Pezron's (Abbe) Origin of ancient nations.
Pickering's (Cha.) Races of man.
Pike's Origin of the English.
Pococke's (E.) India in Greece. (Sources of the Hellenistic race, coloniz. of Egypt.)
Shuckford's Connect. of sac. and prof. hist.
Smith's (C. H.) Nat. hist. of the hum. species.
Stillingfleet's Origines Sacræ.
Taylor's (W. C.) Natural history of society.
Well's Geography of the Old Testament.
Wilson's Prehistoric Man.
Winder's History of Knowledge.

Origin of Writing. See WRITING.

Over-Righteousness.

Allen's (John) Sermons.
Barrow's (William) Sermons.
Bateman's (Edward) Sermons.
Cunningham's (J. W.) Sermons.
D'Oyly's (George) Sermons.
Fiddes' (Richard) Sermons.
Jortin's (John) Sermons.
Law's Earnest and serious answer to Trapp's discourse on the danger of being, &c.
Romaine's (William) Sermons.
Stillingfleet's (Bp.) Sermons.
Trapp's (Dr. Jos.) Sermons. (4 on this subj.)
Whitefield's Sermons. (The danger of not being righteous enough.)

Overcoming the World. See ARMOR, FIGHT OF FAITH, WORLDLINESS.

Beveridge's (Bp.) Sermons.
Blencoe's (Edward) Sermons.
Cooper's (Edward) Sermons.
Downame's Christian Warfare.
Gale's Love of the world inconsistent with love to God.
Hampden's (R. D.) Sermons.
Hopkins' (Bp.) Sermons.
Maltby's (Edward) Sermons.
Nichols' (Benjamin E.) Essays.
Oakley's (Frederick) Sermons.
Ward's (Richard) Sermons.

Oxford Theology. See DEVELOPMENT OF DOCTRINE, TRADITION.

Pro.

Essays and Reviews. (By F. Temple, R. Williams, Baden Powell, H. B. Wilson, C. W. Goodwin, M. Pattison, B. Jowett.)
Gladstone on Church and State.
Hook's Call to Union.

Oxford Theology—*continued.*

Pro.

Hurrell's (Rev. Richard) Remains.
Keble's Christian Year.
Manning's Unity of the Church.
——— Oxford Sermons.
Maurice's (F. D.) Religions of the world.
——— Kingdom of Christ.
——— (Other treatises.)
Newman's (J. H.) Parochial Sermons.
——— Prophetic office of the Church.
——— Reply to "Eclipse of faith."
Plain Sermons; by Contributors to the "Tracts for the Times." (About 350 sermons, by Pusey, Newman, &c.)
Powell's (Baden) Evid. of Christianity.
Pusey's (E. B.) Letter to the Bp. of Oxford. (Intended as a full confession of faith.)
——— Vindication of Tract No. 90.
——— Sermons.
——— Reply to Dr. Hampden.
——— Essay on the Eucharist.
——— Councils of the Church, from A.D. 51 to A.D. 381.
Quarterly Review. 63:291. 81:70.
Tracts for the Times. (90 treatises, in 6 vols.)
Ward's Ideal Church.
Wilberforce's Oxford Sermons.
Wiseman's Letters to Newman.

Con.

Alexander's (W. L.) Anglo-Catholicism not Apostolical.
Arnold's (Tho.) Christian Life.
——— Life and Correspondence.
——— Works.
Beamish's Truth spoken in love.
Beaseley's Examination of Tract No. 90.
Bird's Plea for the Reformed Church.
——— Defence of the principles of the Reformation. (A second plea.)
Bricknell's Judgment of the bishops.
——— Is there not a cause?
——— Warrant and effect of preaching.
British and For. Review. 15:293. 16:1,528.
British Quart. Review. 33:3.
Brown's (John) Letters to Dr. Pusey.
Brown's (J. H.) Charge to the Archdeacons of Ely.
Brown's (T. B.) Oxford divines not members of the English Church.
Burgon's (J. W.) Sermons. (Answers Essays and Reviews in 7 Sermons.)
Burnside's Lex Evangelica.
Butler's (W. A.) Letters to Mr. Newman.
Campbell on Puseyism and Popery.
Candlish's Exam. of Essays and Reviews.
Chapman's (J.) Reply to Baden Powell.
Christian Examiner. 27:174. 28:257. 29:138. 30:41. 35:116,273. 38:72.
Christmas' History of the Hampden Controversy.
Collet's Popish frauds exemplified.
Cook's (F. C.) Ideology and Subscription.
Crosthwaite's Modern Hagiology.

Oxford Theology—*continued.*

Con.

Cummings' (J.) Lectures for the times.
D'Aubigné's Puseyism examined.
Davis' (H.) Anti-Essays.
Denison's Analysis of Essays and Reviews.
Eclectic Review. 4th Series. 2:558. 4:223. 7:504. 10:511. 13:654.
Edinburg Review. 66:208. 67:266. 77:264, 501. 80:163. 93:274. 94:270.
Ellicott on Inspiration and the interpretation of the New Testament.
Faber's Provincial letters from Durham.
——— Letters on the Tractarian secession.
——— The three unproved assertions.
Fendall on the Authority of Scripture.
Ferguson's Errors of the times. 1842.
Fish's (H.) Conferences of the Reformer and early divines of the English Church.
Fisher's (Robert) Sermons.
Fitzgerald on Episcopacy, Tradition, &c.
Fletcher's (Joseph) Works.
Frazier's Magazine. 20:549.
Garbett's Doctrine of the Eucharist.
——— Christ as Prophet, Priest, and King.
Godkin's Apostolic Christianity.
Golightly's New and strange doctrines.
Goode's Divine rule of faith and practice.
——— Reply to Pusey's letter to the Abp. of Canterbury.
——— Several pamphlets.
Gouldburn's Education of the world.
Graham's (James) Essays.
Green & McGill's Popery and Puseyism.
Griffin's Seven answers to the seven Essays and Reviews.
Gurney's Puseyism traced to its root.
Haddam's (A. W.) Rationalism.
Halley (Robt.) on the Sacraments.
Hamel's Tractarian tendencies of the age.
Hampden's Inaugural Lecture. (This lecture gave rise to "The Hampden Controversy," which produced many pamphlets, pro and con, in 1836 and 1837.)
Hare's (Archdeacon) Charges.
——— Contest with Rome.
——— Miscellaneous Pamphlets.
Harrison's Who are the Fathers?
Holden's Authority of tradition.
Howard's Scripture opposed by Puseyism.
Huertley (C. A.) on Miracles.
Hughes' Voice of the Anglican Church. (Cites many Bishops and Archbishops.)
Hughes' (J. G.) Philosophy of Puseyism.
Irons' Idea of a National church.
Jelf's (R. W.) Unsoundness of the Essays, &c.
Jelf's (W. E.) Supremacy of Scripture.
Jordan (J.) on Tradition.
Joyce's (J. W.) The National Church.
Lawrence's Examination of the theories of absolution.
Lee's (W.) Examination of B. Powell on the evidences of Christianity.
Livingston's Remarks on Oxford Theology.
London Rev. 14:512. 20:193. 69:291. 81:70.

Oxford Theology—*continued.*

Con.

McIlvaine's (Bp.) Oxford divinity compared with that of the Roman and Anglican Churches.
Madge on High-church principles.
Mansell's Theories of the history of man.
Methodist Quart. Rev. 1:58. 2:272.
Miller's Bible inspiration vindicated.
Neville's Observations on the Oxford tracts.
New Englander. 5:452.
New York Eclectic Museum. 2:354.
New York Review. 5:136. 6:198.
North Brit. Review. 3:166. 5:418.
Oakley's Tract No. 90 historically refuted.
Page's Position of the Church of England.
Palmer's Letters to Wiseman.
Peace's Phases of Tractarianism.
Poole's (Rich.) Grand Contrast.
Princeton Review. 10:84. 33:59.
Rawlinson on the Pentateuch.
Rogers' Eclipse of faith.
——— Defence of Do.
——— Essays; selected from contributions to the Edinburg Magazine.
Robins' Defence of the faith.
Rorison's The Creative Week.
Rose's (H. J.) Bunsen and Dr. Williams.
Scollard's Rome weighed in the balance.
Sewell's (W.) Letters to Pusey.
Shuttleworth's Not tradition, but Scripture.
Simons' (C.) Answer to Essays and Reviews.
Smith's (Geo. S.) Tractarian System.
Spurgin's (J.) Anti-tractarian tracts.
Stowell's (H.) Tractarianism tested.
Taylor's (Isaac) Ancient Christianity.
Taylor's (C. B.) Sermons.
——— Tractarianism not of God.
Thompson's Bampton Lectures. 1853.
[Trimyard's] Life of Bp. Bonner. (Ironical.)
Turton's Doctrine of the Eucharist.
——— Observations on Wiseman's reply.
Universalist Quarterly. 1:48.
Vaughn's (Robt.) Essays on Theology.
Weaver's (Rich.) View of Puseyism.
Wordsworth on the Interp. of Scripture.

A multitude of *pamphlets* on this subject have been published, especially between 1832 and 1852.

Paganism. See BUDHISM, DRUIDS, IDOLATRY, MYTHOLOGY, SALVATION OF THE HEATHEN, FETICHISM.

Arnobius adversus Gentes.
Athenagoras, Legatio pro Christianis.
Athanasius, contra Gentes.
Augustine, contra Paganos.
Basil, Homiliæ in Hexameron.
Chrysostom, contra Julianum.
Clemens Alex., Sermones.
Cyril, Opera.
Eusebius, Preparatio Evangelica.
Gregory Nys., adversus Græcos.
Justin M., Apologia.
Lactantius, Institutiones.

Paganism—*continued.*

Origen, contra Celsum.
Tertullian, de Superstitione.
Adami Exercitationes. Exerc. V.
Buddei (Fr.) Theses Theologicæ.
Buddeus (Gul.) de Transitu Hellenismi.
Classenii Theologia Gentilis.
Commodiani Instructiones.
Hottingeri Thesaurus Philologicus.
Kortholt, de Religione Ethnica.
Nahuys, de Ethnicismo.
Pfanneri Systema theologiæ gentilis.
Rechenbergii (Adam.) Dissertationes.
Rudiger, de Statu Paganorum sub imperat. Christianis post Constantinum.
St. Croix, Mystères du Paganisme.
Tzchirner's Fall des Heidenthum.
Van Dale, Dissertationes.
Voetii Dissertationes Theologicæ.

Appleton's Works. Lect. 15,16.
Brucker's History of Philosophy.
Campbell's Necessity of Revelation.
Cave's Primitive Christianity. (Appendix.)
Dollinger's Judaism and Paganism.
Enfield's History of Philosophy.
Fiddes on Moral Virtue.
Ireland's P. and Christianity compared.
Leland's Advant. and Neces. of revelation.
Malcom's Travels in S. Eastern Asia. 1839. (Describes the religion of the Burmans.)
Monthly Review. 2:153.
Pritchard's Egyptian Mythology. (Designed to illustrate the *origin* of Paganism.)
Tholuck's Nature and moral influence of P.
Warburton's Divine legation of Moses.

Pain.

Butler's (P. E.) Sermons.
Butt's (Thomas) Sermons.
Locke on the Understanding.
Watts on the Passions.

Palestine. See DEAD SEA, GEOGRAPHY, JERUSALEM.

Ætsingeri Terra promissionis. 1582
Allatii Symmictus. 1620.
Bachiene's Historisch und geogräphisch Beschreibung von P. 1766.
Baumgarten, Peregrinatio in P. 1594.
Bisselii P. Topothesia. 1659.
Bourasse, Voyage dans la Judea. 1860.
Breydenbachii Peregrinationes. 1486.
Brocardi Descriptio Terræ Sanctæ. 1519.
Brocquiere, Voyage a P. 1432.
Cattovici Itenerarium. 1617.
Chateaubriand, Iteneraire. 1811.
Cottard, la Judee au temps de J. C.
Fabii (F. T.) Peregrinationes. 1845.
Geramb, Pelerinage a Jerusalem. 1833.
Gesta Dei per Francos. 1611. (Gives the exact religious and social condition.)
Hasselquist, Voyages dan le Levant. 1749.
Heidmanni Palestina. 1650.
Kuttner's Geographie von Palästina. 1861.

Palestine—*continued.*

Kraft's Topographie Jerusalem. 1846. (Gives the descriptions of Jerus. from Josephus, Tacitus, and New and Old Testament.)
La Roque, Voyage dans la Palestine. 1718.
Lamprecht's Palästina. 1846.
Lucas, Voyage dans la Palestine. 1720.
Munk, Descrip. geograph., histor., etc. 1845.
Oumantz, Voyage au Sinai. 1850.
Pierotti, La P. actuelle dans ses rapports avec la P. ancienne. 1865.
Rathburger's P.; Land und Volk. 1850.
Raumer's Palästina. 1838.
Relandi P. ex monumentis veteribus illustrata. 1714.
Reybaud, la Syria, et Palestine, considerées sous leur rapport historique archæologique, etc. 1835.
Ritche's (W.) Azuba. 1852.
Roger, La Terre Sainte. 1664. (A minute topographical description.)
Saulcy, Syrie et Palestine. 1855.
Schwarze's Heilige Land. 1852.
Teuschert's Pilgerreise. 1858.
Theoderici Libellus de locis sanctis. 1172. Reprinted 1865.
Thevenot, Voyage au Egypte, etc. 1664.
Völter, das Heil. Land Wanderung. 1855.
Waltoni Adparatus ad polyglotta. 1673.
Zeigleri Terræ Sanctæ descriptio. 1536.

Aiton's Lands of the Messiah. 1851.
——— Paul and his localities, as lately visited. 1856.
Amer. Bibl. Repos. 2d Series. 1:400. 6:419. 8:219.
Amer. Eclectic Rev. 3:369.
Anderson's Wanderings in Israel. 1851.
Arundale's Picturesque tour, &c. 1837.
Aveling's Voice of many waters. 1855.
Bannister's Holy Land. 1844. Maps.
Bartlett's Footsteps of our Lord. 1855.
Benjamin's (Rabbi) Itenerary. (Accurate in the 12th cent. An abridgment is given in Pinkerton's voyages.)
Bibliotheca Sacra. 1:221.
Bonar's Land of Promise. 1858.
Brocquiere's Travels in Palestine. 1432.
Bruin's Voyage to the Levant. 1825.
Bulfinch's Holy land. 1834.
Burckhard's Travels in Palestine. 1822.
Carnes' Syria and the Holy Land. 1837.
Cheyne's Mission to the Jews. 1837. (900 references to Scripture.)
Christian Examiner. 27:88,245. 28:89,224. 31:222. 53:178. 63:211.
Clarke's Travels in the Holy land. 1800.
Crosby's (H.) Lands of the Moslem. 1851.
Drew's Scripture lands in connection with their history. 1860.
Durbin's Observations on the East. 1845.
Eclectic Review. New Series. 1:1,626.
Egerton's Tour in the Holy land. 1840.
Fiske & Hershell's Palestine. 1842.
Formby's Visit to the Holy land. 1843.

Palestine—*continued.*

Foster's Norrisean Cambridge Prize Essay. (On the mode of illustrating S. Scripture from the relation of travellers.)
Graham's Topographical Dictionary of P (Made to illustrate the Bible.)
Hackett's Tour in the Holy land. 1855.
Hardy's Places mentioned in S. S. 1835.
Hasselquist's Natural History of P. 1745.
Hibbard's Geog. and History of P. 1851.
Joliffe's Letters from Palestine. 1820.
Jowett's Syria and the Holy Land. 1825.
Kelly's Syria and the Holy Land. 1844.
Kitto's History of P. to the present. 1852.
——— Scripture lands. 1850. Atlas.
La Roque's Voyage to Syria. 1722.
Lamartine's Pilgrimage to Palestine. 1832.
Landseer's Sabæan Researches. 1823.
Leigh's Scripture Atlas.
Lightfoot's Chorography of Canaan. 1684.
Lynch's Exped. to the Jordan and Dead Sea.
Maddox's Travels in Turkey and P. 1827.
Mandeville's Holy land. 1564.
Margoliouth's Pilgrimage. 1850. Plates.
Maundrell's Journey to Jerusalem. 1697. ("A little book, but worth a folio."—Bp. Newton.)
Methodist Quart. Rev. 2:5.
Newman's From Dan to Beersheba. 1864.
North Amer. Rev. 53:174.
North British Rev. 2:215. 8:57.
Olin's (Steph.) Travels in Palestine. 1843.
Osborne's P., past and present. 1858.
Petachia's (Rabbi) Travels. (12th century.) Tr. by A. Benisch. 1856.
Pocock's Travels. 1743.
Porter's Five years in Damascus.
Princeton Review. 1:155. 13:583.
Quarterly Review. 2:150. 54:155.
Ransom's Biblical Topography.
Roberts' Holy land. 1846.
Robinson's (Ed.) Bib. Researches in P. 1838.
——— Later Researches. 1852. Maps.
Robinson's (Geo.) Palestine and Syria. 1837.
Rohr's Palestine in the time of Christ.
Russell's Palestine from the earliest period to the present. 1832. Plates.
Sepp's Jerusalem and the Holy land. 1864.
Smith's (J. V. C.) Pilgrimage to P. 1852.
Southern Quart. Rev. 9:285.
Spencer's Egypt and the Holy land. 1850.
Stanley's Sinai and P. 1856. Maps, plates.
Stent's Holy land. 1843.
Taylor's (B.) Lands of the Saracen. 1855.
Thompson's The Land and the Book. 1859.
Tobin's Land of inheritance. 1863.
Walch's Amer. Rev. 1:89.
Whitby's Table of places mentioned in the New Testament. 1718.
Wilson's (John) Lands of the Bible. 1847.
Wilson's (W. R.) Travels in P. 1826.
Wright's Early travels in P. (Comprises the narratives of Arculf, Willibald, Bernard, Sœwulf, Benjamin, Mandeville, Brocquière, and Maundrell. With notes.)

Woodcock's Scripture lands. 1349.

This copious list is given, with dates, that the curious may trace the changes in the condition of the people.

Pandects. See CANON LAW.

Pantheism. See ATHEISM.

Papal Bulls. See DECRETALS.

Ballerin de Potestate eccles. S. Pontificum.
Benedicti Bullarium.
Bullarium Magnum Romanorum: studio Coquelines, et aliorum. 39 vols. 1849.
Cherubini Bullarium Romanorum.
Dupuy, les Libertés d'eglise Gallican.
Eisenschmid's Romisches Bullarium.

There are numerous collections of Bulls, and many of them with commentaries.

Papias.

Grabii Fragmenta librorum Papiæ. (In his *Spicilegium S. S. Patrum.* These "fragments" are all that remain of this Father, and are gathered out of Eusebius, Ireneus, and others.)

Lardner's Credibility. (Translates some of the Fragments, and is the only English version.)

Parables.

Bonneti (G.) Dissert. philol. theologicæ.
Brouer de Parabolis Christi.
Eilert's Homilien über die Parabeln Jesu.
Grossmanni P. Christi ex rebus Romanis illustrata.
Lisco's Parabeln Jesu bearbeitet.
Rettburg de Parabolis J. C.
Schulteni (W.) Diatribe de parabolis.
Schultze de Parabolarum J. C.
Unger de Parab. J. C. indole poetica.

Arnot's Parables of our Lord.
Bailey's (Dr. J.) Mysteries of the kingdom.
Bailey's (B.) Exp. of the parables.
Bourn (Sam.) on the Parables.
Bragge on the Parables.
Bulkley's (Benj.) Sermons on the Parables.
Burns' (Jabez) Sermons on the Parables.
Chris. Monthly Spect. 1:505.
Christian Rev. 8:199,588.
Close (Dean Francis) on the Parables.
Collyer's (W. B.) Lectures on the Parables.
Cumming's (John) Foreshadows. (Poor.)
Dodd's (Wm.) Miracles and par. of Christ.
Drummond's Engravings of the New Test.
Farrar's (John) Sermons on the Parables.
Gray's (A.) Delineation of the P. of Christ.
Greswell on the P. ("Sterling."—LOWNDES. "Great and learned."—BRITISH CRITIC.)
Grinfield's (E. W.) Sermons on the Parables.
Guthrie on the Parables. 1865.
Horlock's Exposition of the Parables.
Jortin's (S. F.) Sermons.
Kirk's (Ed. N.) Lectures on the Parables.
Knight's (James) Discourses on the P.

Parables—*continued.*

Krummacher on the P. Trans. by Johnson.
Keach's (Ben.) Gospel mysteries unveiled. ("Every time my attention is drawn to it, it enhances its value."—VALPY. "A book without which no minister's library is complete."—DE COETLOGON.)
Lisco's P. of Jesus. Trans. by Fairbairn.
Lonsdale's Exposition of the Parables.
Mackensie's (L. J.) Lectures on the P.
Moore's (Hannah) Works.
Neander on the Parables of Christ.
Norris' (William) Sermons.
Ogilvie's Bampton Lectures. 1836.
Oxenden's Parables of our Lord.
Princeton Rev. 5:481.
Proudfit's (Alex.) Lectures on the Parables.
Roberts' (Arthur) Sermons on our Lord's P.
Scriver (Chr.) on Select P. Tr. by Berinstoff.
Short's (Wm.) Sermons.
Stanhope's Practical explanation of the P.
Stanley's Conversations on the Parables.
Stevens' (W. B.) P. of the New Testament.
Stakes' (Dr. G.) Sermons.
Trench on the Parables of our Lord.
Trinder's (W. M.) Sermons on the Parables.
Upjohn's Parables of Christ.
Westcott's Elements of the Gospel harmony.
Wilson's Questions and answers on the P.

In addition to the above on the parables in general, are the following on particular parables.

BARREN FIG TREE.

Augustini Sermones.
Adams', Tho., Sermons at St. Paul's church.
Bishop's, William, Sermons.
Bunyan's Works.
Clarkson's, David, Sermons.
Fell's, Hunter, Sermons.
Hunter's, Henry, Sermons.
Hutton's, F. H., Discourses.
Jay's, William, Sermons.
Jortin's, John, Sermons.
Lawson's, Charles, Sermons.
Marriot's, Harvey, Sermons.
Muir's, James, Sermons.

DISCREET HOUSEHOLDER.

Hobart's, Bp. J. H., Sermons.
Theol. and Literary Journal. 7:600.

GOOD SAMARITAN. See LOVE TO NEIGHBOR.

Atterbury's, Bp., Sermons.
Baxter's, Arthur G., Sermons.
Brougham's, John, Sermons.
Cennick's, John, Sermons.
Girdlestone's, Charles, Sermons.
Heber's, Bp., Sermons.
Hewlett's, John, Sermons.
Hoadley's, Bp., Sermons.
Jones', William of Nayland, Sermons.
Jortin's, John, Sermons.
Marriot's, Charles, Sermons.
Nares', Edward, Sermons.
Newton's, Bp., Sermons.

Parables.

GOOD SAMARITAN—*continued.*

Sherlock's, Bp., Sermons.
Spencer's, Aubrey, Sermons.
Vincent's, John, Sermons.
Williams', William, Sermons.

GOOD SHEPHERD.

Bowdler's, Thomas, Sermons on the character of Christ.
Brown's, John, Sermons.
Luther's, Martin, Sermons.
McGill's, Stephenson, Sermons.

HID TREASURE.

Cennick's, John, Sermons.
Enfield's, William, Sermons.
Lord's Theol. and Lit. Journal. 7:591.

IMPORTUNATE WIDOW.

Goode's, Francis, Sermons.
Howe's, John, Sermons.

INESTIMABLE PEARL.

Butcher's, Edmund, Sermons.
Cappe's, Newcombe, Practical Discourses.
Fawcett's, John, Sermons.
Stebbings', Henry, Sermons. 2 on this subj.
Theol. and Lit. Journal. 7:594.

LABORERS IN VINEYARD.

Blencoe's, Edward, Sermons.
Bradley's, Charles, Sermons.
Butler's, W. J., Sermons.
Girdlestone's, Charles, Sermons.
Hoadly's, Bp., Sermons.
Knight's, Samuel, Sermons.
Le Bas, Charles W., Sermons.
Pyles', Philip, Sermons.
Short's, William, Sermons.
Van Mildert's, Bp., Sermons.
Whately's, Richard, Sermons.

LOST SHEEP.

Bradley's, Charles, Sermons.
Cennick's, John, Sermons.
Luther's, Martin, Sermons.
Short's, William, Sermons.
Van Mildert's, Bp., Sermons.
Wordsworth's, Christopher, Sermons.

MARRIAGE SUPPER. See SUPPER.

MUSTARD SEED.

Knight's, James, Discourses.
Maurice's, Frederick D., Sermons.
Styles, John, Sermons.

PHARISEE AND PUBLICAN.

Barker's, John, Sermons.
Bishop's, William, Sermons.
Buckminster's, Joseph S., Sermons.
Bunyan's Works.
Burder's, George, Village sermons.
Collison's, M. A., Sermons.
Gatty's, Alfred, Sermons.
Hammond's, Henry, Sermons.
Hastings', H. J., Parochial Sermons.
Heber's, Bp., Sermons.
Heylin's, John, Sermons.

Parables.

PHARISEE AND PUBLICAN—*continued*

Jones', of Nayland, Sermons.
Jortin's, John, Sermons.
Le Bas', Charles W., Sermons.
Marriot's, Charles, Sermons.
Mills', W. H., Sermons.
Noel's, Gerard T., Sermons.
Smith's, Sydney, Sermons.
Sterne's, Lawrence, Sermons.
Tilly's, William, Sermons.
Townsend's, George, Sermons and charges.
Waterland's, Daniel, Sermons.
Whitefield's, George, Sermons.

POLITIC STEWARD. See RICHES.

Gelpke, P. de Œconomo injusto.
Hartmanni Commentatio.
Niedner's Commentar.
Schulz, über die P. vom verwalter.
Anderson's, J. S., Sermons.
Arnold's, Thomas, Sermons.
Butts', Thomas, Sermons.
Chillingworth's, William, Sermons.
Cooper's, Edward, Sermons.
Coppleston's, Edward, Sermons.
Ellis', Clement, Discourses.
Enfield's, William, Sermons.
Fowles', F. W., Sermons.
Fuller's, And., Contrib. to the Evangel. Mag.
Girdlestone's, Charles, Sermons.
Graves', Richard, Sermons.
Hampden's, R. D., Sermons.
Hastings', H. J., Parochial sermons.
Hewlett's, John, Sermons.
Hugh's, Henry, Sermons.
Ibbot's, Benjamin, Sermons.
Jortin's, John, Sermons.
Kennaway's, Charles E., Sermons.
King's Morsels of criticism.
Le Bas', Charles W., Sermons.
Leland's, Dr. Thomas, Sermons.
Lloyd's, Pearson, Sermons.
Nares', Edward, Sermons.
Oakley's, Frederick, Sermons.
Potts', J. H., Sermons.
Sanderson's, Bp., Sermons.
Shuttleworth's, P. N., Sermons.
Skelton's, Philip, Sermons.
Tyndale's, Wm., P. of the wicked Mammon, (The favorite book of Ann Boleyn.)
Van Mildert's, Bp., Sermons.

PRODIGAL SON. See YOUTH.

Alison's, Archib., Sermons. (3 on this subj.)
Baddelly's, Geo., Sermons. (3 on this subj.
Bishop's, William, Sermons.
Blencoe's, Edward, Sermons.
Boyse's, Joseph, Sermons.
Burder's, George, Village sermons.
Cawood's, John, Sermons.
Cooper's, Edward, Sermons.
Cosens', Dr. John, Sermons.
Dwight's, Timothy, Sermons.
Francklin's, Thomas, Sermons.
Goodman's, John, Penitent pardoned.

Parables.

PRODIGAL SON—*continued.*

Grant's, Robt., Lectures on the prod. son.
Graves', Richard, Sermons.
Green's, Samuel, Sermons.
Grew, Obadiah, on the Prodigal son.
Heylin's, Dr. John, Sermons.
Horne's, Bp., Discourses.
Howe's, John, Reformed prodigal.
Jones', Th., Prodigal's pilgrimage and back.
Jortin's, John, Sermons.
Kelly's, Dennis, Practical sermons.
Laurie's, Dr. Thomas, Sermons.
Mackenzie's Lectures on the prodigal son.
Maitland, C. D., on the P. son. (7 sermons.)
Marriot's, Harvey, Sermons.
Mount's Lectures on the prodigal son.
Neves', Timothy, Sermons.
Plumtree's, H. S., Lectures.
Powell's, Samuel, Sermons.
Rogers', Nehemiah, Indulgent Father.
Short's, William, Sermons.
Smith's, Samuel Stanhope, Sermons.
Sterne's, Lawrence, Sermons.
Thornton's, John, Youth admonished.
Vaughn's, Henry, Sermons.
Wallin's, Benjamin, Sermons.
Walton, Jonathan, on Repentance.
Waters', Edward, Sermons.
Wilks', Samuel C., Sermons.

RICH FOOL. See RICHES.

Blencoe's, Edward, Sermons.
Marriot's, Harvey, Sermons.
Milner's, Joseph, Sermons.
Muir's, George, Sermons.
Sherlock's, Bp., Sermons.
Walker's, Bp., Sermons.

RICH MAN AND LAZARUS.

Chrysostom, Homiliæ quartuor.
Klinckhardt, super Parab. de homine divite.
Bishop's, William, Sermons.
Blencoe's, Edward, Sermons.
Bradley's, Charles, Sermons.
Broughton's, Thomas, Sermons.
Bunyan's Sighs from Hell.
Burder's, George, Sermons.
Clarke's, Dr. Samuel, Sermons.
Cruso's, Tim., Sermons. (11 on this subject.)
D'Oyley's, George, Sermons.
Dwight's, Timothy, Sermons.
Ellis', Clement, Discourses.
Fawcett's, John, Sermons.
Francklin's, Thomas, Sermons.
Gilpin's, William, Sermons.
Gregory's, George, Sermons.
Hewlett's, John, Sermons.
Heylin's, John, Theological Lectures.
Hilyard's, James, Sermons. (5 on this subj.)
Hunter's, Henry, Sermons.
Jortin's, John, Sermons.
Laurie's, Thomas, Sermons.
Le Bas', Charles W., Sermons.
Logan's, John, Sermons.
Methodist Quart. Review. 41:414.

Parables.

RICH MAN AND LAZARUS—*continued.*

Milner's, Joseph, Sermons.
Muir's, James, Sermons.
Russell's, Alexander R., Sermons.
Sterne's, Lawrence, Sermons.
Tillotson's, Abp., Sermons.
Trapp's, Joseph, Sermons.
Van Mildert's, William, Sermons.
Walker's, Samuel, Abraham's bosom.
Wesley's, John, Sermons.
Wordsworth's, Christopher, Sermons.
Yonge's, James, Sermons.

SOWER.

Augustine, Sermones.
Arnold's, of Rugby, Sermons.
Beveridge's, Bp., Sermons.
Bird, Charles, on the Parable of the Sower.
Bishop's, William, Sermons.
Brougham's, John, Sermons.
Brown's, Robert, Exposition.
Bulkley's, Benjamin, Sermons.
Burder's, George, Sermons.
Cennick's, John, Sermons.
Clarke's, Dr. Samuel, Sermons.
Francklin's, Thomas, Sermons.
Gifford on the Parable of the Sower.
Girdlestone's, Charles, Course of sermons.
Graves', Dr. Richard, Works.
Hankinson's, Thomas E., Sermons.
Heylin's, John, Sermons.
Hoole's, Joseph, Sermons.
Irving's, Edward, Sermons. (Six on this subject, of great merit.)
Jebb's, Bp., Practical Theology.
Jortin's, John, Sermons.
Jowett's, Joseph, 52 sermons.
Le Bas', C. W., Sermons bef. the University.
Lloyd's, J. C., Lectures on the P. of the S.
Lowel's, Samuel, Sermons.
Marriot's, Harvey, Sermons.
Muir, George, on the P. of the Sower.
Sheppard's, Tho., Parable of the S. opened. 1660. (Edited by Dr. Foote. 1853.)
Short's, William, Sermons.
Stebbins', Henry, Sermons.
Stennett's, Samuel, Parable of the Sower.
Summerfield's, John, Sermons.
Taylor's, Dr. G., Sermons.
Taylor's, Tho., Expos. of Luke viii. 1634.
Wheatly's, Charles, Sermons.

SUPPER.

Arnold's, Thomas, Sermons.
Berriman's, William, Sermons.
Brougham's, John, Sermons.
Crumpton on the great Supper.
Francklin's, Thomas, Sermons.
Girdlestone's, Charles, Sermons.
Glazebrook's, James, Sermons.
Latimer's, Bp., Sermons.
Marriot's, Harvey, Sermons.
Potts', J. H., Sermons.
Short's, William, Sermons.
Whitefield's, George, Sermons.

Parables.

TALENTS.

Augustine, Sermones.
Carr's, George, Sermons.
Enfield's, William, Sermons.
Gilpin's, William, Sermons.
Glass', John, Notes on scripture texts.
Horberry's, M., Sermons.
Lit. and Theol. Journal. 8:193.
Loveday's Alarm to slumbering Christians.
Marriot's, Harvey, Sermons.
Muir's, James, Sermons.
Munkhouse's, Richard, Sermons.
Newton's, Bp., Dissertations.
Rogers', John, Sermons.
Seabury's, Bp., Sermons.
Summerfield's, John, Sermons.
Wilson's, Bp. Thomas, Sermons.

TARES AND WHEAT.

Bishop's, William, Sermons.
Bradley's, Charles, Sermons.
Busfield's, Dr. J., Sermons.
Carrington's, James, Sermons.
Cowes', James, Sermons.
Francklin's, Thomas, Sermons.
Girdlestone's, Charles, Sermons.
Gisbourne's, Thomas, Sermons.
Hastings', H. J., Parochial sermons.
Hewlett's, John, Sermons.
Heylin on the Parable of the Tares. (Ten excellent sermons.)
Latimer's, Bp., Sermons.
Lowth's, Bp., Sermons.
Mills', William H., Sermons.
Muir's, Geo., Sermons. (21 on this parable.)
Newton's, Bp., Dissertations.
Potts', J. H., Sermons.
Short's, William, Sermons.
Shuttleworth's, P. N., Sermons.
Slade's, James, Sermons.
Van Mildert's, William, Sermons.
Venn's, John, Sermons.
Wheatly's, Charles, Sermons.
Wilson's, William, Sermons.
Wordsworth's, Christopher, Sermons.

TEN VIRGINS.

Augustine, Sermones.
Bradley's, Charles, Sermons.
Broughton's, Thomas, Sermons.
Burder's, Henry F., Sermons.
Clowes on the Parable of the Virgins.
Colman's, Benj., Sermons. (Several on this subject, sometimes published separately.)
Dibden's, T. F., Sermons.
Elliot, R., on the Ten virgins.
Ellis', Clement, Discourses.
Erskine's, Eben., Discourses. (6 on this P.)
Kelly's, Dennis, Sermons.
Kennaway's Sermons.
Lavington's, Samuel, Sermons.
Logan's, John, Lectures.
Loveday's Alarm to slumbering Christians.
Maitland's, C. D., Sermons on the P. of V.
Reader, Samuel, on the P. of the Virgins.

Parables.

TEN VIRGINS—*continued.*

Seabury's, Bp., Sermons.
Seiss' P. of the ten virgins. (6 discourses.)
Shepard, Tho., on the P. of the virgins. ("A rich fund of experimental and practical divinity."—WILLIAMS.)
Stebbings', Dr. Henry, P. of the 10 virgins.
Stoneham's Parable of the 10 virgins.
Tillotson's, Abp., Sermons.
Whitefield's, George, Sermons.
Wood's, James, Sermons on the P. of the V

TRUE VINE.

Bowdler on the Character of Christ.
Kelly's, Dennis, Practical sermons.
Merrick's Sermons.
Trench's, R. C., Sermons.

TWO SONS.

Enfield's, William, Sermons.
Faber's, George S., Sermons.
Goodman's, J., Penitent pardoned.
Grew's, Obadiah, Sermons.
Hewlett's, John, Sermons.
Jay's, William, Sermons.
Melville's, Henry, Sermons.
Short's William Sermons.

UNJUST STEWARD. See POLITIC STEWARD.

UNMERCIFUL SERVANT.

Hastings', H. J., Parochial sermons.
Haverfield's, T. T., Sermons.
Lord's Theol. and Lit. Journal. 7:602.
Pyle's Philip, Sermons.
Short's, William, Sermons.
Slade's, James, Sermons.
Wordsworth's, Christopher, Sermons.

WEDDING GARMENT.

Benson's Hulsean Lectures. 1820.
Bradley's, Charles, Sermons.
Brameld's, G. W., Practical sermons.
Butler's, William A., Sermons.
Cooper's, Edward, Sermons.
Dibdin's, Thomas F., Sermons.
Elliot's, John, Sermons.
Garbett's, James, Sermons.
Garrow's, D. W., Sermons.
Gatty's, Alfred, Sermons.
Hastings', H. J., Parochial sermons.
Lord's Theol. and Lit. Journal. 8:177.
Smith's, Henry, Sermons.
Spencer's, Bp., Sermons.
Wesley's, John, Sermons.

WICKED HUSBANDMEN.

Dodd's, William, Discourses.
Jacobson's, William, Sermons.

Paracelsists.

Boulay, Hist. Academiæ Paris. Tom. VI.
Fludd, Philosophia Mosaica.
Guntheri (Wolfgang) Hist. Sac. et Prof.
Hoffmanni (Dan.) Opera.
Hoffmanni (S. F. G.) Lexicon Bibliograph.
Molleri Cimbria Literata.
Severini (Ioann.) Opuscula.
Wood's Athenæ Oxioniensis.

Paradise. See EDEN, HEAVEN, INTERMEDIATE STATE, TREE OF LIFE.

Parallelisms. See ANALYSES, QUOTATIONS.

Claude, de Parallelismo Script. Sacræ.
Dorosii Biblia Numerata.
Drusii Parallela Sacra.
Junii Sacra Parallela. (One of the earliest, 1613, and still one of the best.)
Krebsii Observationes in Nov. Testam.
Kypei Observationes Sacræ. (Excellent.)
Loesneri Observationes in Nov. Test.
Neuman, de Parallelismo Scripturæ.
Perkins, Specimen digesti.
Rambach de Parallelismo Scripturæ.
Ravenelli Thesaurus Script. canonicæ.
Surenhusii ΒΙΒΛΟΣ ΚΑΤΑΛΛΑΓΗΣ.
Vogel's Schatzkammer der heiligen Schrift.
Witt, Repertorium Biblicum.
Wollii Commentatio de parallelismo N. T.

Blunt's Scripture coincidences.
Boy's Tactita Sacra. (Highly useful.)
Boyse's (Tho.) Key to the Book of Psalms.
Broughton's Concent of Scripture. 1588.
Cooper's (Oliver) 400 Texts, and their corresponding passages.
Crutwell's Concordance of parallels. (Immense learning and labor; embracing twelve languages.)
Forbes' Symmetrical structure of Scripture.
Fox's (Francis) New Testament. (References at full length under each text.)
Gersham's Anti-typical parallelisms.
Kitto's Journal. 6:179. 8:184.
McCorkle's Collateral Bible. Similar to Fox's.
Platt's Self-interpreting New Testament.
Roe's Arrangement of Sacred Scripture.
Scientia Biblica. (A copious collection of parallel passages in the N. Test., printed in full, in Greek and English, with various readings, &c. &c.)
Simcoe's Epistle to the Ephesians. (Parallel texts inserted at length.)
Smith's (Jas.) Orig. and connect. of the gosp.
Wilson's Scripture Directory.

Parental Duties.
See EDUCATION, FAMILY RELIGION, MATERNAL DUTIES, RELATIVE DUTIES.

Francke's Unterricht von der Kinderzucht.
Stoltii (Ernest.) Pædagogia Christiana.

Baker's Address to Fathers.
——— " " Mothers.
Benson's (Joseph) Sermons.
Burton's (Hezekiah) Discourses.
Butler's (Bp.) Discourses.
Charlesworth's (J.) Sermons.
Christian Examiner. 43:435.
Christian Review. 3:20. 12:25.
Church Review. 1:228.
Collyer's Lectures on Script. duties. Lec. 12.
Craig's (William) Discourses.
Davies' (William) Discourses.
Dawson's (Benjamin) Sermons.
Delany's (Patrick) Discourses.
Doddridge's (Philip) Discourses.

Parental Duties—*continued.*

Doddridge's Lectures. Part 3, prop. 62.
Dwight's (Theod.) Father's book.
Eaton's (Samuel) Sermons.
Fleetwood's (Bp.) Practical Discourses.
Gahan's (William) Sermons.
Guyse's (John) Discourses.
Harris' (Samuel) Sermons.
Holden's (Lawrence) Sermons.
Hole's (Matthew) Sermons.
Holland's (John) Sermons.
Hopkins' (William) Sermons.
Horne's (Thomas) Sermons.
Hunt's (Jeremiah) Sermons.
Jerment on Parental duties.
Kendall on Parental education.
Lawson on Parental duties.
Morning Exercises at Cripplegate.
Morrison's Parent's Friend.
Muzzey's Christian parent.
Nelson on the Government of children.
Newcombe's (Peter) Discourses.
New England Magazine. 5:613.
New Englander. 6:121.
Palfrey's (Dr. John) Sermons.
Penn's (Jas.) Discourses.
Princeton Review. 35:77.
Searle's Christian Parent.
South's (Robert) Sermons.
Thompson's Address to Christian parents.
Tillotson's (Abp.) Sermons.
Tucker's (Joseph) Sermons.
Wayland's Elements of moral science. Bk.
White's Duties of fathers and mothers.

Parsees. See MAGI, ZENDAVISTA.

Bournouf, Comment. sur le Yaçna.
Hyde, Historia religionis vet. Persarum.
Lord, Religion des anciens Parsis.
Rhode's Zend-Volks.
Tholuck, Ssufismus.

Bibliotheca Sacra. 1:148.
Bleek's Trans. of the P. sacred books.
Bunsen's Egypt's place in history.
Butler's Horæ Biblicæ.
Framjee's Manners and religion of the P.
Grove's Voyage to the East Indies.
Haug's Religion of the Zoroastrians.
Penrose's Bampton Lectures. 1808.
Wilson's Parsee religion refuted.

Partaking of other Men's Sins.

Cooper's (Edward) Sermons.
Morning Exercises at Cripplegate. Vol. (Sermon by J. Kitchin.)

Partial Propagation of Christianity.

Bourne's (Samuel) Sermons.
Breckell's (John) Sermons.
Dewar's (Daniel) Discourses.
Doddridge's Lectures. Part 7.
Foster's Reply to Tindall.
Hodge's (John) Sermons on the principal evidences of the Christian religion.

Jenkins on Christianity.
Law's Theory of Religion.
Ridley on the Spirit.
——— on the Christian Revelation.
Waterland's Scripture vindicated.
Young's Idolatrous corruptions of religion.

Particular Atonement. See DEFINITE.

Party Spirit. See SECTARIANISM.

Passions.

Belouino Des passions dans les rapport avec la religion, etc.
Cartesii Opera omnia. Tom. 4.
Malebranche, Recherche de la verité.
Baxter's (Rich.) Practical Works. (Government of the passions.)
Bragge (Francis) on the Passions.
Carleton's Natural history of the passions.
Carr's (George) Sermons.
Clarke's Effect of the P. on human bodies.
Clarke's (Dr. Sam.) Sermons.
Cogan's Ethical treatise on the passions.
——— Philosophical " "
Cosins' (Dr. John) Sermons. (Gov. of the P.)
Doddridge's Lectures. Part 1, prop. 14.
Evans on the Christian Temper.
Fourier's Passions of the soul, and their influence on society and civilization.
Gregory's (Geo.) Sermons. (Gov. of the P.)
Hanway's Virtue in humble life.
Hussey's (Christoph.) Sermons. (Gov. of P.)
Hutchinson's Nature and conduct of the P.
Le Brun's Character of the passions.
Locke's Essay on the mind.
Malebranche's Search after truth.
Marshall's (Nathaniel) Sermons.
Millingen on Mind and matter, and hereditary insanity.
Newman's (J. H.) Sermons.
Priestley's (Joseph) Essays on Hartley's theory of mind.
Reynolds' (Bp. E.) Discourses.
Saurin's Sermons.
Senault on the Use of the passions.
Southern Review. 6:116.
Spectator. No. 255.
Trapp's (Jos.) Sermons.
Tucker's Light of nature. Ch. 21.
Watts' Doctrine of the Passions.
Wilberforce's View of Christianity. Chap. 3.

Passive Obedience to Kings. See BANGOREAN CONTROVERSY, DIVINE RIGHT OF KINGS.

Pro.

Baylie's Royal charter granted unto kings.
Berkeley's (Bp.) Works. (Three sermons on Romans 13:2.)
Delany's (Bp. Patrick) Sermons.
Filmer's Anarchy of a mixed monarchy.
——— Power of the King of England.
——— Patriarchal Scheme.
——— Origin of Government.
Hicks' (Geo.) Jovian. (Reply to Johnson.)
History of Passive obedience. Anonymous.

Passive Obed. to Kings—*continued.*

Pro.

Hobbes' Elements of moral and political law.
——— Leviathan.
Long's (Tho.) Vind. of primitive Christians.
Parker's (Bp.) Religion and Loyalty.
Potter (Abp.) on Church government.
Salmasius' Defence of Charles I.
Sherlock (Bp.) on Resistance to the supreme power.
Usher's (Abp.) Power communicated from God to the Prince.
Williams' (Bp.) Jura majestas.

Con.

Grotius de Imperio summarum potestatum.
Blennerhasset's (Thomas) Sermons.
Bradbury's (Thomas) Sermons.
Burnett (Bp.) on Submission to authority.
——— Letter on the oath of allegiance.
Collier's (Jer.) Measure of submission, &c.
——— Animadversions on the law of Henry II, &c.
Ellerby on the Doct. of passive obedience.
Goodman's (Chris.) How far superior powers ought to be obeyed.
Hutchinson (John) on Power.
Johnson's (Rev. Sam.) Julian the Apostate.
——— Reply to Constantius and Jovian.
——— Reflections on passive obedience.
Jurieu's Judgment of the Church on defending our religion by arms.
Kettlewell's Measure of Christian obedience
Milton's Tenure of kings and magistrates.
——— Defence of the people of England.
Rutherford's Lex Rex.
Seller's History of self-defence.
Sherlock's Allegiance due to sovereigns.
——— Vindication of Do.
Somers' Rights, powers, and prerogatives of kings. (Said to have been written by Daniel De Foe.)
Sydney (Algernon) on Government.
Wilson's Falsity and vanity of "The history of passive obedience."

Passover.

Bartolocci Bibliotheca Rabbinica.
Cloppenburgius de Controv. inter Baronium et Cassaubonum.
Danzii Memorabilia circa festum P.
Dassovius de Accubitu ad agnem Paschalem.
Frischmuthii Dissertationes. (Utrum agnum pasc. salvator noster, eodem die cum judæis comederit.)
Goldner de Agno Paschali.
Harduinus de Supremo Christi paschate.
Lamy, Traite historique de l'ancienne paque.
Schomeri Diss. de sacramentis Vet. Testam.
Strauch, de Paschate primo.
Chevallier's Hulsean Lectures. 1826.

Pastoral Theology. See PREACHING, VISITING THE SICK.

Ambrose, de Officiis clericorum.

Pastoral Theology—*continued.*

Chrysostom, de Sacerdotio.
Gregory Naz., de Cura pastorali.
Jerome, de Cura pastorali.
Augustine, de Pastoribus.

Borottii Synopsis theologiæ pastoralis.
Erasmi Ecclesiastes.
Frankii (A. H.) Monita pastoralia.
Hartmanni Pastorale evangelicum.
Hemmingii de Pastor. optimo vivendi modo.
Hintenberger's Handb. der Pastoraltheolog.
Kortholti (C.) Pastor fidelis.
Langii Institutiones pastorales.
Palmer's Evangelische Pastoraltheologie.
Quenstedii Ethica pastoralis.
Reichenberger's Pastoral Anweisung, etc.
Seckendorfii Prudentia pastoralis.
Tossani Pastor evangelicus.
Widmer's Pastoraltheologie.

Amer. Biblic. Repos. 3d Series. 1:36.
Atkins' Donnelian Lectures. 1860.
Barrett's (A.) Essay on the Pastoral office.
Baxter's (Rich.) Reformed Pastor.
Best's Parochial Ministrations.
Bibliotheca Sacra. 12:20.
Brown's (John) Pastor's manual.
Bogue's (David) Lectures.
Bulkley's Christian Minister.
Burnett on the Pastoral care.
Campbell (G.) on the Pastoral character.
Canon's (Dr. J. S.) Lectures.
Cecil's Remains.
Christian Rev. 3:218.
Church Rev. 2:348.
Clergyman's Instructor. (Contains treatises by Bull, Burnett, Booth, Doddridge, Cecil, Mason, Watts, Erskine, &c.)
Doke's Sermons on ministerial duties.
Dallas on Pastoral superintendence; its motives and detail.
Deyling's Institutes of Pastoral prudence.
Disney's (John) Sermons.
Edwards' Christian Preacher.
Erskine's (John) Discourses.
Flavel's Evangelical Pastor.
Fordyce's Ordination Sermons.
Gerard's Pastoral care. (Highly prized.)
Griffith's Difficulties of the min. office.
Hall's (Robert) Sermons.
Herbert's Country parson.
Hill (Geo.) on the Pastoral office.
Hill (M.) on the Pastoral function; deduced from Scripture.
Holmes' Clergyman reminded of his duties.
Humphrey's 34 Letters to a son in the ministry.
Hussey's Monitor for young ministers.
Jesse's Parochialia; or letters, &c.
Jowett's (Wm.) Helps to pastoral visitation.
Kortholt's Faithful Pastor.
MacGill's Considerations for a clergyman.
Mason's Student and pastor.
Mather's Student and pastor.
Miller on Clerical Habits.

Pastoral Theology—*continued.*

New York Review. 1:178.
Oxenden's Duties, diffic., and privileges, &c.
Pond's (E.) Lectures on pastoral duties.
Princeton Rev. 13:11,45.
Quenstedt's Pastoral Ethics.
Reynolds' (Bp.) Sermons.
Robinson's Clergyman's assistant.
Rogue's Evangelical Pastor.
Rose's (H. J.) Sermons before the University of Cambridge.
Ryland's (Dr. John of Bristol) Pastoral memorials.
Shedd's Pastoral Theology and Homiletics.
Skinner's (Tho. H.) Pastoral Theology.
Smith's (John) Lectures on the sacred office.
Sumner's (Bp.) Sermons.
Taylor's (Jer.) Visitation Rules.
Thompson's (H.) Pastoralia.
Townsend's Pastoralia.
Venn's Duties of a Parish priest.
Vinet's (Alex.) Pastoral Theology.
Wilson's (Bp.) Sacra Privata.
——— Parochialia.

A great amount of excellent counsel on this subject may be found in Episcopal and Archdeaconal charges, which are annually printed. An extensive list of these is given in HORNE's *Cat. of Queen's College Library.*

Pastoral Visiting. See MINISTRY, VISITING THE SICK.

Baxter's Reformed Pastor.
Bridges on the Christian ministry.
Browning's Aids to pastoral visitation.
Bull's (John) Clergyman's Companion.
Dodwell's Clergyman's Assistant.
Jowett's Helps to pastoral visiting.
Leechman's Duties of a Christian minister.
Mant's Clergyman's obligations.
New York Review. 1:198.
Osterwald's Lectures to young ministers.
Paley's Clergyman's Assistant.
Thompson's Pastoralia. Chap. 3.

Paterines. See WALDENSES.

Patience. See RESIGNATION.

Chrysostom, Homiliæ.
Cyprian, Epistolæ.

Abernethy's, John, Sermons.
Adams', Thomas, Sermons.
Arnold's, Thomas of Rugby, Sermons.
Barrow's, Bp., Sermons.
Baxter's, Richard, Practical works. (Twenty illustrative instances.)
Blair's, Hugh, Sermons.
Butcher's, Edmund, Sermons.
Cave's Primitive Christianity. Part 2.
Conybeare's, Dr. John, Sermons.
Cyprian on Patience. Trans. by Marshall.
Evans on Christian temper.
Gardner's, John, Sermons.
Hall's, Robert, Notes of sermons.
Heylin's, John, Select discourses.

Patience—*continued.*

Homes', Nathaniel, Sermons.
Hopkins, Bp., Works.
Horne's, Bp., Discourses.
Hutchinson's, Roger, Works.
Hunt's, Jeremiah, Sermons.
Medley's, John, Sermons.
Shorthose's, Hugh, Sermons.
Summerfield's, John, Sermons.
Vaughn's, Henry, Sermons.
Wesley's, John, Sermons.

Patience of God. See ATTRIBUTES.

Abernethy's, John, Sermons.
Bradley's, Charles, Sermons.
Christ. Monthly Spect. 8:382.
Clarke's, Samuel, Sermons.
Cooper's, Edward, Sermons.
Gale's, Dr. John, Sermons.
Harte's, Wm. M., Sermons.
Holland's, John, Sermons.
Hopkins', William, Sermons.
Hunt's, Jeremiah, Sermons.
Kollock's, Shepard K., Sermons.
Leng's, Bp., Sermons.
Marriot's, Wm. H., Sermons.
Noel's, G. T., Sermons.
Saurin's, James, Sermons.
Taylor's, William, Sermons.
Tillotson's, Abp., Sermons.
Walker's, Robert, Sermons.
Warren's, John, Sermons.
Wisheart's, William, Sermons.

Patriarchs. See FAITH OF THE PATRIARCHS.

Gramberg's Religionsideen d. alt. Test.
Heideggeri Historia Patriarcharum. (Containing 47 elaborate dissertations.)
Hess' Gesch. der Patriarchen.
Matthiæ Historia Patriarcharum.
Perionius de Vita sanctorum virorum, etc.
Walchii (C. G. F.) Historia Patriarcharum.

Craig's Patriarchal piety.
Fountain's Lives of Old Testament saints.
Hunter's Sacred biography.
Kitto's Bible Illustrations.
Maurice's P. and Lawgivers of the O. Test.
Meth. Quart. Rev. 11:601.
Page's (Tho.) Discourses on the Types.
Pfeiffer's Dubia Vexata Scripturæ.
Princeton Rev. 27:24.
Smith's (Geo.) Patriarchal age.
Taylor's Scheme of Scripture Divinity.
Wemyss' Job and his times.

Patriotism. See LOVE OF COUNTRY.

Patronage. See ESTABLISHMENTS, PLURALITIES, SIMONY.

Cawdrey's Inquiry into the origin, &c.
Park's Rights and liberties of the Church.
Thompson's View of Dissenters and their present duty. 1839.

Patripassians. See SABELLIANS.

Epiphanius, de Hæresibus.
Hippolytus, contra Noetum.
Tertullian, Liber contra Praxeam.
Theodoret, Hæret. Fabul. Lib. 3, cap. 3.
Wesselingii Probabilia. Cap. XXVI.

Paul. See CONVERSION OF PAUL.

Beets' Augenblicken Leben u. Wirkens P.
Bergeri (Io. Guil.) Dissertationes.
Blochii Chronotaxis scriptorum Pauli.
Brantii Vita Pauli.
Danz de Loco Euseb. H. E. 2,21, qui de altera P. captivitate agit.
Deylingii (Salom.) Observationes.
Flechere, Vie de St. Paul.
Gelpke de Familiaritate quæ P. cum Seneca intercessisse traditur verisimillima.
Heumanni Schediasma de conjuge Pauli.
Ichrammius de eruditione Paulli.
Kirchmayer de Eloquentia Paulli.
Kochii Paulli conjugium, scripturæ dictis, patrum, et rentior. doctorum demonstrat.
Kunze, Testimonia eccles. patrum quæ ad mortem P. spectant.
Langius de Vita et Epistolis Pauli.
Pearsonii Annales P. ex temporis illust.
Scharling de P: ejusque adversariis.
Schrader's Leben des Apostle P.
Schrammii Sermo acad. de eruditione P.
Schurzfleischii Dissertationes.
Spier, Diss. hist. de P. itenere in Hispan.
Strohbachii (J. D.) Dissertationes. (Learning of Paul.)
Walchii (Io. E. I.) de Vinculis apostoli P.
Witsii Meletemata.
Wolf (E. F. R.) de altera P. apost. captivit.
——— Dissertatio de loco 2 Cor. 12:7–9.

Aiton's Paul and his localities in their past and present state. Plates. 1856.
Am. Bibl. Repos. 4:138. 10:142.
Baptist Quarterly. 1:154.
Benson's Life of St. Paul. (In the language of Scripture, with the Epistles inserted in their proper places.)
Besser's St. Paul the Apostle.
Bevan's (J. G.) Life of Paul, with the Epistles in their order.
Biblioth. Sacra. 7:743.
Bloomfield's (Bp.) Lectures.
Blunt's (Henry) Lectures on the life of Paul.
Chris. Disciple. 2:89.
Chris. Examiner. 51:89.
Chris. Month. Spect. 5:453. 6:449. 10:418.
Chris. Review. 15:95.
Conybeare's (W. J.) Life and Epistles of J.
Dehon's (Bp. T.) Sermons.
Eadie's (John) Paul the Preacher.
Eclec. Rev. 4th Series. 10:253. N. S. 5:513.
Ellerton's Conduct, character, &c.
Fletcher's (J. W.) Portrait of St. Paul.
Gilpin's Portrait of St. Paul.
Hall's (Robt.) Notes of sermons.
Howson's Hulsean Lectures. 1862.
Jeacocke's Vindication of the character of Paul against Bolingbroke and Middleton.
Kitto's Journal. 7:292.

Paul—*continued.*

Lewin's (Tho.) Life and Epistles of Paul.
Locke on the Life of St. Paul.
McKnight on the Epistles. (End of last vol.)
Milner's (Joseph) Practical Sermons.
Monod's (Adolph) Sermons on St. Paul.
More's (Hannah) Char. and writings of St. P.
Pearson's Annales Paulinæ.
Quar. Reg. 15:181.
Reade's Christian experience as shown in the life and writings of Paul.
Roberts' Life of St. Paul.
Robinson's (Prof.) Serm. on the char. of P.
Smith's (Sydney) Sermons.
Smith's (J.) Shipwreck of Paul, with dissertations on the sources of his writings, and the ships of the ancients.
Stillingfleet's (Bp.) Sermons.
Tate's History of the Apostle Paul.
Tholuck's Life, character, and style of Paul.
Walker's (James) Sermons.
Whately's Difficulties in the writings of P.

Paul and James Reconciled.

Altingii Doctrina Apost. Jacobi, etc.
Baierus de Connexione fidei et operum.
Bullii Harmonia Apostolica.
——— Apologia pro harmonia. (Ag. Tully.)
Capellus, (J.) Observationes in Nov. Test.
Drusii Parallela Sacra.
Gatakeri Animadversiones.
Knappe, Scripta varii argumenti.
Millii Prolegomena ad Nov. Testamentum.
Misleri Harmonia Pauli et Jacobi.
Niemani Diss. de fide incarnata.
Pitcairnii Harmonia Evangelica.
Turretini Concordia Jacobi et Pauli.
Vorstius in Ratione apost. Pauli et Jacobi.
Willii Symphonia Pauli et Jacobi.
Workenii Meditationes Privatæ.

Barlow's (Bp.) Letters. (Powerful.)
Benson's Crit. dissertations on the epistles.
Blackall's (Dr. O.) Sermons.
Bull's Apostolical Harm. Tr. by Wilkinson.
——— Letter to Nelson.
Cave's Apostolical Antiquities.
Christian Review. 1:511.
Dwight's Theology. Ser. 68.
Edwards' Doctrine of faith and justification.
Erskine on Faith. (Appendix.)
Gataker's (Chas.) Way of truth and peace. (Sometimes printed at the end of Thomas Gataker's Antidote to error.)
Hoadley (Bp.) on the Terms of acceptance.
Hopkins' (Ezekiel) Discourses on sin.
Kitto's Journal of Sac. Lit. 3:237.
MacKnight on the Epistles.
Molina's Account of the several advances the Church of England hath made towards Rome for these hundred years. 1680.
Owen on Justification.
Pitcarne's Evangelical Harmony.
Richardson's (William) Sermons.
Robinson's Christian System. Ess. 45.
Tillotson's Sermons.
Truman's Endeavor to rectify some prevailing opinions.
Tully on Justification without works.
Wood's (Prof.) Works.

Paul of Samosata. See SAMOSATIANS.

Paulicians. See WALDENSES.

Cedreni Compendium Historiæ.
Geiseler, Studien und Kritiken.
Gregoire, Histoire des Sects.
Limborch, Historia Inquisitionis.
Muratori Antiquitat. Italiæ medii ævi.
Neander's Kirchengeschichte.
Photius, contra Manichæos.
Schmid, Hist. Paulicianorum Orientalium.
Siculus, Historia Manichæorum.
Wolfii Manichæismus ante Manichæos.

Pauperism. See POOR LAWS.

Fregier, Classes dangereuses dans les grand villes.
Modeste, Paupérisme: — etat en France, causes, remèdes, etc.
Reboul, Pauperisme et Bienfaisance.

Blackwood's Magaz. 27:748.
Bosanquet's Rights of the poor.
Chalmers' (Thomas) Christian polity of a nation. (Speaks of wages, strikes, poor rates, savings banks, &c.)
——— Political Economy.
Chevallier's The Labor question.
Foreign Quart. Rev. 15:159.
Knight on Capital and Labor.
Mease on Loan offices and Savings funds.
Pamphleteer. 11:133.
Quarterly Review. 64:188.

Peace. See CONGRESS OF NATIONS.

Pecqueur, de la Paix, de son principe, etc.
——— des Armées dans leur rapport avec industrie, etc.

Advocate of Peace. Period. Boston, U. S.
Beckwith's Peace Manual.
Book of Peace. (A collection of tracts.)
Burroughs' Irenicum.
Christ. Disciple. 5:67.
Christ. Rev. 12:441. 14:306.
Christ. Examiner. 26:179. 33:291. 34:114. 41:173. 44:356.
Democratic Review. 10:107.
Dymond on War.
Edinb. Review. 20:213.
Foster's (Dr. James) Discourses.
Fuller on the Means of universal peace.
Hancock on Peace.
Haweis on the Blessing of peace.
Herald of Peace. Periodical. London.
Jay's Review of the Mexican War.
Kempis' Imitation of Christ.
Knickerbocker Mag. 3:333,401.
Macnamara's P., permanent and universal.
North Am. Review. 6:25.
North Brit. Rev. 16:1.
Parsons' Christianity a system of peace.

Tracts by the London Peace Society.
Tracts by the American Peace Society.
Upham's Peace Manual.
Worcester's (Dr.) Friend of peace.

Peaceableness. See CONTROVERSY.

Adams' (Thomas) Sermons.
Atterbury's (Francis) Sermons.
Blair's (Hugh) Sermons.
Brooks' (H.) Practical Essays.
Cave's Pri · itive Christianity. Part 3, ch. 2.
Evans on Christian Temper. (Nothing better, as a whole, in the language.)
Gale's (Dr. John) Sermons.
Grove's (Henry) Sermons and Tracts.
Howe's (John) Sermons.
Johnson's (Dr. Sam.) Sermons.
Jortin's (John) Sermons.
Owen on Love, Peace, and Unity.
Sterne's (Lawrence) Sermons.
Trimnel's (Charles) Sermons.

Peace-Makers. See BEATITUDES.

Abernethy's (John) Sermons.
Brereton's Sermons.
Dehon's (Bp. T.) Sermons.
Echlin's (John) Sermons.
Hale's (Jas.) Sermons.
Reynolds' (Bp.) Sermons. (Peace of the Ch.)

Peace of Mind. See CONTENTMENT.

Lombez, Lettres spirituelles.
Seneca de Tranquilitate animi.

Addington on Christian peace.
Barrow's (William) Sermons.
Baxter's Right method for a settled peace of conscience.
Brady's (Nicolas) Sermons.
Carter's (Nicholas) Sermons.
Charnock's Works.
Durham's (James) Sermons.
Dwight's Theology. Ser. 84.
Edwards' (Pres.) Works. (Sermons.)
Gilpin's (William) Sermons.
Graves' (Richard) Sermons.
Hall's (Bp.) Practical Works.
Jones' (Wm. of Nayland) Sermons.
Stillingfleet's (Bp.) Sermons.
Trebeck's (Andrew) Sermons.
Vaughn (Henry) on the Fruits of the Spirit.

Pelagianism.

Pro. See writers against DECREES, and ORIGINAL SIN.

Pelagii Epistolæ.
Whitby on the Imputation of Adam's sin.

Con.

Augustin, de Peccatorum meritis, etc.
——— de Gestis Pelagii.
——— de Gratia Christi, etc.
——— de Natura et gratia.
——— de Perfectione, justitia, etc.
——— de Libero arbitrio.
——— de Corruptione et gratia.
——— de Dono perseverantia.
Jerome, Epistola ad Ctesiphontem.

Pelagianism—*continued.*

Anselm de Concordia gratiæ Dei cum libero arbitrio.
Bradwardin, de Causa Dei.
Horne de Sententiis patrum.
Jansenii Augustinus. (This great work collects all that Augustine wrote touching Pelagianism, even every scattered sentence. In an appendix is collated all the passages, in the other Fathers, relating to this controversy. It occupied the author twenty years.)
Noris, Vindiciæ Augustinianæ.
Marii Opera. (The best edition is that of Baluze. 1684.)
Mercatoris (Marii) Opera.
Vossii (G. J.) Theses Theologicæ.
Wiggers' Darstellung d. Augustinismus und Pelagianismus.

Beza's Popery in patched Pelagianism.
Biblioth. Sac. 5:205.
Christian Rev. 3:411.
Knox's (John) Answer to the blasphemous cavillations, &c.
Lit. and Theol. Rev. 4:469. 5:38.
Methodist Quar. Rev. 8:436.
Short's Bampton Lecture. 1846.
Skepp (John) on Divine energy.
Wiggers on Augustanism and Pelagianism.
Williams' (John) Dissertation on P.

The writers of the 5th century on this controversy, are mentioned by BUDDEUS, in his *Isagoge*, Tom. II. The following historical works sufficiently set forth the chief arguments.

Pelagians, History of.

Alvarez de orgine Pelag. hæres. et ejus progressu et damnatione.
Buddei Isagoge ad Theologiam.
Daniel, Histoire du Concile de Diospolis. (In his Opuscula.)
Garnerii Supplementum Oper. Theodoreti.
Jacobi die Lehre des Pelagius.
Lilienthali Miscellanea Sacra.
Longueval, Historia Pelagiana.
Noris, Diss. de Synodo Quinta Œcumenica. (A famous work, by a papal writer.)
Petavii Pelagianorum dogmatum historia.
Vossii Hist. Pelagiana. (Apologetical.)
Walchii (J. G.) Miscellanea Sacra.

Fairbairn's Theological Essays.
Le Clerc's Life of Clemens Alexandrinus.
Norris' (Robt.) History of Pelagianism.
Usseri Antiquitates Ecclesiasticæ.
Wall's History of Infant Baptism. Chap. 19.
Wigger's History of Augustinism and Pelagianism, from original sources. Translated by R. Emerson.

Penance. See POPERY.

Dallæus de Pœnis et Satisfactione.
Ledrou, Diss. IV de contritione.

Penance—*continued.*

Morinus de Disciplina pœnitentiæ. ("A work which contains whatever can be said on the subject."—DUPIN.)
Suiceri Observationes Sacræ.
Butler's (Alban) Sermons.
Cave's Primitive Christianity. Part 3, ch. 5.
Gahan's (William) Sermons. (Papal.)
Salter's Hall Sermons. Ser. by Dr. Hunt.
Sterne's (Lawrence) Sermons.
Taylor's (Jer.) Polemic Sermons.
Wharton (C. H.) on Penance.

Penitent Thief.

Bateman's (Josiah) Sermons.
Blunt's (Henry) Sermons.
Dealtry's (William) Sermons.

Penn, William. See FRIENDS.

Marsillac, Vie de Guil. Penn.
Penn's (Wm.) Works. 2 vols., folio. 1756.
Analytical Mag. 2:442.
Bess' Confut. of the charge of Deism agt. P.
Christ. Rev. 17:555.
Democratic Rev. 29:130.
Eclec. Mag. 21:433. 23:115.
Edinb. Rev. 21:444. (Jeffrey.) 94:116,229.
Life of Penn; by Clarkson.
——— —— by D'Aubigné.
——— —— by Dixon.
——— —— by Ellis.
——— —— by Janney.
Littell's Living Age. 8:617. 27:304. 29:297. 30:419.
Meth. Quart. Rev. 12:119.
N. Am. Rev. 65:109.
Paget's Inquiry into the charges brought by Lord Macaulay against W. Penn.
Sparks' American Biography.
Westminster Rev. 54:117.

Pentateuch. See SAMARITAN PENTATEUCH.

Arnaud, le Pent. defendu contre les attaques de la critique négative.
Arnheim's Anmerkungen.
Frazzeni Disquisitiones Biblicæ.
Gesenius de Pentateucho.
Grandpierre, Essais sur la Pentateuque.
Hartmann, Hist. kritische forschungen, etc.
Hengstenberg's Geschichte des P. erwiesen.
——— Authentie des Pentateuchs.
Hufnagle de Pent. versione Alexandrinæ.
Koolhaas, Observ. philologico-exegeticæ.
Levi, Nouvelle traduction Française.
Meklenburgii (J. Z.) Scriptura ac traditio.
Mendelssohn's Einleitung in Pentat. Mosis.
Paulus, Commentatio critica vers. Pent.
Robertsoni Clavis Pentateuchi. (The words in their order, with Latin and English versions, notes, &c. New Edition by Kinghorn. 1824.)
Rosenmüller, de Versione Pent. Persica.
Theineri Descriptio codicis manuscripti qui vers. P. Arabici continet.
Toepler de P. interpretatione Alexandrina.
Tychseni Disputat. histor. philol. critica.

Pentateuch—*continued.*

Alexander's (W.) P. illustrated. (Historical, geographical, and explanatory.)
Allix's Reflections on the books of Moses.
Amer. Bib. Repos. 2:681. 11:416. 12:458.
Amer. Quart. Register. 9:59.
Bibliotheca Sac. 2:356,668. 4:188.
Blunt's Hulsean Lectures. 1832.
——— Veracity of the P. argued from undesigned coincidences.
Brightwell's (T.) Notes on the Pentateuch.
Brownson's Quart. Rev. 2d Series. 2:507.
Caunter's Poetry of the Pentateuch.
Christ. Exam. 28:147. 29:63.
Eclec. Rev. 4th Ser. 9:415. 15:267. 28:594.
Exeter Hall Lectures to young men.
Faber's (Geo. S.) Bampton Lectures. 1801.
Graves' Lectures on the Pentateuch.
Grinfield's Apology for the Pentateuch.
Green's (W. H.) Pentateuch vindicated. (Reply to Colenso.)
Hamilton's P. and its assailants. (Meets every form of modern objection. 1852.)
Havernick's Introduction to the Pentateuch. Translated by W. L. Alexander.
——— ——— Trans. by Thomson.
Hengstenberg's Genuineness, &c. Translated by J. E. Ryland.
Jamieson's Use of sacred history. (Two preliminary dissertations.)
Le Clerc's Twelve Dissertations.
Lit. and Theol. Rev. 2:171.
MacDonald's Introduct. to the P. (Discusses the genuineness, authority, and design.)
N. Amer. Rev. 22:274.
Palfrey's Academical Lectures.
Parker's Bibliotheca Biblica. (A Comm. on the Pentat. from the writings of the early Fathers, with a catalogue of heretics censured by them. This huge work is accompanied by many Dissertations by DR. HEYWOOD, on the more curious and uncommon subjects.)
Popham's Extracts from the P., compared with passages in Greek and Latin authors.
Porter's Pentateuch and the Gospels.
Princeton Review. 2:549. 10:542.
Smith's (Geo.) Lectures on the P. (Special reference to recent objections. 1863.)
Thompson's Guide to the study of the P.
Townsend's (George) Pentateuch and Job arranged in chronological order.
Yeates' Collation of an Indian copy of the Hebrew Pentateuch.

Pentecost. See GIFT OF TONGUES, SPIRITUAL GIFTS.

Perfectability of Man. See HUMAN PROGRESS.

Perfection, Christian.

Its attainableness in this life.

Pro.

Macarii Homiliæ.
Osorio de Justitia Cœlesti.

Perfection, Christian—*continued.*

Osorio de Nobilitate Christiana.
Rodriguez, Idea perfectionis Christianæ.
Baker's (A.) Sermons on the affections.
Barclay's Apology.
Besse's Defence of Quakerism.
Caussin's (Nicholas) Holy Court.
Couling (Nich.) on the Saints' perfection.
Fenelon on Christian Perfection.
Finney's (Cha. G.) Lectures to Christians.
Fitch (Charles) on Christian perfection.
Fletcher's Checks to Antinomianism.
Harrison on Entire Sanctification.
Hunt on Entire Sanctification.
Law (Wm.) on Christian Perfection.
Life of Wesley; by Coke.
Lucas' (Dr. Rich.) Practical Christianity.
Mahan on Christian Perfection.
Methodist Quart. Review. 1:123,307. 3:447. 8:293. 9:484.
Oberlin Evangelist. Periodical.
Peck's Doct. of P. stated; with a critical and historical exam. of the controversy.
——— Central idea of Christianity.
Penn's (G.) Institutes of Macarius.
Summerfield's (John) Sermons.
Treffry on Christian Perfection.
Wesley's (John) Sermons.

Con.

Gahn, de Causis cur homo ad perfectam sanctitatem non pervenit.
Melancthonis Loci communes.
Amer. Biblical Repos. 5:166,406. 2d Series. 1:44. 2:143. 4:408.
Augsburg Confession of faith.
Ball's (Nathaniel) Sermons.
Bates' Spiritual perfection unfolded.
Cappe's (Newcombe) Practical Discourses.
Christian Rev. 7:222. 9:232,481.
Christian Quart. Spect. 1:1.
Clarke's (Dr. Samuel) Sermons.
Doddridge's Commentary on 1 John 3:9.
Edinb. Review. 21:8.
Enfield's (William) Sermons.
Fox's (John) Reply to Osorio. (Powerful.)
Gale's (Dr. John) Sermons.
Hale's Methodism inspected.
Lit. and Theol. Rev. 1:554. 3:5.
Lucas' (Richard) Sermons.
New Englander. 1:216. 6:177.
Princeton Rev. 13:231. 14:426.
Selections from Edinb. Review. 3:214.
Snodgrass' Scripture doct. of Santification.
Upham on Christian Perfection.
Waterland's (Daniel) Sermons.
Watmough's Practical Essays.
Wood's (Leonard) Works.

Period of Christ's Ministry. See CHRONOLOGY, DURATION.

Period of 1260 years. See ANTICHRIST, DANIEL, MILLENNIUM, PROPHECY.

Brown's (John Aquila) Eventide.
Christian Observer. 14:427. 28:396.
Cunningham on the Seals and Trumpets.
Digby on the 1260 years.
Ettrick's Second Exodus.
——— Season and Time.
Faber's (Geo. S.) Sacred Calendar.
Habersham on the Prophetic Scriptures.
Maitland's Inquiry into the grounds on which the prophetic periods of Daniel and John are supposed to consist of 1260 years.
——— Second Inquiry.
——— Letter to Rev. W. Digby.
——— Reply to Cunningham.
Manchester's (Geo.) Times of Daniel.
Whitaker on Prophecy. (Opposes Faber.)

Perjury. See OATHS, THIRD COMMANDMENT.

Puffendorf de Leg. Naturæ. Lib. IV, cap. 2.
Barrow's Works.
Blair's (James) Sermons.
Burnet's (Gilbert) Sermons.
Disney's Crying sin of Perjury.
Doddridge's Lectures. Part 2, prop. 56.
Fisher's Guilt and danger of perjury.
Green (Bp.) on the Wickedness of perjury.
Paley's Moral Philosophy.
Wake's (Abp.) Sermons.
Whitaker's (Edw. W.) Sermons.

Persecution.

Augustine, Opera.
Athanasius, Apologetici duo.
Athenagoras, Legatio pro Christianis.
Clemens Alex., Opera quæ extant.
Justin M., Apologiæ duæ.
Origen, Exhortatio ad martyrium.
Tertullian, de Præscriptione Hæreticorum.
Abernethy's (Dr. John) Tracts.
Bayle's Philosophical Com. on Luke 14:23. "Compel them to come in."
Bray on Papal Usurpation.
Childs' Mischief of persecution.
Christian Observer. 10:13.
Clarke's (Dr. Sam.) Sermons.
——— Looking-glass for persecutors.
Cotton's Bloody tenet washed. (Justifies.)
Dick's Philosophy of Religion. Ch. 4.
Doddridge's (Philip) Sermons.
Doddridge's (J.) Lectures. Part 3. prop. 77.
Duncan on Persecution for opinion's sake.
Eclectic Rev. New Series. 7:573.
Edwards' (Thomas) Dissertations.
Emlyn's (Thomas) Tracts.
Evans' Peace and Persecution inconsistent.
Faringdon's (Anthony) Sermons.
Foster's (James) Sermons.
Fox (Geo.), Concerning P. in all ages.
——— Moderation of the heathen Emperors.
Francowitz's Witnesses of the truth.
Grosvenor's (Benjamin) Sermons.
Hickes's (Dr. Geo.) Sermons. (What is P.?)
Horneck's (Anthony) Sermons.
Humphreys' (W. G.) Hulsean Lectures. 1850.
Jortin's (John) Sermons.
——— Life of Erasmus. (Has some fine passages touching the iniquity of Protestants persecuting Baptists.)

Persecution—*continued.*

Lactantius on the Deaths of persecutors. Translated by Burnet.
Limborch's History of the Inquisition. (Introduction.)
Martin Marprelate's Dialogue, wherein is laid open the tyrannical dealings of the Lord Bishops, &c.
——— Arraignment of Mr. Persecution.
Masillon's Sermons.
Montesquieu's Spirit of Laws.
Moyle's Posthumous Works.
Plitt's Evangelical Christendom.
Price's Morals.
Salter's Hall Sermons. Ser. by Grosvenor.
Shaftesbury's Characteristics of men, &c.
Sumner's (Bp.) Sermons.
Taylor's (Jer.) Liberty of prophecying.
Watson's Apology for the Bible.
Wickliffe (J.) on Persecution.
Williams' (Roger) Bloody tenet.
——— Essays on religious liberty.
——— Bloody tenet more bloody. (Reply to Cotton.)

Persecution, History of.

Cyprian, de Mortibus persecutorum.
Lactantius, de Mortibus persecutorum.

Benkendorf's Kurtzgefasste Historie.
Camboline, Hist. d. evenemens, etc. (France.)
Cellarii Dissert. Academicæ. (Under Nero.)
Claude, Tableau de la P. sous Louis XIV.
Comenii Hist. persec. ecclesiæ Bohemicæ.
Coquerel, les Forçats pour la Foi.
Eusebius de Martyribus Palestinæ.
Fabricii Lux Evangelii Salutaris. Cap. 25,26.
Heumani Disputationes. (Under Trajan.)
Huldricus de calumniis Gentilium in Chris.
Kirchmayeri Dissertationes. (Under Trajan.)
Kortholti Paganus obtrectator.
——— Persec. eccles. primitivæ.
Lazari Diss. selectæ. (Apostolic age.)
Ruinarti Hist. persecutionis Vandalicæ.
Simonetta Hist. des persecutions.
Tesmari Processus Gentilium in Christianos.
Walch, Christianorum sub Diocletiano P.
——— P. Neronianæ Explicatio.

Aikman's Annals of P. in Scotland.
Aretius' History of Valentinian.
Backus' (Isaac) History of New England.
Bathumley's Material passages of Ch. Hist.
Benedict's History of the Baptists.
Besse's Sufferings of the Quakers.
Bion's Torments of French Protestants aboard the Galleys. 1712.
Bowers' Lives of the Popes.
Bray's Papal Usurpations.
Bungener's Priest and the Huguenot.
Bowers' Lives of the Popes.
Burman on the Persecution of Diocletian.
Chandler's Hist. of persecution. (From the patriarchal age, by Heathen, Papists, and Protestants, to George II.)
Ciocci's P. at Rome in the 19th century.
Clark's (Sam.) General Martyrology. Plates.

Persecution, History of—*continued.*

Comenius' Hist. of the Bohemian persecut.
Coverdale's (Miles) Godly, fruitful, and comfortable Letters. (Contains letters of Cranmer, Ridley, Hooper, Philpot, Bradford, Lady Grey, and many others. Deserves to be reprinted.)
Crosby's History of the Baptists.
De Castro's Persecution of Spanish Protest.
Eclectic Rev. 4th Ser. 8:423. (Madagascar.)
Ellis' Visits to Madagascar. 1850 to 1856.
Enaroll's P. of Protestants in France.
Fish's (H. C.) Price of soul liberty, and who paid it.
Fox's (John) Acts and Monuments.
Gibbon's (Tho.) Oppress. of French Protest.
Gough's History of the Quakers.
History of the Edict of Nantes. (Being an account of all the persecutions that have been in France from its first publication to the present time. 1694.)
Howie's Scotch Worthies.
Ivemy's History of the Baptists.
Lactantius' Death of persecutors. Trans. by Bp. Burnet.
——— ——— Tr. by Lord Hailes.
——— ——— Tr. by Dalrymple. (The best.)
Lardner's Jewish and Heathen testimonies.
Lloyd's Memoirs of the lives, actions, sufferings, &c., of those who have suffered for the Protestant religion.
Lockman's History of Popish persecutions.
Lombard's Ancient and modern persecutions.
Marolle's Persecution of Prot. in France.
McCoan's Protestant endurance under Popish cruelty.
Neal's History of the Puritans.
Niles' Register. 18:82.
Rey's Persecutions by the French clergy.
Robinson's (Anth.) History of Persecution.
Schoberl's Intolerance of the Ch. of Rome.
Simpson's Voice from the desert. (Persecution in Scotland.)
Symson's Persec. of the first 6 centuries.
Taylor's (M.) England's bloody tribunal. Many plates.
Westminster Rev. 2:1.
Wilkes' History of the persecution of Protestants in France in 1814–1840.
Woodrow's Sufferings of the Ch. of Scotland.
Wright's History of Religious P., from the Apostolic age to the present. 1816.

Perseverance of the Saints.

Abbot (R.) de Perseverantia Sanctorum.
Acta Synodi Dordrect.
Kendall (G.) Sanctis Sancti.
Markii Medulla. Cap. XXVII.
Prideaux Lectiones de controversis.
Stapferi Theologiæ Institutiones.
Tarnovii Exercitationes Biblicæ. Appendix.
Witsii Economia Fœderis. Lib. III.
Zanchii Opera theologica. Vol. VII.
Backus' (Isaac) Sermons.
Baxter's End of Controversy.

Perseverance—*continued.*

Brackenbury's (Edward) Discourses.
Crisp's (Tobias) Christ alone exalted.
Dawson's Vindication of the saint's P.
Doddridge's Lectures. Part 8.
Dwight's Theology. Disc. 87.
Edwards' (John) Theologia reformata.
——— Veritas redux.
Edwards' (Pres.) Works. (Sermons.)
Evans (J. H.) on the Doct. of final persev.
Gill's Sermons and tracts. (Very clear.)
Hale's Golden Remains.
Hall (Tho.) on Final Perseverance.
Hall's (Bp.) Polemic works.
Hall's (Robt. Sen.) Help to Zion's travellers.
Horne's (Bp.) Discourses.
Howe's Living Temple.
Kendall's Doct. of the P. of the saints vind.
Knowles' (Thomas) Sermons.
Lime Street Lectures.
Maurice's Sermons.
Mavor's (William) Sermons.
Oliver's (Tho.) Refutation of the Doct., &c.
Owen (John) on the P. of the saints.
Paige on the Perseverance of the saints.
Park Street Lectures. Lect. 11.
Prynne's Perpetuitie of a regenerate man's estate.
——— God no deluder.
Ryder's (Bp.) Sermons.
Saurin's Sermons.
Spurgeon's (C. H.) Sermons. 8th Series.
Stennet's (Samuel) Sermons.
Taggart's (Sam.) Vind. of the doctrine of P.
Toplady's Works.
Tyler's Doctrine of the Persev. of Saints.
Tyndall's (Wm. the Martyr) Works.
Whately's (Abp.) Essays. Ess. 4.
Whitby's Discourse on the five points.
Williston's Sermons.
Zanchius' Three tracts.

Personal Identity.

Butler's Analogy of relig. and nat. Diss. 1.
Doddridge's Lectures. Proposition 11.
Le Clerc's Ontology. Chap. 2.
Locke's Essays. Bk. 2, chap. 27.
Reid's Intellectual Powers.
Watts' Essays. Ess. 12.

Personal Reign of Christ. See MILLENARIANS, SECOND ADVENT.

Personal Religion. See PRACT. PIETY, and the various graces, and duties, under their proper heads.

Personality of the Holy Ghost. See HOLY SPIRIT.

Deutschius de Personalit. Spiritus S.
Doederlini Theologia.
Dorschei (Ioann. Geo.) Dissertationes.
Gerhardi Loci Theologici.
Melancthonis Opera.
Noeselti Opuscula.

Christian Review. 17:213.
Dwight's Theology. Ser. 70.

Personality of the H. G.—*continued.*

Hawker's Sermons.
Jenkins on the Holy Spirit.
Middleton on the Greek article.
Owen on the Holy Spirit.
Pierce's (S. E.) Scripture Testimonies.
Scott's (Tho.) Theological Essays. Ess. 13.
Smith's (John Pye) Sermons.
Stephens (Will.) on the Holy Spirit.
Vaughn's (J.) Lectures. Lect. 8.
Wardlaw's (Ralph) Discourses.

Perverseness.

Nance's (John) Sermons.
Parry's (Joshua) Sermons.

Peshito Version. See SYRIAC.

Pestilence.

Wedelii (G. W.) Exercitationes decades.

Andrews' (Bp.) Sermons.
Bridges' (Wm.) Works. (Expos. of Ps. 91.)
Grindall's Remarks. (Parker Soc. publ.)
Hooper's (Bp.) Homily. (In his works edited by L. Richmond.)
Scott's (John) Narrative of the great plague of London, with remarks on religious preparation for pestilence.

Peter. See BIOGRAPHY.

Clemens Rom., de Rebus gestis, peregrinationibus, etc., Petri.

Bibliander, de Vita, doctrina, operibus.
Ellendorf, ist P. in Rom und Bischof d. Rom. Kirche gewesen?
Kortholti Dissertationes.
Passaglia de prerogativis Petri. (Collects all the incidents in Peter's life, Canonical, Apocryphal, and Traditional, which seem to favor the doctrine of his supremacy over the other Apostles.)
Sanctorii Acta Sancti Apostoli Petri.
Spanheim de Ficta profectione P. in Rom.
Stengelii Com. rerum gestar. principis P.
Strauchii Diss. historico-theologica.
Veleni Tract. quo 18 argum. adserunter Petrum nunquam Romæ fuisse.
Xavier (Hier.), Historia sancti Petri.

Abernethy's (John) Sermons.
Blunt's Lectures on the history of Peter.
Brown's (J. H.) Peter never at Rome.
Christ. Monthly Spectator. 4:1. 10:172.
Dehon's (Bp. T.) Sermons.
Graves' (Richard) Sermons.
Lake's (Bp.) Sermons.
Lee's (Bp. Alfred) Practical Discourses. (His life of Peter is also printed separately.)
North British Rev. 10:39. (On the question Was Peter ever at Rome?)
Scheller's Was Peter ever at Rome?
Sherlock's (Bp.) Sermons.
Simon's Miss. and Martyrdom of Peter. (Preface, &c., by McCaul and Cumming.)
Taylor's Norrisean Cambridge prize essay.
Thompson's (F. E.) Lent Lectures. Lect. 10.

Peter's Dissimulation.

Bradford's (Charles) Sermons.
Gilpin's (William) Sermons.
Jay's (W.) Short sermons for families.
Mason's (John) Sermons.
McGill's (Stephenson) Sermons.
Quenstedt's Dissertations.
Rees' (Abraham) Sermons.
Richter on Paul's Rebuke to Peter.
Taylor's (T. G.) Conduct and char. of Peter as giving evidence of the Chris. religion.

Peter the Hermit.

Oultreman, Vie de Pierre l'hermit.

Petrobrusians. See COUNCIL OF PISA.

Bassnage, Histoire des Eglises Reformées.
Codex Inquisitionis Tolosanæ.
Heckerus de Testibus veritatis. Sec. XII.
Heltneri Petrobrusiani et Henriciani Testes veritatis. Seculo XII.
Mabilloni Annales Benedictini.
Meisneri (Ioann.) Dissertationes.

London Baptist Mag. July, 1862.

Pharaoh, Hardening of.

Bloomfield's (Bp.) Sermons.
Bradley's (Charles) Sermons.
Fleetwood on Miracles.
Limborch's Theology. Bk. 6, ch. 9.
Milner's (Joseph) Sermons.
Saurin's Dissertations.
Sherlock on Prophecy.

Pharisees. See JUDAISM, SECTS.

Brend's Unterscheid der Moral Christi und der Pharisæer.
Grossmann de Collegio Pharisæorum.
Josephus de Bello Judaico.
Opitii (H.) Exercitationes.
Reschenbergii (L. A.) Dissertationes.
Schmidii (Ioann.) Dissertationes.
Ugolini Trihæresium.

Beausobre's Introduction to the New Test.
Wotten's (Wm.) Miscellaneous Discourses.

Philistines.

Hitzig's Urgeschichte und Mythologie.

Philanthropy. See BENEVOLENCE.

Horsford's P. the genius of Christianity. (With sketches of the most eminent philanthropists.)

Philo Alexandrinus.

Kühn, Spicilegium Observ. ad N. Test.
Loesneri Observ. ad Nov. Test. e Philone.

Philo Judæus.

Philonis Judæi Opera. (Nearly coinciding in date with the first promulgation of the gospel; and throwing much light on the Jewish and Heathen literature of that era, and its influence on Christianity. The best edition of its time is that of MANGEY, 1742. The most complete is that of RICHNER, 1829. There are several others.)
Bellier, Œuvres de Philon.
Carpzovii (J. B.) Exercitationes Sacræ. (Prolegomena.)
Dahlii Chrestomathia Philoniana.
Fabricii (F. A.) Opusculorum Sylloge P.
Grossmanni Questiones Philoneæ.
Hornemanni Observationes de Canone V. T.
Müller (J. G.) über die Textkritik der schriften des P.
Scheffer de Usu P. in interpret. N. Test.
Bryant (Jacob) on the Logos. (Gives large extracts from Philo, on the doctrines of Christianity.)
Jones' (John) Ecclesiastical Researches. (Proves him to be a historian of Christ.)
Morgan on the Trinity of Philo and Plato. (Discusses the influence of these writers on the Christian Fathers.)
Princeton Review. 23:624.
Yonge's Trans. of the works of Philo. 1855.

Philology. See AFFILIATION OF LANGUAGES, BIBLICAL CRITCIISM, DIALECTS, DIFFICULTIES, HEB. LANGUAGE, HERMENEUTICS, IDIOMS, ORIGIN OF LANGUAGES, POETRY OF THE HEBREWS, STYLE OF INSPIRED WRITERS, VARIOUS READINGS, VOWEL POINTS.

Adami Observationes Theologicæ.
——— Exercitationes Exegeticæ.
Adelung (J. C.), Mithridates. (Contains much curious matter. Among other things, the Lord's prayer, in 500 languages.)
Alberti Observationes Philologicæ in N. T.
Almeloveeni Amœnitates Theologicæ.
Baueri Dicta classica V. T. notis illustrata.
Bengelii Apparatus criticus ad N. T.
Biel, Thesaurus Philologicus. ("Necessary to the biblical student."—DIBDIN.)
Bocharti Phaleg and Canaan.
Bode (C. A.), Pseudo critica Millio-Bengeliana. ("Indispensable to those who use Mills' Greek testament, but are unacquainted with the Syriac and Arabic."—MICHAELIS. He insists that Mill and Bengel are often misled by Oriental vers.)
Bonfrerii Prolegomena.
Bos, Exercitationes Philologicæ in quibus N. T. loca auctoribus Græcis illustrantur.
——— Ellipses Græcæ. Cura Michaelis.
——— ——— Ed. Schæfer, quibus adduntur pleonasmi Græci B. Weiske, una cum G. Hermanni diss. de elipsi et pleonasmo Græcæ.
Bretschneideri Lexicon manuale N. Test.
Bulleri Dissertationes Sacræ.
Burtoni Græcæ linguæ Historia.
Buxtorfii Lexicon Chaldaicum, Talmudicum, et Rabbinicum.
Castellii Lexicon Heptaglotton. (Hebrew, Chaldee, Syriac, Arabic, Samaritan, Ethiopic, and Persian.)
——— Harmonia Grammat. Heb., Chaldee, Syriac, Samar., Ethiop., Arabic, et Persic.
Cawton, de usu ling. Heb. in philologia theoretica.
Cellarii Philolog. sac. ling. Orientalium.

Philology—*continued.*

Cornelius a Lapide, Prolegomena.
Crenii Collectiones variæ exercitationes philologicarum. (20 vols., folio.)
Curtii Vind. textus N. T. contra Harduinum.
De Dieu, Grammatica linguar. Orientalium.
Delrii Adagia Sacra Vet. et Nov. Test.
Drusii Critica Sacra.
Du Cange de Causis corruptæ inf. Græcitat.
——— Glossarium ad script. inf. Græcitatis.
——— ——— ——— Latinitatis.
Ernesti Opuscula. (Very valuable.)
Eschenbach, Syntagma.
Fabricii Opera varia.
Fagii Compendiaria Isagoge in ling. Heb.
Fischeri Prolusiones. (Useful for his able judgment of various lexicons, previous to 1790, and exhibition of their errors.)
Franzii Interpretatio Scripturæ Sacræ.
Gesenii Thesaurus philologico-criticus.
Glassii Philologia Sacra.
Hackspanii Diss. philol. et theol. sylloge.
Hassæi et Lampii Bibliotheca Philologica.
Hoogeveen de Particulis ling. Græcæ.
Hottingeri Thesaurus Philologicus.
——— Dissertationes.
Houbiganti Prolegomena. (Unsafe.)
Hunt, de Usu dialectorum Orientalium, ac præcipue Arabicæ, in Hebr. codice interp.
Illirici Clavis Scripturæ.
Iablonski Collectio et explicatio vocum Ægyptiacorum quarum mentio apud scriptores veteres occurrit.
Koecheri Analecta philologica. (A necessary addition to Wolf.)
Koolhaas, Dissertationes grummatico-sacræ. ("Excellent."—Dr. Parr.)
La Crozianarum Thesaurus Epistolarum. (Contains a great number of letters from the cotemporaries of La Croze: e. g., Bengel, Bentley, Brucker, Elsner, Franke, Hase, Lampe, &c.)
Lakemackeri Observationes Philologicæ. ("Exquisite."—Riemmann.)
Leighii Annotationes in N. T.
Leusdeni Opera.
Mayii Introd. ad studium philologicum.
Michaelis (J. G.) Exercitationes.
Mori Acroases Academicæ.
——— Dissertationes.
Morini Explicationes Sacræ.
Mosheimii Cogitationes in N. T.
Naekii Opuscula philologica.
Oudini (Casim.) Dissertationes.
Palairet Observationes philologico-criticæ.
Pfeifferi Opera Philologica.
Raphelii Annotationes in N. Test. (Illustrates by extracts from pure Greek writers, such as Xenophon, Polybius, Arrian, &c.)
Ravii Exercitationes Philologicæ. (Combats Houbigant's Prolegomena.)
Rhenferdii Opera Philologica.
——— Rudimenta gram. harmonia.
Salmasius de Lingua Hellenistica.
Scheidii Dissertationes Exegeticæ.

Philology—*continued.*

Schelling, Descriptio cod. MSS. biblic.
Schottii Adagia sacra Nov. Test.
——— Opuscula critica.
Schleusneri Thesaurus philologico-criticus: sive Lexicon in LXX.
——— Lexicon Græco-Latinum in N. Test. (Almost indispensable.)
Schnurrer, Dissertationes.
Schotti (And.) Observationes.
Schrœderi Institutiones ad fundamenta linguæ Heb.
Schultens (J. J.), de Utilitate dialectorum Orientalium.
Schultens (Albert), Origines Hebrææ.
——— Animad. ad varia loca V. T.
Schulzii Scholia et critica in V. T. (A vast collection of extracts from able philologists; chiefly German.)
Simonis Onomasticum V. et N. Test.
Stockii Clavis ling. sanct. V. et N. Test.
Suiceri Thesaurus eccles. e patribus Græcis.
Tarnovii Exercitationes. (Very useful.)
Tholuck's Spracherklärung d. N. Test.
Tychsen Tentamen de variis codicum Hebr. lectionibus.
Ulmanni Deliciæ rurales.
Van der Leluw de Usu verborum cum propositionibus compositorum in Nov. Test.
Van Voorst, Animad. de usu verborum, etc.
Vitringæ Dissertationes sacræ.
Wagenseilii Exercitationes.
Wahlii Clavis N. Test. philologica.
Waltoni Introd. ad lectionem ling. Orient.
——— Diss. de linguis Orientalibus.
——— Prolegomena.
Werenfelii Opuscula philosoph. et philolog.
Whitby, Observationes philologico-criticæ.
Wildeshausen Bibliotheca disp. theologico-philologicarum.
Winkleri Disquisitiones.
Wolfii Curæ philologicæ et criticæ. (Defends the text, notices the principal criticisms of learned men, and will always be a work of great value.)
Wyttenbachii Bibliotheca critica.
Zimmermanni (Mat.) Florilegium.

American Biblical Reposit. 1:638. (Style.) 3:45. (Greek prepositions.) 8:448. (Lexicography.) 11:131. (Heb. tenses.) 12:113. (Study of Hebrew.) 2d Series. 10:190. (Heb. philology.) 3d Series. 3:1. (Other valuable articles.)
Bates' Reply to Sharp on the word *Berith.*
Biblioth. Sacra. Periodical. N. York.
Blackwall's Sacred Classics.
Black's (Jos.) Palæoromaica. (Historical and critical disquisitions; inquiring whether the Hellenistic style is not Latin-Greek, and whether the Greek text of many MSS. is not a retranslation from the Latin.)
Bloomfield's Greek Testament, with notes. (Exceedingly valuable.)
Christ. Exam. 22:124. 3:247.

Philology—*continued.*

Christ. Rev. 2:136. 16:461.
Collier's Sacred Interpreter.
Conybeare's Lectures at Bristol Coll. 1832,3.
Cook's Enquiry into the books of the N. T.
Cramp's (W.) Philosophy of language.
Crane's (G.) Principles of language.
Crosby's (Howard) Notes on the N. T.
Deyling's Sacred Observations.
Doig's Philological Works.
Doughty's Analecta Sacra.
Eclectic Rev. 2d Series. 17:310.
Ellis' Fortuita Sacra.
Gale's Court of the Gentiles. Part 1.
Gerard's Institutes of Biblical criticism.
Gesenius' Hebrew Lexicon; with geographical names and Chaldee words. (Conant's edition is the best.)
Green's Grammar of the New Test. dialect.
Guichard's Etymological harmony of lang.
Harper's Powers of the Greek tenses.
Harris' Hermes. (Admirable philosophical analysis.)
Heidegger's Dissertations.
Hellenistic Greek Testament. London. 1843. (Shows the connection between the LXX. and the Greek Testament.)
Horne's Introduction to the study of S. S.
Jamieson's Hermes Scythiæus.
Jebb's Sacred Literature.
Kavenaugh on the Science of language.
Kennicott's State of the printed text.
King's Morsels of Criticism.
Kitto's Journal. 4:308. 5:194. 6:193,484. 7:216,469.
Lamy's Biblical Apparatus.
Leigh's Critica Sacra. (Observations on every Hebrew and Greek root in the Bible.)
Manne's Critical notes on some passages, &c. (Comparing them with anc. versions.)
Marshman's Chinese Grammar and dissert.
May's Dissertations; philolog. and critical.
Michaelis' Introd. to the N. T. (Unsafe.)
Middleton's Doctrine of the Greek article.
Mitford on the Principles of harmony.
Nolan's Integrity of the Greek Vulgate. (Classes the Greek MSS., and vindicates the received text.)
North Am. Rev. 24:142. 64:373. 72:261.
Paul's (W.) Structure of the Heb. language.
Pfannkouche On the language of Palestine.
Philological Society's Proceedings. London. From 1842 to the present. 16 volumes.
Pirie's Dissertation on Hebrew roots.
Planck's Sacred Philology and interpretat.
Porson's (Rich.) Tracts.
Princeton Rev. 2:293. 13:250. 36:629.
Pritchard's Eastern origin of Celtic nations, proved by a comparison of their dialect with the Sanscrit, Greek, Latin, and Teutonic languages. (Edited and brought down to the present state of philological learning, by R. G. Latham. 1857.)
Reeves' (John) Collation of the Hebrew and Greek texts of the Psalms.

Philology—*continued.*

Roberts' (F.) Key to the Bible. (A comprehensive digest of the best observations of critics previous to 1665.)
Roberts' Inquiry into the original language of St. Matthew's gospel.
Schimmelpennick's Biblical Fragments.
Sharp's (Archdeacon Thomas) Works.
Sharp (Granville) On the definite Greek article.
Sievwright's Hebrew text considered.
Simpson's Essays on the lang. of Scripture.
Smith's Miscellanea.
Souciet's 12 Critical dissertations.
Stuart's Greek syntax of the New Testament.
Taylor's (John) Power of the Greek article.
Titman's Synonyms of the New Testament.
Walton's Prolegomena.
Wemyss' Biblical Gleanings. (Corrects the translation of many important passages in the English version.)
Wilson's Hist. and compar. view of languages.
Winning's Manual of comparative philology.

For an extensive view of Grammars, Lexicons, Chrestomathies, &c., Greek and Latin, published between 1750 and 1852, see ENGELMAN'S *Bibliotheca Philologica.*

Philosophical Necessity.
See NECESSITY.

Philosophy of the Mind. See MIND.

Philosophy of Religion.

Bilroth über d. Religions-philosophie.
Cocquii Observ. de philosophia morum N. T.
Eschenmayer's Religionsphilosophie.
Gaussenii Diss. de studii theol. ratione et de utilitate philosophiæ in theologia.
Lassus, Comm. sur l'evangile de Jean. Pref.
Miles' (J. W.) Philosophische Theologie: oder d. letzen grunde alles religiosen Glaubens in d. vernunft beruhend.
Ritter's Christliche Phil. nach ihrem Begriff.
Schaumann's Philosophie der Religion.
Scheuchzerus de Usu matheseos in theologia.
Brownson's Quar. Rev. 2d Series. 4:159.
Cheyne's Philosophical principles of religion.
Chris. Exam. 47:247.
Church Rev. 2:226.
Davies' Estimate of the human mind.
Dick's Works. Vol. 3.
Fearn's Essay on the philosophy of faith.
Jebb's (Dr.) Friend and Guide.
Kitto's Journal. 4:58.
Knox's (Alexander) Remains.
Laws' (Edmund) Considerations.
Literary and Theol. Jour. 2:349,525.
Mannyngham's Use of specul. philos. in rel.
Meth. Quar. Rev. 10:349,509.
Morell's (J. D.) Philosophy of Religion.
New Englander. 7:566.
North Brit. Rev. 11:1,157,253.
Pitt's (C.) Philosophy of Christianity.
Powell's (B.) Connect. of Nat. and Div. truth.

Renou's Delineations, physical, intellectual, and moral.

Photinians. See TRINITY.

Calovii (Abrah.) Dissertationes.
Fickleri Hæreticorum novorum Photinian.
Gerhardi Harmonia P. et Pontificorum.
Haberkornii Collegium geminum Anti-Phot.
Himmelii Controversiæ Theologicæ.
Hunnii Examen errorum Photinianorum.
Ittigius de Hæresiarchis ævi Apostolici.
Kesleri Logicæ Photinianæ Examen.
Larroquani de Phot. et ejus condemnatione.
Matthiæ Exercitationes.
Petavii (Dionys.) Dissertationes.
Schallingii Synopsis Doctrinæ veræ et falsæ.
Sirmondi (Iacob.) Opera.
Stegmanni Photinianismus.
Weinrichii (Ioann. Mich.) Dissertationes.

Phrenology.

Azais de la Phrenologie, et de la folie.
Flourens, de la Phrenologie.
Noel (R. R.) Grundzüge der Phrenologie.
Scheve's Katechismus d. P. mit Abbildung.

Amer. Monthly Rev. 2:365.
Amer. Quart. Rev. 20:366.
Amer. Whig Review. 3:32. 12:190.
Blackwood's Magazine. 1:35,365. 10:73,682. 13:100,199.
Boardman's Defence of Phrenology.
Brit. and For. Rev. 12:142.
Brit. Quar. Rev. 4:397.
Chris. Quar. Spectator. 7:274.
Chris. Review. 1:348. 2:536.
Chris. Exam. 16:221. 17:249.
Clarke's (H.) Christian Phrenology; or the teachings of the New Testament respecting the nature of man.
Combes' System of Phrenology.
——— Lectures on Phrenology.
Cowan's Science and Revelation.
Eclectic Mag. 10:188.
Edinburg Rev. 2:147. 25:227. 44:253. 45:248. 74:201.
Epps' Evidences of Christianity from P.
Flourens' Phrenol. examined. Tr. by Meigs. (Powerful attack on the system.)
Foreign Quart. Rev. 2:1.
Foreign Rev. 4:263.
Fowler's Education Complete.
——— P. proved, illustrated, and applied.
——— Various other works.
Frazier's Magaz. 22:509.
Gall's (Dr. John J.) Works.
Grimes' Etherology.
Journal of Science. 39:65.
Knickerbocker's Mag. 2:103. 11:623. 13:308.
Lit. and Theol. Rev. 5:641.
McNish's Introduction to Phrenology.
Meth. Quar. Rev. 7:165,557.
Monthly Rev. 94:395,517. 118:534.
Morel's (J. D.) Strictures.
New Eng. Mag. 6:467. 7:432.

Phrenology—*continued.*

North Am. Rev. 37:59. 45:505. 51:173.
North Brit. Rev. 17:22.
Pamphleteer. 5:219.
Phrenological Journal. Periodical. N. Y. 1824 to the present.
Pierpont's Phrenology and the Scriptures.
Princeton Rev. 10:279. 18:354.
Quar. Rev. 13:159. 57:92.
Rice's (N. L.) Phrenology inconsistent with physiology and Christianity.
Scott's (William) Harm. of P. and Scripture.
Sewall's (Tho.) Examination of Phrenology.
Slade's Conversations with Dugald Stewart.
South. Lit. Journal. 1:393. 2:479.
South. Review. 1:134. 6:265.
Spurzheim's Doctrine of mental phenomena.
——— Outlines of phrenology.
——— Lectures.
Tupper's Inquiry into Gall's system.
United States Lit. Gazette. 6:124.
Weaver's Mental Science.

Phrygians. See MONTANISTS.

Phylacteries.

Beck, de usu Phylacteriorum Judaicorum.
Hiller, de Vestibus Hebræorum.
Lampe, de Sacco, cinctura, etc., Hebræorum.
Leydekker, de Ornamentis Hebræorum.

Wotton's Jewish usages in the time of Christ.

Picards. See WALDENSES.

Pietists. See BOURIGNONISTS, MYSTICS, QUIETISTS.

Arndt's Gleichnissreden Jesu.
Binder's Pietism und d. moderne Bild.
Buddæi Recitationes hist. ecclesiasticæ.
Duttenhofer's Freimüthige Untersuchungen.
Francké, Pietas Hallensis.
Langii Theologia pseudorthoxa.
Loescher's Vollstandiger Tim. Verinus.
Marklin's Darstellung u. kritik d. Pietism.
Schelvigii Synopsis controv. sub pietatis pretextu motarum.
Schmid (H.) Geschichte des Pietismus.
Spener's Theologische Bedenken.
——— Natur und Gnade.
Wurster's Betrachtungen über Pietisten.
Zentgravii Dissertationes.

Francké, Life of.
Gillies' Historical Collections.
Pusey's Historical Enquiry.
Spener (Thomas), Life of; by Hossbach.
Upham's Life of Lady Guion.
Vaughn's Hours with the Mystics.

The controversy on this subject elicited hundreds of books about the beginning of the 18th century, many of which are named by SCHELVIGIUS, above quoted; and still more by WALCH, in his *Einleitung in die religionstreitigk. der evang. Luth. Kirche.*

Pilgrim Fathers.

Backus' Hist. of New England. 1620 to 1804.
Bailey's History of New Plymouth.
Bartlett's Founders of New England.
Bradford's Hist. of Plymouth plantations.
Cheever's Journal of the Plymouth pilgrims in 1620. Reprinted from the original, with notes, 1848.
Christian Disciple. 4:374.
Christian Quart. Spectator. 3:358.
Eclectic Magazine. 5:318.
Elton's Life of Roger Williams.
Hunter's Collections concerning the congregation formed at Scrooby, in England, in the time of James I.
Hutchinson's Colony of Mass'ts. 1628–1691.
——— ——— Continued to 1750.
Knowles' Memoir of Roger Williams.
Matther's Magnalia Dei. 1620 to 1698.
Mial's Footsteps of our Forefathers.
Morse's History of New England.
Neal's History of the Puritans.
New York Review. 9:395.
North Amer. Review. 53:264.
Raffles (Tho.) on the Pilgrim Fathers.
Stéel's Life and times of Brewster.
Uden's New England Theocracy.
Vaughn's (Robt.) Essays on hist. and theol.
Winthrop's (Gov.) Journal. To 1644.
——— History of New England. To 1649.
Young's (A.) Pilgrim Fathers.
——— Chronicles of Massachusetts Bay. 1623 to 1635.

Pilgrimages.

Gregory Nys., Orationes.
Jerome, de Institutio Monachis.

Benzelii Dissertationes Academicæ.
Godsfred ad Codicum Theodosianum.
Gretser de sacris peregrinationibus. Papal.
——— Examen tractatus molinæi.
Heideggeri Diatriba.
Staleni Vind. peregrinantium. Papal.
Wesseling, de Causis peregrinationis Hieros.

Salter's Hall Sermons. Ser. by Dr. Hunt.

Pillar Saints. See SIMONIANS.

Place of Heaven. See HEAVEN.

Broughton's Prospect of futurity.
Carlisle's Station and occupation in heaven.
Doddridge's Lectures. Part 10.
Enty's Reply to Hallet's Notes on Scripture.
Hallet's Notes on Scripture.
Lister's Physico-prophetical Essays.
Watts' Death and Heaven.

Place of the Damned. See HELL.

Blackburn's Review of the controversy concerning the dead.
Broughton's Prospect of futurity. Disc. 4.
Dawes on Hell.
Reynolds' Angelic World.
Swinden on Hell.

Places of Worship.
See CHURCH ARCHITECTURE, WORSHIP.

Ciampini Synopsis hist. de sacris ædificiis de Constantino constructis.
Fabricius de Templis vet. Christianorum.
Hospinian de Origine, progressu, usu, et abusu, templorum.
Siberi Schediasma de templorum ac dedicandorum ritibus.
Voightii Thysiasteriologia.

Bentham's Origin of Christian temples.
Bisse's (Dr. Thomas) Sermons.
Hall's (Robt.) Works. Vol. 3.
Hook's (Walter F.) Sermons.
Mede's Works.
Owen's (James) Temples and Altars.
Sherlock's (Bp.) Sermons.
Sterne's (Lawrence) Sermons.
Trebeck's (Andrew) Sermons.
Wheeler's Primitive Christian temper.

Plagues of Egypt.

Bryant on the Plagues of Egypt.
Stackhouse's History of the Bible.

Planting of Christianity. See APOSTLES, CHRISTIAN ANTIQUITIES, COMMENTATORS ON ACTS, JULIAN, MISSIONS.

Blumhardt's Missions Geschichte.
Buddæi Ecclesia Apostolica.
Bullet, de l'Etabliss. du Christianisme.
Carpzovii de Septem Asiæ ecclesiis.
Cellarii Disputationes Academicæ.
Chateaubriand, Etudes Historiques.
Clerici Hist. eccles. duorum prim. sæculorum.
Crusius de Statu Ephesianorum, ante, in, et post, conversionem.
Fabricii Dux evangelii toti orbi.
Gudeus de Ecclesiæ Ephesianæ statu.
Hartman de Rebus gestis Christianorum sub apostolis. Ch. 7. (Gives the names of the churches planted, &c.)
Kopkii Status Christianor. sub imperator.
Lehmann's (H.) Studien zur gesch. d. apostol. zeitalter.
Manso's Leben Constantin.
Neander's Pflanzung u. Leistung der kirche.
Noack's Ursprung d. Christenthums.
Picteti Diss. de religione Christiana.
Rothe's Anfänge d. christl. kirche.
Schmid (J. A.) Hist. sec. 4. fabulis maculata.
Smithi Septem Asiæ ecclesiarum et Constantinopleos notitia.
Socrates, Historia ecclesiastica.
Sozomen, Historia ecclesiastica.
Stoschius de Ecclesia Thyatarena.
Usserii Dissertatio de Asia, Lydiana, etc.
Volkmann's Ausbreitung des Christenthums.

Apthorpe's (East) Letters. (Very valuable.)
Benson's Planting of the Christian religion. (Dull, but useful as explaining the book of Acts.)
Bingham's Origines Ecclesiasticæ.
Boyle Lectures. 1707,1730,1736,1738.

Planting of Christianity—*continued.*

Bullet's History of the establishment of Christianity. (Compiled from Jewish and Heathen authors only.)
Burton's Eccl. history of the first centuries.
Collinson's Preparation for the Gospel, and its progress, to the end of the 1st century.
Craddock's Apostolical History.
Cureton's Ancient Syriac documents.
Dollinger's Foundation of the Church.
Hale's (Wm.) Origin of the Church in Britain.
Hey's Lectures. Chap. 18.
Hind's Rise and early progress of Christ'y.
Humphreys' Hulsean Lectures. 1851.
Isaacson's Works.
Langton's Rise and progress of Christianity.
Lardner's Jewish and Heathen testimonies.
Littleton on the Conversion of Paul.
Lyall's (W. R.) Design of the Old Testament.
MacKnight on the Truth of Christianity.
Merivale's Boyle Lectures. 1865.
Millar's Hist. of the propagation of Christ'y.
Milman's Hist. of the Church, to the abolition of Paganism in the Roman Empire.
Neander's Planting and training of the Ch.
Povah's (Rich.) Establishment of the Chur.
Schaaf's History of the Apostolic Church.
Smith's (Tho.) Seven churches of Asia.
Thompson on Select passages in the Acts of the Apostles.
Tillemont's Memoires pour servir, etc.
Walch's Ancient coins, medals, and gems.
Watson's Apology for Christianity.
Witherspoon's Works. Lect. 7.
Wright's Early Christianity in Arabia.

Platonism.

Platonis Opera. Ed. Tiedman. 12 v. 8vo. 1781.
——— ——— cum notis. Ast. 10 v. 8vo. 1829.
Ackerman's Christliche im Platon.
Bassnage, Histoire de Juifs. Lib. IV, cap. 4.
Bekkeri (Imm.) Platonis.
Benii Platonis et Aristotelis theologia.
Bessarion in Calumniatorem Platonis.
Crispii de Ethnic. philosoph. caute legendis.
Daille de veterum usu patrum.
Dionysii (Areop.) Opera.
Fabricii (F. A.) Opusculorum Sylloge.
Ficini (M.) Opera.
Fleury (Abbe), Opuscules.
Grotefend, Doct. P. cum chris. comparatur.
Hanchii Diatribe de Enthusiasmo.
Hermann's Gesch. d. Platonischen philos.
Heusdeni Initia philosophiæ Platonicæ.
Janus de Trinitate Platonismi.
Keilii Commentationes. (Sometimes bound up with his Opuscula.)
Le Clerc, Epistolæ Criticæ. Ep. VII.
Lescaloperi Comm. in Ciceronis, lib. de Nat. Deorum.
Loffler, Ueber d. Platonism. d. Kirchenvater.
Meiner's Hist. de doctrinæ de vero Deo.
Porphery de Abstinentia.
Puffendorfii Opuscula.
Souverain, Platonison devoilé.

Platonism—*continued.*

Stallbaum, Platonis opera omnia. (Adds 4 vols. of notes, which are much esteemed.)
Stäudlini (C. F.) Philos. Platon. cum relig. chris. cognitione.
Stein's (H.) Gesch. des Platonismus.
Stephani Theologia Hippocratis.
Tenneman's System der Platonisch. Philos.
Trevnervs de Platonis et Aristotelis.
Vieri Compendium doctrinæ Platonicæ.
Wucherus de Defectis theologiæ Platonicæ.

Ackerman's Christian element in Plato.
Bibliotheca Sacra. 2:527,649.
Brucker's History of Philosophy.
Bull's Defence of the Nicene creed.
Butler's (W. A.) Sermons. (Diss. prefixed.)
Casaubon on Credulity and Incredulity.
Cudworth's Intellectual System. (Mosheim's Latin translation has some admirable notes on this subject.)
Edinburg Review. 123:153.
Hey's (J.) Lectures. Bk. 4.
Lewis' P. against the Atheists. (A comparison between Platonism and some modern theology.)
Mills on the Belief of Plato and Aristotle as to a future state.
Morgan's Effects of P. on the Christian Fathers. ("Admirable."—CONYBEARE.)
New York Review. 9:336.
Ogilvie's Theology of Plato.
Patrick's Mysteries of Plato.
Plato's Works. Tr. by Carey & Davis.
——— ——— Tr. by Dacier.
——— ——— Tr. by Sydenham & Taylor. (Said to be the best edition in English.)
Pond (Enoch) on the Life and influ. of P.
Presbyterian Review. 3:53,378.
Princeton Review. 36:1.
Proclus' Philosophical Commentaries. Tr. by Taylor.
Quarterly Review. 61:256.
Schleiermacher's Introd. to the dialogues of P.
Stanford's Tr. of P. on immortality.
Taylor's (Tho.) Miscellanies.

Many other works on Platonism, and commentaries on the works of Plato, are extant in the principal languages of Europe. Those who desire to consult them, will find a list in TENNIMAN'S *History of philosophy*.

Pleasure. See LOVE OF PLEASURE.

Abernethy's (John) Sermons.
Ashton's (Thomas) Sermons.
Boston's (Tho.) Sermons.
Brown's (John) Sermons.
Cole's (Thomas) Sermons.
Collier's Essays. Part 2.
Dalton's (John) Sermons.
Ferguson's Principles of Moral Science.
Hart's (John) Sermons.
Hoadley's (Bp.) Sermons.
Houghton's (Pendlebury) Sermons.

Pleasure—*continued.*

Hurd's (Bp.) Sermons.
Lucas' (Richard) Posthumous sermons.
Orr's (Dr. John) Sermons.
Pearce's (Bp.) Sermons.
Platt's P. of life examined, and the mistakes respecting pleasure and happiness.
Porteus' (Bp.) Sermons.
Reeve's (William) Sermons.
Seed's (Jeremiah) Sermons.
Sharp's (Gregory, LL.D.) Sermons.
Smith's (S. Stanhope) Sermons.
Tottie's (John) Sermons.
Wesley's (John) Sermons.
Young's (Edward) Centaur not fabulous.

Pleasures of Piety. See WISDOM OF BEING RELIGIOUS.

Abernethy's (John) Sermons.
Atkinson's (Christopher) Sermons.
Baddely's (George) Sermons.
Barnes' (William) Sermons.
Barrow's (Isaac) Sermons.
Bentley's Confutation of Atheism.
Beveridge's (Bp.) Sermons.
Blackley's (Thomas) Sermons.
Burder's (Henry F.) Lectures.
Cookesley's (W. G.) Sermons.
Cooper's (Edward) Sermons.
Enfield's (Wm.) Sermons.
Erskine's (Ralph) Sermons. (5 on this subj.)
Foster's (James) Sermons.
Fothergill's (George) Sermons.
Francklin's (Thomas) Sermons.
Gisbourne's (Thomas) Sermons.
Hammond's (Henry) Sermons.
Henry's (Matt.) Pleasures of a religious life.
Hoadley's (Benjamin) Sermons.
Horneck's (Anthony) Sermons.
Jortin's (John) Sermons.
Killingbeck's (John) Sermons.
Lawson's (Dr. John) Sermons.
Newlin's (Thomas) Sermons.
Newton's (John) Sermons.
Oakes' (John) Sermons.
Pearson's (William) Sermons.
Seed's (Jeremiah) Sermons.
South's (Robert) Sermons.
Stennett's (Samuel) Sermons.
Tillotson's (Abp.) Sermons.
Wesley's (John) Sermons
Wilder's (John) Sermons.

Pluralities. See PATRONAGE.

Black Book, The. (A curious enumeration of the benefices, incomes, &c., in the English Church, as they stood in 1820.)
Christian Observer. 28:438.
Gibson's Codex juris eccles. Anglicani.
Newton's (Rich.) Pluralities indefensible.
Ken's (Bp.) Expostularia; or complaints of the Church of England.
Townsend's Plan for abolishing pluralities.
Wharton's Defence of the Church of England.

Plurality of Worlds.

Pro.

Barel, Discours sur la pluralité, etc. 1657.
Bouvier, sur la Pluralité des Mondes.
Flammarion, la Pluralité des M. habitué.
Fontènelle, sur la Pluralité des Mondes.
Schudt, de Probabilitate mundorum plural.
Brewster's (David) More worlds than one.
Carey's Amer. Museum. 12:241.
Christian Examiner. 57:208.
Copland's Exis. of other worlds, peopled, &c.
Dick's (Thomas) Works.
Dublin Univ. Mag. 44:257. 53:330.
Eclectic Review. New Series. 7:513.
Fontenelle on a Plurality of worlds.
Herschell's (John) Astronomy.
Jacob (W. S.) on the Plurality of worlds.
Jenkins' Reasonableness of Christianity.
London Literary Gazette. 1854.
Nares' Consistency of the notion of a plurality of worlds with the lang. of Scripture.
North British Rev. 21:1.
Powell's (Baden) Inductive philosophy
Presbyterian Review. 3:572.

Con.

Maxwell (Alex.) on a Plurality, &c.
[Whewell's] Plurality of worlds.
——— Dialogue on Do. (Replies to various criticisms on the previous work.)

Plymouth Brethren.

Carson's (James C. L.) Heresies of the P brethren.
Cottles' Strictures on the P. Antinomians.

Podoniptæ. See MENNONITES.

Poetry of the Hebrews.

Aviani Clavis poeseos sacræ.
Barker, Poesis vetus Hebraica restituta.
Beckius de Parallismo membror. in P. Hebr.
Bellerman, einer Metrik der Hebraer.
Bengelii Introd. in Psalmen. (Supplement.)
Clericus [or Le Clerc] de Poesi Hebr.
Danhaveri (J. C.) Oratio Pentecostalis.
Eberti Poetica Hebræica.
Edwards (J.), Prolegomena in Vet. Test.
Eichhorn, de Propheticâ poesi Hebræorum.
Ewald's Poetischen Bücher d. A. T.
Fleury (Abbé) Opuscules.
Genebrand, de Metris Hebræorum.
Gomari Davidis Lyra.
Gügler's Kunst der Hebräer.
Güte Einleitung in die Psalmen.
Herder, Geist der Hebraischen Poesie.
Hermanni Elementa doctrinæ metricæ.
Leutwein's Versuch einer richtigen Theorie von der biblischen Verskunst.
Lowth de Sacra poesi Hebræorum.
Lyseri (P.) Dissertationes.
Meibonii Psal. x et xii Heb. metro restituit.
Mezzer de Poesi Hebraica.
Pfeifferi (A.) Diatribe de poesi Hebræor.
Saalschütz's Form und Geist d. Heb. Poesie.

Poetry of the Hebrews—*continued.*

Schrammii (J. C.) Dissertationes.
Vogel, in Dialectum poeticum V. Test.

Amer. Bibl. Repos. 3d Series. 3:223.
Blackwood's Magazine. 24:917.
Bibliotheca Sacra. 5:58.
Calmet's Dissertations. Trans. by N. Tindal.
Caunter's Poetry of the Pentateuch.
Christian Examiner. 64:74.
Clarke's Hebrew criticism and poetry.
Garnett's Dissertations on the book of Job.
Geist's Spirit of Hebrew poetry.
Gilfillan's Bards of the Bible.
Herder's Oriental Dialogues.
——— Spirit of Heb. poetry. Tr. by Marsh.
Hutchinson's Music of the Bible.
Jebb's (Bp.) Sacred Literature. (Controverts many of the criticisms of Lowth.)
Keble (John) on Sacred poetry.
Kitto's Journal. 1:94,295.
Knickerbocker Mag. 6:189.
Lowth's Sacred Poetry of the Hebrews.
——— Confutation of Bp. Hare's system of Hebrew meter.
Month. Rev. 114:143.
New Eng. Mag. 1:97.
North Am. Rev. 31:337. 35:473. 63:201.
Palfrey's (J. G.) Academical Lectures.
Princeton Rev. 2:323. 3:429.
Quar. Rev. 32:211. 78:13.
Sarchi's Hebrew poetry, ancient and modern.
Taylor's Spirit of Hebrew poetry. (An admirable work to be read in connection with Lowth and Gilfillan.)
Williams on the Song of Solomon. (Introd.)

Polemic Theology. See CONTENDING FOR THE FAITH, HIST. OF DOCTRINES.

Affelmanni Syntagma exercitat. academicar.
Alberti Interesse præcip. relig. Christianor.
Alstedii Theologia Polemica.
Altingii Theologia Elenchtica Nova.
Arnoldi Lux in Tenebris.
Baumgarten (S. J.) Begriff d. theol. Streitigk.
Beckmani Theologia Polemica.
Bellarmin (Card.), Disputationes. ("The most acute, comprehensive, and candid of Papal controversialists."—BP. MARSH.)
Buddei Programma de theol. polem. studio.
Callixti Judicium de controversiis theologus.
——— Disputationes de præcipuis Chris. relig. capitibus.
Calovii de Modo docendi et disputandi.
Carpzovii Disputationes Academicæ.
Dannhaveri Polemosophia.
Essenii Synopsis controversiarum theolog.
Foerstchius de moderatione in controversiis.
Franzii Syntagma controv. theol. Disp. XII.
Gerhardi (Ernest.) Sylloge theologicarum.
Gerhardi (Io.) Disputat. theologicarum.
Hoenegg, de Disputationibus theologicis.
Himmellii Methodus tractandarum controv. theologicæ.
Hoornbeckii Summa controv. religionis.
Hulsii Systema controversiarum theolog.

Polemic Theology—*continued.*

Hunnii Disputationes Theologicæ.
Krackewitsii Disp. de præc. capitibus, etc.
Laurentius de publicis disputationibus, et controv. de religione.
Le Vassor de la Maniere d'examiner les differens de religion.
Loescheri Prenotiones Theologicæ.
Melancthonis Consilium de moderandis controversiis relig. *Acta eruditor.*
Mosheimius de Theolog. non contentioso.
——— Streittheologie.
Muratorius de Ingeniorum negotio.
Neumani Theologia Aphoristica.
Olearii Synopsis controv. selectiorum.
Osiandri Enchiridion controv. religionis.
Petavii Theologia Polemica.
Pfaffius de Prejudiciis theologicis.
Prideaux, Manductio ad theolog. polemicam.
Quistorpii Aphorismi.
Reinhardi Theologia polemica.
Rumpæi Introductio in theol. controversar.
Sack's Christliche Polemik.
Schuberti Institutiones theol. polemicæ.
Schulteti Steroma doctrinæ evangelicæ.
Sirmondi Opera. (A very extensive collection of patristic and other treatises.)
Spanheimii Elenchus controversiarum.
Stapferi Inst. theolog. polemicæ universæ. ("Luculentum."—WALCH. "A masterpiece."—WILLIAMS.)
Turretini Institutiones theol. elencticæ.
Usher, Hist. controv. inter orthod. et pontif.
Van Till, Πρῶτα ψεύδη adversariorum.
Vitringæ Hypotyposis Theologiæ.
Vossii (G. J.) Hist. de Controversiis.
Weidneri Collegium disput. theologicum.
Wernsdorf, de Fervore, tepore, et frigore, theol.
Wildeshausen Biblioth. Disp. theologicæ.
Witsii Oratio de theologo-modesto.

Bechman's Polemic Theology.
Chemnitz's Exam. of the Council of Trent.
Fabricius' Consid. of various controversies.
Hagenbach's History of doctrines.
Hey's (Dr. J.) Lectures. Bk. 2, ch. 1.
Luther's Works. (Generally.)
Miller's Compend of polemic theology.
Mosheim's Controversies of Christians.
Osiander's Manual of controversies.
Schmidt's Breviary.
Schubert's Institutes of polemic theology.
Van Mildert's Bampton Lectures. 1814.
Wolfang on Religious Controversy.

Political Economy. See CIVIL GOVERNMENT, PROPERTY, SOCIALISM.

Baudrillart, Etudes de philosophie morale.
Blanqui, Hist. de l'economie pol. en Europe.
Colins, Science sociale.
Julius, Vorles. über die Gefangnisskunde.
Le Lievre, Principes Economique.
Roscher, Principes d'Economie politique.
Rossi, Cours d'Econ. politique. 1841.
Roussell, les Nations Catholiques et Protestants comparé. 1854.

Political Economy—*continued.*

Say, Traité d'Economie politique. 1815.
Sismondi, Nouveau Principes, etc.
Storch, Cours d'Econ. politique. 1823.

American Quart. Review. 1:309. 2:47.
Atkinson's Principles of P. Econ. as developed by the Christian law of government.
Bailey's (S.) Political Economy and Morals.
Bastiat's Harmonies of Political Economy.
Beddome's State of nations, past and present.
Bentham's Chrestomathia.
——— on Civil legislation.
Blackwood's Magaz. 12:505. 15:222. 16:34. 17:207. 26:510. 27:22.
Bowen's Principles of Political Economy.
Broadhurst's Political Economy.
Brougham's (Lord) Four Essays. 1818.
Burton's Polit. and Social Economy. 1849.
Carey's (H. C.) Principles of P. Econ. 1837.
——— Harmony of interests.
——— Rate of wages.
——— (Other treatises.)
Cantillon's Analysis of trade, coin, &c., 1759, as developed by Christian law.
Chalmer's (Tho.) Political Economy.
Cobbett's Political works. 1801.
Cooper's (Tho.) Lectures on Polit. Economy.
Corbaux on a National debt.
Craig's Elements of Political science.
De Quincy's Logic of Political Economy.
Democratic Review. 8:291.
Deponté's Social Reform in England. 1806.
De Tocqueville's Democracy in Amer. 1830.
Dick's (And. C.) Nature and offices of the state.
Dove's Elements of Political Economy.
Edinburg Review. 52:337. 56:52. 57:1. 73:29. 85:223.
Edmonds' (T.) Political Economy. 1828.
Evans' Political institutions of America.
Federalist, The. 1788.
Foreign Quart. Review. 15:241.
Franklin's (Ben.) Works.
Ganilh on the Various syst. of P. E. 1812.
Gibbons' (Alex.) Nature of taxation.
Humphrey's Manual of Political science.
Innis' (Wm.) Political Economy.
Joplin's (T.) System of Political Economy.
Laing on the Causes and remedies of national distress.
Lauderdale's Nature and origin of public wealth. 1804.
Lawson's Political Economy.
Lawton's (Edward) Lectures. Lect. 3.
Lieber's Essay on property and labor.
——— Political Ethics. 1840.
——— Political Hermeneutics.
Liszt's National system of P. Economy.
Macinnon's Wealth and power of nations.
Macleod's (H. D.) Elements of P. E. 1858.
McCulloch's (J. R.) Principles of P. E. 1824.
——— Influences of taxation and the funding system.
McCullogh's (W. T.) Industrial history of free nations.

Political Economy—*continued.*

Macindoe's Application of Scripture principles to Government essential to prosperity.
McIniscon's Principles of P. Economy.
McVickar's Outlines of P. Economy. 1825.
Maitland's Nat. and origin of pub. wealth.
Malthus' Principles of Political Economy.
Mills' (J.) Elements of Political Economy. (A good school-book.)
Mills (J. S.) on Unsettled questions. 1821.
More's (Sir Tho.) Utopia.
Newman's Lectures on Political Economy.
New York Review. 3:1.
North Amer. Review. 47:73.
North Brit. Review. 2:1.
Ouseley's Political institutions of America.
Pamphleteer. 11:403. 17:289. (Political economy of the Bible. 29:33.)
Purvess (G.) on National wealth.
Rae's Political Economy.
Ramsay (G.) on the Distribution of wealth.
Reed (S.) on National wealth.
Ricardo's Principles of Political Economy.
Ross' Examination of the opinions of several writers on Political Economy.
Say's (J. B.) Political Economy.
Scrope's Elements of Polit. Economy. 1833.
Sedwick's (Theod.) Public and private econ.
Seward's (W. H.) Works. 1855.
Smith's Causes of the Wealth of nations.
Spence's Tracts on political economy.
Stuart's (James) Principles of P. E. 1770.
Thompson on the Distribution of wealth
Torrens on the Production of wealth.
Tracey's (De Strut) Political economy.
Urquehart's Wealth and Want.
Vethake's Principles of Political Economy.
Walch's Review. 4:306.
Wayland's Elements of Political Economy.
Webster's (P.) Essays; published during the American war, and to the present time. 1791.
Westminster Review. 84:48.
Weyland's Population and production as affected by the progress of Society.
Williams' (Nassau) Political economy.
Yates' (R.) Basis of national welfare.

The European Bibliography of this subject may be found in the 2d vol. of BLANQUI, *Hist. de l'Economie politique en Europe.* 1842.

Politeness. See CLERICAL HABITS, COURTESY.

Chesterfield's Letters to his son.
Hogg's Lay Sermons.
Knox's (Vicessimus) Sermons.
Miller's Letters to a young clergyman.
Trusler's Principles of politeness.

Political Responsibility.

Am. Bibl. Repos. 3d Series. 2:602.
Am. Quar. Observer. 1:1.
Am. Whig Rev. 14:357.
Bates' (Ely) Christian politics. (Highly praised in the CHRISTIAN OBSERVER.)

Political Responsibility—*continued.*

Baxter's (Rich.) Christian Directory.
Bibliotheca Sacra. 23:73.
Bullar's (John) Lay Lectures. Lect. 10.
Christ. Exam. 10:327. 26:32.
Christmas' (Henry) Christian Politics. (Reviews Paley.)
Croxall's Scripture Politics.
Cunningham's (J.) Political duties of ministers in times of great national excitement.
Democratic Rev. 24:99.
Dury (John) On ministers meddling with State matters, in or out of their sermons.
Eclectic Mag. 3:145.
Eclectic Rev. 4th Series. 8:401. New Series. 1:148.
Edinb. Rev. 73:29.
Frazier's Mag. 14:657. 15:423. 34:618.
Gresley's (William) Sermons.
Hague's Christianity and Statesmanship.
Lieber's Manual of political ethics.
Miall's Politics of Christianity.
Month. Rev. 108:365.
Morier's What has relig. to do with politics?
New England Mag. 1:142.
North British Rev. 6:133,256.
Robinson's (Robt.) Miscellaneous Works.
Sewall's (Wm.) Christian Politics.
Sheppard's (John G.) Christian obligations of citizenship.

Polycarp. See FATHERS.

Polycarpi Epistola ad Philippenses.
Balthasaris Doctrina Polycarpi.
——— Vita Polycarpi.
Bullialdi Dissertationes.
Cottelerii Patres Apostolicæ.
Crucigeri Oratio de Polycarpi vita.
Groddeck, de Anno passionis P.
Kortholtus de Persecutione eccl. primævæ.
Moyne, Prolegomena ad varia sancta.
Nourrii Dissertatio de Epistola P.
Ruinarti Acta sincera martyrum.
Tentzelii (G. E.) Exercitationes.
Usseri Dissertationes.

Cave's Translation of P.'s epistle.
Chevalier's Translation of the epistle of P.
Clementson's New trans. of the epistle of P.
Elborowe's Epistles of Polycarp & Ignatius, with their lives and deaths.
Wake's Epistles of the Fathers.

Polygamy. See MARRIAGE, MORMONS.

Pro.

Freudenhoefer's Eroerterung der Frage, etc.
Lyser, Kurtzes Gespräch von der P.
——— Discursus de P. (Answers replies.)
Madan's Thelypthora.
Willenbergii Præsidia juris Divini.
——— Schediasma de Finibus polygamiæ licitæ.

Burnet's (G.) Defence of polygamy.
Hanger's Life and opinions.

Con.

Bezæ Tractationes Theologicæ. Vol. 2.

Polygamy—*continued.*

Con.

Calovii (Abr.) Disputationes.
Heideggeri Historia Patriarcharum.
[Lyserus] Kurtzes Gespræch von der P.
Michaelis (J. D.) Paralipomena.
Musæi (Io.) Dissertationes.
Puffendorf de Jure.
Seldeni Uxor Hebraicas.
Wernsdorfii Doctrina de polygamia.
Zeidler, Tractatio de polygamia.

Baxter's Works.
Beattie's Elements of moral science.
——— On the attachments of kindred.
Bowers' History of the Popes.
Cookson on Polygamy.
Delany's Reflections on Polygamy.
Doddridge's Lectures. Part 3, prop. 59.
Dunton's Young Student's Library.
Dwight's (Tim.) System of theol. Ser. 121.
Dwight's (S. E.) Hebrew Wife.
Haweis' Refutation of Thelypthora.
Hill's Blessings of P. (Replies to Madan.)
Lit. and Theol. Rev. 4:182.
Monthly Rev. Vol. 63. (2 capital articles.)
Ochinu's Dialogues. Trans. from the Italian.
Paley's Moral Philosophy. Book 3, part 3.
Palmer's Exam. of Thelypthora.
Penn's Remarks on Thelypthora.
Salmon on Marriage.
Shorthose's (Hugh) Sermons.
Smith's Polygamy indefensible.
Towers' (J.) Polygamy unscriptural.
Wills' (T.) Remarks on P. (Rep. to Madan.)

Polytheism. See IDOLATRY, MYTHOLOGY.

Pool of Bethesda.

Arnold, Dissertationes philologicæ.
Frischmuthi Dissertatio Philologica.
Outrein de Piscina probatica. (In Biblioth.)
Wendeler, Dissert. de Piscina probatica, etc.
Witsii Miscellanea Sac. Exercit. XI, cap. 54.

Hall's (Bp.) Contemplations. Book 4, sec. 11.
Jennings' Jewish Antiquities.
Kollock's Sermons.
Latter-Day Luminary. Periodical. Vol. 2.

Poor Laws. See POLITICAL ECONOMY, PAUPERISM.

Amer. Quart. Review. 14:66.
Analytical Mag. 2:17. 10:265.
Blackwood's Mag. 8:1. 9:217,563. 10:49,509. 11:133,373. 13:113. 16:457. 23:923. 33:811. 43:489. 51:518. 60:555. 61:261.
Bosanquet's Rights of the poor.
British and For. Rev. 4:1.
Chalmer's (Tho.) Political economy.
——— Sufficiency of parochial relief without poor laws.
Christian Observer. 17:30,236.
Cooper's (Sam.) Definitions and axioms.
Dublin Univ. Mag. 30:606. 33:215,340,401, 656.
Dunlop on the Poor law of Scotland.
Ellis (Wm.) on Education.

Poor Laws—*continued.*

Edinburg Rev. 6:160. 22:181. 33:91. 36:110. 47:303. 59:227. 63:256. 74:1. 75:253. 77:207. 84:139.
Frazier's Mag. 9:507. 70:373.
Mahon (J.) on Poor laws.
Martineau's (H.) Poor laws and Paupers.
Monthly Review. 87:201. 102:181. 121:309. 129:495. 130:593.
Nichols' Hist. of English poor laws. 1854.
——— " Scotch " 1855.
——— " Irish " 1856.
North Brit. Rev. 2:471. 12:21.
Page's Principle of the English poor laws.
Pamphleteer. 8:385. 9:217,563. 10:49,509. 11:133,373,551. 13:113. 21:391.
Parliamentary Reports of England.
Pashley's Pauperism and the poor laws.
Quarterly Rev. 8:319. 14:120. 18:259. 19:79. 28:351. 33:429. 48:320. 50:347. 52:123. 53:249.
Reports of the P. law commissioners in Eng.
Richards' (Geo.) Sermons. (The immoral effect of poor laws.)
Sedgwick on the Repeal of poor laws.
Torrens' Poor laws of Ireland.
Westminster Rev. 18:427. 26:357.

Poor Men of Lyons. See WALDENSES.

Pope Joanne.

Pro.

Artopoei Dissertationes.
Bassnage, Histoire de l'eglise.
Blasci, Diatribe de Joanna papissa.
Capelli (Rudolph) Discursus Historicus.
Carionis, Chronicon.
Congnard, Traité si une femme? etc.
Cook, la Papesse Jeanne.
Deckerus de Papa et Papissa Romana.
Ehinger's altes und neues Pabstthum.
Grim's Panselicke Heiligheit.
Kleine's (G.) Papstinn Johanna keine Fabel.
Lehmanni Infelix puerpera Joannes VIII.
L'Enfant; Histoire de la Papesse Joan.
Maresii Joanna papissa, restituta.
Montagne, la Papesse Jeanne.
Nichols' vom Pabst Johanne.
Papa Mulier; sive vera narratio de P. Jo.
Platinæ Vita Christi ac Pontificum omnium. (All that relates to Pope Joanne was suppressed after the first edition.)
Smetz, Mährchen von der Pap. Johanna.
Spanheimii (F.) Disquisitiones historiæ. (Highly commended.)
Voetii Spicelegium.
Wagenseilii Dissertatio de Joanna Papissa. (Gives a candid view of the arguments on both sides.)
Witekindi Jesuitæ.

Cook's Dialogue concerning P. J. (Proofs from Popish writers.)
Mayo's Pope's Parliament.
North British Review. 12:192.
Rutherford on Church Gov. Ch. 8, sec. 8.

Pope Joanne—*continued.*

Pro.

Toplady's (Aug. M.) Works.
Ware's Pope Joan. (Proofs from **Romish** authors previous to Luther.)

Con.

Allatii Confutatio fabulæ, etc.
Baronii Annales. ("Makes havoc of primitive history."—DOWLING.)
Bayle, Dictionaire. Art. *Papesse.*
Bellarmini Opera.
Blondell, Eclaircissement de la question.
Eckhardt, Hist. Franciæ Orient. Lib. XXX.
Heumani Dissertatiônes Sacræ. Par. II.
Labbei Cenotaphium Joannæ.
Leibnitzii Flores sparsi in tumulum Papissæ.
Maresius [or Maret] de Papissa.
Palthenius de Papissa.
Raymond, Erreur populaire de la Papesse.
Schottii Physica curiosa. (Numerous curious dissertations on curious themes.)

Littell's Living Age. 25:193. (The same as in North British Review.)
North British Review. 12:354. (Adduces the arguments pro and con.)

Various writers of eminence mention the female Pope as a fact of history, without discussing the proofs—such as Marian, a Scotch monk, 1060; Martin Polaccus, Abp. of Cosenza, 1277; Amabric, an Augustine Prior, 1362; and Korner, a Dominican, 1435. See a collection of the arguments by all the principal writers who reject the story of Pope Joanne, in Allatius, named above.

Popery. See ABSOLUTION, AURICULAR CONFESSION, ANTICHRIST, CELIBACY, COUNCIL OF TRENT, DECRETALS, IMAGES, INDULGENCES, INFALLIBILITY, JUSTIFICATION, KEYS OF THE CHURCH, MASS, MIRACLES, PENANCE, PERSECUTION, POPES, PRAYER FOR THE DEAD, PROPHECY, PURGATORY, REFORMATION, RELICS, SUPREMACY, SACRAMENTS, TRANSUBSTANTIATION.

Pro.

The symbolical books of the Roman Church are: The Decrees and Catechism of the Council of Trent, and the Symbol of Pius IV.
Arnauld, Œuvres. (Powerful. Boileau calls him "the most learned man that has ever written.")
Arsdekini Theologia Universa. (A great storehouse of authorities.)
Becani Manuale Controversiarum.
Beelingii Vindiciæ Catholicæ Hiberniæ.
Bellarmini Opera. (In the judgment of Bayle, the ablest defender of the Roman Church.)
Bossuet, Expos. de la doct. de l'Eglise.
——— Hist. des variations de l'Eglise Protestantes. (Numerous other treatises, in the 59 volumes of his works.)
Cassandri Defensio traditionum Patrum.
Catharini Apologia pro veritate fidei.

Popery—*continued.*

Campiani Rationes propositæ in causam fidei. ("The Romanists account it an epitome of all their doctrine."—A. WOOD.)
Cochlæus cont. Augustinam confessionem.
——— de Actis et scriptis Lutheri.
Cotoni Institutio Catholica.
D'Antecourt, Defense de l'Eglise.
Dens, Manuale Theologicum.
Dollinger's Kirche und Kirchen.
Emser's Wieder das unchristliche Buch M. Luther.
Fabri Antilogiarum Lutheri Babylonia.
Haunoldus de Infallibilitate eccles. Romanæ.
Henrici VIII, Assertio septem sacramentorum adversus Mart. Lutherum.
Hosii Conf. Cathol. (A standard authority.)
Mesnilii Doctrina et disciplina ecclesiæ.
Nicolas, du Protestantisme précédé de l'examen d'un ecrit. de M. Guizot.
Pole pro Unitate Ecclesiastica.
Rocaberti Bibliotheca. (A collection, in 21 volumes, folio, of the principal papal writers previous to 1700.)
Sardagna, Theologia dogmatico-polemico.

Balmez's Comparison of Prot. and Popery, in their effects on civilization.
Berrington & Kirk's Faith of the Catholics.
Bossuet's Doctrine of Catholic Church.
——— Variations of Protestant Churches.
Brownson's Quarterly Review.
Butler's (Chas.) Book of the Church.
——— Vindication of Do.
Campian's Ten reasons for embracing the Catholic faith.
Catholic World. Periodical.
Chaloner's Grounds of the old religion.
Den's Moral Theology. (Standard work.)
Dollinger's Church and the Churches. Trans. by McCabe.
Dupin on Ecclesiastical and temporal power.
Fisher's (John) Challenge to Protestants.
——— Conference with Abp. Laud.
Gother's Papist misrepresented.
Husenbeth's Faberism exposed and refuted.
Keeling's Alliance of heresy with Deism.
Kellison's Gag of the deformed gospel.
——— Examen Reformationis.
——— Hierarchy of the Church.
Kerrick's (Bp.) Primacy of the Apostolic see.
Knott's Infidelity unmasked. (Reply to Chillingworth.)
——— Protestantism unrepented destroys salvation.
Lingard's Review of anti-Catholic publicat.
Milner's (John) End of relig. controversy.
Stapleton's (Thos.) Works.
Ward's Errata of the Protestant Bible.
Worseley's Protestantism without principles.
White's (Alex.) Confutation of Church-of-Englandism.

Con.

Albert's Wiederlegung einer Pæbstichen Bucher.

Popery—*continued.*

Con.

Amesii (The Puritan) Bellarminus enervatus.
Antonii Pontificiorum doctrina publica.
Balduini Diatriba Theologicæ.
Bassnage, Traité des prejuges faux et legit.
——— Hist. des Eglises reformés. (Answers Bossuet's "Variations.")
Baur's Gegensatz des Katholicismus und Protestanten.
Baxteri Clavis Catholicorum.
Bezæ Opera.
Beyer's Unterscheidungslehren d. Evang. u. Rom. Kirche.
Botsacci Demonstratio quod Ecclesia Romano papistica non sit sancta.
Bucer adv. Axioma Catholicum.
Buddei Miscellanea Sacra.
Bullengerii Antithesis evangelicæ et papisticæ doctrinæ.
Bungener, Rome et le cœur humaine.
Calovii Matæologia Papistica.
Calvini Institutiones.
Capelli Disputationes.
Cassandri Consult. de artic. religione inter Catholicos et Protestantes controversis.
Chamieri Panstratiæ Catholicæ. ("A perfect encyclopedia on all subjects relating to the Popish controversy."—PALMER.)
Coci Censura quorundum scriptorum qui a Pontificiis citari solent. (A most convenient work.)
Cranmeri Defensio veræ et Catholicæ doctr.
Dallæi Opera. (Voluminous and powerful.)
Danhaveri Opera.
Dassovii Disputationes.
De Croy de les Trois conformites, etc.
Deyling, de Insignioribus Rom. ecclesia variationibus.
Dominis (De) de Republica ecclesiastica. ("Of great use."—FULLER. "One of the most illustrious victims of the Inquisition."—PEIGNOT.)
Drelincourt, Abrégée des controverses.
Dresseri Observationes miscellaneæ.
Drieri Controversiæ precipuæ.
Eckhardi Pandectæ Controversiarum.
Flacii Com. de Synodo VI Carthaginensi.
——— Historia de primatu Papæ.
——— Protestatio contra Conc. Tridentum.
——— Catalogus testium veritatis.
——— Various other treatises.
Franckii Dissertationes.
Furmanni Sanctitatis eccl. Rom. eversio.
Gaupp, die Romische Kirche.
Gomari Enchiridion controversiarum.
Guntheri Demonstratio solida.
Haberkorn's Gründlichen Wiederlegung.
Heilbrunner's (J.) Uncatholisch. Pabsthum.
Heshusius de Erroribus Pontificiæ ecclesiæ.
——— de Vera Ecclesia.
Hieronymi (Pragensis) Opera. (Noble.)
Hinckelmanni Papismi errores præcipui.
Hoenegg's Evangelisches Handbüchlein.
Hoepfneri Saxonia Evangelica.

Popery—*continued.*

Con.

Hospiniani Opera. (Learned elucidations of the *history* of the errors of Popery.)
Hunnii Opera. (Greatly prized.)
Hussi (Ioann.) Scripta.
Illyrici Opera. (Discusses most of the points in controversy.)
Illyrici Catalogus testium veritatis. (Written to show what learned and pious men had admitted concerning the corruption of the Roman Church, before Luther.)
Jameson, Roma-racoviana, et Racovia-rom.
James (Tho.), Bellum Papale. (Shows 2000 instances in which the two "infallible" Papal editions of the Vulgate contradict each other.)
Jewelli Apologia Ecclesiæ Anglicanæ.
Jurieu, Systéme de l'Eglise.
——— la Morale des Reformés.
Kesleri Bellum religiosum Petri ac Papæ.
Koecheri Biblioth. Theol. Symbol. (List of authors against the Council of Trent.)
——— Observationes Selectæ.
Kortholti Papa Schismaticus.
——— Disquisitionés.
Krackewitzius de Ecclesiæ Rom. apostasia.
Kromayer, de Ecclesiæ Romanæ apostasia.
La Motte, les Fourberies de l'Eglise.
Le Blanc, Theses Theologicæ.
Leopard (C.), Le Glaive du géant Goliah. (Highly commended.)
Leydekker de Veritate religionis Reformatæ.
Lutherus, Opera varia.
Maccovii Πρωτον ψευδος Pontificiorum.
Magnin, La Papautè considerée dan son origine, development, et etat actuel. 1841
Megandri Petrus nec papa nec papistica.
Meisneri (Balthas.) Consultatio Catholica.
——— Prælectiones.
Meisneri (Jo.) Dissertationes.
Melancthonis Opera.
Molinæi Jugulum causæ pontificiæ.
Morgenstern, de Eccl. vera et Catholica.
Mori Inquisitio in mysterium iniquitatis.
——— Antidotus adversus Idolatriam.
——— Magni mysterii pietatis explanatio.
Mornæi (Phil.) Tractatus de ecclesia.
——— Mysterium Iniquitatis.
Mylii Disquisitiones theologicæ de ecclesia.
Neumannus de Petro a Petro alieno.
——— Dissertationes.
Osiandri Opera. ("Papa non papa." "De antichristus," etc.)
Pfaffii Demonstrationes solidæ.
Pictet, la Religion des Protestants.
Placette, Œuvres. (Greatly esteemed.)
Puffendorf, von der geistliche Monarchie.
Rainoldus de Romanæ eccl. idolatria.
Richter's Evangelische und Roemische Kirchen Lehre.
Riveti Catholicum orthodoxum.
Salmasius de Episcopiis et Presbyteris.
Scherzeri Dissertationes Theologicæ.
Schmidii (Sebast.) Syncresis.

Popery—*continued.*

Con.

Schmidii (Sebast.) Petrus non Papa.
Schulteti Panoplia Sacra.
——— Medulla theologica patrum.
Seldii Papismi et gentilismi comparatio.
Spanheimii (Senior.) Epitome panstratiæ chamieri.
Spanheimii (Junior.) Dissertationes.
Speneri Opera varia.
Steinbergii Anatome papismi.
Stillingfleet, Opera varia.
Taxe, des Parties casuelles de la boutique du Pape. (A damning exposure of corruptions as existing in 1564.)
Turretini (Alph.) Pyrrhonismus Pontificius.
Turrettini (Franc.) Institutiones.
Usseri Hist. controv. inter orthodos et pont.
Van Till, de Petro non Pontifice.
Viret, la Physique papale.
——— la Nécromance papale.
Voetii Disputationes Theol. Pars 1.
Vorstii Anti-Bellarminus.
Wylie's Geschichte, Lehren, Geist, und Aussichten des Papstthums. (Prize essay.)
Zuinglii Opera.

Abbott's Roman and English hierarchies, and the abuses of Episcopacy.
Achilli's Papal Rome, her priests and her Jesuits.
Abernethy's Letters to Bp. Hay.
About, The Roman question. Translated by A. T. Wood.
Allwood's Prophecies relating to the Church.
——— Papal Claims.
Amer. Biblical Repository. 2:546. 4:252. 11:363. 2d Series. 10:159. 3d Series. 4:252.
Amer. Eclectic Review. 2:446.
Ame's (The Puritan) Reply to Bellarmin.
Ashwell on the Roman Church.
Bagge's Development of the Roman system not consistent with the welfare of the state.
Balme's Protest. and Popery compared, in their effects on the civilization of Europe.
Barbeyrac's Spirit of the Ecclesiastics.
Barlow's Principles and positions of the Church of Rome.
Barnard's Rhemes against Rome.
Barrow's (Isaac) Works.
Baxter's (Richard) Works.
Beard's (John R.) The Confessional. (Extracts from Papal sources.)
Beecher's (Edw.) Papal conspiracy exposed.
Becon's Display of the Popish Mass.
Bedell's (Bp.) Life and Letters.
Bell's (James) The Mystery unveiled.
Bennet's (W. J. E.) Distinctive errors of Popery.
Bennet's (Tho.) Confutation of Popery.
Bentley's (Rich.) Doctrinal corruptions of Popery.
Beza's Ten discourses.
——— Patched Pelagianism.
Bibliotheca Sacra. 2:451,757. 8:64.

Popery—*continued.*

Con.

Bicheno's Signs of the times. 1805.
Birbeck's Protestant's evidence. (From the Fathers.)
Blackmoor on the Present state of the controversy between Protestants and Papists. 1765.
Blackwood's Edinb. Magaz. 3:535. 25:331. 44:494.
Blair's Letters to Wilberforce.
Blakeney's Awful disclosure of the principles taught by the Church of Rome: being extracts from the Moral theology of Alphonsus Liguori.
Boyd's Fathers not Papists.
Bramhall's Safeguards against Popery. (A great collection of treatises by eminent divines of the 17th century.)
Bray's Papal Usurpation in anc. and mod. times. (Contains much curious matter, especially in relation to ye old Waldenses.)
Brit. and For. Review. 6:420. 7:457. 8:1.
Brogden's Catholic Safeguards. (A very large collection of tracts by distinguished writers of the 17th century.)
Brownlee on the Rom. Catholic controversy.
——— Popery an enemy to civil liberty.
Bull's Corruptions of the Church of Rome.
Burnap's Superstitions of the Ch. of Rome.
Burnett's (Bp.) Discourses.
Burroughs' (Joseph) Creed of Pope Pius IV.
Burton's Truth's triumph over Trent.
Campbell's (John) Popery; anc. and mod.
Capper's Acknowledged doctrines of the Church of Rome, as set forth by its standard writers. 1849.
Cardwell's Enchiridion. (A collection of important tracts in 3 volumes.)
Cartwright's Pope's deadly wound.
——— Sermons at the Jews' Chapel.
Cheever on the Mixture of civil and eccles. power. (Reply to Bp. Hughes of N. York.)
Chillingworth's Safe way to heaven. ("That masterpiece of human reasoning."—Warburton.)
Christian Examiner. 2:353. 14:371. 39:284. 48:227,341. 56:223. 65:1.
Churchman Armed. (A collection of effective treatises.)
Clagget's (William) Works.
Clarkson's Practical divinity of Papists destructive of Christianity.
Claude's Posthumous Works.
Cobbin's (Ingram) Book of Popery.
Collette's Novelties of Romanism.
——— Popish frauds exemplified in Dr. Wiseman's Lectures.
Comber's Forgeries in the Councils of the first four centuries.
Cox's (John E.) Protestantism contrasted with Popery. (Consists of quotations from authors on both sides.)
Cramp's Text-book of P. (Very useful.)
Cranmer's Works.

Popery—*continued.*

Con.

Croft's (Bp.) Naked Truth.
Culbertson's Lectures on the Apocalypse.
Cullen's (J. E.) Voice of truth. (Small, but effective.)
Cunningham's Apostacy of the Ch. of Rome.
Curtis' Mystery of Iniquity.
Dalton's Word of God vindicated.
De Coetlogon's Sermons.
De Croy's Harmony of the Roman Church with Gentilism, Judaism, and ancient heresies.
De Foe's Curse of Popery. (Powerful.)
De Sanctis' Rome. (As in 1857.)
Dillingham's Mystery of Iniquity.
Dodwell's Fundamental principles of P.
Drelincourt's Summary of Popish errors.
Dublin University Mag. 7:437. 12:548,686. 16:197,511. 23:715. 36:494. 38:369,719.
Du Moulin's Keys of the Church.
——— History of Monks.
——— Defence of the Reformed churches.
Eclectic Review. 4th Series. 11:103. 22:299. 29:97. 30:296. New Series. 6:33.
Edgar's Variations of Popery. (Very able.)
Edinburg Rev. 72:119.
Elliot's (Charles) Delineation of Romanism. (Drawn from acknowledged standards of the Papal Church.)
Elliott's (E. B.) Warburton Lectures. 1856.
Emlin's Frauds of monks and priests.
Enchiridion Theologicum. (Tracts by Taylor, Barrow, &c.)
Erskine's Spirit of Popery.
Evangelical Review. 1:561.
Evans' (B.) Modern Popery. 1855.
Faber's Difficulties of Romanism.
Fleming's (Robt.) Apocalyptical Key.
Fletcher's (Jos.) Works. (His Lectures on Popery are highly praised by Robert Hall and J. Pye Smith.)
Foreign Quarterly Rev. 27:184. 1:515.
Foulis' History of Romish treasons and usurpations, collected out of their own approved authors.
Fox's Book of Martyrs.
Foye's Romish offices, legends, &c., literally translated.
Fulke's Rhemish and Prot. translations of New Test. side by side; with a confutation, &c. (Embodies the whole Popish controversy respecting the Scriptures.)
Garbett's Nullity of the Roman faith.
Gautt's P. the man of sin. (Prize ess. 1854.)
Gavin's Master Key to Popery.
Geddes' Miscellaneous Tracts.
Gibbings' P. falsifications of records.
Gibson's Preservatives against P. (The treatises are mostly those published during the reign of James II. The whole 18 vols. have been lately reprinted.)
——— Supplement to Do. 8 vols. 1849.
Gilley's Vigilantius and his times.
Gray's Bampton Lectures. 1796.

Popery—*continued.*

Con.

Giustiniani's Papal Rome. (Dr. G. was a Romish priest.)
Gordon's (J.) Lives of Alexander VI. and his son, Cesar Borgia.
Gordon's (W.) Popery against Christianity. (Describes the condition of the City of Rome in 1719.)
Grier's Ans. to Milner's End of controversy.
Groser's (W.) Lectures at Maidstone.
Glanvill's Less heeded dangers of Popery. 1681.
Gurney's (John H.) Sermons at St. Mary's.
Halifax's 12 Sermons on prophecy.
Hall's (Bp.) Polemic Works.
Hamilton's (Archibald) Tracts.
Harness' Errors of the Roman Creed.
Harrison's (E.) Protestant Instructor.
Heshusius On the true Church.
Horne's (T. H.) P. the enemy and falsifier of Scripture.
——— Popery delineated. (As in 1848.)
Horneck's Tracts.
Howell's (L.) View of the Pontificate.
Howick's Triple Crown.
Hulme's Comparison of P. and Christianity.
Jackson's (Dr. Tho.) Works. ("I have not read so hearty and vigorous a champion against Rome."—Geo. Herbert. "The most valuable of all our English divines." —Robt. Southey.)
James' Corruptions of the Councils, Fathers, and Scriptures, for the maintenance of P.
——— Defense of the Bellum Papale.
——— Table of books first approved and then censured by Papists.
Jewell's Apol. for the Church. (Powerful.)
Johnson's Julian. (Learned, but violent.)
Jurieu's Council of Trent.
——— Pastoral Letters. (The sophistries and inexpressible cruelties of Papists laid open.)
Keach's Antichrist stormed.
Keary's Commonplace book to the Fathers. (A selection of anti-papal passages.)
Kidd's (Rich.) 14 Lectures on Romanism.
Kirwan's Letters to Bp. Hughes of N. York.
——— Letters to Hon. R. B. Taney.
Knowles' (J. Sheridan) Rock of Rome.
Le Blanc, Theses Theologicæ.
Le Mesurier's (T.) Works.
Leslie's Case truly stated.
Lloyd's Popery no Christianity.
——— True way to suppress Popery.
Lorrain's (H.) Sermons.
Lorrin's (P.) Christianity vs. Paganism.
Lovell's (Edward) Sermons.
Lowman's Principles of P. schismatical.
Luscombe's Church of Rome. Tr. by Wright.
Luther's (Martin) Works.
Malan's (C.) Church of Rome examined.
Mariot (H.) on the Catholic religion.
Marsh's (H.) Comparative view of the Churches of England and Rome.

Popery—*continued.*

Con.

Marvel's Rehearsal transposed. (Very keen.)
Massey's Secret history of Romanism.
Matthias' (B. W.) Popery not Catholicism.
McGavin's (W.) Protestant. Comprehensive.
——— Strictures on Milner's End of controversy.
Mendham's Spiritual venality of Rome.
Middleton's Letters from Rome. (Comparison of Popery and Paganism.)
Milton (John) On true religion.
Morning Exercises at Cripplegate. (Discourses by Bates, Calamy, Howe, Poole, Owen, Baxter, Tillotson, &c.)
Morris' Arraignment of Popery.
Murray's (James) Sermons.
Mussard's Modern and ancient ceremonies. (To prove that the papal ceremonies are derived from the pagan.)
New Englander. 2:333,414,568. 3:125,172. 5:136.
New York Review. 2:146.
Nightingale's Portraiture of Catholicism. (Gives the history, doctrines, and present state. 1812.)
Nolan's Catholic Christianity.
North Brit. Review. 10:21. 11:254. 15:257. 17:56,258.
Olmsted's Picture of Popery.
Ormerod's Picture of a Papist.
Ouseley's Old Christianity. (Replies to Milner's End of controversy.)
Owen's Church of Rome. (Powerful.)
Palmer's Letters on Romanism.
Pamphleteer. 2:71.
Patrick's (Symon) Sermons.
Percy's Romanism as it exists in Rome. 1847. (In an appendix the original documents are given.)
Philpot's Theological Letters.
Pike's Curse of Christendom.
Placette's Incurable skepticism of Rome.
Poole's (M.) Blow at the root.
Poole's (Geo. A.) Testimony of Cyprian.
Poole's (Matt.) Nullity of the Roman faith.
Pope's (R. T.) Misquotations, &c.
Porteus' Brief confutation, &c.
Powel's Roman fallacies and Catholic truths.
Poynder's Popery allied with heathenism.
Price's (E. S.) Is it not written?
Princeton Review. 5:229. 9:230,487. 18:320. 19:196. 26:454. 35:177.
Prior's Popery not Christianity.
Protestant, The. Pub. at New York from 1830 to 1834, by Rev. G. Bourne and Dr. Brownlee. (Violent.)
Protestant Herald. Periodical.
Pryce's Testimonies of Scripture.
Prynne's Tracts. (Powerful.)
Pyle's Paraph. and notes on the Apocalypse.
Quarterly Rev. 3:114. (Demands of Irish Catholics.) 33:134. 58:502. (Schisms in.) 70:108. (Antichrist.) 89:233.
Reformation Society's Tracts. London.

Popery—*continued.*

Con.

Rice's (N. L.) Romanism not Christianity.
Richardson's Popery unmasked.
Rivaloro's Echo from the Vatican.
Robinson's (C.) Impending doom of Papacy.
Robins' (Sanderson) Claims of the Roman Church. (A storehouse of facts.)
Rogers' P. unreasonable, unscript., and novel.
Roussel's Catholic and Protestant nations compared in relation to wealth, knowledge, and morality. 1855.
Sandford's Romanism considered.
Salter's Hall Sermons. (Discourses by distinguished men. "Inestimable."—LOWNDES.)
Scolland's Ch. of R. weighed in the balances.
Secker's (Abp.) Works.
Seward's (Tho.) Popery and Paganism.
Seymour's Mornings among the Jesuits.
——— Evening with the Romanists.
Sherlock's (Bp.) Works.
Smith's (Jas.) Errors of the Romish Church.
Smith's (Sir C. E.) Romanism of Italy.
Soll's True Catholic and Apostolical faith.
Sortain's (Joseph) Lectures.
Sparry's Mysteries of Romanism.
Steinmetz's Novitiate. ("A revealer of secrets, and full of materials of thought; written with every appearance of truthfulness."—QUARTERLY REVIEW.)
Stephens' Spirit of the Roman Church.
Steel's Account of the Roman Cath. religion throughout the world. 1715.
Stewart's Conformity of P. and Paganism.
Stillingfleet's Idol. and fanat. of the Ch. of R.
Stopford's Pagano-Papismus. (A parallel between Rome Pagan and Rome Papal.)
Stovel's (Cha.) Popery in England. 1840.
Stowell's (Hugh) Blots on the escutcheon of Rome.
Sturgess' Defence of Protestantism.
——— Principles and institutions of P.
Taylor's (Jer.) Dissuasive against Popery.
——— (Other powerful tracts.)
Thorold's View of Popery.
Tennison's Popery not found in Scripture.
——— Incurable skepticism of Ch. of Rome.
The Protestant. Periodical.
Tillotson's (Abp.) Works.
Tindal's Rights of the Christian Church.
Tottle's (Archdeacon) Charges.
Trahern's Roman Forgeries.
Trapp's Popery truly stated and confuted.
Urwick's Triple Crown.
Venn's (Henry) Sermons.
Warburtonian Lectures.
Warburton's Portrait of Popery.
Weaver's Popery calmly considered.
Wesley's (John) Works.
Whately's (Abp.) Errors of Romanism traced to their origin in human nature.
Whichcot's (Bp.) Sermons.
Whitaker's Reply to Stapleton & Bellarmin.
Whitby's Idolatry of the Church of Rome.
White's (Blanco) Evidences agt. Catholicism.

Popery—*continued.*

Con.

Williams' Popery unmasked.
Willet's Synopsis Papismi. (10 volumes of important tracts, ancient and modern.)
Winter's Present state of Popery. 1800.
Wylie's The Papacy; its genius, dogmas, history, and prospects. 1851.
Young's Chief points of controversy, &c.

At the Reformation, writers on this subject were innumerable. Just after the Reformation, most theological writers handled the question, more or less. When Papacy seemed about to be restored in England, another multitude of works, on both sides of the subject, appeared. The above extensive list comprises most of the best treatises now accessible. Those who desire to look further into the controversy will find hundreds of other writers on both sides in PECK'S *Complete catalogue of all the discourses written for and against Popery in the time of James II.*, 1779; CLAGGETT'S *Present state* (1687) *of the controversy between the Church of England and the Church of Rome;* and in LOWNDES' *British Librarian.* The last named quotes over 900 *English* writers on the subject.

Popery, History of. See POPES.

Bacchinii de Eccles. hierarchiæ originibus.
Beaufort, Histoire des Papes.
Dauz, Libri symbolici Eccles. Cath. Lect.
Forbesii Instructiones Historico-theologicæ.
Goebelii Cæsareo-papia Romana.
Hamelli Theolog. speculativa et practica.
Heideggeri Historia Papatus.
Helyott, Histoire des ordres monastique.
Lisle, Monumenta vetera Anglo-Saxonica.
Molinæus in Novitate papismi.
Mornæ Mysterium iniquitatis.
Puffendorfii Introductio in historiam, etc.
Seckendorfii Commentarius historicus.
Spanheimii Christianæ religionis apud Genevos restitutæ historia.
Streitwolf, Libri symbol. Ecc. Catholicæ.
Wagenseilii Dissertationes.
Wylie's Gesch. Lehren, Geist. u. Aussichten.
Butler's English, Scotch, and Irish P. 1822.
Dodd's Church History of England. (Intended as an antidote to Burnett.)
Greenwood's Cathedra Petri. (Political. 1858.)
Gavin's History of Popery.
Gill's Rise and progress of Popery.
Gillies' Vigilantius and his times.
Howell's View of the Pontificate.
Hussey's (Robt.) Rise of Papal power.
Lathbury's State of Popery in England, from the Reformation to 1829.
Milman's History of Latin Christianity, including that of the Popes to Nicholas V.
Montgomery's Popery as it exists in Great Britain and Ireland. 1854.

Popery, History of—*continued.*

Moehler's Symbolism. (Appendix containing the state of Protestantism and Popery since 1740.)
Mornay's Mystery of Iniquity. Translated by Lennard.
Murray's (N.) Romanism at home. 1850.
O'Sullivan's Popery in Ireland.
Paul's (Father) Hist. of the Coun. of Trent.
Petrie's Hist. of the Catholic Church, from 600 to 1600. (An able Protestant work.)
Riddle's History of the Papacy.
Sleidan's History of the Reformation.
Soame's Latin Ch. in Anglo-Saxon times.
Stephens' Popery in Foreign parts. 1728.
Townsend's Accusations of history.
Turnley's (Jos.) Popery in power. Plates.
Weekly Packet of advice from Rome. (A series of 240 pamphlets, begun in 1678. Reprinted, 1735, under the title of "History of Popery.")

Popes. See TEMPORAL POWER.

Anastasii Hist. Vitis Rom. Pontif. a Petro ad Nicolaum I.
Artaud, Hist. du Pape Pie VII.
Baille, Vie des papes de Rome.
Barnes, Vitæ Romanorum Pontificum.
Barraterii Successio antiquissima Episc. Romanorum, a Petro usque ad Victorem.
Bartholomæi Vitæi pontificorum.
Bonanni Historia Pontificum.
[Bruys] Histoire des Papes. (To Benoit XIII. Satirical, and often abusive.)
Burmanni Analecta de Hadriano VI.
Carrierii Hist. Chronologica Pontificorum.
Ciaconii Vitæ et res gestæ P. gestis.
Danzii Analecta crit. de Hadriano VI.
Dollinger, d. Papst fabeln des mittelalters.
Du Chesne, Hist. des Papes et Souverains chefs de l'Eglise, jusqu aujourdhui. 1646.
Eccardi Corpus histor. medii ævi.
Glen, Histoire Pontificale.
Guarnacci Vitæ et res gestæ Pont. Rom. (From Clement X to Clement XII.)
Herter's P. Innocenz III. u. seiner. Zeitg.
Keuffelii Hist. Pontificatus Romani.
Krug's (W. T.) Gregor VII. u. Gregor XVI.
Laviconterie Les crimes des Papes.
Lippold (G. H.), Gesch. des Papstthums.
Maimbourg, Pontificat. de Leon le grand.
Mirbach, Papst Clemens XIV.
Montor, Hist. des pontifes. To Pius VI.
Palatii Gesta Pontificum. To Innocent XI.
Papebrochii Conatus chronico-historicus.
Pearsonii Dissertationes.
Platina de Vit. pontif. omnium.
Poloni Chronicon summorum pontificam.
Ranke die Romische Papste.
Sandini Vitæ Pontificum Romanorum.
Schelstrate, Antiquit. ecclesiæ illustrata.
Simon (E. O.), Urbani II. Papæ, vita.
Spittler's Geschichte des Papstthums.
Stellæ Vitæ 230 summorum pontificum.
Voigt's Gregor VII und sein Zeitalter.

Popes—*continued.*

Walch (C. G. F.), Vollständigen Hist., etc.
Amer. Eclec. Rev. 1:229.
Baille's Lives of the Popes.
Bowden's Life of Gregory VII.
Bower's Lives of the Popes. To 1749.
Bruy's History of the Popes.
Cormenin's History of the Popes. To 1840.
Foulis' History of Romish usurpations.
Howell's History of the Pontificate. (To the end of the Council of Trent.)
Leti's Pope Pius V. (Valuable.)
——— Pope Sextus V.
Lit. and Theol. Rev. 2:239.
Mendham's Life of Pius V.
Mills' History of the Popes.
Mornay's Mystery of Iniquity.
Morton's History of the Popes.
Museum of For. Lit. 28:543.
New York Review. 8:157.
Nicolini's Pontificate of Pius IX.
Puffendorf's History of Popedom.
Quar. Rev. 55:287. 58:371.
Ranke's History of the Popes.
Roscoe's (Wm.) Life of Leo X.
Walch's (C. W. F.) Hist. of the P. To 1755.
White's (Joseph B.) Works.
Wilks' (G. A. F.) The Popes. To Pius IX.
Wiseman's Recollections of the last 4 Popes, and of Rome in their time. 1858.

Popes of Avignon.

Baluzii Vitæ paparum Avenionensium.
Dupuy, Histoire generale du schisme, etc.
Frizonii Gallia Purpurata.
Imberdis, Hist. des guerres religieuses.
Maimbourg, Grande Schisme d'Occident.
Mittler, de Schismate in Eccles. Roman.
Tessier, Hist. des soverains Pontifes.
Wagenseilii Exercitat. de Romanis pontifici.
Wietrowski, Hist. de magno schismate.

Very many other histories of the Popes, general and particular, are cited by BRUNET, in his *Manuel de libraire.*

Poplicans. See WALDENSES.

Popularity.

Oxford Prize Essays. 1793.

Population of the World.
See DECREASE OF MANKIND.

Alison's (A.) Principles of pop., and their connection with human happiness.
Black's Comp. view of the mortality of the human species, in all ages.
Bridges' (Sir E.) Population and riches of nations considered together.
Cheyne's Philosophical Principles.
Doubleday's (T.) Law of population.
Goodwin's (W.) Inquiry concerning increase of population.
Graham's (J.) Principles of Population.
Hume's Essay on the populousness of ancient nations.

Population of the World—*continued.*

Malthus' Principles of population.
Moreton (A. H.) on Civilization. (Analyses the natural laws which regulate popul'n.)
Petty (Wm.) on the Multiplicat. of mankind.
Place's (F.) Principles of population.
Purves' (G.) Principles of P. and production.
Ross' Examination of the "Principles, &c.," by Malthus.
Sadler's (M. T.) Law of population.
Wallace's Diss. on the numbers of mankind.
Westminster Review. New Series. 1:468.
Weyland's (J.) Principles of population.

Port Royal. See JANSENISTS, SORBONNE.

Besogne, Hist. de Port Royal.
Clemenset, Hist. de P. R. jusqu'a son entiere destruction.
Du Fosse, Memoires de Port Royal.
Fontaine, Memoir pour servir a l'histoire de Port Royale.
Le Maitre [Commonly called De Sacy], Lettres Chrétiennes.
Memoires de Port Royal.
Moleon, Voyages Liturgiques.
Nicole, Essais de morale.
[Nogent], Hist. de l'Abbaye de Port Royal.
Pinault, Hist. abrégée de la derniére persecution de Port Royal.
Racine, Histoire de Port Royal.
Reuchlin's Geschichte von Port Royal.
Tillemont, Memoires pour servir, etc.
Vie de Maria Angelique D'Arnaud.
Vies des Religieuses de Port Royal.

Edinb. Review. 73:167.
Pascal's Provincial Letters.
Schimmelpennick's Narrative of the destruction of the monastery of Port Royal, including biographical memoirs of its latter inhabitants.
Stephens' (Jas.) Essays in Eccl. biography.

Positive Precepts.

Benson's (Charles) Lectures.
Booth's Infant Baptism examined.
Burroughs' Diss. on positive institutions.
——— Defence of Dissertations.
Butler's Analogy of religion to nature.
Carr's (George) Sermons.
Clagget's Preservative against Popery.
Clarke's (Dr. Samuel) Sermons.
Doddridge's Lectures. Lect. 158.
Gerard's (Alexander) Sermons.
Grosvenor's Obligatión of positive precepts.
Hallet on Scripture.
Hicks' (Dr. Geo.) Posthumous Discourses.
Hoadley's Nat. and end of the Lord's supper.
Hunt's (Jeremiah) Sermons.
Leland against Tyndall. (Preface.)
Owen on the Holy Spirit. Bk. 1, ch. 3.
Reeve's Apologies of Justin Martyr, Tertullian, and Minucius Felix.
Robinson's Claude on the comp. of a sermon.
Rogers' (John) Sermons.
Taylor's Ductor Dubitantium.
Waterland's Comparative view of moral and positive duties.
Weston's (Bp.) Sermons.

Posture in Public Prayer.
See PRAYER.

Caswall's (E.) Sermons.
Christian Observer. 24:9,150.

Poverty See AGUR'S PRAYER.

Baxter's (Arthur G.) Sermons.
Brown's (Will. L.) Sermons.
Collier's (Jeremy) Essays. Essay 6.
Conybeare's (Bp.) Sermons.
Donne's (John) Sermons.
Dyke's (Oswald) Sermons.
Erskine's Sermons.
Evans' (Arthur) Nine plain sermons.
Exeter Hall Lectures to young men.
Gresley's (William) Sermons.
Mant's (Bp.) Duties of the poor.
McCall's (Alex.) Practical sermons.
Melville's (Henry) Sermons.
Norden's Poor man's rest.
Oliver (Benj.) on the Pursuit of happiness.
Secker's (Abp.) Sermons.

Poverty of Spirit.
See BEATITUDES, MEEKNESS.

Blackall's, Bp., Sermons.
Blair's, James, Sermons.
Clarke's, Samuel, Sermons.
Cobden's, Edward, Sermons.
Dawes', Abp., Sermons.
Dunlop's, William, Sermons.
Francklin's, Thomas, Sermons.
Grove's, Henry, Sermons.
Harris', Robert, Sermons.
Horneck's, Anthony, Sermons.
Kimber's, Isaac, Sermons.
Littleton's, Adam, Sermons.
Orr's, John, Sermons.
Pascal's Thoughts.
South's, Robert, Sermons.
Sumner's, John Bird, Sermons.
Thayer's, Elihu, Sermons.
Young's, Edward, Sermons.

Power of the Keys. See KEYS.

Practical Piety. See DEPORTMENT, QUIETNESS, RELIGION AND BUSINESS.

Basil, Homiliæ de diversis.
——— Ascetica.
Jerome, de Vitis Apostolorum.
Augustine, Sermones.
Ebelli[illegible]gii Ethica Christiana.
Erasmi Enchiridion militis Christiani.
Moulin, Traité de la paix de l'ame.
Palingenii Zodaicus vitæ. (Translated into many languages.)
Pfaffii Institutiones.
Poiret, Œconomia Divina.
Sacy [or De Sacy], Lettres Chrétiennes.
Saint Marthe, Lettres. (Precious.)
Abbott's (Jacob) Corner-stone.

Practical Piety—*continued.*

Abbott's (Jacob) Young Christian.
Adams' Private Thoughts. (A selection of precious sentences from his works.)
Addington on a Devout life.
Allen's (Tho.) Practice of a holy life.
Amer. Bibl. Repos. 2d Series. 3:91.
Amer. Quart. Register. 2:1. 7:1. 9:150.
Arnold's (Dr. Tho.) Miscellaneous Works.
Atterbury's (Bp.) Sermons and Miscellanies. ("Nothing dark, nothing redundant, nothing misplaced."—DODDRIDGE.)
Bacon's (Leonard) Christian Self-culture.
Bailey's (Lewis) Practice of piety. (Many editions, and several translations.)
Bates' (Ely) Rural philosophy. ("A very valuable specimen of the moral literature of the 19th century."—BP. BURGESS.)
Baxter's (Rich.) Christian Directory.
——— Saint's everlasting rest. (One of the best books in existence.)
Beveridge's Private Thoughts.
Binsley's The true watch and rule.
Bogatzky's Golden Treasury.
Boardman's (W. E.) Higher Christian life.
Boston's Fourfold State.
Bradley's Select British divines. (Comprises in 25 vols. the devotional works of Beveridge, Leighton, Henry, Flavel, &c., &c.)
Brooks on Assurance.
Brown's Select Remains.
Buck (C.) on Religious Experience.
Bunyan's Pilgrim's Progress.
——— Holy war.
——— (Many other precious treatises.)
Cattermole & Stebbing's Sacred classics. (A choice selection from 40 writers of the 17th century.)
Christian Disciple. 1:110.
Christian Exam. 38:108. 4:4.
Chris. Quart. Spectator. 5:552. 6:267. 7:546. 8:663.
Christian Review. 8:50.
Clarkson's This world or the next? The possibility of making the best of both.
Coles on the Divine sovereignty. ("One of the most useful books in our language."—RYLAND.)
Duchall's (James) Sermons.
Eastcheap Lectures. (Delivered between 1708 and 1717, in London.)
Edwards on the Religious Affections.
Evans' (Arthur B.) Sermons on the Christian life and character.
Evans' (John) on the Christian temper.
Fellows' Manual of Piety.
Fish's (H. C.) Prim. piety revived. Prize Ess.
Flavel's Saint indeed.
——— Providence. (Works.)
Fuller's (Thomas) Works.
Godwin's Child of light walking in darkness.
Gouge (T.) on Walking with God.
Goulburn (E. M.) on Personal Religion.
Gurnall's Christian Armor.
Hallet's (J.) Consistent Christian.

Practical Piety—*continued.*

Hall's (Bp.) Works.
Hawker's Zion's Pilgrim.
Hill's (Rowland) Village Dialogues.
Hinton's Active Christian.
——— Lectures on Revivals.
Hoare's (Cha. J.) Sermons on Chris. charac.
Hodge's Way of Life.
Horneck's Great law of Consideration.
Howe's (J.) Practical Works.
James' (John A.) Christian Professor
Jay's Exercises for the closet.
——— Christian contemplated.
Jebb's (Bp.) Piety without Asceticism.
Jowett's Manual of instruction on the use of time and temper.
Kempis' Imitation of Christ. (Malcom's ed.)
Krummacher's Dew of Israel.
Law's Serious call to a holy life.
Mallary's Soul prosperity.
Mason's (John) Select Remains. (Very precious.)
Mason (Grandson of preceding) on Self-knowledge.
Mason's (Will.) Spiritual Treasury.
Mastricht's Theologia Practica.
Meade's Almost Christian.
Mitchell's Guide to young Christians.
Moore's Practical Piety.
New Englander. 3:373.
Norris' (J. A.) Religion and business; or spiritual life in its secular department.
Palingin's Life of man.
Parsons' Christian Directory.
Pascall's Thoughts.
Phillip on Manly Piety.
Plumpton's Sermons on Christian duty.
Poiret's Divine Economy.
Rauch's Inner life of the Christian.
Romaine's Life, walk, and triumph of faith.
Rutherford's Letters. (Exceedingly devout, but badly edited, and full of repetitions.)
Sale's Introduction to a holy life.
Scott's (John) Christian life.
Scougal's Life of God in the soul.
Scudder's Christian's daily walk.
Secker's Non-such Professor. (Precious.)
Serles' Christian Remembrancer.
Sibbe's Soul's comfort and victory.
——— Evangelical sacrifices.
Spirit of the Pilgrims. 5:277.
Spring's (Gardner) Traits of Chr. character.
Spurgeon's Smooth stones from ancient brooks.
Stennet's Discourses on personal religion.
Stuckley's Gospel Glass. ("Pungent, heart-searching."—DR. JOHN RYLAND.)
Sturm's Reflections.
Swinnock's (Geo.) Christian man's calling.
Taylor's (Jer.) Holy Living.
——— Religious Wisdom.
[Venn's] Complete duty of man. (Millions of this precious book have been printed, but the author remains unknown.)
Walker's (O.) Motives to holy living.

Practical Piety—*continued.*

Walker's (S.) Practical Christianity.
Watson's Divine Cordial.
Wayland's (Francis) Sermons.
Welsford's Lights and shadows of spirit. life.
Wilberforce's Practical view of the religious system of professed Christians in the higher and middle classes, contrasted with real Christianity. 1797.
Williams (W. R.) on Religious Progress.
Wilmot's (R. A.) Christian Life.
Winslow's (Octavius) Man of God.
Wright's Great concern of life.
Wynyard's Sermons on Christian duty.
Zollikoffer's Exercises of piety.

Pragmatic Sanction.

De Boulay, Hist. Academie de Paris.
Harduini Conciliæ Collectio.
Koch, Sanctis Prag. Germanorum illustrata.
Leibnitz, Mantissa codicis diplomat.

Burnet's (Bp.) Hist. of the right of Princes.
Heylin's History of France.

Praise. See THANKSGIVING.

Atterbury's (Francis) Sermons.
Barrow's (Isaac) Sermons.
Christian Observer. Vol. 1.
Fowler's (Bp.) Discourses.
Hewlett's (John) Sermons.
Hunter's (Henry) Sermons.
Reynolds' (Bp.) Sermons.
Smallridge's (Bp.) Sermons.
Smith's (Samuel S.) Sermons.
Vance's (W. F.) Sermons.
Van Mildert's (Bp.) Sermons.
White's (Hugh) Sermons.

Praise, Love of. See LOVE OF PRAISE.

Prayer. See ANSWERS TO PRAYER, DEVOTION, FORMS, LITURGIES, LORD'S PRAYER, PRAYER BOOKS, PRAYER FOR THE DEAD, SECRET PRAYER.

Augustine, Opera.
Chrysostom, Orationes.
Cyprian, de Oratione Dominica.
Gregory Nys., de Oratione Dominica.
Origen, de Oratione.
Tertullian, de Oratione.

Amyraldus in Orationem.
Hildebrandi de Precibus vet. Christianorum.
Rechenbergii (Adam.) Dissertationes.
Thomas, de Ritu veterum Christianorum.
Zornii Delineatio theologiæ patristicæ.

Abernethy on the Divine Attributes.
Adey's (William) Sermons.
Allestree's (Richard) Sermons.
Amory's (Thomas) Sermons.
Andrews' (Bp.) Manual of private devotions.
——— Sermons.
Archer's (John) Essay on Prayer.
Baine's (James) Sermons. (Earnest prayer.)
Baker's Motives to daily prayer.
Barrow's (Isaac) Works.

Prayer—*continued.*

Ben Mordecai's Apology.
Bennett's (Benj.) Christian Oratory.
Bennett's (Thomas) Devotions of the Closet.
Beveridge's Adv. and necessity of public P.
Bickersteth (Edward) on Prayer.
Blackall's (Bp.) Sermons.
Bloomfield's (Bp.) Sermons.
Boston's (Thomas) Sermons.
Bradford's (The Martyr) Works.
Bullinger's Decades. (Parker Soc. publ.)
Burnett's (Mrs.) Method of Devotion.
Chalmers' Natural Theology.
Charlesworth on Private prayer.
Charnock's (Stephen) Works.
Christian Disciple. 1:21. 4:186. 5:9,359.
Chris. Month. Spect. 2:352,522. 5:113. 6:393.
Chris. Quart. Spect. 4:251. 5:46. 6:250.
Chris. Observer. 11:555,626. 12:753. 17:430.
Clarke's (Samuel) Sermons.
Clowes' (J.) Sermons on Prayer.
Cooper's (Edward) Sermons.
Crossinge on the Great duty of prayer.
Dallas' (A.) Sermons on Prayer.
Donne's (John) Sermons.
Dwight's Theology. Sermons 139–144.
Eastcheap Lectures. Part 2. (Discourses on this subject by Bradbury, Earle, Harris.)
Edwards' (Pres.) Works.
Emmon's (Nathaniel) Sermons.
Fiddes' (Richard) Sermons.
Francklin's (Thomas) Sermons.
Gill's (Dr.) Sermons and Tracts.
Goodwin's (Tho.) Select Cases. Case 2.
Goodrich's Bible history of prayer. (A collection of the prayers recorded in Scripture, in chronological order.)
Grove on Secret prayer.
Hale's (Sir M.) Contemplations. Part 2.
Harrison's (Thomas) Divine Logic.
Hastings' (Henry J.) Parochial sermons.
Heles' Offices of private devotion.
Henry (Matt.) on Prayer. (Very useful for young Christians.)
Hinton's Guide to prayer.
Holdsworth's (R.) Sermons.
Horlock's (H. D.) Sermons.
Horneck on the Exercise of P. (Many edit.)
Howe's (John) Works. ("I have learned more from John Howe than from any other author."—ROBT. HALL.)
Ibbot's (Benjamin) Sermons.
Innett's Guide to the devout Christian.
Jebb's (Bp.) Sermons.
Johnson's (Dr. Sam.) Prayers and meditat.
Jones' (Joseph) Sermons on prayer.
Jortin's (John) Sermons.
Kettlewell's (John) Sermons.
Knight's (James) Sermons on prayer.
Law's Serious call to a holy life.
——— Spirit of prayer.
Leighton's Lectures on the 1st Epistle of Peter. (Chap. 3, verse 12.)
Lucas' (Richard) Sermons.
MacDonough's Fourteen Discourses.

Prayer—*continued.*

Magee on Atonement. No. 8.
Mann (Tho.) On the gift of prayer.
Mant's (Bp.) Sermons.
Masillon's Sermons.
Mason's Student and Pastor.
Milner's (Isaac) Sermons.
Milner's (Joseph) Sermons.
Moore's (Hannah) Spirit of prayer.
Moore's (H.) Reflections on prayer.
Nance's (J.) Sermons on prayer.
Newman's (J. H.) Sermons.
Ogden's (Samuel) Sermons.
Orr's (John) Sermons.
Orton's Religious Exercises.
Owen on Spiritual-mindedness. (Nature and use of mental prayer and forms.)
Paley's Moral Philosophy. Book 5, ch. 2–5.
Pettis on Prayer.
Porter's (Prof.) Lectures.
Potts' (J. H.) Sermons.
Price's (Rich.) Dissertations. Diss. 2.
Prime's Power of prayer. (Many editions.)
Princeton Rev. 19:61. 35:353. 37:69.
Rowsell's (T.) Sermons on prayer.
Scott's Essays. Ess. 23.
Shepherd's Persuasives to private devotions.
Sherlock's Practical Discourses.
Smallridge's (Bp.) Sermons.
Smith's System of prayer.
Spring's (Gardner) Essays. Ess. 11.
Stanhope's (George) Sermons.
Stillman's (Samuel) Sermons.
Tappan's (David) Sermons.
Taylor's (Jer.) Christian consolation.
——— Sermons.
Taylor's (John) Scripture account of prayer.
Thompson's The Mercy Seat.
Thornton's Discourse on prayer.
Topping's Whole duty of prayer.
Townsend's Nine sermons on prayer.
Vincent on the Nature and kinds of prayer.
Walker's (Dr. James) Sermons.
Watts' Guide to prayer.
Wayland's Elements of Moral Science.
Webster's (William) Sermons.
West's Nat., design, tendency, &c., of prayer.
Weston's (Bp.) Sermons.
Wettenhall's Enter into thy closet.
Whitefield's Sermons.
White's (Hugh) Meditations and Addresses.
Wilkins' Gift of preaching and praying.
Witherspoon's Works.

Prayer Books. See FAMILY WORSHIP, FORMS OF PRAYER, LITURGIES.

Andrews' Private Devotions.
Arnold's Garden of Paradise.
Baird's Book of public prayer. (Compiled from authorized formularies of the Presbyterian Church, as prepared by Calvin, Knox, Bucer, &c.)
Barnes' Prayers for the use of families.
Bean on Family worship. (Prayers for every day in the year.)

Prayer Books—*continued.*

Beard's Family prayers.
Bennett's (B.) Christian Oratory.
Bennet's (Thos.) Daily Devotions.
Bernay's Family prayers.
Bloomfield's (Bp.) Family prayers.
Bowdler's Prayers for the household.
Brooks' (C.) Family prayers.
Burnet's Rules of holy living.
Carpenter's Family prayers.
Clapham's Prayers, selected from the works of Jeremy Taylor.
Clishold's Prayers of eminent persons.
Cochrane's Manual of devotion. ("None better."—CHALMERS.)
Codrington's Family prayers.
Cotterill's (T.) Family prayers.
Crossman's (F. C.) Family prayers.
Day's Christian prayers. 1569. (Out of ancient writers: commonly called Queen Elizabeth's Prayer Book.)
Enfield's Family prayers.
Evans' Family prayers.
Fletcher's (W. K.) Liturgical prayers.
Gilderdale's Family prayers.
Gladstone's Family prayers.
Gray's Family prayers.
Hamilton's Family prayers.
Hardman's Family prayers.
Hinton's (Jas.) Guide to prayer.
Hook's (W. F.) Family prayers.
Horsfall's Manual of family prayer.
Jay's Prayers for families.
Jenks' Offices of devotion.
Johnson's (Dr. Sam.) P. and Meditations.
Kennaway's Family prayers.
Kent's (Bp.) Manual of prayer.
Kingsbury's Prayers for families.
Mant's Book of family prayers.
May's (R.) Family prayers.
Morrison's Family prayers. (Recommended by Wardlaw and Raffles.)
Murray's Prayers from Calvin.
Murey's Closet devotions in Scripture expressions.
Palmer's (J.) Family prayers.
Palmer's (S.) Family prayers.
Parr's (Cath.) Prayers and Meditations
Patrick's Devout Christian.
Pearson's (E.) Family prayers.
Plumer's (J. J.) Family prayers.
Poppewel's Family assistant.
Richardson's (J.) Family prayers.
Rogers' (T.) Family prayers.
Sheppard's (J.) Family prayers.
Sibthorpe's (R. W.) Family liturgy.
Soltan's Family prayers.
Spinke's Manual of private devotion.
Sutcliffe's (W.) Family prayers.
Swete's Family prayers.
Taylor's (Jer.) Golden Grove. 1650. (30 ed.)
Temple's (E.) Family prayers.
Thornton's (H.) Family prayers.
Toplady's Family P. for each day in the week.
Wainwright's Family prayers.

Whitmore's Family prayers.
Wilberforce's (W.) Family prayers.

Books of prayers are very numerous. More than four hundred are mentioned in booksellers' catalogues. Very few of them are valuable.

Prayer for the Dead.

Frantz's Gebet für die Todten, in seinen zusammenhange m. schriften Augustinus.
Hildebrandi Offertorium Primitivum.
Klüpfel, Tractatus Theologicus.
Pfaffi Opera.

Bradford's (The Martyr) Works.
Butler on Praying for the dead.
Cameron's (Bp.) Primitive doctr. reviewed.
Hall's (W. J.) Doctrine of Purgatory.
Paget's (F. E.) Sermons.
Usher's (Abp.) Works.
Wake's (Abp.) Works.

Prayer Meetings. See SOCIAL WORSHIP.

Preaching. See EXTEMPORE PREACHING.

Augustine, de Doctrina.

Ammon, Gesch. der Homiletik, von Huss, bis Luther.
——— Anleitung zur Kanzelberedsamkeit.
Baur's Grundlage zur Vorlesungen über Homiletik.
Chemnitii Methodus Concionandi.
Erasmi Ecclesiastes.
Fabricii Orator sacer.
Ferrarius de Ritu sacrarum eccles. veterum concionum.
Gaussen de Ratione Concionandi.
Gerard, Rechtfertigung d. Predigerstandes.
Hildebrandi Diss. de veterum concionibus.
Hollebek de Optimo concionum genere.
Hoornbeck de Ratione concionandi.
Houdry, Biblioth. des prédicateurs. (23 quarto volumes.)
Hulsemanni Oratoria Ecclesiastica.
Joly, Hist. de la Prédication.
Knibbii Manductio ad oratoriam sacram.
Lampii Methodus concionandi.
Langii Oratoria Sacra.
Lentz's Gesch. der Christlichen Homiletik.
Maitre, Reflex. sur la maniero de prêcher.
Marheinecke's Grundlage des Homiletik.
Matthiæ Concionadi ratio et causa eloquent.
Melancthonis de Arte concionandi.
Osiander de Ratione Concionandi.
Pfenninger, von der Popularität. im Predig.
Placette sur le Maniere de prêcher.
Schubert, de Abusu philosophiæ in orationibus sacris.
Schuler's Gesch. d. Veranderung d. Geschmacks im Predigen.
Tharin, Atlas des prédicateurs. (A mass of good plans of sermons, or skeletons.)
Titmann's Lehrbuch der Homiletik.
Van Till, Methodus Concionandi.
Vinet, Histoire de la prédication parmi les reformés de France au 17 siècle.

Preaching—*continued.*

Vitringæ Animadversiones.
Zuinglii Ecclesiastes.

Alexander's (J. W.) Thoughts on preaching.
Amer. Bibl. Repos. 2d Series. 2:139,330. 1:341. 3:78,569. 4:9. 5:317,384. 12:85. 3d Series. 7:221.
Amer. Quart. Observer. 1:80. 2:325.
Amer. Presb. and Theol. Review. 3:384. 4:9.
Arthur's (Will.) Tongue of fire.
Barecroft's Instructions to young students.
Bonnett's (James) Lectures on the preaching of Christ.
Benson's Christian preaching considered.
Beveridge's Thesaurus Theologicus. (A great aid.)
——— Sermons.
Bibl. Sacra. 2:12,683. 4:96,247. 5:731. 14:1, 282. 18:610. 24:95.
Bickersteth (Ed.) on Preaching and Hearing.
Blackwell's Method of preaching.
Blair's Lectures on Rhetoric.
Boggs' (James) Art of preaching.
Bray's Pastoral Letters.
Bricknell's Warrant and effect of preaching. (A review of "Tracts for the Times.")
Casaubon on Preaching. (Excellent.)
Chandler's (S.) Letter to Rev. John Guyse.
——— Second letter to Do.
Christian Disciple. 5:427.
Christian Examiner. 29:19. 35:385. 37:80. 38:107. 41:49. 45:427. 78:157. New Series. 3:51.
Christian Monthly Spect. 1:341. 6:131,527. 9:327. 10:635.
Christian Observer. 11:1. 16:651. 20:548,680. 19:495. 22:15. 28:506.
Christian Review. 4:481. 10:609. 14:381.
Claude on the Composition of a sermon.
Close's (Francis) Sermons on the Liturgy.
Cook's (Jas.) Preacher's Assistant. (A series of texts.)
Democratic Rev. 17:31.
Dublin University Mag. 61:131.
Dwight's Theology. (Preaching of Christ and the Apostles.)
Eclectic Rev. 4th Series. 5:20. 10:121. New Series. 7:220.
Edinburg Rev. 64:228. 72:34.
Edwards' Christian Preacher.
——— Vindication. (Reply to Lightfoot.)
Enfield's Preacher's Directory. (A series of topics, with appropriate texts.)
Fordyce's Dialogue on the art of preaching.
Franck's (Prof.) Useful way of preaching.
Frank's (J. C.) Hulsean Lectures. 1823. (Evidences of Christianity from the preaching of the Apostles.)
Fuller's (And.) Works.
Glanvill's Essay concerning preaching.
Gouldburn's (Edward M.) Sermons.
Gregory on the Composition and delivery of a sermon.
Gresley's (W.) Ecclesiastes Anglicanus. (On P. as adapted to Ch. of England pulpits.)

Preaching—*continued.*

Henley on Action in preaching.
Holden's (G.) Ordinance of P. considered.
Jennings' (John) Discourses.
Kidder's (D. P.) Homiletics.
Knickerbocker Mag. 4:13.
Knox's (V.) Essays.
Langhorne's Eloquence of the pulpit.
Leifchild (John) on Preaching and preachers.
Lightfoot's (R.) Remarks on some passages in Dr. Edwards' preacher.
——— Dr. E.'s vindication considered.
Lloyd's (R.) Best mode of preaching Christ.
London Quart. Rev. 5:179.
Maberly's Preach the word; or preaching considered.
Mainwaring's Sermons. (Appendix contains a good dissert. on the comp. of sermons.)
Meth. Quart. Rev. 1:283. 7:63.
Moore's Thoughts on preaching, especially in relation to the requirements of the age. 1861.
Moore's (Steph.) Wise gospel preacher.
Murray's (N.) Preachers and Preaching.
New Englander. 3:548, (Use of imagination.) 5:90.
North Amer. Rev. 19:297.
North British Rev. 28:423.
Petherick on Primitive preaching.
Pike's Essay on preaching.
Placette's Advice on preaching.
Porter's (E.) Lectures on preaching.
Princeton Rev. 10:33. 20:463. 24:533. 26:454. 27:1. 28:655. 35:117. 38:513.
Reybaz on the Art of preaching.
Robertson's (John) Sermons.
Ryland's (Dr.) Sermons.
Sedwick on Evangelical preaching.
Sharp's (Abp.) Discourses on preaching.
Short's (T. V.) Sermons.
Stevens' Essays on the preaching required by the times: with illustrations of Methodist preaching. 1855.
Stillman's (Sam.) Sermons. (3 on this subj.)
Stuart's (Prof.) Preacher's Manual.
Sturtevant's Preacher's Manual.
Styles' Nature and effect of evangelical P.
Sumner (Bp.) on the Epistles of Paul.
Venn's (John) Sermons.
Vinet's Homiletics. Tr. by T. H. Skinner. (On the *theory* of preaching.)
——— History of preaching among the Reformed churches of France in the 19th cent.
Warner on Evangelical preaching.
Weale's Christian Orator.
Wilkins' (Bp.) Ecclesiastes.
Williams' Christian Preacher. (A collection of treatises by Wilkins, Jennings, Franck, Claude, &c.)
Wilson's (Wm.) Popular preachers of the ancient church.

As model sermons, there are none better than those of Robert Walker, of Edinburg, 3 vols. 8vo. "Walker is Whitefield polished by Blair."—Dr. Williams.

Pre-Adamites. See TRADUCTION.

Pro.

Peyrerii Præ-Adamitæ, aut Exercitatio super Rom. 5:12–14. (This famous book, published 1645, was refuted by a crowd of authors. It was sentenced to be burnt by the common hangman.)
——— Systema theol. ex præadimitarum hypothesi.
Beecher's (Edward) Concord of ages.
Berrow's (Capel) Lapse of souls. (Attempts to account for original sin.)
Huxley's Origin and antiquity of man.
Lyell's Geological evidences of the antiquity of man.
Peyrere's Man before Adam.
Preadamite Man. Anonymous. 1860.

Con.

Calovii Biblia Illustrata.
Crameri (L. D.) Dissertationes.
Danhaveri Præ-adamitæ fabulæ explosa.
Felgenhaver, Prufung über des lateinische Buch preadamitæ.
Gregoire, Histoire des sectes.
Maresii Refutatio fabulæ præadamiticæ.
Micrælius, Monstrosæ de præad. opinionis.
Petit Didier, Dissertationes. Diss. XXII
Priorii Animadversiones in librum præad.
Pythii Responsio Exetastica.
Quenstedtii Dissertationes.
Schelvigius de Præ-adamitis.
Ursinus de novo Prometheus.
British Quart. Review. April, 1863.
Christian Examiner. 55:394.
North Brit. Rev. 27:226. (Very strong.)
Parker's (Benj.) Review of the antediluvian world.
Parker's (H.) Harmony of ages.

Precepts of Noah.

Buddeus, Introd. ad hist. philosophiæ Heb.
Fabricius, Apocryph. Veteris Testamenti.
——— Bibliographia Antiquaria.
Frischmuthii Diss. theol. philol. Diss. 2.
Leidekker de Vario Reipublicæ Hebr. statu.
Selden de Jure Nat. et Gentium.

Predestination. See CALVINISM, DECREES, ELECTION.

Predictions by Christ.

Vinke, Vaticin. C. de perpessionibus suis.
Allix's Reflections.
Greenhill's (Jos.) Prophecies of the N. Test.
Hodge's (John) Sermons.
Holmes' Bampton Lectures. 1782.
Jenkins' Certainty of the Christian religion.
Jortin's Remarks upon ecclesiastical history.
Kidder's Demonstration of the Messiah.
Lardner's Jewish and heathen testimonies.
Limborch's Colloquy with a Jew.
Mede's (Joseph) Works.
More's (Dr. Henry) Works.
Myers' (Tho.) Proph. delivered by Christ.

Newton (Bp.) on the Prophecies.
Newton's (J.) Dissertations on prophecy.
Sharp's Rise and fall of the Holy city.
Tillotson's Sermons.
Warburton's Julian.
Whitby's General preface to Annotations.
——— Annotations.

Pre-Existence of Christ's Human Soul. See ARIANISM, HYPOSTATIC UNION.

Pro.

Alderson's (Jos.) Pre-existence of Christ.
Allen on the Pre-existence of Christ.
Fawcett (Benj.) on the Doct. of the Trinity.
Flemming's Christology.
Glanvill's Lux Orientalis.
Hawker on the Divinity of Christ.
Jortin's (John) Works.
Magee on Atonement. No. 1.
Parkhurst on the Divinity of Christ.
Robinson's Plea for the divinity of Christ.
Rudd's (Sayer) Sermons.
Simpson on the Trinity.
Stevens' Script. display of the Triune God.
Stockwell on the Pre-existence of Christ.
Watts' Glory of Christ.

Con. Unitarian and Socinian writers in general, whenever they allude to this topic.

Carpzovius de Anima Christi.
Hagemanni Dissertationes.
Markius de Anima Christi.

Edwards' (Pres.) Works.
Grotius' Commentary.
Haynes on the Attributes of God.
Lardner on the Logos.
Lindsey's Works.
Priestley's History of corruptions.
Taylor's (Abr.) Reply to Watts' Glory, &c.
Whiston's Primitive Christianity.

Pre-Existence of Human Souls. See PRE-ADAMITES, TRADUCTION.

Pro. All the ancient Pythagoreans and Platonists.

Justin Martyr, Origen, Methodius.

Arnobius adversus Gentes.
Aristotle de Generatione et corruptione.
Beausobre, Hist. de Manicheeism.
Ciceronis Tusc. Disputat. Lib. 1, cap. 3.
Mori Opera philosophica.
Origen de Principiis.
Peyrere, Exercit. super Rom. 5:12–14.
Platonis Phædo.
Reynaud, Philosophie religieuse.
Sandius de Origine Animæ.
Sibbern, de Præexistentia.

Beecher's (Edw.) Conflict of Ages.
——— Concord of Ages.
Benneck's Exposition of the Epistle to the Romans.
Berrow's (C.) Lapse of souls.
Colliber's (S.) Theological Treatises.
Glanvill's Lux Orientalis. (Exhibits the opinions of Eastern philosophers.)

Pre-Existence, &c.—*continued.*

Pro.

Helmont's (F. M.) Works. Ch. 46.
Hume's (David) Essays.
More's (Henry) Works. (As able as any on this side of the question.)
Rust's (Bp.) Discourses on truth. (Generally bound up with Glanvill.)

Con.

Augustine, contra Manichæos.
Cyril Alex., Epistolæ Canonicæ.

Bebelii (Balthasar.) Exercitationes.
Bertram's Prüfung der Meinung von der präexistenz, etc.
Cramer, de Doctrina Judæorum.
Pereira, Antoniana Margaritta.
Thomasius de Præexistentia animarum.

Barrow's Works. (Answer to More.)
Baxter's Placid collation with Dr. H. More.
Bibliotheca Sacra. 12:156.
Christian Exam. 54:419.
Cudworth's Intellectual System. Bk. 1, ch. 1.
Dunton's (J.) Visions of the soul. (Ironical.)
Hale's Origin of Mankind.
Leland's Adv. and nec. of Revel. Pt. 3, ch. 5.
Parker on the Platonic philosophy.
Presbyterian Quart. Review. 11:546.
Warren (Edw.) on the Pre-existence, &c.
Watts' Ruin and Recovery. Question 2.

Prejudice.

Biblical Repos. April, 1840.
Christian Observer. 2:405.
Cooper's (Edward) Sermons.
Du Marsais on Prejudice.
Foster's (James) Sermons. (John 1:45–47.)
Horberry's (Matt.) Sermons.
Hurd's (Bp.) Sermons.
[Kennedy's (A. H.)] Letters on prejudice in religion.
Lindsley (Philip) on Religious prejudices.
Mason on Self-knowledge. Ch. 9.
Meth. Quart. Rev. 7:53.
Retrospective Rev. 1:70.
Simondi on Prejudice.
Stebbing's (Henry) Sermons. (Prejudices of education.)
Tottie's (John) Sermons before the University of Oxford.
Williamson's Boyle Lectures. 1788. (Prejudices of the learned.)

Presbyterians.

Pro.

Blondel, de Episcopis et Presbyteris. ("The most learned work in favor of Presbyterianism."—DARLING.)
Catechismus Genevensis.
——— Palatinus.
Confessio Helvetica.
——— Tetrapolitana.
Consensus Tigurini.
Heideggeri Corpus Theologiæ.
Mollinæus de Munere pastorali.

Presbyterians—*continued.*

Pro.

Picteti Medulla.
Riveti (And.) Opera.
Vitringæ de Synagoge vetere.
Zuinglii Fidei Ratio.

Amer. Bibl. Repos. (Various articles.)
Amer. Presbyterian and Theolog. Review.
Anderson (John) on Church government, &c.
Ayton's Constitut. of the Christian Church.
Barnes' (A.) Organization of the Apostolic Church.
Baird's (Sam.) Collection of Acts, &c., of the General Assembly; with notes. 1856.
Blondell on Bishops and Presbyters.
Brown's Vind. of the Scotch form of ch. gov.
——— Letters to King James.
Calamy (Edmund) on Church government.
Calderwood's Hist. of the Chur. of Scotland.
Campbell's (Dr. W.) Presbyterians of Ireland. 1787.
Clarkson on Episcopacy.
Dickinson's Defence of Presb. ordination.
Durell on the Govt. and worship of the Ch.
Edwards' Reasons against the independent form, &c.
Forrester (T.) on the Claims of hierarchical bishops.
Gillespie's (Geo.) Aaron's rod blossoming.
Hall's (Archib.) Const. and order of the Ch.
Harrington's Notes on the Ch. of Scotland.
Hill's (Geo.) Theological Institutes.
——— Constitution of the Ch. of Scotland.
Hodge's (Cha.) What is Presbyterianism?
Jameson's Sum of the Episcopal controversy.
Jamieson's Nazienzeni querula.
Killen's Const. and worsh. of the ancient Ch.
King's (Dav.) Exposition of the P. form, &c.
London Minister's Jus Divinum.
Love's Main points of Church government.
Mason's (Dr. John) Essays on the Church.
Miller's (Prof.) Letters on Ch. government.
——— Primitive order of the Ch. vindicated.
Paget (John) on Church government.
Pierce's Defence of the dissenting ministry.
Pon's Doctrine of the Church of Geneva.
Presbyterian Review. Edinburg. 1828 to the present.
Princeton Rev. 15:286. 21:355,542. 26:377. And others.
Robinson's (Prof. S.) Church of God.
Rockwell's (J. E.) Sketches of the Presbyterian Church. (For youth.)
Rule's Vindication of the Ch. of Scotland.
Rutherford's Government of the Church.
——— Divine right of Presbyteries.
Schlater's Original draft of the primitive church.
Skinner's Truth and Order.
Smyth's (Thomas) Presbytery the primitive policy, &c.
Westminster Catechism and Confession.
Wilson's (J. P.) Primitive government, &c.
Wood's Old and New Theology.

Presbyterians—*continued.*

Con. See APOSTOLICAL SUCCESSION, CONGREGATIONALISM, EPISCOPACY.

Campegii Utriengiæ Archisynagogus.
Hammond adversus Blondellum.
Pearson, Vindic. Ignatii Epistolarum.
Usserus de Eccles. successione.

Ashton (Sir T.) on Presb. government. ("A remonstrance by divers of the nobilitie." 1641.)
Bancroft's Survey of the pretended holy discipline.
——— Dangerous positions and proceedings.
Bellamy's Impossibility of being Presbyterians and not Rebels.
Beveridge (Bp.) on the Apostolical Canons.
Bilson's Government of the Church.
Bingham's Origines Ecclesiasticæ.
Birkenhead's Assembly-man. (Bitter satire.)
Boyd on Episcopacy and Presbytery.
Brokesby's Govt. of the primitive church.
Carson (Alex.) on Church Government.
——— Reply to Brown's Vindication.
——— Reply to Ewing.
Cook's Invalidity of Presb. ordination.
Ferne's Presbytery considered.
Fitz's Modern Presbyt. unmasked. 1830.
[Grey's (Zech.)] Presb. ordination null.
Hall's (Bp.) Lay eldership contrary to Scripture and antiquity.
Hooker's Ecclesiastical Polity.
Jackman's P. ordination presumptuous.
Jaques' Ordination by P. null and void.
King's (Sir P.) Const. of the primitive chur.
Lloyd on Church Government.
Maurice's Defence. (Reply to Clarkson.)
Maxwell's (Bp.) Tyrannical power and practice of Presb. government in Scotland.
Milbourne's Legacy to the Ch. of England.
Owen's (Dr. John) Works.
Parker's (Henry) Trojan Horse.
Sage's Fundamental charter of Presbytery.
Saltmarsh's Divine right of Presbytery.
——— Presbyterian groans.
Skinner's (John) Primitive truth and order.
Stillingfleet's Origines Sacræ.
Stock on Presbyterian principles. (Reply to Campbell.)
Thorndike's Armor for churchmen.
——— Rights of the church.
Wells' Theses. (Reply to Pierce.)
Woodhead on Ancient Church Government.

Presbyterianism, History of.

Acts and Testimonies of the Gen. Assembly.
Alexander's (S. D.) History of the P. Church in Ireland. (An abridgment of Reid.)
Baird's Acts and testimonies of the General Assembly of the United States. (From the beginning to 1856.)
Basier's Hist. of English and Scotch Presb.
Brown's Vind. of the abrogation of the plan of union by the P. Church of the U. S.
Brown's Hist. of the P. Church in the U. S.

Presbyterianism, Hist. of—*continued.*

Cheeseman's Differences between old and new school Presbyterians.
Crocker's Catastrophe of the P. Ch. in 1837.
Davidson's (R.) P.; its place in history.
——— Hist. of the P. Church in Kentucky.
Dundas' Acts of the Gen. Assembly of the Ch. of Scotland. (From 1638 to 1720.)
Engles' Presb. Church in the United States.
Foote's Sketches of Virginia.
Gillett's P. Church of the United States.
Heylin's History of the P. (1536 to 1647.)
Hill's Rise and prog of Amer. P. (To 1839.)
History of the Division of the P. Church, by a committee of the Synods of New York and New Jersey. 1832.
Hodge's Hist. of the P. Ch. in the U. S. 1788.
Hotchkin's History of the Presbyterian Church in New York. 1848.
Laird's History of early American Presbyt.
Minutes of the Gen. Assembly of the P. Ch.
Moore's Digest of the acts and deliverances of the General Assembly of the U. S.
Nevin's Church of the Valley. (Interior of Pennsylvania.)
Peterkin's Records of the Kirk. 1638–1843.
Quart. Christian Spectator. 9:597. 10:337.
Presbyterian Review. (Many valuable articles. Very full on the separation of Amer. Presbyterians into new and old school.)
Records of the P. Ch. of U. S. 1706 to 1788.
Reid's History of Irish Presbyterians. 1833.
——— ——— Continued to 1853, by W. D. Killen.
Rockwell's Sketch of the P. Church.
Smith's Old Redstone. (A history of P. in Western America, to 1854.)
Spence's (Irving) Letters. (P. in America.)
Webster's (Rich.) Pres. Church in America. (With Biographical sketches. 1850.)
Wilson's History of the principles, opinions, and usages of the English Presbyterians.
Wood's (Henry) History of the Presbyterian controversy. (In America.)
Wood's (James) Doctrinal differences which have divided the Presb. Church. 1853.

Present State of the Jews. See JEWS, PRESENT CONDITION.

Presumption.

Adams' (Thomas) Sermons.
Austin's Presumptuous man's mirrour.
Brady's (Nicolas) Sermons.
Burnside's Religion of mankind.
Charnock's Works.
Fuller's (Andrew) Sermons.
Hall's (Bp.) Practical Works.
Hoole's (Joseph) Sermons.
Lucas' (Dr. Richard) Sermons.
Marshall's (Nathaniel) Sermons.
Milner's (Joseph) Sermons.
Morning Exercises at Cripplegate. (Sermon by T. Cole.)
Orr's (Dr. John) Sermons.
Parry's (Joshua) Sermons.
Sacheverille on Presumptuous sins.
Smith's (Elisha) Sermons.
South's (Robert) Sermons.
Sumner's (Samuel) Sermons.
Thomson's (Thomas) Sermons.
Waterland's (Daniel) Sermons.

Presumptuous Sins. See WILFUL SINS.

Pride. See HUMILITY, MEEKNESS.

Balguy's (John) Sermons.
Bell's (William) Sermons.
Brady's (Nicholas) Sermons.
Brown's (Will. Laurence) Sermons.
Charnock's Works.
Collier's (Jer.) Essays on moral subjects.
Edwards' (Pres.) Works.
Francklin's (Thomas) Sermons.
Gisbourne's (Thomas) Sermons.
Hall's (Bp.) Sermons.
Hewlett's (John) Sermons.
Hooker on the Nature of Pride.
Hussey's (Robert) Sermons.
Johnson's (Dr. Samuel) Sermons.
Lamont's (David) Sermons on preval. vices.
Mant's (Bp.) Sermons.
Marriot's (Harvey) Sermons for families.
Placette on Pride.
Rees' (Abraham) Practical Sermons.
Seed's (Jeremiah) Sermons.
Skelton's (Philip) Sermons.
Taylor's (John) Sermons.
Vincent's (John) Sermons.
Waterland's (Dean) Sermons.
Wheatland's Sermons.

Priestcraft.

Barbeyrac's Spirit of the Ecclesiastics in all ages.
Hickeringill's (Edm.) Miscellaneous Tracts. (A powerful exposure by an Episcopal clergyman.)
Howitt's Hist. of P. in all ages and nations.
[Macgowan's] P. defended. (Satirical.)
Mills' (J. B.) History of the Christian priesthood. (Reply to Howitt.)

Priesthood, Jewish. See JUDAISM.

Carpzovius de Pontificis Hebræorum.
Deckeri Catalogus Pontificium vet. legis.
Dodwell de Uno Sacerdotio et uno altare
Selden de Successione in sacordot. Hebr.
Ziegra de Ordinatione sacerdotum Hebr.
Calmet's Commentary on Judith. (Preface.)
Prideaux's Orations. Orat. 2.
Sheringham's Codex Talmudicus.
Tholuck's Priesthood of the Old Testam. (A diss. at the end of his Com. on Hebrews.)

Priesthood of Christ. See JESUS CHRIST.

Primitive Christianity. See CHRISTIAN ANTIQUITIES, HISTORY OF DOCTRINES.

Hagenbach's Vorlesungen über d. Kirchengeschichte.
Rothe, die Aufaenge der Christlichen Kirche in ihrer Verfassung.

Baynes' (H. S.) Church at Philippi.
Hall's (Bp.) Important points.
Holcombe's Lectures on Prim. Christianity.
Kett's Bampton Lectures. 1790.
Knowles' Primitive Christianity.
Semler's State of the early Church.
Whately's Rise and corruption of church.

Primitive Language.
See ORIGIN OF LANGUAGE.

Primitive State of Man.
See STATE OF INNOCENCE.

Primogeniture. See POLITICAL ECONOMY.

Pro.

Puffendorf de Jure. Lib. IV.
Fleetwood on Relative Duties.
Paley's Principles of moral philosophy.

Con.

Condorcet's Life of M. Turgot.

Printed Editions of Scripture.

Adleri Biblioth. Biblica. 1770. (An extensive catalogue of Bibles in various languages.)
Baumgarten (M.), Vindiciæ textus Nov. Test. 1836.
Bibliotheca Sussexiana. (A descriptive cat. of Hebrew, Greek, and Samaritan Bibles.)
Crow, Elenchus scriptorum in S. S. 1672.
De Rossi, de Heb. textus editionibus. 1780. (Republished with a valuable appendix by Marsh. 1784.)
Kortholtus de variis Scripturæ editionibus, et translationibus. 1686.
Le Long, Biblioth. Sacra. 1723. (There is scarcely an edition, Hebrew, Gr., Latin, or Polyglott, then extant, but is here accurately described. Edited, with important additions, by A. G. Marsh. 1785.)
Lorck's Bibelgeschichte.
Simoni Disquisitiones de variis editionibus, etc. 1684.
Winer's Handbuch d. theol. Litteratur. 1842.

Bates' (Julius) Integrity of the Hebrew text. (Opposes many of the constructions of Kennicott.)
Butler's (Cha.) Horæ Biblicæ.
Cotton's (Henry) List of editions of the Bible and parts of it, from 1520 to 1820.
Dibdin's Acc. of Polyglotts, Heb. and Greek Bibles, portions of the Bible, &c. 1827.
Horne's Biblical Bibliography. 1814.
Kennicott's State of the printed Hebrew text. 1754.
Lowndes' British Librarian. 1832.
Nolan on the Text of the N. Test. 1815.
O'Callahan's List of Bibles printed in Amer.
Orme's Biblioth. Biblica. 1824. (Enumerates not only the editions of Hebrew and Greek Scripture, but of the lexicons and concordances.)
Pilkington's Errors in the Hebrew text and versions.

Printed Editions—*continued.*

Reeves' Collation of the Hebrew and Greek texts of the Psalms. 1800.
Simon's Critical enquiries into the various editions of the Bible. 1680.
——— Critical history of the text of Old and New Testaments. 1689.
Tregelles' Account of the printed text of the N. T. (With a collation of the texts of Griesbach, Scholz, Lachman, and Tischendorf.)

See LOWNDES' *British Librarian*, JOHNSON'S *Catalogus Biblioth. Harleianae*, and especially BRUNET'S *Manuel du libraire.*

Priscillianists. See HERESY.

Assemanni Biblioth. Orientalis Vaticana.
Augustinus ad Orosium contra Priscill.
Beausobre, Histoire de Manicheisme.
Calogeia, Opusculum Scientificum.
Girvesii Historia Priscill. chronologica.
Lubbertus de Hæresi P. de fontibus denuo collatis. 1840.
Raccoltæ Opuscula.
Sulpitii (Severi) Historia Sacra. (Valuable for little else than its account of this sect.)
Uries, de Priscillianistis eorumque fatis, doctrinis, et moribus.
Voigtii Biblioth. Historica.

Prisoners. See PRISON DISCIPLINE.

Adshead on Prisons and Prisoners.
Brewster's (John) Sermons for prisoners.
Chesterton's Revelations of prison life.
Christian Observer. 17:446.
Clay's Prison Chaplain.
Dodd's Prison Thoughts.
Edinburg Review. 85:320.
Edwards' (David) Sermons.
Russel's Prisoner's Directory.

Prison Discipline.

Brissot, Bibliotheque Philosophique.
Julius, Vörlesungen ü. d. Gefängnisskunde.

Adshead on Prisons and Prisoners.
Amer. Quart. Review. 14:228. 18:451.
Beaumont on the Penitentiary system of the United States. Trans. by Lieber. 1833.
Beccaria on Crime and Punishment. 1780.
Bentham's (Jer.) Rationale of punishment. 1818.
Blackwood's Magazine. 42:145.
Breton on the Defects of prisons.
British Quarterly Review. 1863.
Burt's Results of solitary confinement.
Buxton (Sir Tho. F.) on the Present system of prison discipline. 1818.
Chesterton's Revelations of P. life. 1856.
Christian Examiner. 3:203. 10:15. 16:251. 20:376. 26:54. 27:381. 40:122.
Christian Quarterly Spectator. 2:201.
Christian Observer. 13:234.
Clay's Prison Chaplain. (English prisons in 1801.)
Democratic Rev. 19:129. 20:172.

Prison Discipline—*continued.*

De Toqueville on the P. system of the U. S.
Dix (Miss) on Prisons. 1855.
Dixon's John Howard and the prison world of Europe. 1850.
Eclec. Rev. 4th Series. 4:568. 22:455. 27:280. N. S. 12:560.
Edinb. Rev. 22:385. 30:463. 35:286. 36:353. 64:169.
Elmes' Hints for the improv. of pris. 1823.
Field's (I.) Life of John Howard. 1855.
——— Advantages of separate confinement.
For. Quarterly Rev. 12:49.
Fry (Mrs. E,) on Prisons. 1845.
——— On female associations for pris. 1848.
Fry's (H. P.) System of penal discipline; with a report on the treatment of prisoners in Great Britain and Van Diemen's Land. 1843.
Gould on the Regimen suited to prisoners.
Gray's P. discipline in America. 1845.
Gurney's Notes on prisons.
Howard's (Jno.) State of prisons in England. 1784.
——— Account of the principal lazarettos in Europe.
Jebb on the Construction, policy, &c., of P.
Journal of Prison discipline and philanthrophy. Periodical. Philadelphia.
Kingsmill on Prisons and Prisoners.
Lofft's (Capel) Works.
Macgill's Remarks on prisons.
Mease on the Penit. system of Pennsylvania.
Month Rev. 89:199. 97:427. 106:311. 130:421.
Mynshul on Prisons and Prisoners.
New York Rev. 6:124.
N. Amer. Rev. 37:117. 47:452. 49:1. 66:145.
North Brit. Rev. 10:1.
Oscar on Prisons and Punishments.
[Packard's] Alleged tendency of solitary confinement to insanity. 1849.
Pamphleteer. 6:473. 15:228,415. 16:98. 18:148. 23:289.
Princeton Rev. 21:331.
Reports of the Inspectors of prisons in Mass., Penna., New York, New Jersey, &c.
Reports of American Prison Disc. Society. (From 1826 to the present.)
Roscoe on Penal jurisprudence and the reformation of criminals.
Sampson on Crime and its treatment.
Sergeant on the Design of punishment.
Timson's Memoirs of Mrs. Fry.
U. S. Lit. Gaz. 4:176.
Westminster Rev. 3:420.

Private Baptism.

Strong's (Dean) Indecency and unlawfulness of baptizing children in private.

Private Communion.

Biedenweg der Rettung des œffentlichen Nachtmalgebrauchs.
Diecmann's Gebrauch der privat Communion betreffende Gewissens Fragen.

Private Communion—*continued.*

Hermann's Gedancken über d. privat Com.
Mencken, Unterricht von de privat Comm.
——— (Several other treatises on the subj.)
Paschius der Unordentlichen Kirchenord.
Schroerus (Geo. Frider.) Dissertationes.
Schweigger de Privato sacræ cœnæ usu.
Ulich Bedencken was von der privat Communion zu halten.
Werner de Loco administr. cœnæ ordinaris.
Wilckius de Communione privata.

Christian Observer. 13:1,345.
Humphrey's Diatribe.
Saunders' Apology. (Reply to Humphrey.)

Private Judgment in Religion.
See FREEDOM OF OPINION, READING THE BIBLE.

Ibbott's Boyle Lectures. 1727.
Kidder's (Richard) Sermons.
McCann's Lectures on Christian liberty.
Morgan on the Right of private judgment.
Rogers' (Henry) Essays.

Probabilities, Doctrine of.
See NECESSITY, SCIENTIA MEDIA.

La Place, Theorie analytique d. probabilités.
Amer. Quart. Rev. 11:473.
Boole on the Laws of Thought.
Eclectic Rev. 4th Series. 25:600.
Edinb. Rev. 23:320. 92:1.
Library of Useful knowledge.
Morgan's Essay on probabilities.
Pascal's Provincial Letters.
Quetelet on the Doctrine of probabilities.

Procession of the Holy Ghost.

Allatii Græciæ Orthodoxæ. (A collection of ecclesiastical writers of the Greek Ch.)
Buttstett Schriftmæsige Abhandlung von dem Ausgang des heilige Geiste.
Cundisii Orthod. doct. de processione Sp. S.
Dannhaveri (Ioann. C.) Dissertationes.
Faydit, Hist. controv. Græc. Latinorumque.
Haberkornius de Processione Spiritus Sanc.
Pfaffii Hist. succincta Controversiæ.
Walchii Hist. controversiæ Græc. et Latin.
Wegnerus de Processione Spiritus Sancti.

Burnett (T.) on the Trinity.
Emlyn's (Thomas) Tracts.
Hurrion on the Spirit.
Mosheim's Eccles. History. Cent. 8, part 2.
Neale's History of the Eastern Church.
Pearson on the Apostles' Creed.
Ridgeley's Body of Divinity.
Scott's (D. D.) Essay on the Trinity.
Watts' (Isaac) Works.

Procrastination. See DECISION, DEATHBED REPENTANCE.

Allestree's, Richard, Sermons.
Barrow's, Isaac, "
Berriman's, William, "
Brown's, W. L., "
Burnet's, Bp., "

Procrastination—*continued.*

Carmichael's, Fred., Sermons.
Christian Month. Spect. 5:421.
Cooper's, Edward, Sermons.
Day's, Henry T., "
Fuller's, Andrew, "
Graves', Richard, "
Hampden's, Bp., "
Hobart's, Bp., "
Knowles', Thomas, "
Lardner's, Nathaniel, "
Lowell's, Samuel, "
Monkhouse's, Richard, "
Parry's, Joshua, "
Reese's, Abraham, "
Saurin's, James, "
Scott's, John, "
Shuttleworth's, P. N., "
Skelton's, Philip, "
Smallridge's, George, "
Tillotson's, Abp., "
Wake's, Abp., "
Weston's, Stephen, "
Whichcot's, Bp., "
Wilson's, Bp., "
Wroughton's, Charles, "

Prodigality. See FRUGALITY, MODERATION, SELF-DENIAL.

Agutter's (William) Sermons.
Dwight's Theology. Ser. 122.
Hewlett's (John) Sermons.
Kettlewell's (John) Discourses.

Prodigies.

Julius de Prodigiis. (Various editions.)
Lavaterus, De spectris variisque præsagitionibus.
Salverte, du Sciences occultes.

Farmer on Miracles.
Lavater of Ghosts, strange noyses, crackes, and sundrie forewarnyges, which commonly happen before the dethe of menne, and alterations of Kyngdomes.
Spencer on Prodigies, Presages, &c.
Warburton's Critical and philosoph. enquiry into the causes of prodigies and miracles, as related by historians.

Profaneness. See OATHS.

Baumgarten-Crusii Theses theologicæ.
Barrow's (Isaac) Sermons.
Becon's (Thomas) Works.
Beveridge's (Bp.) Sermons.
Bishop's (William) Sermons.
Bourne's (Samuel) Sermons.
Boyle's (Robt.) Dissuasive from cursing.
Christian Observer. 18:15.
Cooper's (Edward) Sermons.
Disney's Ancient laws agt. profaneness, &c.
Evans' (R. W.) Sermons.
Fleming's (Caleb) Works.
Foster's (Dr. James) Sermons.
Francis' (Dr. John) Sermons.
Gahan's (W.) Sermons.

Profaneness—*continued.*

Gibson's Admonition to swearers.
Hall's (Bp.) Practical Works.
Hall's (Robt.) Notes of Sermons.
Lamont's (David) Sermons on preval. vices.
Morning Exercises at Cripplegate. (Duty of magistrates to suppress it.)
Newton's (Bp.) Dissertations.
Paley's (William) Sermons.
Reading's (William) Sermons.
Riddock's (James) Sermons.
Secker's (Abp.) Sermons.
Sharp's (Abp.) Sermons.
Smith's (Sydney) Sermons.
Stonehouse's Admonition against swearing.
Tombs' Sepher Sheba.
Wake's (Abp.) Discourses. (Several.)
Walker's (Samuel) Essays.
Woodward's Kind caution to swearers.

Profession of Religion.

Beveridge's, Bp., Sermons.
Buckminster's, Joseph, "
Cooper's, Edward, "
Hurd's, Bp., "
Lewis', W. H., "
Rogers', John, "
Secker's, Abp., "
Slade's, James, "
Stillingfleet's, Bp., "

Progress of Sin. See TEMPTATION.

Gerard's (Alex.) Sermons.
Venn's (John) Sermons.
Young's (Dr. Edw.) Sermons.

Progress of Society. See HUMAN PROG.

Progressive Friends.

Christian Exam. 61:1.
Minutes of the Yearly meetings of the "Friends who have adopted the congreg. order of church government." Since 1848.

Prohibition of Blood.

Danæus in Consilium Jerusalem.
Deylingii Observationes Sacra.
Dorschei (I. G.) Dissert. (Rep. to Grotius.)
Grotius de Sanguine et Suffocato.
Heideggeri Libertas Christianorum et lege.
Nitzch, de Sensu et consilio decreti apostol. Acts xv.
Spencer, de Legibus Hebræorum.
Witsii Miscellanea Sacra.

Barrington's Miscellanea Sacra. Ess. 4.
Bloomfield on the Lawfulness of eating blood.
Christian's Magazine. 3:559.
Delany's (P.) Abstinence from blood defended. (Sometimes appended to his Revelation examined with candor.)
Gale's (Dr. John) Sermons. (Six against the lawfulness of eating blood.)
Glas' (John) Works.
Hooker's Ecclesiastical Polity.
Jenning's Jewish Antiquities.

Prohibition of Blood—*continued.*

Lardner's Remarks on Ward's Dissertation.
Maimonides' Reasons for the law of Moses.
Moore's Moses revived.
Newman's Perpetuity of baptism. Appendix.
Pirie's (A.) Posthumous Works.
Sharp (Tho.) on the Lawfulness, &c.
Shuckford's Connexion of sac. and prof. hist.
Stackhouse's Hist. of the Bible. Bk. 2, ch. 1.
Ward's Dissertations.

Prohibitory Index. See INDEX.

Promises. See VOWS.

Cicero de Officiis. Lib. I.
Grotius de Jure. Lib. II, cap. XI.
Puffendorf de Legibus Nat. Lib. III, C. VI.
Sanderson (Bp.) de Juramento.

Doddridge's Lectures. Part 3, Lect. 69.
Godwin on Political Justice.
Grove's Ethics.
Leigh (Edward) on the Divine promises.
Watts' (Isaac) Sermons.

Promises of the Gospel.

Carter's (N.) Sermons.
Clarke (Sam.) on the Promises. (A small but convenient commonplace book.)
Colquhoun's Treatise on the Promises.
Leigh on the Divine promises.
Patrick's (Bp.) Sermons.
Spurstow's Wells of Salvation.

Propagation of the Soul. See TRADUCTION.

Property, Right of. See SOCIALISM, POLITICAL ECONOMY.

Angel on Corporations and Limitations.
Bingham on Infancy.
Blackwood's Mag. 21:74.
British and For. Rev. 16:30.
Chitty on Pleading.
——— on Contracts.
Collinson on Idiots and Lunatics.
Dalrymple on Feudal Property.
Democratic Rev. 16:17. 27:291.
For. Quart. Rev. 4:484,
Gilbert on Rents.
Humphreys on Real property.
Hunt's Merchant's Mag. 1:484.
Jones' Theory of Rent.
Kyd on Awards.
Lieber's (Francis) Essays.
Long on Sales.
New Englander. 8:220.
N. A. Rev. 67:119.
Patton's Effects of property upon society and Government.
Preston on Estates.
Quarterly Rev. 36:391. 46:81. 83:97.
Reeve's Domestic Relations.
Roberts on Frauds.
Roper on Husband and Wife.
——— on Legacies.
Shelford on Lunatics,
Story on the Conflict of laws.
Wayland's Moral Science. Book 2.
Woodfall's Landlord and Tenant.

Prophecy. See DOUBLE SENSE, NUMBER 666, PERIOD OF 1260 YEARS, SEALS AND TRUMPETS, SEVENTY WEEKS, SIGNS OF THE TIMES.

Baltus la Relig. chrét. prové par les proph.
Carpzovii Introd. ad libros propheticos.
Crameri Schola Prophetica.
——— Isagoge ad libros propheticos.
Crusii (C. A.) Hypomnemeta.
Dupin, Prolegomena sur la Bible.
Frankii Introd. ad lectionem propheticarum.
Gulick, Theol. prophetica de rebus V. Test.
Gurtleri Systema theologiæ propheticæ.
Hengstenberg's Christologie des A. Test.
Hulsii Nucleus propheticæ Script.
Jurieu d'Accomplissement de prophéties.
Maii Theol. proph. ex select V. T. oraculis.
Van Till, Phosphorus propheticus.
Vitringæ Typus doctrinæ propheticæ.

Abbadie's P. accomplished in Christ.
Addis' Theory of prophecy.
Aiton's Drying-up of the Euphrates.
Am. Bibl. Repos. 5:33. 2d Series. 3:35.
Appleton's Works. Lect. 23,24.
Arnold on the Interpretation of prophecy.
Auberlin's P. of Daniel and John viewed in their connection. Tr. by Adolph Saphir.
Barker's P. concerning Messiah.
Bates' Use and intent of prophecy.
Bentley's Remarks on free-thinking.
Bicheno's Signs of the times.
Bickersteth's Guide to the prophecies.
Bonnet's Enquiry. Bk. 4.
Bouchier on P. and its fulfilment.
British Critic. 7:328.
Brooks' (J. W.) Elements of prophetical interpretation. (A convenient compend.)
Browne's (E. H.) P. relating to the Messiah.
Brown's (J.) Harmony of prophecy.
Bullock's Reasoning of Christ and the Apos.
Burton on the Numbers of Daniel and John.
Butler's Analogy. Part 2, ch. 7.
Butler's (W. J.) Testimony of History.
Caulfield's Fall of Babylon.
Chandler's Antiq. and auth. of the P. of Dan.
Chauncey (W. S.) on Unaccomplished P.
Clarke's (S.) Connexion of the prophecies.
Clayton's Dissertations on prophecy.
Cobb's Bampton Lectures. 1783.
Cole (J. W.) on the Prophecies.
Collyer's (Wm. B.) Lectures on prophecy.
Cudworth's Intellectual System. Bk. 1, c. 5.
Cumberland's Origines Gentium.
Cunningham's Remarks on David Levi.
——— (Several other treatises.)
Curtis' Folly and danger of Infidelity.
Davidson's (D.) Test of prophecy.
De Burgh's Early prophecies of a Redeemer.
Dobb's Prophecies which have been fulfilled.
Duffield (Geo.) on the Prophecies.
Durell's Parallel proph. of Jacob and Moses.
Elliott's Warburton Lectures. 1849 to 1853.

Prophecy—*continued.*

Eclectic Rev. 4th Series. 16:625. N. Series. 7:69.
Ellis' (W. W.) Proph. relating to Christ.
Faber's Calendar of the P. (Chiefly those which relate to Antichrist.)
——— P. relating to the Jews.
Fairbairn on P. (Its nature, functions, &c.)
Frazer's Key to the unaccomplished P.
Frere's Combined view of Esdras, Daniel, and John.
Fry (John) on the Unfulfilled prophecies.
Fry's (T.) Scripture prophecies.
Gill's Preface to Vol. 5 of Commentary.
Greenhill's (Jos.) Proph. of the N. Testam.
Habershon's Connection of prophecies of the Apocalypse and Daniel.
——— on the Chronological prophecies.
Hale's (Wm.) Dissertations.
Hardy's Prophecies of the Bible, particularly those of John.
Hengstenberg's Nature of the prophecies.
Hey's Lectures. Bk. 1, ch. 17.
Holmes' (Robt.) Bampton Lectures. 1782.
Hoare's (W. H.) Harmony of the Apocalypse with other prophecies; with an outline of the various interpretations.
Horsley's (Bp.) Sermons. Ser. 15–18.
——— Prophecies of Messiah dispersed among the heathen.
Hurd's Introd. to the study of the prophecies. (Chiefly those relating to Popery.)
Jeffries on the Perfection of religion.
Jennings' Jewish Antiquities.
Jones' Key to prophetical language.
Jortin's Boyle Lectures. 1730.
Jurieu on the Accomplishment of prophecy. (A strong attack on Popery.)
Keith's (A.) Signs of the times. 1833.
——— On the Prophecies.
Ketts' History the interpreter of prophecy. ("Written with great elegance and judgment."—Bp. Tomline.)
Kelly's (James) Lectures on subjects connected with prophecy.
King's (Edward) Morsels of criticism.
Kitto's Journal. 6:389. (Literal interp.)
Lardner's Destruction of Jerusalem.
Leach's Lectures on fulfilled prophecies.
Lee's (S.) Sermons and Dissertations. (Takes the ground that all the prophecies of the Apocalypse are fulfilled.)
Lyall's Propædia Prophetica.
McCaul's Warburton Lectures. 1846. (Prophecy as a proof of Christianity.)
McLaurin on the P. relating to Messiah.
McLeod on the Principal prophecies.
Maitland's Connected view of prophecy. (A valuable collection of authorities from the Fathers down to 1849.)
Marsh's Lectures. Lect. 20,21.
Mead on the Prophecies.
Meth. Quarterly Rev. 4:364.
Morning Watch; a quarterly journal. From 1828 to 1834. London.

Prophecy—*continued.*

Monthly London lectures on prophecy. (Able sermons by Collier, Bird, Pye Smith, Fletcher, Orme, &c.)
New Englander. 1:103.
Newton (Bp.) on P. which have been fulfilled.
Newton (Sir I.) on Daniel and the Apocal.
Nolan's (F.) Warburton Lectures. 1837.
Penn's (Granville) Christian Survey.
Philips (J. S.) on the Interpretation of P.
Princeton Rev. 4:358,511. 29:598.
Purves on Prophetic time.
Randolph's Prophecies cited in the N. Test. compared with the Hebrew original.
Roberts' Manual of prophecy. (Compares the prophecies with the events which fulfilled them.)
Robinson's Prophecies of the Messiah.
Rule's Calculations of time, &c.
Sharp (Granville) on Several important P.
Sherlock's Use and intent of prophecy.
Simpson's Key to the P. (Many editions.)
Smith's (J. Pye) Dissertations.
——— Discourses.
Smith's (Dr. John) Summary view of prophecy. (A good abstract from Lowth, Newcombe, Newton, and Blaney.)
Southwark Morning Lectures. (By Baxter, Fowler, Manton, Poole, Owen, &c.)
Taylor's Comp. of Revelations with Daniel.
Theol. and Lit. Journal. (Many articles.)
Thompson (Ed.) on Prophecy and Miracles.
Thurston's Researches on P.
Tower's Illustrations of prophecy.
Townsend's Illustrations of prophecy.
Turner's Origin, character, and interp. of P.
Twell's Boyle Lectures. 1733.
Van Mildert's Boyle Lectures. 1802–4.
Vint's Dissertations on prophecy.
Waugh's (J. S.) Diss. on the prophecies.
Ward's (Wm.) Declensions and restorations of the church.
Wellwood on Prophecy.
Whiston's Boyle Lectures. 1707.
Whitaker's General and connected view.
White's Christianity and Mahometanism.
Whiteley's Scheme and completion of P.
Williams' Boyle Lectures. 1695.
Wilkin's Hist. of the destruction of Jerusalem, as connected with prophecy.
Winchester on the Prophecies.
Zouch's Attempt to illustrate some of the prophecies. (Learned and cautious.)

A "Dictionary of writers on the prophecies," with the titles, was published in 1835 by the Editor of the London Investigator—M. Brooks.

Prophecy as a Proof of Revelation.

Baltus, La Religion chretienne prouvé par l'accomplishment des prophecies.

Bates' Div. of the Christian religion. Ch. 4.
Berriman's (William) Sermons.
Bonnet's Enquiries.

Prophecy as a Proof, &c.—*continued.*

Boyle on the Fulfilment of Script. prophecy.
Brown's Harmony of Scripture prophecies.
Chalmers' Evidences of Christianity.
Chandler's (Bp.) Defence of Christianity.
Conybeare's (Bp.) Sermons.
Flemming's Fulfilling of Scripture.
Gordon's Christianity supported by P.
Hey's Lectures. Chap. 1
Horsley's (Bp.) Sermons.
Hurd's Lectures on prophecy.
Jenkins' Reasonableness of Christianity.
Keith's Truth of the Christian religion as derived from P., especially as illustrated by travellers. 1830.
La Pluches' Truth of the Gospel.
Lardner's Works. (Destruct. of Jerusalem.)
Newton's (Bp.) Boyle Lectures. 1756.
Paley's Evidences. Part 2, ch. 1.
Powell's (Samuel) Sermons.
Sherlock's Use and intent of prophecy.
Skelton's (P.) Sermons.
Warburton Lectures, viz.:
Allwood, 1815. Apthorp, 1786. Bagot, 1780. Davidson, 1824. Halifax, 1776. Hurd, 1772. Nares, 1805. Nolan, 1837. Pearson, 1811.
Watson's Tracts.
Weaver's (Robt.) Fulfilling of Scripture.
Wellwood's Discourses.
Whiston's Boyle Lectures. 1707.
Wilkinson on the Insp. of the Holy Script.
Wilkins' Hist. of the destruct. of Jerusalem.

Propitiation. See ATONEMENT.

Proprieties of Worship.

Barrow's (William) Sermons.
Buddicom's (Robert P.) Sermons.
Hall's (Bp.) Practical works.
Hewlett's (John) Sermons. (2 on this subj.)

Proselyte Baptism.

Pro. i. e. *that there was such a thing.*

Bengel (E. G.) über d. Proselytentaufe.
Benzelii Syntag. Diss. in Academ. Lundensi.
Butcher, de Initiis baptismi initiationis Judæorum.
Danz, Baptismus proselytorum Judaicus. (Ugolini.)
Reiskii (Ioann.) Dissertationes.
Schneckenburger's Alter der jüdischer Proselytentaufe.
Spencer (J.) de Lustrationibus et purif. Heb.
Lightfoot's Miscellanies, Christian and Judaical.
Selden's Works.
Wall's History of Baptism.

Con.

Buddei Inst. theol. dogmaticæ. Lib. V, c. 1.
Carpzovii (B. D.) Exercitationes.
Engerer's Jüdisch. Tauf betrug aufgedrecht.
Maii Diss. de lustrationibus et purificationibus Hebr. (Against Spencer.)

Proselyte Baptism—*continued.*

Con.

Matthies, Baptismatis Expos. bibl. hist. dogmatica.
Mulleri (J. G.) Dissertationes.
Schyn, Historia Mennonitarum.
Slevogtii Dissertationes.
Van Dale, Diss. super Aristea de LXX, etc.
Venemæ Institutiones historicæ.
Vitringæ Observationes Sacræ.
Wernsdorfius de baptismi Christianorum origine.

Benson's Paraph. and notes on the Epistle of Paul. Diss. 8, part 2.
Gale's Reflections on Wall's Hist. of baptism.
Gibbs on Baptism.
Gill's (Dr. John) Body of Divinity.
——— Preface to Com. on the N. Test.
Jennings' Jewish Antiquities.
Knatchbull's Annotations on difficult texts.
Owen's (John) Exercitations. Exerc. 8.

Proselytes, Jewish. See JEWISH ANTIQ.

Maimonides de Proselytos.
Van Dale (Ant.), Dissertationes.

Beausobre & L'Enfant's Introd. to Old Test.
Jennings' Jewish Antiquities.
Josephus' Jewish Antiquities.

Proseuchæ.

Bennet's (Benj.) Christian Oratory.
Coleridge's Dissertations on Judges 17, 18.

Prosperity. See RICHES, POWER.

Bates' (Will.) Discourses.
Bull's (Bp.) Sermons.
Burnett's (Gilbert) Discourses.
Downame (John) on Contempt of the world.
Fell's (Hunter F.) Sermons.
Hastings' (H. J.) Sermons.
Heurtly's (Cha. S.) Sermons.
Jackson's (Miles) Sermons.
Jortin's (John) Sermons.
Mason's (John) Sermons.
Monsel's (C. H.) Sermons.
Moroney's (Joseph) Sermons.
Oakley's (Fred.) Sermons.
Roe's Sermons.
South's (Robt.) Sermons.
Trebeck's (Andrew) Sermons.
Witherspoon's (Dr. John) Sermons. (Two on this subject.)

Prostitution. See ADULTERY, CHASTITY, FORNICATION, SEDUCTION, UNCLEANN.

Protestantism.

Baur (F. Ch.) Gegensatz d. Kath. and Prot. nach d. Principien der Lehrbegriffe.
Calvini Opera.
Evenii Demonstratio Apologetica.
Guntheri Demonstratio solida.
Handeshagen, der deutsche Protestatismus.
Illyricus de Voce et re Fide.

Protestantism—*continued.*

Larroque, Conformité de la discipline eccl. de Protestantes avec celle des anciens Chrêtiens.
Morneus de Ecclesia.
Mylii Dissertationes.
Planck, Gesch. d. Entstehung, etc., d. protest. Lehrbegriffs.
Schenkel, das Wesen d. Protestantismus.
——— d. Princip. d. Protestantismus.
Spanheimii Dissertationes.
Vorstius contra Bellarminum.

Baird's Protestantism in Italy; past and present. 1847.
Barrow's (Isaac) Works.
Birbeck's Evidence from the Fathers.
Chillingworth's Religion of Protestants.
Christian Examiner. 41:1. 48:341.
Coquerel's History of P. in France.
Du Moulin's Defence of the Reformed Chur.
Eclectic Rev. 4th Series. 15:713.
Edinburg Review. 54:238. (Rev. of Hugh Rose.)
Felice's Hist. of the Protestants of France.
Jewell's (Bp.) Works.
MacGavin's Protestant. (Very useful.)
Marsh's Hist. of the Protestants of France.
Meth. Quart. Rev. 3:69.
New Englander. 2:66.
Princeton Review. 9:1. 17:626.
Rose's (Hugh) Sermons before the Cambridge University in 1828.
Schaff's (P.) Principles of P. as related to the present state of the church. Trans. by J. W. Nevin. 1845.
Smedley's Hist. of the Protestants of France.
Sturgess' Defence of Protestantism.
Tillotson's Works.

Proverbs. See COMMENTATORS.

Crenii Opusculorum Fasciculus.
Debrii Adagialia Vet. et Nov. Testament.
Drusii Adagia Hebraica.
Schottii Adagialia sacra Nov. Test.
Vorstii Diatribe de adagiis Nov. Test.

Providence of God. See CHANCE, FATE, GOVERNMENT OF GOD, UNEQUAL DISTRIBUTION OF GOOD AND EVIL.

Lactantius, de Mortibus Persecutorum.
Theodoret, Oratio de Providentia.
Basil, Conciones.
Chrysostom, de Providentia Dei.

Backerus de Dei providentia circa mala.
Bairus de Prov. Dei circa peccata hominum.
Beza de Prov. Dei circa res temporale.
Bormann's Lehre der Vorsehung.
Burmanni Dissertationes quatuor.
Danhaveri Disputationes Theologicæ.
De Vries, Exercitationes Rationales.
Gomari Concillatio doct. orthodoxæ de P.
Heinii Dissertationes.
Maii Œconomia temporum Vet. Test.
Martinii Com. de gubernatione mundi.
Rechenburgius de Prov. Dei circa minima.

Providence of God—*continued.*

Reynoldi Dissertationes Philosophicæ.
Spanheimii Dissertationes theol. miscel.
Turrettini Dissertationes. Diss. iv, v, vi.
Twisse, Vindicatio Providentiæ Dei.
Viret, de la Providence.
Weismannus de Prov. Dei contra malum.
Wittichii Exercitationes Theologicæ.
Zuinglii Sermones.

Abernethy's (John) Sermons.
Appleton's (Pres.) Works. Lect. 8.
Arnold's (Frederick) Sermons.
Arrowsmith's (John) Discourses.
Atterbury's (Bp.) Sermons.
Balguy's (Dr. Thomas) Discourses.
Balmer's Academic Lectures.
Barrow (Isaac) on the Creed.
Baxter's (Richard) Works.
Bennet's (Benjamin) Sermons.
Berriman's (William) Sermons.
Beveridge's (Bp.) Sermons.
Bidlake's Bampton Lectures. 1811.
Binnings' (Hugh) Sermons.
Bledsoe's Theodicy.
Boston's (Tho.) Sermons.
Bull's (Bp.) Sermons.
Bullinger's Decades. (Parker Society publ.)
Bundy's (Richard) Sermons.
Burnet (Bp.) On the 39 articles.
Cappe on the Government of God.
Carr's (George) Sermons.
Carson's (Alex.) Works.
Cawton on Divine providence.
Chace's Relation of Div. P. to physical laws.
Chandler's (Samuel) Discourses.
Charnock's Works. (Extremely clear.)
Cheyne's Philosophical Principles.
Christian Month. Spect. 9:175
Christian Quart. Spect. 8:1.
Christian Observer. 1:54.
Clarke's (Adam) Discourses.
Clarke's (Samuel) Discourses.
Colling's (Dr. Jno.) Sermons on Providence. ("Well done."—COTTON MATHER.
Conybeare's (Bp.) Sermons.
Craddock's (Z.) Sermons.
Crane's Prospect of Divine Providence.
Croley on Divine Providence.
Crombie's Natural Theology. Essay 2.
Crosthwaite's History of Esther.
Cudworth's Intellectual System. Bk. 1, ch. 5.
Davies' (Samuel) Sermons.
Dewdney on Special providences.
Doddridge's Sermons.
——— Lectures.
Dowling's (J. G.) Sermons.
Dwight's (Tim.) Theology. Disc. 26 to 34.
Duncanson's P. manifested in natural law.
Fawcett on Divine Providence.
Field on Divine Government.
Flavel's Works. (Exceedingly precious.)
Forsyth on Divine Providence.
Foster's (Dr. James) Discourses.
Gifford's (G.) Great mystery of Providence.
Gilpin's (William) Sermons.

Providence of God—*continued.*

Goodman's (Dr. John) Sermons.
Gordon's Particular providence in distinction from general.
Hakewell on Providence. (Highly commended by DUGALD STEWART.)
Hastings' (H. J.) Sermons.
Holwell on Divine Providence.
Hook's (Walter F.) Sermons.
Hopkins' (Bp.) Works.
Horne's (Bp.) Sermons.
Horsley on Providence and free agency.
Hunter's Moral Discourses.
Jackson's Prophecies viewed in the light of Scripture.
Jamieson's Sacred History.
Jenkins' Reasonableness of Christianity.
Jortin's (John) Sermons.
Kattern's (Dan.) Sermons.
Kitto's Journal of Sac. Lit. 6:422.
Kollock's (Shepard K.) Sermons.
Leland's (Thomas) Sermons.
Marshall's (Nathaniel) Sermons.
McBrier's Goodness of Providence.
McCosh's Method of Divine government. (Great.)
Methodist Quarterly. 11:292.
Moore's Divine dialogues.
Natural history of enthusiasm.
New Englander. 6:249.
Parker on God and Divine Providence.
Pilkington (Geo.) on Particular Providence.
Plummer's (W. S.) Jehovah Jireh.
Price's (Rich.) Four Dissertations. Diss. 1.
Princeton Rev. 21:97. 30:319.
Reynolds' (Bp.) Works.
Rutherford's Scholastic Disputations concerning Prophecies.
Sedgewick's Shepherd of Israel.
Seed's (Jeremiah) Sermons.
Sharp's (Abp.) Sermons.
Sherlock's (Dean) Discourses.
South's (Robert) Sermons.
Spurgeon's (Charles H.) Sermons. 1st and 6th Series.
Stebbing's (H.) Sermons.
Sterne's (Lawrence) Sermons.
St. Pierre's Vindication of Divine P.
Stokes' Doct. of special Providence.
Taylor's (Joseph) Remarkable Providences.
Topping's Certainty of an overruling P.
Townsend's (G. F.) Warnings from the past.
Tucker's Light of nature pursued.
Turner's Hist. of remarkable providences.
Watts' Essays.
Welsted's Scheme of Providence.
Whitaker's (Edw. W.) Sermons.
Wilcox's (Daniel) Sermons.
Wilkins on the Beauty of Providence.
Williams' Equity of the Divine government.
Wisheart's (William) Sermons.
Wollaston's Religion of nature.

See an extensive list of Latin and German writers of the last century on this subject, in ARPE, *Theatrum Fati.*

Province of Reason in Religion.

See DEISM, HARMONY OF REASON AND FAITH, PHILOSOPHY OF RELIGION, WEAKNESS OF HUMAN REASON.

Conradus de Rationis usu in religione.
Crusius de Usu et limitibus rationis.
Ernesti (Jo. Aug.) Prolusiones. (Discards philosophy in the interpretation of the sacred writings.)
Friedmann's Christenthum. und Vernunft.
Mayeri (Jac.) Dissertationes.
Michaelis de Distinctione inter ea quæ supra et contra rationem sunt.
Musæus de Usu principiorum rationis et philos. in controversiis theologicis.
Reinhold: d. alte Frage—was ist Wahrheit?
Salat's (Joseph) Sokrates.
Schmidius de Usu principiorum rationis.
Schramm, de Principiorum rationis in theologia valore.
Schulz's Selbstständigkeit u. Abhangigkeit.
Velthusius de Usu rationis in rebus theol. et præsertim in interpretatione S. S.
Voetius de Ratione humana in rebus fidei.
Weidner, de Limitibus rationis in theol. definend.
Wendt, de Ratione inter relig. et philosoph.
Witsius de Usu et abusu rationis.

Abercrombie's Intellectual Powers.
Baker's Reflections upon Learning.
Balguy's (John) Discourses.
Bourn's (Samuel) Sermons.
Boyle's Use of reason in religion.
Brown's Procedure and extent of the human understanding.
[Calamy's (Ed.)] Philologus' Use and abuse of reason.
Campbell (Abp.) on the Necessity of Revelat.
Clark's (John) Office of reason in religion.
Croft's Bampton Lectures. 1786.
Curry's Confirmation of faith.
Davies' (J.) Estimate of the human mind.
Eclectic Review. 1859:225.
Ellis' Knowledge of Divine things.
Ferguson's Interest of reason in religion.
Gale's Court of the Gentiles. Part 3.
Gilderdale on Natural Religion.
Glanvill's Vanity of dogmatizing.
Holden's (Lawrence) Sermons.
Letters Between Ant. Tuckey & B. Whichcot.
Manning's (James) Sermons.
Manningham's Use of speculative philosophy in religion.
Mansel's Bampton Lectures. 1858.
Nelson's (G.) Use of human reason. (Written against the Methodists.)
Newton's (Bp.) Dissertations.
Norris' Mysteries of Christianity.
Princeton Review. 32:648.
Rust on the Use of reason.
Sharp's (Abp.) Sermons.
Sherlock's Danger of corrupting religion by philosophy.
Smallridge's (George) Sermons.
Smith's True Method of obtaining divine knowledge.

Province of Reason—*continued.*

Stephens' Human nature delineated.
Stone's (Edward) Sermons.
Tucker's Light of nature pursued.
Tuckey's Letters.
Twinning's Reason in regard to revelation.
Van Mildert's Boyle Lectures. 1802.
Wardlaw's Christian Ethics.
Whately's (Bp.) Sermons.
Whichcot's Aphorisms in religion.
Whiston's Reason and philos. no enemies.
Witsius on the Abuse of reason.
Worseley's P. of reason in religion deduced from the Sermon on the Mount.
Young's Province of reason. (An able criticism on Mansell.)

Prudence. See DISCRETION.

Diogenes Laertii Apothegmata clarissimor. Philosophorum.
Plutarch de Digne scitis regum.
——— Apothegmata Laconica.
Stobæus de Prudentia.
Abernethy's (Dr. John) Sermons.
Bright (G.) on Christian Prudence.
Burgh's Dignity of human nature.
Cappe's (Newcombe) Practical Discourses.
Carleton's (George) Sermons.
Chris. Rev. 6:213.
Dodwell's (William) Sermons.
Enfield's (Wm.) Sermons.
Evans on Christian Temper. Ser. 19.
Kettlewell's (John) Sermons. (Prudence distinct from craft.)
Lawrence's (J.) Beauty of a Christian life.
Mason's (John) Sermons.
Norris on Christian Prudence.
Paley's (Wm.) Sermons.
Pott's (Archdeacon) Sermons.
Taylor's (Jer.) Sermons.
Tucker's Light of nature pursued. Ch. 30.

Prudentius.

Gundlingii Observationes selectæ.
Le Clerc, Vie de Prudence.
Ludovici (Io. Pet.) Opusculæ Miscellaneæ.
Manutii Vita P. ejus operibus præmissa.

Psalmody. See HYMNOLOGY, INSTRUMENTAL MUSIC, SINGING.

Athanasius, Epist. ad Marcellinum.
Augustine, Confessiones. Lib. IX, c. 6.
Basil, Homiliæ in Psalmos. Hom. I.
Chrysostom, Homiliæ in Epist. ad Rom. Hom. XXVIII.
Lactantius, Institutiones. Lib. VI, c. 21.
Knapp's (A.) Evangelischer Leiderschatz.
Schurzfleischii Disputationes.
Allen's Essay on Singing.
Am. Bibl. Repos. 2d Series. 7:361. 11:425.
Am. Quart. Register. 5:25.
Atterbury's (Francis) Sermons.
Baird's (T. D.) Inquiry into the duty of the church in the exercise of praise.
Baxter's (Arthur G.) Sermons.
Beachcroft's (Robt. P.) Sermons.

Psalmody—*continued.*

Bennet's Christian Oratory.
Blackwood's Mag. 9:565. 41.479.
Boyse (Gilbert) on Singing in pub. worship.
Brown's Natural and revealed religion.
Burne's (Richard) Sermons.
Christian Disciple. 3:360.
Chris. Exam. 3:489. 4:67,300. 6:189. 13:163. 21:254. 29:337. 38:1. 39:102. 40:29. 41:422. 46:88. 47:204. 59:221. 65:230. 69:402.
Chris. Month. Spect. 3:526. 6:544. 7:34. 8:46. 9:378,604.
Chris. Quart. Spect. 3:526. 6:208.
Chris. Review. 2:421.
Clarke's (W. B.) Sermons.
Close's (Francis) Sermons on the liturgy.
Cole's View of modern Psalmody.
Collyer's Practical Discourses.
Dehon's (Dr. T.) Sermons.
Eastcheap Lectures. 1708–17.
Eclectic Rev. 10:535.
Edinb. Rev. 95:64.
Edwards (John) on the Creed. Art. 9.
Emmons' (Nathaniel) Sermons.
Engel's (C.) Reflections on church music.
Exeter Hall Lectures to young men.
Frazier's Mag. 44:609.
Gill's Body of Divinity.
Gould's (N. D.) Church music in America; its history, peculiarities, &c.
Grosvenor's (Benjamin) Sermons.
Hastings on Musical taste.
Henry's (Matt.) Miscellaneous Works.
Horne's (Bp.) Sermons.
Hughes (Henry) on Congregational P.
Kidder's (Bp.) Sermons.
Latta (Dr.) on Psalmody.
Law's Serious call. Ch. 15.
Lit. and Theol. Rev. 3:66. 4:59. 6:360.
Littell's Living Age. 25:241.
London Quart. Review. 38:16.
Mason's (Wm.) Hist. and critical Essays.
Meth. Quart. Review. 2:245. 4:165. 8:283, 602. 9:662.
New Englander. 2:335. 4:312. 6:424. (T. Hastings.) 7:55,350.
N. A. Rev. 11:38. (E. Everett.) 15:402.
Pierce's Vindication of Dissenters.
Princeton Rev. 15:88.
Rawlin's (Richard) Sermons.
Ridgeley's Body of Divinity.
Romaine's (W.) Essay on Psalmody.
Stillingfleet on Church music.
Stone's (Abp.) Sermons.
Taswell's (Will.) Sermons.
Taylor's (Jno.) Spirit and practice of P.
Vincent's (William) Sermons.
Westminster Review. 38:76.

About 90 hymn books are mentioned by LOWNDES, and nearly 2000 by SEDGWICK, in his Catalogue of hymn books. DR. WATTS says: "Of all our religious solemnities, psalmody is the most unhappily managed." He himself did more to remedy this evil than all other writers.

Psychology. See MIND.

Psychodunamy. See ANIMAL MAGNETISM.

Psychopannychy.
See SLEEP OF THE SOUL.

Public Charities.
See BENEVOLENT SOCIETIES, ENDOWMENTS, VOLUNTARY ASSOCIATIONS.

Public Worship. See PLACES OF WORSHIP, PROPRIETIES, WORSHIP.

Harenbergii Theologia dogmatica ex monumentis patrum.
Mercier (L.), sur le Culte public.

Atterbury's (Lewis) Sermons.
Barbauld's Remarks on Wakefield's enquiry.
Baxter's (Rich.) Christian Ecclesiastics.
Bennett's (Benj.) Sermons on Chris. Order.
Beveridge's Neces. and adv. of public prayer.
Bruckner's Thoughts on public worship.
Burgess' Reply to Wakefield.
Burnett's (Gilbert) Sermons.
Carr's (George) Sermons.
Charlesworth on Public worship.
Clagget's (Nicholas) Sermons.
Clarke's (Stephen) Sermons.
Clarkson's (David) Sermons.
Clayton's (Thomas) Sermons.
Craig's (William) Sermons.
Fothergill's (George) Sermons.
Gardner's Duties of public worship.
Gill's (John) Occasional Sermons.
Jones' (Herbert) Sermons.
Jortin's (John) Sermons.
Kinghorn on Public worship.
Knowles' (Thomas) Sermons.
Langhorne's (J.) Sermons.
Maynard's (Edward) Sermons.
Mede's (Joseph) Sermons.
Mudge's (Zachary) Sermons.
Munton's (Anthony) Sermons.
Newman on Early attendance.
Nott's Sermons on P. W. suited to the times.
Parry's Vind. of P. W. (Rep. to Wakefield.)
Pope's P. W. founded in nature. (Do.)
Priestley's Letters to a young man.
Rogers' (Dr. John) Sermons.
Saunders on Public worship.
Sharp's (Thomas) Sermons.
Stillingfleet's (John) Shekinah.
Talbert's Duty of frequenting P. worship.
Toulmin's (J.) Sermons.
Trapp's (J.) Duties of public worship.
Wakefield's Enquiry, &c. (Against P. W.)
Waples' (Edward) Sermons.
Wilson's Def. of P. W. (Rep. to Wakefield.)
Wisheart's (William) Sermons.

Pulpit Eloquence. See ELOQUENCE.

Punctuality. See PROCRASTINATION.

Punishment.
See JUSTICE, PRISON DISCIPLINE.

Amer. Bibl. Repos. 2d Series. 10:1.
Bentham's (Jer.) Rationale of punishment.
Sampson on Crime and its treatment.

Purgatory. See INTERMEDIATE PLACE, SPIRITS IN PRISON.

Allatii de Utriusque ecclesiæ occidentalis et orientalis perpetua in dogmate de Purgatorio consensione. (Papal.)
Austin, Cura de Mortuis.
Beckers' Mittheilungen aus d. merkwurdigst.
Blondel (D.), de la Creances des pères touchant l'etat des ames d'aprés cette vie.
Britzer, Quid doceat eccl. de P.? (Papal.)
Calixti (Georg.) Dissertationes.
Calixti (Ulric.) Dissertationes.
Chytræus de Animarum immortalitate.
Du Moulin, les Eaux de Siloé.
Faber, Disputationes Theologicæ.
Forbesii Considerationes modestæ.
Godeschalci Confessionale.
Hoffner die Shicksale der Seele.
Hulsemanni (Ioann.) Dissertationes.
Kortholti Disquisitiones anti Baronianam.
Laurentius in Fabula Papistica.
Le Quien, Oriens Christianus.
Lensæus de Fidelium animarum purgatorio.
Lutheri Opera.
Meisneri (Io. H.) Dissertationes.
Quenstedius de Ecclesiarum Orient. et Lat. dissensione.
Scherzeri Fasciculus Diss. theologicarum.
Schröckh's Kirchengeschichte.
Thummii Ignis purgat. Pontificii fatuus.
Wallenburch, Tractatus de sanctis.
Wesselii (Ioann.) Opera.
Wetstein, de Vanitate Purgatorii.

Allen's Defence of purgatory.
Beza on the Pope's Canons.
Billingsley's (John) Sermons.
Bradford's (The Martyr) Works.
Bunn's Reasons why Protestants reject the doctrine of purgatory.
Burnet on the 39 Articles.
Collet's Popish frauds exemplified.
Deacon's P. proved to be contrary to Catholic tradition. (Cites many authors.)
Donne's (John) Sermons.
Fletcher's (Jos.) Lectures on the Roman religion.
Fulke (Wm.) on Popery.
Geddes' Miscellaneous Tracts.
Grotius' Collection of the Fathers.
Hall's (Wm. J.) Doctrine of purgatory.
Hey's (Dr. J.) Lectures. Bk. 4.
Johnson's (Sam.) Purgatory proved by miracles. (Satirical.)
Kitto's Journal of Sac. Lit. 1:289
Latimer's (Bp.) Works.
Limborch's Theology.
Marshall's Doct. of P. patriarchal, papistical, and rational.
Morning Exercises at Cripplegate. (Sermon by Edw. West.)
Rogers (Tho.) on the 39 Articles.
Salter's Hall Sermons. Ser. by Dr. Earle.
Stillingfleet on the Satisfaction of Christ.
Tillotson's Sermons.
Tuckney's Prelectiones.

Wake's (Abp.) Discourses.

On the history of this doctrine, see VALVERDE, *Ignis purgatorius assertus*, BELLARMINE, *de Controversiis fidei*, on one side; and USHER's *Answer to a Jesuit's challenge*, and HALL's (W. J.) *Doctrine of Purgatory*, on the other.

Puritans. See HALF-WAY COVENANT, PILGRIM FATHERS.

Niemeyer, Puritanorum libri symbolici.

Ames' English Puritanisme. (Severe.)
Amer. Bibl. Repos. 2d Series. 2:217. 11:77. 3d Series. 2:226. 4:1.
Backus' Hist. of New England. (To 1784.)
Bradshaw's (William) English Puritanism; containing the opinions, &c. (Valuable as showing the difference between ancient and modern Nonconformists. 1605.)
Brook's Lives of the Puritans. (Professes to be "*drawn from 55 vols. in folio, 26 in quarto, 36 in octavo, besides various manuscripts;*" and gives memoirs of nearly 500 persons, with lists of their writings.)
Cambridge University Transactions in the 16th and 17th centuries. Collected by J. Heywood and Tho. Wright.
Chris. Exam. 38:126.
Chris. Observer. 14:386,449.
Chris. Review. 8:481.
Church Rev. 2:370. 3:208,559. 4:203.
Coit's History of P. (A bitter invective.)
Eclec. Rev. 4th Series. 24:219. New Series. 5:213.
Edinburg Rev. 42:338.
Grey's Exam. of 2d vol. of Neal's history.
Hall's (Edwin) Puritans and their principles.
Headley's Life of Cromwell.
Heywood's Cambridge Univer. Transactions during the Puritan controversy.
Hopkins' (Samuel) The Puritans. (Traces them from their origin to 1575.)
Hutchinson's History of Massachusetts.
Hubbard's " " To 1683.
Knickerbocker Mag. 33:508.
Knowles' Memoir of Roger Williams. (Many valuable documents.)
Lee's The family and its duties.
Lond. Quart. Rev. 78:94.
Marsden's History of the early Puritans.
——— History of the later Puritans.
Mather's Magnalia Dei Americana. To 1698.
Meth. Quar. Rev. 5:54. 6:534. 9:217.
Morse's History of New England.
Neal's History of the Puritans.
New Englander. 1:352. 4:288. 9:531.
New York Review. 6:48.
Nichols' (Josiah) Plea for the innocent.
North Am. Rev. 50:432. 51:252. 60:214.
Princeton Rev. 17:1. 18:133.
Quar. Review. 10:90.
Stoughton's Two hundred years ago. (Sketches of the Puritans and Spiritual heroes of 1660 to 1663.)
Stowell's Hist. of the Puritans in England.
Trumbull's (Benj.) History of Connecticut.
Tulloch's Eng. Puritanism and its leaders.
Uhden's New England Theocracy.
Wilson's History of the Pilgrim Fathers.
Winthrop's (Gov.) Journal. To 1644.
Young's Chronicles.

Purity of Heart. See BEATITUDES, GOVERNMENT OF THE HEART, THOUGHTS.

Abernethy's (John) Sermons.
Alford's Hulsean Lectures. 1842.
Beveridge's (Bp.) Sermons.
Blackley's (Thomas) Sermons.
Bloomfield's (Cha. J.) Sermons.
Burton's (Hezekiah) Sermons.
Cook's (John) Sermons.
Cooper's (Edward) Sermons.
Evans on Christian Temper. Ser. 4.
Gale's (John) Sermons.
Hincks' (John) Sermons.
Horsley's (Bp.) Sermons.
Nicholson's (William) Sermons.
Paley's (William) Sermons.
Pyle's (Philip) Sermons.
Saurin's Sermons.
Smallridge's (Bp.) Sermons.
South's (Robert) Sermons.
Spencer's (Bp.) Sermons.
Stebbings' (Henry) Sermons.
Stennett on the Moral law.
Sumner's (John Bird) Sermons.
Wesley's (John) Works.
Whitaker's (Edward W.) Sermons.
Witherspoon's (Dr. John) Sermons.

Puseyism. See OXFORD THEOLOGY.

Pyrrhonism.

Crouza, Examen du P. ancien et modérn.

Quenching the Spirit. See GRIEVING THE SPIRIT.

Boyse's (Joseph) Sermons.
Bragge (Francis) on Undissembled religion.
Dyke's (Jeremy) Discourses.
Greenham's (Richard) Sermons.
Polwheel on Quenching the Spirit.
Sumner's (John Bird) Sermons.
Winslow's Practical view of the Holy Spirit.

Quietists. See BOURIGNONISTS.

Pro.

Abelly, Meditations.
Ameline de l'Amour de souverain bien.
Brisaceriusin, de Jansenismo.
Croizet, Exercises de piété.
Cibole, la Sainte meditation sur soimême.
Dupont, Meditations sur les mystères.
Fenelon, Œuvres. (Almost every volume contains more or less of this phase of piety.)
Malaval, Pratique facile pour elevér l'ame.
Molinosi Opera.
Palamas, Orationes duæ.
[Pean,] le Combat du Molinisme contre le Jansenisme.
Poiret, de Œconomia Divina.

Quietists—*continued.*

Pro.

Poiret, Cogitationes rationales de Deo.
——— de Eruditione triplici: solida, superficiaria, et falsa.
——— (Many other treatises.)
Scharling's Michael de Molinos: ein Bild aus der kirchengesch. des 17 Jahrh.
Theologia Germanica. (Edited by Arndt and others, at different times, and thought by Bp. Jebb to be the source of German Quietism. To these volumes Dr. H. Moore attributes his "deepest and happiest views of religion.")

Amour's Journal of the disputes between the Jansenists and Molinists.
Burnet's (Bp.) Lectures.
Butler's Life of Fenelon.
Fenelon's (Abp.) Works.
Memoirs of Mad. Guion. (A very precious book, though containing many errors.)
Molinos' Works. (M. is generally regarded as the founder of Quietism. For his writings he was condemned to perpetual imprisonment.)

Con.

Acindyni Carmen Jambicum. (Reply to Palamas.)
Argentre, Collectio judiciorum de novis erroribus.
Aurignis, Memoires chronologiq. et dogmat.
Bossuet, Instruction sur les etats d'oraison.
——— Relation sur le Quietisme.
——— (Many other treatises, contained in vols. 30, 40, 42, and 50 of the Versailles edition of his works.)
Carpzovii Disputationes Academicæ.
Colberg's Platonisch-hermetisches Christenthum.
Foertschii Breviar. select. theol. Par. II.
Gregoire, Histoire des Sectes.
Hases' Zeugniss der Wahrheit.
Jaegeri Historia Ecclesiastica.
——— Examen Quietismi.
Langii Dissertationes.
Mayeri Dissertationes Selectæ.
Schmidius de Quietismi revolutione, etc.
Weismanni Hist. ecclesiastica. Sæc. XVII.

Eclectic Review. New Series. 10:437.

See a very full, if not complete, catalogue of books written by Quietists, in the Memoirs of J. P. NICERON. A large list is also given by FLACIUS, *Catal. testium veritatis.*

Quietness of Spirit. See RESIGNATION, PEACEABLENESS.

Quotations from the O. Testament by New Testament Writers.

Altingii Parall. vaticinorum V. T.
Drusii Parallela Sacra.
Frisii Demonstratio Exegetica.
Hottinger, de Usu scriptorum Ebraicum in Nov. Test.

Quotations—*continued.*

Hoffmanni Demonstratio Evangelica. (Every quotation recited in full: 1st, as quoted; 2d, as in the original; and 3d, as in the Septuagint version.)
Keslerus de Dictorum V.T. allegatione in N. T.
Knappii Recensus locorum, etc. (Appended to his edition of the New Testament.)
Melchoir, Paral. locorum Vet. Test. in novo citorum.
Pfaffii (Christop.) Dissertationes.
Sontagius de Allegatis apocryphis, etc.
Surenhusii Βιβλος καταλλαγης.
Workenii Harm. vet. et novi Test.

Rabbinical Literature.

Abarbaneli Opera.
Aben Ezra, Comm. in aliquot libros biblicos.
Ben Gerson, in Pentateuchum.
Biblia Hebraica; cum utraque Masora et Targum; item cum Comment. Rabbinorum. Studio J. Buxtorfii.
Biblia Hebraica magna Rabbinica.
Bombergii Biblia cum Rabbinorum Com.
Cellarii Institutio Rabbinica.
Eisenmeyer's Endecktes Judenthum.
Genebrardi Isagoge.
Hottinger, de Usu script. Ebraicor. in N. T.
Jarchi Com. in Vet. Testamentum.
Kimchi Com. in aliquot libros, etc.
Lightfoot, Horæ Ebraicæ.
Lipmanni Liber Nizachon.
Maimonides Opera Varia.
Meuschenii N. Test. ex Talmude illustratum.
Plantevitii Florilegium Biblicum.
Relandi Analecta Rabbinica.
Rhenferdi Syntagma Dissert. philolog.
Schoettgenii Horæ Ebraicæ et Talmudicæ.

See EISENMEYER, above cited, who gives a list of one hundred and ninety-three Jewish writers. "Stupendum hoc est opus."—RIEMMAN. DR. GILL, in his Commentary, brings to the service of New Testament criticism, about as much Rabbinical literature as is useful.

Races of Men. See ETHNOLOGY.

Rapture of St. Paul.

Ludwig (A. C.), Disputationes Theologicæ.

Rash Judgment.

Balguy's (John) Sermons.
Blair's (James) Sermons.
Brackenbury's (Edward) Sermons.
Enfield's (William) Sermons.
Gale's (John) Sermons.
Haggitt's (George) Sermons.
Hill's (Bryan) Sermons.
Jortin's (John) Dissertations. Diss. 3.
Kollock's (Shepard K.) Sermons.
Mason's (John) Lord's day entertainments.
Norris' (John) Sermons.
Wesley's (John) Sermons.
Wilder's (John) Sermons.

Rationalism. See NEOLOGY.

Pro.

Ammon's Entwarf einer Wissenschaftlich Theologie.
——— Abhandlungen zur Erläuterung, etc.
——— Handbuch d. chris. Sittenlehre.
——— (Other works.)
Bauer's Christliche Gnosis.
——— Untersuchungen über d. Evangelien.
——— Lehrbuch der Dogmengeschichte.
Compte, Systéme universel des conceptions.
De Wette, Kurzgefasstes Exegetiches.
——— Biblische Dogmatik.
——— Religion und Theologie.
Eichhorn's Einleitung ins Alte Test.
——— (Other works.)
Flugge's Versuch einer Darstellung, etc.
Gesenius' Thesaurus philolog. criticus.
Gieseler's Lehrbuch d. Kirchengeschichte.
Hase, die Leipziger Disputation.
——— Streitschriften.
——— die Tubingen Schule.
Kant's Sammtliche Werke.
Michaelis' Vermischte Schriften.
Michelet's Philosophischen Moral.
——— Philosophie vom Kant bis Hegel.
Noach's Biblische Theology.
——— Freidenker in der Religion.
Reinhard's System d. Christlichen Moral.
Schmidt's (J. E. C.) Kirchengeschichte.
Spittler's Grundes d. Gesch. der Kirchen.
Staudlin's Ideen sur Kritik der religion.
——— Dogmengeschichte.
Strauss, das Leben Jesu.
——— Predigten.
Tieftrunk's Versuch einer Kritik d. religion.
——— Dilucidationes.
——— Religion der Mundigen.

Bohlen's [or Van Bolen] Introd. to Genesis.
Combe's Vestiges of the history of Creation.
De Wette's Introduction to S. Scripture.
Donaldson's Jasher.
Essays and Reviews. (By Temple, Pattison, Powell, Wilson, Goodwin, Jowett, &c.)
Hase's Life of Jesus.
Powell's (B.) Claims of Revelation.
Williams' (R.) Rational Godliness.

Con.

Baumgarten (M.) Theologischer Commentar.
——— Apostelgeschichte.
Eschenmeyer's Religions-philosophie.
Glaseri (C.) Dissertationes.
Grimm's Glaubenswuerdigkeit.
Grohmann, Kritik d. Christl. Offenbarung.
Guerické's Gesammt-geschichte des N. T.
Hahnii (A.) Dissertationes.
Harless' Bearbitung des Leben Jesu von Strauss.
Hug, über d. Leben Jesu von Strauss.
Korner's Philosophie d. Rationalismus.
Kuhn's Philos. und Theol. Rationalismus.
Maret, Theodocée Chrétienne.
Müller's Wahren und Gewissen.
Röhr's Brief über d. Rationalismus.

Rationalism—*continued.*

Con.

Rosenkranz's Principien der Strauss.
Sack's Bemerkungen über d. Standpunct der Schrift.
Schäffer's Apologie der Offenbarung.
Schirmer's Würddigung d. Supernaturalis.
Schott, Isagoge in libros N. T. sacros.
Thiersch, über die Aechtheit der N. Test.
——— (Other works.)
Tholuck's Glaubwuerdigkeit d. evangelischen Geschichte.
——— Predigten.
——— Theologische u. exeget. Schriften.
Titman, über Rationalismus u. Atheismus.
Uhlig's Wahre Rationalismus.
Uster's Comm. über den Brief an die Galater.
Vater's Gefuhlsreligion u. Christenthum.
Weber, Libri symbolici eccl. Lutheranæ.

Alford's Principles of the oracles of God.
Amer. Eclectic Rev. 2:545.
Amer. Quart. Rev. 2:171. 3:150. 4:157.
Biblical Repos. 2d Series. 2:198.
Brownson's Review. 2d Series. 2:143. 6:248.
Christian Quart. Spect. 6:509.
Christian Rev. 2:171. 4:370. 5:243,533. 6:269.
D'Aubigné on the Authority of God.
——— Rationalism and Popery.
Democratic Review. 12:467.
Eclectic Mag. 19:289.
Eclectic Review. New Series. 11:105.
Edinburg Rev. 7:13. 46:304. 63:232. 90:155.
Frazier's Mag. 4:53.
Gasparin's Schools of doubt.
Irons' (W. J.) Sermons.
Kitto's Journal. 1:126,257.
Lee's (Prof.) Dissertations.
Littell's Living Age. 24:1.
Literary and Theol. Journal. 3:122.
London Quart. Rev. 2:1. 7:1.
MacCaul's Thoughts on Revelation. (Gives the state of religion in Germany in 1849.)
Monthly Rev. 114:322. 116:305. 117:447.
Neander's Life of Christ. (Written against Eichhorn, but not much more orthodox.)
Parkinson's Hulsean Prize Essay. 1837.
Plank's Introd. to Theological literature.
Princeton Review. 26:689.
Vaughn's (Robert) Essays.

Rationalism differs from Neology chiefly in that it is the more recent form of the Theology which has prevailed for some years in Germany. I distinguish Rationalists from Atheists in that they acknowledge a Supreme Power; and from Deists in that they are professed Christians. The writers cited are a mere specimen, but are more than sufficient.

It is not possible to draw an exact line between Neology and Rationalism, as they are but phases of the same thing. For other writers, see SAINTE, *Histoire critique de Rationalismus*, jusq. 1841; and STAUDLIN'S *Geschichte d. Rationalismus.*

Rationalism, History of.

Gieseler's Lehrbuch d. Kirchengeschichte.
Rosenbaum, de Controv. inter Rationalismum et Supernaturalismum.
Schwarz's Gesch. der neusten Theologie.
Stäudlin's Gesch. u. Geist d. Skepticismus.
——— Rationalismus u. Supernaturalismus.
Tafel's Gesch. u. Kritik d. Skepticismus.
Tholuck's Borgeschichte des Rationalism.

Beard's Crit. history of German Rationalism.
Cottrell's Religious movement in Germany in the 19th century.
Hagenbach's History of the Church in the 18th and 19th centuries.
Kahnis' History of German Protestantism.
Pusey's (H. B.) Causes of the rationalist character of late German theology. 1830.
Rose's (Hugh J.) Works.
St. Armand's Critical history of Rationalism in Germany. (To 1849.)

Reading the Scriptures. See STUDY OF THE SCRIPTURES, USE OF THE BIBLE IN SCHOOLS.

Augustine, Homiliæ.
Bibliandri "Quo modo oportet legere S. S.?"
Hyperius de S. Scripturæ lectione.
Kortholtus de Lectione Bibl. in linguis vulgo cognitis.
Loescheri (Jac.) Philomusi vatis.
Usseri Historia dogmatica controversiæ orthodoxos et Pontificos, de Scripturis vernaculis. (Proves that from the first, Christians read the Scriptures in the common language; and that public worship was not conducted in Latin till the time of Charlemagne.

Adams' (T.) Select Sermons.
Amory's (Thomas) Sermons.
Barker's (C.) Sermons.
Baxter's (Rich.) Practical Works.
Beren's (Edward) Village Sermons.
Bernard's Rhemes against Rome.
Billingsley's Right of the people to read.
Burrows' (William) Sermons.
Carrington's (James) Sermons.
Clay's (John) Sermons.
Collyer's (W. Bengo) Practical discourses.
Cotton's (R. L.) Sermons.
Craig's (Dr. W.) Sermons.
Cranmer's (Abp.) People's right to read.
Cunningham's (J. W.) Sermons.
D'Oyly's (George) Sermons.
Eveleigh's (John) Sermons.
Foster's (James) Sermons.
Fowles' (F. W.) Sermons.
Frank's (J. C.) Hulsean Lectures. 1821.
Frost's (John) Sermons.
Graves' (Richard) Sermons.
Hawkins on the Object and uses of the historical books of the Old Testament.
Hervey's (James) Sermons.
Hewlett's Duty of studying the Scriptures.
Irving's (Edward) Orations.
Jewell's (Bp.) Works.

Reading the Scriptures—*continued.*

Maturin's (C. R.) Sermons.
Millar's Right of the people to search the Scriptures.
Newton's (John) Sermons.
Nourse's (P.) Sermons.
Patrick's Duty of Christians to read.
Ravenscroft's (Bp.) Works.
Roberts' (Arthur) Plain sermons.
Smith's (Will.) Sermons.
Sterne's (Lawrence) Sermons.
Stratford's People's right to read.
Taylor's (C.) Sermons.
Twells' Boyle Lectures.
Whately's Mode of conveying moral precepts in the N. T.
White's Directions for reading.
Whitefield's (George) Sermons.
Whitgift's (Abp.) Works.
Williams' Scripture rule of faith.

Reading Sermons. See EXTEMPORE PR.

Realists. See NOMINALISTS.

Real Presence. See CONSUBSTANTIATION, LORD'S SUPPER, MASS, TRANSUBSTANTIATION.

Reason. See MIND, PROVINCE OF REASON.

Reasoning. See LOGIC, PROV. OF REASON.

Rechabites. See TEMPERANCE.

Bartolocci Dissertatio de Rechabitis.
Drusius de Sectis Judaicis.
Maimonides Opera.
Witsii (H.) Exercitationes Sac. Exerc. IV.

Calmet's Preface to Jeremiah.
Foster's (John) Broadmead Lectures.
Heber's (Bp.) Parish Sermons.
Mill's (W. H.) Lent Sermons.
Potts' (J. H.) Sermons.
Reading's (W.) Sermons.
Townson's History of the Rechabites.
Warter's (J. W.) Sermons.

Reciprocal Influence of Mind and Body.

Bacon (Lord), de Augmentis Scientiarum.
Leuret, Anatomie comparée du systéme nerveux.

American Institute of Instruction. Periodical. (Several articles.)
Barlow's Connection between physical and intellectual philosophy.
Brodie on Matter and mind.
Carpenter's Principles of human physiology.
Cheyne's Philosophical principles of religion. Ch. 3, sec. 39.
Christian Spect. April, 1826, and April, 1827.
De Cartes on the Passions.
Doddridge's Lectures. Prop. 3.
Eclectic Review. 4th Series. 31:422.
Falconer on the Infl. of climate, food, &c., on the temper, laws, and relig. of mankind.
Flavel's Pneumatics.

Reciprocal Influence—*continued.*

Gregory on the Duties and qualifications of a physician.
Haller's Elements of Physiology.
Hervey's (James) Contemplations.
Holland's Medical notes and reflections.
——— Mental Physiology.
Lee's Animal Magnetism.
Locke on the Understanding. Bk. 3, ch. 1.
Mayo's Lectures on medical testimony in cases of lunacy.
Moore's Power of the soul over the body, in relation to health and morals.
Newnham's Reciprocal influence of body and mind.
Quarterly Review. 45:341.
Southern Review. 6:116.
Vizard's Principles of philos. and religion.
Wilkinson on the Human body.
Willis on Cerebral Anatomy.
——— on the Minds of brutes.

Reciprocity. See LOVE OF NEIGHBOR.

Recognition of friends in Heaven.

Christian Exam. 18:222.
Christian Review. 7:47.
Gisbourne's (Tho.) Essays.
Harbaugh's Recog. of friends in Heaven.
Mant's Happiness of the blessed.
Meek on the Felicity of glorified saints.
Muston's Friendship on earth perpetuated.
Partridge's (Samuel) Discourses.
Thompson's (A. C.) The Better land. Ch. 5.

Reconciliation. See ATONEMENT.

Reconciliation of Paul and James. See PAUL AND JAMES.

Recreation. See AMUSEMENTS.

Balguy's (Thomas) Sermons
Baxter's (Rich.) Practical Works.
Blair's (Hugh) Sermons.
Bruder on Amusements.
Grove on Diversions.
Watts on the Improvement of the mind.
——— on the Passions.

Redemption. See ATONEMENT.

Davenantii Dissertationes duæ.
Harenbergii Theologia dogmatica.
Balguy's Essay on Redemption.
Bates' Harmony of the Divine attributes.
Bather's (Edward) Sermons.
Bennet on the Apostles' Creed.
Berriman's Boyle Lectures. 1730.
Bowdler's Sermons.
Broughton's (Bp.) Sermons.
Burnett on Redemption.
Charnock's Works.
Clarke's (A.) Sermons.
Cotton's (R. L.) Sermons.
Creighton's (R.) Sermons.
Cruso's (Timothy) Sermons.
Doddridge's Lectures. Part 8.
Edwards' (Pres.) History of Redemption.

Redemption—*continued.*

Erskine's Harmony of the Divine attributes.
Faber's (Geo. S.) Sermons.
Felton's (H.) Sermons.
Fuller's Gospel worthy of all acceptation.
Haldane's (F. A.) Works.
Hamilton's Scheme of human redemption.
Hill's (John) Sermons.
Hill's (Bryan) Sermons.
Hopkins' (S.) Sermons.
Hurrion on Particular Redemption.
Hussey's (Christopher) Sermons.
Knowles' (Thomas) Sermons.
Lawrence's Bampton Lectures.
Lime Street Lectures.
Magee on Atonement.
Meyrick's Christian Faith.
Moore's (Geo.) Sermons.
Morton's (Joshua) Sermons.
Owen's (John) Death of death.
——— Meditations.
Parkinson's (R.) Sermons.
Pennington's Rise and progress of the Christian religion.
Rawbone's Path to Liberty.
Rennel's (Thomas) Sermons.
Riche on the Doctrines of Revelation.
Richardson's (W.) Sermons.
Rymer on Revealed Religion.
Seed's (Jeremiah) Sermons.
Smith's (John Pye) Sermons.
Smith's (Theyre) Sermons.
Still's (John) Sermons.
Strong on the Two Covenants.
Sykes on Redemption.
Townsend's (George) Sermons.
Tucker's Light of Nature.
Turner's Boyle Lectures. 1708.
Wardlaw on the Socinian Controversy.
Watts' (Isaac) Ruin and Recovery.
Wintle's Bampton Lectures. 1794.
Woodward's Boyle Lectures. 1710.
Worthington's Scheme of Redemption.

See critical and bibliographical notices in the supplement to JOHN PYE SMITH'S *Four Discourses on the Priesthood of Christ.*

Reformation. See CHURCH HISTORY, FORERUNNERS, LUTHER.

Bassnage, Histoire des Eglises Reformé.
Beausobre, Hist. de la Reformation.
Corse, Instructiones historico-theologicæ.
Fuesslin's Erläuterung d. Ref. Gesch.
Gerdesii Annales Evangelii. Sec. XVI. (Gives original documents.)
Gieseler's Lehrbuch d. Kirchengeschichte.
Hagenbach's Vorlesungen über Wesen u. Geschichte der R.
Hase's Kirchengeschichte.
Hermanni Concilium provinciale Coloniense.
Jurieu, Histoire du Calvinisme.
Kreussler's Denkmaler der Reformation.
Lubienetski, Hist. Reform. Polonicæ.
Musæus de Statu Relig. seculo XVII.
Myconii Historia Reformationis.

Reformation—*continued.*

Pellicani Opera.
Planck's Gesch. des protestantischen Lehrbegriffs und d. Entstehung, etc.
Porta, Hist. R. ecclesiarum Raeticarum. (The only history of the Grison Ref.)
Rank's Deutsche Geschichte.
Ruchat, Hist. de la R. de la Swisse.
Rudelbach's Lutherum und Union.
Scaliger, Hist. Confessionis Augustanæ.
Schlegel's Kirchen und R. Geschichte.
Schenkel's Reformatoren im Zammenhange mit d. evangelischen Kirche, etc.
Seckendorf, Commentarius historicus. (Gives Papal as well as Protestant accounts.)
Sleidan, de Statu religionis Carolo V. (Gives original documents entire.)
Villers, sur l'Esprit et l'Influence de la R.
Amer. Bibl. Repos. 9:332. 10:104. 2d Series. 11:65.
Beausobre's History of the Reformation. Trans. by T. Macauley.
Biblioth. Sacra. 1:425. 2:201.
Bird's Defence of the Principles of the Ref.
Blunt's History of the Reformation. (A mere compend.)
Bower's History of the Popes.
——— Life of Luther.
Brandt's Ref. in the Low Countries. (Great.)
British Foreign Review. 15:101.
Burnett's History of the Ref. in England.
Calderwood's True History of the Church of Scotland from the beginning of the Ref. to the end of the reign of James VI.
Cantu's History of the Reformation.
Casaubon's Necessity of Reformation in and before Luther's time.
Christian Examiner. 14:273. 28:20. 32:19. 35:521. 37:130.
Christian Monthly Spectator. 4:142.
Chris. Quart. Spect. 6:169. (Influence of.)
Claude's Defence of the Reformation.
Cook's (Geo.) Reformation in Scotland.
Cox's Life of Melancthon.
D'Aubigne's History of the Reformation.
Eclectic Rev. 4th Series. 5:485. (Bohemia.) 8:186. (France.) 12:106. (Poland.) 16:329. (England.)
Frazier's Mag. 24:479. 26:1.
Fuller's Worthies.
Gilpin's Lives of Wickliffe, Cranmer, Latimer, etc.
Gray's Bampton Lectures. 1796.
Heeren's Treatise on the Reformation.
Hermann's Consultation by what means a reformation, &c., may be accomplished. (A remarkable Papal work of 1555.)
Herveis' (J. O. W.) Elizabethan age.
Heylin's Reformation in England.
Horne's Bampton Lectures. 1828.
——— Protestant Memorial.
Jortin's Life of Erasmus.
Knox's History of the Ref. in Scotland.
Krasinhi's Rise, progress, and decline of Reformation in Poland.

Reformation—*continued.*

Lavalle's Hist. of the Reformation in France.
Mackay's Effect of the Reformation on civil society in Europe.
Massingberd's English Reformation.
McCrie's Reformation in Italy.
——— ——— Spain.
McGee's History of the attempt to establish the Ref. in Ireland, from 1540 to 1830.
Middleton's Biographia Brittanica.
North Amer. Rev. 44:153. *Italy.*
Paul's (Father) Hist. of the Council of Trent.
Princeton Review. 8:115. *Geneva.* 9:153. *Hungary.*
Quart. Rev. 37:50. *Italy.*
Quick's Synodican. *France.*
Reuchlin's Life and Times. *Germany.*
Robertson's History of Charles V.
Ruchat's History of the R. in Switzerland.
Russel's English and Scotch Reformers.
Scott's Lives of Reformers in Scotland.
Seckendorf's History of the Reformation.
Simes' History of the Reformation.
Sleidan's History of the Reformation.
Smedley's History of the R. in France.
Soame's Elizabethean religious history.
Stewart's History of the R. in Scotland.
Strype's Annals. *England.*
Villers' Influence of the Reformation.
Waddington's History of the Reformation on the Continent.
Warner's Eccles. history of England.
Westminster Review. 37:177.

Reformed [Dutch] Church.

Articles of the Synod of Dordrecht.
Belgic Confession of Faith.
Berg's Review.
Christian Intelligencer.
Demarest's History and characteristics of the Reformed Protestant Dutch Church.
Dewitt's History of the Collegiate Reformed Dutch Church. New York.
Heidelberg Catechism.
History and Literature of the Ref. D. Chur.
History of the Synod of Dort.
Mark's (John) Theology.
Motley's Rise of the Dutch Republic.
New American Encyclopedia.
New Brunswick Review.
Presbyterian Quarterly Review. 1866.
Ursinus on the Catechism.

Reformed Presbyterians. [Cameronians.]

Adams' Religious world displayed.
Blackwood's Mag. 6:169,513,663. 7:48,157, 277,374,482,508.
Charteris' Discourse of the Centenary of the Revolution.

Regeneration.

Grebenitzii Dissertationes de Regeneratione.
Haferungius de nomine Regenerationis ejusque usu et abusu.
Henrici Tractatus de Regeneratione.

Regeneration—*continued.*

Krackewitz, de Regeneratione.
Maccovii Loci Communes.
Meisneri Fasciculus Disp. Theologicæ.
Neumanus de Differentia regeneratione, justificatione, et sanctificatione.
Perkinsii Theologia Metaneologia.
Reuchlinus de Nova Creatione.
Wilckius de Regeneratione et Regenitis.

Allen (Thos.) on the New Birth.
Amer. Bibl. Repos. 3d Series. 1:493. 2:633.
Appleton's Works. Lect. 26 to 41.
Backus' 5 Sermons on Regeneration.
Bates' (W.) Works.
Bellamy's Glory of the Gospel.
——— True Religion delineated.
Beveridge's Private Thoughts. Inestimable.
Boston's Fourfold State.
Charnock's Sermons.
Christian Month. Spect. 1:169,287. 5:118.
Christian Quart. Spect. 7:301,591.
Christian Review. 11:510.
Coles (E.) on Divine Sovereignty.
——— on Regeneration. (Both excellent works.)
Close's (Francis) Sermons.
Cutler's (B. C.) Sermons.
Davies' (Pres.) Sermons.
Dickinson on the Five Points.
Doddridge's Sermons on R. (Many editions.)
Draper (H.) on Regeneration.
Duffield's (Geo.) Spiritual life.
Dwight's Theology. Ser. 70–75.
Edwards' (Pres.) Works.
Emmon's (Nath.) Sermons.
Faber's (G. S.) Primitive doctrine of R.
——— Friendly letters to the author of "Plain Tracts."
Fenner's (William) Sermons.
Flavell's Touchstone of sincerity.
Fuller's Works. (Essays.)
Griffin's Park Street Lectures.
Hall's (Robt.) Notes of Sermons.
Hebden on Regeneration.
Hopkins' (Dr. S.) Works.
Howe (John) on Regeneration.
Jamieson's Use of Sacred History.
Law's Grounds and Reasons of Christian R.
Leighton's Lectures on 1st Peter. Lectures 15 and 16.
Literary and Theol. Review. 5:333.
Owen on the Spirit.
Princeton Review. 8:477.
Quincy's (S.) Sermons.
Robinson's Christian System.
Simeon's (C.) Christians born of God.
Spirit of the Pilgrims. 2:595.
Spring's (Gardner) Essays.
Stanhope's (George) Sermons.
Stoddart's Nature of Conversion.
Sutcliffe's Sermons on Regeneration.
Swinnock's Door of Salvation.
Theological Essays: reprinted from the Princeton Review.
Tillotson's Works.

Regeneration—*continued.*

Waterland's Regeneration stated and explained.
Wesley's (John) Sermons.
Whitby's Discourses.
Williams' (Isaac) Sermons.
Wilson's (D.) Sermons bef. the Univ. 1817.
Witherspoon's Works. (Excellent.)
Witsius on the Covenants.
Wright on the Doctrine of the New Birth. (Gone through very many editions.)

Regium Donum.

Eclectic Review. 15:181.

Reign of Christ. See MILLENNIUM.

Relative Duties. See FAMILY RELIGION, FEMALE SEX, FIFTH COMMANDMENT, FILIAL DUTIES, HUSBANDS, PARENTAL DUTIES, SERVANTS, WIVES, YOUTH.

Adams' Duties of Parents, Children, &c.
Baxter's (Rich.) Practical Works. (All the relations.)
Beattie's Elements of Moral Science.
Bishop's (Charles) Village Sermons.
Clarke's (Dr. Sam.) Sermons.
Delany's 15 Sermons on Relative Duties.
Doddridge's Lectures. Part 3, prop. 62,63.
Elliott's Advice to Christian Parents.
Evans' (A. B.) Plain Sermons.
Evans' (Dr. John) Christian Temper.
Fleetwood's 16 Discourses on Relat. Duties.
Foster's (Dr. James) Discourses.
——— on Social Virtue.
Francklin's Sermons on Relative Duties.
Gisbourne's Duties of persons in the higher and middle classes.
——— Duties of Women.
Gouge's Domestic Duties.
Hanway's Virtue in humble life.
Jackson's (A.) Pious Prentice.
James' Family Monitor.
Jay's Mutual Duties of husbands and wives.
Jerment's Parental Duties.
Kitchener's Letters on Marriage.
Lewis' Christian Duties.
Nichols' Duty of Inferiors toward Superiors.
Paley's Principles of Moral Philosophy.
Puffendorf's Offices.
Risley on Family Religion.
Saunders' Domestic Charge.
Stennett's (Sam.) Disc. on Domestic Duty.
Waugh's Duties of apprentices and servants.

Relics.

Agricola de Reliquis sanctorum.
Bochart, de l'Origine du service des reliques.
Calvini Admonitio. (In tract. theolog.)
Dorchæi Specimen sceletomaniæ pontificæ.
Kortholti (Christian.) Disquisitiones.
Mabillon, de la Veneration rendue aux reliq.
Molinæi Thesaurus Disput. theol. Sedanus.
Rainold, de Romanæ eccles. idolatria.
Stengelius de Reliquiarum cultu.
Vossii Historia de Controversiis, etc.

Calvin's (John) Treatise declaring what great profit might come to all Christendom if there was a *register* of all the saints' bodies and other relics!
Evans' Modern Popery. 1855.
Wythers on Saints' bodies and other relics.

Relief Kirk.

Adams' Religious World.
Eclectic Rev. 4th Series. 15:319.
Edinburg Theolog. Rev. 1830.
Princeton Review. 18:26.
Smith's History of the Relief Church.

Religion of Nature. See LAW OF NATURE, LIGHT OF NATURE, NAT. THEOLOGY.

Religions. See BUDHISM, FETICHISM, HINDUISM, IDOLATRY, JUDAISM, PARSEES, MAHOMETANISM, MYTHOLOGY, &c.

Creuzer, Religions de l'Antiquité. (Also in German.)
Dupuis, l'Origine de tous les cultes. ("The ne plus ultra of infidelity."—PRIESTLEY.)
Hyde, Historia religionis vet. Persarum.
Jamblicus de Vita Pythagoricæ.
Jessin, de Finnorum, Lapponumque, Norwegicorum religione.
Jowett, Hist. des relig. de tous les royaumes.
Jurieu, Hist. critique des dogmes.
Lindeman's Gesch. d. Meinungen. (Egypt, Persia, Chaldea, Phœnicia, Greece, &c.)
Müller's Geschichte der Americanischen Urreligionen. (Highly valued.)
Meyeri Historia Religionum.
Niemeyer, Collectio confessionum fidei. (The creeds of all the Reformed Churches.)
Picart, Hist. des ceremon. mœurs, et coutumes relig. du Monde. Plates.
Richter's altesten Religionen d. Orients.
Sagittarii Hist. Eccles. (Introductio.)
Schlegel's Geist der Religionstatt alter Zeiten und Volker.
Simon, Fides Ecclesiast. Oriental.
Sinnerti Exercitationes historico-theol.

Adams' (H.) View of all religions.
Adams' (Robt.) Religious world displayed.
Alley's Genius and temper of the Roman, Greek, Hindu, and Mahometan religions.
Bellamy's (John) History of all Religions.
Benedict's History of all Religions.
Boone's Book of Churches and Sects. (Points out about 200 passages of the N. T. which give rise to conflicting interpretations.)
Brerewood on the Diversities of language and religion.
Broughton's Historical Dictionary of all Religions to the present time. 1742.
Brown's (Dr. Will.) View of Christianity and other forms of religion, with regard to their moral tendency.
Conder's View of all Religions.
De Foe's Dictionary of all Religions.
Duncan's Religions of profane antiquity.
Enfield's History of Philosophy.
Gladwin's Lux Orientalis.

Religions—*continued.*

Heckford's Account of all religions and sects. (Small, and of small use.)
Hurd's Universal History of Religious rites.
Jones' Dictionary of religious opinions.
Jurieu's Crit. hist. of doctrines and worship from Adam to Christ. (With the origin of the various idolatries.)
Malcolm's History of Persia.
Marsden's History of Churches and sects from the earliest times. (To 1855.)
Maurice's Indian Antiquities.
——— Religions of the world and their relations to Christianity.
Mitford's Observations on Christianity and on the primeval Judaic and Heathen religions. (Learned.)
Morrison's (D.) Religious history of Man.
More's Divine Dialogues.
Nightingale's Rites, ceremonies, faith, &c.
Phillips' Learning and Manners of Malabar.
Picart's Religious ceremonies of all ages.
Potter's Grecian Antiquities.
Prichard's Analysis of Egyptian mythology.
Quarterly Review. 28:1,493.
Robinson's Theological Dictionary.
Ross' View of Church government, religions, and heresies in all ages. (To 1690.)
Rupp's Hist. of Religious Denominations.
Ryan's History of the effects of Religion on mankind. (Embraces ancient and modern, barbarous and civilized countries.)
Simons' (Father) Critical History of the Religions and customs of Eastern nations.
Smith's (George) Gentile nations. (Egypt, Babylon, &c.)
Stanley's History of Philosophy.
Taylor on the Eleusinian and Bacchic Mysteries.
Turner's History of all religions from the Creation. (To 1695.)
Ward's Hist., Lit., and Relig. of the Hindus.
Wilkes' State of man in all ages.
Williams' Dictionary of all Religions and Religious denominations.
Williamson's Four principal Religions.

Religious Affections.

Buckminster's (Jos. S.) Sermons.
Edwards on the Affections.
Maclaurin's Essays.
Pike & Hayward's Cases of Conscience.
Tottie on Sympathizing affection.
Watts on the Passions.
Winslow on the Declension and revival of religion in the soul.

Religious Controversy. See POLEMICS.

Religious Declension. See BACKSLIDING.

Religious Intercourse. See COMPANY, SOCIAL INTERCOURSE, VISITING.

Religious Liberty. See CHRISTIAN.

Religious Orders. See MONASTICISM, CARMELITES, DOMINICANS, JANSENISTS.

Remission of Sins. See FORGIVENESS.

Remonstrants. See SYNOD OF DORT.

Pro. See ARMINIANS.

Confessio: sive Declaratio sententiæ pastorum in Belgio.
Cattenburgii Spicilegium Theologiæ.
Curcellæi Opera Theologica.
Drieberge, de Predestinatione.
Grotii Opera Theologica.
Herbert (Herm.) de Predestinatione.
Limborch, Theologia Christiana.
Molinæus, (Io.) Armamentarium Spirituale.
Vorstius, de Natura et attributis Dei.
——— (Opera Omnia.)

Con. See CALVINISTS, DECREES, ELECTION, and the various other subjects on which Calvinists and Armenians disagree.

For a great list of Remonstrant writers see CATTENBURG, *Bibliotheca Scriptorum Remonstrantium*, and THEODOCTUS, *Secta Belgii*.

Remorse. See REPENTANCE.

Repentance. See CONVERSION, DEATHBED REPENTANCE, PARAB. OF PRODIG. SON.

Basil, ad Amphilochium.
Chrysostom, de Compunctione cordis.
Tertullian, de Pœnitentia.

Antoninus de Contritione salutari.
Bebellii Disputationes Theologicæ.
Breithauptus de Contritione.
Eckhardi Dilucidatio Controv. Theol.
Hoffmani Commentatio de Pœnitentia.
Kortholti Disputationes Theologicæ.
Mayi Comm. in VII Psalmos pœnitentiales.
Molinæus de Pœnitentia et Clavibus.
Perkinsii Theologia Metanæologia.
Reudenii Sciagraphia loci de pœnit. et ejus fructibus.
Riveti Com. in VII Psalmos pœnitentiales.
Sennerti " " "
Sontagii Disputationes Theologicæ.
Tarnovii Comm. in VII Psal. pœnitentiales.
Titii Disputationes Theologicæ.

Abernethy's (Dr. John) Sermons.
Alison's (Archibald) Sermons.
Allen's (Joshua) Sermons.
Allix (Peter) on Repentance. (Against Papists.)
Ambrose's (Isaac) First, middle, and last things.
Arnold's (of Rugby) Sermons.
Bailey (B.) on the Lost piece of money.
Baker's (Arthur) Sermons on the saintly character.
Balguy on Redemption.
Baxter (R.) on the Penitential psalms.
——— Persuasions to a sound conversion.
——— Saint's Everlasting Rest.
Bellamy's Nature of the Gospel.

Repentance—*continued.*

Bern's Lectures on the penitential psalms.
Beveridge's (Bp.) Sermons.
Biddulph on the 51st Psalm.
Blencoe's (Edward) Sermons.
Bloomfield's (G. B.) Sermons.
Boston's Repentance unto Life.
Bradford's (The Martyr) Good old way.
Brewster's Meditations.
Bulkley's (C.) Discourses.
Bull's (J.) Sermons on the 51st Psalm.
Bullinger's Decades.
Carter's (John) Sermons.
Case's Sermons.
Chandler's (S.) Sermons.
Charnock's Works.
Clay's (John) Sermons.
Cole's (Thos.) Discourses. ("Highly evangelical and judicious."—WILLIAMS.)
Colquhoun's Treatise on Repentance.
Cooke's (W. G.) Sermons.
Cooper's (William) Sermons.
Davis' (Pres.) Sermons.
Davies' (S.) Nature and Necessity of R.
Decoegleton's Portrait of the Christian Penitent.
Dickinson's Letters. Let. 9.
Dickson's Therapeutica Sacra.
Edwards' (Pres.) Works.
Ellis' Necessity of serious consideration and Repentance.
Evans' (R. W.) Parochial Sermons.
Finney (C. G.) on True and false Repent.
Fisher on the Seven penitential psalms.
Fuller's Gospel worthy of all acceptation.
Gilpin's (Will.) Sermons.
Goodman's (John) Penitent pardoned.
Graham's Only condition of final acceptation.
Grant's (Johnson) Sermons.
Gregory's (Thomas) Sermons.
Grinfield's (E. W.) Sermons.
Hall's (Robt.) Notes of Sermons.
Hammond on R. (Practical Discourses.)
Hervey's (J.) Sermons.
Heylin's (John) Prodigal Son.
Hildersham on the 51st Psalm.
Hobart's (Bp.) Sermons.
Hooker on Contrition.
Hopkins' Body of Divinity.
Howe's Living Temple.
Hunt's (Jeremiah) Sermons.
Hutton's (F. H.) Sermons.
Jackson's (Dean Tho.) Lent Sermons.
Jebb's (Bp.) Angelic Joy.
Kennaway's (C. E.) Sermons.
Le Bas' (C. W.) Sermons.
Logan's (John) Sermons.
Magee on Atonement. Nos. 4, 5.
Manston's Lectures to young persons.
Margoliouth's Genuine R. and its effects.
Milner's (Joseph) Sermons.
Morgan's Exposition of the 51st Psalm.
Morton's (J.) The Penitent's prayer.
Moss' (Robert) Sermons.
Noel's (D.) Berry Street Sermons.

Repentance—*continued.*

Noel's (G. T.) Sermons.
Osterwald's Theology.
Owen on the 130th Psalm.
Patrick's (Bp.) Sermons.
Paley's (William) Sermons.
Payne on Repentance.
Payson's (Edward) Works.
Pearson's (H.) Sermons.
Penn's (James) Sermons.
Pratt's (C. O.) Sermons.
Pyles' (J.) Sermons.
Robinson's Christian System. Ess. 40.
Ross' (John) Sermons.
Saurin's Sermons.
Scott's (Tho.) Theological Essays.
——— Sermons.
Secker's (Abp.) Sermons.
Sellon's (W.) Sermons.
Sheppard's Sound Believer.
Short's (William) Sermons.
Smith (Sam.) on the 51st Psalm.
Smith's (H.) Sermons.
Spring's (G.) Essays. Ess. 7.
Stillingfleet's (James) Sermons.
Styles' (John) Sermons.
Swinnock's Door of Salvation.
Sykes on Redemption.
Taylor's (Jer.) Doctrine and practice of R.
——— Life of Christ. Discourse 9.
——— Holy Living.
Taylor's (John) Sermons.
Thompson's (T.) Sermons.
Toplady's (A.) Joy in heaven over a repenting sinner.
Trench's (R. C.) Notes on the Parables.
Usher's (Abp.) Sermons. (18 admirable discourses on this topic.)
Van Mildert's Parable of the lost sheep.
Walters' Discourses.
Waterland's (Dan.) Sermons.
Watson's Doctrine of Repentance.
Watson's (Alexander) Sermons.
Wells' (C.) Sermons.
Westby's Helps to Repentance.
Whitfield's (George) Sermons.
Wilson's (John) Conversion of Zaccheus.
Wilson's (W. C.) Sermons.
Witsius on the Covenants.
Wordsworth's Parable of the lost sheep.
Wrangham's (Francis) Sermons.
Wright On being born again. (Highly commended by Dr. Doddridge.)
Wynyard's (John M.) Sermons.
Zollikoffer's Festivals and Fasts.

Repining. See CHEERFULNESS, CONTENTMENT, PATIENCE, RESIGNATION, SUBMISSION.

Reprobation. See DECREES, ELECTION, FREE WILL, MORAL ABILITY, &C.

I know of no book advocating the doctrine f absolute reprobation as a corollary to the doctrine of election. The nearest approach to it is by TWISSE, in his *"Riches of God's love unto the vessels of mercy."*

Reproof. See ADMONITION.

Blackall's (Bp.) Sermons.
Blair's (James) Sermons.
Finney's (C. G.) Lectures.
Hall's (Bp.) Sermons.
Hopkins' (Bp. E.) Works.
McDonald's (A.) Sermons.
Moss' (Robert) Sermons.
Pyle's (Philip) Sermons.
Simeon's (C.) Works.
Smith's (Elisha) Sermons.
Stebbings' (Henry) Sermons.
Wesley's (John) Sermons.

Republic of the Jews. See JEWS, HISTORY OF.

Bertram, de Reipublica Hebræorum.
Castellionis Reip. Heb. ex Josepho excerpta.
Coringii (Herman.) Disputationes.
Cunæus de Republica Ebræorum.
Leydekeri Opera. ("Immense."—ORME.)
Menochius de Republica Ebræorum.
Sigonius de Repub. Ebr. (Acta erud.)
Ugolini Thesaurus antiquitarum sacr.
Witsius de Theocratia Israelitarum.
Zeltner, de Adoloscentia repub. Israel.

Homes' Scripture history of the Jews.
Jahn's Hebrew Commonwealth.
Lewis' Hebrew Republic.

Reputation. See AMBITION, FAME, HONOR, LOVE OF PRAISE.

Resentment. See FORGIVENESS.

Butler's (Alban) Sermons.
Christian Rev. 9:212.
Hey on the Malevolent sentiments.

Resignation. See CONTENTMENT.

Adey's (William) Sermons.
Anderson's (James S.) Sermons.
Atterbury's (L.) Discourses.
Barrow's (Isaac) Sermons.
Bates' Works. Disc. 3.
Berens' (Edw.) Village Sermons.
Brinsley's Drinking of the bitter cup.
Brooks' Mute Christian under the smarting rod.
Buchanan (James) on Affliction.
Burroughs on Resignation and Contentment.
Carr's (George) Sermons.
Chappelow's Silence a Christian duty.
Charlesworth's (John) Practical Sermons.
Clagget's (William) Discourses.
Clarke's (Samuel) Sermons.
Coney's (Thomas) Sermons.
Crawford's (W.) Sermons.
Dickson's (David) Sermons.
Dwight's Theology. Ser. 95.
Emmon's (Nath.) Sermons.
Faringdon's (Anthony) Sermons.
Fowler's (Bp.) Sermons.
Gerard's (Alex.) Sermons.
Horne's (Bp.) Sermons.
Jortin's (John) Sermons.
Messinger's Sentiments on Resignation.

Resignation—*continued.*

Newnham's Tribute of Sympathy.
Patrick's (Bp.) Sermons.
Penn's (John) Sermons.
Simeon's (C.) Works.
Smart's Duty of Christian people.
South's (Robert) Sermons.
Stewart's (J. H.) Discourses.
Summerfield's (John) Sermons.
Wilcox's (Daniel) Sermons.
Worthington's Great duty of Resignation.

Resisting Evil.
See FRIENDS, REVENGE, WAR.

Restitution.

Bertheau's (Charles) Sermons.
Beveridge's (Bp.) Sermons.
Burns' (Richard) Sermons.
Chillingworth's Works.
Davies' (Tho.) Sermons.
Ford's (Robt.) Sermons.
Heylin's (John) Theological Lectures.
Kidder's (Bp.) Sermons.
Partridge's (S.) Sermons.
Placette on Restitution.
Ridgeley's Body of Divinity.
Tucker's (John) Sermons.

Restorationists. See UNIVERSALISTS.

Pro.

Gerardi (Lud.) Systema Αποκαταστασεως: das est, ein Volständiger Lehrbegriff des ewigen Evangelii, etc.

Atkins on Universal Redemption.
Bourne (Sam.) on Future punishment.
Brown's Restitution of all things.
Burnett on the State of the dead.
Clarke's (Rich.) Vind. of the honor of God.
Hartley on Man.
Newton on the Final condition of men.
Petitpierre's Thoughts on Divine goodness.
Ramsay's Philosophical principles. (Maintains the doctrine of metempsychosis.)
Stonehouse on Universal Restitution.
Universalist Quarterly. 4:329.
Vidler's Letters to Fuller.
Whiston on the Eternity of hell torments.
White's Restitution of all things.
Winchester's Outcasts comforted.
——— Dialogues.
——— (Various other treatises.)

Con. See ETERNITY OF HELL TORMENTS.

Brandani (H. Gebhardi) Amica disquisitio de diabolorum, etc. (Able reply to Gerard. Scores of other answers appeared, chiefly in the German language.)
Goetzii Observationes Sacræ.
Iänichen's grundlicher Beweis, etc.
Klausing, de Eternis peccatorum pœnis.
Lampii (F. A.) Dissertationes.
Sinsart, Défense du dogme catholique.
Vossius, Bekentniss der Liebe Gottes nach der Wahrheit, etc.
Wernsdorfius de Restitut. rerum omnium.

Appleton's (Pres.) Works. Lect. 47–49.
Edwards against Chauncy.
Erskine's Church History.
Horberry's Script. doct. of fut. punishment.
Isaac (Dan.) on Universal restoration.
Lampe's Dissertations.
Marston on Universal restoration.

There is no denomination of this name. Those who hold the doctrine of future punishment for a finite period, and those who believe that all retribution for sin is inflicted in this life, are generally included in the name "Universalists."

Restoration of the Jews to Canaan.
See CONVERSION OF THE JEWS.

Altingii Spes Israelis.
Burnett, de Restoratione futura, etc.
Calvert, Napthali: seu Collectiones, etc.
Daguet, Traditiones des S. S. péres.
Lightfoot, Promissiones Divinæ.
Willet, de Judæorum vocatione.

Barrington on the Divine dispensations.
Bibliotheca Sacra. 4:337.
Bicheno's R. of the J. the crisis of nations.
Bickersteth on the Restoration, &c.
Blaney's New translation of Jeremiah.
Burnett (Bp.) on the Restoration, &c.
Chris. Monthly Spect. 8:57,502.
Clarke on the Promises.
Clayton on Prophecy. (Makes it to occur A.D. 2015.)
Crool's Restoration of the Jews.
Doddridge's Lectures. Lect. 228.
Draxe's World's Resurrection.
Durell's Parallel proph. of Jacob and Moses.
Ettrick's Reflections on the prophecies.
Eyre on the Restoration of Israel.
Faber's (G. S.) Downfall of the Turkish power.
Faber's Connected view of the P. relating to the restoration of Israel.
Fleming's Apocalyptic Key.
Fletcher's Israel Redux.
Friend of Israel. Periodical.
Hershell's State and prospects of the Jews.
Jewish Repository. Periodical.
Lardner's (Nath.) Discourses.
Lord's Lit. and Theol. Journ. 2:15,240,253.
McNeil's (H.) Lectures on the prophecies.
Maitland's View of prophecy.
Maurice on the Appearing of the Tribes.
Mayer on the Prophecies.
Morning Watch. Periodical.
Pirie's (Alex.) Works.
Tyso's Inquiry as to Prophetic truth.
Whiston on the Restoration of the Jews.
Whitaker on the Prophecies relating to the restoration of the Jews.
Wood's Believers' guide to prophecy.

Resurrection. See IDENTITY.

Athenagoras, de Resurrectione.
Chrysostom, Homiliæ.
Origen, contra Celsum.
Tertullian, de Resurrectione carnis.

Resurrection—*continued.*

Bebelius de R. infantum nondum genitorum.
Bernholdi Dissertationes Theologicæ.
Beza, Homiliæ.
Callixtus de Resurrectione carnis.
Calovii (Abrah.) Dissertationes.
Danhaveri (Ioann. C.) Dissertationes.
Fabricii de Relig. Christi. Cap. XLV.
Gerhardi Loci Communes.
Haberkorn, de R. efficacia et fructu.
Hottingeri Diss. theolog.-polemicarum.
Mosheim, de Statura corporum beatorum.
Segerus de Resurrectione embryorum.
Teller de Dogm. R. per iv priora secula.
Wegneri de R. impiorum.
Zornii Delineatio theologiæ Patristicæ.

Amer. Bibl. Repos. 3d Series. 1:212.
Arnold's (Dr. Tho.) Sermons.
Barrow (Isaac) on the Creed.
Baxter on the Soul.
Boston's Fourfold State.

Resurrection of Christ. See ASCENSION, DESCENT INTO HELL.

Calovius de Christi Resurgentis majestate.
Carpzovii Discussio difficilium quorundam de morte et R. Christi.
Daillé, sur la R. de Christ.
Gerardus de Gloria R. Christi.
Hottinger, de Resurrectione Christi.
Meyerus, utrum R. Christi pertineat ad opus redemptionis?
Quenstedius de Fundamento R. Christi.
Wesselius de veritate R. Christi.

Adey's (William) Sermons.
Arnold's (Thomas) Sermons.
Atterbury's (Lewis) Sermons.
Benson's History of the Life of Christ.
——— Evidences of Christ's resurrection.
Burder's Village Sermons.
Butcher's (William) Sermons.
Chandler's Witnesses of Christ's resurrection re-examined.
Clarke's (Dr. Sam.) Sermons.
Cook's (Geo.) Illustrations of Christ's R.
Coverdale's (Miles) Remains.
Dimock's (Henry) Sermons.
Ditton on Christ's Resurrection.
Dore's Essay on the R. of Christ.
Edwards' (Pres.) Works.
Garbent's Demonstration of the R. of C.
Grove's Evidences of our Saviour's R.
Hall's (Bp.) Contemplations. Bk. 4.
Hopkins' (Bp.) Works.
Horsley's (Bp.) Nine Sermons.
Jackson's (John) Address to Deists.
Lardner's Remarks on our Lord's R.
Newcombe (Bp.) on the Difficulties in the Gospel History, &c.
Perkins' (Joseph) Sermons.
Priestley on the Resurrection.
Saurin's Sermons.
Secker's (Abp.) Lectures on the Catechism. Lect. 16,17.
Sherlock's Trial of the Witnesses. Admirable.
Townson on the Evangelical Histories.
West's Hist. and Evidences of the Resurrection of Jesus Christ. (One of the best on the subject, if not the best.)
Whitby's Resurrection of Christ.

Retirement. See MEDITATION, SOLITUDE.

Revelation. See AUTHENTICITY.

Ernest, de Verbo Dei Scripto.
Gerhard de Verbo Dei.
Sandius de Verbo Dei.
Vossius de Idolatria.
Wald, de Origine religionis Christianæ.

Baker's Insufficiency of Learning.
Barrow's (W.) Bampton Lectures.
Barrington's Relation between Natural and Revealed Religion.
Bennet's (Benjamin) Discourses.
Berriman's Gradual revelation of the Gospel.
Blackall's (Bp.) Sermons.
Boyle Lectures. (From 1693 to the present.)
Broadley's Religion of Moses.
Chalmers' Astronomical Discourses.
Chapman's Eusebius.
Clark's History of Christian Revelation.
Collyer's (W. Bengo) Lectures.
Conybeare on Revealed Religion.
Dewar on Divine Revelation.
Edwards' (John) Authority and perfection of Revelation.
Ellis' Knowledge of Divine things. (Ranks next to Butler's Analogy.)
Elwin's (F.) Sermons.
Forbes' (Duncan) Thoughts on Religion.
Goodwin's Charter of the world's blessedness.
Haldane on Revelation.
Halyburton on Natural Religion.
Hey's Lectures.
Jew's Letters to Voltaire.
Leland's Divine authority, &c.
Lloyd's Christian Theology.
Marsh's Bampton Lectures.
Owen's (John) Reason of faith.
Redford on the Holy Scriptures.
Ritchie's Peculiar doctrine of Revelation.
Rogers' (John) Sermons.
Ross' (John) Sermons.
Ryland's (John) Sermons.
Saurin's Sermons.
Squier's Natural and Revealed religion.
Stevens' (Dr. W.) Sermons.
Storr's Christian Doctrine.
Watson's Theological Tracts.
West's Defence of Christian Revelation.
Wettenhall on Scripture Revelation.
Wilks' (S. C.) Christian Essays.
Williams' Boyle Lectures. 1695.

Revenge. See FORGIVENESS.

Abercrombie's Philos. of the moral feelings.
Balguy's (John) Sermons.
Blackall's (Bp.) Sermons.
Boston's (Thomas) Works.
Delaune's (W.) Sermons.
Grant's (Johnson) Sermons.

Hurd's (Bp.) Sermons.
Mainwaring's (John) Sermons.
Marriott's (C.) Sermons.
Moss' (Robert) Sermons.
Paley's Moral Philosophy.
Payne's (John) Evangelical Sermons.
Stratford's Dissuasive from revenge.
Waugh's Sermons.

Revision of the English Bible. See ENGLISH BIBLE.

Revivals of Religion.

Amer. Quart. Register. 5:210. 9:117. 12:305.
Bradley's History of Revivals.
Christian Disciple. 5:321.
Christian Monthly Spect. 9:295. 10:174.
Christian Quarterly Spect. 2:434. 4:25,277. 5:20. 10:131,387.
Christian Review. 2:405.
Duncan's Hist. of R. in the British Isles.
Edwards' (Jonathan) Thoughts on the revival of religion. 1742.
——— Narrative of the work of God in Northampton. 1736.
——— Attempt to promote prayer for the revival of religion.
Eclectic Rev. 4th Series. 8:41.
Finney's (C. G.) Lectures on Revivals.
Fish's Primitive piety revived.
Gillies' Historical Collections.
Lit. and Theol. Rev. 2:667. 6:469.
Meth. Quart. Rev. 2:594, and elsewhere.
New Englander. 2:175.
Princeton Rev. 7:626. 14:1.
Spirit of the Pilgrims. 1:37,74,145,248. 4:405,467,556. 5:256,315,378. 6:125,467.

Revocation of the Edict of Nantes. See HUGUENOTS, PERSECUTION.

Ancillon, l'Irrevocabilité de l'Edit de N.
Benoist, Hist. de l'Edit de Nantes jusq'a l'edit de revocation en 1683, avec ce qui a suivi jusque a present. (1693.)
Daniel, Histoire de France.
Frazier's Mag. 22:307.

Rhetoric. See ELOQUENCE.

Condillac, Traité de l'art d'ecriture.
Schott's Theorie der Beredsamkeit.
St. Real, de la Critique.
Barrett's Analysis of sublimity of style.
Blair's Lectures.
Campbell's Philosophy of rhetoric.
Gibbons' Rhetoric.
Hobbes' (Thos.) Translation of Aristotle's Rhetoric.
Irving's Elements of English composition.
Kaimes' Elements of Criticism.
Langley's Manual of the figures of Rhetoric.
Lowth's Introduction to the Eng. grammar.
McGill's Lectures on rhetoric and criticism.
Melmoth's Letters of Fitz-Osborne.
Newman's Practical system of rhetoric.
Taylor's (Thos.) Translation of the Rhetoric and Ethics of Aristotle.
Whateley's Rhetoric.

Riches. See AGUR'S PRAYER, PARABLES, COVETOUSNESS.

Andrews' (Bp.) Sermons.
Arnot's Race for Riches; and some of the pits into which the runners fall.
Baker's (D. B.) Sermons.
Barrow's (William) Sermons.
Baxter's (Rich.) Practical Works.
Bell's (William) Sermons.
Berriman's (William) Sermons.
Beveridge's Private Thoughts.
Blair's (Hugh) Sermons.
Boston's (Tho.) Works.
Boyse's (C. S.) Charge to the Rich.
Bradford's (Samuel) Sermons.
Bradley's (Charles) Sermons.
Brady's (Nicholas) Sermons.
Browne's (W. L.) Sermons.
Burnett's (G.) Practical Sermons.
Carter's (B.) Discourses.
Chalmer's Commercial Discourses.
Charter's (S.) Sermons.
Christian Examiner. 22:218.
Cummings' (J.) Foreshadows.
Cunningham's (J. W.) Sermons.
D'Oyly's (George) Sermons.
Dumoulin's (P.) Sermons.
Durand's (J. F.) Sermons.
Enfield's (Will.) Sermons.
Ferguson on Civil Liberty.
Francklin's (Thomas) Sermons.
Fronde's (R. H.) Remains.
Furlong's (C. J.) Sermons.
Gale's (John) Sermons.
Garbet's (I.) Sermons.
Gisbourne's (Thomas) Sermons.
Hall's (Bp.) The Righteous Mammon.
Hewlett's (John) Sermons.
Heylin's (J.) Theological Lectures.
Hough's (John) Sermons.
Hurd's (Bp.) Sermons.
Knight's (Titus) Sermons.
Langehorne's (J.) Sermons.
Lowell's (Samuel) Sermons.
Maltby's (B.) Sermons.
Markland's (Abp.) Sermons.
Marshall's (Nath.) Sermons.
Matthews' (George) Sermons.
McCaul's (Alex.) Plain Sermons.
Medley's (Bp.) Sermons.
Oliver's (B. L.) The Pursuit of Happiness.
Parsons' (J.) Sermons.
Pascall's Discourses.
Pearson's (Hugh) Sermons.
Penn's (J.) Sermons and Tracts.
Phelan's (W.) Remains.
Reynolds' (Bp.) Sermons.
Richardson's (W.) Sermons.
Ringer's (Thomas) Sermons.
Rowlatt's (W. H.) Sermons.
Seed's (Jeremiah) Discourses.
Secker's (Abp.) Sermons. (3 on this subject.)
Sellon's (W.) Sermons.
Sharp's (Abp.) The Rich Man's Duty.
Simeon's (C.) Works.

Riches—*continued.*

Smith's (Sydney) Sermons.
Spencer's (A. G.) Sermons.
Sumner's (Abp.) Duty of beneficence.
Talbot's Use and Abuse of Riches.
Wamford's (R.) Sermons.
Watts' (Isaac) Sermons.
Wesley's (John) Sermons.
Westoby's Helps to Repentance.
Witherspoon's (J.) Sermons.
Zollikoffer's (G. J.) Dignity of man.

Right Use of the Fathers. See USE.

Rights of Conscience. See CONSCIENCE, FREEDOM OF OPINION, LIBERTY, PERSECUTION, PRIV. JUDGMENT, TOLERATION.

Rights of Man. See CIVIL GOVERNMENT.

Rights of Property. See PROPERTY, POLITICAL ECONOMY, SOCIALISM.

Rites and Ceremonies.

Assemanus de Sacris ritibus.
Encyclopedie Théologique.
Euchologion Magnum. (Ritual of the Greek Church.)
Gavanti Thesaurus sac. rituum.
Gavanti Thesaurus additionibus Merati.
La Croix, le Parfait Ecclesiastique. (Directions for every ceremony of the Roman Church; and for the size, shape, &c., of altars, vestments, implements, ornaments.)
Lorenzana, Breviarum Gothicum.
Martene, de Antiq. ecclesiæ ritibus.
Missale Romanum.
Polydori Historia Anglic.
Rogers, de Ceremoniis et ritibus omnium populorum.
Vinitoris Compendium Ceremoniarum.
Zacariæ Bibliotheca Ritualis.

Ames on Ceremonies.
Hurd's Rites and Ceremonies of all nations.
Lewis' Bible, Missal, and Breviary.
Trollope's Encyclopædia Ecclesiastica.
Townley's Essays on various subjects.

Rosecrucians.

Andreæ Invitatio ad fraternitatem Christi. (Andreas is by some regarded as the founder of this sect.)
Campis dem Send-brief an alle, etc.
Colberg, Platonisch.-hermetisch. Christenth.
Florentini Rosa florescens.
Fludd (Robt.), Apologia Compendiara.
Heiden's Unbetriegliche Grundsätze.
Kazaveri Disputationes.
Maieri Themes aurea.
Meder's Christlichen Bedencken.
Naude, sur la Verité de l'histoire des frères de Rosecroix. (Considers them impostors.)
Staurophor's Philosophischer Offenbarung and die Fraternitæt Rosæ-crucis.
Tschirness' Schnelle Botschaft.

Rubrics. See LITURGIES, MISSAL.

Rulers. See CIVIL GOVERNMENT, DIVINE RIGHT OF KINGS, MAGISTRACY, PASSIVE OBEDIENCE, RELATIVE DUTIES.

Rules of Interpretation. See HERMENEUTICS.

Ruling Elders. See EPISCOPACY, PRESBYTERIANISM.

King's Ruling Eldership.
Miller on Presbyterianism.
——— Office of Ruling Elder.
Princeton Review. 15:313,432. 17:276. 19:42.

Ruth.

Edwards' (Jon.) Ruth's resolution.
Hall's (Bp.) Contemplations.
Hughes' (H.) Female Characters.
Hughes' (J.) Ruth and her kindred.
Jenkins' (J.) Discourses.
McGowan's (Dr. John) Works.
Milner's (J.) Sermons.
Sullivan's (H. W.) Sermons.
Topsell's Lectures on Ruth.
Tyng's (S. H.) The Rich Kinsman.
Wilson's (Dan.) Sermons.

Sabbatarians.

Pro.

Alsop's Traditions of men.
Bamfield's All in One. (Art. Sabbath.)
Burnside on the Diff. sentiments of Christians as to the weekly Sabbath.
Carlew's Truth defended.
Cornthwaite's Reflect. on Wright's Treatise.
——— on the Seventh day of the week.
——— Essay occasioned by publications of Hallet, Jepson, Chubb, Watts, and others.
——— Further Vindication.
Davis' Last Legacy.
Elwell on the Lord's Day.
James' (John) Narrative.
Maulden's Threefold Dialogue.
Sellers' Examination of a late book by Dr. Owen.
Slater's (Thos.) Sermon on the Church.
Soursby on the Sabbath.
Stennet's (Edw.) Royal law contended for.
Stennet's (Jos.) Answer to Russon.
Tamar's History of Sabbatarian Churches. (Embracing those of Armenia, East India, Abyssinia, &c.)
Tillam's Present from prison.
Wincup's Remarks on Dr. Wright.

Con. See CHANGE OF SABBATH.

Ben's Answer to Bamfield.
Edmonds' Sabbatarians weighed in their own balance.
Evanson's Attempt to prove that there is no authority for the Christian Sabbath.
G. T. on the Christian Sabbath.
Ives' Saturday no Sabbath.
Keach's Jewish Sabbath abrogated.
Wallace's Defence of the Sabbath.
Ward's Discourses on the Sabbath.
White (Bp. Francis) on the Sabbath day.
Wright on the Lord's day.

Sabbath. See COMMANDMENTS, CHANGE OF SABBATH, LORD'S DAY, SABBATARIANS.

Chytræi Dispositio Epistolarum.
Gomarus de Origine Sabbati.
Grotius de Veritate Religionis.
Scaliger, de Emendatione temporum.
Scholugii Sabb. lege morali mandato.
Selden, de Jure Gentium.
Spencer de Legibus.
Strychius de Jure sabbati.

Abbot's Vindiciæ Sabbati.
Amer. Bibl. Repos. 9:235.
Amner (Rich.) on Positive Institutions.
Bernard's Threefold Treatise.
Biblioth. Sacra. 1:526.
Brerewood's Treatise on the Sabbath.
Brown's (W. A.) Five Tracts.
Byfield on the S. (Reply to Brerewood.)
Carrington's (J.) Sermons.
Chandler's Origin and Institution of the S.
Clark's (Sam.) Sermons.
Cleandon on the Sabbath.
Cox's (Robt.) Sabbath laws and S. duties.
Eclectic Rev. 4th Series. 22:697.
Edwards' (Pres.) Works.
Estrange's S. before and after the law.
Fleming on the Fourth Commandment.
Hamilton (Winter) on the Revealed S.
Heylin's (P.) History of the Sabbath.
Howarth's Moral laws of Moses.
Hughes (Geo.) on the S. and the 92d Ps.
Jennings' Jewish Antiquities. Bk. 3, ch. 3.
Jordan's (J.) Scripture views of the S.
Kennicott's Sermon on the Sabbath.
——— Dialogue on the Sabbath.
King's Morsels of Criticism.
Kitto's Journal. 2:128. 8:70.
Leland's Advantage and necessity of Revel.
Lightfoot's Discourses. Vol. 2.
Macbeth's Dissertations.
Mallet's Northern Antiquities.
Maxon & Parkinson's Debate on the origin, perpetuity, &c.
Meth. Quart. Rev. 9:21.
Mover on the Sabbath.
Newcombe's (P.) Discourses.
North British Review. 9:1.
Nourse's (Peter) Discourses.
Orton's Religious Exercises.
Paley's Moral Philosophy. Bk. 5, ch. 6,7,8.
Palmer on the Sabbath.
Piggot's (Edward) Discourses.
Piret's Ethics on the Sabbath. (Argues for the S. not from Scripture nor experience, but from the dictates of conscience.)
Porteus' (Bp.) Sermons.
Prideaux's Testimony of anc. and modern on the origin and nature of the Sabbath.
Robinson's Christian System.
Seabury's (Bp.) Discourses.
Seller's Exam. of Owen's book on the S.
Skeeler's (Tho.) Sermons.
Smith's Sabbath of Rest.
Toogood's Seventh day a day of rest.
Watts' Sermons.
Wayland's Elements of Moral Science. Bk. 2, ch. 4.
Whiteley on the Difficulties of Paul's Epist.
Wilder's (John) Discourses.

A very extended list of authors on this subject, mostly controversial, in LOWNDES' *British Librarian.* HOLDEN, *on the Christian Sabbath,* names 146 writers.

Sabbath Schools. See SUNDAY SCHOOLS.

Sabellians.

Athanasii Oratio contra gregales Sabellii.
Bazilii Homilia. Hom XXXII.
Calvini Defensio Orthodoxæ fidei.
Eusebii Eccles. Historia. Lib. VI.
Mosheimii Comm. de rebus Christianis.
Mosheimii Institutiones Hist. Ecclesiastica.
Schleiermacher, Gegensatz Zwicken der S.
Servetus de Trinitatis erroribus. Lib. VII.
Wormii Historia Sabelliana. (Extends to the beginning of the 5th century.)

Bayle's Dictionary. (Art. Sabellius.)
Berriman on the Trinity.
Collier's Dictionary. (Art. Sabellius.)
Hale (Dr. Wm.) on the Holy Trinity.
Lardner's Credibility of the Gospel.
Whiston's True origin of the Sab. doctrines.

Sacraments. See EFFICACY OF SACRAM.

Sacramentarians.

Brentii Opera Polemica.
Laveretus de Origine et progressu controversiæ Sacramentariæ.

Sacred Music. See PSALMODY.

Sacrifice.

Cloppenburgii Scholia S. Patriarchalis.
Deylingius de Authore Sacrificiorum.
Eusebii Preparatio Evangelica.
Franz, Scholia Sacrificiorum Patriarcharum.
Frischmuth, de S. primorum hominum.
Kurtz, das Mosaische Opfer.
Maimonides de Sacrificiis.
Meyer de Sacrificiis.
Outram de Sacrificiis. (Cont. Socinum.)
Saubertus de Sacrificiis Vetrum.
Spenceri de Legibus Hebræosum.
——— de Origine Sacrificiorum.
Witsii Egyptiaca.

Benson's Hulsean Lectures. 1822.
Charnock's Works.
Christian Disciple. 4:332.
Davison (John) on Primitive Sacrifice.
Davidson's (J.) Remains.
Delany's Revelation Examined.
Dodwell's One Altar.
Edwards' History of Redemption.
Faber's (G. S.) Horæ Mosaicæ.
——— Origin of Expiatory Sacrifices.
Felton's (H.) Institution of sacrifice.
Findlay's Vindication of the sacred books.
Hall's (Robt.) Sermons. (Sermon on the Lamb of God.)

Sacrifice—*continued.*

Hallett on Scripture.
Hawkins' Efficacy of Mosaic atonements.
Hobhouse's Origin and intention of sacrifice. (Hulsean Prize Essay.)
Jennings' Jewish Antiquities.
Kennicott's Oblation of Cain and Abel.
Lightfoot's Miscellaneous Works.
Litton's Divine origin of sacrifices.
Magee on Atonement.
Mather on Figures and Types.
Maurice's Doctrine of Sacrifice.
McEwen on the Types.
Molesworth's Reply to Davison.
Nichols' Conference with a Theist.
Owen's Sacrifices of the old law.
Outram's (W.) Dissertations. Most excel'nt.
Philo Judæus' Works.
Portall's Scripture account of sacrifices.
Ricaultoun's (Robt.) Essays.
Ridley's Origin and use of sacrifice.
Ritchie's Peculiar doctrines of Revelation. ("Satisfactory."—MAGEE.)
Shuckford's Connect. of sac. and prof. hist.
Simeon's Use of typical purifications.
Stackhouse's History of the Bible.
Sykes on Sacrifices.
Taylor on Deism.
Tholuck on Sacrifice and Priesthood.
Tillotson's Sermons.
Veysie's Bampton Lectures.
Warburton's Divine Legation.
Wells on Offerings and Sacrifices.
Woodward's Archæologia.

Sadducees. See SECTS.

Barthel Sched, Hist. de Sadducæis.
Calmet, Dissertationes.
Slevogtius de Metempsychosi Hebræorum.
Ugolini Thesaurus.

Jortin's Remarks on Eccles. History.
Josephus' Antiquities of the Jews.
Lightfoot on Matthew. 3:7.
Simon's Crit. history of the New Test.

Sadness. See DESPONDENCY.

Safety of the Church.

Beveridge's (Bp.) Works.
Calamy's (Edmund) Sermons.
Cawood's (John) Sermons.
Clagett's (William) Sermons.
Cochrane (J.) on Difficult texts.
Draper (D.) on the Collects.
Enfield's (William) Sermons.
Gatty's (Alfred) Sermons.
Nicholson (Bp.) on the Apostles' Creed.
Plumtree's Christian's Guide.
Reynolds' (Bp.) Sermons.

Saints Judging the World. See JUDGMENT.

Boullier, les Privilèges des saints.

Cawdrey's (D.) Sermons.
Gahan's (Will.) Sermons.
Garbett's (James) Christ on earth.
Jenner's (W.) Works.
Lightfoot's (John) Sermons.
Massilon's Sermons.

Salvation. See CHRISTIANITY, GRACE, REDEMPTION, REMISSION OF SINS, SATISFACTION OF CHRIST, UNIVERSALISM.

Balguy's Visitation Charges.
Beddome's Short Discourses.
Blackley's The Rejected Stone.
Burton's (Ed.) Family Sermons.
Caddel's (H.) Sermons.
Carr's (Samuel) Sermons.
Chandler's (Samuel) Sermons.
Dunlop's (W.) Sermons.
Evans' (R. W.) Sermons.
Farmer's (John) Sermons.
Finney's (C. J.) Lectures.
Fuller's Great Question answered.
Fuller's Gospel worthy of all acceptation.
Gilpin's (William) Sermons.
Gisbourne's (Thomas) Sermons.
Gleig's (George) Sermons.
Gresley's (Wm.) Parochial Sermons.
Halyburton's Great Concern.
Hare's (J. C.) Sermons.
Hopkins' (W.) Sermons.
Horberry's (Matthew) Sermons.
Hunter's (Henry) Sermons.
Kay's (Bp.) Sermons.
Kingsley's (C.) Sermons.
Lardner's (Nathaniel) Sermons.
Lawson's (C.) Sermons.
Mandell's (William) Sermons.
Mant's (Bp.) Sermons.
Ravenscroft's (Bp.) Sermons.
Ryland's Scheme of Infidelity ruined forever.
Snowden's (W.) Sermons.
Vaughan's Salvation in Christ only.
Witherspoon's (John) Essays and Sermons.
Wrangham's (Francis) Sermons.
Zinzendorf's Discourses.

Salvation of Heathen as such.

Collins de Animabus Paganorum.
Curcellius de Necessitate cognitione Christ. Sec. VI.
Müller (J. G.) de Paganorum post mortem conditione.
Turretini Theologia Elenctica. Ques. IV.

Arnold, Dr., Life of.
Barclay's Apology.
Baxter's Saint's Rest.
Bradford's Boyle Lectures. Appendix.
Breckell's (John) Sermons.
Doddridge's Lectures. Lect. 240.
Goodwin's (John) Pagan Debt and Dowry.
Grove's Moral Philosophy.
McKnight's Preliminary Essays.
Mede's Works.
Newton's Messiah.
Owen on the Spirit.
Rymer's Representation of Revealed religion. Ch. 5.

Saurin's Sermons.
Scott's Christian Life.
Staynoe's Salvation by Christ alone.
Taylor's Key to Romans. Ch. 13.
Watt's Strength and Weakness of Human reason.

Samaritans.

Antonii Observationes Theologicæ.
Cellarii Collectanea Historiæ Samaritanæ.
Freiderich, Christologia Samaritanum.
Gesenius de Samaritanorum Theologia.
Hottingeri Thesaurus Philologicus.
Iuynbolli Chronicon.
Rehlingii Dissertatio Critica de S.
Reland, de Inscriptionibus nummorum.
Rhenferd, de Judæorum Hæresibus.
Sacy, l'Etat actuel des S. (17th century.)
Weiss, de Jurejurando per Deum.

Amer. Eclectic Review. 2:249,481.
Bassnage's History of the Jews. Bk. 8.
Simon's Dissertations on the Caraites and Samaritans.

Samaritan Pentateuch. See PENTAT.

Gesenius de P. Samar. origine, indole, etc.
Hassencamp de Pentateucho.
Hottingeri Exercitationes anti-Morrisianæ.
Houbiganti Prolegomena.
Kennicott's Dissertationes.
Lightfoot, Collatio Hebr. cum Samaritico.
Morini Exercitationes in Samaritan. Pent.
Simonis Hist. Critic. de Vet. Testam.
Waltoni Prolegomena ad Bib. Polyglot.
Wineri de Vers. Pent. Samar. indole.

Biblical Repository. 1832. (Prof. Stewart. Reprinted from N. Amer. Review.)
Brett's Dissertations on ancient versions.
Gerard's Institutes of Biblical Crit. Ch. 1.
Hamilton's General introduction to the study of the Hebrew Scriptures.
North Amer. Review. 22:274. (By Professor Stewart. A comprehensive and scholarly digest of about all that is known on this subject.)
Owen's (H.) Comparison of the Hebrew and Samaritan Pentateuchs.
Whiston's Essay toward restoring the text of the O. T. (In an appendix is an English version of all the passages in which the Samaritan Pent. differs from the Hebrew. Mr. W. is sharply answered by CARPZOW, in his *Critica Sacra.*)
Yeates' (Thos.) Collation of an Indian Copy. (Valuable preliminary remarks.)

Samosatenians.

Athanasius de Incarnatione.
Baieri Dissertationes Theologicæ.
Ehrlichii Miscellanea Sacra.
Feverlinus de Hæresi Pauli Samosateni.
Schnizlini Dissert. de Hæresi Pauli S.
Schwab, Pauli Samos. vita et doctrina.
Thillii Dissertationes Theologicæ.
Trechsel's Gesch. des Antitrinitarismus.
Walchii Miscellanea Sacra.

Sanctification.

Hulsemanni Breviarum Theologicum.
Mayerus de Sanctificatione.
Quistorpii (Ioann.) Dissertationes.
Walchii Miscellanea Sacra.

Adams' (Will.) Sermons.
Bates' (William) Works.
Benson's (Joseph) Sermons.
Biber's (G. E.) Sermons.
Blunt's (Henry) Posthumous Sermons.
Boucher's (J.) Sermons.
Broughton's (Bp.) Sermons.
Carr's (Samuel) Sermons.
Cawood's (John) Sermons.
Cooper's (Edward) Sermons.
Dugard's Nature of the Divine law.
Dwight's Theology. Ser. 83.
Fessenden's Science of Sanctity.
Fowler's (Bp.) Design of Christianity.
Frazier's Expos. of Romans, ch. 6, 7, and 8. (Combats the sentiments on this subject of Grotius, Hammond, Locke, Whitby, Taylor, and others, in a learned and candid manner.)
Gregory's (Thomas) Sermons.
Knight's (Robert) Sermons.
Lit. and Theol. Review. 1:103.
Lucas on Gospel holiness.
Manton's (Thomas) Sermons.
Marsh's Bampton Lectures. 1848.
Marshall on Sanctification. ("Were I to be banished to a desolate island with but two books beside my Bible, this should be one of them."—HERVEY.)
Moore's Mystery of godliness.
Owen on the Spirit.
Payson's (Ed.) Sermons. (Amiable instincts not holiness.)
Taylor's (Jer.) Holy Living.
——— Christian Consolations.
Vaux's (W.) Sermons.
——— Bampton Lectures.
Walker's Christ the Sanctifier.
Witsius on the Covenants.

Sandemanians.

Pro.

Sandeman's Letters on Theoron and Aspasio.
——— Epistolary Correspondence.
——— Discourses, Essays, and Letters.
Cooper's (M.) Letters.
Ecking's (Sam.) Essays on grace and faith.
Glass' Testimony of the King of Martyrs. (A strong book.)
——— Whole Works. (5 vols., 8vo. 1760.)

Con.

Backus on Faith.
Bellamy's Nature and glory of the Gospel.
Fuller's (And.) Works. Vol. 2.
Hervey's Letters of Theoron and Aspasio.
Wilson's Palæmon's creed examined.

Satan.

Mayeri (J. G.) Historia Diaboli.
Millii (D.) Dissertationes.

Satan—*continued.*

[Schmid, (J. W.)] de Doctrina de Diabolo.
Schulz's (J. C. F.) Bedentung des Wort S.
Simon's Alt. u. neu. Gesch. d. Glaubens, etc.
Zentgravii Dissertationes. (One on Satan's transforming himself into an angel of light.)
Allestree's (Richard) Sermons.
Ashdowne Concerning the Devil or Satan.
Bloomfield's (G. B.) Sermons.
Brooks on Satan's Devices.
Boyse's (William) Works.
Bulkeley's Economy of the Gospel.
Campbell on the Four Gospels.
Carson's (Alexander) Works.
Charnock's Works.
Christian Review. 9:349.
Close's (Francis) Sermons.
Coleman's (J. N.) Sermons.
Cook's (John) Sermons.
De Foe's Political History of Satan.
Dublin University Mag. 52:421.
Edwards' (John) Critical and Historical Exercitations.
Fawcett's (John) Sermons.
Gilpin on Temptation.
Grant's (Johnson) Course of Sermons.
Hall's (Robt.) Personality of Satan.
Heber's (Bp.) Parish Sermons.
Howe's Works.
Hunt's Historical Essay on Lucifer.
Hurd's (Bp.) Sermons.
Munkhouse's (R.) Sermons.
Porteus' (Bp.) Sermons.
Ransom on Satanic influence.
Reynolds on Angels.
Roberts' (Arthur) Village Sermons.
Scoresby's (W.) Discourses to Seamen.
Simpson (John) on the words שטן, Σαταν, Διαβολος, and synonymous expressions.
Smith's (Henry) Sermons.
Tweedie's Satan as revealed in Scripture.
Vaughn's (Cha. John) Sermons.
Vaughn's (J.) Lectures. Lect. 11.

Satire. See RIDICULE.

Oxford Prize Essays. 1786.

Satisfaction of Christ. See ATONEMENT, REDEMPTION, SUBSTITUTION, SUFFERINGS.

Scandal. See EVIL SPEAKING, OFFENCES, SLANDER, TONGUE.

Alsop on Scandal.
Bossuet's Sermons.
Bourdaloue's Sermons.
Butler's (Alban) Sermons.
Chapman's (J.) Essays.
Durham on Scandal.
Dyke's (Jer.) Sermons.
Ford's Sinfulness of a defamatory tongue.
Gahan's (William) Sermons.
Hammond (H.) on Scandal.
Hole's (Matthew) Sermons.
Tombes' (Jno.) Christ's commination against scandalizers.

Scape-Goat. See TYPES.

Deylingii (Solom.) Dissertationes.
Frischmuthii (Ioann.) Dissertationes.
Schmidt de Hirco apopompeo.
Spencer de Legibus. Diss. VIII.
Bradley's (Charles) Sermons.
Kennaway's (C. E.) Sermons.
Simeon's (C.) Works.

Scepter of Judah. See SHILOH.

Cellarii Dissertationes de Pompeii magni.
Deylingii (D. S.) Observationes.
Dieterici (J. C.) Antiquitates.
Grævii Syntagma dissert. rariarum.
Helvici Sceptrum Judæ.
Phaletranius de Principatu Maccabæorum.
Platneri Pharo Veteris Testamenti.
Wagenseilii (J. C.) Dissertationes.
Wernsdorfii Commentatio de fide historica librorum Maccabæorum.
Beveridge's (Bp.) Thesaurus.
Faber's (Geo. S.) Dissertations.
Hawker's (Robert) Works.
Jackson's (W. F.) Sermons.
Le Clerc's (John) Dissertations.
Mountain's (J. H. B.) Sermons.
Robinson (T.) on Scripture prophecies.
Sharp (Granville) on Important prophecies.
Toplady's (A. M.) Christmas Meditations.
Wilson's (Thomas) Sermons.

Schism.

Cyprian de Unitate Ecclesiæ.
Bennett on Schisms.
Buck's (James) Sermons.
Campbell's Preliminary Dissertations.
Caudry on Schism.
Daubeny's (A.) Nature, &c., of Schism.
Dodwell's One altar and one priesthood.
Firmin on Schism.
Foster's (Dr. Jas.) Sermons.
Garscome's Ans. to Tallent's Short history.
Hale's Treatise on schism and schismatics.
Hall's View of a Gospel Church.
Harness' (Wm.) Two Sermons on schism.
Henry's Enquiry into the nature of schism.
Hody's Treatise out of ecclesiastical history.
Hoppus' (J.) Schism in these times. 1839.
Ling's Primitive Church.
Le Messurier's Bampton Lectures. 1807.
Long's Examination of Hale's Treatise.
Owen's (Cha.) Plain Dealing.
——— Vindication of Do.
Owen's (John) Discourses. (Rep. to Caudry.)
Page's Animadversions on Hale's Treatise.
Polhill on Schism.
Sherlock's Defence of Stillingfleet.
Spofford's Weapons of Schism.
Stillingfleet's Mischief of Separation.
——— Unreasonableness of Do.
Tallent's Short history of Schism.
——— Considerations on Garscome's Ans.
Tate's Cure of Contention.
Wesley's (John) Sermons.
Whately's Bampton Lectures. 1822.
Woodgate's Bampton Lectures. 1838.

Scholasticism. See THOMISTS.

Alberti Magni Opera.
Alesii Summa universæ theologiæ.
Annati Apparatus ad positivam theologiam methodicus.
Arnauld, Œuvres.
Baur's Lehre von der Versohnung.
Bruckeri Historia Philosophiæ.
Bulæi Historia Universitatis Parisiensis.
Cajetani Commentaria.
Damascenus de Fide orthodoxa.
Duns Scotus, Opera.
Durandi Commentaria.
Engelhardt's Dogmengeschichte.
Erhard's Geschichte des Wiederaufblühens wissenschaftlicher Bildung.
Estii Commentaria. (An excellent account of scholastic divinity.)
Faber's (B.) Thesaurus eruditionis scholast.
Fabricii Bibliotheca mediæ ætatis.
Heeren's Geschichte der Philosophie.
Hegel's Geschichte der Philosophie.
Jourdain la Philosophie de St. Thomas.
Lombardi Opera. ("There is hardly a useless question which is not here discussed."—LOWNDES.)
Melancthonis Didymi Faventini. (Powerful exposure of scholastic nonsense.)
Occamii Opera.
Peter (of Poictiers) Libri Sententiarum.
Raimondi Theologia Naturalis.
Roscellini Opera.
Schettgenii Opera.
Schleiermacher's Kirchengeschichte.
Spizelii Templum honoris referatum.
Tanneri Theologia ad methodum S. Thomæ.
Tenneman's Geschichte der Philosophie.
Thomasii (Aquin.) Opera.
Tribbechovius de Doct. scholast. et corrupta per eos divinar. et human. rerum scientia.
Walteri (St. Victoire) contra Manifestas et damnatas etiam in conciliis hæreses.
——— super Sententias Lombardi.

Amer. Biblical Repos. 3d Series. 3:143.
Edinburg Review. 68:337.
Hampden's Bampton Lectures. 1832. (The relation of scholastic philosophy to Christian theology.)
Princeton Rev. 18:191.
Robins' Defence of the faith.

A great list of Scholastic writers is given in LOWNDES' *British Librarian.*

Schools of the Prophets.

Alting, Hist. Acadamiarum Hebræorum.
Calmet, les Ecoles des Hébreux.
Fabricii (F.) Oratio de scholis prophetarum.
Huebneri (J. L.) Dissertationes. (Ugolinus.)
Othonis Hist. doctorum Misnicorum.
Ugolini Thesaurus antiq. sacrarum.
Ursini Antiquitates Hebræicæ.

Schwartz.

Episc. Magazine. 1:37,69,191,132.
Jones' Christian Biography.
Panoplist. New Series. 3:123.
Pearson's Life and correspondence of S. (With a sketch of the history of Christianity in India.)

Schwinkfeldians.

Pro.

Schwinkfeld, de Cursu verbi Dei.
——— Catechismus.
——— Quæstiones vom Erkantniss J. C.
——— Deutsche Theologie.
——— Von der Speyse des ewigen Lebens.
——— Auslegung des Evangelisten.
——— Vom Worte Gottes.
——— (Numerous other treatises.)
Arnold's Kirchen und Ketzer Historie.
Crautwald, Bericht von der Weise, etc.
——— de Neuse meusch.
Friderick, Geheimniss der Prüfung.
Fueslini Epistolæ.
Herxheimer Bekenntniss Christl. Glaubens.
Hilliger de Vita, fatis, et scriptis, ect.
Salig, Histor. August. confessionis.
Werneri Catechismus.

Con.

Coccoii Disputationes.
Faber de Presentia corporis et sanguinis J. C. in sacramento.
Flaccius von der Heiligen Schrift.
Lutheri Epistolæ.
——— Scheda.
Melancthonis Dissertationes.
Osiandri Disputationes.
Wigandi Schwenckfeldiana.
Winklemani Disputationes.

Schwinkfeldians, History of.

Arnold's Kirchen und Ketzer Historie.
Cruse, Leben Caspar von Schwenkfeld.
Kocheri Biblioth. theologiæ symbolicæ.
Planck, Gesch. der protestantis. Theologie.
Salig, Hist. August. confessionis. Lib. XI.
Schlusseburgi Catalogus Hæreticorum.

Science. See HARMONY OF REASON AND FAITH, HARMONY OF SCIENCE AND RELIGION, PHILOSOPHY OF RELIGION, PROVINCE OF REASON, VAIN PHILOS.

Scientia Media. See CONTINGENCY.

Annatus de Scientia media.
Borulli (Matt.) Dissertationes.
Crellius de Deo.
Herrera, de Voluntate Dei.
Molinæ Liberi arbitrii cum gratiæ donis divina præscientia prædest. concordia.
Platellii (Iacob.) Dissertationes.
Ramirez de Scientia Dei.
Reginaldi Theses Apologeticæ.
Suarezius de Scientia Dei futurorum.
Twisse, adversus Bellarminum.
——— de Scientia Media. (Cont. Suarez.)
Zimmerman, de Effectibus casualibus.

Abernethy's Sermons.
Clarke's (S.) Boyle Lectures. 1704,1705.
——— Posthumous Sermons.

Jackson on Human Liberty.
Le Blanc's Theses.
Twisse's Dissertations.

Scoffers.

Alexander's (J. W.) Sermons.
Arnold's (Frederick) Sermons.
Bather's (Edward) Sermons.
Berens' (Edward) Sermons.
Blair's (Hugh) Sermons.
Carr's (George) Sermons.
Clarke's (Samuel) Sermons.
Clements' (B.) Sermons.
Cooper's (Edward) Sermons.
Coyle's (Tobias) Sermons.
Davies' (Thomas) Sermons.
Fell's Character of the last days.
Fiddes' (Richard) Sermons.
Foster's (James) Sermons.
Francis' (Dr. John) Sermons.
Glanvil's (Joseph) Discourses.
Hammond's (Henry) Sermons.
Hurd's (Bp.) Sermons.
Johnson's (Dr. Samuel) Sermons.
Kearney's (John) Sermons.
Knagg's (Thomas) Sermons.
Rogers' (John) Sermons.
Stillingfleet's (Bp.) Sermons.
Sutton's (W.) Sermons.
Tillotson's (Abp.) Sermons.
Tottie's (John) Sermons.
Trapp's (Joseph) Preservative.
Van Mildert's Boyle Lectures.
Whichcot's (B.) Sermons.

Scotists.

Duns Scoti opera omnia. (12 v. fol.)
Frassenii Scotus Academicus.
Hackhofferi Compendium alphabeticum.
Hermanni Tractatus Theologici.
Krisperi Theologia.
Opstraeti Theologia.
Schopenii Universa Theologia.
Varesii Promptuarium.

Scribes. See JEWISH ANTIQUITIES.

Hechtius de Secta Scribarum.
Ugolini Thesaurus antiq. sacrarum.

Beausobre & L'Enfant's Introd. to N. Test.
Calmet's Sects of the Jews.
Lightfoot's Commentary. Matt. 2:14.
Tomline's (Bp.) Christian Theology.
Wells' Help to understanding the Scriptures.
Wotton's Miscellaneous Discourses.

Scripture Biography. See BIOGRAPHY.

Scripture Natural History. See NATURAL HISTORY OF THE BIBLE.

Seal of the Spirit. See WITNESS.

Seals and Trumpets. See COMMENTAT. ON THE APOCALYPSE.

Cunninghame on the Seals and Trumpets.
Gascoine's (R.) New Solution, &c. 1847.
Glass' (John) Five Letters.
Hardy (S.) on the Principal prophecies.
Harrison's (B.) Warburton Lectures.
Markwick's (D. W.) Six Tracts.
Moule's (Henry) Lectures. (First 6 seals.)

Seamen.

Abbot's (A.) Sermons to Mariners.
Bains' Naval Discourses.
Bassnet's (C.) Sermons.
Blackwood's Mag. 9:414.
Burder's (Geo.) Twelve Sermons to sailors.
Christian Quart. Spect. 3:253.
Clarke's (J. S.) Naval Sermons. (Character and duties of Seamen.)
Flavel's Navigation spiritualized.
Hanway's Seamen's Christian friend.
Harris' (Dr. John) Brittania. (A prize essay. 1837.)
Hayward's (S.) Sermons.
Maddock's Sermons to seamen.
Mark's Sea Sermons.
Philips' Bethel Flag.
Ramsey's Sermons for the Navy.
Reports of the various Seamen's Friend Soc.
Ryther's Seamen's Preacher.
Scoresby's Discourses to Seamen.
Stockdale's (Percival) Sermons. (13 to S.)
Wood's (J.) True honor of navigation. (Quaint.)

Searching the Scriptures. See READING.

Amory's (Thomas) Sermons.
Clapp's (J.) Sermons.
D'Oyly's (George) Sermons.
Eveleigh's (John) Sermons.
Fowle's (F. W.) Ten plain sermons.
Frost's (John) Sermons.
Gibbs' (Jos.) Directions for searching the S.
Gilpin's (William) Sermons.
Hervey's (James) Sermons.
Nourse's (P.) Discourses.
Patrick's (Bp.) Sermons.
Scott's (John) Sermons.
Scobel's (Edward) Sermons.
Shuttleworth's (P. N.) Sermons.
Skelton's (Philip) Sermons.
Sterne's (Lawrence) Sermons.
Williams' (Bp.) Sermons.

Seat of the Soul.

Des Cartes de Passionibus.
Vitringæ Dissertationes.
Doddridge's Lectures. Propos. 4.
Moore on the Immortality of the soul.
Vitringa's Observations on obscure texts.
Watts' Essays. Essay 3.

Secession Church.

Anderson's (John) Works.
Brown's (John) Gospel truth stated.
——— Rise and progress of Secession.
——— History of British Churches.
Dick's (John) Lectures.
Eclectic Review. 4th Series. 17:695.
Erskine's (Ebenezer) Works.

Secession Church—*continued.*

Erskine's (Ralph) Works.
Ferrier's Memoir of Rev. W. Wilson. (Contains a very good account of the origin of the Secession Church.)
Frazier's Memoir of Ebenezer Erskine.
Gibbs' Display of the Secession Testimony.
Graham on Ecclesiastical Establishments.
Hetherington's Hist. of the Ch. of Scotland.
McCrie's Unity of the Church.
McKerrow's Secession Ch. 1847. (Very satisfactory, though Gibbs is more copious.)
Robertson's Hist. of the Secession Church.
——— Hist. of the S. Ch. missions to Nova Scotia and Prince Edward's Island.
Struthers' History of Scotland.
Wilson's Def. of Reformation principles.

Second Adam.

Edge's (W. J.) Lectures.

Second Advent of Christ.
See MILLENARIANS, MILLERISM.

Chrysostom de Secundo adventu.
Cyril (Hieros.) Catecheses.
Cyril (Alex.) de Exitu animi, etc.

Bengel's Erklärte Offenbarung Johannis. (In this and several other works he endeavors to prove the time to be 1836.)
Böhm's Zeichen der Zeit.
Ephraem Syrus, Opera.
Henke Lineamenta. (Explains it away.)
Hoelemann's Stellung Pauli zu der Frage um d. Zeit d. Wiederkunst Christi.
Schott (H. A.), Comm. in eos J. C. sermones qui de reditu ejus, etc.
Stilling's Siegsgeschichte der Kirche.
Vossius de Adventu Christi ultimo.

Abdiel [J. W. Brooks] on the Kingdom of Christ.
Bayford's Messiah's Kingdom.
Benson's (Joseph) Sermons.
Bloomfield's Lent Lectures. (Ten volumes of discourses by England's ablest divines.)
Bosthwick's Lectures.
Brookes' (J. W.) Essays.
Burgh's [or De Burgh] Lectures.
Burroughs' Jerusalem's Glory.
Caswall's (E.) Sermons.
Chalmers' (Tho.) Sermons.
Christian Observer. 28:226,450.
Christian Review. 9:597.
Chace's (Samuel) Messiah's advent.
Coleman's Redeemer's Triumph.
Cotton's (R. L.) Sermons.
Crosby (Alpheus) on the Second advent.
Doddridge's (Philip) Sermons.
Dodsworth on the Second advent.
Dowling's Reply to Miller's Lectures.
Drummond's Defence of the students of prophecy.
Duffield (Geo.) on the Proph. relating, &c.
Durant's Salvation of the Saints.
Fleming's Christology.
Foster's (Dr. James) Sermons.

Second Advent—*continued.*

Fry's (John) Glorious Epiphany of Christ.
Gale on Christ's coming.
Guild's Harmony of all the prophets.
Hatherell's (J. W.) Words of Jesus applied to our own times. 1858.
Hodgkinson on Whether the apostles believed the day of judgment to be at hand.
Hook's (William F.) Sermons.
Horseley's (Bp.) Sermons.
Jewish Expositor. (Several articles of great value.)
Kapff on the Coming of the Lord.
Lavington's (Samuel) Sermons.
Lee's (Sam.) Eschatology.
Litch (J.) on the Second coming 1838. (Makes it to be in 1843.)
Lord's Theo. and Lit. Journal. 2:563. 3:262. 4:1,233.
Madden on the Nature, time, &c.
Mandeville's Things hoped for.
McCheyne's (Robt. M.) Sermons.
McNeil's (Hugh) Sermons.
Mede on Peter's prophecy.
Miller's Lectures on the Second coming, &c.
Newman's (Thomas) Sermons.
Newton's (John) Sermons.
Noel's (Gerard T.) Prospects of the Church.
Philpot's Bloomsbury Lectures.
Reynolds' Parochial discourses.
Riddle's (J. E.) Sermons.
Rogers' End of the world.
Saville on the First and second advent.
Seiss' (Jos. A.) The Last times.
Stewart's (Jas. H.) Sermons. (A calm and profitable discussion of the subject.)
Tillinghast's Knowledge of the times.
Tillotson's Sermons.
Trigg's Analysis of Matt. xxiv.
Universalist Quarterly. 1:381.
Urwick's Blessed hope of the Church.
Walker's (Robert) Sermons.
White (Hugh) On the second advent.
Witherby's Review of Scripture.
Wood's (Walter) The last things.
Worthington on Redemption.
Young's (John) Sermons. (3 on this subj.)

Second Commandment.
See COMMANDMENTS, COUNCIL IV. OF CONSTANTINOPLE, ICONOCLASTS, IMAGE WORSHIP.

Marshall's (Nath.) Sermons.
Ogden's (Samuel) Sermons.
Paley's (William) Sermons.
Sanderson's (Bp.) Sermons.

Second Marriages.

Ambrose de Viduis.
Ripa de Secundis nuptiis.

Secret Faults. See SELF-EXAMINATION, SINS OF IGNORANCE.

Barnes' (Albert) Practical Sermons.
Benson's (Jos.) Sermons.
Burgess' (Anth.) Sermons.

Secret Faults—*continued.*

Chevallier (Temple) on Prayer for deliverance from sin.
Hewlett's (John) Sermons.
Newman's (John H.) Sermons.
Paley's (Will.) Sermons.
Payson's (Edward) Works.
Reynerd's Sermons.
Sedwick's (O.) Anatomy of secret sins.
Sherlock's (Bp.) Sermons.
Spurgeon's (Cha. H.) Sermons. 3d Series.
Sullivan's (Henry W.) Sermons.
Tappan's (David) Sermons.

Secret Prayer. See PRAYER.

Blair's (James) Sermons.
Barnes' (Albert) Practical sermons.
Butler's (Bp.) Sermons.
Cookesley's (W. G.) Sermons.
Grove's (Henry) Sermons.
Heywood's (Oliver) Tracts and Sermons.
Hyatt's (John) Sermons.
Jay's Christian in the Closet.
Jowett's (Joseph) Sermons.
Kattern's (Daniel) Sermons.
Kollock's (Shepard K.) Sermons.
McGill on Secret prayer.
Morris' (Joseph) Sermons.
Newman's (J. H.) Parochial Sermons.
Ninds' (W.) Sermons.
Noel's (Gerard T.) Sermons.
Orton's (Job) Discourses.
Slade's (James) Sermons.
Stebbings' (Henry) Sermons.
Townsend's (John) Sermons.
Trapp (Jos.) on Private devotion.
Young's (W. T.) Sermons.

Sectarianism. See CHRISTIAN UNION, HERESY, UNITY.

Allen's Persuasive to peace and unity.
Balguy's (John) Sermons.
Blakie's Philosophy of Sectarianism. (Gives a classified view of Christian sects in the United States. 1854.)
Bolton's True grounds of Christian freedom.
Chris. Exam. 21:291.
Christian Monthly Spect. 4:460.
Christian Observer. 3:730. 16:569.
Howe (John) on Christian Union.
James on Party distinctions in religion.
New Englander. 5:78.
Princeton Rev. 12:465.
Trapp on Want of principles in religion.
Universalist Quarterly. 6:15.
Whately's (Abp.) Bampton Lectures. 1822.
Wilson's (H. B.) Bampton Lectures. 1851.
Wylie's (A.) Sectarianism is Heresy.

Sects. See HISTORY OF DOCTRINES, RELIGIONS, SCHISM, SECTARIANISM.

Arnold's (G.) Hist. d. Kirchen, etc. (Numerous portraits. Begins with the first century, and gives the details of all the sects up to the year 1700.)

Sects—*continued.*

Erbkam's Geschichte d. Sekten, in Zeitalter d. Ref.
Gregoire, Histoire des Sectes religieuses. (A copious and very useful digest.)
Ittigii Diss. de hæres. ævi apostolor.
Jaegeri Hist. Ecclesiastica. 1714. (Relates chiefly to sects which have risen since the Reformation.)
Scaligeri Trihæræsium liber. 1630. (Very valuable.)
Schmidt (T.), Dissertationes.
Voetii Bibliotheca historica. 1631.
Walch's (C. G. F.) Hist. der Ketzereien. 1750. (Extensive [11 vols.], reaching to the Reformation.)
Zeltneri Breviarium controversiarum. 1724.
American Christian Record. (A convenient manual of confessions and statistics.)
Blakie's Philos. of Sectarianism. (A classified view of the sects in the U. States.)
Boone's Book of churches and sects. 1836.
Eadie's Ecclesiastical Cyclopedia. 1856.
Evans' Sketch of all denominations. 1794.
Gorries' Churches and Sects of the United States. 1850.
Greenleaf's History of all the Churches of New York. 1850.
Gregoire's Hist. of the religious sects which have sprung up, been modified, or extinguished, in the 18th century.
Marsden's Hist. of Churches and S. 1855.
Pagitt's Christianography. 1640.
——— Sectaries of these times. 1645.
Ross' Relig. and Heresies in all ages. 1690.
Rupp's Relig. Denom. in the U. S. 1844.
Staudlin's Ecclesiastical geography and statistics. 1804.
Tomline on the Jewish Sects.
Wells' Help for understanding Scripture.
Williams' Dictionary of Denominations.
Winebrenner's Rel. Denom. of the U. S. 1849.

Secularism. See ATHEISM.

Secundians. See VALENTINIANS.

Bassnage, Histoire des Juifs. Tom. III.
Faydit, Eclaircissemens sur les deux premier siècles.
Vitringa Observationes Sacræ.

Seduction.

Barnaby's (A.) Sermons.
Burton's (John) Sermons.
Christian Examiner. 15:158.
Dwight's (T.) Discourses. (Very powerful.)
Edwards' (Bp.) Body of Divinity.
Madan's Thelypthora. (On female ruin. Thinks polygamy tolerable.)
——— Answers to various Reviews.
Pyle's (Philip) Character of Joseph.
Smith's (Mary, a penitent) on Seduction and prostitution, and their consequences.
Tait's Magdalenism.
Wardlaw's Lectures on Female prostitution.
Whitaker's (Edw. W.) Sermons.

Selah. See BIBLICAL CRITICISM, PHILOLOGY.
Bartolocci Excerpta. (Ugolinus, vol. 32.)
Calmet (A.) de סלה.
Heumann de סלה Heb. interject. musica.
Michaelis (J. G.) Exercitationes Theologicæ.
Paschii de סלה philologica enucleatio.
Pfeiffer, de Voce vexata סלה.
Reine (M. H. C.) de סלה. (Ugolinus, tom. 32.)
Calmet's Dissertations.
Danville Review. June, 1864.
Jebb's Trans. of the Psalms. (Appendix.)

Self-Conceit. See CONCEIT, HUMILITY, VAINGLORY, VANITY.

Self-Confidence.
Barrow's (Isaac) Sermons.
Bateman's (Josiah) Sermons.
Bather's (Edward) Sermons.
Bell's (William) Sermons.
Boston's (T.) Happiness of fearing always.
Christian Observer. 14:155.
Disney's (John) Sermons.
Enfield's (William) Sermons.
Fawcett's (Joseph) Sermons.
Free's (John) Sermons.
Henry's (Matthew) Sermons.
Hill's (John) Sermons.
Hoole's (Joseph) Sermons.
Jackson's (Miles) Sermons.
Johnson's (Dr. S.) Sermons.
Langhorne's (John) Sermons.
Lardner's (Nath.) Sermons.
Mant's (Bp.) Lectures.
Martin's (S.) Sermons.
Milner's (Joseph) Sermons.
Moore's (Hannah) Practical Piety.
Parkinson's (R.) Sermons.
Rogers' (John) Sermons.
Shuttleworth's (P. N.) Sermons.
Skelton's (Philip) Works.
Smith's (Henry) Sermons.
Taylor's (C.) Sermons.
Vincent's (John) Sermons.
Webster's (James) Sermons.
Wheatland's (Thomas) Sermons.

Self-Culture.
Amer. Bibl. Repos. 5:75.
Amer. Monthly Rev. 1:504.
Analytical Magazine. 16:481.
Bacon's (Leonard) Christian self-culture.
Beard (J. R.) on Self-culture.
Burder (H. F.) on Mental discipline.
——— Sermons. (Self-discipline.)
Channing's (Will. E.) Essays.
Christian Examiner. 2:412. 9:70. 11:295. 37:331. 51:185.
Democratic Review. 5:85.
Foster's (John) Essays. (Admirable.)
Grey's Thoughts on self-culture.
Mason on Self-knowledge.
Monthly Chris. Spectator. 8:388.
Taylor's Hints to a youth leaving school.

Self-Deception. See DECEITFULNESS OF THE HEART.
Alexander's (J. A.) Sermons.
Arnold's (Frederick) Sermons.
Baxter's Mischief of self-ignorance.
Black's (David) Sermons.
Blair's (James) Sermons.
Bourn's (Samuel) Sermons.
Burgess' (A.) Spiritual Refinings.
Butler's (Bp.) Sermons.
Butler's (Will. A.) Sermons.
Christian Observer. 1:638,696. 20:150.
Christian Quar. Spect. 9:42.
Cooper's (Edward) Sermons.
Danberry's Trial of the spirits.
Dykes' Mystery of self-deceiving.
Ellis' (C.) Self-deceiver discov'd to himself.
Enfield's (Will.) Sermons.
Evans on Christian temper.
Fawcett's (Joseph) Sermons.
Fawcett's (John) Sermons.
Finney's (C. G.) Lectures to profess. Chris.
Hall's (Bp.) Sermons.
Haweis' (T.) Sermons.
Hort's (Josiah) Sermons.
Howe's Living Temple. (Ed. by Chalmers.)
Jamieson's (John) Sermons.
Johnson's (Dr. Sam.) Sermons.
Lamont's (David) Sermons.
Mason on Self-knowledge.
McGill's (Stephenson) Sermons.
Morgan's (J. P.) Sermons.
Sharpe's (Wm.) Sermons before the University at Cambridge.
Smith's (Sydney) Sermons.
Spurgeon's (Cha. H.) Sermons. 7th Series.
Stebbings' Sermons.
Taylor's (Bp.) Sermons.
Vincent's (John) Sermons.
Wesley's (John) Sermons.
Yonge's (James) Sermons. 3d Series.

Self-Dedication.
Bibliotheca Sacra. 18:143.
Chandler's (Sam.) Sermons.
Christian Observer. 20:737.
Cooper's (Edward) Sermons.
Davies' (Sam.) Sermons.
Doddridge's Rise and progress of religion in the soul.
Dow's (W.) Discourses.
Edwards' (Pres.) Memoirs.
Evans' (Dr. John) Discourses.
Fish's Primitive piety revived. Ch. 3.
Gold and the Gospel. (Prize Essays on giving in proportion to income, by Constable, Morgan, Spence, Ross, and others. 1856.)
Hardwick's Christ and other Masters.
Harris (Dr. Will.) on Personal self-dedicat.
Howe's (John) Works. Vol. 1.
Lavington's (Samuel) Sermons.
Le Bas' (C. W.) Sermons.
Short's (Bp.) Sermons.
Watts on Prayer.
Worthington's (John) Select Discourses.

Self-Defence. See DUELLING.

Ballou's Christian non-resistance defended.
Blackall's (Bp.) Sermons.
Christ. Exam. 31:164.
Clagget's (William) Sermons.
Coleman's (C.) Sermons.
Dodd's (Will.) Sermons to young men.
Gresley's (William) Sermons.
Grove's Moral Philosophy.
Miles' (Cornelius) Sermons.

Self-Denial. See SENSUALITY.

Wahrenburg (C. H. W.) de Abnegatione sui.
Windischmann Vorlesungen über Ethik.

Abernethy's (John) Sermons.
Ashwood's Heavenly Trade.
Atterbury's (Lewis) Sermons.
Bather's (Edward) Sermons.
Baxter's (Rich.) Treatise on self-denial.
Bloomfield's (G. B.) Sermons. (Self-crucifix.)
Calvin's Institutes of Theology.
Campbell (G.) on Temperance and Self-den.
Cappe's Practical Discourses.
Channing's (Will. E.) Sermons.
Craig's (Edward) Sermons.
Crisp's (Tobias) Christ alone exalted. (Very superior.)
Dowling's (John G.) Sermons.
Edwards' (Dr. John) Theologia Reformata.
Erskine's (Dr. John) Sermons.
Fawcett's (John) Sermons.
Firmin's Real Christian.
Fish's (H. C.) Prim. piety revived. Ch. 4.
Foster (Dr. J.) on Self-gov't and Self-denial.
Gilpin's (William) Sermons.
Hale's (Sir Matt.) Contemplations.
Hill's (G. D.) Wayfarings in Christ.
Hooker's Treatise on Self-denial.
Horne's (Bp.) Discourses.
Jelf's (R. W.) Sermons.
Jones' (Wm. of Nayland) Sermons.
Jortin's (John) Sermons.
Kempis' Imitation of Christ.
Mason on Self-knowledge. Part 2, ch. 7.
McLean's Apostolical Commission. (Exc't.)
Moncreiff's (H. W.) Sermons.
Muir's (James) Sermons.
Newman's (John H.) Sermons.
Nicholson's (Will.) Sermons.
Noel's (G. T.) Sermons.
Polwheele on Self-denial.
Preston's Life Eternal.
Reynolds' (Bp.) Sermons.
Scott's (John) Sermons.
Serle's Christian Remembrancer.
Spring's (Gardner) Essays. Ess. 10.
Tucker's Light of nature pursued.
Wesley's (John) Sermons.
Whately's (Rich.) Essays on var. passages.
Whitby's Annotations on Luke 9:23.
——— Sermons.
Whitefield's Sermons.
Wilson's (Thomas) Sermons.
Yonge's (James) Sermons. 3d Series.
Young's (Dr. Edward, Sen.) Sermons.

Self-Examination.

Abbadie, l'Art de la connaitre soi meme.
Adey's (Wm.) Sermons.
Atkinson's (Christopher) Sermons.
Balguy's (John) Sermons.
Barker's (John) Sermons.
Barr's Help to professing Christians.
Baxter's Mischief of self-ignorance.
Berens' (Edward) Sermons for a sick-room.
Boyce's Ground of hope.
Brewster's Meditations.
Brooks' Unsearchable Riches.
——— on Holiness.
Buck's Dictionary. Art. "Self-Deception."
Buddicom's (Robt. P.) Sermons.
Burder's (Henry F.) Sermons.
Burgess (Ant.) on Self-judging.
Charnock's (S.) Works.
Christian Observer. 2:205,408. 11:416. 20:1, 121,477,743.
Colquhoun on Spiritual Comfort.
Corbet's Self-employment in secret.
Dibden's (R. W.) Sermons.
Drysdale's (Dr. John) Sermons.
Dyke's Mystery of self-deceiving.
Edwards' (Pres.) Works.
Ellis' Self-deceiver discovered to himself.
Fenelon's Spiritual Works.
Firmin's Real Christian.
Fowle's (F. W.) Sermons.
Gilpin's (William) Sermons.
Gouge's Christian Directions.
Goodhue's The Crucible. (Not always judicious.)
Gurnall's Christian Armor. (Capital.)
Guthrie's Trial of a saving interest in Christ.
Haldane's (J. A.) Works. (Excellent.)
Hale's (Judge) Contemplations.
Hastings' (H. J.) Parochial Sermons.
Hoare's (C. J.) Sermons.
Jacomb on Holy Dedication.
Jenks' Meditations.
Johnson's (Dr. S.) Sermons.
Lavington's (Samuel) Sermons.
Leland's (Dr. Thomas) Sermons.
Malan's Theogones; or answer to the question, "Am I a child of God?"
Mason on Self-knowledge.
Mead's Almost Christian discovered.
Milner's (Isaac) Sermons.
Muston's (C. R.) Sermons.
Newlin's (Tho.) Sermons before the University of Oxford.
Newnham's Tribute of sympathy.
Palmer's Gospel new creature.
Pattison's (E.) Sermons.
Price's (Richard) Sermons.
Rowe's Devout Christian.
Scudder's Christian's daily walk.
Secker's (Abp.) Sermons.
Shepherd's Sincere Convert.
Sherlock's Mercurius Christianus.
Skelton's (Philip) Sermons.
Smith's (Sydney) Sermons.
Sterne's (Lawrence) Sermons.

Self-Examination—*continued.*

Still's Horæ Privatæ.
Thomas' (Bp.) Sermons.
Trail's Guide to Communicants.
Trapp's (Joseph) Sermons.
Valdeso's Divine Considerations.
Vincent's True Christian Love.
Waples' (Edward) Sermons.
Warren's (Samuel) Sermons.
Woodhouse's (G. W.) Practical Sermons.
Zollikoffer's Sermons on the evils that are in the world.

Self-Existence of God. See EXISTENCE OF GOD, INDEPENDENCE.

Self-Government.

Abernethy's (John) Sermons.
Barker's (John) Sermons.
Buckminster's (Joseph S.) Sermons.
Claggett's (William) Sermons.
Edmondson's Concise system of self-gov't.
Foster's (Dr. James) Discourses.
Gouge's Christian Directions.
Hewlett's (John) Sermons.
Horneck's Law of Consideration.
Ibbot's (Benj.) Sermons.
Maurice's (F. D.) Sermons.
Oakeley's (Frederick) Sermons.
Wallin's (B.) Sermons.

Selfishness.

Abernethy's (Bp.) Sermons.
Christian Observer. 20:378,507.
Enfield's (William) Sermons.
Finney's (Cha. G.) Sermons.
Guyse's (John) Sermons.
Hare's (J. C.) Victory of faith.
Harris' Mammon; or, Covetousness the sin of the Church.
Manning's (H. E.) Sermons.
Müller's Doct. of sin. Tr. by Pulsford.
Richardson's (William) Sermons.
Sartain's (Joseph) Sermons.
Simeon's (C.) Works.
Spencer's (Bp.) Sermons.
Spirit of the Pilgrims. 6:623.
Stennett's (Joseph) Sermons.

Self-Knowledge. See SELF-DECEPTION, SELF-EXAMINATION.

Abbadie, L'art de se connoitre soi-meme. (The author makes self-love the highest principle of virtue.)
Wigandi Γνωθι Σεαυτον. (Contemplates man as innocent, fallen, renewed, and glorified.)

Abbadie's Art of knowing one's self.
Baxter's (Rich.) Mischief of Self-ignorance.
Blunt's (Henry) Sermons.
Buckminster's (Joseph S.) Sermons.
Drew's Principles of Self-knowledge.
Finche's Elements of Self-knowledge.
Foster's (John) Essays.
Frith's (John, the Martyr) Works.

Self-Knowledge—*continued.*

Hickman's (Bp.) Sermons.
Langhorne's (W.) Sermons.
Langhorne's (J.) Sermons.
Locke on the Human understanding.
Mason On the benefit of self-knowledge.
Noel's (Gerard T.) Sermons.
Nichols' (Benj. E.) Sermons.
Porteus' (Bp.) Sermons.
Ravenell's [or Ravenhill] Nosce teipsum; or the sure foundation of true religion.
Sterne's (Lawrence) Sermons.
Watts on the Improvement of the mind.
——— Logic.
Zollikoffer's (Geo. J.) Sermons on prevalent errors and vices.

Self-Love.

Abercrombie's Moral Philos. Part 1, sec. 3.
Barrow's (Isaac) Sermons.
Butler's (Bp.) Sermons.
Christ. Quart. Spectator. 7:564.
Darnell's (W. N.) Sermons.
Doddridge's Lectures. Part 1.
Foster (James) on Self-love and its excess.
Jortin's (John) Sermons.
Kirwan's (W. B.) Sermons.
Müller's Christian doctrine of sin.
Newton's (Bp.) Dissertations.
Tennison's (Abp.) Treatise against self-love.
Waterland's (Bp.) Sermons.
Wayland's Elements of moral science.

Self-Reliance. See SELF-CONFIDENCE.

Am. Monthly Rev. 1:504.
Christ. Exam. 37:331.

Self-Righteousness.

Bather's (Edward) Sermons.
Bellamy's Nature and glory of the Gospel.
Burgess' (Anthony) Sermons.
Christ. Month. Spectator. 5:124.
Crisp's (T.) Sermons.
Glass' (John) Works.
Jenks on Submission to the righteousness of God.
Keach (Benj.) on Justification.
Mather's (N.) Sermons.
Milne's (James) Sermons.

Semi-Arians. See ARIANS, EUNOMIANS, TRINITY, &c.

Semi-Pelagians. See SYNERGISTS.

Buddei Hist. crit. theologiæ dogmaticæ.
Geffkenii Hist. Semipelagian. antiquissima.
Morainis Anti-Jansenius. (Full of valuable quotations.)
Neander's Denkwürdigkeiten.
Prosperi Epistola ad Augustinam.
Vossii Historia Pelagiana.
Walch's Historie der Ketzereien.

Wall's History of infant baptism.
Wiggers' Augustanism and Pelagianism.

Sensuality. See LOVE OF PLEASURE, MORTIFICATION, PLEASURE, SELF-DENIAL, SOBRIETY, &c.

Baxter's (Rich.) Christian Ethics.
Case's Sensuality dissected; or the epicure's motto opened and censured.
Drysdale's (Dr. John) Sermons.
Fordyce's Folly and misery of unlawful pleasures.
Fowle's (F. W.) Ten plain sermons.
Parsons' (J.) Sermons.
Spencer's (Aubrey G.) Sermons.
Taylor's (Jer.) Holy living.
Tottie's (John) Sermons before the University of Oxford.
Wise's (Thomas) Sermons.
Zollikoffer's (Geo. J.) Sermons.

Septuagint.

Aristeæ Historia LXX. (This author is said to have been one of the Seventy. His history is regarded as authentic by Vossius, Walton, Whiston, Brett, and others; but is rejected by Van Dale, Hody, and others.)
Capelli Epistola ad Usserum. 1651.
Eichorn's Einleitung ins Alte Test. 1795.
Ernesti Institutiones. 1760.
Fischeri Prolusiones de vers. Græcis. 1772.
Frankel's Histor. kritische Studien zu der Sept. 1841.
Geret, de Causis discrepantiarum vers. LXX a textu originali.
Grabii Dissertat. de variis vitiis LXX ante Originis ævum illatis. 1707.
Henckius de Usu LXX in N. Test. 1711.
Hody contra Hist. Aristeæ de LXX. 1680.
——— de Bibliorum textibus vers. Græcis. 1705. ("This is the classical work on the LXX."—MARSH.)
Holmes et Parsons Vet. Test. Græcum. 1798. (See an extended notice of this splendid work in the Eclectic Review. Vol. 2.)
Hornemanni Specimen Exerc. in LXX. 1773.
Jahn's Einleitung in Alte Test. 1813.
Landschreiber's Quellen zu Text, etc. 1857.
Morini Prolegomena et Exercitationes. 1586.
Mücke de Origine vers. LXX. 1788.
Rosenmuller's Handbuch für Litteratur der biblischen Kritik u. Exegese. 1830.
Scharfenbergii Animadversiones. 1776.
Schleusneri Opuscula Critica. 1802.
Simonis Histori Crit. de Vet. Test. 1741.
Usseri de Græca vers. syntagma. 1650.
Valesii Epistola de Versione Septuaginta. 1770. (Reply to Usher.)
Van Dale, Diss. super Aristeam. (Great.)
Vossii (I.) Dissertationes. 1640
Waltoni Biblia Polyglott. 1655. (Prolegom.)

Aristeus' Hist. of the Sept. Tr. by Donne.
Blair (Dr. John) on the Canon of Scripture. (Has a learned dissertat. on this subject.)
Brenton's LXX. (With chronology, tables.)
Brett's Dissertations. 1715. (On the difference between our English Bible and the Sept., though both translated from the Hebrew. In Watson's Tracts.)

Septuagint—*continued.*

Butler's Horæ Biblicæ.
Christian Examiner. 54:165.
Christian Month. Spect. 6:404.
Christian Observer. 20:543,610,646,746.
Cruwys on the Archetype of the Sept. 1774.
Ernest's Principles of interpretation. Trans. by Terrot. 1835.
Grabb's Preface to his edition of the Sept.
Gregory (John) on the Septuagint. 1674.
Grinfield's Apology for the Septuagint. 1774. (Asserts its biblical and canon. authority.)
[Hayes' (Cha.)] Vindication of the S. (From Scaliger, Dupin, Hody, &c.)
Hertzog's Real Encyclopedia. (Very full.)
Hey's (John) Lectures. Bk. 1.
Holmes' (R.) Annual accounts of the collation of MSS. of the LXX. (Great.)
Kitto's Journal. 2:324. (Samaritan text.)
Owen's (H.) Histor. and crit. account of the S., with a diss. on the comparative excellence of the Heb. and Samar. Pent. 1787.
——— Present state of the S. version. 1769.
Princeton Rev. 22:541. (Rev. of Grinfield.)
Spearman's Letters on the LXX. 1759.
Thomson's (Cha.) English vers. of the Sept.
Tischendorf's Septuagint. 1854.
Wall's (Wm.) Critical Notes on the N. Test. 1720. (Preface.)

For a full account of editions of the Septuagint in Greek, and in Greek and Latin, see DIBDEN'S *Greek and Latin Classics.* 1808.

Septuagint Chronology.

Pro.

Capelli Critica Sacra.
Morini (Ioann.) Exercitationes.
Pezron, l'Antiq. des temps rétablie.
——— Defence de Do.
Vossii Diss. de vera ætate mundi.
Waltoni Biblicus Adparatus.

Brett's Essay on Chronology. (Reprinted in Watson's Tracts.)
Hale's (Will.) New analysis of chronology.
[Hayes' (Cha.)] Vind. of the Sept. history.
——— Supplement to Vindication.
Rouse's (N.) Sacred Chronology.
Squiers' on the Greek Chronology.

Con.

Boniour, Dissertationes selectæ.
Bootii Apodixis Apologetica.
Buxtorfii Anti-critica.
Hottingeri Dissertationes de Pent. Samar.
——— Dissertationum Biblico-chronolog.
Le Quien, Défense du texte Hébreu.
Marshamus Diatriba Chronologica.
Martianay, Défense du texte Hébreu.
Meyeri Chronicon Ebræorum.
Muis, Adsertio veritatis Ebraicæ, etc.
Ravii Chronologia Biblica.
Rerr's Beweis das die Zeitrechnung, etc.
Scaliger de Emendatione temporum.
Taylori Examen prefationis Morini.
Wasmuthi Vindiciæ sacræ Ebrææ Script.

Septuagint Chronology—*continued.*

Con.

Wasmuthi Heutontimorumenos.

Bedford's Chronology demonstrated by astronomical calculations.
Clayton's Hebrew chronology vindicated.
Hody's Dissertat. against Aristeus. (Attacks Vossius also.)
Kennedy on the Chron. of the Hebrew text.
Martianay's Defence of the Hebrew text. (Reply to Pezron.)
Prideaux's Connection of the Old and New Testament.
Squiers' Diss. on the Hebrew text.
Usher's Annals of the Old and New Test.

Sepulchre of Christ.

Cellarii (Balthas.) Disquisitiones.
Cypriani (Ernest.) Dissertationes.
Kirchmayeri (Geo. Guil.) Dissertationes.
Millii Miscellanæ Philologicæ.
Nicolas de Sepulchris Hebræorum.
Petzchius de Sepulcro Christi.
Rabenieri Amœnitates historic. philolog.
Schmidii (Andr.) Dissertationes.
Seligmanni Programma.
Zornii (Petri) Dissertationes.

Seraphim.

Goulburn's Parochial Sermons.
Simpson's Essays on the lang. of Scripture.

Sermon on the Mount.
See BEATITUDES.

Augustine, Opera.

Arndt's Bergpredigt Jesu.
Braune's Bergpredigt unser Herrn J. C.
Nielsen's Seligpreisungen unsers Herrn.
Pott, Diss. de indole orationis montanæ.
Rau's Untersuchungen, ect.
Tholuck's Auslegung der Bergpredigt.

Blackall's (Dr. O.) Practical discourses.
Blair's (Jas., of America) Sermon on the M. 1722. ("Best extant."—DODDRIDGE.)
Brewster's (J.) Lectures on the sermon, &c.
Butcher's (Edm.) Discourses on the ser., &c.
Cobbold's Voice from the Mount.
Crum's (G. C.) Mount of blessing.
Cunningham's Morning Thoughts.
Fiddes' Body of Divinity.
Gardner's Expos. of the Ser. on the Mount.
Good's (J. E.) 46 Sermons. (Very able.)
Graves' (Richard) Sermons.
Hill (D. H.) on the Sermon on the Mount.
Horneck's 39 Sermons on Matt. v.
MacKay's (M.) Practical Exposition.
McIntyre's (Wm.) Exposition.
Norris' Practical Discourses.
Ogle's Sermon on the Mount. (A system of Ethics.)
Penington's (John) Exposition. 1656.
Perkins' (Wm.) Exposition. 1611.
Pitman's (John R.) Practical Com. 1852.
Tholuck's Exposition. Tr. by R. L. Brown.

Sermon on the Mount—*continued.*

Thornton's Family Com. on Christ's sermon.
Todd's (J.) Com. on the Ser. on the Mount.
Trench's (R. C.) Expos. of the Serm. on the M.; drawn from the writings of Augustine.
Warner's (R.) Discourses on the Sermon on the Mount.
Watson's (Thomas) Discourses.
Wesley's (John) Discourses on the Sermon on the Mount.
Worsley's Province of the intellect in matters of religion.

Serpent, Worship of. See OPHITES.

Kochii (J. C.) Dissertationes.

Bellamy's (John) The Ophion.
Bibliotheca Sacra. 21:163.
Dean's Worship of the Serpent traced throughout the world.
Dimock's Notes on Genesis. (An able diss. on this subject in the appendix.)
Franklin's Tenets and doctrines of the Jains.
Robinson's (N.) Dissertations.
Sydenham's (J.) Dissertations.
Tait's Exp. of the bk. of Numbers. Ch. 21.

Servants. See RELATIVE DUTIES.

Baxter's (Rich.) Practical Works.
Baylis' Rights and duties of servants.
Blencoe's (Edward) Sermons.
Bloomfield's (Geo. B.) Sermons.
Chalmers' (Tho.) Posthumous Sermons.
Church Rev. 4:368.
Delany's (Dean) Sermon on Social duties.
Defoe's Family Instructor.
Dodd's Advice to apprentices.
Knowles' (Thomas) Sermons.
Knox's (Vicessimus) Sermons.
Lewis' (T.) Christian Duties. Disc. 4.
Lucas' Duty of servants. (With forms of prayer.)
Riddock's (James) Sermons.
Seaton on the Duties of servants.
Stennett's (Sam.) Sermons.
Taylor's Present of a mistress to a young servant.
Watson's (J. W.) Sermons.
Willis' (W. D.) Sermons for servants.

Servetus.

Allwoerdini Hist. M. Serveti. (Very full and accurate, and quite sufficient on this subject.)
Senebier, Hist. de Genève. (Exculpates Calvin.)
Servetus de Trinitatis erroribus.

Benson's (Dr. Geo.) Works.
Biblical Repository. 3:51.
Mosheim's Life and death of Servetus.
Sigmond's Unnoticed theories of Servetus.
Tweedie's Calvin and Servetus. (The share of Calvin in the trial and condemnation of Servetus.)
Wright's Apology for Servetus. (A full account of his life and writings.)

Sethians.

Rhenferdi (Jacob.) Opera philologica.

Seven Churches of Asia.
See COMMENTATORS ON APOCALYPSE.

Carpzovius de VII Asiæ ecclesiis.
Theime, Commentatio de septem Epistolis.
Witsii Miscellaneæ.

Allen's (Tho.) Christian's sure guide.
Arundell's Visit to the 7 churches. 1827.
Biber's (G. E.) Seven voices of the Spirit.
Bibliotheca Sacra. 12:339.
Blunt's Seven Churches of Asia.
Carr's (Tho. W.) Sermons on Rev. Ch. 2, 3.
Chamberlain's Seven ages of the Church.
Cotterel's Histor. Expos. of the 7 epistles.
Cummings' (John) Apocalyptic Sketches.
Girdlestone's Analytical Commentary, &c., on the Seven epistles.
Hyatt's (John) Sermons.
Kittle's Crit. and pract. lect. on the 7 Epist.
McFarlane's History of the seven churches.
Maguire's (Robt.) Seven churches. Plates.
Miller's (Ebenezer) Voice of Christ to the Churches.
Milner's (Tho.) History of the 7 churches.
Milner's (Jos.) Sermons on the Epistles to the seven churches.
More's (Henry) Theological Works.
Muir's (William) Sermons.
Museum of For. Literature. 18:142.
Parker's Interpretation of the prophecy, &c.
Slade's (James) Lent Lectures.
Smith's (Tho.) Manners of the Turks.
Statham's (F. F.) Message of the Spirit.
Stuart (Moses) on the Apocalypse.
Taylor's (Tho.) Lectures on the 7 Epistles.
Trench's Commentary on the 7 Epistles.
Wadsworth (J.) on the Apoc. Epistles.
Wallace's Commentary on Rev. Ch. 2, 3.
West's 19 Discourses on the Apoc. epistles.
Wills' Seven Churches of Asia. (Gives a historical and geographical account of each place, as illustrating the prophecies concerning them.)
Withey's (H.) Lectures on Rev. Ch. 2, 3.

Seventh Commandment. See ADULTERY, CHASTITY, FORNICATION, LEWDNESS, PURITY, UNCLEANNESS.

Seventh-Day Baptists.
See SABBATARIANS.

Seventy Weeks of Daniel.

Abrami Pharus. Lib. XIV, XV.
Ayroli Liber LXX hebdomadum resignatus.
Bartolocci Bibliotheca Rabbinica.
Calovii Biblia Illustrata.
Derodoni (David.) Disputationes.
Frischmuthii Thesaurus Philologicus.
Helvicus de LXX Hebdomadibus.
Kluitii Vaticinum de Messia duce primarium.
Michælis (J. D.) Epistolæ de LXX hebdom.
Moore, Prophetæ de LXX hebd. explicatio.
Strauchius de LXX hebdomadis Danielis.

Seventy Weeks—*continued.*

Allwood's Proph. of Daniel and John comp.
Blackley on the Seventy Weeks, &c.
Blaney on the Seventy Weeks. (Controverts MICHAELIS. Learned and temperate.)
Bosanquet's Times of Daniel, Ezra, and Nehemiah.
Brightman's Revelation revealed.
Broughton's (Hugh) Visions of Daniel.
Burton's Reconciliation of Daniel and John.
Caverhill on the Seventy weeks. (Gives the chronology of the Jews.)
Eyton's Dates in Daniel and John.
Faber's (Geo. S.) Dissertations.
Farmer on Daniel's seventy weeks.
Foster (Benj.) on the Prophecies.
Frere's Combined view of Daniel and John.
Girdlestone's (W.) Visions of Daniel.
Greswell's (Edw.) Dissertations.
Hengstenberg's Christology.
Hershell's (R.) Prospects of the Jews.
Hinton's (Isaac T.) Daniel and John illustr.
Holmes on Ezek., Daniel, and Revelations.
Howard (Dr. John) on the Seventy weeks.
Jewish Repos. Period. London. 1813, et seq.
Johnson (John) on Daniel's seventy weeks.
Lancaster's (P.) Chronological Essay.
Lee's (Prof.) Visions of Daniel and John.
Lloyd (Bp.) on Daniel's seventy weeks.
——— Letter to Dr. Prideaux.
Macqueen's Observations on Daniel's weeks.
Magee's Interpretation of the seventy weeks. (In an appendix, many different schemes which have been proposed, are described.)
Manchester's (Geo.) Times of Daniel.
Marwick (N.) on Difficult chapters in Daniel and the Apocalypse.
Marshall (Benj.) on the Seventy weeks.
Mede (Jos.) on Daniel's weeks.
Monthly Review. 53:487.
Moore's (John) Explication.
More (Henry) on the Apocalypse.
Parry on Daniel's seventy weeks.
Roos on Certain prophecies of Daniel. Translated by Henderson.
Simons' (B. A.) Hope of Israel.
Stegart's (John) Sermons.
Stonard on the LXX weeks. (Elaborate.)
Thomas' (Bp.) Sermons.
Thorald on the Seventy weeks.
Winter's (Rich.) Nine sermons upon, &c.

Shakers. See MILLENNIAL CHURCH.

Shame. See FALSE SHAME.

Newton's (Bp.) Dissertations.

Shekinah.

Barrington on the Divine dispensations.
Lowman's Tracts. Tract 2. (Describes all the Divine appearances mentioned in Scripture.)
Sewall's Scripture account of the Shekinah.
Skinner's (John) Dissertations.
Whitley's Scheme of prophecy. (Appendix.)

Shem. See ETHNOLOGY, ORIGIN OF NATIONS.

Perkins' Genealogical and topographical exposition of Genesis, ch. 10.

Shiloh. See MESSIAH, SCEPTER.

Altingii Vaticinum Jacobi.

Beveridge's Thesaurus.
Christian Review. 14:285.
Edwards' (Dr. John) Enquiry, &c.
Erskine's (Ralph) Sermons.
Harris' (Wm.) Sermons on the Messiah.
Mede's (Jos.) Works.
Sherlock (Bp.) on Prophecy.
Simeon's (C.) Works.

Shortness of Life.

Barrow's, Isaac, Sermons.
Conant's, Dr. John, Sermons.
Crowes', William, Sermons.
Dunlap's, William, Sermons.
Hastings', H. J., Sermons.
Haverfield's, T. T., Sermons.
Hawker's, Robert, Sermons.
Hobart's, John H., Sermons.
Hoole's, Joseph, Sermons.
Johnson's, Dr. S., Sermons.
Leighton's (Abp.) Works.
Littleton's, Adam, Sermons.
Newman's, J. H., Sermons.
Rogers', T., Lectures.
Shorthose's, Hugh, Sermons.
Simeon's, C., Works.
Tidcombe's, J., Sermons.
Tillotson's, Abp., Sermons.
Townsend's (George) Sermons.
Warren's, Robert, Sermons.
Wilson's, Thomas, Sermons.

Sibylline Oracles. See ORACLES.

Sibyllina Oracula. (Several editions.)
Assemanni Bibliotheca.
Baltus, Réponse a l'hist. de Fontenelle.
Betulii Oracula Græca.
Blondel, des Sybylles célebrées.
Cellier, Hist. generale des auteurs.
Crasseus de Carminibus, etc.
Fontenelle, Histoire des Oracles.
Friedliebii Orac. Sib. prætextis prolegomenis illustravit, adnotationes, etc.
Galleus de S. eorumque oraculis.
Markius de S. oraculis. (Ag. Crasseus.)
Schmidtii Versio N. T. (Appendix.)
Van Dale de Oraculis Ethnicorum.
Vossius de S. Oraculis aliisq. quæ christi natalem processerunt.

Beaumont's Gleanings of antiquities.
Blondel on the Sibyls, and the influence of their books on the Christian religion. (This book is all that most persons need examine on this subject.)
Bradford (J.) on the Truth of Christianity.
Chandler (Edw.) on Christianity.
Christian Review. 13:81.
Cudworth's Intell. system. Ch. 4, sec. 16.
Doddridge's Lectures. Part 6.

Sibylline Oracles—*continued.*

Floyer's S. Oracles translated and compared with Scripture. (Strongly maintains the authenticity of these fables.)
Galles on the S. oracles.
Jortin's Remarks on ecc. hist. (Takes as much pains to destroy their credit, as Floyer does to support it.)
Napier on the Apocalypse. (Appendix.)
Simon on the Various editions of the Bible. (Reviews the position of Vossius.)
Van Dale's History of Oracles.
Whiston's Vind. of the S. oracles, with the oracles themselves, and ancient quotations from them, in the originals and in English.
Yelverton on the Sibyls. (Asserts their authority, and replies to Casaubon, Blondel, and others.)

These are not the S. oracles of the Romans, which, from the time of Tarquin, were preserved by the Quindecemviri, but are generally supposed to have been forged in the 2d century. Many books have been written for and against their genuineness.

Sickness. See VISITING THE SICK.

Bouvier, Lettres d'un malade au malade.
Villethierry, le Chrétien dan la tribulation.

Asheton's Devotions for sick people.
Bacon's (H. B.) Lectures.
Baxter's (Rich.) Works.
Becon's (Thomas) Works.
Beren's Seven sermons for a sick-room.
Bourdillon's Bedside Readings.
Brown's Religio Medici.
Buckminster's (Jos. S.) Sermons.
Burnham's Pious Memorials.
Cappe's Devotional Discourses.
Clarke's (Adam) Christian Directory.
Coleridge's Advice to attendants on the sick.
Coney's Companion for the sick.
Dodwell's Sick man's companion.
Edwards' (Bp.) Body of Divinity.
Fawcett's Sick man's employment.
Fry's (John) Sick man's friend.
——— Present for the convalescent.
Gibson's (Bp.) Serious Advice.
Gilbert's (Mrs.) Convalescent.
Girdlestone's (Charles) Sermons.
Girl's Duty of Relations.
Harris' (Robt.) Sermons.
Huntingford's Manual for the sick
James (J.) on Christian Watchfulness.
Kollock's (S. K.) Sermons.
Lavington's (Samuel) Sermons.
Mackenzie's Handbook for the sick.
Newman's (J. H.) Sermons.
Noel's (B. W.) Meditations for the sick.
Oemler's Pastor at the sick bed.
Partridge's (S.) Sermons. (Recovery.)
Plummer's Clergyman's assistant.
Rogers' (Tim.) Practical Sermons.
Sanderson's (A. R.) Thoughts on Sickness.
Secker's (Abp.) Sermons.

Sickness—*continued.*

Simeon's (C.) Works. Grateful recollections.
Stanhope's (M.) Sermons.
Stonehouse's Sick man's assistant.
Taylor's (Jer.) Holy living.
Thornton's Companion for the sick.
Venning's Sick-bed studies.
Victor's Minister's Manual.
Wilson's (R.) Sick-bed studies.
Winchester's (S.) Counsels to the sick.

Signs of the Times.

Bunsen's Zeichen der Zeit. 1855.
Gasparin, Perspectives du temps present. 1861.
Gurtleri Theologia prophetica. 1705.
Löwe's Offenbarung u. Fragen d. Zeit. 1842.
Meulini Signa temporum.

Bicheno's Address to the Jews. 1808.
——— Fulfilment of prophecy.
Bickersteth's Signs in the East. 1840.
Bloomsbury's Lent Lectures. 1854.
Bunsen's Signs of the times. Tr. by Winkworth. (Dangers to religious liberty.)
Burgess' Tendency of the times. 1820.
Cecil's (Rich.) Sermons. 1800.
Cooper's (Edw.) The Crisis. 1825.
Cuyler's (C. C.) Signs of the times. 1839.
Davis' (Sam.) Sermons. 1755.
Dodsworth's Signs of the times. 1848.
Erskine's (Ralph) Signs of the times. 1742.
Evans' (R. W.) Sermons. 1830.
Galloway On such prophecies as refer to the present times. 1802.
Glass' (John) Notes on Script. texts. 1765.
Habershon on the Apocalypse. 1844.
Hale's (Wm.) Dissertations. 1808.
——— on the Chronological prophecies.
Hall's (Robt.) Sermons. 1825.
Hastings' (H. L.) Signs of the times. 1863.
Irving (Edw.) On the last days. 1850.
Jurieu on Prophecy. 1687.
Keith's (Alex.) Signs of the times. 1823.
Kett's Hist. the interpreter of proph. 1801.
King's (Edw.) Signs of the times. 1799.
Linn's (Wm.) Discourses. 1794.
Lit. and Theol. Journal. 3:302. 5:275.
Marriott's (Harvey) Sermons. 1813.
Monsell's (C. H.) Sermons. 1845.
Morell's Tendencies of the age. 1846.
Morgan's Bampton Lectures. 1819.
Morning's Pantheistic tendency of Christianity. 1846.
Nance's (John) Sermons. 1807.
Princeton Review. 12:1.
Rice's (N. L.) Signs of the times. 1855.
Scott's Scripture system of prophecy. 1844.
Smith's (Sydney) Sermons. 1840.
Vane's (Sir Harry) Works. 1650.
Warburton Lectures for 1833.
Wesley's (John) Sermons. 1780.
Whitaker's (Edw. W.) Sermons. 1801.

Silence.

Christian Observer. 17:439.

Simonians, or Stylites.

Assemanni (S. E.) Acta Sanctorum.
Horbii (Ioann. H.) Disquisitiones.
Mosheimii Dissertationes.
Siberi (Gothofr.) Dissertationes.
Tillemont, Memoires pour servir a l'hist. etc.

Simon Magus.

Andreæ Disquisitiones.
Calmet, Dissert. (Prefixed to Com. on Matt.)
Grabbei Spicilegium S. S. Patrum.
Helwigius de Primo Novi Test. hæretico.
Horbii Disquisitiones.
Mosheimii (Io. L.) Dissertationes.
Schotani (Chr.) Disputationes.
Vogtii Bibliotheca historiæ hæresologiæ.
Wonnæ Exercitationes.

Simony. See INVESTITURES.

Gersoni (Joh.) Tractatus de Simonia.
Goldasti Replicatio contra Gretserum.
Gretseri Apologia pro Gregorio VII.
Humbertus adversus Simoniacos.
Iageri Dissertationes.
Molinei Dissertationes.
Pertschii Commentatio de crimine Simoniæ.
Schotani (Chr.) Disputationes.

Burton's (Henry) Censure of Simony.
Cawley's Nature and kinds of Simony.
Cunningham's Law of Simony (Relates all the English statutes on this subject.)
Fowle's Church Nepotism.
Ken's (Bp.) Complaints of the Ch. of Engl.
Lowth's (Robt.) Letter to the London clergy. (Works.)

Simplicity. See SINCERITY.

Sin. See BESETTING SINS, DEADLY SINS, DECEITFULNESS OF SIN, ORIGINAL SIN, ORIGIN OF EVIL, SINS OF BELIEVERS, SINS OF IGNORANCE, SINS OF INFIRMITY, VENIAL SIN, WILFUL SINS.

Buys de Induratione peccatoris.
Callixti Dissertationes.
Deutchmannus de Peccatis natura.
Hunnius de Peccato.
Lagarce, le Péché considere dans ses effets.
Müller's Christl. Lehre von der sünde.
Musæi Dissertationes Theologicæ.
Reuserus de Peccati definitione.
Schumacher's Erbsünde und Erbschuld.
Tholuck's Lehre von der Sünde, und vom Versöhner.
Umbreit's Beitrag zur Theologie des A. T.

Aires on Natural sins and the causes.
Am. Bibl. Repos. 8:310.
Bates' (William) Sermons.
Bellamy's Nature and glory of the Gospel.
Biblioth. Sac. 5:499. 8:594. 22:486.
Bloomfield's (G. B.) Sermons. (Temporal consequences of sin.)
Bullinger's Decades. (Pub. of Parker Soc.)
Burroughs' Evil of Evils.
Channing's (W. E.) Sermons.
Charnock's Works.

Sin—*continued.*

Christian Monthly Spect. 6:177,293. 9:17.
Christian Quarterly Spect. 2:529. 4:465,614.
Cotton's (Rich. L.) Sermons.
Collison's (Bp.) Sermons.
Dana's (Dr. James) Letters.
Dodd on the Miracle of the leper.
Goodman's Efficacy of repentance.
Hall's (Robt.) Works. (Spiritual leprosy.)
Howe's Living Temple.
Jackson's Sinfulness of little sins.
Liter. and Theol. Rev. 5:418.
Müller's Chris. doct. of sin. Tr. by Pulsford.
Owen on Indwelling sin.
Panoplist. 11:213.
Princeton Rev. 5:521. 11:590.
Reynolds' (Bp.) Sermons.
Sheldon's (D. M.) Sin and redemption.
Smith on the Permission of evil.
Spurgeon's (Cha. H.) Sermons. 7th Series.
Styles' (John) Sermons.
Tuckney's Prelections.
Venn's (John) Sermons.
Watson's Mischief of sinne.
Watts' Ruin and Recovery.
Wenning's Sin the worst of evils.
Williams' Reply to Belsham.

Sincerity. See CANDOR.

Atterbury's (Francis) Sermons.
Bowers' (Dean) Sermons.
Carr's (George) Sermons.
Cookesley's (Will. G.) Sermons.
Cooper's (E.) Doctrinal Sermons.
Evans on Christian Temper.
Foster's (James) Sermons.
Foster's (John) Lect. at Broadmead Chapel.
Hickman's (Bp.) Sermons.
Kelty on Straightforwardness.
Knowles' (Thomas) Sermons.
Lockyer's Divine discovery of sincerity.
Newlin's (Tho.) Eighteen Sermons.
Paley's (William) Sermons.
Penrose on Christian Sincerity.
Slade's (James) Sermons.
Smallridge's (George) Sermons.
Taylor's (Jer.) Sermons.
Tillotson's Sermons.
Thornwell's (J. H.) Discourses on truth.
Verschoyle's (Hamilton) Sermons.
Williams' (Alfred) Sermons.
Zollikoffer's Sermons on prevalent vices.

Sinful Thoughts. See GOVERNMENT OF THE HEART, THOUGHTS.

Singing in Public Worship.
See PSALMODY.

Pro.

Clemens Alexand., Pædagogus. Lib. II.

Allen on Singing psalms with conjoined voices.
Anderson's (Abr.) Vindiciæ Cantus.
Cotton's (John) Singing of psalms a Gospel ordinance. (1st. The duty. 2d. The matter. 3d. The singers. 4th. The manner.)

Singing—*continued.*

Pro.

Ford's (Thomas) Singing psalms a duty. (Five sermons on Eph. v. 19.)
Hitchin's Scripture proof for singing.
Keach's (Benj.) Breach in God's worship repaired.)
Reynolds' (Tho.) Eastcheap Lectures. 1708.
Ridgeley's Divinity. Question 154.
Sidenham's Sober and plain exercitations on the grand controversy of these times—Infant baptism, and the singing of psalms. 1653. (Recites all the main arguments on both sides.)
Taylor's (Dan.) Dissertation on singing.
——— Second Do.

Con.

Claridge on Singing in public worship.
Russell's (Wm.) Reply to Allen's Essay on Singing.

Sinless Perfection. See PERFECTION.

Sinners without excuse.

Appleton's Works.
Burder's (George) Village Sermons.
Croft's (G. D.) Sermons.
Davies' (T.) Discourses.
Edwards' (Jon.) Works.
Grose's (John) Sermons.
Landon's (W.) Sermons.
Potts' (J. H.) Sermons.
Ravenscroft's (Bp.) Sermons.
Sandercock's (E.) Sermons.
Scott's (B.) Sermons.
Turner's (W. H.) Sermons.
Wilson's (Bp.) Sermons.
Young's (E.) Sermons.

Sins of Believers.
See SINS OF INFIRMITY.

Basnage, Sermons. (One on Rom. 7:24.)
Callixtus de Renatis ex Deo, an peccant?
Keislingii de Renatorum Ἀναμαρτησια.
Quenstedius de Peccato reliquo in renatis.

Barrow's (William) Sermons.
Blunt's (Henry) Sermons.
Chevalier's Hulsean Lectures. 1827.
Coxe's (R. C.) Sermons.
Grove's (Henry) Sermons. (3 on this subj.)
Ibbot's (Benjamin) Sermons.
Kidder's (Bp.) Sermons.
Morris' (Geo.) The sins of God's people.
Ryland's (John) Contemplations.
Turner's (I.) Sermons.
Wesley's (John) Sermons.

Sins of Ignorance.
See SELF-EXAMINATION, WILFUL.

Burgess' (Anthony) Sermons.
Coney's (Thomas) Sermons.
Hoole's (Joseph) Sermons.
Newman's (John Henry) Sermons.
Nichols' (Benj. E.) Sermons.
Pascall's Provincial Letters.

Potts' (J. H.) Sermons.
Secker's (Abp.) Sermons.
Warter's (John W.) Sermons.

Sins of Infirmity. See SINS OF IGNORANCE, WILFUL SINS.

Bridges' (William) Sermons.
Carr's (George) Sermons.
Fowle's (W. S.) Sermons.
Hoole's (Jos.) Sermons. (2 on this subject.)
Manning's (H. E.) Sermons.
Newman's (John Henry) Sermons.
Smallridge's (Bp.) Sermons.
Taylor's (Bp.) Sermons.
Waterland's (Daniel) Sermons.

Sins of Omission.

Bennet's (Wm.) Miscellaneous Sermons.
Burrows' (E.) Hours of Devotion.
Irving's (Edward) Sermons.
Morris' (Joseph) Sermons.
Prideaux's (Bp.) Sermons.
Robinson (C.) on Future happiness.
Simeon's (C.) Works.
Stillingfleet's (Bp.) Sermons.
Walker's (James, D.D.) Sermons.
Walker's (Robert) Sermons.

Sixth Commandment. See DUELLING, MURDER, SUICIDE, WAR.

Slander. See CENSORIOUSNESS, DETRACTION, EVIL SPEAKING, SCANDAL, TONGUE.

Baxter's (Rich.) Christian Directory.
Blackwood's Magazine. 2:400. 3:388.
Brackenbury's (Edward) Sermons.
Chapman's (J.) Essays.
Clarke's (Dr. Samuel) Nature of things indifferent.
Cooper's (Edward) Sermons.
Cosen's (Dr. John) Sermons.
Down's (John) Sermons and Tracts.
Dwight's (Tim.) Theology. Ser. 128.
Falkner on Reproach and Censure.
Fiddes' (Richard) Sermons.
Foster's (Dr. Jas.) Sermons.
Fowler's (Bp.) Sermons.
Hammond's (H.) Sermons.
Hopkins' (Bp.) Sermons.
Investigator. 6:124.
Leighton's (Abp.) Works.
Massillon's Sermons.
Moss' (Robert) Sermons.
Ogden's (Samuel) Sermons.
Paley's Moral Philosophy. Bk. 3, part 2.
Panoplist. 9:402.
Poole's (Matt.) Sermons.
Quincey's Sermons.
Seed's (Jeremiah) Sermons.
Smith's (Sam. S.) Sermons.
Taylor's (Jer.) Life of Christ. Ser. 7.
Tottie's (John) Sermons.
Vaughn's (Sir W.) Arraignment of slander, blasphemy, &c.
Wilder's (John) Sermons.

Slavery. See JEWISH ANTIQUITIES, MORAL PHILOSOPHY, SLAVE-TRADE.

Pro.

Armstrong's Christian doctrine of S. 1857.
Christie's (David) Pulpit Politics. 1862.
Dew (Tho. R.) on Slavery. 1853.
England's (Bp.) Letters on Slavery. 1840.
Este's S. as it exists in the U. S. 1846.
Fletcher's (John) Studies on Slavery. 1852.
Franklin's (G.) Answer to Clarkson on the slave-trade.
Hammond's (James H.) Letters on Slavery.
Harper's (Robt. G.) Works. 1814.
Hopkins' (Bp. of Vermont) The American Citizen. 1845.
How's (S. B.) Slaveholding not sinful. 1850.
Priest's (Rev. J.) Origin, fortunes, and history of the negro race. 1852.
Pro-Slavery Argument, The. (A collection of treatises.)
Raphael's Bible view of slavery. 1861.
Ross' (F. A.) Slavery ordained of God. 1857. (As able as any on this side.)
Sawyer (Geo. S.) on Southern Institutions.
Seabury's Amer. slavery distinguished from the slavery of English theorists. 1861.
Sloan's (J. A.) Great question answered.
Stringfellow (Thornton) on Slavery. 1856.
Styles' (Jos. C.) Modern reform examined.
Thornton's (T. C.) History of Slavery. 1841.

Con.

Beaumont, l'Esclavage aux Etats Unis. 1842.
Borde's Grausamkeit der Neger auf St. Domingo. 1792.
Brissot, Mem. sur les Noirs d'Amerique.
Castelli, Esclavage et Emancipation. 1844.
Cochin, l'Abolition de l'esclavage. (A great storehouse of facts.)
Fernaud, l'Esclavage-servage.
Froissard, La cause des esclaves negres, portee au tribunal de la justice, religion, etc. 1789.
Gasparin, Esclavage et l'affranchissement.
Jollivet, sur l'Abolition immediate.
Larroque, de l'E. chez les nations chrétiennes.
Puffendorf de Jure Naturæ.
Reichard's Negersklav. in Westindien. 1779.
Sismondi Traite des Négres.
Therow, le Christianisme et l'Esclavages.
Wallon, Histoire de l'E. de l'antiquité.

Abolitionist, The. Period. Boston. 1833.
Abstract of the evidence before the Com. of the House of Commons. 1790,1791. Plates.
Adams' (W.) Slavery in British India.
African Observer. Periodical. Phila.
African Repository. Periodical. Washington. 1826 to the present.
Amer. Bibl. Repos. 2d Series. 11:302.
Amer. Quart. Observer. 1:83. 3:20.
Amer. Quart. Rev. 2:237. 12:189,379. 13:436. 14:54.
Analytic Magaz. 10:1.
Anti-Slavery Advocate. London. Period.
Anti-Slavery Quart. Mag. London.
Anti-Slavery Recorder. London.

Slavery—*continued.*

Con.

Atkins' Voyage to Guinea. 1735.
Aughey's Iron Furnace. (Amer. S. in 1863.)
Babington's (C.) Hulsean prize Essay. 1846.
Ball's (Cha.) Slavery in the U. S. 1837.
Bandinell on Slavery. London. 1842.
Barclay's State of S. in the W. Indies. 1801.
Barnes' (Albert) Slavery in its scriptural aspects. 1855.
——— The Church and Slavery. 1857.
Beard's (J.) Life of Toussaint l'Ouverture; with a history of Hayti to the present period. 1860.
Beckford's Situation of negroes in Jamaica. 1788.
Benezet's Warning to Great Britain. 1767.
——— Historical account of Guinea. 1772.
Beecher (C. E.) on the Slave question.
Biblioth. Sac. 12:739. 13:1,359,575. 19:563.
Bicknell's West Indies as they are. 1825.
Bigelow's Effects of freedom in Jamaica. 1851.
Blackwood's Mag. 32:87.
Blair's State of S. among the Romans.
Bleby's Death struggles of S. (Historical.)
Bledsoe on Liberty and Slavery.
Booth's (Abraham) Sermons. (Able.)
Bourne's Picture of S. in the U. S. 1834.
——— The Book and S. irreconcilable.
Branagan's Serious Remonstrance.
Brisbane (W. H.) on Slavery. 1847.
Brown's Address to the Presbyterians of Kentucky. 1836.
Buckingham's Slave States of America. 1842.
Burgess' (Dr. Tho.) Considerations on S.
Buxton's S. and freedom in the West Indies.
Cabinet of Freedom. Periodical.
Cairn's Char. and career of the slave power.
Carey's (Matt.) American Museum. 4:414.
Carey's (H. C.) Domestic and foreign slavery. 1853.
Chambers on American Slavery. 1857.
Chamerovzow's Slave-life in Georgia. 1855.
Channing's (W. E.) Letter to Jona. Phillips.
——— Essay on negro slavery. 1835.
Chase's (Henry) The North and the South. 1856.
Cheever's (Geo. B.) God against S. 1857.
Christian Examiner. 2:457. 4:201. 11:109. 26:301. 29:128. 34:29. 36:263. 40:156. 43:223. 44:46. 57:225. 61:211,389. 63:166. 66:246. 68:67.
Christian Observer. 20:36,416.
Christian Spectator. 5:145. 6:332. 8:112.
Clarkson's Condition of slaves in the West Indies. 1808.
——— (Several works on the slave-trade.)
Cobb's History of slavery.
Cochin's Results of S. Tr. by Miss Booth.
——— Results of Emancipation.
Conway's Testimonies concerning slavery.
Copley's Hist. of S. and its abolition. 1839.
Danville Review. December, 1864.
Debates in the British Parliament. 1823.
Debate between Brownlow and Pryne.
Democratic Review. 19:241.
Dick's (David) Modern slavery indefensible.
Dickson's (Wm.) Letters on Slavery. 1789. ("Irresistible."—Cobbin.)
——— Mitigations of Slavery. 1789.
Dudley on the Merchandise of men.
Eclectic Review. 4th Series. 3:54,458. 7:685. 8:227. 9:33. 11:370. 13:673. 21:1. New Series. 2:424. 12:323.
Edinburg Rev. 4:476. 7:224. 8:384. 38:168. 39:118. 41:195. 46:490. 55:144.
Eliot's (Archdeacon) Lectures on S. 1833.
Emancipationist. Periodical. New York.
Fawke's Englishman's Manual. 1817.
Fedrick's Slave life in Virginia. (A narrative of 50 years' life of slavery.)
Frazier's Mag. 1:610. 2:334.
Freeman (O. S.) on Slavery. (Reviews it in all ages and nations.)
Fuller & Wayland's Discussion on Slavery.
Garrison's History of the anti-slavery struggle. 1866.
Gasparin's Uprising of a great people. (America in 1861.)
Geddes' Apology for Slavery. (Ironical.)
Genius of Universal Emancipation. Periodical by Garrison. Baltimore.
Gibbon's Decline and fall of Roman empire.
Gisbourne's Moral Philosophy.
Godwin's (B.) British colonial slavery.
Goodell's The Amer. slave code illustrated by facts. 1845. (Statutes, judicial decisions.)
——— Slavery and anti-slavery. 1855. (Historical.)
Grahame (J.) on American Slavery.
Greeley's History of the struggle for slavery extension in the U. States. 1787 to 1856.
Grimke's Letter to Miss Beecher.
Grosvenor's (C. P.) Slavery vs. the Bible.
Hague's (Dr. W.) Review of Fuller and Wayland.
Hall's (Robt.) Works.
Hargrave's Argument in the case of the negro Somerset. 1772. (This was the case which decided the unlawfulness of slavery in England.)
Harris' Popery and slavery displayed.
[Help's] Conquerors of the new world. 1848. (Origin of American slavery.)
Helper's Impending crisis at the South. 1857. (Statistical and sober.)
Henderson's Condition of negroes in the British colonies. 1816.
Hickeringill's Sin of man-catching. 1681.
Hildreth's Despotism in America. 1854.
Hodge's (Charles) Essays and Reviews.
Hodgson's Truths from the W. Indies. 1838.
Holders' (H. E.) S. in Barbadoes. 1788.
Hopkins' (Sam.) System of Doctrines. 1793.
Hovey's Letters from the West Indies.
Humbolt's (Baron) Political Essays. 1811
Investigator. 7:122.

Slavery—*continued.*

Con.

Jamieson's Sorrows of Slavery.
Jay's (W.) Character of the American Colonization Society. 1837.
——— Government action in behalf of S.
——— Slavery in America. 1850.
Jeremie on Colonial Slavery.
Kennedy on the Abolition of Slavery.
Lawton's (Edward) Lectures.
Lay's (Benj.) All slaveholders apostates.
Liddon's Cruelty inseparable from S. 1792.
Living Age. 1:422. 12:433.
London Review. 13:509. 14:111. 17:252.
Long's Pictures of S. in Ch. and State. 1857.
Lord's Lit. and Theol. Rev. 3:121. 6:41.
Macauley's (T. B.) Historical Essays. 1841.
Massachusetts Quart. Review. 1:145,273. 2:32,487.
Matlack's Amer. S. and Methodism. 1849.
Mattison's Impending crisis of 1860.
McDonald's Enquiry into negro slavery.
McGill's American Slavery as acted on by the Presbyterian Church of America.
McMahon's Jamaica plantership. 1839.
Memoirs of Sir T. F. Buxton. 1846.
Miller's (Dr. Sam.) Disc. before the N. York Society for the manumission of slaves.
Mitchell's Underground Railway.
Montesquieu's Spirit of Laws. 1748.
Monthly Rev. 24:160.
Munkhouse's Discourses.
Murray's Lands of the slave and the free. 1857. (Cuba, and the United States.)
Museum of For. Lit. 5:427.
New Englander. 2:589. 3:567. 4:45,384.
Niles' Register. 13:200. 18:278,307. 20:106, 357. 21:23. 22:325. 23:12,17. 24:285. 25:77. 26:226,346. 28:58,114. 33:9. 34:386. 36:345. 41:130. 44:295. 49:10.
Noel's (Baptist W.) Freedom and Slavery in the United States.
North Amer. Rev. 39:413. 41:170. 71:1. 73:347.
North Brit. Rev. 2:168. 11:245. 19:445.
Olmsted's Journey in the seaboard Slave States. 1856.
Owen's (Robt. D.) Wrong of Slavery.
Paley's Moral Philosophy. Bk. 3.
Pamphleteer. 4:227,407. 7:315. 8:305. 14:417.
Parsons' Fireside view of slavery. 1855.
Paulding's (J. K.) Slavery in the United States. 1836.
Paxton's (J. D.) Letters on Slavery. 1833. Lexington, Ky.
Phelps' (Amos) Lectures. 1834.
Phillippo's History, &c., of Jamaica. 1830.
Porteus' (Bp.) Sermons.
Priestley's Discourse on Abolition.
Princeton Review. 8:268. 18:420. 21:582. 34:524. 36:529. (Record of Presbyterian utterances on the subject.)
Proceedings of the anti-slavery convention held in London, June, 1840.
Puffendorf's Law of nature and nations.

Slavery—*continued.*

Con.

Quar. Register. 26:51. 28:161. 34:579. 55:134.
Ramsay's Essays. 1812.
Rankin (John) on American Slavery.
Renny's (Robt.) History of Jamaica. 1807.
Reports of African Institution. London. From 1807.
Rice's (David) S. unjust and impolitic.
Robinson's (John) Testimony and practice of the Presbyterian Church in the United States in reference to Slavery.
Robinson's (Robt.) Miscellaneous Works.
Robinson's (J. B.) Pictures of Slavery.
Rushton's (E.) Letter to Gen. Washington. 1797.
Sharp's (Granv.) Injustice and danger of S.
——— Warning to Great Britain.
——— on Passive Obedience.
——— Law of Retribution.
——— (Other works, about A. D. 1800.)
Stanford's Mystery of Iniquity.
Stevens' (Sir Geo.) Anti-slavery Recollections. 1854.
Stephens' War in disguise. (Slavery in the British West Indies, as in 1824. Able, legal, and dispassionate.)
Steward's 22 years a slave, and 40 y. a man.
Stowe's (H. B.) Uncle Tom's Cabin. 1853.
——— Dred. 1856.
Stroud's Slave laws in the slave States. 1856.
Stuart's West India Question.
Sturge & Hervey's West Indies.
Sumner's (Cha.) White slavery in the Barbary States.
Sunderland's (Le Roy) Testimony of God against Slavery.
Telfair's Slavery in the Mauritius.
Thompson on American Slavery.
Thompson's (Geo.) Lectures. 1836.
Torrey's (J.) Domestic S. in the U. S. 1817.
Tower's (Philo) Slavery unmasked. 1856. (A journal of three years' residence in the Southern States.)
Tucker's (G.) Diss. on S., and proposal for its abolition in Virginia. 1796.
Underhill's Emancipation in the W. Indies. (A faithful and minute account of the condition of emancipated slaves, as it was in 1860.)
Wadstrom's (C. B.) Coast of Guinea. 1789.
Webster's (Noah) Effects of S. on morals and industry. 1793. (Contains a speech by Pinkney, observations by Priestly, &c.)
Wesley's (Jno.) Thoughts on slavery.
Westminster Rev. 1:337. 3:125. 11:275. 84:1.
Whitaker's Review of Gibbon's Rome.
Wigham's Anti-slavery cause in America, and its martyrs.
Wilberforce's Appeal in behalf of slaves.
Winn (T. S.) on West India slavery.

Slave-Trade.

Alexander's (G.) Letters on the S. trade.
Badinell on the Slave-trade.

Slave-Trade—*continued.*

Benezet's Account of Guinea.
Bisset's History of the Slave-trade.
Blackwood's Mag. 63:5,220,235.
British and For. Review. 9:466.
Buxton (Tho. F.) on the Slave-trade.
Carey (H. C.) on the S. trade. (Treats the subject purely as one of political economy.)
Cheever's God against slavery.
Clarkson (Tho.) on the Slave-trade.
Dannet's Exam. of Harris on slavery.
Dublin University Mag. 21:439.
Dudley on the Merchandise of men.
Falconbridge's S. tr. on the coast of Africa.
Gaisford (S.) on the Slave-trade.
Gregory's (George) Essays.
Harris on the Slave-trade.
Hill's Voyage to the slave coast. 1849.
——— Fifty days in a slave ship. 1853.
Jamieson's Sorrows of slavery.
Museum of For. Literature. 2:147. 20:92.
Nichols on the Slave-trade.
North British Rev. 11:245.
Paley's Political Economy.
Pamphleteer. 4:227.
Panoplist. 4:407, 7:135. 14:417.
Princeton Review. 12:516.
Ramsay's Exam. of Harris on slavery.
Raynal's European settlements in the West Indies.
Roscoe's Wrongs of Africa.
——— Slave-trade.
Snelgrave's Guinea.
Thorp's View of the slave-trade.
Torrey on the Amer. slave-trade. (Showing that free negroes are taken from Northern States and sold at the South. 1822.)
Turnbul's Slave-trade in Cuba.
Westminster Review. 34:125.
Wilberforce's Speeches in the House of Commons.
Winchester's (E.) Reigning abominations.

Sleep. See DREAMS, MIND.

Bichat, Recherches physiologique.
Binn's (E. E.) Anatomy of sleep.
Burnet's Theory of the Earth.
Christian Examiner. 57:364.
Elwin's Operations of the mind in sleep.
Holland's Mental Physiology.
Lime Street Lectures.
Macnish's Philosophy of sleep.
Phillips' (A. P. W.) on the Nature of sleep and death.
Rohault's Physics.

Sleep of the Soul.
See INTERMEDIATE STATE.

Pro.

Heym's Theologische Streitigkeiten.
Parker (Bp.) de Descensu ad infernum.
Reinhard's Dogmatik.
Stegmani Disquisitio brevis. (Reply to Valerian.)
Balfour's (Walter) Three Essays.

Sleep of the Soul—*continued.*

Pro.

Blackburn's Historical view of the controversy concerning a future state.
Burgh's Dignity of human nature.
Combe's (J.) Teaching of the O. and N. T.
[Coward's] Thoughts on the soul. (Published under the name of Estibius Psychalethes.)
——— Second Thoughts, &c.
Dehon's (Bp. T.) Sermons.
Hallet's Future state of the soul.
Kenrick's (Timothy) Discourses.
Law's (Bp.) Theory of Religion. Appendix.
Lawton's Search after souls. (Answers separately Broughton, Nichols, and Turner.)
Monthly Review. 1787. (Notice of Steffer.)
Oliver on the Pursuit of happiness.
Peckard on the Intermediate state.
——— Reply to Fleming
——— Reply to Morton.
——— Further observations.
(Peckard is as able as any writer on this side of the question.)
Tyndall's (Wm.) Works. (Replies to Sir T. Moore.)
Wadsworth's Αντιψυχοθανασία.
Wettstein's (J. J.) Prolegomena.

Con.

Calvin, Traité par lequel est prouvé que les ames viellant et vivant, etc. (Trans. into Latin, and published under the title of Psychopannychia.)
Capellus de Hominum post mortem statu.
Schubert (J. E.), de Animis defunctorum.
Valerian (Mag.) de Acatholicorum regula credendi.

Austin's (Gilbert) Sermons in Dublin.
Broughton's (John) Psychologia.
Bull's (Bp.) Sermons.
Calvin's Tracts. ("Psychopannychia.")
——— Sermons. (Ser. on Immortality.)
Campbell's Dissertations. Diss. 6.
Christian Review. 20:383.
Fleming's (Caleb) Survey of the "Search after souls."
Goddard on the Inter. state. (Rep. to Law.)
Groves on the Fut. state. (Reply to Hallet.)
Howe's (John) Works.
Huntingford's State of the soul after death.
Jortin's (J.) Sermons.
Kitto's Journal. April, 1853.
Month. Rev. 130:525.
Moore's (Sir T.) Dialogues.
More's (Henry) Grand mystery of godliness.
Morton's Queries to Dr. Law.
——— Remarks on Mr. Peckard.
Nichols' Conference with a Theist.
Norton's (John) Orthodox Evangelist.
Polwhele's (R.) State of the soul after death.
Secker (Abp.) on the Catechism.
Steffer's Letters to Bp. Law.
Turner's Exist. of the soul. Rep. to Coward.
Warburton's Divine Legation of Moses.
Watts' Philosophical Essays.

Whiston's (Wm.) Sermons and Essays.

A very sufficient account, not only of the writers on this subject, but of the opinions of eminent divines who incidentally mention it, will be found in BLACKBURN, cited above.

Sloth. See DILIGENCE, INDUSTRY, NEW YEAR, REDEEMING TIME, TIME, ZEAL.

Smalcald Articles.

Articuli qui dicunter Smalcaldici e Palatino codice editi. 1817.
B[illegible]ni Disputationes XXII.
Be[illegible]m's Gesch. des Symbol. d. Schmalk.
Deutchmanni (Ioann.) Dissertationes.
Fabricii Harmonia Confessionis.
Francke, Libri symbolici eccles. Lutheranæ.
Guhlingii Prefatio Historica ad artic. Sm.
Hanei Orationes.
Iahn's Gesch. d. Schmalkaldischen Krieges.
Kahleri Dissertationes XXII.
Marheinecke in Artic. qui dicuntur Smalc.
Mundenii Prefatio historica ad artic. Smalc.
Plitt, de Auctoritate articulorum S. symbol.
Salthenii Dissertationes Historicæ.
Sauberti Synopsis et partitio artic. Smalc.
Schmidii Prefatio historica ad art. Smalc.
Schrammii Disputationes.
Seeleni (J. H.) Observationes.
Selneccer's Smalcald. Artickel.

Sobriety. See AMUSEMENTS, MODERATION, MIRTH, SELF-DENIAL, WATCHFULNESS.

Atterbury's (Lewis) Sermons.
Barrow's (S.) Sermons.
Beveridge's (Bp.) Sermons.
Calamy's (Edmund) Sermons.
Cave's Primitive Christianity.
Christian Review. 3:559.
Clark's (John) Sermons.
Craig's (William) Sermons.
Dwight's (Timothy) Sermons.
Fawcett's (John) Sermons.
Foster's (John) Lectures. Lect. 1.
Grove's (Edward) Sermons.
Henry (Matt.) on Sobermindedness.
Hunter's (Thomas) Sermons.
Icter's (J. B.) Sermons.
Kennett's (Basil) Sermons.
Manton's (Thomas) Sermons.
Markland's (Abr.) Sermons.
Mayhew's (Jonathan) Sermons.
Price's (S.) Berry Street Sermons.
Rees' (Abraham) Sermons.
Secker's (Abp.) Sermons.
Snowden's (W.) Sermons.
Spirit of the Pilgrims. 4:9.
Taylor's (Jeremy) Holy living.
Watts' (Isaac) Sermons.
Zollikoffer's Sermons on prevalent vices.

Socialism.

Pro.

Bastiat, Harmonies Economiques.
Bauer's (Bruno) Burgerliche Revolution in Deutschland.

Socialism—*continued.*

Pro.

Blanc (Louis) Organization du Travail.
——— Le Socialisme.
Chevalier, sur l'Organization du Travail.
Fröbels' System der sozialen Politik.
Fourrier (C.) Theorie des quatre movements.
——— Nouveau monde industriel.
——— Traite de l'Association.
——— (Various other works.)
Garnier, le Droit au travail.
Grun's Soziale Bewegung in Frankreich.
Le Producteur. Periodical. Paris.
Proudon, Qu'est-ce que la proprieté?
——— Du principe fédératif.
Reybaud, les Reformateurs contemporain.
Sand (Geo.) [Mrs. Dudevant], Lettres au peuple.
St. Simon, Œuvres.
Thomas, Histoire des Ateliers nationaux.

Annet's (Peter) Works. (In these are the germs of modern Socialism. 1739.)
London Phalanx. Periodical.
More's Utopia.
Owen's (Robt.) Regeneration of Society.
Owen's (R. D.) Book of the new moral world.
Promethian, The. Period. Lond. 1842 et seq.
Spirit of the Times. Period. London.

Con.

De Lustrac, Christianisme et Socialisme.
Grotius de Jure belli et pacis.
Mosheimii Dissertationes.

Amer. Eclectic Rev. 4:91.
Amer. Whig. Rev. 2:80. 5:492,545. 7:632.
Balou (A.) on Christian Socialism.
Blackwood's Mag. 56:588.
Bray's Outlines of social systems.
Brit. Quart. Rev. 2d Series. 3:438.
Brownson's Quart. Rev. 1:450.
Channing (W. H.) on Fourierism.
Christ. Exam. 45:194,204. 37:57.
Democratic Rev. 8:451. 10:30. 11:481. 12:129 16:17. 18:142.
Eclectic Mag. 14:333. 16:470. 17:374,545. 21:522.
Eclectic Rev. New Series. 1:66. 2:327.
Edinb. Review. 90:260. 93:1.
Ewing's (Alex.) Discourses.
Fisher's Exam. of R. Owen's view of society.
Frazier's Mag. 2:520. 5:666. 27:609.
Gamond's (Mad.) Fourier and his System.
Hall's (Robt.) Sermons.
Hennel's Outline of the various social systems and communities which have been founded on the principle of co-operation.
Littell's Living Age. 15:4. 18:4.
Locke on Government.
Meth. Quar. Rev. 5:545. 8:29.
New Englander. 4:56.
New York Rev. 7:525.
North Amer. Review. 10:141. 11:218. 12:47. 67:119. 69:277.
North Brit. Rev. 9:115. 10:141. 12:86.
Pamphleteer. 10:280.

Quar. Rev. 45:407. (R. Southey.) 65:485.
Thornton's Lectures on Socialism.
United States Lit. Gaz. 2:61.
Univ. Quarterly. 2:52,136.
Ward (Jas.) on the Working classes.
Westminster Rev. 16:279.

Social Intercourse. See COMPANY, CHRISTIAN INTERCOURSE, VISITING.

Plutarchi Opera.
Angus' (Jos.) The Church the noblest form of social life.
Annet's (Peter) Lectures.
Christian Observer. 18:625.
Collyer's Lectures on Script. duties. Lec. 10.
Delany's (Patrick) Sermons on social duties.
Drummond's Social duties on Christian principles.
Dwight's Theology. Ser. 145.
Foster's (Jas.) Discourses on natural relig.
Girdlestone (Charles) on Christian conduct.
Hall's (Robt.) Sermons. (Ser. on the Influence of Christianity on society.)
Jortin's (John) Sermons.
Leland's (Thomas) Sermons.
Norris' (John) Sermons.
Percival's (G. C.) Sermons.
Stebbings' Sermons.
Stokes' (Gabriel) Serm. *Unguarded speech.*
Wallis' (John) Sermons.
Whitefield's Sermons.
Wood's (William) Sermons.
Zollikoffer's (Geo. J.) Sermons.

Social Nature of Man.

Brisbane's Social destiny of man.
Butler's (Bp.) Sermons.
Christ. Exam. 11:70.
Delany's (Patrick) Sermons.
N. Brit. Rev. 15:151.

Social Virtue. See RELATIVE DUTIES, VIRTUE.

Atterbury's (Bp.) Sermons. *Doing as we would be done by.*
Beattie's Elements of moral science.
Beveridge's (Bp.) Sermons. *Doing as we would be done by.*
Butler's (Alban) Sermons.
Carey's (H. C.) Principles of social science.
Carter's (N.) Sermons.
Delany's (Patrick) Sermons.
Doddridge's Lectures. Lect. 65.
Evans on the Christian temper.
Huntingdon's Divine aspects of human society.
Hutcheson's Inquiry into the ideas of beauty and virtue. Ess. 2.
Piggott's (S.) Guide to families.
Secker's (Abp.) Sermons. *Doing as we would be done by.*

Social Worship.

Beattie's Elements of Moral Science.
Christ. Monthly Spect. 5:403.
Colliber on Natural and Revealed religion.

Social Worship—*continued.*

Haldane's (J. A.) View of social worship as observed by the first Christians. (Exc'nt.)
Moore's Scriptural authority for social wor.
Morrice's Social religion exemplified. ("That inimitable book."—J. A. JAMES.)
Pope's Vindication of social and public W.
Price's Dissertations.
Townsend's (John) Sermons.
Young's Importance of prayer-meetings.

Society. See CIVIL GOVERNMENT, DIVINE RIGHT OF KINGS, MAGISTRACY, ORIGIN OF LAWS, ORIGIN OF NATIONS, PASSIVE OBEDIENCE, SOCIALISM, SUBMISSION TO RULERS.

Socinians. See CREEDS, JESUS, DEITY OF, PHOTINIANS, SACRIFICES, TRINITY, UNITARIANS.

Pro.

Catechismus Racoviensis, ac Confessio. (The great standard.)
Bibliotheca Fratrum Polon. (Containing the works of Socinus, Crellius, Slichtingius, Walzogen, &c.)
Borellii Concatenatio Aurea.
Brenii Adnotationes in Vet. et Nov. Test.
Conf. Fidei Christianæ: ed. Schlichtingius.
Crellii (Sam.) Fides primorum Christianor.
Crellii (Joh.) Opera Exegetica et polemica. (In Biblioth. fratrum.)
Crellii (Chr.) Disputationes.
——— Opera omnia.
Eneidini Explicationes locorum Scripturæ.
Goslavii Disputationes.
Huthmanni Prodomus Novi Foederis.
Langendult's (P.) Aanteekeningen ouer het geheele N. T.
Modrevius de Tribus personis Dei.
Moormanni Opera posthuma.
Moscorovii Sublatio pudefactionis.
——— Refutatio libri de baptismo Smiglecii.
Ostorod der Gottheit Christi.
Pisekii Responsio ad E. Campianum.
Sandii (C. C.) Bibliotheca Antitrintitarum.
——— Opera. (Voluminous.)
Schlichtingii Dissertatio de Trinitate.
Serveti Opera.
Sluteri Propylæ historiæ Christianæ.
Smalcii (V.) Disputationes.
Socini (Fausti) Opera omnia. (Contained in the second and third volumes of the "Bibliotheca Fratrum.")
Stegmanni Dissertationes.
Stoinii Disputationes.
Volkelius de Vera religione.
——— Dissolutio nodi gordii.
Walzogenii Preparatio ad utilem lectionem N. T.
——— de Uno Deo in essentia.
——— Compendium religionis Christi.
Zuickeri Opera.
Ashdowne's Unitarian, Arian, and Trinitarian opinions examined.
Belsham's Answer to Wilberforce.
——— Epistles of Paul. Trans. with notes.

Socinians—*continued.*

Pro.

Biddle's Catechism.
——— 12 Reasons from Sacred Scripture.
Bury's Naked Gospel. (Produced many pamphlets for and against him, from 1690 to 1700.)
Cardale's True doctrine of the N. T. concerning Christ.
——— Comment. on Christ's last prayer.
——— Treatise on certain terms applied to Socinianism.
Carpenter's (Lant.) Reply to Veysie's preservative
——— View of Unitarianism.
——— Strictures on Bp. Magee.
Christie's Discourses on the unity of God.
Clarke's Defence of the unity of God.
Collins' Defence of Unitarian faith.
Cornish on the Pre-existence of Christ.
Eme's Deist turned Christian.
Firmin's Brief history of Unitarians.
Fox's (W. F.) Sermons on the mission, character, and doctrines of Christ.
——— Lectures on the corruption and genuine influence of Christianity.
Frend's (William) Works.
Hobhouse on Heresy and Blasphemy.
——— Reply to Randolph.
Lardner on the Logos.
——— on the Holy Spirit.
——— Divine unity asserted.
Porter's Answer to Hawker.
Recovian Catechism. Tr. by T. Rees, with notes and illustrations, and a sketch of Unitarianism in Poland.
Ritter's Brief Demonstration.
Smith's Letter to a member of the Church of England.
Sykes' Doctrine of Redemption.
Toland's Christianity not mysterious.

Con. See ATHANASIUS, SONSHIP.

Abbadie, Traité de la divinité de J. C.
Alstedius contra Catechismum Racoviensem.
Ames, de Incarnatione Verbi.
Amyraldus de Trinitate.
Arnoldus contra Catechismum Racoviensem.
——— Lux in Tenebris.
Ashwell, de Socino et Sociniauismo.
Balduinus contra Catechismum Racovien.
Bertram's Triumph der Wahren.
Besenbeck über die Dreieinigkeit Gottes.
Bullii Defensio Synodi Nicenæ.
——— Judicium Ecclesiæ de necessitate credendi Jesum esse verum Deum.
Calovii Anti Sociniana. (Acta erud.)
Calvini Defensio orthodoxæ fidei.
Comenii de Christianorum uno Deo.
Crocii Anti Socinianismus contractus.
Deutschmanni Examen Synopticum.
Durrii Christianismi per Socin. eversio.
Franckii Demonstratio deitatis Christi.
Franzius contra Catechismum Racoviensem.
Gardner (S.), Hypotyposis.

Socinians—*continued.*

Con.

Grosse, Dem Socinianischen Glaubens-bekæntniss, etc.
Grotii Defensio fidei Catholicæ.
Hoornbeckii Socinianismi confutatio.
Jameson, Romam Racovianam, et Racoviam Romanam.
Jurieu, le Tableau de Socinianisme.
Langii Causa Dei ac religionis.
——— Refutatio Catech. Racoviensis.
——— Jesus Typicus.
Le Blanc, Principes contre les Sociniens.
Maccovii Πρωτα ψευδη.
Maresii Hydra Socinianismi expugnata.
Mayeri (J. F.) Dissertationes.
Nicolaides (Tho.) Dissertationes.
Prodæi Matæologia Sociniana.
Rambachii Refutatio catech. Racoviensis.
——— Character Lælii und Socini.
Scherzeri Collegium anti-Socinianum.
Smiglecius de Erroribus nov. Arianorum.
——— de Christo.
Sonntagii Refutatio catech. Racoviensis.
Spener, Zeugnisses, etc.
Widde [or De Widde], Confut. Socinianismi.
Wren, Increpatio Bar Jesu.
Wyttenbachii (D.) Tentamen Theologiæ.
Zanchius de Tribus Elohim.

Alderson on the Pre-existence of Christ.
Allix's Fathers vindicated.
Arnauld's Examinator.
Barclay's Socinian. and Irvingism refuted.
Barlow's (Bp.) Remains.
Bingham's Doct. of the Church of England.
Burgess' Doctrine of original sin.
Cheynell's Rise, growth, and danger of S.
Cloppenburg's Compendium on Socinianism.
Cottle's (Joseph) Essays.
Dod's Preservative against Socinianism.
——— Foreign and English Socinians.
——— S. creed tending to Atheism.
Edwards' (Jonathan, of Eng.) S. unmasked.
Fletcher's Socinianism unscriptural.
Fowler's Descent of Christ.
Fox's (Jos.) Lectures. (On the modern phase. 1824.)
Freeston's Nature and effects of modern S.
Fuller's Calvinistic and S. syst. compared.
——— Reply to Toulmin and Kentish.
Gaillard's Socinian heresy disproved.
——— Spirit and principles of Socinianism.
Gregory's Divine Antidote.
Hall's (Robt.) Notes of Sermons.
Hare (Edw.) on Socinianism.
Hawker's (R.) Sermons on the Div. of Chr.
——— Evidences of plenary inspiration.
——— Letter to Thomas Porter.
Hawkins on Scripture Mysteries.
——— Expostulat. address to Dr. Priestley.
Howe's Critical Observations.
Hussey's Glory of Christ unveiled.
Jerram on the Atonement.
Jones' (Sir W.) Preservative agt. modern S

Socinians—*continued.*

Con.

Kett's Bampton Lectures. 1790.
Lamothe on the Divinity of Christ.
Lawrence's Dissertations on the Logos.
Leslie's Short Method with Socinians.
——— S. controversy discussed; wherein the chief Socinian tracts are considered.
Magee on Atonement and sacrifice.
Mann's (Isaac) Essay on the Atonement.
——— Strictures on N. T. Heineken.
Milbourn's Vindication of mysteries in religion.
Morning Exercises at Cripplegate.
Nichols' Short history of Socinianism.
Nye (S.) on the Trinity.
Owen's Exercitations. (Prefixed to Commentary on the Hebrews.)
——— Mystery of the Gospel vindicated. (Reply to Biddle.)
Parkhurst's Demonstrations from Scripture. (Reply to Priestley.)
Prideaux's Life of Mahomet.
Randolph's Letter to Dr. Priestley.
——— Reply to Lindsay.
——— Scriptural revision of the arguments of Socinians. (Reply to Hobhouse.)
Shepherd's Free examination of the first verses of John's Gospel.
Sherlock's Vindication of the doctrine of the Trinity.
(An answer to several Socinian writers.)
——— Apology for writing agt. Socinians.
——— Defence of the Apology.
——— Danger of corrupting faith by philosophy.
——— Present state of the Socinian controversy. 1698. (Sherlock was opposed by Dr. South and others, and a warm controversy was kept up from 1690, till stopped by royal authority, some years after.)
Shuttleworth's Consistency of revelation with itself and with human reason.
Smith's (J.) End of the S. controversy.
Smith's (J. Pye) Scripture testimony to the Messiah.
Stebbing's Person and mission of Christ.
Stillingfleet on Christ's satisfaction.
——— Sermon on the mysteries of faith.
——— Vindication of the Trinity.
Veysie's Doctrine of the Atonement.
——— Preservative against Socinianism.
Whitaker's Dialogues on the Trinity.
——— Origin of Arianism.
Williams' Vindication of the Archbishops.
Wisheart's (George) Sermons. (Great.)
Wynperse on the Divinity of Christ. (Small book, but powerful.)

See Sandii *Bibliotheca Antitrinitariana;* Webster's *Account of English writers in the Socinian controversy,* 1728; Barlow's *Directions for the choice of books.* It is not possible to make an accurate division between Socinian and Unitarian writers.

Socinianism, History of.

Acta Eruditorum.
Adelt, Historia de Arianismo.
Bockii Hist. Socinianismi Prussici.
Buddeus de Origine Socinianismi.
Calovii Decas dissertationes de pseudo-theologiæ Socinianæ, ortu, et progressu.
Cloppenburg de Origine ac progressu S.
Engelkenii Dissertationes.
Guichard, Hist. du Socinianisme.
Hoornbeckii Adparatus ad controversias S.
Horbii Historia hæreseos Unitariorum.
Lauterbachii Ariano-Socinianismus olim in Polonia.
Lubiencii Hist. reformationis Polonicæ.
Mayer de Controversiis Antitrinitariis.
Morscovii Politia Ecclesiastica.
Sandii Bibliotheca Antitrinitariorum.
Stoinii Epitome hist. orig. Unitariorum in Polonia.

Addison's History of Socinianism.
Ashwell's Socinus and Socinians.
Chewney's Lives of the chief Socinians.
Cheynel's Rise, growth, and danger of S.
Lindsey's Histor. view of doct. and worship.
Nichols' Short history of Socinianism.
Owen's (John) Vindiciæ Evangelicæ.
Sherlock's State of the S. controv. 1698.
Webster's History of Arianism and Socinianism. To 1730.

Socinus, Faustus.

Socini Opera.
Chris. Examiner. 50:212.

The works of Socinus are given in the first two volumes of the "Fratres Poloni;" with a life of the author.

Sodom. See GEOGRAPHY OF SCRIPTURE.

Cellarii (C.) Dissertationes.
Clerici [or Le Clerc] Dissertationes.
Collyer on Scripture facts.
Gisbourne's (T.) Sermons.
Gunn's (W. A.) Sermons.
Hall's (Bp.) Contemplations.
Rose's (Sir G.) Scripture Researches.
Saurin's (James) Historical Sermons.
Sewall's (Steph.) Origin of the Salt Sea.
Whately's (William) Prototypes.

Solfidians. See ANTINOMIANS.

Solitude. See MEDITATION.

Groschii Orationes.
Mackenzie (Geo.) on Preferring solitude to public employment.
Meikle's Solitude sweetened.
Orton's Discourses to the aged.
Ranew's Solitude improved.
Reade's Christian Meditations.
Winslow's (O.) Midnight Harmonies.
Woodward's (Henry) Essays.
Zimmerman on Solitude.
Zollikoffer's (Geo. J.) Sermons.

Solomon. See BIOGRAPHY.

Alexander, de Salomone.
Chorsey, Vie de Salomon.
Cognatus de Prosperitate et exitio S.
Pineda, de Rebus Salomonis.

Alison's (Archibald) Sermons.
Beza's (Theodore) Sermons.
Christian Month. Spect. 4:131.
Close's (F.) Typical persons of the O. Test.
Critical Review. Vol. 15. (Appendix.)
Hall's (Bp.) Contemplations.
Kitto's Bible Illustrations.
Maurice's (F. D.) Prophets and Kings.
May's (W.) Sermons to the Young.
Milner's (Joseph) Sermons.
Saurin's (James) Sermons.

Sonnites. See MAHOMETANISM.

Sale's Dissertations prefixed to his translation of the Koran.

Sonship of Christ. See ETERNAL GENERATION.

Dorschei Dissertationes Theologicæ.
Driessenii Generatio filii Dei Divina.
Rittangelii Libræ veritatis.
Wayen, Dissertationes. (Adv. Clericum.)
Wetstenius de Jesu Christo.
Wigandus Rationes pro et contra generat. filii Dei, etc.

Christ. Quar. Spect. 6:156.
Hawtrey's Appeal to the New Testament.
Kidd (J.) on the Sonship of Christ.
McLean (A.) on the Sonship of Christ.
Mayer (D.) on the Sonship of Christ.
Millar's (Dav.) Co-essential sonship of C.
Miller's (Sam.) Letters.
——— on Unitarianism.
Taylor's (H.) Opinions of learned Christians, ancient and modern, concerning the generation of Christ.
Treffry's Inquiry into the doctrine of the eternal Sonship, &c.
Wallin's Ten discourses on the filiation, &c.
Watson (Rich.) on the Eternal sonship of Christ.
Webb's (F.) Sermons.

Song of Deborah.

Coceeii Com. in Canticum Deboræ.
Gumpach, das Triumphleid Debora's.
Holmanni Com. philol.-crit. in carmen D.
Kalkar, de Cantico Deboræ.
Muis, Selecta Cantica V. Test.
Schaurrieri Dissertationes.

Biblical Repository. Vol. 1.
Bibliotheca Sacra. 12:597.
Cleeves' (C.) Song of D. paraphrased.
Cooper's (Bp.) Expos. of the song of D.
Doughty's (John) Analecta Sacra.
Green's New tr. and Com. on the song of D.
Horsley's (Bp.) Song of Deborah.
Reading's (W.) Sermons.
Weston's Trans. and Exp. of the song of D.

Sorbonne. See PORT ROYAL.

Coringii Antiquitates Academicæ.
Du Boulay, Hist. Academiæ Paris.
Duvernet's Gesch. der Sorbonne.
——— Histoire de la Sorbonne.
Hemeræus de Academia Parisiensi.
Schelhornii Antiquitates literariæ.

Beza's Ten discourses on the Pope's canons.
Du Fresner's Life of St. Lewis.

Sorcery. See MAGIC, WITCHCRAFT.

Sorrow. See AFFLICTION, WOUNDED SPIRIT.

Abernethy's (John) Sermons.
Collins on the Providence of God.
——— Cordial for a fainting spirit.
Colquhoun on Spiritual Comfort.
Elliot's (Wm. G.) Discipline of sorrow.
Grandpierre's (J. H.) Sermons.
Hooker's Remedy against sorrow and fear.
Jacomb's Treatise of Holy Dedication.
Jelf's (R. W.) Sermons preached abroad.
Morning Exercises at Cripplegate. Sermon by Rich. Baxter.
Newnham's Tribute of sympathy.
Orton's Discourses to the Aged.
Polhill's Armatura Dei.
Rowe's Saint's temptations.
Stow's (Mrs.) Minister's Wooing.
Traughton's Cause and cure of disconsolate thoughts.
Tulloch's Theism.
Williams' Voices from the silent land.

Soul. See MATERIALISM.

Augustin, Epistolæ.
Tertullian, de Anima.
Gregory Nys., de Anima.
Gregory Thau., ad Tatianum.

Beck's Biblische Sittenlehre.
Feverlini (J. C.) Dissertationes.
Kliefoth (T.), das Zeugniss der Seele.
Laugel, le Problème de l'âme.
Ludovici de Mente humana.
Melancthon, Commentaria de anima.
Nemesius de Natura hominis. Cap. 1.
Olshausen, Opuscula.
Poiretus de Anima.
Quandt's Wissen und Sein.
Schubert's Geschichte der Seele.
Tissot, la Vie dans l'homme.

Baptist Quarterly. 1:177.
Baxter on the Nature of the human soul.
Beveridge's (Bp.) Sermons.
Broughton's (John) Psychologia.
Chambers' Cyclopædia. Art. "Soul."
Clerke's (Richard) Sermons.
Cousin's Psychology.
Cudworth's Intellectual system. Bk. 1, ch. 5.
Delitsch's Psychology.
Doddridge's Lectures. Part 1.
Dwight's Sermons. Ser. 22 to 24.
Flavel's (John) Pneumatologia.
Heard's Tripartite nature of man.
Hill's Treatise on the Soul.

Soul—*continued.*

Law's (Bp. Ed.) Sermons. (Use of the word in Sacred Scripture.)
Mason on Self-knowledge.
Newman's (John H.) Sermons.
Potts' (J. H.) Sermons.
Rausch's Psychology.
Redford's (Geo.) Body and Soul.
Storr's (Rich.) Constitution of the soul.
Tillotson's (Abp.) Sermons.
Warburton's Divine Legation of Moses.
Watts' Ontology.

Souls of Brutes. See INSTINCT, METEMPSYCHOSIS.

Aubrey, de l'Ame des bêtes. (Maintains their immortality.)
Buckii Commentatio Psychologica.
Des Cartes, de Methodo.
Dieterici (J. G.) Dissertationes.
Gimma (G.) Dissertationes Academicæ.
Guillemont, de Principiis rerum corporeal.
Henrichii Sylloge script. de spiritibus.
Kluge's Vernünftige Seele.
Meieri (Gerhard.) Dissertationes.
Meier's (Geo. F.) Seelen der Thiere. (Maintains their immortality.)
Pardies, sur la Connaisance des brutes.
Sbarragii Entelechia. (Ag. Descartes.)
Schoock (Mart.), Dissertat. (Ag. Descartes.)
Sennert, de Orig. et nat. animarum in brutis.
Willis (Tho.), Exercitationes.

Balguy's (John) Sermons.
Baxter on the Nature of the soul.
Bayle's Dictionary. Articles *Pereira, Rosarius*, and *Sennertus*.
Beattie's Dissertations.
Cheyne's Philosoph. Principles. Ch. 3, § 10.
Christian Examiner. 74:199.
Colliber's Enquiry into the existence, &c.
Coxe's (John Redman) Considerations.
Dean (Rich.) on the Future life of brutes.
Des Cartes on the Passions.
Ditton on the Resurrection.
Edwards' Critical and philos. exercitations.
Hewlett's (J. T.) Penscelwood Papers.
Hume's Philosophical Essays. Ess. 9.
Le Grand's Philosophy. Tr. by R. Blome.
Locke on the Understanding. Book 2.
Middleton on the Future life of brutes.
Morer's (T.) Sermons.
North Amer. Review. 63:91.
Polignac's Anti-Lucretius.
Polwhele's (R.) Discourses.
Priestley's (Joseph) Essays on the theory of mind.
Ramsay's Philosophical Principles.
Rothwell's Letter to the Rev. Mr. Dean.
Search's Light of Nature. Chap. 12.
Spectator. No. 120.
Wagstaffe on the Immortality of brutes.
Watts' Philosophical Essays. Ess. 9.
Willis (Tho.) on the Souls of brutes. Tr. by S. Pordage. (Discusses the subject—1st, physiologically; and 2d, pathologically.)

Southcot.

Southcot's (Joana) Book of Wonders.
——— Testimony of the Lord.
——— The sealed Prophecies.
——— Letters and Communications.
Hughson's History of religious impostors.
Lane's (Sam.) Joana Southcot detected.
Matthias' Case of Joana Southcot.
Observations on the Divine claims of J. S.

Sovereignty of God. See ELECTION.

Brown's Natural and revealed religion.
Burder's (Henry F.) Sermons.
Charnock's Sermons.
Coleman's (J. N.) Sermons.
Coles on God's sovereignty. (Practical.)
Creassy (R.) on the Sovereignty of God.
Davies' (Pres.) Sermons.
Dixon's Sov. of the Divine administration.
Dwight's Theology. Ser. 16.
Gearing on God's sovereignty.
Jamieson's Sacred History.
Payne's (George) Lectures.
Silver (F.) on the Sovereignty of God.
Williams' Equity of the Divine government.
Wilson's (Robt.) Divine sovereignty.

Space.

Clarke's Boyle Lectures. 1705, 1706.
Doddridge's Lectures. Part 2, prop. 40.
Jackson on the Existence and unity of God.
Law's (Ed.) Enquiry into the idea of space.
Leibnitz's Theodicee.
Locke's Essays. Book 2.
Ramsay's Philosoph. principles. Prop. 24.
Waterland's Diss. on the argument *a priori*.
Watts' Ontology. Ch. 4 and 12.
——— Essays. Ess. 1.
Wollaston's Religion of nature.

Spinoza. See SPINOCISM.

Coler, Vie de Spinoza.
Niceron, Memoires pour servir a l'histoire des hommes illustre.

Christian Examiner. 74:313.

Spinocism. See ATHEISM, SPINOZA.

Pro.

Spinoza, Opera. Ed. Paulus. 1802.
——— ——— Ed. Bruder. 1846.
Bekker (Balthas.) die bezauberte Welt.
Bredenburgii Principia.
Cuffeleri Ars ratiocinandi.
Hobessii Elementa Philosophica.
Knutsii Epistola amici ad amicum.
Leenhof, der Himmel auf Erden.

The sentiments of Spinoza, though not stated in form, are developed, and more or less adopted, in the writings of Fichté, Hegel, Paulus, Schelling, Strauss, Wegscheider, and others.

Con.

Blyenburg's Wederlegging de zede-kunst von Spinoza.

Spinocism—*continued.*

Con.

Batalerii Vindiciæ miraculorum.
Bredenburgii Enervatio tractatus Theol. politici.
Brun, Veritable religion des Hollandois.
Buddei Dissertationes.
——— Spinocismus ante Spinozam.
Coler, de Resurrection de Jesus Christ.
Cuperi Arcana Atheismi detecta.
Horschii Investigationes circa orig. rerum.
Huet, La conformité de la raison avec la foi.
Jacquelot, Dissertationes.
Jensii Examen ethices Spinozæ.
Kortholtus de Tribus impostoribus magnis.
Lamy, Nouvelle Atheisme renversé.
Mansvelt adv. Theologico-politicum.
Melchoiris Religio Naturæ.
Musæi Tract. Theol. polit. Examinatus.
Nieuwentyt's Gronden van Zekerheit.
Orobius adversus Bredenburgii principia.
Pererius de Communibus principiis.
Poireti Fundamenta Atheismi eversa.
Staalkopfii Animadversiones succinctæ.
Velthuysii Tractatus de cultu naturali.
Weidneri Dissertationes.
Wittichii Anti Spinoza.
Wittigii Examen ethices Benedicti de Spin.
Wolfii Theologia Naturæ. Sect. 716.
Yvon, L'impiete Convaincu.

Buddeus' Spinocism before Spinoza.
Clark's Being and attributes of God.
Earbery's Deism answered and confuted.
Howe's Living Temple.

Spinocism, History of.

Coler, Vie de Spinoza.
Feverlinus in quantum Cartesis Atheismus imputandus.
Gundlingii Observationes Selectæ.
Jaegerus de Spinocismo, cum vita, etc.
Jenichen, Historia Spinozismi.
Kettnerus de duobus Impostoribus. (Spinoza et Bekker.)
Kortholtus de tribus Impostoribus. (Herbert, Hobbes, and Spinoza.)
Lampe, Bibliotheca Bremensis.
Orell's Spinoza's Leben und Lehre.
Sigwart's Spinozismus historisch und philos. Erläutert.
Staalkopfius de Spinozismo post Spinozam.
Werder (J. F.) de Spinozismo ante Spinozam.

Buchanan's (J.) Modern Atheism. Ch. 3.
Christian Examiner. 74:313.

Spirit of Adoption. See ADOPTION.

Breithaupt, de Spiritu adoptionis.
Deutchmanni (Ioann.) Dissertationes.
Olearius de Spiritu servit. et adoptionis.

Beddome's (B.) Discourses.
Beveridge's (Bp.) Thesaurus.
Evans' (John) Discourses.
Gresley's (W.) Parochial Sermons.
King's (Henry) Sermons.

Spirit of Adoption—*continued.*

Muir (W.) on the Holy Spirit.
Noel's (G. T.) Sermons.
Pierce's (S. E.) Sermons.
Scattergood's Operations of the Holy Spirit.
Stewart's (J. H.) Sermons.
Wallis' (John) Sermons.
Walton on the Witness of the Spirit.
Wesley's (John) Sermons.
Williams' (Isaac) Sermons.
Wilson's Nature and Privileges of adoption.

Spirit-Rapping. See SPIRITUALISM.

Spirits in Prison.
See DESCENT INTO HELL.

Limborch, Theologia Christiana.

Barrow on the Creed.
Benson's (Geo.) Dissertations on the Catholic faith. Diss. 2.
Bibliotheca Sacra. 1:708. 19:1.
Brackenbury's (Edward) Sermons.
Brown's (Dr. John) Bibliotheca Sacra.
Burnett's (Bp.) Four Dissertations.
Cochrane's Sermons on difficult texts.
Hobart's (Bp.) Sermons.
Kitto's Journal. New Series. Vol. 3.
Miles' Christ preaching to the Spirits, &c.
Moore's (Dr.) Theological Works.
Parker's (Benj.) State of the antediluvian world.
Pearson on the Creed.
Pirie's (Alex.) Critical Observations.
Puckle on the Intermediate State.
Wheatland's (Thomas) Sermons.
Woodward's (Henry) Essays.

Spiritual Death.

Armstrong's (John) The new life.
Bellamy's Nature and glory of the Gospel.
Cunningham's (J. W.) Sermons.
Davies' (Sam.) Sermons.
Davy's (C.) Cottage Sermons.
Doddridge's Character of the unregenerate.
Flavel's Method of grace in the gospel.
Hall's (Robt.) Notes of Sermons.
Martyn's (Henry) Sermons.
Muller's Christian doctrine of sin.
Payson's (Edward) Works.
Preston's (John) A lifeless life.
Sibbs' Beams of Divine light.
Trenchard's (W. E.) Sermons.
Usher's (Abp.) Sermons.
Waples' (Edward) Sermons.
West on Moral Agency.

Spiritual Gifts. See OPERATIONS OF THE HOLY GHOST.

Kurzman de Interpretatione locorum N. T. in quibus donorum S. S. extraord. mentio injicitur.
Wernsdorfii Dissertationes. Diss. 3.
Witsii Miscellanea Sacra. (Beautiful.)

Benson's (Dr. Geo.) Critical Dissertations.
Bloomfield's (Bp.) Sermons.

Spiritual Gifts—*continued.*

Briggs' (F. W.) Pentecost and the founding of the Church.
Clarke's (Samuel) Sermons.
Collyer (W. B.) on Miracles.
Cooper's (Edward) Doctrinal Sermons.
D'Oyly's (George) Sermons.
Faringdon's (Anthony) Sermons.
Frazier's Mag. 4:754. (Ed. Irving.)
Goode's (Wm.) Modern claims to extraordinary gifts examined.
Goodwin On being filled with the Spirit.
Gregory's (Thomas) Sermons.
Hawker on the Holy Spirit.
Jortin's (John) Sermons.
MacDonald's (W.) Sermons.
Macleod's (Alex.) View of inspiration.
Moberly's (G.) College Sermons.
Muir on the Holy Spirit.
Norris' (W.) Sermons.
Robertson's (F. W.) Sermons.
Sanderson's (Bp.) Sermons.
South's (Robert) Sermons.
Thompson (J. P.) on the Christian graces.
Warburton on the Doctrine of grace.
Yonge's (James) Sermons.

Spiritual Life. See HEAVENLY-MINDEDNESS, WALK OF FAITH.

Buchanan's Office and Work of the Spirit.
Christian Review. 15:543.
Davies' (Sam.) Sermons.
Gilfillan's (Sam.) Practical Discourses.
Literary and Theol. Rev. 4:40.
Owen on Spiritual-mindedness.
Priestley's (Tim.) Christian's looking-glass.
Princeton Rev. 18:275.
Simeon's (Charles) Sermons.
Upham's (T. C.) Interior life.
——— Life of faith.
——— Religious maxims.
Wesley's (John) Sermons.
Wills' Defence of experimental religion.

Spiritual Mindedness. See HEAVENLY.

Spiritual Pride. See PRIDE.

Charlesworth's (John) Practical Sermons.
Collyer's Scr. Parables. *Pharisee and Publ.*
Dodd's (W.) Pharisee and Publican.
Fuller's (And.) Occasions, causes, and effects of highmindedness in religion.
Graves' (Richard) Sermons.
Mills' (W. H.) Sermons.
Miller's (Edward) Sermons.
Pyle's (Philip) Sermons.
Tilly's (William) Sermons.

Spiritual Warfare. See FIGHT OF FAITH.

Spiritualism. See CLAIRVOYANCE.

Pro.

Augues, Spiritualisme.
Cahagnet (L. A.), Magnétisme.
——— Arcanes de la vie future.
Journal du Magnétisme. 1845–1867.

Spiritualism—*continued.*

Pro.

Adams' Rivulets from the ocean of truth.
Ambler's Spiritual Teacher.
Barth's Mesmerist.
Brittain's "Sheckinah."
Cahagnet's Celestial Telegraph.
Davis' (And. J.) Penetralia.
——— The great Harmonia.
——— Other publications.
Debate between J. Tiffany and J. Erret. 1856.
Dee's Relation of what passed between himself and some spirits. (Has a confirmatory preface by Casaubon. 1659.)
Dexter on Spiritualism.
Edmonds (J. W.) on Spiritualism.
Hammond's Communication from the spirit of Tho. Paine.
Hare's (R.) Experimental Investigations.
Home's (D. D.) Incidents of my life.
Howitt's History of the supernatural.
Jung Stilling's Pneumatology. Translated by S. Jackson.
Linton's Healing of the nations.
Longshore's Hist. of recent developments. 1851.
Parker's Prospect intô the Spir. world. 1770.
Rogers' Philosophy of mysterious agents.
Ross' Spiritual World.
Spiritual Herald. Period. New York. 1856.
Spiritual Magazine. Lond. 1860 to present.
Spiritual Telegraph. Periodical. New York. 1853 to 1856.
Townsend's (C. H.) Facts in Mesmerism.
Tuttle's Clairvoyant Physician.
——— Other treatises.
Wilkinson's Spirit Drawings.
——— The Revival.

Con.

Blasche's Kritik d. modernen Geisterglaub.
Chevreul, de la Bagnette divinatoire.
Horst's Theurgie.
Schiff, les Esprits frappeurs.
Beecher's (Cha.) Review of S. manifestations.
Begbee on Supernatural Illusions.
Berg's (J. F.) Demons and Guardian angels.
Billington's Lectures on manifestations.
Bird's (Geo.) Scripture Principles.
Blackwood's Mag. 73:629.
Blakeman on Credulity.
Byre's Naturalism and Spiritualism.
Capron (E. W.) on Spiritualism.
Christian Examiner. 61:352.
Daniels' Spiritualism versus Christianity.
De Boisment on Hallucination.
Dod (J. B.) on Spirit Manifestations.
Edinburg Review. 122:287.
Gasparin on Modern Spiritualism.
Gordon's Spiritualism examined.
Kitto's Journal. (Numerous articles.)
McDonald on Spiritualism.
Mackay on Popular Delusions.
Mahan's Modern mysteries explained.
Mattison's Origin, hist., &c., of sp. rappings.

North British Review. 39:174.
Oldfield's "To Damonion."
Pritchard's Sober words of table talk.
Quarterly Review. 114:179.
Ramsay (David) on Spiritualism.
Spicer's (H.) Sights and Sounds.
Vaughn's (Robt.) Letter and Spirit.

Spirituality. See HEAVENLY MINDEDNESS.

Spirituality of God. See ATTRIBUTES.

Limborch, Theologia Christiana.

Atterbury's (Lewis) Sermons.
Binning's (Hugh) Sermons.
Charnock's Works.
Clarke's (Dr. Samuel) Sermons.
Doddridge's Lectures. Lect. 47.
Foster's (Dr. James) Discourses.
Gill's Body of Divinity.
Hall's (Robt.) Sermons.
Paley's Natural Theology.
Styles' (John) Sermons.

Spoiling the Egyptians. See BORROWING.

Spontaneous Generation. See EQUIVOCAL GENERATION.

Stability. See DECISION.

Stage Plays.

Bossuet, Maximes et Réflections.
Concinna (Dan.), Dissertationes.
Conti, de la Comédie.
[D'Abignac], Condemnation des Théâtres.
Dräseke's Heiligen auf der Bühne.
Desprez de Boissy, Lettres.
Le Brun, sur la Comédie.
[Less], Bedenken der Theol. Facultat zu Göttingen. 1769.
Tholuck, Stimme wider d. Theaterlust.
Voisin, Défence du Prince de Conti.

Amer. Biblical Repository. 2d Series. 1:449. (Ancient Greek drama.)
Amer. Quart. Review. 1:331.
Amer. Whig Review. 2:117.
Bedford's Blasphemies of the playhouse, from seven thousand instances. 1719.
Bellowes' Relation of public amusements to public morality.
Best's (T.) Sermons on Amusements.
Blackwood's Mag. 7:387. 11:440. 14:421,723. 23:33. 59:54.
Brit. and For. Review. 2:568.
Bunn (Alfred) on the Stage.
Chris. Monthly Spect. 9:411.
Chris. Observer. 18:166.
Chris. Quart. Spect. 10:557.
Chris. Review. 2:393.
Collier's (Jer.) Immorality of the English stage. 1699.
——— Defence of Do.
——— Second Defence of Do.
——— Further vindication.
——— Dissuasive from the Playhouse.
Dwight's Essay on the Stage.

Stage Plays—*continued.*

Dennis' Defence of the Stage. (Reply to Collier.)
East's Letters to young ladies.
Eclectic Rev. 4th Series. 26:129.
Edinburg Review. 57:281. 78:204.
Episcopal Magazine. 2:56.
Foster's (Jno.) Contrib. to the Eclectic Rev.
Fuller's (Dr.) The Theatre.
Gosson's Schoole of abuse. (This effective treatise against the stage, 1579, is reprinted in the Sommers Collec. of tracts.)
Green's (J.) Refutation of the "Apology for actors." 1615.
Hill's (Rowland) Expostulatory Letter.
——— Aphoristic Observations.
Kendell on Stage entertainments.
Law's Unlawfulness of stage entertainments.
Macdonnell's Oxford Prize Essay. 1820.
Macnicoll on the Influence of the stage.
More (Hannah) on Amusements.
Museum of For. Liter. 6:355. 9:247. 12:661.
Orton's (Job) Discourses.
Oxford Prize Essays. 1820.
Plumtree's (James) Discourses.
Prynne's Histrio Mastix. (For writing this proper but dull book, which was declared to be a libel on the Queen, who patronized theatres, Prynne was punished [1633] by the pillory and whipping, the loss of both his ears, and perpetual imprisonment.)
Rankin's Mirror of Monsters.
Raynolds' Overthrowe of stage playes. (One of the strongest writers of the 17th cent.)
Schleiermacker's Christian Morals.
Sewell's Vindication of the English stage.
Simpson's (David) Select Works.
Styles' (John) Character and tendency of the stage. 1838.
Turnbull on the Theatre.
Thompson's (J. P.) Lectures to young men.
Ware's (Sam.) Remarks on Theatres.
Winchester's (S. G.) The Theatre.
Wilkes' (John) General view of the Stage.
Witherspoon's Serious enquiry into the nature and effect of stage plays.
——— Letter respecting play actors.

Star of Bethlehem.

Callixti (Geo.) Historia Magorum.
Cellarii (Christ.) Diss. Academicæ.
Elswichius de Magis stella duce Bethlehem. profectis.
Olearii Adsertionum Philologicarum heptas.

Blackley's (T.) Sermons.
Gell's (R.) Remains.
Hall's (Bp.) Contemplations.
Hastings' (H. J.) Sermons.
Trench's (R. C.) Star of the wise men.

State Churches. See ESTABLISHMENTS.

State of Innocence.

Callixtus de Vario hominis statu.
Himmelii (Ioann.) Dissertationes.
Kippingii Exercitationes Sacræ.

State of Innocence—*continued.*

Mayeri (Io. Frider.) Dissertationes.
Meisneri (Balthas.) Dissertationes.
Osiandri (Luc.) Dissertationes.
Sontagii (Christoph.) Dissertationes.
Zeæmannus de Primo homine statu.

Am. Bibl. Repos. 2d Ser. 3:277. 6:1. 11:274.
Hale's (Sir M.) Primitive organization of mankind.
Pirie's Posthumous Works.
Princeton Rev. 16.67.

Steadfastness. See CONSTANCY, DECISION, INCONSTANCY.

Berriman's, William, Sermons.
Beveridge's, Bp., Sermons.
Bloomfield's, Bp., Sermons.
Cunningham's, J. W., Sermons.
French's, John, Sermons.
Fuller's, Andrew, Sermons.
Gisbourne's, Thomas, Sermons.
Hayward's Sermons.
Miller's, James, Sermons.
Newman's, J. H., Sermons.
Riddock's, James, Sermons.
Russell's, Alex. R., Sermons.
Tate's, Thomas, Sermons.
Wake's, Abp., Sermons.
Waterland's, Daniel, Sermons.
Watson's, Thomas, Sermons.
Wilder's, John, Sermons.
Young's, John, Sermons.

Stercorianists.

Bassnage, Histoire de l'Eglise.
Mabillon, Prefatio ad acta Benedictorum. Sec. IV.
Pfaffii (Christoph.) Dissertationes.

Stewardship. See PARABLES.

Stoicism.

Bruckeri Hist. philosoph. literariæ criticæ.
Fabricii (F. A.) Sylloge. (Every thing from the pen of Fabricius is erudite and critical.)
Klippel, Doctr. stoic. ethicæ atque Christ. exposit. et comparata.
Lescaloperii Commentarius in libros Ciceronis, etc. (An exhibit of the philosophy not only of Cicero, but of Homer, Thales, Pythagoras, Plato, Aristotle, Zeno, and many others.)
Lipsii Philosophia Stoica.
Meyeri Doct. Stoicorum ethica, cum Christ. comparata.
Sluiteri Idea theologiæ Stoicæ.

Brucker's History of Philosophy.
Burgess' (Bp.) Christianity of Stoicism.
Cudworth's Intel. system of the universe.
Duvaix's Moral philosophy of the Stoics.
Enfield's History of Philosophy.
Hume's (David) Essays.
James' Moral Philosophy of the Stoics. Bk. 1, chap. 4.
Tenniman's History of Philosophy.
Tiedmann's Syst. of the Stoical philosophy.
Ward's (Seth) Philosophical Essays.

Strife. See CONTENTION, PEACE.

Striving of the Spirit. See GRIEVING.

Study of Theology. See EDUCATION SOCIETIES, HISTORY OF DOCTRINES, MINISTERIAL EDUCATION, PROVINCE OF REASON, THEOLOGY.

Alihn's Einleitung in das studium d. Dogm.
Bartholini Consilium de stud. theologico.
Bebelii Methodus studii theologici.
Beck's (J. T.) Einleitung in d. system d. Chris. Lehre.
Bennetti Introd. in studium theol. syst.
Bertholdt's Theolog. Wissenschaftskunde.
Buddei Isagoge historico-theologica.
Bulfinger de Legibus studii theol.
Bullinger Ratio studiorum theologicorum.
Burmanni Consilium de studio theol.
Callisen's Anweisung für Theol. studirende.
Callixti Adparatus Theologicus.
Callovii Isagoge ad sacram theologiam.
Chytræus de Studio theologicæ recte.
Danz's Encyklop. und methodol. der theol. Wissenschaften.
Dorscheus de Conformatione studii theol.
Dupin, Methodus studii theologici.
Eckhardi Monita ad theol. stud. auspiciend.
Franckii (A. H.) Methodus studii theologici.
Franke (G. S.), Theolog. Encyklopädie.
Hagenbach's Encyklop. und methodol. d. theologische Wissenschaften.
Heideggeri Typus studii theologici.
Hulsemanni Methodus studii theologici.
Junius de Ortu, natura, formis, et modo, etc.
Melancthon, Ratio discendæ theologiæ.
Meyerus de Studio theologiæ.
Olearii Methodus theologici studii.
Osiandri Admonitiones.
Owen (J.), Theologoumena pantolapa.
Pfaffii Introd. ad historiam theologiæ.
Rambach's Wohlunterrichtete stud. Theol.
Reinhardus de Methodo studii theologici.
Welleri Consilium de stud. theol. rite instituendo et feliciter continuando.
Winer's Handbuch der theol. Literatur.

Barlow's (Bp.) Directory for the choice of books in the study of divinity. (Reaches only to 1690.)
Barrington's Sermons and Charges.
Bennet's Directions for studying Divinity.
Bentham's Reflections on the study of Div.
Bickersteth's Christian Student.
Bruce's (A.) Lectures to young men.
Christian Disciple. 2:233,417. 3:1,81,171.
Dodwell's Two letters of advice.
Dupin's Method of studying divinity.
Eclectic Review. N. S. 1:172.
Gleig's Letters from a bishop to his son.
Herder's Lectures on the study of theology.
Leighton's (Abp.) Prælectiones Theologicæ.
Marsh (Bp.) on Theological study.
Owen's (Henry) Directions for candidates.
Phillips' Study of sacred literature.
Plumptree's (E. H.) Sermons. (3 on this.)
Porteus' (Bp.) Letters to his clergy.

Study of Theology—*continued.*

Powell's (W. S.) Discourses.
Preston's Student's theological manual; compiled from standard authors.
Randolph's (Jno.) Enchiridium theologicum.
Rose (Hugh) on the Study of divinity.
Smith's (John) Select Discourses.
Tate's Suggestions to the theol. student.
Warburton's Directions for the study of theol.
——— Divine Legation of Moses. Bk. 9.
Wardsworth's (Chris.) Christian Institutes.
Waterland's Advice to a student.
Watts' (I.) Works. (Questions for students.)
Whiston's Advice for the study of divinity.
Williams' Christian Preacher.
Witherspoon's Works.
Wotton's Method of studying divinity.

Study of the Fathers. See USE.

Study of the Scriptures. See INTRODUCTIONS, READING THE SCRIPTURES.

Calmeti Prolegomena.
Delrii Pharus sacræ Scripturæ.
Drusii Animadversiones.
Ederi Œconomia Bibliorum.
Erasmus de Ratione studii, etc.
Gaussenius (Steph.) de Ratione studii, etc.
Gerhardi Methodus studii theologici.
Grotius de Studiorum ratione, etc.
Hardy, Biblia Græca, cum notis theol.
Hyperius de S. S. lectione et meditatione.
Le Long, Bibliotheca Sacra.
Ravenelii Thesaurus Scripturæ canonicæ.

Amory's (Thomas) Sermons.
Barker's (C.) Sermons.
Barlow's (Bp.) Remains.
Burder's Duty and means of ascertaining the genuine sense.
Byfield's Directions for the private reading of the Scriptures.
Campbell's Preliminary Dissertations.
Carington's (James) Sermons.
Christian Observer. 20:406,597.
Clarke's (Dr. A.) Clavis Biblica.
Clay's (John) Sermons.
Collyer's (David) Sacred Interpreter.
D'Oyly's (George) Sermons.
Dodwell's Letters of Advice.
Foster's (James) Sermons.
Fowle's (F. W.) Sermons.
Franck on the Study of the Scriptures. ("Full of good sense and piety."—DODDRIDGE.)
Fuller's Miscellanea Sacra.
Graves' (Richard) Sermons.
Irving's (Edward) Oracles of God.
Lee's (Prof. S.) Six Sermons. (Superior.)
Litton's Guide to the study, etc.
Lowth's Directions for the profitable reading. ("Very excellent."—ORME.)
Maturin's (C. R.) Sermons.
Nourse's (P.) Discourses.
Strype's Genuine remains of Dr. Lightfoot.
Wayland's (Francis) Discourses.

Style of Inspired Writers. See BIBLICAL CRITICISM, DIALECT OF THE NEW TESTAMENT, IDIOMS, PHILOLOGY.

Alberti Periculum criticum in Vet. et N. T.
——— Observationes Philologicæ.
Bebelius de Phrasi Nov. Test.
Beckii (F.) Observationes.
Beza de Dono linguæ, et apostol. sermone.
Boecleri Dissertatio de stylo N. Test.
Cocceus de Puritate linguæ Nov. Test.
Draudius de Stylo Nov. Testamenti.
Gataker (T.), Adversaria Miscellanea.
——— Dissertationes de stylo N. T.
Gaultheri Sylloge vocum exoticarum.
Georgii Vindiciæ N. T. ab Hebraismis.
Glassii Philologia Sacra. Lib. I and II.
Grinfield, Biblia Hellenistica.
Hoffman, de Stylo apost. Pauli.
Honerti Dissertationes de Stylo N. Test.
Hurgronje, de Parallelismo membror. in J. C. dictis observando.
Lamy, de Eruditione Apostolorum.
Leighii Annotationes in Nov. Testam.
Michaelis de Textu Nov. Test. Græco.
Morii Acroas. academ. sup. hermeneut. Nov. Test. (Valuable for containing the opinions on this subj. of various eminent writers.)
Mullerus de Stilo idiotico Nov. Test.
Olearius de Stylo Novi Testamenti.
Palairet, Observationes in Nov. Test.
Pfochenus de Stylo N. T. (Written to prove that there are no Hebraisms in the Greek Testament, but that the expressions so considered are purely classic!)
Planck de Vera, natura, et indole orationis N. Test.
Rhenferdi Dissertationes. (Collects the opinions of the best writers on this subject.)
Schwarzius in Solecismis Nov. Testamenti.
Solanus de Stilo Nov. Test.
Stephani Prefatio ad N. Test. (Sustains Beza in maintaining that the style of the Apostles is inimitably elegant.)
Stolbergii Exercitationes. (Points out what he considers the solecisms, barbarisms, &c., of the New Testament.)
Vorstius de Hebræismis N. T. Commentar.
Wyssii Dialectologia Sacra.

Amer. Biblic. Repos. 1:638.
[Black's (John)] Palæoromaica.
Blackwall's Sacred Classics. (Great.)
Boyle (Robt.) on the Style of Scripture.
Brown on the Characteristics, &c. Ess. 3.
Burnet on the 39 Articles.
Butler's Horæ Biblicæ.
Campbell's (Geo.) Preliminary Dissertations.
Edwards' (J.) Style and perfections, &c.
——— Exercitations.
Elwin's Style of the Scriptures considered.
Field's Edit. of the Septuagint. (Preface.)
Gataker's (Tho.) Dissertations. (Defends the purity of the New Testament from Hebraisms and Barbarisms.)
Jenkins' Reasonableness of Christianity.
La Mothe on Inspiration.

Style of Inspired Writers—*continued.*

Lowth on Inspiration.
——— Prelections.
Michaelis' Introduction; with Marsh's notes.
Nichols' Conference with a Deist.
Owen on Scripture.
Princeton Rev. 1:395.
Rymer on Revelation.
Spectator. No. 405.
Warburton's Doctrine of Grace.
Whitby's Preface to the New Testament.
Williams (Isaac) on the Study of the Script.
Winer's Greek Grammar of the New Test.

Stylites. See SIMONIANS.

Sublapsarians. See SUPRALAPSARIANS.

Submission. See RESIGNATION.

Submission to Kings. See MAGISTRACY, CIVIL GOVERNM'T, PASSIVE OBEDIENCE.

Subscription to Creeds.
See ESTABLISHMENTS, USE OF CREEDS.

Pro.

Abernethy's (John) Tracts and Sermons.
Balguy's (Thomas) Discourses.
Biddulph (Tho.) on the Oath of canonical obedience.
Burnaby's (And.) Sermons and Charges.
Burnet on the 39 Articles.
——— History of his own times.
Christian Observer. 1:92.
Clarke's (Jos.) Church of England vindicated. (Reply to Chandler.)
Clarke (S.) on the Trinity. (Introduction.)
Conybeare's (John) Sermons. (1 Tim. 6:3,4.)
Dunlop's Preface to the Scottish Confessions.
Dyer on the Nature of subscription.
Ellis' Plea for the Test.
Halifax's (Bp.) Sermons and Charges.
Hardy (S.) on Subscription to creeds.
Harvest's Defence of the Church of England.
Hebert (C.) on Clerical subscription.
Hey's (Will.) Tracts and Essays.
Ibbotson on Subscription to the 39 Articles.
Law (Edmund) on Requiring sub. to creeds.
London Quart. Rev. 116:231. 117:221.
Mozley (J.) on Subscription to creeds.
Napier's Letter to the Dean of St. Paul's.
Oulton's Vindication, &c. (Against Wesley.)
Paley's Moral Philosophy. Bk. 3, ch. 22.
——— on Requiring subscription to creeds.
Patrick (Bp.) on Conformity.
Powell (W. S.) on Subscription to creeds.
——— Reply to Blackburne.
Princeton Rev. 30:669.
Randolph on Subscription to creeds.
Rotherham on Religious Establishments.
Rutherforth's (T.) Visitation Charge.
——— Defence of the Charge.
——— Second Defence.
Toplady's Sermons.
——— Essay on subscription to creeds.
Tottie on the 39 Articles.
Tucker's Apology for the Ch. of England.

Subscription to Creeds—*continued.*

Pro.

Waterland's (D.) Case of Arian subscription considered.
——— Supplement to Do.
White's Letter to Mr. Chandler.

Con.

Bremensii Defensio denegatæ subscriptionis.

Benson's Hardship of subscription to creeds.
Blackburne's Remarks on Dr. P.'s discourse.
——— Confessional. (This powerful treatise gave rise to more than a hundred answers, for and against it.)
Bristed's Scripture the only text.
Cartwright's Admonit. to the people of Eng.
Cave on Human authority in matters of religion.
Chandler (Sam.) on Subs. to articles of faith.
Christian Disciple. 4:147.
Clayton (Robt.) on Subscription to creeds.
Dawson's (B.) Free and candid disquisition.
——— Short and safe expedient for terminating the controversy.
——— Examination of Dr. Rutherforth.
——— Letter to Dr. R., occasioned by his vindication, &c.
Durette on the Abuse of Confessions.
Dyer on Subscription to creeds.
Evans' Scripture Standard.
Firebrace's Letter to Ibbetson.
——— (Various other tracts.)
Fowne on the Principles of Toleration.
Frend's (Wm.) Thoughts on religious tests.
Furneaux's Letters to Judge Blackstone.
Gale's (Dr. John) Sermons.
Halliday (Sam.) on Subscription to creeds.
Heywood's Rights of Dissenters.
Hopkins' (Wm.) Letter to Dr. Tucker.
——— (Several other able tracts.)
Jebb's (John) Reasons for resigning, &c.
Jenkins' (Jos.) Dissenting minister's reasons for an application to Parliament, &c.
Jukes' (And.) Way which some call Heresy.
Kippis' Vindication of dissenting ministers.
Norman on Subscription to creeds.
Panoplist. 1:162.
Pearce on the Test Act.
Priestley's Sermons.
——— Considerations on church authority.
Radcliffe's (Eben.) Works.
Robinson's (Robt.) Miscellaneous Works.
Seagrave's Principles of liberty.
Talbot (Earl of Shrewsbury) on the Test oath.
Toulmin's Letters to dissenting ministers.
——— Letters to Dr. Sturges.
Wakefield's Addresses.
Williams' Earnest and serious address.
Wilton's Statement of some of the 39 articles.
Wollaston's Address to the clergy of England.

See a copious list of other authors on this subject in HORNE'S *Catalogue of Queen's College Library*. A full enumeration of the tracts on both sides of the controversy, up to

1775, was published anonymously by JOHN DISNEY. A large list of pamphlets and anonymous books may be found in the *Gentleman's Magazine*, vols. 41 and 42.

Substitution. See ATONEMENT, DEFINITE ATONEMENT, IMPUTATION, SACRIFICE, REDEMPTION, SUFFERINGS OF CHRIST.

Dreschlerus, An Ima gutta sanguinis Christi satisfacere potuerit pro peccatis totius mundi?

Boston's (Thomas) Works.
Clarke's (John) Sermons.
Fuller's (And.) Works. (Dialogue between Peter, James, and John.)
Gilbert (Joseph) on the Atonement.
Hall's (Robert) Sermons.
Hull's (W.) Discourses.
Kirkus' Christianity, theoret. and practical.
Lloyd's (J. C.) Sermons.
Lucas' (Richard) Sermons.
Morning Exercises at Cripplegate. (Sermon by M. Poole.)
Raphelius' Annotations on Rom. 5:8.
Robertson's (F. W.) Sermons.
Simeon's The Believer's security.
Stillingfleet's Sermons. (2 on this subject.)

Succoth Benoth. See JEWISH ANTIQ.

Crausii (J.) Dissertationes.
Ugolini (B.) Thesaurus antiq. sacrarum.

Sudden Death. See DEATH.

Burrows' (E. J.) Hours of devotion. ("Is a lingering or a sudden death to be preferred?")
Christian Observer. 18:499.
Dupree's (Dr. John) Discourses. (Advantages and disadvantages.)
Granville (A. B.) on Sudden death.
Harris' (Robert) Sermons.
Lucas' (Richard) Sermons.
Milner's (Joseph) Sermons.
Simeon's (C.) Works.

Sufferings of Christ.

Athanasii Homiliæ.
Bechmanni de Acerbissima Christi passione.
Bezæ Homiliæ in Histor. passionis Domini.
Blocksdorf's der Sohn Gottes unser Hoherpriester, etc.
Bugenhagii Conciliatio historia passionis et glorif. Christi.
Bullii Defensio fidei Nicenæ.
Bynæi Libri tres de Morte Jesu.
Dorscheus de Admirandis mortis Christi.
Feri Hist. passionibus Jesu Christi ex evangelistis. (A series of eloquent discourses.)
Haferungius De sanguine Jesu Christi.
Lyseri Paraphrasis in hist. passionis.
Mayeri (Jo. Frider.) Disputationes.
Mulleri (Hen.) Disputationes.
Quenstedtii (Ioann.) Dissertationes.
Sagittarii Harmonia hist. pass. J. C.

Amer. Bibl. Repos. 5:294.
Arnold's (Dr. Thomas) Sermons.

Sufferings of Christ—*continued.*

Baker's Sermons on the saintly character.
Balguy on Redemption.
Barrow's (Isaac) Sermons.
Bilson's Survey of Christ's sufferings.
Bloomfield's (Bp.) Sermons.
Charnock's Works.
Chenie's (J.) Meditations.
Clunie's (J.) Sufferings of Christ.
Cooper's (Edward) Sermons.
Coverdale's (Miles) Remains.
Davies' (Pres.) Sermons.
Dehon's (Bp.) Sermons.
Deyling's Sacred Observations.
Durer (A.) on the Sufferings of Christ.
Fleming's Christology.
Hacket's (Bp.) Five sermons.
Hall's (Bp.) Contemplations. (Precious.)
——— Sermons.
Hanna's (Wm.) Last days of our Lord.
Hewitt's Points of Christian doctrine.
Hopkins' (Benjamin) Sermons.
Jones' (Wm. of Nayland) Sermons.
Knowles on the Passion of Christ.
Krummacher's Suffering Saviour.
——— The Martyr Lamb.
Le Bas' (Cha. W.) Sermons.
Milner's (Joseph) Sermons.
Milner's (Isaac) Sermons.
Pearson on the Apostles' Creed.
Porteus' (Bp.) Sermons.
Priestley's History of early opinions.
Rambach's Meditations.
Sandford's (Bp.) Lectures. (Very popular.)
Scott's Christian Life.
Stanhope's (Dean) Holy Week.
Stillingfleet on the Sufferings of Christ.
Sturm's Contemplations.
Tholuck's Light from the cross.
Williams' (Griffith) Sermons.
Williams (I.) on our Saviour's passion.
Wilson's (Bp.) Sermons.

Sufficiency of God.

Barrow's (Isaac) Works.
Harris' Pre-Adamite Earth.
——— Man primæval.
Ridgeley's Body of Divinity.
Saurin's Sermons.

Suggestions of Satan. See SATAN, TEMPTATION.

Suicide.

Demas, Traité de Suicide.
Puffendorf de Jure. Lib. II, cap. IV.
Reinardi Opuscula Academica.
Robeck de Ευλογω Εξαγωγη.

Adams' (John) Essay on Self-murder.
Am. Whig Rev. 6:137.
Ayscough's (Francis) Sermons.
Booker's (Dr. Luke) Sermons.
Clarke on Natural and revealed religion.
Denny's (Sir Wm.) Pelecanicidium.
De Stael (Madam) on Suicide.
Doddridge's Lectures. Part 3, prop. 8.

Suicide—*continued.*

Donne (John) on Self-homicide. (Maintains it to be not invariably sinful.)
Dwight's System of Theology. Ser. 117.
Eclectic Museum. 3:395.
Edinb. Rev. 21:424.
Fleetwood's (Bp.) 3 Sermons on self-murder.
Francis' (Dr. John) Sermons.
Grove's Moral Philosophy.
Hey's (Richard) Dissertations.
Hume's Essays.
Jeffery's (Dr. John) Sermons and Tracts.
Knagg on Self-murder.
Knox's (Vicessimus) Sermons.
Matthews' (G.) Sermons.
Miller's (Joseph) Sermons.
Montesquieu's Spirit of laws.
Monthly Rev. 118:159.
More (C.) on Suicide. (Admirable.)
Paley's Moral Philosophy. Bk. 4, chap. 3.
——— Sermons.
Pamphleteer. 23:365.
Pearce's (Bp.) Sermons.
Piggott's Suicide and its antidotes. (A series of actual narratives.)
Plotinus on Suicide. Trans. by T. Taylor. (With notes from Porphyry, Proclus, and Olympiodorus.)
Prince's Self-murder a heinous crime.
Ryland's (John) Discourses. (On Ex. 20:13.)
Smith's (Sydney) Sermons.
Stevens' (Dr. W.) Sermons.
Toogood's (Charles) Sermons.
Turner's (Lewis) Sermons.
Vaughn's (Cha. John) Sermons.
Watts' Defence against temptations to S.
Winckler on Suicide.
Winslow's Anatomy of suicide.
Wrangham's (Francis) Sermons.

Sulpicius (Severus).

Breithauptii (Christ.) Dissertationes.
Le Clerc, Remarques sur la vie de Sulpice.
Tricautii Vita et scriptis Sulpicii.
Welleri Diss. de perpetui silentii votum.

Sunday. See LORD'S DAY.

Sunday Laws. See LORD'S DAY, SABBATH.

Fisher's History of the Sabbath day.
McFarlane on the Sabbath.
Princeton Rev. 31:733.

Sunday Schools.

Alexander's (J. W.) S. S. and its adjuncts.
Am. S. S. Magazine. Periodical. Philad.
American S. S. Union Reports.
Amer. Quar. Register. (Valuable statistics.)
Barclay's (Hugh) Thoughts on S. Schools.
Brit. Quar. Rev. 5:491.
Christian Examiner. 53:387.
Chris. Month. Spect. 1:346,403.
Chris. Quar. Spect. 2:425. 9:457.
Church of Eng. S. S. Quarterly. 1848 to pres.
Eclectic Rev. 4th Series. 15:304.
Gilbert's Christian Benevolence.

Sunday Schools—*continued.*

Hart's (John S.) Thoughts on S. Schools.
Hill's (Rowland) Apology for S. Schools.
James' Sunday School Teacher's guide.
Knowles (Dr.) on Charity and S. Schools.
Lloyd's Teacher's Manual. (Very useful.)
McCrae's Address to S. S. children.
New Englander. 5:162.
Princeton Rev. 8:96. (Books.)
Raikes, Life of; by W. F. Lloyd.
Southern Lit. Messenger. 4:224.
Sunday School Times. Periodical. Phila.
Todd's Sunday School Teacher.
Tyng's Forty years' experience in S. S.
Watson's History of the S. S. Union. 1853.
Wilson's (Bp.) Sermons.

Sun standing still.

Aberbanel de Miraculosa statione solis.
Abichtii (Ioann. Geo.) Dissertationes.
Alexander (N.), Historia Ecclesiastica.
Alexander (F.) Dissertationes. Diss. 13.
Calmet, Dissertations.
Deylingii (D. S.) Observationes.
Didièr, Dissertations. Diss. 22.
Werchau, de Statione solis; Josh. 10:12.

Am. Bibl. Repos. 4:721. (Hengstenberg.)
Bryant's Observ. on some passages of S. S.
Calmet's Diss. Prefixed to Com. on Joshua.
Collyer's Lectures on miracles. Lec. 6.
Cowie's Hulsean Lectures. 1853.
D'Oyly's (George) Sermons.
Kitto's Journ. 3:136. 4:148. 5:225. 6:208,459.
Oakes (A.) on the Sun standing still.
Rawlinson's Bampton Lectures. 1859.
Reading's (William) Sermons.

Supererogation. See GOOD WORKS, JUSTIFICATION, POPERY.

Smythæi de Missæ sacrificio enarratio.

Chauncey's Doctrine according to godliness.
Coles on Divine sovereignty.
Hey's (Dr. John) Lectures. Bk. 4.
Leighton's Meditations on the 130th Psalm.
Moore's Grand mystery of godliness.
Morning Exercises at Cripplegate. (Sermon by Tho. Lye.)

Superstition. See APPARITIONS.

Baumgarten-Crusii Theses Theologicæ.
Bonnet de Causis S. inter Christianos.
Buddæi Theses Theologicæ.
Crusius (C. A.) de Dissimilitudine inter religionem et superstitionem.
Encyclopedie Theologique.
Gerson contra Superstitiosos dierum observ.
Le Brun, Hist. des practiques superstitieuse.
Matthæi Analecta veteris ævi.
Picart, Superstit., Anciennes et Modernes.
Thier, Traité des Superstitions.
Werenfels (S.), Dissertations.

Am. Quar. Rev. 3:423.
Atterbury's (Lewis) Sermons.
Bigland's Essays. Ess. 6.
Blakeman's (Dr. E.) Philosophical Essays.

Superstition—*continued.*

Blackwood's Mag. 3:188. (Welch.) 47:553. (Modern.) 61:368,432,541,547,673. 62:166.
Brown's Vulgar Errors.
Buck's (Cha.) Religious Anecdotes.
Calvin (John) on Relics.
Chandler's (Dr. Samuel) Discourses.
Cheke, Life of; by Strype.
Claude on the Composition of a sermon.
Cooke's (John) Sermons.
Delolme's Memorial of Superstition.
Dodwell's (Will.) Sermons.
Durand's (Jas. F.) Sermons. Translated by Munkhouse.
Durant's Memoirs of an only son.
Edwards' (Bp.) Theologia Reformata. (On the 1st commandment.)
Evans' Unhappy effects of superstition.
Fellowes' (Robt.) Religion without cant.
For. Quar. Rev. 2:556. (Naples.)
Foster's (John) Contributions to the Eclectic Review.
Fox's Book of Martyrs.
Frazier's Mag. 11:218. 73:705.
Grant's Superstitions of the Highlanders.
Graves' (Richard) Sermons.
Gregory's Essays. Ess. 3.
Hewlett's (John) Sermons.
Hoadley's (Bp.) Sermons.
Hospinian on Popery.
Ibbot's (Benjamin) Sermons.
Leighton's (Abp.) Sermons. (Sermon on Heavenly Wisdom.)
Limborch's Theologia Christiana.
Littell's Living Age. 13:105,518. 14:83. 22:423.
Lowell's (Samuel) Sermons.
McDonald (J. M.) on Credulity.
Manningham's Nature and effects of S.
Marshall's (N.) Sermons.
Museum of For. Lit. 3:372. (Popular.) 15:299. (Italian.) 26:15. (Scotch.)
Naylor's Insanity and mischief of vulgar S.
Newnham's Effects of physical influence on the mind, in producing visions, &c.
North Amer. Rev. 34:198.
Orr's (John) Sermons.
Pagitt's Christianography.
Payne's (W.) Discourses.
Quar. Rev. 29:440.
Radcliffe's Fiends, Ghosts, and Spirits.
Retrospective Rev. 11:66. (Welch.)
Riddle's Bampton Lectures. 1852.
Saurin's Sermons.
Shelton's (William) Discourses.
Skinner's Attempt to discover truth.
Smedley's Traditions and S. of past times.
Southern Lit. Mess. 2:198. 8:1,169. (Maltese Superstitions.)
Stillingfleet's (Bp.) Sermons.
Taswell on Superstition.
Trenchard's Natural history of superstition.
Voltaire on Toleration.
Warburton's Divine legation of Moses.
Westminster Review. 17:382.

Support of Ministers.
See ESTABLISHMENTS, MINISTRY.

Barnaby's (A.) Sermons.
Hutcheson's (Francis) Moral Philosophy.
Mede's (Joseph) Works.
Princeton Review. 11:180.
Rees on the Maintenance of ministers.
Spry (John) on Ministerial maintenance.

Suppression of the Jesuits.

Collombet, Hist. de la suppresion, etc.
D'Alembert, La destruction d. J. en France.
St. Priest, Hist. de la chute des J.
Wolf's (P. P.) Geschichte der Jesuiten.
D'Alembert's Destruc. of the J. in France.
Steinmetz's History of the Jesuits. To 1848.

Supralapsarians. See DECREES, FALL, GRACE, SYNOD OF DORT.

Pro.

Bezæ Opuscula.
Calvini Opera.
Maccovii Questiones Theologicæ.
Naude's Theologische Gedancken über den Entwurf, etc.
Viti Apologia.
Voetii Exerc. studiosi theologiæ.
——— Disputationes Theologicæ.
Brine (John) on the Supralapsarian scheme.
Gill's (John) God's everlasting love.
——— Truth defended.
Twisse's Riches of God's love.
——— Vindication of grace.

Con.

Amyrald, Traité de la predestination.
Capelli Prelectiones Theologicæ.
Davenant, Dissertationes de morte Christi.
Drusii Confutatio Viti litigationum.
Hochsetteri Schediasma philos.-theologicum.
Mosheim de Auctoritate concil. Dordraceni.
Œderi Responsio ad S. Viti librum.
Placette, Eclairciss. sur quelques diffic.
Spanheim de Gratia et libero arbitrio.

Most Calvinistic writers reject supralapsarian views.

Supremacy of the Pope.
See TEMPORAL POWER.

Pro.

Bellarmini Opera.
Cenni Monumenta. (A full collection of documents relating to this subject.)
Chamieri Disputationes.
Dupanloup, La Souveraineté pontificale.
Eckius de Primatu Petri.
Marcæ (P.) Dissertationes.
Mathieu, Le Pouvoir temporel, etc.
Rocaberti Bibliotheca. (A collection of 120 treatises.)
Zacaria, Anti Febronius.
Kenrick's (Bp.) Primacy of the Pope.

Con.

Barclai de Potestate Papæ.
Blondell de Primatu en l'eglise.
Brockmandi Dissertationes.

Supremacy of the Pope—*continued.*

Cameronis Opera Theologica.
Cranmeri (Abp.) Opera.
Dominis, de Repub. Ecclesiastica.
Febronius [Bp. Hontheim] de Statu ecclesiæ.
——— Gouvernement de l'eglise.
Gieseler's Kirchengeschichte.
[Gosselin,] Pouvoir du Pope au moyen age.
Gualtheri Problemata.
Heideggeri Historia Papatus.
——— Diatribe.
Hugo de St. Victor, Opera.
Huss (John), de Ecclesia.
Lubbertus de Papa Romana.
Mornæi Historia Papatus.
Neigebauer, der Papst und sein Reich.
Schroeck's Kirchengeschichte.

Barrow (Isaac) on the Sup. of the Pope.
——— Sermons.
Barwick (Edw.) on the Church.
Berriman's (Will.) Sermons.
Clarendon's Religious and civil policy.
Clenche on the Supremacy of St. Peter.
Donne's Pseudo-Martyr. (Unanswerable.)
Geddes' Miscellaneous Tracts.
Hawkins' (T.) Power of the Pope.
Hey's (J.) Lectures. Bk. 4.
James (King of Eng.) on the S. of the Pope.
McCaul on Papal Supremacy.
Neal on the Supremacy of Peter.
Stephenson's (Geo.) Romish Church.

Swearing. See OATHS, PERJURY, PROFANENESS, THIRD COMMANDMENT.

Swedenborgianism. See NEW JERUSALEM CHURCH.

Symbolical Language. See FIGURATIVE LANGUAGE, TYPES.

Symmetry of Character. See CONSISTENCY, HARMONY.

Sympathy. See MOURNERS, PASSIONS.

Gaskin's (John) Sermons.
Greene's (Samuel) Sermons.
Mariott's (Harvey) Sermons.
Newnham's Tribute of sympathy.
Priestley's (Joseph) Essays.
Rees' (Abrm.) Practical Sermons.
Simeon's (C.) Works.
Slade's (James) Sermons.
Stevens' Person, char., and gov't of Christ.
Summerfield's (John) Sermons.
Tottie's (John) Sermons.
Trench's (Francis) Sermons.

Synagogue. See JEWISH ANTIQUITIES.

Cyril Alex., de Judæorum synagoga.

Benzelius de Synedrio magno Rabbinorum.
Bucher, Synedrium magnum. (Ugolinus.)
Clodius de Synagogis Judæorum.
Dassovii (T.) Dissertationes.
Hold, de Synagogis Judæorum.
Le Clerc, de Synedrio LXX virorum.
Polemanni (N.) Dissertationes.

Synagogue—*continued.*

Rhenferdi (J.) Dissertationes.
Sauberti (J.) Dissertationes.
Vitringæ Dissertationes.
Vorstii (Ioann.) Dissertationes.
Witsii Miscellanea Sacra.

Bassnage's History of the Jews.
Harby on the Jewish Synagogue.
Neander's Planting of Christianity.
Smyth's Prelacy and Presbytery.
Whately's Kingdom of Christ. (Appendix.)

Syncretists. See INDIFFERENTISTS.

Bruckeri Historia critica Philosophiæ.
Buscheri Crypto-papismus novæ theologiæ Helmstadiensis.
Callixti (Fred. U.) Opera.
Callixti (Geo.) Disputationes. (The originator of this once important controversy.)
Callovii (Abrah.) Dissertationes.
Cass' Callixtus und der Syncretismus.
Danhaveri Disputationes Theologicæ.
Ketneri Exercitationes.
Kromayeri Loci anti-syncretistici.
Niceron, Memoires des hommes illustres.
Perei Irenicon.
Placcii Theatrum pseudonymorum.
Postelli Opera.
Rangonis Hist. syncretismi a mundo condito.
Scharfii Protestatio adversus Callixtum.
Schmid's (H.) Geschichte der syncretischen Streitigkeiten in d. Zeit d. G. Callixt.
Schröckh's Kirchengeschichte seit der Ref.
Strauchii (Ægid.) Dissertationes.
Thomasii Orationes.
Zentgravii (Io. Ioach.) Dissertationes.

Synergists.

Alvarez de Auxiliis divinæ gratiæ.
Arnoldi Hist. ecclesiastica. Lib. 16, c. 29.
Bezæ Vita Calvini.
Flacii Dissertationes.
Leuckfeldii Hist. Spangenbergensis.
Melancthoni Opera et vita.
Micrælii Syntagma hist. ecclesiastica.
Musæi Prelectiones in Formulam Concordiæ.
Salig, Hist. August. confessionis.
Strigelii (Victor.) Opera.

Bayle's Dictionary. Art. *Synergists*, and *Strigelius.*

This controversy, confined almost to Germany, brought out a host of writers. Those who wish to examine further, may consult ARNOLD, CAROLUS, WALCH, and WEISMAN; and especially the third volume of *Cimbria Litterata*, by MOLLERUS; in each of which there are plenty of other writers named.

Synods. See COUNCILS, DORT.

Acta Synodi Dordrecht.
Acta Synodalia ministrorum Remonstrant.
Acta Synodi nationalis eccles. Belgicarum.
Amesii Anti-Synodalia.
Aymon de Synodes nationaux des Eglises Réformées de France. To 1710.

Synods—*continued.*

Corpus de Syntagma conf. fidei quæ in diversis nationibus fuerint edita, in celeberrimus Conventionibus.
Gomari Opera. (Chiefly Synod of Dort.)
Hilarii Opera.
Ittigii Hist. Synodorum in Gallia.
Le Long, Bibliotheca Historica Galliæ.
Linwood, Provinciale. (Synods in England.)
Mansi Collectio nova.
Peterfy, Concilia in regno Hungariæ.
Saens, Collectio Concil. Hispaniæ.
Sirmondi Concilia Galliæ.
Spelmanni Concilia Brittanica.
Wilkins, Concilia magnæ Britt. et Hiberniæ.
Cardwell's Synodalia. (Gives the Canons, &c., in the province of Canterbury, from 1547 to 1717; with notes.)
—— Annals of the Reformed Church of England.
Hody's English councils and convocations.
Joyce's Hist. of all the councils held in Eng.
Quick's Synodicon. (Acts, Decisions, &c., of the Reformed Churches in France.)
Sparrow's Canons of the Church of England.
Wilkins' Councils of Britain and Ireland.

Synonyms. See PARALLELISMS.

Brissonius de Verborum significatione.
Iohlson's Biblisch-Hebräisches Wörterbuch.
Reuschi Syrius interpretes, cum fonte N. T.
Roubard, Synonymes.
Bennet's Concordance of Bible synonyms.
Biblical Cabinet. Vol. 4.
Campbell's (Geo.) Dissertations.
Lond. Quart. Review. 7:406.
Tittman's Synonyms of the N. T. Trans. by E. Craig. (All that a student needs, as to the New Testament.)
Trench's Synonyms of the New Testament.
——— ——— Second Series. 1863.
Trussler's Distinction between words that seem synonymous.

Syriac Version.

Adleri Nov. Test. versiones Syriacæ.
Bocharti (Sam.) Opera.
Breytherus de Vi quam antiquissimæ vers. habeant.
Cawtoni Disputationes.
Erpenii Psalmi Davidis lingua Syriaca.
Fabricii (Joh. A.) Bibliotheca Græca.
Fabricii (Iohan.) Historia Bibliothecæ Fabricianæ.
Gerhard, Exercitatio ad N. T. Syr. spectans.
Hirzelii de Indole comment. crit.-exegetica.
Kirsch, Pentat. Syr. ex polyglot. Angl. edid.
Lee (Prof.) Vet. Testamentum Syriacum.
Michælis, Curæ in vers. Syr. actuum apost.
Middledorpfii Codex Syriaco-Hexaplaris.
Norbergii Codex Syriaco-hexaplaris Ambros. Mediolanensis.
Ridley de Syriaca N. Test. versione.
Schaffii Nov. Testamentum Syriacum.
Storr, Observationes super N. Test.

Syriac Version—*continued.*

White, Sac. Evangelium, versio Syriaca. ("An accurate text and version."—ORME.)
——— Actuum Apost. et Epist. catholicar.
Widmanstadt, Liber sacros evanglii ling. S.
Winer de Vers. N. T. Syr. usu critico.
Butler's Horæ Biblicæ.
Journal of Amer. Oriental Soc. Vol. 2.
Murdock's Trans. of the Syriac N. Testam.
Oliver's Trans. of the S. vers. of the Psalms.

Syrian Christians. See JACOBITES, MONOPHYSITES, NESTORIANS, &c.

Assemanni Biblioth. Orientalis. (Furnishes all we need to know on this subject.)
Christian Observer. 16:302.
Etheridge's Syrian Churches. 1846. (Embraces the historical literature, &c.)
Hough's History of Christianity in India.
Robinson's Later Biblic. Researches. 1854.
Southgate's Visit to Mesopotamia, and the present state of Christ'y in Turkey. 1844.

Systematic Theology. See THEOLOGY.

Tabernacle.

Clemens (H. G.) Dissertationes.
Habichhorstii Thesaurus.
Ham, Exercit. philol. sacræ.
Hasæi (T.) Dissertationes.
Lamy, de Tabernac. fœd., et de templo.
Peringeri Historia Tabernaculi Mosaici.
Rau (J. E.), Dissertationes Sacræ.
Van Till, Commentarius de Tabernac. Mosis.
Witsii Miscellanea Sacra.
Ziegra Thesaurus theolog. Philologica.
Herschell's (R. H.) Golden Lamp.
Mudge's (Wm.) Sixteen discourses.
Newton's Jewish T. in its typical teachings.
Rhind's (W. G.) Tabernacle in the wilderness.
Soltau's Exposition of the tabernacle.

Taborties. See HUSSITES.

Tale-Bearing. See DETRACTION.

Fawcett's (John) Sermons.
Frost's (R.) Sermons.
Ridgeley's Body of Divinity.

Talmuds. See CABALA.

Talmud Babylonicum. (Various editions. One in 1760, 15 vols., fol. One in 1846, 24 vols., 8vo. A translation of the first part was issued in German, by Pinner, in 1842.)
Talmud Hierosolymitanum. (Has never all been published uniformly. Separate portions are common, and have been commented on extensively.)
Mishna: Sive totius Hebræor. juris, rituum, ac legum oralium, Systema.
Bashuisen, Clavis Talmudica.
Ben Boas, Commentaria in T. Babylonici.
Cocceii [or Kock] Sanhedrim et Maccoth. cum versione et commentariis.

Talmuds—*continued.*

Goldenthal (J.), Clavis Talmudica.
Jeshuæ Clavis Talmudica.
Joma, Codex Talmudicus.
Lewysohn's Zoologie des Talmuds.
Lightfoot, Horæ Hebr. et Talmudicæ.
Maimonides Peruschim.
——— Yad Hachazaka. (A compend of the decisions of the Rabbis.)
Rabe's Talmudische tractat. Brachoth.
Samuel's (Rabbi) Agadoth. ("A subtle and acute commentary on the Jerusalem Talmud."—WOLF.)
Schœtgenii Horæ Hebraicæ et Talmudicæ.
Wineri Chrestomathia Talmud. et Rabbin.

Butler's Horæ Biblicæ.
Mishna. Eighteen treatises. Translated by De Sola & Raphall. (The only English translation.)
Stehelin's Traditions of the Jews. ("Curious and melancholy."—ORME.)
Wotton on the Usages of the Scribes and and Pharisees, in the time of Christ.

Targum. See CHALDEE PARAPHRASE.

Taste. See RHETORIC.

Bouterwick's Æsthetik.
Dacier, les Causes de la corruption du gout.

Alexander on Taste.
Alison's Nature and principles of taste.
Amer. Bibl. Repos. 3d Series. 3:524.
Amer. Eclectic Rev. 4:38.
Blackwood's Mag. 13:385. 14:672.
Blair's Lectures on Rhetoric.
British and For. Rev. 13:1.
Burke on the Sublime and Beautiful.
D'Alembert on the Use and Abuse of Philosophy in matters of Taste.
Edinburg Rev. 7:307. 18:1.
Fisgrave's (Anthony) Midas.
Gerard on the Principles of Taste.
Gregory (Geo., D.D.), Letters on Literature.
Hegel's Æsthetics.
Hogarth's Elements of beauty.
Kames' Elements of criticism.
Knickerbocker Mag. 24:103.
Knight's Analysis of the principles of Taste.
Knox's (Alex.) Remains. (Appendix.)
Longinus on the Sublime.
McDermot's (Martin) Critical Dissertation.
McKensie's Taste founded on Association.
Montesquieu's Productions of taste in nature and art.
North Amer. Rev. 7:1.
Payne's (Rich.) Principles of taste.
Pope's Essay on Criticism.
Princeton Rev. 21:251.
Savarin's Physiology of Taste.
Spectator. From No. 411 to No. 422.
Warton's History of Poetry.
Westminster Rev. 53:1.

Tatian.

Tatiani Harmonia Evangelica.

Tatian—*continued.*

Tatiani Oratio ad Græcos.
(Of the numerous works of Tatian, only these are extant. There is no English translation of either. Whether he wrote the harmony is doubtful.)
Longerve, (Ludovic. de Tour) Dissertationes.
Nourry, (Nicol.) Dissertationes.
Tentzellii Exercitationes Selectæ.
Vogtii (Ioann.) Bibliotheca.

Conybeare's Bampton Lectures. 1839.
Lardner's Credib. of the gospel hist. Part 2.

Temperament.

Combe on the Management of infants.
New York Review. 8:74.
Stokes' (Wm.) Theory and pract. of physic.

Temperance. See DRUNKENNESS.

American Almanac. 1830, p. 125.
American Monthly Rev. 2:45.
Amer. Quart. Observer. 1:58. 3:46.
Arthur's Ten nights in a bar-room.
——— Temperance Tales.
Baker's Intemp. the idolatry of Gt. Britain.
Baird's Hist. of Temp. Societies. To 1836.
Beecher's (Lym.) Sermons. (Very effective.)
Browne on Drinking healths.
Brownrig's (Bp.) Sermons.
Buckingham's History and progress of the Temperance Reformation in Gt. Britain.
Burne's Teetotaller's Companion.
Campbell (G.) on Temperance and self-denial.
Carpenter's Physiology of temperance.
Christ. Disciple. 1:55. 2:207. 4:235. 5:446.
Christ. Examiner. 3:291. 5:209. 9:236. 12:243. 14:24. 31:243.
Christ. Monthly Spect. 9:587,645. 10:243.
Christian Observer. 1:430.
Christ. Quart. Spect. 6:371,593.
Chubb's Results of prohibition in Connec't.
Church of England Temp. Mag. London.
Couling's Maine law the only hope of Engl.
Cross' History of the T. reformation.
De Bow's Commercial Rev. 13:397.
Dodwell's (William) Sermons.
Drake (D.) on Intemperance.
Dunlop's Compulsory drinking usages.
Dyke's (Oswald) Sermons.
Eclectic Rev. 4th Series. 10:313.
Edinburg Total Abstinence Soc. Reports.
Edwards' Temperance Manual.
Ellis' Hist. of the order of the "Sons of T." from its organization. 1842.
Encyclop. Americana. (History of the Ref.)
Encyclopedia of Religious Knowledge.
Gregory's (George) Sermons.
Grindrod's Bacchus. (A Prize Essay.)
Guthrie's Plea in behalf of drunkards.
Harwood's (Dr. Ed.) Treatise on T. 1774.
Hitchcock on Dyspepsia.
Journal of Am. Temperance Union.
Journal of Health. Periodical.
King (Bp.) on the Great evil of the prevailing custom of drinking healths. 1716.

Temperance—*continued.*

Knickerbocker Mag. 1828.
Lee's Argument for legislative prohibition. London. 1856.
Limborch's Christian Theology.
McNish's Anatomy of Drunkenness.
Meth. Quarterly Rev. 2:91.
Miller's (J.) Alcohol; its place and power.
——— Nephalism; the temperance of Scripture, science, and experience.
Morewood's Philos. history of inventions, ancient and modern, in the making and use of inebriating liquors.
Nott's (Eliphalet) Lectures.
N. Am. Rev. 36:188. 39:494.
Panoplist. (Many articles.)
Parsons' Anti-Bacchus.
Permanent Temperance Documents. By the American Temperance Society.
Princeton Rev. 13:267,471.
Proceedings of the World's Temperance Convention. London.
Prynne's (Wm.) Great evil of health-drinking. 1684.
Rush's (Benj.) Works.
Sargeant's Temperance Tales.
Scottish T. League Register. Periodical.
Temperance Recorder.
Temperance Herald.
Temperance Intelligencer.
Temperance Journal.
Temperance Almanacs.
Temperance Documents. (A vol. of important papers, pub. by the Amer. Tract Society.)
The Prohibitionist. Periodical. New York.
Thompson (J. P.) on the Christian graces.
Tryon's Way to health, long life, and happin.
Tucker's Light of nature pursued. Ch. 32.
Tweddie on Temperance and Exercise.
U. S. Literary Gazette. 4:331. 6:184.
Wayland's (Pres.) Discourses.
White's (P. S.) War of 4000 years. (History of efforts to suppress intemperance.)
Wisdom's Voice to the rising generation.
Wooler's Philosophy of Temperance.

Temple of Ezekiel.

Haffenrefferi Templum Ezechielis.
Mayeri Dissertationes.
Radi Commentatio in Ezechielem.
Ricardus de Templo Ezechielis.
Sturmii Sciagraphia templi.
Venemæ Lectiones Academicæ.
Villalpandi in Ezechielem Explicationes.
Vitringæ Dissertationes.

Bennet's (Solomon) Temple of Ezekiel.

Temple of Jerusalem.
See JERUSALEM, JEWISH ANTIQUITIES.

Bähr, der Mosaischen Kultus.
Capelli Templi Hierosolymitani Delineatio.
Hospinianus de Origine, progressu, usu, et abusu Templorum.
Keil's Tempel: eine archäol. Untersuchung.
Kirchner's Tempel d. Juden zu Jerusalem. (Extensive and valuable.)

Temple of Jerusalem—*continued.*

Kopp's (E.) der Tempel Salomons.
Lightfoot, Descriptio templi Hierosol.
Maimonides de Constitutione T. vasis, etc.
Opitii Dissertationes.
Relandi Prolusiones. (Notes by Schulze.)
Schlichteri (C. L.) Dissertationes.
Spencer, de Legibus Hebræorum.
Ugolini (B.) Dissertationes.

Bunyan's Solomon's temple spiritualized.
Lee's (Samuel) Orbis miraculum.
Lightfoot's Temple and temple service in the time of Christ.
Newton's (Sir I.) Description of the Temple.
Outram on Sacrifices.

Temporal Benefits of Christianity.
See INFLUENCE OF CHRISTIANITY.

Temporal Power of the Pope.
See SUPREMACY.

Pro. Most Papal writers take the affirmative on this question. The following contain the strength of the argument.

Bellarmin de Potestate Pontificis.
Bozzius de Monarchia Ecclesiæ.
Carrerius de Potestate Pontificis.
Grassii Opuscula.
Maimbourg, Traite des prerogatives de l'eglisse et ses eveques.
Sanctarellus de Hæresi, Scismate, etc.
Sanderus de Visibili eccles. monarchia.
——— de Militantis eccles. potestate.
Stephanus de Potestas coactiva, etc.

Con.

Alban's Pæbstische Anatomie.
Banckius de Tyrannide Papæ.
Barclaius (G.) de Potestate Papæ.
——— de Puissance du Pape.
Buckeridge de Potestate Papæ.
Crakanthorpii Defensio ecc. Anglicanæ.
Dresseri Observationes Miscellaneæ.
Evenii Demonstratio apologetica.
Goebelii [vel Gibelini] Cæsareo-papia Rom.
Gosselin, Pouvoir du Pape au moyen age.
Guicciardinus de Origine potestat. secularis.
Henricus VIII de Primatu Romani Pontif.
Lairitz's Rœmischer Papsts Thron.
Mollinæus de Monarchia Pontificis.
Pressense, Le pouvoir temporel, est il nécessaire?
Siricii Idolum Papale.
Steinbergii Anatome Papismi.
Tillii Christi vicariorum exempla.

Bray's Papal usurpation and persecution.
Christian Examiner. 69:40.
Döllinger's The Church and the Churches.
[Gosselin's] Power of the Pope in the middle ages. Tr. by M. Kelly. (The origin of his temporal power, his deposition of sovereigns, &c.)
North British Rev. 11:135. 12:76,141.

Many hundred volumes on this controversy have been published, but few are now extant, and some of the above are rare. The subject has been disputed in the Roman Church itself, ever since the assumption of this power; and many of its greatest writers, such as Bossuet, Dupin, De Marca, and Natalis, have denied it.

Temptation. See WATCHFULNESS.

Chrysostom, Homiliæ.

Acontius de Stratagematibus Satanæ.
Fechtius de Suggestionibus Satanæ.
Gerson de Diversis Diaboli temptationibus.

Abernethy's (Bp.) Sermons.
Atterbury's (Lewis) Sermons.
Balguy's (John) Sermons.
Barry's (J.) Reviving Cordial.
Bolton's Instruct. for afflicted consciences.
Boston's Crook in the lot. (Excellent.)
Brooks' Precious remedies against Satan's devices.
Capel's Nature, danger, and cure of T.
Cecil's (Richard) Sermons.
Christ. Disciple. 3:106.
Clarke's (Samuel) Sermons.
Farmer on Temptation.
Flavel on Keeping the heart.
Gillespie's Treatise on Temptation.
Gilpin's (Rich.) Demonologia Sacra. (Exc't.)
Graves' (Richard) Sermons.
Gurnall's (Wm.) Christian Armor.
Haynes' Illustrations of faith and practice.
Hickes' (Geo.) Sermons.
Jackson's (Miles) Sermons.
Kattern's (Daniel) Sermons.
Kirk's (John) Trials of the heart.
Littell's Living Age. 11:522,545.
Luther's (Martin) Sermons.
Marshall's (Nathaniel) Sermons.
Mason on Self-knowledge. Chap. 8.
Montgomery's (Robt.) God and Man.
Mountain's (J. H. B.) Sermons.
Owen's (John) Works.
Parsons' (Will. L.) Satan's devices.
Porteus' (Bp.) Sermons.
Ransom's Treatise on Temptation.
Robertson's (F. W.) Sermons at Brighton.
Scattergood's (Samuel) Sermons.
Scobel's (Edward) Sermons.
Skelton's (Philip) Sermons.
Smith's (Sydney) Sermons.
South's (Robt.) Seven Sermons on Temptat.
Sparstow's Wiles of the Devil.
Taylor's (Jer.) Life of Christ. Ch. 5.
Trapp's (Joseph) Sermons.
Ward's (Richard) Sermons.
Wesley's (John) Sermons.
Wharton's Manifold T. of Christians.
Whately's Good and evil Angels.
Williston's Sermons.

Temptation of Christ.

Deylingii Observationes Sacræ.

Andrews (Bp.) on Import. passages of Scrip.
Bagot's T. of Christ in the wilderness.
Barret's (J. T.) T. of Christ in the wilderness.

Temptation of Christ—*continued.*

Bibliotheca Sacra. 22:127.
Bloomfield's (G. B.) Sermons.
Bradley's (Cha.) Sermons.
Calthorp's (G.) Sermons.
Capp on Important passages of Scripture.
Chandler's (Samuel) Sermons.
Christian Disciple. 1:254.
Christian Examiner. 32:37. 56:297.
Christian Quart. Spect. 5:332.
Clarke's (Samuel) Sermons.
Cookesley's (W. G.) Sermons.
Davies' (Tho.) Sermons.
Dehon's (Bp.) Sermons.
Dyke on Repentance. (Often reprinted.)
Eyre's (Dr. Robt.) 4 Serm. on Matt. 4:1–10.
Faringdon's (Anthony) Sermons.
Farmer's Nat. and design of the T. of Christ.
Fleming's Temptation in the wilderness.
Fletcher's (Joseph) Posthumous Sermons.
Garbett's (Archdeacon) Parochial Sermons.
Hacket's 21 Sermons on Matt. 4:1–11.
Hall's (J. C.) Sermons.
Hall's (Bp.) Contemplations. Bk. 2, sec. 3.
Hewlett's (John) Sermons.
Hill's (D. G.) Wayfarings in Christ.
Hutton's (F. H.) Discourses.
Huxtable on the Temptation of our Lord.
Jenkins' Reasonableness of Christianity.
Kirby's (Wm.) Sermons. (7 on this subject.)
Krummacker's Sermons on the temptations.
Manton's (Dr. Thomas) Works.
Mills' (W. H.) Five Sermons.
Monod's Jesus tempted.
Newton's (Bp.) Essays on parts of the N. T.
Perkins' Combat betw. Christ and the Devil.
Potts' (J. H.) Sermons.
Ridgeley's Body of Divinity. Ques. 48.
Scobell's (Edward) Sermons.
Scott (Rev. Walter) on Evil Spirits.
Shuttleworth's (P. N.) Sermons.
Smith's (T. Tunstall) Lectures.
Stebbings' (Henry) Sermons.
Taylor's (Dr. T.) Sermons.
Taylor's (Jer.) Life of Christ.
Taylor's (Tho.) Exposition of Christ's combat and conquest.
Townsend's (George) Sermons.
Van Mildert's Sermons at Lincoln's Inn.
Wheatly's (Charles) Sermons.
Whitefield's Sermons.
Wiseman's (L. H.) Christ in the wilderness.

Tenth Commandment.
See COMMANDMENTS, COVETOUSNESS.

Ten Tribes of Israel. See RESTORATION.

Calmet, Diss. sur le pays, etc. (Comm.)
——— —— Si les dix tribus sont revenues?
Calvert, Naphtali: seu Collectationes Theol.
Lumnius de Extremo Dei judicio. (Considers the N. Am. Indians to be the lost tribes.)
Rabaneri quinque Decades.
Witsii Egyptiaca.
Boudinot's Star in the West. *Amer. Indians.*

Ten Tribes of Israel—*continued.*

Buchanan's Researches in Asia.
Crawford's (C.) Propagation of the Gospel. *American Indians.*
Durell's Parallel prophecies of Jacob and Moses. (Gives the Hebrew text, with a translation and notes of such parts as relate to the different tribes.)
Edrehi's Hist. acc. of the ten tribes. (Finds them beyond the Sambotyan in the East.)
Elliott's (The Missionary) Jews in America.
Ewing's (Greville) Essays.
Fletcher's (Giles) Israel Redux. *Tartars.*
Grant's (Ariel) Nestorians, or lost tribes.
Ingraham's Ten Tribes. *American Indians.*
Jewish Repository. (Afterwards, "Friend of Israel." Periodical, begun 1813, by the London Society for promoting, &c.)
Jones' Hist. of anc't America. *Am. Indians.*
Latter-day Luminary. Periodical. 1:77.
L'Estrange's (H.) Americans no Jews.
Moore's (Geo.) The lost tribes. *Saxons.*
Sailman's Researches in the East. (An acct. of the ten tribes to the 17th century.)
Samuels' Israel's hiding discovered. *The Jews of Daghiston, on the Caspian Sea.*
Simons' The Hope of Israel. *Amer. Indians.*
Thorowgood's Jews in America.
Whiston's Memoirs. Vol. 1. *Tartars.*
Worsley's American Indians.

Teraphim. See JEWISH ANTIQUITIES.

Hildebrandi (Ioach.) Antiquitates Selectæ.
Jahn's Biblische Archæologie.
Lightfoot, Horæ Hebræicæ.
Marckii Scripta in Selecta Scripturæ.
Pfeifferi (A.) Exercitationes.
Schulzii Compend. Archæologiæ Hebraicæ.
Wichmanshausenii (J. C.) Dissertationes.

Calmet's Sacred and profane antiquities.

Terms of Communion. See CLOSE COMMUNION.

Tertiaries. See BEGHARDS.

Tertullian. See FATHERS.

Tertulliani Opera. (Various editions.)
Allixius de T. vita et scriptis.
Ballenstädt's T. Geistesfähigk. und Theol.
Blumenbach de Senatus Consulto.
Hoffmanni (J. W.) Dissertationes.
La Motte, Histoire de T.
Mosheimii Dissertationes.
Neander's (A.) Einleitung in Schriften T.
Noesselti Dissertationes. (True time of the the writings ascribed to Tertullian.)
Nourrii Adparatus ad biblioth. maximum patrum.
Rechenbergii (Adami) Dissertationes.
Zentgravii Exercitationes hist.-theol.
Zimmermanni (Matth.) Dissertationes.

Amer. Quar. Church Rev. 18:525.
Betty's Trans. of the "Prescriptions" and other tracts, with notes and dissertations.
Brown's Trans. of Tertullian's "Apology."
Chevalier's Trans. of Tertullian's "Apology."
Conybeare's Bampton Lectures. 1839.
Dodson's Translation of the works of T.
Kaye's Ecc. hist. of the 2d and 3d centuries, illustrated from the works of Tertullian.
Neander's Antignostikus.
Reeves' Tr. of Tertullian's "Apology."
Woodham's Introd. and notes to T.'s "Apol."

Testament of the 12 Patriarchs.

Grabii Spicelegium.
Nitzschii Commentatio critica.

Grosthead's Test. of the 12 Patriarchs.
Tertullian's Apology. Trans. by J. Betty.
Whiston's Authentic records.

Test Act. See CORPORATION.

Testimony of Josephus. See JOSEPHUS.

Arnoldi Epistolæ Philologicæ. (Given in Havercamp's edition of Josephus.)
Bossii Exercitationes Criticæ.
Daubuz, Test. Josephi de Jesu Christu.
Eichstadt, Testimonia de Jesu Christu.
Frickii Exercitationes Historicæ.
Ittigii Prolegomena ad Josephi opera.
Martin, Dissertations Critique.
Schoedelii Joseph. de Christo testatus.
Strettenberg de Test. de J. C. Josephi.

Testimony of Profane Authors to Christianity.

Buddei Dissertationes.
Colonie, Religion Chrétienne autorisée, etc. (Quotes Marcellinus, Plutarch, Strabo, Lucian, Macrobius, Tacitus, Pliny, and many others.)
Cuper, Lettres de critiq. de litterat. et d'histoire, etc.
Du Clot, La sainte Bible vengée des attaques de l'incredulité.
Eckhardi Testimonia non-Christianorum.
Ernesti (J. C. G.) Epistola ad Schleusnerum. (Shows the great utility of Suidas.)
Guberti Apologeticon.
Gudei Paganus Chris. laudator et fautor.
Hase de Decreto Tiberii quo Christum referre voluit in numerum deorum.
Heumannus de Chresto Suetonii.
Iselin, sur le Projet, concu par le Tibere, de mettre notre Seigneur au nombre des dieux.
Mulleri Dissertationes.
Nuscheleri Tentamen verit. doctrina Christo confirmandæ.
Plinii (Junioris) Epistolæ.
Raphelii Annotationes in N. T. ex Xenophonte collectæ.
——— ——— ex Polybio collectæ.
——— ——— ex Herodoto collectæ.

Addison (Joseph) on the Christian religion.
Biscoe's Boyle Lectures. 1736–8.
Browne's (Tho.) Testimony of heathen writers of the first two centuries.
Bryant's Authenticity of the Scriptures.

Testimony, &c.—*continued.*

Bullet's Estab. of Christianity. (Compiles the hist. of the establishm. of Christianity wholly from Jewish and Heathen authors.)
Campbell's (John) History of the Bible.
Carwithen's Bampton Lectures. 1809.
Dawson's Test. of Heathen and Jew. writers.
Evidence of prof. hist., &c. (Anon. Able.)
Faber's Horæ Mosaicæ. (Bamp. Lect. 1801.)
Finch's Bampton Lectures. 1797.
Fletcher's (Joseph) Posthumous Sermons.
Gray's Connection between the sacred writings and the literature of Jewish and Heathen authors. ("Indispensable to the biblical student."—British Critic.)
Lardner's Credibility of the Gospel history. (Sufficient of itself on this subject.)
Rawlinson's Bampton Lectures. 1859.
Sharp's (Gregory) Defence of Christianity; from the testimony of the most ancient adversaries—Jews, Pagans, Philosophers, and Historians.
Whiston's Testimony of Phlegon. (In relation to the darkness and earthquake at our Saviour's crucifixion.)

Tetragramaton. See NAME OF GOD.

Teutonic Knights. See KNIGHTS.

Duelli Historia ordinis Teutonici.
Dusburg, Chronicon Prussiæ.
Heylot, Histoire des Ordres, etc.
Ludewig de Reliquiis manuscriptorum.
Matthæi Analecta veteris ævi.

Thammuz.

Braunius de Fletu super Thammuz.
Deylingii (S.) Disputationes. (Disput. in Ezekiel 8:14.)
Fludd, Dissertationes.
Chowlson's Thammuz, and man-worship among the ancient Babylonians.

Thankfulness. See GRATITUDE.

Thanksgiving.

Allestree's, Richard, Sermons.
Alison's, Archib., Sermons. (3 on this subj.)
Apthorp's, East, Sermons.
Arrowsmith's, John, Sermons. *For victory.*
Atterbury's, Francis, Sermons.
Bennet's Christian Oratory.
Beveridge's, Bp., Sermons.
Biddulph's, T. T., Sermons.
Blakeney's, John B., Sermons.
Bowen's, Thomas, Sermons.
Bradford's, The Martyr, Sermons.
Brady's, Nicholas, Sermons. *For peace.*
Bramhall's, Abp., Sermons.
Bulman's, John, Sermons.
Burnett's, Gilbert, Sermons.
Burton's, John, Sermons.
Chandler's, Samuel, Sermons.
Clarke's, Dr. Samuel, Sermons.
Craddock's, William, Sermons.
Davies', Pres., Sermons.

Thanksgiving—*continued.*

Dehon's, Bp., Sermons.
Evans', John, Sermons.
Fiddes', Richard, Sermons.
Fothergill's, George, Sermons.
Fowler's, Bp., Sermons.
Francklin's, Thomas, Sermons.
Gibson's, Bp., Sermons.
Hale's, Sir M., Contemplations.
Hare's, Bp., Sermons.
Hobart's, Bp., Sermons.
Holdsworth's, R., Sermons.
Horne's, Bp., Sermons.
Howe's, John, Sermons.
Jones', William, Sermons.
Jortin's, John, Sermons.
Kennett's, Bp., Sermons.
Kollock's, S. K., Sermons.
Leighton's, Abp., Sermons.
Lucas', Richard, Sermons. *For victory.*
Maddox's, Bp., Sermons.
Mayhew's, J., Sermons.
McCheyne's, Robt. M., Sermons.
Nares', Edward, Sermons.
Neve's, Timothy, Sermons.
Rogers', John, Sermons.
Scott's, John, Sermons.
Secker's, Abp., Sermons.
Sharp's, Abp., Sermons.
Sherlock's, Bp., Sermons.
Smallridge's, Bp., Sermons.
Spurgeon's, Ch. H., Sermons. Vols. 2 and 9
Stanhope's, George, Sermons. *For victory.*
Stillman's, Sam., Sermons.
Talbot's, Bp., Sermons.
Tillotson's, Abp., Sermons.
Warburton's, Bp., Sermons.
Ware's, Henry, Sermons.
Watts', Isaac, Sermons.
Wesley's, John, Sermons.
White's, Bp., Sermons.
Williams', D., Sermons. *For victory.*
Wingfield's, T., Sermons.
Wright's, Sam., Sermons.

Theatre. See STAGE PLAYS.

Theban Legion.

Baldensani Historia legionis Thebanæ.
Bourdieu, Diss. historique et critique.
D'Lisle de la Legion Thebeéne.
Füssly's Christ ein Soldat.
Rivaz (Jos.), Eclaircissements.
Burton's Bampton Lectures. 1829.

Theft. See COMMANDMENTS.

Abercrombie on the Church Catechism.
Beveridge's Thesaurus.
Beddome's Expos. of the Baptist Catechism.
Brackenbury's (Edward) Sermons.
Clarke (Sam.) on the Church Catechism.
Delany's (Pat.) Sermons.
Edwards' (Jonathan) Works.
Edwards' (John, D.D.) Theologia Reformata.
Enfield's (William) Sermons for families.

Theft—*continued.*

Foster's (Dr. James) Sermons.
Haggitt's (George) Sermons.
Hole (Matt.) on the Church Catechism.
Piggot's (S.) Sermons.
Secker (Abp.) on the Church Catechism.
Sherlock's (Bp.) Discourses.
Vincent (Nath.) on the Church Catechism.
Whitaker's (E. W.) Sermons.
Wilson's (Bp.) Sermons.

Theism. See DEISM.

Theodore of Mopsuetia.

Brett de Fragmentis Theod. Mopsuetii.
Corderii Catena.
Kleneri Symbolæ liter. ad T. pertinentes.
Langles, Rituel des Tartares.
Photii Bibliotheca.
Siefferti T. Vet. Test. sobrie interp. vindex.

Theodoret.

Theodoreti Opera omnia. (Cura Sirmondi, Soc. Jesu. 5 vols., fol. 1648.
Garneri Dissertationes quinque.
Oudini (Casimeri) Dissertationes.
Richter de T. epistolæ Paulinarum interp.
Sirmondi Vita Theodoreti.
Sommer, Oratio de St. Theodoret.
Strigelii Vita Theodoreti; ex Evagrio, Nicephoro, et aliis, collecta.
Lardner's Credibility. Part 2.

Theological Seminaries. See EDUCATION SOCIETIES, MINISTERIAL EDUCATION, STUDY OF THEOLOGY.

Assemanni Bibliotheca Orientalis.
Eusebii Hist. Ecclesiastica. Lib. V, cap. 20.
Schmidii Schola catechetica Alexandrina.
Eclectic Review. N. S. 1:99.
Knight's Utility of Theolog. seminaries.
Mosheim's Eccles. history. Cent. 1, part 2.

Theology. See FUNDAMENTALS, HERESY, HISTORY OF DOCTRINES, NATURAL THEOLOGY, POLEMICS, SCHOLASTICISM, STUDY OF THEOLOGY.

Alberti Magni Opera. 1651.
Alstedii Theologia Didactica. 1630.
Altingii Methodus theol. didacticæ. 1654.
Amesii Medulla theologica. 1628.
Aquinatis (Tho.) Summa theologiæ. 1512.
Aretii Loci communes. 1604.
Arsdekini Theolog. tripartita. 1682. (Held in great esteem by Romanists, and truly valuable as a great magazine of authorities.)
Beconi Principia relig. Christianæ. 1564.
Binchii Mellificium Theologicum. 1658. (Comprises the marrow of the orthodox writers of his day.)
Boylii Summa theol. Christianæ. 1681.
Braunii Doctrina Fœderum. 1700.
Breithaupti Institutiones Theologicæ. 1695.
Brockmandi Universæ theol. systema. 1633.
Buddei Inst. theol. dogmaticæ. 1723.
Bullingeri Compendium Chris. relig. 1559.
Callixti Epitome Theologiæ. 1656.

Theology—*continued.*

Callovii Theologia positiva. 1682.
——— Systema locorum theologicor. 1691.
Calvini Institutiones. 1536.
Carpzovii Systema Theologicum. 1795.
Chenevierre, Dogmatique Chrétienne. 1840.
Coccei Summa Doctrinæ. 1660.
Colleti Institutiones Theologicæ. 1777.
Danhaveri Hodosophia Christiana. 1649.
Davenantii Determinationes. 1631.
Doderleini Institutiones. 1785.
Dorschei Aphorismi theologici. 1702.
Ebrard's Christliche Dogmatik. 1850.
Episcopii Institutiones Theol. 1650.
Erasmi Ratio: seu methodus, etc. 1530.
Fabricii Prelectiones Theologicæ. 1729.
Gass' Gesch. d. Protest. Dogmatik in ihrem Zusammenhange mit der Theologie überhaupt.
Gerhardi Loci Theologici. 1610.
——— Exegesis: seu Explicationes, etc. (G. was one of the greatest of Lutheran writers.)
Gomari Opera Theologica. 1630.
Gousset, Théologie Dogmatique. 1853.
Heideggeri Dissertationes theol. Died 1698.
——— Medulla theologiæ. 1700.
Hoffmanni Synopsis theologiæ. 1754.
Hollasii Examen theologicum. 1741. (The frequent reprints show a high esteem of this work.)
Honerti (Joh.) Theol. didactico-elencticæ. 1730.
Hoornbeckii Theologia practica. 1660.
Hottingeri Typus doct. Christianæ. 1650.
Iaegeri Syst. theol. dogmatico-polemicum. 1715.
Klupfelii Instit. theol. dogmaticæ. 1810.
Knapp's (G. C.) Vorlesungen über die Christliche Glaubenslehre. 1827.
Knoll, Institutiones theol. theoreticæ. 1660.
Koeckeri Conspectus Theologiæ. 1749.
Kromayeri Theologia positivo-polem. 1666.
Langii Œconomia salutis. 1720.
Leighton, Prelectiones theologicæ. 1693.
Leydekkeri Synopsis theologiæ. 1712.
Liebermanni Institutiones. 1836.
Loescheri Nucleus theologiæ. 1717.
Lutheri Loci communes. 1527.
Lutzelberger's Grundzüge d. Paulinischen glaubens. 1854.
Lyseri Systema thetico-exegeticum. 1699.
Maii Synopsis theologiæ. 1709.
Markii Compendium. 1686.
Mastrichtii Theol. theoretico-practica. 1724.
Melancthonis Loci communes. 1521. (This book passed through seventy editions before the end of the century, besides numerous translations. Edited with valuable dissertations by J. C. G. Augusti. 1821.)
Mori Epitome theol. 1797. (Once very popular.)
Mosheim (J. L.), Elementa Theologiæ. 1766.
Neandri (M.) Theol. script. patrum Græcorum et Latinorum. 1595.

Theology—*continued.*

Olearii Theologia Universa. 1674.
Opitii Theol. Thetica, methodo analytica. 1700.
Osiandri Theol. positivo-acromatica. 1576.
Parei Decuria collegiorum theologicorum. 1620. ("Incomparabilis Theologus."—SPANHEIM.)
Petavii Dogmata. 1700. (A huge collection of the sentiments of the Fathers, lucidly arranged.)
Pfaffii Institutiones Theologicæ. 1720.
Pictet, Theologie. 1696. (Admirable.)
Piscatoris Theses Theologicæ.
Placette de la Foi divine. 1735.
Quenstedtii Theologia. Died 1688.
Reinhardi Instit. theol. dogmat. 1770.
Scherzeri Definitiones, etc. 1680.
Schmidii (And.) Comp. theol. per thesin et antithesin. 1699.
Schuberti Inst. theol. dogmaticæ. 1749.
Selnecceri Inst. Chris. religionis. 1579.
Stohlii Dogmatische Theologie. 1752.
Storr, Doctrina Christ. theoret. 1807.
Strigelii Enchiridion theol. 1541.
Thummii Synopsis præcip. art. fidei. 1721.
Turretini (J. A.) Dilucidationes. 1695.
Turretini (F.) Institutiones theolog. 1679.
Twesten's Vorlesungen über d. Dogmatik. 1826.
Tzschirner's Glaubenslehre. 1829.
Usseri Corpus Theologiæ. 1660.
Van Till, Theol. Compendium. 1704.
Viret, Expos. de la foi Chrétienne. 1543.
Vitringa, Doct. rel. per aphorismos. 1702. (Admirable text-book, full of quotations.)
Voget, Institutiones. 1736.
Vossii (Gerard.) Theses Theologicæ. 1640.
Walch (C. W. F.), Breviarum Theol. dogmaticæ. 1775.
Weismanni Theol. exegetico-dogmat. 1739.
Wigandi Corpus Doctrinæ. 1564.
Witsii Œconomia Fœderum. 1700.

Baxter's Catholic Theology. 1675.
Bennett's Theol. of the early church. 1841.
Beveridge's Thesaurus Theologicus. 1710.
Beza's Golden Chain, &c. 1575.
——— Confession of faith.
Bickersteth's Christian Student. 1832.
Boston's Doctrine of religion. 1773.
Boyle's (Robt.) Excellency of theology. 1774.
Breckenridge's (Robert) Knowledge of God objectively considered. 1858.
Brown's System of nat. and rev. relig. 1780.
Burrows' Summary of faith and practice. 1822.
Calvin's Institutes of Religion. 1560.
Campbell's (Dr. Geo.) Systematic Theology. 1807.
Chalmers' (Tho.) Institutes of Theology.
Craddock's Knowledge and Practice. 1702. ("One of the best systems of divinity which a plain man can read."—BOGUE.)
Dagg's Manual of Theology. 1857.
Davy's (W.) System of Divinity. 1785.

Theology—*continued.*

Dick's (J.) Lectures on Theology. 1834.
Doddridge's Lectures. 1763. (Nothing superior to it as a text-book.)
Doolittle's Complete Body, &c. 1723.
Doutrin's Scheme of Divine truth. 1713.
Dwight's Theology. 1823. (Lucid and pious.)
Edwards' (Bp.) Theologia Reformata. 1713.
Farrar's Study of T. (Highly suggestive.)
Fiddes' Theological Speculations. 1718.
Fisher's Marrow of modern divinity. 1646.
Gill's Body of Divinity. 1765.
Gregory's (Olinthus) Letters on Relig. 1810.
Heylin's (John) Theol. Lectures. 1755.
Heylin (Peter) on the Creed. 1660.
Hey's Lectures in Divinity. 1796.
Hill's (Dr. Geo.) Theolog. Institutes. 1803.
Jebb's (Bp.) Practical Theology. 1830.
Jackson's (Tho.) Works. (Has the highest praise of OLEY and BP. HORNE.)
Knapp's Lectures. Trans. by L. Woods.
Leigh's Body of Divinity. 1662.
Leighton's Theological Lectures. 1675.
Limborch's System of Divinity. Trans. by W. Jones. 1715. (The first system of divinity according to Armenianism.)
Lincoln's (Bp. of) Elements of Christian T.
Marsh's Systematic arrangement of the several branches of divinity.
Milton (Jno.) on Christian doctrine. 1650.
Morren's Biblical Theology. (Includes annotations of recent German critics, and notices of many authors, and disquisitions by De Wette, Neander, Storr, Winer, and many others.)
Owen's (John) Nature, rise, progress, and study of true theology. 1680.
Payne's (Geo.) Lectures on Theology. 1846.
Pearson on the Creed. 1741.
Pictet's Theology. Trans. by Reyroux.
Ridgeley's Body of Divinity. 1731.
Roberts' Marrow of the Bible. 1657.
Robinson's Christian System. 1805.
Schmucker's Popular Theology.
Scott's (John) Christian Life. ("One of the best schemes of Divinity in any language." —ADDISON.)
Scrivener's Course of Divinity. 1674.
Smith's (J. Pye) First lines in theology.
Stackhouse's Body of Divinity. 1729.
Storr & Flatt's Bible Theology. Translated by Schmucker.
Taylor's (John) Scheme of Script. divinity. 1753. (Watson's Tracts.)
Usher's (Abp.) Body of Divinity. 1648.
Venema's Institutes of Theology. 1715.
Vinet's Outlines of Theology. Translated by Astie. 1865.
Warden's System of revealed religion. 1769.
Wardlaw's Systematic Theology.
Warner's System of Divinity, compiled from eminent divines. 1750.
Watson's (Rich.) Theological Institutes.
Watson's (Tho.) 175 Sermons on the Shorter Catechism. 1662.

Witsius' Economy of the Covenants. 1700.

Scarcely a third of the books of this sort, which have fallen under my notice, are here given; but the list is more than sufficient, and comprises the best.

Theopaschites. See MONOPHYSITES.

Assemani Bibliotheca Orient. Vatican.
Giesseleri Commentatio.
Iablonski Dissert. de henotico Zenonis.
Münscher's Ordnung des deutschen Amts zu Alsted.
Norris, de Uno ex Trinitate.
Titii (Ger.) Disputationes.

Theophilanthropists.

Gregoire, Histoire des Sectes religieuses.

Manual of the Theophilanthropists, or adorers of God. Translated by Walker.
Paine's (Tho.) Discourse before the Society of Theophilanthropists.
Quarterly Review. 28:493. 30:113.

Theophylus Antiocenus.

Theophyli Libri ad Autolycum.
——— Commentaria in Evangelium.
——— Commentaria in Canticum.
Grabeneri Dissertationes.
Monarchi Prefatio ad Justini M. opera.
Tentzelii (Guil. Ernest.) Exercitationes.
Walpergeri (Christoph.) Comment. de T.

Betty's Translation of the Works of T.

Theories of the Earth. See CREATION, DELUGE, GEOLOGY.

On the side of Scripture.

Analytical Mag. 13:26.
Bugge (George) on Geological phenomena. (Replies to Cuvier.)
Chalmers' (Tho.) Tracts and Essays.
Edinburg Review. 22:454.
Edwards' (J.) Remarks on Whiston's theory.
Emlyn's Examinat. of Burnet's new theory.
Grew's (Neh.) Cosmographia Sacra.
Howard's History of the earth and of mankind compared with other cosmographies.
Kirwan's Geological Essays.
Littell's Living Age. 14:516.
Monthly Review. 126:371.
Nichols' Conference with a Theist.
North Amer. Rev. 18:266.
Pierre's (St.) Theory of the Earth.
Ray's Physico-Theological Essays.
Southern Rev. 8:69.
Universal History. (Introduction.)
Warren's Geologia. (Opposes Burnet.)
Woodward's Natural history of the earth.
Worthington's Theory of the Earth, throughout all its revolutions, and all periods of its existence.

Contrary to Scripture.

Burnet, Telluris theoria sacra.
Delance, Theorie de la terre.

Buffon's Theory of the earth.
Burnet's (Tho.) Sacred theory of the earth.
Cuvier's Theory of the earth.
Hutton's Theory of the earth.
Keill's Examination of Burnet and Whiston.
Knight's Facts and Observations, &c.
Whiston's New Theory of the earth.
——— Vindication of the "Theory."
——— Second Vindication.

Theosophists. See PARACELSISTS.

Bruckeri Historia Critica. (A full account of the lives and writings of these philosophers.)

Therapeutæ. See ESSENES.

Fabricii Lux salutaris evangelii. (Gives a list of writers on this subject in chap. 4.)

Third Commandment. See COMMANDMENTS, OATHS, PROFANENESS.

Blackall's (Bp.) Sermons.
Blencoe's (Edward) Sermons.
Brackenbury's (Edward) Discourses.
Bradbury's (Thomas) Sermons.
Carr's (George) Sermons.
Clapp's (John) Sermons.
Clarke's (Dr. Samuel) Discourses.
Copner's (James) Sermons.
Dwight's (Tim.) Discourses. (3 on this subj.)
Fleetwood's (Bp.) Discourses.
Foster's (James) Sermons.
Haggitt's (George) Sermons.
Hall's (Bp.) Practical Works.
Hall's (Robert) Notes of Sermons.
Hole on the Catechism.
Marriot's (Harvey) Sermons.
Newton's (John) Sermons.
Nourse's (Peter) Discourses.
Ogden's (Samuel) Sermons.
Paley's (Will.) Sermons.
Parsons on the Catechism.
Partridge's (Samuel) Sermons.
Pearce's (John) Discourses.
Secker on the Catechism.
Skelton's (Philip) Sermons.
Smith's (Sam. Stanhope) Sermons.
Smith's (Sydney) Sermons.

Thirty-nine Articles.

Ellis, Articulorum XXXIX Defensio.
Ford, Christianæ religionis.

Bennett's Introd. to the study of theology.
Beveridge's Doct. of the Church of England.
Bingham's Apology for the Ch. of England.
Blunt's Discourses on the doctrinal articles
Blythe's Thirteen Conferences.
Boyse's Genuine sense of the 39 articles.
Brown's (G. H.) Expos.; hist. and doctrinal.
Burnet's (Gilbert) Exposition.
Cary's Testimony of the Fathers.
Collins' Histor. and crit. essay on the 39 art.
Dimock (J. F.) on the 39 Articles. (Compared with the other authorized formularies and the liturgy.)
Hall's (Bp. John) Parochial Discourses.
Hervey's Elementa Christiana.

Thirty-nine Articles—*continued.*

Hull on the Expediency of changes, &c.
Jewell's Apology for the Church of England.
Kidd's Testimonies and authorities in confirmation, &c.
Kipling's Articles of the Ch. not Calvinistic.
Lamb's Historical account of the 39 articles, from their first promulgation in 1553, to their final establishment in 1571, with exact copies of the Latin and English MSS., &c.
Lawrence's (Abp.) Attempt to illustrate those articles of the Ch. of England which are improperly considered as Calvinistic.
Lincoln's (Bp.) Elements of Theology.
McBride's (J. D.) Lectures on the 39 art.
O'Donahue on the 39 Articles.
Page's Burnet's Exp. revised and corrected; with notes, references, &c.
Rogers' (Dr.) Analysis of the 39 articles.
Tomline's (Bp.) Expos. of the 39 articles.
——— The same, with notes, by R. B. Paul.
Veneer's Exposition. (From the Sac. Scriptures and fathers of the first 3 centuries.)
Waite's Sermons; Practical and Explanatory. (Half-way Calvinism.)
Welshman's 39 Art. illustrated with notes.
Wilson's 39 Art. illustrated from the liturgy, homilies, Jewell's Apology, &c.
Wix's (Sam.) Illustrations of the 39 articles.

A cloud of writers on the 39 articles, some of them not inconsiderable, have passed into oblivion; and many yet extant are superseded by the above.

Thomas. See BIOGRAPHY, SCRIPTURE.

Stapleton, de Tribus Thomis.
Adams' (W.) Warnings.
Berriman's (William) Sermons.
Bourdaloue's Sermons.
Clark's (R.) Sermons.
Horsley's (Bp.) Sermons.
McCrie's (Thomas) Sermons.
South's (Robert) Sermons.
Whately's (Richard) Sermons.

Thomas Aquinas. See THOMISTS.

Aquinatis Opera Omnia. Cum Cajetani, Commentariis. 18 v., fol. 1570.
——— cum Vita, etc. 28 v., 4to. 1788.
Boetii Opera.
Touron, La vie de S. Thomas d'Aquin.
Vielmii Doctrina et scriptis Tho. Aquin.

Thomists. See DOMINICANS.

Billuarti Cursus Theologiæ.
Cerboni Institutiones Theologicæ.
Daniel, le Parallele de la doctrine des Thomistes avec celle des Jesuites.
Iacobatius de VII Sacramentis.
Serry (Iacob. Hyacinth.) Prelectiones.
Silvii Comment. in totam summam Thomæ.
Vasquez, Disputationes et Commentarii.
Ysamberti (Nicol.) Disputationes.

See a great list of Thomist writers in MOLAN'S *Bibliotheca Interpretum.*

Thorn in the Flesh.

Atterbury's (Lewis) Sermons.
Boston's (Thomas) Works.
Bull's (Bp.) Works.
Funch's (J.) Sermons.
Hordern's (Joseph) Sermons.
Jacobson's (W.) Sermons.
Jay's (William) Short Discourses.
Jortin's (John) Sermons.
Jowett's (J.) Sermons.
Morus' (Alex.) Sermons. (2 on this subject.)
Muller's (Edw.) Sermons. (3 on this subject.)
Princeton Review. 35:521.
Rose's (Hugh) Sermons.
Rowe's (John) The Saints' temptations.
Slade's (J.) Sermons.
Walker's (Robert) Sermons.
Wilcox's (Daniel) Sermons.

Thoughtlessness. See CONSIDERATION, MEDITATION, PRUDENCE.

Howe's (John) Sermons.
Jay's (W.) Works. (The secure alarmed.)
Knowles' (T.) Discourses.
Knox's (Vicessimus) Sermons.

Thoughts, Government of. See GOVERNMENT OF THE HEART.

Arwaker's Thoughts well employed.
Baxter's (Rich.) Christian Ethics.
Blair's (James) Sermons.
Calamy's (Edmund) Sermons.
Chevalier's (T.) Hulsean Lectures. 1827.
Fawcett's (James) Sermons.
Gell's (Robert) Sermons.
Horne's (Bp.) Discourses.
Hussey's (Christopher) Sermons.
Morning Exercises at Cripplegate. Vol. 2. (Sermon by S. Charnock.)
Newton's (Bp.) Dissertations.
Seed's (Jeremiah) Sermons.
Sharp's (John) Sermons.
Stebbings' (Henry) Sermons.
Trapp's (Joseph) Sermons.
Tullie on the Government of the thoughts.
Walker's (Dr. James) Sermons.

Three Witnesses. See GENUINENESS OF 1 JOHN V. 7.

Thundering Legion.

Pro, i. e. that the story is true.

Baumgarten de Miraculo, etc. (Refutes Woolston.)
Whiston, de Legione fulminatrice.
Witsii Ægyptiaca. (Appendix.)
King's (Rev. Mr.) Dissertations. (Replies to Moyle.)

Con.

Boysenii Dissertatio.
Iablonski Spicilegium.
——— de Legione fulminatrice. (Reprinted in vol. 8 of Miscellanea Leipsiensia.)
Larroque, Adversaria Sacra. (Appendix.)
Mosheim (J. L.), Observationes, etc. (Appended to his diss. "Ad disciplinos.")

Richardson (J.), Prælectiones Ecclesiasticæ.
Lardner's Testimony of ancient heathens.
Moyle's Posthumous Works. (The letters on this subject are translated into Latin by Mosheim, and published at the end of his Syntagma.)
Woolston's (Tho.) The Miracle of the T. L.

WITSIUS, at the end of his *Ægyptiaca*, recites the opinions of many learned men on this subject.

Time. See NEW YEAR, REDEEMING TIME, VANITY OF THE WORLD.

Alison's (Archibald) Sermons.
Ambrose's (Isaac) Sermons.
Appleton's (Pres.) Works.
Atterbury's (Lewis) Sermons.
Barrow's (Isaac) Sermons.
Baxter's (A. G.) Sermons.
Blair's (Hugh) Sermons.
Butcher's (Edmund) Sermons.
Carr's (George) Sermons.
Close's (Francis) Sermons.
Edwards' Posthumous Sermons.
Evans' (R. W.) Parochial Sermons.
Fawcett's (Joseph) Sermons.
Fox on Time.
Gatty's (Alfred) Sermons.
Hale's (Sir M.) Contemplations.
Hervey's Meditations.
Hewlett's (J. P.) Sermons.
Jenyn's (Soame) Disquisitions. Disq. 4.
Law's (Edmund) Enquiry into the ideas of space, time, &c.
Le Clerc's Logic.
Locke on the Human understanding.
Masillon's Sermons.
Milner's (Joseph) Sermons.
Neve's (Timothy) Sermons.
Reid's Intellectual Powers.
Secker's (Abp.) Sermons.
Sharpe's (Wm.) Sermons before the University of Cambridge.
Showers' Reflections on time and eternity.
Sterne's (Lawrence) History of Jacob.
Taylor's (Jer.) Holy Living.
Tucker's Light of Nature.
Watts on the Improvement of the mind.
——— Ontology. Ch. 12.
Young's Night Thoughts.
Zollikoffer on the Festivals and Fasts.

Tithes. See CHURCH RATES.

Pro.

Blackwood's Mag. 33:321. 41:682.
Burgess on Bishop's lands and tithes.
Collins' (Tho.) Divine right of tithes.
Comber (T.) On the right of tithes.
Delany's (Patrick) Sermons. (Appendix.)
Elderfield's Civil right of tithes.
Frazier's Mag. 5:476. 9:379. 11:457. 15:146.
Hale's (Wm.) Observations on tithes.
Heylin's Undeceiving of the people.
——— Historical and miscellaneous tracts.

Tithes—*continued.*

Pro.

Howlett on the Influence of Tithes.
Montague's Diatribe. (Reply to Selden.
Nortcliffe on the Divine right of tithes.
Pagitt on the Provision for the ministry.
Poyntell on Tithes.
Prideaux's Origin and right of tithes.
Poyntell on Tithes.
Quarterly Rev. 42:105. 57:198.
Spelman (Sir Henry) on Tithes.

Con.

Applegate on Tithes.
Atkinson's Testimony concerning tithes.
Cove on the Revenues of the Ch. of England.
Eclectic Review. 4th Series. 1:290. 2:109.
Ellwood's Foundation of tithes.
Flower (R.) on the Abolition of tithes.
Fox's (George) Reply to Burgess on tithes.
Gentleman's Mag. 42:347.
Gibson's Tithes ended by Christ.
Gratton on the Divine right of tithes.
Lindley's Cerinthus and Ebion. 1708.
Pamphleteer. 7:1. 8:337. 12:493. 15:293. 27:305.
Pearson's Great case of Tithes truly stated.
Selden's History of tithes. (This book was so offensive to the English that the author was compelled to retract it.)
Stratten's English and Jewish tithe systems compared.
Thompson's (Tho.) Origin and effects of T.
Toller on the Law of tithes.
Watkins on Tithes and Oaths.
Westwood on Tithes.
Whitaker's Unjust plea confuted. (Reply to Poyntell.)

Tithes, Jewish.

Amama de Decimis.
Hottingerus de Decimis Judæorum.
Quenstedtii (Ioann.) Dissertationes.
Scaligeri (J. J.) Opuscula.
Spenceri (J.) Dissertationes.

Tithes, History of.

Comber on the Divine right of tithes. (Gives the practice of Jews, Gentiles, and Christians, in all ages.)
Dalton's Hist. of tithes and church benefices.
Selden's History of tithes.

Titles of Christ.

Bloomsbury Lent Lectures. For 1857.
Dyer's (William) Sermons.
Flavel's Method of Grace.
Goode's (Wm.) Essays. (All sufficient on this subject. Gives *all* the Scripture names of Christ.)
Mylne's (J. G.) Titles and offices of Christ.
Randall's Titles of C., adopted by himself.
Serle's (Ambrose) Horæ Solitariæ.
Spear's (C.) Titles and names of Christ.
Steward on Mediatorial Sovereignty.

Titles of the Psalms.

Fenwick on the Heb. titles of the Psalms. (The only treatise on the subject, in the language. Intended to show that Christ or the Church is the burden of all the psalms.)

Tobacco.

American Quart. Rev. 9:136.
Budgett's Tobacco question, morally, socially, and physically considered.
Clarke (Adam) on the Use and abuse of T.
Fairholt's History of T. and its use in all countries and ages. 100 cuts.
James I. (King of Eng.), Counterblast.
Knickerbocker Magaz. 24:307.
Paul (S.) on Tobacco, Tea, and Coffee.
Rush's (Benj.) Essays. (A medical authority of the highest value.)
Trask's Series of tracts on tobacco and rum.
Venner (Tobias) on the Use of Tobacco.

Toleration. See CHRISTIAN LIBERTY, CORPORATION AND TEST ACTS, LIBERTY OF CONSCIENCE, ESTABLISHMENTS, PERSECUTION, PRIVATE JUDGMENT.

Pro.

Tertullian, ad Scapulam.
Forbesii (Jo.) Irenicum.
Grotius de Imperio potestatum summarum.
Saueri Christus præstantissimum exemplum.
Spinozæ Tractatus Theologico-politicus.
Vossii (Gerard.) Dissertationes.
Zwickeri Irenicum Irenicorum.
——— Irenicomastix.
Baldwin's Essay on Christianity.
Bayle's (Peter) Philos. Com. on Luke 14:23.
Brakenridge's (William) Sermons.
Brooks' History of religious liberty in Great Britain, from the introduction of Christianity to the death of George III.
Capes' (J. M.) Use of church authority.
Cartwright's (Tho.) Truth on Toleration.
Clarke's (J. E.) History of Intolerance.
Clarendon's (Edw.) Religion and Policy.
Cobbet on the Power of magistrates.
Colebrooke on Intolerance; ancient and modern.
Davenant's Exhort. to brotherly communion.
Dicks (A. C.) on Church Polity.
Dublin University Mag. 41:638.
Edinb. Review. 16:413. 17:393. 19:149. 26:51. 27:159. 76:382.
Farnsworth on Christian Toleration.
Fellowes' Religion without cant.
Fowne on the Principles of toleration.
Francklin's (Thomas) Sermons.
Furneaux's (P.) Essay on Toleration.
——— Letters to Blackstone.
Goodwin's Rights of civil magistrates.
Gregory's (G.) Sermons.
Grosvenor's Cruelty in rel. no service to God.
Hall's (Bp.) Contemplations.
Hall's (Robt.) Works.
Hammond's (Henry) Sermons.
Jortin's (John) Sermons.
Kidder on Private judgment in religion.

Toleration—*continued.*

Pro.

Lake's (Bp. Arthur) Sermons.
Laurie's (Dr. Thomas) Sermons.
Locke's Letters on Government.
Mills' Principles of Toleration.
Milton's (Jno.) Civil power in eccl. causes.
North British Rev. 5:222.
Owen (Dr. John) on Church government.
——— Truth and innocence vindicated. (Reply to Bp. Parker.)
Paley's Moral Philosophy. Book 6.
Richardson on Religious toleration.
Robinson's Claude.
Sage on Toleration.
Salter's Hall Sermons.
Saurin's Sermons. (Preface to vol. 3.)
Smith's (Sydney) Sermons.
Spinoza on the Use of natural reason.
Stillingfleet's Irenicum.
Sturgeon's Plea for toleration.
Sturges' (John) Discourses.
Taylor's (Jer.) Liberty of prophecying.
Taylor's (M.) England's bloody tribunal.
Voltaire on Toleration. Tr. by Williams.
Watts on Civil power in things sacred.
Webb's (Francis) Sermons.
Wellesly (Sir Cha.) on Liberty of conscience.
West's (W.) Sermons.
Whiston's Serious address to the Princes of Europe. 1716.
White's (Jer.) Persuasives to moderation.
Whitefield's (Thomas) Discourses.
Williams' (Roger) The bloody tenet.
Wyvill's (Chris.) Letters on toleration.
Zollikoffer on the Festivals and Fasts of the Church.

Con.

Comenii Admonitio. (Reply to Zwicker.)
Asheton's (W.) T. disproved and condemned.
Blackstone on the Act of Toleration.
Cartwright (Thomas) on Toleration.
Edwards (Tho.) on Toleration and liberty of conscience.
Fosdick on Toleration.
Hammond on the Power of the magistrate.
Holdsworth's Answer without a question
Mather's The bloody tenet washed white.
[Parker's (Bp.)] Ecclesiastical polity. (Exhibits the mischiefs of toleration, and answers "the pretences for liberty of conscience.")
Stahl (Prof.) on Toleration.
Synge's (Abp.) Address to Nonconformists.
Tomkins on Toleration.
Warburton's Alliance between Ch. and State.

See J. JOHNSON'S *List of pamphlets on Toleration published between* 1772 and 1790. Professes to be complete.

Tongue. See SOCIAL INTERCOURSE, VAIN WORDS.

Adams' (Thomas) Sermons.
Ball's (The Puritan) Power of godliness.

Tongue—*continued.*

Baxter's (Rich.) Christian Ethics.
Bloomfield's (G. B.) Sermons. (Judged by our words.)
Blunt's (J. J.) Sermons.
Boston's (Thomas) Sermons.
Boys' (Dr. H.) Sermons.
Brailsford's (J.)) Sermons.
Brinsley's (Wm.) Sermons.
Butler's (Bp.) Sermons.
Collyer (W. B.) on Scripture duties. Lec. 15.
Dawes' (Abp.) Sermons.
Eden's (C. P.) Sermons.
Fawcett's (John) Sermons.
Fiddes' (Richard) Sermons.
Gisbourne's (Tho.) Sermons.
Gleig's (George) Sermons.
Goodwin's (H.) Sermons.
Gregory's (George) Sermons.
Horton's Discourses on practical subjects.
Hurd's (Bp.) Sermons.
Irving's (Edward) Sermons.
Jackson (Bp.) on Little sins.
Lardner's (Nath.) Sermons.
Leland's (Thomas) Sermons.
Morning Lectures at Cripplegate. (Sermon by Edw. West.)
Newton's (Bp.) Dissertations.
Oakley's (Frederick) Sermons.
Peters' (Charles) Sermons.
Pittman's Sermons from eminent divines.
Reyner's Rules for the gov't of the tongue.
Robertson's (F. W.) Sermons.
Rogers' (John) Sermons.
Secker's (Abp.) Sermons.
Sherlock's (Bp.) Sermons.
Shorthose's (Hugh) Sermons.
Simeon's (C.) Works.
Tappan's (David) Sermons.
Taylor's (Jer.) Sermons. (4 on this subject.)
Trench's (Richard C.) Sermons.
Ward's (Richard) Theological Lectures.
Watson's (Thomas) Sermons.
Whitaker's (Edward W.) Sermons.
Whitty's (John) Sermons.
Wynyard's (John M.) Sermons.

Total Depravity. See HUMAN DEPRAV.

Tower of Babel. See CONF. OF TONGUES.

Calmeti Dissertationes.
Deylingii Observationes Sacræ.
Hoynovius de Structura turris Babel.
Kircheri (Athanas.) Dissertationes.
Zentgravius de Turri Babel.

Bedford's Chronology. (Appendix.)
Jones' (J.) Tower of Babel.
Mede's (Bp.) The Bible and the Classics.

Tractarians. See OXFORD THEOLOGY.

Tradition. See COUNCIL OF TRENT, POPERY, RABBINICAL LITERATURE, TARGUM.

Pro.

Baronii Dissertationes Theologicæ.
Bellarmin, de Verbo Dei non scripto.
Bossuet, de la Tradition.

Tradition—*continued.*

Pro.

Lensius de Verbo Dei.
Varenii pro Catholica fide libellus. ("The great champion of T."—NEWMAN.)
Brett's T. necessary to interpret Scripture.
——— Further proof of the necessity, &c.
Eyre (F.) on T. (Reply to Churton.)
Hampden's Lectures at Oxford.
Hawkins on Unauthoritative tradition.
Holden (Geo.) on the Authority of T.
Hook's (Walter) Sermons.
Hooker's (Richard) Works.
Keble's (J.) Sermons.
Newman's (J. H.) Sermons.
Palmer (Will.) on the Church.
Russell's (F.) Judgment of the Anglican Ch.
Sandis' (Abp.) Tracts of the Anglic. fathers.
Soames' (Henry) Bampton Lectures.

Con.

Aslaci Theses de Scriptura.
Christman's Tradition und Schrift.
Hackspanius de Libertate Christiana.
Hannekenii (M.) Examen manualis Becani.
Hannekenii (Phil.) Jesuita conversus.
Heilbruneri Synopsis errorum Pontificorum.
Holtzmann's Kanon und Tradition.
Hunnii Prima controversia cum Bellarmino.
Hussius (Joann.) de Abolendis sectis.
Kromayer de Traditionibus.
Loescheri Sorex Romanus.
Molina, La perfectione de l'ecriture sainte.
Molitor's Philosophie der Geschichte.
Pictet, Sermons sur divers sujets.
Turrettini (Jo. Alphon.) Cogitationes.
Urbani Notæ in Bellarmino.
Wahlenburg de Traditionibus.
Wegellini Trophæum Augustanum.
Weinman's Streitfrage über die Tradition.

Baxter's (Rich.) Tradition examined.
Beaufort's Norrisian Prize Essay. 1841.
Bennett's (W. J. E.) Distinctive errors of Popery.
Case on Human authority in religion.
Churton on the Value of Tradition.
Davies' (J.) Supremacy of the Scriptures.
Fletcher's (Jos.) Lectures on Romanism.
Goode's (W.) Divine rule of faith and pract.
Hampden (R. D.) on Tradition.
Hey's (Dr. John) Lectures. Bk. 4.
Jordan's (J.) Review of Tradition, as taught in the "Tracts for the Times."
Jackson's (Thomas) Works.
King's (Bp.) Inventions of men in the worship of God.
Peck's (Geo.) Appeal from T. to Scripture.
Powell's (Baden) Tradition unveiled.
Quarterly Review. 21:352.
Salter's Hall Sermons. (Ser. by Dr. Wright.)
Shirley's Bampton Lectures. 1847.
Shuttleworth's (Bp.) Works.
Stehelin's (J. P.) Rabbinical Literature.
Stillingfleet's (Bp.) Sermons.
Wotton's (Will.) Miscellaneous Discourses.

Traduction of the Soul. See ORIGINAL SIN, PRE-ADAMITES, PRE-EXISTENCE.

Tertullian, de Anima.
Plutarch, de Procreatione animi.

Baltzer, de Modo propagationis animarum.
Beausobre, Hist. de Manicheisme. Lib. 7, c. 5.
Callixti Disputationes de præcipuis Christianæ religionis capitibus.
Delitzsch's Syst. d. biblischen Psychologie.
Frenzelius de Origine animæ.
Kemnerus de Propagatione animæ.
Langii (J.) Dissertationes.
Lovensenius de origine Animæ.
Menzelii Dissertationes Theologicæ.
Molitor's Philosophie der Geschichte.
Planck's Gesch. der Protestantism.
Pfanerus de Animæ humanæ propagatione.
Schaffer, de Peccato.
Sennerti Physica Hypomnemata.
Zeishold, de Generatione hominis.

Baxter on the Soul.
Chambers' Dictionary. Art. *Generation.*
Coward's Thoughts on the human soul.
Drake's Anatomy. Chap. 24.
Gale's Court of the Gentiles.
[Glanvil's] Lux Orientalis. Cap. 2, 3.
Hagenbach's Hist. of doctrines. Sec. 247.
Hill's (H.) Infancy of the soul.
Le Clerc's Pneumatics. Part 1, ch. 8.
Ramsay's Man's dignity and perfect. vindic.
Vilvain's Theological Treatises. (An abridgment of Woolnor, Thorndike, Bp. Cowper, Baily, Hakewell, and others.)
Watts' Philosophical Essays. Ess. 9.
Wollaston's Religion of Nature.
Woolnor's Extraction of man's soul.

See a great list of writers on this subject in ALGER'S *History of the doctrine of a future life.* Appendix.

Trance.

Gualtperius in Acta Apostol. x. 10.

Edinburg Encyclopedia.
Flavel's Works. (Pneumatics.)
Locke on the Mind. Bk. 2, ch. 9.
Tennent, Memoirs of.

Tranquility. See PEACE OF MIND.

Transcendentalism. See ATHEISM, NEOLOGY, RATIONALISM.

Abicht, de Philosophia Kantiana.
Bernhard's Darstellung d. Kantisch. Lehren.
Borrowski über Imm. Kant; Darstellung des Lebens und character.
Fichté's Anweisung zum seligen Leben, etc.
Hegel's System des transcend. Idealism.
Kant's Sammtliche Werke.
Koppen's Schelling's Lehre.
Ratze's Betrachtungen über d. Kantische Religionslehre.
Rosencranz's Gesch. d. Kantischen Philos.
Schad's Darstellung des fichteschen System.
Schulze's Bemerkung. ü. Kant's phil. Relig.
Storr's Bemerkung. ü. Kant's Religionslehre.

Transcendentalism—*continued.*

Amer. Biblical Repository. 2d Series. 8:195. 3d Series. 1:64.
Amer. Eclectic Rev. 1:276. (V. Cousin.)
Amer. Whig Rev. 1:233.
Blackwood's Mag. 28:244.
Brownson's Quart. Rev. 2:273,409.
Chalybaus' Hist. survey of speculat. philos.
Christian Examiner. 21:371. 23:170. 28:378. 30:189.
Edinburg Rev. 1:253.
Fairbairn's Theological Essays.
Foreign Quart. Review. 2:307.
Haywood's Analysis of Kant's critic of pure reason.
Kant's Critic of pure reason. Tr. by Semple.
——— Metaphysics. Tr. by Richardson.
Knickerbocker Magaz. 23:205.
Methodist Quart. Review. 5:43.
Müller's Christian doctrine of sin.
New Englander. 1:502.
North Amer. Review. 49:44.
Pamphleteer. 23:151.
Panoplist. 32:151.

Transfiguration of Christ.

Chrysostom, Homiliæ.
Cyril (Alex.), Homiliæ.

Olearii Observationes.
Sonntagii Observationes Miscellanea.

Appleton's (Pres.) Works. Vol. 2.
Bagot's Treatise on the transfiguration.
Bragge (Francis) on Miracles.
Brownrig's (Bp.) Sermons.
Christian Exam. 42:270.
Faber's (G. S.) Sermons.
Felton's (George) Sermons.
Fonsecca's Devout Contemplations.
Goulburn's (E. M.) Parochial Sermons.
Hackett's (Bp.) Sermons.
Hall's (Bp.) Contemplations.
Hawker's (Robert) Works.
Henderson's (John) Illustration of the T.
Hobart's (John H.) Sermons.
Kennaway's (Cha. E.) Sermons at Brighton.
Laurie's (Dr. Thomas) Sermons.
Leland's (John) Discourses.
Manton's (Dr. Tho.) Works.
Porteus (Bp.) on the T. of Christ.
Russell's (Fred.) Expository Sermons.
Saurin's Historical Discourses.
Sharpe's (William) Sermons.
Thomson's (Thomas) Sermons.
Townsend's (George) Sermons.
Van Mildert's Sermons at Lincoln's Inn.
Whitefield's Sermons.
Williams' (Alfred) Sermons.

Translations of Scripture. See ENGLISH BIBLE, NEW VERSION OF ENG. BIBLE, SEPTUAGINT, VULGATE.

Adleri Bibliotheca Biblica. ("Great merit.")
Bernstein's Heilige Evang. Joannis Syrisch.
Bindseil's Verz. d. orig-ausgaben d. Lutherischen Bibelübersetzung.

Translations of Scripture—*continued.*

Bos, Prolegomena. (Exceedingly valuable.)
Castellionis Biblia Sacra Latina. (Elegant, and with valuable prolegomena.)
——— Defensio suarum translationum.
Clerici et Hammondi Versio, cum paraphr., Dissertat., et tabulis chronol. et geograph.
Dupin, Bibliothèque Nouvelle.
Gesenius' Isaia Uebersetz. mit Commentar.
Hirzel, de Pentateucho vers. Syriacæ quam Peschito vocant.
Hodius de Bibliorum textibus orig. versionibus Græcis et Latina vulgata.
Hottingeri Dissertationes. (Extensive and varied information.)
Jaspis, Versio Latina Epistolarum N. T.
Junii Acta Apost. ex Arabica transl. Latine reddita.
Le Clerc, Biblioth.; ancienne et moderne.
Le Long, Biblioth. Sacra: seu syllabus omnium fere S. S. editionum et versionum.
Louette, Hist. des traductions Françoises.
Michaelis Introductio ad Nov. Test.
Palm's Historie der M. Luther's Bibel.
Scaligeri Notæ in Nov. Testamentum.
Simonis Hist. critica Vet. Testamenti.
——— Disquisitiones Criticæ.
Usseri Hist. dogmatica de Scripturis.
Waltoni Prolegomena.

Amer. Bibl. Repos. 6:451.
Beausobre & L'Enfant's Introduction.
Bibliotheca Sacra. 15:261. 16:56.
Brett's Ancient Versions. (Watson's Tracts.)
Brief view of Baptist trans. in India. 1815.
Brown's Hist. of the Propag. of the Gospel.
Buchanan's Notices of Oriental translations.
Butler's Horæ Biblicæ. (An account of the text, early versions, and printed editions.)
Davidson's (S.) Biblical Criticism. *Peshito, Gothic, Syriac, Æthiopic, Armenian,* and other versions.
Eclectic Review. 4th Series. 23:315. *Gothic.*
Encyclopedia Brittanica.
Foster's Contributions to the Eclectic Rev.
Gerard's Institutes of Biblical Criticism.
Gyle's (J. F.) Essays.
Hamilton's Crit. hist. of the versions of the Pentateuch and the Chaldee paraphrase.
Henderson's View of Icelandic translations.
Hewlett's Holy Bible with notes. (Introd.)
Horne's Introduction. *English translations.*
Kennicott's Dissertations.
Kidder's Remarks on Castellio's version.
Kitto's Journal. 3:320. *Gothic version.*
Lamy's Biblical Apparatus.
Lincoln's Elements of Christian Theology.
Llewellyn's History of the Welch versions.
Long's Bibliotheca Sacra.
MacGill's (S.) Lectures.
MacKnight on the Epistles. (General pref.)
Marsh's History of translations, from the earliest period to the present. 1812.
Orme's Historical sketch of the translation and circulation of the Scriptures, to the present. 1815.

Translations of Scripture—*continued.*

Period. Accounts of the Baptist Miss. Soc.
Quar. Rev. 1:276.
Reports of the Brit. and For. Bib. Society.
Serampore Memoirs of Oriental translations. 1834.
Simons' Crit. hist. of Scripture versions.
Spearman's Letters on the Septuagint.
Stuart's (E. C.) The Bible and its Versions.
Thomson & Orme's History of the translation and circulation of S. S. 1815.
Townley's Illustration of Biblical literature.
——— Introd. to the liter. hist. of the Bible.
Tytler (A. F.) on the Principles of Translat.
Wrangham on the Oriental translations.

For valuable notices of translators and biblical scholars, see TOWNLEY's *Illustrations of Biblical Literature,* 3 vols., 1821; ADLER's *Bibliotheca Biblica,* 1789; L. LONG, *Bibliotheca Sacra,* 1723; T. H. HORNE's *Manual of Biblical Bibliography.* For recent translat. into foreign languages, see Reports of British and For. Bible Society, and American and Foreign Bible Society.

Transmigration of Souls.
See METEMPSYCHOSIS.

Transubstantiation.

Albertinus de Eucharistia. ("The best."—WISEMAN.)
Allix, Prefatio historica de dogmate transub.
Anselm, de Corpore et Sanguine Domini.
Bebelii Antiquitates Ecclesiæ.
Beranger, de Sacra Cœna.
Buddei Institutiones Theologiæ Dogmaticæ.
Bullingeri Opera.
Chamieri Dissertationes.
Chemnitii Loci Theologici.
Claude, Traite de l'Eucharist.
Cosini Hist. transubstantiat. papalis.
Dallei Dissertationes.
Derodon, le Tombeau de la messe.
Feverlini Dissertationes.
Flaccus Illyricus, Dissertationes.
Gerhardi Loci Theologicæ.
Hoepfneri Dissertationes.
Hutteri Dissertationes.
Ittigii Select. Hist. Ecclesiast. capita.
Maresii Disputatio Apologetica.
Marheinecke, Hist. tripartita Eucharistiæ.
Moulin, Abregé des controverses.
Œcolampadius de Eucharistia.
Pfaffii Foetus polemicus Lud. Rogerii.
Pictet, Theologie Chrétien.
Placette, l'Autorité des sens. (Acta erud.)
Radberti (P.) Opera. (The first writer [A.D. 850] in favor of transubstantiation. He was answered by many: e. g., Ratram, John Scott, and Rabanus Maurus, Archbishop of Mentz, who denounced the doctrine as an error and a novelty.)
Ratrami Opera. (Quotes Ambrose, Jerome, Isidore, Fulgentius, Augustine, &c., showing that the doct. was unknown to them.

Transubstantiation—*continued.*

Turretini Institutiones Theologicæ.
Vannii de Missa Historia.
Van Till, Disputationes historico-theologica.
Verini (sive Salmasius) Liber de Transub.
Walchii (Geo.) Hist. transubstantionum.
Walchii (J. G.) Miscellanea Sacra.

Abernethy's Dialogues.
——— Remarks on transubstantiation.
Allibond (Peter) on Transubstantiation.
Beveridge's Thesaurus Theologicus.
Beza's True meaning of "This is my body."
Bibliotheca Sacra. 1:110,225.
Bradford's (The Martyr) Works.
Brown on Natural and revealed religion.
Burnet (Bp.) on Idolatry.
Carson's (Alex.) Transubstant. impossible.
Cornthwaite's Trans. impartially considered.
Cosin's Hist. of transubs. ("Cosin was the Atlas of the Protestant religion."—THOS. FULLER. A new edit., by Rev. J. S. Brewer, 1850, gives the authorities at full length.)
Cranmer's (Abp.) Works.
Du Moulin's Apology for the Eucharist.
Faber's (G. S.) Christ's discourse at Capernaum fatal to the doctrine of transubstantiation on the very principle of exposition adopted by Papal divines.
Featley's Transubstantiation exploded.
Gataker on Transubstantiation.
Geddes' Miscellaneous Tracts.
[Goodwin's] T. a peculiar article of the Roman Ch., never owned by the Ancient Ch.
Ingram's Doctrine of Transub. refuted.
Jewell's (Bp.) Works. (Parker Society pub.)
Johnson's Absolute impossibility of T.
Kidder's Demonst. of the Messiah. Part 3.
Knowles' (J. Sheridan) The idol demolished by its own priests. (A strong exhibit.)
More (Dr. Henry) on the Real presence.
Moulin's Apology for the Lord's Supper.
Nelson's Transub. contrary to Scripture.
Newcombe (H.) on Transubstantiation.
Patrick's (Bp.) Works.
Placette's Testimony of sense against T.
Randolph's Enchiridion Theologicum.
Ridley's (Bp.) Works. (Parker Soc. publ.)
Salter's Hall Sermons. (Ser. by Dr. Harris.)
Smith's Errors of the Roman Church.
Stillingfleet's Doctrine of the Trinity.
Taylor's (J.) Polemic Discourses. (Several.)
Tillotson's (Abp.) Sermons.
Turner's (John) Sermons.
Wake's (Abp.) Treatise concerning T.
Whitby's Derision of the breaden God.

This article might be indefinitely enlarged. See MEIER'S *Gesch. der Transubstationslehre; mit Abhandlung von* H. E. G. PAULUS.

Trappists. See CISTERCIANS.

Du Bois, Hist. civile, religieuse, et litteraire, de l'Abbaye de la Trappe.
Felibien, Descrip. de l'Abbaye de la T.
Gaillardin, l'Ordre des Citaux. To 1844.

Trappists—*continued.*

Rance, Règlemens de la Trappe.
Règlemens de la Maison Dieu de Notre Dame de la Trappe.
Ritsert's Orden der Trappisten.
Sartorii Historia Bis tertium.

Fellows' Visit to the Monastery of La Trappe. Plates. 1817.

For a full account of Trappist writers, see DU BOIS, above quoted.

Tree of Knowledge.

Eleutherus de Arbore scientiæ, etc.
Barrington on the Various dispensations.
Baseley's (T.) Sermons.
Burnet's Boyle Lectures. 1724, 1725.
——— on the 39 Articles.
Delany's Revelation examined. Diss. 1.
Gilbert's (N.) Sermons.
Heylin's (John) Theological Lectures.
Horne's (Bp.) Discourses.
King's (Abp.) Origin of evil.
Manston's (Jos.) Lectures to young persons.
Page (Thomas) on the Types.
Pirie's (Alex.) Miscellaneous Works.
Raleigh's (Sir W.) History of the world.

Tree of Life.

Turretini Institutiones.
Witsii Œconomia Fœderis.
Ziegra, Thesaurus.

Arrais' Physical account of the tree of life.
Eliot's (W. L.) Discourses.
Horne's (Bp.) Discourses.
Kennicott's (Benj.) Dissertations.
Lee's (Francis) Dissertations.
Page (T.) on the Types connected with the patriarchal covenant.
Raleigh's (Sir W.) History of the world.

Trent. See COUNCILS.

Tribulation. See AFFLICTION, ANXIETY, MOURNERS, PATIENCE, RESIGNATION, TROUBLE, TRUST.

Trinity.

Athanasius, Orationes. (And other works.)
Augustine, de Trinitate.
Ambrose, Lectiones.
Justin Martyr. Opera quæ extant.
Epiphanius, adversus Hæreses.
Hilary, Libri XII de Trinitate.
Chrysostom, Homiliæ.
Irenæus Detectio: seu contra hæreses.
Cyprian, Epistolæ.
Cyril Alex., de Trinitate.

Alesii (Valentini) Confutatio, etc.
Allix, Judicium veteris Ecclesiæ Judaicæ.
Amyraldus de Mysterio Trinitatis.
Amyrant, de Mysterio Trinitatis.
Boethii Opera Theologica.
Bretschneider's Systematische Entwickelung.

Trinity—*continued.*

Burcher de Deo triuno. (A small but convenient work, made up of extracts from Polycarp, J. Martyr, Irenæus, Tatian, Theophilus, Athenagoras, &c., in the original Greek, with a Latin version.)
Callixti (F. U.) Dissert. de questione, num mysterium sanc. Trinitatis e Vet. Testam. libris possit demonstrari.
Capelli Critica Sacra.
Carpzovii de Sanc. Trinitatis mysterio.
Danæi Synopsis Doct. de Trinitate.
Deylingii Revelat. mysterii sacro-sanc. Tr.
Dorner's Entwickelung-Geschichte der Lehre der person Christi. (Refutes Bauer's History of the Trinity.)
Estius in Præcipua difficiliora S. Scrip.
Hunnii Questiones et Responsiones.
Hyperii Theses Theologicæ.
Misleri (Ioann. Nicol.) Theognosia.
Oehmbs de Deo. (A collection of all the passages, both of Scripture and of the Fathers, arranged under heads in refutation of the several Anti-trinit. doctrines.)
Osiandri Aug. Trin. myst. ex utriusque Vet. et Nov. Test. libris adumbratum.
Quenstedtii (Ioann.) Disputationes.
Sandii Bibliotheca Anti-Trin., etc. To 1684.
Somneri Specimen Theologiæ Soharicæ.
Stapferi Institutiones. Cap. II, sec. 16.
Witsii Exercitationes.
Zanchius de Tribus Elohim.

Allix's Testimony of the Jewish Church.
——— Fathers vindicated.
Am. Bibl. Repos. 4:204.
Am. Monthly Rev. 4:29.
Arnold's (Thomas) Sermons.
Barrow's Defence of the Holy Trinity.
Bates' Works. Chap. 5.
Baxter's End of Controversy.
Bedford's (A.) Defence of the doctrines, &c.
Berriman's Moyer Lectures. 1723, 1724. (Historical.)
Biblioth. Sac. 3:499,760. 4:25.
Bradbury's Mystery of Godliness.
Bull's (Bp.) Defence of the Nicene Creed.
Burgess' (Bp.) Introd. to the doct. of the T.
Burgess' Collection of Tracts.
Burton's Testim. of Ante-Nicene Fathers.
Butler's (Wm. Archer) Sermons.
Bushnel's Christian T. a practical truth.
Calamy's (Edm'd) Sermons at Salter's Hall.
Chapman's (Dr.) Miscellaneous Tracts.
Cheyne's Doctrine of the Holy Trinity.
Christ. Month. Spect. 8:257.
Christ. Quart. Spect. 6:259.
Clarke's (Sam.) Scripture doctrine of the T.
Cleland's Unitarianism Unmasked.
Clements' Moyer Lectures. 1757.
Croft's Bampton Lectures. 1786.
Crosthwaite's (J. C.) Sermons.
Cudworth's Intellec. system of the universe.
D'Oyly's (Dr. George) Sermons.
Drumond (W. H.) on the Trinity.
Eveleigh's (J.) Bampton Lectures. 1792.

Trinity—*continued.*

Faber's Apostolicity of Trinitarianism. (The testimony of history to the antiquity of the doctrine.)
Fuller's (Andrew) Works.
Gastrell on the Trinity, and the way of managing that controversy.
Gill's (John) Sermons and Tracts.
——— Treatise on the Trinity.
Gilpin's (William) Sermons.
Graves' (R.) Scripture Proof, &c.
Hale (Dr. Wm.) on Faith in the Holy T.
Hartley's (T.) Trinity defended.
Hayward's Sermons.
Hey's Lectures in Divinity.
Holden's (Geo.) Scripture Testimony.
Holden's (Henry E.) Doct. of the Trinity.
Hope's (C. D.) Catholic Doctrine.
Horne's Scripture doctrine of the Trinity.
Horsley's (Sam.) Tracts. (Controversy with Priestley.)
Howard's (Leonard) Sermons.
Howard (J.) on the Trinity.
Howell's (W.) The Trinity proved.
Huntingford's Thoughts on the Trinity.
Jackson (J.) on the Trinity.
Jamieson's Sacred History.
Jennings' (D.) Berry St. Lectures. 1733.
Jones' (Wm. of Nayland) Ans. to Clayton on the Spirit. (Gives a particular account of the Hermetic, Pythagorean, and Platonic Trinities.)
——— Catholic doct. of the T. (Sufficient.)
——— Preservative agt. modern Socinians.
Jones' (Sir Wm.) Doctrine of the Trinity.
Kidd's Essay on the Trinity. (Reasons from reason, duration, space, tradition, &c.)
Kidder on the Messias.
Kirby's Philosophical demonst. of the T.
Lady Moyer's Lectures. By Waterland, Berriman, Trapp, Browne, Seed, Bedford, Wheatly, Ridley, Clement, Morell, and others. These lectures were established in 1719, and continued to 1774. They are printed separately.
Marsh's (Bp.) Letters to Archdeacon Travis.
Marshall's (N.) Sermons.
Maurice on the Oriental Trinities.
Morgan on the Effect of the writings of Plato and Philo Judæus on the principles and reasonings of the Fathers of the Ch.
Mortlock's Scripture doct. of the Trinity.
Murray's (A.) Clear display of the Trinity.
Nelson's Doctrine of the Trinity vindicated. (Reply to Clarke.)
New Englander. Periodical. Various pieces.
Norton's Reasons for not believing the doct.
Nye's Doctrine of the Holy Trinity.
Owen's (John) Vindic. of the doct. of the T.
Panoplist. Periodical. Many articles.
Parker's Tr. of the orations of Athanasius.
Pearson on the Creed.
Randolph's Vind. of the doctrine of the T.
Ryland's Life of Hervey.
Scott's (Thomas) Essays.

Trinity—*continued.*

Scott's (Daniel) Demonstration of the Scripture Trinity.
Serle's Horæ Solitariæ. (Appendix.)
Sherlock on the Trinity.
Simpson's True Scripture doct. of the T.
Skelton's (Philip) Sermons.
Spirit of the Pilgrims. 3:225,287,344, et alia.
Stillingfleet's Vind. of the doctrine of the T.
Stuart's Letters to Channing.
Taylor's (Abraham) Scripture doct. of the T.
Tolley's Explanatory View.
Trapp on the Doct. of the Trinity. (Ably answers the strongest objections.)
Tucker's Light of nature pursued.
Vogan's Bampton Lectures. 1837. (Considers the main objections.)
Wallis' Letters on the Trinity.
Waterland (D.) on the Trinity.
Wheatly (Cha.) on the Nicene and Athanasian creeds so far as they express a co-equal Trinity explained and confirmed by the Holy Scriptures.
Whitby's (D.) Thoughts on the Trinity.

For a full list of Antitrinitarian writers, see SAND, *Biblioth. Antitrinitariorum Scriptorum*, 1684; BOCK, *Hist. Antitrinit.*, in 3 vols., folio, with notices of authors, synods, disputations, &c., 1784. Also, THOMAS HEARNE'S *Acct. of all the considerable books and pamphlets concerning the Trinity, between* 1712 and 1720.

Tritheists.

Assemanni Bibliotheca Orientalis.
Cottelerii Monumenta Eccl. Græcæ.
Damascenus de Heresibus.
Harduini Concilia.
Harenburgii Dissertationes.
Rinkius de Orig. et progressu Tritheismi.

Trouble. See AFFLICTION, ANXIETY, RESIGNATION, TRUST.

Allestree's (Richard) Sermons.
Baddelly's (George) Sermons.
Bingham's (Richard) Sermons.
Brady's (Nicholas) Sermons.
Bridge's (W.) Saints' hiding-place.
Coles' (Thomas) Sermons.
Cotton's (John) Mercy mixed with Justice.
Cruden's (W.) Sermons.
Hale's (James) Sermons.
Halyburton's (Thomas) Works.
Horne's (Bp.) Sermons.
Howe's (John) Sermons.
Hurd's (Bp.) Sermons.
Ibbot's (Dr.) Sermons.
Jones' (William) Sermons.
Leightonhouse's Sermons.
McNeile's (Hugh) Sermons.
Newton's (Benjamin) Sermons.
Paterson's (Jas.) Advantages of adversity.
Patrick's (Bp.) Sermons.
Polhill's (E.) Preparation for suffering.
Reynolds' (John) Sermons.
Rogers' (Timothy) Sermons.
Seed's (Bp.) Sermons.
Smith's (Sydney) Sermons.
Toplady's (A. M.) Essays.
Welch's (John) Sermons.

Trust in God.

Abernethy's, John, Sermons.
Adey's, William, Sermons.
Atkinson's, Christopher, Sermons.
Atterbury's, Lewis, Sermons.
Bentley's, Richard, Sermons.
Beveridge's, Bp., Sermons.
Bishop's, William, Village Sermons.
Bowdler's Theological Essays.
Bradley's, Cha., Sermons.
Bull's, Bp., Sermons.
Burder's, H. F., Sermons.
Carr's, George, Sermons.
Charnock's, Stephen, Sermons.
Christian Observer. 11:631.
Close's, F., Sermons.
Coney's, Dr. Thomas, Sermons.
Cooper's, Edward, Sermons.
Cotes', Henry, Sermons.
Crosthwaite's, J. C., Sermons.
Donne's, John, Sermons.
Drysdale's, Dr. John, Sermons.
Duché's, Jacob, Sermons.
Gibbs', John, Sermons.
Heurtley's, Cha. A., Sermons.
Johnson's, Dr. Sam., Sermons.
Jortin's, John, Sermons.
Langhorne's, William, Sermons.
Leighton's, Abp., Sermons.
Leland's, Thomas, Sermons.
Leng's, John, Sermons.
Lucas', Richard, Sermons.
Masillon's Sermons.
Mason's, John, Christian Morals.
Milner's, Joseph, Sermons.
Morehead's, Robert, Discourses.
Morning Exercises at Cripplegate. (Sermon by Sylvester.
Moss', Robt., Sermons.
Neal's, D., Berry Street Sermon.
Newlin's, Thomas, Sermons.
Pierce's, Sam. Eyles, Sermons.
Reeves', William, Sermons.
Rogers', John, Sermons.
Scattergood's, Samuel, Sermons.
Seed's Posthumous Sermons.
Sharp's, Abp., Sermons.
Smallridge's, Geo., Sermons.
Smith's, Samuel S., Sermons.
Stebbings', Henry, Sermons.
Taylor's, John, Sermons.
Toulmin's, J., Sermons.
Trebeck's, Andrew, Sermons.
Venn's, John, Sermons.
Wilcox's, Dan., Sermons.
Witherspoon's, Dr. John, Sermons.

Truth. See LYING, PROMISES.

Arnauld, des Vrayes et des fausses idées. (Against Malebranche on Truth.)
——— Défence contre la réponse, etc.

Truth—*continued.*

Cartesii Meditationes.
Grotius de Jure. Lib. III.
Malbranche, Recherche de la Verité.

Balguy's Law of Truth.
Barbeyrac's Notes on Puffendorf.
Beattie on the Nature of Truth.
Buffier's First Truths.
Butler's Analogy of religion and nature.
Dwight's Theology. Disc. 125.
Edwards' (John) Truth and Errors in relig.
Follet's Origin, science, and end of moral T.
Fuller's Essay on Truth.
Grindall's (Abp.) Remains. (Publication of the Parker Society.)
Hawkins' Bampton Lectures. 1840.
Haynes' Illustrations of faith and practice.
Johnson's (Dr. Sam.) Sermons.
Locke on the Human understanding.
New Englander. 2:359. 3:66.
New England Mag. 7:302.
Oswald on Common Sense.
Powell (Baden) on Natural and Divine T.
Puffendorf's Law of Nature. Bk. 4.
Rose's Duty of maintaining truth.
Saurin's Sermons. (Buying the truth.)
Stennet's (Jos.) Sermons. (Nature of truth.)
Stennet's (Sam.) Sermons. (Propagat. of T.)
Tatham's Chart and Scale of truth.
Thornwell's (J. H.) Discourses on truth.
Tillotson's Sermons.
Van Mildert's (Bp.) Sermons.
Watts' (Isaac) Sermons.
Whately's (Abp.) Essays. Ess. 1.
Wilkins' Nature of Religion.
Wollaston's Religion of Nature.

Truth of God. See FAITHFULNESS.

Tunkers. See GERMAN BAPTISTS.

Two Witnesses. [REV. 11:3.]

Prideaux, de Duobus testibus.

Beith's The two witnesses traced in history.
Bridge's (W.) Works.
Charter's (S.) Sermons.
Elliot's Warburton Lectures.
Glas' (John) Works.
Harrison's Warburton Lectures. 1849.
Homes' Revelation revealed.
Tillinghast's (John) Generation works.
Todd's Donnellan Lectures. 1841.
Worthington's Boyle Lectures.

Types. See under the several types, as BRAZEN SERPENT, SCAPE-GOAT, &c.

Bacmeisteri Explicatio typorum V. Test.
Balduini Passio Christi typica.
Biermanni Moses et Christus.
Cremeri Prodromus typicus.
——— de Typorum usu et abusu.
Driesenii Diatribe de principiis emblemat.
Ewald, Emblemata Sacra.
Glassii Philologia Sacra.
Hiller's Neues system aller Vorbilder J. C.

Types—*continued.*

Honerti Institutiones theologiæ typicæ.
Hulsii Nucleus prophetiæ.
Langii Mysterium Christi. (*Acta erud.*)
Maii Synopsis Theologiæ Symbolicæ.
Michaelis Entwurf der typischen, etc.
Outram de Sacrificiis Judæorum. (Superior.)
Rappolti (Frideric.) Dissertationes.
Rudelbach, de Symbolis ac Typis.
Snabellii Amœnitates Theologiæ.
Weisman, de Sensu spirituali Vet. Test.

Aitkin's Teachings of the Types.
Bates' (Julius) Evid. of types vindicated.
Brown's (John) Sacred Tropology.
Burns' Sermons on Types and Metaphors.
Cecil's Remains. *Mode of explaining.*
Chevalier's Hulsean Lectures. 1826.
Close (Francis) on the Typical persons.
Crombie's Character and offices of Christ.
Dickie's Typical forms and special ends in Creation.
Doddridge's Lectures. Part 9.
——— Ten Sermons.
Eclectic Review. 4th Series. 26:194.
Edwards' (Jonathan) Works.
Fairbairn's Typology of Scripture. ("Learned and judicious."—J. PYE SMITH.)
Guild's Moses pourtrayed.
Hawkins' (Dr. Edward) Sermons.
Hill's Testimony to the Messiah. (Not controversial, but forestalls the "Essays and Reviews.")
Juke's (Andrew) Types of Genesis.
Keach's Key to Scripture metaphors.
Lavington's Nature and use of a type.
Le Bas' Scripture fulfilled.
Lee's Orbis miraculum.
Lond. Quart. Rev. 10:382.
Lord's Literary and Theol. Journal. 5:353.
Ludlam on Scripture Metaphors.
Mather's (Cotton) Types of the Old Test.
Mather (Sam.) on the O. and N. Test. types.
McCosh's Typical forms in creation.
McEwen's Grace and Truth.
McKnight on the Language of Scripture.
Muenscher on Typical Interpretation.
Newton's (Rich.) Jewish Tabernacle.
Outram on Sacrifices.
Page (T.) on the Types.
Piers' Typical illustration considered.
Ridgeley's Body of Divinity.
Seiss' (Jos. A.) Holy Types; or the Gospel in Leviticus.
Scott's (John) Christian Life.
Simpson's (F. G.) Lent Lectures.
Slye's (Jas.) The old mine explored.
Smith's (G. B.) Typical parts of Christ's teaching.
Steward on Mediatorial Sovereignty.
Taylor's (Dr. Tho.) Moses and Aaron.
——— Christ revealed.
Thompson's (Edw.) Evidences of Christ'y.
Townley's Maimonides.
Trevor's Types and Antitypes.
Tyng's Rich Kinsman; or History of Ruth.

Types—*continued.*

Vertue's (H.) Christ and the Church.
Warburton's Divine Legation of Moses.
Wemyss' Key to the symbolical language of Scripture.
West's Figures and Types of the O. Test.
Wilson's (John) Doct. of Scripture types.
Wood's (J.) Nature and use of figures. (Chiefly extracted from Keach.)
Worden's Types unveiled; or the gospel picked out of the legal ceremonies.

Unbelief. See FAITH, INFIDELITY.

Abernethy's Evil heart of incredulity.
Alexander's (J. W.) Sermons.
Bridge's (W.) Works.
Case's (Thomas) Sermons.
Chalmers' (Thomas) Sermons.
Charnock's (Stephen) Works.
Churchill on Unbelief.
Clerke's (Richard) Sermons.
Davy's (C.) Sermons.
Donne's (John) Sermons.
Erskine's (Ebenezer) Sermons.
Fearn (J.) on Belief and Unbelief.
Gresley's (William) Sermons.
Hannam's Compendium.
Jamieson's (John) Sermons. (8 on this subj.)
Lamb's (Robert) Sermons.
Lucas' (Richard) Sermons.
Melville's (Henry) Sermons.
Mills' (Tho.) Absurdity of unbelief.
Milner's (Joseph) Sermons.
Moberly's (G.) Sermons at Winchester.
Owen's Reasons of faith.
Panoplist. 4:247.
Payson's (Edward) Sermons.
Porteus' (Bp.) Sermons.
Pyle's (T.) Sermons.
Rees' (Abraham) Sermons.
Scattergood's (Sam.) Sermons.
Seabury's (Bp.) Sermons.
Sherlock's Sermons.
Shuttleworth's (P. N.) Sermons.
Spurgeon's (Cha. H.) Sermons. 2d Series.
Tillotson's Sermons.
Trench's (Richard C.) Sermons.
Venn's (Henry) Sermons.
Welch's (John) Sermons.
Willison's (John) Works.

Uncertainty of Life. See FRAILTY PROCRASTINATION.

Blair's (Hugh) Sermons.
Bramston's (William) Sermons.
Calthrop's (John) Sermons.
Edwards' (Jonathan) Works.
Fawcett's (John) Sermons.
Francklin's (Thomas) Sermons.
Jones' (Walter) Sermons.
Leightonhouse's (W.) Sermons.
Moss' (Robert) Sermons.
Morton's (Edward) Sermons.
Parkinson's (R.) Sermons.
Stebbings' (Henry) Sermons.

Uncharitableness. See CENSORIOUSNESS, CHRISTIAN UNION, EVIL SPEAKING, FELLOWSHIP, RASH JUDGMENT, SECTS, UNITY.

Watts' Orthodoxy and charity united.

Uncleanness. See CHASTITY.

Brydane, Conférence sur l'Impurité.
Lebrun, Electuaire souverain.
Picard, le Fouet des paillards.

Barlow (W.) on Fornication.
Becon's (Tho.) Works. (Parker Soc. pub.)
Blair's (James) Sermons.
Burnet's (Gilbert) Sermons.
Collier's (Jeremy) Essays on moral subjects.
Cosens' (John) Sermons.
Evans' (Dr. John) Sermons.
Garbent's Testimony against whoremongers.
Goodwin's (H.) Parish Sermons.
Holbrook's (Anthony) Sermons.
Osterwald on the Nature of uncleanness.
Scott's (John) Sermons.
Southgate's (Richard) Sermons.
Spectator. No. 286.
Stebbings' (Henry) Sermons.
Warter's (John W.) Sermons.
Zollikoffer on Prevalent vices.
——— on Fasts and Festivals.

Unequal Distribution of Good and Evil. See INEQUALITIES, &c.

Ashburnham's, William, Sermons.
Bather's, Edward, Sermons.
Du Moulin's, Peter, Sermons.
Gresley's, William, Sermons.
Hill's, George, Sermons.
Landon's, W., Sermons.
Maltby's, Bp., Sermons.
Moss', Robert, Sermons.
Nares', R., Sermons.
Phillips', R., Sermons.
Pyle's, Philip, Sermons.
Saurin's Sermons.
Warter's, John W., Sermons.
Yonge's, James, Sermons.
Zollikoffer's Sermons on Education.

Unigenitus. See PAPAL BULLS.

D'Alembert, Essai sur la destruction des Jesuites.
Dubois, Collectio actor. publ. Clement XI.
Fehmelii (A. G.) Dissertationes.
Fricke (J.) die Bulle unigenitus.
Jenichii (G. F.) Historia et examen bullæ Clementis XI contra Quesnellum.
Lafiteau, Hist. de la constit. Unigenitus.
Marmontel, Régence du Duc d'Orleans.
[Nivelle,] la Constitution Unigenitus.
Noailles, Memoires et instructions secrets.
Pfaffii Acta publica a Clemente XI.
Schillingii Hist. bullar. Clementis VI et XI.
[Villefore,] Anecdotes: ou memoires secréts.
Gordon's Famous bull U. impartially related; wherein the absurdities and delusions of Popery are laid open.
Whately's Parallel bet. Pagans and Jesuits.

Union of Church and State.
See ESTABLISHMENTS.

Union with Christ.
Albertus de modo Unionis mysticæ.
Basnage, l'Union de l'âme avec Jésus.
Breithaupti Inst. theolog. de credendis et agendis.
Carpovii Theologia revelata dogmatica.
Klemius de Unione S. S. cum fidelibus.
Quistorpius de Conjugio mystico.
Scharfius de Mystico J. C. adventu infideles.
Schelvigii (Sam.) Dissertationes.
Schmidtius (Seb.) de Conjugio mystico.
Schomeri Differentia unionis personalis et mysticæ.
Barker's (John) Morning Exercises.
Bayley's (B.) Sermons.
Dealtry's (Archdeacon) Sermons.
Dickinson's Letters. Letter 17.
Dorney's Divine Contemplations.
Ferguson's (Robt.) Lectures.
Flavel's Method of grace in the gospel.
Gammon's Christ's a Christian life.
Hall's Help to Zion's pilgrims. Chap. 4. (A very valuable little manual for young Christians.)
Harte's (W. M.) Sermons.
Heurtley's (C. A.) Sermons.
Marshall on Sanctification. (Famous.)
McGill's (W.) Sermons.
Murray's Christian's Pattern.
Polhill's Christus in Corde.
Sherlock's Knowledge of Jesus Christ.
Simeon's (C.) Works.
Watts' (Isaac) Sermons.
Wilberforce's (R. S.) Sermons.
Williams' (John) Sermons.
Yonge's (James) Sermons.

Union, Christian. See CHRISTIAN UNION.

Unitarians. See ARIANS, ATONEMENT, GENUINENESS OF 1 JOHN V. 7, LOGOS, JESUS CHRIST, SOCINIANS, &c.

Pro.

Bidelii Rationes duodecem.
Eniedini Explicatio locorum S. S. ex quibus trinitatis dogma stabiliri solet.
Franzii Disputationes.
Ritteri Demonstratio quod Christus non sit ipse Deus.
Sandii Bibliotheca Antitrinitarum.
Schaffer's Kurtzer Bericht auf die Frage, etc.
Servetus de Trinitatis Erroribus.
Alexander's (John) Crit. notes on 1 Cor. xv.
Alger's (W. R.) History of the Cross.
Allen (J. H.) on Orthodoxy.
Amner (Rich.) on the Prophecies of Daniel.
Aspland's (Robt.) Works.
Bartol's Sermons.
Barlee's Review of Trinitarianism; chiefly as it appears in the writings of Pearson, Bull, Waterland, Sherlock, and Howe.
Brooks (Cha. T.) on Christ's teaching.
Burnap's Christianity—its essence, &c.
Cappe's Crit. remarks on important texts.

Unitarians—*continued.*

Pro.

Carpenter's (Lant.) View of Unitarianism.
——— Proofs from Scripture.
——— Letters to Dr. Vessie.
——— (Other treatises.)
Channing's (Wm. E.) Works.
Christian Disciple. Periodical. 1819–1824.
Chris. Exam. Period. Boston. Since 1824.
Chris. Reformer. Periodical. Since 1834.
Collins' (Ant.) Defence of the U. faith.
——— Supreme deity of the Father.
Dewey's (Orv.) Discourses and Discussions.
Disney's Letters to Dr. Knox.
——— Sermons.
Drummond's (W. H.) Doct. of the Trinity.
Durnap on Unitarianism.
Eddowe's (Ralph) Sermons.
Eddy's Reasons for becoming a Unitarian.
Emlyn's (Thomas) Works.
Elliot's (W. G.) Doctrines of Christianity.
Evanson's Doct. of the Trinity examined.
——— Letter to the Bp. of Gloucester.
Frothingham's (N. L.) Sermons.
Furness' (W. H.) Genius of Christianity.
——— History of Jesus.
Grundy's Evang. Christianity considered.
Harrington's (Joseph) Sermons.
Hawthorne (G. S.) on the Trinity.
Haynes on the Attributes of God.
Hedge's Reason in Religion.
Hopkins' Appeal to common sense.
Hyndman's Principles of Unitarianism.
Jardine on the Love of God.
——— Sermons. Edited by J. P. Estlin.
Kenrick's Exposition of the New Testament.
Kentish's Principles of Unitarians.
Lamson's Church of the first 3 centuries.
Lindsay's Apol. on resigning his vicarage.
——— Against Robt. Robinson of Camb.
——— Address to Oxford students.
——— on Praying to Christ.
——— Sequel to the Apology.
(Mr. L. was a notable champion of Unitarianism, and wrote several other treatises. A list of writers in opposition to him, is given by DR. KIPPIS, in one of his notes to Doddridge's Lectures.)
Livermore's Com. on the Ep. to the Romans.
Madge on the Personality of the H. Ghost.
Martineau's Studies of Christianity.
Maurice on the Unitarian faith.
Morrison's Notes on the Gospels.
North's Theological Essays.
Norton's (Andrews) Statement of reasons, &c.
Noyes' Theological Essays.
Peabody's (A. P.) Sermons.
Pierce's Tracts. (These produced a fruitful controversy in 1720, an account of which is given in Bogue & Bennet's History of Dissenters.)
Porter's Lectures on Christian doctrine.
Priestley's History of early opinions.
——— Appeal to professors of Christianity.
——— Illustrations of Scripture.

Unitarians—*continued.*

Pro.

Priestley's Corruptions of Christianity.
——— (Other treatises in his "Works.")
Scott's Effect of the creation of J. Christ.
Sears (E. H.) on Regeneration.
Servetus (or Reves) on the Trinity.
Smith's Design and end of the controversy.
Sparks (J.) on the Moral tendency of U.
——— Unitarian Miscellany.
Taylor's Key to the Apostolical writings.
——— Scripture doctrine of the Atonement.
Taylor's (H.) Letters of Ben Mordecai.
Taylor's (James) Faith and Duty.
Theological Repository. Periodical.
Toulmin's Efficacy of Unitarian doctrine.
——— Exhortation to Christian people.
——— Life of Socinus.
——— Life of Biddle.
Tracts of the Unitarian Association. 15 vols.
Wakefield's Enquiry into early opinions.
——— Trans. of the N. Test. and notes.
Ware's (Henry, Sen.) Sermons.
Ware's (Henry, Jun.) Letters to Trinitarians.
Whiston's Primitive Christianity revived. (This book called out many replies. See a list of such as were published between 1711 and 1740, in HORNE's *Catalogue of Queen's College Library.*)
Whitmarsh's Catechism.
Wilson's (John) Scripture proofs and illustrations.
——— Concessions of Trinitarians. (Extracts from eminent critics and commentators.)
Worcester on Atonement and Sacrifice.
Yates on Unitarianism. (Rep. to Wardlaw.)
——— Sequel to Do.

Brief treatises advocating Unitarian sentiments are extant, by Acton, Aspland, Barrington, Bakewell, Bennet, Bromhead, Colman, Elton, Fellowes, Francklin, Fullagan, Garnham, Harris, Howe, Hunter, Kenrick, Mardon, Phillips, Platt, Rowe, &c.

Con. See ATONEMENT, SACRIFICE.

Calovii Systema locorum theologicarum.
——— XXIX Disputationes.
Hoornbeckii Sociniasmus confutatus.
Masii Synopsis Theologiæ.
Olearii Synopsis Errorum.
——— Dissertationes.
Thummii Majestas Jesu Christi.
Turretinus de Satisfactione Christi.
Whitby, de vera Christi Deitate.

Allwood's Lectures on Prophecy.
Baker (G. A.) on Unitarianism.
Baylee (Joseph) on Unitarianism.
Bedford's Testimony of the ancient Jews.
Bibliotheca Sacra. 15:726.
Brown's (John) Eight Sermons.
Bull's Opinion of the Ch. for the first 3 cent.
Burgh's Belief of Christians in the first 3 centuries. (Reply to Lindsay.)
Burton's Testim. of the Ante-Nicene Fathers.
Chamberlain's Christian verity stated.

Unitarians—*continued.*

Con.

Christian Observer. 17:1, 205, 345, 417, 561, 624, 697, 769.
Clelland's Unitarianism unmasked.
Cooper's (C.) Veil turned aside.
Daubeny's Scripture its own interpreter.
——— Remarks on the Unitarian method of interpreting Scripture.
Easton's Hist., doct., and tendencies of U.
Felton on the Christian faith.
Garbett's Unitarianism indefensible.
Geddes' Letter to Priestley.
Hampton's Remarks on Taylor's Discourse.
——— Answer to Priestley on Atonement.
Hawker on Plenary Inspiration. (Reply to Porter.)
Horsley's Tracts. (On the historical question of the belief of the early Christians.)
Jamieson's Vindication of Script. doctrine.
Knight on the Old Testament proof, &c.
Knowles' Primitive Christianity.
Kohlman's Unitarianism philosophically and theologically examined.
Law's (Jos.) Review of Unitarianism. (Reply to Hyndman.)
——— Doctrine of the Divine unity.
Macgowan's (John) Works.
Magee's (Abp.) Discourses and Dissertations.
Miller's Letters to the Baltimore Church.
Moyer Lectures. (A series of discourses delivered in London from 1719 to 1774.)
Moysey's Bampton Lectures. 1818.
Nares' Remarks on the Unitarian New Test.
Noel's (B. W.) Christianity comp'd with U.
Norris' Account of reason and faith.
Powell's (Baden) Rational Relig. examined.
Presbyterian Review. (Numerous articles.)
Princeton Review. (Numerous articles.)
Ridley on the Div. of the Holy Ghost.
Seed's (Jeremiah) Eight Sermons.
Stuart's (Moses) Reply to Channing.
Trapp's Moyer Lectures. 1729.
Twell's Sermons. (24 at the Boyle Lecture, and 8 at the Moyer.)
Wardlaw's Unitarianism incapable of vindication. (Reply to Yates.)
——— Nature and extent of the Atonement.
Wheatley on the Athanasian and Nicene Creeds.
Wood's (Dr. L.) Letters to Unitarians.
——— Reply to Dr. Ware.

A copious list of books on the U. controversy, published anterior to 1750, is given by WALCH, *Bibliotheca Theologica.*

Unitarians, History of.
See HISTORY OF DOCTRINES.

Boch, Historia anti-Trinitariorum.
Lange's Gesch. u. Lehrbegriff d. Unitarier vor d. Nicaenischen Synode.
Martin's Gesch. d. Dogma v. d. Gottheit C. in d. 4 ersten Jahrh.
Purmann's Gesch. d. Glaubens an einen Gott.
Ritteri Eusebii de divinitate C. sententia.

Unitarians, History of—*continued.*

Stoinii Historia originis Unitariorum.
Vogelsangii Fides Nicena de filio Dei, etc., 3 primis sæculis.
Walchii (J. G.) Vindiciæ Origenis de div. Christi.
Zeltneri Historia Crypto-Socinismi.

American Quart. Register. 1832.
Beard's U. in its actual state. 1862.
Berriman's History of the controversy.
Bogue & Bennet's History of Dissenters.
Christian Disciple. (Many articles.)
Christian Examiner. 2:264. 3:337. 4:197,291. 9:348. 38:291. 40:303. 42:378. 60:64. And other articles.
Chris. Monthly Spect. 10:86.
Christian Reformer. London. 1834, till now.
Eaton's Hist., doctrines, and tendency of U.
Ellis' Half century of the Unitarian controversy among the Congregationalists of Massachusetts. 1857.
Firmin's History of the Unitarians.
Martineau's (Jas.) Studies of Christianity.
Monthly Journal. Periodical. Boston.
Quarterly " Predecessor of the Monthly.
Nye's History of Unitarianism.
Princeton Review. 37:575.
Spirit of the Pilgrims. 2:65,122,177,289. 3:113,337,503. 4:31,80. 5:20,145.
Sprague's Annals of the Am. pulpit. Vol. 8.
Taylor's (G. G.) Retrospect of religious life in England. 1845.
Wallace's (Rob.) Antitrinitarian Biography.
——— History of Unitarianism in Europe, to the close of the 17th century.
Ware (Henry), Memoir of.

Unitarians are often called, by their opponents, Socinians; though not so often as formerly. I have enumerated writers under both heads. The division is unsatisfactory, but no inconvenience can result to the reader. On the continent of Europe the term Socinian is commonly applied to all classes of Antitrinitarians.

United Associate Church. See SECESSION.

United Brethren. See MORAVIANS.

United Presbyterian Church.

Formed by the junction, in America, of the "Associate," and "Associate Reformed" Churches.

Blakie's (Dr. A.) The Organ.
——— The Schools.
Christian Instructor.* Periodical. Philada.
Evangelical Repository.* " " 1821 to the present.
McKerrow's Hist. of the Secession Church.
Presbyterian Witness. Period. Cincinnati.
Ritchie's Pastor's Gift-book.
——— Christian's Friend.

* These were conjoined in 1862.

The Testimony of the United Presbyterian Churches. Philadelphia. 1859.
Thomson (J. R.), Life of, and Sermons.
Union Presbyterian. Periodical. Cincinnati.
United Presbyterian Rev. Pittsburg. Penna.
United Secession Magazine.

Unity of God. See POLYTHEISM.

Cyril Alex., Opera. Cura et studio Auberti. (The only complete edition.)
Cyril Hieros., Catecheses.
Behmii Disputationes de Deo.
Calovii Theol. naturalis et revelata de theognasia.
Grotius de Veritate Christianæ religionis.
Osiandri Exercit. de nominibus Divinis.
Abernethy's (John) Sermons.
Atterbury's (Lewis) Sermons.
Boston's (Thomas) Sermons.
Brown's Philos. of the mind. Lect. 93.
Burnet on the 39 Articles.
Clarke's Demonstration. Prop. 7.
Clay's (J.) Sermons.
Cudworth's Intellectual System. Ch. 4.
Dwight's Theology. Disc. 4.
Fiddes on the Decalogue.
Foster's (James) Sermons.
Foster's Natural Religion. Ch. 2.
Fotherby's (Bp.) Atheomastix.
Gifford's Elucidation of the unity of God.
Hallet's (Joseph) Works.
Hole on the English Liturgy.
Horsley's Tracts on the Socinian controv.
Howe's (John) Works.
Hunt's (Jeremiah) Sermons.
Jackson on the Existence and Unity of God.
Jamieson's Use of Sacred History.
Knowles' (Thomas) Sermons.
Lowman's Unity of God. (The argument *a priori.*)
Parsons' Catechetical Lectures.
Secker's (Abp.) Works.
Sherlock's Vindication. Sec. 4.
Skelton's (Philip) Sermons.
Slade's (James) Plain Sermons.
Stuart's Letters to Channing.
Taylor (Abraham) on Faith.
Tillotson's (Abp.) Works.
Vaughn's (J.) Lectures. Lect. 5.
Warburton's Divine Legation. Lib. II.
Wardlaw's Discourses. Disc. 1.
Wesley's (John) Sermons.
Whitaker's (Ed. W.) Sermons.
Wilkins on Natural Religion.
Wisheart's (William) Sermons.
Witherspoon's Works. Lect. 9.

Unity of the Human Race. See MAN.

Pro.

De Salles, Hist. genérale d. races humaines.
Humbolt's Ansichtender Natur.

Agassiz's Origin of the human races. (Maintains that all mankind are of one species, but did not originate from one pair.)
Amer. Biblical Repos. 2d Series. 10:29.

Unity of the Human Race—*continued.*

Pro.

Bachman's Doct. of the unity, &c., examined on the principles of science.
Cabell's Testimony of modern science to the unity of mankind.
Caldwell's Unity of the race of man.
Christian Examiner. 49:111.
Christian Quart. Spect. 3:56.
Christian Review. 16:226.
Dawson's (J. W.) Archaia.
Democratic Review. 11:111.
Hamilton's Pentateuch and its assailants.
Johnes' Philological proofs of the recent origin of the human race. (From a comparison of the languages of Europe, Asia, Africa, and America.)
Kames' Origin and diversity of mankind.
Knox's Races of men.
Latham's Varieties of mankind.
——— Man and his migrations.
Lord's Theol. and Lit. Journal. 3:424.
Meade's (Bp.) The Bible and the Classics.
Monthly Review. 119:18.
North Amer. Rev. 73:163.
North British Rev. 4:177.
Pickering on the Races of men.
Presbyterian Quarterly Review. 3:177.
Prichard's Physical history of mankind.
Princeton Rev. 21:159. 22:313,603. 31:103.
Prot. Episc. Monthly Review.
Quarterly Review. 3:68.
Smith's (Sam. S.) Causes of the diversity of figure, color, &c.
——— Strictures on Lord Kames.
Smyth's (Tho.) Unity of the human race. (Reviews Agassiz.)
Tullidge's (Henry) Triumphs of the Bible.
Van Arminge's Natural history of man.
Wartz's Anthropology of the uncivilized races.

Con.

Gobineau's Moral and intellectual diversity of races. Tr. by Hotz; with notes.
Morton's (Dr. S. G.) Types of mankind.
——— Archæology of the Amer. Indians.
——— Hybridity in men and animals.
——— Crania Ægyptiaca.
Nott & Gliddon's Types of mankind.
——— Indigenous races of the earth.

Unity of Sense. See DOUBLE SENSE.

Universal Language.

Beck's Universal language by which all nations may understand each other.
Wilkins'

Universalists.

Pro.

Petersenii Opera. (Mostly published, at various times, in German.)
Austin's (J. M.) Review of J. S. Backus.
——— Debate with Holmes.

Universalists—*continued.*

Pro.

Balfour's Letters. (Reply to Hudson.)
——— Letters to Moses Stuart.
——— on Sheol, Hades, and Gehenna.
Ballou's (Hosea, Sen.) Sermons.
——— Review of Dr. Hawes.
——— on the Atonement.
——— on Divine benevolence.
——— on the Parables.
Berean, The. Periodical. 1802 to 1810.
Bourne (Sam.) on Future punishment.
Brooks' Universalism a practical power.
Brown's (James) Scripture redemption.
Browne's (L. C.) Review of M. Hale Smith.
Canfield's Review of Joel Hawes.
Chauncy's Salvation of all men.
——— Mystery hid from ages.
——— on the Fall and its consequences.
——— View of Episcopacy.
——— Benevolence of the Deity.
Chris. Ambassador. Period. 1851 to present.
Clapp's (Theod.) Theological Views.
Clark's (Rich.) Vind. of the honor of God.
Cogan's Characteristics of Christianity.
Davis (Tho.) on Endless sufferings.
Dobney's Doctrine of future punishment.
Dutton's (Salmon) Thoughts on God.
Flanders' Review of Alex. Hall.
Foster's (Dan.) Exam. of Nathan Strong.
Gospel Banner. Period. 1834 to the present.
Grinfield's (Edw. W.) Image of God in man.
——— Nature and extent of the Christian dispensation.
Harris' (J.) The future life.
Huntingdon's (Joseph) Calvinism improved.
King (T. S.) on Endless punishment.
Kingsford's Appeal to the Scriptures.
Kneeland's (Abner) Lectures.
Lake (E. H.) on Endless Punishment.
Livermore's Bible doctrine of hell.
——— Guide to Universalist theology.
——— Proof texts examined.
Morse's (Pitt) Vindication. (Agt. Parker.)
——— Answer to Johnson.
Murray's (John) Vind. of Universalism.
——— Letters and Sermons.
New Covenant. Period. —— to the present.
Paige's Select. from eminent commentators.
Pingrees' Debate with N. L. Rice.
Pitrat's Pagan origin of Partialist doctrines.
Relly's Affinity bet. Christ and his Church.
——— Sadducee detected.
Rogers' Pro and Con of Universalism.
Sawyer's Letters to Remington.
——— Review of Hatfield.
Simpson on Future punishment.
Skinner's Universalism illustrated.
Smith (T. S.) on Divine Government.
Stafford's Thoughts on the life to come.
Star in the West. Period. 1837 to present.
Streeter's Familiar Conversations.
Thayer's Theology of Universalism.
——— Origin and history of the doctrine of endless punishment.

Universalists—*continued.*

Pro.

Thompson on Universal grace and atonem't.
——— on Eternal Penalty.
Townsend's (Shippie) Gospel News.
Trumpet, The. Period. 1828 to the present.
Universalist Expositor. Period. 1832–1840.
——— Miscellany. " Lond. 1797–1805.
——— Magazine. " 1819–1828.
——— Quarterly. " 1844 to present.
——— The. " 1864 to present.
Watson (Richard) on Redemption.
Whiston's Primitive Christianity.
Whittemore's Hist. of Universalism. 1830.
Williamson's (Isaac D.) Sermons.
Wilson's Reasons for our hope.
Winchester's (E.) Lectures on the prophecies.
——— Dialogues.
——— (Other works.)
Wistanley's New law of righteousness.
Young's Calvinism and U. contrasted.

Con.

Delbut, la Certitude d'un enfer.
Grappii (Zech.) Disputationes.
Ittigii (T.) Exercitationes Theologicæ.
Portzig's Triumphirende Wahrheit.
Wolf's Anmerkungen ü. d. Frage, etc.

Alexander's (Archib.) Universalism false.
Amer. Biblical Repos. 12:70. 2d Series. 4:1. 3d Series. 1:52. 5:651. 6:75.
Andrews' Moral tendency of the doctrine of Universalism.
Bartlett's Lectures on modern U. 1856.
Bates' (Bp.) Works.
Christian Quart. Spectator. 5:266.
Cook's (Parsons) Universalism Exposed.
Coon on the Doct. of endless punishment.
Crowell on Universal Salvation.
Davis' Universalism Unmasked.
Dexter's (H. M.) Verdict of Reason.
Douglas' (Neil) Antidote to Deism.
Edwards' (Jon.) Salvation of all men examined. (Reply to Chauncy.)
Emmons' (Nathaniel) Sermons.
Fuller's (Andrew) Letters to Vidler.
——— Gospel its own Witness.
George's Universalism not of the Bible.
Haldane (J. A.) on Universal pardon.
Hall's (Alex.) Universalism against itself.
Hamilton's (J. L.) Scheme of Redemption.
Hamilton (R. W.) on Rewards and punishm.
Hamilton (W.) on Opinions recently propagated. 1725.
Hare's (Edw.) Preservative ag. Socinianism.
Hatfield's Universalism as it is. 1841.
Hawes' Reasons for not being a Universalist.
Hopkins (Sam.) on a Future state.
Isaac on the Doct. of universal restoration.
Jerram's Letters to a Universalist.
Knowlton's Elements of mod. materialism.
Lee's (L.) Universalism examined.
Lupton's (William) Sermons.
——— on Future punishment.
McCalla on the Salvation of all men.

Universalists—*continued.*

Con.

McLeod's Modern Universalism. 1837.
Marsom (John) on Universal restoration.
Mather (S.) on the Salvation of all men.
Methodist Quar. Review. 2:81.
New Englander. 1:35. 9:186.
Parker's (Joel) Lectures on Universalism.
Pond's (Enoch) Probation.
Powers (J. H.) on Universal salvation.
Priest's Anti-Universalist.
Princeton Review. 8:327. 15:507.
Remington's Anti-Universalist.
Rice's Debate with E. M. Pingree.
Royse's Universalism a modern invention.
Rust (Bp.) on Origen's opinions.
Serpent Uncoiled.
Smith's (M. Hale) U. renounced. (Gives the experience of the author, and other Universalist ministers, as to the tendency of the system.)
——— Universalism not of God.
Smyth (John) on the Forgiveness of sin.
Spalding's U. confounds and destroys itself.
Spirit of the Pilgrims. 2:406.
Spurgeon's (C. H.) Sermons. First series.
Stearn's (J. G.) Antidote to the doctrine, &c.
Strong's (Nath.) Doct. of eternal misery.
Strong's (Will.) Sermons.
Stuart's (Moses) Exegetical Essays.
Taylor's (D.) Eternity of fut. pun. asserted.
——— " " " reasserted.
Theolog. and Literary Journal. 3:395.
Thompson's Doctrine of universal pardon.
Todd's Renunciation of Universalism.
Whitman's (Bernard) Friendly Letters.
Wright's Eternity of hell torments.

Universalism, History of.

Balfour, Life of; by Whittemore.
Ballou (H.), Life of; by his son Maturin.
Ballou's (H., Jun.) Ancient history of U.
Brown's Origin and prog. of the doct., &c.
Hatfield's Universalism as it is. 1841.
Murray (Rev. John), Life of; by himself.
Smith's (S. R.) Establishment and progress of Universalism in New York.
Stacey (Nathaniel), Life of; by himself.
Winchester, Life of; by Vidler.
Whittemore's History of Universalism, from the Reformation to the present. 1829. (A new and enlarged edition, 1860.)

University Degrees.

Malden on the Origin of University degrees.

Unjust Steward. See PARABLES.

Unpardonable Sin.

Athanasius, Epistolæ.
Augustine, Sermones.
Jerome, ad Marcellam.

Amyraldi Theses de Peccato.
Botsac's Sünde in den Heiligen Geist.
Bugenhagius de Peccato contra S. Sp.

Unpardonable Sin—*continued.*

Calmeti Dissertationes. (Pref. to Mark.)
Carpovii Illust. incredulitatis finalis.
Hageman's Sünde wider den Heiligen Geist.
Hoornbeckii Theologia Practica.
Klaiber's Neutest. Lehre von der Sünde.
Maresii Disputationes Theologicæ.
Markius de Blasphemia.
Musæi (J.) Dissertationes.
Nitzsch de Peccato homini cavendo, etc.
Osiandri (Luc.) Dissertationes.
Œttingenii de Peccato in S. Sp. Disputatio.
Rathlef's Laster des H. Geist.
Schaff die Sünde wider den H. Geist.
Walch (J. E. I.) Dissertationes.

Augustin's (St.) Sermons on Matthew.
Baxter's (Richard) Sermons.
Bridges' (William) Sermons.
Burnet's (Bp.) Sermons.
Burton's (Edward) Sermons.
Carr's (Samuel) Sermons.
Chalmers' (Thomas) Sermons.
Christian's Magazine. 3:46.
Clarke's (Dr. Samuel) Sermons.
Cockrane's (James) Sermons. (3 on this sub.)
Cookesley's (W. G.) Sermons.
Cosens' (John) Sermons.
Cowie's Hulsean Lectures. 1854.
Disney's (John) Sermons.
Donne's (John) Sermons.
Emmon's (Nathaniel) Sermons.
Fisk's (George) Sermons.
Fuller's (Andrew) Works. (Takes up all the passages of Scrip. relating to the subject.)
Gilpin's (William) Sermons.
Green's (James) Sermons.
Gregory's (Thomas) Sermons.
Goodwin's (H.) Sermons.
Hale's (John of Eton) Tracts. (Several on this subject.)
Hare's (Julius C.) Sermons.
Hoole's (Joseph) Sermons.
Horberry on Future Punishment.
Howe's Works.
Jortin's (John) Sermons.
Kollock's (S. K.) Sermons.
Lambe's (Charles) Sermons.
Lamont's (David) Sermons.
Lightfoot's (John) Sermons.
Marsden's Hulsean Lectures.
Marshall's (Nathaniel) Sermons.
Martin on the Sin against the Holy Ghost. (Reviews Bayle's reasonings on the entrance of sin into the world.)
Mortimer's (Thomas) Lectures.
Muir (W.) on the Holy Spirit.
Müller's Christian doct. of sin. (Appendix.)
Newton's (Bp.) Dissertations on parts of the New Testament.
Ninds' (William) Sermons.
Orme (Wm.) on Divine influence.
Owen's (John) Pneumatologia. ("Worth its weight in gold."—RYLAND.)
Pearce's (Bp.) Sermons.
Princeton Review. 16:376. 18:376.

Unpardonable Sin—*continued.*

Pusey's (E. B.) Sermons.
Russel't Seven sermons on the sin, &c.
Saurin's Sermons.
Secker's (Abp.) Sermons.
Sedgwick's Anatomy of sins.
Sharp's (Abp.) Sermons.
Stephens' (Robt.) Sermons.
Taylor's (Jer.) Liberty of Prophecying.
——— Deus Justificatus.
Tillotson's (Abp.) Sermons.
Waterland's (Daniel) Sermons.
Whitby's Appendix to Commentary on the 12th chapter of Matthew.

Unthankfulness. See INGRATITUDE.

Uprightness. See INTEGRITY.

Barrow's (Isaac) Sermons.
Bates' (W.) Works.
Beveridge's Thesaurus Theologicus.
Clarke's (Samuel) Sermons.
Craig's (William) Sermons.
Duke's (Richard) Sermons.
Grosvenor's (Benj.) Sermons to the Young.
Jortin's (John) Sermons.
Newcome (P.) on Bosom Sins.
Newton's (Benj.) Sermons.
Oldfield's Way to Heaven.
Saville's (D.) Dissertations.
Simeon (C.) on Besetting Sins.
South's (Robt.) Sermons.
Strong's (W.) Sermons.

Ur of the Chaldees. See GEOGRAPHY.

Baumgarten (M. A.) Peregrinationes. 1667
Bonfrerii Onomasticon locorum Scripturæ.
Buntingii Itenerarium biblicum.
Wagneri (Chr.) Dissertationes.

Urim and Thummim.

Bellermann's Urim und Thummim.
Buxtorfii (Jno.) Exercitationes. (Ugolinus.)
Carpzovii (J. B.) Conjecturæ quid fuerint.
Deylingii Observationes.
Hottingeri Dissertationes.
Polemanni Dissertationes.
Riboudeald, Dissertationes. (Cont. Spencer.)
Schmidt (Seb.) de Urim et Thummim.
Spenceri (J.) Dissertationes.
——— de Legibus Hebræorum.
Villeri Lux in tenebris.

Christian Observer. 11:136.
Gill's (John) Occasional Sermons.
Glas' (John) Notes on Scripture texts.
Parkhurst's Heb. Lexicon. (On the word.)
Senner on the Urim and Thummim.
Tillotson's Works.

Use of Creeds. See CREEDS, SUBSCRIPTION.

Baumgarteni Necessitas librorum symbolic.
Bernhold de Formul. Augustanæ usu.
Chastel, de l'Usage des conf. de fois.
Chricton de Fide humana.
Du Viel, Epistola ad Robert. Boyle. (A most masterly work.)

Use of Creeds—*continued.*

Edzardi Vindiciæ librorum symbolicorum.
Feldmann, über Symbolzwang.
Heyer, Coup d'oeil sur les conf. de foi.
Höfling de Symb. natura, necess., atque usu.
Kieslingii Historia Symbolorum.
Loescheri Hypomnemata.
——— Parallipomena.
Meyer, de Utilit. et histor. symb. ecclesiæ.
Muhlii Dissertationes.
Neislingius de Usu symbolorum.
Rumpæus de Symbolis.
Seligmani Exercitationes.
Wernsdorfii Auctoritas librorum symbolicor.
Widburg de Auctoritate librorum symbolicorum et juramento.

Ballentine on Confessions of faith.
Bates' (S.) Creeds and Confessions defended.
Blackburn's Confessional. (A work which excited much controversy.)
Card's Use of the Athanasian creed.
Carlisle's (Jas.) Use and Abuse of creeds.
Church Review. 1:352.
Duncan (J. M.) on Conf. of faith. (Against.)
Dunlop's Ends and uses of Conf. of faith.
Durette on the Abuse of Creeds.
Glass' Works.
Harthouse on Creed-making.
Hook on the Use of the Athanasian Creed.
Millennial Harbinger. Period. (Against.)
Miller on Conf. of faith. (Reply to Duncan.)
Panoplist. Vol. 3.
Pressly on Church Fellowship.
Wheatly's (Charles) Sermons at the Moyer Lectures.

Use of the Bible. See READING.

Use of the Bible in Schools.

Bibliotheca Sacra. 13:724. 17:323.
Breckenridge on Denominational education.
Cheever's Right of the Bible in com. schools.
Clarke's (R. W.) Romanism in America. Ch. 9, 10.
Colwell's Position of Christianity in the United States.
Grimke's (Thomas S.) Works. (Address at Columbia, S. C., 1830.)
Princeton Review. 26:504.
Reports of the Board of Education of the Presbyterian Church. Reports 33 and 34.
Tyler's (R. H.) The Bible and Social reform.

Use of the Fathers. See TRADITION.

Augusti Chrestomathia Patristica.
Buddei Isagoge ad Theologiam. Lib. II.
Cave, Epistola Apologet. adv. Clerici Epist.
Clerici Epistolæ criticæ et ecclesiasticæ.
Daillé, de l'Emploi des péres pour le jugement des differences en religion.
Ernesti Institutiones.
Forbesii Instructiones historico-theologicæ.
Freppel, les Pères apostolique.
Gerardi Methodus studii theolog. Pars III.
Hottingeri Introd. ad lectionem patrum.
——— Dissertationes. (Defends Daillé.)

Use of the Fathers—*continued.*

Hulseman's Calixtinischer Gewissenswurm.
Ittigii Exercitationes. (Defends Daillé.)
Marèchal, Concordances des S. Péres.
Mariæ Animadversiones in usum critices.
Molineus de Usu Patrum. (Defends Daillé.)
Perkensii Propædia ad lect. patrum.
Rivetus de Patrum auctoritate.
Schleusneri Opuscula Critica. (Chiefly as tc the readings of the LXX.)
Scrivneri Apologia pro patribus. (A reply to Daillé, and a good specimen of a host of opponents of that author.)
Voetii Dissertat. Selectæ. (Defends Daillé.)
Whitby, Dissertationes. (A convincing exhibit of the incapacity of the Fathers for Biblical interpretation.)
Zornii Opuscula. (Defends Daillé.)

Blunt's Right use of the early fathers.
Boyd's (H. S.) The Fathers not Papists.
British Critic. October, 1834.
Byrth's The Fathers destitute of authority.
Church Review. 4:497.
Collinson's Bampton Lectures. 1813.
Daillé on the Right use of the Fathers. Tr. by T. Smith, and edited in 1841 by Jekyll. ("Brought the Fathers from the bench to the table."—WARBURTON. A work of uncommon learning and strength.)
Edinburg Review. 24:58.
Edwards on the Authority of the Fathers.
Reeves' Translat. of the Apologies of Justin Martyr. (In a dissertation at the end, he endeavors to confute Daillé.)
Selections from the Edinb. Rev. 2:480.
Wickham (J. A.) on Baptism. (Introduction.)
Woodhouse's Hulsean Prize Essay. 1842.

Use of the Roman Alphabet.

That is, in reducing to writing unwritten languages.

Lapsius' Standard alphabet for reducing unwritten languages to writing.
Lobscheid's Chinese English Grammar. 1865.
London Quart. Review. 11:143.
Malcom's (Howard) Travels in Southeastern Asia. (Appendix.)
Muller (Max.) on the Use of the Roman alphabet.
Princeton Review. 10:396.
Trevelyan on the Application of the Roman letters to unwritten languages.

Use of the World. See WORLDLINESS.

Bisse's Christian use of the world.
Blair's (Hugh) Sermons.
Bridge's (W.) Works.
Brown's (David) Memorial Sketches.
Carter's (B.) Discourses.
Clapp's (J.) Sermons.
Dawes' (Abp.) Works.
Dunlop's (William) Sermons.
Elwin's (F.) Sermons.
Hoadly's (Bp.) Sermons.
Mason's (William) Works.

Use of the World—*continued.*

Moss' (Robert) Sermons.
Norris' (John) Practical Discourses.
Orr's (John) Sermons.
Pearson's (W.) Sermons.
Sibbs' (Rich.) Spiritual man's aim.
Simeon's (C.) Works.'
Smith's (Sydney) Sermons.
Taylor's (Thomas) Works.
Tucker's (Josiah) Sermons.
Venn's (John) Sermons.
Warneford's (R.) Sermons.
Webb's (Francis) Sermons.

Usury.

Ambrose, Scripta Moralia.
Chrysostom, Homiliæ.
Grotius de Jure Belli et Pacis.
Joly, Traité des Restitutions.
La Porte, Principes Théologiques.
Leotardus de Usuris et contractibus.
Luzerne, le Prêt de commerce.
Rullié, Théorie de l'interêt de l'argent.
Amer. Quart. Review. 21:145. 22:177.
Analytical Mag. 10:194.
Banker's Magazine. 4:581,683. 5:712,781,842.
Bentham's (Jer.) Works. (Shows the impolicy of legal restraint.)
Blackall's (Dr. O.) Sermons.
Blackwood's Mag. 24:68.
Blaxton's English Usurer. (Quotes many eminent divines as opposed to usury.)
Byles' Observations on the Usury laws.
Cæsar's (Philip) Damnable sect of Usurers.
Capel (Edw.) on Temptations.
Democratic Rev. 27:221,328.
Downhame on the 15th Psalm.
Eclectic Mag. 24:345,455.
Edinburg Rev. 27:339.
Edwards' Body of Divinity. (8th comm'dt.)
Fenton (Roger) on Usury.
Filmer on Taking use for money
Gregory on Usury.
Holmes' Usury is Injury.
Hunt's Merchant's Mag. 2:16. 3:516. 5:40, 115. 9:243. 24:59.
Jellinger's (C.) Sermons.
Mosse's (M.) Arraignment of Usurie.
Museum of For. Literature. 8:507.
Niles' Register. 24:143.
North Am. Review. 39:68. (Alex. Everett.)
Ord's (Mark) Essay on Usury.
Pamphleteer. 11:165. 13:139. 23:421.
Plowden on Usury and Annuities.
Puffendorf on the Law of Nature.
Smith's (Henry) Sermons.
Turnbull's (R.) Expos. of the 15th Ps. 1606.
Whitehook upon Usury and its effects.

Utility as a Moral Guide.

Bentham's Introd. to Moral Philosophy.
Brown's Lectures on Mental Science.
Dymond's Principles of Morality.
Edinburg Rev. 49:159,273. 50:99. 61:195.
Hume on the Principles of Morals.
New Eng. Magazine. 4:208,290.
New York Review. 1:58.
North Amer. Rev. 35:466.
Paley's Moral Philosophy.
Smith's Theory of Moral Sentiments.
Southern Rev. 7:261.
Westminster Rev. 11:254,526. 12:246.

Vain Glory. See PRIDE.

Laget, Sermons sur divers sujets.
Blair's (James) Sermons.
Boone's (James S.) Sermons.
Bull's (Bp.) Sermons.
Calamy's (Benjamin) Sermons.
Charters' (S.) Sermons.
Cooper's (Edward) Sermons.
Goodwin's (H.) Sermons.
Hunt's (Jeremiah) Sermons.
Hurd's (Bp.) Sermons.
Le Bas' (Cha. W.) Sermons.
Milner's (Joseph) Sermons.
Morison's (John) Sermons.
Moss' (Robert) Sermons.
Tillotson's (Abp.) Sermons.
Tilly's (William) Sermons.
Ward's (Richard) Sermons.
Whichcot's (Bp.) Sermons.

Vain Philosophy.
See PROVINCE OF REASON.

Bilstone's (John) Sermons.
Boys' (Henry) Sermons.
Buddicome's (Robt. P.) Sermons.
Burton's (E.) Bampton Lectures. 1829.
Delany's (Pat.) Discourses. (2 on this subj.)
Disney's (John) Sermons.
Durand's (James F.) Sermons.
Dwight's Theology.
Halifax's (Bp.) Sermons.
Kennedy's (Baillie J.) Donnellan Lectures.
Markham's (Abp.) Concio ad Clerum.
Moysey's Bampton Lectures. 1818.
Parry's (J.) The Rudiments of the world.
Partridge's (S.) Sermons.
Patten's Opposition between the Gospel, and what is called the religion of Nature.
Pearson's (Bp.) Minor Works.
Purkis' Present pursuits in learning as they affect religion, considered. 1786.
Sherlock's (W.) Sermons.
South's (Robert) Sermons.
Sydenham's (Humphrey) Sermons.
Townsend's (J.) Sermons.
Trapp's Danger of fallacious reasoning.
Twisleton's Self-sufficiency incompatible with Christianity.
Vaughn's (Henry) Sermons.
Watson (T.) on False Philosophy.
Wilkins' (Bp.) Sermons.

Vain Thoughts. See THOUGHTS.

Arnold's (Fred.) Sermons.
Barrow's (Isaac) Sermons.
Burder's (Henry F.) Sermons.
Craig's (James) Sermons.
Dorrington's Sermons.

Vain Thoughts—*continued.*

Fiddes' (Richard) Sermons.
Foster's (John) Lectures.
Goodwin's (Thomas) Vanity of thoughts discovered and cured.
Gordon's (D. W.) Sermons.
Jowett's (Jos.) Fifty-two short sermons.
Osterwald on Uncleanness.
Richardson's (William) Sermons.
Taylor's (R.) Sermons.

Vain Words. See SOCIAL INTERCOURSE, TONGUE.

Villars, Contre les vain sermons, etc.

Barrow's (Isaac) Works.
Bather's (Edward) Sermons.
Dawes' (Abp.) Works.
Flavel's Works. ("Cautions.")
Gale's (John) Sermons.
Girdlestone's (Charles) Sermons.
Goode's (Francis) Sermons.
Gouldburn's Essays.
Lardner's (Nathaniel) Sermons.
Littleton's (E.) Sermons.
Melvill's (Henry) Sermons.
Newman's (T.) Sermons.
Oakley's (F.) Sermons.
Rogers' (A.) Advantages of good discourse.
Shorthose's (Hugh) Sermons.
Stebbings' (Henry) Sermons.
Stokes' (Dr. J.) Sermons.
Tillotson's (Abp.) Sermons.
Vaughn's (C. J.) Sermons.
Whitaker's (E. W.) Family Sermons.

Valentinians. See GNOSTICS.

Irenæus, contra Hæreses. Lib. V.
Clemens Alex., Stromata.
Tertullian, adversus Valentinianos.

Valentini Opera.
Acta Eruditorum. MDCCXII. p. 183.
Bassnage, Histoire des Juifs.
Beausobre, Histoire du Manicheisme.
Buddæi Dissertatio de Hæresi Valentini.
Faydit, Hist. eccles. d. deux premiers siècles.
Grabbii Spicelegium Patrum. Secul. II.
Hooper (Bp.) de Valentinianorum Hæresi.
Lodbergii Disquisitio Historica de V.
Losii Fasciculus considerationum de diversis materiis.
Souverain, Platonisme devoilé. Chap. 8.
Vitringæ Observationes Sacræ. Lib. I.

Hooper's Heresy of the Valentinians.

Value of the Soul. See SOUL.

Barker's (John) Sermons.
Bishop's (William) Sermons.
Blencoe's (Edward) Sermons.
Bunyan's (John) Works.
Burder's (George) Village Sermons.
Clarke's (Samuel) Sermons.
Clerke's (R.) The Careless Merchant.
Crossthwaite (J. C.) Sermons.
Duchall's (James) Sermons.
Fiddes' (Richard) Sermons.

Value of the Soul—*continued.*

Graves' (Richard) Sermons.
Henry's (Matthew) Works. (6 Sermons.)
Hyatt's (John) Sermons.
Kattern's (Daniel) Sermons.
Kennet's (Basil) Sermons.
May's (William) Sermons.
Moss' (Robert) Sermons.
Newman's (J. H.) Sermons.
Oakley's (Fred.) Sermons.
Paley's (Will.) Sermons.
Pyle's (Philip) Sermons.
Quincy's (S.) Sermons.
Reynolds' (Bp.) Sermons.
Saurin's Sermons.
Scott's (John) Christian life.
Snowden's (W.) Sermons.
Stillingfleet's (Bp.) Sermons.
Taylor's (Jer.) Sermons.
Talbot's (Bp.) Sermons.
Wesley's (John) Sermons.

Value of Time. See PROCRASTINATION, NEW YEAR, REDEEMING TIME, TIME.

Vanity. See HUMILITY, PRIDE, SELF-CONFIDENCE, VAIN GLORY.

Dunlop's (William) Sermons.
Erskine's (Ralph) Sermons.
Francklin's (Thomas) Sermons.
Hill's (G. D.) Practical Sermons.
King's (Abp.) Sermons.
Lamont's (David) Sermons.
Preston's Golden scepter held out to the humble.
Smith's (Sydney) Sermons.
Young's (Dr. John) Sermons.
Zollikoffer's (Geo. J.) Sermons.

Vanity of Man. See BREVITY OF LIFE, FRAILTY.

Bingham's (Richard) Sermons.
Bradley's (Charles) Sermons. (Funeral sermon on Princess Charlotte.)
Clarke's (Dr. Samuel) Sermons.
Collet's (J.) Sermons. (3 on this subject.)
Du Moulin's Heraclitus. Trans. by Darcie.
Fernie's (John) Sermons.
Grove's (Henry) Sermons.
Hall's (Robt.) Works. (Sermons.)
Howe's Theological Treatises.
Laurie's (Dr. Thomas) Sermons.
Leighton's (Abp.) Expository Lectures on Psalm 39. Lecture 2.
Mandel's (William) Sermons.
Mason's (John) Sermons.
Mayhew's (Jonathan) Sermons.
Newman's (J. H.) Sermons.
Norris' (John) Sermons.
Paget's (F. E.) The Living and the Dead.
Quincey's (Samuel) Sermons.
Reeves' (W.) Sermons.
Reynolds' (W.) Vanity of Man.
Slade's (James) Sermons.
Vane's Retired man's Meditations.
Warneford's (John) Sermons.

Vanity of the World. See USE OF THE WORLD, WORLDLINESS.

Berriman's (William) Sermons.
Blair's (Hugh) Sermons.
Beeston's (Edw.) Sermons.
Bryson's (James) Sermons.
Chalmers' (Thomas) Sermons.
Conybeare's (Bp.) Sermons.
Crowe's (Dr.) Sermons.
Denison's (E.) Sermons.
Doddridge's (Philip) Sermons.
Emlyn's (T.) Works.
Erskine's (Ralph) Sermons.
Foster's (John) Lectures at Broadmead.
Grove's (Henry) Sermons.
Hobart's (Bp.) Sermons.
Hopkins' (Bp. E.) Sermons.
Howe's Vanity of man as mortal.
Hunter's (Henry) Sermons.
Johnson's (Sam.) Sermons.
Langhorne's (W.) Sermons.
Laurie's (T.) Sermons.
Lucas' (Richard) Sermons.
Markland's (Abraham) Sermons.
Marshall's (Nath.) Sermons.
Marriott's (Harvey) Sermons.
Newman's (J. H.) Sermons.
Newman's (T.) Sermons.
Pierce's (John) Sermons.
Pyle's (Philip) Sermons.
Reynolds' (Bp.) Sermons.
Riddock's (James) Sermons.
Sharp's (Abp.) Sermons.
Slade's (James) Sermons.
Snowden's (B. C.) Sermons.
Tuckney's (Anthony) Sermons.
Warneford's (John) Sermons.
Zollikoffer's (George J.) Sermons on the dignity of man.
——— on the Festivals and Fasts.

Varieties of Human Condition. See INEQUALITIES OF CONDITION, UNEQUAL DISTRIBUTION OF GOOD AND EVIL.

Various Readings. See MANUSCRIPTS, SAMARITAN PENTATEUCH.

Amamæ Keri et Chetib.
Amersfoordtii Dissertationes Philologicæ.
Baieri Dissertationes. (The use and abuse of various readings.)
Bengelii Gnomon Novi Test. (Admirable.)
——— Apparatus Criticus.
Birch, Var. Lect. ad textum Nov. Test. (A very sufficient book for most clergymen.)
Bode, Pseudocritica Millio-Bengeliana.
Buxtorfii Tiberias.
——— Anticritica. (Reply to Capellus.)
Capelli Critica Sacra.
Carpzovii Critica sacra Vet. Test.
Clerici Ars critica.
Danzii Sinceritas scripturæ Vet. Test.
De Rossi, Specimen var. lectionum S. S. (The result of a collation of 825 MSS. and 375 printed editions. A great treasure, conveniently arranged.)

Various Readings—*continued.*

Dermoutii Collecta Critica in Nov. Test.
Elias Levita, Opera.
Fry, de Variis lectionibus Nov. Test.
Grabe, de Variis vitiis LXX.
Griesbachii Nov. Testamentum Græcum. Prolegomena.
——— Symbolæ Criticæ.
Hilleri Arcanus Keri et Kethib.
Hottingeri (Io. Heinric.) Dissertationes.
Kennicott, Dissertationes. (Probably the best work on the subject for students. It has set at rest the controversy between Buxtorf and Capellus, with their allies, as to the purity of the Hebrew text.)
Klemm, Critica Sacra Nov. Test.
Laymari Animadversiones Massoreti.
Luderi Dissert. de causis variantium, etc.
Michaelis (C. B.) de Variis lect. Nov. Test. colligendis et dijudicandis.
Michaelis (J. D.) Introductio.
Millii Novum Testamentum. (Next in importance to Wetstein.)
Montfaucon, Hexapla Origenis.
Montani (A.) Apparatus Biblicus.
Morini Exercitationes Biblicæ.
Osiandri Oratio et Disputatio.
Pfaff, de Genuinis lectionibus Nov. Testam. (Pfaff was the first [1716] to write systematically on the use of various readings.)
Rechenbergii (Adami) Dissertationes.
Reinhardus de Notis marginalibus sacri codicis Ebræi.
Rinkii Lucubratio critica.
Sauberti Variæ lect. textus Græci Matthei.
Schroederi Dissertationes.
Schulteus Dissertationes.
Scholz's Biblisch-kritische Reise.
Scholz, Nov. Test. Græce. (Contains the various readings of 674 manuscripts, of which 322 are here first collated.)
Schulze de Codice IV Evangelistæ. Proleg.
Shnurer, de Codicum Hebr. V. Test. ætate.
Tischendorfii Nov. Testamentum. Prolegom.
——— Anecdota.
Usseri Epistola ad Ludov. Capellum.
Van Mastrichi, Prolegomena.
Waltoni Biblia Polyglotta. Prolegomena.
Wetstein, Nov. Testamentum. Prolegomena.
White, Criseos Griesbachianæ. (Convenient.)
Whitby, Examen Millii variantium lect.
Wolfii (Io. Christop.) Bibliotheca.

Baruh's Critica Sacra examined. (Shows these readings to be no mark of corruption or mistake.)
Bates' Integrity of the Heb. text. (Contends with Kennicott on various passages.)
Blackwall's Sacred Classics.
Bloomfield's Gr. Testament, with notes, &c.
Boothroyd's Hebrew Bible. (An approved selection from Kennicott.)
Butler's Horæ Biblicæ. Chap. 17.
Danville Review. June, 1863.
Davidson's Text of the O. Test. revised.
Edinburg Rev. 94:1.

Various Readings—*continued.*

Edwards' (T.) Dissertations.
Green's (T. S.) Course of developed criticism.
Gyle's (J. F.) Authent. of the N. T. with an acc. of anc. versions and the princip. MSS.
Hey's (Dr. John) Lectures. Bk. 1, ch. 8.
Jenkins' Reasonableness of Christianity.
Jowett's New Test. of Scholz; with the readings of Griesbach, Stephens, Beza, and the Elzevir, with the English version, and its marginal readings.
Kennicott's State of the Heb. printed text.
Macgill on the Manuscripts of the Old Test.
Marsh's Michaelis' Introd. to the New Test.
May's Exam. of Simons' Critical history.
Montfaucon's Origens Hexapla.
Nolan's Integrity of the Greek Vulgate. (Pub. in 1815, and with valuable additions in 1830. Notices of this excellent work appeared in the BRITISH CRITIC, New Series, Vol. 1, and in the QUARTERLY REVIEW, 26:328, in which last some of his positions are refuted.)
Platt's (Jno.) Self-interpreting New Testam. (A valuable collection of criticisms from approved authors.)
Pocock's (Edw.) Works.
Quarterly Review. June, 1863.
Rogers' (J.) Various readings of the Hebrew Bible.
Scrivener's Introd. to the New Testament.
Simons' Crit. hist. of the New Test. text.
Tregelles' Introduction to the textual criticism of the New Testament.
Wall's (Will.) Critical notes on the N. Test.

Vaudois. See WALDENSES.

Vedas. See HINDUISM.

Venial Sins. See SINS OF IGNORANCE, SINS OF INFIRMITY.

Billingsley's (John) Sermons.
Jackson's (John) Six sermons preached in Lent. (All on "little sins.")
Morning Exercises at Cripplegate. (Sermon by W. Jenkins.)
Müller's Christian doctrine of sin. Translated by Pulsford. (Appendix.)
Smallridge's (G.) Sermons. (No sins venial.)
Spurgeon's (C. H.) Sermons. 6th Series.

Veracity of God. See FAITHFULNESS.

Versions of Scripture. See ENGLISH BIBLE, NEW VERSION, SYRIAC VERSION, REVISION, SEPTUAGINT, TRANSLATIONS, VULGATE.

Vestments, Ministerial. See RITES.

Braunius de Vestitu sacerdotum Hebræor.
Buxtorfiii (J.) Dissertationes.
Dieterici Vestitus Sacerdotum.
Picart, Ceremonies et costumes religieuses. (11 vols., folio. 243 plates.)
Prideaux, de Vestibus Aaronis.
Rabanus Maurus de Ceremoniis ecclesiasticis.
Tiron, Hist. et costumes des ordres religieux, civiles, et militaires.

Vestments, Ministerial—*continued.*

Wichmanshausenii Dissertationes.
Bullinger's Judgment that it is lawful for ministers of the Church of England to wear the apparel prescribed by law.
Gylbyes' "Epistel to my louynge brethren that is troubled about ye Popishe apparel." 1566.
Roberts' (Jos.) Oriental illustrations of S. S.
Satchwell's Scripture Costumes.
Scripture Costumes, engraved under the superintendence of Benjamin West, with historical remarks.
Soltau on the Tabernacle, priestly vestm., &c.

A controversy on the subject of clerical vesture, prolific in books and pamphlets, was rife in England in the 16th century, and is now renewed with warmth.

Vicarious Suffering. See IMPUTATION, JUSTIFICATION, SUBSTITUTION, &c.

Balguy on Redemption.
Bates' Works. Chap. 13.
Berry Street Lectures.
Collis' Three Tribunals.
Disney's (John) Sermons.
Edwards on Original Sin.
Evans (Caleb) on the Atonement.
Hampton on Atonement. (Reply to Taylor.)
Hey's Lectures.
Knight's (Titus) Sermons.
Ludlam's Essays. Ess. 4.
Magee on Atonement.
Mann's (Isaac) Theological Essays.
Portal on Sacrifices. Part 4.
Robinson's Christian System. Essay 28.
Simeon's (Cha.) Works.
Taylor's Apology of Ben Mordecai.
Vesie's Bampton Lectures. 1795.
Wardlaw's Discourses. Disc. 7.
West on the Atonement. Chap. 3.

Vice. See SIN.

Tzschirner Ueber d. moral. indifferentism.
Balguy's (John) Discourses.
Fawcett's (Joseph) Sermons.
Foster's (Dr. James) Discourses.
Hall's (Bp.) Practical Works.
Hall's (Joshua) Charac. of virtues and vices.
Lamont's Sermons on prevalent vices.
Newman's (T.) Sermons in Carter lane.
Peckhard's (Peter) Sermons.
Rees' (Abr.) Sermons. (Progress of vice.)
Tilley's Vice the cause of ignorance in relig.
Zollikoffer's Sermons on prevalent vices.

Virtue. See MORALITY, MORAL PHILOSOPHY, MOTIVES.

Cumberland, de Legibus Naturæ.
Montaigne, Essais.
Puffendorf de Jure.
Adams' Nature and obligation of virtue.
Adamson on Moral Virtue.
Balguy's (Moral and Theological Tracts. (Replies to Hutchinson and Shaftesbury.)

Virtue—*continued.*

Beattie's Elements of Moral Science.
Becon's (Tho.) Works. (Parker Soc. pub.)
Bibliotheca Sacra. 22:477.
Botts' Answer to Warburton.
Brown's Ans. to Shaftesbury's Characterist.
Campbell (Archibald) on Moral Virtue.
Chalmer's (Thomas) Sermons.
Clapp (T.) on Moral Virtue.
Colston's (Alexander) Essays.
Cumberland's Law of Nature. Ch. 1, sec. 4.
Doddridge's Lectures. Part 3, prop. 48–51.
Edwards (Pres.) on the Nature of virtue.
Evans on Christian Temper.
Ferguson's Principles of Moral Science. (As distinguished from Christian holiness.)
Foster's (James) Sermons.
Grove's Moral Philosophy.
——— Wisdom of God.
Hall's (Bp.) Practical Works.
Hall's (Josh.) Charac. of virtues and vices.
Hallywell's Excellence of moral virtue.
Hopkins on Holiness.
Howe's Blessedness of the Righteous.
Hume's (David) Essays.
Hutcheson's Enquiry into the idea of virtue.
——— on the Passions.
Innes on the Origin of moral virtue.
Jameson on the Obligation of virtue.
Kames on the Principles of morality.
King's Origin of Evil. (Preliminary Dissert.)
Lime Street Lectures.
Mills' (W.) Theory of moral obligation.
Mole's (Thomas) Sermons. (Nature of V.)
Nettleton (W.) on Virtue and Happiness.
Paley's Moral Philosophy.
Park Street Lectures.
Pinto's Essay on Luxury.
Pope's Essays.
Price's Review of the principal questions and difficulties in morals.
Rutherforth's Nature and obligations of V.
Scott's Christian Life. Ch. 4.
Shaftesbury's Characteristics of men, &c.
——— Enquiry after virtue.
Smith's (Adam) Theory of moral sentiments. (Cites various theories.)
Thompson (J. P.) on the Christian Graces.
Tidcombe's Sermons. (Tendency of virtue.)
Tillotson's (Abp.) Works.
Tucker's Light of Nature pursued. Ch. 29.
Warburton's Divine Legation. Lib. I.
Wardsworth's Christian Institutes.
Watts' Essays. (V. and self-love reconciled.)
Wilkins' Religion of Nature.
Wollaston's Religion of Nature.
Wright's Answer to Mole's Sermon.

Vision of Constantine.
See CONSTANTINE'S VISION.

Visions. See APPARITIONS.

Amortius de Revelationibus et visionibus.
Brierre, des Hallucinations.
Gerson de Discernendis veris visionibus a falsis.
Nider, de Visionibus ac Revelationibus.
Hawker's (R.) Operations of the H. Ghost.
Lee (W.) on the Inspiration of Scripture.
Torquemado's Garden of curious flowers. (A curious account of strange events.)

Visiting. See SOCIAL INTERCOURSE.

Visiting the Sick.
See PASTORAL VISITING.

Gregorii (Mag.) Pastoralis. Pars III.
Lohneri Instructiones practica.
Stearn de Visitatione infirmiorum.

Addington on Visiting the sick.
Berens' (Edward) Lent Lectures.
Calvin's Tracts. Trans. by H. Beveridge.
Cecil's Remains.
Comber on the Offices for visiting the sick.
Cox's (Wm.) Offices for the visiting, &c.
Darnell's (W. N.) Sermons.
Francklin's (Thomas) Sermons.
Mant's (Bp.) Order for visitation of the sick.
Morning Exercises at Cripplegate. (Sermon by Matt. Poole.)
Paley's Clergyman's Assistant.
Searle's (Tho.) Sick visitor's Assistant.
Spinckes' Sick man visited. (With meditations and prayers.)
Stonehouse's Offices for the visitation, &c.
Taylor's (Jer.) Holy Living.
Victor's Manual for visiting the sick.
Wesley's (John) Sermons.

Works on this subject are numerous, but contain few directions of much value. Paley's is most esteemed, but is very defective, both as to instruction, and emotional interest; and does not refer to appropriate portions of Scripture.

Vocation. See EFFECTUAL CALLING.

Baumgarten de Vocatione Dei ad salutem, variis ejus gradibus, etc.
Calovii Dissertationes.
Kahlii Predicatio evangelii universalis.
Schafii Fides Catholica.
Wagneri Dissertationes.

Bennett on the Gospel Dispensation.
Black's (David) Sermons.
Bloomfield's (Geo. B.) Sermons.
Booth's Reign of Grace.
Bunyan's Water of Life.
Clarke's (F. F.) Sermons.
Fuller's Gospel worthy of all acceptation.
Griffith's (Thomas) Sermons.
Hooker's Soul's vocation.
Jowett's (Joseph) Sermons.
Marsh's (E. G.) Brief Survey, &c.
Martyn's (Henry) Sermons.
Matthias' (B. W.) Sermons.
Muir's (James) Sermons.
Owen on the Spirit.
Russell's (F.) Sermons.
Sumner's (Samuel) Sermons.
Whitty's (John) Sermons.
Witsius on the Covenants.

Voluntary Associations. See BENEVOLENT INSTITUTIONS, ESTABLISHMENTS, ENDOWMENTS, SOCIALISM.

Amer. Bibl. Repos. 9:485. 12:257.
Blackwood's Mag. 40:787.
Christian Disciple. 2:368.
Christian Examiner. 8:321. 13:337.
Christian Review. 8:321.
Christian Quar. Spect. 4:142.
Dunlop's Tendency of mankind to association analyzed and illustrated.
Eclectic Rev. 4th Series. 6:545. 7:38. 8:207.
Lord's Liter. and Theol. Rev. 4:81,393. 5:5.
Maitland (S. R.) on the Voluntary system.
Miall's Views of the voluntary principle.
Princeton Review. 9:101.
Quar. Review. 53:94.

Vowel Points. See MASSORA.

Pro.

Bootius de text. Heb. V. Test. certitudine et authentia.
Buxtorfii (Pater.) Tiberias.
Buxtorfius (Filius) de Auctoritate Punctorum.
——— Anticritica. (Reply to Capel.)
Cooper (Jos.), Domus Mosaicæ Clavis. ("More zeal on this subject than knowledge."—ORME.)
Dashellii Biblia Ebraica accentuata.
Daserus de Origine punctorum, etc.
Glassii Philologia Sacra.
Juarus de Punctationis Ebræicæ antiquitate.
Leusdeni Philologus Hebræus.
Michaelis de Punctorum Ebræic. antiquitate.
Raadt de Punctationis Hebr. natura.
Scaligeri Opuscula Varia.
Spitzneri Vindiciæ auctoritatis punct.
Wasmuthii Vindiciæ S. Scrip. Ebrææ.
Wolfius (N.) de Accentuum in V. T. origine.
Boston's (Tho.) Tractatus Stigmologicus.
Cross' (Walter) The Taghmical Art.
Dunton's Author. of the points and accents.
Gell (P.) on the Hebr. language and letters. (Said to be the ablest defence of points.)
Gesenius' Doctrine of the accents.
Gill (John) on the Hebrew language.
Moncrieff (John) on the Vowel points.
Owen's (Henry) Introd. to Heb. criticism.
Wall's Critical notes on the Old Testament. (Introduction.)
Whitfield (P.) on the V. points. (Says all that can be said in their favor.)

Con.

Aben Ezra, Commentatio.
Capelli (Lud.) Arcanum punct. revelatum.
——— Arcani punctationis vinditiæ.
——— Diatriba de veris et antiquis Ebræorum literis. (Agt. Buxtorf and Scaliger.)
Capelli (Jacobi) Observationes.
Masclef, Gram. Heb. a punctis, etc., libera. (Gilbert Wakefield [Life of, vol. 1, p. 100] warmly praises this book, and contemns the points. He says he acquired a good knowledge of Hebrew, without points, in ten days.)

Vowel Points—*continued.*

Con.

Elias Levita, in Massora.
Houbiganti Prolegomena in Scrip. sacram.
Molleri Mare Masoreticum insidium.
Morini (Steph.) Exercitationes.
Pfeifferi Critica Sacra.
Prideaux (Joh.) Viginti duæ lectiones.
Schultens, Institutiones Gram. Hebr.
Vossii Hist. critica Vet. Testamenti.
Waltoni Prolegomena ad Biblia polyglot.
Wolfii (Christop.) Bibliotheca Ebraica.
Bates' (Julius) Hebrew English Dictionary. (The preface is a very able discussion of this subject.)
Bayley's Hebrew Grammar.
Breckell (John) on the Hebrew tongue. ("Sensible."—ORME.)
Burgess' (Bp.) Hebrew elements and primer. (An excellent and easy introduction to the language.)
Butler's (Cha.) Horæ Biblicæ.
Calmet's Dictionary of the Bible. Under "Letters."
Danton on the Antiq. and authority, &c.
Gerard's Institutes of Biblical criticism.
Grey's (Dr. Rich.) Method of learning Heb.
Howerth's (Will.) Sermons.
Lowth's Preliminary Dissertations.
Pike's (Sam.) Hebrew Lexicon.
Prideaux's Connection. Bk. 5. (Gives the arguments pro and con.)
Robertson's Hebrew Grammar.
——— True and ancient manner of reading Hebrew.
Sharpe's (Gregory) Dissertations on lang.
Sievwright's Hebrew text considered.
Wall's (C. W.) Proofs of the interpolation of the points in the Hebrew Bible; and hence the necessity of a revised English translation. 1857.
Weemse's (John) Dissertations.
Whiston's Essay toward restoring the true text.
Wilson's (James P.) Hebrew Grammar.

Among the opponents of the Massoretic points are also Bochart, Calvin, the Casaubons, De Dieu, Drusius, Erpen, Grotius, Heise, Luther, Masius, Olivetan, Zuingle, Boothroyd, and other eminent Oriental scholars.

Vows.

Krafft de Votis, eorumque sanctimonio.
Baxter's (Rich.) Christian Ecclesiastics.
Calamy's (Edm.) Practical treatise on vows. (With special reference to baptism and the Lord's Supper.)
Davis on Religious Vows.
Edwards' (John) Theologia Reformata.
Foyster's (J. G.) Sermons.
Hurst's (Henry) Sermons.
Lightfoot's (J.) Sermons.
Randolph on Jephthah's vow. (Appendix.)

Sharpe's (Gregory) Dissertations.
Shower's (John) Sacramental Discourses.
Simeon's (C.) Works.
Slade's (James) Sermons.
Smallridge's (Bp.) Sermons.
Thomson's (Thomas) Sermons.
Thornwell's (J. H.) Discourses.

Vulgate Bible.

Blanchini Vindiciæ Vulgatæ.
Brunatus de Nomine, auctore, etc., Dissert.
Calmeti Dissertationes.
Du Hamel, Bib. lat. vulg. cum annot. proleg.
James (Tho.), Bellum Papale: sive concordia discors, etc. (Shows the discrepancies of the "authentic editions" of Sextus V, Clement VIII, etc.)
Menochii Biblia Sac. Lat. cum commentariis.
Müller de Usu vers. Latinæ in interp. S. S.
Panzeri Bibliotheca.
Riegler's Kritisch Gesch. der Vulgata.
Van Ess, Pragmatisch-kritische G. d. Vulg.

Butler's Horæ Biblicæ. Chap. 14.
Campbell's Preliminary Dissertations.
Hamilton's Introd. to the Heb. Scriptures.
Hey's (Dr. John) Lectures. Bk. 1, ch. 9.
Marsh's Michaelis' Introduction.
——— Bibliotheca Sacra.
Orme's Bibliotheca Biblica.
Simon's Critical hist. of the Old Testament.

Numerous editions of the Latin Vulgate are described by Dr. Clarke, in his *Bibliographical Dictionary*. 1802.

Wages of Sin.

Baxter's (Arthur G.) Sermons.
Cawood's (John) Sermons.
Garbett's (J.) Sermons.
Hincks' (John) Sermons.
Pearce's (Innes) Sermons.
Reay's (William) Sermons.
Saville's (David) Discourses.
Sharp's (William) Sermons.
South's (Robert) Sermons.
Tuson's (Fred. E.) Sermons.
Warren's (Robert) Sermons.
Watts' (Isaac) Berry Street Sermons.
Wintle's (T.) Christian Ethics.

Waldenses. See ALBIGENSES, PERSECUTION, PETROBRUSIANS.

Andoque, Histoire de Languedoc.
Apologia Veræ doctrinæ eorum qui vulgo adpellantur Waldenses.
Arnaud, Histoire de la glorieuse rentrée des Vaudois dans leur vallées.
Battus de Veritate Cœlesti.
Bender's Geschichte der W. (Map.)
Benoist, Hist. de Vaudois, ou Barbets.
Bernard, adversus Waldensium sectam.
Bossuet, Hist. de variations, etc. Livre XI.
Boyer, Abregé de l'histoire des Vaudois.
Brez [or Bresse], Histoire des Vaudois. (An abridged translat. of this book is given by the translator of Arnaud.)

Waldenses—*continued.*

[Camuzatio] Histoire des Albigeois.
Charvaz, Recherches historique, etc. 1836.
Chassanion, des A. (Doct., sufferings, &c.)
Codex Inquisitionis Tolosanæ.
Colvorii Fissuræ Sionis. Lib. XII.
Confessio fidei fratrum Waldensium. (Extat in "Sylvii libris de Concilio Basiliæ.")
Danhaveri Eccles. Waldensium orthodoxæ.
Dieckhoff, die Wald. in Mittelalter.
Dieterich's Waldenser und ihre Verhältnisse.
Flaccii Catalogus testium veritatis. (A noble work.)
Frossard (Pastor) les Vaudois de Provence.
Gilly's Histoire eccles. des eglises Vaudoises. (From 1160 to 1643.)
Grattii Fasciculus rerum expendendarum.
Hahn's Geschichte der Waldenser.
Heber's Waldo; und älteren Waldenser.
Hederici Notationes confessionis Voldensicæ.
Herzog, de Origine Waldensium.
Herzog's Vorreformat. Zustande u. Lehren.
Hesterbergii Ecclesia Waldensium.
Hockii Dissertationes. (Valuable.)
Honerti Orationes Bohemorum.
Jas (P.), Disputatio Academica. (Shows the distinction between Waldenses and Albigenses.)
Kiesling, de Variis Wald. veritatis testium nominibus et sectis.
Langlois, Hist. des Croisades.
Leger's Schweiz u. d. verfolgten Waldenser.
——— Geschichte der Waldenser.
——— Hist. générale des eglises Vaudois.
Limborch, Historia Inquisitionis.
Lydii Conservatio veræ ecclesiæ.
Maranda, Tableau du Piédmont. 1803.
Maresii (Samuel.) Disputationes.
Martene, Thesaurus Anecdotorum.
Mayerhoff's Wald. in unsern Tagen. 1834.
Monastier, Hist. de V. jusq. nos jours. 1847.
Moser's Geschichte d. Waldenser.
Muratori Antiquitates Ital. medii ævi.
——— Scriptores Rerum Italicarum.
Muston, l'Israel des Alpês. Plates. To 1851.
——— La foi dans les epreuves. (Persecution of 1560.)
——— La Gossen opprimée.
——— Les Néhémites. 1686 to 1690.
——— La Couronne dépines.
——— (Other treatises.)
Netteri Doct. antiquitatum fidei eccles. cath.
Pelegrin's Korte schets van de Geschiedenis.
Perrin, Hist. des Vaudois et des Albigeois.
Petrus, Monachus des vallées Sernay.
Picolomini Com. de Concilia Basiliæ.
Raineri Rerum Bohemicarum Script.
Réponse pour les eglises des Vallées de Piedmont, au Sieur Faverot, ou sont refutées les erreurs de l'eglise Romaine, et des chicanes des missionaires. (Geneva. 1697.)
Richard, Guerres contre les Vaudois.
Roman, Essai historique sur les Vaudois de Provence.

Waldenses—*continued.*

Saxius ad Sigonium de regno Italiæ.
Schmidt's Uebersicht einiger zur Kentness des relig. Leben in Mittelalter, etc.
Schmidt (C.), Hist. et doct. de la secte des Cathares, ou Albigeois. 1850.
Seckendorf, Hist. de la Reform. (Appendix.)
Simleri Descriptio Vallesiæ.
Sismondi, les Croisades contre les Albigois.
Usserus (Abp.) de Ecclesiarum successione.
Vaisette, Hist. de Languedoc. (Gives an account of the Waldenses under the Counts of Toulouse.)
Waldenser Chronick. 1160 bis 1655.
Weihenmaieri Dissertatio Historica.
Weismanni Hist. eccles. revisa. (Refutes Bossuet on this subject.)
Weiss' (J. H.) Kirchenverfassung d. Piemontertschen Waldensergemeinden. 1844.
Wengerseii Ecclesiæ Sclavonicæ.
Wesenbecius de Walden. et Abigens. 1585.
Ziegleri Confessio Valdensium.

Abbot's History of the massacre in the Valtoline.
Acland's Present condition of the W. 1825.
Allix's Ancient churches of Piedmont.
Arnaud's Hist. of the glorious return of the Vaudois to their valleys in 1689.
Baird's Protestantism in Italy. 1851.
Beattie's Protestant valleys of Piedmont.
Blair's Christian churches in France. 1833.
Boyer's History of the Vaudois. (Traces through them the preservation of the true church from the days of the Apostles.)
Bray's Papal dominion and persecutions.
Brown's (John) Compendious Chur. history. (Gives a brief connected history of the W.)
Chastamion's History of the Vaudois.
Christian Month. Spect. 5:337.
Christian Quart. Spect. 10:505. 1837.
Christian Observer. 20:792.
Devisme's State of the Waldenses. 1753.
Faber's Hist. and theology of the ancient W.
Gilly's Excursion to the valleys of Piedmont. 1823.
——— Second excursion to Do. 1830. (Two important books, containing copies of manuscripts and documents illustrating the antiquities of the W. Church. See Quart. Review. 33:134.)
Henderson's Observ. on the Vaudois. 1844.
Jackson's (J. L.) Remarks on the Vaudois. 1826.
Jones' (W.) History of the Waldenses. (Eminently clear and satisfactory.)
Latter day Luminary. 1:225.
Lennard's Hist. of the W. and Albigenses.
Lond. Quart. Rev. 9:
Lowther's Present state of the W. 1821.
Maitland's Tracts and documents, illustrating the history, doctrines, &c., of the W.
Matchlesse Crueltie declared in the history of the W., wherein is related their piety and purity of doctrine. (Published by command of Cromwell. 1655.)

Waldenses—*continued.*

McCrie's Reformation in Italy.
Monastier's History of the Vaudois Church, from its origin to the present. 1847.
Moreland's History of the Waldenses.
Muston's Israel of the Alps. Tr. by Hazlitt.
——— ——— Tr. by Montgomery.
Perrin's (J. P.) Luther's Forerunners.
Peyran's (J. A.) Historical defence of the Waldenses. Tr. by S. Leonard.
——— Luther's Forerunners. (Showing that for centuries before Luther the Waldenses opposed Popery.)
Princeton Review. 15:557. 23:656.
Quart. Review. 33:134.
Sim's Apology for the Waldenses.
Sismondi's Hist. of the Crusades agt. the W.
Todd's Discourses on Antichrist.
Todd's (James H.) Books of the Vaudois. (The Waldensian MSS. of Trinity College, Dublin, and other Waldensian literature recently discovered. 1865.)
Willyam's Hist. of the W. Church. To 1855.

The majority of the writers in the above long list were malignant enemies of this people. The principal Waldensian writers on all subjects are enumerated by MONASTIER and FLACCIUS, referred to above; but scarcely any of them are to be had.

Walk of Faith. See PRACTICAL PIETY, HEAVENLY-MINDEDNESS.

Abernethy's (John) Sermons.
Anderson's (Geo. W.) Way and Walk.
Baxter's (Rich.) Christian Ethics.
——— on the Divine life.
Bolton's (Robt.) Lectures on Genesis.
Brameld's (G. W.) Sermons. 2d Series.
Burrows' (Jeremiah) Sermons.
Butler's (Wm. A.) Sermons.
Cooper's (Edward) Sermons.
Davy's (C.) Sermons.
Evans' (R. W.) Parochial Sermons.
Faringdon's (Arthur) Sermons.
Fuller's (And.) Sermons.
Graves' (Richard) Sermons.
Hickman's (Bp.) Sermons.
Hobart's (Bp.) Sermons.
Hordern's (Joseph) Sermons.
Knowles' (Thos.) Sermons. (3 on this subj.)
Martyn's (Henry) Sermons.
McCheyne's (Robt. W.) Sermons.
Nares' (R.) Sermons.
Norris' (John) Practical Sermons.
Owen's (John) Sermons.
Pyle's (Philip) Sermons.
Romaine's Works.
Searle's (Ambrose) Way of life.
Secker's (Abp.) Non-such Professor.
Sibbs' (Rich.) Sermons.
Stewart's (Jas. H.) Sermons.
Taylor's Circumspect walking described.
Tillinghast's (John) Life of Faith.
Toulmin's (Joshua) Sermons.
Wallin's (Benjamin) Christian Life.

Watson's (Tho.) Sermons.
Watson's (Alex.) Sermons.
Wesley's (John) Sermons.
Whitefield's Sermons.

Walloon Churches.

Burns' Hist. of the French refugees in Engl.
Lange's (Joshué T.) Sermons. (A very good acc. of these churches is given at the end.)
Weiss' Hist. of French Protestant refugees. (From the revocation of the edict of Nantes, to 1857.)

Wandering Thoughts. See GOVERNMENT OF THE HEART, THOUGHTS.

Adams' (J.) Sermons.
Atterbury's (Lewis) Ten Sermons.
Barrow's (Isaac) Works.
Beveridge's (Bp.) Works.
Craig's (James) Sermons.
Fawcett's (James) Sermons.
Hollingsworth's (J. B.) Sermons.
Horne's (Bp.) Sermons.
Lavington's (Samuel) Sermons.
Morning Exercises at Cripplegate. Sermon by Manton.
Steele's Remedy for wandering thoughts.
Tenison's (Abp.) Sermons.
Vincent's (Nathan) Sermons.
Wesley's (John) Sermons.

War. See CONGRESS OF NATIONS, PEACE.

Pro.

Carmichael's Sermons on War.
Chris. Monthly Spect. 1:459.
Chris. Observer. 3:399.
Chris. Review. 13:345.
Cousin's Introd. to the hist. of philosophy.
Godwin on Political Justice.
Grotius on the Law of Peace and War.
Henderson's Lawfulness of defensive arms.
Jones on Defensive war in a just cause.
Law's (Bp. Henry) Doctrine of Christianity on the subject of war.
McLeod's Five Sermons on war.
Paley's Moral and Political philosophy.
Puffendorf on the Laws of Nations.
Tennent on Defensive War.
Vattell's Law of Nations.

Con.

Erasmi Anti Polemus: seu belli detestatio.
Fichté, Grundlage des Naturrechts. 1776.
Gabinus de Wal. disputatio philosophico juridica de conjunctione populorum ad pacem perpetuam. 1808.
Kant's Idee zu einer allgemein. Gesch., etc.
——— Metaphysiche Anfangsgründe der Rechtslehre.
——— Zum Ewigen Frieden. 1796.
La Motte. Utrum pax perpetua pangi possit?
Lilienfel's Neues Staatsgebande. 1767.
Schwabe, Ueber das unvermeidliche Unrecht. 1804.
Totze, Ewiger u. Allgemeiner Friede, etc.
Advocate of Peace. Periodical. Boston.

War—*continued.*

Con.

Aiken's War, religiously and historically considered.
Appleton's Works.
Banker's Mag. 1:582.
Benezet's (Anth.) Works. (Excellent.)
Brown's (James) Distress and misery the constant effect of war, both to conqueror and conquered. (A brief sketch, &c., from the earliest times of history.)
Chalmers' (Thomas) Sermons.
Channing's (W. E.) Essays and Discourses.
Christian Examiner. 4:83. 7:338. 18:368. 27:72. 42:157. 44:124.
Clarkson's Sentiments of early Christians.
Cone's War and Christianity.
Davies' (Pres. S.) Sermons.
Dublin University Mag. 39:747.
Dymond's Inquiry into the accordance of war with Christianity.
Eclectic Rev. 4th Series. 26:236.
Essays of Philanthropos.
Evans' Sermons.
Geree's Red Horse; or the Bloodiness of W.
Hall's (Robt.) Sermons.
Herald of Peace. Periodical. London.
Holcombe's Lectures on primitive theology.
Knox's Trans. of Erasmus' Antipolemus.
Law's (George) Sermons.
Law's (William) Thoughts on War.
Leng's (Bp.) Sermons.
Littell's Living Age. 28:362.
Morgan's Facts addressed to the people of Great Britain.
North Amer. Rev. 3:33.
North Brit. Rev. 16:1.
Parsons' Christianity a system of peace.
Raleigh's (Walter) Reliquæ.
Scott's W. inconsistent with Christianity.
Sheppard's Duty of Christians as to war.
Smith's Doct. of Christianity vindicated.
Stone's Sermons on War.
Sumner's (Hon. Chas.) Address on Peace.
The Friend of Peace. Periodical. London.
Thrush's Reasons for withdrawing from the Army.
——— Causes and Evils of war.
Upham's (Prof.) Manual of Peace.
Warner's War inconsistent with Christ'y.
[Wemyss' (Thomas)] Pictures of war from authentic narratives.
Whelply's Letters to Gov. Strong.

Warfare. See FIGHT OF FAITH.

Washing the Disciples' Feet.

Rauschius de Pedilavio, etc.
Röpe, Dass das Mahl d. Fusswaschens m. dem Paschamahl nicht, etc.

Brown's (John) Discourses of Jesus.
Evangelical Review. 1:434.
Fuller's (And.) Miscellaneous Works.
Harn on Washing of feet.
Kemp's (H. W.) Sermons.

Watchfulness. See TEMPTATION.
Adey's (Wm.) Sermons.
Alleine's Instructions about heart-work.
Atterbury's (Lewis) Sermons.
Bishop's (Will.) Sermons.
Boston's (Tho.) Sermons.
Bowers' (Dean) Sermons.
Calthrop's (John) Sermons.
Cecil's (Rich.) Sermons.
Christian Observer. 14:8.
Christian Review. 6:213.
Doddridge's (Philip) Sermons.
Dowling's (A. G.) Sermons.
Faringdon's (Anthony) Sermons.
Fiddes' (Dr. Richard) Sermons.
Fothergill's (George) Sermons.
Fowle's (F. W.) Ten plain sermons.
Francklin's (Thomas) Sermons.
Gataker's (Tho.) Sermons.
Gregory's (George) Sermons.
Hale's (Sir Matt.) Contemplations.
Hampden's (R. D.) Sermons.
Hoole's (Joseph) Sermons.
James' (John) Christian Watchfulness in prospect of sickness, mourning, and death.
Johnson's (John) Sermons.
Kennaway's Sermons.
Lavington's (Samuel) Sermons.
Leighton on 1 Peter 1:3 and 5:8.
Morrison's (Robert) Sermons.
Newman's (J. H.) Sermons.
Riddock's (James) Sermons.
Romaine's (William) Sermons.
Skelton's (P.) Sermons.
Slade's (James) Sermons.
Smith's (Sam. Stanhope) Sermons.
Stillingfleet's (Bp.) Sermons.
Spurgeon's (C. H.) Sermons. Vol. 2.
Wilson's (Will. C.) Sermons.
Woodhouse's Careless Christian.

Waterlandians. See MENNONITES.

Weak Christians.
Baxter's (Rich.) Directions for weak Chris.
Bedford's (Arth.) Case of a weak conscience.
Chalmers' (Tho.) Congregational Sermons.
Davies' (President) Sermons.
Disney's (John) Sermons.
Hales' (John) Golden Remains.
Law's Serious Call to Christians.
Scott's (David) Discourses.
Spurgeon's (C. H.) Sermons.
Thorndike's (H.) Works.

Weakness of Human Reason.
See PROVINCE OF REASON.
Antonii Estimatio rationis humani.
Beckmanni Affectatio rationis captivato.
Collier's (Jer.) Essays on moral subjects.
Gale's Court of the Gentiles. Part 2.
Newlin's (Tho.) Sermons before the University of Oxford.
Van Mildert's Boyle Lectures. 1802.

Wealth. See POLITICAL ECONOMY, RICHES.

Weanedness from the World. See AMUSEMENTS, FASHION, HEAVENLY-MINDEDNESS, MORTIFICATION, SELF-DENIAL, SELF-DEDICATION, WALK OF FAITH, WORLDLINESS.
Biddulph's (Tho. T.) Sermons.
Bisset's (Thomas) Sermons.
Bradley's (Cha.) Sermons.
Brown's (Bp.) Sermons.
Cooper's (Edward) Sermons.
Delany's (Patrick) Discourses.
Downame (John) on Contempt of the world.
Gale's Love of the world inconsistent with love of God.
Gell's (R.) Remains.
Griffith's (T.) Lectures.
Hambleton's (John) Seven Sermons.
Hunt's (Jer.) Sermons.
Le Bas' (Cha. W.) Sermons.
Maltby's (Edw.) Sermons at Lincoln's Inn.
Oakley's (Fred.) Sermons.
Stewart's (James H.) Sermons.
Vance's (W. T.) Sermons.
Walker's (Robert) Sermons.
Wilkinson's (Henry) Sermons.

Weekly Communion.
See LORD'S SUPPER.

Pro.

Dodsworth's (Wm.) Discourses.
Grant's Plea for weekly communion.
Haldane (R.) on the Lord's Supper.
Millennial Harbinger. Periodical. Bethany, Va. (Many articles.)
Ridley's (W. H.) Preparation for the Comm.

Much has been written on this subject, but almost all in pamphlets and single sermons.

Weigelians.

Pro.

Weigelii Opera.
Held, Algemeiner Friede mit Jesu.
Hilliger, de Vita, fatis, et scriptis Weigelii.
Lohman, Autwort auf Herzogs, etc.
Methus, Epzählung der Ursachen.
Stiefel's Christ und Gottselige Tractætlein.
Tetingii Prodomus Apologeticus.
——— Vermanungschreiben, etc.

Con.

Balduini Disputationes.
Colberger's Platonisch-hermet. Christenth.
Crockii Anti Weigelius.
Feurbonii Diss. de distinctis relig. capit.
Gerhardi Disputationes Theologicæ.
Hoornbeckii Comm. de paradoxis, etc.
Hunn, Bericht von d. neuen Propheten relig
——— de Principiis theologiæ fanaticæ.
Müller, der Vertheidigung des Berichts.
Piscator, der Warnung. (Contra Stiefel.)
Theobald's Bericht von der Wiedertæuffern.
Thumii (Theodori) Considerationes.
Weberi Censura Stiefelianismi.

A full list of the numerous writings of Weigelius is given by WALCH, *Bibliotheca.*

Weigelians, History of.

Foertschii Observatio de Val. Weigelio.
Hilligeri Diss. de vita, fatis, et scriptis, etc.

Weights and Measures. See ARCHÆOLOGY, JEWISH ANTIQUITIES, &c.

Bernard de Mensuris et ponderibus Antiquis. (Attacks Cumberland.)
Brerewood de Ponderibus et pretiis Hebraic. (Inserted by Walton in his prolegomena.)
Eisenschidius de Ponderibus et mensuris Rom., Græc., Hebr., etc. (Ugolinus.)
Garnier, sur les Monnaies dè l'antiquité.
Queipo, Systèmes mêtriques et monitaires des anciens peuples.
Waltoni Supplementum.

Alexander's Dictionary of weights and measures, ancient and modern.
Arbuthnot's Ancient weights and measures.
Cumberland's Jewish weights and measures.
Godwin's Moses and Aaron.
Hindmarsh's Weights, &c., of the Bible.
Hooper's Anc. Measures, especially Jewish.
Jervis' Records of ancient science.
Kelly's Universal Cambist.

Wesley, John.

Wesley, John, Life of; by Bradbury.
———— ——— by Clarke.
———— ——— by Coke.
———— ——— by Colet.
———— ——— by Dove.
———— ——— by Drew.
———— ——— by Emory.
———— ——— by Hampsen.
———— ——— by Holmes.
———— ——— by Larrabie.
———— ——— by Moore.
———— ——— by Southey.
———— ——— by Taylor.
———— ——— by Watson.
———— ——— by Whitehead.
Am. Bibl. Repos. 2d Series. 9:388.
Chris. Disciple. 2:44.
Chris. Exam. 43:1. 76:157.
Chris. Month. Spect. 3:471,530.
Episcopal Mag. 2:224,263,296.
Kitto's Journal. 3:1.
McBriar's Apology for Wesley. (Reply to Taylor.)
Meth. Quarterly Rev. 8:406,455.
Month. Rev. 96:26.
Quarterly Rev. 1:38. 24:1.

Wesleyans. See METHODISTS.

Westminster Confession. See CREEDS, CONGREGATIONALISM.

Whitefield.

Tholuck's (A.) Leben G. Whitefield.

Am. Bibl. Repos. 2d Series. 7:302.
Am. Quar. Reg. 4:297.
Chris. Exam. 25:85.
Chris. Month. Spect. 3:471,530.
Chris. Quar. Spect. 6:88.
Chris. Rev. 3:264.
Eclec. Rev. 4th Series. 3:520.
Frazier's Mag. 17:133.
Newell's Life of Whitefield.
New Englander. 3:24.
North Am. Rev. 48:478.
Ryle's (J. C.) Priest, Puritan, and Preacher.
Stevens' Relig. movement of the 17th cent.
Theol. and Lit. Review. 5:468.

White Stone.

Bibliotheca Sacra. 1:461.

Whitsunday Sermons. See FESTIVALS.

Andrewes', Bp., Sermons.
Arnold's, Thomas, Sermons.
Barrow's, Isaac, Sermons.
Berriman's, William, Sermons.
Beveridge's, Bp., Sermons.
Brownrig's, Bp., Sermons.
Cooper's, Edward, Sermons.
Dehon's, Bp., Sermons.
Delany's, Patrick, Sermons.
Donne's, John, Sermons.
Faringdon's, Anthony, Sermons.
Gordon's, Adam, Sermons.
Hacket's, Bp., Sermons.
Lake's, Bp., Sermons.
Le Bas', Cha. W., Sermons.
Newman's, J. H., Sermons.
Potts', J. H., Sermons.
Secker's, Abp., Sermons.
Smallridge's, Bp., Sermons.
Stillingfleet's, Bp., Sermons.
Van Mildert's, Bp., Sermons.
Weston's, Bp., Sermons.

Wickliff.

Jäger's J. Wicliff, und seine Bedentung für d. Reformation.
Lechler's Wiclif als Vorlaufer der Reformat.
Winkelmanni (J.) Gerson, Wiclef, Hus, inter se comparati.

Wickliff's Works.
Amer. Monthly Rev. 2:189.
British Critic. 5:389.
Christian Examiner. 51:53.
Christian Review. 6:115.
Eclectic Mag. 50:307.
Edinb. Rev. 56:221.
Frazier's Mag. 5:177.
Gilpin's Lives of the Reformers.
Hanna's (W.) Wycliffe and the Huguenots.
Henthorn's Apology for Lollard doctrines, attributed to Wickliffe. With Introduction and notes.
Le Bas' Life of Wickliffe.
Lewis' Life and sufferings of Jno. Wickliff.
Littell's Living Age. 1:655.
Meth. Quar. Rev. 2:234.
North British Rev. 20:110.
Pond's (E.) Wickliffe and his times.
Sumner's Life and times of John de W.
Vaughn's Life and opinions of W. (Principally from his unpublished manuscripts.)

Wicklifites. See HUSSITES.

Grassi Historia de ortu ac progressu, etc.
Hardt, Magnum Œcumenicum Constansiense Concilium.
Varillase du Wicklifianisme, avec les guerres de Boheme, qui en ont eté les suites.
Zitte's Gesch. d. Eng. reform. J. Wicleff.
Mackay's Wicklifites in the 19th century.

Wilful Sins. See DEADLY SINS.

Blunt's (Henry) Sermons
Brady's (Nicholas) Sermons.
Burgess' (Anth.) Sermons. (3 on Ps. 19:13.)
Cooper's (Edward) Sermons.
Fenner's (William) Sermons.
Gresley's (William) Sermons.
Hammond's (Henry) Works.
Hoole's (Joseph) Sermons.
Kidder's (Bp.) Works.
Littleton's (Adam) Sermons.
Marshall's (Nath.) Sermons.
Milner's (Joseph) Sermons.
Orr's (John) Sermons.
Owen's (J.) Display of Arminianism.
Pyle's (Philip) Sermons.
Quincey's (Samuel) Sermons.
Rogers' (John) Sermons.
Sacheverell (Henry) on Presumptuous sins.
Sanderson's (Bp.) Sermons.
Scott's (John) Sermons.
Sedwick's (Obadiah) Sermons.
Sharp's (Abp.) Sermons.
Smith's (Elisha) Sermons.
Sumner's (Samuel) Sermons.
Thompson's (Thomas) Sermons.
Turner's (John) Sermons.
Walker's (Robert) Sermons.
Warren's (Dr. J.) Sermons.
Waterland's (Dan.) Sermons.

Will. See FREE AGENCY, MORAL ABILITY, HUMAN RESPONSIBILITY.

Augustin, de Libero arbitrio.
Amyraldi (Mos.) Dissertationes.
Andala Disputationes.
Anselm, Concordia præscientia, predestinatione, et gratiæ, cum libertate.
Calvini Opera.
Drexellii Heliotropium.
Erasmus de Libero arbitrio.
Feder's Untersuch. üb. d. menschl. Willen.
Haberkorn, Vindicatio libri beati Lutheri.
Leibnitz, Essai sur l'origine du mal.
Luther, de Servo arbitrio. (Agt. Erasmus.)
Masii (H. G.) Dissertationes.
Morus Victoria Gratiæ.
Placæi Opera. (One of the strongest writers of the 17th century.)
Quenstedii (Ioann.) Dissertationes.
Quistorpius de Viribus liberi arbitrii.
Thummii (Theod.) Dissertationes.
Zornei Delineatio Theologiæ patristicæ.

Abercrombie's Philos. of the moral feelings.
Abernethy's (John) Sermons.
Alger on the Will.

Will—*continued.*

Am. Bibl. Repos. 2d Series. 7:330,411. 9:33. 3d Series. 1:709.
Blakeley on our Notions of good and evil.
Burgess on Original Sin.
Butterworth on Moral government.
Charnock's Works.
Clarke's Enquiry into the cause of evil.
Day (Jeremiah) on the Will.
Doddridge's Lectures.
Edwards (Pres.) on the Will. ("I consider Jonathan Edwards the greatest of the sons of men. He ranks with the brightest luminaries of the Christian church, not excluding any country or age since the apostolic."—ROBERT HALL.)
Emmon's (Nath.) Sermons.
Erskine's Uncondit. freeness of the Gospel.
Fuller's (And.) Dialogues. Dial. 2.
——— Gospel worthy of all acceptation.
——— Essays.
Gill's Cause of God and Truth.
Grove's Moral Philosophy.
Hazard (R. G.) on the Will.
Hervey's Theoron and Aspasio.
Hey's Lectures on Divinity.
Hoadly on Acceptance with God.
Jackson's Defence of human liberty.
King's Essay on the origin of evil.
Luther (M.) on the Will. Tr. by H. Cole.
Marriott's Sermons on the Will.
New Englander. 5:337.
Palmer on the Liberty of man.
Pitt's Philosophy of Christianity. (In the preliminary Dissertations.)
Reid on the Active powers of the mind.
Saurin's Sermons.
Solly's The Will, Divine and human.
Spring's (Gardner) Essays.
Stewart's Philosophy of the mind.
Tappan's Review of Edwards on the Will.
Theological Essays reprinted from the Princeton Review.
Theol. and Lit. Rev. 1:521. 2:148.
Toplady's Sermon on free-will.
Upham on the Will.
Watts' Works.
West on Moral Agency.

Winebrennarians. See CHURCH OF GOD.

Wisdom. See DISCRETION, PRUDENCE.

Bishop's (W.) Sermons.
Crabb's (Habak.) Sermons.
Dowling's (John G.) Sermons.
Doyley's (Bp.) Sermons.
Fothergill's (George) Sermons.
Gibbon's (Thomas) Sermons.
Gouldburn's (E. M.) Sermons.
Hall's (Robt.) Notes of Sermons.
Henry's (Matt.) Miscellaneous Works.
Holland's (Philip) Sermons.
Horne's (Bp.) Sermons.
Hough's (John) Sermons.
Hurd's (Bp.) Sermons.
Jortin's (John) Sermons.

Wisdom—*continued.*

Langhorn's (William) Sermons.
Leighton's (Abp.) Works.
Millar's (James) Sermons.
Morehead's (Robert) Sermons.
Moss' (Robert) Sermons.
Newman's (John H.) Sermons.
Scott's (J. N.) Sermons.
Skelton's (Philip) Sermons.
Townson's (George) Discourses.
Vincent's (William) Sermons.
Welb's (F.) Sermons.
Whitefield's (Henry) Sermons.

Wisdom of being Religious. See PLEASURES OF PIETY, YOUTH.

Abernethy's (John) Sermons.
Barnes' (William G.) Sermons.
Batty's (Adam) Sermons.
Beveridge's (Bp.) Sermons.
Bourn's (Samuel) Sermons.
Burnaby's (Andrew) Sermons.
Carr's (George) Sermons.
Clarke's (Samuel) Sermons.
Davies' (Samuel) Sermons.
Fisher's (Nathaniel) Sermons.
Foster's Preface to Doddridge's Rise and Progress.
Gilbert's (John) Sermons.
Holden's (Lawrence) Sermons.
Horton's (Thomas) Sermons.
Hunter's (Thomas) Sermons.
Meyrick's (Frederick) Sermons.
Peters' (C.) Sermons.
Savage's (S. M.) Sermons.
Smith's (Henry) Sermons.
Synge's (Abp.) Sermons.
Tillotson's (Abp.) Sermons.
Young's (E.) Sermons.
Zollikoffer's Sermons.

Wisdom of God. See ATTRIBUTES.

Abernethy's (John) Sermons.
Appleton's (Pres.) Works. Lect. 2 and 3.
Bates' (William) Works.
Bentley's Boyle Lectures. 1692.
Blair's (Hugh) Sermons.
Chalmer's (Thomas) Sermons.
Chevalier's Hulsean Lectures. 1827.
Clarke's (Dr. Samuel) Sermons.
——— Boyle Lectures. 1706.
Derham's Boyle Lectures. 1727.
Dwight's Theology. Ser. 13.
Fenelon's Demonst. of the wisdom of God.
Foster on Natural Religion.
Foster's (Dr. James) Discourses.
Groves On the first spring of action in the Deity.
McCullock's (Dr. John) Sermons.
Monthly Rev. 131:187.
Nieuentyt's Religious Philosopher.
Ray's Wisdom of God in Creation.
Rieman on Natural Religion.
Saurin's Sermons.
Towne's Chemistry, as exemplifying the wisdom of God.
Turner's Boyle Lectures. 1709. (Ag. Deists.)
Tyerman's (Daniel) Essays.
Wilkins' (Bp.) Natural Religion.
——— World in the moon.

Wit.

Fordyce's Dialogues on Education.
Kames' Elements of Criticism. Vol. 2, ch. 13.
Spectator. Nos. 58–63.
Stewart's Philosophy of the Mind.

Witchcraft. See MAGIC.

Bekker, die Bezauberte Welt.
Boissard, de Divinatione et magicis.
Delrii Disquisitionum magicarum.
Edwardus de Natura Dæmonorum.
Lavater de Spectris.
Limborch, Theologia Christiana.
Massé de l'Imposture et tromperie des enchanteurs, necromanciers, etc.
Mengi (H.) Flagellum Dæmonum.
Selden de Diis Syriis, Syntagma.
Taisneri Opus Mathematicum. (Describes various arts and experiments.)
Turretini Institutiones Theol. Locus V.
Wieri Opera. (Very superstitious, but allows that some were burnt for witches in his day [1660] who were harmless hypochondriacs.)
Zanchius de Dæmonibus.

Ady's Candle in the dark. 1656. (Very good.)
Am. Bibl. Repos. 2d Series. 7:129,253.
Am. Whig Review. 3:60.
Aubrey on Magic, Charms, and Apparitions.
Bacon's (Peter) Witchcraft detected and prevented. (Wood cuts.)
Beaumont's Treatise on Spirits. (An account of genii, apparitions, magic, &c., maintaining the reality of such things.)
Becker's Enchanted world. (Denies the truth of witchcraft.)
Bovet's Pandemonium. (Holds the existence of witches.)
Burnett's Boyle Lectures. 1724.
Calef's More wonders of the invisible world. (An able answer to Cotton Mather.)
Calmet (Father) on Apparitions, Demons, Vampires, &c.)
Casaubon (Meric.) on Credulity and incredibility. (Holds the existence of witches, &c.)
Chris. Exam. 11:240.
Danæus on Witches. ("Wherein is declared whatever may be required touching that matter." 1564.)
Dwight's (Pres.) Travels in New England.
Edwards' (Bp.) Body of Divinity.
Edwards' (John) Exercitations.
Encyclopedia Brittanica.
For. Quart. Review. 6:1.
Gage's Survey of the West Indies. 1677.
Glanvill's Blow at Modern Sadducism.
——— Full and plain Evidence.
Hallywell's Kingdom of darkness.
Hawkins' Sermons on Witchcraft.
Holland's (Henry) Satanical operations truely proued.

Witchcraft—*continued.*

Howe's Works.
Hutchinson's (F.) Historical account of W. (A chronological history of many English witch trials, and other curious cases; and also of the witches of Boston and Salem.)
International Magazine. 5:198.
Lawson's Christ's fidelity our only shield.
Le Clerc's Pneumatics.
Mackay's Extraordinary popular delusions.
Man's Discouerie of the three witches of Warbois, executed at Huntingdon. 1593.
Mather's (Cotton) History of New England.
——— Wonders of the invisible world.
Mather's (Increase) Cases of Conscience.
——— Memorable Providences.
——— Account of trial of certain witches.
Mitchell & Dickie's Philosophy of W.
More's Theological Works.
Nicholson's (Isaac) Sermons.
Perkins' Damned art of witchcraft.
Perrerius' Vanity of star-gazing.
Pickering on Witchcraft.
Potts' Trial of 19 witches at Lancaster, Eng.
Quitman on Magic.
Retrospective Rev. 5:87.
Ross' Advertisement to the Jurymen of Eng.
Scott's (Sir W.) Demonology and Witchcraft.
Scott's (R.) Discovery of Witchcraft.
Sibley's History of the occult sciences.
Sinclair's Satan's invisible world discovered. (Relations of witches, spirits, &c.)
Thatcher's Witchcraft delusion at Salem, in 1692.
Upham's Lectures on the Salem witchraft.
Wagstaff's Question of witchcraft debated.
Webster's (John) Display of supposed witchcraft. (Learned. Written in opposition to Glanvill, and More the Platonist.)
Williams' (Howard) Superstitions of W.
Wright's Dialogue on witches and witchcraft. (Fine exhibition of the state of feeling in the age of Elizabeth. Reprinted 1842.)
Young on Idolatry.

See a great list of Latin and German works on this subject, previous to the year 1700, in THOMASIUS, *Dissertatio de processus inquisitorii contra sagas.*

Witch of Endor.

Gregory Nyssen, de Pythonissa.
Origen, de Engastrimytho.

Arcularii Disputationes Theologicæ.
Buddei Historia Ecclesiastica. (An able dissertation on the Pythonis at the end of the 2d volume.)
Deylingii Observationes Sacræ.
Eustathius de Engastrimytho. (Refutes Origen, and proves that the ghost of Samuel was not really raised.)
Gerhardi (J. E.) Disputationes.
Heideggeri Dissertationes.
Ianzonius de Pythonisa Endorensi.
Marckii Scripta in selecta Scripturæ.

Witch of Endor—*continued.*

Schotti (Soc. Jesu) Physica curiosa.
Strauchii Dissertationes.

Brevint's Saul and Samuel at Endor.
Calmet's Preface to Comm. on 1st Sam.
Dawson's (T.) Dissertations.
Edwards' (Dr. John) Critical Exercitations.
Hall's (Bp.) Contemplations.
Hughes' Female characters.
Le Bas' (C. W.) Sermons.
Lindsay's (H.) Lectures.
Miller's (Joseph) Sermons.
Muggleton's True interp. of the witch of E.
Osgood's (David) Sermons.
Penn's (James) Miscellaneous Tracts.
Ridgley's Body of Divinity.
Sharp's (Granville) Case of Saul
Waterland's (Daniel) Works.

Witness of the Spirit.
See ASSURANCE, SPIRIT OF ADOPTION.

Guntheri (Ioann.) Dissertationes.
Noesselt, de Interno testimonio Sp. Sancti.
Schranckenmüller, de Spiritus testimonio.
Stoeberus de Spiritus Testimonio.
Wernsdorfii (Gottl.) Dissertationes. Diss. 2.

Alston's (P. W. W.) Sermons.
Barrington's Miscellanea Sacra. Essay 1. (This ess. is reprinted in *Watson's Tracts.*)
Benson's Reasonableness of Christianity.
Burder's (Henry F.) Sermons.
Burder's (Geo.) Village Sermons.
Cawood's (John) Sermons.
Cooper's (Edward) Sermons.
Cunningham's (J. W.) Sermons.
Dickinson's (Jonath.) Sermons and Tracts.
Doddridge's (Philip) Sermons.
Edwards' (Pres.) Works.
Fuller's (Andrew) Expository Notes.
Jackson's (Dr. John) Sermons.
Leifchild's (John) Discourses.
Lloyd's (J. C.) Sermons.
Muir on the Holy Spirit.
Secker's (Abp.) Sermons.
Sharp's (Abp.) Sermons.
Short's Bampton Lectures. 1846.
Usher's (Abp.) Sermons.
Vaughn's (Cha. John) Sermons.
Warburton's Doctrine of Grace.
Watts' Ordinary and extraordinary witness of the Spirit.
Wesley's (John) Sermons.
Wilson's (William) Parochial Sermons.

Wives. See FEMALE SEX, MATERNAL DUTIES, MARRIAGE.

Bishop's (William) Sermons.
Boston's (Tho.) Sermons.
Calvert's Wife's Memorial.
Collyer's (W. B.) Lectures on Script. duties.
Creffeild's A good wife a great blessing.
Dowling's (J. G.) Sermons.
Dyke's (Oswald) Sermons.
Erskine's (Ralph) Works.
Ford's (John) Two discourses.

Wives—*continued.*

Fordyce's (James) Sermons.
Gataker's (Thomas) Sermons.
Grant's (Johnson) Discourses.
Hackett's Wedding Sermon.
Hole on the Liturgy.
Jay on Marriage.
Leighton on 1st Peter, Ch. 3, v. 1–6.
Manton's (Dr. Thos.) Sermons.
Melville's (Henry) Lectures.
Morgan's (Lady) Woman and her Master.
Phelps' Maternal influence on Sons.
Secker's (William) Sermons.
Shepard's (Thomas) Sermons.
Shuttleworth's (P. N.) Sermons.
Taylor's (J.) Conjugal Ring. (Beautiful.)
Tuthill's Perthes; the Christian Wife.
Watts' (Isaac) Sermons.

Wolsey.

Cavendish's Life of Cardinal Wolsey. (Ably edited, with notes, by S. W. Singer; and with additional notes by J. Holmes.
Fiddes' Life of Cardinal Wolsey.
Galt's Life and administration of Wolsey.
Howard's Wolsey and his times.
Knickerbocker Mag. 6:401.
Museum of For. Liter. 3:105,208. 22:116.
Quarterly Review. 8:163.

Woman. See FEMALE SEX.

Woman's Rights.

Amer. Quart. Rev. 18:289.
Beecher's (Cath.) True remedy for women's wrongs.
Burnap's Sphere and duties of woman.
Christian Exam. 52:194. 56:1.
Crocker (H. M.) on the Rights of woman.
Democratic Rev. 14:477.
Eclectic Mag. 4:403.
Edinburg Rev. 73:99.
Grimke (Sarah) on the Equal. of the sexes.
Hale's (Mrs.) Woman's Record.
Landals on Woman's sphere.
Masters' Woman's rights commensurate with her obligations.
North Amer. Rev. 42:489.
Ossolis' (Marg.) Women in the 19th cent.
Quart. Review. 75:50.
Smith's (Rev. R.) Ecclesiazusæ; or the Female parliament.
Tonno's (Charlotte) Wrongs of women.
Westminster Rev. 34:254.
Wharton's Exp. of the laws of Eng. relating to women; showing their rights, remedies, and responsibilities.

Works. See GOOD WORKS.

Worldliness. See ANXIETY, HEAVENLY-MINDEDNESS, OVERCOMING THE WORLD, SPIRITUALITY, VANITY OF THE WORLD, WEANEDNESS FROM THE WORLD.

Alexander's (J. W.) Sermons.
Alston's (P. W. W.) Sermons.

Worldliness—*continued.*

Ball's (Nathaniel) Sermons.
Bell's (William) Sermons.
Biddulph's Conformity to the world inconsistent with a profession of Christianity.
Bisset's (Tho.) Sermons.
Blackall's (Bp.) Sermons.
Blair's (Hugh) Sermons.
Bradley's (Charles) Sermons.
Burnside's Religion of Mankind.
Burroughes on Earthly-mindedness.
Butler's (Alban) Sermons.
Carpenter's (B.) Sermons. (4 on this subj.)
Chalmer's (Tho.) Congregational Sermons.
Christian Observer. 14:75. 16:9. 20:137,739.
Colquhoun's World's religion contrasted with Christianity.
Dibden's (T. F.) Sermons.
Dwight's (Timothy) Sermons.
Finney's (C. G.) Lectures to Christians.
Girdlestone's Social conduct of a Christian.
Jackson's (Dr. John) Sermons.
Jelf's (R. W.) Sermons.
Jortin's (J.) Sermons.
Judd (H.) on Conformity to the world.
Knox's (Vicessimus) Sermons.
Lavington's (Samuel) Sermons.
Law's Serious call to Christians.
Le Bas' (Cha. W.) Sermons.
Lee's The family and its duties.
Lucas' Enquiry after happiness.
Miller's (John) Sermons.
Milner's (Isaac) Sermons.
Morning Exercises at Cripplegate. Sermon by T. Gale.
Princeton Review. 30:226.
Ray's Persuasive to a holy life.
Rogers' (John) Sermons.
Rowlatt's (Will. H.) Sermons.
Scobel's (Edw.) Sermons.
Scott's (Dr. John) Christian life.
Sharp's (Abp.) Sermons.
Skelton's (P.) Sermons.
Smith's (Theyre) Sermons.
Stennet's (Samuel) Sermons. (Precious.)
Stubbs (Henry) on Conformity to the world.
Tappan's (David) Sermons.
Tate's (T.) Sermons.
Tillotson's Sermons.
Walker's (Robt.) Sermons. (Models.)
Wesley's (John) Sermons.
Wilson's (W. C.) Sermons.

Worship. See LITURGIES, PROPRIETIES, PLACES OF WORSHIP, PUBLIC WORSHIP, RITES AND CEREMONIES, SOCIAL WORSH.

Augustin, Opera.

Abeken's Gottesdienst der alten kirche.
Alt (H.) der Christliche Cultus: historisch Dargestellt.
Bahr's [Baierus] Symbolik der Mosaischen cultus.
Dupin's (C. F.) Origine de tous les culte. (10 vols., 4to.)
——— Abrégé. (1 vol., 8vo.)

Worship—*continued.*

Durandi Rationale divinorum officiorum. (The great ceremonial law of Romanists.)
Ehrenfeuchter's Theorie des Christl. cultus.
Harnack's Gemeine-Gottesdienst im apostolischen Zeitalter.
Herrliberger's Gottesdienstliche ceremonien. (Describes the worship of Romanists, Waldenses, Protestants, Mahometans, Hindus, Africans, American Indians, &c. Plates.)
Hofling's (J. W. F.) Lehre d. ältest. kirche.
Hospinianus de Templis. (Origin, use, and abuse of temples.)
Jurieu, Hist. critique de cultes, bon et mauvais; depuis Adam, jusqu'a Jesus Christ. ("Perspicuous, terse, elegant." REIMMAN.)
Klöpper's Theorie der stehenden Cultusform.
Martene de Antiquis ecclesiæ disciplina. ("Most valuable."—PALMER.)
Meyer's (K.) Verhältniss der kunst zum Cultus.
Ritter's (J.) Protest. Gottesdienst und die kunst in ihrem gegenseitigen Verhältniss.
Turrettini (Io. A.) Cogitationes.
Vetter's Lehre vom Christlichen Cultus.
Vitringa de Vetere Synagoga. (Written to show that the rites of the synagogue were translated into the Christian Church.)
Walter's (R.) Æsthetischen in der religion.

Abernethy's (John) Sermons.
Atkinson's (Wm.) The Church. (On the wide-spread error of substituting worship for religion. A very extensive and able survey.)
Atterbury's (Francis) Sermons.
Baptist Quarterly. 1:191.
Barrow's (Isaac) Sermons.
Barrow's (Wm.) Sermons. (Several on this subject.)
Baxter's (Arthur G.) Sermons.
Beachcroft's (Robt. P.) Sermons.
Beveridge's Thesaurus Theologicus.
Bibliotheca Sacra. 22:529.
Bingham's Antiquities of the Church.
Blissard's (W.) Moral influence of religious worship.
Bowers' (Dean) Sermons.
Boyse's Remarks on a late discourse, &c. (Reply to Bp. King.)
Brownrig's (Bp.) Sermons.
Bunsen's Hippolytus and his age. (An able comparison of the modern with the ancient worship.)
Cardale's (P.) The Gospel Sanctuary.
Carr's (George) Sermons.
Cave's Primitive Christianity. Part 1, ch. 9.
Charnock's Works. *Spiritual worship.*
Christ. Exam. 37:350.
Clark on Worship.
Clarke's (A.) Sermons.
Close's (Francis) Sermons.
Crosthwaite's (J. C.) Sermons.
Dehon's (Bp.) Sermons.
Evert's (W. W.) Bethel.

Worship—*continued.*

Gill's Sermons and Tracts.
Haldane's (James A.) Social worship and ordinances of the first Christians. (Exc't.)
Hall's (Bp.) Practical Works.
Hall (Archd.) on Gospel worship.
Horseley's (Bp.) Sermons.
Jones' (Wm. of Nayland) Sermons.
Jurieu's Crit. Hist. of worship from Adam to Christ; with an account of all the idolatries of ancient Pagans.
King's Inventions of men in the W. of God.
Marshall's (N.) Sermons.
Masillon's Sermons.
Melvill's (Henry) Sermons.
Miller's Religious worship as directed in the Holy Scripture.
Orton on Christian Worship.
Owen on Hebrews, Ch. i. 7 and viii. 6.
Pearsol on Public Worship.
Pope's Vindic. of public and social worship.
Price's (S.) Berry Street Sermon.
Princeton Rev. 13:407.
Riddle's Manual of Christian antiq. Preface.
Robinson's Serious Call.
Rogers' (John) Sermons.
Spurgeon's (C. H.) Sermons. Vol. 3.
Tappan's (David) Sermons.
Templer on the Worship of God.
Wakefield (Gilbert) on Public Worship.
Watts' Holiness of times and places.
Wayland's (Francis) Sermons.
Webster's (Wm.) Sermons.
Wesley's (John) Sermons.
Wilson's (Bp.) Sermons.

Worship of Angels.

Clotz, de Angelolatria.
Heideggeri Disputationes.
Remigii Demonolatria.
Voetii Disputationes Theologicæ.
Geddes' Miscellaneous Tracts.
Powell's (H. T.) Roman Fallacies.

Worship of Saints. See INVOCATION.

Worship of Spirits. See DEMONS.

Septchenes de la religion des anciennes.
Barrier's Mythol. and fables of the ancients.
Body's Demonology.
Callaway's Yakkun Nattanawa. (A translation of a Cingalese work.)
Farmer on the Worship of human spirits.
Pfanner's Theology of the Pagans.

Worship of the Serpent. See SERPENT.

Worship of the Virgin. See MARIOLATRY.

Worth of the Soul. See VALUE.

Wounded Spirit. See CONSCIENCE.

Blair's, Hugh, Sermons.
Bolton's Instructions for the right comforting of afflicted consciences.

Wounded Spirit—*continued.*

Carr's, Dr. Samuel, Sermons.
Dawes', Abp., Works.
Elsmere's, S., Sermons.
Fiddes', Richard, Sermons.
Francklin's, Thomas, Sermons.
Gibbe' , Charles, Sermons.
Greenham's, R. A., Works.
Grose's, J., Sermons.
Harris', Robert, Works.
Pyle's, Thomas, Sermons.
Rees', Abraham, Sermons.
Sherlock's, William, Sermons.
Snape's, Andrew, Sermons.
South's, Robert, Sermons.
Townley's, James, Sermons.
Trapp's, Joseph, Sermons.
Waterland's, Daniel, Sermons.
Wilcox's, Daniel, Sermons.

Writing.

Fortia, l'Origine de l'Ecriture.
Gebelin, Monde Primatif.
Hugo (Hern.) de Origine Scribendi.
Silvestre, Paléographie Universelle.
Urban, l'Origine de l'Ecriture.
Wailley, Eléments de Paléographie.

Astle's Origin and progress of writing.
British Mag. Jan., 1836.
Carmichael on the Invention of alphabetical writing.
Fry's Pantographia. (Copies all the known alphabets in the world, and gives in English the force of each letter.)
Johnson's (John) Sermons. (No alphabet before Moses.)
Latter-day Luminary. 2:165.
[Massay's] Origin and progress of alphabetical writing.
More (Sam.) on the Invention of writing.
Princeton Review. 26:624.
Sharp's (Gregory) Dissertations. (Original powers of letters.)
Wall's (T.) Ancient orthog. of the Jews, the original state of the Hebrew text, and the propagation of alphabets.

Xabatatenses. See WALDENSES.

Xavier.

Bartol, Vie de St. Xavier.
Bonhours, Vie de St. Xavier.
Pagès, Lettres de St. Xavier.
Turselin, Vie de St. Xavier.

Bartol's Life of X. Trans. by Faber.
Bonhours' Life of X. Trans. by Dryden.
Morgan's Life of Xavier.

Yoke of Christ. See PLEASURES OF PIETY.

Bean's (James) Sermons.
Beveridge's (Bp.) Sermons.
Bishop's (William) Sermons.
Caswall's (E.) Sermons.
Christian Observer. 20:438.
Cooper's (Edward) Sermons.

Yoke of Christ—*continued.*

Denham's (J. E.) Sermons.
Denison's (Edward) Sermons at Oxford.
Gilpin's (Wm.) Sermons.
Girdlestone's (Charles) Parochial Sermons.
Green's (Samuel) Sermons.
Hewlett's (John) Sermons.
Hoadley's (Bp.) Sermons.
Le Bas' (Cha. W.) Sermons.
Mede's (Joseph) Sermons.
Newton's (John) Sermons.
Nicholson's (John) Sermons.
Nicholson's (William) Sermons.
Oakeley's (Frederick) Sermons.
Shuttleworth's (P. N.) Sermons.
Sumner's (John B.) Sermons. (3 on this sub.)
Tillotson's (Abp.) Sermons.
Van Mildert's Sermons at Lincoln's Inn.
Wilson's (W. C.) Sermons.
Witherspoon's (John) Sermons.

Youth. See CATECHIZING, EARLY PIETY, PLEASURES OF PIETY, WISDOM OF BEING RELIGIOUS.

Abbott's (John S.) Practical Christianity.
Abbott's (Jacob) Young Christian.
Alexander's (Arch.) Counsels of the aged.
Alison's (Archibald) Sermons.
Appleton's Works.
Bacon's (Leonard) Christian self-culture.
Balguy's (Tho.) Sermons.
Barton's (Lucy) History of our Lord.
Batchelder's Young men of America. (Prize Essay.)
Baxter's (Rich.) Counsels to young men.
Beecher's (Henry Ward) Lectures to young men.
Belfrage's Pract. discourses for the young.
Berens' Sermons for youth of the higher classes.
Binney's (Thomas) Wise Counsels.
Blyth's (G. B.) Sermons to children.
Bourn's (S.) Lectures.
Bowden's Dialogues.
Bridges' (Cha.) Manual for the young.
Brooks' Apples of Gold.
Brodum's Guide to old age.
Brown's Expos. of the Shorter Catechism.
Bruce's Lectures to young men.
Buckland on Early rising.
Burrows' (W. F.) Pastoral Advices.
Burney's (T.) Is it possible to make the best of both worlds?
Butterworth's Introduction to Christianity.
Calamy's (Edmund) Sermons. *On Obadiah.*
Chalmer's Posthumous Sermons.
Christian Observer. 20:551.
Clark (Rufus) on the Formation of character.
Clunie's Path of life. (Small, but good.)
Cobbet's (Wm.) Advice to young men.
Coetlogan's Sermons.
Cooper's (Edward) Sermons.
Cox's (F. A.) Our young men. (Prize essay.)
Crossman's Young man's Monitor.
Culverwell's (Matthew) Sermons.

Youth—*continued.*

Dana's (Jas.) Sermons to Young people.
Davies' Appeal in behalf of young men.
Dohon's Selections of Sermons.
Dodd's (Wm.) Sermons to young men.
Doddridge's (P.) Sermons.
——— Sermons to young persons.
Duchall's (Dr. James) Sermons.
Eddy's (A. D.) Duties and dangers of youth.
Eddy's (D. C.) Young man's Friend.
Elliot's Lectures to young men.
——— ——— young women.
Enfield's (William) Sermons.
Evans' (John) Discourses to young people.
Fawcett's Sermons at the Old Jewry.
Fletcher's (Alex.) Addresses to the Young.
Fordyce's Sermons to young men.
——— Sermons to young women.
Gilbert's (John) Sermons.
Gouge's (Thomas) Young man's Guide.
Greene's (John) Sermons.
Greenwood's Affect. address to the young.
Guyse's (John) Sermons to young men.
Hague's (Joseph) Sermons.
Hale's (Sir M.) Contemplations.
——— Counsels of a Father.
——— Advice to Grandchildren.
Hampden's (R. D.) Sermons.
Harness' Boyle Lectures. 1821.
Harvey's (W. W.) Sermons to young men.
Hesketh's Importance of religion.
Hewlett's Thought upon Thought.
Hickman's (Bp.) Sermons.
Hooper's (J.) Addresses to young people.
Horne's (Bp.) Sermons.
Hotchin's (B. B.) Manliness.
James' (John A.) Young man's Friend.
——— Young man from home.
——— Young woman's Friend.
——— Sermons to young men.
Jennings' (D.) Discourses.
Jewsbury's (Maria) Letters to the young.
Jortin's (John) Sermons.
Keach's (Benj.) War with the Devil.
Kennaway's (C. E.) Sermons to the young.
Kennet's (Basil) Sermons.
Kidder's Young man's duty.
Lamb's (Robert) Sermons.
Lardner's Counsels of prudence. (Fifty-two selected sermons.)
Lavington's (S.) Sermons to young people.
Lee's Sunday Lectures.
Leechman's (William) Sermons.
Lynch (T. C.) on Self-improvement.
Magie's (David) Spring-time of life.
Marsh's Early life of Christ.
May's Sermons to young people.
Mayhew's (Jon.) Sermons to young people.
McAll's Address to the young.
Milner's (John) Sermons. (6 on this subj.)
Morehead's (R.) Discourses.
Morrison's (John) Counsels to young men.
Nelson's (Valentine) Sermons.
Newcombe's (H.) Life and its Duties.
Oakes' (John) Sermons.

Youth—*continued.*

Orton's Discourses to the aged. Disc. 1.
Panoplist. New Series. 3:64.
Pike's Persuasives to early piety.
Preston's (M. M.) Sermons to young people.
Ranyard's The Book and its story.
Scott's Daniel a model for young men.
Secker's (Abp.) Sermons.
Sewell's Sermons to young men.
Smith's (Henry) Sermons.
Sprague's Letters to young men.
Stillman's (Samuel) Sermons.
Strype's (John) Sermons.
Taprell's Lectures on the Lord's prayer.
——— Advice to young people.
Taylor's (Isaac) Advice to the Teens.
——— Advice to young men.
——— Twelve addresses to young persons.
Taylor's (Mrs.) Hints to young females.
Thayer's (Elihu) Sermons.
Thomas' (David) The Crisis of Being.
Thomson's Warnings against the enticements of sinners.
Thornton's Counsels and Cautions. (Exc't.)
——— Maxims and Directions.
Toulmin's (J.) Sermons.
Trapp's (Joseph) Sermons.
Trench (R. C.) on the Lessons in Proverbs.
Turner's Religious and Moral Letters.
West's (Mrs.) Lectures on import. subjects.
White's Letters from a father to a son.
Wilcox's (Daniel) Sermons.
Wordsworth's (Cha.) Christian boyhood at a public school. (Two volumes of discourses on topics appropriate to boys.)

Zabians. See ASTROLOGY.

Burckhardt, les Nazarreens.

Townley's Essays on various subjects.

Zeal.

Adams on False zeal.
Bishop's (William) Sermons.
Bundy's (Richard) Sermons.
Christian Rev. 9:37.
Clarke's (Dr. Samuel) Sermons.
Cook's (John) Thirty-nine Sermons.
Cooper's (Edward) Sermons.
Delany's (Patrick) Sermons.
Edwards' (Dr. John) Theologia Reformata.
Enfield on Religious Zeal.
Evans' (B.) Hints to young Christians.
Evans' Christian Temper.
Fish's Primitive piety revived. Ch. 6.
Foster's (John) Lectures at Broadmead Chapel.
Galloway's (J. C.) Lectures.
Gatty's (Alfred) Sermons.
Gill's Body of practical divinity.
Gisbourne's (Thomas) Sermons.
Godwin's Sermons on religious zeal.
Grant's (Johnson) Sermons.
Gresley's (William) Sermons.
Haynes' Illustrations of faith and practice.

Zeal—*continued.*

Hill's (Brian) Christian zeal enforced.
Hinton's (J. H.) Active Christian.
Hoadly's (Bp.) Sermons. (False zeal.)
Hughes' Sermon on Christian zeal.
Jewell's (Bp.) Sermons.
Kirwan's (W. B.) Sermons.
Knowles' (Thomas) Discourses.
Lambe's (Henry) Sermons.
Lamont's (David) Sermons on prevalent vices.
Logan's (John) Sermons.
Maltby's (Edward) Sermons at Lincoln's Inn.
Mason's Christian Morals.
Mather's Essays to do good.
Noel's (Gerard T.) Sermons.
Orton on Sacred Zeal.
Rees' (Abraham) Practical Sermons.
Reed's Advancement of religion the claim of the times.
Reynolds' (Bp.) Sermons.
Robertson's (Theodore) Obligations of Christians.
Spratt's (Bp.) Sermons.
Tappan's (David) Sermons.
Walker's (Robert) Sermons.
Wake's (Wm.) Sermons. (Misguided zeal.)
Webb's (Francis) Sermons.
Wesley's (John) Sermons.
Young's (W. T.) Sermons.

Zendavista. See ZOROASTER.

Bergmanni (J. P.) Dissertationes.
Bournouf, Traduction et Commentaire.
Fechner's Zendavista. (A German translat.)
Haugh's Gatha d. Zaratrastra. (A German trans. of some portions, with notes.)
Hyde, Hist. religionis veterum Persarum.
Perron, Zendavista de Zoroastre.
Tholuck, Theosophia Persarum pantheistica.
Westergaard, Zendavista.

Bibliotheca Sacra. 1:148. 3:540.
British Quarterly. 7:49.
Butler's (Cha.) Notes on the Zendavista.
Christian Examiner. 1:35.
Eclectic Mag. 14:476.
Jones' (Sir W.) Letter to M. A. Du Perron.
Wesley's (John) Sermons.
Wilson's Parsee religion contrasted with Christianity.

Zinzendorf. See MORAVIANS.

Zinzendorfii Opera.
Duvernoy's Lebensgeschichte des Z.
Jung's Leben und Lehren von Z.
Schrantenbach's Z. und die Brüdergemeine v. seiner zeit.
Schroeder's Z. und Herrnhut.
Spangenberg's Leben des Grafen von Z.
Vanhagen's Leben des Zinzendorf.
Verbech d. Z. Leben und Charakter.
Winkler's Z.'s Unternehmungen.
Wolderhausen's Leben des Herrn. Grafen Z.

Bovet's The Banished Count.
Jackson's Life of Zinzendorf.
James's Lives of eminent Christians.
Latrobe's Life of Zinzendorf.
Spangenberg's Life of Z. Trans. by Jackson.
Wolderhausen's Life of Zinzendorf.

Zoroaster. See PARSEES.

Zuingle.

Zuinglii Opera. (Ed. Schulero et Schulthesio. 1828-1842. 8 vols., 8vo.)
Bullinger's Reformations Geschichte.
Hess' Leben des U. Zuingli.
Hottinger, Evangelische Kirchengeschichte.
——— Zuingli und seine Zeit.
Hundeshagen, die Conflicte des Zuinglianismus, Lutherthums, und Calvinismus in Berne.
Müller's Ulrick Zuingli Denkmal
Myconii Vitæ quartuor Reformatorum.
Nuscheler's Leben Ulrick Zuingli.
Richard's U. Z. Biographie Geschildert.
Rothermund's Leben des Reformator U. Z.
Schulleri Vita Zuinglii.
Sigwart's U. Zuingli. (Reply to Zellers.)
Zellers' Theologische Syst. Z. Dargestelt.

Biblioth. Sacra. 8:563,675.
Blackwood's Mag. 24:194. 48:740.
Christian Disciple. 3:125.
Christian Examiner. 45:170.
Chris. Monthly Spect. 6:246.
Christoffel's Z. and the Swiss reformation.
Hess' Life of Z. Trans. by Aikin.
Hottinger's Life of Z. Trans. by Porter.
London Review. 12:209.
Princeton Review. 13:197.
Sigwart's Character and theology of Z.
Zeller's Theology of Zuingle.

HEADS

UNDER WHICH BOOKS GIVING THE BIBLIOGRAPHY OF THE SUBJECT ARE NAMED.

Adiaphorists.
Adoptians.
Anabaptists.
Anointing the Sick.
Apocrypha.
Archæology.
Armenianism.
Arianism.
Atheism.
Augustine.

Bangorean Controversy.
Baptismal Regeneration.
Baptists.
Barnabas.
Benedictines.
Berengarians.
Biblical Criticism.
Book of Common Prayer.

Calvinism.
Canon Law.
Capucins.
Cartesians.
Catechisms.
Catenæ.
Christianity.
Christology.
Church History, General.
——— ——— Africa.
——— ——— Denmark.
——— ——— England.
Church of England.
Cistercians.
Clemens Romanus.
Coins.
Commentators.
Corporation and Test Acts.
Creeds.

Decretals.
Descent into Hell.
Deism (Polemic).
Deism (Historical).
Dionysius Areop.
Dominicans.

Egypt.
Election.
Eunomians.

Fate.
Fathers.
Formula Concordia.
Franciscans.
Freemasonry.
Friends (Quakers).
Funeral Sermons.
Future State.

Genuineness of 1 John 5:7.
Gnostics.

Halfway Covenant.
Hebraisms.
Hermeneutics.
Hinduism.
Hymnology.

Ignatius.
Image Worship.
Immortality of the Soul.
Imputation.
Indexes Expurgatory.
Indulgences.
Infant Baptism.
Infidelity.
Interim.
Intermediate Place.
Intermediate State.

Jansenists.
Jasher.
Jesuits.
Jewish Antiquities.
Jewish Controversy.
Josephus.
Judaism.

Knights of St. John.

Lapsed Christians.
Liturgies.
Logic.
Lord's Supper.
Luther.

Macedonians.
Magic.
Mahomotenism.
Manuscripts.
Marriage.
Martyrology.
Mass.
Methodism.
Middle Ages.
Ministerial Education.
Missal.
Monasticism.
Monothelites.
Moravians.
Mystics.

Nestorians.

Origin of Evil.

Pastoral Theology.
Philology.
Pietists.
Platonism.
Political Economy.
Popery.
Popes of Avignon.
Pope Joan.
Printed Editions.
Prophecy.
Providence.
Psalmody.
Purgatory.

Quietists.

Rabbinical Literature.
Rationalism.
Redemption.
Remonstrants.
Sabbath.
Scholasticism.
Septuagint.
Socinianism.
Subscription to Creeds.
Synergists.

Theosophist.
Therapeutæ.
Thomists.
Thundering Legion.
Toleration.
Traduction of the Soul.
Translations.
Transubstantiation.
Trappists.
Trinity.

Unitarians.

Vulgate Bible.

Waldenses.
Weigelians.
Witchcraft.

THEOLOGICAL INDEX.

BY

HOWARD MALCOM, D.D.

One Volume, Royal Octavo. $4.00.

This important production has been almost the life-work of Dr. Malcom, and no Library can hereafter be deemed *complete* which does not include this work.

COMMENDATORY NOTICES

FROM DISTINGUISHED SCHOLARS WHO HAVE EXAMINED THE PROOF-SHEETS OF THIS WORK.

From Pres. Walker, of Harvard College.

"In looking over the advance sheets of your Theological Index, I have been struck with the amount of labor it must have required, to collect and classify so many titles of books on theoretical and practical religion, and the kindred topics. But, it bears no proportion to the labor it will save others. The need of such a work is more and more felt. Some theologians, as you say in your preface, may perhaps wonder at some of your omissions. But the index is not intended for them so much as for the working clergy, who, in consulting or purchasing books, need just such a guide, and will be greatly helped by the one you have provided."

From Charles Hodge, D.D., of Princeton Theological Seminary.

I have examined the sheets of your Theological Index, for which I thank you. The work of Winer on the same general plan is not adapted to American students, as his references are so generally to works not accessible to them.

I have no doubt that your book will be found adapted to meet a want long and widely felt, and prove useful in a high degree.

From Geo. R. Bliss, D.D., University at Lewisburg, Pa.

Your book will certainly fill a place now *entirely unoccupied*, and will be indispensable to all studious clergymen, to libraries, and to scholars generally. You have facilitated the labors of a multitude of Christian scholars, through generations to come.

From Prof. Hackett, D.D., Newton Theological Institution.

I have examined your sheets with much interest. I think well of the plan. The book will enable those who wish to form a library to select books judiciously, and afterward to use them with advantage. It is not enough to have books in our possession; we need also an index of their contents, at the right moment, to show us whether the information we seek is within our reach. Your book supplies that want. I am sure it will lay very many persons under lasting obligations to your industry, skill, and scholarship.

From S. S. Schmuker, D.D., Emeritus Professor of Theology in the Theological Seminary of the Lutheran Church, Gettysburg, Pa.

After having examined the several sheets of your Bibliographical Manual or Lexicon, which you kindly sent me, I take great pleasure in bearing testimony in favor of its diversified and decided utility.

This work differs from the more systematic productions of Noesselt and Winer, in that it does not follow the *authors' names*, nor give the authors' birth and death, as well as the offices they sustained. But it makes a selection of several thousand *topics*, embracing every important subject on which students may desire information, and under each of these arranges the authors who discuss that subject.

While, therefore, the work does not furnish as much material to gratify the curiosity of the critical, it affords a vast amount of information more valuable to students, pastors, and preachers, because more available for the purposes of professional life. One who has access to but a moderate library will, by the aid of this work, seldom fail to find important material for his purpose, and I cannot doubt it will meet a cordial reception from those whose benefit it contemplates.

Valuable Works,

PUBLISHED BY

GOULD AND LINCOLN,

59 Washington Street, Boston.

HAMILTON'S LECTURES, embracing the METAPHYSICAL and LOGICAL COURSES; with Notes, from Original Materials, and an Appendix, containing the Author's Latest Development of his New Logical Theory. Edited by Rev. HENRY LONGUEVILLE MANSEL, B. D., Prof. of Moral and Metaphysical Philosophy in Magdalen College, Oxford, and JOHN VEITCH, M. A., of Edinburgh. In two royal octavo volumes, viz.,

I. METAPHYSICAL LECTURES. Royal octavo, cloth, 3.50.

II. LOGICAL LECTURES. Royal octavo, cloth, 3.50.

☞ G. & L., by a special arrangement with the family of the late Sir William Hamilton, are the authorized, and only authorized, American publishers of this distinguished author's *matchless* LECTURES ON METAPHYSICS AND LOGIC.

The above have already been introduced into nearly all our leading colleges.

LOOMIS' ELEMENTS OF GEOLOGY; adapted to Schools and Colleges. With numerous Illustrations. By J. R. LOOMIS, President of Lewisburg University, Pa. 12mo, cloth, 1.25.

"It is surpassed by no work before the American public."—*M. B. Anderson, LL. D., President Rochester University.*

PEABODY'S CHRISTIANITY THE RELIGION OF NATURE. Lectures delivered before the Lowell Institute in 1863, by A. P. PEABODY, D. D., LL. D., Preacher to the University, and Plummer Professor of Christian Morals, Harvard College. Royal 12mo, cloth, 1.50.

A masterly production, distinguished for its acuteness and earnestness, its force of logic and fairness of statement, written in a style of singular accuracy and beauty.

PALEY'S NATURAL THEOLOGY: Illustrated by forty Plates, with Selections from the Notes of Dr. Paxton, and Additional Notes, Original and Selected, with a Vocabulary of Scientific Terms. Edited by JOHN WARE, M. D. Improved edition, with elegant illustrations. 12mo, cloth, embossed, 1.75.

MANSEL'S PROLEGOMENA LOGICA; the Psychological Character of Logical Processes. By HENRY LONGUEVILLE MANSEL, B. D. 12mo, cloth, 1.25.

YOUNG LADIES' CLASS BOOK: a Selection of Lessons for Reading in Prose and Verse. By EBENEZER BAILEY, A. M. Cloth, embossed, 1.25.

MILLER'S CRUISE OF THE BETSEY; or, a Summer Ramble among the Fossiliferous Deposits of the Hebrides. With Rambles of a Geologist; or, Ten Thousand Miles over the Fossiliferous Deposits of Scotland. 12mo, pp. 524, cloth, 1.75.

MILLER'S ESSAYS, Historical and Biographical, Political and Social, Literary and Scientific. By HUGH MILLER. With Preface by Peter Bayne. 12mo, cloth, 1.75.

MILLER'S FOOT-PRINTS OF THE CREATOR; or, the Asterolepis of Stromness, with numerous Illustrations. With a Memoir of the Author, by LOUIS AGASSIZ. 12mo, cloth, 1.75.

MILLER'S FIRST IMPRESSIONS OF ENGLAND AND ITS PEOPLE. With a fine Engraving of the Author. 12mo, cloth, 1.50.

MILLER'S HEADSHIP OF CHRIST, and the Rights of the Christian People, a Collection of Personal Portraitures, Historical and Descriptive Sketches and Essays, with the Author's celebrated Letter to Lord Brougham. By HUGH MILLER. Edited, with a Preface, by PETER BAYNE, A. M. 12mo, cloth, 1.75.

MILLER'S OLD RED SANDSTONE; or, New Walks in an Old Field. Illustrated with Plates and Geological Sections. NEW EDITION, REVISED AND MUCH ENLARGED, by the addition of new matter and new Illustrations, &c. 12mo, cloth, 1.75.

MILLER'S POPULAR GEOLOGY; With Descriptive Sketches from a Geologist's Portfolio. By HUGH MILLER. With a Resume of the Progress of Geological Science during the last two years. By MRS. MILLER. 12mo, cloth, 1.75.

MILLER'S SCHOOLS AND SCHOOLMASTERS; or, the Story of my Education. AN AUTOBIOGRAPHY. With a full-length Portrait of the Author. 12mo, 1.75.

MILLER'S TALES AND SKETCHES. Edited, with a Preface, &c., by MRS. MILLER. 12mo, 1.50.

Among the subjects are: Recollections of Ferguson — Burns — The Salmon Fisher of Udoll — The Widow of Dunskaith — The Lykewake — Bill Whyte — The Young Surgeon — George Ross, the Scotch Agent — M'Culloch, the Mechanician — A True Story of the Life of a Scotch Merchant of the Eighteenth Century.

MILLER'S TESTIMONY OF THE ROCKS; or, Geology in its Bearings on the two Theologies, Natural and Revealed. "Thou shalt be in league with the stones of the field." — *Job.* With numerous elegant Illustrations. One volume, royal 12mo, cloth, 1.75.

HUGH MILLER'S WORKS. Ten volumes, uniform style, in an elegant box, embossed cloth, 17; library sheep, 20; half calf, 34; antique, 34.

MACAULAY ON SCOTLAND. A Critique from HUGH MILLER'S "Witness." 16mo, flexible cloth. 37 cts.

LIFE, TIMES, AND CORRESPONDENCE OF JAMES MANNING, AND THE EARLY HISTORY OF BROWN UNIVERSITY. By REUBEN ALDRIDGE GUILD. With Likenesses of President Manning and Nicholas Brown, Views of Brown University, The First Baptist Church, Providence, etc. Royal 12mo, cloth, 3.00.

A most important and interesting historical work.

MEMOIR OF GEORGE N. BRIGGS, LL. D., late Governor of Massachusetts. By W. C. RICHARDS. With Illustrations. Royal 12mo. 2.50

THE LIFE OF JOHN MILTON, narrated in connection with the POLITICAL, ECCLESIASTICAL, AND LITERARY HISTORY OF HIS TIME. By DAVID MASSON, M. A., Professor of English Literature, University College, London. Vol. I., embracing the period from 1608 to 1639. With Portraits and specimens of his handwriting at different periods. Royal octavo, cloth, 3.50.

LIFE AND CORRESPONDENCE OF REV. DANIEL WILSON, D. D., late Bishop of Calcutta. By Rev. JOSIAH BATEMAN, M. A., Rector of North Cray, Kent. With Portraits, Map, and numerous Illustrations. One volume royal octavo, cloth, 3.50.

☞ An interesting life of a great and good man.

THE LIFE AND TIMES OF JOHN HUSS; or, The Bohemian Reformation of the Fifteenth Century. By Rev. E. H. GILLETT. Two vols. royal octavo, 7.00.

"The author," says the *New York Observer*, "has achieved a great work, performed a valuable service for Protestantism and the world, made a name for himself among religious historians, and produced a book that will hold a prominent place in the esteem of every religious scholar."

The *New York Evangelist* speaks of it as "one of the most valuable contributions to ecclesiastical history yet made in this country."

MEMOIR OF THE CHRISTIAN LABORS, Pastoral and Philanthropic, of THOMAS CHALMERS, D. D. L.L. D. By FRANCIS WAYLAND. 16mo, cloth, 1.00.

The moral and intellectual greatness of Chalmers is, we might say, overwhelming to the mind of the ordinary reader. Dr. Wayland draws the portraiture with a master hand. — Method. Quart. Rev.

LIFE OF JAMES MONTGOMERY. By Mrs. H. C. KNIGHT, author of "Lady Huntington and her Friends," etc. Likeness, and elegant Illustrated Title-Page on steel. 12mo, cloth, 1.50.

DIARY AND CORRESPONDENCE OF AMOS LAWRENCE. With a brief account of some Incidents in his Life. Edited by his son, WM. R. LAWRENCE, M. D. With elegant Portraits of Amos and Abbott Lawrence, an Engraving of their Birthplace, an Autograph page of Handwriting, and a copious Index. One large octavo volume, cloth, 2.50.

THE SAME WORK. Royal 12mo, cloth, 1.75.

DR. GRANT AND THE MOUNTAIN NESTORIANS. By Rev. THOMAS LAURIE, his surviving associate in that Mission. With a Likeness, Map of the Country, and numerous Illustrations. Third edition. Revised and improved. 12mo, cloth, 1.75. ☞ A most valuable memoir of a *remarkable man.*

WAYLAND'S LETTERS ON THE MINISTRY OF THE GOSPEL. By FRANCIS WAYLAND, D.D. 16mo, cloth, 90 cts.

WAYLAND'S SALVATION BY CHRIST. A Series of Discourses on some of the most Important Doctrines of the Gospel. By FRANCIS WAYLAND, D.D. 12mo, cloth, 1.50; cloth, gilt, 2.25.

THE LIFE OF TRUST; being a Narrative of the Dealings of God with the REV. GEORGE MÜLLER. Edited and condensed by Rev. H. LINCOLN WAYLAND. With an Introduction by FRANCIS WAYLAND, D.D. Cloth, 1.75.

This work has a peculiar charm, as an unadorned story of the experience of a Christian man who believed in the mighty power of prayer, who gave a literal interpretation to the precept, "Take no thought for the morrow," and lived by daily faith in God's providence and grace.

THE YEAR OF GRACE: a History of the Great Revival in Ireland in 1859. By Rev. WILLIAM GIBSON, Professor of Christian Ethics in the Presbyterian College, Belfast. 12mo, cloth, 1.75.

A remarkable book on a remarkable subject. Next to a visit to the scenes of the Revival, nothing can give so adequate an idea of the wonderful work as the thrilling narrative of Prof. Gibson.

MEMORIALS OF EARLY CHRISTIANITY; Presenting, in a graphic, compact, and popular form, Memorable Events of Early Ecclesiastical History, etc. By Rev. J. G. MIALL, author of "Footsteps of our Forefathers." With numerous Illustrations. 12mo, cloth, 1.50.

FOOTSTEPS OF OUR FOREFATHERS; What they Suffered and what they Sought. Describing Localities, and Portraying Personages and Events, conspicuous in the Struggles for Religious Liberty. By JAMES G. MIALL. Containing thirty six Illustrations. 12mo, cloth, 1.50.

MODERN ATHEISM; Under its forms of Pantheism, Materialism, Secularism, Development, and Natural Laws. By JAMES BUCHANAN, D. D., LL. D. 12mo, cloth, 1.75.

"The work is one of the most readable and solid which we have ever perused." — *Hugh Miller.*

MORNING HOURS IN PATMOS. The Opening Vision of the Apocalypse, and Christ's Epistle to the Seven Churches of Asia. By Rev. A. C. THOMPSON, D. D., author of "The Better Land," "Gathered Lilies," etc. With beautiful Frontispiece. 12mo, cloth, 1.50.

FIRST THINGS; or, the Development of Church Life. By BARON STOW, D. D. 16mo, cloth, 90 cts.

THE GREAT CONCERN; or, Man's Relation to God and a Future State. By NEHEMIAH ADAMS, D. D. 12mo, cloth, 1.25.

"Pungent and affectionate, reaching the intellect, conscience, and feelings; admirably fitted to awaken, guide, and instruct. Just the thing for distribution in our congregations." —*N. Y. Observer.*

EVENINGS WITH THE DOCTRINES. By Rev. NEHEMIAH ADAMS, D. D. Royal 12mo, cloth, 1.75.

TRUTHS FOR THE TIMES. By NEHEMIAH ADAMS, D. D., Pastor of Essex-street Church, Boston. 12mo, paper covers, 15 and 30 cts.

THE PURITANS; or, The Court, Church, and Parliament of England, during the reigns of Edward VI. and Elizabeth. By SAMUEL HOPKINS, author of Lessons at the Cross," etc. In 3 vols. Octavo, cloth, per vol., 3.00; sheep, 4.00; half calf, 6.00.

It will be found the most interesting and reliable History of the Puritans yet published, narrating, in a dramatic style, many facts hitherto unknown.

THE PREACHER AND THE KING; or, Bourdaloue in the Court of Louis XIV.; being an Account of the Pulpit Eloquence of that distinguished era. Translated from the French of L. F. BUNGENER, Paris. Introduction by the Rev. GEORGE POTTS, D. D. *A new, improved edition*, with a fine Likeness and a BIOGRAPHICAL SKETCH OF THE AUTHOR. 12mo, cloth, 1.50.

THE PRIEST AND THE HUGUENOT; or, Persecution in the Age of Louis XV. From the French of L. F. BUNGENER. Two vols. 12mo, cloth, 3.00.

☞ This is not only a work of thrilling interest, — no fiction could exceed it, — but, as a Protestant work, it is a masterly production.

THE PULPIT OF THE AMERICAN REVOLUTION; or, The Political Sermons of the Period of 1776. With an Historical Introduction, Notes, Illustrations, etc. By JOHN WINGATE THORNTON, A. M. 12mo, cloth, 1.75.

THE LEADERS OF THE REFORMATION. LUTHER, CALVIN, LATIMER, and KNOX, the representative men of Germany, France, England, and Scotland. By J. TULLOCH, D. D., Author of "Theism," etc. 12mo, cloth, 1.50.

A portrait gallery of sturdy reformers, drawn by a keen eye and a strong hand. Dr. Tulloch discriminates clearly the personal qualities of each Reformer, and commends and criticises with equal frankness.

THE HAWAIIAN ISLANDS; their Progress and Condition under Missionary Labors. By RUFUS ANDERSON, D. D., Foreign Secretary of the American Board of Commissioners for Foreign Missions. With Maps, Illustrations, etc. Royal 12mo, cloth, 2.25.

WOMAN AND HER SAVIOUR in Persia. By a RETURNED MISSIONARY. With beautiful Illustrations and a Map of the Nestorian Country. 12mo, cloth, 1.25.

LIGHT IN DARKNESS; or, Christ Discerned in his True Character by a Unitarian. 16mo, cloth, 90 cts.

LIMITS OF RELIGIOUS THOUGHT EXAMINED, in Eight Lectures, delivered in the Oxford University Pulpit, in the year 1858, on the "Bampton Foundation." By Reu. H. LONGUEVILLE MANSEL, B. D., Reader in Moral and Metaphysical Philosophy at Magdalen College, Oxford, and Editor of Sir William Hamilton's Lectures. With Copious NOTES TRANSLATED for the American edition. 12mo, cloth, 1.50.

THE CRUCIBLE; or, Tests of a Regenerate State; designed to bring to light suppressed hopes, expose false ones, and confirm the true. By Rev. J. A. GOODHUE, A. M. With an introduction by Rev. E. N. KIRK, D. D. 12mo, cloth, 1.50.

SATAN'S DEVICES AND THE BELIEVER'S VICTORY. By Rev. WILLIAM L. PARSONS, D. D. 12mo, cloth, 1.50.

CRUDEN'S CONDENSED CONCORDANCE. A Complete Concordance to the Holy Scriptures. By ALEXANDER CRUDEN. Revised and re-edited by the Rev. DAVID KING, LL. D. Octavo, cloth arabesque, 1.75; sheep, 2.00.

The condensation of the quotations of Scripture, arranged under the most obvious heads, while it *diminishes the bulk* of the work, *greatly facilitates* the finding of any required passage.
"We have in this edition of Cruden the *best* made *better.*"—*Puritan Recorder.*

EADIE'S ANALYTICAL CONCORDANCE OF THE HOLY SCRIPTURES; or, the Bible presented under Distinct and Classified Heads or Topics. By JOHN EADIE, D. D., LL. D., Author of "Biblical Cyclopædia," "Ecclesiastical Cyclopædia," "Dictionary of the Bible," etc. One volume, octavo, 840 pp., cloth, 4.00; sheep, 5.00; cloth, gilt, 5.50; half calf, 6.50.

The object of this Concordance is to present the SCRIPTURES ENTIRE, under certain classified and exhaustive heads. It differs from an ordinary Concordance, in that its arrangement depends not on WORDS, but on SUBJECTS, and the verses *are printed in full.*

KITTO'S POPULAR CYCLOPÆDIA OF BIBLICAL LITERATURE. Condensed from the larger work. By the Author, JOHN KITTO, D. D. Assisted by JAMES TAYLOR, D. D., of Glasgow. With over five hundred Illustrations. One volume, octavo, 812 pp., cloth, 4.00; sheep, 5.00; half calf, 7.00.

A DICTIONARY OF THE BIBLE. Serving also as a COMMENTARY, embodying the products of the best and most recent researches in biblical literature in which the scholars of Europe and America have been engaged.

KITTO'S HISTORY OF PALESTINE, from the Patriarchal Age to the Present Time; with Chapters on the Geography and Natural History of the Country, the Customs and Institutions of the Hebrews. By JOHN KITTO, D. D. With upwards of two hundred Illustrations. 12mo, cloth, 1.75.

☞ A work admirably adapted to the Family, the Sabbath School, and the week-day School Library

WESTCOTT'S INTRODUCTION TO THE STUDY OF THE GOSPELS. With HISTORICAL AND EXPLANATORY NOTES. By BROOKE FOSS WESTCOTT, M. A., late Fellow of Trinity College, Cambridge. With an Introduction by Prof. H. B. HACKETT, D. D. Royal 12mo, cloth, 2.00.

☞ A masterly work by a master mind.

ELLICOTT'S LIFE OF CHRIST HISTORICALLY CONSIDERED. The Hulsean Lectures for 1859, with Notes Critical, Historical, and Explanatory. By C. J. ELLICOTT, B. D Royal 12mo, cloth, 1.75.

☞ Admirable in spirit, and profound in argument.

RAWLINSON'S HISTORICAL EVIDENCES OF THE TRUTH OF THE SCRIPTURE RECORDS, STATED ANEW, with Special reference to the Doubts and Discoveries of Modern Times. In Eight Lectures, delivered in the Oxford University pulpit, at the Bampton Lecture for 1859. By GEO. RAWLINSON, M. A., Editor of the Histories of Herodotus. With the Copious NOTES TRANSLATED for the *American edition* by an accomplished scholar. 12mo, cloth, 1.75.

"The consummate learning, judgment, and general ability, displayed by Mr. Rawlinson in his edition of Herodotus, are exhibited in this work also."—*North-American.*

HACKETT'S COMMENTARY ON THE ORIGINAL TEXT OF THE ACTS OF THE APOSTLES. By HORATIO B. HACKETT, D. D., Prof. of Biblical Literature and Interpretation in the Newton Theol. Institute. ☞ A new, revised, and enlarged edition. Royal octavo, cloth, 3.00.

☞ This most important and very popular work has been thoroughly revised; large portions entirely re-written, with the addition of *more than one hundred pages of new matter*; the result of the author's continued investigations and travels since the publication of the first edition.

HACKETT'S ILLUSTRATIONS OF SCRIPTURE. Suggested by a Tour through the Holy Land. With numerous Illustrations. A new, Improved, and Enlarged edition. By H. B. HACKETT, D. D., Prof. of Biblical Literature in the Newton Theol. Institution. 12mo, cloth, 1.50.

FINE EDITION, TINTED PAPER. Square 8vo, cloth, red edges, 2.50; cloth, gilt, 3.50; half calf, 5.00; full Turkey mor., 7.50.

Prof. Hackett's accuracy is proverbial. We can rely on his statements with confidence, which is in itself a pleasure. He knows and appreciates the wants of readers; explains the texts which need explanation; gives life-like pictures, and charms while he instructs. — *N. Y. Observer.*

MUSIC OF THE BIBLE; or, Explanatory Notes upon all the passages of the Sacred Scriptures relating to Music. With a brief Essay on Hebrew Poetry. By ENOCH HUTCHINSON. With numerous Illustrations. Royal octavo, 3.25.

This book is altogether a unique production, and will be found of interest not only to Biblical scholars and clergymen generally, but also to Sabbath-school teachers, musicians, and the family circle. It is illustrated with numerous engravings.

MALCOM'S NEW BIBLE DICTIONARY of the most important Names, Objects, and Terms found in the Holy Scriptures; intended principally for Sabbath-School Teachers and Bible Classes. By HOWARD MALCOM, D. D., late President of Lewisburg University, Pa. 16mo, cloth, 1.00.

☞ The former Dictionary, of which more than *one hundred thousand copies* were sold, is made the basis of the present work.

PATTISON'S COMMENTARY ON THE EPISTLE TO THE EPHESIANS, Explanatory, Doctrinal, and Practical. With a Series of Questions. By ROBERT E. PATTISON, D. D., late President of Waterville College. 12mo, cloth, 1.25.

RIPLEY'S NOTES ON THE GOSPELS. Designed for Teachers in Sabbath Schools and Bible Classes, and as an Aid to Family Instruction. By HENRY J. RIPLEY, Prof. in Newton Theol. Inst. With Map of Canaan. Cloth, embossed, 1.75.

RIPLEY'S NOTES ON THE ACTS OF THE APOSTLES. With a beautiful Map, illustrating the Travels of the APOSTLE PAUL, with a track of his Voyage from Cesarea to Rome. By Prof. HENRY J. RIPLEY, D. D. 12mo. cloth, embossed, 1.25

RIPLEY'S NOTES ON THE EPISTLE OF PAUL TO THE ROMANS. Designed for Teachers in Sabbath Schools and Bible Classes, and as an Aid to Family Instruction. By HENRY J. RIPLEY. 12mo, cloth, embossed, 90 cts.

The above works by Prof. Ripley should be in the hands of every student of the Bible, especially every Sabbath-school and Bible-class teacher. They contain just the kind of information wanted.